Dear West Customer:

West Academic Publishing has changed the look of its American Casebook Series®.

In keeping with our efforts to promote sustainability, we have replaced our former covers with book covers that are more environmentally friendly. Our casebooks will now be covered in a 100% renewable natural fiber. In addition, we have migrated to an ink supplier that favors vegetable-based materials, such as soy.

Using soy inks and natural fibers to print our textbooks reduces VOC emissions. Moreover, our primary paper supplier is certified by the Forest Stewardship Council, which is testament to our commitment to conservation and responsible business management.

The new cover design has migrated from the long-standing brown cover to a contemporary charcoal fabric cover with silver-stamped lettering and black accents. Please know that inside the cover, our books continue to provide the same trusted content that you've come to expect from West.

We've retained the ample margins that you have told us you appreciate in our texts while moving to a new, larger font, improving readability. We hope that you will find these books a pleasing addition to your bookshelf.

Another visible change is that you will no longer see the brand name Thomson West on our print products. With the recent merger of Thomson and Reuters, I am pleased to announce that books published under the West Academic Publishing imprint will once again display the West brand.

It will likely be several years before all of our casebooks are published with the new cover and interior design. We ask for your patience as the new covers are rolled out on new and revised books knowing that behind both the new and old covers, you will find the finest in legal education materials for teaching and learning.

Thank you for your continued patronage of the West brand, which is both rooted in history and forward looking towards future innovations in legal education. We invite you to be a part of our next evolution.

Best regards,

Heidi M. Hellekson
Publisher, West Academic Publishing

EDUCATION AND THE LAW

Second Edition

■ ■ ■

By

Stuart Biegel

University of California, Los Angeles

AMERICAN CASEBOOK SERIES®

WEST®

A Thomson Reuters business

Mat #40730545

American Casebook Series is a trademark in the U.S. Patent and Trademark Office.

© West, a Thomson business, 2006
© 2009 Thomson Reuters

    610 Opperman Drive
    St. Paul, MN 55123
    1–800–313–9378

Printed in the United States of America

ISBN: 978-0-314-19108-3

 TEXT IS PRINTED ON 10% POST CONSUMER RECYCLED PAPER

To my students—past, present, and future.

*

Preface to the Second Edition

This edition of *Education and the Law* is being published three years after the first edition. Reflecting the extent to which new developments have arisen in the field, approximately 20% of the content is brand new.

The book retains the structure of the first edition, focusing on both K–12 and higher education. It includes the same basic chapter topics and the same inquiry-based approach. In addition to the updated analytical questions contained throughout the text, over fifty major hypothetical problems are provided for those who wish to conduct additional exploration of relevant legal and public policy considerations.

The casebook is designed to be used in different ways and in different settings. The materials are arranged in a manner that would enable them to be employed in both traditional law school settings and in a variety of education and public policy school settings ranging from theoretical doctoral level courses to programs that train practitioners to become leaders in their respective fields.

In addition, the updates continue to contemplate the additional use of this work as a reference book and a treatise. Indeed, the materials are designed to be a resource both for scholars in the area generally and for those whose work places them within the legal, education, and/or public policy communities.

From novel issues generated by new technologies to reform efforts designed to reshape societal norms, Education Law continues to reflect the times we live in. Thus, as much as possible, the casebook is centered in the present, informed by the past, but pointing toward a better future.

****

In addition to recognizing once again the contributions of all those listed in the 2006 acknowledgments section, I would like thank those who have contributed to this second edition.

I have benefited greatly from the insights and perspectives of the following people, whose work during this era has focused to such a great extent on the intersection of law and education: Patricia Gándara, Maya Harris, Michael Harris, Marilyn Korostoff, Bill Koski, Holning Lau, Catherine Lhamon, Goodwin Liu, Hiroshi Motomura, Doug NeJaime, Michael Olivas, Gary Orfield, Kevin Reed, John Rogers, Victor Saenz, Janeen Steel, Zak Szymanski, John Targowski, Kent Wada, and Perry Zirkel. I would also like to acknowledge the continued and extensive contributions of Michael Hersher, Bob Kim, David Levine, and Kevin Welner to this work.

Many current and former students have also contributed greatly to the second edition updates, both formally as research assistants and informally in the course of daily events. In particular, I would like to thank Bram Alden, Paul Astin, Roberto Baeza, Maureen Carroll, Lisa Concoff, Ryan Dunn, Logan Elliott, Stephanie Enyart, Shawn Kravich, Kevin Minnick, Victor Pineda, Megan Roberts, Rene Tiongquico, Felipe Velez, Ryan White, Debra Weinberg, and Desmund Wu. I am not only grateful for their contributions, but I continue to be inspired by their commitment to a brighter future for everyone.

STUART BIEGEL

Spring 2009

ACKNOWLEDGMENTS

I would like to thank the many people who have contributed—directly or indirectly—to the completion of this casebook project. The project reflects twenty years of personal involvement with Education Law issues, in an academic context and in the real world of public education. During these years, I have benefited greatly from the insights, encouragement and support of my colleagues at UCLA and from so many members of both the legal community and the education community.

In particular, I would like to express my gratitude to the following current and former colleagues: Lynn Beck, Megan Franke, Kris Gutierrez, Harry Handler, John McNeil, Ted Mitchell, Danny Solorzano, Jim Trent, Concepcion Valadez, Amy Stuart Wells, and Buzz Wilms at the UCLA Graduate School of Education & Information Studies; and Michael Asimow, Paul Bergman, David Binder, Gary Blasi, Ken Karst, Chris Littleton, Grant Nelson, Gary Rowe, Bill Rubenstein, Gary Schwartz, Kirk Stark, and Eugene Volokh at the UCLA School of Law.

I would also like to express my enduring gratitude to Kristin Crosland, Amanda Datnow, Hoover Liddell, Octavio Pescador, Eric Rofes, and Kevin Welner from the education community; and the Honorable William H. Alsup, Kelly Rozmus Barnes, David Campos, Charles Forster, Ben Fox, Robin Johansen, Bob Kim, Tom Klitgaard, David Levine, David G. Lim, Shannon Minter, Thuy Thi Nguyen, The Honorable William H. Orrick, Jason Snyder, Joe Symkowick, and Ryan Tacorda from the legal community.

****

This casebook, and the accompanying teacher's manual, could not have been completed without the invaluable efforts of six outstanding research assistants: Allen Chiu and Jennifer Gin Lee in 2004–2005, Elizabeth Oh and Arvin Tseng in the Summer and Fall of 2005, and Jacob Foster and Jonathan Kuai in 2005–2006. I would also like to acknowledge with gratitude the assistance, support, and professionalism of the Thomson/West editorial team, and in particular the two editors I have worked most closely with, Staci Herr and Kathleen Vandergon.

Finally, special thanks should go to the following people, who have contributed directly to the completion of this project on so many levels over time: Ryan Christopher Fox, Joel Handler, Michael Hersher, Daniel Javitch, Jerry Kang, Allan Keown, Patricia McDonough, Rick Mintrop, Jeannie Oakes, Brad Sears, Diane Steinberg, Richard Steinberg, Dylan Vade, and Jonathan Zasloff.

In sum, this was not a project I could have completed on my own. I have been truly fortunate to have met so many wonderful people over such an extended period of time who have given so much on both a professional and a personal level.

STUART BIEGEL

Spring 2006

Summary of Contents

———

	Page
Preface to the Second Edition	v
Acknowledgments	vii
Table of Cases	xxi

Chapter I. Introduction: Context for Examining Education–Related Disputes — **1**
A. Sources, Interdisciplinary Features, & Unique Characteristics of Education Law — 1
B. Patterns, Trends, and Casebook Organization — 2
C. The Challenge of Effecting Change in an Education Setting — 4
D. The Right to an Education — 6

Chapter II. Campus Safety and Privacy — **12**
A. Liability for Injuries at the K–12 Level — 13
B. Liability for Injuries at the College & University Level — 46
C. Search and Seizure, Drug Testing, and Related Fourth Amendment Concerns — 71
D. Student Records — 95
E. Privacy and Technology in the Information Age — 104

Chapter III. Student Freedom of Expression — **118**
A. Basic First Amendment Principles Applicable in All Settings — 119
B. "Freedom of Expression" at the K–12 Level: The *Tinker* Rule and Campus Safety — 127
C. The Evolution and Refinement of K–12 "Freedom of Expression" Rules — 135
D. Conceptualizing the Parameters of the Right to Be "Out" — 169
E. Higher Education "Freedom of Expression" Controversies Generally — 186
F. Hate–Related Speech Controversies at the Higher Education Level — 204

Chapter IV. Combating Threatening Behavior, Peer Harassment, and Peer Mistreatment — **226**
A. Threatening Activity Generally — 227
B. First Amendment Issues in a Threat–Related Context — 249
C. Peer Harassment and Mistreatment — 278

Chapter V. The Right to Equal Educational Opportunity — **303**
A. Admissions, Placement, and Race — 307
B. The Persistence of the Standardized Testing Controversy — 375
C. Interscholastic and Intercollegiate Athletics Generally — 382
D. Gender Equity in the Education Process — 396
E. The Rights of Undocumented Students — 416

Page

Chapter VI. Educational Quality and the Law **426**
A. Defining and Identifying Quality Education 427
B. The U.S. "No Child Left Behind" Act 461
C. School Choice, Vouchers, and Privatization 482
D. Charter Schools 497

Chapter VII. The Rights of Students With Particular Needs:
    English Learners & Students With Disabilities **505**
A. Bilingual Education and Other Programs for English Learners 506
B. Special Education and Other Programs for Students With Disabilities 549
C. Higher Education and Disability Rights 596

Chapter VIII. Religion and Public Education: Determining the
    Shifting Contours of Establishment Clause Jurisprudence **622**
A. The Evolving Inquiry Into Purpose & Effects 625
B. The Endorsement Inquiry 637
C. The Coercion Inquiry 654
D. Applying the Neutrality Principle: Public Funding for Private Religious Education 674

Chapter IX. Morality, Values, and Educational Policy **695**
A. The Right to Alternative Models of Education 696
B. Patriotism, Religion, and Freedom of Expression: The Flag Salute Controversies 705
C. Disputed Access to Campus Forums and Facilities 720
D. The Parameters of the Right to Receive Information & Ideas 745
E. Sex Education 783
F. Internet Filtering and the Safety of Children in Cyberspace 791

Chapter X. Copyright Issues in Education **809**
A. Basic Principles of U.S. Copyright Law 810
B. Ownership of Copyright and Related Matters 812
C. The Parameters of the Fair Use Doctrine 821
D. Prosecutions Under the "No Electronic Theft" Act 852
E. Assessing the Parameters of the Digital Millennium Copyright Act 864
F. Peer-to-Peer File Sharing and Other Internet–Related Disputes 872

Chapter XI. The Rights of Educators **887**
A. Perspectives on Labor Relations in Public Education 887
B. The Right to Acquire & Retain Tenure 906
C. Disputes Regarding the Dismissal Process Generally 911
D. First Amendment Rights of Educators 927
E. Employment Discrimination 971

INDEX 989

TABLE OF CONTENTS

_____

		Page
PREFACE TO THE SECOND EDITION		v
ACKNOWLEDGMENTS		vii
TABLE OF CASES		xxi

Chapter I. Introduction: Context for Examining Education–Related Disputes — **1**

A. Sources, Interdisciplinary Features, & Unique Characteristics of Education Law — 1

B. Patterns, Trends, and Casebook Organization — 2

C. The Challenge of Effecting Change in an Education Setting — 4

D. The Right to an Education — 6

　　PROBLEM 1: The Fundamental Right to an Education — 10

Chapter II. Campus Safety and Privacy — **12**

A. Liability for Injuries at the K–12 Level — 13

　PROBLEM 2: Green v. Suburbia Sch. Dist. — 13

　1. State Negligence Law Principles — 14

　　A. Extent of the Duty to Supervise — 15

　　　Glaser v. Emporia Unified Sch. Dist. No. 253 — 15

　　　Notes — 19

　　　PROBLEM 3: The Marbury Middle School Lawsuits — 21

　　B. Supervision During Extracurricular Activities — 23

　　　Cerny v. Cedar Bluffs Junior/Senior Pub. Sch. — 23

　　　Notes — 27

　　C. School Shootings — 29

　　　PROBLEM 4: The Tragic Events at Columbine High School — 29

　　　From Columbine High School Complaint — 30

　　　Notes — 36

　　D. Issues Relating to Race and Ethnicity — 36

　　　Ties That Bind, Forces That Divide: Berkeley High School and the Challenge of Integration — 37

　　　Notes — 42

　2. The "Right to Safe Schools" Under State Law — 42

　3. Relevant Federal Statutes and Case Law — 43

　　A. Federal Gun–Free Requirements in Elementary & Secondary Schools, 20 U.S.C. § 7151 — 43

　　　Notes — 44

　　B. The "Unsafe School Choice Option" Under the "No Child Left Behind Act" (2001), 20 U.S.C. § 7912 — 44

　　　Notes — 45

B. Liability for Injuries at the College & University Level — 46

　1. Higher Education Negligence–Related Controversies Generally — 46

Page

B. Liability for Injuries at the College & University Level—Continued
    PROBLEM 5: Perot v. Univ. of Eldorado at Emerald City 46
    Peterson v. San Francisco Cmty. Coll. Dist. 47
    Notes 52
    PROBLEM 6: The Tragic Events at Virginia Tech 55
    Note 59
    Brueckner v. Norwich Univ. 60
    Notes 64
  2. Negligence and Intercollegiate Athletics 66
    Kavanagh v. Trustees of Boston Univ. 66
    Notes 70
C. Search and Seizure, Drug Testing, and Related Fourth Amendment
    Concerns 71
  1. The Doctrine of in Loco Parentis 71
  2. K–12 Search & Seizure Case Law Generally: The Continuing
    Vitality of *New Jersey v. T.L.O.* 72
    PROBLEM 7: The Suburbia Lawsuits (Continued) 72
    New Jersey v. T.L.O. 73
    Notes 84
  3. Drug Testing of Students 87
    PROBLEM 8: Drug Testing and Nirvana Macro Systems 87
    Board of Educ. of Indep. Sch. Dist. No. 92 v. Earls 88
    Notes 95
D. Student Records 95
  1. The Family Educational Rights and Privacy Act (FERPA) and
    Related Federal Statutes 95
    Notes 97
  2. Determining the Parameters of FERPA in the U.S. Supreme
    Court 99
    Owasso Indep. Sch. Dist. No. I–011 v. Falvo 99
    Notes 103
E. Privacy and Technology in the Information Age 104
    PROBLEM 9: Driver's Licenses for the Information Superhighway 105
    Reconstructing Electronic Surveillance Law 106
  1. Monitoring of Student Activity Generally 110
    Privacy v. Piracy 110
    Notes 111
  2. The Prospective Applicability of the Right to Anonymity 113
    Mcintyre v. Ohio Elections Comm'n 113

Chapter III. Student Freedom of Expression **118**
A. Basic First Amendment Principles Applicable in All Settings 119
    *Highlights of U.S. First Amendment Law: Basic Principles and Major
    Exceptions* 119
B. "Freedom of Expression" at the K–12 Level: The *Tinker* Rule and
    Campus Safety 127
    PROBLEM 10: The Coalition to Resist Political and Social Indoctrination 127
    Tinker v. Des Moines Indep. Cmty. Sch. Dist. 129
    Notes 134
C. The Evolution and Refinement of K–12 "Freedom of Expression"
    Rules 135
  1. The *Fraser* Decision: Identifying Society's Interest in "Teaching
    the Boundaries of Socially Appropriate Behavior" 136
    Bethel Sch. Dist. No. 403 v. Fraser 136

Page

C. The Evolution and Refinement of K–12 "Freedom of Expression"
    Rules—Continued
    2. *Hazelwood v. Kuhlmeier*: Limiting Expressive Activities That the
        Public "Might Reasonably Perceive to Bear the Imprimatur of
        the School" -- 141
        Hazelwood v. Kuhlmeier --- 141
        Notes -- 145
    3. *Morse v. Frederick*: Reassessing the Applicability of *Tinker* and Its
        Progeny -- 146
        PROBLEM 11: Jamie and His Friends—The Sequel ----------------- 146
        Morse v. Frederick -- 148
        Notes -- 157
    4. The "T–Shirt" Cases: Addressing Inflammatory Slogans and Im-
        ages on Student Clothing-- 157
        A. The *Boroff* Case: Restricting Ostensibly Anti–Religious Ex-
            pression --- 158
        B. *Chambers, Harper*, and *Nuxoll*: Restricting Ostensibly Anti–
            Gay Expression--- 159
            Notes-- 161
            PROBLEM 12: T–Shirts in New Tuolumne --------------------- 163
    5. Challenges Posed by Online and Wireless Technologies: Deter-
        mining the Extent to Which Students Can Be Held Accountable
        for Electronic Communication Outside of School -------------------- 164
        Doninger v. Niehoff--- 164
        Note--- 169
D. Conceptualizing the Parameters of the Right to Be "Out" -------------- 169
    Fricke v. Lynch--- 171
    Colin v. Orange Unified Sch. Dist. ------------------------------------- 175
    Boyd County High Sch. Gay Straight Alliance v. Board of Ed.------- 180
    Notes --- 182
    Henkle v. Gregory --- 183
    PROBLEM 13: Further Variations on the Events at Southern Valley High ----- 186
E. Higher Education "Freedom of Expression" Controversies Generally 186
    PROBLEM 14: The Alistaire & Georgina Jones Cases ----------------- 186
    Healy v. James -- 188
    Notes --- 192
    Rosenberger v. Rector & Visitors of Univ. of Va. --------------------- 192
    Husain v. Springer -- 197
F. Hate–Related Speech Controversies at the Higher Education Level ---- 204
    PROBLEM 15: Hate-Related Web Site Activity ----------------------------- 204
    Doe v. University of Mich. -- 205
    Rights in Conflict: The First Amendment's Third Century -------------- 212

**Chapter IV. Combating Threatening Behavior, Peer Harass-
    ment, and Peer Mistreatment** --- **226**
A. Threatening Activity Generally-- 227
    PROBLEM 16: Zero Tolerance for Threats I ------------------------------- 227
    1. Addressing Threats Under Negligence Law -------------------------- 227
        Tarasoff v. Regents of Univ. of Cal. ---------------------------------- 227
        Notes -- 232
    2. Relevant Statutory Prohibitions Addressing Threats Under Fed-
        eral & State Law --- 233
        California Penal Code § 422.6-- 234
        Missouri Rev. Stat. § 565.090 (2008) ----------------------------- 235

Page

A. Threatening Activity Generally—Continued
    H.R. 6123 (Sanchez–Hulshof) 236
    3. Criminal Law Cases Addressing Threatening Activity 237
        Commonwealth v. Milo M., A Juvenile 237
        In re George T. 243
        Notes 248
B. First Amendment Issues in a Threat–Related Context 249
    1. Construing the "True Threat" Doctrine in a Higher Education
        Setting 250
        PROBLEM 17: The Alistaire Jones Litigation, Part II 250
        United States v. Alkhabaz, Also Known as Jake Baker 251
        Notes 260
    2. Construing the "True Threat" Doctrine in a K–12 Setting 261
        PROBLEM 18: Zero Tolerance for Threats II 261
        Doe v. Pulaski County Special Sch. Dist. 261
    3. Applying Tinker & its Progeny to K–12 Threat–Related Situations 267
        Wisniewski v. Bd. of Educ. of the Weedsport Cent. Sch. Dist. 267
        Ponce v. Socorro Indep. Sch. Dist. 271
        Notes 278
C. Peer Harassment and Mistreatment 278
    1. Liability for Peer-to-Peer Sexual Harassment 278
        PROBLEM 19: Maxwell v. Valhalla Unified School District 278
        PROBLEM 20: Student Teaching at McKinley High 280
        Hostile Environment Sexual Harassment Law 282
        Davis v. Monroe County Bd. of Ed. 283
        Notes 289
    2. Liability for Mistreatment of Lesbian, Gay, Bisexual, & Transgen-
        der (LGBT) Students 290
        Nabozny v. Podlesny 291
        Flores v. Morgan Hill Unified Sch. Dist. 296
        Notes 301
        PROBLEM 21: Nabozny and Flores as Hypotheticals 302

Chapter V. The Right to Equal Educational Opportunity **303**
A. Admissions, Placement, and Race 307
    1. The Evolution of Basic Fourteenth Amendment Doctrine 307
        Brown v. Board of Educ. 307
        San Antonio Indep. Sch. Dist. v. Rodriguez 309
        Notes 316
    2. Affirmative Action in Higher Education Admissions 317
        PROBLEM 22: Meglino v. Regents of Atlantis State Teachers College 318
        Grutter v. Bollinger 319
        Notes 332
        The California Civil Rights Initiative (Proposition 209) (1996) 334
        PROBLEM 23: The New Mendocino Professional Development Program .. 336
    3. Sorting Out the Parameters of K–12 Desegregation Law in the
        Aftermath of Grutter and Seattle-Louisville 337
        PROBLEM 24: The Vista Creek School District–University Partnership 338
        Parents Involved in Community Schools v. Seattle School District No. 1 ... 339
        Notes 354
    4. The San Francisco Unified School District Consent Decree: A
        Case Study 356
        Court-Mandated Education Reform: The San Francisco Experience and
        the Shaping of Educational Policy after Seattle-Louisville and Brian Ho
        v. SFUSD 356

Page

A. Admissions, Placement, and Race—Continued
    5. Within–School Segregation, Tracking, & Homogeneous Ability
         Grouping 363
         Hobson v. Hansen 364
         Closing the Achievement Gap by Detracking 370
         Note 374
         PROBLEM 25: Tracking & Ability Grouping 374
B. The Persistence of the Standardized Testing Controversy 375
     Debra P. v. Turlington 375
     Notes 379
C. Interscholastic and Intercollegiate Athletics Generally 382
     PROBLEM 26: School Sports, Testing, and Related Academic Issues 382
    1. Equal Educational Opportunity Issues in School Sports 383
         Steffes v. California Interscholastic Fed'n 383
         Note 386
         Washington v. Indiana High Sch. Athletic Ass'n, Inc. 387
         PROBLEM 27: Cooper v. Clarion Unified School District (CUSD) 390
    2. Title IX Issues in School Sports 391
         Neal v. Board of Trustees of the Cal. State Univs. 391
D. Gender Equity in the Education Process 396
    1. Separating Students on the Basis of Gender 396
         PROBLEM 28: Admissions and Gender 396
         United States v. Virginia 397
    2. Differential Treatment in K–12 Settings 402
         Gender Equity in the Classroom 402
    3. Legal and Policy Perspectives on Transgender Issues 405
         Doe v. Yunits 409
         Notes 413
E. The Rights of Undocumented Students 416
     Plyler v. Doe 416
     League of United Latin Am. Citizens v. Wilson 421
     Notes 424

Chapter VI.   Educational Quality and the Law 426
A. Defining and Identifying Quality Education 427
    1. Educational Malpractice Litigation 428
         Peter W. v. San Francisco Unified Sch. Dist. 428
         Note 431
         *Report 18: The Annual Report of the San Francisco Consent Decree
            Monitoring Team* 431
    2. Federal Court Efforts to Define Educational Quality in a Desegre-
         gation Context 433
    3. Conceptualizing Educational Quality in a School Finance Context 435
         Educational Adequacy: A Theory and its Remedies 435
         State Education Articles 437
         Rose v. Council for Better Ed., Inc. 439
         Notes 444
         PROBLEM 29: The Peter W. Education Articles Lawsuit 446
         Achieving "Adequacy" in the Classroom 446
    4. Construing Educational Quality Under an Individual State's Fun-
         damental Right to an Education 449
         T. K. Butt v. California 449
         Note 454
         Williams v. State 455
         PROBLEM 30: Amending the U.S. Constitution 459

Page

A. Defining and Identifying Quality Education—Continued
  House Joint Resolution 29 (Jackson) ---- 459
  PROBLEM 31: Educational Quality Issues in the State of Ocean Wave ---- 460
B. The U.S. "No Child Left Behind" Act ---- 461
  Challenging Racial Disparities: The Promise and Pitfalls of the No Child Left Behind Act's Race–Conscious Accountability ---- 465
  Key Statutory Provisions: The "No Child Left Behind" Act ---- 470
  PROBLEM 32: Challenging the Implementation of the NCLB in Ocean Wave 477
  Qualifications for Educators Under the "No Child Left Behind" Act ---- 477
  Note ---- 482
C. School Choice, Vouchers, and Privatization ---- 482
  PROBLEM 33: Choice for Literacy in the 21st Century ---- 482
  1. School Choice Generally ---- 483
   Reforming School Reform ---- 483
   Notes ---- 492
  2. The School Choice Provisions of NCLB ---- 492
  3. Obligations of Private Institutions Under Public Law if They Accept Public Funding ---- 495
   Note ---- 496
D. Charter Schools ---- 497
  The Politics of Charter Schools ---- 497
  Notes ---- 500
  PROBLEM 34: Litigating Educational Quality at Glen Park Charter High School ---- 502

Chapter VII. The Rights of Students With Particular Needs: English Learners & Students With Disabilities ---- **505**
A. Bilingual Education and Other Programs for English Learners ---- 506
  PROBLEM 35: The Community Language Academy ---- 508
  1. Basic Federal Doctrine ---- 509
   Lau v. Nichols ---- 509
   Notes ---- 512
   Flores v. Arizona ---- 513
   United States v. Texas ---- 519
  2. California Proposition 227 ---- 526
   California Education Code, Title 1, Division 1, Part 1, Chapter 3 ---- 527
   Notes ---- 529
   PROBLEM 36: The New Mendocino Education Code Litigation ---- 530
   Defining an Adequate Education for English Learners ---- 531
  3. English Learners and Within-School Segregation Issues ---- 538
   Bilingual Education and Resegregation: Reconciling the Apparent Paradox Between Bilingual Education Programs and Desegregation Goals 538
B. Special Education and Other Programs for Students With Disabilities 549
  1. Federal Special Education Law Generally ---- 551
   The Individuals With Disabilities Education Act: Why Considering Individuals One at a Time Creates Untenable Situations for Students and Educators ---- 551
   PROBLEM 37: Johnson v. Sutter Springs Unified School District ---- 558
  2. "Appropriateness" of the Special Education: An Increasing Focus on Educational Quality ---- 560
   Board of Education v. Rowley ---- 560
   Notes ---- 571

Page

B. Special Education and Other Programs for Students With Disabilities—Continued
   3. Within–School Segregation Issues in Special Education 572
     A. Disputes Regarding Inclusion, Mainstreaming, and the Least Restrictive Environment Generally................................ 572
       Sacramento City Unified Sch. Dist. v. Rachel H. 572
       Beth B. v. Van Clay 578
     B. Disproportionate Representation of Minority Students in Separate Special Education Classrooms........................ 583
       Larry P. v. Riles 583
   4. Standardized Testing and K-12 Students With Disabilities 584
     Larry P. v. Riles 584
     Connecticut v. Spellings 591
C. Higher Education and Disability Rights 596
   Southeastern Cmty. Coll. v. Davis 598
   Zukle v. Regents of the Univ. of Cal. 604
   Steere v. George Washington University School of Medicine and Health Sciences 612
   Notes 619

Chapter VIII. Religion and Public Education: Determining the Shifting Contours of Establishment Clause Jurisprudence 622
PROBLEM 38: United Parents of Newman County v. NCUSD 625
A. The Evolving Inquiry Into Purpose & Effects........................ 625
   Engel v. Vitale 626
   Notes 630
   Wallace v. Jaffree 631
   Notes 634
   Agostini v. Felton 635
B. The Endorsement Inquiry 637
   Doe v. Duncanville Indep. Sch. Dist. 639
   PROBLEM 39: Re-litigating Doe v. Duncanville Today 644
   Borden v. Sch. Dist. of the Township of East Brunswick 644
C. The Coercion Inquiry 654
   Lee v. Weisman 655
   Note 662
   Mellen v. Bunting 664
D. Applying the Neutrality Principle: Public Funding for Private Religious Education 674
   PROBLEM 40: The Eldorado Teacher Education Institute............... 674
   Zobrest v. Catalina Foothills Sch. Dist. 676
   Zelman v. Simmons–Harris 678
   Notes 691
   Bush v. Holmes 691

Chapter IX. Morality, Values, and Educational Policy 695
A. The Right to Alternative Models of Education.................... 696
   Wisconsin v. Yoder 696
   Notes 703
B. Patriotism, Religion, and Freedom of Expression: The Flag Salute Controversies 705
   West Virginia State Bd. of Educ. v. Barnette 705
   PROBLEM 41: Deciding Newdow Under the Establishment Clause............ 709
   Elk Grove Unified School Dist. v. Newdow 710
C. Disputed Access to Campus Forums and Facilities 720
   1. Access to Forums 720
     Rosenberger v. Rector & Visitors of Univ. of Va. 720

C. Disputed Access to Campus Forums and Facilities—Continued
    Note ---- 723
    Peck v. Baldwinsville Central Sch. Dist. ---- 724
  2. Access to Campus Facilities ---- 732
    Good News Club v. Milford Central Sch. ---- 732
    Notes ---- 737
    Equal Access to Public School Facilities Under the "No Child Left Behind" Act ---- 738
    Gilles v. Blanchard ---- 742
D. The Parameters of the Right to Receive Information & Ideas ---- 745
    PROBLEM 42: Montoya v. Gold Coast Unified School District ---- 745
    PROBLEM 43: The Columbia Education Initiatives ---- 746
  1. The Right to Receive Information ---- 747
    Board of Educ., Island Trees Union Free Sch. Dist. No. 26 v. Pico ---- 747
    Edwards v. Aguillard ---- 755
    Notes ---- 759
  2. The Right Not to Receive Information ---- 763
    Mozert v. Hawkins County Bd. of Educ. ---- 763
    Parker v. Hurley ---- 772
    Notes ---- 781
    PROBLEM 44: Curriculum Disputes in Moss Grove ---- 782
    PROBLEM 45: The Changing Nature of the Family and Its Impact on the Curriculum ---- 783
E. Sex Education ---- 783
    PROBLEM 46: The Riverview Lawsuits ---- 783
    The California Sex Education Statutes ---- 786
F. Internet Filtering and the Safety of Children in Cyberspace ---- 791
    Just How Different Is Cyberspace? ---- 791
    PROBLEM 47: The Marbury Student Council Community Web Site ---- 794
    Mainstream Loudoun v. Board of Trustees of the Loudoun County Library ---- 795
    Notes ---- 801
    United States v. American Library Ass'n, Inc. ---- 801
    Notes ---- 807
    PROBLEM 48: Cleaning Up the Inconsistencies in Current Age Requirements ---- 808

Chapter X. Copyright Issues in Education ---- **809**
A. Basic Principles of U.S. Copyright Law ---- 810
B. Ownership of Copyright and Related Matters ---- 812
    Williams v. Weisser ---- 812
    Weinstein v. University of Illinois ---- 815
    Shaul v. Cherry Valley–Springfield Cent. Sch. Dist. ---- 819
    Note ---- 821
C. The Parameters of the Fair Use Doctrine ---- 821
    Marcus v. Rowley ---- 823
    PROBLEM 49: Cadillac University ---- 828
    PROBLEM 50: ETS v. Wong ---- 829
    Educational Testing Servs. v. Katzman ---- 829
    Chicago Bd. of Educ. v. Substance, Inc. ---- 832
    Princeton Univ. Press v. Michigan Document Servs. ---- 836
    Note ---- 847
    A.V. v. iParadigms ---- 848
D. Prosecutions Under the "No Electronic Theft" Act ---- 852
    PROBLEM 51: Fighting "Electronic Theft" ---- 852
    A Road to No Warez: The No Electronic Theft Act and Criminal Copyright Infringement ---- 854
    Notes ---- 862

Page

E. Assessing the Parameters of the Digital Millennium Copyright Act 864
　PROBLEM 52: Fighting "Electronic Burglary" ------------------------------ 864
　The Digital Millennium Copyright Act: Provisions on Circumventing Protection Systems and Limiting Liability of Service Providers ------------- 864
　Note--- 868
　PROBLEM 53: Linking and Related Activities at Educational Institutions..... 871
F. Peer-to-Peer File Sharing and Other Internet–Related Disputes -------- 872
　Metro–Goldwyn–Mayer Studios v. Grokster------------------------------------ 873
　Note--- 879
　The U.S. Higher Education Opportunity Act -------------------------------- 885

Chapter XI.　The Rights of Educators --------------------------------- **887**
A. Perspectives on Labor Relations in Public Education -------------------- 887
　1. Collective Bargaining and the Education Process --------------------- 887
　　Public Employees' Right to Strike: Law and Experience ---------------- 895
　2. The Perceived Tension Between Reform Efforts and the Rights of Educators-- 896
　　From the Statehouse to the Schoolhouse: How Legislatures and Courts Shaped Labor Relations for Public Education Employees During the Last Decade -- 896
　　Notes --- 905
B. The Right to Acquire & Retain Tenure ---------------------------------- 906
　Perry v. Sindermann --- 907
C. Disputes Regarding the Dismissal Process Generally---------------------- 911
　PROBLEM 54: Teacher Dismissal at the K–12 Level -------------------------- 911
　Morrison v. State Bd. of Educ. --- 913
　Head v. Chicago Sch. Reform Bd. of Trustees------------------------------- 920
D. First Amendment Rights of Educators ----------------------------------- 927
　　A. U.S. Supreme Court Doctrine Generally -------------------------- 927
　　　Pickering v. Board of Educ. of Township High Sch. Dist. 205---------- 927
　　　Connick v. Myers --- 931
　　B. "Academic Freedom" at the K–12 Level ---------------------------- 941
　　　Cockrel v. Shelby County Sch. Dist.--------------------------------- 941
　　　Notes-- 953
　　　Weingarten v. Board of Education of the City School District of the City of New York --- 954
　　　Notes-- 959
　　C. "Academic Freedom" at the Higher Education Level ------------ 960
　　　Urofsky v. Gilmore -- 960
　　　PROBLEM 55: Disciplinary Sanctions at the Higher Education Level 970
E. Employment Discrimination -- 971
　1. Race/Ethnicity --- 971
　2. Gender --- 972
　3. LGBT Status --- 975
　4. Religion -- 979
　5. Age -- 981
　6. Disability -- 983

INDEX--- 989

*

TABLE OF CASES

The principal cases are in bold type. Cases cited or discussed in the text are in roman type. References are to pages. Cases cited in principal cases and within other quoted materials are not included.

Agostini v. Felton, 521 U.S. 203, 117 S.Ct. 1997, 138 L.Ed.2d 391 (1997), **635**

Alkhabaz, United States v., 104 F.3d 1492 (6th Cir.1997), **251**

Allegheny, County of v. American Civil Liberties Union, 492 U.S. 573, 109 S.Ct. 3086, 106 L.Ed.2d 472 (1989), 635, 638

American Library Ass'n, Inc., United States v., 539 U.S. 194, 123 S.Ct. 2297, 156 L.Ed.2d 221 (2003), **801**

A&M Records, Inc. v. Napster, Inc., 239 F.3d 1004 (9th Cir.2001), 872

Ashcroft v. American Civil Liberties Union, 542 U.S. 656, 124 S.Ct. 2783, 159 L.Ed.2d 690 (2004), 807

Ashcroft v. Free Speech Coalition, 535 U.S. 234, 122 S.Ct. 1389, 152 L.Ed.2d 403 (2002), 807

A.V. v. iParadigms, Ltd. Liability Co., 544 F.Supp.2d 473 (E.D.Va.2008), **848**

Baker, United States v., 890 F.Supp. 1375 (E.D.Mich.1995), 260

Beard v. Whitmore Lake School Dist., 402 F.3d 598 (6th Cir.2005), 87

Benefield ex rel. Benefield v. Board of Trustees of University of Alabama at Birmingham, 214 F.Supp.2d 1212 (N.D.Ala.2002), 290

Beth B. v. Van Clay, 282 F.3d 493 (7th Cir.2002), **578**

Bethel School Dist. No. 403 v. Fraser, 478 U.S. 675, 106 S.Ct. 3159, 92 L.Ed.2d 549 (1986), **136**

Board of Curators of University of Missouri v. Horowitz, 435 U.S. 78, 98 S.Ct. 948, 55 L.Ed.2d 124 (1978), 66

Board of Education of Independent School District No. 92 of Pottawatomie County v. Earls, 536 U.S. 822, 122 S.Ct. 2559, 153 L.Ed.2d 735 (2002), **88**

Board of Educ., Island Trees Union Free School Dist. No. 26 v. Pico, 457 U.S. 853, 102 S.Ct. 2799, 73 L.Ed.2d 435 (1982), **747**

Board of Educ. of Hendrick Hudson Central School Dist., Westchester County v. Rowley, 458 U.S. 176, 102 S.Ct. 3034, 73 L.Ed.2d 690 (1982), 549, **560**

Borden v. School Dist. of Tp. of East Brunswick, 523 F.3d 153 (3rd Cir.2008), **644**

Boroff v. Van Wert City Bd. of Educ., 220 F.3d 465 (6th Cir.2000), 158

Bowers v. Hardwick, 478 U.S. 186, 106 S.Ct. 2841, 92 L.Ed.2d 140 (1986), 979

Bown v. Gwinnett County School Dist., 112 F.3d 1464 (11th Cir.1997), 635

Boyd County High School Gay Straight Alliance v. Board of Educ. of Boyd County, KY, 258 F.Supp.2d 667 (E.D.Ky. 2003), **180**

Brown v. Board of Ed. of Topeka, Shawnee County, Kansas, 347 U.S. 483, 74 S.Ct. 686, 98 L.Ed. 873 (1954), 304, **307, 972**

Brown v. Hot, Sexy and Safer Productions, Inc., 68 F.3d 525 (1st Cir.1995), 784

Brueckner v. Norwich University, 169 Vt. 118, 730 A.2d 1086 (Vt.1999), **60**

Bush v. Holmes, 919 So.2d 392 (Fla.2006), 492, **691**

Butt, T.K. v. State of California, 15 Cal. Rptr.2d 480, 842 P.2d 1240 (Cal.1992), 8, **449**

Cain v. Horne, 218 Ariz. 301, 183 P.3d 1269 (Ariz.App. Div. 2 2008), 492

Carlson ex rel. Stuczynski v. Bremen High School Dist. 228, 423 F.Supp.2d 823 (N.D.Ill.2006), 87

Castaneda v. Pickard, 648 F.2d 989 (5th Cir. 1981), 513

Casterson v. Superior Court, 123 Cal.Rptr.2d 637 (Cal.App. 6 Dist.2002), 21

Caudillo ex rel. Caudillo v. Lubbock Independent School Dist., 311 F.Supp.2d 550 (N.D.Tex.2004), 183

Cerny v. Cedar Bluffs Junior/Senior Public School, 267 Neb. 958, 679 N.W.2d 198 (Neb.2004), **23**

Chalifoux v. New Caney Independent School Dist., 976 F.Supp. 659 (S.D.Tex.1997), 135

Chambers v. Babbitt, 145 F.Supp.2d 1068 (D.Minn.2001), 159

Chandler v. McMinnville School Dist., 978 F.2d 524 (9th Cir.1992), 134

Chicago Bd. of Educ. v. Substance, Inc., 354 F.3d 624 (7th Cir.2003), **832**

Child Evangelism Fellowship of New Jersey Inc. v. Stafford Tp. School Dist., 386 F.3d 514 (3rd Cir.2004), 737

Christian Legal Society v. Walker, 453 F.3d 853 (7th Cir.2006), 723

Clark v. Dallas Independent School Dist., 806 F.Supp. 116 (N.D.Tex.1992), 135

Cleveland Bd. of Educ. v. LaFleur, 414 U.S. 632, 94 S.Ct. 791, 39 L.Ed.2d 52 (1974), 972

Cockrel v. Shelby County School Dist., 270 F.3d 1036 (6th Cir.2001), **941**

Colin ex rel. Colin v. Orange Unified School Dist., 83 F.Supp.2d 1135 (C.D.Cal. 2000), **175**

Commonwealth v. _____ (see opposing party)

Connecticut v. Spellings, 549 F.Supp.2d 161 (D.Conn.2008), 463, **591**

Connick v. Myers, 461 U.S. 138, 103 S.Ct. 1684, 75 L.Ed.2d 708 (1983), **931**

Cornfield by Lewis v. Consolidated High School Dist. No. 230, 991 F.2d 1316 (7th Cir.1993), 87

Corso v. Creighton University, 731 F.2d 529 (8th Cir.1984), 66

County of (see name of county)

Crook v. Baker, 813 F.2d 88 (6th Cir.1987), 66

Curtis v. Board of Educ. of Sayre Public Schools, 914 P.2d 656 (Okla.1995), 28

Davis v. Monroe County Bd. of Educ., 526 U.S. 629, 119 S.Ct. 1661, 143 L.Ed.2d 839 (1999), **283**

Debra P. v. Turlington, 644 F.2d 397 (5th Cir.1981), **375**

DePinto v. Bayonne Bd. of Educ., 514 F.Supp.2d 633 (D.N.J.2007), 157

DHX, Inc. v. Allianz AGF MAT, Ltd., 425 F.3d 1169 (9th Cir.2005), 160

Diamond v. Chakrabarty, 447 U.S. 303, 100 S.Ct. 2204, 65 L.Ed.2d 144 (1980), 810

Doe v. Archbishop Stepinac High School, 286 A.D.2d 478, 729 N.Y.S.2d 538 (N.Y.A.D. 2 Dept.2001), 21

Doe v. Duncanville Independent School Dist., 70 F.3d 402 (5th Cir.1995), **639**

Doe v. Hillsboro Independent School Dist., 113 F.3d 1412 (5th Cir.1997), 46

Doe v. Pulaski County Special School Dist., 306 F.3d 616 (8th Cir.2002), **261**

Doe v. University of Michigan, 721 F.Supp. 852 (E.D.Mich.1989), **205**

Doe ex rel. Doe v. Yunits, 2000 WL 33162199 (Mass.Super.2000), **409**

Doninger v. Niehoff, 527 F.3d 41 (2nd Cir. 2008), **164**

Douglas D., In re, 243 Wis.2d 204, 626 N.W.2d 725 (Wis.2001), 250

Downs v. Los Angeles Unified School Dist., 228 F.3d 1003 (9th Cir.2000), 781

East High Gay/Straight Alliance v. Board of Educ. of Salt Lake City School Dist., 81 F.Supp.2d 1166 (D.Utah 1999), 182

Edgewood Independent School Dist. v. Kirby, 777 S.W.2d 391 (Tex.1989), 445

Educational Testing Services v. Katzman, 793 F.2d 533 (3rd Cir.1986), **829**

Edwards v. Aguillard, 482 U.S. 578, 107 S.Ct. 2573, 96 L.Ed.2d 510 (1987), **755**

E.E.O.C. v. Bd. of Regents of University Of Wisconsin System, 288 F.3d 296 (7th Cir. 2002), 981

Elk Grove Unified School Dist. v. Newdow, 542 U.S. 1, 124 S.Ct. 2301, 159 L.Ed.2d 98 (2004), **710**

Engel v. Vitale, 370 U.S. 421, 82 S.Ct. 1261, 8 L.Ed.2d 601 (1962), **626**

Fewless v. Board of Educ. of Wayland Union Schools, 208 F.Supp.2d 806 (W.D.Mich. 2002), 87

Fields v. Palmdale School Dist., 427 F.3d 1197 (9th Cir.2005), 785

Fitzgerald v. Barnstable School Committee, 504 F.3d 165 (1st Cir.2007), 289

Flores v. Arizona, 516 F.3d 1140 (9th Cir. 2008), **513**

Flores v. Morgan Hill Unified School Dist., 324 F.3d 1130 (9th Cir.2003), **296**

Foraste v. Brown University, 290 F.Supp.2d 234 (D.R.I.2003), 821

Forest Grove School Dist. v. T.A., ___ U.S. ___, 129 S.Ct. 987 (2009), 572

Franklin Central Gay/Straight Alliance v. Franklin Tp. Community School Corp., 2002 WL 32097530 (S.D.Ind.2002), 183

Freeman v. Pitts, 503 U.S. 467, 112 S.Ct. 1430, 118 L.Ed.2d 108 (1992), 434

Fricke v. Lynch, 491 F.Supp. 381 (D.R.I. 1980), **171**

Furek v. University of Delaware, 594 A.2d 506 (Del.Supr.1991), 64

Garcetti v. Ceballos, 547 U.S. 410, 126 S.Ct. 1951, 164 L.Ed.2d 689 (2006), 953

Gay–Straight Alliance Network v. Visalia Unified School Dist., 262 F.Supp.2d 1088 (E.D.Cal.2001), 183

Gay–Straight Alliance of Okeechobee High School v. School Bd. of Okeechobee County, 483 F.Supp.2d 1224 (S.D.Fla.2007), 183

George T., In re, 16 Cal.Rptr.3d 61, 93 P.3d 1007 (Cal.2004), **242**

Georgia State Conference of Branches of NAACP v. State of Georgia, 775 F.2d 1403 (11th Cir.1985), 380

Gilles v. Blanchard, 477 F.3d 466 (7th Cir. 2007), **742**

Glaser v. Emporia Unified School Dist. No. 253, 271 Kan. 178, 21 P.3d 573 (Kan. 2001), **15**

Glover v. Williamsburg Local School Dist. Bd. of Educ., 20 F.Supp.2d 1160 (S.D.Ohio 1998), 975

Gonzaga University v. Doe, 536 U.S. 273, 122 S.Ct. 2268, 153 L.Ed.2d 309 (2002), 103

Good News Club v. Milford Central School, 533 U.S. 98, 121 S.Ct. 2093, 150 L.Ed.2d 151 (2001), **732**

Gorman v. University of Rhode Island, 837 F.2d 7 (1st Cir.1988), 66

Goss v. Lopez, 419 U.S. 565, 95 S.Ct. 729, 42 L.Ed.2d 725 (1975), 44

Gratz v. Bollinger, 539 U.S. 244, 123 S.Ct. 2411, 156 L.Ed.2d 257 (2003), 333

Grutter v. Bollinger, 539 U.S. 306, 123 S.Ct. 2325, 156 L.Ed.2d 304 (2003), **319**

Harper v. Poway, No. 04CV1103 JAH (POR) (S.D.Cal.2008), 157

Harper v. Poway Unified School Dist., 445 F.3d 1166 (9th Cir. 2006), 160

Hazelwood School Dist. v. Kuhlmeier, 484 U.S. 260, 108 S.Ct. 562, 98 L.Ed.2d 592 (1988), **141**

Head v. Chicago School Reform Bd. of Trustees, 225 F.3d 794 (7th Cir.2000), **920**

Healy v. James, 408 U.S. 169, 92 S.Ct. 2338, 33 L.Ed.2d 266 (1972), **188**

Helena Elementary School Dist. No. 1 v. State, 236 Mont. 44, 769 P.2d 684 (Mont.1989), 445

Henkle v. Gregory, 150 F.Supp.2d 1067 (D.Nev.2001), **183**

Hill v. National Collegiate Athletic Assn., 26 Cal.Rptr.2d 834, 865 P.2d 633 (Cal.1994), 95

Hobson v. Hansen, 269 F.Supp. 401 (D.D.C 1967), **364**

Hoff v. Vacaville Unified School Dist., 80 Cal. Rptr.2d 811, 968 P.2d 522 (Cal.1998), 14, 20

Horton v. Meskill, 172 Conn. 615, 376 A.2d 359 (Conn.1977), 445

Hosty v. Carter, 412 F.3d 731 (7th Cir.2005), 146

Husain v. Springer, 494 F.3d 108 (2nd Cir. 2007), **197**

Ingraham v. Wright, 430 U.S. 651, 97 S.Ct. 1401, 51 L.Ed.2d 711 (1977), 44

In re (see name of party)

Jacobs v. Clark County School Dist., 526 F.3d 419 (9th Cir.2008), 146

James v. Board of Ed. of Central Dist. No. 1 of Towns of Addison et al., 461 F.2d 566 (2nd Cir.1972), 957

Jenkins v. Talladega City Bd. of Educ., 95 F.3d 1036 (11th Cir.1996), 87

J.N.Y., In re, 931 A.2d 685 (Pa.Super.2007), 87

Jonathan L. v. Superior Court, 81 Cal.Rptr.3d 571 (Cal.App. 2 Dist.2008), 703

Kahn v. East Side Union High School Dist., 4 Cal.Rptr.3d 103, 75 P.3d 30 (Cal.2003), 27

Karp v. Becken, 477 F.2d 171 (9th Cir.1973), 134

Kavanagh v. Trustees of Boston University, 440 Mass. 195, 795 N.E.2d 1170 (Mass. 2003), **66**

K.C.B., In re, 141 S.W.3d 303 (Tex.App.-Austin 2004), 87

Kentucky Retirement Systems v. E.E.O.C., ___ U.S. ___, 128 S.Ct. 2361, 171 L.Ed.2d 322 (2008), 983

Kitzmiller v. Dover Area School Dist., 2005 WL 3565563 (M.D.Pa.2005), 759

Konop v. Northwestern School Dist., 26 F.Supp.2d 1189 (D.S.D.1998), 87

Lamb v. Holmes, 162 S.W.3d 902 (Ky.2005), 87

Larry P. v. Riles, 343 F.Supp. 1306 (N.D.Cal. 1972), **583**

Larry P. By Lucille P. v. Riles, 793 F.2d 969 (9th Cir.1984), **584**

Lau v. Nichols, 414 U.S. 563, 94 S.Ct. 786, 39 L.Ed.2d 1 (1974), **509**

LaVine v. Blaine School Dist., 257 F.3d 981 (9th Cir.2001), 134

Lawrence v. Texas, 539 U.S. 558, 123 S.Ct. 2472, 156 L.Ed.2d 508 (2003), 301, 975

League of United Latin American Citizens v. Wilson, 908 F.Supp. 755 (C.D.Cal. 1995), **421**

Lee v. Weisman, 505 U.S. 577, 112 S.Ct. 2649, 120 L.Ed.2d 467 (1992), **655**

Leebaert v. Harrington, 332 F.3d 134 (2nd Cir.2003), 785

Lloyd v. Alpha Phi Alpha Fraternity, 1999 WL 47153 (N.D.N.Y.1999), 65

Lopez v. Southern Cal. Rapid Transit Dist., 221 Cal.Rptr. 840, 710 P.2d 907 (Cal.1985), 14

Lynch v. Donnelly, 465 U.S. 668, 104 S.Ct. 1355, 79 L.Ed.2d 604 (1984), 638

Mainstream Loudoun v. Board of Trustees of Loudoun County Library, 24 F.Supp.2d 552 (E.D.Va.1998), 801

Mainstream Loudoun v. Board of Trustees of Loudoun County Library, 2 F.Supp.2d 783 (E.D.Va.1998), **795**

Marcus v. Rowley, 695 F.2d 1171 (9th Cir. 1983), **823**

Martinez v. Regents of University of California, 83 Cal.Rptr.3d 518 (Cal.App. 3 Dist. 2008), 425

Mayer v. Monroe County Community School Corp., 474 F.3d 477 (7th Cir.2007), 954

Mayer v. Monroe County Community School Corp., 2006 WL 693555 (S.D.Ind.2006), 954

McDuffy v. Secretary of Executive Office of Educ., 415 Mass. 545, 615 N.E.2d 516 (Mass.1993), 445

McIntyre v. Ohio Elections Com'n, 514 U.S. 334, 115 S.Ct. 1511, 131 L.Ed.2d 426 (1995), **113**

Mellen v. Bunting, 327 F.3d 355 (4th Cir. 2003), **664**

Metro–Goldwyn–Mayer Studios Inc. v. Grokster, Ltd., 545 U.S. 913, 125 S.Ct. 2764, 162 L.Ed.2d 781 (2005), 872, **873**

Milo M., Commonwealth v., 433 Mass. 149, 740 N.E.2d 967 (Mass.2001), **237**

Morrison v. State Board of Education, 82 Cal.Rptr. 175, 461 P.2d 375 (Cal.1969), **913**

Morse v. Frederick, ___ U.S. ___, 127 S.Ct. 2618, 168 L.Ed.2d 290 (2007), **148**

Morse v. Lower Merion School Dist., 132 F.3d 902 (3rd Cir.1997), 46

Mozert v. Hawkins County Bd. of Educ., 827 F.2d 1058 (6th Cir.1987), **763**

Nabozny v. Podlesny, 92 F.3d 446 (7th Cir. 1996), **291**

Neal v. Board of Trustees of California State Universities, 198 F.3d 763 (9th Cir. 1999), **391**

New Jersey v. T.L.O., 469 U.S. 325, 105 S.Ct. 733, 83 L.Ed.2d 720 (1985), **73**

Nichol v. ARIN Intermediate Unit 28, 268 F.Supp.2d 536 (W.D.Pa.2003), 979

Nuxoll v. Indian Prairie School Dist. # 204, 523 F.3d 668 (7th Cir.2008), 157, 161

Owasso Independent School Dist. No. I–011 v. Falvo, 534 U.S. 426, 122 S.Ct. 934, 151 L.Ed.2d 896 (2002), **99**

Parents Involved in Community Schools v. Seattle School Dist. No. 1, ___ U.S. ___, 127 S.Ct. 2738, 168 L.Ed.2d 508 (2007), **339**

Parents United For Better Schools, Inc. v. School Dist. of Philadelphia Bd. of Educ., 148 F.3d 260 (3rd Cir.1998), 784

Parker v. Hurley, 514 F.3d 87 (1st Cir.2008), **772**

Pauley v. Kelly, 162 W.Va. 672, 255 S.E.2d 859 (W.Va.1979), 445

Peck ex rel. Peck v. Baldwinsville Central School Dist., 426 F.3d 617 (2nd Cir.2005), **724**

Perry v. Sindermann, 408 U.S. 593, 92 S.Ct. 2694, 33 L.Ed.2d 570 (1972), **907**

Peterson v. San Francisco Community College Dist., 205 Cal.Rptr. 842, 685 P.2d 1193 (Cal.1984), **47**

Peter W. v. San Francisco Unified Sch. Dist., 60 Cal.App.3d 814, 131 Cal.Rptr. 854 (Cal.App. 1 Dist.1976), **428**

Phaneuf v. Fraikin, 448 F.3d 591 (2nd Cir. 2006), 87

Pickering v. Board of Ed. of Tp. High School Dist. 205, Will County, Illinois, 391 U.S. 563, 88 S.Ct. 1731, 20 L.Ed.2d 811 (1968), **927**

Pitts v. Freeman, 887 F.2d 1438 (11th Cir. 1989), 433

Plyler v. Doe, 457 U.S. 202, 102 S.Ct. 2382, 72 L.Ed.2d 786 (1982), **416**

Ponce v. Socorro Independent School Dist., 508 F.3d 765 (5th Cir.2007), 157, **271**

Princeton University Press v. Michigan Document Services, Inc., 99 F.3d 1381 (6th Cir.1996), **836**

Redding v. Safford Unified School Dist. No.1, 531 F.3d 1071 (9th Cir.2008), 84

Reno v. American Civil Liberties Union, 521 U.S. 844, 117 S.Ct. 2329, 138 L.Ed.2d 874 (1997), 807

Robinson v. Cahill, 62 N.J. 473, 303 A.2d 273 (N.J.1973), 445

Romer v. Evans, 517 U.S. 620, 116 S.Ct. 1620, 134 L.Ed.2d 855 (1996), 979

Rose v. Council for Better Educ., Inc., 790 S.W.2d 186 (Ky.1989), **439**, 444

Rosenberger v. Rector & Visitors of Univ. of Va., 515 U.S. 819, 115 S.Ct. 2510, 132 L.Ed.2d 700 (1995), **192, 720**

Rothberg, United States v., 2002 WL 171963 (N.D.Ill.2002), 863

Sacramento City Unified School Dist., Bd. of Educ. v. Rachel H., 14 F.3d 1398 (9th Cir.1994), **572**

San Antonio Independent School Dist. v. Rodriguez, 411 U.S. 1, 93 S.Ct. 1278, 36 L.Ed.2d 16 (1973), **309, 455**

San Francisco NAACP v. San Francisco Unified School Dist., 576 F.Supp. 34 (N.D.Cal. 1983), 431

Santa Fe Independent School Dist. v. Doe, 530 U.S. 290, 120 S.Ct. 2266, 147 L.Ed.2d 295 (2000), 648, 662

Saxe v. State College Area School Dist., 240 F.3d 200 (3rd Cir.2001), 134

School Bd. of Nassau County, Florida v. Arline, 480 U.S. 273, 107 S.Ct. 1123, 94 L.Ed.2d 307 (1987), 983

School District of City of Pontiac v. Secretary of United States Dept. of Educ., 512 F.3d 252 (6th Cir.2008), 463

Serrano v. Priest (Serrano II), 135 Cal.Rptr. 345, 557 P.2d 929 (Cal.1976), 445, 455

Shaul v. Cherry Valley–Springfield Cent. School Dist., 218 F.Supp.2d 266 (N.D.N.Y. 2002), **819**

Sony Corp. of America v. Universal City Studios, Inc., 464 U.S. 417, 104 S.Ct. 774, 78 L.Ed.2d 574 (1984), 811

Southeastern Community College v. Davis, 442 U.S. 397, 99 S.Ct. 2361, 60 L.Ed.2d 980 (1979), **598**

Steere v. George Washington University School of Medicine and Health Sciences, 439 F.Supp.2d 17 (D.D.C.2006), **612**

Steffes v. California Interscholastic Federation, 176 Cal.App.3d 739, 222 Cal.Rptr. 355 (Cal.App. 2 Dist.1986), **383**

Straights and Gays for Equality (SAGE) v. Osseo Area Schools–Dist. No. 279, 471 F.3d 908 (8th Cir.2006), 183

Tanja H. v. Regents of University of California, 228 Cal.App.3d 434, 278 Cal.Rptr. 918 (Cal. App. 1 Dist.1991), 53

Tarasoff v. Regents of University of California, 131 Cal.Rptr. 14, 551 P.2d 334 (Cal. 1976), **227**

Texas, United States v., 572 F.Supp.2d 726 (E.D.Tex.2008), **519**

Thomas v. Clayton County Bd. of Educ., 94 F.Supp.2d 1290 (N.D.Ga.1999), 87

Thomas v. Roberts, 261 F.3d 1160 (11th Cir. 2001), 87

Tinker v. Des Moines Independent Community School Dist., 393 U.S. 503, 89 S.Ct. 733, 21 L.Ed.2d 731 (1969), **129, 134**

Turner v. Association of American Medical Colleges, 85 Cal.Rptr.3d 94 (Cal.App. 1 Dist. 2008), 619

United States v. _____ (see opposing party)
Universal City Studios, Inc. v. Corley, 273 F.3d 429 (2nd Cir.2001), 869
Universal City Studios, Inc. v. Reimerdes, 111 F.Supp.2d 294 (S.D.N.Y.2000), 868
University of Colorado v. Derdeyn, 863 P.2d 929 (Colo.1993), 95
Urofsky v. Gilmore, 216 F.3d 401 (4th Cir. 2000), **960**

Valeria v. Davis, 320 F.3d 1014 (9th Cir.2003), 529
Valeria v. Davis, 307 F.3d 1036 (9th Cir.2002), 529
Virginia, United States v., 518 U.S. 515, 116 S.Ct. 2264, 135 L.Ed.2d 735 (1996), **397**

Wallace v. Jaffree, 472 U.S. 38, 105 S.Ct. 2479, 86 L.Ed.2d 29 (1985), **631**
Washakie County School Dist. No. One v. Herschler, 606 P.2d 310 (Wyo.1980), 445
Washington v. Indiana High School Athletic Ass'n, Inc., 181 F.3d 840 (7th Cir. 1999), **387**
Weaver v. Nebo School Dist., 29 F.Supp.2d 1279 (D.Utah 1998), 976
Weingarten v. Board of Educ. of City School Dist. of City of New York, 2008 WL 4620573 (S.D.N.Y.2008), **954**

Weinstein v. University of Illinois, 811 F.2d 1091 (7th Cir.1987), **815**
West v. Derby Unified School Dist. No. 260, 206 F.3d 1358 (10th Cir.2000), 135
West Virginia State Board of Education v. Barnette, 319 U.S. 624, 63 S.Ct. 1178, 87 L.Ed. 1628 (1943), **705**
Williams v. State, Cal. Super. Ct. No. 312236 (Filed May 2000, Settled August 2004), **455**
Williams v. Weisser, 273 Cal.App.2d 726, 78 Cal.Rptr. 542 (Cal.App. 2 Dist.1969), **812**
Williams by Williams v. Ellington, 936 F.2d 881 (6th Cir.1991), 87
Wisconsin v. Yoder, 406 U.S. 205, 92 S.Ct. 1526, 32 L.Ed.2d 15 (1972), **696**
Wisniewski v. Board of Educ. of Weedsport Cent. School Dist., 494 F.3d 34 (2nd Cir.2007), **267**
Wygant v. Jackson Bd. of Educ., 476 U.S. 267, 106 S.Ct. 1842, 90 L.Ed.2d 260 (1986), 971

York v. Wahkiakum School Dist. No. 200, 163 Wash.2d 297, 178 P.3d 995 (Wash.2008), 95
Young v. Montgomery County (Alabama) Bd. of Educ., 922 F.Supp. 544 (M.D.Ala.1996), 386

Zelman v. Simmons–Harris, 536 U.S. 639, 122 S.Ct. 2460, 153 L.Ed.2d 604 (2002), 492, **678**
Zobrest v. Catalina Foothills School Dist., 509 U.S. 1, 113 S.Ct. 2462, 125 L.Ed.2d 1 (1993), **676**
Zukle v. Regents of University of California, 166 F.3d 1041 (9th Cir.1999), **604**

*

EDUCATION AND THE LAW
Second Edition

*

CHAPTER I

INTRODUCTION: CONTEXT FOR EXAMINING EDUCATION-RELATED DISPUTES

■ ■ ■

Education Law has emerged today as a bona fide area of specialization, both within the legal community and within the education community. Its major topical areas, which continue to grow and change, are derived from some of the most volatile controversies of our times. The primary focus of the field is public education, with issues spanning both the K–12 and the higher education sectors.

Almost every education-related legal dispute is accompanied by important public policy considerations. These considerations include not only the general policy context for the dispute, but also the policy implications of any proposed resolution. Thus it is not surprising that a rich body of Education Law scholarship can be identified, with cutting-edge literature continuing to be published in both legal and education journals, and significant books being written about these issues on a regular basis.

Education continues to be a central area of concern for political leaders, policy makers, and of course individuals across the nation, with legal issues comprising an integral part of almost every area of education today. Given the ongoing increase in education-related litigation and legislation, it is also not surprising that the opportunities for practicing in this area continue to grow exponentially. It is an area rich with possibility, and there is great opportunity for creativity on all levels.

A. SOURCES, INTERDISCIPLINARY FEATURES, & UNIQUE CHARACTERISTICS OF EDUCATION LAW

In general, the sources of Education Law include constitutions, statutes, case law, regulations, and policies. This list does constitute a hierarchy, with the constitution, for example, superseding any inconsistent statutes, case decisions, regulations, and policies. International treaties

1

and collective bargaining agreements may also need to be factored in, depending on the nature of the particular dispute.

Education Law is an interdisciplinary field, and education-related cases can generate issues in a number of traditional legal areas simultaneously. A large percentage of the disputes fall within the category of constitutional law, and other areas that might be implicated include criminal law and procedure, torts, and remedies. In addition, particularly in the employment context, issues of contract law and civil procedure may arise. The interface between case law and statutory frameworks is often at the heart of the dispute, with questions of statutory interpretation sometimes playing a central role.

Unless a controversy is specifically covered by statute, the relevant legal principles are typically the same at both the K–12 and the higher education levels. Yet these principles are often applied in very different ways depending on the setting and the age of the students. Often the question arises as to the precedential value of a given case decision at a grade level other than the one addressed. Sometimes, for example, the courts have recognized the applicability of major K–12 decisions to higher education disputes, and sometimes higher education cases have been deemed directly applicable at the K–12 level. Other times, however, the courts distinguish cases based on which grade level was initially addressed, on the grounds that the settings are very different. Patterns are often difficult to discern in this regard.

Finally, it is important to note that while education was traditionally seen as primarily the province of the states, there has been a major shift in this regard in recent years, particularly at the K–12 level. Education is not even mentioned in the U.S. Constitution, while it is typically a central feature of individual state constitutions. There was no separate U.S. Department of Education until the late 1970's. Yet with the passage of the bipartisan "No Child Left Behind" legislation by Congress in 2001, the entire dynamic shifted. Suddenly the federal government was seeking to play a central role in public education, defining the obligations of state and local educational agencies, and establishing draconian penalties for the failure to comply. This new and dramatic story is still continuing to unfold.

B. PATTERNS, TRENDS, AND CASEBOOK ORGANIZATION

Education Law is an evolving field, and the controversies that are being addressed today are often very different from those education-related issues that were being confronted by the legal community twenty and thirty years ago. The controversies may also be much broader in scope, embodying the range of "front-burner" disputes that are on the minds of many Americans on a day-to-day basis. The organization of this casebook is designed to reflect these emerging patterns and trends.

Each of the ten substantive chapters in the casebook is designed to stand on its own, and the inquiry in any given chapter is not necessarily dependent on having first read the material in the previous chapters. But Chapters 2–9 can be viewed as constituting three clearly defined thematic groupings that exemplify recent developments. And the ten chapters together reflect five major areas of inquiry, as follows:

- *Chapters 2, 3 & 4*
  campus safety issues and related efforts to protect student privacy and freedom of expression in that context

- *Chapters 5, 6 & 7*
  parameters of the right to equal educational opportunity and related efforts to increase educational quality for all students

- *Chapters 8 & 9*
  religion, morality, and values in public education

- *Chapter 10*
  intellectual property issues in education, as reflected in volatile disputes regarding copyright in the higher education community

- *Chapter 11*
  rights of educators in the interrelated areas of labor relations, tenure, dismissal, academic freedom, and employment discrimination

The casebook begins with a focus on campus safety, because if the schools are not safe, then arguably little else matters. Chapter 2 also introduces the range of privacy-related issues that arise in education, and the built-in tension between efforts to maximize safety and efforts to address privacy interests. Chapter 3 provides an overview of First Amendment student "freedom of expression" principles, and highlights the extent to which safety concerns are reflected in the legal frameworks that have emerged. Chapter 4 then turns to the changing nature of efforts to combat threatening behavior, peer harassment, and peer mistreatment, and notes just how much this relatively new area of the law has been fueled by such watershed events as the tragic school shootings at Columbine High School and the September 11, 2001 attacks on the nation.

Chapter 5 shifts the focus to the right to equal educational opportunity, and to the range of disputes that continue to be litigated in that context, including but not limited to ongoing efforts to maximize equal access and equal treatment for students on the basis of race, ethnicity, and gender. Chapter 6 turns to the related topic of educational quality, documenting an emerging area of the law that is reflected in efforts—sometimes at cross purposes—to ensure educational "adequacy" through school finance litigation, guarantee accountability through the U.S. "No Child Left Behind" Act, increase school choice through charter schools or even vouchers, and facilitate privatization across the board. Chapter 7 follows by examining the legal and policy debates regarding the unmet needs of English learners and students with disabilities, debates that encompass issues of equity *and* educational quality.

Chapter 8 provides an overview of First Amendment principles in the area of religion, and documents the central role of education-related disputes in shaping Establishment Clause jurisprudence, especially with regard to school prayer and public funding for private sectarian education. Chapter 9 then turns to recent debates relating to "morality" and values, focusing in particular on paradigmatic controversies such as the text of the flag salute, disputed access to campus forums and facilities, the context for the teaching of evolution, the nature of the values that should be taught in public schools, the extent to which certain topics should be included in the curriculum, and the parameters of sex education in general.

Chapter 10 addresses copyright issues in education, a topic that exemplifies an increasing focus on intellectual property disputes in this country generally. The chapter provides an overview of basic principles in this area, examines traditional disputes regarding ownership and fair use, and then turns to the range of unresolved controversies relating to the digitization of information that have emerged over the past twenty years as the Internet became a central feature of virtually everyone's daily life in higher education.

Chapter 11 concludes with a separate inquiry into the panoply of educator rights that have been recognized through collective bargaining laws, tenure statutes, protections against arbitrary dismissal, victories in First Amendment cases, and noteworthy prohibitions against employment discrimination. Academic freedom emerges as a surprisingly complex topic in this area, with the parameters of the "freedom" neither as precise nor as sweeping as many educators believe.

Over fifty hypothetical problems are included throughout the case-book, designed to help focus the inquiry and supplement the questions raised in the materials generally. While most of these are traditional legal hypotheticals, many contain related policy questions that seek to highlight important contextual issues. And in certain instances, a given hypothetical may focus directly on educational policy matters that are at the very heart of a particular controversy.

C. THE CHALLENGE OF EFFECTING CHANGE IN AN EDUCATION SETTING

The study of Education Law would be incomplete without an acknowledgment of the complexities that are often prevalent behind the scenes. Particularly when change is sought with regard to how institutions operate and how educators act on a day-to-day level, these complexities can make it very difficult to effect any sort of lasting transformation.

Thus it is important to recognize that victories in the legal arena do not necessarily translate into substantive and effective change in the education arena. Indeed, a legal victory is often the first of many steps that may be necessary before stated goals are actually accomplished.

Not only do many educators distrust attorneys and question their understanding of education issues, but the educational system—as commentators have noted—is particularly resistant to change. For example, in certain settings, so many people may need to be informed of a legal requirement and so many levels of bureaucracy may be implicated that too often the persons who have the ability to actually make the changes may not be aware of what needs to be done. In addition, education officials responsible for monitoring relevant activity and enforcing compliance may have so many other responsibilities that it may not be humanly possible to do all that is being asked of them.

For many reasons, then, an education-related law may be "on the books," but there may be no mechanism in place for its enforcement. And even if strategies are developed and implemented to address compliance with court orders, decrees, statutory mandates, and regulatory requirements, these strategies may prove ineffective. For example:

- Funding may be unavailable to fully implement the strategies.

- Accountability measures designed to facilitate monitoring may be linked to standardized tests that provide a distorted or incomplete picture of day-to-day realities.

- Self-reporting mechanisms can lead to incomplete or even incorrect depictions of what is actually taking place.

- Sanctions, if implemented, may do more harm than good.

- External monitoring, if required, may be resisted, obfuscated, or even blocked... sometimes in subtle ways that are difficult to discern.

- Independent reports documenting failure to act or even a lack of compliance may end up sitting on the proverbial shelf, gathering dust, for example, in a court clerk's office, as months and years go by.

- Motions to enforce provisions of court orders or decrees pursuant to findings in legally mandated reports may be denied by courts.

- Political forces may compromise the ability of well-meaning people to act.

- The adversarial system may lead to educational institutions bringing in highly skilled attorneys to help them resist efforts to change.

None of these examples should discourage continued efforts to use the legal system to shape educational policy and improve quality of life for those involved. Indeed, much has changed in education as a result of efforts by members of the legal community. Education-related litigation has led to noteworthy victories, and education-related statutory schemes have proliferated. The impact of the law in this setting has indeed been far-reaching.

And often the lasting changes that do actually occur are the result of attorneys and educators working together—and not at cross purposes—to make those changes happen.

D. THE RIGHT TO AN EDUCATION

Many of the legal disputes that reach the courts in this field continue to directly or indirectly implicate the right to an education. Everyone agrees that there is such a right, but there is ongoing disagreement over its parameters.

The sources of the right to an education are many and varied. While the U.S. Constitution does not specifically mention education, many U.S. Supreme Court cases have determined—particularly under the First, Fourth, and Fourteenth Amendments—that students have the right to certain protections and guarantees in an education setting. On occasion, the Court actually does speak very precisely about both the content and the quality of the education that is expected, especially at the K–12 level.

One of the most widely recognized rights in this context is the right to equal educational opportunity. Consider the following description of the parameters of this right, originally written in 1989. What, if anything, would you change today?

The Continuing Vitality of the Right to Equal Educational Opportunity[a]

In *Brown v. Board of Education*, the Court held that under the Equal Protection Clause "the opportunity of an education . . . is a right which must be made available to all on equal terms." Most commentators and jurists have determined that this language validates a "right" to some form of "equal educational opportunity," with the subsequent debates centering on the definition of the term and on the extent to which a legal system can require or enforce equality of opportunity.

More than three decades later, Justice Marshall relied heavily on the language of Brown in his *Kadrmas* dissent, reproducing the most famous paragraph from Chief Justice Warren's opinion and concluding that the North Dakota statute authorizing the imposition of fees for transporting students infringes upon the right to equal opportunity. "In allowing a State to burden the access of poor persons to an education," he declared, "the Court denies equal opportunity and discourages hope. I do not believe the Equal Protection Clause countenances such a result." * * *

Marshall's focus on the right to equal educational opportunity as the key interest at stake in the North Dakota case reflects the continuing vitality of this right in the American legal system today. Indeed, the

---

a. *From* Stuart Biegel, *Reassessing the Applicability of Fundamental Rights Analysis: The Fourteenth Amendment and the Shaping of Educational Policy after Kadrmas v. Dickinson Public Schools,* 74 CORNELL L. REV. 1078, 1081–1084 (1989).

controversy regarding the parameters of the right has been at the center of many school-related disputes. Although not always mentioned explicitly, "denial of equal opportunity" is typically a central, underlying concern in fourteenth amendment litigation that involves such volatile areas as school desegregation, school finance, [the rights of students with disabilities] * * *, standardized testing, and bilingual education. * * *

The right to equal educational opportunity has become a strong and multi-faceted interest * * * When federal legislation establishing a separate Department of Education included a declaration that the new cabinet post had been set up "to strengthen the federal commitment to ensuring access to equal opportunity for every individual," Congress was simply affirming that this recognized right now occupied a position of central importance in educational policy making.

As discussed above, one of the most significant changes in this area has been the passage of the "No Child Left Behind" Act at the federal level. While this legislation has engendered great controversy, particularly with regard to its "accountability" provisions, many who join in criticism of certain provisions also believe that its focus on raising the bar for all students will serve to enhance the right to equal educational opportunity. In addition, commentators have suggested that the Act's explicit requirement that every school work toward proficiency for every student has strengthened the right to a quality education as well.

Other federal statutes, along with their accompanying regulations, continue to play an important role in guaranteeing rights for students. Civil rights statutes generally have been of central importance in guaranteeing equal access, and statutes addressing particular areas of education—including but not limited to the Individuals with Disabilities Education Act (IDEA)—have provided road maps that have led to significant improvement in many settings.

At the state court level, additional rights have been recognized under individual state constitutional provisions guaranteeing the availability of public education until a certain age. In addition, states have sometimes recognized broader protections for individual rights in this area, protections that go beyond the federal baseline. For example, while the U.S. Supreme Court, by a vote of 5–4, determined that education was not a fundamental right under the Fourteenth Amendment, a number of state courts have come to an opposite conclusion under their own constitutions.

The California Supreme Court was one of these institutions, holding in 1976 that education would be considered a fundamental right in California, at least within the context of equalizing public school finance. In 1992, the same Court was presented with the question of whether this fundamental right could be deemed to have broader applicability, beyond the narrower fact pattern of the 1970's litigation.

What might be the implications of a recognition that education is a fundamental constitutional right? Consider the following excerpt from the opinion of that Court, *Thomas K. Butt v. State of California,* 4 Cal.4th 668, 15 Cal.Rptr.2d 480, 842 P.2d 1240 (1992):

> In late April 1991, after a period of mounting deficits, the Richmond Unified School District (District) announced it lacked funds to complete the final six weeks of its 1990–1991 school term. The District proposed to close its doors on May 1, 1991.
>
> [A group of parents, represented by pro bono attorneys from the San Francisco office of Morrison Foerster and acting in concert with the California Department of Education's legal team, challenged the proposed closure as violative of the children's fundamental right to an education and obtained a preliminary injunction from Contra Costa County Superior Court. The injunction directed the State of California (State), its Controller, and its Superintendent of Public Instruction (SPI) to ensure that the District's students would receive a full school term or its equivalent.
>
> Rather than complying, the State of California, represented by the Governor and the Attorney General, chose to file an appeal.]
>
> We declined to stay implementation of the plan pending the State's appeal. However, we transferred the appeal here in order to decide an important issue of first impression: Whether the State has a constitutional duty, aside from the equal allocation of educational funds, to prevent the budgetary problems of a particular school district from depriving its students of "basic" educational equality.
>
> We affirm the trial court's determination that such a duty exists under the California Constitution.
>
> * * *
>
> Since its admission to the Union, California has assumed specific responsibility for a statewide public education system open on equal terms to all. The Constitution of 1849 directed the Legislature to "provide for a system of common schools, by which a school shall be kept up and supported in each district ...." That constitutional command, with the additional proviso that the school maintained by each district be "free," has persisted to the present day.
>
> * * * [T]he State itself has broad responsibility to ensure basic educational equality under the California Constitution. Because access to a public education is a uniquely fundamental personal interest in California, our courts have consistently found that the State charter accords broader rights against State-maintained educational discrimination than does federal law. Despite contrary federal authority, California constitutional principles require State assistance to correct basic "interdistrict" disparities in the system of common schools, even when the discriminatory effect was not produced by the purposeful conduct of the State or its agents. * * *

Hence, * * * [we declared, in 1976, that] "[i]n applying our state constitutional provisions guaranteeing equal protection of the laws we shall continue to apply strict and searching judicial scrutiny" to claims of discriminatory educational classifications. More recent cases confirm that education is a fundamental interest under the California equal protection guaranties and that the unique importance of public education in California's constitutional scheme requires careful scrutiny of state interference with basic educational rights.

* * * It therefore appears well settled that the California Constitution makes public education uniquely a fundamental concern of the State and prohibits maintenance and operation of the common public school system in a way which denies basic educational equality to the students of particular districts. The State itself bears the ultimate authority and responsibility to ensure that its district-based system of common schools provides basic equality of educational opportunity.

The State claims it need only ensure the six-month minimum term guaranteed by the free school clause. This contention, however, misconstrues the basis of the trial court's decision. Whatever the requirements of the free school guaranty, the equal protection clause precludes the State from maintaining its common school system in a manner that denies the students of one district an education basically equivalent to that provided elsewhere throughout the State. * * *

The State suggests there was no showing that the impact of the threatened closure on District students' fundamental right to basic educational equality was real and appreciable. Of course, the Constitution does not prohibit all disparities in educational quality or service. Despite extensive State regulation and standardization, the experience offered by our vast and diverse public school system undoubtedly differs to a considerable degree among districts, schools, and individual students. These distinctions arise from inevitable variances in local programs, philosophies, and conditions. "[A] requirement that [the State] provide [strictly] 'equal' educational opportunities would thus seem to present an entirely unworkable standard requiring impossible measurements and comparisons...." Moreover, principles of equal protection have never required the State to remedy all ills or eliminate all variances in service. * * *

Even unplanned truncation of the intended school term will not necessarily constitute a denial of "basic" educational equality. A finding of constitutional disparity depends on the individual facts. Unless the actual quality of the district's program, viewed as a whole, falls fundamentally below prevailing statewide standards, no constitutional violation occurs.

Here, however, plaintiffs' preliminary showing suggested that closure of the District's schools on May 1, 1991, would cause an extreme and unprecedented disparity in educational service and progress. District students faced the sudden loss of the final six weeks, or almost one-fifth, of the standard school term originally intended by the District and provided everywhere else in California. The record indicates that the decision to close early was a desperate, unplanned response to the District's impending insolvency and the impasse in negotiations for further emergency State aid. Several District teachers declared that they were operating on standard-term lesson schedules made at the beginning of the school year. These declarants outlined in detail how the proposed early closure would prevent them from completing instruction and grading essential for academic promotion, high school graduation, and college entrance. Faced with evidence of such extensive educational disruption, the trial court did not abuse its discretion by concluding that the proposed closure would have a real and appreciable impact on the affected students' fundamental California right to basic educational equality. * * *

In addition to the decisions of state courts, state legislatures have also delineated rights for students in the area of education beyond the federal baseline. These rights have included, but are not limited to, protection against discrimination and mistreatment on the basis of race, ethnicity, gender, age, disability, religion, and lesbian, gay, bisexual, and transgender (LGBT) status. State legislation and accompanying regulations also provide many specific programmatic guarantees, both in the area of curriculum generally as well as with regard to students with additional needs. The scope of state education codes, in particular, is typically very broad and wide-ranging.

Consider the following hypothetical, which takes place in the fictional state of Eldorado. Given the range of protections and guarantees that are available for students, what are your initial reactions to the questions presented?

PROBLEM 1: THE FUNDAMENTAL RIGHT TO AN EDUCATION

The Rainbow Ridge Unified School District grants permission to the Nanotech Valley Consortium to establish five charter schools for economically disadvantaged students. As envisioned, these schools would serve as models for the integration of wireless computer technology into the daily education program. Yet once the schools are open they are not only plagued by inconsistent connections, but they are constantly in the process of repairing unreliable equipment (much of it donated and relatively outdated). In addition, the faculty appears to have abandoned the teaching of basic skills in favor of an Internet-based curriculum which emphasizes analysis, synthesis, and creative problem solving.

When the state-mandated standardized test results are released the following summer, the students in all five charter schools score—on the average—in the 35th percentile in reading and in the 38th percentile in math (based on national percentile rankings). A group of parents, infuriated by these test results and by what they perceive to be a second rate education for their students, consult you for the purpose of filing a lawsuit on the grounds that their children's *fundamental right to an education* has been violated.

What arguments might you consider setting forth? What additional factual information might you wish to obtain? What would be an appropriate remedy under the circumstances? Or would you even consider taking such a case? Why?

CHAPTER II

CAMPUS SAFETY AND PRIVACY

■ ■ ■

This chapter addresses basic issues of safety in the education community. We begin with safety, because if campuses are not safe, little else matters. Education is invariably ineffective in an atmosphere of fear and distrust. But an analysis of safety issues, particularly in this era, is incomplete without a concurrent examination of privacy concerns. Indeed, both under the law and as a matter of policy, a perennial ongoing tension between safety concerns and privacy concerns continues to be evident in this country.

This tension is especially apparent in school settings, and has only increased after the 1999 shootings at Columbine High School and the attacks against the nation on September 11, 2001. And privacy issues have become even more pressing with the advent of the information age and continued advances in surveillance technology.

Chapter 2 begins with an examination of negligence, which continues to be the main area of the law implicated in a school safety context. Part A addresses liability at the K–12 level, and Part B addresses liability at the higher education level. Related statutes at both the federal and the state levels are also referenced in these sections. These include zero-tolerance statutes addressing weapons on campus and safety-related requirements under the "No Child Left Behind" Act.

The second half of the chapter focuses on privacy interests that may be compromised by efforts to maintain or increase campus safety. Part D addresses search and seizure issues, including but not limited to drug testing. Part E addresses student records, focusing in particular on the scope of protections available under the Family Educational Rights and Privacy Act (FERPA). Part F then turns to technology and privacy, examining both the range of Internet-related issues that continue to arise as well as recent developments in offline surveillance that will invariably lead to novel legal disputes.

It is important to note that incidents affecting campus safety often implicate multiple areas of the law. In addition to negligence, for example, issues may arise under the First Amendment Free Speech Clause, under threat law generally, and under laws specifically addressing peer harassment and mistreatment. We examine these additional areas of the law in the two chapters that follow.

A. LIABILITY FOR INJURIES AT THE K–12 LEVEL

PROBLEM 2: GREEN V. SUBURBIA SCH. DIST.

As the Suburbia High Senior Class Cabinet assembled in Room 190 for their weekly lunchtime meeting, Class Sponsor Fred Brown realized that he had forgotten to pack a sandwich. Having left these meetings several times before, Coach Brown did not hesitate to do so now. After all, the only people in the room were the school's top student leaders.

While he was in the cafeteria purchasing lunch, however, Sherry Marvin passed around a vial of cocaine and a silver spoon. Six of the eight students in the room (including Class President Amanda Green) ingested several "doses" of cocaine while Coach Brown was gone.

Amanda, who had permission to leave school to pick up supplies for the Senior Class Dance, departed before Coach Brown returned. Eight blocks from school, however, she drove her new 4Runner into a tree and suffered a variety of injuries, including a whiplash and a broken leg. She was hospitalized for three days, and missed two weeks of school.

Amanda "confessed" to her parents that she had indeed been under the influence of cocaine when the accident occurred. She also explained that this was the third time she had ingested cocaine . . . all three times coming on the Suburbia campus. In September, a classmate had shared the substance with her while they were dressing in the girls locker room after P.E., and in October a fellow class officer had given her several "hits" while seated in the bleachers watching a football game.

A.   What arguments would the Green family set forth under a negligence theory in a lawsuit against the Suburbia School District?

B.   Would the plaintiff's case be stronger or weaker if the following happened instead? Why? If the case went to trial, what result? Discuss.

   1. Students were sixth graders rather than high school seniors, and Amanda rode on roller skates instead of in her car. All other facts were the same.

   2. Coach Brown actually was in the room when the cocaine was ingested. All other facts were the same.

   3. Coach Brown left and an earthquake occurred; some students were injured.

   4. A gun was passed around, not cocaine; Amanda was injured in her car when the gun went off while she was examining it.

   5. A gun was passed around, not cocaine; a student was accidentally shot.

   6. It was not lunchtime, but class time. Coach Brown left the class with a student teacher in charge. All other facts were the same.

7. Two school dropouts (former students of Coach Brown) came into the room while he was gone. A fight ensued, and several students were injured.

1. STATE NEGLIGENCE LAW PRINCIPLES

Negligence cases are typically decided in state courts, under principles that are generally similar from place to place. Negligence has been defined as the breach of a duty of care, owed to the plaintiff, that is the actual and proximate cause of plaintiff's injury.

While school districts in general are no longer immune from lawsuits in this area, both the type and the extent of "sovereign immunity" protection vary from state to state. For example, in Illinois, immunity is granted in those situations where state actors are deemed to have been in a position where they were "exercising discretion." In Mississippi, immunity is granted if educators are deemed to have been using ordinary care in controlling students. In South Carolina, a public school district is generally not liable for injuries resulting from negligent supervision unless the supervising educator is "grossly negligent."[a] In California, however, if statutory liability can be established under provisions of the state's Government Code, a successful cause of action can often be maintained. As the California Supreme Court has stated, "the rule is liability; immunity is the exception."[b]

Assuming that the doctrine of sovereign immunity does not apply, educational institutions can generally be found liable for the negligence of their employees under the traditional doctrine of *respondeat superior*.[c]

At the K–12 level, on school grounds and during school hours, duty is typically not an issue. There is both a common law duty to supervise, and—in many states—a statutory duty to supervise. In general, the standard of care in carrying out this duty is deemed to be identical to that required of school personnel in the performance of their other duties. As a general rule, adults in these settings are held to that degree of care which a person of ordinary prudence, charged with comparable duties, would exercise under the same circumstances. These cases, therefore, often turn on an analysis of breach. If one student is injured by another (the most typical fact pattern), a breach of the school district's duty of care can generally be found in one of two ways: (1) failure to exercise proper

---

a. Todd A. DeMitchell, *The Educator and Tort Liability*, 154 ED. LAW REP. 417 (2001).

b. Lopez v. Southern Cal. Rapid Transit Dist., 40 Cal.3d 780, 792, 221 Cal.Rptr. 840, 710 P.2d 907, 914 (1985). In California, all government tort liability must be based on statute, and an aggrieved party must show that the District acted in violation of at least one provision "designed to protect against the risk of ... [that] particular kind of injury...." CAL. GOV'T CODE § 815.6 (West 2005). *See generally id.* at §§ 810–895.8.

c. *See, e.g.,* Hoff v. Vacaville Unified Sch. Dist., 19 Cal.4th 925, 80 Cal.Rptr.2d 811, 968 P.2d 522 (1998) (Mosk, J., concurring) ("[A] school district may be liable for the acts or omissions of school employees within the scope of employment 'if the act or omission would, apart from this section, have given rise to a cause of action against that employee.'").

supervision, and (2) directing or permitting pupils to engage in activities that might reasonably be foreseen to result in injuries.

Duty can be a major issue, however, if the injuries occur before school, after school, or near school, or if the injured party is not a student. Injuries during extracurricular activities can also raise troublesome questions regarding the duty owed. And circumstances surrounding a school shooting can be particularly complex in this regard.

The cases and problems that follow wrestle with the parameters of the duty owed in these types of situations.

A.   EXTENT OF THE DUTY TO SUPERVISE

GLASER v. EMPORIA UNIFIED SCH. DIST. NO. 253

271 Kan. 178, 21 P.3d 573 (2001)

ALLEGRUCCI, J.:

This is a personal injury action brought on behalf of Todd Glaser, a seventh-grader at Lowther Middle School in Emporia, Kansas. When he was chased by another student, he ran off school grounds into a public street. He was injured in a collision with a car driven by Patricia Gould–Lipson. Glaser settled his claims against the driver, [but prosecuted a lawsuit against the District]. * * *

* * * The only factual findings the district court determined to be necessary to its decision are the following:

1.   The plaintiff was injured when he collided with an automobile on the 22nd day of December 1993.

2.   Prior to the collision, the plaintiff was on school property that was unsupervised by Emporia Unified School District No. 253 employees.

3.   The collision between the plaintiff and an automobile driven by Patricia Gould–Lipson occurred prior to classes beginning, and the collision occurred on a public street adjacent to school property.

The district court also noted that it was undisputed that the school district "does not exercise supervision before school until a student is in the building."

On appeal, both parties supply additional facts with references to the record. The following "additional facts" are not disputed:

On December 22, 1993, Glaser was a 12-year-old seventh-grade student at Lowther South. He lived approximately a 15- to 20-minute walk from school, and he normally got to school by walking. School began at 8:10 a.m. On the day he was injured, Glaser arrived at school between 7:30 a.m. and 7:45 a.m.

A school district policy, which was approved June 22, 1993, provided: "Teachers who observe students in a potentially dangerous situation should attempt, as they are reasonably able, either to halt or prevent injury to students or property."

The sole issue on appeal is whether the school district owed a duty to Glaser under the circumstances.

* * *

Cases cited by Glaser from other jurisdictions include *Raymond v. Paradise Unified School Dist.*, 218 Cal.App.2d 1, 31 Cal.Rptr. 847 (1963); *Tymkowicz v. San Jose, Etc. Unified School Dist.*, 151 Cal.App.2d 517, 312 P.2d 388 (1957); * * * *Titus v. Lindberg*, 49 N.J. 66, 228 A.2d 65 (1967); and *Rice v. School District No. 302, Pierce Co.*, 140 Wash. 189, 248 Pac. 388 (1926). The general principle for which Glaser cites these cases is that schools and school personnel have a duty to protect the safety of students.

In the New Jersey case, a 9-year-old student named Titus was on the grounds of his school, headed for the rack to put up the bicycle that he had ridden there, when he was struck by a paper clip shot from an elastic band by 13-year-old Lindberg. The principal of Titus' school "stated flatly that he maintained 'supervision outside the building on the grounds between eight and 8:30.' " For the reason that the principal "assumed the responsibility for supervising the school grounds beginning at 8 a.m.," the New Jersey court rejected the argument that his responsibilities did not begin before 8:15. The New Jersey court gave an additional reason:

They customarily began coming at 8 a.m and that was reasonable. Smith [, the principal,] undoubtedly knew of their coming and of their 'keep away' games. When all this is coupled with the fact that Fairview was also a pickup site for the older students, the dangers and the need for reasonable supervision from 8 a.m. on were entirely apparent.

Titus could be distinguished from the present case on the ground that Lowther Middle School was not a designated pickup site for older students. * * *

In *Tymkowicz*, a 10-year-old student died from injuries sustained on the school grounds while he was engaged in a game with other students. The object of the game was to render a participant unconscious. The principal admitted knowing that the game was played, and there was no evidence of any efforts by school authorities to stop the game. The California Education Code contained a provision requiring that "[e]very teacher in the public schools shall hold pupils to a strict account for their conduct ... on the playgrounds, or during recess." The distinction with the present case is obvious. The injury occurred during recess, on school grounds, and we have no comparable statute.

* * *

In *Raymond*, a 7-year-old boy waited on the grounds of the high school for the school bus that took him to his elementary school. He was injured when he ran toward the bus before it came to a halt, placed his left hand on the side of the bus, and fell backward on the sidewalk. The jury found that the school district was negligent in failing to provide for supervision of the bus boarding area. A basis on which the appellate court affirmed the judgment were statutory provisions obliging the school district, once it furnished transportation for students, to provide a reasonably safe system. Other considerations were: (1) that supervision of the bus stop on the grounds of the high school rather than in an isolated place was a practical possibility for the school district, (2) that it was a very busy stop, with up to three busloads of students arriving and departing there at peak periods, and (3) that small children were present.

Although there are some similarities between the present case and *Raymond,* differences prevail. The injured student in the California case, Raymond, was 7, and Glaser was a seventh-grader. Raymond was injured at a school district designated bus stop, and Glaser was injured when he ran off school grounds into a public street.

In *Rice,* an 11-year-old student was severely shocked and burned on the school grounds before classes began when he pulled on a radio aerial wire, which had broken after being installed for a PTA entertainment, and the radio wire dropped on electric wires. Earlier, several teachers passed by, saw Rice and other boys tugging on the broken wire, and told them to play elsewhere. In response, Rice played football for awhile before returning to the wire. School policy provided playground supervision for one-half hour before classes, but there was no supervision at the time of the injury. There was disputed evidence about whether the injury occurred within the period that should have been supervised. The disposition of the case in the student's favor, however, did not turn on the issue of supervision. The school district was charged with the duty "from the time the defendant had knowledge that the wire was dangling down and reaching the ground where pupils might take hold of it" to put the school grounds in a reasonably safe condition.

The present case does not involve an extraordinary, dangerous condition on the school grounds such as the one that existed in *Rice.* Nonetheless, Glaser quotes Section 364 of the Restatement (Second) of Torts, Creation or Maintenance of Dangerous Artificial Conditions (1964). Generally stated, § 364 provides that a landholder is subject to liability for injuries caused by a structure or other artificial condition created by the landholder or with his permission. Proximity to the public street and the absence of a fence seem to be the conditions complained of by Glaser. Neither would seem to be a structure or other artificial condition within the meaning of § 364. With regard to this claim, the trial court stated that Glaser "provides no evidence that would meet [this] duty * * *."

   * * *

Glaser asserts that his classroom was locked at the time of his injury, thus forcing him to remain outside on the unsupervised school grounds. There is nothing in the district court's findings of fact that would support the assertion. Nor does Glaser supply a reference to the record where his assertion is supported. The school district, on the other hand, furnished a reference to the record where there is evidence that Glaser had the option of waiting inside the school building where the school provided supervision before classes began. * * *

The district court found that neither the school district nor [teacher Douglas] Epp had assumed a duty to supervise Glaser. Glaser's contention that they had assumed a duty to supervise rests on written school district policies, including the following provisions: "Students shall be under the supervision of appropriate school personnel at all times when they are under the jurisdiction of the school," and "[t]eachers who observe students in a potentially dangerous situation should attempt, as they are reasonably able, either to halt or prevent injury to students or property." Glaser contends that the policies constitute "clear evidence" that the duty to prevent injury was not limited to the interior of the building or the time when classes are in session. He further contends that the policies demonstrate that the school district assumed a duty to protect students in any potentially dangerous situation. We disagree.

* * *

> Plaintiff would add that * * * [p]rior to the accident, a teacher for Lowther Middle School, Douglas Epp, observed Todd and Justin playing and running in an area not ten feet away from Congress street. Despite observing the students in a potentially dangerous situation, he took no action. He simply kept walking, even though he would later admit to Pagan Glaser that he thought "somebody was going to run out in that street and get hit by a car."

* * * [However,] the issue for this court is simply whether the school district, by adopting its written policies, assumed to protect the safety of students gathered on the school grounds before classes began. Epp's presence and conduct are not relevant to the court's review of the trial court's entry of summary judgment on the assumption of duty question.

The legal basis for Glaser's contention is Restatement (Second) of Torts § 324A (1964), and its interpretation in *Honeycutt* [*v. City of Wichita*, 251 Kan. 451, 836 P.2d 1128 (1992)] * * *.

[*Honeycutt* was a personal injury action brought on behalf of a minor in which summary judgment was granted in favor of the school district. This court affirmed. Jeremy Honeycutt attended morning kindergarten. Railroad tracks ran between his house and the school. He usually was taken or escorted to school by an adult, but on March 5, 1987, Jeremy and another student were walking home after school unaccompanied by an adult. Jeremy ran alongside a moving train and fell under the wheels.

Jeremy argued that the school district owed him three duties: "(1) to retain him until an authorized adult took custody of him, (2) to retain him on school property through a 'hold back' policy in the event of a train operating off school property, and (3) to establish a safety patrol at the railroad crossing." His bases for arguing that the school district owed him those duties were that the student-school district relationship created a duty and that the school district assumed a duty by its conduct and written policies.]

In [*rejecting plaintiff's argument*], the [*Honeycutt*] court engaged in an extensive discussion of § 324A * * * [.]

This court has accepted § 324A's theory of liability and established the following principles:

"The threshold requirement for the application of the Restatement (Second) of Torts § 324A (1964) is a showing that the defendant undertook, gratuitously or for consideration, to render services to another. In order to meet this requirement, the evidence must show the defendant did more than act, but *through affirmative action* assumed an obligation or intended to render services for the benefit of another.

"A duty is owed to third persons by one who undertakes, *by an affirmative act,* to render aid or services to another and then is negligent in the performance of that undertaking." "For a defendant to meet the threshold requirements of § 324A, the defendant must not only take affirmative action to render services to another, but the person to whom the services are directed *must accept such services* in lieu of, or in addition to, such person's obligation to perform the services."

"The extent of the undertaking should define the scope of the duty."

"[O]ne who does not assume an obligation to render services does not owe a duty to third persons."

* * *

In *Honeycutt,* the court rejected plaintiff's argument that the school district assumed a duty by its written policies.

Here, as in *Honeycutt,* the injury occurred off school premises and at a time when the student was not on school property or in school custody. Todd was injured after he ran off the school grounds, across a parking area and into a city street. The school district never undertook to render services calculated to protect or supervise Todd, either by affirmative acts or promise to act, nor was Todd under the control or in the custody of the school district. Thus, as in *Honeycutt,* there has been no showing that a student-school district duty existed.

Affirmed.

Notes

1. State courts are typically very deferential to school districts in negligence cases. As a general rule, only the most egregious set of circumstances result in school district liability. The principle that schools cannot be "insurers of safety" is articulated over and over again in case decisions. Courts

decide cases in this area on practical grounds, determining whether or not a school could reasonably be expected to prevent the particular injury under all the circumstances of the case. And implicit in these decisions is the recognition that educational institutions are almost always financially strapped, especially at the K–12 level.

2. In *Glaser,* the Kansas Court appeared to determine that the cases from other jurisdictions cited by the plaintiff were relatively easy to distinguish. Was this analysis justified? Why?

3. Would the Court have come to the same conclusion if the plaintiff had been in kindergarten rather than in seventh grade? Should it have come to the same conclusion?

4. Assume the same set of facts, except that instead of being hit by a car off school grounds, the plaintiff was hit by a car on school grounds. Would the decision have been the same? Should the decision have been the same? In light of this inquiry, should *Glaser* be characterized as a broad ruling, or a narrow and fact-specific ruling, in the end?

5. In *Hoff v. Vacaville Unified School District,* 19 Cal.4th 925, 80 Cal.Rptr.2d 811, 968 P.2d 522 (1998), the California Supreme Court considered the question of whether the school district owed a duty of care to a non-student who was walking across the street from the high school and sustained serious injuries when a 16-year-old student lost control of his car and slammed into him:

> In exiting the lot, Lozano had "floor[ed]" the accelerator, "peeled out" with the wheels "screeching," "fishtailed," and jumped the curb and hit Hoff, who was walking on the sidewalk across the street. Lozano had been driving for six months, had no history of misbehavior, and obeyed his school supervisors. *Id.* at 930.

The Court determined that neither a common law duty nor a state statutory duty ran to Hoff. Under common law, the Court analogized to the duty of parents to control their children:

> California follows the Restatement rule (Rest.2d Torts, § 316), which finds a "special relationship" between parent and child, and accordingly places upon the parent "a duty to exercise reasonable care so to control his minor child as to prevent [the child] from intentionally harming others or from so [behaving] * * * as to create an unreasonable risk of bodily harm to them, if the parent (a) knows or has reason to know that he has the ability to control his child, and (b) knows or should know of the necessity and opportunity for exercising such control." * * * Thus, knowledge of dangerous habits and ability to control the child are prerequisites to imposition of liability. * * * Only the manifestation of specific dangerous tendencies * * * triggers a parental duty to exercise reasonable care to control the minor child in order to prevent * * * harm to third persons. * * *

> * * * At common law, "[s]chool officials are said to stand *in loco parentis,* in the place of parents, to their students, with similar powers and responsibilities." Moreover, by statute, we measure school personnel's criminal liability for exercising physical control over students by the

standard applicable to parents. Given these similarities, any duty that school employees owe off-campus nonstudents should at least be no greater in scope than the duty that parents owe third persons. Accordingly, school personnel who neither know nor reasonably should know that a particular student has a tendency to drive recklessly owe no duty to off-campus nonstudents. *Id.* at 934–35.

Hoff was not referenced in *Glaser*. Would the decision have helped either party, or are the facts easily distinguishable?

6. Field trips and other school-sponsored, off-campus excursions and activities have long been a complex area of dispute within the parameters of negligence law. While the basic general rule is that school officials are not absolved of their responsibility to supervise students under such circumstances, the possibility of unfamiliar situations arising and unforeseen events occurring in field trip settings can make supervision much more challenging than it might be in the well-known and clearly delineated world of the school campus. Many districts have sought to limit or perhaps even absolve themselves of liability in this context by requiring parents to sign "permission slips" or "release forms." However, as Perry Zirkel explains, such forms do "not necessarily" protect a school and its employees from liability:

> [T]he form would have to be carefully drafted to waive liability and some states regard such waivers as void, based on public policy. For example, in [*Doe v. Archbishop Stepinac High Sch.*, 729 N.Y.S.2d 538 (App. Div. 2001),] a case where a student was injured on an overseas field trip, the court concluded that the release form was unenforceable because it did not clearly and unequivocally express the intention of the plaintiffs to relieve the school defendants from negligence liability. Perry A. Zirkel, *Liability for Field Trips: An Update*, Principal Magazine, Vol. 86, No. 5, at 12–14 (May/June 2007).

State legislatures, however, can take the affirmative step of creating absolute statutory immunity for injuries occurring during a field trip. California Education Code Section 35330, for example, provides such immunity, which has been construed as extending not only to school districts but also to district employees. *See Casterson v. Superior Ct.*, 101 Cal.App.4th 177, 123 Cal. Rptr.2d 637 (2002). Arguably implicit in such statutory schemes is the goal of encouraging educational institutions to continue to provide the unique learning opportunities for students that arise from exciting trips to new and different places. Too often, during this era, as Zirkel reports, school officials have hesitated to plan field trips because of fear of liability. *See id.*

PROBLEM 3: THE MARBURY MIDDLE SCHOOL LAWSUITS

Over a twenty-year period, Marbury Middle School—a fictional urban campus—developed a unique relationship with the Fred Korematsu Public Library. Both the school's main office and classroom facility and the public library were situated in the same complex, and when a combination of overcrowding and budget cutbacks led to the dismantling and closing down of the school's own library collection, a close working arrangement was established between the two separate institutions. Under this informal arrangement, all Marbury students received automatic borrowing privileges, later expanded to include free and unlimited use of the 15 computer terminals. Teachers brought their classes to the library on a regular basis pursuant to a schedule worked out by Korematsu librarians. And when the library installed unrestricted Internet access on all the terminals, students were able to benefit from this additional service as well.

In early February 2006, a major incident took place at the library involving Mrs. Parks' eighth grade English class and resulting in both computer damage and injuries. Parks, a tough disciplinarian whose calm and supportive personality meshed well with the 39 high-energy students, never had any trouble in class. The incident took place, however, on a day when she was not in school, due to an unexpected family emergency linked to the high winds that were buffeting the area. At the last minute, the school office contacted Mr. Purview, a retired teacher who sometimes assisted in the reading recovery classes. Purview was not walking well, but he agreed to come in and take the class for the day, knowing that Parks always left detailed lesson plans for substitutes in the unlikely event that she could not be there.

Things went fairly well throughout the morning, but everything changed when Purview took the 5th period eighth graders to the library after lunch as scheduled. Students jostled each other as they walked over, and several yelled so loudly that two other teachers had to leave their classrooms to quiet them down. In the library, they quickly ran over to the terminals, and some pushing occurred as students vied for the best seats. But before too long things had settled down, and most students worked on their Internet research projects. Purview, however, suddenly remembered that he needed to call his son to schedule a ride home, and asked Morrie to watch the students while he went to retrieve his cell phone. Morrie—a Korematsu employee and part-time poet—was everyone's favorite librarian.

Three minutes after Purview had left the room, Janie—angry at a Web site she had come across that questioned the war policies of the Bush Administration—gestured clumsily at the computer screen and accidentally knocked it over. The monitor fell to the floor, and landed on Sally's foot. Sally and Janie, who feuded constantly over everything from boyfriends to politics, immediately began pushing and shoving each other, knocking over three other monitors in the process. Several other students joined in the melee, including five members of the junior wrestling team. According to Morrie, it was unclear how many were actually fighting and how many were simply playing. Yet numerous injuries did occur, including one broken arm (Sally), and several cuts requiring stitches. In addition, Julio—a two-year-old who was in the library with his mother while these events occurred—was knocked out of his mother's arms and fell against a broken computer monitor, suffering injuries that required an overnight stay in the local hospital.

Negligence lawsuits are filed against the school district by both Sally's family and Julio's family. What arguments would be set forth by the plaintiffs in these respective lawsuits? What result?

B. SUPERVISION DURING EXTRACURRICULAR ACTIVITIES

CERNY v. CEDAR BLUFFS JUNIOR/SENIOR PUB. SCH.

267 Neb. 958, 679 N.W.2d 198 (2004)

Miller–Lerman, J.

* * *

[Cerny, a high school football player, brought this action against the school district, seeking damages for the alleged negligence of his coaches in allowing him to reenter a game after suffering a head injury, and then allowing him to participate in contact drill practice several days later.]

II.   Statement of Facts

* * *

In the fall of 1995, Cerny was a student at the School and a member of its football team. On the evening of Friday, September 15, 1995, he participated in a football game between Cedar Bluffs and Beemer high schools. Mitchell R. Egger was the head coach of the Cedar Bluffs team, and Robert M. Bowman was the assistant coach. Both held Nebraska teaching certificates with coaching endorsements.

Cerny fell while attempting to make a tackle during the second quarter of the Beemer game, striking his head on the ground. Although he felt dizzy and disoriented after the fall, Cerny initially remained in the game but took himself out after a few plays. He returned to the game during the third quarter. Subsequently, during football practice on Tuesday, September 19, Cerny was allegedly injured again when his helmet struck that of another player during a contact tackling drill.

There was conflicting evidence at trial regarding the symptoms experienced and communicated by Cerny during and after the Beemer game. Cerny testified that when he came out of the game, he told Egger and Bowman that he felt dizzy, disoriented, and extremely weak. Egger stated that Cerny complained of dizziness when he came off the field during the Beemer game. He also noted that Cerny was short of breath and had a tingling sensation in his neck. Egger stated that Bowman continued to monitor Cerny.

Bowman testified that Cerny did not complain of a headache when he left the game, but did state that he felt fuzzy or dizzy, that he had some burning in his shoulder, and that he could not catch his breath. Bowman attributed Cerny's dizziness to hyperventilation, not a head injury. Bowman stated that when Cerny came out of the game, Cerny made normal eye contact with Bowman and Cerny's speech and movement appeared normal. After catching his breath, Cerny appeared to Bowman to be in a normal emotional state. However, Bowman did recommend to Egger that

Cerny should get medical attention, but to his knowledge, no medical personnel examined Cerny that evening.

When Cerny asked to re-enter the game during the third quarter, Bowman observed that he seemed completely normal, exhibiting neither confusion, disorientation, nor abnormal speech. Bowman also noted that Cerny did not complain of a headache. Egger allowed Cerny to re-enter the game after observing that his color looked good, his eyes looked clear, and his speech was normal.

Cerny testified that he had a headache continuously from Friday night until the practice on Tuesday. However, there is conflicting evidence as to whether he reported this to his coaches. Cerny testified he told Bowman he had a headache during the bus ride home after the Beemer game. However, Bowman testified that during the bus ride, he asked Cerny how he felt, and Cerny replied "I feel good, Coach" and did not complain of a headache. . . . Cerny testified that he told his coaches before the Tuesday practice that he had a nagging headache all weekend, but on cross-examination, he admitted that he did not remember if he had told the coaches that he was feeling bad before practice. Egger testified that he did not talk to Cerny before the Tuesday practice and permitted him to participate because "I thought he was okay, just—he was okay Friday. At least in our eyes he was okay."

Dr. Thomas A. McKnight, a family practice physician who has treated Cerny since September 1995, and Dr. Richard Andrews, a neurologist to whom Cerny was referred by McKnight, both expressed opinions that Cerny suffered a concussion during the Friday night game; that he was still symptomatic at the practice on the following Tuesday; and that during the practice, he suffered a closed-head injury with second concussion syndrome. Andrews testified that the second blow to the head sustained during the practice was "the principal cause of [Cerny's] traumatic brain injury, and the sequelae as [they] exist now."

Cerny filed a personal injury action against the School under the Political Subdivisions Tort Claims Act, and in his amended petition (petition) alleged that the School, acting through its coaches, was negligent in a number of particulars, including "failing to adequately examine [Cerny] following his initial concussion . . . to determine the need for immediate qualified medical attention" and "allowing [Cerny] to return to play . . . without authorization from qualified medical personnel and without verifying it was safe to do so."

* * *

V.   ANALYSIS

* * *

2.   DISTRICT COURT'S FINDINGS OF FACT

* * * Cerny asserts that the district court erred (1) in its finding of fact as to what conduct was required to meet the applicable standard of care, (2) in its finding of fact that the coaches' decision to permit Cerny to reenter the game did not violate the applicable standard of care, and (3) in its resolution of the question of fact that the School was not negligent. Cerny is asserting on appeal that the evidence shows that Cerny's coaches, Mitchell Egger and Robert Bowman, acted negligently in failing to keep Cerny out of competition until after he had received clearance from a physician to play. * * *

As noted above, in *Cerny I,* we set forth the standard of care to be applied in this case. We stated that determining the standard of care to be applied in a particular case is a question of law, and we concluded that in the instant case, "[t]he applicable standard of care by which the conduct of the School's coaching staff should be judged is that of a reasonably prudent person holding a Nebraska teaching certificate with a coaching endorsement." Under the law-of-the-case doctrine, the applicable standard of care that the School's coaches were required to meet in this case has been conclusively established.

* * *

(a) Conduct Required to Meet Standard of Care

As noted above, on remand, after reviewing the evidence, the district court found that the conduct required of a reasonably prudent person holding a Nebraska teaching certificate with a coaching endorsement in 1995, when a player has sustained a possible head injury, was (1) to be familiar with the features of a concussion; (2) to evaluate the player who appeared to have suffered a head injury for the symptoms of a concussion; (3) to repeat the evaluation at intervals before the player would be permitted to reenter the game; and (4) to determine, based upon the evaluation, the seriousness of the injury and whether it was appropriate to let the player reenter the game or to remove the player from all contact pending a medical examination.

* * *

(b) Conformance With Standard of Care

In its evaluation of whether the coaches' conduct conformed to the standard of care, we note that the district court found that the evidence in the case showed that Bowman was familiar with the signs of a concussion. The district court found additional facts that showed that the coaches met the standard of care regarding evaluating Cerny at intervals and making their determination whether to permit Cerny to reenter the game.

The facts found by the district court include the following: The district court found that when Cerny removed himself from the game, he told Bowman that he was fuzzy and had tingling in his neck. The district court found that Bowman talked to Cerny continuously for 5 to 6 minutes and observed that Cerny did not have a vacant stare, responded normally to conversation, did not appear to be disoriented or confused, and did not complain of nausea, headache, or blurred vision. The district court also found that the record demonstrated that Bowman observed and talked to Cerny approximately 15 minutes after his initial evaluation and that during this second observation, Bowman noted that Cerny was oriented, breathing normally, speaking coherently, and not complaining of headache, dizziness, vision problems, or nausea. The district court also found that Bowman observed Cerny on the sidelines during the third quarter and that Bowman noted that Cerny appeared to be "100% normal"; that his responses were appropriate; that he did not seem confused or disoriented; that his speech was not incoherent or slurred; that his emotions were appropriate; that he did not complain of dizziness, unsteadiness, nausea, or headache; and that he told the coach he felt "fine." Based upon the foregoing, the district court found that Bowman evaluated Cerny for symptoms of a concussion and that Cerny was evaluated at intervals. Further, the district court found that Cerny was properly allowed to reenter the game.

With regard to whether the conduct of the coaches met the standard of care, we note that the record contains Stineman's testimony, in which he stated that the evaluations and actions taken by Egger and Bowman regarding Cerny were reasonable for Nebraska endorsed coaches on September 15, 1995. According to Stineman, Bowman's evaluation of Cerny during the Beemer football game and Egger's decision to permit Cerny to reenter the game were the actions that would have been taken by a reasonable Nebraska endorsed football coach under similar circumstances in 1995.

Given its findings of fact summarized above, the district court determined, inter alia, that "the conduct of the coaches in this matter comported with the standard of care required of reasonable [sic] prudent persons holding a Nebraska teaching certificate with a coach's endorsement. The court finds no negligence on the part of [the School]."

Although we recognize that the record contains evidence that could controvert the district court's findings of fact, we are required to consider the evidence in a light most favorable to the School. The district court's findings that the coaches' conduct met the standard of care and that the School was not negligent are supported by evidence and are not clearly wrong. Pursuant to our standard of review, we determine that there is sufficient evidence to sustain the district court's judgment.

Cerny's second, third, and fourth arguments are without merit. Further, we have considered all of Cerny's remaining arguments on appeal and determine that they are without merit.

VI. Conclusion

For the reasons stated above, the decision of the district court finding in favor of the School and dismissing Cerny's petition is affirmed.

AFFIRMED.

NOTES

1.   Not only have courts been much more likely to rule in favor of school districts generally in negligence cases, but they have also shown great deference to coaches, athletic directors, and sports programs . . . unless the actions in question vary dramatically from common practice. In a sense, it can be argued that the courts have deferred to the will of the majority in this context, given that so many Americans—particularly in certain parts of the country—love athletic competition and follow the exploits of individuals and teams with great interest on a regular basis. Yet many have argued that the legislatures and the courts need to dissociate themselves from the majority in this area and provide greater protection for young people whose sports-related injuries too often lead to devastating disabilities when they reach middle age. *See, e.g.*, Matthew J. Mitten, *Emerging Legal Issues in Sports Medicine*, 76 ST. JOHN'S L. REV. 5, 48–57 (2002).

2.   In *Kahn v. East Side Union High School District*, 31 Cal.4th 990, 4 Cal.Rptr.3d 103, 75 P.3d 30 (2003), the California Supreme Court considered the case of a 14-year-old plaintiff who, while participating in a competitive swim meet as a member of the junior varsity team, executed a practice dive into a shallow racing pool and broke her neck. Plaintiff "alleged that the injury was caused in part by the failure of her coach, a district employee, to provide her with any instruction in how to safely dive into a shallow racing pool. She also alleged lack of adequate supervision and further that the coach breached the duty of care owed to her by insisting that she dive at the swim meet despite her objections, her lack of expertise, her fear of diving, and the coach's previous promise to exempt her from diving." *Id.* at 995.

Showing the traditional deference to coaches and school sports programs, the Court explained that "because a significant part of an instructor's or coach's role is to challenge or 'push' a student or athlete to advance in his or her skill level and to undertake more difficult tasks, and because the fulfillment of such a role could be improperly chilled by too stringent a standard of potential legal liability, we conclude that the same general standard should apply in cases in which an instructor's alleged liability rests primarily on a claim that he or she challenged the player to perform beyond his or her capacity or failed to provide adequate instruction or supervision before directing or permitting a student to perform a particular maneuver that has resulted in injury to the student. A sports instructor may be found to have breached a duty of care to a student or athlete only if the instructor intentionally injures the student or engages in conduct that is reckless in the sense that it is 'totally outside the range of the ordinary activity' involved in teaching or coaching the sport." *Id.* at 996.

Even under this stringent standard, however, the Court concluded that "the totality of the circumstances precludes the grant of defendants' motion for summary judgment. Specifically, we refer to evidence of defendant coach's failure to provide plaintiff with training in shallow-water diving, his awareness of plaintiff's intense fear of diving into shallow water, his conduct in lulling plaintiff into a false sense of security by promising that she would not be required to dive at competitions, his last-minute breach of this promise in the heat of a competition, and his threat to remove her from competition or at least from the meet if she refused to dive. Plaintiff's evidence supports the conclusion that the maneuver of diving into a shallow racing pool, if not done correctly, poses a significant risk of extremely serious injury, and that there is a well-established mode of instruction for teaching a student to perform this maneuver safely." *Id.*

3. In *Curtis v. Board of Education of Sayre Public Schools*, 914 P.2d 656 (1995), the Oklahoma Supreme Court considered whether that state's very forgiving rules regarding immunity applied to protect the school district in a sports-related negligence lawsuit. Plaintiff parents sought damages against the school district after their twelve-year-old son was "severely injured when he was hit in the mouth with a baseball bat." *Id.* at 657. Apparently the student was instructed by his teacher to play the position of catcher, but was not supplied with a catcher's mask.

Ruling in favor of the school district, the Court—by a 5–4 vote—found that § 155(20) of the Oklahoma Governmental Tort Claims Act did in fact protect the District in this instance. § 155(20) provides:

> A political subdivision shall not be liable if a loss or claim results from:
> 20. Participation in or practice for any interscholastic *or other athletic contest* sponsored or conducted by or on the property of the state. * * *

The Court determined that "[a] physical education class softball game, sponsored by a public school and conducted on school property falls within the parameters of § 155(20), and the school is shielded from liability for losses resulting therefrom." *Id.* at 660.

4. The National Center for Catastrophic Sport Injury Research at the University of North Carolina, Chapel Hill, has been focusing on catastrophic football injuries since the 1970s. Its *Annual Survey of Catastrophic Football Injuries* "is part of a concerted effort put forth by many individuals and research organizations to reduce the steady increase of football head and neck injuries taking place during the 1960s and 1970s. The primary purpose of the research * * * is to make the game of football a safer sport."

The Center's *Annual Survey* for the years 1977–2007 tracks the incidence of different types of football injuries, with its greatest focus on injuries that cause permanent disabilities and what might be done proactively to prevent such injuries. It also tracks participation in football competition at all levels, and documents the extent to which students playing high school football continue to be at risk. For example, the survey found that:

> [over] the past 31 years there have been a total of 278 football players with incomplete neurological recovery from cervical cord injuries. Two hundred and twenty-nine of these injuries have been to high school players, thirty-three to college players, six to sandlot players and ten to professionals. This data indicate a reduction in the number of cervical cord injuries with incomplete neurological recovery when compared to data published in the early 1970s. National Center for Catastrophic Sport Injury Research, Annual Survey of Catastrophic Football Injuries (1977– 2007), University of North Carolina, Chapel Hill, www.unc.edu/depts/ nccsi/ (last accessed November 15, 2008).

While the data showed a disproportionate number of high school players being injured in this manner, the survey also found that a much larger number of students play football at the high school level. Indeed, "The latest participation figures show 1,500,000 players participating in junior and senior high school football and 75,000 in college football." Thus the incidence rate of spinal cord injuries is the more telling figure. And the survey found that "[i]n looking at the incidence rates for the past 30 years, the high school incidence is 0.52 per 100,000 participants and the college incidence is 1.41 per 100,000 participants." *See id.*

The Annual Survey continues the Center's tradition of making recommendations and setting forth strategies for making participation in football safer, both with regard to the training of coaches and referees and with regard to what should and should not be allowed. Its work has resulted in key changes in the rules, particularly those that apply to blocking and tackling, the two areas that result in the greatest number of injuries.

5.   For a discussion of sports-related negligence issues within the context of higher education, *see infra,* Liability for Injuries at the Higher Education Level.

C. SCHOOL SHOOTINGS

PROBLEM 4: THE TRAGIC EVENTS AT COLUMBINE HIGH SCHOOL

On April 20, 1999, at Columbine High School in Littleton, Colorado, two seniors—Eric Harris and Dylan Klebold—fatally shot fourteen fellow students and one teacher and wounded at least twenty-three others before taking their own lives.

According to news reports, the young men, armed with guns and explosives, entered the school from the back parking lot at about 11:30 a.m. Wearing ski masks, they first went upstairs to the library, firing semiautomatic weapons at students and teachers and throwing explosives. Then they went back downstairs to the cafeteria, still shooting. Finally they returned to the library, where they later killed themselves. During these events, which together comprised a five-hour siege, students reported hiding throughout the school.

At least 13 bombs were found in the school, and one, set with a timer, exploded at night. Three automobiles were also found rigged with bombs, one of which exploded. The bodies of the gunmen and some of their victims also appear to have been wired with explosives. *See, e.g.,* James Brooke, *Terror in Littleton: The Overview,* New York Times, April 21, 1999.

Extensive details emerged regarding the extent to which Harris and Klebold had themselves been victims of bullying by fellow students. They apparently banded together with a small group of others, calling themselves the "trench coat mafia" and wearing dark gothic-style clothing. From all evidence, it appears that during the attacks they specifically targeted athletes and those who had bullied or otherwise mistreated them in the past.

Not long after the attacks, it also became clear that many signs of the violence to come had been evident, or should have been evident, to school officials and members of the community for some time. CNN reported, for example, that "Harris' and Klebold's interest in Hitler and World War II was well-known around school. They played war games and bragged about their guns. The two sometimes spoke German in the hallways and made references to '4–20,' Hitler's birthday. * * * The massacre took place on the anniversary of Hitler's birthday." CNN, *Harris Hinted at Violence to Come*, Apr. 21, 1999. The *Washington Post* reported "[c]onfrontations with kids they disdained. A fascination with Nazism and automatic weapons. A video made for a class project months ago in which the real-life shooters play trench-coated trigger-men who mow down athletes in a school hallway." Kevin Merida, *Not Telling Anymore: Fearful Kids Keep a Code of Silence*, WASH. POST, Apr. 27, 1999.

All the lawsuits that followed were ultimately settled. But had a negligence lawsuit against school officials proceeded to trial, given these facts and the additional evidence presented in the Castaldo Complaint that follows, would the school district officials have been found liable for negligence? What are the arguments that would be set forth by the respective sides?

FROM COLUMBINE HIGH SCHOOL COMPLAINT

Plaintiff Richard R. Castaldo
DISTRICT COURT, COUNTY OF JEFFERSON, STATE OF COLORADO
Civil Action No. 2000CV921, Division 6

General Allegations

1.   Plaintiff Richard R. Castaldo was a student at Columbine High School in Jefferson County, Colorado on April 20, 1999, when he was shot and seriously injured. At the time of his injuries, Richard R. Castaldo was a minor, aged 17.

* * *

9.   Defendant Frank DeAngelis was, at all material times, Principal of Columbine High School.

* * *

11.   Defendant Garrett Talocco was, at all material times, a teacher at Columbine High School. In one of Defendant Talocco's classes, Eric Harris (Harris) presented a videotape depicting himself and Dylan Klebold (Klebold) enacting revenge shootings of other Columbine High School students. This video depicted Harris and Klebold in possession of guns enacting the killing of other Columbine students.

12.   Defendant Judy Kelly was, at all material times, a teacher at Columbine High School who taught Eric Harris and Dylan Klebold in a creative writing class.

13.   Defendant Tom Johnson was, at all material times, a teacher at Columbine High School who taught Eric Harris and Dylan Klebold in a psychology class.

14.   John or Jane Does 11 through 30 were, at all material times, deans, administrators, counselors, teachers or staff members at Columbine High School who knew of the Eric Harris Web site described elsewhere in

this Complaint, or of any of the violent videotapes made by or depicting Harris and Klebold, or of the violent writings and discussions of Harris and Klebold which depicted themes of murder, suicide, possession and use of firearms, and desire and intent to kill and injure others, including fellow Columbine students.

* * *

20.   On the morning of April 20, 1999, at approximately 11:20 a.m. local time, at Columbine High School in Jefferson County, Colorado, at a location outside near the rear door to the cafeteria, the Plaintiff Richard R. Castaldo was shot approximately nine times by one Dylan Klebold and/or Eric Harris with a 9 millimeter weapon or weapons.

21.   At the said time and place, Dylan Klebold and Eric Harris were students at Columbine High School and were co-conspirators in a plot and scheme to assault, terrorize and kill fellow students at Columbine High School. Their plot and its execution included multiple random killings and infliction of severe injuries by gunshots and placement of multiple explosive devices inside the school building.

22.   The plot and scheme of Harris and Klebold was planned for more than a year and involved meticulous planning and extensive preparation, including selection of a date, design of a scheme, surveillance of school activities, acquisition of bomb-making supplies, construction and testing of bombs, acquisition of firearms, modification of firearms, shooting practice, transportation and delivery of bombs to Columbine High School, and numerous other steps.

23.   The lengthy preparation for the April 20, 1999 attack was accompanied by multiple disclosures and announcements by Harris and Klebold of their evil desires and intent, in the form of a Web site, videotapes, writings and verbal statements.

24.   The plot and scheme carried out by Harris and Klebold resulted in the deaths of 12 students and one teacher, and in physical injuries to at least 26 others, many of which were life-threatening, catastrophic, or serious.

25.   The plot and scheme created by Harris and Klebold and which they attempted to execute, was calculated to cause hundreds of deaths and serious injuries. Hundreds of deaths and serious injuries were averted because large explosive devices planted in the cafeteria malfunctioned.

First Claim for Relief
(Willful and wanton conduct against the Sheriff Defendants)

* * *

45.   In approximately February of 1998, the Jefferson County Sheriff's Department acquired knowledge that, on or about January 30, 1998, Harris and Klebold broke into a van to steal tools. Thereafter, Harris and Klebold were defendants in the Jefferson County justice system and,

commencing approximately March 25, 1998, were placed in a Jefferson County juvenile offender diversion program.

46. On or about March 18, 1998, Defendant Mark M. Miller, while acting within the course and scope of his employment, was notified by one Randall P. Brown, a citizen of Jefferson County, that Harris had repeatedly threatened to kill Mr. Brown's son, that Harris often talked about making pipe bombs and using them to kill numerous people, and that Klebold knew of Harris' bomb-making activity. Mr. Brown also told Defendant Miller that Harris maintained an Internet Web site, a hard copy of which was printed out by Mr. Brown and provided to Defendant Miller. The Web site contained death threats and statements that Harris and Klebold were planning to use pipe bombs to kill numerous people. The Web site included: description of a pipe bomb detonation by Harris and Klebold; detailed descriptions of multiple pipe bombs that were built by Harris and Klebold; explicit threats to shoot and kill people; reference to killing using a sawed-off shotgun; threatening to "go to some downtown area in some big . . . city and blow up and shoot everything I can"; threatening to rig up and detonate explosives and shoot numerous people; and similar threats and statements of intent. The Web site printout was attached to Defendant Miller's Report of his contact with Mr. Brown and became part of the Jefferson County Sheriff Department's records available thereafter to any Jefferson County Sheriff's deputy charged with investigating Harris and Klebold. [A copy of Deputy Miller's Report and the printed Web site are attached to the original Complaint as Exhibit A.]

47. The existence and address of the Web site was disclosed to Brooks Brown by Dylan Klebold.

* * *

50. Defendant Neil Gardner also knew, or in the exercise of reasonable care should have known information available to Columbine teachers and school officials about the bizarre, hate-filled and threatening behavior of Harris and Klebold. Upon information and belief, this information included, but was not limited to, video tapes made by Harris and Klebold showing: Harris and Klebold in possession of firearms; Harris and Klebold in a mock attack on Columbine High School students; an enactment portraying Harris and Klebold killing Columbine students. The said information known to school personnel also included hateful, threatening writings and similar verbal statements by Harris and Klebold. * * *

Second Claim for Relief
(Willful and wanton conduct against the School Defendants)

* * *

80. The videotapes produced by Eric Harris for Defendant Talocco's class were violent, threatening, and a representation and foreshadowing of the assault of April 20, 1999.

81. In the creative writing class taught by Defendant Judy Kelly, Eric Harris and Dylan Klebold produced writings and other presentations

which also described or demonstrated some or all of the following: their hatred, anger, possession and use of firearms, and desire and intent to kill and injure others, including fellow Columbine students.

82. In the psychology class taught by Defendant Tom Johnson, Harris and Klebold produced writings and other presentations which also described or demonstrated some or all of the following: their hatred, anger, possession and use of firearms, and desire and intent to kill and injure others, including fellow Columbine students.

83. Harris and/or Klebold produced or appeared in, and presented in classes at Columbine High School, other videotapes depicting themselves in possession of firearms enacting violence on others including fellow Columbine students.

84. Harris and Klebold at various times and on multiple occasions in classes not specifically known to these Plaintiffs writings and verbal statements describing irrational hatred, obsession with guns, bombs and violence, and their desire and intent to harm or kill others, including fellow Columbine students.

85. Taken together, and in many instances taken separately, the Web site, videotapes, writings and verbal statements of Harris and Klebold demonstrated, revealed and conveyed to the School Defendants information which any reasonable person would perceive and understand as serious threats to the safety of students at Columbine High School.

86. Other malevolent writings of Harris and Klebold were stored on the school's network server.

87. The School Defendants, and each of them, at all material times, by virtue of their positions in a public school, had a relationship with all Columbine students, including Eric Harris, Dylan Klebold, and Richard R. Castaldo, in the nature of an *in loco parentis* relationship.

88. By virtue of the relationship in the nature of *in loco parentis*, the School Defendants, and each of them, owed a duty to all Columbine students to discipline those students who presented a threat of harm to other students and to provide a safe learning environment for all students while on school premises.

89. The duty of the School Defendants included a duty not to act in a willful and wanton manner in reckless disregard of the rights of Columbine High School students.

90. This duty included a responsibility to confer and consult with each other, other school personnel including teachers involved with Harris and Klebold, counselors, administrators, deans and the school resource officer and security personnel about the disturbing behavior of Harris and Klebold and to report the disturbing videotapes, writings and Statements of Harris and Klebold to other teachers, counselors, administrators, deans, the school resource officer and security personnel.

91. The School Defendants' duty also included a responsibility to initiate, investigate, and implement contact with the parents of Harris and Klebold and other intervention, including law enforcement intervention concerning the behavior of Harris and Klebold.

92. The School Defendants, and each of them, made a conscious decision not to report, consult, confer, or intervene at all or any further concerning the behavior of Harris and Klebold.

93. The decisions of the School Defendants, and each of them, in view of the nature and seriousness of the threats and magnitude of the harm threatened by Klebold and Harris to other Columbine students, was willful, wanton and reckless.

94. To an extent not specifically known to Plaintiffs at this time, the School Defendants consciously conspired in their decision to decline to pursue reports or intervention concerning the behavior of Harris and Klebold.

95. The said Web site, videotapes, writings and verbal statements of Harris and Klebold announced predicted, foretold and made foreseeable the events of April 20, 1999. Between the time the School Defendants became aware of the disturbing behavior of Harris and Klebold and April 20, 1999, the School Defendants, acting independently or in conjunction with law enforcement authorities, had ample opportunity to intervene and interrupt the nefarious plans of Harris and Klebold.

96. Had the School Defendants, or any of them, acted in a manner that was not reckless, willful and wanton and pursued further reporting or intervention concerning Harris and Klebold's behavior, the attack at Columbine High School on April 20, 1999 would have been prevented.

97. Therefore, the injuries and damages to Plaintiffs as more fully described in paragraph 74, above, are a direct and proximate result of the reckless, willful and wanton conduct of the School Defendants and each of them.

* * *

Sixth Claim for Relief
(42 U.S.C. § 1983 against School Defendants)

* * *

128. The School Defendants had a duty to Richard R. Castaldo which included, but is not limited to, obligations to:

a) Contact the parents of Harris and Klebold concerning the contents of videotapes, writings and verbal statements known to the School Defendants;

b) To refer these matters to higher level administrators or directly intervene, or both;

c) To report these matters to the School Resource Officer or other law enforcement personnel;

d) To initiate or conduct disciplinary proceedings against Harris and Klebold;

e) To elicit information from the School Resource Officer concerning his knowledge of Harris and Klebold;

f) To otherwise intervene or set in motion a process that would result in effective intervention to interrupt the plan and scheme of Harris and Klebold;

g) To take whatever reasonable measures necessary to protect the safety and security of Columbine High School students.

129.   The School Defendants breached their duty, and in so doing violated the United States Constitution depriving Plaintiffs of their Federal Rights and subjecting the School Defendants to liability pursuant to 42 U.S.C. § 1983.

130.   The practical manifestation of the rights of Richard R. Castaldo that were violated as a result of the Sheriff Defendants' breach, i.e. the right to be physically safe at his public school, was a well known right clearly protected by the Constitution.

131.   The savagery and seriousness of the threats by Harris and Klebold, and the extreme potential for harm, demanded serious attention and investigation.

132.   The School Defendants made deliberate and conscious decisions not to further investigate or intervene as to Harris and Klebold and not to take any of the measures outlined in paragraphs 90 and 128, above.

133.   These deliberate and conscious decisions were in reckless indifference and disregard of the safety of Columbine students, including Richard R. Castaldo.

134.   The School Defendants' deliberate indifference, reckless, willful and callous disregard to their duties, which created a substantial risk of injury to Plaintiffs, deprived Plaintiff of his Constitutional Rights in a manner which shocks the conscience. The failure to address the threatening behavior of Harris and Klebold in any meaningful way showed a conscious and unreasonable disregard of the substantial risk of serious immediate and proximate harm to students at Columbine including Plaintiff and the failure to take action by the School Defendants shock the conscience.

135.   For the foregoing deprivations of Richard R. Castaldo's constitutional rights to life, liberty and personal security, the School Defendants are liable in their individual capacities for compensatory and punitive damages as well as reasonable attorney's fees and costs under 28 U.S.C. § 1988 in an amount to be proven at trial.

136.   As a direct and proximate result of the violations of his Civil Rights, Richard R. Castaldo and his parents suffered the injuries and damages described in paragraph 74, above.

NOTES

1. While Problem 4 raises the question of negligence, the complaint actually sought damages for "willful, wanton, and reckless conduct." The rules and the terminology may vary slightly from state to state, but in general negligence is viewed as synonymous with inadvertent or unintentional action, with a failure to take precautions, and/or as reflecting a certain level of incompetence. Willful and wanton conduct, on the other hand, is more egregious, going far beyond mere inadvertence. It is typically characterized as reflecting a conscious choice of a course of action with a knowledge of the serious danger to others.

Some state courts have recognized a sliding scale in this context. In Illinois, for example, the distinction between negligence and willful and wanton conduct is sometimes seen as only slight, and in other instances willful and wanton acts may be only degrees less than intentional wrongdoing.

A key question, then, in Problem 4 is whether the acts of the school officials even constituted basic negligence. If so, then an additional question is whether the actions went beyond negligence and rose to the level of willful and wanton conduct.

In the end, the Columbine cases all settled, and the questions remain hypothetical from a legal perspective.

2. The tragic events at Columbine High School, however, continue to remain very compelling from both a legal and a policy perspective all these years later, for so many reasons, and on so many fronts.

Among other things, the events at Columbine have raised issues regarding: (a) race (racial epithets were reportedly shouted by at least one of the white perpetrators when an African American football player was shot and killed), (b) gender (a videotape recorded by the perpetrators the night before the killings and subsequently transcribed in Time Magazine included highly offensive comments about women), (c) bullying (the perpetrators and their friends had apparently been victimized repeatedly by campus bullies), (d) Neo–Nazism (the perpetrators dressed in black trench coats, often greeted each other and their friends with the expression "heil Hitler," and planned the killings to take place on Hitler's birthday), (e) parenting (many have wondered how the perpetrators could have stockpiled so many weapons and communicated so extensively regarding their plans without their parents finding out or intervening), (f) side effects of anti-depressant drugs (Eric Harris had apparently been taking anti-depressant drugs, and experts were ready to testify in a lawsuit against drug companies that these drugs sometimes amplify suicidal tendencies), and (g) gun control (the young perpetrators in suburban Denver appear to have been able to obtain an arsenal of weapons all too easily).

D. ISSUES RELATING TO RACE AND ETHNICITY

No discussion of campus safety issues in the public schools at the K–12 level would be complete without addressing the dynamic of race and the role that relationships between and among students of different races and ethnicities can and does play in this context.

Consider the following excerpts from a piece published in 1995 by Education Professor Pedro Noguera. In it, Dr. Noguera reflects on his experiences as the only African American person on the Berkeley School Board during a time of significant racial tension at Berkeley High School. In light of more recent events in cities across the country, what conclusions can be drawn regarding prospective legal and policy initiatives that might be implemented in this context?

TIES THAT BIND, FORCES THAT DIVIDE: BERKELEY HIGH SCHOOL AND THE CHALLENGE OF INTEGRATION

Pedro A. Noguera
29 U.S.F. L. Rev. 719 (1995)

* * *

Left on their own to figure out how to create an educational environment where respect and tolerance for difference supersedes racial antagonisms and hostilities, many schools have settled for a less ambitious goal: minimizing racial conflict. In several schools this has meant allowing students to resegregate themselves within the school in order to create social harmony. * * *

Despite the adverse consequences that often accompany segregation within schools, many administrators have tacitly supported this development out of fear that forcing greater interaction might increase the likelihood of interracial conflict. For this reason, instead of being truly integrated, many desegregated schools continue to be racially fragmented and polarized.

* * * This Essay presents a case study analysis of the challenges encountered by a school that has been called "the most integrated high school in America." Berkeley High School ("BHS") has attained this distinction because its student population is racially, ethnically and socio-economically diverse. Drawing many of its white students from middle and upper-middle class neighborhoods in the Berkeley hills, and many of its minority students from low income flatland neighborhoods, BHS has served as the single public institution that attempts to meet Berkeley's divergent needs. * * *

* * *

III.   * * * THE SUPPRESSION OF DISCOURSE ABOUT RACE

* * *

On issues like school violence, * * * [m]y experience has led me to conclude that all groups at BHS are engaged in an ongoing struggle for ownership of the victim mantle, because with it comes sympathy, understanding and, occasionally, resources. Labeling themselves as victims allows minority students to avoid taking responsibility for failing a class or starting a fight. This victimization also makes it possible for white students to ignore the privileges of attending a school where most teachers and administrators are white, and the cultural bias of the school curriculum clearly favors the white middle class. Moreover, racial conflicts at BHS more frequently take a political, not physical, form. Because of the school's paralysis in addressing racial issues, competition over who the true victims and villains really are tends to become the primary focus of discourse about race.

The school's inability to deal effectively with racial issues negatively affects many aspects of its daily operations. The difficulties BHS has experienced in responding to the growing problem of violence provides a prime example of this paralysis. Over the last four years, there have been shootings, stabbings and some evidence of gang violence at the school. Although most violence among students occurs within racial groups, the occurrence of racially motivated assaults upon white students has generated the greatest degree of concern.

In response to demands from parents and teachers for tough action, the BHS administration adopted a fairly traditional approach to the problem in 1991. Police officers were hired to patrol the campus, fences were built to secure the perimeter from outsiders and hidden security cameras were installed in an attempt to identify some of the perpetrators. The school board's adoption of these measures was no small feat, given the existence of considerable opposition within some segments of the community to any tactic which could be construed as a violation of students' civil liberties. However, given the depth of concern about school safety and the consequences that continued negative publicity might have on future white student enrollment, the security measures were adopted with minimal opposition.

Interestingly, during the many public meetings that were held on the subject of school violence, there was never any discussion on the causes of violent conflicts between minority and white students. There were indirect references to race, such as a comment by one black parent that white teachers at the school were "unable to deal with this problem because they lacked moral authority in their relations with black students." However, the question of why students who had attended integrated schools all of their lives would engage in unprovoked attacks that appeared to be racially motivated was not discussed. The merits of metal detectors and strategies for graffiti removal were hotly debated, but the cause of racial violence went largely unexplored, at least during the public meetings.

IV. CREATING SPACE FOR DISCUSSIONS ABOUT RACE

While most adults connected to BHS have been unwilling or afraid to discuss racial issues openly in racially mixed groups, students generally have not. Left to interpret and give meaning to the reality of race which confronts them on a daily basis, students have devised their own means to add fuel to racial conflict, and occasionally to create space for productive dialogue.

An example of the former can be seen in the publication and distribution of *The God Knows Truth* and student reaction to it on the campus. During the spring of 1992, a newsletter began appearing at BHS with an explicit focus on racial issues. Clandestinely published and distributed, the paper contained personal attacks on individuals the authors accused of racism or "selling out." Topics covered in the first issue of *The God Knows Truth* included the following: 1) an article on how the spread of homosexuality was sterilizing the black population; 2) an article which argued that black women who perm their hair deserve to be burned and; 3) an article which suggested that the Rodney King beating was understandable "because police were created to brutalize, capture, and lynch black people."

Another article directly addressed the issue of racial violence at BHS. * * *

While administrators attempted to downplay the newsletter's significance and dismiss it as the rantings of a few extremists, other students reacted with anger and put forward arguments that matched the hostility of the first issue. * * * [All this] * * * prompted the publishers of *The God Knows Truth* to become even more provocative and extreme. * * *

As the attacks increased, the administration began to take the newsletter more seriously and attempted to identify the authors by offering rewards to anyone who would provide information. Although none of the individuals behind the publication was ever apprehended, outrage over the newsletter created the opportunity for heated discussion among students. In mixed groups, students began discussing what it meant to act white or black. They argued about why racial violence at BHS had increased and what could be done to curtail it. They also debated how their racial identities influenced their options and opportunities for the future. These discussions took place in classrooms, hallways and on school grounds. While the tenor of debate was often intense, for the first time in many years students of different races were openly communicating with one another about issues that had previously been treated as taboo in public conversation.

Reactions to clandestine publications have not been the only cause for dialogue about racial issues among BHS students. In the spring of 1990, a group calling itself STOP (Students Together Opposing Prejudice) called upon the School Board to establish a mandatory ethnic studies course that would compel students to learn about different racial and ethnic groups. In a presentation before the School Board, STOP argued:

> At Berkeley High there are tremendous barriers that separate the students, one of the most pervasive being tracking.... Required history courses at BHS fail to do a thorough job of educating students about non-Whites as well as working class Euro–Americans. We would

like to see a course that gives us a chance to learn about each other, not just historical events, but learning about culture.

The School Board responded favorably to the students' demand and, despite opposition from teachers, established a mandatory ethnic studies class for ninth grade students. However, the fact that the course had been imposed upon the school made its implementation initially difficult. Most teachers refused to teach the new classes, so new teachers, most of whom lacked experience, were assigned. Furthermore, only a small amount of funding was allocated to support curriculum development for the course, and the new teachers were not hired until September, making prior planning impossible.

Given the obstacles encountered at the inception of the course, it is not surprising that the first year was anything but successful. Teachers complained about the lack of materials and the absence of a coherent curriculum. Students complained that the course, rather than a means of reducing prejudice, actually served as a forum for students to vent racist opinions. Parents also became concerned that poor management of the course was fueling hostility between students, and some petitioned the School Board to eliminate the course so that students could enroll "in more important elective courses like a foreign language or vocational class."

Despite growing opposition, the School Board refused to rescind the course and in the spring of 1993 directed the newly hired principal to take measures to insure that past mistakes were not repeated. Taking advantage of the summer, the principal was able to hire teachers who had the experience and desire to teach the ethnic studies class. Together, they were able to use part of the summer to develop a common approach to teaching the class and began to devise an appropriate curriculum.

Now that it is in its fourth year of existence, opposition to the ethnic studies course has subsided and many regard it as a major success. Despite continued opposition from some teachers and parents, many students enrolled in the course have expressed support for its continued existence. Student responses to an anonymous survey revealed that eighty-two percent of those enrolled in the spring of 1994 believed the course was a "worthwhile and valuable learning experience." Similarly, sixty-eight percent of those polled claimed that "the course had substantially changed the way [they] think about other racial groups." Commenting on what he had gained from taking the course, ninth grader Peter Graham claimed the class helped him "communicate with people that [he] thought [he] couldn't talk to." In an attempt to explain why the class had made such a change possible, classmate Jose Perez explained that "[o]ne of the best ways for us to break through the stereotypes and generalizations about other people is for us to get to know each other ... then all the labels you have on them have to fall away."

CONCLUSION

The experience of integrated schools like BHS provide a valuable source of information on race relations in schools and in society. Left on their own to figure out how to make integration work, such schools have been forced to grapple with difficult issues with minimal support. Particularly as support for the goal of integration in public education diminishes, the successes and failures of schools like BHS will be seen by others as evidence for abandoning the effort or pressing on toward integration.

It is easy to point out the many ways in which integration is not working at BHS. The producers of *School Colors* did so dramatically through their PBS documentary on the school. Although the drop-out rates for all students are relatively low, black and Latino students leave the school in large numbers prior to graduation. Moreover, despite the school's proclaimed commitment to equality, many white and Asian students graduate with honors and attend elite colleges and universities, while few black and Latino students follow a similar path. As is true in many other schools across the country, racial tensions among students, between students and teachers, and between parents and school personnel, continue to be a major problem plaguing BHS.

While these issues are by no means minor, over the years BHS has demonstrated a commitment to confronting them. Too often however, reforms that have been initiated to address the educational needs of minority students have not been well thought out or well planned. Berkeley's willingness to embrace innovation and to concede quickly to the demands of organized groups has at times exacerbated the school's educational problems. Still, no one can claim that efforts have not been undertaken to reform educational inequality at BHS and to improve race relations among its students.

Given its many problems, how do we explain the school's popularity among students? Each year, hundreds of students of all races from communities throughout the Bay Area petition the Berkeley Unified School District for admission to BHS. Perhaps the attraction is the reputation BHS has developed as a liberal school with lax discipline policies. However, the security measures that were adopted in 1991 have led to much stricter enforcement of school discipline policies and substantially reduced the degree of freedom enjoyed by students at the school. Perhaps it is the outstanding academic programs and extracurricular activities that have brought numerous awards to the school. While this is also likely, it seems that the school's diversity adds to its appeal and is perceived as an advantage by prospective students.

Undoubtedly, some of those students admitted to BHS on intradistrict transfers are quickly disappointed by the reality of race relations at the school. BHS is not one big happy family. Conflicts and tensions are a real and ever present part of the school. But where do we find schools or communities in the United States that have created alternatives to the conflicts that abound at BHS? Again, this is not simply a matter of racial diversity, but of diversity based upon socioeconomic status as well as race. Most demographic indicators point to greater racial separation in the United States, not only in public schools, but also in communities, churches and social organizations. Fear of difference, distrust of the "other" and plain old-fashioned bigotry, continue to drive ethnic groups apart.

Schools like BHS, which struggle to make diversity an asset rather than a weakness, need support. They are engaging in an effort that most of the nation has abandoned. These schools are swimming against the tide and their failure will represent more than just another example of public school incompetence; it may serve as further evidence that the promise of racial equality in the United States cannot be fulfilled.

NOTES

1. Not only are racial tensions still at the heart of campus disputes in many parts of the country from time to time, but a lack of cultural sensitivity and the concurrent prevalence of low expectations and negative stereotyping in both classroom placement and the discipline process only serve to exacerbate these tensions. *See, e.g.,* Russell J. Skiba, Robert S. Michael, Abra Carroll Nardo, and Reece L. Peterson, *The Color of Discipline: Sources of Racial and Gender Disproportionality,* 34 Urban Review 317 (2002).

2. Is it possible for you to posit a hypothetical fact situation where school officials might be deemed negligent for not taking affirmative, proactive steps to address racial/ethnic issues in particular settings? How might this fact pattern look?

2. THE "RIGHT TO SAFE SCHOOLS" UNDER STATE LAW

A handful of states have added explicit "right to safe schools" provisions to their own bodies of law. In California, Article I, Section 28 (c) was added to the Constitution by the voters in 1982. Originally a little-noticed portion of a high-profile ballot initiative entitled "The Victim's Bill of Rights," the provision soon became the subject of extended controversy, as the legal and education communities wrestled with its prospective applicability.

California Constitution, Article I, Section 28 (c) provides:

All students and staff of public primary, elementary, junior high and senior high schools have the inalienable right to attend campuses which are safe, secure, and peaceful.

While some commentators and legal activists sought to use this "safe schools" provision to make it easier to find school districts liable for injuries, in the end the California Courts of Appeal determined that Article I, Section 28 (c) was not self-executing, and that unless the Legislature identified specific additional requirements, there would be no change in the liability laws.

Article I, Section 28 (c) is often referenced by attorneys and jurists in a school safety context, but it is questionable, all these years later, whether it has had any impact whatsoever. At best, it remains an important mission statement.

More recently, the Rhode Island State Legislature voted to include a version of the California provision in its General Laws. Section 16–2–17 of the Rhode Island General Laws now provides that "[e]ach student, staff member, teacher, and administrator has a right to attend and/or work at a school which is safe and secure."

For an overview of the Rhode Island legislation and its prospective implications, as well as a retrospective on the California "safe schools" provision twenty years down the road, see Kyle Zambarano, *Rhode Island's Right to a Safe School: A Means to an End, or an End Without Means?*, 8 WILLIAMS U. L. REV. 383 (2003).

3. RELEVANT FEDERAL STATUTES AND CASE LAW

A. FEDERAL GUN–FREE REQUIREMENTS IN ELEMENTARY & SECONDARY SCHOOLS, 20 U.S.C. § 7151

(a) Short title.

This subpart [this section] may be cited as the "Gun–Free Schools Act".

(b) Requirements.

(1) In general. Each State receiving Federal funds under any title of this Act [20 USC §§ 6301 et seq.] shall have in effect a State law requiring local educational agencies to expel from school for a period of not less than 1 year a student who is determined to have brought a firearm to a school, or to have possessed a firearm at a school, under the jurisdiction of local educational agencies in that State, except that such State law shall allow the chief administering officer of a local educational agency to modify such expulsion requirement for a student on a case-by-case basis if such modification is in writing.

(2) Construction. Nothing in this subpart [this section] shall be construed to prevent a State from allowing a local educational agency that has expelled a student from such a student's regular school setting from providing educational services to such student in an alternative setting.

* * *

(g) Exception.

Nothing in this section shall apply to a firearm that is lawfully stored inside a locked vehicle on school property, or if it is for activities approved and authorized by the local educational agency and the local educational agency adopts appropriate safeguards to ensure student safety.

(h) Policy regarding criminal justice system referral.

(1) In general. No funds shall be made available under any title of this Act [20 USC §§ 6301 et seq.] to any local educational agency unless such agency has a policy requiring referral to the criminal justice or juvenile delinquency system of any student who brings a firearm or weapon to a school served by such agency.

NOTES

1. The U.S. "Gun–Free Schools Act" is a prime example of the zero tolerance statutes that have been added to federal and state codes in recent decades. Many of the initial statutes of this type focused on drug abuse. But as weapons-related incidents became more prevalent in the early 1990's, guns became a greater concern in K–12 schools nationwide. Zero tolerance statutes remain controversial, however, as they significantly limit the ability of school site administrators to address particular problems in a manner that might best meet the needs of both the students and the community. *See, e.g.,* Avarita L. Hanson, *Have Zero Tolerance School Discipline Policies Turned into a Nightmare?* 9 U.C. DAVIS J. JUV. L. & POL'Y 289 (2005).

2. Two major U.S. Supreme Court decisions addressed the interrelated areas of discipline and punishment in the 1970s: *Goss v. Lopez,* 419 U.S. 565, 95 S.Ct. 729 (1975), and *Ingraham v. Wright,* 430 U.S. 651, 97 S.Ct. 1401 (1977).

In *Goss,* the Court determined that the procedural due process rights of K–12 students would be violated if they were suspended from school without notice and an opportunity to be heard. As a result of this decision, states found themselves obligated to revise their education codes and provide extensive guidance for school officials regarding the suspension and expulsion process.

In *Ingraham,* the Court ruled that the Cruel and Unusual Punishment Clause of the Eighth Amendment did not apply to disciplinary corporal punishment. Many states have thus been able to continue some level of corporal punishment, although many others have moved to end the practice since that time. *See, e.g.,* Deana Pollard, *Banning Child Corporal Punishment,* 77 TULANE L. REV. 575, 586 (2003) (documenting the change from 1986, when only five states had banned corporal punishment, to 2003, when this number had grown to 27 states and the District of Columbia).

3. It should be noted in this context that school districts may be liable for excessive corporal punishment, even in states where the practice has not been prohibited by statute.

B. THE "UNSAFE SCHOOL CHOICE OPTION" UNDER THE "NO CHILD LEFT BEHIND ACT" (2001), 20 U.S.C. § 7912

(a) Unsafe School Choice Policy

Each State receiving funds under this Act shall establish and implement a statewide policy requiring that a student attending a persistently dangerous public elementary school or secondary school, as determined by the State in consultation with a representative sample of local educational agencies, or who becomes a victim of a violent criminal offense, as determined by State law, while in or on the grounds of a public elementary school or secondary school that the student attends, be allowed to attend a safe public elementary school or secondary school within the local educational agency, including a public charter school.

(b) Certification

As a condition of receiving funds under this Act, a State shall certify in writing to the Secretary that the State is in compliance with this section.

NOTES

1. It is important to recognize that, consistent with the structure of the "No Child Left Behind" Act (NCLB) generally, each state gets to determine its own definition of "persistently dangerous." And not only do these definitions vary significantly from state to state, but in most cases the definitions have been criticized for being far too lax. *See, e.g.,* Nelson Hernandez, *'No Child' Data on Violence Skewed: Each State Defines 'Dangerous School,'* Washington Post, November 18, 2007.

2. The "Unsafe School Choice Option" is one of several key NCLB provisions that set forth school choice as a remedy for parents whose children attend "unacceptable" schools. It is indeed striking to note just how central school choice principles (underlying the school voucher movement) were to this legislation. For an extensive overview and analysis of the NCLB, *see infra,* Chapter 6.

3. The question of parental "notice" also arises in this context. What requirements exist, if any, regarding the notification of parents under the statute? Or are things left completely to the discretion of individual states and local districts?

4. The entire question of notice in Education Law is arguably highly significant but often relatively unexplored. It arises not only in a NCLB context, but in other education-related settings as well ... including, but not limited to, "failure to warn" disputes, the right to opt out of bilingual education programs, the choices available to parents under District-wide student assignment plans, and issues relating to opt-out provisions in the sex education curriculum. In this context, it should be noted that there is also a requirement of notice and opportunity to be heard for suspended students under the procedural due process requirements of the Fourteenth Amendment.

5. If school districts fail to provide adequate notice/warning under the NCLB, might liability be found if someone gets hurt? Might this constitute an argument for expanding the "duty to warn" in a school setting? *See* Melissa

L. Gilbert, *Time-Out for Student Threats: Imposing a Duty to Protect on School Officials,* 49 UCLA L. Rev. 917 (2002).

6.   While issues relating to liability for injuries at the K–12 level continue to arise primarily within the context of state law, several federal courts of appeal have considered the question of whether school districts should be held liable under a Fourteenth Amendment Due Process Clause theory. *See, e.g., Doe v. Hillsboro Indep. Sch. Dist.,* 113 F.3d 1412 (5th Cir. 1997), *Morse v. Lower Merion Sch. Dist.,* 132 F.3d 902 (3d Cir. 1997)

B.   LIABILITY FOR INJURIES AT THE COLLEGE & UNIVERSITY LEVEL

In cases involving injuries at colleges and universities, courts look to the same basic negligence principles discussed above. Given the difference in setting, age, and circumstances, however, the application of these principles may be very different.

Duty is almost always an issue at the higher education level. And injuries in these cases are often much more egregious. Disputes relating to alcohol abuse, hazing, suicide, and sexual assault continue to recur with troubling regularity in this setting.

The typical legal analysis in this context is derived from the special relationship doctrine, with state courts engaging in a case-by-case determination of whether the facts give rise to a higher duty of care. Factors to be considered in this analysis depend on an individual state's case law, and on the type of relationship that is identified. Some disputes may be decided under the rubric of the university-student relationship, for example, while others may look to a *dangerous condition* analysis under rules pertaining to landowner and invitee. *See, e.g.,* Peter F. Lake, *The Special Relationship(s) Between a College and a Student: Law and Policy Ramifications for the Post In Loco Parentis College,* 37 Idaho L. Rev. 531 (2001). *See generally* Joseph Beckham & Douglas Pearson, *Negligent Liability Issues Involving Colleges and Students: Does a Holistic Learning Environment Heighten Institutional Liability?* 175 Ed. Law Rep. 379 (2003).

1.   HIGHER EDUCATION NEGLIGENCE– RELATED CONTROVERSIES GENERALLY

Problem 5: Perot v. Univ. of Eldorado at Emerald City

On March 21st, Maria (a former student who had recently withdrawn from the University of Eldorado at Emerald City in good standing) attended UEEC's "Spring Fling." She was accompanied by three of her former high school friends who were currently in the United States Marine Corps. The annual event, organized by the university's fraternities and sororities, was designed to help raise money for various UEEC programs. As usual, the festivities took place adjacent to the rural campus in a privately owned meadow that was made available to the students at no cost. The only access to the meadow was through a gate at the northern edge of the campus.

The group of four (two men and two women) soon began drinking heavily. They each purchased several beers at the refreshment stand, and then proceeded to consume the hard liquor that they had brought with them.

Later that evening, one of Maria's friends observed his former fiancée walking arm-in-arm with Fraternity President Lance Perot III, accompanied by several other fraternity members who had also been drinking heavily. Words were exchanged, and a fight soon broke out. One of the students was so badly injured that he required surgery on his shoulder and could not return to school until the following fall. After finally recovering, the student filed a negligence lawsuit against the university in Eldorado state court.

What legal arguments will the injured fraternity member set forth? What result? Discuss. (Assume that no affirmative defenses will be raised by the university.)

PETERSON v. SAN FRANCISCO CMTY. COLL. DIST.

36 Cal.3d 799, 205 Cal.Rptr. 842, 685 P.2d 1193 (1984)

BROUSSARD, JUSTICE.

This case presents the question whether a community college district and its agents have a duty to exercise due care to protect students from reasonably foreseeable assaults on the campus. We conclude that the district does owe such a duty to its students. As we shall explain, we also conclude that while the district is immune from liability for failure to provide adequate police protection, it is not immune for failure to warn its students of known dangers posed by criminals on the campus.

Plaintiff Kathleen Peterson brought this action for damages under California's Tort Claims Act (Gov. Code, § 810 et seq.)[1] against the San Francisco Community College District, a state agency, and its agents. The plaintiff, a student, sustained injuries as a result of an attempted daylight rape in the parking lot area of the City College of San Francisco campus. * * *

The complaint consists of two causes of action. In the first cause of action plaintiff alleges that by virtue of a special relationship between the defendant district and herself, the defendants had a duty to protect her and/or to warn her of danger. In her second cause of action plaintiff alleges that defendants are liable under section 835 for maintaining a dangerous condition of property which together with the criminal act of a third party caused her injuries.

FACTS

* * *

On April 25, 1978, plaintiff, a student at City College of San Francisco, was assaulted while ascending a stairway in the school's parking lot.

---

1. All further statutory references are to the Government Code unless specified otherwise.

An unidentified male jumped from behind "unreasonably thick and untrimmed foliage and trees" which adjoined the stairway and attempted to rape her. The assailant used a modus operandi which was similar to that used in previous attacks on the same stairway. The defendants were aware that other assaults of a similar nature had occurred in that area and had taken steps to protect students who used the parking lot and stairway. Plaintiff relied upon this increased protection.

Plaintiff had been issued a parking permit by the college in return for a fee. Defendants did not publicize the prior incidents or in any way warn the plaintiff that she was in danger of being attacked in that area of campus. Plaintiff sustained physical and emotional injuries and economic loss as a result of the assault.

Although plaintiff has chosen to proceed under two different theories, the primary question before us is whether under the facts as alleged the defendants owed her a duty of care. The question then becomes whether this duty is affected by the fact that the defendants here are a public entity and its agents. Accordingly, we proceed to consider the nature of the relationship between plaintiff and defendants and the duty, if any, which the defendants owed her.

DUTY

Plaintiff alleges that the following circumstances placed upon the defendants an affirmative duty to exercise due care for her protection: "Having invited [her] onto the campus property, having enrolled her as a student, having issued to [her] a permit to park and use the parking lot and stairway in question in exchange for . . . payment of a fee, having undertaken to patrol the parking lot and stairway in question in the light of the prior incidents of violence in the area, and having induced [her] to rely and depend upon this protection, a special relationship existed between Plaintiff and Defendants pursuant to which Defendants were obliged to take reasonable protective measures to ensure Plaintiff's safety against violent attacks and otherwise protect her from foreseeable criminal conduct and/or to warn her as to the location of prior violent assaults in the vicinity of the subject parking lot and stairway."

We have observed that the question of a duty " ' . . . is a shorthand statement of a conclusion, rather than an aid to analysis in itself . . . [b]ut it should be recognized that 'duty' is not sacrosanct in itself, but only an expression of the sum total of those considerations of policy which lead the law to say that a particular plaintiff is entitled to protection.' " In considering whether one owes another a duty of care, several factors must be weighed including among others: " '[T]he foreseeability of harm to the plaintiff, the degree of certainty that the plaintiff suffered injury, the closeness of the connection between the defendant's conduct and the injury suffered, the moral blame attached to the defendant's conduct, the policy of preventing future harm, the extent of the burden to the defendant and consequences to the community of imposing a duty to exercise care with resulting liability for breach, and the availability, cost, and prevalence of insurance for the risk involved.' '' When public agencies are involved, additional elements include 'the extent of [the agency's] powers, the role imposed upon it by law and the limitations imposed upon it by budget; ...' * * *

As a general rule one has no duty to control the conduct of another, and no duty to warn those who may be endangered by such conduct. * * * A duty may arise, however, where "(a) a special relation exists between the actor and the third person which imposes a duty upon the actor to control the third person's conduct, or (b) a special relation exists between the actor and the other which gives the other a right to protection." Among the commonly recognized special relationships are that between a common carrier and its passengers, that between an innkeeper and his or her guests, and that between a possessor of land and members of the public who enter in response to the landowner's invitation.[3]

There is no question that if the defendant district here were a private landowner operating a parking lot on its premises it would owe plaintiff a duty to exercise due care for her protection. * * * It has long been recognized that "a possessor of land who holds it open to the public for entry for business purposes is subject to liability to members of the public while they are upon the land for such a purpose, for physical harm caused by the accidental, negligent or intentionally harmful acts of third persons ... and by the failure of the possessor to exercise reasonable care to (a) discover that such acts are being done or are likely to be done, or (b) give a warning adequate to enable the visitors to avoid the harm, or otherwise to protect them against it." Liability will normally be imposed in circumstances where the possessor has reasonable cause to anticipate the misconduct of third persons.

* * *

---

3. We have also observed that in some instances the relationship of a school district to its students gives rise to a duty of care. In *Dailey v. Los Angeles Unified School District* (1970) 2 Cal.3d 741, 87 Cal.Rptr. 376, 470 P.2d 360, we stated: "While school districts and their employees have never been considered insurers of the physical safety of students, California law has long imposed on school authorities a duty to 'supervise at all times the conduct of the children on the school grounds and to enforce those rules and regulations necessary to their protection. [Citations.]' '' (*Taylor v. Oakland Scavenger Co.* (1941) 17 Cal.2d 594, 600 [110 P.2d 1044]; Ed.Code, § 13557.) [Citations.] The standard of care imposed upon school personnel in carrying out this duty to supervise is identical to that required in the performance of their other duties. This uniform standard to which they are held is that degree of care 'which a person of ordinary prudence, charged with [comparable] duties, would exercise under the same circumstances.' [Citations.] Either a total lack of supervision [citation] or ineffective supervision [citation] may constitute a lack of ordinary care on the part of those responsible for student supervision...." (*Id.*, at p. 747, 87 Cal.Rptr. 376, 470 P.2d 360.)

Dailey arose in the context of a secondary school where a 16-year-old was killed while engaging in a "slap boxing match." We observed that children of that age "should not be expected to exhibit that degree of discretion, judgment, and concern for the safety of themselves and others which we associate with full maturity." *Id.*, at p. 748, 87 Cal.Rptr. 376, 470 P.2d 360. The present case, by contrast, does not implicate the duty to supervise the activities of students who are too immature to exercise judgment for their personal safety. Rather, the issue here is the extent of the school's duty to provide safe premises.

Under the circumstances of this case, plaintiff, an enrolled student using the parking lot in exchange for a fee, was an invitee to whom the possessor of the premises would ordinarily owe a duty of due care.[6] * * * The question remains whether the provisions of the Tort Claims Act preclude the imposition of such a duty on the defendants under the circumstances of this case.

THE TORT CLAIMS ACT

Turning to the Tort Claims Act, we note initially that public entity liability is statutory in nature. (§ 815.)[7] Its provisions, however, are to be read against the background of general tort law. "The conceptual theory of statutory liability under the act is keyed to the common law of negligence and damages...." * * *

Section 835 is the principal provision addressing the circumstances under which the government may be held liable for maintaining a dangerous condition of public property. It provides in relevant part: "Except as provided by statute, a public entity is liable for injury caused by a dangerous condition of its property if the plaintiff establishes that the property was in a dangerous condition at the time of the injury, that the injury was proximately caused by the dangerous condition, that the dangerous condition created a reasonably foreseeable risk of the kind of injury which was incurred, and that either:

"(a) A negligent or wrongful act or omission of an employee of the public entity within the scope of his employment created the dangerous condition; or

"(b) The public entity had actual or constructive notice of the dangerous condition under Section 835.2 a sufficient time prior to the injury to have taken measures to protect against the dangerous condition." Section 830 defines a "dangerous condition" as: "... a condition of property that creates a substantial (as distinguished from a minor, trivial or insignificant) risk of injury when such property or adjacent property is used with due care in a manner in which it is reasonably foreseeable that it will be used."

* * *

The majority of cases which have construed these provisions have concluded that third party conduct by itself, unrelated to the condition of the property, does not constitute a "dangerous condition" for which a public entity may be held liable. * * * The cases so holding have relied

---

6. The characterization of students as invitees is not a novel proposition. In *Vreeland v. State Board of Regents* (1969) 9 Ariz. App. 61 [449 P.2d 78], *Jesik v. Maricopa County Community College Dist.* (1980) 125 Ariz. 543 [611 P.2d 547] and *Relyea v. State* (Fla. 1980) 385 So.2d 1378, students were characterized as invitees to whom a duty was owed to make the premises reasonably safe. In both *Jesik* and *Relyea* the danger to the students arose because of criminal conduct by a third party.

7. Section 815 provides in relevant part: "Except as otherwise provided by statute: [#] (a) A public entity is not liable for an injury, whether such injury arises out of an act or omission of the public entity or a public employee or any other person."

primarily on policy considerations and the definition of dangerous condition as a "condition of *property*" for the conclusion that a defect in property is necessary in order to state a cause of action based on the wrongful conduct of third parties. Nothing in the provisions of section 835, however, specifically precludes a finding that a public entity may be under a duty, given special circumstances, to protect against harmful criminal conduct on its property.

    * * *

    * * * [I]ntervening criminal conduct cannot absolve the defendant of liability where as here the plaintiff alleges that defendants maintained the property in such a way so as to increase the risk of criminal activity. In *Slapin v. Los Angeles International Airport*, 65 Cal.App.3d 484, plaintiff was attacked in a parking lot. Plaintiff alleged that prior to the incident, defendants were aware that the parking lot was unsafe unless properly supervised and maintained. Moreover, plaintiff alleged that defendants " 'carelessly, negligently, and improperly owned, operated, managed, maintained, supervised, controlled, lighted, and secured [the] parking area … so as to maintain a dangerous condition of property….' " The Court of Appeal held that the trial court erred in sustaining defendant's demurrer to the dangerous condition theory. "That a mugger thrives in dark public places is a matter of common knowledge. If defendant so poorly lighted the parking lot as to create a substantial risk of muggings, plaintiffs may be able to establish the elements of a cause of action under section 835."

    The instant case is indistinguishable from *Slapin*. The court in *Slapin* recognized that a defendant may not escape liability by claiming that plaintiff's injuries were caused by a criminal agency when the basis of plaintiff's cause of action is that the defendant created a reasonably foreseeable risk of that criminal conduct.

    Plaintiff alleges here that the property was in a dangerous condition because the thick and untrimmed foliage and trees around the parking lot and stairway permitted the assailant to perpetrate his crime; she further alleges that defendants were aware of the condition and failed to take reasonable protective measures, including trimming the foliage or warning her of the danger. Defendant's inaction she alleges, created a reasonably foreseeable risk that she and others using the stairway would be injured. In light of the relationship between plaintiff and defendants as well as the facts known to the defendants, we conclude that plaintiff has stated a cause of action under the provisions of the Tort Claims Act.

    * * *

    An examination of the policies discussed in *Rowland v. Christian*, 69 Cal.2d 108, and other cases compels the conclusion that the defendants did in fact owe the plaintiff a duty of care. First, the allegations, if proved, suggest that harm to the plaintiff was clearly foreseeable. In light of the alleged prior similar incidents in the same area, the defendants were on notice that any woman who might use the stairs or the parking lot would be a potential target. Secondly, it is undisputed that plaintiff suffered injury. Third, given that the defendants were in control of the premises and that they were aware of the prior assaults, it is clear that failure to apprise students of those incidents, to trim the foliage, or to take other protective measures closely connects the defendants' conduct with plaintiff's injury. These factors, if established, also indicate that there is moral blame attached to the defendants' failure to take steps to avert the foreseeable harm. Imposing a duty under these circumstances also furthers the policy of preventing future harm. Finally, the duty here does not place an intolerable burden on the defendants.

The fact that the defendants are a public entity and its agents also does not preclude the imposition of a duty of care. As we have often noted, the policy of compensating injured parties is an important one. "Unless the Legislature has clearly provided for immunity, the important societal goal of compensating injured parties for damages caused by wilful or negligent acts must prevail." As a community college district responsible for overseeing the campus, the defendant and its agents are in a superior position to know about the incidences of crime and to protect against any recurrences.

     * * *

* * * [W]e conclude that plaintiff is entitled to prove that the failure to warn, to trim the foliage, or to take other reasonable measures to protect her was the proximate cause of her injuries.

Plaintiff's first cause of action alleges facts which are sufficient to establish a common law duty of care but which are inadequate to state a cause of action against a public entity. Plaintiff's second cause of action, by incorporating by reference the allegations in the first cause of action and by pleading the elements of section 835, states a cause of action against defendants. Thus the judgment of dismissal was entered erroneously. The judgment is reversed.

NOTES

1. The *Peterson* case ultimately stands for the proposition that there is a duty (under a dangerous condition theory) to exercise due care to protect students from reasonably foreseeable assaults on the campus, and that public policy considerations are central to a determination of whether such a duty exists in a given situation.

It is clear from the facts of this case that the San Francisco Community College District "did not publicize the prior incidents or in any way warn the plaintiff that she was in danger of being attacked in that area of campus." Indeed, "plaintiff's complaint . . . alleges not only inadequate police protection but failure to warn her of the known danger and failure to trim the foliage growing by the parking lot stairway."

Arguably, however, the case does not actually rule that a duty to protect would include a duty to warn, but it certainly says that "plaintiff is entitled to prove that the failure to warn, to trim the foliage, or to take other reasonable measures to protect her was the proximate cause of her injuries."

The "duty to warn" issue is directly relevant to our examination of threats, *infra*, Chapter 4, since negligence law is implicated when a threat arises and school officials with knowledge of alleged threats fail to warn. It is important to note, however, that school officials must proceed carefully in this context. Generalized warnings may do nothing more than foster an atmosphere of fear and paranoia, leading to an environment where productive learning cannot easily take place.

2.   *Peterson* is different, however, from the more typical negligence cases in this area, in that both the level of foreseeability and the apparent ability of the educational institution to take reasonable steps to address the problem led to a clear decision in favor of the plaintiff. In most cases, particularly where one student is injured by another, courts continue to be very deferential to institutions of higher education in this context. Indeed, even in the prototypical situation where excessive alcohol in consumed and students may be seriously injured or even killed, colleges and universities are often found not liable, absent additional facts.

3.   For example, in *Tanja H. v. Regents of Univ. of Cal.*, 228 Cal.App.3d 434, 278 Cal.Rptr. 918 (Cal. App. 1991) the apparent victim of a highly publicized gang rape by male football players in a UC Berkeley dormitory argued that the university should be found negligent for failing to protect her against this activity. The California Court of Appeal, however, citing well-established case law in this area, ruled against her and in favor of the university:

> Relevant authority indicates universities are not generally liable for the sometimes disastrous consequences which result from combining young students, alcohol, and dangerous or violent impulses. * * *

> We agree with the assessment of [the university] that it could 'not have prevented this [violent] incident from taking place except *possibly* by posting guards in each dorm room on a 24–hour, 365–day per year basis.' * * *

> As campuses have * * * moved away from their former role as semi-monastic environments subject to intensive regulation of student lives by college authorities, they have become microcosms of society; and unfortunately, sexually degrading conduct or violence in general—and violence against women in particular—are all too common within society at large. College administrators have a moral duty to help educate students in this respect, but they do not have a legal duty to respond in damages for student crimes.

> We agree with appellant that it may be—in some sense not relevant here—foreseeable that a group of football players could rape a fellow student after a party where alcohol was served. The problem of gang rape, rape by acquaintances, and alcohol abuse on campuses is heinous. It is also foreseeable that there will always be criminals among us. The relevant issue here, however, is the one posed by the courts in [other recent cases]: Should a duty be imposed which would make colleges liable

for damages caused by third parties, unless colleges impose onerous conditions on the freedom and privacy of resident students—which restrictions are incompatible with a recognition that students are now generally responsible for their own actions and welfare? * * * In these circumstances, the courts can establish the criminal and civil liability of the perpetrators of crimes; but the courts with good reason have been unwilling to shift moral and legal responsibility away from student perpetrators and onto the heads of college administrators. *Id.* at 437–39.

4. Sexual assault cases such as *Tanja H.* are not the only examples of decisions by the courts that even in the most tragic of circumstances liability for injuries will not necessarily be found. In *Jain v. State,* the Iowa Supreme Court held that the University was not liable for the death of a freshman student who had committed suicide in his dormitory room. The family had sued the university for wrongful death, claiming it "negligently failed to exercise reasonable care and caution for the student's safety." In particular, plaintiffs claimed "that if the university had followed its policy of notifying parents of a student's self-destructive behavior, the suicide could have been prevented."

On the university's motion for summary judgment, the district court had dismissed the suit. It concluded the university owed no legal duty to Sanjay Jain to prevent him from harming himself, nor did it breach any legally recognized duty of care by failing to notify his parents of an earlier suicide attempt. The state supreme court affirmed.

5. The ongoing prevalence of sexual assault issues on college and university campuses continues to disproportionately impact female students. In late 2003, for example, a civilian commission report documented the existence of frequent and unpunished sexual assaults on female cadets at the Air Force Academy over time. It charged that "since at least 1993, the highest levels of Air Force leadership have known of serious sexual misconduct problems at the academy," but failed to take effective action. *See* Diana Jean Schemo, *Air Force Ignored Sex Abuse At Academy, Inquiry Reports,* N.Y. TIMES, Sept. 23, 2003.

6. In August 2005, a Pentagon task force focusing on the U.S. Military Academy at West Point and on the Naval Academy in Annapolis concluded that hostile attitudes and inappropriate treatment of women persist on these campuses. *See* John J. Lumpkin, *Sexual Harassment, Assault, Not Adequately Addressed by Military Academies,* ASS. PRESS, Aug. 26, 2005.

7. *Peterson* is not only noteworthy as an exception to the rule that colleges and universities are not typically found liable for sexual assault or attempted sexual assault absent additional facts, but it also is an example of a negligence case that had an impact on policy decisions throughout the state. After the decision, colleges and universities statewide trimmed back bushes and foliage, increased lighting, and implemented campus escort services. In addition, the momentum of these actions and the concurrent efforts of the women's rights movement led to the establishment of women's resource centers and women's studies departments on campuses. All of these efforts together have had an important and often-significant impact, although there is still agreement that much work remains to be done.

8. While negligence law in and of itself may not require colleges and universities to do any more than they have been doing today, emerging legal principles under threat law and harassment law arguably require a higher baseline of protection for students today.

PROBLEM 6: THE TRAGIC EVENTS AT VIRGINIA TECH

Consider the following questions in light of the key findings set forth below in excerpts from the August 2007 Governor's panel report on the tragic events at Virginia Tech, where student Seung–Hui Cho killed 32 people and wounded many others before taking his own life.

1. In a hypothetical lawsuit filed by the family of a Virginia Tech victim under principles of negligence law set forth in the *Peterson* case and other relevant higher education-related decisions, would the university be found liable:

   a. For failing to take action to protect students, faculty, and staff when the parameters of Seung–Hui Cho's mental condition became apparent?

   b. For failing to take action to protect Seung–Hui Cho when the parameters of his mental condition became apparent?

   c. For failing to take immediate action and employ available technology to warn the campus community and otherwise limit any additional violence after the initial killings in the dormitories had been reported?

2. Would you support a legal mandate that would require K–12 and higher education officials to implement relevant interventions (including but not limited to those described in Paragraph 128 of the *Castaldo* complaint, *supra*) when and if it becomes apparent that particular students are at risk and might pose a danger to themselves and/or to others? Why or why not?

3. Should the current systems of record-keeping and reporting be adjusted to require K–12 schools to disseminate information to institutions of higher education regarding the existence of certain emotional disabilities that could–if not addressed–endanger the lives of both the students with the disabilities themselves and the lives of others? Why or why not?

From the Report of the Virginia Tech Review Panel, Released August 30, 2007

● *from* SUMMARY OF KEY FINDINGS

The panel conducted over 200 interviews and reviewed thousands of pages of records, and reports the following major findings:

1. Cho exhibited signs of mental health problems during his childhood. His middle and high schools responded well to these signs and, with his parents' involvement, provided services to address his issues. He also

received private psychiatric treatment and counseling for selective mutism and depression.

In 1999, after the Columbine shootings, Cho's middle school teachers observed suicidal and homicidal ideations in his writings and recommended psychiatric counseling, which he received. It was at this point that he received medication for a short time. Although Cho's parents were aware that he was troubled at this time, they state they did not specifically know that he thought about homicide shortly after the 1999 Columbine school shootings.

2. During Cho's junior year at Virginia Tech, numerous incidents occurred that were clear warnings of mental instability. Although various individuals and departments within the university knew about each of these incidents, the university did not intervene effectively. No one knew all the information and no one connected all the dots.

3. University officials in the office of Judicial Affairs, Cook Counseling Center, campus police, the Dean of Students, and others explained their failures to communicate with one another or with Cho's parents by noting their belief that such communications are prohibited by the federal laws governing the privacy of health and education records. In reality, federal laws and their state counterparts afford ample leeway to share information in potentially dangerous situations.

4. The Cook Counseling Center and the university's Care Team failed to provide needed support and services to Cho during a period in late 2005 and early 2006. The system failed for lack of resources, incorrect interpretation of privacy laws, and passivity. Records of Cho's minimal treatment at Virginia Tech's Cook Counseling Center are missing.

5. Virginia's mental health laws are flawed and services for mental health users are inadequate. Lack of sufficient resources results in gaps in the mental health system including short term crisis stabilization and comprehensive outpatient services. The involuntary commitment process is challenged by unrealistic time constraints, lack of critical psychiatric data and collateral information, and barriers (perceived or real) to open communications among key professionals.

6. There is widespread confusion about what federal and state privacy laws allow. Also, the federal laws governing records of health care provided in educational settings are not entirely compatible with those governing other health records.

7. Cho purchased two guns in violation of federal law. The fact that in 2005 Cho had been judged to be a danger to himself and ordered to outpatient treatment made him ineligible to purchase a gun under federal law. * * *

10. On April 16, 2007, the Virginia Tech and Blacksburg police departments responded quickly to the report of shootings at West Ambler Johnston residence hall, as did the Virginia Tech and Blacksburg rescue squads. Their responses were well coordinated.

11.   The Virginia Tech police may have erred in prematurely concluding that their initial lead in the double homicide was a good one, or at least in conveying that impression to university officials while continuing their investigation. They did not take sufficient action to deal with what might happen if the initial lead proved erroneous. The police reported to the university emergency Policy Group that the "person of interest" probably was no longer on campus.

12.   The VTPD erred in not requesting that the Policy Group issue a campus-wide notification that two persons had been killed and that all students and staff should be cautious and alert.

13.   Senior university administrators, acting as the emergency Policy Group, failed to issue an all-campus notification about the WAJ killings until almost 2 hours had elapsed. University practice may have conflicted with written policies.

14.   The presence of large numbers of police at WAJ led to a rapid response to the first 9–1–1 call that shooting had begun at Norris Hall.

15.   Cho's motives for the WAJ or Norris Hall shootings are unknown to the police or the panel. Cho's writings and videotaped pronouncements do not explain why he struck when and where he did. * * *

• *From* TIMELINE OF EVENTS–4/16/07

6:47 a.m. Cho is spotted by a student waiting outside the West Ambler Johnston (WAJ) residential hall entrance, where he has his mailbox.

7:02 a.m. Emily Hilscher enters the dorm after being dropped off by her boyfriend (the time is based on her swipe card record).

About 7:15 a.m. Cho shoots Hilscher in her room (4040) at WAJ. He also shoots Ryan Christopher Clark, an RA. Clark, it is thought, most likely came to investigate noises in Hilscher's room, which is next door to his. Both of the victims' wounds prove to be fatal. * * *

7:40 a.m. VTPD Chief Flinchum is notified by phone of the WAJ shootings.

7:51 a.m. Chief Flinchum contacts the Blacksburg Police Department (BPD) and requests a BPD evidence technician and BPD detective to assist with the investigation.

7:57 a.m. Chief Flinchum notifies the Virginia Tech Office of the Executive Vice President of the shootings. This triggers a meeting of the university's Policy Group.

8:00 a.m. Classes begin. Chief Flinchum arrives at WAJ and finds VTPD and BPD detectives on the scene and the investigation underway. A local special agent of the state police has been contacted and is responding to the scene. * * *

8:25 a.m. The Virginia Tech Policy Group meets to plan on how to notify students of the homicides.

8:52 a.m. Blacksburg public schools lock their outer doors upon hearing of the incident at WAJ from their security chief, who had heard of the incident on police radio.

9:00 a.m. The Policy Group is briefed on the latest events in the ongoing dormitory homicide investigation by the VTPD.

9:01 a.m. Cho mails a package from the Blacksburg post office to NBC News in New York that contains pictures of himself holding weapons, an 1,800–word rambling diatribe, and video clips in which he expresses rage, resentment, and a desire to get even with oppressors. He alludes to a coming massacre. Cho prepared this material in the previous weeks. The videos are a performance of the enclosed writings. Cho also mails a letter to the English Department attacking Professor Carl Bean, with whom he previously argued.

9:05 a.m. Classes begin for the second period in Norris Hall.

9:15 a.m. Both police ERTs are staged at the BPD in anticipation of executing search warrants or making an arrest.

9:15–9:30 a.m. Cho is seen outside and then inside Norris Hall, an engineering building. He chains the doors shut on the three main entrances from the inside. No one reports seeing him do this. * * *

9:26 a.m. Virginia Tech administration sends e-mail to campus staff, faculty, and students informing them of the dormitory shooting. * * *

About 9:40 a.m. until about 9:51 a.m. Cho begins shooting in room 206 in Norris Hall, where a graduate engineering class in Advanced Hydrology is underway. Cho kills Professor G. V. Loganathan and other students in the class, killing 9 and wounding 3 of the 13 students. Cho goes across the hall from room 206 and enters room 207, an Elementary German class. He shoots teacher Christopher James Bishop, then students near the front of the classroom and starts down the aisle shooting others. Cho leaves the classroom to go back into the hall. Students in room 205, attending Haiyan Cheng's class on Issues in Scientific Computing, hear Cho's gunshots. (Cheng was a graduate assistant substituting for the professor that day.) The students barricade the door and prevent Cho's entry despite his firing at them through the door. Meanwhile, in room 211 Madame Jocelyne Couture–Nowak is teaching French. She and her class hear the shots, and she asks student Colin Goddard to call 9–1–1. A student tells the teacher to put the desk in front of the door, which is done but it is nudged open by Cho. Cho walks down the rows of desks shooting people. Goddard is shot in the leg. Student Emily Haas picks up the cell phone Goddard dropped. She begs the police to hurry. Cho hears Haas and shoots her, grazing her twice in the head. She falls and plays dead, though keeping the phone cradled under her head and the line open. Cho says nothing on entering the room or during the shooting. (Three students who pretend to be dead survive.)

9:41 a.m. A BPD dispatcher receives a call regarding the shooting in Norris Hall. The panel estimates that the shooting began at this time based on the time it took for the students and faculty in the room next door to recognize that the sounds being heard were gunshots, and then make the call to 9–1–1. The dispatcher initially has difficulty understanding the location of the shooting. Once identified as being on campus, the call is transferred to VTPD.

9:42 a.m. The first 9–1–1 call reporting shots fired reaches the VTPD. A message is sent to all county EMS units to staff and respond.

9:45 a.m. The first police officers arrive at Norris Hall, a three-minute response time from their receipt of the call. Hearing shots, they pause briefly to check whether they are being fired upon, then rush to one entrance, then another, and then a third but find all three chained shut. Attempts to shoot open the locks fail.

About 9:45 a.m. * * * Back in room 207, the German class, two uninjured students and two injured students go to the door and hold it shut with their feet and hands, keeping their bodies away. Within 2 minutes, Cho returns. He beats on the door and opens it an inch and fires shots around the door handle, then gives up trying to get in. Cho returns to room 211, the French class, and goes up one aisle and down another, shooting people again. Cho shoots Goddard again twice more. A janitor sees Cho in the hall on the second floor loading his gun; he flees downstairs. Cho tries to enter room 204 where engineering professor Liviu Librescu is teaching Mechanics. Librescu braces his body against the door yelling for students to head for the window. He is shot through the door. Students push out screens and jump or drop to grass or bushes below the window. Ten students escape this way. The next two students trying to escape are shot. Cho returns again to room 206 and shoots more students.

9:50 a.m. Using a shotgun, police shoot open the ordinary key lock of a fourth entrance to Norris Hall that goes to a machine shop and that could not be chained. The police hear gunshots as they enter the building. They immediately follow the sounds to the second floor. Triage and rescue of victims begin. A second e-mail is sent by the administration to all Virginia Tech e-mail addresses announcing that "A gunman is loose on campus. Stay in buildings until further notice. Stay away from all windows." Four loudspeakers out of doors on poles broadcast a similar message. Virginia Tech and Blacksburg police ERTs arrive at Norris Hall, including one paramedic with each team.

9:51 a.m. Cho shoots himself in the head just as police reach the second floor. Investigators believe that the police shotgun blast alerted Cho to the arrival of the police. Cho's shooting spree in Norris Hall lasted about 11 minutes. He fired 174 rounds, and killed 30 people in Norris Hall plus himself, and wounded 17.

NOTE

1. In late June 2008, the Chronicle of Higher Education reported that 28 of the 32 families whose relatives were killed in the April 2007 shootings at

Virginia Tech had reached final settlements with the Commonwealth of Virginia that preclude their filing lawsuits alleging that the state or the university is to blame:

> The terms of the settlement, which were announced by Gov. Timothy M. Kaine in April, offer the families financial compensation and other benefits. In final, public form, it grants each family $100,000; additional compensation for medical and mental-health expenses; meetings with state-government and university officials; and joint access to a $3.7–million "public purpose" fund for campus-safety projects, memorial activities, and alleviation of severe personal hardships related to the killings.
> * * *
>
> In the settlement, both Virginia and Virginia Tech officially deny all liability related to the events of April 16, 2007, in which a gunman killed 32 people on the campus before taking his own life. * * * In a public hearing last week, a state judge in Richmond approved 24 of the settlements, with the remaining four delayed for administrative reasons. The terms of all of the settlements are identical, except that one also offers immigration assistance to a victim's relative, a source close to the families said. Two families never filed wrongful-death claims against the state, and two others opted out of the settlement, reserving their right to sue.
>
> State officials also announced that they had settled all 18 personal-injury claims filed by survivors of the shootings. Each survivor will receive up to $100,000, state-employee health insurance, free or reduced-fee treatment at two public-university hospitals, and access to the same meetings and public-purpose fund as was given to the families of the victims.
>
> Under the settlement, the combined group of 18 survivors and 28 families will meet three times with Governor Kaine before his term concludes, in 2010. The agreement states that "the meetings will provide opportunities to review and discuss legislative and administrative accomplishments and strategies in response to the tragedy," as well as the "suggestions of the report of the Virginia Tech Review Panel."
>
> Governor Kaine, a Democrat, signed into law this spring two dozen bills crafted in response to the shootings. Over the past year, the university has weighed hundreds of related recommendations, many of them from the state panel mentioned in the settlement.
>
> * * * Under the terms of the settlement, the university must also develop an electronic archive of written records related to the shootings and give survivors and victims' families remote access to it. Sara Lipka, *28 Families Reach Final Settlements With Virginia Tech and the State,* Chronicle of Higher Education, June 27, 2008.

BRUECKNER v. NORWICH UNIV.

169 Vt. 118, 730 A.2d 1086 (1999)

AMESTOY, C.J.

Norwich University appeals from the denial of its post-trial motions for judgment as a matter of law, or in the alternative, for a new trial, following a jury verdict finding it liable and awarding compensatory and punitive damages on several tort claims arising from incidents of hazing suffered by plaintiff while a freshman. * * * We affirm the court's rulings on liability and lost earnings damages, but reverse the award of punitive damages because there was an insufficient showing of malice to support the award.

* * * In August 1990, plaintiff William C. Brueckner, Jr. arrived as an incoming freshman, or "rook," at the Military College of Vermont of Norwich University (Norwich). At the time, he was a twenty-four year old, five-year veteran of the United States Navy, having been awarded a four-year naval ROTC scholarship in the amount of $80,000 to attend Norwich. Under the authority and training of Norwich and its leadership, certain upperclassmen were appointed by the university to indoctrinate and orient the incoming rooks, including plaintiff. These upperclassmen were known as the "cadre."

Plaintiff attended Norwich for only sixteen days as a result of his subjection to, and observation of, numerous incidents of hazing. In those sixteen days, plaintiff withstood a regular barrage of obscene, offensive and harassing language. He was interrogated at meals and thereby prevented from eating. He was ordered to disrobe in front of a female student, although he did not follow the order. He was prevented from studying during some of the assigned study periods and, on several occasions, cadre members destroyed his academic work with water. Members of the cadre also forced him to squat in the hall as they squirted him with water. He was forced to participate in unauthorized calisthenic sessions, despite an injured shoulder. He was slammed into a wall by a cadre member riding a skateboard in the hall. After cadre members vandalized his room by dumping water in it, plaintiff was ordered to clean up the mess. On two occasions, plaintiff was prevented from attending mandatory ROTC study hall on time, leading him to believe his scholarship status was endangered. One morning, as plaintiff walked along the corridor in the dormitory, he encountered two cadre members, one of whom asked plaintiff where plaintiff's name tag was. When plaintiff responded that he had forgotten it, one cadre member hit plaintiff hard in the shoulder, which was injured and in a sling. After the other cadre member told the hitter to stop, the hitter struck plaintiff again in the same shoulder, causing pain and bruises. After reporting the hazing problems to Norwich officials, plaintiff left the campus, believing that his situation would not improve. He returned briefly once more, then withdrew from Norwich, his scholarship terminated. Norwich investigated plaintiff's complaints and, as a result, several cadets were disciplined.

Plaintiff brought this action against Norwich for assault and battery, negligent infliction of emotional distress, intentional infliction of emotional distress and negligent supervision. * * *

A. VICARIOUS LIABILITY * * *

Norwich claims error in the court's entry of judgment on the claims of assault and battery, as well as negligent and intentional infliction of emotional distress, because those claims are premised on acts of the cadre members that were not authorized and did not occur within the scope of their employment. Norwich claims it should not be held vicariously liable for the cadre's hazing.

Under the settled doctrine of respondeat superior, an employer or master is held vicariously liable for the tortious acts of an employee or servant committed during, or incidental to, the scope of employment. Norwich concedes that cadre members acted as its agents in "indoctrinating and orienting" rooks such as plaintiff. Norwich claims, however, that the tortious acts complained of were not committed within the cadre members' "scope of employment." Whether a given act is committed within the scope of employment is properly determined by the finder of fact after consideration of the attendant facts and circumstances of the particular case.

To be within the scope of employment, conduct must be of the same general nature as, or incidental to, the authorized conduct. Conduct of the servant falls within the scope of employment if: (a) it is of the kind the servant is employed to perform; (b) it occurs substantially within the authorized time and space limits; (c) it is actuated, at least in part, by a purpose to serve the master; and (d) in a case in which the force is intentionally used by the servant against another, it is not unexpectable by the master. Conduct of a servant is not within the scope of employment if it is different in kind from that authorized, far beyond the authorized time and space limits, or too little actuated by a purpose to serve the master.

Here, the cadre were authorized by Norwich to indoctrinate and orient rooks through activities performed at various times of the day and night. A jury could reasonably find members of the cadre were acting in furtherance of their general duties to indoctrinate and orient the rooks and thus within their "scope of employment" at the time of the hazing incidents of which plaintiff complains.

Norwich argues that, because it had adopted policies against hazing and had instructed the cadre to refrain from mistreating the rooks, the tortious conduct was outside the scope of employment. Norwich contends that *McHugh v. University of Vermont* supports this result. In *McHugh*, the Second Circuit Court of Appeals, applying Vermont law, concluded that an employee who sexually and religiously harassed a fellow employee was not acting within the scope of employment. There, a major in the United States Army and an employee at the University of Vermont's Department of Military Studies told plaintiff, a female secretary, that his definition of a "secretary" was a "paid whore." The employee repeatedly joked about plaintiff contracting AIDS, stating that he hoped she would be able to avoid infection. The employee also told plaintiff that it was "a good day to watch Catholic babies burn." *Id.* at 68–69. The court rejected the argument that the employee's conduct was within his scope of employment because it was within that scope for him to talk with the plaintiff, either to give instructions or to avoid the awkwardness of silence at work. It held: "It can hardly be contended that [the employee's] alleged conduct furthered the business" of his employer.

The same cannot be said of this case, where the actions involved in hazing rooks may fairly be seen as qualitatively similar to the indoctrination and orientation with which the cadre members were charged. Indeed, Norwich described some of the acts of which plaintiff complained, such as forced calisthenics and questioning at mealtime, as not far removed from the official system of military discipline and training which recruits are expected to endure. The evidence supported the jury's conclusion that the cadre members were acting within the scope of employment.

     * * *

iii. NEGLIGENT INFLICTION OF EMOTIONAL DISTRESS

Norwich claims that it was error for the court to uphold the jury's finding of liability for the claim of negligent infliction of emotional distress. To establish a claim for negligent infliction of emotional distress, a plaintiff must make a threshold showing that he or someone close to him faced physical peril. The prerequisites for establishing a claim differ according to whether plaintiff suffered a physical impact from an external force. If there has been an impact, plaintiff may recover for emotional distress stemming from the incident during which the impact occurred. If plaintiff has not suffered an impact, plaintiff must show that: (1) he was within the "zone of danger" of an act negligently directed at him by defendant, (2) he was subjected to a reasonable fear of immediate personal injury, and (3) he in fact suffered substantial bodily injury or illness as a result.

In this case, plaintiff withstood at least two incidents of physical impact by a cadre member. Plaintiff testified about the fear of personal injury he felt in connection with a cadre member's careening down the dormitory hallway on a skateboard and "plowing" into rooks. On one such occasion, the cadre member ran into plaintiff. Plaintiff also testified as to the fear and apprehension he felt when struck twice in the shoulder he had previously injured. Plaintiff's doctor testified that plaintiff suffered from post-traumatic-stress disorder and a major depressive disorder as a result of his perception that he was at risk of serious physical injury during the incidents just described. The evidence at trial fairly and reasonably supported the jury's verdict on negligent infliction of emotional distress.

B.   DIRECT LIABILITY—NEGLIGENT SUPERVISION

Norwich argues it was not liable to plaintiff for negligent supervision of the students in the cadre because it owed no duty of care to plaintiff. Norwich's claim is premised on the fact that the hazing in question came at the hands of fellow students. It cites *Smith v. Day* for the proposition that Norwich owed no duty to control the actions of Norwich students for the protection of plaintiff. We disagree because, unlike the *Smith* case, Norwich specifically charged cadre members with "indoctrinating and orienting" plaintiff.

A principal may, in addition to being found *vicariously* liable for tortious conduct of its agents, be found *directly* liable for damages resulting from negligent supervision of its agents' activities. Norwich's claim that it owed no duty to plaintiff under the circumstances of this case fails under these established principles. Under the Restatement, "[a] person conducting an activity through servants or other agents is subject to liability for harm resulting from his conduct if he is negligent or reckless . . . in the supervision of the activity." According to the Restatement's drafters, § 213 "is a special application of the general rules stated in the Restatement of Torts. . . . Liability exists only if all the requirements of an action of tort for negligence exist." In this instance, the cadre members, and by extension Norwich, owed plaintiff at minimum the duty to use reasonable care to avoid harming him. "One who engages in an enterprise is under a duty to anticipate and to guard against the human traits of his employees which unless regulated are likely to harm others. He is likewise required to make such reasonable regulations as the size or complexity of his business may require." Norwich, therefore, owed plaintiff a duty of reasonable care in the control and supervision of the cadre.

In the instant case, the court correctly instructed the jury that Norwich owed plaintiff a duty to use reasonable care in avoiding harm to plaintiff, and the evidence in the record fairly and reasonably supports the jury's finding of liability.

* * *

The judgment of punitive damages is reversed. The judgment is affirmed in all other respects.

NOTES

1. At the higher education level, hazing injuries often occur in a fraternity context, as they have for a very long time, raising issues of university jurisdiction over such extracurricular (and sometimes off-campus) events.

2. In *Furek v. University of Delaware*, 594 A.2d 506 (Del. 1991), a student who had entered the university on a full football scholarship suffered permanent injuries during "Hell Night," "an extended period of hazing during which [he and other pledges to the local chapter of Sig Ep were] physically and emotionally abused." As part of the ritual, the pledges were "escorted into the kitchen blindfolded, and pancake batter, ketchup and other foodstuffs were poured on their heads. During this process, [a fraternity member] poured a container containing a lye-based liquid oven cleaner over the back and neck" of the plaintiff, who was "permanently scarred, subsequently withdrew from the University and forfeited his football scholarship."

"Although official policy directives from the University and the National Fraternity forbade hazing, Sig Ep and other fraternities on the Newark campus had engaged in various forms of hazing for at least five years previous to the incident in question.''

Plaintiff brought a negligence action in state court, seeking to hold the university liable for the failure to protect him from the hazing activities of Sig Ep and its members. The Delaware Supreme Court ruled in his favor.

3. In *Lloyd v. Alpha Phi Alpha Fraternity,* 1999 WL 47153 (N.D.N.Y. 1999), plaintiff student sought to hold Cornell University liable for ''various forms of physical beatings and torture, psychological coercion and embarrassment'' suffered during hazing activities. In that case, however, the federal court in a diversity action found neither actual nor constructive knowledge of the events, and ruled for the university.

4. Knowledge of the specific fraternity hazing activities appears to have been a central factor in both *Furek & Lloyd.* The University of Delaware apparently had knowledge that these specific activities were taking place, while Cornell apparently did not. But location also appeared to play a major role in the Delaware case. What if the Delaware fraternity had been located off-campus, on private property, but all other facts were the same? Would the legal result have been different? Should the legal result have been different?

5. Colleges and universities nationwide often voluntarily ''exercise'' their jurisdiction over off-campus events and activities that pertain to students. This is typically done formally, with guidelines included in written campus policies. And it may also involve the establishment of a relationship between campus police and the local community police department.

A 2003 University of North Carolina policy, for example, provides the following broad, general, guiding principles:

> Conduct by students on University premises or the premises of groups affiliated with the University, as well as conduct that occurs elsewhere, may give rise to offenses prohibited by this Instrument if University interests are implicated. Determinations of whether such conduct should be addressed pursuant to this Instrument in instances in which University interests are implicated is reserved to the discretion of the Student Attorney General and campus authorities with associated responsibilities.

The 2005–2006 UC Riverside Student Conduct Policy, on the other hand, provides a much greater degree of specificity:

> 3.30 Off Campus Jurisdiction. Student conduct that occurs off University property is subject to UCR Standards of Conduct where it 1) adversely affects the health, safety, or security of any member of the University community, or the mission of the University, or 2) involves academic work or any records, or documents of the University. In determining whether or not to exercise jurisdiction over such conduct, the University shall consider the seriousness of the alleged offense, the risk of harm involved, whether the victim(s) are members of the campus community and/or whether the off-campus conduct is part of a series of actions, which occurred both on and off University property. Recommendations to extend jurisdiction will be reviewed by the Assistant Vice Chancellor for Student Affairs.

The University may also exercise jurisdiction over student conduct that occurs off campus where, the conduct compromises University neighbor relations.

For examples of such policies nationwide, *see* Information on Off–Campus Behavior Policies, National Association of State Universities and Land Grant Colleges (NASULGC), http://www.nasulgc.org/CSA/Off-campus.pdf (last visited Sept. 2, 2005).

6.   Disciplinary action against students at public institutions of higher education is, of course, subject to the Due Process Clause. And similar protections are granted to students at many private colleges and universities as a matter of policy. Other legal issues may also arise in this context, some similar to those that have arisen at the K–12 level, but many others very different. For an example of a safety-related suspension/expulsion case with parallels to K–12, *see Gorman v. Univ. of Rhode Island,* 837 F.2d 7 (1st Cir. 1988). For an example a degree-revocation case that is more uniquely higher education, see *Crook v. Baker,* 813 F.2d 88 (6th Cir. 1987).

7.   A distinction has been identified at the higher education level between academic discipline and non-academic discipline. *See Board of Curators, Univ. of Miss. v. Horowitz,* 435 U.S. 78, 98 S.Ct. 948 (1978) (actions of public university under the Fourteenth Amendment); *Corso v. Creighton University,* 731 F.2d 529 (8th Cir. 1984) (actions of private university under policies set forth in the student handbook). *See generally* Jayme L. Butcher, MIT v. Yoo*: Revocation of Academic Degrees for Non–Academic Reasons,* 51 Case W. L. Rev. 749 (2001).

2.   NEGLIGENCE AND INTERCOLLEGIATE ATHLETICS

KAVANAGH v. TRUSTEES OF BOSTON UNIV.

440 Mass. 195, 795 N.E.2d 1170 (2003)

SOSMAN, J.

Having been punched by an opposing Boston University player during an intercollegiate basketball game, the plaintiff brought suit against the trustees of Boston University (university) and the coach of the university's team, contending that the university was vicariously liable for the conduct of its "scholarship athlete," and that the university and its coach were negligent in that they "took no steps to prevent this act." Against the coach, Kavanagh also alleged both negligent and intentional infliction of emotional distress. * * *

1.   *Facts.* On December 22, 1998, the university hosted a men's intercollegiate basketball game against Manhattan College. The plaintiff, Kenneth Kavanagh, was a member of the Manhattan College team. Following a contested rebound during the second half, the referee blew his whistle to signal a foul, and some elbowing and shoving ensued among a few of the competing players. When Kavanagh intervened to break up a developing scuffle between one of his teammates and a university player,

he was punched in the nose by another university player, Levar Folk. Folk was immediately ejected from the game. Kavanagh was treated for what turned out to be a broken nose and returned to play later in the same game.

* * * Until the incident involving Kavanagh, Folk had not been involved in any physical altercation during a game and had never been ejected from a game. He had no prior history of physical confrontations or fights with either his own teammates or opposing players.

[However, i]n his junior year, one year prior to the assault on Kavanagh, Folk had had an argument with Coach Wolff about his manner of play (Wolff believed that Folk was taking too many shots) and about an academic issue (Wolff was concerned that Folk had missed an examination and had tried to secure an excuse for having done so). The argument was heated, but involved no physical contact. Wolff suspended Folk for a period of several games, and Folk resumed team play thereafter without incident until the December, 1998, game against Manhattan College.

Folk's disciplinary history with the university included the imposition of two periods of "residence probation" for violation of the university's policies on noise and alcohol. Neither infraction involved any act of violence or threatened violence.

Although Kavanagh characterizes the December 22, 1998, game as "the most physical" he ever played, the number of penalties called by the referees was within a normal range. Up until the time he struck Kavanagh during the second half, no technical fouls had been called on Folk, and no university players had been ejected. Kavanagh describes the university team's play as follows: "with reckless abandon," "elbows to people's faces, trying to steal the ball," "after plays, bumping people," "holding you with both their hands, walking by, getting the elbow." He also claimed that Coach Wolff incited the team's aggressiveness by yelling encouragement from the sideline, not substituting for players who were allegedly elbowing opposing players, and calling out praise for his players, despite the fact that they were, in Kavanagh's view, committing fouls. Wolff denied that he had ever instructed Folk (or any other player) to hit or fight with any opposing player, and Kavanagh presented no contrary evidence.

* * * When Wolff talked to Folk about the incident sometime after the game, Folk's explanation for his misconduct was that he "lost it."

2. *Discussion.* a. *Vicarious liability.* Kavanagh contends that Folk's status as a scholarship athlete playing for the university made him an agent of the university and that the university is therefore vicariously liable for any torts committed by Folk while playing for the university's basketball team. We reject the proposition that the doctrine of respondeat superior renders schools liable for the acts of their students, and decline to treat scholarship students any differently from paying students for these purposes.

* * *

b. *Negligence.* Kavanagh also claims that the university breached a duty to protect him from the allegedly foreseeable assault and battery by Folk. He acknowledges that, as a general rule, there is no duty to protect another from the criminal conduct of a third party. However, such a duty arises when there is a "special relationship" between the defendant and the injured victim. "[S]pecial relationships exist in several situations, based either on responsibilities imposed by statute or common law (or both). A special relationship, when derived from common law, is predicated on a plaintiff's reasonable expectations and reliance that a defendant will anticipate harmful acts of third persons and take appropriate measures to protect the plaintiff from harm." * * * Kavanagh contends that his status as a student athlete on an opposing team created such a special relationship between himself and the university.

In recent years, courts and commentators have taken differing views as to what duties schools have to the scholarship athletes that they have recruited. Some are of the view that the unequal bargaining power in the recruitment process, the degree of influence that a school and its coaches have over a student athlete's daily life, the pressures placed on student athletes to win at all costs (which may cause some students to risk their own health and safety), and the enormous sums of money schools now reap from their successful teams, are such that schools should be deemed to have a "special relationship" with their own scholarship athletes and a corresponding duty to protect those athletes from injury. * * * Others have rejected that theory on the ground that there is "nothing different about a student athlete's relationship with a university which would justify the conclusion that a student athlete is a custodial ward of the university while the non-athlete student is an emancipated adult." * * *

For purposes of this case, we need not enter that debate, as none of the authorities favoring such a "special relationship" has opined that that relationship extends to athletes from another school. Here, the university did not recruit Kavanagh; Kavanagh did not depend on the university nor the university on him for any benefit; and the university did not exert any form of control or influence over Kavanagh, or affect his ability or motive to protect himself. In short, Kavanagh had no relationship with the university, special or otherwise, and the sources he cites would, if accepted as law here in Massachusetts, place a duty on his own school, Manhattan College, not on the university.

Kavanagh's negligence claim also fails on the ground that any duty to protect him from the harm of another's criminal acts extends only to those acts that are reasonably foreseeable. However, "where there has been a showing that the risk of a criminal assault is foreseeable, the exact nature and source of the assault need not be shown in order for liability to attach." In a general sense, one can always foresee that, in the thrill of competition and the heat of battle inherent in a contact sport, any player might some day lose his or her temper and strike an opposing player. If that possibility alone sufficed to make an assault on the field of play reasonably "foreseeable," schools and coaches would face liability every time they allowed their enthusiastic players to take the field against an opposing team. For these purposes, foreseeability must mean something more than awareness of the ever-present possibility that an athlete may become overly excited and engage in physical contact beyond the precise boundaries of acceptably aggressive play. Rather, a defendant would have to have specific information about a player suggesting a propensity to engage in violent conduct, or some warning that a player or players appeared headed toward such conduct as the game progressed.

No such evidence has been presented here. On the undisputed facts, neither the university nor its coach had any reason to foresee that Folk would engage in violent behavior. He had never done so before, he had no history suggestive of potential violence on or off the basketball court,[7] and nothing in his conduct during the earlier part of the game provided any warning signal that Folk was on the verge of a violent outburst. Neither the university nor its coach had any duty to protect Kavanagh from a harm that they could not have reasonably foreseen.

Kavanagh's final theory of negligence alleges that Folk's attack was incited by Coach Wolff's own aggressive demeanor on the sidelines. Kavanagh has no evidence that Wolff instructed or expressly encouraged Folk to hit an opposing player. Rather, he contends that Wolff's animated style of coaching effectively pushed Folk beyond the boundaries of aggressive physical play into criminal violence. We agree with the motion judge that the record fails to support Kavanagh's theory.

We must first address what standard is to be applied to claims that coaches are liable for causing their players to injure other players. Recognizing that, by their nature, competitive sports involve physical contact between opposing players, and that some degree of aggressiveness in play is essential to athletic competition, we have held that mere negligence on the part of a player does not suffice to impose liability for injuries inflicted by that player during competition. Rather, an injured player must show that the other player's conduct amounted to recklessness before the law will impose liability. Utilizing a standard of recklessness, as opposed to mere negligence, "furthers the policy that '[v]igorous and active participation in sporting events should not be chilled by the threat of litigation.'" Just as players are entitled to play aggressively without fear of liability, a coach properly may encourage players to play aggressively. Indeed, a coach's ability to inspire players to compete aggressively is one of a coach's important attributes. The mere possibility that some players might overreact to such inspiration or encouragement should not, by itself, suffice to impose liability on a coach. As we do with the players themselves, we must impose liability only where a coach's behavior amounts to at least recklessness.

---

7. While Kavanagh makes much of the fact that Folk had previously been suspended from the team, and had been disciplined by university authorities, none of those prior incidents had anything to do with violence or threats of violence.

Here, Kavanagh cannot demonstrate any recklessness on the part of Coach Wolff. To the extent that Wolff's demeanor was excited and aggressive, that is demeanor appropriate for a coach during a game. As to Kavanagh's contention that Wolff encouraged violence by failing to send in substitute players for players who were allegedly committing fouls, that contention would effectively require Wolff to be more sensitive to possible fouls than the referees. Under the rules of any sport, fouls or other violations carry their own penalties, and it is up to the officials refereeing the competition to enforce those rules and impose those penalties. It is not up to a coach to remove a player who may, conformably with the rules of the sport and the judgment of the referees, remain in the game despite the infractions allegedly committed. Finally, Kavanagh contends that Wolff yelled encouragement to aggressive players, praising their play when those same players were, in Kavanagh's judgment, committing fouls. Again, the policing of fouls is up to the referees, and the mere fact that a player has committed a foul, or even multiple fouls, does not preclude a coach from encouraging that player to play aggressively. Coach Wolff's behavior, viewed in the light most favorable to the plaintiff, amounted to nothing more than aggressive coaching. It did not amount to reckless conduct.

Judgments affirmed.

NOTES

1. Perhaps the most highly publicized incident involving injury to a college athlete in this era was the tragic death of Hank Gathers, star basketball player for an outstanding Loyola Marymount team (LMU) that was headed for a top seed in the men's NCAA playoffs. Gathers, a high scoring and inspirational forward, would have been one of the top draft picks in the National Basketball Association. As described in the following law journal excerpt, a series of interrelated and troubling issues were raised by the death:

> On the afternoon of March 4, 1990, * * * Hank Gathers * * * collapsed after scoring a basket. Less than two hours later he was dead, a victim of idiopathic cardiomyopathy, a heart disorder. As a result of Gather's death, a $32.5 million lawsuit [was] filed by his family * * *.

> Defendants in the suit include Loyola Marymount University, Loyola Marymount's athletic director, its team trainer, and the former coach. Also named as defendants [were] several physicians who were treating Gathers for an irregular heartbeat discovered after he collapsed during a game on December 9, 1989. Among the allegations raised by the Gathers family [were] that the team coach induced the physicians into lowering the dosage of medication Gathers was taking to control his heart condition; that the physicians failed to adequately monitor the effects of the changed dosage; and that they failed to fully disclose the nature, extent, and effects of Gathers' heart disease and the consequences of his returning to play basketball with such a condition. The complaint also [raised] the issue of whether Gathers should have been allowed to continue his basketball career at all after the heart condition was discovered months before his death.

On its face, *Gathers* appears to be another case of alleged medical malpractice raising concerns about the treatment provided to a heart patient. However, because Hank Gathers was a major college basketball star playing for a school that allegedly hoped to parlay his athletic abilities into millions of dollars and national exposure for itself, *Gathers* raises deeper, and indeed more troubling, questions concerning relationships among athletic teams, their players, and the team physicians who must serve them both. A reexamination of the relationship of the team physician to both the team and the athletes he or she serves is one of the most important issues raised by Gathers' death. A team physician's professional obligations are confronted by both the triangular nature of the relationships and the pressures raised by the competition and money involved in high-stakes sports. Craig A. Isaacs, *Conflicts of Interest for Team Physicians: A Retrospective in Light of* Gathers v. LMU, 2 ALBANY L.J. SCI. & TECH. 147, 148–49 (1992).

While the case ultimately settled, many believe that the alleged conduct of the treating physicians, if proven, would have constituted actionable negligence.

What are the lessons that might be drawn from this incident today, legally and as a matter of policy?

C. SEARCH AND SEIZURE, DRUG TEST-ING, AND RELATED FOURTH AMEND-MENT CONCERNS

1. THE DOCTRINE OF *IN LOCO PARENTIS*

As referenced above under a negligence law analysis, the doctrine of *in loco parentis* has had a significant impact on the laws relating to campus activity. The doctrine is predicated on the idea that educators should be viewed as standing *in loco parentis* (in the place of parents) in a school setting, and should therefore have the same rights and responsibilities as parents. This reasoning has not only impacted the scope of the duty of care under negligence law, but has been used to justify limiting student rights under the First and Fourth Amendments. Just as parents are legally entitled to silence their children at the dinner table, for example, educators were once able to silence their students in a similarly arbitrary fashion. And just as parents are able under the law to search their children's rooms and belongings without permission, so too were educators able to search their students indiscriminately.

It is unclear today just exactly where the doctrine stands, and the picture may be different depending on the area of the law impacted, the geographical location, and of course the age of the students. For the youngest students, few would argue that the school does not stand in the place of the parent today for all intents and purposes. For graduate students, few would argue the opposite.

As a general rule, however, the doctrine has arguably gained renewed force in recent decades, after having been all but completely abrogated by the courts in the 1960's, 1970's, and 1980's. Even at the higher education level, both legislators and jurists have shown an increasing tendency to place additional responsibilities on the educational institutions, particularly with regard to campus safety.

Consider the materials in the second half of this chapter in light of the meaning, rationale, and arguably renewed vigor of the *in loco parentis* doctrine. What are the implications for student privacy rights, particularly in an era of increasing electronic and digital surveillance across the board? What can or should be done to address these trends?

2. K–12 SEARCH & SEIZURE CASE LAW GENERALLY: THE CONTINUING VITALITY OF *NEW JERSEY v. T.L.O.*

PROBLEM 7: THE SUBURBIA LAWSUITS (CONTINUED)

SUBURBIA HIGH, NOVEMBER 4th: Senior Class Sponsor Fred Brown, on his way to the teacher's cafeteria, realized that he had forgotten his wallet and returned to his room to retrieve it. As he walked into the room, where several Senior Class officers were participating in a lively impromptu debate, he saw Sherry Marvin dip a key into a small vial of white powder and bring it up to her nose.

There were various interpretations as to what happened next. All agreed that "Coach" Brown yelled "What is going on here?" and that in the ensuing commotion the vial disappeared from view. The students had been sitting in somewhat of a semicircle, with several backpacks and purses lying around (some open, the others closed). It appeared to Brown that at least three students reached for backpacks, and it seemed to him that one or two packs or purses (he could not be sure) were either exchanged or at least shuffled around under the desks. Then the room became silent. Coach Brown explained that he had to take Sherry to the Assistant Principal.

As Sherry and Coach Brown began walking out of the classroom, Senior Class President Amanda Green suddenly became visibly agitated. "Sherry," she yelled, "you don't need to go with him." A large crowd of students gathered, and followed Amanda, Sherry, and Brown to the office building. Just before they entered the building, Amanda shouted: "Sherry, would you please give me back my purse!" The action was so dramatic that not only did everyone hear Amanda, but everyone saw Sherry hand over the purse.

Once inside the office building, Assistant Principal Margie Cole asked Amanda to leave, but she insisted on waiting to see what would happen to Sherry (who seemed to have disappeared). Cole hesitated, then asked Amanda and Brown to come into her private office. After repeated unsuccessful attempts to convince Amanda to hand over the purse, Ms. Cole forcefully took it and opened it up. Inside was a plastic bag containing white powder, and three small, empty vials. The police were called, Amanda was arrested, and lab tests later revealed that the white powder was in fact 7.5 grams of high quality cocaine.

NOVEMBER 5th: While all the students were in their Period 2 classes, Principal Arthur Ramsey ordered a search of the lockers of all Suburbia High Senior Class officers. Although no additional cocaine was found, two marijuana cigarettes were found in one locker, and one Jack Daniel's Country Cocktail in another. The police were called, and the students whose lockers had been searched were arrested. (When students were assigned lockers in September, no notice of any kind was provided regarding the possibility of locker searches. In fact, this was the first time in the history of Suburbia High that student lockers had been "searched.")

NOVEMBER 6th: Sherry Marvin, after two sleepless nights, contacted the local newspaper and in a shocking interview, admitted that she was in fact a Suburbia Police Officer who was only posing as a student. She also announced that she was checking herself into a drug rehabilitation center.

What arguments should be set forth in the following lawsuits? What result? Discuss.

Amanda Green v. Suburbia School District (alleging that the search of Amanda's purse violated her constitutional rights)

Suzukida v. Suburbia School District (alleging that the locker search violated the students' constitutional rights)

NEW JERSEY v. T.L.O.

469 U.S. 325, 105 S.Ct. 733 (1985)

JUSTICE WHITE delivered the opinion of the Court.

* * *

I

On March 7, 1980, a teacher at Piscataway High School in Middlesex County, N.J., discovered two girls smoking in a lavatory. One of the two girls was the respondent T.L.O., who at that time was a 14-year-old high school freshman. Because smoking in the lavatory was a violation of a school rule, the teacher took the two girls to the Principal's office, where they met with Assistant Vice Principal Theodore Choplick. In response to questioning by Mr. Choplick, T.L.O.'s companion admitted that she had violated the rule. T.L.O., however, denied that she had been smoking in the lavatory and claimed that she did not smoke at all.

Mr. Choplick asked T.L.O. to come into his private office and demanded to see her purse. Opening the purse, he found a pack of cigarettes, which he removed from the purse and held before T.L.O. as he accused her of having lied to him. As he reached into the purse for the cigarettes, Mr. Choplick also noticed a package of cigarette rolling papers. In his experience, possession of rolling papers by high school students was closely associated with the use of marihuana. Suspecting that a closer examination of the purse might yield further evidence of drug use, Mr.

Choplick proceeded to search the purse thoroughly. The search revealed a small amount of marihuana, a pipe, a number of empty plastic bags, a substantial quantity of money in one-dollar bills, an index card that appeared to be a list of students who owed T.L.O. money, and two letters that implicated T.L.O. in marihuana dealing.

Mr. Choplick notified T.L.O.'s mother and the police, and turned the evidence of drug dealing over to the police. At the request of the police, T.L.O.'s mother took her daughter to police headquarters, where T.L.O. confessed that she had been selling marihuana at the high school. On the basis of the confession and the evidence seized by Mr. Choplick, the State brought delinquency charges against T.L.O. in the Juvenile and Domestic Relations Court of Middlesex County. Contending that Mr. Choplick's search of her purse violated the Fourth Amendment, T.L.O. moved to suppress the evidence found in her purse as well as her confession, which, she argued, was tainted by the allegedly unlawful search.

* * *

II

In determining whether the search at issue in this case violated the Fourth Amendment, we are faced initially with the question whether that Amendment's prohibition on unreasonable searches and seizures applies to searches conducted by public school officials. We hold that it does.

It is now beyond dispute that "the Federal Constitution, by virtue of the Fourteenth Amendment, prohibits unreasonable searches and seizures by state officers." Equally indisputable is the proposition that the Fourteenth Amendment protects the rights of students against encroachment by public school officials * * *.

* * *

III

To hold that the Fourth Amendment applies to searches conducted by school authorities is only to begin the inquiry into the standards governing such searches. Although the underlying command of the Fourth Amendment is always that searches and seizures be reasonable, what is reasonable depends on the context within which a search takes place. The determination of the standard of reasonableness governing any specific class of searches requires "balancing the need to search against the invasion which the search entails." On one side of the balance are arrayed the individual's legitimate expectations of privacy and personal security; on the other, the government's need for effective methods to deal with breaches of public order.

We have recognized that even a limited search of the person is a substantial invasion of privacy. We have also recognized that searches of closed items of personal luggage are intrusions on protected privacy interests, for "the Fourth Amendment provides protection to the owner of every container that conceals its contents from plain view." A search of a child's person or of a closed purse or other bag carried on her person,[5] no less than a similar search carried out on an adult, is undoubtedly a severe violation of subjective expectations of privacy.

Of course, the Fourth Amendment does not protect subjective expectations of privacy that are unreasonable or otherwise "illegitimate." To receive the protection of the Fourth Amendment, an expectation of privacy must be one that society is "prepared to recognize as legitimate." * * *

Although this Court may take notice of the difficulty of maintaining discipline in the public schools today, the situation is not so dire that students in the schools may claim no legitimate expectations of privacy. * * * We are not yet ready to hold that the schools and the prisons need be equated for purposes of the Fourth Amendment.

Nor does the State's suggestion that children have no legitimate need to bring personal property into the schools seem well anchored in reality. Students at a minimum must bring to school not only the supplies needed for their studies, but also keys, money, and the necessaries of personal hygiene and grooming. In addition, students may carry on their persons or in purses or wallets such nondisruptive yet highly personal items as photographs, letters, and diaries. Finally, students may have perfectly legitimate reasons to carry with them articles of property needed in connection with extracurricular or recreational activities. In short, schoolchildren may find it necessary to carry with them a variety of legitimate, noncontraband items, and there is no reason to conclude that they have necessarily waived all rights to privacy in such items merely by bringing them onto school grounds.

Against the child's interest in privacy must be set the substantial interest of teachers and administrators in maintaining discipline in the classroom and on school grounds. Maintaining order in the classroom has never been easy, but in recent years, school disorder has often taken particularly ugly forms: drug use and violent crime in the schools have become major social problems. Even in schools that have been spared the most severe disciplinary problems, the preservation of order and a proper educational environment requires close supervision of schoolchildren, as well as the enforcement of rules against conduct that would be perfectly permissible if undertaken by an adult. "Events calling for discipline are frequent occurrences and sometimes require immediate, effective action." Accordingly, we have recognized that maintaining security and order in

---

5. We do not address the question, not presented by this case, whether a schoolchild has a legitimate expectation of privacy in lockers, desks, or other school property provided for the storage of school supplies. Nor do we express any opinion on the standards (if any) governing searches of such areas by school officials or by other public authorities acting at the request of school officials. Compare *Zamora v. Pomeroy,* 639 F.2d 662, 670 (CA10 1981) ("Inasmuch as the school had assumed joint control of the locker it cannot be successfully maintained that the school did not have a right to inspect it."), and *People v. Overton,* 24 N.Y.2d 522, 249 N.E.2d 366, 301 N.Y.S.2d 479 (1969) (holding that school administrators have power to consent to search of a student's locker), with *State v. Engerud,* 94 N.J. 331, 348, 463 A.2d 934, 943 (1983) ("We are satisfied that in the context of this case the student had an expectation of privacy in the contents of his locker.... For the four years of high school, the school locker is a home away from home. In it the student stores the kind of personal 'effects' protected by the Fourth Amendment.").

the schools requires a certain degree of flexibility in school disciplinary procedures, and we have respected the value of preserving the informality of the student-teacher relationship.

How, then, should we strike the balance between the schoolchild's legitimate expectations of privacy and the school's equally legitimate need to maintain an environment in which learning can take place? It is evident that the school setting requires some easing of the restrictions to which searches by public authorities are ordinarily subject. The warrant requirement, in particular, is unsuited to the school environment: requiring a teacher to obtain a warrant before searching a child suspected of an infraction of school rules (or of the criminal law) would unduly interfere with the maintenance of the swift and informal disciplinary procedures needed in the schools. Just as we have in other cases dispensed with the warrant requirement when "the burden of obtaining a warrant is likely to frustrate the governmental purpose behind the search," we hold today that school officials need not obtain a warrant before searching a student who is under their authority.

The school setting also requires some modification of the level of suspicion of illicit activity needed to justify a search. Ordinarily, a search—even one that may permissibly be carried out without a warrant—must be based upon "probable cause" to believe that a violation of the law has occurred. However, "probable cause" is not an irreducible requirement of a valid search. The fundamental command of the Fourth Amendment is that searches and seizures be reasonable, and although "both the concept of probable cause and the requirement of a warrant bear on the reasonableness of a search, . . . in certain limited circumstances neither is required." Thus, we have in a number of cases recognized the legality of searches and seizures based on suspicions that, although "reasonable," do not rise to the level of probable cause. Where a careful balancing of governmental and private interests suggests that the public interest is best served by a Fourth Amendment standard of reasonableness that stops short of probable cause, we have not hesitated to adopt such a standard.

We join the majority of courts that have examined this issue in concluding that the accommodation of the privacy interests of schoolchildren with the substantial need of teachers and administrators for freedom to maintain order in the schools does not require strict adherence to the requirement that searches be based on probable cause to believe that the subject of the search has violated or is violating the law. Rather, the legality of a search of a student should depend simply on the reasonableness, under all the circumstances, of the search. Determining the reasonableness of any search involves a twofold inquiry: first, one must consider "whether the . . . action was justified at its inception,"; second, one must determine whether the search as actually conducted "was reasonably related in scope to the circumstances which justified the interference in the first place." Under ordinary circumstances, a search of a student by a teacher or other school official will be "justified at its inception" when there are reasonable grounds for suspecting that the search will turn up evidence that the student has violated or is violating either the law or the rules of the school.[8] Such a search will be permissible in its scope when the measures adopted are reasonably related to the objectives of the search and not excessively intrusive in light of the age and sex of the student and the nature of the infraction.

This standard will, we trust, neither unduly burden the efforts of school authorities to maintain order in their schools nor authorize unrestrained intrusions upon the privacy of schoolchildren. By focusing attention on the question of reasonableness, the standard will spare teachers and school administrators the necessity of schooling themselves in the niceties of probable cause and permit them to regulate their conduct according to the dictates of reason and common sense. At the same time, the reasonableness standard should ensure that the interests of students will be invaded no more than is necessary to achieve the legitimate end of preserving order in the schools.

IV

* * * Our review of the facts surrounding the search leads us to conclude that the search was in no sense unreasonable for Fourth Amendment purposes.[10]

The incident that gave rise to this case actually involved two separate searches, with the first—the search for cigarettes—providing the suspicion that gave rise to the second the search for marihuana. Although it is the fruits of the second search that are at issue here, the validity of the search for marihuana must depend on the reasonableness of the initial search for cigarettes, as there would have been no reason to suspect that T.L.O. possessed marihuana had the first search not taken place. Accordingly, it is to the search for cigarettes that we first turn our attention.

* * * T.L.O. had been accused of smoking, and had denied the accusation in the strongest possible terms when she stated that she did not smoke at all. Surely it cannot be said that under these circumstances, T.L.O.'s possession of cigarettes would be irrelevant to the charges against her or to her response to those charges. T.L.O.'s possession of cigarettes, once it was discovered, would both corroborate the report that she had been smoking and undermine the credibility of her defense to the charge

---

8. We do not decide whether individualized suspicion is an essential element of the reasonableness standard we adopt for searches by school authorities. In other contexts, however, we have held that although "some quantum of individualized suspicion is usually a prerequisite to a constitutional search or seizure[,] . . . the Fourth Amendment imposes no irreducible requirement of such suspicion." Exceptions to the requirement of individualized suspicion are generally appropriate only where the privacy interests implicated by a search are minimal and where "other safeguards" are available "to assure that the individual's reasonable expectation of privacy is not 'subject to the discretion of the official in the field.' " Because the search of T.L.O.'s purse was based upon an individualized suspicion that she had violated school rules, *see infra,* at 745–46, we need not consider the circumstances that might justify school authorities in conducting searches unsupported by individualized suspicion.

10. Of course, New Jersey may insist on a more demanding standard under its own Constitution or statutes. In that case, its courts would not purport to be applying the Fourth Amendment when they invalidate a search.

of smoking. To be sure, the discovery of the cigarettes would not prove that T.L.O. had been smoking in the lavatory; nor would it, strictly speaking, necessarily be inconsistent with her claim that she did not smoke at all. But it is universally recognized that evidence, to be relevant to an inquiry, need not conclusively prove the ultimate fact in issue, but only have "any tendency to make the existence of any fact that is of consequence to the determination of the action more probable or less probable than it would be without the evidence." The relevance of T.L.O.'s possession of cigarettes to the question whether she had been smoking and to the credibility of her denial that she smoked supplied the necessary "nexus" between the item searched for and the infraction under investigation. * * *

* * * Mr. Choplick's suspicion that there were cigarettes in the purse was not an "inchoate and unparticularized suspicion or 'hunch,' " [R]ather, it was the sort of "common-sense conclusio[n] about human behavior" upon which "practical people"—including government officials—are entitled to rely. Of course, even if the teacher's report were true, T.L.O. *might* not have had a pack of cigarettes with her; she might have borrowed a cigarette from someone else or have been sharing a cigarette with another student. But the requirement of reasonable suspicion is not a requirement of absolute certainty: "sufficient probability, not certainty, is the touchstone of reasonableness under the Fourth Amendment. . . ." Because the hypothesis that T.L.O. was carrying cigarettes in her purse was itself not unreasonable, it is irrelevant that other hypotheses were also consistent with the teacher's accusation. Accordingly, it cannot be said that Mr. Choplick acted unreasonably when he examined T.L.O.'s purse to see if it contained cigarettes.

Our conclusion that Mr. Choplick's decision to open T.L.O.'s purse was reasonable brings us to the question of the further search for marihuana once the pack of cigarettes was located. The suspicion upon which the search for marihuana was founded was provided when Mr. Choplick observed a package of rolling papers in the purse as he removed the pack of cigarettes. Although T.L.O. does not dispute the reasonableness of Mr. Choplick's belief that the rolling papers indicated the presence of marihuana, she does contend that the scope of the search Mr. Choplick conducted exceeded permissible bounds when he seized and read certain letters that implicated T.L.O. in drug dealing. This argument, too, is unpersuasive. The discovery of the rolling papers concededly gave rise to a reasonable suspicion that T.L.O. was carrying marihuana as well as cigarettes in her purse. This suspicion justified further exploration of T.L.O.'s purse, which turned up more evidence of drug-related activities: a pipe, a number of plastic bags of the type commonly used to store marihuana, a small quantity of marihuana, and a fairly substantial amount of money. Under these circumstances, it was not unreasonable to extend the search to a separate zippered compartment of the purse; and when a search of that compartment revealed an index card containing a list of "people who owe me money" as well as two letters, the inference that T.L.O. was involved in marihuana trafficking was substantial enough to justify Mr. Choplick in examining the letters to determine whether they contained any further evidence. In short, we cannot conclude that the search for marihuana was unreasonable in any respect.

Because the search resulting in the discovery of the evidence of marihuana dealing by T.L.O. was reasonable, the New Jersey Supreme Court's decision to exclude that evidence from T.L.O.'s juvenile delinquency proceedings on Fourth Amendment grounds was erroneous. Accordingly, the judgment of the Supreme Court of New Jersey is

Reversed.

JUSTICE POWELL, with whom JUSTICE O'CONNOR joins, concurring.

I agree with the Court's decision, and generally with its opinion. I would place greater emphasis, however, on the special characteristics of elementary and secondary schools that make it unnecessary to afford students the same constitutional protections granted adults and juveniles in a nonschool setting.

In any realistic sense, students within the school environment have a lesser expectation of privacy than members of the population generally. They spend the school hours in close association with each other, both in the classroom and during recreation periods. The students in a particular class often know each other and their teachers quite well. Of necessity, teachers have a degree of familiarity with, and authority over, their students that is unparalleled except perhaps in the relationship between parent and child. It is simply unrealistic to think that students have the same subjective expectation of privacy as the population generally. But for purposes of deciding this case, I can assume that children in school—no less than adults—have privacy interests that society is prepared to recognize as legitimate.

* * *

The special relationship between teacher and student also distinguishes the setting within which schoolchildren operate. Law enforcement officers function as adversaries of criminal suspects. These officers have the responsibility to investigate criminal activity, to locate and arrest those who violate our laws, and to facilitate the charging and bringing of such persons to trial. Rarely does this type of adversarial relationship exist between school authorities and pupils. Instead, there is a commonality of interests between teachers and their pupils. The attitude of the typical teacher is one of personal responsibility for the student's welfare as well as for his education.

The primary duty of school officials and teachers, as the Court states, is the education and training of young people. A State has a compelling interest in assuring that the schools meet this responsibility. Without first establishing discipline and maintaining order, teachers cannot begin to educate their students. And apart from education, the school has the obligation to protect pupils from mistreatment by other children, and also to protect teachers themselves from violence by the few students whose conduct in recent years has prompted national concern. For me, it would be unreasonable and at odds with history to argue that the full panoply of constitutional rules applies with the same force and effect in the school-house as it does in the enforcement of criminal laws.

In sum, although I join the Court's opinion and its holding, my emphasis is somewhat different.

JUSTICE BLACKMUN, concurring in the judgment.

I join the judgment of the Court and agree with much that is said in its opinion. I write separately, however, because I believe the Court omits a crucial step in its analysis of whether a school search must be based upon probable-cause. The Court correctly states that we have recognized limited exceptions to the probable-cause requirement "[w]here a careful balancing of governmental and private interests suggests that the public interest is best served" by a lesser standard. I believe that we have used such a balancing test, rather than strictly applying the Fourth Amendment's Warrant and Probable–Cause Clause, only when we were confronted with "a special law enforcement need for greater flexibility." I pointed out in *United States v. Place*:

> While the Fourth Amendment speaks in terms of freedom from unreasonable [searches], the Amendment does not leave the reasonableness of most [searches] to the judgment of courts or government officers; the Framers of the Amendment balanced the interests involved and decided that a [search] is reasonable only if supported by a judicial warrant based on probable cause.

Only in those exceptional circumstances in which special needs, beyond the normal need for law enforcement, make the warrant and probable-cause requirement impracticable, is a court entitled to substitute its balancing of interests for that of the Framers.

      * * *

The Court's implication that the balancing test is the rule rather than the exception is troubling for me because it is unnecessary in this case. The elementary and secondary school setting presents a special need for flexibility justifying a departure from the balance struck by the Framers. As Justice POWELL notes, "[w]ithout first establishing discipline and maintaining order, teachers cannot begin to educate their students." Maintaining order in the classroom can be a difficult task. A single teacher often must watch over a large number of students, and, as any parent knows, children at certain ages are inclined to test the outer boundaries of acceptable conduct and to imitate the misbehavior of a peer if that misbehavior is not dealt with quickly. Every adult remembers from his own schooldays the havoc a water pistol or peashooter can wreak until it is taken away. Thus, the Court has recognized that "[e]vents calling for discipline are frequent occurrences and sometimes require immediate, effective action." Indeed, because drug use and possession of weapons have become increasingly common among young people, an immediate response frequently is required not just to maintain an environment conducive to learning, but to protect the very safety of students and school personnel.

Such immediate action obviously would not be possible if a teacher were required to secure a warrant before searching a student. Nor would it be possible if a teacher could not conduct a necessary search until the teacher thought there was probable cause for the search. A teacher has neither the training nor the day-to-day experience in the complexities of probable cause that a law enforcement officer possesses, and is ill-equipped to make a quick judgment about the existence of probable cause. The time required for a teacher to ask the questions or make the observations that are necessary to turn reasonable grounds into probable cause is time during which the teacher, and other students, are diverted from the essential task of education. A teacher's focus is, and should be, on teaching and helping students, rather than on developing evidence against a particular troublemaker.

Education "is perhaps the most important function" of government, *Brown v. Board of Education,* 347 U.S. 483, 493, 74 S. Ct. 686, 691 (1954), and government has a heightened obligation to safeguard students whom it compels to attend school. The special need for an immediate response to behavior that threatens either the safety of schoolchildren and teachers or the educational process itself justifies the Court in excepting school searches from the warrant and probable-cause requirement, and in applying a standard determined by balancing the relevant interests. I agree with the standard the Court has announced, and with its application of the standard to the facts of this case. I therefore concur in its judgment.

JUSTICE BRENNAN, with whom JUSTICE MARSHALL joins, concurring in part and dissenting in part.

I fully agree with Part II of the Court's opinion. Teachers, like all other government officials, must conform their conduct to the Fourth Amendment's protections of personal privacy and personal security. * * *

I do not, however, otherwise join the Court's opinion. Today's decision sanctions school officials to conduct full-scale searches on a "reasonableness" standard whose only definite content is that it is *not* the same test as the "probable cause" standard found in the text of the Fourth Amendment. In adopting this unclear, unprecedented, and unnecessary departure from generally applicable Fourth Amendment standards, the Court carves out a broad exception to standards that this Court has developed over years of considering Fourth Amendment problems. Its decision is supported neither by precedent nor even by a fair application of the "balancing test" it proclaims in this very opinion.

* * *

On my view, the presence of the word "unreasonable" in the text of the Fourth Amendment does not grant a shifting majority of this Court the authority to answer *all* Fourth Amendment questions by consulting its momentary vision of the social good. Full-scale searches unaccompanied by probable cause violate the Fourth Amendment. I do not pretend that our traditional Fourth Amendment doctrine automatically answers all of the difficult legal questions that occasionally arise. I do contend, however, that this Court has an obligation to provide some coherent framework to resolve such questions on the basis of more than a conclusory recitation of the results of a "balancing test." The Fourth Amendment itself supplies that framework and, because the Court today fails to heed its message, I must respectfully dissent.

JUSTICE STEVENS, with whom JUSTICE MARSHALL joins, and with whom JUSTICE BRENNAN joins as to Part I, concurring in part and dissenting in part.

* * *

The State of New Jersey sought review in this Court, first arguing that the exclusionary rule is wholly inapplicable to searches conducted by school officials, and then contending that the Fourth Amendment itself provides no protection at all to the student's privacy. The Court has accepted neither of these frontal assaults on the Fourth Amendment. It has, however, seized upon this "no smoking" case to announce "the proper standard" that should govern searches by school officials who are confronted with disciplinary problems far more severe than smoking in the restroom. Although I join Part II of the Court's opinion, I continue to believe that the Court has unnecessarily and inappropriately reached out to decide a constitutional question. More importantly, I fear that the concerns that motivated the Court's activism have produced a holding that will permit school administrators to search students suspected of violating only the most trivial school regulations and guidelines for behavior.

* * *

Justice Brandeis was both a great student and a great teacher. It was he who wrote:

"Our Government is the potent, the omnipresent teacher. For good or for ill, it teaches the whole people by its example. Crime is contagious. If the Government becomes a lawbreaker, it breeds contempt for law; it invites every man to become a law unto himself; it invites anarchy." Those of us who revere the flag and the ideals for which it stands believe in the power of symbols. We cannot ignore that rules of law also have a symbolic power that may vastly exceed their utility.

Schools are places where we inculcate the values essential to the meaningful exercise of rights and responsibilities by a self-governing citizenry. If the Nation's students can be convicted through the use of arbitrary methods destructive of personal liberty, they cannot help but feel that they have been dealt with unfairly. The application of the exclusionary rule in criminal proceedings arising from illegal school searches makes an important statement to young people that "our society attaches serious consequences to a violation of constitutional rights," and that this is a principle of "liberty and justice for all."

* * *

In arguing that teachers and school administrators need the power to search students based on a lessened standard, the United States as *amicus curiae* relies heavily on empirical evidence of a contemporary crisis of violence and unlawful behavior that is seriously undermining the process of education in American schools. A standard better attuned to this concern would permit teachers and school administrators to search a student when they have reason to believe that the search will uncover *evidence that the student is violating the law or engaging in conduct that is seriously disruptive of school order, or the educational process.*

* * *

Like the New Jersey Supreme Court, I would view this case differently if the Assistant Vice Principal had reason to believe T.L.O.'s purse contained evidence of criminal activity, or of an activity that would seriously disrupt school discipline. There was, however, absolutely no basis for any such assumption—not even a "hunch."

In this case, Mr. Choplick overreacted to what appeared to be nothing more than a minor infraction—a rule prohibiting smoking in the bathroom of the freshmen's and sophomores' building. It is, of course, true that he actually found evidence of serious wrongdoing by T.L.O., but no one claims that the prior search may be justified by his unexpected discovery. As far as the smoking infraction is concerned, the search for cigarettes merely tended to corroborate a teacher's eyewitness account of T.L.O.'s violation of a minor regulation designed to channel student smoking behavior into designated locations. Because this conduct was neither unlawful nor significantly disruptive of school order or the educational process, the invasion of privacy associated with the forcible opening of T.L.O.'s purse was entirely unjustified at its inception.

A review of the sampling of school search cases relied on by the Court demonstrates how different this case is from those in which there was indeed a valid justification for intruding on a student's privacy. In most of them the student was suspected of a criminal violation; in the remainder either violence or substantial disruption of school order or the integrity of the academic process was at stake. Few involved matters as trivial as the no-smoking rule violated by T.L.O. The rule the Court adopts today is so open-ended that it may make the Fourth Amendment virtually meaningless in the school context. Although I agree that school administrators must have broad latitude to maintain order and discipline in our classrooms, that authority is not unlimited.

IV

The schoolroom is the first opportunity most citizens have to experience the power of government. Through it passes every citizen and public official, from schoolteachers to policemen and prison guards. The values they learn there, they take with them in life. One of our most cherished ideals is the one contained in the Fourth Amendment: that the government may not intrude on the personal privacy of its citizens without a warrant or compelling circumstance. The Court's decision today is a curious moral for the Nation's youth. Although the search of T.L.O.'s purse does not trouble today's majority, I submit that we are not dealing with "matters relatively trivial to the welfare of the Nation. There are village tyrants as well as village Hampdens, but none who acts under color of law is beyond reach of the Constitution." *West Virginia State Board of Education v. Barnette,* 319 U.S. 624, 638, 63 S. Ct. 1178, 1185 (1943).

I respectfully dissent.

NOTES

1. The numerous opinions filed by the justices in *T.L.O.* reflect the multi-dimensional and highly nuanced nature of the issues raised. As referenced below, Justice Blackmun's concurrence arguably has had the greatest impact on the development of the law (with regard to the special needs doctrine) over time; but the respective dissenting opinions of Justices Brennan and Stevens highlight the dilemmas educators face in trying to teach values, dilemmas that are equally compelling today. *Cf infra,* Ch. 9. And the Powell/O'Connor concurrence raises important privacy issues that remain very much unresolved.

2. It is important to note the changing nature of the law in the area of criminal procedure generally, with the pendulum swinging from the 1960s and 1970s—where many Americans fought for greater protection from searches and seizures—to a willingness of the same Americans to retain less rights in the decades that followed as concerns regarding safety, on campus and in society as a whole, increased.

3. Footnote 8 of the majority opinion raises the important question of whether and to what extent a requirement of individualized suspicion must be met before individual students can be searched under the Fourth Amendment. For an overview of developments in this area in the aftermath of *T.L.O.,* and a summary of issues that remained unresolved 15 years down the road, see Jason E. Yearout, *Individualized School Searches and the Fourth Amendment: What's a School District to Do?*, 10 WM. & MARY BILL RTS. J. 489 (2002).

4. In early January 2009, the U.S. Supreme Court granted certiorari in *Safford Unified Sch. Dist. v. Redding*, a case involving the question of whether the "strip search" of a female student in an Arizona middle school was constitutional under the reasonableness test set forth in *T.L.O.* The Ninth Circuit, rehearing the case *en banc,* had reversed its earlier decision on behalf of the school district and ruled 6–5 in favor of the plaintiff. *Redding v. Safford Unified Sch. Dist.,* 531 F.3d 1071 (9th Cir. 2008).

The details of the search of thirteen-year-old Savana Redding (an honor-roll student with no prior discipline problems) were described by the original Ninth Circuit panel as follows:

[Vice Principal Kerry] Wilson * * * showed Redding the pills he had seized from [her apparent friend] Marissa and asked her what she could tell him about them. After Redding denied having knowledge of the pills, Wilson told Redding that he had received a report that she had been passing the pills out to her classmates and asked Redding if she would object to being searched. Redding denied bringing pills to school, denied distributing pills to her classmates, and told Wilson that she did not mind being searched. Wilson then invited [Administrative Assistant Helen] Romero into his office, and together, they conducted a search of Redding's backpack. After the search proved fruitless, Wilson asked Romero to take Redding into the nurse's office and conduct a search of her person [as they had done with Marissa]. Romero complied.

Romero took Redding into the nurse's office and again invited [school nurse Peggy] Schwallier to observe. At the time of the search, Redding was wearing "stretch pants without pockets and a T-shirt without pockets." In Schwallier's presence, Romero asked Redding to: (1) remove her jacket, shoes, and socks, (2) remove her pants and shirt, (3) pull her bra out and to the side and shake it, exposing her breasts, and (4) pull her underwear out at the crotch and shake it, exposing her pelvic area. The search did not produce any pills. Immediately after it had concluded, Defendants returned Redding's clothes and allowed her to get dressed. At no point during the search did either Schwallier or Romero touch Redding. Prior to the search, no attempt was made to contact Redding's mother. 504 F.3d 828, 831 (9th Cir. 2007).

Judge Wardlaw, writing on behalf of the *en banc* majority, inquired whether under *T.L.O.* the search was (a) "justified at its inception" and (b) "reasonably related in scope to the circumstances which justified the interference in the first place":

[As to the justification,] [a]bsent the sort of physical evidence found in *T.L.O.*, the primary purported justification for the strip search was Marissa's statement that Savana had given her the ibuprofen that she was caught with in violation of the school's rule. This self-serving statement, which shifted the culpability for bringing the pills to school from Marissa to Savana, does not justify initiating a highly invasive strip search of a student who bore no other connection to the pills in question. * * * At a minimum, Assistant Principal Wilson should have conducted additional investigation to corroborate Marissa's "tip" before directing Savana into the nurse's office for disrobing. 531 F.3d at 1082–1083.

* * * [As to the scope of search], the public school authorities adopted a disproportionately extreme measure to search a thirteen-year-old girl for violating a school rule prohibiting possession of prescription and over-the-counter drugs. We conclude the strip search was not reasonably related to the search for ibuprofen, as the most logical places where the pills might have been found had already been searched to no avail, and no information pointed to the conclusion that the pills were hidden under her panties or bra (or that Savana's classmates would be willing to ingest pills previously stored in her underwear). Common sense informs us that directing a thirteen-year-old girl to remove her clothes, partially revealing

her breasts and pelvic area, for allegedly possessing ibuprofen, an infraction that poses an imminent danger to no one, and which could be handled by keeping her in the principal's office until a parent arrived or simply sending her home, was excessively intrusive. *Id.* at 1085.

The *en banc* majority added that n]owhere does the *T.L.O.* Court tell us to accord school officials' judgments unblinking deference

> Nor does *T.L.O.* provide blanket approval of strip searches of thirteen-year-olds remotely rumored to have had Advil merely because of a generalized drug problem. Rather, the Court made it clear that while it did not require school officials to apply a probable cause standard to a purse search, it plainly required them to act "according to the dictates of reason and common sense." * * * [T]he public school officials who strip searched Savana acted contrary to all reason and common sense as they trampled over her legitimate and substantial interests in privacy and security of her person. *Id.* at 1080.

Judge Gould, dissenting, wrote that while he agreed with the majority that "although the Supreme Court precedent in [*T.L.O.*] and common sense show that the strip search of Savana was unreasonable and unconstitutional," he would find that the defendants were entitled to qualified immunity "because the law heretofore did not give adequate guidance to the school officials." *Id.* at 1089–1091.

> Judge Hawkins, dissenting, began by asserting that he "would reserve the term 'strip search' for a search that required its subject to fully disrobe in view of officials," and that in his view "it is useful to maintain the distinction so that we can distinguish such searches from the one in this case." *Id.* at 1091, note 1.

> As to the first prong of the *T.L.O.* reasonableness test, Hawkins would find the search to be justified at its inception because additional evidence of a relationship between Savana and Marissa had been uncovered that indicated the possibility that they were selling these pills in violation of school rules:

> Indeed, information uncovered at the meeting actually *increased* the likelihood that Redding had supplied Marissa with the pills. By conceding that she had lent Marissa [a] planner, Redding established a crucial link between the two girls, enabling Wilson to reasonably conclude that Redding and Marissa were friends. *Id.* at 1101.

As to the second prong, Judge Hawkins wrote:

> The measures adopted in this case were reasonably related to finding ibuprofen. * * * Wilson had reason to believe that Redding possessed small pills. There was no indication where those pills might be, however. A search of Redding's backpack turned up nothing, and she was wearing clothes without any pockets that day. There is no question that the pills could physically be concealed in Redding's underwear in a way that would avoid superficial observation.

> Absent evidence that pills were not under Redding's clothes, it hardly seems irrational that they might be concealed in places that only a more intrusive search would uncover. * * * *Id.* at 1106.

5. While two appellate panels in the years immediately following *T.L.O.* had upheld the constitutionality of certain strip searches in K–12 settings (*see Williams v. Ellington,* 936 F.2d 881 (6th Cir. 1991); *Cornfield v. Consolidated H.S. Dist.,* 991 F.2d 1316 (7th Cir. 1993)), the trend at both the federal and state court levels over the past fifteen years has been to find strip searches unconstitutional.

Indeed, the number of courts that have found strip searches unconstitutional in K–12 public schools under the Fourth Amendment has grown incrementally over time. At the federal court of appeals level, they include *Jenkins v. Talladega City Bd. of Ed.,* 95 F.3d 1036 (11th Cir. 1996), *Thomas v. Roberts,* 261 F.3d 1160 (11th Cir. 2001), *Beard v. Whitmore Lake Sch. Dist.,* 402 F.3d 598 (6th Cir. 2005), and *Phaneuf v. Fraiken,* 448 F.3d 591 (2d Cir. 2006). At the U.S. District Court level, they include *Konop v. Northwestern Sch. Dist.,* 26 F.Supp.2d 1189 (D. S.D. 1998), *Thomas v. Clayton County Bd. of Ed.,* 94 F.Supp.2d 1290 (N.D. Ga. 1999), *Fewless v. Board of Educ. of Wayland,* 208 F.Supp.2d 806 (W.D. Mi. 2002), and *Carlson v. Bremen High School,* 423 F.Supp.2d 823 (N.D. Il. 2006). At the state court level, they include *Matter of K.C.B.,* 141 S.W.3d 303 (Tx. Ct. App. 2004), *Lamb v. Holmes,* 162 S.W.3d 902 (Ky. 2005), and *In re J.N.Y.,* 931 A.2d 685 (Pa. Super. Ct. 2007).

It should be noted that some of the cases finding Fourth Amendment violations ultimately found for defendants under a qualified immunity theory. These include *Beard, Thomas v. Clayton,* and *Lamb.*

For a comprehensive overview of Fourth Amendment issues raised in the aftermath of the *Redding* decision, *see* Ralph D. Mawdsley & Joy Cumming, *Student Informants, School Strip Searches, and Reasonableness: Sorting Out Problems of Inception and Scope,* 230 Ed. Law Rep. 1 (2008).

3. DRUG TESTING OF STUDENTS

PROBLEM 8: DRUG TESTING AND NIRVANA MACRO SYSTEMS

The following hypothetical is set in the fictional state of Nirvana.

In response to the increasing demand for distance education programs linked to the interrelated areas of home schooling, charter schooling, and the "No Child Left Behind" Act, Nirvana Macro Systems (NMS, a private, entrepreneurial company) develops a full-featured program that can lead to the attainment of a high school diploma online. NMS educational materials, accessible only after registration and the payment of a fee, range from text and picture files to MP3 files, streaming video, and webcasting. In addition, registrants can benefit from personal feedback regarding their work, feedback provided by NMS "educational advisers" via e-mail.

A highly effective marketing team succeeds in getting the NMS program endorsed by a significant number of educators and political leaders, and before too long it is serving a significant student population. But noted policymakers are quick to criticize the quality of the program, questioning in particular the loose nature of the registration system, the professional background of the educational advisers, and the boilerplate materials that focus primarily on basic skills ... to the exclusion of inquiry, analysis, problem solving, and other higher level cognitive abilities.

After a series of reports in local newspapers documenting allegations that a significant percentage of NMS students are using recreational drugs before, during, and after participating in the online activities. NMS, in conjunction with participating local school districts, implements a requirement that all NMS students residing in the relevant geographical areas served by these districts be randomly drug tested.

The district-mandated and publicly funded drug testing program is challenged by the local branch of the ACLU, on behalf of several students who refuse to be tested.

What arguments will be set forth by the ACLU? What result? Discuss.

BOARD OF EDUC. OF INDEP. SCH. DIST. NO. 92 v. EARLS

536 U.S. 822, 122 S.Ct. 2559 (2002)

JUSTICE THOMAS delivered the opinion of the Court.

* * *

I

The city of Tecumseh, Oklahoma, is a rural community located approximately 40 miles southeast of Oklahoma City. The School District administers all Tecumseh public schools. In the fall of 1998, the School District adopted the Student Activities Drug Testing Policy (Policy), which requires all middle and high school students to consent to drug testing in order to participate in any extracurricular activity. In practice, the Policy has been applied only to competitive extracurricular activities sanctioned by the Oklahoma Secondary Schools Activities Association, such as the Academic Team, Future Farmers of America, Future Homemakers of America, band, choir, pom-pom, cheerleading, and athletics. Under the Policy, students are required to take a drug test before participating in an extracurricular activity, must submit to random drug testing while participating in that activity, and must agree to be tested at any time upon reasonable suspicion. The urinalysis tests are designed to detect only the use of illegal drugs, including amphetamines, marijuana, cocaine, opiates, and barbituates, not medical conditions or the presence of authorized prescription medications.

At the time of their suit, both respondents attended Tecumseh High School. Respondent Lindsay Earls was a member of the show choir, the marching band, the Academic Team, and the National Honor Society. Respondent Daniel James sought to participate in the Academic Team. Together with their parents, Earls and James brought a Rev. Stat. § 1979, 42 U.S.C. § 1983, action against the School District, challenging the Policy both on its face and as applied to their participation in extracurricular activities. They alleged that the Policy violates the Fourth Amendment as incorporated by the Fourteenth Amendment and requested injunctive and declarative relief. They also argued that the School District failed to identify a special need for testing students who participate in extracurricular activities, and that the "Drug Testing Policy neither addresses a proven problem nor promises to bring any benefit to students or the school."

   * * *

II

The Fourth Amendment to the United States Constitution protects "[t]he right of the people to be secure in their persons, houses, papers, and effects, against unreasonable searches and seizures." Searches by public school officials, such as the collection of urine samples, implicate Fourth Amendment interests. We must therefore review the School District's Policy for "reasonableness," which is the touchstone of the constitutionality of a governmental search.

In the criminal context, reasonableness usually requires a showing of probable cause. * * * [However,] [t]he Court has * * * held that a warrant and finding of probable cause are unnecessary in the public school context because such requirements " 'would unduly interfere with the maintenance of the swift and informal disciplinary procedures [that are] needed.' "

Given that the School District's Policy is not in any way related to the conduct of criminal investigations, * * * respondents do not contend that the School District requires probable cause before testing students for drug use. Respondents instead argue that drug testing must be based at least on some level of individualized suspicion. It is true that we generally determine the reasonableness of a search by balancing the nature of the intrusion on the individual's privacy against the promotion of legitimate governmental interests. But we have long held that "the Fourth Amendment imposes no irreducible requirement of [individualized] suspicion." "[I]n certain limited circumstances, the Government's need to discover such latent or hidden conditions, or to prevent their development, is sufficiently compelling to justify the intrusion on privacy entailed by conducting such searches without any measure of individualized suspicion." Therefore, in the context of safety and administrative regulations, a search unsupported by probable cause may be reasonable "when 'special needs, beyond the normal need for law enforcement, make the warrant and probable-cause requirement impracticable.' "

Significantly, this Court has previously held that "special needs" inhere in the public school context. While schoolchildren do not shed their constitutional rights when they enter the schoolhouse, see *Tinker v. Des Moines Independent Community School Dist.*, 393 U.S. 503, 506, 89 S. Ct. 733 (1969), "Fourth Amendment rights ... are different in public schools than elsewhere; the 'reasonableness' inquiry cannot disregard the schools' custodial and tutelary responsibility for children." In particular, a finding of individualized suspicion may not be necessary when a school conducts drug testing.

In *Vernonia,* this Court held that the suspicionless drug testing of athletes was constitutional. The Court, however, did not simply authorize all school drug testing, but rather conducted a fact-specific balancing of the intrusion on the children's Fourth Amendment rights against the promotion of legitimate governmental interests. Applying the principles of *Vernonia* to the somewhat different facts of this case, we conclude that Tecumseh's Policy is also constitutional.

A

We first consider the nature of the privacy interest allegedly compromised by the drug testing. As in *Vernonia,* the context of the public school environment serves as the backdrop for the analysis of the privacy interest at stake and the reasonableness of the drug testing policy in general. * * *

A student's privacy interest is limited in a public school environment where the State is responsible for maintaining discipline, health, and safety. Schoolchildren are routinely required to submit to physical examinations and vaccinations against disease. Securing order in the school environment sometimes requires that students be subjected to greater controls than those appropriate for adults.

Respondents argue that because children participating in nonathletic extracurricular activities are not subject to regular physicals and communal undress, they have a stronger expectation of privacy than the athletes tested in *Vernonia.* This distinction, however, was not essential to our decision in *Vernonia,* which depended primarily upon the school's custodial responsibility and authority.

In any event, students who participate in competitive extracurricular activities voluntarily subject themselves to many of the same intrusions on their privacy as do athletes. Some of these clubs and activities require occasional off-campus travel and communal undress. All of them have their own rules and requirements for participating students that do not apply to the student body as a whole. For example, each of the competitive extracurricular activities governed by the Policy must abide by the rules of the Oklahoma Secondary Schools Activities Association, and a faculty sponsor monitors the students for compliance with the various rules dictated by the clubs and activities. This regulation of extracurricular activities further diminishes the expectation of privacy among schoolchildren. * * * We therefore conclude that the students affected by this Policy have a limited expectation of privacy.

B

Next, we consider the character of the intrusion imposed by the Policy. Urination is "an excretory function traditionally shielded by great privacy." But the "degree of intrusion" on one's privacy caused by collecting a urine sample "depends upon the manner in which production of the urine sample is monitored."

Under the Policy, a faculty monitor waits outside the closed restroom stall for the student to produce a sample and must "listen for the normal sounds of urination in order to guard against tampered specimens and to insure an accurate chain of custody." The monitor then pours the sample into two bottles that are sealed and placed into a mailing pouch along with a consent form signed by the student. This procedure is virtually identical to that reviewed in *Vernonia,* except that it additionally protects privacy by allowing male students to produce their samples behind a closed stall. Given that we considered the method of collection in *Vernonia* a "negligible" intrusion, the method here is even less problematic.

In addition, the Policy clearly requires that the test results be kept in confidential files separate from a student's other educational records and released to school personnel only on a "need to know" basis. Respondents nonetheless contend that the intrusion on students' privacy is significant because the Policy fails to protect effectively against the disclosure of confidential information and, specifically, that the school "has been careless in protecting that information: for example, the Choir teacher looked at students' prescription drug lists and left them where other students could see them." But the choir teacher is someone with a "need to know," because during off-campus trips she needs to know what medications are taken by her students. Even before the Policy was enacted the choir teacher had access to this information. In any event, there is no allegation that any other student did see such information. This one example of alleged carelessness hardly increases the character of the intrusion.

Moreover, the test results are not turned over to any law enforcement authority. Nor do the test results here lead to the imposition of discipline or have any academic consequences. Rather, the only consequence of a failed drug test is to limit the student's privilege of participating in extracurricular activities. Indeed, a student may test positive for drugs twice and still be allowed to participate in extracurricular activities. After the first positive test, the school contacts the student's parent or guardian for a meeting. The student may continue to participate in the activity if within five days of the meeting the student shows proof of receiving drug counseling and submits to a second drug test in two weeks. For the second positive test, the student is suspended from participation in all extracurricular activities for 14 days, must complete four hours of substance abuse counseling, and must submit to monthly drug tests. Only after a third positive test will the student be suspended from participating in any extracurricular activity for the remainder of the school year, or 88 school days, whichever is longer.

Given the minimally intrusive nature of the sample collection and the limited uses to which the test results are put, we conclude that the invasion of students' privacy is not significant.

C

Finally, this Court must consider the nature and immediacy of the government's concerns and the efficacy of the Policy in meeting them. This Court has already articulated in detail the importance of the governmental concern in preventing drug use by schoolchildren. The drug abuse problem among our Nation's youth has hardly abated since *Vernonia* was decided in 1995. In fact, evidence suggests that it has only grown worse.[5] As in *Vernonia*, "the necessity for the State to act is magnified by the fact that this evil is being visited not just upon individuals at large, but upon children for whom it has undertaken a special responsibility of care and direction." The health and safety risks identified in *Vernonia* apply with equal force to Tecumseh's children. Indeed, the nationwide drug epidemic makes the war against drugs a pressing concern in every school.

Additionally, the School District in this case has presented specific evidence of drug use at Tecumseh schools. Teachers testified that they had seen students who appeared to be under the influence of drugs and that they had heard students speaking openly about using drugs. A drug dog found marijuana cigarettes near the school parking lot. Police officers once found drugs or drug paraphernalia in a car driven by a Future Farmers of America member. And the school board president reported that people in the community were calling the board to discuss the "drug situation." We decline to second-guess the finding of the District Court that "[v]iewing the evidence as a whole, it cannot be reasonably disputed that the [School District] was faced with a 'drug problem' when it adopted the Policy."

Respondents consider the proffered evidence insufficient and argue that there is no "real and immediate interest" to justify a policy of drug testing nonathletes. We have recognized, however, that "[a] demonstrated problem of drug abuse . . . [is] not in all cases necessary to the validity of a testing regime," but that some showing does "shore up an assertion of special need for a suspicionless general search program." The School District has provided sufficient evidence to shore up the need for its drug testing program.

Furthermore, this Court has not required a particularized or pervasive drug problem before allowing the government to conduct suspicionless drug testing. For instance, in *Von Raab*, the Court upheld the drug testing of customs officials on a purely preventive basis, without any documented history of drug use by such officials. In response to the lack of evidence relating to drug use, the Court noted generally that "drug abuse is one of the most serious problems confronting our society today," and that programs to prevent and detect drug use among customs officials could not be deemed unreasonable. Likewise, the need to prevent and deter the substantial harm of childhood drug use provides the necessary

---

5. For instance, the number of 12th graders using any illicit drug increased from 48.4 percent in 1995 to 53.9 percent in 2001. The number of 12th graders reporting they had used marijuana jumped from 41.7 percent to 49.0 percent during that same period. *See* DEP'T OF HEALTH & HUMAN SERVICES, MONITORING THE FUTURE: NATIONAL RESULTS ON ADOLESCENT DRUG USE, OVERVIEW OF KEY FINDINGS (2001) (Table 1).

immediacy for a school testing policy. Indeed, it would make little sense to require a school district to wait for a substantial portion of its students to begin using drugs before it was allowed to institute a drug testing program designed to deter drug use.

Given the nationwide epidemic of drug use, and the evidence of increased drug use in Tecumseh schools, it was entirely reasonable for the School District to enact this particular drug testing policy.

* * *

Respondents also argue that the testing of nonathletes does not implicate any safety concerns, and that safety is a "crucial factor" in applying the special needs framework. They contend that there must be "surpassing safety interests," or "extraordinary safety and national security hazards," in order to override the usual protections of the Fourth Amendment. Respondents are correct that safety factors into the special needs analysis, but the safety interest furthered by drug testing is undoubtedly substantial for all children, athletes and nonathletes alike. We know all too well that drug use carries a variety of health risks for children, including death from overdose.

We also reject respondents' argument that drug testing must presumptively be based upon an individualized reasonable suspicion of wrongdoing because such a testing regime would be less intrusive. In this context, the Fourth Amendment does not require a finding of individualized suspicion, and we decline to impose such a requirement on schools attempting to prevent and detect drug use by students. Moreover, we question whether testing based on individualized suspicion in fact would be less intrusive. Such a regime would place an additional burden on public school teachers who are already tasked with the difficult job of maintaining order and discipline. A program of individualized suspicion might unfairly target members of unpopular groups. The fear of lawsuits resulting from such targeted searches may chill enforcement of the program, rendering it ineffective in combating drug use. * * *

Finally, we find that testing students who participate in extracurricular activities is a reasonably effective means of addressing the School District's legitimate concerns in preventing, deterring, and detecting drug use. While in *Vernonia* there might have been a closer fit between the testing of athletes and the trial court's finding that the drug problem was "fueled by the 'role model' effect of athletes' drug use," such a finding was not essential to the holding. *Vernonia* did not require the school to test the group of students most likely to use drugs, but rather considered the constitutionality of the program in the context of the public school's custodial responsibilities. Evaluating the Policy in this context, we conclude that the drug testing of Tecumseh students who participate in extracurricular activities effectively serves the School District's interest in protecting the safety and health of its students.

III

Within the limits of the Fourth Amendment, local school boards must assess the desirability of drug testing schoolchildren. In upholding the constitutionality of the Policy, we express no opinion as to its wisdom. Rather, we hold only that Tecumseh's Policy is a reasonable means of furthering the School District's important interest in preventing and deterring drug use among its schoolchildren. Accordingly, we reverse the judgment of the Court of Appeals.

It is so ordered.

* * *

JUSTICE O'CONNOR, with whom JUSTICE SOUTER joins, dissenting.

I dissented in *Vernonia School Dist. 47J v. Acton*, and continue to believe that case was wrongly decided. Because *Vernonia* is now this Court's precedent, and because I agree that petitioners' program fails even under the balancing approach adopted in that case, I join Justice GINSBURG's dissent.

JUSTICE GINSBURG, with whom JUSTICE STEVENS, JUSTICE O'CONNOR, and JUSTICE SOUTER join, dissenting.

Seven years ago, in *Vernonia School Dist. 47J v. Acton*, this Court determined that a school district's policy of randomly testing the urine of its student athletes for illicit drugs did not violate the Fourth Amendment. In so ruling, the Court emphasized that drug use "increase[d] the risk of sports-related injury" and that Vernonia's athletes were the "leaders" of an aggressive local "drug culture" that had reached " 'epidemic proportions.' " Today, the Court relies upon *Vernonia* to permit a school district with a drug problem its superintendent repeatedly described as "not . . . major," to test the urine of an academic team member solely by reason of her participation in a nonathletic, competitive extracurricular activity—participation associated with neither special dangers from, nor particular predilections for, drug use.

"[T]he legality of a search of a student," this Court has instructed, "should depend simply on the reasonableness, under all the circumstances, of the search." *New Jersey v. T.L.O.*, 469 U.S. 325, 341, 105 S. Ct. 733 (1985). Although " 'special needs' inhere in the public school context," those needs are not so expansive or malleable as to render reasonable any program of student drug testing a school district elects to install. The particular testing program upheld today is not reasonable; it is capricious, even perverse: Petitioners' policy targets for testing a student population least likely to be at risk from illicit drugs and their damaging effects. I therefore dissent.

* * *

NOTES

1.   It is instructive to trace the development of the "special needs" doctrine from Justice Blackmun's concurrence in *New Jersey v. TLO,* to the *Earls* decision, seventeen years later. *See, e.g.*, Fabio Arcila, Jr., *Special Needs and Special Deference: Suspicionless Civil Searches in the Modern Regulatory State,* 56 ADMIN. L. REV. 1223, 1228 (2004).

2.   In 2008, the Washington Supreme Court ruled unanimously that the Wahkiakum School District's policy of suspicionless urine testing for students who participate in extracurricular athletic activities violated the state constitution's privacy clause. The drug testing policy had been adopted in 1999 without any convincing evidence that there was a significant problem among students with the use of illegal drugs. Article I, Section 7 of the Washington Constitution provides that "No person shall be disturbed in his private affairs, or his home invaded, without authority of law," and the state's courts have consistently found that it provides broader protections for privacy than its federal counterpart. *See York v. Wahkiakum Sch. Dist. No. 200,* 163 Wash.2d 297, 178 P.3d 995 (2008).

3.   Drug testing of student athletes at the higher education level— particularly the testing program mandated by the NCAA—was challenged by plaintiffs in the late 1980s and early 1990s. *See University of Colorado v. Derdeyn,* 863 P.2d 929 (Colo. 1993), *Hill v. NCAA,* 7 Cal.4th 1, 865 P.2d 633, 26 Cal.Rptr.2d 834 (1994). After the NCAA prevailed in the *Hill* case, drug testing became standard procedure for intercollegiate athletics, not only under NCAA mandates, but under programs implemented by individual colleges and universities.

Today, these higher education programs are generally accepted as legal, and little debate regarding their efficacy is evident. Yet it must be noted that even with extensive testing of student athletes, abuses of steroids and related substances continue to be a major problem in organized athletic competition, at both the amateur and the professional level. Many believe that the prototypical drug testing programs at colleges and universities are not focusing in on the heart of the problem in this context, and that they are not having the sort of deterrent effect that many might have hoped.

D.   STUDENT RECORDS

1.   THE FAMILY EDUCATIONAL RIGHTS AND PRIVACY ACT (FERPA) AND RELATED FEDERAL STATUTES

From Electronic Privacy Information Center, *Student Privacy,*
at http://www.epic.org/privacy/student/ (2005)

[Federal Statutes Relating to Privacy of Student Records Generally]

* * * The most prominent of the federal protections for student privacy is the Family Educational Rights and Privacy Act (FERPA), also known as the "Buckley Amendment," "FERPA protects the confidentiality of student records to some extent, while also giving students the right to review their own records."

Students' personal information is often collected through in-school surveys, sometimes for commercial use. Congress most recently addressed such surveys in the No Child Left Behind Act, a broad federal educational act. The Act provides parents and students the right to be notified of, and consent to, the collection of student information. However, the Act includes many exceptions to this right.

* * * Another provision of No Child Left Behind mandates that high schools turn over student contact information to military recruiters, unless parents or students explicitly opt out of such disclosure. And in 2002, Congress amended FERPA, via the USA Patriot Act, to require schools to transmit information about immigrant students to the INS. Under this program, the Student and Exchange Visitor Information System, schools had to begin in 2003 reporting immigrants' academic information, such as disciplinary actions or changes in programs of study.

Family Educational Rights and Privacy Act

The FERPA protects the confidentiality of student educational records. The Act applies to any public or private elementary, secondary, or post-secondary school and any state or local education agency that receives federal funds. All public schools and virtually all private schools are covered by FERPA because they receive some sort of federal funding.

The Act has two parts. First, it gives students the right to inspect and review their own education records, request corrections, halt the release of personally identifiable information, and obtain a copy of their institution's policy concerning access to educational records. (20 U.S.C.S. § 1232g(a)). Second, it prohibits educational institutions from disclosing "personally identifiable information in education records" without the written consent of the student, or if the student is a minor, the student's parents. (20 U.S.C.S. § 1232g(b)). Schools that fail to comply with FERPA risk losing federal funding.

However, there are several exceptions that allow the release of student records to certain parties or under certain conditions. Records may be released without the student's consent: (1) to school officials with a legitimate educational interest; (2) to other schools to which a student seeks or intends to enroll; (3) to education officials for audit and evaluation purposes; (4) to accrediting organizations; (5) to parties in connection with financial aid to a student; (6) to organizations conducting certain studies for or on behalf of a school; (7) to comply with a judicial order or lawfully issued subpoena; (8) in the case of health and safety emergencies; and (9) to state and local authorities within a juvenile justice system. (20 U.S.C.S. § 1232g(b)(1)).

In addition, some records maintained by schools are exempt from FERPA, including: (1) records in the sole possession of school officials; (2)

records maintained by a law enforcement unit of the educational institution; (3) records of an educational institution's non-student employees; and (4) records on a student who is 18 years of age or older or who attends a post-secondary institution that are maintained by a health professional. (20 U.S.C.S. § 1232g(a)(4)(B)). In addition, FERPA allows, but does not require, schools to release "directory information," including students' names and addresses, to the public. (20 U.S.C.S. § 1232g(a)(5)(A)). However, this exception was modified in 2002, and high schools are now required to provide students' names, addresses and telephone numbers to military recruiters, unless a student or parent opts out of such disclosure.

NOTES

1. In 2007, H.R. 2220 was introduced in the U.S. Congress. The legislation, entitled the "Mental Health Security for America's Families in Education Act of 2007," would have amended FERPA to provide that "an educational agency or institution of higher education may disclose, to a parent or legal guardian of a student who is a dependent, * * * information related to any conduct of, or expression by, such student that demonstrates that the student poses a significant risk of harm to himself or herself, or to others, including a significant risk of suicide, homicide, or assault." Written certification of such risk by a licensed mental health professional would have been required before such disclosure could be made.

While H.R. 2220 did not move forward as of early 2009, there was much activity in this area during this time. In April 2008, for example, the U.S. Department of Education proposed "the most comprehensive update of its regulations" for FERPA in two decades:

> The more than 30 pages of proposed rules include protections for educators who seek to share information to protect a student's health or safety, new guidelines for school districts on sharing student data with educational researchers, and a proposed requirement that schools safeguard electronic and other records, including from some school staff members. Several of the proposed changes * * * stem from problems with FERPA identified by federal and state investigations into the massacre at [Virginia Tech] in April 2007 * * * . Alyson Klein, *New Rules on School Privacy Law Proposed: FERPA Regulations Seek to Clarify That Data on Dangers May Be Shared*, Education Week, April 2, 2008.

In addition, some of the H.R. 2220 language was incorporated into The Higher Education Opportunity Act (H.R. 4137), signed into law in the Summer of 2008. Section 825 of the Act requires the Secretary of Education to:

> (a) * * * continue to provide guidance that clarifies the role of institutions of higher education with respect to the disclosure of education records, including to a parent or legal guardian of a dependent student, in the event that such student demonstrates that the student poses a significant risk of harm to himself or herself or to others, including a significant risk of suicide, homicide, or assault. Such guidance shall further clarify that an institution of higher education that, in good faith,

discloses education records or other information in accordance with the requirements of this Act and section 444 of the General Education Provisions Act (the Family Educational Rights and Privacy Act of 1974) shall not be liable to any person for that disclosure.

(b) Information to Congress-The Secretary shall provide an update to the authorizing committees on the Secretary's activities under subsection (a) not later than 180 days after the date of enactment of the Higher Education Opportunity Act.

The U.S. Department of Education now posts several publications addressing issues relating to FERPA and campus safety at both the K–12 and the higher education levels. *See Safe Schools and FERPA: Guidance on Emergency Management* (publications for K–12 schools, colleges and universities, and parents), available at www.ed.gov/policy/gen/guid/fpco/ferpa/safeschools/index. html (accessed November 15, 2008).

2.   In a related matter, the Office of Civil Rights (OCR) in late 2008 issued guidance on the extent to which certain records of students with disabilities at the K–12 level are protected under Section 504 of the Rehabilitation Act of 1973, the Americans with Disabilities Act of 1990 (Title II), the Individuals with Disabilities Education Act (IDEA), and FERPA. The guidance addressed report cards and transcripts:

* * * [R]eport cards are made available to parents, not to postsecondary institutions, potential employers, and others outside the [school district]. In contrast, a student's transcript generally is intended to inform postsecondary institutions or prospective employers of a student's academic credentials and achievements. Accordingly, there is an expectation that a student's transcript could be shared with persons other than the student and the student's parents.

* * * [U]nder federal disability discrimination laws, the general principle is that report cards may contain information about a student's disability, including whether that student received special education or related services, as long as the report card informs parents about their child's progress or level of achievement in specific classes, course content, or curriculum, consistent with the underlying purpose of a report card.

However, transcripts may not contain information disclosing students' disabilities. Transcripts are provided to persons other than the student and the student's parents to convey information about a student's academic credentials and achievements. Information about a student's disability, including whether that student received special education or related services due to having a disability, is not information about a student's academic credentials and achievements. Therefore, transcripts may not provide information on a student's disability. * * * Office of Civil Rights, "Dear Colleague Letter", Report Cards and Transcripts for Students with Disabilities, October 17, 2008, www.ed.gov/about/offices/list/ocr/letters/colleague–20081017.html (accessed November 15, 2008).

3.   A related issue that has moved to the proverbial "front burner" in recent years is the responsibility of educational institutions regarding data flow and data protection. As the country moves increasingly toward the

digitization of all records, the difficulties inherent in trying to secure these records and protect the privacy of all those involved has moved to the forefront. When institutional records were all on paper, stored in locked file cabinets, securing those documents was generally a much simpler operation than it has become today. This is an area that will undoubtedly be the focus of greater attention on the part of both the legal and the educational policy communities. In light of the principles identified in this portion of Chapter 2, and the interrelated issues that have emerged, what might an appropriate response entail? Are there additional legal protections that can or should be put in place? What technological challenges must be faced in this context?

2. DETERMINING THE PARAMETERS OF FERPA IN THE U.S. SUPREME COURT

OWASSO INDEP. SCH. DIST. NO. I–011 v. FALVO

534 U.S. 426, 122 S.Ct. 934 (2002)

JUSTICE KENNEDY delivered the opinion of the Court.

Teachers sometimes ask students to score each other's tests, papers, and assignments as the teacher explains the correct answers to the entire class. Respondent contends this practice, which the parties refer to as peer grading, violates the Family Educational Rights and Privacy Act of 1974 (FERPA or Act), 88 Stat. 571, 20 U.S.C. § 1232g. We took this case to resolve the issue.

I

Under FERPA, schools and educational agencies receiving federal financial assistance must comply with certain conditions. § 1232g(a)(3). One condition specified in the Act is that sensitive information about students may not be released without parental consent. The Act states that federal funds are to be withheld from school districts that have "a policy or practice of permitting the release of education records (or personally identifiable information contained therein ...) of students without the written consent of their parents." The phrase "education records" is defined, under the Act, as "records, files, documents, and other materials" containing information directly related to a student, which "are maintained by an educational agency or institution or by a person acting for such agency or institution." The definition of education records contains an exception for "records of instructional, supervisory, and administrative personnel ... which are in the sole possession of the maker thereof and which are not accessible or revealed to any other person except a substitute." The precise question for us is whether peer graded classroom work and assignments are education records.

Three of respondent Kristja J. Falvo's children are enrolled in Owasso Independent School District No. I–011, in a suburb of Tulsa, Oklahoma. The children's teachers, like many teachers in this country, use peer grading. In a typical case the students exchange papers with each other and score them according to the teacher's instructions, then return the work to the student who prepared it. The teacher may ask the students to report their own scores. In this case it appears the student could either call out the score or walk to the teacher's desk and reveal it in confidence, though by that stage, of course, the score was known at least to the one other student who did the grading. Both the grading and the system of calling out the scores are in contention here.

Respondent claimed the peer grading embarrassed her children. She asked the school district to adopt a uniform policy banning peer grading and requiring teachers either to grade assignments themselves or at least to forbid students from grading papers other than their own. The school district declined to do so, and respondent brought [this] class action * * *.

　　* * *

We granted certiorari to decide whether peer grading violates FERPA. Finding no violation of the Act, we reverse.

II

At the outset, we note it is an open question whether FERPA provides private parties, like respondent, with a cause of action enforceable under § 1983. We have granted certiorari on this issue in another case. See *Gonzaga Univ. v. Doe*, [534 U.S.] 1103, 122 S. Ct. 865 [(2002)]. * * * In these circumstances we assume, but without so deciding or expressing an opinion on the question, that private parties may sue an educational agency under § 1983 to enforce the provisions of FERPA here at issue. * * *

The parties appear to agree that if an assignment becomes an education record the moment a peer grades it, then the grading, or at least the practice of asking students to call out their grades in class, would be an impermissible release of the records under § 1232g(b)(1). Without deciding the point, we assume for the purposes of our analysis that they are correct. The parties disagree, however, whether peer graded assignments constitute education records at all. The papers do contain information directly related to a student, but they are records under the Act only when and if they "are maintained by an educational agency or institution or by a person acting for such agency or institution."

Petitioners, supported by the United States as *amicus curiae*, contend the definition covers only institutional records—namely, those materials retained in a permanent file as a matter of course. They argue that records "maintained by an educational agency or institution" generally would include final course grades, student grade point averages, standardized test scores, attendance records, counseling records, and records of disciplinary actions—but not student homework or classroom work.

Respondent, adopting the reasoning of the Court of Appeals, contends student graded assignments fall within the definition of education records. That definition contains an exception for "records of instructional, supervisory, and administrative personnel ... which are in the sole possession of the maker thereof and which are not accessible or revealed to any other person except a substitute." The Court of Appeals reasoned that if grade books are not education records, then it would have been unnecessary for Congress to enact the exception. Grade books and the grades within, the court concluded, are "maintained" 939 by a teacher and so are covered by FERPA. The court recognized that teachers do not maintain the grades on individual student assignments until they have recorded the result in the grade books. It reasoned, however, that if Congress forbids teachers to disclose students' grades once written in a grade book, it makes no sense to permit the disclosure immediately beforehand. The court thus held that student graders maintain the grades until they are reported to the teacher.

The Court of Appeals' logic does not withstand scrutiny. Its interpretation, furthermore, would effect a drastic alteration of the existing allocation of responsibilities between States and the National Government in the operation of the Nation's schools. We would hesitate before interpreting the statute to effect such a substantial change in the balance of federalism unless that is the manifest purpose of the legislation. This principle guides our decision.

Two statutory indicators tell us that the Court of Appeals erred in concluding that an assignment satisfies the definition of education records as soon as it is graded by another student. First, the student papers are not, at that stage, "maintained" within the meaning of § 1232g(a)(4)(A). The ordinary meaning of the word "maintain" is "to keep in existence or continuance; preserve; retain." Even assuming the teacher's grade book is an education record—a point the parties contest and one we do not decide here—the score on a student graded assignment is not "contained therein," until the teacher records it. The teacher does not maintain the grade while students correct their peers' assignments or call out their own marks. Nor do the student graders maintain the grades within the meaning of § 1232g(a)(4)(A). The word "maintain" suggests FERPA records will be kept in a filing cabinet in a records room at the school or on a permanent secure database, perhaps even after the student is no longer enrolled. The student graders only handle assignments for a few moments as the teacher calls out the answers. It is fanciful to say they maintain the papers in the same way the registrar maintains a student's folder in a permanent file.

The Court of Appeals was further mistaken in concluding that each student grader is "a person acting for" an educational institution for purposes of § 1232g(a)(4)(A). The phrase "acting for" connotes agents of the school, such as teachers, administrators, and other school employees. Just as it does not accord with our usual understanding to say students are "acting for" an educational institution when they follow their teacher's direction to take a quiz, it is equally awkward to say students are "acting for" an educational institution when they follow their teacher's direction to score it. Correcting a classmate's work can be as much a part of the assignment as taking the test itself. It is a way to teach material again in a new context, and it helps show students how to assist and respect fellow pupils. By explaining the answers to the class as the students correct the papers, the teacher not only reinforces the lesson but also discovers whether the students have understood the material and are ready to move on. We do not think FERPA prohibits these educational techniques. We also must not lose sight of the fact that the phrase "by a person acting for [an educational] institution" modifies "maintain." Even if one were to agree students are acting for the teacher when they correct the assignment, that is different from saying they are acting for the educational institution in maintaining it.

Other sections of the statute support our interpretation. FERPA, for example, requires educational institutions to "maintain a record, kept with the education records of each student." This record must list those who have requested access to a student's education records and their reasons for doing so. The record of access "shall be available only to parents, [and] to the school official and his assistants who are responsible for the custody of such records."

Under the Court of Appeals' broad interpretation of education records, every teacher would have an obligation to keep a separate record of access for each student's assignments. Indeed, by that court's logic, even students who grade their own papers would bear the burden of maintaining records of access until they turned in the assignments. We doubt Congress would have imposed such a weighty administrative burden on every teacher, and certainly it would not have extended the mandate to students.

Also, FERPA requires "a record" of access for each pupil. This single record must be kept "with the education records." This suggests Congress contemplated that education records would be kept in one place with a single record of access. By describing a "school official" and "his assistants" as the personnel responsible for the custody of the records, FERPA implies that education records are institutional records kept by a single central custodian, such as a registrar, not individual assignments handled by many student graders in their separate classrooms.

FERPA also requires recipients of federal funds to provide parents with a hearing at which they may contest the accuracy of their child's education records. The hearings must be conducted "in accordance with regulations of the Secretary," which in turn require adjudication by a disinterested official and the opportunity for parents to be represented by an attorney. It is doubtful Congress would have provided parents with this elaborate procedural machinery to challenge the accuracy of the grade on every spelling test and art project the child completes.

Respondent's construction of the term "education records" to cover student homework or classroom work would impose substantial burdens on teachers across the country. It would force all instructors to take time, which otherwise could be spent teaching and in preparation, to correct an assortment of daily student assignments. Respondent's view would make it much more difficult for teachers to give students immediate guidance. The interpretation respondent urges would force teachers to abandon other customary practices, such as group grading of team assignments. Indeed, the logical consequences of respondent's view are all but unbounded. At argument, counsel for respondent seemed to agree that if a teacher in any of the thousands of covered classrooms in the Nation puts a happy face, a gold star, or a disapproving remark on a classroom assignment, federal law does not allow other students to see it.

We doubt Congress meant to intervene in this drastic fashion with traditional state functions. Under the Court of Appeals' interpretation of FERPA, the federal power would exercise minute control over specific teaching methods and instructional dynamics in classrooms throughout the country. The Congress is not likely to have mandated this result, and we do not interpret the statute to require it.

For these reasons, even assuming a teacher's grade book is an education record, the Court of Appeals erred, for in all events the grades on students' papers would not be covered under FERPA at least until the teacher has collected them and recorded them in his or her grade book. We limit our holding to this narrow point, and do not decide the broader question whether the grades on individual student assignments, once they are turned in to teachers, are protected by the Act.

The judgment of the Court of Appeals is reversed, and the case is remanded for further proceedings consistent with this opinion.

It is so ordered.

NOTES

1. In *Gonzaga Univ. v. Doe*, 536 U.S. 273, 122 S.Ct. 2268 (2002), the Court considered the question of whether a student may sue a private university for damages under 42 U.S.C. 1983 to enforce provisions of FERPA. The Court found that relevant provisions of FERPA create no personal rights in this context:

> Our conclusion that FERPA's nondisclosure provisions fail to confer enforceable rights is buttressed by the mechanism that Congress chose to provide for enforcing those provisions. Congress expressly authorized the Secretary of Education to *"deal with violations"* of the Act, 1232g(f) (emphasis added), and required the Secretary to "establish or designate [a] review board" for investigating and adjudicating such violations, 1232g(g). Pursuant to these provisions, the Secretary created the Family Policy Compliance Office (FPCO) "to act as the Review Board required under the Act [and] to enforce the Act with respect to all applicable programs." The FPCO permits students and parents who suspect a violation of the Act to file individual written complaints. If a complaint is timely and contains required information, the FPCO will initiate an investigation, notify the educational institution of the charge, and request a written response. If a violation is found, the FPCO distributes a notice

of factual findings and a "statement of the specific steps that the agency or institution must take to comply" with FERPA. *Id.* at 289–290.

E. PRIVACY AND TECHNOLOGY IN THE INFORMATION AGE

The rapid growth of digital and electronic surveillance technology over the past two decades, and the proliferating use of this technology in both the public and the private sector, have led many people to focus on privacy issues in this context.

Indeed, for those who have conceptualized technology-related legal issues as a separate and emerging body of law, privacy is considered a major area of focus. Whether the field is characterized in a more limited fashion as *Online Law* or *Internet Law,* or more broadly as *Cyberspace Law* or *Information Technology (IT) Law,* most scholars see it as encompassing at least four primary areas: free speech issues, intellectual property issues, computer crime, and privacy.

The emergence of this field of law is typically tied to the growth and development of the post–1980s Internet, which includes but is not limited to the World Wide Web and related technologies. In this manner, the field can be seen as unfolding over the course of two decades: 1990–1999 and 2000–2009. During the second decade, the Internet became less of a luxury and more of a necessity for a large percentage of the population. Yet the area still retained a quality of adventure and opportunity. As technology improved and communication alternatives expanded, everything from business opportunities to alternative "publishing" options to social networking possibilities multiplied. Information gathering was enhanced dramatically by the fine-tuning of the powerful *Google* search engine and the explosive popularity of *Wikipedia*. The emergence of blogs changed the nature of journalism, the development of *YouTube* changed the dynamics of both political campaigns and the entertainment industry, and the growth of social networking sites such as *Facebook* and *MySpace* and virtual reality sites such as *Second Life* continued to change the way people interacted with each other. And breakthrough products such as the iPhone enabled more and more people to carry full versions of the Internet with them wherever they went.

Much of the second decade in this field was dominated by the aftermath of the September 11, 2001 attack on the nation, and by the ongoing concerns that not only was the online world vulnerable to cyberterrorism but that cyberspace could be used by lawbreakers to plan attacks and in other ways wreak havoc on civilized society. In ever-increasing numbers, law enforcement officials began patrolling cyberspace. The USA Patriot Act and other related federal and state legislation served to further regulate the territory, and these statutes themselves became the subject of new litigation, scholarship, and ongoing debate.

It is difficult to determine the extent to which lawlessness of every kind persisted in cyberspace during the second decade of Information Technology Law. The types of crimes arguably changed, with fewer large-scale hacking attacks but an increasing number of schemes that sought to take advantage of the more vulnerable members of our society. Cyberstalking and cyberbullying also increased in both quantity and scope, leading to additional efforts on the part of lawmakers to bring this area under a greater level of control.

By the end of the second decade, however, many believed that privacy issues had become perhaps the most compelling of all the topic areas in IT Law. It may be the case, for example, that every time anyone in any country chose to go online in 2009, information was being collected–actively and/or passively–about the person and his or her activities. The aggregate amount of such information, most of which, in the offline world and in another era, might have been private, raises a host of unresolved issues and concerns. Who is collecting the information? How legal is such collection? Who has the information? Where is it stored? How, if at all, is it accessed? How, if at all, is it protected? How, if at all, should it be protected?

Finally, it has also become clear after twenty years that much remains to be learned from the way that the law has interacted with the new Internet technologies from 1990–2009. Indeed, by identifying policy imperatives, representative patterns, and guiding principles, members of the legal and public policy communities will be better able to address new and unregulated technologies in the future. These technologies might include, but are certainly not limited to, artificial intelligence, robotics, surveillance technology, the technology of war, nanotechnology, cloning, and genetic engineering.

Most of these new technologies can and in numerous instances already have raised issues within education communities, impacting everything from the way interactions might be monitored to the way research can be conducted. The interrelated challenges posed by the ongoing imperatives of record keeping, data protection, and both online and offline security continue to raise privacy concerns throughout both the K–12 and the higher education sectors. Regulations and policies will need to be promulgated, and inevitable disputes are certain to be litigated.

Consider the materials in this sub-section in light of recent privacy-related developments. Given the perspectives presented by the commentators, and the relevant legal principles that are identified, what predictions might you make regarding how all this will look in 5–10 years? How will educational institutions be impacted? What can or should be done in this area at the present time?

PROBLEM 9: DRIVER'S LICENSES FOR THE INFORMATION SUPERHIGHWAY

Consider the efficacy of the following proposed federal legislation, designed to implement a hypothetical international treaty.

To increase online safety, protect online users, & enhance Internet commerce, the legislation would mandate the creation of a National Internet Clearinghouse (akin to a national DMV) which would issue driver's licenses for the Information Superhighway. Access to the Internet in the U.S. would be limited to those who do not have a criminal record and who pass a written test regarding a new, international "acceptable use policy." The license must be renewed every four years, and can be revoked if an Internet-related crime is committed. The latest in biometric technology will be used to make sure that when a person logs on, his or her license number will be correctly identified.

1.   In light of your analysis of (a) the regulatory design and (b) whether the plan is likely to achieve its purpose, would you recommend passage of such a bill? Why? Alternatively, could you support a modified version of this bill? If so, what modifications might be appropriate?

2.   Instead, might you support a more limited version of this legislation that would impact only students?

3.   Alternatively, assuming the existence of the technology, could you support the creation of a private Internet for educational institutions only, where students would be required to comply with the above guidelines and obtain "driver's licenses" before they could access this private Internet? Or might there be a better way to accomplish the same safety-related purposes and goals?

4.   Assume that a version of this bill passes that impacts only students, and that it is challenged as violative of their right to privacy. What arguments might be set forth? What result? Discuss.

RECONSTRUCTING ELECTRONIC SURVEILLANCE LAW

Daniel J. Solove
72 GEO. WASH. L. REV. 1264 (2004)

* * *

Today, technology has given the government an unprecedented ability to engage in surveillance. New X-ray devices can see through people's clothing, amounting to what some call a "virtual strip-search." Thermal sensors can detect movement and activity via heat patterns. Telephone calls can be wiretapped; places can be "bugged" with hidden recording devices; and parabolic microphones can record conversations at long distances. A device known as Carnivore developed by the Federal Bureau of Investigation ("FBI") can scan through all of the e-mail traffic of an internet service provider ("ISP"). Keystroke logger devices can record every keystroke typed on one's computer, and these devices can be installed into a person's computer by e-mailing a computer virus called "Magic Lantern." Tracking devices can relay information about a person's whereabouts. One can trace cell phone calls to a person's particular location.

Surveillance cameras have become ubiquitous. Britain has erected an elaborate system of video cameras which enable officials to monitor city streets through closed circuit television. Called CCTV, this system has grown rapidly ever since it was first used in 1994 in response to terrorist bombings. By 2001, according to estimates, Britain had one half million surveillance cameras, one for every 120 people. The United States has begun moving toward the British model. In 2002, the U.S. National Park Service installed surveillance cameras around national monuments in Washington, D.C.

Surveillance technology can be a useful law enforcement tool, for it provides the government with the power to watch people's activities and listen to their conversations. These profound powers, however, raise difficult problems. As with many countries throughout the world, the United States has enacted a series of laws to balance the benefits and dangers of surveillance.

* * *

I. THE PURPOSE AND HISTORY OF ELECTRONIC SURVEILLANCE LAW

In order to examine the effectiveness of electronic surveillance law and the methods by which to improve it, we must first articulate the goals that we want the law to achieve. At a very general level, the law of electronic surveillance recognizes two things: that government surveillance is good and that it is bad. Surveillance is an important law enforcement tool, and it can be highly effective at solving and preventing crimes. Thus, we want the government to be able to engage in certain forms of surveillance. But surveillance is also a very dangerous tool, with profound implications for our freedom and democracy. Hence, we also want government surveillance to be tightly controlled.

Our electronic surveillance law was created in response to specific problems. It was thus borne out of experience, and it is designed to redress these problems. In this Part, I discuss the animating problems and concerns of surveillance law. I examine the costs and benefits of electronic surveillance as well as the history of how and why surveillance law developed the way it did.

A. SURVEILLANCE: THE GOOD AND THE BAD

Electronic surveillance is one of the central tools of modern law enforcement. It can aid significantly in the investigations of crimes, for it allows the government to watch and listen to people during their unguarded moments, when they may speak about their criminal activity. Video cameras may capture criminals in the act and aid in their identification and arrest. Surveillance can also assist in preventing crimes because it enables the government to learn about criminal activity that is afoot and to halt it before it happens. Few would argue that these are not significant benefits.

Surveillance can also prevent crime in another way. In 1791, Jeremy Bentham imagined a new architectural design for a prison which he called the Panopticon. As Michel Foucault describes it:

[A]t the periphery, an annular building; at the centre, a tower; this tower is pierced with wide windows that open onto the inner side of the ring; the peripheric building is divided into cells, each of which extends the whole width of the building. . . . All that is needed, then, is to place a supervisor in a central tower and to shut up in each cell a madman, a patient, a condemned man, a worker or a schoolboy. By the effect of backlighting, one can observe from the tower, standing out precisely against the light, the small captive shadows in the cells of the periphery. They are like so many cages, so many small theatres, in which each actor is alone, perfectly individualized and constantly visible.

The Panopticon achieves obedience and discipline by having all prisoners believe they could be watched at any moment. Their fear of being watched inhibits transgression. Surveillance can thus prevent crime by making people decide not to engage in it at all. More generally, surveillance is good because it is a highly effective tool for maintaining social order. We want to foster a society where people are secure from theft, vandalism, assault, murder, rape, and terrorism. We thus desire social control, and surveillance can help achieve that end.

But surveillance is bad for the very same reason. George Orwell's Nineteen Eighty–Four chronicles a totalitarian government called "Big Brother" that aims for total social control. Everyone is under constant fear of being watched or overheard, and everything that people do is rigidly controlled by the government. In contrast to the society depicted in Orwell's novel, our society aims to be free and democratic, and our government is a far cry from Big Brother. The goal is not to suppress all individuality, to force everybody to think and act alike. Our government, however, has some of the same surveillance capabilities as Big Brother. And even when the government does not aim for total social control, surveillance can still impair freedom and democracy.

Surveillance has negative side effects that affect both the observed and the observers. For the observed, surveillance can lead to self-censorship and inhibition. According to Julie Cohen: "Pervasive monitoring of every first move or false start will, at the margin, incline choices toward the bland and the mainstream." Monitoring constrains the "acceptable spectrum of belief and behavior," and it results in "a subtle yet fundamental shift in the content of our character, a blunting and blurring of rough edges and sharp lines." Surveillance "threatens not only to chill the expression of eccentric individuality, but also, gradually, to dampen the force of our aspirations to it." Paul Schwartz argues that surveillance inhibits freedom of choice, impinging upon self-determination. Surveillance rigidifies one's past; it is a means of creating a trail of information about a person. Christopher Slobogin argues that being placed under surveillance impedes one's anonymity, inhibits one's freedom to associate with others, makes one's behavior less spontaneous, and alters one's freedom of movement. Surveillance's inhibitory effects are especially potent when people are engaging in political protest or dissent. People can face persecution, public sanction, and blacklisting for their unpopular political beliefs. Surveillance can make associating with disfavored groups and causes all the more difficult and precarious.

For the observers, surveillance presents a profound array of powers that are susceptible to abuse. As Raymond Ku notes, the Framers of the Constitution were concerned about "unfettered governmental power and discretion." The Framers were deeply opposed to general warrants and writs of assistance. General warrants "resulted in 'ransacking' and seizure of the personal papers of political dissidents, authors, and printers of seditious libel." Writs of assistance authorized "sweeping searches and seizures without any evidentiary basis." As Patrick Henry declared: "They may, unless the general government be restrained by a bill of rights, or some similar restrictions, go into your cellars and rooms, and search, ransack, and measure, every thing you eat, drink, and wear. They ought to be restrained within proper bounds." The problem, in short, is with the government having too much power.

Electronic surveillance presents additional problems. It is a sweeping form of investigatory power. It extends beyond a search, for it records behavior, social interaction, and everything that a person says and does. Rather than a targeted query for information, surveillance is often akin to casting a giant net, which can ensnare a significant amount of data beyond that which was originally sought. As James Dempsey notes, electronic surveillance captures a wide range of communications, "whether they are relevant to the investigation or not, raising concerns about compliance with the particularity requirement in the Fourth Amendment and posing the risk of general searches." Moreover, unlike a typical search, which is often performed in a short once-and-done-fashion, electronic surveillance "continues around-the-clock for days or months." Additionally, in a regular search, the government comes to a suspect's house and often searches while the suspect is present; on the other hand, "the usefulness of electronic surveillance depends on lack of notice to the suspect." As Justice Douglas observed, wiretapping can become "a dragnet, sweeping in all conversations within its scope."

Dissenting from *Lopez v. United States*, where the Court upheld the use of a pocket wire recorder to record a conversation, Justice Brennan observed that surveillance "makes the police omniscient; and police omniscience is one of the most effective tools of tyranny." As Justice Brandeis observed:

> Whenever a telephone line is tapped, the privacy of the persons at both ends of the line is invaded and all conversations between them upon any subject, although proper, confidential and privileged, may be overheard. Moreover, the tapping of one man's telephone line involves the tapping of the telephone of every other person whom he may call or who may call him. As a means of espionage, writs of assistance and general warrants are but puny instruments of tyranny and oppression when compared with wire tapping.

Furthermore, information collected by electronic surveillance can potentially be abused. Even if abuses are rare or the risk of abuse is low, the existence of legal protection is comforting and freedom-enhancing. People need a degree of control over the government in order to feel free. Freedom is not just the absence of restraints; it is a mental state, a felt reality in both structure and sentiment. Like insurance, protections against surveillance provide a sense of security.

Surveillance gives significant power to the watchers. Part of the harm is not simply in being watched, but in the lack of control that people have over the watchers. Surveillance creates the need to worry about the judgment of the watchers. Will our e-mail be misunderstood? Will our confidential information be revealed? What will be done with the information gleaned from surveillance?

Thus, the goal of surveillance law is to ameliorate these problems while at the same time allowing for effective law enforcement. This can be accomplished by providing for the oversight of government surveillance, accountability for abuses and errors, and limits against generalized forms of surveillance.

* * *

1. MONITORING OF STUDENT ACTIVITY GENERALLY

PRIVACY v. PIRACY

Sonia K. Kaytal
7 YALE J. L. & TECH. 222 (2005)

* * * Today, the Recording Industry Association of America (RIAA) and other copyright owners maintain automated Web crawlers that regularly survey and record the Internet Protocol addresses of computers that trade files on peer to peer networks. After the RIAA's initial victories, hundreds of subpoenas were issued—sometimes numbering seventy-five per day—each unveiling the digital identities of various Internet subscribers. Schools, responding to threats from the recording industry, have implemented programs that track and report the exchange of copyrighted files. A few have even decided to audit and actively monitor files traded by their students, at the RIAA's request. * * *

This outcome is not solely attributable to the development of peer-to-peer technologies, or the explosion of piracy in cyberspace, as some might suggest. Rather, the outcome involves the comparatively more subtle failure of law to resolve the troubling and often rivalrous relationship between the protection of intellectual property and privacy in cyberspace. The irony, of course, is that both areas of law are facing enormous challenges because of technology's ever-expanding pace of development. * * *

B.   SPECTERS OF PIRACY SURVEILLANCE

In August 2001, the Ninth Circuit, in a debate of unprecedented visibility, refused to install certain software that would enable monitoring of their computers to detect the downloading of music, streaming video, and pornography. The software was a filtering device ostensibly designed to prevent overloading the network system—but the judges believed that the alleged purpose behind its installation was broader. They feared that third parties would use such "content-detection" monitoring policies to identify individuals who engaged in file sharing or other potentially nefarious activities at work. A firestorm of controversy ensued. The judges ultimately defied the administrative order, disabled the software, and issued a host of statements publicly criticizing the administrative decision. As Judge Alex Kozinski put it:

> At the heart of the policy is a warning—very much like that given to federal prisoners—that every employee must surrender privacy as a condition of using common office equipment. Like prisoners, judicial employees must acknowledge that, by using this equipment, their "consent to monitoring and recording is implied with or without cause." . . . The proposed policy tells our 30,000 dedicated employees that we trust them so little that we must monitor all their communications just to make sure they are not wasting their work day cruising the Internet.

Even though the larger policymaking body of the federal court system, the Judicial Conference, disagreed with the Ninth Circuit, and chose to continue using the monitoring software, its decision angered some federal workers, highlighting the tradeoffs that many universities and employers have made in order to prevent being saddled with a lawsuit for contributory liability.

As this example demonstrates, the problem of piracy has led some private entities to respond even more forcefully than necessary, seeking to destroy not only the peer-to-peer networks that have sprouted across the Internet, but the very boundaries of privacy, anonymity, and autonomy in cyberspace. * * * [F]ear of suits for contributory infringement has led to regimes of institutional monitoring from ISPs, colleges, and private entities. Some schools have utilized monitoring regimes that bar students from sharing certain types of files; others undertake less invasive bandwidth monitoring practices; and still others continue to closely monitor students' and employees' activity out of fear of suits for contributory liability.

The result is a protracted, and largely invisible, web of surveillance[.]
* * *

NOTES

1. Preventing copyright infringement and any prospective liability (under the DMCA and related statutes) is only one of many purposes articulated

by those who argue for increased monitoring of student online activity. Other purposes may include protecting students from Internet predators, protecting students from inappropriate content (such as violence or obscenity), protecting students from each other (*cf* Columbine, Virginia Tech), protecting everyone from terrorism (*cf* the Patriot Act), and law enforcement generally.

2. Issues relating to the monitoring of student online activity interface with the materials in several other chapters of this book, including Chapter 3 (student "freedom of expression" rights), Chapter 4 (combating threatening activity and peer mistreatment), Chapter 9 (morality and values), and Chapter 10 (copyright issues in education).

3. The Children's Online Privacy Protection Act (COPPA) was passed by the U.S. Congress in 1998 for the purpose of protecting against the disclosure of personal information by children under the age of 13. The Act became effective in 2000, and the Federal Trade Commission ("FTC") was given the power to enforce it. As was the case with just about every piece of Internet-related legislation adopted by the federal government in that era, the Act engendered much debate. *See, e.g,* Danielle J. Garber, *COPPA: Protecting Children's Personal Information on the Internet,* 10 J. L. & POL'Y 129 (2001)(arguing that "although the COPPA presents some enforcement problems, such as the inability to detect whether children are truthfully disclosing their age, it will likely prove to be effective in making the Internet a more private and safe place for children"); *see also* Melanie A. Hersh, *Is COPPA a Cop Out? The Child Online Privacy Protection Act as Proof That Parents, Not Government, Should Be Protecting Children's Interests on the Internet* (asserting that "in light of COPPA's shortcomings and faulty attempts to emulate regulations of other media, the government should step back and allow parents to maintain the bulk of regulatory responsibility").

4. As Internet use becomes increasingly more commonplace among young people, parents may be less engaged in monitoring the online activities of their children. For example, a 2004 survey commissioned by a non-profit marketing research board in New York found that about 75 percent of the parents of children under 18 who have home Internet access remained in the room while their children used the Internet. *See* Jessica L. Tonn, *Online Monitoring,* ED. WEEK, Jan. 19, 2005. However, a 2005 study by Cox Communications in partnership with the National Center for Missing and Exploited Children found that 42% of parents surveyed did not review the content of their teenagers' communication in chat rooms or via Instant Messaging, and that 51% of parents either did not have or did not know whether they had monitoring software installed on their computers. See Parents' Internet Monitoring Study, www.netsmartz.org/pdf/takechargestudy.pdf (accessed November 15, 2008). Arguably, with the incremental growth of social networking sites in the years that followed, the ability of parents to monitor their children's Internet usage may have become an even greater challenge.

5. With regard to the monitoring of e-mail, it should be noted that under federal statutory law, the Electronic Communications Privacy Act (ECPA), which originally served as an anti-wiretapping act, has been expanded to include electronic communication. But commentators have pointed out that this statute is filled with exceptions and provides a significantly lower

level of protection for e-mail users than it does for others employing electronic transmission devices. In the workplace, for example, it is generally agreed by both commentators and jurists that employers may monitor employee e-mail communication.

6.   Particularly at the postsecondary level, educational institutions have moved an increasingly larger percentage of their daily communication to the Internet. In light of the fact that virtually all educational institutions have retained the ability to access back-up copies of e-mail sent and received through their servers, what are the implications of this activity today, legally and as a matter of policy?

2.   THE PROSPECTIVE APPLICABILITY OF THE RIGHT TO ANONYMITY

A related legal principle in the area of privacy in the right to anonymity. This limited right, recognized by the U.S. Supreme Court within the context of political speech, has been referenced subsequently in a variety of online disputes.

Particularly in an education setting, the parameters of the right remain unclear. And it must be recognized that students are not generally expected to anonymous in educational institutions. In fact, educators are invariably urged to do all they can to fight against anonymity in such settings. On the other hand, students do have privacy rights, and the right to anonymity has been recognized in the highest courts of the land.

Consider the following opinion in the *McIntyre* case. While not an education law case per se, *McIntyre* sets forth basic principles regarding the relative right to anonymity under First Amendment law. To what extent might this case be applicable in an education setting? To what extent might it be distinguishable? Why?

McINTYRE v. OHIO ELECTIONS COMM'N

514 U.S. 334, 115 S.Ct. 1511 (1995)

JUSTICE STEVENS delivered the opinion of the Court.

The question presented is whether an Ohio statute that prohibits the distribution of anonymous campaign literature is a "law . . . abridging the freedom of speech" within the meaning of the First Amendment.

I

On April 27, 1988, Margaret McIntyre distributed leaflets to persons attending a public meeting at the Blendon Middle School in Westerville, Ohio. At this meeting, the superintendent of schools planned to discuss an imminent referendum on a proposed school tax levy. The leaflets expressed Mrs. McIntyre's opposition to the levy. There is no suggestion that the text of her message was false, misleading, or libelous. She had composed and printed it on her home computer and had paid a professional printer to make additional copies. Some of the handbills identified her as the author; others merely purported to express the views of "CONCERNED PARENTS AND TAX PAYERS." Except for the help provided by her son and a friend, who placed some of the leaflets on car windshields in the school parking lot, Mrs. McIntyre acted independently.

While Mrs. McIntyre distributed her handbills, an official of the school district, who supported the tax proposal, advised her that the unsigned leaflets did not conform to the Ohio election laws. Undeterred, Mrs. McIntyre appeared at another meeting on the next evening and handed out more of the handbills.

The proposed school levy was defeated at the next two elections, but it finally passed on its third try in November 1988. Five months later, the same school official filed a complaint with the Ohio Elections Commission charging that Mrs. McIntyre's distribution of unsigned leaflets violated § 3599.09(A) of the Ohio Code. The commission agreed and imposed a fine of $100.

* * *

Mrs. McIntyre passed away during the pendency of this litigation. Even though the amount in controversy is only $100, petitioner, as the executor of her estate, has pursued her claim in this Court. Our grant of certiorari reflects our agreement with his appraisal of the importance of the question presented.

II

Ohio maintains that the statute under review is a reasonable regulation of the electoral process. The State does not suggest that all anonymous publications are pernicious or that a statute totally excluding them from the marketplace of ideas would be valid. This is a wise (albeit implicit) concession, for the anonymity of an author is not ordinarily a sufficient reason to exclude her work product from the protections of the First Amendment.

"Anonymous pamphlets, leaflets, brochures and even books have played an important role in the progress of mankind." Great works of literature have frequently been produced by authors writing under assumed names.[4] Despite readers' curiosity and the public's interest in identifying the creator of a work of art, an author generally is free to

---

4. American names such as Mark Twain (Samuel Langhorne Clemens) and O. Henry (William Sydney Porter) come readily to mind. Benjamin Franklin employed numerous different pseudonyms. *See* 2 W. BRUCE, BENJAMIN FRANKLIN SELF REVEALED: A BIOGRAPHICAL AND CRITICAL STUDY BASED MAINLY ON HIS OWN WRITINGS, ch. 5 (2d ed. 1923). Distinguished French authors such as Voltaire (Francois Marie Arouet) and George Sand (Amandine Aurore Lucie Dupin), and British authors such as George Eliot (Mary Ann Evans), Charles Lamb (sometimes wrote as "Elia"), and Charles Dickens (sometimes wrote as "Boz"), also published under assumed names. Indeed, some believe the works of Shakespeare were actually written by the Earl of Oxford rather than by William Shaksper of Stratford on Avon. *See* C. OGBURN, THE MYSTERIOUS WILLIAM SHAKESPEARE: THE MYTH & THE REALITY (2d ed. 1992); *but see* S. SCHOENBAUM, SHAKESPEARE'S LIVES (2d ed. 1991) (adhering to the traditional view that Shakespeare was in fact the author). *See also Stevens, The Shakespeare Canon of Statutory Construction*, 140 U. PA. L. REV. 1373 (1992) (commenting on the competing theories).

decide whether or not to disclose his or her true identity. The decision in favor of anonymity may be motivated by fear of economic or official retaliation, by concern about social ostracism, or merely by a desire to preserve as much of one's privacy as possible. Whatever the motivation may be, at least in the field of literary endeavor, the interest in having anonymous works enter the marketplace of ideas unquestionably outweighs any public interest in requiring disclosure as a condition of entry.[5] Accordingly, an author's decision to remain anonymous, like other decisions concerning omissions or additions to the content of a publication, is an aspect of the freedom of speech protected by the First Amendment.

The freedom to publish anonymously extends beyond the literary realm. In *Talley*, the Court held that the First Amendment protects the distribution of unsigned handbills urging readers to boycott certain Los Angeles merchants who were allegedly engaging in discriminatory employment practices. Writing for the Court, Justice Black noted that "[p]ersecuted groups and sects from time to time throughout history have been able to criticize oppressive practices and laws either anonymously or not at all." Justice Black recalled England's abusive press licensing laws and seditious libel prosecutions, and he reminded us that even the arguments favoring the ratification of the Constitution advanced in the Federalist Papers were published under fictitious names. On occasion, quite apart from any threat of persecution, an advocate may believe her ideas will be more persuasive if her readers are unaware of her identity. Anonymity thereby provides a way for a writer who may be personally unpopular to ensure that readers will not prejudge her message simply because they do not like its proponent. Thus, even in the field of political rhetoric, where "the identity of the speaker is an important component of many attempts to persuade," the most effective advocates have sometimes opted for anonymity. The specific holding in *Talley* related to advocacy of an economic boycott, but the Court's reasoning embraced a respected tradition of anonymity in the advocacy of political causes.[6] This tradition is perhaps best exemplified by the secret ballot, the hard won right to vote one's conscience without fear of retaliation.

---

5. Though such a requirement might provide assistance to critics in evaluating the quality and significance of the writing, it is not indispensable. To draw an analogy from a nonliterary context, the now pervasive practice of grading law school examination papers "blindly" (i.e., under a system in which the professor does not know whose paper she is grading) indicates that such evaluations are possible—indeed, perhaps more reliable—when any bias associated with the author's identity is prescinded.

6. That tradition is most famously embodied in the *Federalist Papers*, authored by James Madison, Alexander Hamilton, and John Jay, but signed "Publius." Publius' opponents, the Anti–Federalists, also tended to publish under pseudonyms: prominent among them were "Cato," believed to be New York Governor George Clinton; "Centinel," probably Samuel Bryan or his father, Pennsylvania judge and legislator George Bryan; "The Federal Farmer," who may have been Richard Henry Lee, a Virginia member of the Continental Congress and a signer of the Declaration of Independence; and "Brutus," who may have been Robert Yates, a New York Supreme Court justice who walked out on the Constitutional Convention. 2 THE COMPLETE ANTI FEDERALIST (H. Storing ed. 1981). A forerunner of all of these writers was the pre-Revolutionary War English pamphleteer "Junius," whose true identity remains a mystery. *See* ENCYCLOPEDIA OF COLONIAL AND REVOLUTIONARY AMERICA 220 (J. Faragher ed. 1990) (positing that "Junius" may have been Sir Phillip Francis). The *"Letters of Junius"* were "widely reprinted in colonial newspapers and lent considerable support to the revolutionary cause."

III

California had defended the Los Angeles ordinance at issue in *Talley* as a law "aimed at providing a way to identify those responsible for fraud, false advertising and libel." We rejected that argument because nothing in the text or legislative history of the ordinance limited its application to those evils. We then made clear that we did "not pass on the validity of an ordinance limited to prevent these or any other supposed evils." The Ohio statute likewise contains no language limiting its application to fraudulent, false, or libelous statements; to the extent, therefore, that Ohio seeks to justify § 3599.09(A) as a means to prevent the dissemination of untruths, its defense must fail for the same reason given in *Talley*. As the facts of this case demonstrate, the ordinance plainly applies even when there is no hint of falsity or libel.

Ohio's statute does, however, contain a different limitation: It applies only to unsigned documents designed to influence voters in an election. In contrast, the Los Angeles ordinance prohibited all anonymous handbilling "in any place under any circumstances." For that reason, Ohio correctly argues that *Talley* does not necessarily control the disposition of this case. We must, therefore, decide whether and to what extent the First Amendment's protection of anonymity encompasses documents intended to influence the electoral process.

* * *

* * * [A]s we have explained on many prior occasions, the category of speech regulated by the Ohio statute occupies the core of the protection afforded by the First Amendment[.] * * *

* * * Indeed, the speech in which Mrs. McIntyre engaged—handing out leaflets in the advocacy of a politically controversial viewpoint—is the essence of First Amendment expression. * * * No form of speech is entitled to greater constitutional protection than Mrs. McIntyre's.

When a law burdens core political speech, we apply "exacting scrutiny," and we uphold the restriction only if it is narrowly tailored to serve an overriding state interest. * * *

* * *

VI

Under our Constitution, anonymous pamphleteering is not a pernicious, fraudulent practice, but an honorable tradition of advocacy and of dissent. Anonymity is a shield from the tyranny of the majority. It thus exemplifies the purpose behind the Bill of Rights, and of the First Amendment in particular: to protect unpopular individuals from retaliation—and their ideas from suppression—at the hand of an intolerant society. The right to remain anonymous may be abused when it shields fraudulent conduct. But political speech by its nature will sometimes have unpalatable consequences, and, in general, our society accords greater weight to the value of free speech than to the dangers of its misuse. Ohio has not shown that its interest in preventing the misuse of anonymous election related speech justifies a prohibition of all uses of that speech. The State may, and does, punish fraud directly. But it cannot seek to punish fraud indirectly by indiscriminately outlawing a category of speech, based on its content, with no necessary relationship to the danger sought to be prevented. One would be hard pressed to think of a better example of the pitfalls of Ohio's blunderbuss approach than the facts of the case before us.

The judgment of the Ohio Supreme Court is reversed.

It is so ordered.

CHAPTER III

STUDENT FREEDOM OF EXPRESSION

■ ■ ■

The nature and extent of student "free speech" rights under the First Amendment is both one of the most vibrant and one of the most difficult areas of constitutional law. Not necessarily difficult doctrinally, since rules have been articulated to address a wide range of fact patterns, but difficult in that the disputes often involve rights in conflict and gut-wrenching compromises. In addition, as a matter of policy, the correct course of action in these disputes is often unclear.

In the 1960s and 1970s, free speech issues were at the forefront of education-related debates, with students asserting themselves in ways they never had before. After a period of relative calm in the 1980s and early 1990s, free speech disputes flared up again, and by the early twenty-first century, they had once again become among the most compelling of all the controversies in the education community.

It is often impossible to separate free speech issues from campus safety concerns, and students accused of threatening or harassing behavior often seek to rely on the protections of the First Amendment. In addition, freedom of expression principles are often at the center of controversies in areas relating to curriculum, religion, morality, and values.

This chapter is designed to serve as an introduction to the large body of law that has emerged in this area. It highlights the major U.S. Supreme Court decisions that first recognized broad protections for student freedom of expression at both the K–12 and higher education levels, and provides examples of cases over the next several decades that clarified the parameters of those protections. In this manner, it points toward a further examination of complex First Amendment disputes in Chapter 4 (combating threats and peer harassment) and Chapter 9 (morality and values).

It can be argued, in this regard, that a key principle implicit in Education Law—and especially in First Amendment speech and religion cases—is the principle of *respect*. Although rarely stated explicitly, U.S. law appears to require that every person attending public schools be treated with respect. Factoring in the equal protection guarantees, the principle can be expanded to embody a requirement that all persons be treated with equal respect and equal dignity.

Consider the materials in this chapter in light of this argument. What evidence can you find that a *respect principle* does in fact exist? What evidence is there that this may not necessarily be the case, at least at the present time, and at least in certain instances? If a *respect principle* is indeed evident, what are its parameters? What guidelines are people expected to follow? What are the accompanying rights and responsibilities?

A. BASIC FIRST AMENDMENT PRINCIPLES APPLICABLE IN ALL SETTINGS

HIGHLIGHTS OF U.S. FIRST AMENDMENT LAW: BASIC PRINCIPLES AND MAJOR EXCEPTIONS

From Beyond Our Control? Confronting
the Limits of Our Legal System
In the Age of Cyberspace
Stuart Biegel
MIT Press (2001)

Two basic principles of U.S. free speech law as interpreted by the courts under the Constitution are particularly relevant [in an education-related context]. * * * The first is that statutes and policies designed by public entities to regulate speech are unconstitutional if vague or overbroad.[1] The second is that speech cannot generally be regulated on the basis of its content, unless the regulation falls within some recognized exception or some other related rule of law.

Under well-settled constitutional law, a statute or policy is unconstitutionally *vague* "when men of common intelligence must necessarily guess at its meaning.... [It] must give adequate warning of the conduct which is to be prohibited and must set out explicit standards for those who apply it."[2] A statute or policy regulating speech will be deemed *overbroad* "if it sweeps within its ambit a substantial amount of protected speech along with that which it may legitimately regulate."[3] * * *

Any attempt by a governmental entity to restrict speech on the basis of its * * * content would be deemed *content-based regulation,* a type of regulation that is disfavored and presumed unconstitutional under First Amendment law.[4] Yet speech can indeed be regulated on the basis of its content if it is found to be (1) obscene, (2) child pornography, (3) fighting

---

1. *See, e.g.,* UWM Post v. Bd. of Regents of the Univ. of Wis. Sys., 774 F. Supp. 1163 (E.D. Wis. 1991); Doe v. Univ. of Mich., 721 F. Supp. 852 (E.D. Mich. 1989).

2. *See Doe,* 721 F. Supp. at 866–67.

3. *Id.* at 864; *see also UWM Post,* 774 F. Supp. at 1169.

4. Under First Amendment case law, it is often useful to identify two types of speech regulation: content-based regulation and content-neutral regulation. Content-neutral regulation can generally be regulated under reasonable time, place, and manner restrictions. But content-based regulation can only be regulated if the speech falls within one or more recognized exceptions or can be prohibited under other relevant laws. *See, e.g.,* LAURENCE H. TRIBE, *AMERICAN CONSTITUTIONAL LAW,* Chapter 12, *Rights of Communication and Expression* (2d ed. 1988).

words, (4) incitement to imminent lawless conduct, (5) defamation (libel or slander), (6) an invasion of privacy under tort law, (7) harassment, (8) a true threat, (9) copyright infringement, or (10) another recognized tort or crime. * * *

1/ Obscenity—While Justice Potter Stewart's famous line "I know it when I see it" is still quoted in this context, the U.S. Supreme Court in the 1973 case of *Miller v. California*[5] developed a three-part test for obscenity that is still being used today. A Court will inquire whether:

> (a) " 'the average person applying contemporary community standards' would find that the work, taken as a whole appeals to the prurient interest";

> (b) it "depicts or describes, in a patently offensive way, sexual conduct specifically defined by applicable state law"; *and*

> (c) "the work, taken as a whole, lacks serious literary, artistic, political, or scientific value."

2/ Child Pornography—The definition of child pornography, as set forth by the U.S. Congress, was originally limited to visual depictions of real children. It was expanded in 1996, however, to include both "computer-generated images" and pictures of people who only appear to be under 18. Under Title 18 of the U.S. Code, § 2256, child pornography is defined as "any visual depiction, including any photograph, film, video, picture, or computer or computer generated image or picture, whether made or produced by electronic, mechanical, or other means, of sexually explicit conduct, where

> (a) the production of such visual depiction involves the use of a minor engaging in sexually explicit conduct;

> (b) such visual depiction is, or appears to be, of a minor engaging in sexually explicit conduct;

> (c) such visual depiction has been created, adapted, or modified to appear that an identifiable minor is engaging in sexually explicit conduct; or

> (d) such visual depiction is advertised, promoted, presented, described, or distributed in such a manner that conveys the impression that the material is or contains a visual depiction of a minor engaging in sexually explicit conduct."

In [2002, however, the U.S. Supreme Court in *Ashcroft v. The Free Speech Coalition,* held that "the prohibitions of §§ 2256(8)(B) and 2256(8)(D) are overbroad and unconstitutional.[6]"]

3/ Fighting Words—The U.S. Supreme Court in the 1942 case of *Chaplinsky v. New Hampshire* set out a two-part definition for fighting words:

---

5. 413 U.S. 15 (1973).

6. 535 U.S. 234 (2002).

(a) words which by their very utterance inflict injury and

(b) words which by their very utterance tend to incite an immediate breach of the peace.[7]

Since *Chaplinsky,* the Supreme Court has narrowed and clarified the scope of the fighting words doctrine in at least three ways. First, the Court has arguably limited the fighting words definition so that it now only includes its second half. Second, the Court has stated that in order for words to meet the second half of the definition they must "naturally tend to provoke violent resentment." Finally, the Court has held that fighting words must be "directed at the person of the hearer."[8]

Chaplinsky himself was distributing religious literature on public sidewalk and was led away by the City Marshal because of fear that his acts were causing or would cause a public disturbance. As he was led away, he called the Marshal a "G-damned racketeer and a damned fascist." His breach of peace conviction was upheld because of the danger that listener of his words would be incited to violence. The test was whether or not men of common intelligence would understand the words as likely to cause the average addressee to fight. For speech to be restricted under this doctrine, it had to be "words and expressions which by general consent are fighting words when said without a disarming smile." And the Court referred to words that would produce an "uncontrollable impulse."

It must be noted that since *Chaplinsky* not one conviction under the fighting words exception has been upheld by the U.S. Supreme Court.[9] And after the Court's decision in the 1992 case of *R.A.V. v. City of St. Paul,*[10] many commentators argued that the fighting words doctrine had become a relic of another age. Yet the doctrine has not been explicitly overruled, and it remains on the books as a recognized exception to the rule that speech cannot be regulated on the basis of its content.

4/ *Incitement to Imminent Lawless Conduct*—Under the rule set forth by the U.S. Supreme Court in *Brandenburg v. Ohio,* speech can be restricted on the basis of its content if it is "directed to inciting or producing imminent lawless action and is likely to incite or produce such action."[11] As the Court further explained in a subsequent case, "we have not permitted the government to assume that every expression of a provocative idea will incite a riot, but have instead required careful consideration of the actual circumstances surrounding such expression."[12]

Brandenburg focused on circumstances surrounding a rally and speeches by members of the Ku Klux Klan. During the rally, "reven-

---

7. 315 U.S. 568, 571–72 (1942).

8. *See also UWM Post,* 774 F. Supp. at 1169–72.

9. *See* Nadine Strossen, *Regulating Racist Speech On Campus: A Modest Proposal,* 1990 DUKE L.J. 484, 508–14.

10. 505 U.S. 377 (1992).

11. 395 U.S. 444, 447 (1969).

12. *Texas v. Johnson,* 491 U.S. 397 (1989).

geance" was threatened, and the defendant—who had organized the event—added that "the n----r should be returned to Africa" and "the Jew returned to Israel." Defendant was convicted under a 1919 Ohio statute which forbid "advocating ... the duty, necessity, or propriety of crime, sabotage, violence, or unlawful methods of terrorism as a means of accomplishing industrial or political reform." In a relatively short opinion, the Court found in favor of the defendant, holding that the statute was unconstitutional because the First Amendment does not permit a state "to forbid or proscribe advocacy of the use of force or of law violation except where such advocacy is directed to inciting or producing *imminent* lawless action and is likely to incite or produce such action."[13]

Commentators have noted that the distinction drawn between "mere advocacy" and "incitement to imminent lawless action" parallels the reasoning in *Chaplinsky* and indicates that in the U.S. the "public peace" can only be protected against speech which is likely to produce immediate violence.[14]

5/ Defamation—In general, defamatory statements—which include libel (the written word) and slander (the spoken word)—are not protected by the First Amendment. Rules of defamation have evolved under the common law and vary from state to state, but typically, to qualify as defamation, a statement must be

(a) a defamatory communication about the plaintiff,

(b) published to third persons,

(c) which was false at the time it was made.[15]

A *defamatory communication* has been defined as one which "tends so to harm the reputation of another as to lower him in the estimation of the community or to deter third persons from associating or dealing with him."[16] *Published to third persons* means that the communication (oral or written) must be to someone other than the person allegedly defamed. As to the *falsity* requirement, virtually all states today require that the communication be untrue before a defamation action can proceed.

---

13. *Brandenburg*, 395 U.S. at 447 (emphasis added).

14. *See generally* Friedrich Kubler, *How Much Freedom for Racist Speech? Transnational Aspects of a Conflict of Human Rights*, 27 HOFSTRA L. REV. 335 (1998).

15. John Faucher explains that, according to the general rule,

[T]o prevail in a defamation action, the plaintiff must show that: (1) the defendant published the statement by showing or saying it to a third party, (2) the statement identified the plaintiff, (3) the statement put the plaintiff in a bad light, and (4) it was false at the time that it was made.

Though law schools teach the same defamation law from Hawaii to Maine, state laws vary widely. In particular, state laws vary on standards of fault, distinctions between fact and opinion, application of rules of libel per se and per quod, availability of punitive damages, and statutes of limitations. Any of these laws could affect the outcome of a case.

John D. Faucher, *Let the Chips Fall Where They May: Choice of Law in Computer Bulletin Board Defamation Cases*, 26 U.C. DAVIS L. REV. 1045, 1052–54 (1993).

16. RESTATEMENT (SECOND) OF TORTS, § 559 (1977).

[While at one time the U.S. courts recognized a cause of action for "group defamation," this doctrine has been discredited over time, and is generally not viewed as either a viable avenue of litigation today or a valid justification for the restriction of speech on the basis of its content.]

Over the years, the law of defamation has been bolstered by many special rules. For example, under the First Amendment, if the subject of the communication is a public figure, defendant can be held liable for defamation only if the statement was made with actual malice or reckless disregard for the truth.[17] Even if the subject is a private figure, media defendants focusing on matters of *public concern* must also have acted with actual malice or reckless disregard for the truth to be found liable.[18]

In addition, a statement that is only an opinion—and not fact—cannot be considered defamatory under the First Amendment if it

(a) addresses matters of public concern,

(b) is expressed in a manner that is not provably false, and

(c) cannot be reasonably interpreted as stating actual facts about a person.[19]

Finally, it should be noted that a "republisher" of defamatory statements is also liable under the basic framework outlined here. *Republishers* are "those who participate in distributing a libel," and can include, for example, newspapers that print op-ed pieces or even letters to the editor. As a general rule, if the original author is liable for defamation, republishers can also be found liable for defamation for the same defamation.[20]

6/ Invasion of Privacy—Statements that constitute an invasion of privacy under tort law are also not protected by the First Amendment. Four separate torts (or civil wrongs) have actually emerged in this context over the past 100 years. They include *appropriation* of a person's picture or name, *intrusion* upon a person's private affairs or seclusion, publication of facts placing a person in a *false light,* and public disclosure of *private facts*. Each tort has its own basic requirements.[21]

An *appropriation* is an unauthorized use by defendant of plaintiff's picture or name for commercial advantage. Plaintiff can be a celebrity or a private person, but a celebrity typically stands a better chance of winning

---

17. New York Times v. Sullivan, 376 U.S. 254 (1964).

18. Gertz v. Robert Welch, 418 U.S. 323 (1974).

19. Milkovich v. Lorain Journal Co., 497 U.S. 1, 17–21 (1990). In determining whether a statement is intended to convey an actual fact about a person, the Court will look at (1) whether the language loose, figurative, or hyperbolic, which would negate the impression that the speaker was seriously maintaining the truth of the underlying facts, (2) whether the general tenor of the article negate the impression that the speaker was seriously maintaining the truth of the underlying fact, and (3) whether the connotation sufficiently factual to be susceptible of being proved true or false. *Id.* at 21.

20. *See generally* Eugene Volokh, *Freedom of Speech in Cyberspace from the Listener's Perspective: Private Speech Restrictions, Libel, State Action, Harassment, and Sex*, 1996 U. CHI. LEGAL F. 377. Other rules under the law of defamation include certain "privileges" that defendants may invoke against claims of defamation in certain circumstances.

21. In addition, like defamation, certain arguments have been recognized as providing valid defenses to invasion of privacy claims.

a large monetary award by suing not under this right of privacy but under the related "right of publicity."[22]

An *intrusion* is an intentional or negligent act of prying or intruding by the defendant into a private area of plaintiff's life. The intrusion must be something that would be objectionable to a reasonable person. It can be physical (such as entering private property uninvited), or nonphysical (such as repeatedly calling a person late at night). In any case, plaintiff cannot prevail in such a lawsuit unless it can be shown that a person could reasonably expect that he or she would not be intruded upon in this manner by someone in defendant's position.

False light invasion of privacy is the publication of facts about the plaintiff placing him or her in a false light in the public eye. As with an intrusion, it must be objectionable to a reasonable person under the circumstances. False light invasion of privacy may include views that a person does not hold, or a description of actions that he or she did not take. It should be noted that such behavior may also constitute defamation if the falsity affects a person's reputation.

Public disclosure of private facts is the disclosure of private information about the plaintiff. Disclosure must be highly offensive, such that a reasonable person of ordinary sensibilities would object to having it made public. Private facts under this tort must involve those aspects of plaintiff's private life that have not already received some publicity and are not left open to public observation. Thus a magazine selling mailing lists of subscribers has been held not to have publicly disclosed private facts within the meaning of this rule.[23]

Any statements that fall within the definitions of one or more of these four torts can be restricted by governmental entities without violating the First Amendment.

*7/ **Harassment***—Rules prohibiting racial, religious, or sexual harassment evolved in the workplace under Title VII of the U.S. Civil Rights Act of 1964. At this point in time, sexual harassment laws are arguably the most highly developed,[24] and they include prohibitions against both *quid pro quo* harassment and *hostile environment* harassment.

Hostile environment claims were first recognized by the U.S. Supreme Court in 1986,[25] and over the next 10–15 years the rules were fine tuned by subsequent judicial opinions. 1998 proved to be a turning point, with the Court deciding four sexual harassment cases in one year.[26] Commenta-

---

22. *See generally* Cristina Fernandez, *The Right of Publicity on the Internet,* 8 Marq. Sports L.J. 289 (1998).

23. Shibley v. Time, Inc., 40 Ohio Misc. 51 (1974).

24. In *Faragher v. Boca Raton,* 524 U.S. 775 (1998), the U.S. Supreme Court noted that hostile environment sexual harassment claims had actually developed from the earlier racial and national origin harassment cases.

25. *See* Meritor Savings Bank v. Vinson, 477 U.S. 57 (1986).

26. The four cases were *Oncale v. Sundowner Offshore Services,* 523 U.S. 75 (1998), *Gebser v. Lago Vista Independent School District,* 524 U.S. 274 (1998), *Faragher v. City of Boca Raton,* 524 U.S. 775 (1998), and *Ellerth v. Burlington Industries,* 524 U.S. 951 (1998).

tors have raised questions in recent years regarding the extent to which the First Amendment can or should be employed to limit the scope of harassment law,[27] but as of the Year 2000—as long as certain expression falls within the definitions outlined by the Court—it is not protected speech and can be restricted accordingly.

The basic hostile environment claim under Title VII can only be filed by a person who alleges harassment in the workplace. Sexual harassment is not a crime, but an act or a series of acts that can lead to large monetary awards for aggrieved employees who have sued their employers under Title VII. * * *

To establish actionable hostile environment harassment, plaintiffs must prove that the activity in question was unwelcome and that it constituted "a sexually objectionable environment" which was

(a) objectively offensive and

(b) subjectively offensive.

An environment is deemed *objectively offensive* if a "reasonable person" would find it to be hostile or abusive, and it will be found *subjectively offensive* if the victim in fact perceived it to be so.

A version of this framework has recently been applied by the Courts in federally funded education programs under Title IX of the Education Amendments of 1972 to the Civil Rights Act of 1964. In *Davis v. Monroe County Board of Education,* the Court held that educational institutions can be held liable for peer-to-peer hostile environment sexual harassment "that is so severe, pervasive, and objectively offensive that it effectively bars the victim's access to an educational opportunity or benefit." But even if plaintiff can meet the requirements of this stringent test for actionable harassment, he or she can only prevail if the education officials in charge acted "with deliberate indifference to known acts of harassment."[28]

*8/ **True Threats**—*As discussed in earlier chapters, threatening speech can be restricted by governmental entities only if it constitutes a "true threat." The U.S. courts have disagreed over the years regarding the exact contours of an appropriate test to determine whether words amount to a *true* threat, but there is general agreement in most jurisdictions regarding certain basic principles.

(a) The threat must be "against the physical safety or freedom of some individual or class of persons,"[29] and

---

27. *See, e.g.,* Eugene Volokh, *Freedom of Speech and Workplace Harassment,* 39 UCLA L. REV. 1791 (1992).

28. *See* Davis v. Monroe County Bd. of Educ., 526 U.S. 629, 633 (1999).

29. U.S. v. Alkhabaz, 104 F.3d 1492, 1506 (6th Cir. 1997) (Krupansky, J., dissenting). This requirement is generally satisfied "irrespective of the identity of the person or group threatened, the originator's motivation for issuing the threat, or the existence or nonexistence of any goal pursued by the threat."

(b) The communication * * * would lead a reasonable, objective re-cipient to believe that the person expressing the threat "was serious about his threat ... regardless of the subjective intent of the speaker to make an actual threat or whether anyone actually felt frightened, intimidated, or coerced by the threat."[30]

As with many other legal tests, then, the Courts here inquire into the state of mind of a hypothetical objective reasonable person. The key question is whether such a hypothetical person would feel threatened, regardless of whether the real-life recipient of the threat actually did. If the communication is objectively threatening, it is deemed to be a true threat.

9/ *Copyright Infringement*—On some level, copyright laws act to restrict freedom of expression on the basis of content, because limitations on expressive activity that infringes one or more of the five exclusive rights of a copyright owner have of course been deemed acceptable if they reflect the balance of interests required by the U.S. Constitution.

There has been a significant amount of scholarship over the years addressing the interface between First Amendment law and copyright law. Certain disputes have been characterized as pitting one body of law against the other, and commentators have set out a range of very interesting positions in these debates * * * some favoring the primacy of the free speech guarantees and others favoring the primacy of intellectual property protection. While interpretations still vary, most believe that the U.S. Supreme Court decision in *Harper & Row v. Nation Enterprises*[31] ended this debate, or at least significantly limited the impact of any future arguments in favor of loosening copyright restrictions on free speech grounds.

In *Harper,* defendants—who had reproduced excerpts of President Ford's biography in their magazine prior to the biography's formal publi-cation—invoked First Amendment principles in an effort to excuse their actions.[32] The Court rejected their argument, finding that current copy-right law "strikes a definitional balance" in this context "by permitting free communications of facts while still protecting an author's expres-sion."

An early cyberlaw case, *Religious Technology Center v. Netcom,*[33] also addressed the viability of First Amendment arguments by defendants accused of copyright infringement. Netcom—an Internet Service Provid-er—had been charged by the Church of Scientology with contributory copyright infringement for the posting of protected church documents via its server. * * *

---

30. *Id.*

31. 471 U.S. 539 (1985).

32. *See id.* at 555–56.

33. 907 F. Supp. 1361 (N.D. Cal. 1995).

Netcom argued in part that if it were found liable for copyright infringement, First Amendment principles would be contravened * * * "as it would chill the use of the Internet because every access provider or user would be subject to liability when a user posts an infringing work to a Usenet newsgroup." The court, however, disagreed, declaring that "while an overbroad injunction might implicate the First Amendment . . . imposing liability for infringement where it is otherwise appropriate does not necessarily raise a First Amendment issue."[34] * * *

[In general, then] * * * words constituting copyright infringement can still be restricted as they have been in the past despite the imperatives of recent free speech law.

10/ Another Recognized Tort or Crime—Other expressive activity can also be regulated on the basis of its content if it is a crime and/or a tort under U.S. law. The crimes and torts discussed in this section are typically among the most prominent examples, but different circumstances may trigger the application of other legal principles in this area.

Beyond these ten categories, additional restrictions on freedom of expression may be implemented in certain special circumstances, such as on K–12 public school campuses. While the U.S. Supreme Court has indeed recognized that students do not "shed their constitutional rights to freedom of speech or expression at the schoolhouse gate," student speech may be regulated if it materially and substantially interferes with schoolwork, discipline, or the rights of others.[35] * * *

Finally, it must be noted again that all these First Amendment rules and exceptions generally apply only in the public sector. Non-public entities such as private universities, corporations, and [Internet Service Providers] are not typically under any obligation to comply with the limits imposed by case law in this context. As a matter of policy, however, most private institutions of higher education and a good number of ISPs do in fact choose to follow these same rules and regulations.

B. "FREEDOM OF EXPRESSION" AT THE K–12 LEVEL: THE *TINKER* RULE AND CAMPUS SAFETY

PROBLEM 10: THE COALITION TO RESIST POLITICAL AND SOCIAL INDOCTRINATION

Assume that all the events in this hypothetical take place in a publicly funded education setting.

In response to the announcement of the new "Groundhog Day" humani-

---

34. *See id.* at 1377.

35. Tinker v. Des Moines Indep. Cmty. Sch. Dist., 393 U.S. 503 (1969).

ties unit (as it came to be called),[a] Jamie—an eleventh grader who has consistently been an outspoken student activist on a range of political and social issues since entering Southern Valley High in the ninth grade—organizes the Coalition to Resist Political and Social Indoctrination (CRI). Meetings of the CRI attract significant numbers of students, many of whom dress differently and have been consistent victims of bullying perpetrated by apolitical students showing off for their friends. Jamie himself takes pride in defying the culture of the school, dressing flamboyantly, and being perennially provocative.

An activist agenda is developed at the CRI meetings to protest what the organization believes to be "one-sided" education. The protest activities are slated to include the distribution of fliers on and off campus, the creation of a Web site, and plans for picketing the school. But before any of these activities can be implemented, Principal Madeline Arthur announces that the organization will be prohibited from meeting on campus or distributing any materials online or offline relating to the announced agenda, and that any picketing will result in the immediate suspension of all those participating. At the next faculty meeting, Dr. Arthur asserts that there were two reasons behind the decision to restrict this expression "Not only am I concerned," she said, "that many of the CRI students—who have been victims of peer harassment and mistreatment in the past—would be vulnerable to further bullying as a result of their protest activities, but I simply do not believe that students have the right to question the curricular decisions of the faculty on a high school campus."

Represented by the ACLU, Jamie and two fellow CRI members file a lawsuit challenging the principal's restrictions as violative of their free speech rights. In addition, Jamie and several of his peers choose to defy the principal by wearing CRI buttons. As the four are walking down the hall one day, dressed flamboyantly and wearing the buttons, they are accosted by six well-known and aggressive seniors, whose trademark "practical jokes" include "going bowling" with fellow students. A teacher assigned to "hall duty" views the interaction from a distance, but she is simultaneously involved in a discussion with two other students about an upcoming trip to the Mediterranean and chooses not to intercede. Events move quickly, and before Jamie and his friends can respond or leave, the seniors squirt baby oil on the hallway floor and send Jamie and his friends sliding into other students and crashing into lockers. Three adults hear the crashing and rush to the scene, but it is too late. Several students suffer injuries requiring significant medical treatment.

---

a. As envisioned, the new four-week unit would be taught once a year to all students in the humanities program. Designed by the English and social studies teachers of Southern Valley High's award-winning humanities program, the unit is built around a study of "the central importance of morality, truth, justice, and patriotism in literature and history."

The unit would begin each year with a showing of the popular 1993 film, *Groundhog Day*. Discussions and activities would flow from the viewing of that film, and appropriate readings would be assigned. These readings would include, but would not be limited to, primary religious texts. Every year, students in the program would be expected to spend 3–5 days reading from a different primary religious text, until they had been exposed to the holy books of Judaism, Christianity, Islam, Hinduism and Buddhism.

What arguments should the respective parties set forth in the free speech lawsuit filed by the ACLU on behalf of the students in the CRI?

TINKER v. DES MOINES INDEP. CMTY. SCH. DIST.

393 U.S. 503, 89 S.Ct. 733 (1969)

MR. JUSTICE FORTAS delivered the opinion of the Court.

Petitioner John F. Tinker, 15 years old, and petitioner Christopher Eckhardt, 16 years old, attended high schools in Des Moines, Iowa. Petitioner Mary Beth Tinker, John's sister, was a 13-year-old student in junior high school.

In December 1965, a group of adults and students in Des Moines held a meeting at the Eckhardt home. The group determined to publicize their objections to the hostilities in Vietnam and their support for a truce by wearing black armbands during the holiday season and by fasting on December 16 and New Year's Eve. Petitioners and their parents had previously engaged in similar activities, and they decided to participate in the program.

The principals of the Des Moines schools became aware of the plan to wear armbands. On December 14, 1965, they met and adopted a policy that any student wearing an armband to school would be asked to remove it, and if he refused he would be suspended until he returned without the armband. Petitioners were aware of the regulation that the school authorities adopted.

On December 16, Mary Beth and Christopher wore black armbands to their schools. John Tinker wore his armband the next day. They were all sent home and suspended from school until they would come back without their armbands. They did not return to school until after the planned period for wearing armbands had expired—that is, until after New Year's Day.

This complaint was filed in the United States District Court by petitioners, through their fathers, under § 1983 of Title 42 of the United States Code. It prayed for an injunction restraining the respondent school officials and the respondent members of the board of directors of the school district from disciplining the petitioners, and it sought nominal damages. After an evidentiary hearing the District Court dismissed the complaint. It upheld the constitutionality of the school authorities' action on the ground that it was reasonable in order to prevent disturbance of school discipline. The court referred to but expressly declined to follow the Fifth Circuit's holding in a similar case that the wearing of symbols like the armbands cannot be prohibited unless it "materially and substantially interfere(s) with the requirements of appropriate discipline in the operation of the school."

On appeal, the Court of Appeals for the Eighth Circuit considered the case *en banc*. The court was equally divided, and the District Court's decision was accordingly affirmed, without opinion. We granted certiorari.

* * *

First Amendment rights, applied in light of the special characteristics of the school environment, are available to teachers and students. It can hardly be argued that either students or teachers shed their constitutional rights to freedom of speech or expression at the schoolhouse gate. This has been the unmistakable holding of this Court for almost 50 years. * * *

In *West Virginia State Board of Education v. Barnette*, this Court held that under the First Amendment, the student in public school may not be compelled to salute the flag. Speaking through Mr. Justice Jackson, the Court said:

> The Fourteenth Amendment, as now applied to the States, protects the citizen against the State itself and all of its creatures—Boards of Education not excepted. These have, of course, important, delicate, and highly discretionary functions, but none that they may not perform within the limits of the Bill of Rights. That they are educating the young for citizenship is reason for scrupulous protection of Constitutional freedoms of the individual, if we are not to strangle the free mind at its source and teach youth to discount important principles of our government as mere platitudes. 319 U.S. at 637.

On the other hand, the Court has repeatedly emphasized the need for affirming the comprehensive authority of the States and of school officials, consistent with fundamental constitutional safeguards, to prescribe and control conduct in the schools. Our problem lies in the area where students in the exercise of First Amendment rights collide with the rules of the school authorities.

II.

The problem posed by the present case does not relate to regulation of the length of skirts or the type of clothing, to hair style, or deportment. It does not concern aggressive, disruptive action or even group demonstrations. Our problem involves direct, primary First Amendment rights akin to "pure speech."

The school officials banned and sought to punish petitioners for a silent, passive expression of opinion, unaccompanied by any disorder or disturbance on the part of petitioners. There is here no evidence whatever of petitioners' interference, actual or nascent, with the schools' work or of collision with the rights of other students to be secure and to be let alone. Accordingly, this case does not concern speech or action that intrudes upon the work of the schools or the rights of other students.

Only a few of the 18,000 students in the school system wore the black armbands. Only five students were suspended for wearing them. There is no indication that the work of the schools or any class was disrupted. Outside the classrooms, a few students made hostile remarks to the children wearing armbands, but there were no threats or acts of violence on school premises.

The District Court concluded that the action of the school authorities was reasonable because it was based upon their fear of a disturbance from the wearing of the armbands. But, in our system, undifferentiated fear or apprehension of disturbance is not enough to overcome the right to freedom of expression. Any departure from absolute regimentation may cause trouble. Any variation from the majority's opinion may inspire fear. Any word spoken, in class, in the lunchroom, or on the campus, that deviates from the views of another person may start an argument or cause a disturbance. But our Constitution says we must take this risk; and our history says that it is this sort of hazardous freedom—this kind of openness—that is the basis of our national strength and of the independence and vigor of Americans who grow up and live in this relatively permissive, often disputatious, society.

In order for the State in the person of school officials to justify prohibition of a particular expression of opinion, it must be able to show that its action was caused by something more than a mere desire to avoid the discomfort and unpleasantness that always accompany an unpopular viewpoint. Certainly where there is no finding and no showing that engaging in the forbidden conduct would "materially and substantially interfere with the requirements of appropriate discipline in the operation of the school," the prohibition cannot be sustained.

In the present case, the District Court made no such finding, and our independent examination of the record fails to yield evidence that the school authorities had reason to anticipate that the wearing of the armbands would substantially interfere with the work of the school or impinge upon the rights of other students. Even an official memorandum prepared after the suspension that listed the reasons for the ban on wearing the armbands made no reference to the anticipation of such disruption.

On the contrary, the action of the school authorities appears to have been based upon an urgent wish to avoid the controversy which might result from the expression, even by the silent symbol of armbands, of opposition to this Nation's part in the conflagration in Vietnam.[4] It is revealing, in this respect, that the meeting at which the school principals decided to issue the contested regulation was called in response to a student's statement to the journalism teacher in one of the schools that he wanted to write an article on Vietnam and have it published in the school paper. (The student was dissuaded.)

It is also relevant that the school authorities did not purport to prohibit the wearing of all symbols of political or controversial significance. The record shows that students in some of the schools wore buttons relating to national political campaigns, and some even wore the Iron

---

4. The District Court found that the school authorities, in prohibiting black armbands, were influenced by the fact that "(t)he Viet Nam war and the involvement of the United States therein has been the subject of a major controversy for some time. When the arm band regulation involved herein was promulgated, debate over the Viet Nam war had become vehement in many localities. A protest march against the war had been recently held in Washington, D.C. A wave of draft card burning incidents protesting the war had swept the country. At that time two highly publicized draft card burning cases were pending in this Court. Both individuals supporting the war and those opposing it were quite vocal in expressing their views."

Cross, traditionally a symbol of Nazism. The order prohibiting the wearing of armbands did not extend to these. Instead, a particular symbol—black armbands worn to exhibit opposition to this Nation's involvement in Vietnam—was singled out for prohibition. Clearly, the prohibition of expression of one particular opinion, at least without evidence that it is necessary to avoid material and substantial interference with schoolwork or discipline, is not constitutionally permissible.

In our system, state-operated schools may not be enclaves of totalitarianism. School officials do not possess absolute authority over their students. Students in school as well as out of school are "persons" under our Constitution. They are possessed of fundamental rights which the State must respect, just as they themselves must respect their obligations to the State. In our system, students may not be regarded as closed-circuit recipients of only that which the State chooses to communicate. They may not be confined to the expression of those sentiments that are officially approved. In the absence of a specific showing of constitutionally valid reasons to regulate their speech, students are entitled to freedom of expression of their views. As Judge Gewin, speaking for the Fifth Circuit, said, school officials cannot suppress "expressions of feelings with which they do not wish to contend."

In *Meyer v. Nebraska*, Mr. Justice McReynolds expressed this Nation's repudiation of the principle that a State might so conduct its schools as to "foster a homogeneous people." He said:

> In order to submerge the individual and develop ideal citizens, Sparta assembled the males at seven into barracks and intrusted their subsequent education and training to official guardians. Although such measures have been deliberately approved by men of great genius, their ideas touching the relation between individual and State were wholly different from those upon which our institutions rest; and it hardly will be affirmed that any Legislature could impose such restrictions upon the people of a state without doing violence to both letter and spirit of the Constitution.

This principle has been repeated by this Court of numerous occasions during the intervening years. In *Keyishian v. Board of Regents*, Mr. Justice Brennan, speaking for the Court, said:

> The vigilant protection of constitutional freedoms is nowhere more vital than in the community of American schools. The classroom is peculiarly the "marketplace of ideas." The Nation's future depends upon leaders trained through wide exposure to that robust exchange of ideas which discovers truth out of a multitude of tongues, [rather] than through any kind of authoritative selection.

The principle of these cases is not confined to the supervised and ordained discussion which takes place in the classroom. The principal use to which the schools are dedicated is to accommodate students during prescribed hours for the purpose of certain types of activities. Among those activities is personal intercommunication among the students. This is not only an inevitable part of the process of attending school; it is also an important part of the educational process. A student's rights, therefore, do not embrace merely the classroom hours. When he is in the cafeteria, or on the playing field, or on the campus during the authorized hours, he may express his opinions, even on controversial subjects like the conflict in Vietnam, if he does so without 'materially and substantially interfere[ing] with the requirements of appropriate discipline in the operation of the school' and without colliding with the rights of others. But conduct by the student, in class or out of it, which for any reason—whether it stems from time, place, or type of behavior—materially disrupts classwork or involves substantial disorder or invasion of the rights of others is, of course, not immunized by the constitutional guarantee of freedom of speech.

Under our Constitution, free speech is not a right that is given only to be so circumscribed that it exists in principle but not in fact. Freedom of expression would not truly exist if the right could be exercised only in an area that a benevolent government has provided as a safe haven for crackpots. The Constitution says that Congress (and the States) may not abridge the right to free speech. This provision means what it says. We properly read it to permit reasonable regulation of speech-connected activities in carefully restricted circumstances. But we do not confine the permissible exercise of First Amendment rights to a telephone booth or the four corners of a pamphlet, or to supervised and ordained discussion in a school classroom.

If a regulation were adopted by school officials forbidding discussion of the Vietnam conflict, or the expression by any student of opposition to it anywhere on school property except as part of a prescribed classroom exercise, it would be obvious that the regulation would violate the constitutional rights of students, at least if it could not be justified by a showing that the students' activities would materially and substantially disrupt the work and discipline of the school. In the circumstances of the present case, the prohibition of the silent, passive "witness of the armbands," as one of the children called it, is no less offensive to the constitution's guarantees.

As we have discussed, the record does not demonstrate any facts which might reasonably have led school authorities to forecast substantial disruption of or material interference with school activities, and no disturbances or disorders on the school premises in fact occurred. These petitioners merely went about their ordained rounds in school. Their deviation consisted only in wearing on their sleeve a band of black cloth, not more than two inches wide. They wore it to exhibit their disapproval of the Vietnam hostilities and their advocacy of a truce, to make their views known, and, by their example, to influence others to adopt them. They neither interrupted school activities nor sought to intrude in the school affairs or the lives of others. They caused discussion outside of the classrooms, but no interference with work and no disorder. In the circumstances, our Constitution does not permit officials of the State to deny their form of expression.

We express no opinion as to the form of relief which should be granted, this being a matter for the lower courts to determine. We reverse and remand for further proceedings consistent with this opinion.

Reversed and remanded.

NOTES

1. Subsequent cases have clarified the parameters of the *Tinker* rule, and how it might play out on a day-to-day level at individual school sites. The basic principle is that educators do not have to wait for the "disruption" to happen before the expressive activity can be restricted,[a] but at the same time "undifferentiated fear" of disruption is not sufficient.[b]

Recent Ninth Circuit decisions, for example, provide relevant guidelines for school site administrators seeking to ascertain the nature and extent of the prospective disruption. In a 2001 case addressing a dispute over a student poem that the school believed might constitute a threat in the highly charged aftermath of the tragic shootings at Columbine, the court synthesized the set of rules that govern the application of *Tinker*.[c] Judge Fisher explained that if school officials wish to "suppress speech" in anticipation of disruption that has not yet occurred, they must "justify their decision by showing facts which might reasonably have led school authorities to forecast substantial disruption of or material interference with school activities." He noted that this standard "does not require certainty that disruption will occur," and that it contemplates an analysis based on the "totality of the facts."[d]

On the other hand, it is clear from *Tinker* and its progeny that "undifferentiated fear or apprehension of disturbance is not enough to overcome the right to freedom of expression."[e] In a 2001 decision addressing the constitutionality of a "campus speech code" at the high school level, the Third Circuit summarized the applicable case law in this regard.[f] It cautioned that, "[a]s subsequent federal cases have made clear, *Tinker* requires a specific and significant fear of disruption, not just some remote apprehension of disturbance."[g] And the court cited numerous examples of fact patterns where administrators acted incorrectly under this standard to restrict student expression when in fact the fear was indeterminate and the perceived danger was remote. These examples included the failure of an Oregon school district "to present any evidence" that the wearing of buttons supporting striking

---

a. Chandler v. McMinnville Sch. Dist., 978 F.2d 524, 529 (9th Cir. 1992); Karp v. Becken, 477 F.2d 171, 175 (9th Cir. 1973).

b. Tinker v. Des Moines Indep. Cmty. Sch. Dist., 393 U.S. 503, 508, 89 S.Ct. 733 (1969).

c. LaVine v. Blaine School District, 257 F.3d 981 (9th Cir. 2001). In synthesizing these principles, the Ninth Circuit also looked to its 1992 decision, *Chandler v. McMinnville Sch. Dist.*, 978 F.2d 524, where middle school students had been disciplined for wearing provocative political buttons that supported striking teachers and criticized "scabs" during a bitter school strike.

d. "In applying *Tinker*, we look to the totality of the relevant facts. We look not only to James' actions, but to all of the circumstances confronting the school officials that might reasonably portend disruption." *LaVine*, 257 F.3d at 989.

e. *Tinker*, 393 U.S. at 508.

f. Saxe v. State College Area Sch. Dist., 240 F.3d 200 (3d Cir. 2001).

g. *Id.* at 211.

teachers were "inherently disruptive" to school activities,[h] the finding of both "insufficient evidence of actual disruption" and the lack of "substantial reason to anticipate a disruption" when a Texas high school prohibited a devoutly religious student from wearing a rosary to school on the ground that some gangs had adopted the rosary as their identifying symbol,[i] and the insufficient nature of the Dallas Independent School District's attempt to rely on "the objection of several other students" to justify its prohibition of the distribution of religious tracts on school grounds.[j]

And even when the Tenth Circuit did in fact rule on behalf of a school district in this context, such a ruling—according to the 2001 Third Circuit panel—only "confirms *Tinker's* requirements of specificity and concreteness." The Tenth Circuit panel had determined that the suspension of a middle school student "for drawing a Confederate flag in math class" was justified by the district's demonstration of "a concrete threat of substantial disruption"— the fact that the district had already experienced "a series of racial incidents [including 'hostile confrontations' and at least one fight] that year, some of which were related to the Confederate flag."[k]

In sum, all the recent cases in this area have made clear that the mere desire to avoid "discomfort" or "unpleasantness" is not enough to justify restricting student speech under *Tinker*. However, if a school can point to a well-founded expectation of disruption—especially one based on past incidents arising out of similar speech—the restriction may pass constitutional muster.[l]

C. THE EVOLUTION AND REFINEMENT OF K–12 "FREEDOM OF EXPRESSION" RULES

After *Tinker,* it was not until the mid to late 1980s that the U.S. Supreme Court agreed to address student freedom of expression issues, deciding *Bethel v. Fraser* in 1986 and *Hazelwood v. Kuhlmeier* in 1988. And almost twenty more years then passed before the Court considered the applicability of *Tinker* and its progeny once again, granting certiorari in *Morse v. Frederick*.

As the first decade of the Twenty-first Century drew to a close, the mainstream view of how these four cases fit together was that each of the latter three constituted narrow exceptions to the broad general rule set forth in *Tinker*. *Fraser* enabled K–12 schools to restrict sexually inappropriate speech, *Hazelwood* granted broad power to administrators to limit school-sponsored expressive activity, and *Morse* held that expression rea-

---

h. *Chandler*, 978 F.2d at 530.

i. Chalifoux v. New Caney Indep. Sch. Dist., 976 F.Supp. 659, 667 (S.D.Tex.1997).

j. Clark v. Dallas Indep. Sch. Dist., 806 F.Supp. 116, 120 (N.D.Tex.1992).

k. West v. Derby Unif. Sch. Dist. No. 260, 206 F.3d 1358, 1366 (10th Cir. 2000) ("The history of racial tension in the district made administrators' and parents' concerns about future substantial disruptions from possession of Confederate flag symbols at school reasonable.").

l. *Saxe*, 240 F.3d at 212.

sonably perceived to be advocating illegal drug use could be regulated. In all three cases, such limits on speech were deemed constitutional even if there was no material and substantial disruption and no interference with the rights of others.

Yet not everyone agreed that such an analytical construct appropriately reflected the direction of First Amendment jurisprudence in this context. Debates continued, for example, regarding the scope of each decision, both within the federal courts and in the scholarly literature. Some courts found the *Fraser* rule applicable to allegedly inappropriate speech that may not have been sexual in nature at all. Other courts applied *Hazelwood* to *educator* freedom of expression in rulings that significantly limited the First Amendment rights of K–12 teachers on school grounds and during school time.

It was the *Morse v. Frederick* decision, however, that appeared to provide the most fuel for the controversy regarding the primacy of *Tinker* and the correct method of applying the four K–12 student freedom of expression cases to future disputes. While Justices Alito and Kennedy warned in their concurrence that they only joined the *Morse* majority on the understanding that the ruling was limited to a very narrow set of facts, subsequent decisions in the lower courts began to identify various ways that the decision could be applied more broadly than it may have originally been intended. Indeed, some began to see in *Morse* a vehicle for perhaps casting *Tinker* aside.

Consider these debates in light of the materials that follow. Does *Tinker* still constitute the broad, general rule, taking priority over the other three Supreme Court cases, or has *Morse* begun to take on a stature that would lead it to be viewed as much more than simply one more narrow exception to *Tinker*?

1. THE *FRASER* DECISION: IDENTIFYING SOCIETY'S INTEREST IN "TEACHING THE BOUNDARIES OF SOCIALLY APPROPRIATE BEHAVIOR"

BETHEL SCH. DIST. NO. 403 v. FRASER
478 U.S. 675, 106 S.Ct. 3159 (1986)

CHIEF JUSTICE BURGER delivered the opinion of the Court.

We granted certiorari to decide whether the First Amendment prevents a school district from disciplining a high school student for giving a lewd speech at a school assembly.

I.

A.

On April 26, 1983, respondent Matthew N. Fraser, a student at Bethel High School in Pierce County, Washington, delivered a speech[2] nominat-

---

2. The Court speculates that the speech was "insulting" to female students, and "seriously damaging" to 14-year-olds, so that school officials could legitimately suppress such expression in

ing a fellow student for student elective office. Approximately 600 high school students, many of whom were 14–year-olds, attended the assembly. Students were required to attend the assembly or to report to the study hall. * * * Students who elected not to attend the assembly were required to report to study hall. During the entire speech, Fraser referred to his candidate in terms of an elaborate, graphic, and explicit sexual metaphor.

Two of Fraser's teachers, with whom he discussed the contents of his speech in advance, informed him that the speech was "inappropriate and that he probably should not deliver it," and that his delivery of the speech might have "severe consequences."

During Fraser's delivery of the speech, a school counselor observed the reaction of students to the speech. Some students hooted and yelled; some by gestures graphically simulated the sexual activities pointedly alluded to in respondent's speech. Other students appeared to be bewildered and embarrassed by the speech. One teacher reported that on the day following the speech, she found it necessary to forgo a portion of the scheduled class lesson in order to discuss the speech with the class.

* * *

The morning after the assembly * * * Fraser was * * * suspended for three days, and * * * his name [was] removed from the list of candidates for graduation speaker at the school's commencement exercises.

* * *

II.

* * * The marked distinction between the political "message" of the armbands in *Tinker* and the sexual content of respondent's speech in this case seems to have been given little weight by the Court of Appeals. * * *

III.

The role and purpose of the American public school system were well described by two historians, who stated: "[P]ublic education must prepare pupils for citizenship in the Republic.... It must inculcate the habits and manners of civility as values in themselves conducive to happiness and as indispensable to the practice of self-government in the community and the nation." In *Ambach v. Norwick,* we echoed the essence of this statement of

order to protect these groups. There is no evidence in the record that any students, male or female, found the speech "insulting." And while it was not unreasonable for school officials to conclude that respondent's remarks were inappropriate for school-sponsored assembly, the language respondent used does not even approach the sexually explicit speech regulated in *Ginsberg v. New York,* or the indecent speech banned in *FCC v. Pacifica Foundation.* Indeed, to my mind, respondent's speech was no more "obscene," "lewd," or "sexually explicit" than the bulk of programs currently appearing on prime time television or in the local cinema. Thus, I disagree with the Court's suggestion that school officials could punish respondent's speech out of a need to protect younger students.

the objectives of public education as the "inculcat[ion of] fundamental values necessary to the maintenance of a democratic political system."

These fundamental values of "habits and manners of civility" essential to a democratic society must, of course, include tolerance of divergent political and religious views, even when the views expressed may be unpopular. But these "fundamental values" must also take into account consideration of the sensibilities of others, and, in the case of a school, the sensibilities of fellow students. The undoubted freedom to advocate unpopular and controversial views in schools and classrooms must be balanced against the society's countervailing interest in teaching students the boundaries of socially appropriate behavior. Even the most heated political discourse in a democratic society requires consideration for the personal sensibilities of the other participants and audiences.

In our Nation's legislative halls, where some of the most vigorous political debates in our society are carried on, there are rules prohibiting the use of expressions offensive to other participants in the debate. The Manual of Parliamentary Practice, drafted by Thomas Jefferson and adopted by the House of Representatives to govern the proceedings in that body, prohibits the use of "impertinent" speech during debate and likewise provides that "[n]o person is to use indecent language against the proceedings of the House." The Rules of Debate applicable in the Senate likewise provide that a Senator may be called to order for imputing improper motives to another Senator or for referring offensively to any state. Senators have been censured for abusive language directed at other Senators. Can it be that what is proscribed in the halls of Congress is beyond the reach of school officials to regulate?

The First Amendment guarantees wide freedom in matters of adult public discourse. A sharply divided Court upheld the right to express an antidraft viewpoint in a public place, albeit in terms highly offensive to most citizens. It does not follow, however, that simply because the use of an offensive form of expression may not be prohibited to adults making what the speaker considers a political point, the same latitude must be permitted to children in a public school. In *New Jersey v. T.L.O.*, we reaffirmed that the constitutional rights of students in public school are not automatically coextensive with the rights of adults in other settings. As cogently expressed by Judge Newman, "the First Amendment gives a high school student the classroom right to wear Tinker's armband, but not Cohen's jacket."

Surely it is a highly appropriate function of public school education to prohibit the use of vulgar and offensive terms in public discourse. Indeed, the "fundamental values necessary to the maintenance of a democratic political system" disfavor the use of terms of debate highly offensive or highly threatening to others. Nothing in the Constitution prohibits the states from insisting that certain modes of expression are inappropriate and subject to sanctions. The inculcation of these values is truly the "work of the schools." *Tinker,* 393 U.S. at 508. The determination of what manner of speech in the classroom or in school assembly is inappropriate properly rests with the school board.

The process of educating our youth for citizenship in public schools is not confined to books, the curriculum, and the civics class; schools must teach by example the shared values of a civilized social order. Consciously or otherwise, teachers—and indeed the older students—demonstrate the appropriate form of civil discourse and political expression by their conduct and deportment in and out of class. Inescapably, like parents, they are role models. The schools, as instruments of the state, may determine that the essential lessons of civil, mature conduct cannot be conveyed in a school that tolerates lewd, indecent, or offensive speech and conduct such as that indulged in by this confused boy.

The pervasive sexual innuendo in Fraser's speech was plainly offensive to both teachers and students—indeed to any mature person. By glorifying male sexuality, and in its verbal content, the speech was acutely insulting to teenage girl students. The speech could well be seriously damaging to its less mature audience, many of whom were only 14 years old and on the threshold of awareness of human sexuality. Some students were reported as bewildered by the speech and the reaction of mimicry it provoked.

This Court's First Amendment jurisprudence has acknowledged limitations on the otherwise absolute interest of the speaker in reaching an unlimited audience where the speech is sexually explicit and the audience may include children * * * These cases recognize the obvious concern on the part of parents, and school authorities acting *in loco parentis,* to protect children—especially in a captive audience—from exposure to sexually explicit, indecent, or lewd speech.

We have also recognized an interest in protecting minors from exposure to vulgar and offensive spoken language. * * *

We hold that petitioner School District acted entirely within its permissible authority in imposing sanctions upon Fraser in response to his offensively lewd and indecent speech. Unlike the sanctions imposed on the students wearing armbands in *Tinker,* the penalties imposed in this case were unrelated to any political viewpoint. The First Amendment does not prevent the school officials from determining that to permit a vulgar and lewd speech such as respondent's would undermine the school's basic educational mission. A high school assembly or classroom is no place for a sexually explicit monologue directed towards an unsuspecting audience of teenage students. Accordingly, it was perfectly appropriate for the school to disassociate itself to make the point to the pupils that vulgar speech and lewd conduct is wholly inconsistent with the "fundamental values" of public school education. Justice Black, dissenting in *Tinker,* made a point that is especially relevant in this case:

I wish therefore * * * to disclaim any purpose * * * to hold that the Federal Constitution compels the teachers, parents, and elected school officials to surrender control of the American public school system to public school students. 393 U.S. at 526.

* * *

The judgment of the Court of Appeals for the Ninth Circuit is

Reversed.

* * *

JUSTICE BRENNAN, concurring in the judgment.

Respondent gave the following speech at a high school assembly in support of a candidate for student government office:

> I know a man who is firm—he's firm in his pants, he's firm in his shirt, his character is firm—but most . . . of all, his belief in you, the students of Bethel, is firm. Jeff Kuhlman is a man who takes his point and pounds it in. If necessary, he'll take an issue and nail it to the wall. He doesn't attack things in spurts—he drives hard, pushing and pushing until finally—he succeeds.
>
> Jeff is a man who will go to the very end—even the climax, for each and every one of you.
>
> So vote for Jeff for A.S.B. vice-president—he'll never come between you and the best our high school can be.'

The Court, referring to these remarks as "obscene," "vulgar," "lewd," and "offensively lewd," concludes that school officials properly punished respondent for uttering the speech. Having read the full text of respondent's remarks, I find it difficult to believe that it is the same speech the Court describes. To my mind, the most that can be said about respondent's speech—and all that need be said—is that in light of the discretion school officials have to teach high school students how to conduct civil and effective public discourse, and to prevent disruption of school educational activities, it was not unconstitutional for school officials to conclude, under the circumstances of this case, that respondent's remarks exceeded permissible limits. Thus, while I concur in the Court's judgment, I write separately to express my understanding of the breadth of the Court's holding.

The Court today reaffirms the unimpeachable proposition that students do not "shed their constitutional rights to freedom of speech or expression at the schoolhouse gate." If respondent had given the same speech outside of the school environment, he could not have been penalized simply because government officials considered his language to be inappropriate; the Court's opinion does not suggest otherwise. Moreover, despite the Court's characterizations, the language respondent used is far removed from the very narrow class of "obscene" speech which the Court has held is not protected by the First Amendment. It is true, however, that the State has interests in teaching high school students how to conduct civil and effective public discourse and in avoiding disruption of educational school activities. Thus, the Court holds that under certain circumstances, high school students may properly be reprimanded for giving a speech at a high school assembly which school officials conclude disrupted the school's educational mission. Respondent's speech may well have been protected had he given it in school but under different circumstances, where the school's legitimate interests in teaching and maintaining civil public discourse were less weighty.

In the present case, school officials sought only to ensure that a high school assembly proceed in an orderly manner. There is no suggestion that school officials attempted to regulate respondent's speech because they disagreed with the views he sought to express. *Cf. Tinker.* Nor does this case involve an attempt by school officials to ban written materials they consider "inappropriate" for high school students, cf. *Board of Education v. Pico,* 457 U.S. 853 (1982), or to limit what students should hear, read, or learn about. Thus, the Court's holding concerns only the authority that school officials have to restrict a high school student's use of disruptive language in a speech given to a high school assembly.

* * *

* * * Under the circumstances of this case * * * I believe that school officials did not violate the First Amendment in determining that respondent should be disciplined for the disruptive language he used while addressing a high school assembly. Thus, I concur in the judgment reversing the decision of the Court of Appeals.

2. *HAZELWOOD v. KUHLMEIER*: LIMITING EXPRESSIVE ACTIVITIES THAT THE PUBLIC "MIGHT REASONABLY PERCEIVE TO BEAR THE IMPRIMATUR OF THE SCHOOL"

HAZELWOOD v. KUHLMEIER

484 U.S. 260, 108 S.Ct. 562 (1988)

JUSTICE WHITE delivered the opinion of the Court.

This case concerns the extent to which educators may exercise editorial control over the contents of a high school newspaper produced as part of the school's journalism curriculum.

I.

Petitioners are the Hazelwood School District in St. Louis County, Missouri; various school officials; Robert Eugene Reynolds, the principal of Hazelwood East High School; and Howard Emerson, a teacher in the school district. Respondents are three former Hazelwood East students who were staff members of Spectrum, the school newspaper. They contend that school officials violated their First Amendment rights by deleting two pages of articles from the May 13, 1983, issue of Spectrum.

Spectrum was written and edited by the Journalism II class at Hazelwood East. The newspaper was published every three weeks or so during the 1982–1983 school year. More than 4,500 copies of the newspaper were distributed during that year to students, school personnel, and members of the community.

* * *

The practice at Hazelwood East during the spring 1983 semester was for the journalism teacher to submit page proofs of each Spectrum issue to Principal Reynolds for his review prior to publication. On May 10, Emerson delivered the proofs of the May 13 edition to Reynolds, who objected to two of the articles scheduled to appear in that edition. One of the stories described three Hazelwood East students' experiences with pregnancy; the other discussed the impact of divorce on students at the school.

Reynolds was concerned that, although the pregnancy story used false names "to keep the identity of these girls a secret," the pregnant students still might be identifiable from the text. He also believed that the article's references to sexual activity and birth control were inappropriate for some of the younger students at the school. In addition, Reynolds was concerned that a student identified by name in the divorce story had complained that her father "wasn't spending enough time with my mom, my sister and I" prior to the divorce, "was always out of town on business or out late playing cards with the guys," and "always argued about everything" with her mother. Reynolds believed that the student's parents should have been given an opportunity to respond to these remarks or to consent to their publication. He was unaware that Emerson had deleted the student's name from the final version of the article.

Reynolds believed that there was no time to make the necessary changes in the stories before the scheduled press run and that the newspaper would not appear before the end of the school year if printing were delayed to any significant extent. He concluded that his only options under the circumstances were to publish a four-page newspaper instead of the planned six-page newspaper, eliminating the two pages on which the offending stories appeared, or to publish no newspaper at all. Accordingly, he directed Emerson to withhold from publication the two pages containing the stories on pregnancy and divorce.[1] He informed his superiors of the decision, and they concurred.

* * *

II.

Students in the public schools do not "shed their constitutional rights to freedom of speech or expression at the schoolhouse gate." *Tinker*, 393 U.S. at 506. They cannot be punished merely for expressing their personal

---

1. The two pages deleted from the newspaper also contained articles on teenage marriage, runaways, and juvenile delinquents, as well as a general article on teenage pregnancy. Reynolds testified that he had no objection to these articles and that they were deleted only because they appeared on the same pages as the two objectionable articles.

views on the school premises—whether "in the cafeteria, or on the playing field, or on the campus during the authorized hours," 393 U.S. at 512–513—unless school authorities have reason to believe that such expression will "substantially interfere with the work of the school or impinge upon the rights of other students."

We have nonetheless recognized that the First Amendment rights of students in the public schools "are not automatically coextensive with the rights of adults in other settings," *Bethel School District No. 403 v. Fraser,* 478 U.S. 675, 682 (1986) and must be "applied in light of the special characteristics of the school environment." *Tinker,* 393 U,S, at 506. A school need not tolerate student speech that is inconsistent with its "basic educational mission," *Fraser,* 478 U.S. at 685, even though the government could not censor similar speech outside the school. Accordingly, we held in *Fraser* that a student could be disciplined for having delivered a speech that was "sexually explicit" but not legally obscene at an official school assembly, because the school was entitled to "disassociate itself" from the speech in a manner that would demonstrate to others that such vulgarity is "wholly inconsistent with the 'fundamental values' of public school education." * * *

A.

We deal first with the question whether Spectrum may appropriately be characterized as a forum for public expression. The public schools do not possess all of the attributes of streets, parks, and other traditional public forums that "time out of mind, have been used for purposes of assembly, communicating thoughts between citizens, and discussing public questions." Hence, school facilities may be deemed to be public forums only if school authorities have "by policy or by practice" opened those facilities "for indiscriminate use by the general public," or by some segment of the public, such as student organizations. If the facilities have instead been reserved for other intended purposes, "communicative or otherwise," then no public forum has been created, and school officials may impose reasonable restrictions on the speech of students, teachers, and other members of the school community. "The government does not create a public forum by inaction or by permitting limited discourse, but only by intentionally opening a nontraditional forum for public discourse."

The policy of school officials toward Spectrum was reflected in Hazelwood School Board Policy 348.51 and the Hazelwood East Curriculum Guide. Board Policy 348.51 provided that "[s]chool sponsored publications are developed within the adopted curriculum and its educational implications in regular classroom activities." * * *

School officials did not deviate in practice from their policy that production of *Spectrum* was to be part of the educational curriculum and a "regular classroom activit[y]." * * *

* * * School officials did not evince either "by policy or by practice," any intent to open the pages of Spectrum to "indiscriminate use," by its

student reporters and editors, or by the student body generally. Instead, they "reserve[d] the forum for its intended purpos[e]," as a supervised learning experience for journalism students. Accordingly, school officials were entitled to regulate the contents of *Spectrum* in any reasonable manner. It is this standard, rather than our decision in *Tinker,* that governs this case.

B.

The question whether the First Amendment requires a school to tolerate particular student speech—the question that we addressed in *Tinker*—is different from the question whether the First Amendment requires a school affirmatively to promote particular student speech. The former question addresses educators' ability to silence a student's personal expression that happens to occur on the school premises. The latter question concerns educators' authority over school-sponsored publications, theatrical productions, and other expressive activities that students, parents, and members of the public might reasonably perceive to bear the imprimatur of the school. These activities may fairly be characterized as part of the school curriculum, whether or not they occur in a traditional classroom setting, so long as they are supervised by faculty members and designed to impart particular knowledge or skills to student participants and audiences.

Educators are entitled to exercise greater control over this second form of student expression to assure that participants learn whatever lessons the activity is designed to teach, that readers or listeners are not exposed to material that may be inappropriate for their level of maturity, and that the views of the individual speaker are not erroneously attributed to the school. Hence, a school may in its capacity as publisher of a school newspaper or producer of a school play "disassociate itself," *Fraser,* 478 U.S. at 685, not only from speech that would "substantially interfere with [its] work . . . or impinge upon the rights of other students," *Tinker,* 393 U.S. at 509, but also from speech that is, for example, ungrammatical, poorly written, inadequately researched, biased or prejudiced, vulgar or profane, or unsuitable for immature audiences. A school must be able to set high standards for the student speech that is disseminated under its auspices—standards that may be higher than those demanded by some newspaper publishers or theatrical producers in the "real" world—and may refuse to disseminate student speech that does not meet those standards. In addition, a school must be able to take into account the emotional maturity of the intended audience in determining whether to disseminate student speech on potentially sensitive topics, which might range from the existence of Santa Claus in an elementary school setting to the particulars of teenage sexual activity in a high school setting. A school must also retain the authority to refuse to sponsor student speech that might reasonably be perceived to advocate drug or alcohol use, irresponsible sex, or conduct otherwise inconsistent with "the shared values of a civilized social order," *Fraser, 478* U.S. at 683, or to associate the school with any position other than neutrality on matters of political controversy. Otherwise, the schools would be unduly constrained from fulfilling their role as "a principal instrument in awakening the child to cultural values, in preparing him for later professional training, and in helping him to adjust normally to his environment." *Brown v. Board of Education,* 347 U.S. 483 (1954).

Accordingly, we conclude that the standard articulated in *Tinker* for determining when a school may punish student expression need not also be the standard for determining when a school may refuse to lend its name and resources to the dissemination of student expression. Instead, we hold that educators do not offend the First Amendment by exercising editorial control over the style and content of student speech in school-sponsored expressive activities so long as their actions are reasonably related to legitimate pedagogical concerns.

This standard is consistent with our oft-expressed view that the education of the Nation's youth is primarily the responsibility of parents, teachers, and state and local school officials, and not of federal judges. It is only when the decision to censor a school-sponsored publication, theatrical production, or other vehicle of student expression has no valid educational purpose that the First Amendment is so "directly and sharply implicate[d]," as to require judicial intervention to protect students' constitutional rights.

III.

We also conclude that Principal Reynolds acted reasonably in requiring the deletion from the May 13 issue of Spectrum of the pregnancy article, the divorce article, and the remaining articles that were to appear on the same pages of the newspaper.

* * *

The judgment of the Court of Appeals for the Eighth Circuit is therefore

Reversed.

NOTES

1.   In the First Amendment area, individual states are able to go beyond the federal "baseline" and grant their students additional free speech rights. California, for example, provides its students with more free speech protection than the *Tinker-Fraser-Hazelwood-Morse* line of cases. *See, e.g.,* Cal. Educ. Code § 48907 (2005), which provides, in pertinent part:

Students of the public schools shall have the right to exercise freedom of speech and of the press including, but not limited to, the use of bulletin boards, the distribution of printed material or petitions, the wearing of buttons, badges, and other insignia, and the right of expression in official publications, whether or not such publications or other means of expression are supported financially by the school or by use of school facilities, except that expression shall be prohibited which is obscene, libelous, or slanderous. Also prohibited shall be material which so incites students as to create a clear and present danger of the commission of unlawful acts on school premises or the violation of lawful school regulations, or the substantial disruption of the orderly operation of the school.

Student editors ... shall be responsible for assigning and editing the news, editorial, and feature content of their publications subject to the limitations of this section. However, it shall be the responsibility of a journalism adviser ... to maintain professional standards of English and journalism....

Id.; see also CAL. EDUC. CODE § 48950, which provides in pertinent part that "[s]chool districts * * * shall not make or enforce any rule subjecting any high school pupil to disciplinary sanctions solely on the basis of conduct that is speech or other communication that, when engaged in outside of the campus, is protected * * * by the First Amendment."

On the other hand, individual states may mandate dress codes and uniforms without violating First Amendment rights. See, e.g., Jacobs v. Clark County Sch. Dist., 526 F.3d 419 (9th Cir. 2008).

2. Unlike *Tinker* and *Fraser,* which have generally been found applicable only at the K–12 level, *Hazelwood v. Kuhlmeier* has been applied by some courts at other levels and in other contexts. *See, e.g., Hosty v. Carter,* 412 F.3d 731 (7th Cir. 2005) (finding *Hazelwood* applicable to a censorship dispute at the higher education level). In addition, several circuits have relied on *Hazelwood* to limit the in-class First Amendment rights of K–12 educators. *See generally infra,* Chapter 11.

3. *MORSE v. FREDERICK*: REASSESSING THE APPLICABILITY OF *TINKER* AND ITS PROGENY

PROBLEM 11: JAMIE AND HIS FRIENDS—THE SEQUEL

The following hypothetical is a continuation of the events set forth in Problem 10, supra. Assume that the setting is the same publicly funded educational institution, one year down the road.

After years of being bullied by fellow students, and in particular because of the influence of new student Diana, Jamie and his friends developed a multi-faceted plan to "fight back." Among the key strategies for furthering this goal were a strict and highly disciplined weight-lifting regimen, enrollment in martial arts classes, and the formation of a new student group unofficially affiliated with both the National Libertarian Party and the Unitarian Universalist church.[1]

---

1. See www.uua.org/aboutus/index.shtml (last visited June 26, 2008): "The Unitarian Universalist Association (UUA) is a religious organization that combines two traditions: the Universalists, who organized in 1793, and the Unitarians, who organized in 1825. They consolidated into the UUA in 1961... Each of the 1,041 congregations in the United States, Canada, and overseas are democratic in polity and operation; they govern themselves...."

By the beginning of the twelfth grade, Jamie and his friends had bulked up considerably, and several had become quite proficient in the martial arts. Diana, a star athlete in both gymnastics and wrestling, continued to set the tone for the group...which was determined "not to take anything from anybody." On several occasions, in fact, when the apolitical students who had caused trouble in the past began to tease and attempt to bully Jamie and his friends, scuffles had broken out and several of the former bullies had suffered a range of minor injuries. Students from both groups were suspended for "fighting" on more than one occasion.

After the winter break, consistent with the newly revised positions of student libertarian groups nationwide, Jamie, Diana, and their fellow group members adopted a plan to build support at Southern Valley High for two key libertarian policy goals: legalizing all recreational and performance-enhancing drugs, and lowering the drinking age to sixteen. On their group's Web site, they spoke openly of their policy goals, and announced that they planned to disseminate this information offline–on and off campus–through the distribution of fliers, the wearing of buttons, and the circulating of petitions.

At about the same time, Diana began to arouse the concern of her friends when it became clear to them that she was not just talking about drug use, but was actually using both legal and illegal drugs in substantial quantities. After having what she claimed to be a religious experience while using a combination of drugs and alcohol, she drafted a position statement encouraging fellow church-going students to enhance the meaning of their devotion by ingesting drugs. Jamie—a devout Christian who used neither alcohol nor drugs—had strong reservations regarding the position statement. His other friends had reservations as well, but they felt that if they were going to be true to their libertarian principles they needed to distribute it along with the other fliers. And when Diana designed T-shirts that had a drawing of a cross on the front and a collage of National Libertarian Party slogans, marijuana leaves, coca leaves, peyote buttons, and well-known alcoholic beverage advertisements on the back, they agreed to wear them on the first day of their planned offline publicity campaign.

As they began distributing fliers and asking students to sign petitions before First Period, several of the longtime bullies approached the group and began to heckle them. Diana immediately went over and knocked one of them to the ground, and Jamie then shouted that the hecklers had better leave "if they knew what was good for them." A brawl broke out, and several students were injured, including two innocent bystanders. Principal Arthur and other school officials showed up almost immediately and soon restored order. They confiscated all the publicity materials, and then ordered the students to either cover their T-shirts or face the consequences. Jamie, Diana, and five others refused to comply, and they were immediately suspended for the remainder of the week.

"Unitarian Universalism is a liberal religion with Jewish–Christian roots. It has no creed. It affirms the worth of human beings, advocates freedom of belief and the search for advancing truth, and tries to provide a warm, open, supportive community for people who believe that ethical living is the supreme witness of religion."

The next day, a former member of the school board who had once been the Libertarian Party candidate for governor issued a statement in which he strongly criticized the school's administration. "The principal has had it in for these kids from day one," he asserted. "She needs to remember that she is supposed to be there for everyone in the community."

Principal Arthur responded by holding an angry press conference in which she announced that not only would the T-shirts be banned and not only would these students be prohibited from distributing or circulating any other materials relating to their "so-called publicity campaign," but that their school computer privileges would be taken away for the remainder of the year. "Actions have consequences," she asserted. "These students have been continually disruptive, and they consistently interfere with the rights of others. I have consulted with school district attorneys, and they assure me that this event is no different than the *Morse v. Frederick* case recently decided by the Supreme Court in favor of school officials. And I must emphasize that perhaps the most inappropriate aspect of the group's activities is the sacrilegious suggestion that the ingestion of drugs is in any way related to Christian devotion."

The following day, the state's largest newspaper described Arthur's comments as "an unacceptable attempt to censor lawful student expression," and called for the principal to resign. Libertarian bloggers across the country picked up the story, and were virtually unanimous in expressing their contempt for the school officials. Other bloggers hailed the principal for "defending traditional values" and for standing up to "delinquent students."

Later in the week, the President of the local Unitarian Universalist church went on local television and stated the following:

> While I certainly do not condone illegal drug use, beliefs that are sincerely held by members of our church and are marked by devotion to Christian principles should not be so easily dismissed. High school students are still learning many things, and they must be allowed to do so in a supportive manner. I understand that the students are considering a lawsuit against the school district. I would wholeheartedly support such an action.

The students do in fact file a lawsuit, in which they argue that each of the principal's actions–from the confiscation of materials and the suspension to the banning of the T-shirts, the prohibition against further distribution of materials, and the removal of their school computer privileges–constituted a violation of their rights under the First Amendment.

What arguments might the students set forth under First Amendment *freedom of expression* case law? What result? Discuss. (Assume that the viewpoint discrimination doctrine will not be raised in this case).

MORSE v. FREDERICK
___ U.S. ___, 127 S.Ct. 2618 (2007)

Chief Justice ROBERTS delivered the opinion of the Court.

* * *

Our cases make clear that students do not "shed their constitutional rights to freedom of speech or expression at the schoolhouse gate." At the same time, we have held that "the constitutional rights of students in public school are not automatically coextensive with the rights of adults in other settings," and that the rights of students "must be 'applied in light of the special characteristics of the school environment.' " Consistent with these principles, we hold that schools may take steps to safeguard those entrusted to their care from speech that can reasonably be regarded as encouraging illegal drug use. We conclude that the school officials in this case did not violate the First Amendment by confiscating [a] pro-drug banner and suspending the student responsible for it.

I

On January 24, 2002, the Olympic Torch Relay passed through Juneau, Alaska, on its way to the winter games in Salt Lake City, Utah. The torchbearers were to proceed along a street in front of Juneau–Douglas High School (JDHS) while school was in session. Petitioner Deborah Morse, the school principal, decided to permit staff and students to participate in the Torch Relay as an approved social event or class trip. Students were allowed to leave class to observe the relay from either side of the street. Teachers and administrative officials monitored the students' actions.

Respondent Joseph Frederick, a JDHS senior, was late to school that day. When he arrived, he joined his friends (all but one of whom were JDHS students) across the street from the school to watch the event. Not all the students waited patiently. Some became rambunctious, throwing plastic cola bottles and snowballs and scuffling with their classmates. As the torchbearers and camera crews passed by, Frederick and his friends unfurled a 14–foot banner bearing the phrase: "BONG HiTS 4 JESUS." The large banner was easily readable by the students on the other side of the street.

Principal Morse immediately crossed the street and demanded that the banner be taken down. Everyone but Frederick complied. Morse confiscated the banner and told Frederick to report to her office, where she suspended him for 10 days. Morse later explained that she told Frederick to take the banner down because she thought it encouraged illegal drug use, in violation of established school policy. * * * The Juneau School District Board of Education upheld the suspension.

Frederick then filed suit under 42 U.S.C. § 1983, alleging that the school board and Morse had violated his First Amendment rights. He sought declaratory and injunctive relief, unspecified compensatory damages, punitive damages, and attorney's fees. The District Court granted summary judgment for the school board and Morse, ruling that they were entitled to qualified immunity and that they had not infringed Frederick's First Amendment rights. * * * The Ninth Circuit reversed. Deciding that Frederick acted during a "school-authorized activit[y]," and "proceed[ing] on the basis that the banner expressed a positive sentiment about marijuana use," the court nonetheless found a violation of Frederick's First Amendment rights because the school punished Frederick without demonstrating that his speech gave rise to a "risk of substantial disruption." The court further concluded that Frederick's right to display his banner was so "clearly established" that a reasonable principal in Morse's position would have understood that her actions were unconstitutional, and that Morse was therefore not entitled to qualified immunity.

We granted certiorari on two questions: whether Frederick had a First Amendment right to wield his banner, and, if so, whether that right was so clearly established that the principal may be held liable for damages. We resolve the first question against Frederick, and therefore have no occasion to reach the second.

II

At the outset, we reject Frederick's argument that this is not a school speech case-as has every other authority to address the question. The event occurred during normal school hours. It was sanctioned by Principal Morse "as an approved social event or class trip," and the school district's rules expressly provide that pupils in "approved social events and class trips are subject to district rules for student conduct." Teachers and administrators were interspersed among the students and charged with supervising them. The high school band and cheerleaders performed. Frederick, standing among other JDHS students across the street from the school, directed his banner toward the school, making it plainly visible to most students. Under these circumstances, we agree with the superintendent that Frederick cannot "stand in the midst of his fellow students, during school hours, at a school-sanctioned activity and claim he is not at school." * * *

III

The message on Frederick's banner is cryptic. It is no doubt offensive to some, perhaps amusing to others. To still others, it probably means nothing at all. Frederick himself claimed "that the words were just nonsense meant to attract television cameras." But Principal Morse thought the banner would be interpreted by those viewing it as promoting illegal drug use, and that interpretation is plainly a reasonable one.

As Morse later explained in a declaration, when she saw the sign, she thought that "the reference to a 'bong hit' would be widely understood by high school students and others as referring to smoking marijuana." She further believed that "display of the banner would be construed by students, District personnel, parents and others witnessing the display of the banner, as advocating or promoting illegal drug use"-in violation of school policy. (" I told Frederick and the other members of his group to put the banner down because I felt that it violated the [school] policy against displaying ... material that advertises or promotes use of illegal drugs").

We agree with Morse. At least two interpretations of the words on the banner demonstrate that the sign advocated the use of illegal drugs. First, the phrase could be interpreted as an imperative: "[Take] bong hits ..."-a message equivalent, as Morse explained in her declaration, to "smoke marijuana" or "use an illegal drug." Alternatively, the phrase could be viewed as celebrating drug use-"bong hits [are a good thing]," or "[we take] bong hits"-and we discern no meaningful distinction between celebrating illegal drug use in the midst of fellow students and outright advocacy or promotion.

* * *

The pro-drug interpretation of the banner gains further plausibility given the paucity of alternative meanings the banner might bear. The best Frederick can come up with is that the banner is "meaningless and funny", [but] dismissing the banner as meaningless ignores its undeniable reference to illegal drugs.

The dissent mentions Frederick's "credible and uncontradicted explanation for the message-he just wanted to get on television." But that is a description of Frederick's *motive* for displaying the banner; it is not an interpretation of what the banner says. The *way* Frederick was going to fulfill his ambition of appearing on television was by unfurling a pro-drug banner at a school event, in the presence of teachers and fellow students.

Elsewhere in its opinion, the dissent emphasizes the importance of political speech and the need to foster "national debate about a serious issue," as if to suggest that the banner is political speech. But not even Frederick argues that the banner conveys any sort of political or religious message. Contrary to the dissent's suggestion, this is plainly not a case about political debate over the criminalization of drug use or possession.

IV

The question thus becomes whether a principal may, consistent with the First Amendment, restrict student speech at a school event, when that speech is reasonably viewed as promoting illegal drug use. We hold that she may.

In *Tinker,* this Court made clear that "First Amendment rights, applied in light of the special characteristics of the school environment, are available to teachers and students." * * * *Tinker* held that student expression may not be suppressed unless school officials reasonably conclude that it will "materially and substantially disrupt the work and discipline of the school." The essential facts of *Tinker* are quite stark, implicating concerns at the heart of the First Amendment. The students sought to engage in political speech, using the armbands to express their "disapproval of the Vietnam hostilities and their advocacy of a truce, to make their views known, and, by their example, to influence others to adopt them." Political speech, of course, is "at the core of what the First Amendment is designed to protect." The only interest the Court discerned underlying the school's actions was the "mere desire to avoid the discomfort and unpleasantness that always accompany an unpopular viewpoint," or "an urgent wish to avoid the controversy which might result from the expression." That interest was not enough to justify banning "a silent, passive expression of opinion, unaccompanied by any disorder or disturbance."

This Court's next student speech case was *Fraser*. Matthew Fraser was suspended for delivering a speech before a high school assembly in which he employed what this Court called "an elaborate, graphic, and explicit sexual metaphor." Analyzing the case under *Tinker,* the District Court and Court of Appeals found no disruption, and therefore no basis for disciplining Fraser. This Court reversed, holding that the "School District acted entirely within its permissible authority in imposing sanctions upon Fraser in response to his offensively lewd and indecent speech."

The mode of analysis employed in *Fraser* is not entirely clear. The Court was plainly attuned to the content of Fraser's speech, citing the "marked distinction between the political 'message' of the armbands in *Tinker* and the sexual content of [Fraser's] speech." But the Court also reasoned that school boards have the authority to determine "what manner of speech in the classroom or in school assembly is inappropriate." (Brennan, J., concurring in judgment) ("In the present case, school officials sought only to ensure that a high school assembly proceed in an orderly manner. There is no suggestion that school officials attempted to regulate [Fraser's] speech because they disagreed with the views he sought to express").

We need not resolve this debate to decide this case. For present purposes, it is enough to distill from *Fraser* two basic principles. First, *Fraser's* holding demonstrates that "the constitutional rights of students in public school are not automatically coextensive with the rights of adults in other settings." Had Fraser delivered the same speech in a public forum outside the school context, it would have been protected. In school, however, Fraser's First Amendment rights were circumscribed "in light of the special characteristics of the school environment." Second, *Fraser* established that the mode of analysis set forth in *Tinker* is not absolute. Whatever approach *Fraser* employed, it certainly did not conduct the "substantial disruption" analysis prescribed by *Tinker.* * * *

Our most recent student speech case, *Kuhlmeier,* concerned "expressive activities that students, parents, and members of the public might reasonably perceive to bear the imprimatur of the school." Staff members of a high school newspaper sued their school when it chose not to publish two of their articles. The Court of Appeals analyzed the case under *Tinker,* ruling in favor of the students because it found no evidence of material disruption to classwork or school discipline. This Court reversed, holding that "educators do not offend the First Amendment by exercising editorial control over the style and content of student speech in school-sponsored expressive activities so long as their actions are reasonably related to legitimate pedagogical concerns."

Kuhlmeier does not control this case because no one would reasonably believe that Frederick's banner bore the school's imprimatur. The case is nevertheless instructive because it confirms both principles cited above. *Kuhlmeier* acknowledged that schools may regulate some speech "even though the government could not censor similar speech outside the school." And, like *Fraser,* it confirms that the rule of *Tinker* is not the only basis for restricting student speech.

Drawing on the principles applied in our student speech cases, we have held in the Fourth Amendment context that "while children assuredly do not 'shed their constitutional rights . . . at the schoolhouse gate,' . . . the nature of those rights is what is appropriate for children in school." In particular, "the school setting requires some easing of the restrictions to which searches by public authorities are ordinarily subject." *New Jersey v. T.L.O.* See * * * *Board of Ed. of Independent School Dist. No. 92 of Pottawatomie Cty. v. Earls* (* * * "[w]hile schoolchildren do not shed their constitutional rights when they enter the schoolhouse, Fourth Amendment rights . . . are different in public schools than elsewhere. * * *

Even more to the point, these cases also recognize that deterring drug use by schoolchildren is an "important-indeed, perhaps compelling" interest. * * *

Just five years ago, we wrote: "The drug abuse problem among our Nation's youth has hardly abated since * * * 1995. In fact, evidence suggests that it has only grown worse." *Earls.* * * *

The "special characteristics" of the school environment and the governmental interest in stopping student drug abuse—reflected in the policies of Congress and myriad school boards, including JDHS—allow schools to restrict student expression that they reasonably regard as promoting illegal drug use. *Tinker* warned that schools may not prohibit student speech because of "undifferentiated fear or apprehension of disturbance" or "a mere desire to avoid the discomfort and unpleasantness that always accompany an unpopular viewpoint." The danger here is far more serious and palpable. The particular concern to prevent student drug abuse at issue here, embodied in established school policy, extends well beyond an abstract desire to avoid controversy.

Petitioners urge us to adopt the broader rule that Frederick's speech is proscribable because it is plainly "offensive" as that term is used in *Fraser.* We think this stretches *Fraser* too far; that case should not be read to encompass any speech that could fit under some definition of "offensive." After all, much political and religious speech might be perceived as offensive to some. The concern here is not that Frederick's speech was offensive, but that it was reasonably viewed as promoting illegal drug use.

* * *

School principals have a difficult job, and a vitally important one. When Frederick suddenly and unexpectedly unfurled his banner, Morse had to decide to act—or not act—on the spot. It was reasonable for her to conclude that the banner promoted illegal drug use-in violation of established school policy-and that failing to act would send a powerful message to the students in her charge, including Frederick, about how serious the school was about the dangers of illegal drug use. The First Amendment does not require schools to tolerate at school events student expression that contributes to those dangers.

The judgment of the United States Court of Appeals for the Ninth Circuit is reversed, and the case is remanded for further proceedings consistent with this opinion.

It is so ordered.

Justice THOMAS, concurring.

The Court today decides that a public school may prohibit speech advocating illegal drug use. I agree and therefore join its opinion in full. I write separately to state my view that the standard set forth in *Tinker* is without basis in the Constitution. * * *

II

Tinker effected a sea change in students' speech rights, extending them well beyond traditional bounds. * * * Justice Black dissented, criticizing the Court for "subject[ing] all the public schools in the country to the whims and caprices of their loudest-mouthed, but maybe not their brightest, students." He emphasized the instructive purpose of schools: "[T]axpayers send children to school on the premise that at their age they need to learn, not teach." In his view, the Court's decision "surrender[ed] control of the American public school system to public school students."

Of course, *Tinker's* reasoning conflicted with the traditional understanding of the judiciary's role in relation to public schooling, a role limited by *in loco parentis*. Perhaps for that reason, the Court has since scaled back *Tinker's* standard, or rather set the standard aside on an ad hoc basis. * * *

Today, the Court creates another exception. In doing so, we continue to distance ourselves from *Tinker,* but we neither overrule it nor offer an explanation of when it operates and when it does not. I am afraid that our jurisprudence now says that students have a right to speak in schools except when they don't-a standard continuously developed through litigation against local schools and their administrators. In my view, petitioners could prevail for a much simpler reason: As originally understood, the Constitution does not afford students a right to free speech in public schools. * * *

I join the Court's opinion because it erodes *Tinker's* hold in the realm of student speech, even though it does so by adding to the patchwork of exceptions to the *Tinker* standard. I think the better approach is to dispense with *Tinker* altogether, and given the opportunity, I would do so.

Justice ALITO, with whom Justice KENNEDY joins, concurring.

I join the opinion of the Court on the understanding that (a) it goes no further than to hold that a public school may restrict speech that a reasonable observer would interpret as advocating illegal drug use and (b) it provides no support for any restriction of speech that can plausibly be interpreted as commenting on any political or social issue, including speech on issues such as "the wisdom of the war on drugs or of legalizing marijuana for medicinal use."

* * *

I do not read the opinion to mean that there are necessarily any grounds for * * * regulation that are not already recognized in the holdings of this Court. In addition to *Tinker*, the decision in the present case allows the restriction of speech advocating illegal drug use; *Fraser* permits the regulation of speech that is delivered in a lewd or vulgar manner as part of a middle school program; and *Kuhlmeier* allows a school to regulate what is in essence the school's own speech, that is, articles that appear in a publication that is an official school organ. I join the opinion of the Court on the understanding that the opinion does not hold that the special characteristics of the public schools necessarily justify any other speech restrictions.

The opinion of the Court does not endorse the broad argument advanced by petitioners and the United States that the First Amendment permits public school officials to censor any student speech that interferes with a school's "educational mission." This argument can easily be manipulated in dangerous ways, and I would reject it before such abuse occurs.

* * *

The public schools are invaluable and beneficent institutions, but they are, after all, organs of the State. When public school authorities regulate student speech, they act as agents of the State; they do not stand in the shoes of the students' parents. It is a dangerous fiction to pretend that parents simply delegate their authority-including their authority to determine what their children may say and hear-to public school authorities. It is even more dangerous to assume that such a delegation of authority somehow strips public school authorities of their status as agents of the State. Most parents, realistically, have no choice but to send their children to a public school and little ability to influence what occurs in the school. It is therefore wrong to treat public school officials, for purposes relevant to the First Amendment, as if they were private, nongovernmental actors standing *in loco parentis*.

For these reasons, any argument for altering the usual free speech rules in the public schools cannot rest on a theory of delegation but must instead be based on some special characteristic of the school setting. The special characteristic that is relevant in this case is the threat to the physical safety of students. School attendance can expose students to threats to their physical safety that they would not otherwise face. Outside of school, parents can attempt to protect their children in many ways and may take steps to monitor and exercise control over the persons with whom their children associate. Similarly, students, when not in school, may be able to avoid threatening individuals and situations. During school hours, however, parents are not present to provide protection and guidance, and students' movements and their ability to choose the persons with whom they spend time are severely restricted. Students may be compelled on a daily basis to spend time at close quarters with other students who may do them harm. Experience shows that schools can be places of special danger.

* * * [D]ue to the special features of the school environment, school officials must have greater authority to intervene before speech leads to violence. And, in most cases, *Tinker's* "substantial disruption" standard permits school officials to step in before actual violence erupts.

Speech advocating illegal drug use poses a threat to student safety that is just as serious, if not always as immediately obvious. As we have recognized in the past and as the opinion of the Court today details, illegal drug use presents a grave and in many ways unique threat to the physical safety of students. I therefore conclude that the public schools may ban speech advocating illegal drug use. But I regard such regulation as standing at the far reaches of what the First Amendment permits. I join the opinion of the Court with the understanding that the opinion does not endorse any further extension.

Justice STEVENS, with whom Justice SOUTER and Justice GINSBURG join, dissenting.

A significant fact barely mentioned by the Court sheds a revelatory light on the motives of both the students and the principal of Juneau–Douglas High School (JDHS). On January 24, 2002, the Olympic Torch Relay gave those Alaska residents a rare chance to appear on national television. As Joseph Frederick repeatedly explained, he did not address the curious message—" BONG HiTS 4 JESUS"—to his fellow students. He just wanted to get the camera crews' attention. Moreover, concern about a nationwide evaluation of the conduct of the JDHS student body would have justified the principal's decision to remove an attention-grabbing 14–foot banner, even if it had merely proclaimed "Glaciers Melt!"

I agree with the Court that the principal should not be held liable for pulling down Frederick's banner. I would hold, however, that the school's interest in protecting its students from exposure to speech "reasonably regarded as promoting illegal drug use" cannot justify disciplining Frederick for his attempt to make an ambiguous statement to a television audience simply because it contained an oblique reference to drugs. The First Amendment demands more, indeed, much more.

The Court holds otherwise only after laboring to establish two uncontroversial propositions: first, that the constitutional rights of students in school settings are not coextensive with the rights of adults; and second, that deterring drug use by schoolchildren is a valid and terribly important interest. As to the first, I take the Court's point that the message on Frederick's banner is not *necessarily* protected speech, even though it unquestionably would have been had the banner been unfurled elsewhere. As to the second, I am willing to assume that the Court is correct that the pressing need to deter drug use supports JDHS's rule prohibiting willful conduct that expressly "advocates the use of substances that are illegal to minors." But it is a gross non sequitur to draw from these two unremarkable propositions the remarkable conclusion that the school may suppress student speech that was never meant to persuade anyone to do anything.

In my judgment, the First Amendment protects student speech if the message itself neither violates a permissible rule nor expressly advocates conduct that is illegal and harmful to students. This nonsense banner does neither, and the Court does serious violence to the First Amendment in upholding—indeed, lauding—a school's decision to punish Frederick for expressing a view with which it disagreed. * * *

NOTES

1.   The scope of the *Morse v. Frederick* decision arguably remains unsettled. Wrestling with a growing number of free speech disputes in the aftermath of *Morse,* courts are not always agreeing on how far the ruling extends. Some courts have gone no further than the specific language of the decision, as interpreted by the concurring justices. *See, e.g., DePinto v. Bayonne Bd. of Educ.,* 514 F.Supp.2d 633, 639 (D.N.J. 2007) ("*Morse* adds a third exception to *Tinker*, allowing a school to censor student speech that is 'reasonably viewed as promoting illegal drug use.' "). But support has emerged for a broader interpretation of *Morse* that would enable school officials to "insulate vulnerable students from harmful speech" in general. *See, e.g.,* Harper v. Poway, No. 04CV1103 JAH(POR), Order Denying Plaintiff's Motion for Reconsideration (S.D. Cal. 2008), at Pages 6–10 (unpublished order available at www. alliancealert.org/2008/20080213.pdf). *See generally Nuxoll v. Indian Prairie Sch. Dist. #204,* 523 F.3d 668 (7th Cir. 2008), *infra,* sub-section C.4.

2.   The Fifth Circuit has found the *Morse* ruling directly applicable to a dispute regarding the transfer of a high school student to an alternative program based on writings in a journal that allegedly threatened a Columbine style attack. *See Ponce v. Socorro Indep. Sch. Dist.,* 508 F.3d 765 (5th Cir. 2008), *infra,* Chapter 4.

4.   THE "T–SHIRT" CASES: ADDRESSING INFLAMMATORY SLOGANS AND IMAGES ON STUDENT CLOTHING

Controversies regarding messages on T-shirts and similar articles of student clothing have persisted at K–12 school sites throughout the first decade of the new century. Educators and administrators acting in good faith seek to justify restricting such inflammatory slogans and images by asserting that they are inappropriate in a school setting because of "the special characteristics" of the public school environment. The educators also argue that there are legitimate concerns regarding school climate in this area.

Definitions of *school climate* may vary depending on context, but the term is generally seen as encompassing such things as school culture, mood, degree to which people get along, respect for differences, motivation, pride, and vision. The linchpin of a positive school climate is the existence of collaborative and optimistic working relationships between and among all members of the school community, from the youngest students to the most senior faculty and staff. And research invariably points toward the conclusion that the proliferation of such relationships will go a long way toward preventing the type of mistreatment and discriminatory conduct documented in later chapters of this book.

Certain slogans on T-shirts and on other personal possessions can have a decidedly negative impact on a school's culture, and among the most volatile T-shirts in this area are those implicating religion or commenting on homosexuality. Yet even as they legitimately seek to address the prospective negative impact of such shirts on school climate, educators must also be sensitive to student freedom of expression and student freedom of religion under the First Amendment.

A. THE *BOROFF* CASE: RESTRICTING OSTENSIBLY ANTI–RELIGIOUS EXPRESSION

In *Boroff v. Van Wert City Board of Education*, 220 F.3d 465 (6th Cir. 2000), the Sixth Circuit considered a dispute at an Ohio high school regarding commercial T-shirts that promoted the heavy metal rock group Marilyn Manson. Pursuant to its dress code, the District prohibited all types of Marilyn Manson T-shirts after student Nicholas Boroff wore one that had the group's name printed on the front, accompanied by a depiction of "a three-faced Jesus" and the words "See No Truth. Hear No Truth. Speak No Truth." On the back, the word "believe" was spelled out in capital letters, with the letters "lie" highlighted.

Apparently unable to point to any evidence that would justify banning the shirts under the *Tinker* rule, the District successfully invoked the *Fraser* decision. The 2–1 panel majority, determining that "[t]he standard for reviewing the suppression of vulgar or plainly offensive speech is governed by *Fraser*," based its ruling on the fact that the school "found the Marilyn Manson T-shirts to be offensive because the band promotes destructive conduct and demoralizing values that are contrary to the educational mission of the school."

According to the Court, "[t]he principal specifically stated that the distorted Jesus figure was offensive, because '[m]ocking any religious figure is contrary to our educational mission which is to be respectful of others and others' beliefs.'" In addition, the principal believed that wearing such shirts could "reasonably be considered a communication agreeing with or approving of the views espoused by Marilyn Manson" in its "vulgar" lyrics and its pro-drug statements to the press:

> The Supreme Court [in *Fraser*] has held that the school board has the authority to determine "what manner of speech in the classroom or in school is inappropriate." The Court has determined that "[a] school need not tolerate student speech that is inconsistent with its 'basic educational mission ... even though the government could not censor similar speech outside the school.' "In this case, where Boroff's T-shirts contain symbols and words that promote values that are so patently contrary to the school's educational mission, the School has the authority, under the circumstances of this case, to prohibit those T-shirts. *Boroff*, 220 F.3d at 470.

Dissenting Judge Gilman questioned the reasoning of the *Boroff* majority, and disagreed in particular with its definitions of the terms *vulgar* and *offensive*. "In First Amendment cases," he asserted, "those terms refer to words and phrases that are themselves coarse and crude, regardless of whether one disagrees with the overall message that the speaker is trying to convey."

B. *CHAMBERS, HARPER,* AND *NUXOLL*: RESTRICTING OSTENSIBLY ANTI–GAY EXPRESSION

Three cases addressing ostensibly anti-gay expression were also heard by the federal courts in recent years. All three addressed the constitutionality of restricting the expression of conservative Christian students who wore shirts with slogans arguably offensive to gay and lesbian students. Unlike the shirt in *Boroff* that was arguably offensive to religious students, however, all these were "home-made" shirts and all were created in response to events that had taken place at school.

● ***Chambers.*** In *Chambers v. Babbitt*, 145 F.Supp. 2d 1068 (D. Minn. 2001), a 15–year old male student in a Minnesota school district created a "straight pride" sweatshirt and wore it to school after a debate at his high school Christian club regarding how Jesus might view homosexuality. The words "straight pride" were written on the front, and a picture on the back depicted a man and a woman holding hands. Applying the *Tinker* rule, the U.S. District Court ruled in favor of the student, finding that there had been no evidence of material and substantial disruption. The school district did not appeal.

● ***Harper.*** In *Harper v. Poway,* litigation that has persisted over an extended period of time, the courts considered the constitutionality of prohibiting Tyler Chase Harper's home-made T-shirt, which was created in response to a "Day of Silence" demonstration by gay and lesbian students and their allies at a suburban San Diego high school. The demonstration was one of many taking place across the country, part of an annual coordinated national effort by student groups to call attention to ongoing harassment and safety-related concerns negatively impacting gays on public school campuses. *Harper v. Poway,* 345 F.Supp.2d 1096 (S.D. Cal. 2004).

Harper created two versions of the same T-shirt. The first, worn on the same day as the "Day of Silence" protest, had a slogan on the back that read: "Homosexuality Is Shameful. Romans 1:27," while on the front the shirt stated: "I will not accept what God has condemned." The second, worn on the day after the demonstration, had the same slogan on the back, while the slogan on the front now read: "Be ashamed. The school has accepted what God has condemned." The school said nothing to him on the first day, but on the second day he was told that the T-shirt was "too inflammatory" and that he could not wear it. *See generally id.*

Harper challenged the restriction under First Amendment speech and religion grounds, and to date he has not prevailed at any level of the federal court. He lost in the U.S. District Court in 2004 (345 F.Supp.2d 1096), in the Ninth Circuit in 2006 (445 F.3d 1166), and after the Ninth Circuit opinion was vacated on a finding of mootness at the U.S. Supreme Court level (127 S.Ct. 1484), his sister Kelsie Harper lost at the U.S. District Court level in 2008 (No. 04CV1103 JAH(POR), Unpublished Order Denying Plaintiff's Motion for Reconsideration).

In the 2006 decision that was both widely praised and widely criticized, Ninth Circuit Judge Stephen Reinhardt analyzed the facts under *Tinker* on behalf of a 2–1 majority and found that while there was no evidence of material and substantial disruption, *Tinker's* "rights of others" prong had been implicated:

> Public school students who may be injured by verbal assaults on the basis of a core identifying characteristic such as race, religion, or sexual orientation, have a right to be free from such attacks while on school campuses. As *Tinker* clearly states, students have the right to be secure and to be let alone. Being secure involves not only freedom from physical assaults but from psychological attacks that cause young people to question their self-worth and their rightful place in society. *Harper v. Poway,* 445 F.3d 1166 (9th Cir. 2006).

The panel majority also concluded that if the *Tinker* rule is found to be applicable, which it was in this case, viewpoint discrimination cannot be raised by a student plaintiff on his or her behalf.[a]

Although the Ninth Circuit opinion was vacated in 2007, the substantive analysis in an opinion vacated on procedural grounds may still be found applicable in subsequent proceedings.[b] Indeed, both the lower court

---

a. The Ninth Circuit majority in *Harper* concluded that "the Court in *Tinker* held that a school may prohibit student speech, even if the consequence is viewpoint discrimination, if the speech violates the rights of other students or is materially disruptive. *Harper,* 445 F.3d at 1184–1186. See also *Tinker,* 393 U.S. at 511, 89 S.Ct. 733 (stating school cannot prohibit "expression of one particular opinion" unless it makes a specific showing of constitutionally valid reasons)".

b. *See, e.g.,* DHX, Inc. v. Allianz AGF MAT, Ltd., 425 F.3d 1169, 1176 (9th Cir. 2005):

...[A]t minimum, a vacated opinion still carries informational and perhaps even persuasive or precedential value. See U.S. v. Joelson, 7 F.3d 174, 178 n. 1 (9th Cir.1993) (stating that a certain vacated Court of Appeals opinion "has no precedential effect" but citing the vacated

in the 2008 *Harper* ruling and the lower court in the 2007 *Zamecnik-Nuxoll* proceedings discussed below relied at least in part on Judge Reinhardt's reasoning to hold in favor of the school districts.

● ***Nuxoll.*** In *Nuxoll v. Indian Prairie School District,* 523 F.3d 668 (7th Cir. 2008), a young male student continued to pursue the First Amendment litigation originally prosecuted by Heidi Zamecnik when she was prohibited from wearing a T-shirt that read "Be Happy, Not Gay" in response to the "Day of Silence" demonstration at her suburban Chicago high school.[c] After losing at the U.S. District Court level, the students appealed, challenging the constitutionality of both the District's "derogatory comments" policy and the banning of the T-shirt itself.

Writing on behalf of a unanimous panel, Seventh Circuit Judge Richard Posner first upheld the constitutionality of the policy, which prohibited "derogatory comments that refer to race, ethnicity, religion, gender, sexual orientation, or disability." In language that arguably mirrored the verbal assault rule set forth by Judge Reinhardt in *Harper,* Posner wrote:

> People are easily upset by comments about their race, sex, etc., including their sexual orientation, because for most people these are major components of their personal identity—none more so than a sexual orientation that deviates from the norm. Such comments can strike a person at the core of his being. *Nuxoll,* 523 F.3d at 671.

Posner never actually cited to the Reinhardt Ninth Circuit opinion itself. Instead, construing *Morse* as potentially enabling educators to restrict speech that may have negative "psychological effects," Posner wrote that "if there is reason to think that a particular type of students' speech will lead to a decline in students test scores, an upsurge in truancy, or other [similar] symptoms of substantial disruption[,] the school can forbid the speech." *Id.* at 674.

Posner then found that the "Be Happy, Not Gay" T-shirt not only did not violate the District "derogatory comments" policy, but also that it did not implicate the newly articulated "test-score" rule.

NOTES

1. Can these "T-shirt" decisions be reconciled? In all four instances, school officials appeared to be operating in good faith, acting to restrict allegedly inflammatory expression because of valid concerns regarding school climate. Indeed, all the shirts were arguably offensive to at least some people.

---

opinion for its informational and persuasive value); Gould v. Bowyer, 11 F.3d 82, 84 (7th Cir.1993) (noting that a vacated district court opinion carries informational value "even if the reviewing court intoned in its most solemn voice that the district court's decision would have no precedential effect"); County of Los Angeles v. Davis, 440 U.S. 625, 646 n. 10, 99 S.Ct. 1379, 59 L.Ed.2d 642 (1979) (Powell, J., dissenting) (asserting that the opinion of the court of appeals, though vacated, "will continue to have precedential weight and, until contrary authority is decided, [is] likely to be viewed as persuasive authority if not the governing law of the [ ] Circuit"). Beezer, J., concurring.

c. For an overview of the *Zamecnik* litigation, *see generally* 2007 WL 1141597 (N.D. Ill. 2007).

All might have caused bad feelings, ill will, and tension between persons and groups, even though no apparent disruption of a physical nature took place. And all the decisions recognize in their own way the prospective harm of psychological injury. Even the *Chambers* Court and the *Nuxoll* Court, while ruling against the school districts, referenced the sensitivity of the subject matter and the prospective negative implications of exclusionary messages implicitly endorsed by school officials who fail to intervene.

On the other hand, the four opinions arguably represented four very different analytical approaches. In the rulings on behalf of the students, the *Chambers* Court relied upon a traditional application of *Tinker,* while the *Nuxoll* Court appeared to discern a novel "test-score" rule based upon an arguably expansive application of *Morse.* In the rulings on behalf of the school districts, the *Boroff* Court relied on an expansive interpretation of *Fraser,* while the *Harper* Ninth Circuit panel discerned a novel "verbal assault" rule based upon an arguably expansive analysis of *Tinker* rights of others prong.

2. The prospective applicability of *Fraser's* appropriateness test arguably remains unsettled. In light of the analysis set forth in Chief Justice Burger's *Fraser* opinion and Justice Brennan's concurrence, should the *Fraser* rule be deemed applicable to T-shirt disputes such as *Boroff,* or should it in fact be limited to crude, sexually offensive speech of the type present in Matthew Fraser's nominating speech?

3. Longtime Ninth Circuit Judge Stephen Reinhardt and longtime Seventh Circuit Judge Richard Posner are among the nation's most highly respected jurists, even as they often represent opposite sides of the political spectrum. Reinhardt's positions are generally liberal in nature, while Posner is typically characterized as conservative. Yet on key aspects of the issues presented in these T-shirt cases, the two do not appear to be very far apart.

Consider the language of Reinhardt's "verbal assault" rule in *Harper.* Is this a principled application of the *Tinker* "rights of others" prong, or an overly expansive application of existing law? As a matter of policy, would you view this rule as helpful in a K–12 school setting? Or are there unintended negative consequences that may flow from the adoption of this rule by other courts?

Similarly, consider the language of Posner's "test-score" rule in *Nuxoll.* Is this a principled application of *Morse* and other First Amendment principles, or an overly expansive application of existing law? As a matter of policy, would you view this rule as helpful in a K–12 school setting? Or are there unintended negative consequences that may flow from its adoption by other courts?

4. Can it be argued that a pattern may be discerned in all the "T-shirt" cases by analyzing the level of egregiousness reflected in each of the messages? Arguably, the "shameful and condemned by God" shirt and the "three-faced Jesus" shirt are the most egregious, with the "straight pride" shirt arguably the least egregious and the "be happy, not gay" shirt perhaps somewhere in the middle. Thus the students wearing the more egregious shirts lose their lawsuits, while the others prevail.

Might it be possible, then, to delineate an objective standard that would reflect such an analysis, perhaps by devising a statute or a policy that prohibits T-shirt slogans or images that would interfere with the ability of a reasonable person of the implicated group to complete his or her work while confronted with the slogan or image in close classroom quarters? Would you support such a statute or policy at the K–12 level? Why or why not?

PROBLEM 12: T–SHIRTS IN NEW TUOLUMNE

The state of New Tuolumne, located in the Pacific Northwest, is home to a burgeoning collective movement that spearheads a series of highly profitable business ventures. These ventures include agricultural products, natural cleansers, arts, crafts, children's books, teas, microbreweries, and vineyards.

The collectives are united not only by their business interests, but also by a philosophical commitment to a different and—in their view—more natural way of living. The leaders of the collectives have sought to be true to the diverse and interrelated efforts of Thoreau, John Muir, participants in the early communal experiments in rural America, the kibbutz movements in early twentieth-century Palestine, and the "back to nature" movements of the 1960s and 1970s. The collectives are open to anyone of any race, ethnicity, national origin, gender, or religion. Members commit to living a simple life in a natural outdoor setting, and they reject the concept of individual material possessions. All financial resources and all collective profits are combined into communal resource accounts and investments. Finally, all members unite in a commitment to reject the institution of marriage. No one in any of the collectives is allowed to either marry or be married, and all children born on the collectives are viewed as belonging to everyone and raised by everyone over the course of time. As a general rule, no effort is even made to ascertain who the biological father of any individual child might be.

The largest collective in the state is located just outside the city of Moss Grove, and several hundred children from the collective attend the local public schools. The Moss Grove collective has been in existence for over thirty years, and, for the most part, the relationship between its members and other residents of the area is quite good. Some members of the collective work in the city, and some city residents choose to join the collective. Many maintain social contact with each other. However, a certain level of tension has existed all along between the collective and some of Moss Grove's more traditional religious institutions.

* * *

In 2010, an effort is launched by a statewide coalition to "protect traditional marriage" by placing an initiative on the ballot that would prohibit the collectives' practices relating to marriage and procreation. Members of the collectives could be jailed, and the collectives could be shut down, if the initiative passes and is upheld by the courts.

In response to the campaign to collect signatures for the initiative, teenagers from the collective who attend Moss Grove High—along with their friends and allies—get permission to hold a peaceful protest on campus. The protest activities include the distribution of flyers and the wearing of home-made T-shirts with messages supportive of the collective. Several students wear shirts with the slogan "Reject Marriage" on the front and "Back to Nature" on the back, superimposed on a picture of an outdoor scene.

The following day, three students from the city show up at school with their own homemade T-shirts. All have the slogan "Protect Marriage" on the front, while each have different messages on the back. One shirt states "Shame on the Collective," a second reads "Ban the Sinners," and the third reads "End Perversion Now."

Tensions are clearly simmering on campus, angry words are exchanged, and some pushing and shoving takes place between periods. During second period, the three students are called into the office and told that their shirts are too inflammatory and cannot be displayed. When the students refuse to comply, they are suspended and sent home for three days. Mirroring the tension in the larger community, the school climate remains unsettled when the students return, and both faculty and school site administrators must devote extensive efforts to calming things down. Many report having difficulty concentrating and being easily distracted by the ongoing anger on both sides, an anger that is exacerbated by the news that enough signatures have been gathered for the initiative to qualify for the ballot.

The three students who were suspended file a lawsuit against the District. In their complaint, they assert that their freedom of expression rights have been violated, and, in particular, they seek to build on recent approaches employed by U.S. Circuit Courts in analogous T-shirt cases. What arguments should these plaintiffs set forth under Tinker and its progeny? How might the District be expected to respond? What result? Discuss.

5. CHALLENGES POSED BY ONLINE AND WIRELESS TECHNOLOGIES: DETERMINING THE EXTENT TO WHICH STUDENTS CAN BE HELD ACCOUNTABLE FOR ELECTRONIC COMMUNICATION OUTSIDE OF SCHOOL

DONINGER v. NIEHOFF

527 F.3d 41 (2nd Cir. 2008)

LIVINGSTON, Circuit Judge:

* * * [Lewis Mills (LMHS) is a public high school] located in Burlington, Connecticut. At the time of the events recounted here, Avery Doninger was a junior at LMHS. She served on the Student Council and was also the Junior Class Secretary.

This case arises out of a dispute between the school administration and a group of Student Council members * * * over the scheduling of an event called "Jamfest," * * * [which had been postponed a number of times.]

     * * *

Four Student Council members, including Avery, decided to take action by alerting the broader community to the Jamfest situation and enlisting help in persuading school officials to [see to it that the Jamfest took place]. The four students met at the school's computer lab that morning and accessed one of their fathers' email account. They drafted a message to be sent to a large number of email addresses in the account's address book, as well as to additional names that Avery provided. The message * * * requested recipients to contact Paula Schwartz, the district superintendent, to urge that Jamfest be held as scheduled, as well as to forward the email o as many people as you can. All four students signed their names and sent the email. * * *

Both [Superintendent] Schwartz and [Principal] Niehoff received an influx of telephone calls and emails from people expressing concern about Jamfest. Niehoff, who was away from her office for a planned in-service training day, was called back by Schwartz as a result. Later that day, Niehoff encountered Avery in the hallway at LMHS. Avery claimed that Niehoff told her that Schwartz was very upset "and that [,] as a result, Jamfest had been cancelled." The district court found otherwise, however, crediting Niehoff's testimony denying that she ever told Avery the event would not be held.

According to Niehoff, she advised Avery that she was disappointed the Student Council members had resorted to a mass email rather than coming to her or to Schwartz to resolve the issue. She testified that class officers are expected to work cooperatively with their faculty advisor and with the administration in carrying out Student Council objectives. They are charged, in addition, with "demonstrat[ing] qualities of good citizenship at all times." The district court found that Niehoff discussed these responsibilities with Avery in their conversation on April 24. She told Avery that the email contained inaccurate information because Niehoff was, in fact, amenable to rescheduling Jamfest so it could be held in the new auditorium. Niehoff asked Avery to work with her fellow students to send out a corrective email. According to Niehoff, Avery agreed to do so.

That night, however, Avery posted a message on her publicly accessible blog, which was hosted by livejournal.com, a website unaffiliated with LMHS. The blog post began as follows: "jamfest is cancelled due to douchebags in central office." * * *

[The post reproduced the email that the Student Council members sent that morning, and then continued:]

And here is a letter my mom sent to Paula [Schwartz] and cc'd Karissa [Niehoff] to get an idea of what to write if you want to write something or call her to piss her off more. im down.—

Avery testified before the district court that "im down" meant that she approved of the idea of others contacting Schwartz to "piss her off more." She stated that the purpose of posting the blog entry was "to encourage more people than the existing e-mail already encouraged to contact the administration" about Jamfest. The district court concluded that the content of the message itself suggested that her purpose was "to encourage her fellow students to read and respond to the blog." The district court also noted that "[s]everal LMHS students posted comments to the blog, including one in which the author referred to Ms. Schwartz as a 'dirty whore.' "

[The following morning, after receiving more phone calls and email messages regarding Jamfest, Niehoff and Schwartz scheduled a meeting with relevant faculty and staff and the Student Council members who sent the email the day before.] They agreed during this meeting that Jamfest would be rescheduled for June 8, 2007. Niehoff announced this resolution in the school newsletter and the students notified the recipients of the April 24 email. * * * The district court * * * [also] found that, as a result of the Jamfest controversy, both Schwartz and Niehoff were forced to miss or arrived late to several school-related activities scheduled for April 24 and April 25.

* * * Jamfest was successfully held on June 8, with all but one of the scheduled bands participating. Even after this resolution, however, Schwartz and Niehoff, unaware of Avery's blog post, continued to receive phone calls and emails in the controversy's immediate aftermath. According to Schwartz's testimony, she learned of Avery's posting only some days after the meeting when her adult son found it while using an Internet search engine. * * *

On May 17, * * * Niehoff declined to provide an administrative endorsement of Avery's nomination, which effectively prohibited her from running for Senior Class Secretary * * *. [H]er decision was based on: (1) Avery's failure to accept her counsel "regarding the proper means of expressing disagreement with administration policy and seeking to resolve those disagreements"; (2) the vulgar language and inaccurate information included in the post; and (3) its encouragement of others to contact the central office "to piss [Schwartz] off more," which Niehoff did not consider appropriate behavior for a class officer.

As a result of Niehoff's decision, Avery was not allowed to have her name on the ballot or to give a campaign speech at a May 25 school assembly regarding the elections. Apart from this disqualification from running for Senior Class Secretary, she was not otherwise disciplined. * * *

Lauren Doninger filed a complaint in Connecticut Superior Court asserting claims under 42 U.S.C. 1983 and state law. She principally alleged violations of her daughter's rights under the First Amendment * * * and analogous clauses of the Connecticut Constitution. * * *

I. THE FIRST AMENDMENT CLAIM

* * *

The Supreme Court has yet to speak on the scope of a school's authority to regulate expression that, like Avery's, does not occur on school grounds or at a school-sponsored event. We have determined, however, that a student may be disciplined for expressive conduct, even conduct occurring off school grounds, when this conduct "would foreseeably create a risk of substantial disruption within the school environment," at least when it was similarly foreseeable that the off-campus expression might also reach campus. *Wisniewski v. Bd. of Educ.* We are acutely attentive in this context to the need to draw a clear line between student activity that "affects matter of legitimate concern to the school community," and activity that does not. But as Judge Newman accurately observed some years ago, "territoriality is not necessarily a useful concept in determining the limit of [school administrators'] authority." * * * [T]his observation is even more apt today, when students both on and off campus routinely participate in school affairs, as well as in other expressive activity unrelated to the school community, via blog postings, instant messaging, and other forms of electronic communication. It is against this background that we consider whether the district court abused its discretion in concluding that Doninger failed to demonstrate a clear likelihood of success on the merits of her First Amendment claim.

A.

If Avery had distributed her electronic posting as a handbill on school grounds, this case would fall squarely within the Supreme Court's precedents recognizing that * * * offensive forms of expression may be prohibited. [*Fraser*].

To be clear, *Fraser* does not justify restricting a student's speech merely because it is inconsistent with an educator's sensibilities; its reference to "plainly offensive speech" must be understood in light of the vulgar, lewd, and sexually explicit language that was at issue in that case. We need not conclusively determine *Fraser*'s scope, however, to be satisfied that Avery's posting-in which she called school administrators "douchebags" and encouraged others to contact Schwartz "to piss her off more" contained the sort of language that properly may be prohibited in schools. *Fraser* itself approvingly quoted Judge Newman's memorable observation * * * that "the First Amendment gives a high school student the classroom right to wear Tinker's armband, but not Cohen's jacket." *cf. Cohen v. California* (holding that adult could not be prosecuted for wearing jacket displaying expletive). Avery's language, had it occurred in the classroom, would have fallen within *Fraser* and its recognition that nothing in the First Amendment prohibits school authorities from discouraging inappropriate language in the school environment.

B.

It is not clear * * * that *Fraser* applies to off-campus speech. * * * We [find, however, that] * * * the *Tinker* standard has been adequately established here. * * *

Tinker provides that school administrators may prohibit student expression that will "materially and substantially disrupt the work and discipline of the school." In *Wisniewski,* we applied this standard to an eighth grader's off-campus creation and Internet transmission to some fifteen friends of a crudely drawn icon that "depict[ed] and call[ed] for the killing of his teacher." We recognized that off-campus conduct of this sort "can create a foreseeable risk of substantial disruption within a school" and that, in such circumstances, its off-campus character does not necessarily insulate the student from school discipline. We determined that school discipline was permissible because it was reasonably foreseeable that the icon would come to the attention of school authorities and that it would create a risk of substantial disruption.

Applying [this] framework * * *, the record amply supports the district court's conclusion that it was reasonably foreseeable that Avery's posting would reach school property. Indeed, the district court found that her posting, although created off-campus, "was purposely designed by Avery to come onto the campus." The blog posting directly pertained to events at LMHS, and Avery's intent in writing it was specifically "to encourage her fellow students to read and respond." As the district court found, "Avery knew other LMHS community members were likely to read [her posting]." Several students did in fact post comments in response to Avery and, as in *Wisniewski,* the posting managed to reach school administrators. The district court thus correctly determined that in these circumstances, "it was reasonably foreseeable that other LMHS students would view the blog and that school administrators would become aware of it."

Contrary to Doninger's protestations, moreover, the record also supports the conclusion that Avery's posting "foreseeably create[d] a risk of substantial disruption within the school environment." There are three factors in particular on which we rely to reach this conclusion. First, the language with which Avery chose to encourage others to contact the administration was not only plainly offensive, but also potentially disruptive of efforts to resolve the ongoing controversy. Her chosen words-in essence, that others should call the "douchebags" in the central office to "piss [them] off more" were hardly conducive to cooperative conflict resolution. Indeed, at least one LMHS student (the one who referred to Schwartz as a 'dirty whore') responded to the post's vulgar and, in this circumstance, potentially incendiary language with similar such language, thus evidencing that the nature of Avery's efforts to recruit could create a risk of disruption.

Second, and perhaps more significantly, Avery's post used the "at best misleading and at wors[t] false" information that Jamfest had been cancelled in her effort to solicit more calls and emails to Schwartz. * * * Avery herself testified that by the morning of April 25, students were "all riled up" and that a sit-in was threatened because students believed the event would not be held. Schwartz and Niehoff had received a deluge of calls and emails, causing both to miss or be late to school-related activities. Moreover, Avery and the other students who participated in writing the mass email were called away either from class or other activities on the morning of April 25 because of the need to manage the growing dispute * * *. It was foreseeable in this context that school operations might well be disrupted further by the need to correct misinformation as a consequence of Avery's post.

* * *

CONCLUSION

Avery, by all reports, is a respected and accomplished student at LMHS. We are sympathetic to her disappointment at being disqualified from running for Senior Class Secretary and acknowledge her belief that in this case, "the punishment did not fit the crime." We are not called upon, however, to decide whether the school officials in this case exercised their discretion wisely. Local school authorities have the difficult task of teaching "the shared values of a civilized social order" values that include our veneration of free expression *and* civility, the importance we place on the right of dissent *and* on proper respect for authority. Educators will inevitably make mistakes in carrying out this delicate responsibility. Nevertheless, as the Supreme Court cautioned years ago, "[t]he system of public education that has evolved in this Nation relies necessarily upon the discretion and judgment of school administrators and school board members," and we are not authorized to intervene absent "violations of specific constitutional guarantees."

The judgment of the district court is therefore affirmed.

NOTE

1. As the Internet and related technologies continue to become an integral part of daily life for a substantial percentage of the population, the boundaries between the online world and the offline world have been increasingly blurred. Education officials in mounting numbers are therefore faced with the challenge of determining whether and to what extent to hold students accountable for material ostensibly posted outside of school that may have an impact on day-to-day affairs within a school community. In this regard, the Second Circuit opinion in the *Doninger* case may become an important milestone.

D. CONCEPTUALIZING THE PARAMETERS OF THE RIGHT TO BE "OUT"

In the public sector today, every individual has a right to be "out" regarding fundamental aspects of identity, personhood, and group affiliation. Reflecting a classic combination of First Amendment and Fourteenth Amendment principles, it is both a right to express an identity and a right to be treated equally as a result of expressing this identity.

Emerging under both case law and a range of relevant federal and state statutes, the right to be "out" encompasses—but is not limited to—

disclosure of one's race, ethnicity, religion, sexual orientation, gender identity, political views, medical conditions, past experiences, present involvement, and future plans.[a]

Within the lesbian, gay, bisexual, and transgender (LGBT) communities, nothing is more central than the right to be out. To the extent that it is in fact recognized in the U.S. today, it encompasses the right to identify openly as an LGBT person and the right to live openly as an LGBT person . . . without experiencing any negative consequences as a result.

The centrality of this right for LGBT persons can be linked to the fact that not only is there still so much pressure, in so many settings, not to come out, but that as recently as 30–40 years ago the U.S. legal system had set forth such imposing hurdles to living openly that being out was typically not an option. Public school teachers, for example, could lose their jobs if they were openly gay. Bars were actually prohibited from serving drinks to persons who were known homosexuals or openly homosexual. Dancing with same sex partners in public was restricted. And propositioning another person of the same gender was not only a crime but an act that could lead to "sex offender" status and the accompanying loss of employment, legal rights, and social standing in the community.[b]

It is generally agreed that we are currently undergoing a significant transition with regard to issues impacting LGBT persons in this country. The legal terrain is changing dramatically, and the accompanying public policy issues reflect a society that is wrestling openly for the first time in U.S. history with high-profile controversies concerning the role that LGBT persons can and should be playing in daily life. Underlying every one of these controversies is an implicit but not-often-stated tension regarding the nature and extent of the right to be out.

Nowhere is this tension more evident than in our nation's educational institutions. Indeed, particularly at the K–12 level, LGBT students, teachers, and school site administrators have found themselves at the eye of the

---

a. It must be noted, of course, that just as there is a concurrent right, under the First Amendment Free Speech Clause, not to speak, there is also a concurrent right in this context not to be out. Indeed, the right not to be out is an important component of the right to privacy.

b. *See, e.g.,* WILLIAM N. ESKRIDGE, JR., GAYLAW 98, Harvard University Press (1999):

The homosexual in 1961 was smothered by law. She or he risked arrest and possible police brutalization for dancing with someone of the same sex, cross-dressing, propositioning another adult homosexual, possessing a homophile publication, writing about homosexuality without disapproval, displaying pictures of two people of the same sex in intimate positions, [or] . . . operating a lesbian or gay bar . . . Misdemeanor arrests for sex-related vagrancy or disorderly conduct offenses meant that the homosexual might have her or his name published in the local newspaper, would probably lose her or his job, and in several states would have to register as a sex offender. If the homosexual were not a citizen, she or he would likely be deported. If the homosexual were a professional—teacher, lawyer, doctor, mortician, beautician—she or he could lose the certification needed to practice that profession.

LGBT persons of color have often faced additional challenges above and beyond those described above. *See, e.g.,* JOHN D'EMILIO, LOST PROPHET: THE LIFE AND TIMES OF BAYARD RUSTIN, Free Press (2003); BLACK LIKE US: A CENTURY OF LESBIAN, GAY, AND BISEXUAL AFRICAN AMERICAN FICTION, Cleis Press (Devon W. Carbado et al. eds., 2002); *see also* REINALDO ARENAS, ANTES QUE ANOCHEZCA (BEFORE NIGHT FALLS), Penguin Books (1992); RUSSELL LEONG, ASIAN AMERICAN SEXUALITIES: DIMENSIONS OF THE GAY AND LESBIAN EXPERIENCE, Routledge (1995).

proverbial storm as school communities confront the rapidly changing realities in this area. The intensive and ongoing level of personal contact in a setting where certain values are expected to be instilled can and often does lead to high emotions and volatile confrontations. Litigation and legislation addressing these issues has increased substantially in recent years, and a growing body of relevant law has developed as a result.[c]

The material in this section includes decisions that, when taken together, comprise the First Amendment component of the right to be out for LGBT students in the public schools. It also reflects an initial inquiry into the parameters of this emerging right. Additional aspects of the inquiry appear in the Chapter 4 section on peer harassment and mistreatment (addressing the equal protection component of the right to be out), the gender equity section of Chapter 5 (addressing transgender issues in a gender equity context), the *religion, morality, and values* chapters (addressing the debates regarding competing visions of "morality" and the contours of the "wall of separation" between church and state), and the overview of the rights of educators in Chapter 11 (addressing both academic freedom issues and employment discrimination concerns).

FRICKE v. LYNCH

491 F. Supp. 381 (D. R.I. 1980)

PETTINE, CHIEF JUDGE.

Most of the time, a young man's choice of a date for the senior prom is of no great interest to anyone other than the student, his companion, and, perhaps, a few of their classmates. But in Aaron Fricke's case, the school authorities actively disapprove of his choice, the other students are upset, the community is abuzz, and out-of-state newspapers consider the matter newsworthy. All this fuss arises because Aaron Fricke's intended escort is another young man. Claiming that the school's refusal to allow him to bring a male escort violates his first and fourteenth amendment rights, Fricke seeks a preliminary injunction ordering the school officials to allow him to attend with a male escort.

Two days of testimony have revealed the following facts. The senior reception at Cumberland High School is a formal dinner–dance sponsored and run by the senior class. It is held shortly before graduation but is not a part of the graduation ceremonies. This year the students have decided to hold the dance at the Pleasant Valley Country Club in Sutton, Massachusetts on Friday, May 30. All seniors except those on suspension are eligible to attend the dance; no one is required to go. All students who attend must bring an escort, although their dates need not be seniors or even Cumberland High School students. Each student is asked the name of his date at the time he buys the tickets.

* * *

---

c. For examples of an early identification of relevant principles in this area, see, e.g., Kenneth L. Karst, *Myths of Identity: Individual and Group Portraits of Race and Sexual Orientation,* 43 UCLA L. REV. 263, 360 (1995); Kenji Yoshino, *Covering,* 111 YALE L.J. 769 (2002).

The seeds of the present conflict were planted a year ago when Paul Guilbert, then a junior at Cumberland High School, sought permission to bring a male escort to the junior prom. The principal, Richard Lynch (the defendant here), denied the request, fearing that student reaction could lead to a disruption at the dance and possibly to physical harm to Guilbert. The request and its denial were widely publicized and led to widespread community and student reaction adverse to Paul. Some students taunted and spit at him, and once someone slapped him; in response, principal Lynch arranged an escort system, in which Lynch or an assistant principal accompanied Paul as he went from one class to the next. No other incidents or violence occurred. Paul did not attend the prom. At that time Aaron Fricke (plaintiff here) was a friend of Paul's and supported his position regarding the dance.

This year, during or after an assembly in April in which senior class events were discussed, Aaron Fricke, a senior at Cumberland High School, decided that he wanted to attend the senior reception with a male companion. Aaron considers himself a homosexual, and has never dated girls, although he does socialize with female friends. He has never taken a girl to a school dance. Until this April, he had not "come out of the closet" by publicly acknowledging his sexual orientation.

Aaron asked principal Lynch for permission to bring a male escort, which Lynch denied. * * * Lynch gave Aaron written reasons for his action; his prime concern was the fear that a disruption would occur and Aaron or, especially, Paul would be hurt. He indicated in court that he would allow Aaron to bring a male escort if there were no threat of violence.

After Aaron filed suit in this Court, an event reported by the Rhode Island and Boston papers, a student shoved and, the next day, punched Aaron. The unprovoked, surprise assault necessitated five stitches under Aaron's right eye. The assailant was suspended for nine days. After this, Aaron was given a special parking space closer to the school doors and has been provided with an escort (principal or assistant principal) between classes. No further incidents have occurred.

This necessarily brief account does not convey the obvious concern and good faith Lynch has displayed in his handling of the matter. Lynch sincerely believes that there is a significant possibility that some students will attempt to injure Aaron and Paul if they attend the dance. Moreover, Lynch's actions in school have displayed a concern for Aaron's safety while at school. Perhaps—one cannot be at all sure—a totally different approach by Lynch might have kept the matter from reaching its present proportions, but I am convinced that Lynch's actions have stemmed—in significant part—from a concern for disruption.

Aaron contends that the school's action violates his first amendment right of association, his first amendment right to free speech, and his fourteenth amendment right to equal protection of the laws. (The equal protection claim is a "hybrid" one—that he has been treated differently than others because of the content of his communication.)

* * *

* * * [T]he proposed activity has significant expressive content. Aaron testified that he wants to go because he feels he has a right to attend and participate just like all the other students and that it would be dishonest to his own sexual identity to take a girl to the dance. He went on to acknowledge that he feels his attendance would have a certain political element and would be a statement for equal rights and human rights. * * *

Accordingly, the school's action must be judged by the standards articulated in *United States v. O'Brien* and applied in *Bonner*: (1) was the regulation within the constitutional power of the government; (2) did it further an important or substantial governmental interest; (3) was the governmental interest unrelated to the suppression of free expression; and (4) was the incidental restriction on alleged first amendment freedoms no greater than essential to the furtherance of that interest?

I need not dwell on the first two *O'Brien* requirements: the school unquestionably has an important interest in student safety and has the power to regulate students' conduct to ensure safety. As to the suppression of free expression, Lynch's testimony indicated that his personal views on homosexuality did not affect his decision, and that but for the threat of violence he would let the two young men go together. Thus the government's interest here is not in squelching a particular message because it objects to its content as such. On the other hand, the school's interest is in suppressing certain speech activity because of the reaction its message may engender. Surely this is still suppression of free expression.

It is also clear that the school's action fails to meet the last criterion set out in *O'Brien*, the requirement that the government employ the "least restrictive alternative" before curtailing speech. * * * It is, of course, impossible to guarantee that no harm will occur, no matter what measures are taken. But only one student so far has attempted to harm Aaron, and no evidence was introduced of other threats. The measures taken already, especially the escort system, have been highly effective in preventing any further problems at school. Appropriate security measures coupled with a firm, clearly communicated attitude by the administration that any disturbance will not be tolerated appear to be a realistic, and less restrictive, alternative to prohibiting Aaron from attending the dance with the date of his choice.

The analysis so far has been along traditional first amendment lines, making no real allowance for the fact that this case arises in a high school setting. The most difficult problem this controversy presents is how this setting should affect the result. *Tinker v. Des Moines Independent Community School District*, 393 U.S. 503, 89 S. Ct. 733 (1969), makes clear that high school students do not "shed their constitutional rights to freedom of speech or expression at the schoolhouse gate." * * *

It seems to me that here, not unlike in *Tinker*, the school administrators were acting on "an undifferentiated fear or apprehension of disturbance." True, Aaron was punched and then security measures were taken, but since that incident he has not been threatened with violence nor has he been attacked. There has been no disruption at the school; classes have not been cancelled, suspended, or interrupted. In short, while the defendants have perhaps shown more of a basis for fear of harm than in *Tinker*, they have failed to make a "showing" that Aaron's conduct would "materially and substantially interfere" with school discipline. *See Tinker* at 509, 89 S. Ct. at 737. However, even if the Court assumes that there is justifiable fear and that Aaron's peaceful speech leads, or may lead, to a violent reaction from others, the question remains: may the school prohibit the speech, or must it protect the speaker?

It is certainly clear that outside of the classroom the fear—however justified—of a violent reaction is not sufficient reason to restrain such speech in advance, and an actual hostile reaction is rarely an adequate basis for curtailing free speech. * * * Thus, the question here is whether the interest in school discipline and order, recognized in *Tinker*, requires a different approach.

After considerable thought and research, I have concluded that even a legitimate interest in school discipline does not outweigh a student's right to peacefully express his views in an appropriate time, place, and manner. To rule otherwise would completely subvert free speech in the schools by granting other students a "heckler's veto," allowing them to decide—through prohibited and violent methods—what speech will be heard. The first amendment does not tolerate mob rule by unruly school children. This conclusion is bolstered by the fact that any disturbance here, however great, would not interfere with the main business of school—education. No classes or school work would be affected; at the very worst an optional social event, conducted by the students for their own enjoyment, would be marred. In such a context, the school does have an obligation to take reasonable measures to protect and foster free speech, not to stand helpless before unauthorized student violence.

> * * *

The present case is so difficult because the Court is keenly sensitive to the testimony regarding the concerns of a possible disturbance, and of physical harm to Aaron or Paul. However, I am convinced that meaningful security measures are possible, and the first amendment requires that such steps be taken to protect—rather than to stifle—free expression. Some may feel that Aaron's attendance at the reception and the message he will thereby convey is trivial compared to other social debates, but to engage in this kind of a weighing in process is to make the content-based evaluation forbidden by the first amendment.

As to the other concern raised by *Tinker*, some people might say that Aaron Fricke's conduct would infringe the rights of the other students, and is thus unprotected by *Tinker*. This view is misguided, however.

Aaron's conduct is quiet and peaceful; it demands no response from others and—in a crowd of some five hundred people—can be easily ignored. Any disturbance that might interfere with the rights of others would be caused by those students who resort to violence, not by Aaron and his companion, who do not want a fight.

Because the free speech claim is dispositive, I find it unnecessary to reach the plaintiff's right of association argument or to deal at length with his equal protection claim. I find that the plaintiff has established a probability of success on the merits and has shown irreparable harm; accordingly his request for a preliminary injunction is hereby granted.

* * *

COLIN v. ORANGE UNIFIED SCH. DIST.

83 F. Supp. 2d 1135 (C.D. Cal. 2000)

Carter, District Judge.

* * *

In late August 1999, Anthony Colin ("Colin") and his friend Shannon MacMillan ("MacMillan") decided to form a "Gay–Straight Alliance Club" ("GSA") at their school, El Modena High School in Orange, California. Colin, a tenth-grade student, had the idea after Matthew Shepherd, a young man from Wyoming, died after being brutally assaulted due to his homosexuality. Colin testified that he wanted to form the club to promote acceptance among and for gay and straight students at the school. After discussing the idea with friends and family, Colin submitted a club constitution in compliance with school policy during the week of September 7, 1999, the first week of the school year.[a] * * *

* * * Colin asked Mrs. Maryina Herde, a drama and English teacher at the school, to serve as the faculty advisor and she accepted. * * *

Colin and the other founders of the Gay–Straight Alliance had reason to believe that their application would be accepted. Consistent with the policy of the Orange Unified School District's Board of Education ("the Board"), their high school had a policy of allowing student-initiated groups to meet on school grounds during lunch period and to use school facilities to publicize their meetings and activities.[b] * * *

---

a. The mission statement for the club, written by MacMillan, a twelfth grade student, stated the following:

Public schools have an obligation to provide an equal opportunity for all students to receive an education in a safe, nonhostile, nondiscriminatory environment. Our goal in this organization is to raise public awareness and promote tolerance by providing a safe forum for discussion of issues related to sexual orientation and homophobia. We wish to stress the need for people to put aside their personal prejudice and agree to treat everyone with respect when the situation calls for it. We invite ALL students, gay or straight, to join us in discussions, field trips, lectures, and social activities that will counterattack unfair treatment and prejudice. We respect privacy and require NO one to make disclosures regarding his or her own sexual orientation. This is not a sexual issue, it is about gaining support and promoting tolerance and respect for all students.

b. A recent list of the clubs on campus, of which there were 38 in total, included the following noncurriculum related student groups: the Asian Club, Black Student Union, Christian Club,

[The application was denied, however, and Plaintiffs brought this action alleging violations of the Equal Access Act, 20 U.S.C. §§ 4071–4074, the Civil Rights Act of 1871, 42 U.S.C. § 1983, and the Fourteenth Amendment to the United States Constitution. Plaintiffs sought declaratory relief under 28 U.S.C. §§ 2201–2202.]

II. Analysis

A. The Equal Access Act

* * * Under the [U.S. Equal Access Act of 1984], schools that allow student groups whose purpose is not directly related to the curriculum to meet on school grounds during lunch or after school cannot deny other student groups access to the school due to the content of the students' proposed discussions. * * *

* * * As Justice Kennedy pointed out, "one of the consequences of the statute, as we now interpret it, is that clubs of a most controversial character might have access to the student life of high schools that in the past have given official recognition only to clubs of a more conventional kind." * * * Due to the First Amendment, Congress passed an "Equal Access Act" when it wanted to permit religious speech on school campuses. It did not pass a "Religious Speech Access Act" or an "Access for All Students Except Gay Students Act" because to do so would be unconstitutional.[c]

It is against the backdrop of this federal law that this Court must decide whether the locally elected Orange Unified School District Board of Education can vote to deny recognition by the school to one club out of many that have sought to meet on campus.

* * *

C. Plaintiffs Have a Strong Likelihood of Succeeding on the Merits of their Claim for Violation of the Equal Access Act

In order for Plaintiffs to show a likely violation of the Equal Access Act, they must show that El Modena High School accepts federal funds, has a "limited open forum," and has discriminated against students wishing to conduct a meeting within the open forum due to the content of speech that will take place at the proposed meetings. * * * It is undisputed that the Board accepts federal funding.

* * *

[In addition, the Court found that the Board had established a "limited open forum" at El Modena High because it had granted "an

---

Gentlemen's Club, Girls' League, Koinonia (for Catholic students), MECHA (Movimiento Estudiantil Chicano de Aztlan), and Red Cross/Key Club.

c. *See* Bd. of Educ. v. Mergens, 496 U.S. 226 (1990), where the U.S. Supreme Court agreed with the plaintiff that the Equal Access Act, 20 U.S.C. §§ 4071–4074 (2000), prohibits a high school "from denying a student religious group permission to meet on school premises during noninstructional time," and that the Act, so construed, does not violate the Establishment Clause of the First Amendment. In so doing, the Court set forth guidelines for schools to follow pursuant to the Act.

offering to or opportunity for one or more noncurriculum related student groups to meet on school premises during noninstructional time." 20 U.S.C. § 4071(b). Modena "is therefore precluded from discriminating against student groups seeking access to that open forum."]

2. The Gay–Straight Alliance is a "Noncurriculum Related Student Group"

Defendants contend that the Gay–Straight Alliance is not protected by the Act because it is related to the curriculum. Specifically, Board Member Kathy Ward stated in her motion that "the District has a curriculum on sex education, which deals with human sexuality, sexual behavior and consequences, and prevention of sexually transmitted diseases. To the extent that the proposed GSA club intends to discuss these issues related to sexual orientation, the club is a 'curriculum related' club, not covered by the Equal Access Act." * * *

According to Colin, Zetin, and the Mission Statement of the Gay–Straight Alliance, however, they do not intend to discuss topics that are covered under the sex education curriculum. According to the Mission Statement, their goal was to talk about "tolerance," "issues related to sexual orientation and homophobia," the need to "treat everyone with respect," and counterattacking "unfair treatment and prejudice." The Mission Statement emphasizes, in a one-sentence paragraph at the end, that "[t]his is not a sexual issue, it is about gaining support and promoting tolerance and respect for all students." Both Colin and Zetin state in their declarations that the club did not propose to talk about the things that were covered in sex education. Furthermore, none of the classes at El Modena covered discrimination and harassment based on sexual orientation. Zetin testified that "the word homosexual is never even mentioned in our classes." Colin testified that the club was about "acceptance" for gay and straight people, and about helping people deal with being called "fag" or "dyke." Both Colin and Zetin laughed on the stand at the thought of the group discussing the "physiology of the reproductive system" and the other issues covered in Health class. What the students *did* want to talk about is best expressed in their own words. Echoing the Mission Statement, Zetin testified "I want us to talk about the experiences that gay, lesbian and bisexual kids go through in their everyday lives such as harassment, coming out of the closet or telling people that they are gay: the fear and the emotions such as self-hatred or denial that a lot of kids go through and the harassment they get and how to deal with that."

    * * *

* * * A curriculum-related student group is "one that has more than just a tangential or attenuated relationship to courses offered by the school" and "must at least have a more direct relationship to the curriculum than a religious or political club would have." Thus, if a Christian Club prays for abstinence, it is still "noncurriculum related" even though abstinence is a topic covered in the curriculum. Indeed, Zetin testified that she believed in abstinence. Just as with the Christian Club, if discussion of

abstinence were to arise at one of the meetings of the Gay–Straight Alliance, the club would still be "noncurriculum related."

* * *

Finally, even if the Court were to find at trial that the subject matter of the Gay–Straight Alliance was actually taught in a regularly offered course at El Modena, the Equal Access Act does not then allow the Board to withhold official recognition of the group. Whether or not a school recognizes a "noncurriculum related student group" merely determines whether or not the Act's obligations are triggered. Once a school recognizes any such group, it has created a "limited open forum" and the school is prohibited "from denying equal access to *any* other student group on the basis of the content of that group's speech." Contrary to the Board's interpretation of the Act, the Board may not foreclose access to the "limited open forum" merely by labeling a group curriculum-related. The only meetings that schools subject to the Act can prohibit are those that would "materially and substantially interfere with the orderly conduct of educational activities within the school." So long as the Board has a "limited open forum" at El Modena and allows any "noncurriculum related" student groups to meet, it can not prohibit the Gay–Straight Alliance even if its meetings directly relate to the curriculum. Instead, the Board will have to show that meetings will "materially and substantially interfere with the orderly" instruction of students. The Board will not likely be able to show that groups of students discussing homophobia and acceptance of all students regardless of sexual orientation somehow serves as a major disruption to the education of students. Indeed, this club is actually being formed to avoid the disruptions to education that can take place when students are harassed based on sexual orientation.

* * *

The Board Members may be uncomfortable about students discussing sexual orientation and how all students need to accept each other, whether gay or straight. As in *Tinker,* however, when the school administration was uncomfortable with students wearing symbols of protest against the Vietnam War, Defendants can not censor the students' speech to avoid discussions on campus that cause them discomfort or represent an unpopular viewpoint. In order to comply with the Equal Access Act, Anthony Colin, Heather Zetin, and the members of the Gay–Straight Alliance must be permitted access to the school campus in the same way that the District provides access to all clubs, including the Christian Club and the Red Cross/Key Club. Plaintiffs have shown a strong likelihood of succeeding on their claim that Defendants have violated their rights under the Equal Access Act.

D. First Amendment Claim

In finding that the District has likely violated the Equal Access Act, the Court need not reach Plaintiffs' First Amendment claim.

E.   Plaintiffs Will Be Irreparably Injured Absent Preliminary Relief

"The loss of First Amendment freedoms, for even minimal periods of time unquestionably constitutes irreparable injury." * * *

Plaintiffs have been injured not only by the Board's excessive delay, but also by the inability to effectively address the hardships they encounter at school every day. Some students at El Modena do not even feel safe using the school's restrooms. Zetin is often harassed by students calling her a "dyke." While such harms may not be cured by a preliminary injunction, "gay-straight alliance clubs provide a safe place for students ... [and] create a respectful environment where students realize that they have a place at the table ..." * * *

Granting a preliminary injunction would also be in the public interest. Recent California legislation confirms that it is state public policy to prevent discrimination on the basis of sexual orientation. In passing the California Student Safety and Violence Prevention Act of 2000, the California Legislature found that "[v]iolence is the number one cause of death for young people in California and has become a public health problem of epidemic proportion" and "[t]he fastest growing, violent crime in California is hate crime." The Legislature felt that "it is incumbent upon us to ensure that all students attending public school in California are protected from potentially violent discrimination." The California Penal Code already contained a prohibition on hate crimes based on sexual orientation. In passing ch. 587, however, the Legislature added sexual orientation to the list of prohibited forms of discrimination in public schools. In addition to protecting students from hate crimes, the Legislature was also concerned about suicide. * * *

By adding sexual orientation to the list of prohibited forms of in-school discrimination, the Legislature could specifically target the teen suicide rate. According to a Center for Disease Control and Prevention analysis of Massachusetts statistics in 1997, gay students were more than six times as likely to have tried suicide as straight students. This injunction therefore is not just about student pursuit of ideas and tolerance for diverse viewpoints. As any concerned parent would understand, this case may involve the protection of life itself. Since the Gay–Straight Alliance seeks to end discrimination on the basis of sexual orientation, a preliminary injunction requiring the Board to recognize the club would be consistent with state public policy and in the public interest.

In addition to demonstrating a strong likelihood that Defendants have violated the Equal Access Act, Plaintiffs have also shown a significant threat of irreparable injury, greater hardship to Plaintiffs than Defendants, and that the public interest favors granting the injunction. The Court finds that a preliminary injunction is warranted under these circumstances.

BOYD COUNTY HIGH SCH. GAY STRAIGHT ALLIANCE v. BOARD OF ED.

258 F. Supp. 2d 667 (E.D. Ky. 2003)

BUNNING, DISTRICT JUDGE.

I. INTRODUCTION

* * * Plaintiffs claim that Defendants violated their rights under the Equal Access Act, 20 U.S.C. § 4071, *et seq.*, and their First Amendment rights of expression and association by denying the Boyd County High School Gay Straight Alliance the same access to school facilities given to other student groups. * * *

Plaintiffs seek a preliminary injunction requiring Defendants to offer them the same opportunities given to other student groups at Boyd County High School. Plaintiffs assert that affording them the same opportunities includes authorization to meet at school during noninstructional time, to use the school hallways and bulletin boards for posters, and to use the intercom to make club announcements during home room.

* * *

II. FINDINGS OF FACT

* * *

3. In January or February of 2002, students at BCHS circulated a petition to create a GSA Club. * * * The purpose of the GSA Club is to provide students with a safe haven to talk about anti-gay harassment and to work together to promote tolerance, understanding and acceptance of one another regardless of sexual orientation. * * *

4. Anti-gay harassment, homophobia, and use of anti-gay epithets have been and continue to be serious problems at BCHS.[1] One student dropped out of BCHS because of harassment based on sexual orientation and another student dropped out because of both anti-gay harassment at school as well as problems at home. * * *

III. ANALYSIS

* * *

A. *Plaintiffs' Likelihood of Success on the Merits*
* * *

Although the majority of cases defining and interpreting the Equal Access Act involve requests by religious groups to meet on school property

---

1. One example of the harassment includes students in Plaintiff Fugett's English class stating that they needed to take all the fucking faggots out in the back woods and kill them. This occurred in October, 2002. During a basketball game in January 2003, students with megaphones chanted at Plaintiff Reese: "faggot-kisser," "GSA" and "fag-lover." On a regular basis, students call out "homo," "fag," and "queer" behind Plaintiff McClelland's back as he walks in the hallway between classes. On April 10, 2002, during an observance of National Day of Silence, about 25 participants sat in a circle in the front lobby of BCHS. During the lunch hour observance, protesters used anti-gay epithets and threw things at them.

during noninstructional time, several district courts have specifically addressed the more contentious issue of permitting gay rights groups to meet during noninstructional time. For example, in *Colin v. Orange Unified School District,* 83 F. Supp. 2d 1135, 1147 (C.D. Cal. 2000) the court * * * ruled that the GSA Club had been denied access to the school's limited open forum, holding this denial is "exactly the type of content-based restriction that is forbidden by the Equal Access Act." The court granted the injunction, ordering the school district to provide equal access to the GSA Club.

[Also,] * * * [i]n *East High Gay/Straight Alliance v. Board of Education of Salt Lake City School Disrict,* a GSA club was granted injunctive relief, thereby permitting it to meet at the defendant high school. * * *

* * * [H]aving found that the Defendants [in the case at hand] are subject to the EAA by virtue of permitting at least one noncurriculum-related group to meet or use the facilities at BCHS, in order to properly exclude the GSA from having equal access as required by the EAA, Defendants must show that the GSA Club will "materially and substantially interfere with the orderly conduct of educational opportunities within the school," 20 U.S.C. § 4071(c)(4), or will limit the school's ability "to maintain order and discipline on school premises, to protect the well-being of students and faculty . . ."

　　　* * *

In this case, it is obvious that the proposed creation of a GSA Club at BCHS has caused some level of uproar within the local community. It is equally apparent that several school administrators and board members received numerous complaints and questions from parents who were concerned about the approval of the GSA Club and how that approval might affect the safety of their children. Additionally, there were two student protests regarding the approval of the GSA Club, one on October 30, 2002, and the other on November 4, 2002. In short, the disruption to which Defendants were responding when they voted to ban all clubs was caused by GSA opponents, not GSA Club members themselves.

Although there is a relative paucity of case law interpreting what level of disruption is necessary before a school, subject to the obligations of the EAA can deny equal access without violating the Act, a review of what little case law does exist is helpful. The leading case on attempts to suppress speech within the high school setting is *Tinker v. Des Moines Independent Community School Dist.,* 393 U.S. 503, 89 S. Ct. 733 (1969).

　　　* * *

Refusing to allow a "heckler's veto" to justify suppression of student speech, the Court in *Tinker* was careful to focus on whether "*engaging in the forbidden conduct* would materially and substantially interfere with the requirements of appropriate discipline," *id.* at 538, 89 S. Ct. 733

(emphasis added), and concluded that the protesting students' speech was protected because it was "entirely divorced from actually or potentially disruptive conduct *by those participating in it.*"

* * *

Incorporation of the *Tinker* rule into 20 U.S.C. § 4071(f) means that a school may not deny equal access to a student group because student and community opposition to the group substantially interferes with the school's ability to maintain order and discipline, even though equal access is not required if the student group itself substantially interferes with the school's ability to maintain order and discipline. * * * [T]he Equal Access Act permits Defendants to prohibit Plaintiffs from meeting on equal terms with the noncurriculum-related student groups that have been permitted to meet * * * only upon a showing that Plaintiffs' *own* disruptive activities have interfered with Defendants ability to maintain order and discipline. * * * As addressed herein, Defendants have made no such showing in this case.

* * *

While Defendants argue that these protests and the public uproar surrounding the GSA Club have materially and substantially interfered with the orderly conduct of educational activities at BCHS, limited their authority to maintain order and discipline, and limited their ability to protect the well-being of students and faculty, the facts simply do not support such a conclusion. Other than one incident, there have been no documented instances of disruptions caused by GSA members or GSA supporters. * * *

As the district court stated in *Colin, supra:*

> The Board Members may be uncomfortable about students discussing sexual orientation and how all students need to accept each other, whether gay or straight. As in *Tinker,* however, when the school administration was uncomfortable with students wearing symbols of protest against the Vietnam War, Defendants cannot censor the students' speech to avoid discussions on campus that cause them discomfort or represent an unpopular viewpoint. 83 F. Supp. 2d. at 1149.

For these reasons, the Court finds that Plaintiffs have shown a strong likelihood of succeeding on their claim that Defendants violated their rights under the Equal Access Act.

* * *

[The motion for a preliminary injunction was granted.]

NOTES

1. Plaintiffs challenging their school district's decision to ban gay-straight alliances tend to prevail under the Equal Access Act. In addition to *Colin* and *Boyd, see, e.g., East High Gay/Straight Alliance v. Board of*

Education of Salt Lake City Sch. Dist., 81 F. Supp. 2d 1166 (D. Utah 1999); *Gay-Straight Alliance Network v. Visalia Unified School District,* 262 F.Supp.2d 1088 (E.D. Cal. 2001); *Franklin Cent. Gay/Straight Alliance v. Franklin Township Community School Corporation,* 2002 WL 32097530 (S.D. Ind. 2002); *Straights and Gays for Equality (SAGE) v. Osseo Area Schools– District No. 279,* 471 F.3d 908 (8th Cir. 2006); *Gay-Straight Alliance of Okeechobee High School v. School Board of Okeechobee County,* 483 F. Supp. 2d 1224 (S.D. Fla. 2007). *But see Caudillo v. Lubbock Independent School District,* 311 F. Supp. 2d 550 (N.D. Tex. 2004), an exception to this trend. The *Caudillo* court found the other cases to be distinguishable, in part, because it was "unable to find that any of the cases involved a school that maintained an abstinence-only policy and banned any discussion of sexual activity on its campuses."

2. LGBT students in many of the gay-straight alliance cases have benefited from prior efforts by religious students and their affiliated organizations, who lobbied for a federal Equal Access Act and then prevailed in *Board of Education v. Mergens,* the primary case construing the parameters of the Act. These prior efforts played a major role in establishing precedent that gay plaintiffs could rely upon in *Colin.*

3. The reasoning in many of these cases also parallels the reasoning found in the higher education cases of the 1970s and 1980s, where the federal courts ruled, consistently, in favor of gay and lesbian students who were prohibited from starting gay student clubs on campus.

HENKLE v. GREGORY

150 F. Supp. 2d 1067 (D. Nev. 2001)

McQUAID, UNITED STATES MAGISTRATE JUDGE.

BACKGROUND

Plaintiff, Derek R. Henkle, began his freshman year, in 1994, at Galena High School ("Galena") after skipping the eighth grade. In Fall 1995, Plaintiff appeared on the local access channel's program "Set Free" where he participated in a discussion about gay high school students and their experiences. From this point on, the alleged harassment began. Plaintiff alleges that, during school hours and on school property, he endured constant harassment, assaults, intimidation, and discrimination by other students because he is gay and male and school officials, after being notified of the continuous harassment, failed to take any action.

One incident of alleged harassment occurred in Fall 1995. Several students approached Plaintiff, on Galena property, calling him "fag," "butt pirate," "fairy," and "homo." They lassoed him around the neck and suggested dragging him behind a truck. Plaintiff escaped to a classroom and used an internal phone to report the incident to Defendant, Assistant Vice Principal Hausauer. After waiting nearly two hours, Defendant Hausauer arrived and responded with laughter. Defendant, Principal Gregory, was also made aware of the incident, but they took no action against the alleged harassers despite knowing their identities.

Another alleged incident occurred in Plaintiff's English class. Students in the class continuously wrote the word "fag" on the whiteboard and sent him notes calling him "fag." Students also drew sexually explicit pictures and called Plaintiff's attention to them. Defendant Rende, Plaintiff's English teacher, was allegedly aware of the harassment and identity of the harassers. Despite this knowledge, Defendant Rende chose to tell Plaintiff that his sexuality was a private matter that should be kept to himself, rather than end the harassment or discipline the harassers. Plaintiff alleges that Defendants Gregory and Hausauer also knew of this incident, yet did nothing to remedy the situation.

Plaintiff also faced harassment when reporting the incidents to Galena's discipline office. Several students, running by the office and shouting anti-gay epithets, threw a metal object at the Plaintiff that missed him and stuck in the wall. A school administrator witnessed this incident and a report was filed. Again, it is alleged that no investigation was made or discipline taken, despite the fact that school administrators were aware of the incident. Plaintiff suffered an emotional breakdown because of this episode.

At the end of the Fall 1995 semester, Plaintiff asked to leave Galena because he feared further harassment and assaults. Defendant Anastasio decided to transfer Plaintiff to Washoe High School ("Washoe"), an alternative high school. Plaintiff's transfer allegedly was conditioned on the fact that he keep his sexuality to himself. During Plaintiff's time at Galena, he wore buttons on his backpack that said "We are everywhere" and "Out," however, upon his transfer to Washoe, he removed the buttons.

Defendant Floyd was the Principal at Washoe during Plaintiff's tenure from January 1996 to May 1996. Defendant Floyd, on several occasions, allegedly told Plaintiff to keep quiet about his sexual orientation and during one meeting with Plaintiff, Floyd told him to "stop acting like a fag." On some occasions, Plaintiff expressed his viewpoints and identity, but for the most part kept them to himself. Finally, Plaintiff requested a transfer because of the lack of educational opportunities at Washoe. Plaintiff alleges that Floyd initially told him the transfer was not possible because Plaintiff was openly gay and a traditional high school would not be appropriate.

Plaintiff was subsequently transferred to Wooster High School ("Wooster") and, once again, prior to the transfer, was told by Floyd to keep his sexuality to himself. When Plaintiff's classmates, at Wooster, learned his identity and the fact that he was gay, they allegedly harassed and intimidated him during school hours and on school property. Plaintiff reported the incidents several times, however, he alleges the administration took no action.

One particular incident of inaction occurred when Plaintiff was assaulted at Wooster. Several students approached him shouting gay epithets, and one student punched him in the face, calling him "bitch." The other students encouraged the attack. School police, Defendants Ramilo and Selby, allegedly witnessed the attack, but did nothing. In fact, Plaintiff alleges Defendants Ramilo and Selby discouraged him from calling the assault a hate crime and from reporting it to the Reno Police Department. Furthermore, Defendants refused to arrest the attacker despite knowing the identity.

After this incident, Defendants Floyd and Anastasio agreed that Plaintiff should be transferred back to Washoe. However, Floyd later decided not to accept Plaintiff at Washoe despite having room for him. Instead, Defendants placed Plaintiff in an adult education program at Truckee Meadows Community College, thus making Plaintiff ineligible for a high school diploma because he was no longer enrolled in a public high school.

* * *

II. Violation of Plaintiff's First Amendment Rights

Plaintiff's Third and Fourth Claims for Relief allege Defendants violated his First Amendment rights by censoring, chilling, and deterring him from exercising his right to freedom of speech and by retaliating against him when he did exercise his rights.

* * *

In examining a First Amendment retaliation claim, courts engage in [a] three part inquiry. For the first two prongs of the inquiry, plaintiff must demonstrate: (1) the speech at issue was constitutionally protected; and (2) the speech was a substantial or motivating factor in the adverse action. If plaintiff satisfies this burden, the burden shifts to the defendants to demonstrate they would have taken the same actions against plaintiff, even in the absence of his protected conduct.

In light of the previous discussion, Plaintiff satisfied element one by alleging that his speech was constitutionally protected [under *Tinker*]. Thus, we will turn our attention to element two.

Plaintiff alleges several actions and/or inactions by Defendants that warrant the inference that the actions and/or inactions were retaliatory in nature. He alleges that after his appearance on "Set Free" where he participated in a discussion about gay high school students and their experiences, the harassment began at Galena and, ultimately, resulted in his transfer to Washoe, an alternative high school. Plaintiff also alleges, rather than disciplining the harassers, Defendants treated him as the problem and told him numerous times to keep his sexuality to himself. Plaintiff further alleges, his first transfer from Galena to Washoe was conditioned on the fact that he keep his sexuality to himself. In an effort to comply with this request, he removed buttons, pertaining to his sexuality, from his backpack. Moreover, Defendants transferred Plaintiff, a gifted and talented student, to Washoe, and alternative education program. Furthermore, when he asked for a transfer from Washoe because of lack of educational opportunities, Defendant Floyd told him the transfer was not possible because he was openly gay and a traditional high school was not appropriate, but was eventually transferred to Wooster. And finally, after Plaintiff continued to express his sexuality at Wooster, he was denied a transfer back to Washoe, and instead was transferred to an adult education program where he could not receive a high school diploma because he was no longer enrolled in a public high school.

Thus, at this stage of the proceedings, Plaintiff has made sufficient allegations, that his constitutionally protected speech was a substantial motivating factor in adverse action directed at him. Therefore, this court cannot say as a matter of law that Plaintiff failed to state a claim for retaliation for exercising his First Amendment rights.

* * *

In *Tinker,* the Supreme Court clearly established that students in public schools have the right to freedom of speech and expression. This is a broad right that would encompass the right of a high school student to express his sexuality. * * *

PROBLEM 13: FURTHER VARIATIONS ON THE EVENTS AT SOUTHERN VALLEY HIGH

Assume the same facts and circumstances that were originally set forth in Problems 10 and 11, except that, in addition, Jamie is openly gay. How, if at all, might that fact change the analysis in either of the two problems? What additional facts might be needed to complete the analysis of those events?

Assume, in this context, that one or more of the organizations that Jamie and his friends created had been a gay-straight alliance? What additional arguments might be put forth by the respective parties? What result?

E. HIGHER EDUCATION "FREEDOM OF EXPRESSION" CONTROVERSIES GENERALLY

PROBLEM 14: THE ALISTAIRE & GEORGINA JONES CASES

This hypothetical takes place (basically) at public educational institutions in the fictional State of Eldorado.

Early in the fall semester, Alistaire Jones—who had covered campus religious issues at the University of Golden Galleon (UGG) as a freshman cub reporter the previous year—began writing a weekly column on world events. Almost immediately, he chose to focus on the events in Abscella and the interrelated, often-violent disputes regarding land, culture, and religion.

(Abscella is a fictional region that had been controlled by an authoritarian Communist government from 1945 to 1989. At the end of the Cold War, five separate countries had been formed in the region, but three of these countries contained combinations of two ethnic groups (Group A & Group B) that had been at war on and off for eight centuries. While most of the people in Group A were nominal followers of Religion A, 5–10 percent were highly religious and followed fundamentalist teachings which—among other things—promised the entire region of Abscella to them. Most of the people in Group B followed Religion B, but 10–15 percent were highly religious and followed fundamentalist teachings which, among other things, promised eternal paradise to anyone who was killed defending Abscella from "infidels.")

Alistaire, whose mother had been born in Abscella and had been raised as a devout member of Religion B, began to take up the cause of Group B in his columns. Many letters soon appeared in response to Alistaire's writings, some laudatory, but many others angry and emotional. (UGG was home to the largest percentage of students of Abscellan descent in the entire USA).

In response to the letters, Alistaire's columns took on an even more strident tone, and also became more religious in nature. He urged fellow members of Religion B to stand up for their land and their religion, and referred to members of Religion A as infidels. After several of these columns, the faculty journalism advisor called Alistaire into his office and asked him to tone down the columns. Alistaire sat quietly and listened, but then went out and wrote another column that was even more strident. In the column, dated November 8th, he wrote that all self-respecting citizens of the world—upon learning the truth—will learn why members of Group B grow to hate members of Group A and view them as "the animals that they are." He urged student members of Group B to stand up to student members of Religion A, and to use "whatever means might be necessary" to uphold the honor of Religion B.

The next day, Alistaire was informed that his column would be discontinued. He resigned from the *Daily Explorer* staff and proceeded to post all his Abscella-related columns on a new blog site, which was situated on the university server. He was determined to continue writing articles, and planned to "publish" them on his blog.

Two days later, a fundamentalist member of Religion A shot at a group of western tourists in Abscella, killing 25 and injuring 32 others. On November 12th, three fundamentalist members of Religion B strapped explosives to their bodies and entered a shopping mall in a crowded commercial area of Abscella populated almost exclusively by members of Religion A. The explosives were detonated, and hundreds of people were killed. On campus, several fights broke out among students from the two groups, and a number of students were arrested.

On November 14th, Alistaire's cousin Georgina—who attended Sir Francis Drake High School—was caught downloading and printing Alistaire's November 8th article. She was suspended for three days under a school policy that prohibited "the possession and/or dissemination of hate-related literature in school."

On November 15th, Alistaire wrote a new "column," which was clearly his most strident and emotional piece to date. In powerful and highly articulate prose, he wrote approvingly of the suicide bombers and called their actions "an integral part of our holy war against a people of unacceptable moral character who practice a religion of depravity." He urged members of Religion B "wherever in the world they might be located, to fight ceaselessly until our land has been ethnically and religiously cleansed and our temple is rebuilt."

After receiving numerous complaints, the campus network administrator notified Alistaire that—pursuant to the university's acceptable use policy—his Internet access privileges would be suspended for the year and his blog site would be taken down. But before it could be taken down, self-styled "computer commandos" from Group A—infuriated after finding Alistaire's columns posted online—hacked into the university computer system and disrupted operations for several hours before all systems could be restored. During the time that the system was down, previous records for three student patients at the campus medical center were unobtainable, and incorrect medication was administered to all three. As a result, one of the students lapsed into a coma.

Predictably, numerous lawsuits were filed as a result of these events, under a variety of legal principles and theories.

A. In the free speech area, assume that Alistaire and Georgina—represented by the ACLU—file separate lawsuits against their respective educational institutions. Alistaire is prepared to argue that the university unconstitutionally restricted his speech on the basis of its content, and that no recognized exceptions apply. Georgina is prepared to argue that her First Amendment rights were violated, and further, that the district's hate speech policy is in and of itself unconstitutional. What contentions should be set forth by the respective parties? What result?

B. What if Alistare was a K–12 student and all these events (minus campus medical center incidents) took place at the high school level instead of at the university? Would the legal result be the same? Should the legal result be the same?

HEALY v. JAMES

408 U.S. 169, 92 S.Ct. 2338 (1972)

MR. JUSTICE POWELL delivered the opinion of the Court.

This case [arises] out of a denial by a state college of official recognition to a group of students who desired to form a local chapter of Students for a Democratic Society (SDS) * * *.

I.

We mention briefly at the outset the setting in 1969–1970. A climate of unrest prevailed on many college campuses in this country. There had been widespread civil disobedience on some campuses, accompanied by the seizure of buildings, vandalism, and arson. Some colleges had been shut down altogether, while at others files were looted and manuscripts destroyed. SDS chapters on some of those campuses had been a catalytic force during this period. Although the causes of campus disruption were many and complex, one of the prime consequences of such activities was the denial of the lawful exercise of First Amendment rights to the majority of students by the few. Indeed, many of the most cherished characteristics long associated with institutions of higher learning appeared to be endangered. Fortunately, with the passage of time, a calmer atmosphere and greater maturity now pervade our campuses. Yet, it was in this climate of earlier unrest that this case arose.

Petitioners are students attending Central Connecticut State College (CCSC), a state-supported institution of higher learning * * *.

II.

[T]he precedents of this Court leave no room for the view that, because of the acknowledged need for order, First Amendment protections should apply with less force on college compuses than in the community at large. Quite to the contrary, "[t]he vigilant protection of constitutional freedoms is nowhere more vital than in the community of American schools." The college classroom with its surrounding environs is peculiarly the "marketplace of ideas," and we break no new constitutional ground in reaffirming this Nation's dedication to safeguarding academic freedom.

Among the rights protected by the First Amendment is the right of individuals to associate to further their personal beliefs. While the freedom of association is not explicitly set out in the Amendment, it has long been held to be implicit in the freedoms of speech, assembly, and petition. There can be no doubt that denial of official recognition, without justification, to college organizations burdens or abridges that associational right. The primary impediment to free association flowing from nonrecognition is the denial of use of campus facilities for meetings and other appropriate purposes. * * *

Petitioners' associational interests also were circumscribed by the denial of the use of campus bulletin boards and the school newspaper. * * * Such impediments cannot be viewed as insubstantial.

* * * [Also, i]t is to be remembered that the effect of the College's denial of recognition was a form of prior restraint. * * * While a college has a legitimate interest in preventing disruption on the campus, which under circumstances requiring the safeguarding of that interest may justify such restraint, a "heavy burden" rests on the college to demonstrate the appropriateness of that action.

III.

* * * [D]iscounting the existence of a cognizable First Amendment interest and misplacing the burden of proof—require that the judgments below be reversed. But we are unable to conclude that no basis exists upon which nonrecognition might be appropriate. Indeed, based on a reasonable reading of the ambiguous facts of this case, there appears to be at least one potentially acceptable ground for a denial of recognition. Because of this ambiguous state of the record we conclude that the case should be remanded and, in an effort to provide guidance to the lower courts upon reconsideration, it is appropriate to discuss the several bases of President

James' decision. Four possible justifications for nonrecognition, all closely related, might be derived from the record and his statements. Three of those grounds are inadequate to substantiate his decision: a fourth, however, has merit.

A.

From the outset the controversy in this case has centered in large measure around the relationship, if any, between petitioners' group and the National SDS. * * *

Although this precise issue has not come before the Court heretofore, the Court has consistently disapproved governmental action imposing criminal sanctions or denying rights and privileges solely because of a citizen's association with an unpopular organization. * * *

Students for a Democratic Society, as conceded by the College and the lower courts, is loosely organized, having various factions and promoting a number of diverse social and political views only some of which call for unlawful action. Not only did petitioners proclaim their complete independence from this organization, but they also indicated that they shared only some of the beliefs its leaders have expressed. On this record it is clear that the relationship was not an adequate ground for the denial of recognition.

B.

Having concluded that petitioners were affiliated with, or at least retained an affinity for, National SDS, President James attributed what he believed to be the philosophy of that organization to the local group. He characterized the petitioning group as adhering to "some of the major tenets of the national organization," including a philosophy of violence and disruption. Understandably, he found that philosophy abhorrent. In an article signed by President James in an alumni periodical, and made a part of the record below, he announced his unwillingness to "sanction an organization that openly advocates the destruction of the very ideals and freedoms upon which the academic life is founded." He further emphasized that the petitioners' "philosophies" were "counter to the official policy of the college."

The mere disagreement of the President with the group's philosophy affords no reason to deny it recognition. As repugnant as these views may have been, especially to one with President James' responsibility, the mere expression of them would not justify the denial of First Amendment rights. Whether petitioners did in fact advocate a philosophy of 'destruction' thus becomes immaterial. The College, acting here as the instrumentality of the State, may not restrict speech or association simply because it finds the views expressed by any group to be abhorrent. * * *

C.

As the litigation progressed in the District Court, a third rationale for President James' decision—beyond the questions of affiliation and philosophy—began to emerge. His second statement, issued after the court-ordered hearing, indicates that he based rejection on a conclusion that this particular group would be a "disruptive influence at CCSC." Associational activities need not be tolerated where they infringe reasonable campus rules, interrupt classes, or substantially interfere with the opportunity of other students to obtain an education.

The "Student Bill of Rights" at CCSC, upon which great emphasis was placed by the President, draws precisely this distinction between advocacy and action. * * *

* * * [Yet there] was no substantial evidence that these particular individuals acting together would constitute a disruptive force on campus. Therefore, insofar as nonrecognition flowed from such fears, it constituted little more than the sort of "undifferentiated fear or apprehension of disturbance [which] is not enough to overcome the right to freedom of expression." *Tinker v. Des Moines Independent School District*, 393 U.S. at 508.

D.

These same references in the record to the group's equivocation regarding how it might respond to "issues of violence" and whether it could ever "envision . . . interrupting a class," suggest a fourth possible reason why recognition might have been denied to these petitioners. These remarks might well have been read as announcing petitioners' unwillingness to be bound by reasonable school rules governing conduct.

[T]he critical line for First Amendment purposes must be drawn between advocacy, which is entitled to full protection, and action, which is not. Petitioners may, if they so choose, preach the propriety of amending or even doing away with any or all campus regulations. They may not, however, undertake to flout these rules. * * *

Just as in the community at large, reasonable regulations with respect to the time, the place, and the manner in which student groups conduct their speech-related activities must be respected. A college administration may impose a requirement, such as may have been imposed in this case, that a group seeking official recognition affirm in advance its willingness to adhere to reasonable campus law. Such a requirement does not impose an impermissible condition on the students' associational rights. Their freedom to speak out, to assemble, or to petition for changes in school rules is in no sense infringed. It merely constitutes an agreement to conform with reasonable standards respecting conduct. This is a minimal requirement, in the interest of the entire academic community, of any group seeking the privilege of official recognition.

    * * *

IV.

We think the above discussion establishes the appropriate framework for consideration of petitioners' request for campus recognition. Because respondents failed to accord due recognition to First Amendment principles, the judgments below approving respondents' denial of recognition must be reversed. Since we cannot conclude from this record that petitioners were willing to abide by reasonable campus rules and regulations, we order the case remanded for reconsideration. We note, in so holding, that the wide latitude accorded by the Constitution to the freedoms of expression and association is not without its costs in terms of the risk to the maintenance of civility and an ordered society. Indeed, this latitude often has resulted, on the campus and elsewhere, in the infringement of the rights of others. Though we deplore the tendency of some to abuse the very constitutional privileges they invoke, and although the infringement of rights of others certainly should not be tolerated, we reaffirm this Court's dedication to the principles of the Bill of Rights upon which our vigorous and free society is founded.

Reversed and remanded.

NOTES

1. It is important to note the references by the Court to the decision in *Tinker*, delivered only three years earlier, in 1969. Many have come to view *Healy* as the higher education version of the *Tinker* decision.

2. As has been the case in K–12 education, the most controversial student groups at the higher education level over time have not been the political student groups per se, but the religious student groups and the gay student groups. The U.S. Supreme Court addressed the nature and extent of the rights of religious student groups on college and university campuses in *Rosenberger,* the decision that follows.

ROSENBERGER v. RECTOR & VISITORS OF UNIV. OF VA.

515 U.S. 819, 115 S.Ct. 2510 (1995)

JUSTICE KENNEDY delivered the opinion of the Court.

The University of Virginia, an instrumentality of the Commonwealth for which it is named and thus bound by the First and Fourteenth Amendments, authorizes the payment of outside contractors for the printing costs of a variety of student publications. It withheld any authorization for payments on behalf of petitioners for the sole reason that their student paper "primarily promotes or manifests a particular belie[f] in or about a deity or an ultimate reality." That the paper did promote or manifest views within the defined exclusion seems plain enough. The challenge is to the University's regulation and its denial of authorization, the case raising issues under the Speech and Establishment Clauses of the First Amendment.

I.

* * *

Before a student group is eligible to submit bills from its outside contractors for payment by the fund described below, it must become a "Contracted Independent Organization" (CIO). * * *

Petitioners' organization, Wide Awake Productions (WAP), qualified as a CIO. Formed by petitioner Ronald Rosenberger and other undergraduates in 1990, WAP was established "[t]o publish a magazine of philosophical and religious expression," "[t]o facilitate discussion which fosters an atmosphere of sensitivity to and tolerance of Christian viewpoints," and "[t]o provide a unifying focus for Christians of multicultural backgrounds." WAP publishes Wide Awake: A Christian Perspective at the University of Virginia. The paper's Christian viewpoint was evident from the first issue, in which its editors wrote that the journal "offers a Christian perspective on both personal and community issues, especially those relevant to college students at the University of Virginia." The editors committed the paper to a two-fold mission: "to challenge Christians to live, in word and deed, according to the faith they proclaim and to encourage students to consider what a personal relationship with Jesus Christ means." The first issue had articles about racism, crisis pregnancy, stress, prayer, C.S. Lewis' ideas about evil and free will, and reviews of religious music. In the next two issues, Wide Awake featured stories about homosexuality, Christian missionary work, and eating disorders, as well as music reviews and interviews with University professors. Each page of Wide Awake, and the end of each article or review, is marked by a cross. The advertisements carried in Wide Awake also reveal the Christian perspective of the journal. For the most part, the advertisers are churches, centers for Christian study, or Christian bookstores. By June 1992, WAP had distributed about 5,000 copies of Wide Awake to University students, free of charge.

* * *

A few months after being given CIO status, WAP requested the SAF to pay its printer $5,862 for the costs of printing its newspaper. The Appropriations Committee of the Student Council denied WAP's request on the ground that Wide Awake was a "religious activity" within the meaning of the Guidelines, *i.e.,* that the newspaper "promote[d] or manifest[ed] a particular belie[f] in or about a deity or an ultimate reality." It made its determination after examining the first issue. WAP appealed the denial to the full Student Council, contending that WAP met all the applicable Guidelines and that denial of SAF support on the basis of the magazine's religious perspective violated the Constitution. The appeal was denied without further comment, and WAP appealed to the next level, the Student Activities Committee. In a letter signed by the Dean of Students, the committee sustained the denial of funding.

Having no further recourse within the University structure, WAP, Wide Awake, and three of its editors and members filed suit in the United States District Court for the Western District of Virginia * * *.

* * * They alleged that refusal to authorize payment of the printing costs of the publication, solely on the basis of its religious editorial viewpoint, violated their rights to freedom of speech and press, to the free exercise of religion, and to equal protection of the law. * * *

II.

It is axiomatic that the government may not regulate speech based on its substantive content or the message it conveys. Other principles follow from this precept. In the realm of private speech or expression, government regulation may not favor one speaker over another. Discrimination against speech because of its message is presumed to be unconstitutional. These rules informed our determination that the government offends the First Amendment when it imposes financial burdens on certain speakers based on the content of their expression. When the government targets not subject matter, but particular views taken by speakers on a subject, the violation of the First Amendment is all the more blatant. Viewpoint discrimination is thus an egregious form of content discrimination. The government must abstain from regulating speech when the specific motivating ideology or the opinion or perspective of the speaker is the rationale for the restriction.

These principles provide the framework forbidding the State to exercise viewpoint discrimination, even when the limited public forum is one of its own creation. * * * The necessities of confining a forum to the limited and legitimate purposes for which it was created may justify the State in reserving it for certain groups or for the discussion of certain topics. Once it has opened a limited forum, however, the State must respect the lawful boundaries it has itself set. The State may not exclude speech where its distinction is not "reasonable in light of the purpose served by the forum," nor may it discriminate against speech on the basis of its viewpoint. Thus, in determining whether the State is acting to preserve the limits of the forum it has created so that the exclusion of a class of speech is legitimate, we have observed a distinction between, on the one hand, content discrimination, which may be permissible if it preserves the purposes of that limited forum, and, on the other hand, viewpoint discrimination, which is presumed impermissible when directed against speech otherwise within the forum's limitations.

The SAF is a forum more in a metaphysical than in a spatial or geographic sense, but the same principles are applicable. The most recent and most apposite case is our decision in *Lamb's Chapel*. There, a school district had opened school facilities for use after school hours by community groups for a wide variety of social, civic, and recreational purposes. The district, however, had enacted a formal policy against opening facilities to groups for religious purposes. Invoking its policy, the district rejected a request from a group desiring to show a film series addressing various child-rearing questions from a "Christian perspective." There was no indication in the record in *Lamb's Chapel* that the request to use the school facilities was "denied, for any reason other than the fact that the presentation would have been from a religious perspective." Our conclusion was unanimous: "[I]t discriminates on the basis of viewpoint to permit school property to be used for the presentation of all views about family issues and childrearing except those dealing with the subject matter from a religious standpoint."

The University does acknowledge (as it must in light of our precedents) that "ideologically driven attempts to suppress a particular point of view are presumptively unconstitutional in funding, as in other contexts," but insists that this case does not present that issue because the Guidelines draw lines based on content, not viewpoint. As we have noted, discrimination against one set of views or ideas is but a subset or particular instance of the more general phenomenon of content discrimination. And, it must be acknowledged, the distinction is not a precise one. It is, in a sense, something of an understatement to speak of religious thought and discussion as just a viewpoint, as distinct from a comprehensive body of thought. The nature of our origins and destiny and their dependence upon the existence of a divine being have been subjects of philosophic inquiry throughout human history. We conclude, nonetheless, that here, as in *Lamb's Chapel,* viewpoint discrimination is the proper way to interpret the University's objections to Wide Awake. By the very terms of the SAF prohibition, the University does not exclude religion as a subject matter but selects for disfavored treatment those student journalistic efforts with religious editorial viewpoints. Religion may be a vast area of inquiry, but it also provides, as it did here, a specific premise, a perspective, a standpoint from which a variety of subjects may be discussed and considered. The prohibited perspective, not the general subject matter, resulted in the refusal to make third-party payments, for the subjects discussed were otherwise within the approved category of publications.

The dissent's assertion that no viewpoint discrimination occurs because the Guidelines discriminate against an entire class of viewpoints reflects an insupportable assumption that all debate is bipolar and that antireligious speech is the only response to religious speech. Our understanding of the complex and multifaceted nature of public discourse has not embraced such a contrived description of the marketplace of ideas. If the topic of debate is, for example, racism, then exclusion of several views on that problem is just as offensive to the First Amendment as exclusion of only one. It is as objectionable to exclude both a theistic and an atheistic perspective on the debate as it is to exclude one, the other, or yet another political, economic, or social viewpoint. The dissent's declaration that debate is not skewed so long as multiple voices are silenced is simply wrong; the debate is skewed in multiple ways.

* * *

Vital First Amendment speech principles are at stake here. The first danger to liberty lies in granting the State the power to examine publications to determine whether or not they are based on some ultimate idea and, if so, for the State to classify them. The second, and corollary, danger is to speech from the chilling of individual thought and expression. That danger is especially real in the University setting, where the State acts against a background and tradition of thought and experiment that is at the center of our intellectual and philosophic tradition. See *Healy v. James*, 408 U.S. 169, 180–181 (1972). In ancient Athens, and, as Europe entered into a new period of intellectual awakening, in places like Bologna, Oxford, and Paris, universities began as voluntary and spontaneous assemblages or concourses for students to speak and to write and to learn. The quality and creative power of student intellectual life to this day remains a vital measure of a school's influence and attainment. For the University, by regulation, to cast disapproval on particular viewpoints of its students risks the suppression of free speech and creative inquiry in one of the vital centers for the Nation's intellectual life, its college and university campuses.

The Guideline invoked by the University to deny third-party contractor payments on behalf of WAP effects a sweeping restriction on student thought and student inquiry in the context of University sponsored publications. The prohibition on funding on behalf of publications that "primarily promot[e] or manifes[t] a particular belie[f] in or about a deity or an ultimate reality," in its ordinary and commonsense meaning, has a vast potential reach. The term "promotes" as used here would comprehend any writing advocating a philosophic position that rests upon a belief in a deity or ultimate reality. And the term "manifests" would bring within the scope of the prohibition any writing that is explicable as resting upon a premise that presupposes the existence of a deity or ultimate reality. Were the prohibition applied with much vigor at all, it would bar funding of essays by hypothetical student contributors named Plato, Spinoza, and Descartes. And if the regulation covers, as the University says it does, those student journalistic efforts that primarily manifest or promote a belief that there is no deity and no ultimate reality, then undergraduates named Karl Marx, Bertrand Russell, and Jean–Paul Sartre would likewise have some of their major essays excluded from student publications. If any manifestation of beliefs in first principles disqualifies the writing, as seems to be the case, it is indeed difficult to name renowned thinkers whose writings would be accepted, save perhaps for articles disclaiming all connection to their ultimate philosophy. Plato could contrive perhaps to submit an acceptable essay on making pasta or peanut butter cookies, provided he did not point out their (necessary) imperfections.

Based on the principles we have discussed, we hold that the regulation invoked to deny SAF support, both in its terms and in its application to these petitioners, is a denial of their right of free speech guaranteed by the First Amendment. It remains to be considered whether the violation following from the University's action is excused by the necessity of complying with the Constitution's prohibition against state establishment of religion. * * *

To obey the Establishment Clause, it was not necessary for the University to deny eligibility to student publications because of their viewpoint. The neutrality commanded of the State by the separate Clauses of the First Amendment was compromised by the University's course of action. The viewpoint discrimination inherent in the University's regulation required public officials to scan and interpret student publications to discern their underlying philosophic assumptions respecting religious theory and belief. That course of action was a denial of the right of free speech and would risk fostering a pervasive bias or hostility to religion, which could undermine the very neutrality the Establishment Clause requires. There is no Establishment Clause violation in the University's honoring its duties under the Free Speech Clause.

The judgment of the Court of Appeals must be, and is, reversed.

It is so ordered.

HUSAIN v. SPRINGER

494 F.3d 108 (2d Cir. 2007)

CALABRESI, CIRCUIT JUDGE:

In this appeal, we consider whether a public college president's decision to cancel a student government election because of content published in a school newspaper violates the First Amendment rights of the student journalists who produce that publication. We conclude that, in the circumstances presented in this case, the school administrator's actions did violate the First Amendment. * * *

BACKGROUND

I. *Events Giving Rise to the Lawsuit*

A. *The School*

The school newspaper at issue was produced by students at the College of Staten Island ("CSI" or the "College"), which is part of the City University of New York ("CUNY") system. Under state law, the CUNY Board of Trustees (the "CUNY Board") may impose mandatory student activity fees to support student activities and regulate the expenditure of those funds. At all times relevant to this lawsuit, CSI students, as a condition for registering for classes, were required to pay mandatory student activity fees in an amount set by the CUNY Board. * * *

B. *Publications Funded by Student Activity Fees at CSI*

CSI allocates student activity fees to fund a number of student publications, including the one at issue in this litigation, the *College Voice*. The *College Voice* is a student newspaper and political journal that is primarily paid for from student activity fees.[1] The *College Voice* publishes

---

1. The May 1997 issue of the *College Voice,* which is at the heart of this litigation, was funded entirely by student activity fees.

articles and editorials on a wide range of topics, including pieces on CSI, CUNY, local, national, and international affairs, reviews, and poetry. The editors of the *College Voice* choose the material that the newspaper publishes without any supervision or prior review by anyone other than the editors and staff of the newspaper. (The newspaper has a faculty advisor who does not review or approve articles prior to publication.) Participation in the *College Voice* is entirely extracurricular, and the editors and staff do not receive any academic credit for working on the newspaper.

In addition to the *College Voice,* CSI also funds a college radio station and other student media outlets using the student activity fees. The other outlets include the *Banner,* which the student government designated the official campus newspaper, a literary magazine named *The Third Rail,* and various other publications. CUNY and CSI have not placed any restrictions on the subjects that may be covered in the *College Voice* or the *Banner.* These newspapers are not prohibited from publishing articles or editorials expressing opinions or endorsing candidates in student elections. There is no rule or regulation prohibiting or restricting the editors or staff members of the *College Voice,* or other publications, from running for student government positions or from endorsing themselves.

According to the plaintiffs' complaint, in the early 1990s the *College Voice* was designated the official college newspaper of CSI. Several years before the Spring 1997 election, the editors of the *College Voice* began publishing articles that reflected a generally "left-wing" perspective on campus, local, national, and international political issues. Many of the articles and editorials were critical of CUNY and CSI administration officials. These positions prompted some students, who disagreed with the *College Voice*'s editorial policy, to form a second student newspaper at CSI called the *Banner.* The CSI Student Government subsequently revoked *College Voice*'s designation as the "official" CSI student newspaper and gave that status to the *Banner.* In Spring 1997, the *Banner* was the official CSI student newspaper.

C. The Spring 1997 Election

i. The Student Union Slate

In the Fall 1996 term, some CSI students concerned about various student life issues at CSI and CUNY began meeting and formed an organization they called the "Student Union." During the student government elections in the Spring 1997 semester, the Student Union ran a slate of candidates for a total of 37 positions in the Student Senate and other governing organizations. Several editors and staff members of the *College Voice,* including some of the plaintiffs, were among the candidates running on the Student Union slate. The only opposing slate was "Students for Students" ("SFS"), which was composed mainly of incumbent members of the Student Senate seeking re-election. Almost all of the candidates in the Spring 1997 election were affiliated with either the Student Union or SFS slates. * * *

ii.   May 1997 Issue of the College Voice

Prior to the Spring 1997 election, the *College Voice* decided to endorse the Student Union slate. By agreement within the *College Voice* editorial board, the decision about whether or not to endorse candidates, which candidates to endorse if the newspaper decided to do so, and what content to run in the issue was to be made by the members of the board that were not candidates in the Spring 1997 election. The *College Voice* chose to publish a special election issue that the editors intended to have distributed on April 28, 1997, two days before the beginning of the voting period. The timing was a significant aspect of the *College Voice*'s message. An editor of the *College Voice* explained, "an important part [of publication] is not just the content of the newspaper, but timing and placement. And we felt that the timing a few days before the election would be the most opportune time to influence the election."

The May 1997 issue of the *College Voice* consisted of twenty-eight pages. The front page displayed a group photograph of twelve of the candidates running on the Student Union slate under a bold headline, "VOTE STUDENT UNION!" The rear cover of the newspaper featured only the Student Union's twelve-point platform. Page two of the issue contained an editorial entitled "Vote Student Union." Various candidates' platform statements were printed on pages six and seven. The issue also included two articles by two of the plaintiffs criticizing the incumbent members of the student government who were running on the SFS slate, and two articles, one by a plaintiff and the other by a non-plaintiff, criticizing the CUNY chancellor. The remainder of the issue was devoted to articles on a wide variety of other matters, including pieces on international affairs, a New York City mayoral candidate forum, a work requirement for students receiving public assistance, campus security, the history of CUNY, the CUNY faculty union, and tenants' rights. It also included music reviews and poetry.

The *Banner* also published an election issue prior to the May 1997 election that included platform statements from candidates running on both the Student Union and the SFS slates.

iii.   The Actions of the Student Government and CSI Administration

* * * After the *College Voice* was delivered to campus, Andre Woods, an incumbent member of the Student Senate running for re-election on the SFS slate, filed a complaint with the [Student Elections Review Committee (SERC)]. His complaint alleged that the May 1997 issue of the *College Voice* violated Election Rule 2, which provided that "[t]he campus newspaper may not be used as posters on walls, bulletin boards, etc. and may not be used as a means to distribute campaign flyers." * * *

The SERC considered Woods's complaint regarding the alleged Rule 2 violations at a meeting on April 30, 1997, and declined to sustain it. But the SERC passed a resolution declaring that "[t]he *College Voice* used student activity fee funds allocated to promote the election of particular candidates affiliated with the *College Voice*" and adjourned until the next day to consider further action on the complaint. On May 1, the SERC met again and passed a motion "to postpone the election and to consider those ballots cast null and void as it is the committee's decision that the electoral process had been compromised beyond its ability to be fair to all candidates." * * *

iv.   President Springer's Nullification of the Election

On May 6, 1997, President Springer issued a memorandum announcing her decision to affirm the SERC's nullification of the election because of the contents of the May 1997 issue of the *College Voice*.

* * *

DISCUSSION

I. President Springer Violated Plaintiffs' First Amendment Rights

A.   Scope of First Amendment Rights for Student Media Outlets, and the Student Journalists who Produce Them, at Public Universities

Courts have long recognized that student media outlets at public universities, and the student journalists who produce those outlets, are entitled to strong First Amendment protection. These rights stem from courts' recognition that such student media outlets generally operate as "limited public fora," within which schools may not disfavor speech on the basis of viewpoint.

A limited public forum is "is created when the State 'opens a non-public forum but limits the expressive activity to certain kinds of speakers or to the discussion of certain subjects.' ... In limited public fora, the government may make reasonable, viewpoint-neutral rules governing the content of speech allowed." *Peck v. Baldwinsville Cent. Sch. Dist.* (2d Cir. 2005). Once the state has created a limited public forum, however, it must respect the boundaries that it has set. It may not "exclude speech where its distinction is not reasonable in light of the purpose served by the forum, nor may it discriminate against speech on the basis of its viewpoint." *Rosenberger v. Rector & Visitors of the Univ. of Va.* * * *

[A]lthough the treatment of forum analysis with respect to student media outlets at public universities has differed in some respects in the various circuits, *all* the circuits that have considered the issue have determined that, at the very least, when a public university creates or subsidizes a student newspaper and imposes no *ex ante* restrictions on the content that the newspaper may contain, neither the school nor its officials may interfere with the viewpoints expressed in the publication without running afoul of the First Amendment.[a]

---

a. The Court noted a split between the Circuits on certain aspects of the limited public forum analysis:

We agree that, at a minimum, when a public university establishes a student media outlet and requires no initial restrictions on content, it may not censor, retaliate, or otherwise chill that outlet's speech, or the speech of the student journalists who produce it, on the basis of content or viewpoints expressed through that outlet. This holding is fully consistent with and, indeed, substantially follows from, our decisions, and those of the Supreme Court, in other cases addressing limited public fora.

* * *

B.   *Springer's Actions Violated Plaintiffs' First Amendment Rights*
i.   *The College Voice Constituted a Limited Public Forum*

* * * [I]t is clear that the *College Voice* was a limited public forum in which (subject always to the existence of a compelling state interest such as the maintenance of public order) the only permissible restriction was on the speakers who could participate. CSI, through the student government, chartered the *College Voice* and provided the newspaper with most of its funding through the allocation of student activity fees. The defendants agree that neither CUNY nor CSI had placed any restrictions on the subjects that could be covered in the *College Voice* or other student publications. Indeed, in earlier litigation before this court, CUNY "expressly disclaim[ed] any right of the institution to control student publications, such as those financed through student activity fees."

Accordingly, the policy and practice of CSI demonstrate that the school intended to open the pages of the *College Voice* to "indiscriminate use" by the students who serve as its contributors and editors, and that it thereby created a public forum in which the only limit involved the nature of permissible speakers. Because the *College Voice* operated as such a forum, CSI and its officials could not, under the First Amendment, take adverse action against the student newspaper, including engaging in

---

The Fourth, Fifth, and Eighth Circuits * * * have adopted the position that the establishment of a student media outlet, in essence, necessarily involves the creation of a limited public forum where the only restraint is on the speakers who can participate (i.e., students) and where there can be no restrictions on the content of the outlet except with respect to content that threatens the maintenance of order at the university. Two other circuits, while also recognizing that student media outlets often enjoy First Amendment protection from interference by school administrators, have taken a less expansive view. The Sixth and Seventh Circuits agree that the establishment of a student media outlet *can* create a limited public forum but have concluded that the scope of that forum can be restricted by the school. In other words, these courts do not consider the creation of a student media outlet as *categorically* involving the creation of a limited public forum within which students may speak on essentially any subject without fear of reprisal, but rather look to the *context* of the public university's treatment of a student media outlet, including its intent in creating the outlet and practices with respect to the outlet, in order to determine what First Amendment protection the outlet, and those that participate in it, receive. 494 F.3d at 123–124.

Yet the Court found that for purposes of its analysis in the case at hand, given its conclusion that the limited public forum doctrine did in fact apply, it "need not decide in this case which of the two approaches embraced by other circuits governs evaluations of the First Amendment protections afforded student media outlets at public colleges":

Because CUNY had a policy in which it expressly placed no limits on the contents of student publications, under even the less protective contextual approach of the Sixth and Seventh Circuits, it is clear that the *College Voice* was a limited public forum in which there were no restrictions on the subjects that could be addressed. *Id.* at 124–125.

conduct designed to chill the speech contained in future editions, on the basis of the views expressed in the publication unless such action served a compelling government interest. The defendants have offered no arguments that the nullification of the May 1997 election advanced any such interest, and we can conceive of no interest of sufficient import to justify President Springer's actions given the First Amendment concerns involved.

ii. President Springer Canceled the Spring 1997 Election Because of the Viewpoint Expressed in the May 1997 Issue of the College Voice * * *

Remarks and testimony made by President Springer reveal that it was the *College Voice*'s viewpoint on the election-expressed in both the substance of its content and in the manner in which that content was presented-that led her to nullify the election. First, in announcing her decision, Springer noted the aspects of the May 1997 issue of the *College Voice* that caused her to nullify the initial Spring 1997 election included its "cover [that] boldly encourage [ed] a vote for a particular slate of candidates" and her assessment that "much of the issue was devoted to supporting an endorsed slate of candidates."

President Springer's testimony also shows that she nullified the election because of the viewpoint expressed by the *College Voice.* * * * [The] nullification * * * was premised on two types of viewpoint discrimination relating to the subject of student elections. First, Springer's action was driven by her belief that only one perspective was acceptable for speech on student elections in a student newspaper-a viewpoint that reflected a balanced view of the candidates-and that contrary views-including that certain candidates should be elected-were inappropriate. Second, Springer's testimony reveals that her nullification of the initial election was premised on her belief that the *College Voice*'s view as to the importance of electing the Student Union slate, as reflected in the presentation of the content promoting those candidates, was improper and should be excluded from the limited public forum of the student newspaper. * * *

Such viewpoint discrimination is clearly impermissible in a limited public forum open to unrestricted speech on campaigns, candidates, and issues affecting CUNY. Indeed, as the Supreme Court and this court have repeatedly emphasized, once a state institution opens a limited forum to speech on a particular topic, it may not act against a speaker in that forum on the basis of views they express on that topic. * * *

iii. The Defendants' Arguments For Why President Springer's Actions Did Not Violate the First Amendment Are Unavailing

a. The Nullification of the Election Created a Chilling Effect and Thus Violated the First Amendment

Defendants assert that any harm the plaintiffs may have suffered as a result of the nullification of the election does not rise to the level of cognizable constitutional injury. This argument is entirely without merit. When a state university official takes retaliatory action against a newspaper for publishing certain content in an effort to force the newspaper to refrain from publishing that or similar content in the future, the official's action creates a chilling effect which gives rise to a First Amendment injury. Here, the record establishes that Springer's nullification of the election created just such a chilling effect.

As the district court explained, "there was a concrete action taken in nullifying a student election because of a publication supportive of a particular slate of candidates which won the election. The threat or chill that plaintiffs assert they felt regarding future issues of the newspapers is not merely subjective, but has already been experienced." In the wake of President Springer's actions in Spring 1997, the *College Voice* scaled back its coverage of elections and reduced the prominence and extent of its candidate endorsements in an effort to avoid provoking another election nullification. * * *

b. The May 1997 Issue Did Not Constitute Candidate Speech Nor Did Its Content Violate Applicable Election Rules

The defendants contend, however, that the front and back covers of the May 1997 issue of the *College Voice,* as well as the candidate position statements included in the inside of the issue, did not constitute the newspaper's speech, but rather was the speech of the candidates themselves. The defendants argue that President Springer nullified the election because of this method of *candidate* speech, which, they assert, violated the governing election rules by essentially creating 5,000 flyers for the Student Union candidates. This claim is unconvincing. * * * [T]he choice to speak in the way challenged by the defendants was not made by any of the candidates. * * *

In any event, the *College Voice*'s publication of the election-related content in the May 1997 issue did not violate any germane election rules. The two rules that the defendants assert justified President Springer's actions are Elections Rules 2 and 5. Rule 2 provided: "The campus newspaper may not be used as posters on walls, bulletin boards, etc. and may not be used as a means to distribute campaign flyers." Rule 5 stated: "The Student Government will be glad to make you 30 copies of your stamped and approved poster or flyer. All candidates must remove their election materials from the designated areas after the election is over." As the district court clearly and correctly explained, neither of these rules precluded the *College Voice* from publishing the election-related content in its May 1997 issue. * * *

c. President Springer's Actions Cannot Be Justified as Necessary to Ensure Viewpoint Neutrality in the Administration CSI's Student Activity Fees Fund

* * * The defendants are correct that when a state college implements a mandatory student activity fee, its procedure for allocating the

funds that fee generates must be viewpoint neutral. This is totally different from, and in no way means, that the college has a duty to ensure that the positions expressed by the recipients of the fees reflect a balance of viewpoints. Far from it; as long as the availability of the funds to student groups *is not restricted based on their viewpoint,* the college's administration of a mandatory student activity fee complies with the neutrality requirement demanded by the First Amendment. *See Board of Regents v. Southworth.* * * *

* * *

We conclude that President Springer's nullification of the Spring 1997 election violated the plaintiffs' First Amendment rights. * * *

F.   HATE–RELATED SPEECH CONTROVERSIES AT THE HIGHER EDUCATION LEVEL

PROBLEM 15: HATE-RELATED WEB SITE ACTIVITY

Consider the efficacy of the following hypothetical policy, designed to be implemented at a major public university. In light of your legal analysis, would you recommend such a policy? Why? Alternatively, could you support a modified version of this bill? If so, what modifications might be appropriate?

A.   The Regents of the University are concerned about the corrosive effects of hate-related Web sites and believe that such expression in public settings is another form of obscenity, equally offensive and inappropriate.

B.   The purpose of this policy is to prohibit Web-based expression—created and fostered by Web site owners—that (a) includes slurs based on the race, ethnicity, religion, gender, gender identity, and/or sexual orientation of persons or groups; and (b) contains extensive deprecatory remarks and/or highly offensive visual imagery regarding the alleged inferiority of such persons or groups.

C.   In determining whether online expression constitutes *hate-related Web site activity* within the meaning of this policy, campus officials will inquire whether:

1.   the average person applying contemporary community standards would find that the site, taken as a whole, appeals to the bigoted and malevolent interest;

2.   the site embraces, encourages, or sets forth—in an aggressive and patently offensive way—propaganda, invective, and/or activity designed to intimidate others and subject them to hatred; and

3.   taken as a whole, the site lacks serious literary, artistic, political, or scientific value.

DOE v. UNIVERSITY OF MICH.

721 F.Supp. 852 (E.D. Mich. 1989)

COHN, UNITED STATES DISTRICT JUDGE

* * * Recently, the University of Michigan at Ann Arbor (the University), a state-chartered university, adopted a Policy on Discrimination and Discriminatory Harassment of Students in the University Environment (the Policy) in an attempt to curb what the University's governing Board of Regents (Regents) viewed as a rising tide of racial intolerance and harassment on campus. The Policy prohibited individuals, under the penalty of sanctions, from "stigmatizing or victimizing" individuals or groups on the basis of race, ethnicity, religion, sex, sexual orientation, creed, national origin, ancestry, age, marital status, handicap or Vietnam-era veteran status. However laudable or appropriate an effort this may have been, the Court found that the Policy swept within its scope a significant amount of "verbal conduct" or "verbal behavior" which is unquestionably protected speech under the First Amendment. Accordingly, the Court granted plaintiff John Doe's (Doe) prayer for a permanent injunction as to those parts of the Policy restricting speech activity, but denied the injunction as to the Policy's regulation of physical conduct. The reasons follow.

II. FACTS GENERALLY

According to the University, in the last three years incidents of racism and racial harassment appeared to become increasingly frequent at the University. * * *

Following discussions with a national civil rights leader in March of 1987, the University adopted a six-point action plan to remedy the racial problems on campus. This included the adoption of "an anti-racial harassment policy ... as a component of the University's rules and regulations with appropriate sanctions specified."

* * *

III. THE UNIVERSITY OF MICHIGAN POLICY ON DISCRIMINATION AND DISCRIMINATORY HARASSMENT

A. *The Terms of the Policy*

The Policy established a three-tiered system whereby the degree of regulation was dependent on the location of the conduct at issue. The broadest range of speech and dialogue was "tolerated" in variously described public parts of the campus. Only an act of physical violence or destruction of property was considered sanctionable in these settings. Publications sponsored by the University such as the *Michigan Daily* and the *Michigan Review* were not subject to regulation. The conduct of students living in University housing is primarily governed by the standard provisions of individual leases, however the Policy appeared to apply in this setting as well. The Policy by its terms applied specifically to "[e]ducational and academic centers, such as classroom buildings, libraries, research laboratories, recreation and study centers[.]" In these areas, persons were subject to discipline for:

1. Any behavior, verbal or physical, that stigmatizes or victimizes an individual on the basis of race, ethnicity, religion, sex, sexual orientation, creed, national origin, ancestry, age, marital status, handicap or Vietnam-era veteran status, and that

   a. Involves an express or implied threat to an individual's academic efforts, employment, participation in University sponsored extra-curricular activities or personal safety; or

   b. Has the purpose or reasonably foreseeable effect of interfering with an individual's academic efforts, employment, participation in University sponsored extra-curricular activities or personal safety; or

   c. Creates an intimidating, hostile, or demeaning environment for educational pursuits, employment or participation in University sponsored extra-curricular activities.

2. Sexual advances, requests for sexual favors, and verbal or physical conduct that stigmatizes or victimizes an individual on the basis of sex or sexual orientation where such behavior:

   a. Involves an express or implied threat to an individual's academic efforts, employment, participation in University sponsored extra-curricular activities or personal safety; or

   b. Has the purpose or reasonably foreseeable effect of interfering with an individual's academic efforts, employment, participation in University sponsored extra-curricular activities or personal safety; or

   c. Creates an intimidating, hostile, or demeaning environment for educational pursuits, employment or participation in University sponsored extra-curricular activities.

On August 22, 1989, the University publicly announced, without prior notice to the Court or Doe, that it was withdrawing section 1(c) on the grounds that "a need exists for further explanation and clarification of [that section] of the policy." No reason was given why the analogous provision in paragraph 2(c) was allowed to stand.

The Policy by its terms recognizes that certain speech which might be considered in violation may not be sanctionable by stating: "The Office of the General Counsel will rule on any claim that conduct which is the subject of a formal hearing is constitutionally protected by the first amendment."

B. *Hearing Procedures*

Any member of the University community could initiate the process leading to sanctions by either filing a formal complaint with an appropriate University office or by seeking informal counseling with described University officials and support centers. * * *

C. *Sanctions*

The Policy provided for progressive discipline based on the severity of the violation. It stated that the University encouraged hearing panels to impose sanctions that include an educational element in order to sensitize the perpetrator to the harmfulness of his or her conduct. The Policy provided, however, that compulsory class attendance should not be imposed "in an attempt to change deeply held religious or moral convictions." Depending on the intent of the accused student, the effect of the conduct, and whether the accused student is a repeat offender, one or more of the following sanctions may be imposed: (1) formal reprimand; (2) community service; (3) class attendance; (4) restitution; (5) removal from University housing; (6) suspension from specific courses and activities; (7) suspension; (8) expulsion. The sanctions of suspension and expulsion could only be imposed for violent or dangerous acts, repeated offenses, or a willful failure to comply with a lesser sanction. The University President could set aside or lessen any sanction.

D. *Interpretive Guide*

Shortly after the promulgation of the policy in the fall of 1988, the University Office of Affirmative Action issued an interpretive guide (Guide) entitled *What Students Should Know about Discrimination and Discriminatory Harassment by Students in the University Environment.* The Guide purported to be an authoritative interpretation of the Policy and provided examples of sanctionable conduct. These included:

A flyer containing racist threats distributed in a residence hall.

Racist graffiti written on the door of an Asian student's study carrel.

A male student makes remarks in class like "Women just aren't as good in this field as men," thus creating a hostile learning atmosphere for female classmates.

Students in a residence hall have a floor party and invite everyone on their floor except one person because they think she might be a lesbian.

A black student is confronted and racially insulted by two white students in a cafeteria.

Male students leave pornographic pictures and jokes on the desk of a female graduate student.

Two men demand that their roommate in the residence hall move out and be tested for AIDS.

In addition, the Guide contained a separate section entitled "You are a harasser when" which contains the following examples of discriminatory conduct:

You exclude someone from a study group because that person is of a different race, sex, or ethnic origin than you are.

You tell jokes about gay men and lesbians.

Your student organization sponsors entertainment that includes a comedian who slurs Hispanics.

You display a confederate flag on the door of your room in the residence hall.

You laugh at a joke about someone in your class who stutters.

You make obscene telephone calls or send racist notes or computer messages.

You comment in a derogatory way about a particular person or group's physical appearance or sexual orientation, or their cultural origins, or religious beliefs.

It was not clear whether each of these actions would subject a student to sanctions, although the title of the section suggests that they would. It was also unclear why these additional examples were listed separately from those in the section entitled "What is Discriminatory Harassment."

According to the University, the Guide was withdrawn at an unknown date in the winter of 1989, because "the information in it was not accurate." The withdrawal had not been announced publicly as of the date this case was filed.

IV. STANDING

Doe is a psychology graduate student. His specialty is the field of biopsychology, which he describes as the interdisciplinary study of the biological bases of individual differences in personality traits and mental abilities. Doe said that certain controversial theories positing biologically-based differences between sexes and races might be perceived as "sexist" and "racist" by some students, and he feared that discussion of such theories might be sanctionable under the Policy. He asserted that his right to freely and openly discuss these theories was impermissibly chilled, and he requested that the Policy be declared unconstitutional and enjoined on the grounds of vagueness and overbreadth.

* * *

V. VAGUENESS AND OVERBREADTH
* * *

B. *Overbreadth*

1.

Doe claimed that the Policy was invalid because it was facially overbroad. It is fundamental that statutes regulating First Amendment activities must be narrowly drawn to address only the specific evil at hand. "Because First Amendment freedoms need breathing space to survive, government may regulate in the area only with narrow specificity." A law regulating speech will be deemed overbroad if it sweeps within its ambit a substantial amount of protected speech along with that which it may legitimately regulate.

The Supreme Court has consistently held that statutes punishing speech or conduct solely on the grounds that they are unseemly or offensive are unconstitutionally overbroad. * * * These cases stand generally for the proposition that the state may not prohibit broad classes of speech, some of which may indeed be legitimately regulable, if in so doing a substantial amount of constitutionally protected conduct is also prohibited. This was the fundamental infirmity of the Policy.

2.

The University repeatedly argued that the Policy did not apply to speech that is protected by the First Amendment. It urged the Court to disregard the Guide as "inaccurate" and look instead to "the manner in which the Policy has been interpreted and applied by those charged with its enforcement." However, as applied by the University over the past year, the Policy was consistently applied to reach protected speech.

On December 7, 1988, a complaint was filed against a graduate student in the School of Social Work alleging that he harassed students based on sexual orientation and sex. The basis for the sexual orientation charge was apparently that in a research class, the student openly stated his belief that homosexuality was a disease and that he intended to develop a counseling plan for changing gay clients to straight. He also related to other students that he had been counseling several of his gay patients accordingly. The student apparently had several heated discussions with his classmates over the validity and morality of his theory and program. On January 11, 1989, the Interim Policy Administrator wrote to the student informing him that following an investigation of the complaints, there was sufficient evidence to warrant a formal hearing on the charges of sex and sexual orientation harassment. A formal hearing on the charges was held on January 28, 1989. The hearing panel unanimously found that the student was guilty of sexual harassment but refused to convict him of harassment on the basis of sexual orientation. * * *

Although the student was not sanctioned over the allegations of sexual orientation harassment, the fact remains that the Policy Administrator—the authoritative voice of the University on these matters—saw no First Amendment problem in forcing the student to a hearing to answer for allegedly harassing statements made in the course of academic discussion and research. Moreover, there is no indication that had the hearing panel convicted rather than acquitted the student, the University would have interceded to protect the interests of academic freedom and freedom of speech.

A second case, which was informally resolved, also demonstrated that the University did not exempt statements made in the course of classroom academic discussions from the sanctions of the policy. On September 28, 1988, a complaint was filed against a student in an entrepreneurship class in the School of Business Administration for reading an allegedly homophobic limerick during a scheduled class public-speaking exercise which ridiculed a well known athlete for his presumed sexual orientation. The Policy Administrator was able to persuade the perpetrator to attend an educational "gay rap" session, write a letter of apology to the *Michigan Daily*, and apologize to his class and the matter was dropped. No discussion of the possibility that the limerick was protected speech appears in the file or in the Administrator's notes.

A third incident involved a comment made in the orientation session of a preclinical dentistry class. The class was widely regarded as one of the most difficult for second year dentistry students. To allay fears and concerns at the outset, the class was broken up into small sections to informally discuss anticipated problems. During the ensuing discussion, a student stated that "he had heard that minorities had a difficult time in the course and that he had heard that they were not treated fairly." A minority professor teaching the class filed a complaint on the grounds that the comment was unfair and hurt her chances for tenure. Following the filing of the complaint, the student was "counseled" about the existence of the policy and agreed to write a letter apologizing for making the comment without adequately verifying the allegation, which he said he had heard from his roommate, a black former dentistry student.

* * *

The manner in which these three complaints were handled demonstrated that the University considered serious comments made in the context of classroom discussion to be sanctionable under the Policy. The innocent intent of the speaker was apparently immaterial to whether a complaint would be pursued. Moreover, the Administrator generally failed to consider whether a comment was protected by the First Amendment before informing the accused student that a complaint had been filed. The Administrator instead attempted to persuade the accused student to accept "voluntary" sanctions. Behind this persuasion was, of course, the subtle threat that failure to accept such sanctions might result in a formal hearing. There is no evidence in the record that the Administrator ever declined to pursue a complaint through attempted mediation because the alleged harassing conduct was protected by the First Amendment. Nor is there evidence that the Administrator ever informed an accused harasser during mediation negotiations that the complained of conduct might be protected. The Administrator's manner of enforcing the Policy was constitutionally indistinguishable from a full blown prosecution. The University could not seriously argue that the policy was never interpreted to reach protected conduct. It is clear that the policy was overbroad both on its face and as applied.

C. *Vagueness*

Doe also urges that the policy be struck down on the grounds that it is impermissibly vague. A statute is unconstitutionally vague when "men of common intelligence must necessarily guess at its meaning." A statute must give adequate warning of the conduct which is to be prohibited and must set out explicit standards for those who apply it. "No one may be required at the peril of life, liberty or property to speculate as to the meaning of penal statutes. All are entitled to be informed as to what the State commands or forbids." These considerations apply with particular force where the challenged statute acts to inhibit freedoms affirmatively protected by the constitution. * * *

Looking at the plain language of the Policy, it was simply impossible to discern any limitation on its scope or any conceptual distinction between protected and unprotected conduct. The structure of the Policy was in two parts; one relates to cause and the other to effect. Both cause and effect must be present to state a prima facie violation of the Policy. The operative words in the cause section required that language must "stigmatize" or "victimize" an individual. However, both of these terms are general and elude precise definition. Moreover, it is clear that the fact that a statement may victimize or stigmatize an individual does not, in and of itself, strip it of protection under the accepted First Amendment tests.

The first of the "effects clauses" stated that in order to be sanctionable, the stigmatizing and victimizing statements had to "involve an express or implied threat to an individual's academic efforts, employment, participation in University sponsored extra-curricular activities or personal safety." It is not clear what kind of conduct would constitute a "threat" to an individual's academic efforts. It might refer to an unspecified threat of future retaliation by the speaker. Or it might equally plausibly refer to the threat to a victim's academic success because the stigmatizing and victimizing speech is so inherently distracting. Certainly the former would be unprotected speech. However, it is not clear whether the latter would.

Moving to the second "effect clause," a stigmatizing or victimizing comment is sanctionable if it has the purpose or reasonably foreseeable effect of interfering with an individual's academic efforts, etc. Again, the question is what conduct will be held to "interfere" with an individual's academic efforts. The language of the policy alone gives no inherent guidance. The one interpretive resource the University provided was withdrawn as "inaccurate," an implicit admission that even the University itself was unsure of the precise scope and meaning of the Policy.

During the oral argument, the Court asked the University's counsel how he would distinguish between speech which was merely offensive, which he conceded was protected, and speech which "stigmatizes or victimizes" on the basis of an invidious factor. Counsel replied "very carefully." The response, while refreshingly candid, illustrated the plain fact that the University never articulated any principled way to distinguish sanctionable from protected speech. Students of common understanding were necessarily forced to guess at whether a comment about a controversial issue would later be found to be sanctionable under the Policy. * * *

VI. CONCLUSION

* * *

While the Court is sympathetic to the University's obligation to ensure equal educational opportunities for all of its students, such efforts must not be at the expense of free speech. Unfortunately, this was precisely what the University did. * * * [T]here is no evidence in the record that anyone at the University ever seriously attempted to reconcile their efforts to combat discrimination with the requirements of the First Amendment. * * *

RIGHTS IN CONFLICT: THE FIRST AMENDMENT'S THIRD CENTURY

Robert M. O'Neil
65 LAW & CONTEMP. PROBS. 7 (2002)

* * *

III. Civility and Free Speech in an Increasingly Uncivil Society

* * * [M]uch confusion surrounds the constitutional boundaries in the quest for civility. On one hand, the Supreme Court has said that a person can be punished for uttering "fighting words" in a public place.[65] On the other hand, the same person could not be charged for the public display of a taboo or vulgar four-letter word.[66] The tension between two such rulings, and the consequent difficulty of defining the line between protected speech and unprotected epithets, is apparent. The lack of clarity in this area has created much confusion and has led to the adoption of various measures (campus speech codes, for example) that have fared poorly in the courts.[67]

It all began one Saturday afternoon in the town center of Rochester, New Hampshire, shortly before the outbreak of World War II.[68] A Jehovah's Witness named Chaplinsky had unsettled spectators by loudly denouncing mainstream religious faiths.[69] The local constabulary, without making an arrest, escorted him toward the police station.[70] Chaplinsky then turned on the officer and uttered the words which became the basis for an immediate criminal charge and an eventual Supreme Court ruling.[71] The precise words remain in doubt to this day. The arresting officer

---

65. Chaplinsky v. New Hampshire, 315 U.S. 568 (1942).

66. Cohen v. California, 203 U.S. 15 (1971).

67. *See, e.g.*, ROBERT M. O'NEIL, FREE SPEECH IN THE COLLEGE COMMUNITY (1997) [hereinafter O'NEIL, FREE SPEECH].

68. *Chaplinsky*, 315 U.S. at 569.

69. *Id.* at 569–70.

70. *Id.* at 570.

71. *Id.*

insisted that he had been called, to his face, "a damned fascist" and "a God-damned racketeer."[72] Chaplinsky, however, maintained that he had firmly but politely informed the officer that "You, sir, are damned in the eyes of God" and "no better than a racketeer."[73] Whatever he actually said, Chaplinsky was convicted of violating a state law which made it a crime to "address any offensive, derisive, or annoying word to any person who is lawfully in any street or other public place, nor call him by any offensive or derisive name...."[74]

The New Hampshire Supreme Court affirmed the conviction, finding the statute properly limited to "face to face words plainly likely to cause a breach of the peace ... classical fighting words."[75] A unanimous Supreme Court affirmed, including several Justices who had consistently supported free expression in the past.[76] Justice Murphy wrote for the Court, and Justices Black and Douglas joined without comment, a brief opinion that allowed states to punish the utterance of mere words, albeit under unusual conditions.[77] The key to the ruling was the Court's view that "such utterances are no essential part of any exposition of ideas, and are of such slight social value as a step to truth that any benefit that may be derived from them is clearly outweighed by the social interest in order and morality."[78]

So dismissive a view of expression that was both provocative and substantive now seems remarkable; it is even more so given the deeply religious context in which Chaplinsky voiced his disdain for the police.[79] But the Court was convinced that such words lost any claim to First Amendment protection when they were uttered face to face in a manner that was "likely to cause a breach of the peace," even though no disorder actually ensued.[80] The New Hampshire law was deemed "a statute punishing verbal acts," which, through interpretation, had been "limited to define and punish specific conduct lying within the domain of state power."[81] Under such conditions, the words Chaplinsky was charged with speaking seemed provocative enough not to merit any First Amendment protection.[82] Commentators have rightly observed that the decision had two prongs or elements: First, there was an assumption that utterance of epithets under such conditions inherently inflicts injury on a person who

---

72. *Id.* at 569.

73. This alternative version of Chaplinsky's words, advanced in the trial court by the defendant himself, was rejected in the absence of any third-party corroboration. The judge understandably favored the account given by the arresting officer, which provided the record and, in substantial part, the rationale for successive affirmance of Chaplinsky's conviction.

74. *Id.* at 569.

75. *Id.* at 573.

76. *Id.* at 574.

77. *Id.*

78. *Id.* at 572.

79. *Id.* at 570.

80. *Id.* at 573–74.

81. *Id.* at 574.

82. *Id.*

is their target.[83] Second, when such verbal hostility creates an imminent breach of the peace, government may intercede even though only words are involved.[84] Justice Murphy's cryptic opinion offered little guidance to those—law enforcement officers and judges—who would seek after *Chaplinsky* to resolve the inherent tension between the "damaging words" and "breach of peace" theories which the judgment blended.[85]

The *Chaplinsky* decision has caused no end of confusion during the ensuing six decades. This case has been cited with sufficient deference to imply that uttering "fighting words" remains a recognized exception to First Amendment freedoms.[86] As recently as the "hate speech" decision in 1992, the majority assumed *Chaplinsky*'s continuing vitality, stressing only that fighting words which were used to convey particular messages could not be selectively disfavored on a subject-matter basis.[87] Moreover, in that ruling Justice Scalia expressly declined an invitation to "modify the scope of the *Chaplinsky* formulation," a step he deemed unnecessary to the majority's disposition of the case.[88] Rumors of *Chaplinsky*'s demise are, therefore, greatly exaggerated and quite premature.[89]

When it comes to factually similar cases, however, the Justices have consistently distinguished *Chaplinsky*. Even when based on verbal affronts and assaults at least as provocative as the events of that long-ago New Hampshire Saturday afternoon, convictions have been set aside.[90] The lower courts have been understandably confused, however, and have been less reticent to invoke *Chaplinsky* as the basis for affirming the convictions of "in your face" verbal assailants—believing, quite understandably, that the precedent for doing so remained alive, if not in perfect health.[91]

The paradox of civility is not limited to fighting words. At the height of the Vietnam War, Paul Cohen walked about the lobby of the Los Angeles County courthouse wearing a jacket which bore in prominent lettering the words "Fuck the Draft."[92] He was arrested, and charged with violating a California breach of the peace law.[93] The state courts affirmed the conviction, one of several at the time involving the arrest of protestors who had used the same taboo word in public places, including one at the center of the Berkeley campus during the Free Speech Move-

---

83. Note, *The Demise of the Chaplinsky Fighting Words Doctrine: An Argument for Its Interment*, 106 HARV. L. REV. 1111, 1129, 1130–31 (1993) [hereinafter *Demise*].

84. *Id.*

85. *Id.*

86. *See, e.g.*, Martin Redish, *The Value of Free Speech*, 130 U. PA. L. REV. 591, 626 (1982).

87. R.A.V. v. City of St. Paul, 505 U.S. 377, 387 (1992).

88. *Id.* at 381.

89. *Id.* at 399.

90. Lewis v. New Orleans, 415 U.S. 130 (1974); Gooding v. Wilson, 405 U.S. 518 (1972).

91. *E.g.*, Mercer v. Winston, 199 S.E.2d 724 (Va. 1973), *cert. denied*, 416 U.S. 988 (1974).

92. *Cohen*, 403 U.S. at 16.

93. *Id.* at 17.

ment.[94] To the surprise of most observers, the U.S. Supreme Court agreed to review the conviction. Even greater was the surprise at the outcome—a six-to-three reversal of Cohen's conviction, with a ringing defense of free speech in a majority opinion by Justice John Marshall Harlan.[95] * * *

Justice Harlan [made] almost a virtue of the defendant's choice of language when he noted: "[I]t is often true, that one man's vulgarity is another's lyric."[103] If government could ban the public utterance of disfavored language, he warned, those in power "might soon seize upon the censorship of particular words as a convenient guise for banning the expression of unpopular views."[104] Thus it would be unwise and even dangerous for the high Court to assume "that one can forbid particular words without also running a substantial risk of suppressing ideas in the process."[105]

Herein lies the paradox of *Cohen* and its uneasy coexistence with *Chaplinsky* as an arbiter of civility in public discourse. The most persistent question, which the Justices had no occasion to address in *Cohen* and have managed to avoid ever since, is how far this judgment reflects the political context of Cohen's statement and the "unpopular view" whose expression was enhanced by the use of a taboo four-letter word. A few simple variants will suggest how soon we enter a realm of uncertainty. * * * [S]uppose Mr. Cohen had returned to the courthouse to flaunt his Supreme Court triumph, sporting the very same jacket, but having removed "the draft" to leave the offending word in splendid isolation. While charging him with a breach of the peace would still be problematic on the original facts, the gathering of a crowd angered by such language might change the circumstances. Any charge based on the isolated use of a vulgar and taboo word would require some assessment of the anti-war context of the actual *Cohen* case. While there is ample support in Justice Harlan's opinion for a non-contextual view—"one man's vulgarity is another's lyric," most notably—there are also grounds in the opinion for confining its protection of public incivility to the use of a taboo or vulgar term in order to, as the Court put it, "express unpopular views."[106]

The latter, context-driven and narrower, reading of *Cohen* seems recently to have gained favor. The lower federal courts have reviewed a growing number of charges brought against faculty members on the basis of their classroom use of vulgar and taboo language, usually designed to revive flagging student interest in arcane subject matter.[107] The legal fortunes of professors so charged have varied, more on the basis of particular institutional policies invoked than on broad academic freedom

---

94. *Id.*

95. *Id.* at 26.

103. *Id.* at 25.

104. *Id.* at 26.

105. *Id.*

106. *Id.*

107. *E.g.,* Cohen v. San Bernardino Valley College, 92 F.3d 968 (9th Cir. 1996).

or free speech grounds.[108] The latest such ruling does, however, reopen the larger issue of incivility. John Bonnell, a long-time faculty member at a Michigan community college, was suspended for the occasional use of taboo and sexually offensive words in his classroom.[109] The particular choice of language was deemed to violate the college's sexual harassment policy.[110] Bonnell sought redress in federal court and persuaded a district judge that his free speech had been abridged.[111] The Sixth Circuit, however, took a much less sympathetic view than that of the district court, or of other federal courts that have recently assessed such claims.[112] The Sixth Circuit invoked a recent Supreme Court ruling which had sustained curbs on unwelcome approaches to clinic visitors by anti-abortion protestors.[113] In that case, the Supreme Court, in support of a patient's right to be free of unwanted entreaties while seeking clinic access, recalled *Cohen* in this way: "Even in a public forum, one of the reasons we tolerate a protestor's right to wear a jacket expressing his opposition to government policy in vulgar language is because offended viewers can effectively avoid further bombardment of their sensibilities simply by averting their eyes."[114] For the Sixth Circuit, this rather cautious use of *Cohen* buttressed its view that "the context in which a message is delivered is often the pivotal factor when determining whether the speech will be protected"—and held that, in Bonnell's case, the speech was protected.[115]

One citation does not, of course, reflect a trend. Nothing in *Bonnell* necessarily impairs or qualifies *Cohen*'s broad protection for public incivility. On the other hand, there may be some risk in continuing to assume that the unadorned utterance of taboo or vulgar words enjoys full First Amendment protection. That seems to be the premise on which the appellate courts of several states recently relied in the cases noted at the opening of this section.[116] The facts in none of those cases would have met *Chaplinsky*'s test for "fighting words," much less the more stringent test the Supreme Court later imposed on such outbursts.[117] Yet the holdings in these cases have caused uncertainty over the current balance between the contending interests in civility and free expression.[118]

---

108.   1 Silva v. Univ. of N.H., 888 F. Supp. 293 (D.N.H. 1994).

109.   Bonnell v. Lorenzo, 241 F.3d 800, 803 (6th Cir. 2001).

110.   *Id.*

111.   *Id.* at 806–07.

112.   *Id.* at 826–27.

113.   *Id.* at 819.

114.   Hill v. Colorado, 530 U.S. 703, 716 (2000).

115.   *Bonnell*, 214 F.3d at 819.

116.   *E.g.*, Minnesota v. Clay, No. CX–99–343, 1999 Minn. App. LEXIS 1059 (Minn. Ct. App. Sept. 14, 1999); Hamilton v. Johnson, No. CA99–02–025, 1999 Ohio App. LEXIS 5623 (Ohio Ct. App. Nov. 29, 1999).

117.   *Id.*

118.   *See, e.g.*, Melody L. Hurdle, R.A.V. v. City of St. Paul: *The Continuing Confusion of the Fighting Words Doctrine*, 47 VAND. L. REV. 1143 (1994); E. Kenly Ames, Note, *The Fighting Words Doctrine*, 93 COLUM. L. REV. 1473 (1993); *Demise, supra* note 83 at 1111, 1129.

* * * *Cohen* and *Chaplinsky* cannot coexist indefinitely, because one declares that offensive epithets are "no essential part of any exposition of ideas" while the other insists with equal conviction that "one man's vulgarity is another's lyric."

IV. Equality and Free Expression

Patrick Suiter is not the only Idaho resident whose public utterances have incurred legal action. Not many months before Mr. Suiter's outburst, Lonnie Rae had been in the stands at a high school football game in Boise.[120] His wife Kim, a newspaper photographer, tried to photograph the referees in order to illustrate an article.[121] The referees objected, and one of them, an African–American named Ken Manley, tried to take Mrs. Rae's camera.[122] The husband then shouted at Manley, using a racially derogatory and offensive epithet.[123] He was promptly arrested and charged with violating a state hate-crime law, aimed specifically at "malicious harassment," conviction for which could bring a five-year prison sentence.[124] Although no further proceedings have yet been pursued, the Raes' attorney has maintained, and the facts confirm, that "the charge is based solely on the language [my client] used."[125]

Whether such abusive language, uttered at a football game or in any other public place, warrants a criminal sanction poses [another] of our persistent tensions. Here, too, we find continuing ambivalence among our own views and those of the courts—hardly a surprise since we greatly esteem both equality and free expression. For most of the past century, protecting vulnerable religious, ethnic, and other groups from extreme verbal assaults has been a high priority.[126] It has also been a source of much litigation, the results of which are as confusing as our national ambivalence toward the underlying values of equality and expression.[127] On one hand, the Supreme Court a half-century ago held that states may enact and enforce "group libel" laws against purveyors of hostile and demeaning racist tracts and the like.[128] Much more recently, a unanimous Court rendered a remarkable and not easily compatible pair of judgments striking down "hate speech" laws while upholding laws that impose harsher sentences on those who commit "hate crimes."[129] A journey along this tortuous path of First Amendment law concludes our review of

---

120. Aarika Mack, Hate–Crimes Bill Raise First Amendment Concerns for Some, Freedom Forum, *at* http://www.freedomforum.org/templates/document.asp? documentID=13756 (Apr. 23, 2001).

121. *Id.*

122. *Id.*

123. *Id.*

124. *Id.*

125. *Id.*

126. 1 O'NEIL, FREE SPEECH, *supra* note 67 at 5–7.

127. 1 *Compare* Wisconsin v. Mitchell, 508 U.S. 476 (1993) *with* R.A.V. v. City of St. Paul, 505 U.S. 377 (1992).

128. Beauharnais v. Illinois, 343 U.S. 250 (1952).

129. *R.A.V.*, 505 U.S. at 398.

persistent tensions between free expression and other transcendent societal values.

We tend to assume that laws which protect vulnerable groups from verbal assault and abuse have recent origins. In fact, however, the first statute clearly aimed at curbing racist speech was adopted by the New York legislature in 1913.[130] This earliest version of what would come to be known as group libel laws specifically forbade hotels from discriminatory advertising—that is, publicly announcing a refusal to accommodate guests on the basis of race, color, or religion.[131] No concern about free expression was raised at the time; the only opposition came from those who feared hotels might be unable under the law to refuse rooms to persons infected with tuberculosis.[132]

By the mid 1920s, at least seven states had adopted similar anti-discrimination laws that targeted hostile words as well as acts.[133] Concern for the legal protection of minorities was further heightened in the post-war period by anti-Semitic publications, notably Henry Ford's Dearborn Independent and its focus on the allegedly subversive Protocols of Zion. Specific efforts were made by a number of cities, with mixed success, to ban distribution of Ford's newspaper.[134] For the first time, free speech and free press concerns were raised in opposition to such proposals.

The Michigan legislature declined to adopt such a measure largely because of challenge by the state's mainstream media and the fledgling American Civil Liberties Union.[135] A Cleveland, Ohio, ordinance aimed at the Independent was successfully challenged in federal court, producing what is undoubtedly the first judgment invalidating government efforts to suppress racist or ethnically offensive expression.[136] The American Jewish Committee viewed the events which led to such legislation with intense ambivalence, and the prospects for protection from verbal assaults of the Dearborn Independent variety with frustration.[137] The president of the Anti–Defamation League of B'Nai B'rith lamented in 1935 that, although the First Amendment "was never intended as a protection against group libel any more than as an obstacle individual libel," it had nonetheless posed "an insurmountable obstacle in bringing before the bar of justice one of the lowest forms of malefactors."[138]

Events in Europe leading up to World War II would intensify such concerns. The most direct response to the world-wide threat of Nazi

---

130. Evan P. Schulz, *Group Rights, American Jews, and the Failure of Group Libel Laws, 1913–1952*, 66 BROOKLYN L. REV. 71, 92 (2000).

131. *Id.* at 91.

132. *Id.* at 92.

133. *Id.* at 98–99.

134. *Id.* at 102–03.

135. *Id.* at 105.

136. Dearborn Pub. Co. v. Fitzgerald, 271 Fed. 479 (N.D. Ohio 1921).

137. Schultz, *supra* note 130 at 110–11.

138. *Id.* at 111.

propaganda was a two-part article written in 1942 by the young David Reisman, who was a law teacher well before his metamorphosis into the eminent sociologist he became a decade later.[139] Reisman's plea was for the wider enactment and enforcement of group libel laws, which he saw as the most effective antidote to Nazi propaganda.[140] Though he could hardly overlook the potential conflict with free speech and press that such laws would present, he insisted that, in perilous /times, even Bill of Rights guarantees must yield to national exigency: "[I]t is no longer tenable to continue a negative policy of protection from the state ... [which] plays directly into the hands of the groups whom supporters of democracy need most to fear."[141]

In substantial part as a response to Reisman's plea, a number of states did enact laws that specifically targeted racist, anti-religious, and otherwise ethnically demeaning publications.[142] The validity of such laws was bound to reach the Supreme Court, and, in 1951, it did.[143] The specific context was an Illinois law applied to the publications of a racist group known as the White Circle League.[144] The statute imposed penalties on those who published or exhibited material that "portrays depravity, criminality, unchastity, or lack of virtue of a class of citizens, of any race, color, creed, or religion which said publication or exhibition exposes the citizens of any race, color, creed, or religion to contempt, derision, or obloquy or which is productive of breach of the peace or riots."[145]

The officers of the White Circle League were charged with organizing the distribution of a provocative leaflet that urged the Chicago city government to "halt the further encroachment, harassment and invasion of white people, their property, neighborhoods and persons by the Negro" and called upon "one million self respecting white people in Chicago to unite."[146] The leaflet also warned of ominous prospects—" the rapes, robberies, knives, guns, and marijuana of the Negro"—should such pleas not be heeded by the white community.[147]

The Illinois courts sustained the convictions, rejecting First Amendment and due process claims, noting that the statute provided a defense only for publication "with good motives and for justifiable ends."[148] The state courts also rejected the defendants' plea that a "clear and present danger" must exist before such a sanction could be imposed on expression,

---

139. David Reisman, *Democracy and Defamation: Control of Group Libel*, 42 COLUM. L. REV. 727 (1942).

140. *Id.* at 777–78.

141. *Id.* at 779–80.

142. *E.g.*, the Illinois statute which the Supreme Court sustained in *Beauharnais*, 343 U.S. at 251.

143. *Beauharnais*, 343 U.S. at 251.

144. *Id.* at 252–53.

145. *Id.* at 251.

146. *Id.* at 252.

147. *Id.*

148. *Id.* at 254.

however hateful.[149] A sharply divided U.S. Supreme Court in *Beauharnais v. Illinois* upheld the convictions and the validity of group libel laws.[150] The majority found persuasive an analogy to individual civil redress for defamation, and also by recent and earlier racial tensions in Chicago area: "We would deny experience," wrote Justice Frankfurter for the Court, "to say that the Illinois legislature was without reason in seeking ways to curb false or malicious defamation of racial and religious groups, made in public places and calculated to have a powerful emotional impact on those to whom it was presented."[151] Since libel at that time claimed no First Amendment protection, there was no constitutional imperative for a clear and present danger standard.[152]

The dissenters were dismayed by such a ruling; Justice Black (who often cited *Beauharnais* as the Court's very worst judgment during his three and one-half decades) insisted that the majority "acts on the bland assumption that the First Amendment is wholly irrelevant."[153] Even Justice Stanley Reed, seldom counted among champions of free speech, dissented here, albeit more on due process than First Amendment grounds.[154] Justice Robert Jackson, usually found on the other side of such issues after his experience as chief War Crimes prosecutor at Nuremberg, also dissented from what he deemed an unsupportable inference of danger or threat from a misguided racist tract.[155]

Despite universal condemnation in later years[156] and ample opportunity, the Court has never overruled *Beauharnais*. Though one would today rely upon it at very considerable peril, as recently as a decade ago the Court cited *Beauharnais* as illustrative of categories of speech that had been denied First Amendment protection.[157] The central premise of *Beauharnais* may survive in a different and more ominous form. To what extent persistent efforts to curb racist, sexist, anti-religious, and homophobic rhetoric may have taken comfort from the survival of this precedent, albeit without honor, is impossible to tell. The fact remains that the past half-century has been a time of pervasive and recurrent effort to protect vulnerable groups in our society from words that may wound or offend because of racial, religious, ethnic or other differences.[158] This question has taken several forms beyond the criminal sanctions against "group libel" that were theoretically validated in *Beauharnais*.

In the late 1970s, a dozen or so states, including New York and California, did enact laws that imposed civil sanctions on those who

---

149. *Id.*

150. *Id.* at 267.

151. *Id.* at 261.

152. *Id.* at 267.

153. *Id.*

154. *Id.* at 277.

155. *Id.* at 287.

156. *See, e.g.,* HARRY KALVEN, JR., THE NEGRO AND THE FIRST AMENDMENT 15–16, 50–51 (1965).

157. New York v. Ferber, 458 U.S. 747, 763 (1982).

158. *See, e.g.,* O'NEIL, FREE SPEECH, *supra* note 67, at Chapter 1.

uttered racially or religiously hostile words.[159] It was on the basis of such statutes, for example, that an upstate New York gift shop was ordered to remove from its window an abacus device jokingly labeled "Polish calculator"[160] and that a downstate restaurant owner was ordered to apologize in writing to a waitress whom he had denounced publicly as a "Jewish Broad" because she allegedly sought special treatment.[161] While such laws were occasionally challenged, they seem to have remained on the books, largely forgotten and apparently seldom, if ever, enforced.[162]

The ensuing decade saw renewed focus on the protection of vulnerable groups in a very different form. Several hundred colleges and universities, responding both to minority student pressure and to an institutional quest for civility, adopted restrictive speech codes.[163] The precise approach varied substantially from campus to campus. Some such constraints were added to existing harassment codes,[164] while others buttressed anti-bias rules,[165] and a few targeted racially or religiously oriented "fighting words."[166] Legal challenges by civil liberties groups were not far behind.

By the mid 1990s, every speech code challenged in court was found wanting, chiefly because of imprecise language, often drafted in haste, that left the campus community genuinely uncertain about what language was prohibited.[167] Moreover, there was little evidence that the existence of such speech codes genuinely made a difference—either in the sensitivity of the campus racial climate, or in the civility of discourse.[168] Occasionally, even today, a university may consider adopting a speech code in response to racial or other campus tensions despite the dismal record of such regulations in the courts and the meager proof of positive impact.[169]

It is the latest attempt to balance free speech and equality that has produced the Supreme Court's conundrum. Even as speech codes were being challenged, some communities adopted "hate speech" laws.[170] The St. Paul, Minnesota, ordinance, which brought the issue to the high Court, was representative. That law made it a crime to place on public or private property "a symbol, object . . . or graffiti including, but not limited to, a burning cross or Nazi swastika, which one knows or has reasonable

---

159. *E.g.*, N.Y. Exec. Law § 296 (1980).

160. The order was reversed by the Appellate Division, and the reversal was sustained by a sharply divided Court of Appeals. State Div. of Human Rights *ex rel.* Gladwin v. McHarris Gift Center, 419 N.Y.S.2d 405, *aff'd*, 418 N.E.2d 393 (N.Y. 1980).

161. Imperial Diner, Inc. v. State Human Rights Appeals Bd., 417 N.E.2d 525 (N.Y. 1980).

162. *See* Robert M. O'Neil, *Second Thoughts on the First Amendment*, 13 N.M.L. Rev. 577, 588–89 (1983).

163. *See* O'Neil, Free Speech, *supra* note 67, at Chapter 1.

164. *Id.* at 8.

165. *Id.* at 8–9.

166. *Id.* at 9.

167. *E.g.*, Doe v. University of Michigan, 721 F. Supp. 852 (E.D. Mich. 1989).

168. *See* O'Neil, Free Speech, *supra* note 67, at 12–13.

169. For a relatively recent revival of such interest at Rutgers University, see John Carlin, *Racial Slur Sparks Student Revolt Against "PC" Notions*, The Independent, Feb. 19, 1995, at 16.

170. *E.g.*, St. Paul, Minn. Legis. Code § 292.012 (1990).

grounds to know arouses anger, alarm or resentment in others on the basis of race, color, creed, religion or gender."[171] One of the first persons so charged was a juvenile who had burned a cross on the lawn of an African–American family.[172] Although charges for trespass, arson, and other clearly unlawful conduct would have been in order, the prosecutor opted to use the newly enacted ordinance.[173]

Minnesota's courts rejected First Amendment challenges to the law, and the Supreme Court granted certiorari.[174] The unanimity of the Justices in reversing the conviction in *R.A.V. v. St. Paul* masked a deep philosophical division within the Court.[175] For Justice Scalia, writing for the new majority, the fatal flaw of the ordinance was its reliance on content differentiation.[176] Even though the expression involved in such a case might well be less than fully protected—as fighting words, for example—its status did not empower government to "regulate [its] use based on hostility—or favoritism—towards the underlying message expressed."[177] While the City might well have forbidden all expression of a certain type, it could not selectively target only regulable speech which evoked tension or hostility "on the basis of race, color, creed, religion or gender" and not for other reasons or in other realms of advocacy.[178]

For the four Justices who concurred only in the result, such a novel approach departed sharply from familiar First Amendment jurisprudence, and potentially created far more problems than it solved–indeed, for one of these Justices, potentially "an aberration."[179] They were "puzzled" by the notion that otherwise unprotected speech, such as fighting words, might gain protection if targeted because of specific content.[180] For them, the same result should have been reached, and the conviction overturned, because of the overbreadth of the ordinance.[181] Under a narrower and more precise prohibition aimed at such activity, three of the concurring Justices strongly implied they would have been ready to recognize state power to proscribe such hateful activity, even if it incidentally included some expression.[182]

That suggestion soon proved prophetic. In the very next term, again with unanimity, the Court held in *Wisconsin v. Mitchell* that states might decree harsher sentences for those who commit certain criminal acts on

---

171. R.A.V. v. City of St. Paul, 505 U.S. 377, 379 (1992).

172. *Id.*

173. *Id.* at 380.

174. *Id.* at 380–81.

175. *Id.* at 379.

176. *Id.* at 381.

177. *Id.* at 386.

178. *Id.* at 391.

179. *Id.* at 415.

180. *Id.* at 402.

181. *Id.*

182. *Id.* at 417.

the basis of the race of the victim.[183] Many states had, even while rejecting hate speech laws and codes, enacted versions of a model law which required a stiffer sentence if it were proved that the defendant had "select[ed] the person against whom the crime is committed because of the race, religion, color, disability, sexual orientation, national origin or ancestry of that person."[184]

Distinguishing hate crimes from hate speech might have proved an impossible task. The defendant in Mitchell had insisted that a racially hostile motive or animus could be established only by evidence of the very type of speech that *R.A.V.* seemed to protect from direct criminal sanctions.[185] Thus, the precise words that could not be reached directly because of the Court's concern about content selectivity now seemed vulnerable to collateral use for the purpose of justifying a substantially harsher penalty.

The Mitchell Justices were not deterred. The Court reasoned that to the extent that a sentence-enhancement law targeted motive, it was not markedly different from reliance on motive for a host of other purposes.[186] Here the Court invoked two recent rulings that had allowed trial judges to take account of racial animus in the sentencing process and overlooked the difference between what was in those cases a discretionary use of words that revealed bias, and the mandatory use of such evidence under the Wisconsin law.[187] *R.A.V.* was distinguished in a few sentences as an ipse dixit. Although the law struck down the year before "was explicitly directed at expression (i.e., 'speech' or 'messages'), the statute in this case," declared the *Mitchell* opinion, "is aimed at conduct unprotected by the First Amendment."[188] Such a distinction was not satisfying at the time and, though the Court has not revisited the hate speech/hate crime distinction, it remains troubling a decade later.

If perfect consistency in so complex and contentious a field as First Amendment law is unrealistic, the current tension between free expression and equality leaves much to be desired. As though to illustrate, one of the Supreme Court's most recent rulings compounds the confusion. A divided Court ruled that the Boy Scouts of America could not, as a First Amendment matter, be compelled to accept a gay person as a scoutmaster in violation of longstanding policy and its declared mission.[189] In several previous encounters with comparable conflicts between freedom of association and anti-bias laws, the First Amendment claim had been forced to yield to a compelling state interest in equal access to places of public accommodation.[190] Thus, service organizations and even private social

---

183.   508 U.S. 476, 490 (1993).

184.   *Id.* at 483.

185.   *Id.* at 488.

186.   *Id.* at 485.

187.   *Id.* at 486–87.

188.   *Id.* at 487.

189.   Boy Scouts of Am. v. Dale, 530 U.S. 640, 661 (2000).

190.   *E.g.*, Roberts v. United States Jaycees, 468 U.S. 609 (1984).

clubs had been required to admit women despite long traditions as all-male entities.[191] Now, however, the balance tipped the other way. What the Chief Justice found crucial was that compelled acceptance of a gay scoutmaster would "force the organization to send a message" abhorrent to its mission and its traditions.[192] In that respect, the majority found guidance in an earlier judgment which declined to force the organizers of a St. Patrick's Day parade to accept a gay and lesbian contingent, even though state law defined the parade as a "place of public accommodation" for such purposes.[193] In the parade case, the anti-bias law had been stretched well beyond its customary reading, and there was little doubt that having to include an unwelcome group in a two-hour event would have conveyed, if not compelled, an abhorrent message.[194]

Such concerns were substantially muted, however, in the Boy Scout case. To the four dissenters, the private club precedents were dispositive, save for one implicit distinction.[195] "The only apparent explanation for the majority's holding," concluded Justice Stevens, "is that homosexuals are simply so different from the rest of society that their presence alone—unlike any other individual's—should be singled out for special First Amendment treatment."[196] Such a critique seems both harsh and warranted–though no harsher than the claim of Justices Scalia, Thomas, and Kennedy that, in sustaining curbs against anti-abortion protest, the Court has acted "in stark contradiction of the constitutional principles we apply in all other contexts."[197]

The culprit, in the Boy Scout case at least, is in substantial part our deep and persistent ambivalence about equality and expression.[198] Under the First Amendment, we highly value all speech. Almost alone among nations, we extend such protection fully to material that is racist, sexist, anti-Semitic, and homophobic.[199] Even Canada, whose values are remarkably similar to ours in virtually all respects, imprisons virulent anti-Semites and racists.[200] We still insist, at least in theory, that we do not recognize different levels of protection on the basis of favored and disfa-

---

191. *E.g.*, New York State Club Ass'n v. New York, 487 U.S. 1 (1988).

192. *Id*. at 653.

193. *Id*. at 653–54.

194. Hurley v. Irish–Am. Gay, Lesbian & Bisexual Group, 515 U.S. 557, 574–75 (1995).

195. *Dale*, 530 U.S. at 696.

196. *Id*.

197. Hill v. Colorado, 730 U.S. 703, 742 (2000).

198. *See, e.g.*, Steven Shiffrin, *Racist Speech, Outsider Jurisprudence, and the Meaning of America*, 80 CORNELL L. REV. 43 (1994).

199. *See*, ROBERT M. O'NEIL, THE FIRST AMENDMENT AND CIVIL LIABILITY 14–15 (2001).

200. *E.g.*, R. v. Keegstra, [1990] 3 S.C.R. 697. The Canadian Human Rights Commission recently ruled that Holocaust denier Ernst Zundel must close down his Internet Web site because of the hateful messages it contained and disseminated. Noting that, on the Zundelsite, as it is often cited, "Jews are vilified in the most rabid and extreme manner," the Commission answered Zundel's free speech claims by observing that material such as that which he regularly posted "can erode an individual's personal dignity and self worth." See Kirk Makin, *Rights Group Orders Zundel to Kill Hate Site*, TORONTO GLOBE & MAIL, Jan. 19, 2002, at A7 (summarizing a sixty-nine page opinion rendered by the Commission the previous day).

vored messages. Indeed, the teaching of *R.A.V.* is that even material which normally deserves less than full protection may somehow acquire such protection if it is targeted on the basis of its treatment of race, gender, religion, or sexual orientation.

Somehow our view of the relationship between equality and speech remains confused, and the tension unresolved. *Beauharnais*, to the extent it survives, suggests that certain sanctions may be appropriate for such expression where they would not (even a half century ago) have been acceptable for less volatile material. The Court's seemingly clear aversion to hate speech laws was sharply tempered by its readiness to embrace not easily distinguishable hate crime or sentence enhancement provisions. So it has been for well over a half century. Easy answers are not a ready prospect.

CHAPTER IV

COMBATING THREATENING BEHAVIOR, PEER HARASSMENT, AND PEER MISTREATMENT

■ ■ ■

In recent decades, relevant legal doctrine in the area of campus safety has expanded far beyond the traditional negligence inquiry. A number of highly publicized campus shootings in the 1990s led to an increasing focus on threatening activity at the K–12 level, and this focus was ramped up considerably in the aftermath of the September 11, 2001 attacks. New developments in Title VII "hostile environment" law, combined with watershed national events such as the Anita Hill testimony at the confirmation hearings of Justice Clarence Thomas, led to an increasing awareness of peer-to-peer sexual harassment in the schools and widespread litigation seeking to hold educational institutions liable under Title IX. And litigation focusing on the mistreatment of LGBT students by their peers led to greater awareness in this area as well, and to notable rulings under the Equal Protection Clause.

As referenced above in Chapter 2, legal principles impacting campus safety often span a range of interrelated areas. It is not unusual, in this context, for on-campus injuries to raise questions relating to negligence, privacy, freedom of expression, threat law, harassment law, and/or equal protection.

The materials in this chapter reflect these developments and interrelationships. The chapter begins with an inquiry into threatening activity generally, examining relevant statutory language, and exploring examples of threat-related disputes that have arisen under both negligence law and criminal law. It then turns to freedom of expression issues, focusing on how courts have sought to determine whether speech that some find threatening might still be protected under the First Amendment.

In the last section of the chapter, the focus shifts to peer harassment and mistreatment, documenting the significant changes in relevant legal doctrine and the prospects for continued positive change in the future.

A. THREATENING ACTIVITY GENERALLY

PROBLEM 16: ZERO TOLERANCE FOR THREATS I

Belinda—an eleventh grade student at a large public high school in the fictional state of Riverview—sends an e-mail from a school computer to a friend in the fictional state of Floral Valley, which reads in part: "I can't wait until I can kill the people in my class. I'll just go to the entrance of the school on a clear, sunny day and blow up and shoot everything I can." She also sends copies to five friends, one of whom shares it with her parents. The parents report the details to the school, which suspends Belinda for ten days under a new "zero tolerance for threats" policy enacted in the aftermath of the events at Columbine. Belinda is not only suspended from school, she is also arrested by the local police and charged with a violation of Riverview General Law Ch. 275, Section 2, which provides, in pertinent part:

> If complaint is made to any such court or justice that a person has threatened to commit a crime against the person or property of another, such court or justice shall examine the complainant and any witnesses who may be produced, on oath, reduce the complaint to writing and cause it to be subscribed by the complainant.

A. The state is prepared to argue that Belinda is guilty of "threaten[ing] to commit a crime against the person or property of another," and should be adjudicated juvenile delinquent. What arguments might Belinda set forth in her defense? What result? Discuss.

B. Assume that Belinda actually attempts to blow up and shoot everything she can, but is thwarted before any major damage occurs. However, three students are in fact shot, and spend months recovering from their injuries. If a negligence lawsuit is brought against the District, what arguments would be set forth? What result? Discuss.

1. ADDRESSING THREATS UNDER NEGLIGENCE LAW

TARASOFF v. REGENTS OF UNIV. OF CAL.

17 Cal.3d 425, 131 Cal.Rptr. 14, 551 P.2d 334 (1976)

TOBRINER, JUSTICE.

On October 27, 1969, Prosenjit Poddar killed Tatiana Tarasoff. Plaintiffs, Tatiana's parents, allege that two months earlier Poddar confided his intention to kill Tatiana to Dr. Lawrence Moore, a psychologist employed by the Cowell Memorial Hospital at the University of California at Berkeley. They allege that on Moore's request, the campus police briefly detained Poddar, but released him when he appeared rational. They further claim that Dr. Harvey Powelson, Moore's superior, then directed that no further action be taken to detain Poddar. No one warned plaintiffs of Tatiana's peril.

* * *2

We shall explain that defendant therapists cannot escape liability merely because Tatiana herself was not their patient. When a therapist determines, or pursuant to the standards of his profession should determine, that his patient presents a serious danger of violence to another, he incurs an obligation to use reasonable care to protect the intended victim against such danger. The discharge of this duty may require the therapist to take one or more of various steps, depending upon the nature of the case. Thus it may call for him to warn the intended victim or others likely to apprise the victim of the danger, to notify the police, or to take whatever other steps are reasonably necessary under the circumstances.

* * *

2. *Plaintiffs can state a cause of action against defendant therapists for negligent failure to protect Tatiana.*

The second cause of action can be amended to allege that Tatiana's death proximately resulted from defendants' negligent failure to warn Tatiana or others likely to apprise her of her danger. Plaintiffs contend that as amended, such allegations of negligence and proximate causation, with resulting damages, establish a cause of action. Defendants, however, contend that in the circumstances of the present case they owed no duty of care to Tatiana or her parents and that, in the absence of such duty, they were free to act in careless disregard of Tatiana's life and safety.

In analyzing this issue, we bear in mind that legal duties are not discoverable facts of nature, but merely conclusory expressions that, in cases of a particular type, liability should be imposed for damage done. As stated in *Dillon v. Legg*, 68 Cal. 2d 728, 734 (1968): "The assertion that liability must . . . be denied because defendant bears no 'duty' to plaintiff 'begs the essential question—whether the plaintiff's interests are entitled to legal protection against the defendant's conduct. . . . [Duty] is not sacrosanct in itself, but only an expression of the sum total of those considerations of policy which lead the law to say that the particular plaintiff is entitled to protection.' "

In the landmark case of *Rowland v. Christian*, 69 Cal. 2d 108 (1968), Justice Peters recognized that liability should be imposed "for injury occasioned to another by his want of ordinary care or skill" as expressed in section 1714 of the Civil Code. Thus, Justice Peters quoting from *Heaven v. Pender*, 11 Q.B.D. 503, 509 (1883) stated: "whenever one person is by circumstances placed in such a position with regard to another . . . that if he did not use ordinary care and skill in his own conduct . . . he would cause danger of injury to the person or property of the other, a duty arises to use ordinary care and skill to avoid such danger."

---

2. The therapist defendants include Dr. Moore, the psychologist who examined Poddar and decided that Poddar should be committed; Dr. Gold and Dr. Yandell, psychiatrists at Cowell Memorial Hospital who concurred in Moore's decision; and Dr. Powelson, chief of the department of psychiatry, who countermanded Moore's decision and directed that the staff take no action to confine Poddar.

We depart from "this fundamental principle" only upon the "balancing of a number of considerations"; major ones "are the foreseeability of harm to the plaintiff, the degree of certainty that the plaintiff suffered injury, the closeness of the connection between the defendant's conduct and the injury suffered, the moral blame attached to the defendant's conduct, the policy of preventing future harm, the extent of the burden to the defendant and consequences to the community of imposing a duty to exercise care with resulting liability for breach, and the availability, cost and prevalence of insurance for the risk involved."

The most important of these considerations in establishing duty is foreseeability. As a general principle, a "defendant owes a duty of care to all persons who are foreseeably endangered by his conduct, with respect to all risks which make the conduct unreasonably dangerous." As we shall explain, however, when the avoidance of foreseeable harm requires a defendant to control the conduct of another person, or to warn of such conduct, the common law has traditionally imposed liability only if the defendant bears some special relationship to the dangerous person or to the potential victim. Since the relationship between a therapist and his patient satisfies this requirement, we need not here decide whether foreseeability alone is sufficient to create a duty to exercise reasonable care to protect a potential victim of another's conduct.

Although, as we have stated above, under the common law, as a general rule, one person owed no duty to control the conduct of another,[5] nor to warn those endangered by such conduct, the courts have carved out an exception to this rule in cases in which the defendant stands in some special relationship to either the person whose conduct needs to be controlled or in a relationship to the foreseeable victim of that conduct. Applying this exception to the present case, we note that a relationship of defendant therapists to either Tatiana or Poddar will suffice to establish a duty of care; as explained in section 315 of the Restatement Second of Torts, a duty of care may arise from either "(a) a special relation ... between the actor and the third person which imposes a duty upon the actor to control the third person's conduct, or (b) a special relation ... between the actor and the other which gives to the other a right of protection."

Although plaintiffs' pleadings assert no special relation between Tatiana and defendant therapists, they establish as between Poddar and defendant therapists the special relation that arises between a patient and his doctor or psychotherapist.[6] Such a relationship may support affirma-

---

5. This rule derives from the common law's distinction between misfeasance and nonfeasance, and its reluctance to impose liability for the latter.... Morally questionable, the rule owes its survival to "the difficulties of setting any standards of unselfish service to fellow men, and of making any workable rule to cover possible situations where fifty people might fail to rescue...." WILLIAM PROSSER, TORTS § 56, at 341 (4th ed. 1971). Because of these practical difficulties, the courts have increased the number of instances in which affirmative duties are imposed not by direct rejection of the common law rule, but by expanding the list of special relationships which will justify departure from that rule. *See* PROSSER, *supra*, § 56, at 348–50.

6. The pleadings establish the requisite relationship between Poddar and both Dr. Moore, the therapist who treated Poddar, and Dr. Powelson, who supervised that treatment. Plaintiffs also

tive duties for the benefit of third persons. Thus, for example, a hospital must exercise reasonable care to control the behavior of a patient which may endanger other persons.[7] A doctor must also warn a patient if the patient's condition or medication renders certain conduct, such as driving a car, dangerous to others.

Although the California decisions that recognize this duty have involved cases in which the defendant stood in a special relationship *both* to the victim and to the person whose conduct created the danger,[9] we do not think that the duty should logically be constricted to such situations. Decisions of other jurisdictions hold that the single relationship of a doctor to his patient is sufficient to support the duty to exercise reasonable care to protect others against dangers emanating from the patient's illness. The courts hold that a doctor is liable to persons infected by his patient if he negligently fails to diagnose a contagious disease, or, having diagnosed the illness, fails to warn members of the patient's family.

Since it involved a dangerous mental patient, the decision in *Merchants Nat. Bank & Trust Co. of Fargo v. United States*, 272 F. Supp. 409 (D.N.D. 1967) comes closer to the issue. The Veterans Administration arranged for the patient to work on a local farm, but did not inform the farmer of the man's background. The farmer consequently permitted the patient to come and go freely during nonworking hours; the patient borrowed a car, drove to his wife's residence and killed her. Notwithstanding the lack of any "special relationship" between the Veterans Administration and the wife, the court found the Veterans Administration liable for the wrongful death of the wife.

In their summary of the relevant rulings Fleming and Maximov conclude that the "case law should dispel any notion that to impose on the therapists a duty to take precautions for the safety of persons threatened by a patient, where due care so requires, is in any way opposed to contemporary ground rules on the duty relationship. On the contrary, there now seems to be sufficient authority to support the conclusion that by entering into a doctor-patient relationship the therapist becomes sufficiently involved to assume some responsibility for the safety, not only of

---

allege that Dr. Gold personally examined Poddar, and that Dr. Yandell, as Powelson's assistant, approved the decision to arrange Poddar's commitment. These allegations are sufficient to raise the issue whether a doctor-patient or therapist-patient relationship, giving rise to a possible duty by the doctor or therapist to exercise reasonable care to protect a threatened person of danger arising from the patient's mental illness, existed between Gold or Yandell and Poddar. *See* DAVID M. HARNEY, MEDICAL MALPRACTICE 7 (1973).

7. When a "hospital has notice or knowledge of facts from which it might reasonably be concluded that a patient would be likely to harm himself *or others* unless preclusive measures were taken, then the hospital must use reasonable care in the circumstances to prevent such harm."

9. *Ellis v. D'Angelo*, 116 Cal. App. 2d 310 (1953), upheld a cause of action against parents who failed to warn a babysitter of the violent proclivities of their child; *Johnson v. California*, 69 Cal. 2d 782 (1968), upheld a suit against the state for failure to warn foster parents of the dangerous tendencies of their ward; *Morgan v. County of Yuba*, 230 Cal. App. 2d 938 (1964), sustained a cause of action against a sheriff who had promised to warn decedent before releasing a dangerous prisoner, but failed to do so.

the patient himself, but also of any third person whom the doctor knows to be threatened by the patient."

Defendants contend, however, that imposition of a duty to exercise reasonable care to protect third persons is unworkable because therapists cannot accurately predict whether or not a patient will resort to violence. In support of this argument amicus representing the American Psychiatric Association and other professional societies cites numerous articles which indicate that therapists, in the present state of the art, are unable reliably to predict violent acts; their forecasts, amicus claims, tend consistently to overpredict violence, and indeed are more often wrong than right. Since predictions of violence are often erroneous, amicus concludes, the courts should not render rulings that predicate the liability of therapists upon the validity of such predictions.

The role of the psychiatrist, who is indeed a practitioner of medicine, and that of the psychologist who performs an allied function, are like that of the physician who must conform to the standards of the profession and who must often make diagnoses and predictions based upon such evaluations. Thus the judgment of the therapist in diagnosing emotional disorders and in predicting whether a patient presents a serious danger of violence is comparable to the judgment which doctors and professionals must regularly render under accepted rules of responsibility.

We recognize the difficulty that a therapist encounters in attempting to forecast whether a patient presents a serious danger of violence. Obviously, we do not require that the therapist, in making that determination, render a perfect performance; the therapist need only exercise "that reasonable degree of skill, knowledge, and care ordinarily possessed and exercised by members of [that professional specialty] under similar circumstances." Within the broad range of reasonable practice and treatment in which professional opinion and judgment may differ, the therapist is free to exercise his or her own best judgment without liability; proof, aided by hindsight, that he or she judged wrongly is insufficient to establish negligence.

In the instant case, however, the pleadings do not raise any question as to failure of defendant therapists to predict that Poddar presented a serious danger of violence. On the contrary, the present complaints allege that defendant therapists did in fact predict that Poddar would kill, but were negligent in failing to warn.

Amicus contends, however, that even when a therapist does in fact predict that a patient poses a serious danger of violence to others, the therapist should be absolved of any responsibility for failing to act to protect the potential victim. In our view, however, once a therapist does in fact determine, or under applicable professional standards reasonably should have determined, that a patient poses a serious danger of violence to others, he bears a duty to exercise reasonable care to protect the foreseeable victim of that danger. While the discharge of this duty of due care will necessarily vary with the facts of each case,[11] in each instance the adequacy of the therapist's conduct must be measured against the traditional negligence standard of the rendition of reasonable care under the circumstances. As explained in Fleming and Maximov, *The Patient or His Victim: The Therapist's Dilemma*, 62 Cal. L. Rev. 1025, 1067 (1974): "... the ultimate question of resolving the tension between the conflicting interests of patient and potential victim is one of social policy, not professional expertise.... In sum, the therapist owes a legal duty not only to his patient, but also to his patient's would-be victim and is subject in both respects to scrutiny by judge and jury."

* * * Weighing the uncertain and conjectural character of the alleged damage done the patient by such a warning against the peril to the victim's life, we conclude that professional inaccuracy in predicting violence cannot negate the therapist's duty to protect the threatened victim.

The risk that unnecessary warnings may be given is a reasonable price to pay for the lives of possible victims that may be saved. We would hesitate to hold that the therapist who is aware that his patient expects to attempt to assassinate the President of the United States would not be obligated to warn the authorities because the therapist cannot predict with accuracy that his patient will commit the crime.

* * *

NOTES

1. While *Tarasoff* is a state court ruling, it has increasingly taken on the trappings of a national decision, as one court after another adopted its principles and built on its conclusions. Issues continue to arise in this context, as commentators and jurists debate its prospective applicability to new and different fact patterns at both the higher education and the K–12 levels.

2. How relevant is the *Tarasoff* ruling to threat-related issues in the aftermath of Columbine and 9/11/01? Should the courts be applying *Tarasoff* to expand an educational institution's duties? *See* Melissa L. Gilbert, *Time-Out for Student Threats: Imposing a Duty to Protect on School Officials*, 49 UCLA L. REV. 917 (2002).

3. Recall the *Peterson* decision from Chapter 2, *supra*, where several attempted rapes had occurred in the exact spot that plaintiff had been injured. The Court determined that—under the facts of the case—there was a duty to exercise due care to protect students from reasonably foreseeable assaults on the campus. While the case, arguably, does not actually rule that a duty to protect would include a duty to warn, it certainly says that "plaintiff is entitled to prove that the failure to warn, to trim the foliage, or to take other reasonable measures to protect her was the proximate cause of her injuries."

---

11. Defendant therapists and amicus also argue that warnings must be given only in those cases in which the therapist knows the identity of the victim. We recognize that in some cases it would be unreasonable to require the therapist to interrogate his patient to discover the victim's identity, or to conduct an independent investigation. But there may also be cases in which a moment's reflection will reveal the victim's identity. The matter thus is one which depends upon the circumstances of each case, and should not be governed by any hard and fast rule.

Read together in light of current realities, *Tarasoff* and *Peterson* might very well stand for the proposition that in threat-related situations, a higher duty of care is more likely to be found, and that this obligation might often include a duty to warn. This may be particularly true in circumstances similar to those at Columbine, where students communicate through word and deed a desire or propensity to commit violent acts on campus.

4. A duty to warn may also be applicable in other education contexts. For example, an ongoing debate continues to rage in the area of sex education, with advocates of a more explicit curriculum—particularly relating to the threat of HIV—beginning to argue that educators have a legal obligation to warn students of the foreseeable dangers that may await them, and to communicate to them what precautions they could reasonably take to prevent irreversible injuries. *See infra*, Chapter 9.

2. RELEVANT STATUTORY PROHIBITIONS ADDRESSING THREATS UNDER FEDERAL & STATE LAW

At the K–12 level, state education codes generally permit all school districts to suspend students for threatening behavior on campus. Some statutes do not actually define the word *threat,* leaving it to local districts and individual educators to come up with workable descriptions of threatening activity. Others include either an actual definition or at least describe the type of threatening behavior that would be punishable. In certain circumstances—such as threats accompanied by possession of a weapon—suspensions or expulsions may be mandatory.

At the higher education level, threats are generally prohibited in student codes of conduct, and may be the basis for disciplinary action or even dismissal.

In general, both federal law and state law also include broad prohibitions against threatening behavior. These prohibitions are often found in the criminal law, and may sometimes be accompanied by precise definitions. At other times, the prohibitions are very general, leaving it to the courts to articulate tests for determining whether a person's words or actions, in a particular situation, might constitute a threat within the meaning of the statute.

With the increasing focus on hate-related violence in the U.S. over the past several decades, some state legislatures have made an effort to address threatening behavior in this context as well. California, for example, is one of a small but growing number of states that has sought to provide broad protection for all its citizens against threats and related activity on the basis of a person's actual or perceived group affiliation.

Consider the parameters of California Penal Code Section 422.6. Is such a statute important primarily for its symbolic value, or can it truly have a real-life impact?

CALIFORNIA PENAL CODE § 422.6

Interference with exercise of civil rights
because of actual or perceived characteristics of victim

(a) No person, whether or not acting under color of law, shall by force or threat of force, willfully injure, intimidate, interfere with, oppress, or threaten any other person in the free exercise or enjoyment of any right or privilege secured to him or her by the Constitution or laws of this state or by the Constitution or laws of the United States in whole or in part [because of one or more of the following actual or perceived characteristics of the victim: (1) Disability, (2) Gender, (3) Nationality, (4) Race or ethnicity, (5) Religion, (6) Sexual orientation, (7) Association with a person or group with one or more of these actual or perceived characteristics.][a]

(b) No person, whether or not acting under color of law, shall knowingly deface, damage, or destroy the real or personal property of any other person for the purpose of intimidating or interfering with the free exercise or enjoyment of any right or privilege secured to the other person by the Constitution or laws of this state or by the Constitution or laws of the United States, in whole or in part because of one or more of the actual or perceived characteristics of the victim listed in subdivision (a) of Section 422.55.

(c) Any person convicted of violating subdivision (a) or (b) shall be punished by imprisonment in a county jail not to exceed one year, or by a fine not to exceed five thousand dollars ($5,000), or by both the above imprisonment and fine, and the court shall order the defendant to perform a minimum of community service, not to exceed 400 hours, to be performed over a period not to exceed 350 days, during a time other than his or her hours of employment or school attendance. However, no person may be convicted of violating subdivision (a) based upon speech alone, except upon a showing that the speech itself threatened violence against a specific person or group of persons and that the defendant had the apparent ability to carry out the threat.

Especially in the aftermath of Columbine, many people turned their attention to the Internet, seeking to identify ways to combat threatening behavior that may originate online. One particular area of focus was bomb-making activity, since so much information has been made available online regarding weapons, explosives, how to obtain them, and indeed how to make them.

A federal ban on "bomb-making instructions" was indeed passed by Congress as a result of these concerns, but its provisions were significantly limited by First Amendment considerations.

---

a. The complete text of subdivision (a), as amended in 2004, concludes with the following clause: "because of one or more of the actual or perceived characteristics of the victim listed in subdivision (a) of Section 422.55." The characteristics listed in Section 422.55 are therefore included here in brackets.

Consider the language of Section 842, which follows. Given the limiting language regarding knowledge and intent, can such a law play any sort of significant role in combating the very type of threatening behavior that its proponents were hoping to address?

FEDERAL BAN ON "BOMB–MAKING INSTRUCTIONS"
from **18 U.S.C. § 842 (2003)**

(p) Distribution of information relating to explosives, destructive devices, and weapons of mass destruction. * * *

(2) Prohibition. It shall be unlawful for any person—

(A) to teach or demonstrate the making or use of an explosive, a destructive device, or a weapon of mass destruction, or to distribute by any means information pertaining to, in whole or in part, the manufacture or use of an explosive, destructive device, or weapon of mass destruction, with the intent that the teaching, demonstration, or information be used for, or in furtherance of, an activity that constitutes a Federal crime of violence; or

(B) to teach or demonstrate to any person the making or use of an explosive, a destructive device, or a weapon of mass destruction, or to distribute to any person, by any means, information pertaining to, in whole or in part, the manufacture or use of an explosive, destructive device, or weapon of mass destruction, knowing that such person intends to use the teaching, demonstration, or information for, or in furtherance of, an activity that constitutes a Federal crime of violence.

As more and more people use the Internet for a wide variety of day-to-day activities, *cyberbullying*—which often encompasses both threatening behavior and harassment—has become, for many, a major concern. The issue gained national prominence in October 2006 with the tragic suicide of St. Louis area resident Megan Meier. The thirteen-year-old teenager had begun corresponding on MySpace with someone named Josh, and at first the messages were generally positive. But after several weeks, Josh told her he no longer wanted to be her friend, and said very mean-spirited things that apparently led her to hang herself. It was later disclosed that Josh never existed, but was instead a creation of a neighbor who pretended to be Josh in order to see what Megan might have been saying about the neighbor's teenage daughter on MySpace.

In June 2008, Missouri Governor Matt Blunt signed a bill that outlawed "cyberbulling" by updating state laws against harassment:

MISSOURI REV. STAT. § 565.090 (2008)
Harassment

1. A person commits the crime of harassment if he or she:

(1) Knowingly communicates a threat to commit any felony to another person and in so doing, frightens, intimidates, or causes emotional distress to such other person; or

(2) When communicating with another person, knowingly uses coarse language offensive to one of average sensibility and thereby puts such person in reasonable apprehension of offensive physical contact or harm; or

(3) Knowingly frightens, intimidates, or causes emotional distress to another person by anonymously making a telephone call or any electronic communication; or

(4) Knowingly communicates with another person who is, or who purports to be, seventeen years of age or younger and in so doing and without good cause recklessly frightens, intimidates, or causes emotional distress to such other person; or

(5) Knowingly makes repeated unwanted communication to another person; or

(6) Without good cause engages in any other act with the purpose to frighten, intimidate, or cause emotional distress to another person, cause such person to be frightened, intimidated, or emotionally distressed, and such person's response to the act is one of a person of average sensibilities considering the age of such person.

2.   Harassment is a class A misdemeanor unless:

(1) Committed by a person twenty-one years of age or older against a person seventeen years of age or younger; * * *

In such cases, harassment shall be a class D felony. * * *

At the federal level, the following bipartisan legislation was introduced in May 2008 by California Congresswoman Linda Sanchez and Missouri Congressman Kenny Hulshof. In light of your analysis of the regulatory design and whether the plan is likely to achieve its purpose, would you recommend passage of such a bill? Why? Alternatively, could you support a modified version of this bill? If so, what modifications might be appropriate?

H.R. 6123 (SANCHEZ–HULSHOF)

The 'Megan Meier Cyberbullying Prevention Act'
May 2008

* * *

Sec. 2. Findings.

(3) Electronic communications provide anonymity to the perpetrator and the potential for widespread public distribution, potentially making them severely dangerous and cruel to youth.

(4) Online victimizations are associated with emotional distress and other psychological problems, including depression.

(5) Cyberbullying can cause psychological harm, including depression; negatively impact academic performance, safety, and the well-being of children in school; force children to change schools; and

in some cases lead to extreme violent behavior, including murder and suicide.

(6) Sixty percent of mental health professionals who responded to the Survey of Internet Mental Health Issues report having treated at least one patient with a problematic Internet experience in the previous five years; 54 percent of these clients were 18 years of age or younger.

Sec. 3. Cyberbullying. In General—Chapter 41 of title 18, United States Code, is amended by adding at the end the following:

(a) Whoever transmits in interstate or foreign commerce any communication, with the intent to coerce, intimidate, harass, or cause substantial emotional distress to a person, using electronic means to support severe, repeated, and hostile behavior, shall be fined under this title or imprisoned not more than two years, or both. * * *

3. CRIMINAL LAW CASES ADDRESSING THREATENING ACTIVITY

COMMONWEALTH v. MILO M., A JUVENILE

433 Mass. 149, 740 N.E.2d 967 (2001)

IRELAND, J.

Milo M., a juvenile defendant, appeals from the Juvenile Court's adjudication of him as delinquent by reason of threatening his teacher in violation of G.L. c.275, § 2.[a] While public schools remain very safe places for children to be, with respect to this appeal, we face the important and troubling question whether, given recent, highly publicized incidents of school violence, a drawing that depicts a student pointing a gun at his teacher constitutes a threat. We conclude that it does, and thus, affirm the adjudication of delinquency.

1. *Facts and procedural history*

On October 27, 1998, the twelve year old juvenile sat at a desk in the hall directly outside of his classroom and drew a picture. While the juvenile was awaiting the principal's arrival to address with him "some issues from the previous day," a teacher at the school confiscated the drawing and showed it to the juvenile's teacher, Mrs. F. The drawing depicted a violent scene of the juvenile shooting Mrs. F. See Appendix A. Meanwhile, the juvenile left the desk, entered the classroom, took a piece of paper, returned to the desk in the hall and "proceeded to draw another picture." Moments later, the juvenile reentered the classroom and stood near the doorway. He held up the second picture, which depicted the

---

a. Mass. Gen. Law ch. 275, § 2, provides:

If complaint is made to any such court or justice that a person has threatened to commit a crime against the person or property of another, such court or justice shall examine the complainant and any witnesses who may be produced, on oath, reduce the complaint to writing and cause it to be subscribed by the complainant.

juvenile pointing a gun at Mrs. F. See Appendix B. He looked at Mrs. F and in a defiant tone said, "[D]o you want this one too?" From where she was standing, Mrs. F could not see the drawing. However, after seeing the first drawing, and "[f]rom his posture, [and] the look on his face," Mrs. F realized that the juvenile was very upset and very angry. Because she did not want the juvenile to approach her, she instructed him to give the drawing to another student, who then gave it to Mrs. F. The juvenile returned to his desk in the hall without further comment. Mrs. F testified that, after seeing the second drawing, she became "apprehensive" and "[a]fraid for [her] safety." Apparently, as a result of these incidents, the juvenile was suspended immediately for three days and sent home. However, at the end of that same school day, both Mrs. F and the teacher who confiscated the first drawing witnessed the juvenile at the school, loitering very near Mrs. F's car.

Subsequently, the Worcester Division of the Juvenile Court Department issued a complaint, charging the juvenile with threatening Mrs. F in violation of G.L. c. 275, § 2. At trial, the judge adjudicated the juvenile delinquent by reason of threatening his teacher, on the basis of the second drawing.[2] The juvenile appealed, and we transferred the case on our own motion.

2. *The standard applied*

The word "threatened" is not defined in the Massachusetts threat statute, G.L. c. 275, § 2. However, "[t]he elements of threatening a crime include an expression of intention to inflict a crime on another and an ability to do so in circumstances that would justify apprehension on the part of the recipient of the threat."

* * *

There was sufficient evidence to support the judge's finding that the juvenile expressed an intent to commit the threatened crime and an ability to do so in circumstances that would justify apprehension on Mrs. F's part. In making this determination, we consider "the context in which the allegedly threatening [drawing was given to Mrs. F] and all of the surrounding circumstances." The juvenile's intention to carry out the threat may be inferred from several facts. First, the content of each drawing separately evidences his intent.[6] The first drawing portrays a figure, labeled with the juvenile's name, pointing what appears to be a gun at another figure, labeled with Mrs. F's name. The Mrs. F figure has her hands clasped in front of her and is crying and pleading, "Please don't kill me." Drawn directly next to the Mrs. F figure is another unlabeled figure, whose head is falling off to the right. At the bottom of the drawing is the

---

2. The judge found that the first drawing could not have constituted a threat because the juvenile himself did not communicate it to Mrs. F.

6. In finding that the second drawing constituted a threat, the judge considered the first drawing, which he found to "portray[ ] an act of violence being perpetrated upon the teacher." The fact that the judge ruled that the first drawing was not a separate threat because the juvenile did not communicate it to Mrs. F, did not diminish its evidentiary value and he could have inferred the juvenile's intent from it.

word "Blood," written in large letters. The second drawing depicts a figure labeled with the juvenile's name, aiming a gun at another figure, labeled with Mrs. F's name. Directly above the Mrs. F figure are the words "Pissy Pants." The Mrs. F figure is kneeling with her hands clasped in front of her, and appears to have urinated on herself, suggesting her extreme fear of being shot. Some words are written inside a box drawn under the barrel of the gun; one of the words appears to be "Bang." The content of both drawings makes the juvenile's intent to harm Mrs. F clear.[7] Second, the juvenile made not just one, but two drawings, both of which depicted images of himself perpetrating violence upon Mrs. F. The judge could have inferred the juvenile's intent from the number of drawings. Third, the juvenile's intent may be inferred from his very angry demeanor and defiant manner toward Mrs. F when he held out the drawing to her. Thus, there was sufficient evidence to support the judge's finding that the drawing was "an expression of an intention to harm. . . ."

As to the juvenile's present ability to carry out the threat, the juvenile contends that "there was no direct evidence that the [juvenile] had the ability to commit this crime." There was, however, sufficient circumstantial evidence to support this finding. This is not a case where the finding of ability "rest[s] on surmise, conjecture, or guesswork." Indeed, as discussed above, the juvenile held the second of two very violent drawings out to Mrs. F in an angry and defiant manner. Moreover, prior to the incident, the juvenile was sitting out in the hall, awaiting the principal's arrival. Although it is not clear exactly what, if anything, the juvenile had done to warrant this discipline, the teacher who confiscated the first drawing testified that "[u]sually, if a student is outside the room, [the student] had done something to cause that situation. . . ." Thus, the judge could have reasonably inferred that the juvenile was already being disciplined, and that Mrs. F, as his teacher, "was familiar with the [juvenile's] history" at school and in her classroom.

Moreover, although there is no evidence that the juvenile possessed an immediate ability to carry out the threat at the time he communicated the drawing to Mrs. F, this does "not mean that [the juvenile] could not have carried out his threat at a later time." Indeed, the juvenile's ability to carry out the threat in the future could have been inferred from the fact that the juvenile was seen loitering near Mrs. F's car later the same day.

Finally, given the recent highly publicized, school-related shootings by students, we take judicial notice of the actual and potential violence in public schools. Although we note that schools remain very safe places for children to be, such violent episodes are matters of common knowledge, particularly within the teaching community, and thus, are "indisputably

---

7. The intent that must be expressed is an intent to commit a crime. We note that both drawings depict extreme fear on the part of Mrs. F and express the juvenile's desire to instill such fear on her part. Assuming that the drawings should not be interpreted as an intent to actually shoot Mrs. F, an intent to assault her by means of a dangerous weapon would still constitute an intent to commit a crime.

true."[8] Recently, "[o]ther children of like age [have] made similar threats ... and [have] carried them out with tragic consequences for both juveniles and their victims."

These factors, when considered in light of the "climate of apprehension" concerning school violence in which this incident occurred, make Mrs. F's fear that the juvenile could carry out the threat quite reasonable and justifiable.

Finally, we conclude that the record supports the finding that the juvenile communicated the threat, vis-a-vis the second drawing, to Mrs. F. Indeed, the obviously angry juvenile entered Mrs. F's classroom, held out the second violent picture—the content of which was directed at Mrs. F— to her and defiantly asked, "[D]o you want this one too?" Although Mrs. F testified that initially, she could not "really see" the picture, she was able to once she received it from the other student shortly thereafter. From these facts, the judge could have found that the drawing itself, when held out to Mrs. F, communicated the threat. Viewed in the light most favorable to the Commonwealth, the combination of these factors sufficiently supports the finding that the juvenile communicated the threat to Mrs. F.

This evidence, when viewed as a whole "may constitute the requisite expression [of intention to do bodily harm], and may indicate additionally, in these circumstances, ability and apprehension." Thus, we find that sufficient evidence supports the judge's decision that the drawing constituted a threat.

---

8. We take judicial notice of the fact that, prior to this incident, the following highly publicized school shootings had occurred: On February 2, 1996, in Moses Lake, Washington, a fourteen year old fatally shot a teacher and two students and wounded another student; on February 19, 1997, in Bethel, Alaska, a sixteen year old shot and killed his principal and a student, and wounded two other students; on October 1, 1997, in Pearl, Mississippi, a sixteen year old boy shot his mother, and then went to school and shot nine students, two fatally; on December 1, 1997, in West Paducah, Kentucky, a fourteen year old student shot and killed three students and wounded five others; on March 24, 1998, in Jonesboro, Arkansas, two boys, aged eleven and thirteen years, shot to death four girls and a teacher, and wounded ten others during a false fire alarm; on April 24, 1998, in Edinboro, Pennsylvania, a fourteen year old student was charged with fatally shooting his science teacher at an eighth grade dance; on May 19, 1998, in Fayetteville, Tennessee, an eighteen year old honor student allegedly shot his classmate to death in the parking lot of their high school; on May 21, 1998, in Springfield, Oregon, a fifteen year old boy allegedly shot and killed two of his classmates and wounded more than twenty other students; on June 15, 1998, in Richmond, Virginia, a fourteen year old allegedly wounded one teacher and one guidance counselor in a high school. This tragic trend regrettably continued after the incident at issue in this case occurred. On April 20, 1999, at Columbine High School in Littleton, Colorado, two young men fatally shot fourteen students and one teacher and wounded at least twenty-three others, before taking their own lives. *See 25 Feared Dead, 20 Hurt in High School Shooting: Colorado Rampage Ends When 2 Commit Suicide*, COURIER JOURNAL (Louisville, Kentucky), Apr. 21, 1999 at 1A; Haney, *A Timeline of Recent School Shootings* (Apr. 27, 2000); *ABC News, An Explosion of Violence* (Mar. 28, 2000). We also note that, in 1985, the United States Supreme Court noted that "in recent years, school disorder has often taken particularly ugly forms: drug use and violent crime in the schools have become major social problems." New Jersey v. T.L.O., 469 U.S. 325, 339, 105 S.Ct. 733 (1985). Additionally, in 1995, the United States Supreme Court in a dissent by Justice Breyer noted that "reports, hearings, and other readily available literature make clear that the problem of guns in and around schools is widespread and extremely serious." United States v. Lopez, 514 U.S. 549, 619, 115 S.Ct. 1624, 1657 (1995) (Breyer, J., dissenting).

"[T]he First Amendment [to the United States Constitution] does not protect conduct that threatens another." Because we find there was sufficient evidence to support the judge's conclusion that the juvenile's drawing constituted a threat, there is no violation of the juvenile's First Amendment rights.

The adjudication of delinquency is affirmed.

So ordered.

Appendices to *Milo M.*

APPENDIX A

APPENDIX B

IN RE GEORGE T.

33 Cal.4th 620, 16 Cal.Rptr.3d 61, 93 P.3d 1007 (2004)

MORENO, J.

We consider in this case whether a high school student made a criminal threat by giving two classmates a poem labeled "Dark Poetry," which recites in part, "I am Dark, Destructive, & Dangerous. I slap on my face of happiness but inside I am evil!! For I can be the next kid to bring guns to kill students at school. So parents watch your children cuz I'm BACK!!" For the reasons below, we conclude that the ambiguous nature of the poem, along with the circumstances surrounding its dissemination, fail to establish that the poem constituted a criminal threat.

I. FACTS AND PROCEDURAL HISTORY

Fifteen-year-old George T. (minor) had been a student at Santa Teresa High School in Santa Clara County for approximately two weeks when on Friday, March 16, 2001, toward the end of his honors English class, he approached fellow student Mary S. and asked her, "Is there a poetry class here?" Minor then handed Mary three sheets of paper and told her, "[r]ead these." Mary did so. The first sheet of paper contained a note stating, "These poems describe me and my feelings. Tell me if they describe you and your feelings." The two other sheets of paper contained poems. Mary read only one of the poems, which was labeled "Dark Poetry" and entitled "Faces":

> Who are these faces around me? Where did they come from? They would probably become the next doctors or loirs or something. All really intelligent and ahead in their game. I wish I had a choice on what I want to be like they do. All so happy and vagrant. Each origonal in their own way. They make me want to puke. For I am Dark, Destructive, & Dangerous. I slap on my face of happiness but inside I am evil!! For I can be the next kid to bring guns to kill students at school. So parents watch your children cuz I'm BACK!!
>
> by: Julius AKA Angel[1]

Minor had a "straight face," not "show[ing] any emotion, neither happy or sad or angry or upset," when he handed the poems to Mary.

Upon reading the "Faces" poem, Mary became frightened, handed the poems back to minor, and immediately left the campus in fear. After she informed her parents about the poem, her father called the school, but it was closed. Mary testified she did not know minor well, but they were on "friendly terms." When asked why she felt minor gave her the poem to read, she responded: "I thought maybe because the first day he came into our class, I approached him because that's the right thing to do" and because she continued to be nice to him.

After Mary handed the poems back to minor, minor approached Erin S. and Natalie P., students minor had met during his two weeks at Santa Teresa High School. Erin had been introduced to minor a week prior and had subsequently spoken with him on only three or four occasions, whereas Natalie considered herself minor's friend and had come to know him well during their long after-school conversations, which generally

---

1. Minor went by the name "Julius"; misspelled words are in original.

lasted between an hour to an hour and a half and included discussions of poetry. Minor handed Erin a "folded up" piece of paper and asked her to read it. He also handed a similarly folded piece of paper to Natalie, who was standing with Erin. Because Erin was late for class, she only pretended to read the poem to be polite, but did not actually read it. She placed the unread poem in the pocket of her jacket.

* * * Mary remained in fear throughout the weekend because she understood the poem to be personally threatening to her, as a student. Asked why she felt the poem was a threat, Mary responded: "It's obvious he thought of himself as a dark, destructive, and dangerous person. And if he was willing to admit that about himself and then also state that he could be the next person to bring guns and kill students, then I'd say that he was threatening." She understood the term "dark poetry" to mean "angry threats; any thoughts that aren't positive."

* * *

Police officers went to the school the following Monday to investigate the dissemination of the poem. Erin was summoned to the vice-principal's office and asked whether minor had given her any notes. She responded in the affirmative, realized that the poem was still in the pocket of her jacket, and retrieved it. The paper contained a poem entitled "Faces," which was the same poem given to Mary. Upon reading the poem for the first time in the vice-principal's office, Erin became terrified and broke down in tears, finding the poem to be a personal threat to her life. She testified that she was not in the poetry club and had no interest in the subject.

* * *

Natalie did not feel threatened by the poem, rather it made her "feel sad" because "[i]t was kind of lonely." She testified that "dark poetry is * * * relevant to like pure emotions, like sadness, loneliness, hate or just like pure emotions. Sometimes it tells a story, like a dark story." Based on her extended conversations with minor, Natalie found him to be "mild and calm and very serene" and did not consider him to be violent.

Minor testified the poem "Faces" was not intended to be a threat and, because Erin and Natalie were his friends, he did not think they would have taken his poems as such. He thought of poetry as art and stated that he was very much interested in the subject, particularly as a medium to describe "emotions instead of acting them out." He wrote "Faces" during his honors English class on the day he showed it to Mary and Erin. Minor was having a bad day as a consequence of having forgotten to ask his parents for lunch money and having to forgo lunch that day, and because he was unable to locate something in his backpack. He had many thoughts going through his head, so he decided to write them down as a way of getting them out. The poem "Who Am I," which was given to Natalie, was written the same day as "Faces," but was written during the lunch period. Neither poem was intended to be a threat. Instead they were "just creativity."

Minor and his friends frequently joked about the school shootings in Littleton, Colorado.[3] They would jokingly say, "I'm going to be the next Columbine kid." Minor testified that Natalie and Erin had been present when he and some of his friends had joked about Columbine, with someone stating that "I'll probably be the next Columbine killer," and indicating who would be killed and who would be spared. Given this past history, minor believed Natalie and Erin would understand the poems as jokes.

The poems were labeled "dark poetry" to inform readers that they were exactly that and, minor testified, "if anybody was supposed to read this poem, or let's say if my mom ever found my poem or something of that nature, I would like them to know that it was dark poetry. Dark poetry is usually just an expression. It's creativity. It is not like you're actually going to do something like that, basically."

* * *

On cross-examination, minor conceded that he had had difficulties in his two previous schools, including being disciplined for urinating on a wall at his first school and had been asked to leave his second school for plagiarizing from the Internet. He explained that the urination incident was caused by a doctor-verified bladder problem. He denied having any ill will toward the school district, but conceded when pressed by the prosecutor that he felt the schools "had it in for me."

An amended petition under Welfare and Institutions Code section 602 was filed against minor, alleging minor made three criminal threats in violation of Penal Code section 422.[4] * * *

Following a contested jurisdictional hearing, * * * the court adjudicated minor a ward of the court and ordered a 100–day commitment in juvenile hall. Minor appealed, challenging the sufficiency of the evidence to support the juvenile court's finding that he made criminal threats. Over a dissent, the Court of Appeal affirmed the juvenile court. * * * We granted review and now reverse.

II. DISCUSSION

* * * [We have made it clear] ... that not all threats are criminal and enumerated the elements necessary to prove the offense of making criminal threats under section 422. The prosecution must prove "(1) that

---

3. This reference is to the 1999 school shooting at Columbine High School in Colorado involving two student shooters that resulted in the death of 12 fellow students and one faculty member.

4. Section 422 provides in relevant part:

Any person who willfully threatens to commit a crime which will result in death or great bodily injury to another person, with the specific intent that the statement, made verbally [or] in writing ... is to be taken as a threat, even if there is no intent of actually carrying it out, which, on its face and under the circumstances in which it was made, is so unequivocal, unconditional, immediate, and specific as to convey to the person threatened, a gravity of purpose and an immediate prospect of execution of the threat, and thereby causes that person reasonably to be in sustained fear for his or her own safety, shall be punished by imprisonment in the county jail not to exceed one year, or by imprisonment in the state prison.

the defendant 'willfully threaten[ed] to commit a crime which will result in death or great bodily injury to another person,' (2) that the defendant made the threat 'with the specific intent that the statement * * * is to be taken as a threat, even if there is no intent of actually carrying it out,' (3) that the threat—which may be 'made verbally, in writing, or by means of an electronic communication device'—was 'on its face and under the circumstances in which it [was] made, * * * so unequivocal, unconditional, immediate, and specific as to convey to the person threatened, a gravity of purpose and an immediate prospect of execution of the threat,' (4) that the threat actually caused the person threatened 'to be in sustained fear for his or her own safety or for his or her immediate family's safety,' and (5) that the threatened person's fear was 'reasonabl[e]' under the circumstances."

> * * *

* * * Minor challenges the findings with respect to two of the five elements, contending that the poem "was [not] 'on its face and under the circumstances in which it [was disseminated] so unequivocal, unconditional, immediate, and specific as to convey to [Mary and Erin] a gravity of purpose and an immediate prospect of execution of the threat' " and that the facts fail to establish he harbored the specific intent to threaten Mary and Erin.

With respect to the requirement that a threat be "so unequivocal, unconditional, immediate, and specific as to convey to the person threatened a gravity of purpose and an immediate prospect of execution of the threat," we ... [have] ... explained that the word "so" in section 422 meant that " 'unequivocality, unconditionality, immediacy and specificity are not absolutely mandated, but must be sufficiently present in the threat and surrounding circumstances....' " "The four qualities are simply the factors to be considered in determining whether a threat, considered together with its surrounding circumstances, conveys those impressions to the victim." A communication that is ambiguous on its face may nonetheless be found to be a criminal threat if the surrounding circumstances clarify the communication's meaning.

With the above considerations in mind, we examine the poem at issue—"Faces."

Only the final two lines of the poem could arguably be construed to be a criminal threat: "For I can be the next kid to bring guns to kill students at school. So parents watch your children cuz I'm BACK!!" Mary believed this was a threat, but her testimony reveals that her conclusion rested upon a considerable amount of interpretation: "I feel that when he said, 'I can be the next person,' that he meant that he will be, because also he says that he's dark, destructive, and dangerous person. And I'd describe a dangerous person as someone who has something in mind of killing someone or multiple people." The juvenile court's finding that minor threatened to kill Mary and Erin likewise turned primarily on its interpretation of the words, "For I *can* be the next kid to bring guns to kill students at school'' (italics added) to mean not only that minor could do so, but that he would do so. In other words, the court construed the word "can" to mean "will." But that is not what the poem recites. However the poem was interpreted by Mary and Erin, and the court, the fact remains that "can" does not mean "will." While the protagonist in "Faces" declares that he has the potential or capacity to kill students given his dark and hidden feelings, he does not actually threaten to do so. While perhaps discomforting and unsettling, in this unique context this disclosure simply does not constitute an actual threat to kill or inflict harm.

As is evident, the poem "Faces" is ambiguous and plainly equivocal. It does not describe or threaten future conduct since it does not state that the protagonist plans to kill students, or even that any potential victims would include Mary or Erin. Such ambiguity aside, it appears that Mary actually misread the text of the poem. In her e-mail to Rasmussen, she stated that the poem read, "he's *going* to be the next person to bring a gun to school and kill random people.'" (Italics added.) She did not tell Rasmussen that this was her interpretation of the poem, but asserted that those were the words used by minor. Given the student killings in Columbine and Santee, this may have been an understandable mistake, but it does not alter the requirement that the words actually used must constitute a threat in light of the surrounding circumstances.

* * * [In this regard, the note given to Mary] ... is consistent with the contention that the poem did nothing more than describe certain dark feelings. The note asked whether Mary had the same feelings; it did not state or imply something to the effect of, "this is what I plan to do, are you with me."

Of course, exactly what the poem means is open to varying interpretations because a poem may mean different things to different readers. As a medium of expression, a poem is inherently ambiguous. In general, "[r]easonable persons understand musical lyrics and poetic conventions as the figurative expressions which they are," which means they "are not intended to be and should not be read literally on their face, nor judged by a standard of prose oratory." Ambiguity in poetry is sometimes intended: "'Ambiguity' itself can mean an indecision as to what you mean, an intention to mean several things, a probability that one or the other or both of two things has been meant, and the fact that a statement has several meanings." * * *

In short, viewed in isolation the poem is not "so unequivocal" as to have conveyed to Mary and Erin a gravity of purpose and an immediate prospect that minor would bring guns to school and kill them. Ambiguity, however, is not necessarily sufficient to immunize the poem from being deemed a criminal threat because the surrounding circumstances may clarify facial ambiguity. * * *

[However,] [u]nlike some cases that have turned on an examination of the surrounding circumstances given a communication's vagueness, incriminating circumstances in this case are noticeably lacking: there was no history of animosity or conflict between the students.... Thus the circumstances surrounding the poem's dissemination fail to show that, as a threat, it was sufficiently unequivocal to convey to Mary and Erin an immediate prospect that minor would bring guns to school and shoot students.

The themes and feelings expressed in "Faces" are not unusual in literature * * * * "Faces" was in the style of a relatively new genre of literature called "dark poetry" that amici curiae J.M. Coetzee et al. explain is an extension of the poetry of Sylvia Plath, John Berryman, Robert Lowell, and other confessional poets who depict "extraordinarily mean, ugly, violent, or harrowing experiences." Consistent with that genre, "Faces" invokes images of darkness, violence, discontentment, envy, and alienation. The protagonist describes his duplicitous nature—malevolent on the inside, felicitous on the outside.

For the foregoing reasons, we hold the poem entitled "Faces" and the circumstances surrounding its dissemination fail to establish that it was a criminal threat because the text of the poem, understood in light of the surrounding circumstances, was not "so unequivocal, unconditional, immediate, and specific as to convey to [the two students] a gravity of purpose and an immediate prospect of execution of the threat."

This case implicates two apparently competing interests: a school administration's interest in ensuring the safety of its students and faculty versus students' right to engage in creative expression. Following Columbine, Santee, and other notorious school shootings, there is a heightened sensitivity on school campuses to latent signs that a student may undertake to bring guns to school and embark on a shooting rampage. Such signs may include violence-laden student writings. For example, the two student killers in Columbine had written poems for their English classes containing "extremely violent imagery." Ensuring a safe school environment and protecting freedom of expression, however, are not necessarily antagonistic goals.

Minor's reference to school shootings and his dissemination of his poem in close proximity to the Santee school shooting no doubt reasonably heightened the school's concern that minor might emulate the actions of previous school shooters. Certainly, school personnel were amply justified in taking action following Mary's e-mail and telephone conversation with her English teacher, but that is not the issue before us. We decide here only that minor's poem did not constitute a criminal threat.

　　　* * *

NOTES

1.　There are many parallels between the *Milo M.* case and the *George T.* case. In particular, both reflect the efforts of state supreme court justices to wrestle with threat-related issues within a national context in the aftermath of Columbine and related events.

2. Given the parallels and the broad similarities, why did the decisions come out differently? Why did the Massachusetts court rule against the student, while the California court ruled in the student's favor? Can the two opinions be reconciled, or do they ultimately stand as examples of different state courts coming to different conclusions regarding the same issue?

3. It is interesting to note that in *Milo M.,* had it not been for the teacher who came upon the student after he had completed the first drawing, none of the subsequent events would have happened and arguably no threatening behavior would have taken place. Was the court wrong in its decision to apparently pay no attention to the fact that had this other teacher left things alone, the situation might not have careened out of control?

4. In the late 1990s, a series of hate-related e-mail cases led to highly publicized prosecutions of persons at the higher education level. Perhaps the most prominent of these cases was *United States v. Machado,* No. SACR 96–142–AHS (S.D. Cal. 1998). Richard Machado—a former UC Irvine student—was found guilty of violating federal civil rights laws after sending a hateful and threatening e-mail message to 59 UCI students with Asian surnames. The message, signed "Asian Hater," warned that all Asians should leave UC Irvine or the sender would "hunt all of you down and kill your stupid asses." He also wrote: "I personally will make it my life's work to find and kill every one of you personally. OK? That's how determined I am. Do you hear me?" At trial, the defense attempted to portray Machado's actions as "a classic flame," and argued that no reasonable person should have felt threatened by it. But the federal court did not agree. *See also* Davan Maharaj, *Anti-Asian E–Mail Was Hate Crime, Jury Finds,* L.A. TIMES, Feb. 11, 1998, at A1.

A case with many similarities was resolved without a trial in 1999 when Kingman Quon—a Cal Poly Pomona student—pled guilty to seven misdemeanor counts of interfering with federally protected activities. Quon had sent his message to persons with Hispanic surnames across the U.S., including 42 professors at California State University, Los Angeles, 25 students at MIT, and employees of Indiana University, Xerox Corp., the Texas Hispanic Journal, the Internal Revenue Service, and NASA's Ames Research Center. The message was two pages long, strewn with profanity, and began with the words "I hate your race. I want you all to die." It also included such phrases as "kill all wetbacks." David Rosenzweig, *Man Charged in Sending Hate E–Mail to Latinos Across U.S.,* L.A. TIMES, Jan. 29, 1999, at B1.

B. FIRST AMENDMENT ISSUES IN A THREAT–RELATED CONTEXT

Case law regarding threats in an education setting—and indeed threat-related case law in general—remains relatively unsettled at this point in time. Different courts may approach the issues in different ways, and different circuits have set forth different tests for deciding the First Amendment questions.

In sorting through this material, it is useful to divide the cases into two general categories: those that involve actual criminal prosecutions, and those that only involve some sort of administrative/ disciplinary action taken against the student.

In the criminal cases, some courts simply base the inquiry on whether the elements of the criminal statute were violated. This is true for the *Milo M.* and *George T.* cases, above, and for the Sixth Circuit majority in *United States v. Alkhabaz,* below. Other courts link the criminal analysis to whether there was a "true threat" as defined by First Amendment case law. Examples of this are the Sixth Circuit dissent by Judge Krupansky in *Alkhabaz,* and the Wisconsin Supreme Court's opinion in *In re Douglas D., 243 Wis.2d 204, 626 N.W.2d 725 (2001).*

The *Douglas D.* analysis is a particularly good example of how First Amendment doctrine fits into a criminal prosecution:

> [F]or purposes of First Amendment analysis, a "threat" is very different from a "true threat." "Threat" is a nebulous term that can describe anything from "[a]n expression of an intention to inflict pain, injury, evil, or punishment" to any generalized "menace." Under such a broad definition, "threats" include protected and un-protected speech. Thus, states cannot enact general laws prohibiting all "threats" without infringing on some speech protected by the First Amendment. By contrast, "true threat" is a constitutional term of art used to describe a specific category of unprotected speech. This category, although often inclusive of speech or acts that fall within the broader definition of "threat," does not include protected speech. Therefore, states may, consistent with the First Amendment, prohibit all "true threats." *In re* Douglas D., 243 Wis.2d at 230–31, 626 N.W.2d at 739 (2001).

In the disciplinary action cases, First Amendment rights of students are typically *the* central issue. Some courts, such as the Eighth Circuit in *Doe v. Pulaski,* address the question under the true threat doctrine. Others, like the Court in *Wisniewski v. Bd. of Educ.,* below, analyze the facts under the *Tinker* rule alone.

1. CONSTRUING THE "TRUE THREAT" DOCTRINE IN A HIGHER EDUCATION SETTING

PROBLEM 17: THE ALISTAIRE JONES LITIGATION, PART II

The following hypothetical is based on the facts set forth in Problem 14, *supra,* Chapter 3.

Assume that a Joseph, a member of Group A, upon reading Alistaire's November 8th column, posted an open letter to Alistaire on a university-sponsored online discussion forum which castigated him for "stirring up the forces of fascism and repression," and included the following quotes: "I'll meet you, one-on-one, any time and any place. Your words are fighting words, and you need to be prepared to pay. Don't think, for example, that you can ever set foot on this campus again and hope to leave in one piece." Many people were taken aback by these highly publicized comments, especially given the fact that Joseph was a soft-spoken, slightly built young man known mostly for his roles in school dramatic productions, while Alistaire was a former nose guard on his high school football team. Joseph is prosecuted by the local U.S. Attorney under Title 18, Section 875(c) of the U.S. Code. Would the U.S. prevail? Why?

(Assume that this jurisdiction follows Judge Krupansky's view of threat law set forth in the *Alkhabaz* dissent.)

UNITED STATES v. ALKHABAZ, ALSO KNOWN AS JAKE BAKER

104 F.3d 1492 (6th Cir. 1997)

BOYCE F. MARTIN, JR., CHIEF JUDGE.

Claiming that the district court erred in determining that certain electronic mail messages between Abraham Jacob Alkhabaz, a.k.a. Jake Baker, and Arthur Gonda did not constitute "true threats," the government appeals the dismissal of the indictment charging Baker with violations of 18 U.S.C. § 875(c).

From November 1994 until approximately January 1995, Baker and Gonda exchanged e-mail messages over the Internet, the content of which expressed a sexual interest in violence against women and girls. Baker sent and received messages through a computer in Ann Arbor, Michigan, while Gonda—whose true identity and whereabouts are still unknown—used a computer in Ontario, Canada.

Prior to this time, Baker had posted a number of fictional stories to "alt.sex.stories," a popular interactive Usenet news group. Using such shorthand references as "B & D," "snuff," "pedo," "mf," and "nc," Baker's fictional stories generally involved the abduction, rape, torture, mutilation, and murder of women and young girls. On January 9, Baker posted a story describing the torture, rape, and murder of a young woman who shared the name of one of Baker's classmates at the University of Michigan.

On February 9, Baker was arrested and appeared before a United States Magistrate Judge on a criminal complaint alleging violations of 18 U.S.C. § 875(c), which prohibits interstate communications containing threats to kidnap or injure another person. The Magistrate Judge ordered Baker detained as a danger to the community and a United States District Court affirmed his detention. Upon Baker's motion to be released on bond, this Court ordered a psychological evaluation. When the evaluation concluded that Baker posed no threat to the community, this Court ordered Baker's release.

* * * On March 15, 1995, citing several e-mail messages between Gonda and Baker, a federal grand jury returned a[n] * * * indictment, charging Baker and Gonda with five counts of violations of 18 U.S.C.

§ 875(c). The e-mail messages supporting the superseding indictment were not available in any publicly accessible portion of the Internet.

* * * [T]he district court dismissed the indictment against Baker, reasoning that the e-mail messages sent and received by Baker and Gonda did not constitute "true threats" under the First Amendment and, as such, were protected speech. The government argues that the district court erred in dismissing the indictment because the communications between Gonda and Baker do constitute "true threats" and, as such, do not implicate First Amendment free speech protections. * * *

* * * For the reasons stated below, we conclude that the indictment failed, as a matter of law, to allege violations of Section 875(c). Accordingly, we decline to address the First Amendment issues raised by the parties.

* * * Because Congress's intent is essentially a question of statutory interpretation, we review the district court's decision *de novo*.

Title 18, United States Code, Section 875(c) states:

Whoever transmits in interstate or foreign commerce any communication containing any threat to kidnap any person or any threat to injure the person of another, shall be fined under this title or imprisoned not more than five years, or both.

The government must allege and prove three elements to support a conviction under Section 875(c): "(1) a transmission in interstate [or foreign] commerce; (2) a communication containing a threat; and (3) the threat must be a threat to injure [or kidnap] the person of another." In this case, the first and third elements cannot be seriously challenged by the defendant. However, the second element raises several issues that this Court must address. * * *

Although its language does not specifically contain a mens rea element, this Court has interpreted Section 875(c) as requiring only general intent. Accordingly, Section 875(c) requires proof that a reasonable person would have taken the defendant's statement as "a serious expression of an intention to inflict bodily harm."

Additionally, Section 875(c) does not clearly define an actus reus. * * *

* * *

To determine what type of action Congress intended to prohibit, it is necessary to consider the nature of a threat. At their core, threats are tools that are employed when one wishes to have some effect, or achieve some goal, through intimidation. This is true regardless of whether the goal is highly reprehensible or seemingly innocuous.

For example, the goal may be extortionate or coercive. * * *

Additionally, the goal, although not rising to the level of extortion, may be the furtherance of a political objective. * * *

Finally, a threat may be communicated for a seemingly innocuous purpose. For example, one may communicate a bomb threat, even if the bomb does not exist, for the sole purpose of creating a prank. However, such a communication would still constitute a threat because the threatening party is attempting to create levity (at least in his or her own mind) through the use of intimidation.

The above examples illustrate threats because they demonstrate a combination of the mens rea with the actus reus. Although it may offend our sensibilities, a communication objectively indicating a serious expression of an intention to inflict bodily harm cannot constitute a threat unless the communication also is conveyed for the purpose of furthering some goal through the use of intimidation.

Accordingly, to achieve the intent of Congress, we hold that, to constitute "a communication containing a threat" under Section 875(c), a communication must be such that a reasonable person (1) would take the statement as a serious expression of an intention to inflict bodily harm (the mens rea), and (2) would perceive such expression as being communicated to effect some change or achieve some goal through intimidation (the actus reus).

The dissent argues that Congress did not intend to include as an element of the crime the furthering of some goal through the use of intimidation. Emphasizing the term "any" in the language of the statute, the dissent maintains that Congress did not limit the scope of communications that constitutes criminal threats. While we agree that Congress chose inclusive language to identify the types of threats that it intended to prohibit, we cannot ignore the fact that Congress intended to forbid only those communications that in fact constitute a "threat." The conclusion that we reach here is one that the term "threat" necessarily implies. * * *

It is important to note that we are not expressing a subjective standard. * * * [T]he actus reus element of a Section 875(c) violation must be determined objectively, from the perspective of the receiver.

Our interpretation of the actus reus requirement of Section 875(c) conforms not only to the nature of a threat, but also to the purpose of prohibiting threats. Several other circuits have recognized that statutes prohibiting threats are designed to protect the recipient's sense of personal safety and well being. If an otherwise threatening communication is not, from an objective standpoint, transmitted for the purpose of intimidation, then it is unlikely that the recipient will be intimidated or that the recipient's peace of mind will be disturbed.

* * *

Applying our interpretation of the statute to the facts before us, we conclude that the communications between Baker and Gonda do not constitute "communication[s] containing a threat" under Section 875(c). Even if a reasonable person would take the communications between Baker and Gonda as serious expressions of an intention to inflict bodily harm, no reasonable person would perceive such communications as being conveyed to effect some change or achieve some goal through intimidation.

Quite the opposite, Baker and Gonda apparently sent e-mail messages to each other in an attempt to foster a friendship based on shared sexual fantasies.

Ultimately, the indictment against Baker fails to "set forth . . . all the elements necessary to constitute the offense intended to be punished" and must be dismissed as a matter of law. We agree with the district court, that "[w]hatever Baker's faults, and he is to be faulted, he did not violate 18 U.S.C. § 875(c)."

For the foregoing reasons, the judgment of the district court is affirmed.

KRUPANSKY, CIRCUIT JUDGE, dissenting.

The panel majority has ruled that an interstate or international "communication containing any threat" to kidnap or injure another person is criminalized by 18 U.S.C. § 875(c) only when the subject communication was conveyed with the general intent "to effect some change or achieve some goal through intimidation." The majority concludes that because the instant indictment alleges only communications purportedly intended to foster a perverse camaraderie between the correspondents, rather than "to effect some change or realize some goal through intimidation," the indictment must be dismissed because each count fails to allege an essential element of a section 875(c) charge. Because the majority has intruded upon Congressional prerogatives by judicially legislating an exogenous element into section 875(c) that materially alters the plain language and purpose of that section and ignores the prevailing precedents of the Supreme Court and this circuit, I respectfully dissent from the majority's decision.

Jake Baker (also known as Abraham Jacob Alkhabaz), an undergraduate student attending the University of Michigan in Ann Arbor, for some time prior to November 1994 and continuing until February 1995 was a regular contributor of sadistic fictional "short stories" intended for public dissemination and comment via a Usenet electronic bulletin board. The appellate record contains a substantial anthology of Baker's efforts. Overall, these misogynistic articles evince an extreme and morbid fascination with the concept of the physical and psychological abuse and torment of women and young girls, described in lurid detail, and often culminating in murder.[1]

---

1. The "Jane Doe story," which he named after an actual female classmate and which in fact is a relatively mild exemplar of the bestial genre of Baker's fiction, follows:

[LAST NAME OF A SPECIFIC FEMALE CLASSMATE OF BAKER'S OMITTED]

Prologue: The following story start [sic] in media res. The premise is that my friend Jerry and I have broken into the apartment of this girl, [FULL NAME OMITTED], whom I know from call [sic], and are porceeding [sic] to have a little fun with her. ('I' = the protagonist).

[Judge Krupansky then proceeded to quote further from the defendant's exact words, in which he describes in highly graphic detail how he and his friend Jerry will rape, torture, humiliate, and mutilate this woman. This extreme violence culminates with the pouring of gasoline over the woman and setting both her and her apartment on fire.]

By November 1994, Baker's sadistic stories attracted the attention of an individual who called himself "Arthur Gonda,"[2] a Usenet service subscriber residing in Ontario, Canada, who apparently shared similarly misdirected proclivities. Baker and Gonda subsequently exchanged at least 41 private computerized electronic mail ("e-mail") communications between November 29, 1994 and January 25, 1995. Concurrently, Baker continued to distribute violent sordid tales on the electronic bulletin board. On January 9, 1995, Baker brazenly disseminated publicly, via the electronic bulletin board, a depraved torture-and-snuff story in which the victim shared the name of a female classmate of Baker's referred to below as "Jane Doe."[3] This imprudent act triggered notification of the University of Michigan authorities by an alarmed citizen on January 18, 1995. On the following day, Baker admitted to a University of Michigan investigator that he had authored the story and published it on the Internet.

Later that month, pursuant to Baker's written consent, university security personnel searched the defendant's dormitory room, personal papers, and computer files including his unique e-mail compartment. This investigation surfaced a second violent and reprehensible tale featuring Jane Doe's actual name, as well as her accurate residential address. The search of Baker's electronic mailbox disclosed a chilling correspondence between the defendant and Gonda chronicling the two men's plans of abduction, bondage, torture, humiliation, mutilation, rape, sodomy, murder, and necrophilia. Most ominously, these messages cumulated in a conspiracy between the two men to realize their aberrant e-mail discussions and exchanges by implementing an actual abduction, rape, and murder of a female person.

* * *

[Judge Krupansky then proceeded to reproduce extensive portions of the highly offensive e-mail exchange, which focused in great part on what Baker and Gonda wanted to do sexually to young teenage girls. In one exchange, for example, Gonda wrote that "their young bodies would really be fun to hurt." Baker replied: "Oh. They'd scream nicely too!"

Recent "sex slayings" in Canada were also referenced in this context.

On several occasions, specific locations and/or persons were referenced. For example, in one exchange, Baker wrote: "As I said before, my room is right across from the girl's bathroom. Wiat until late at night. grab her when she goes to unlock the door. Knock her unconscious. and put her into one of those portable lockers (forget the word for it). or even a duffle bag. Then hurry her out to the car and take her away * * * What do you think?"

---

2. The true identity and current whereabouts of "Arthur Gonda" are unknown.

3. Although the true name of "Jane Doe" was known to the district court and to this appellate forum, her identity has been concealed to spare this young woman any additional and unnecessary fear, emotional trauma, or embarrassment. The record reflected that during an interview concerning Baker's Jane Doe publication conducted by a University of Michigan investigator, Jane Doe "appeared to be controlling herself with great difficulty[,]" resulting in a recommendation for psychological counseling by University of Michigan personnel.

In another exchange, Gonda wrote: "I had a great orgasm today thinking of how you and I would torture this very very petite and cute, south american girl in one of my classes." To which Baker replied: "Just thinking about it anymore doesn't do the trick * * * I need TO DO IT."

Gonda then wrote back, stating: "My feelings exactly! We have to get together * * * I will give you more details as soon as I find out my situation...."]

  * * *

On April 25, 1995, Baker moved to quash the superseding indictment, averring that the charged communications were not "true threats" as that term has been defined by the Supreme Court and federal appellate courts and hence constituted innocuous speech protected by the First Amendment. The lower court agreed, dismissing all five counts of the superseding indictment. Although the majority of this panel now affirms the judgment of the district court, it has avoided addressing the First Amendment issue. Instead it mandates, by judicial license, that the communications charged in the superseding indictment did not constitute "threats" of *any* kind because the panel majority interprets section 875(c) to require, as a matter of law, that a "threatening" communication must be accompanied by an intent to intimidate or coerce someone to attain some "change" or "goal." It is obvious, however, from the concise language of 18 U.S.C. § 875(c) that Congress refused to include an "intent to intimidate or coerce someone to attain some change or goal" as an element of the criminal act addressed therein:

> Whoever transmits in interstate or foreign commerce any communication containing *ANY threat to kidnap ANY person* or *ANY threat to injure the person of another,* shall be fined under this title or imprisoned not more than five years, or both.

18 U.S.C. § 875(c) (emphases added).

The words in section 875(c) are simple, clear, concise, and unambiguous. The plain, expressed statutory language commands only that the alleged communication must contain *any threat* to kidnap or physically injure *any person,* made for *any reason* or no reason. Section 875(c) by its terms does *not* confine the scope of criminalized communications to those directed to identified individuals and intended to effect some particular change or goal. This circuit has already considered and decided the meaning of section 875(c) in ... a decision in which a member of this panel concurred, wherein it defined, to the exclusion of "intimidation," the three essential elements under 18 U.S.C. § 875(c). * * *

By contrast to section 875(c), a companion statutory provision, 18 U.S.C. § 875(b), *criminalizes similar communications made with the intent to extort money or other value,* coupled with more severe penalties than those appertaining to a threat illegalized by section 875(c). * * *

Patently, Congress sought to punish *all* interstate or international communications containing a threat to kidnap or injure any person; such communications accompanied by an intent to extort value (section 875(b)) could be punished more severely than those which are not coupled with the intent to extort (section 875(c)). * * *

The panel majority attempts to justify its improper fusion of an extra-legislative element re the "intent to intimidate some change or goal" upon section 875(c) by embracing an artificially narrow legal definition of the term "threat." The panel majority posits, "[a]t their core, threats are tools that are employed when one wishes to have some effect, or achieve some goal, through intimidation." However, this interpretation does not comprise the *exclusive* ordinary or legal meaning of the word "threat." Undeniably, a simple, credible declaration of an intention to cause injury to some person, made for any reason, or for no reason whatsoever, may *also* constitute a "threat." For instance, *Black's Law Dictionary* 1480–81 (6th ed. 1990) adopts, among other definitions, the following:

> **Threat**. *A communicated intent to inflict physical or other harm on any person or on property. A declaration of an intention to injure another or his property by some unlawful act. A declaration of intention or determination to inflict punishment, loss, or pain on another, or to injure another or his property by the commission of some unlawful act. . . .*
>
> *The term, "threat" [sic] means an avowed present determination or intent to injure presently or in the future.* A statement may constitute a threat even though it is subject to a possible contingency in the maker's control. The prosecution must establish a "true threat," which means a serious threat as distinguished from words uttered as mere political argument, idle talk or jest. In determining whether words were uttered as a threat the context in which they were spoken must be considered.
>
> (Emphases added & citations omitted).

Although some reported threat convictions have embraced a form or degree of intimidation, this circuit has not previously adopted that element as an essential component of a prosecution under 18 U.S.C. § 875(c). * * *

Thus, the plain language of 18 U.S.C. § 875(c), together with its interpretive precedents, compels the conclusion that "threats" within the scope of the statute in controversy include all reasonably credible communications which express the speaker's objective intent to kidnap or physically injure another person. Whether the originator of the message intended to intimidate or coerce anyone thereby is irrelevant. Rather, the pertinent inquiry is whether a jury could find that a reasonable recipient of the communication would objectively tend to believe that the speaker was serious about his stated intention. * * * There can be no doubt that a rational jury could find that some or all of the minacious communications charged in the superseding indictment against Baker constituted threats by the defendant to harm a female human being, which a reasonable objective recipient of the transmissions could find credible.[11]

Because the communications charged against Baker could be found by a rational jury to constitute "threats" within the ambit of 18 U.S.C. § 875(c), the district court's resolution that a rational jury could not find that any of these communications comprised constitutionally unprotected "true threats" is ripe for review.[12] The Supreme Court has recognized that, while the First Amendment extends varying degrees of protection against government censure to most forms of expression (with political speech receiving the most stringent safeguards), certain forms of speech are deemed unworthy of any constitutional protection and consequently may be criminalized. A "threat" is a recognized category of expression which warrants no First Amendment protection. * * * However, only communications which convey "true threats" (as opposed to, for example, inadvertent statements, mistakes, jests, hyperbole, innocuous talk, or political commentary not objectively intended to express a real threat) are "threats" outside the embrace of the First Amendment's guarantees.

In *Watts,* the Court announced that "threats" against the President were obviously proscribable, but also recognized that, as "pure speech" which may be imbued with protected political commentary, such ostensibly minatory speech must be assessed for its true nature—that is, whether it constituted mere political commentary or hyperbole, which was protected, or constituted a *"true threat"* which is not protected. Watts had stated at a public rally that he would not willingly submit to the draft but, if forced to carry a rifle, "the first man I want to get in my sights is L.B.J." The Court instructed that this statement, in its factual context, was not a "true threat" which could be constitutionally prosecuted, but instead was mere "political hyperbole" immunized by the First Amendment.[13]

     * * *

The majority's disposition leads to absurd results where, as in the case at bench, minacious communications have been made which may satisfy the constitutional "true threat" standard because a reasonable jury could find that those communications contained believable expressions of

---

11. The majority's concern that interpreting 18 U.S.C. § 875(c) to encompass threatening messages sent by persons who did not intend to achieve some coercive result would effectively criminalize the legitimate and innocent reiteration, such as by news reporters, trial watchers, or publishers of judicial opinions, of communications initiated by another, is misplaced. To constitute a threat under section 875(c), the communication at issue must be accompanied by the perpetrator's general intent to kidnap or harm someone. Stated differently, by promulgating the menacing verbiage, the speaker must be expressing a credible intention to perform, or cause to be performed, the forbidden actions. Typically, only the originator of the minatorial communication, or a confederate, could possess or express this intent. By contrast, a person who republishes the threatening language for legitimate or otherwise innocuous purposes cannot reasonably be deemed to have articulated an intent to kidnap or injure any person.

12. The determination whether a communication embodies a "true threat" resides in the fact finder.

13. The Supreme Court has recognized that the considerations which remove threats of violence outside the reach of the First Amendment apply with "special force" to threats which menace the President. By contrast, threats against private individuals are typically devoid of political content and hence should be accorded less stringent First Amendment protection.

an intention to injure a person, yet those same communications are nonetheless deemed beyond the reach of 18 U.S.C. § 875(c) as not constituting "threats" as a matter of law, merely because the subject communications were not made with the intent to realize a specific purpose through intimidation. Although Congress, via section 875(c), clearly intended to punish *every* credible interstate or transnational expression of an intent to kidnap or injure another person, the majority's legally erroneous unduly restrictive interpretation of the word "threat" as used in section 875(c) effectively divests Congress of its constitutional lawmaking authority by artificially confining the intended scope of section 875(c) to a degree not compelled by the First Amendment.

Accordingly, in order to prove a "true threat" proscribed by 18 U.S.C. § 875(c) and unprotected by the First Amendment, the prosecution must evidence to a rational jury's satisfaction *only* the following: (1) that the defendant transmitted the subject communication in interstate or foreign commerce, (2) that the communication contained a threat, (3) that the threat was one against the physical safety or freedom of some individual or class of persons (irrespective of the identity of the person or group threatened, the originator's motivation for issuing the threat, or the existence or nonexistence of any goal pursued by the threat), and (4) that the subject communication in its factual context would lead a reasonable, objective recipient to believe that the publisher of the communication was serious about his threat (regardless of the subjective intent of the speaker to make an actual threat or whether anyone actually felt frightened, intimidated, or coerced by the threat).

Finally, the facts of the instant case justify reversal and remand because they even satisfy the judicially legislated edict articulated in the majority opinion. Assuming *arguendo* that a threat under 18 U.S.C. § 875(c) requires a general intent by the speaker to attain some result or change through intimidation (which it does not), a rational jury could conclude that this element was proved in this case. By publishing his sadistic Jane Doe story on the Internet, Baker could reasonably foresee that his threats to harm Jane Doe would ultimately be communicated to her (as they were), and would cause her fear and intimidation, which in fact ultimately occurred. The panel majority may casually conclude within the security of chambers that Baker's threats conveyed to Jane Doe in his articles published on the Internet were nonintimidating. However, Jane Doe's reaction to those threats when brought to her attention evinces a contrary conclusion of a shattering traumatic reaction that resulted in recommended psychological counseling.

A jury in the instant case could reasonably infer, in the light of all the evidence, that Baker intended the foreseeable, natural, and ordinary consequences of his voluntary actions. Indeed, a rational jury could infer that the reason Baker published his Jane Doe story featuring the actual name of a young woman was the probability that its threats would be communicated to her and cause her to suffer fear, anxiety, and intimidation. Moreover, the e-mail correspondence between Baker and Gonda evidenced overt acts of a conspiracy to violate 18 U.S.C. § 875(c) in that the two men clearly agreed *at the least* to threaten, and otherwise implement their conspiracy by intimidating, one or more women or young girls with physical harm as discussed in their plans.

Accordingly, I would reverse the district court's judgment which dismissed the superseding indictment as purportedly not alleging "true threats," and remand the cause to the lower court. **I DISSENT.**

Notes

1. The Sixth Circuit majority's analysis, including its determination that an "intimidation" element is built into the federal criminal statute, is not reflective of the general trend in this area. In fact, Judge Krupansky's dissent would be considered the more typical, more "mainstream" analysis of these issues in most parts of the country. In your view, which approach is more consistent with the implicit goals of the federal statute? Which approach might be more appropriate as a matter of policy?

2. It is important to note that while both the newsgroup post by Jake Baker and the e-mail exchange between him and Arthur Gonda were referenced in the opinions—and while the newsgroup post, because of its particularly offensive and notorious character—garnered the most publicity in the national media—the U.S. Attorney's Office ultimately prosecuted the defendant only for the e-mail exchange. *See* United States v. Baker, 890 F.Supp. 1375, 1380 n.6 (1995) ("At oral argument on May 26, 1995, the government stated that it abandoned the story as a basis of prosecution because it did not constitute a threat."). Yet for Judge Krupansky, the post provided important context, particularly since the law in this area typically calls for an analysis of context within the totality of the circumstances. Thus, he reproduced this post in its entirety, in Footnote 1 of the dissent.

3. The widely publicized *Alkhabaz* case not only left everyone unsatisfied but also left the larger issue unresolved. Free speech advocates criticized the "persecution" of Jake Baker, who ultimately left the university after undergoing what amounted to a public humiliation. And university officials—justifiably concerned that expressions of intent to commit violent acts are often translated into reality—felt let down by the legal system. In light of this disappointment on all sides, might there have been a better way to handle the dispute?

4. Threats in cyberspace can be a particular challenge for public officials, both in education and in society as a whole. Unlike the real-time, offline world, for example, there are no visual cues and few contextual cues that would help a person to determine whether a particular communication does in fact constitute a threat. In light of the result in *Alkhabaz*, would you conclude that threat law is in need of substantial revision? Is greater precision possible, for example? Or, particularly given the complexities of cyberspace, is this an example of a situation where the limits of the legal system might have been reached?

2. CONSTRUING THE "TRUE THREAT" DOCTRINE IN A K–12 SETTING

PROBLEM 18: ZERO TOLERANCE FOR THREATS II

Belinda—an eleventh grade student at a large public high school in the fictional state of Riverview—sends an e-mail from a school computer to a friend in the fictional state of Floral Valley, which reads in part: "I can't wait until I can kill the people in my class. I'll just go to the entrance of the school on a clear, sunny day and blow up and shoot everything I can." She also sends copies to five friends, one of whom shares it with her parents. The parents report the details to the school, which expels Belinda under a new "zero tolerance for threats" policy enacted in the aftermath of the events at Columbine.

Legal Inquiry

A. Belinda, represented by the ACLU, challenges her expulsion on the grounds that her free speech rights have been violated. The ACLU is prepared to argue that her actions did not constitute true threats. What arguments should the ACLU set forth on her behalf? What result? Discuss.

B. If this case had taken place at a public university instead of at the high school level, would the ACLU make any additional or different arguments? Would the result be any different? Explain.

Policy Inquiry

A. Does the problem of online and offline threats in U.S. high schools today (after Columbine and after 9/11) justify a "zero tolerance for threats" policy in public high schools? Just how bad are things in that regard nationwide? Is "zero tolerance" the answer? Why? If not, what other strategies from both a legal and a policy perspective would you recommend? Why?

B. In light of the fact that there have already been several "online threats" cases at the higher education level in recent years, does this problem justify a "zero tolerance for threats" policy at major public universities? Just how bad are things in this regard nationwide after 9/11? Is "zero tolerance" the answer? Why? If not, what other strategies from both a legal and a policy perspective would you recommend? Why?

DOE v. PULASKI COUNTY SPECIAL SCH. DIST.

306 F.3d 616 (8th Cir. 2002)

HANSEN, CIRCUIT JUDGE.

We granted en banc review to determine whether a school board ran afoul of a student's free speech rights when it expelled him for an offensive and vulgar letter that the student had prepared at home. The expelled student described in the letter how he would rape, sodomize, and murder a female classmate who had previously broken up with him. After a bench trial, the district court ordered the expelled student reinstated, concluding that the letter was not a "true threat" and that it therefore was protected speech under the First Amendment. A divided panel of our court affirmed the district court's decision. We vacated the panel decision, ordered en banc rehearing, and now hold that the school board did not violate the student's First Amendment rights when it expelled him.

I. BACKGROUND AND FACTS

J.M., a male, and K.G., a female, began "going together" during their seventh-grade year at Northwood Junior High School. As one would expect from typical junior high students, the two primarily saw each other at school and church, and their relationship was marked by multiple breakups during the school year. Sometime during the summer vacation after the end of the seventh-grade year, K.G. "broke up" with J.M. for the final time because she was interested in another boy.

Frustrated by the breakup and upset that K.G. would not go out with him again, J.M. drafted two violent, misogynic, and obscenity-laden rants expressing a desire to molest, rape, and murder K.G. According to J.M., he intended to write a rap song with lyrics similar in theme to the more vulgar and violent rap songs performed by controversial "rappers" such as Eminem, Juvenile, and Kid Rock, but found that his "song" fit no particular beat or rhythm. J.M. ultimately penned the documents as letters, signing them at their conclusion. J.M. prepared both letters at his home, where they remained until J.M.'s best friend, D.M., discovered one of them approximately a month before the youths were to begin their eighth-grade year at Northwood.

D.M. found the letter in J.M.'s bedroom while he was searching for something on top of a dresser. Before D.M. had a chance to read the letter, J.M. snatched it from his hand. D.M. asked to read the letter, and J.M. handed it back to him and gave D.M. permission to read the letter. D.M. asked for a copy of the letter, but J.M. refused to give him one.

K.G. also learned about the existence and contents of the letter, but it was not made clear during the trial when or how she learned about it. K.G. testified that she first learned about *a* letter during a telephone conversation with J.M. She claimed that J.M. told her that another boy had written a letter that stated she would be killed. J.M. claimed instead that K.G. learned about the letter from D.M. Either way, the testimony clearly established that J.M. voluntarily discussed the letter with K.G. during two or three telephone conversations and that J.M. admitted to K.G. in their final telephone conversation that he, not another boy, had written the letter.

Concerned about the letter, K.G. enlisted D.M.'s help in obtaining it from J.M. About a week before the start of school, D.M. spent the night at J.M.'s house and took the letter from J.M.'s room on the following morning. D.M. did so without J.M.'s knowledge or permission. D.M. delivered the letter to K.G. on the second day back from summer vacation, and K.G. read it in gym class in the presence of some other students. One of those students went immediately to the school resource officer, Officer James Kesterson, and reported that threats had been made against K.G.

Officer Kesterson accompanied the student back to the gym where he found K.G. frightened and crying. * * *

Bob Allison, the principal, conducted his own investigation and learned that D.M. had taken the letter from J.M. and delivered it to K.G. at school. After the investigation, Principal Allison recommended that J.M. be expelled from Northwood for the remainder of his eighth-grade year. Allison based his recommendation on Rule 36 of the district's Handbook for Student Conduct and Discipline, which prohibits students from making terrorizing threats against others. The rule requires that a violator be recommended for expulsion.

* * *

Upset with the school board's decision ... [expelling J.M. from both Northwood and the alternative school for the remainder of his eighth-grade year] ... , J.M.'s mother filed this lawsuit on her son's behalf. J.M. sought reinstatement at Northwood on the ground that the school board violated his free speech rights when it disciplined him for the letter. * * *

II.   DISCUSSION AND ANALYSIS

* * *

B.   The True Threat Inquiry

* * *

In *Watts v. United States,* 394 U.S. 705, 89 S.Ct. 1399 (1969), the Supreme Court recognized that threats of violence * * * fall within the realm of speech that the government can proscribe without offending the First Amendment. Although there may be some political or social value associated with threatening words in some circumstances, the government has an overriding interest in "protecting individuals from the fear of violence, from the disruption that fear engenders, and from the possibility that the threatened violence will occur." Our task, therefore, is to determine "[w]hat is a threat ... from what is constitutionally protected speech." The Court in *Watts,* however, set forth no particular definition or description of a true threat that distinguishes an unprotected threat from protected speech. Thus, the lower courts have been left to ascertain for themselves when a statement triggers the government's interest in preventing the disruption and fear of violence associated with a threat.

The federal courts of appeals that have announced a test to parse true threats from protected speech essentially fall into two camps * * *. All the courts to have reached the issue have consistently adopted an objective test that focuses on whether a reasonable person would interpret the purported threat as a serious expression of an intent to cause a present or future harm. The views among the courts diverge, however, in determining from whose viewpoint the statement should be interpreted. * * *

Our court is in the camp that views the nature of the alleged threat from the viewpoint of a reasonable recipient. ... [W]e ... [have] ... emphasized the fact intensive nature of the true threat inquiry and held that a court must view the relevant facts to determine "whether the recipient of the alleged threat could reasonably conclude that it expresses 'a determination or intent to injure presently or in the future.' " * * * We ... [have] ... also set forth ... a nonexhaustive list of factors relevant to how a reasonable recipient would view the purported threat. Those factors include: 1) the reaction of those who heard the alleged threat; 2) whether the threat was conditional; 3) whether the person who made the alleged threat communicated it directly to the object of the threat; 4) whether the speaker had a history of making threats against the person purportedly threatened; and 5) whether the recipient had a reason to believe that the speaker had a propensity to engage in violence.

* * * [W]e adhere to ... [this] ... inquiry and hold that a true threat is a statement that a reasonable recipient would have interpreted as a serious expression of an intent to harm or cause injury to another.

C.   Intent to Communicate

Before we address whether a reasonable recipient would view the letter as a threat, we are faced with a threshold question of whether J.M. intended to communicate the purported threat. The district court's conclusion that the letter was protected speech turned on its finding that J.M. never intended to deliver the letter to K.G.; in other words, that J.M. never intended to communicate the purported threat to K.G. In determining whether a statement amounts to an unprotected threat, there is no requirement that the speaker intended to carry out the threat, nor is there any requirement that the speaker was capable of carrying out the purported threat of violence. However, the speaker must have intentionally or knowingly communicated the statement in question to someone before he or she may be punished or disciplined for it. The requirement is satisfied if the speaker communicates the statement to the object of the purported threat *or* to a third party. * * *

Requiring less than an intent to communicate the purported threat would run afoul of the notion that an individual's most protected right is to be free from governmental interference in the sanctity of his home and in the sanctity of his own personal thoughts. * * * It is only when a threatening idea or thought is communicated that the government's interest in alleviating the fear of violence and disruption associated with a threat engages.

We conclude here that J.M. intended to communicate the letter and is therefore accountable if a reasonable recipient would have viewed the letter as a threat. Although J.M. snatched the letter out of D.M.'s hands when D.M. first found it, J.M. handed the letter back to D.M. and *permitted* D.M. to read it. J.M.'s decision to let D.M. read the letter is even more problematic for J.M. given his testimony that he knew there was a good possibility that D.M. would tell K.G. about the letter because D.M. and K.G. were friends. J.M. also discussed the letter in more than one phone conversation with K.G., and J.M. admitted to K.G. that he wrote the letter and that it talked of killing her. J.M. made similar admissions to

K.G.'s best friend who would be likely to convey the information to K.G. One can hardly say, based on J.M.'s willingness to let D.M. read the letter and his overt discussion of the letter and its contents with K.G. and K.G.'s best friend, that J.M. intended to keep the letter, and the message it contained, within his own lockbox of personal privacy.

D.   Reasonable Recipient's Perception of the Letter

We turn next to the question of whether a reasonable recipient would have perceived the letter as a threat. There is no question that the contents of the letter itself expressed an intent to harm K.G., and we disagree entirely, but respectfully, with the district court's assessment that the words contained in it were only "arguably" threatening. The letter exhibited J.M.'s pronounced, contemptuous and depraved hate for K.G. J.M. referred to or described K.G. as a "bitch," "slut," "ass," and a "whore" over 80 times in only four pages. He used the f-word no fewer than ninety times and spoke frequently in the letter of his wish to sodomize, rape, and kill K.G. The most disturbing aspect of the letter, however, is J.M.'s warning in two passages, expressed in unconditional terms, that K.G. should not go to sleep because he would be lying under her bed waiting to kill her with a knife.[3] Most, if not all, normal thirteen-year-old girls (and probably most reasonable adults) would be frightened by the message and tone of J.M.'s letter and would fear for their physical well-being if they received the same letter.

The fact that J.M. did not personally deliver the letter to K.G. did not dispel its threatening nature. Although J.M. did not personally hand the letter to K.G., J.M. titled the letter "F___ that bitch [K.G.]," and he wrote the letter as though he was speaking directly to her. As a consequence, the letter was extremely intimate and personal, and the violence described in it was directed unequivocally at K.G.

There is also no indication that J.M. ever attempted to alleviate K.G.'s concerns about the letter during the period between when he told her about the letter and when she received it at school. Prior to K.G. obtaining the letter, J.M. had discussed its contents with her in phone conversations, and he testified at trial that he knew K.G. might have taken the threat as being truthful. It readily appears that J.M. wanted K.G. to be scared as retribution for her treatment of him. In fact, K.G.'s best friend testified at trial that J.M. told her, before D.M. obtained the letter and delivered it, that J.M. wanted to hide under K.G.'s bed and kill her. J.M. told this to K.G.'s best friend knowing the friend would likely pass the message along to K.G. J.M. also shared the letter with D.M. suspecting that D.M. would pass the information it contained to K.G. J.M. ultimately apologized to K.G., but his apology came only after he was expelled by the school board and during the pendency of the district court

---

3. J.M. argues it would have been improbable for him to harm K.G. in the manner he described because K.G. resided with her parents. However, a threat does not need to be logical or based in reality before the government may punish someone for making it.... It seems quite probable that the threat to hide under a person's bed with a knife would induce fear and apprehension.

proceeding. The crescendoing events that presaged K.G.'s receipt of the actual letter would not have given a reasonable person in K.G.'s shoes much solace that J.M. did not want or intend to harm her.

Based on the tone of the letter, and the situation surrounding its communication, we are not surprised that those who read it interpreted it as a threat. D.M. was concerned enough by the letter that he purloined it from his friend's home because he "felt that something should be done about it." A girl present when K.G. first read the letter immediately went to Officer Kesterson because she thought someone needed to know about the letter and the threats contained therein. * * *[4]

J.M.'s previous portrayal of himself as a tough guy with a propensity for aggression made his threat more credible and contributed to K.G.'s reaction. Before the breakup, J.M. had told K.G., as well as K.G.'s best friend and D.M., that he was a member of the "Bloods" gang. K.G. also testified at trial that J.M. once shot a cat while she was speaking to him on the phone and that J.M.'s penchant for violence towards animals heightened her concern over the letter. The district court excluded the district's evidence of J.M.'s violent propensities on the ground that the evidence was not considered by the school board. We conclude, however, that the evidence is relevant to an understanding of K.G.'s response to the threat and our determination of whether her response was a reasonable one. * * *

Viewing the entire factual circumstances surrounding the letter, we conclude that a reasonable recipient would have perceived J.M.'s letter as a serious expression of an intent to harm K.G. As such, the letter amounted to a true threat, and the school's administrators and the school board did not violate J.M.'s First Amendment rights by initiating disciplinary action based on the letter's threatening content. The district court's contrary conclusion was erroneous. Had we been sitting as the school board, we might very well have approached the situation differently, for it appears to us that the board's action taken against J.M. was unnecessarily harsh. Other options have occurred to us that could have furthered the district's interest in protecting its students, as well as have punished J.M., but also have aided him in understanding the severity and inappropriateness of his conduct. However, "[i]t is not the role of the federal courts to set aside decisions of school administrators which the court may view as lacking a basis in wisdom or compassion." Those judgments are best left to the voters who elect the school board.

III. CONCLUSION

We reverse the judgment of the district court and remand the case to the district court with instructions to dissolve the injunctive relief afforded J.M. and to dismiss J.M.'s First Amendment claim against the school district.

---

4. We find it untenable in the wake of Columbine and Jonesboro that any reasonable school official who came into possession of J.M.'s letter would not have taken some action based on its violent and disturbing content.

HEANEY, Circuit Judge, with whom McMILLIAN, MORRIS SHEP-PARD ARNOLD, and BYE, Circuit Judges, join, dissenting.

Because I believe the majority has undermined the scope of the First Amendment by failing to consider the unique circumstances of speech in a school setting, I respectfully dissent. I believe the proper inquiry before us is 1) whether J.M.'s written expression is protected speech or a true threat; and 2) if it is protected speech, as I believe it is, whether it is subject to regulation because it may cause substantial disruption or interfere with the rights of other students. The majority ignores the school context analysis and creates dangerously broad precedent by holding that *any* private utterance of an intent to injure another person is not entitled to First Amendment protection. I reject this reasoning because it violates the fundamental principles of the First Amendment. I would hold instead that J.M.'s written expression is constitutionally protected speech, but can be *reasonably* regulated by school administrators to prevent substantial disruption in the school setting.

3. APPLYING *TINKER* & ITS PROGENY TO K–12 THREAT–RELATED SITUATIONS

WISNIEWSKI v. BD. OF EDUC. OF THE WEEDSPORT CENT. SCH. DIST.

494 F.3d 34 (2d Cir. 2007)

JON O. NEWMAN, CIRCUIT JUDGE.

This appeal concerns a First Amendment challenge to an eighth-grade student's suspension for sharing with friends via the Internet a small drawing crudely, but clearly, suggesting that a named teacher should be shot and killed. * * * We conclude that the federal claims were properly dismissed because it was reasonably foreseeable that Wisniewski's communication would cause a disruption within the school environment[.] * * * We therefore affirm.

BACKGROUND

Facts of the episode. This case arose out of an Internet transmission by an eighth-grader at Weedsport Middle School, in the Weedsport Central School District in upstate New York. In April 2001, the pupil, Aaron Wisniewski ("Aaron"), was using AOL Instant Messaging ("IM") software on his parents' home computer. Instant messaging enables a person using a computer with Internet access to exchange messages in real time with members of a group (usually called "buddies" in IM lingo) who have the same IM software on their computers. Instant messaging permits rapid exchanges of text between any two members of a "buddy list" who happen to be on-line at the same time. Different IM programs use different notations for indicating which members of a user's "buddy list" are on-line at any one time. Text sent to and from a "buddy" remains on the computer screen during the entire exchange of messages between any two users of the IM program.

The AOL IM program, like many others, permits the sender of IM messages to display on the computer screen an icon, created by the sender, which serves as an identifier of the sender, in addition to the sender's name. The IM icon of the sender and that of the person replying remain on the screen during the exchange of text messages between the two "buddies," and each can copy the icon of the other and transmit it to any other "buddy" during an IM exchange.

Aaron's IM icon was a small drawing of a pistol firing a bullet at a person's head, above which were dots representing splattered blood. Beneath the drawing appeared the words "Kill Mr. VanderMolen." Philip VanderMolen was Aaron's English teacher at the time. Aaron created the icon a couple of weeks after his class was instructed that threats would not be tolerated by the school, and would be treated as acts of violence. Aaron sent IM messages displaying the icon to some 15 members of his IM "buddy list." The icon was not sent to VanderMolen or any other school official.

The icon was available for viewing by Aaron's "buddies" for three weeks, at least some of whom were Aaron's classmates at Weedsport Middle School. During that period it came to the attention of another classmate, who informed VanderMolen of Aaron's icon and later supplied him with a copy of the icon. VanderMolen, distressed by this information, forwarded it to the high school and middle school principals, who brought the matter to the attention of the local police, the Superintendent Mabbett, and Aaron's parents. In response to questioning by the school principals, Aaron acknowledged that he had created and sent the icon and expressed regret. He was then suspended for five days, after which he was allowed back in school, pending a superintendent's hearing. VanderMolen asked and was allowed to stop teaching Aaron's class.

At the same time, a police investigator who interviewed Aaron concluded that the icon was meant as a joke, that Aaron fully understood the severity of what he had done, and that Aaron posed no real threat to VanderMolen or to any other school official. A pending criminal case was then closed. Aaron was also evaluated by a psychologist, who also found that Aaron had no violent intent, posed no actual threat, and made the icon as a joke.

The superintendent's hearing. In May 2001 a superintendent's hearing, regarding a proposed long-term suspension of Aaron, was held before a designated hearing officer, attorney Lynda M. VanCoske. Aaron was charged under New York Education Law § 3214(3) with endangering the health and welfare of other students and staff at the school.

In her decision of June 2001, VanCoske found that the icon was threatening and should not have been understood as a joke. Although the threatening act took place outside of school, she concluded that it was in violation of school rules and disrupted school operations by requiring special attention from school officials, replacement of the threatened teacher, and interviewing pupils during class time. The hearing officer acknowledged the opinions of the police investigator and the psychologist that Aaron did not intend to harm VanderMolen and that he did not pose any real threat, but stated that "intent [is] irrelevant." Citing the evidentiary standard followed in New York suspension hearings, the decision concluded:

Substantial and competent evidence exists that Aaron engaged in the act of sending a threatening message to his buddies, the subject of which was a teacher. He admitted it. Competent and substantial evidence exists that this message disrupted the educational environment. . . .

As a result of the foregoing, I conclude Aaron did commit the act of threatening a teacher, in violation of page 11 of the student handbook, creating an environment threatening the health, safety and welfare of others, and his actions created a disruption in the school environment.

The hearing officer recommended suspension of Aaron for one semester. The recommendation was presented to the district's Board of Education ("Board"), which approved the one semester suspension in late September 2001. Aaron was suspended for the first semester of the 2001–2002 school year. During the period of suspension the school district afforded Aaron alternative education. He returned to school for the spring term. At oral argument, we were advised that because of school and community hostility, the family moved from Weedsport.

* * * In November 2002 Aaron's parents filed on his behalf the current suit against the Board and Superintendent Mabbett, seeking damages under 42 U.S.C. § 1983. The complaint included five counts: the first count claimed that Aaron's icon was not a "true threat," but was protected speech under the First Amendment. It * * * alleged that in suspending Aaron the Board acted in a retaliatory manner in violation of his First Amendment rights. * * *

DISCUSSION

* * * [W]e turn directly to the merits of the Plaintiffs' claim that Aaron's icon was protected speech under the First Amendment.

In assessing that claim, we do not pause to resolve the parties' dispute as to whether transmission of the icon constituted a "true 'threat'" within the meaning of the Supreme Court's decision in *Watts v. United States*. * * * Although some courts have assessed a student's statements concerning the killing of a school official or a fellow student against the "true 'threat'" standard of *Watts, see, e.g., Doe v. Pulaski County Special School District,* * * * we think that school officials have significantly broader authority to sanction student speech than the Watts standard allows. With respect to school officials' authority to discipline a student's expression reasonably understood as urging violent conduct, we think the appropriate First Amendment standard is the one set forth by the Supreme Court in *Tinker*.

* * * In its most recent consideration of a First Amendment challenge to school discipline in response to a student's allegedly protected speech, the Supreme Court viewed the ... [following] ... as *Tinker*'s holding: *Tinker* held that student expression may not be suppressed unless school officials reasonably conclude that it will 'materially and substantially disrupt the work and discipline of the school.' " *Morse v. Frederick.*

Even if Aaron's transmission of an icon depicting and calling for the killing of his teacher could be viewed as an expression of opinion within the meaning of *Tinker,* we conclude that it crosses the boundary of protected speech and constitutes student conduct that poses a reasonably foreseeable risk that the icon would come to the attention of school authorities and that it would "materially and substantially disrupt the work and discipline of the school." For such conduct, *Tinker* affords no protection against school discipline. *See LaVine v. Blaine School District,* 257 F.3d 981 (9th Cir. 2001) (upholding, under Tinker, suspension of high school student based in part on poem describing shooting of students); *Boucher v. School Board,* 134 F.3d 821 (7th Cir. 1998) (upholding, under *Tinker,* one-year expulsion of high school student for writing article in underground newspaper outlining techniques for hacking into school computers); *J.S., a Minor v. Bethlehem Area School District,* 757 A.2d 412 (Pa.Cmwlth. 2000) (upholding, under *Tinker,* permanent expulsion of student for placing on web-site picture of severed head of teacher and soliciting funds for her execution).

The fact that Aaron's creation and transmission of the IM icon occurred away from school property does not necessarily insulate him from school discipline. We have recognized that off-campus conduct can create a foreseeable risk of substantial disruption within a school, *see Thomas v. Board of Education,* 607 F.2d 1043, 1052 n. 17 (2d Cir. 1979) ("We can, of course, envision a case in which a group of students incites substantial disruption within the school from some remote locale."), as have other courts, *see Doe* v. *Pulaski* (letter, written and kept at home, that threatened killing of fellow student); *Sullivan v. Houston Independent School District,* 475 F.2d 1071, 1075–77 (5th Cir. 1973) (underground newspaper distributed off-campus but near school grounds); *J.S.,* 757 A.2d at 418–22 (material created on home computer).

In this case, the panel is divided as to whether it must be shown that it was reasonably foreseeable that Aaron's IM icon would reach the school property or whether the undisputed fact that it did reach the school pretermits any inquiry as to this aspect of reasonable foreseeability. We are in agreement, however, that, on the undisputed facts, it was reasonably foreseeable that the IM icon would come to the attention of school authorities and the teacher whom the icon depicted being shot.[4] The

---

4. Judge Walker, who otherwise fully concurs in this opinion and in the judgment, would hold that a school may discipline a student for off-campus expression that is likely to cause a disruption on campus only if it was foreseeable to a reasonable adult, cognizant of the perspective of a student, that the expression might reach campus. *Cf. Skoros v. City of New York,* 437 F.3d 1,

potentially threatening content of the icon and the extensive distribution of it, which encompassed 15 recipients, including some of Aaron's class-mates, during a three-week circulation period, made this risk at least foreseeable to a reasonable person, if not inevitable. And there can be no doubt that the icon, once made known to the teacher and other school officials, would foreseeably create a risk of substantial disruption within the school environment.

Whether these aspects of reasonable foreseeability are considered issues of law or issues of fact as to which, on this record, no reasonable jury could disagree, foreseeability of both communication to school author-ities, including the teacher, and the risk of substantial disruption is not only reasonable, but clear. These consequences permit school discipline, whether or not Aaron intended his IM icon to be communicated to school authorities or, if communicated, to cause a substantial disruption. As in *Morse,* the student in the pending case was not disciplined for conduct that was merely "offensive," *Morse,* ___ U.S. at ___, 127 S.Ct. at 2629, or merely in conflict with some view of the school's "educational mission," *id.* at 2637 (Alito, J., with whom Kennedy, J., joins, concurring).

     * * *

[I]n the absence of a properly presented challenge, we do not decide whether the length of the one semester suspension exceeded whatever constitutional limitation might exist. We rule only that the First Amend-ment claims against the School Board and the Superintendent were properly dismissed * * *.

CONCLUSION

The judgment of the District Court is affirmed.

PONCE v. SOCORRO INDEP. SCH. DIST.

508 F.3d 765 (5th Cir. 2007)

E. GRADY JOLLY, CIRCUIT JUDGE:

This appeal presents the question of whether student speech that threatens a Columbine-style attack on a school is protected by the First Amendment. Today we follow the lead of the United States Supreme Court in *Morse v. Frederick* and hold that it is not because such speech poses a direct threat to the physical safety of the school population. We therefore VACATE the preliminary injunction entered by the district court and REMAND for further proceedings, if appropriate.

---

23 (2d Cir. 2006) (discussing perspective of reasonable adult who assesses religious display aware that it will be seen primarily by children). He believes that to hold otherwise would run afoul of *Thomas,* 607 F.2d at 1045 (holding that "the arm of [school] authority does not [generally] reach beyond the schoolhouse gate"), and would raise substantial First Amendment concerns, as it might permit a school to punish a student for the content of speech the student could never have anticipated reaching the school, such as a draft letter concealed in his night-stand, stolen by another student, and delivered to school authorities, cf. *Porter v. Ascension Parish School Board,* 393 F.3d 608, 615 n. 22 (5th Cir. 2004) ("[T]he fact that Adam's drawing was composed off-campus and remained off-campus for two years until it was unintentionally taken to school by his younger brother takes the present case outside the scope of [*Tinker*].").

I.

While enrolled as a sophomore at Montwood High School, a minor student identified as E.P. kept an extended notebook diary, written in the first-person perspective, in which he detailed the "author's" creation of a pseudo-Nazi group on the Montwood High School Campus, and at other schools in the Socorro Independent School District ("SISD" or "School District"). The notebook describes several incidents involving the pseudo-Nazi group, including one in which the author ordered his group "to brutally injure two homosexuals and seven colored" people and another in which the author describes punishing another student by setting his house on fire and "brutally murder[ing]" his dog. The notebook also details the group's plan to commit a "[C]olumbine shooting" attack on Montwood High School or a coordinated "shooting at all the [district's] schools at the same time." At several points in the journal, the author expresses the feeling that his "anger has the best of [him]" and that "it will get to the point where [he] will no longer have control." The author predicts that this outburst will occur on the day that his close friends at the school graduate.

On August 15, 2005, E.P. told another student (the "informing student") about the notebook and supposedly showed him some of its contents. * * * [The informing student told a teacher, who then shared the information with Assistant Principal Jesus Aguirre. After speaking with the informing student, Aguirre scheduled a meeting with E.P.]

During the meeting, Aguirre told E.P. that students had complained to him that E.P. was writing threats in his diary. E.P. denied these accusations and instead explained that he was writing a work of fiction. Aguirre asked E.P. for permission to search his backpack and E.P. consented. Aguirre discovered the notebook and briefly reviewed its contents. E.P. continued to maintain that the notebook was a work of fiction.

Aguirre called E.P.'s mother to tell her about the notebook. She too maintained that the notebook was fiction, and explained that she also engaged in creative writing.[a] Aguirre informed her that he would read the

---

a. The District Court opinion added the following relevant facts:

On the inside cover of the notebook, Aguirre observed the title "My Nazi Diary Based on a True Story." When questioned, E.P. professed that the notebook was a work of fiction, and that the words "True Story" referred to *The Life & Death of Adolf Hitler* by Robert Payne—a book E.P. was in the process of reading. In his affidavit, E.P. explained that he became interested in World War II because his grandfather fought in the U.S. Army during World War II, and that before reading Payne's book, he read *June 6, 1944: D–Day These Men Were There.*

Aguirre reviewed the contents of the notebook. He continued to ask E.P. about specific "journal entries," to which E.P. continued to respond "It's all fiction." Shortly thereafter, Aguirre called E.P.'s mother and requested that she meet him at the Montwood High School campus. She agreed to do so. Upon informing her of the notebook, E.P.'s mother told Aguirre that it was all fiction and noted that she, herself, engaged in creative writing. In fact, E.P. claims that he got the idea to write a fictional journal from his mother because she had been taking creative writing courses at the University of Texas at El Paso, and had further suggested that he write a dramatic monologue—a story told from the point of view of one of its characters. Ponce v. Socorro Indep. Sch. Dist., 432 F.Supp.2d 682, 685 (W.D. Tex. 2006).

In addition, the District Court found that "after gathering the facts and conducting a brief investigation, Defendant knew the following, at least: 1) E.P. was a good student without any

notebook in detail and "call her the next day with an administrative decision based on the safety and security of the student body." Aguirre then released E.P. back into the general student population to complete the school day. Aguirre took the notebook home and read it several times. He found several lines in the notebook alarming and ultimately determined that E.P.'s writing posed a "terroristic threat" to the safety and security of the students and the campus.[b]

As a "terroristic threat," Aguirre determined that the writing violated the Student Code of Conduct. He therefore suspended E.P. from school three days and recommended that he be placed in the school's alternative education program at KEYS Academy.[1] E.P.'s parents unsuccessfully appealed the decision to the Principal of the Montwood High School, the Assistant Superintendent of Instructional Services, and finally to the School Board's designated committee. To prevent E.P. from being transferred to KEYS Academy, E.P.'s parents placed him in private school, where he completed his sophomore year without incident.

* * *

E.P.'s parents sued SISD under 42 U.S.C. § 1983 alleging violations of E.P.'s First, Fourth, and Fourteenth Amendment rights and analogous provisions under the Texas Constitution. E.P.'s parents also moved to enjoin the School District: from placing him at KEYS Academy, from informing third parties that E.P. had planned to commit violence, from discussing the contents of his writing without his consent, and from retaining any reference to the infraction in his school record. On May 2, 2006, the district court granted a preliminary injunction on First Amend-

---

history of disciplinary action having been taken against him, 2) E.P. disavowed any of the viewpoints expressed in the notebook, 3) there were no incidents involving E.P. following his immediate release into the general student population, and 4) none of the events involving the pseudo-Nazi party as described in the notebook, at least according to the record before the Court, have or had actually occurred." Id. at 698.

b. According to the District Court opinion, these "several lines" that Aguirre found alarming were never precisely identified:

Aguirre failed to identify the particular lines of concern-a curious omission considering the subject unidentified lines presumably were/are the basis of Defendant's decision to suspend and transfer E.P. from Montwood High School, the very subject of this lawsuit. Id. at 686, n. 3.

In considering the totality of the evidence entered into the record, the District Court found that "Plaintiffs had succeeded in stating a First Amendment claim:

This Court ... holds that Plaintiffs have succeeded in showing a substantial likelihood of success on the merits. Defendant was required to show that it had a reasonable basis to believe that E.P.'s expression would materially and substantially interfere with the operation of the school. However, the facts reveal that after reading E.P.'s notebook, Aguirre did not take immediate action to segregate him from the general student population and that E.P. denied any truth to or belief in the contents of the notebook, professing instead that it was part of a creative writing project. Other than Aguirre's conclusory statement that he based his decision upon "the training I have received as an Administrator within the Socorro Independent School District with regard to protection and safety of students," the record is devoid of any evidence indicating that he has been trained in the elements of what constitutes terroristic threat. Instead, it is clear that Aguirre's decision was based on nothing other than mere supposition or base reaction. *Id.* at 705.

1. The day after reading the notebook, Aguirre called the El Paso Police Department and had E.P. arrested. After reviewing the case, the El Paso County Attorney's Office declined to prosecute.

ment grounds. The court held that under the Supreme Court's *Tinker* standard, the evidence was insufficient to prove that SISD acted upon a reasonable belief that disruption would occur.

* * *

III.

* * * There is not, on the record before us, a substantial likelihood that the Ponces can succeed on the merits of their First Amendment claim.

We are guided by the Supreme Court's recent decision in *Morse v. Frederick.* But before applying *Morse* to the case before us, some extended analysis of the case and particularly of Justice Alito's concurring, and controlling, opinion is necessary. That concurring opinion appears to have two primary purposes: providing specificity to the rule announced by the majority opinion, and, relatedly, ensuring that political speech will remain protected within the school setting. Taken together, the majority and concurring opinions in *Morse* explain well why the actions of the school administrators here satisfy the requirements of the First Amendment.

In *Morse,* a student at Juneau–Douglas High School unfurled a 14–foot banner bearing the phrase "BONG HiTS 4 JESUS" during a school-sanctioned and supervised event. The principal confiscated the banner and suspended Frederick. *Id.* Frederick filed suit * * * against the principal and the School Board, claiming that the principal's actions violated his First Amendment rights. * * *

The Supreme Court [held] * * * that Frederick's suspension violated no constitutional right. In reaching this conclusion, the Court expressly declined to apply the *Tinker* standard of "risk of substantial disturbance" to drug speech. The Court's refusal to apply *Tinker* rested on the relative magnitude of the interest it considered to be at stake, *viz.,* prevention of the "serious and palpable" danger that drug abuse presents to the health and well-being of students. Because the already significant harms of drug use are multiplied in a school environment, the Court found "that deterring drug use by schoolchildren is an 'important-indeed, perhaps compelling' interest," not arising from an "undifferentiated fear or apprehension of disturbance" or "a mere desire to avoid the discomfort and unpleasantness that always accompany an unpopular viewpoint," as was the case in *Tinker.* Accordingly, on the Court's reasoning, school administrators need not evaluate the potential for disruption caused by speech advocating drug use; it is *per se* unprotected because of the scope of the harm it potentially foments.

The Court's evaluation of the harm led to an evidently potent remedy. To the extent that preventing a harmful activity may be classified as an "important-indeed, perhaps compelling interest," speech advocating that activity may be prohibited by school administrators with little further inquiry. But the Court did not provide a detailed account of how the particular harms of a given activity add up to an interest sufficiently compelling to forego *Tinker* analysis. As a result of this ambiguity, speech advocating an activity entailing arguably marginal harms may be included within the circle of the majority's rule. Political speech in the school setting, the important constitutional value *Tinker* sought to protect, could thereby be compromised by overly-anxious administrators.

It is against this background of ambiguity that Justice Alito's concurring opinion opens. It begins by making two interpretive points about the majority opinion:

(a) [the majority opinion] goes no further than to hold that a public school may restrict speech that a reasonable observer would interpret as advocating illegal drug use and (b) it provides no support for any restriction of speech that can plausibly be interpreted as commenting on any political or social issue * * *.

By making these points, the concurring opinion makes clear from the outset that the majority is focused on the particular harm to students of speech advocating drug use; the concurring opinion is not itself announcing a general rule defining the requirements for applying *Tinker* whenever the safety of the school population is threatened in some other context. On this reading, the majority opinion "does not hold that the special characteristics of the public schools *necessarily* justify any other speech restrictions." But importantly, Justice Alito's concurring opinion goes on to expound with further clarity why some harms are in fact so great in the school setting that requiring a school administrator to evaluate their disruptive potential is unnecessary. In doing so it provides the specificity necessary for determining the harms that are so serious as to merit the *Morse* analysis.

The central paragraph of Justice Alito's concurring opinion states:

[A]ny argument for altering the usual free speech rules in the public schools ... must ... be based on some special characteristic of the school setting. *The special characteristic that is relevant in this case is the threat to the physical safety of students.* School attendance can expose students to threats to their physical safety that they would not otherwise face. * * * *Experience shows that schools can be places of special danger.* (emphasis added)

On Justice Alito's analysis, the heightened vulnerability of students arising from the lack of parental protection and the close proximity of students with one another make schools places of "special danger" to the physical safety of the student. *Id.* And it is this particular threat that functions as the basis for restricting the First Amendment in schools: "school officials must have greater authority to intervene before speech leads to violence." *Id.* The limits of that authority are often, but not always, adequately determined by *Tinker,* which "in most cases ... permits school officials to step in before actual violence erupts." *Id.* As such, *Tinker* will not always allow school officials to respond to threats of violence appropriately.

The concurring opinion therefore makes explicit that which remains latent in the majority opinion: speech advocating a harm that is demonstrably grave and that derives that gravity from the "special danger" to the physical safety of students arising from the school environment is unprotected. But, because this is a content-based regulation, the concurring opinion is at pains to point out that the reasoning of the court cannot be extended to other kinds of regulations of content, for permitting such content-based regulation is indeed at "the far reaches of what the First Amendment permits." *Id.* Instead, *Tinker*'s focus on the result of speech rather than its content remains the prevailing norm. The protection of the First Amendment in public schools is thereby preserved.

The constitutional concerns of this case-focusing on content-fall precisely within the student speech area demarcated by Justice Alito in *Morse*. That area consists of speech pertaining to grave harms arising from the particular character of the school setting. The speech in question here is not about violence aimed at specific persons,[2] but of violence bearing the stamp of a well-known pattern of recent historic activity: mass, systematic school-shootings in the style that has become painfully familiar in the United States. * * * Such shootings exhibit the character that the concurring opinion identifies as particular to schools. As the concurring opinion points out, school attendance results in the creation of an essentially captive group of persons protected only by the limited personnel of the school itself. This environment makes it possible for a single armed student to cause massive harm to his or her fellow students with little restraint and perhaps even less forewarning. Indeed, the difficulty of identifying warning signs in the various instances of school shootings across the country is intrinsic to the harm itself. *Cf. LaVine*, 257 F.3d at 987 ("After Columbine, Thurston, Santee and other school shootings, questions have been asked how teachers or administrators could have missed telltale 'warning signs,' why something was not done earlier and what should be done to prevent such tragedies from happening again."). We therefore "find it untenable in the wake of Columbine and Jonesboro that any reasonable school official who came into possession of [E.P.'s diary] would not have taken some action based on its violent and disturbing content." *Doe v. Pulaski County Special Sch. Dist.* Our recent history demonstrates that threats of an attack on a school and its students *must* be taken seriously.[3]

---

2. Two post-*Morse* cases are instructive on this point. In *Boim v. Fulton County School District,* 494 F.3d 978 (11th Cir.2007) and *Wisniewski v. Board of Education of the Weedsport Central School District,* 494 F.3d 34 (2d Cir.2007), threats of violence to individual teachers were analyzed under *Tinker.* Such threats, because they are relatively discrete in scope and directed at adults, do not amount to the heightened level of harm that was the focus of both the majority opinion and Justice Alito's concurring opinion in *Morse.* The harm of a mass school shooting is, by contrast, so devastating and so particular to schools that *Morse* analysis is appropriate.

3. With respect to the reasonableness of an administrator's actions, it is of great import that the *Morse* Court's opinion specifically did not turn on Frederick's motive for displaying the banner, which was that "he just wanted to get on television." *Morse,* 127 S.Ct. at 2625. Instead, the Court considered how the banner would likely be interpreted by its viewers, *id.* at 2624–25, finding that it was reasonable for the principal to conclude that "failing to act would send a powerful message to the students in her charge ... about how serious the school was about the

Lack of forewarning and the frequent setting within schools give mass shootings the unique indicia that the concurring opinion found compelling with respect to drug use. If school administrators are permitted to prohibit student speech that advocates illegal drug use because "illegal drug use presents a grave and in many ways unique threat to the physical safety of students," *Morse,* then it defies logical extrapolation to hold school administrators to a stricter standard with respect to speech that gravely and uniquely threatens violence, including massive deaths, to the school population as a whole.[4]

Of course, we do not remotely suggest that "schools can[ ] expel students just because they are 'loners,' wear black and play video games." *LaVine,* 257 F.3d at 987. We do hold, however, that when a student threatens violence against a student body, his words are as much beyond the constitutional pale as yelling "fire" in crowded theater, *see Schenck v. United States,* 249 U.S. 47, 39 S.Ct. 247 (1919), and such specific threatening speech to a school or its population is unprotected by the First Amendment. School administrators must be permitted to react quickly and decisively to address a threat of physical violence against their students, without worrying that they will have to face years of litigation second-guessing their judgment as to whether the threat posed a real risk of substantial disturbance.

IV.

Because we conclude that no constitutional violation has occurred, our inquiry ends here. Our role is to enforce constitutional rights, not "to set aside decisions of the school administrators which [we] may view as lacking a basis in wisdom or compassion." Because the journal's threatening language is not protected by the First Amendment, SISD's disciplinary action against E.P. violated no protected right and, accordingly, the

---

dangers of illegal drug use." *Id.* at 2629. Thus here, where E.P. contended that his writings were mere fiction that posed no real threat, it was reasonable for Aguirre to conclude that failing to respond to E.P.'s diary would not only place E.P. and other students at risk of physical danger if the intent expressed in the diary was actualized, but would also send a message to E.P. and to the informing student that the school administration would tolerate violent threats against the student body. Aguirre did not punish E.P. for speech because it was in conflict with his vision of the school's "educational mission," *id.* at 2637 (Alito, J., concurring), nor out of a "mere desire to avoid ... discomfort and unpleasantness." *Tinker,* 393 U.S. at 509, 89 S.Ct. 733. He acted in response to a danger that, like drug use, "is far more serious and palpable." *Morse,* 127 S.Ct. at 2629.

4. And in fact, the dissenting justices in *Morse* presumably would agree that the content of E.P.'s speech is unprotected. *See Morse,* 127 S.Ct. at 2644 (Stevens, J., dissenting) ("In my judgment, the First Amendment protects student speech if the message itself neither violates a permissible rule nor *expressly advocates conduct that is illegal and harmful to students.*") (emphasis added). The expressly violent content of E.P.'s diary is not the kind of political speech that "implicat[es] concerns at the heart of the First Amendment." *Id.* at 2626. "The students [in *Tinker*] sought to engage in political speech, using the armbands to express 'their disapproval of the Vietnam hostilities and their advocacy of a truce, to make their views known, and, by their example, to influence others to adopt them.'" *Id.* (quoting *Tinker,* 393 U.S. at 514, 89 S.Ct. 733). In contrast, E.P.'s diary is much more characteristic of threat speech, which the Supreme Court has held that the government may proscribe without offending the First Amendment. *See Watts v. United States,* 394 U.S. 705, 89 S.Ct. 1399, 22 L.Ed.2d 664 (1969).

Ponces have failed to show that they have a "substantial likelihood" of success on the merits.

Accordingly, the preliminary injunction is VACATED and the case is REMANDED to the district court for further proceedings not inconsistent with this holding.

NOTES

1. *Wisniewski* and *Ponce* arguably represent two very different applications of *Tinker* and its progeny to allegedly threatening behavior in the aftermath of *Morse v. Frederick*. The Second Circuit in *Wisniewski* applied the *Tinker* rule itself to rule against the student, while the Fifth Circuit in *Ponce* relied instead on an expansive interpretation of *Morse*. Can these appellate decisions be viewed as consistent with each other, or do they represent the outlines of a circuit split that future courts may need to sort out?

2. Both the *Wisniewski* and the *Ponce* courts not only strive to demonstrate that their rulings are consistent with *Morse,* but both show great deference to Justice Alito's concurring opinion. In *Ponce* the concurrence is actually at the center of the Court's analysis. Many commentators have in fact concluded that it is the Alito concurrence itself that states the rule of the case, but others read the decisions quite differently. *See, e.g.,* Frederick Schauer, *Abandoning the Guidance Function: Morse v. Frederick,* 2007 Sup. Ct. Rev. 205.

3. With Judge Newman's opinion in *Wisniewski* and Judge Calabresi's opinion in *Doninger* (set forth above in Chapter 3), the Second Circuit has taken the lead in finding that school officials have increasingly broad power to hold students accountable for their expression outside of the school setting, online or offline. By extending the reach of school officials to student homes, personal computers, and private lives, might it be argued that the courts are overstepping their bounds? Or do these decisions represent a principled application of First Amendment jurisprudence to the increasingly complex fact patterns that are being litigated today?

C. PEER HARASSMENT AND MISTREATMENT

1. LIABILITY FOR PEER-TO-PEER SEXUAL HARASSMENT

PROBLEM 19: *MAXWELL v. VALHALLA UNIFIED SCHOOL DISTRICT*

This problem is based on the following hypothetical, which focuses on the high school journalism class at Nirvana High, in the Valhalla Unified School District (a public school district located in the fictional state of Columbia).

At the beginning of his third semester in Nirvana High's award-winning journalism program, Joey—a quiet 15–year-old with an interest in pursuing a writing career—was promoted to the position of reporter for the *Nirvana*

News, the official school newspaper. The Nirvana News was produced by students who were enrolled in the journalism production class and were graded by the faculty advisor.

Joey was assigned to work under the supervision of Sheree, a gregarious 17–year-old who served as the paper's front page editor. Sheree followed recent developments nationwide as a matter of course, and she soon became fascinated by the emerging news stories focusing on the Clinton–Lewinsky affair and the investigation by Kenneth Starr.

One day in early February 1998, when they were alone in the production room, Sheree asked Joey what he thought about the alleged events in the Paula Jones lawsuit. "If you came into the room and I was there and started taking off my clothes, what would you do?" she asked him. Embarrassed, Joey did not respond.

As time passed, Sheree began sharing stories and pictures of the Lewinsky affair with all four of her reporters. Yet Joey began to feel that she was sending him more e-mail attachments than she had sent the others. In addition, on several occasions when they were alone in the production room, Sheree brushed up against Joey, and on two occasions patted him on his backside (as coaches often do to their players) to congratulate him on his latest stories for the *Nirvana News*.

Joey, a highly religious young man who lived a very simple life with his foster parents, began to feel that he was being sexually harassed. For weeks he told no one, but finally he confided in his foster father, Mr. Maxwell, a highly respected elder in a local church. Unbeknownst to Joey, Maxwell then scheduled an appointment with the school principal, and demanded that the school do something to stop this "harassment" of his foster son. The principal listened, and then shook his head. "This sounds like normal behavior to me," the principal said. "Sheree is a great kid, and Joey is pretty lucky to be getting this attention, if you ask me."

A week later, Joey and Sheree were working after school, and everybody else had gone home. Joey walked into the back room, and there was Sheree, unbuttoning her shirt and smiling at him. "OK," she said, "I'll be Clinton. Here's the role play come true." Joey bolted out the door, and immediately went to his foster father's office in the church, where he told Mr. Maxwell about the latest incident. Outraged, Maxwell went back to see the principal, insisting that something be done. "At least talk to this girl, and to the journalism advisor," Maxwell exclaimed. "I'm sorry," the principal responded, "but in situations like this it's always one student's word against the other. I just don't see that I can or should get involved."

The next day, Joey withdrew from the journalism program, and Mr. Maxwell visited the local office of the Columbia Legal Foundation, a conservative public interest law firm. A widely publicized lawsuit was filed against the district on Joey's behalf, seeking monetary damages under Title VII principles applicable to the schools through Title IX. A key component of the foundation's argument was that the school would have responded very differently had the alleged harasser been a boy and had the alleged victim been a girl.

What arguments might be set forth by the respective sides? What result?

PROBLEM 20: STUDENT TEACHING AT MCKINLEY HIGH

This hypothetical is set in the fictional state of Valhalla.

Sarah Jackson, a graduate student at the University of Northern Valhalla (a large public university located in an urban setting), was ready to begin the student teaching component of her one-year teacher preparation program. After considerable pressure from friends and family, she decided to carry a small handgun with her when she reported to McKinley High School for her first day of student teaching.

(McKinley High had been in the news often over the previous few months. Not only had there been a shooting incident at a football game, but nine current and former male students had been accused of raping or molesting young girls and keeping an account of their sexual conquests. The boys had all been members of the "Hornets' Nest," a clique of teen-agers who readily acknowledge their desire to have sex with large numbers of young girls.)

As Sarah walked down the hall to her assigned classroom on her first morning, she was greeted by catcalls from several male students, and one student shouted out: "There's number fifty-nine for you, Carl." She soon learned that one of these boys, Carl Haley, was actually in the class that she would be teaching. In addition, she found out that he was the star of the football team ... *and* that he was a member of the Hornets' Nest.

The rest of the day, and indeed the next two weeks, passed without incident. Sarah worked on the observation/participation component of her assignment, and continued to bring the gun with her every day. Two other people found out that she had a gun in her purse: a fellow student teacher (Jamal) whom she had taken into confidence, and Jamal's supervising teacher (Ms. Kelly) (whom Jamal had told). Ms. Kelly kept several weapons at home, and told Jamal that she had considered bringing a gun to school herself.

Finally the time came for Sarah to teach her first lesson. After introductory remarks and a brief discussion, she put the students to work on a written assignment. Things were going just fine until she observed Carl and several of his friends snickering and passing papers in the back of the room. Walking over to them, she discovered that Carl had drawn a lewd and suggestive caricature of her—accompanied by a caption describing all the sexual acts she was allegedly ready to participate in with members of the Hornets' Nest.

Sarah turned back toward her supervising teacher's desk, but Mr. Gonzales had left the room for a few minutes to give Sarah the experience of being alone with the students. Embarrassed and increasingly flustered, she literally ran over to the desk to get Mr. Gonzales' referral slips so that she could send Carl to the office. As she did so, she knocked over her purse, and her gun fell out onto the ground. The room fell silent, but then Carl slowly stood up and began walking toward the desk area—where Sarah was standing next to the fallen purse. Julio, a quiet student who respected and admired Sarah, suddenly got up, pushed Carl aside, and picked up the gun. In the ensuing commotion, the gun went off, seriously wounding Latrice Elliot—who was hospitalized and missed three months of school.

The following events subsequently transpired:

A. After being apprised of all the facts leading up to the shooting incident, Dr. Lisa Caunca (the principal) decided to punish Carl by suspending him for harassing Sarah Jackson within the meaning of Education Code sections 212.5 and 48900.2. The football coach protested, but to no avail. Carl missed the last two games of the season, and the quarterback at arch-rival Harding High won the league's most valuable player award (an award that everyone had expected Carl to win).

B. The Elliot family filed a lawsuit against the school district, arguing under a variety of legal theories that the district was responsible for the injury to Latrice.

C. Carl Haley filed a lawsuit against the school district, arguing that the district had violated his rights by suspending him.

* * *

A. What arguments would the Elliot family be expected to raise in their lawsuit against the district? What result? Discuss.

B. Carl Haley is prepared to argue that he did not commit sexual harassment within the meaning of Education Code sections 212.5 and 48900.2. What contentions would the district be likely to set forth in this regard? What result? Discuss.

Relevant portions of the Valhalla Education Code are reproduced below for reference:

Valhalla Education Code Section 48900.2

[A] pupil may be suspended from school or recommended for expulsion if the superintendent or the principal of the school in which the pupil is enrolled determines that the pupil has committed sexual harassment as defined in Section 212.5.

For the purposes of this chapter, the conduct described in Section 212.5 must be considered by a reasonable person of the same gender as the victim to be sufficiently severe or pervasive to have a negative impact upon the individual's academic performance or to create an intimidating, hostile, or offensive educational environment. This section shall not apply to pupils enrolled in kindergarten and grades 1 to 3, inclusive.

Valhalla Education Code Section 212.5

"Sexual harassment" means unwelcome sexual advances, requests for sexual favors, and other verbal, visual, or physical conduct of a sexual nature, made by someone from or in the work or educational setting, under any of the following conditions:

(a) Submission to the conduct is explicitly or implicitly made a term or a condition of an individual's employment, academic status, or progress.

(b) Submission to, or rejection of, the conduct by the individual is used as the basis of employment or academic decisions affecting the individual.

(c) The conduct has the purpose or effect of having a negative impact upon the individual's work or academic performance, or of creating an intimidating, hostile, or offensive work or educational environment.

(d) Submission to, or rejection of, the conduct by the individual is used as the basis for any decision affecting the individual regarding benefits and services, honors, programs, or activities available at or through the educational institution.

HOSTILE ENVIRONMENT SEXUAL HARASSMENT LAW*

Hostile environment claims were first recognized by the U.S. Supreme Court in 1986,[5] and over the next 10–15 years the rules were fine tuned by subsequent judicial opinions. 1998 proved to be a turning point, with the Court deciding four sexual harassment cases in one year.[6]

The basic hostile environment claim under Title VII can only be filed by a person who alleges harassment in the workplace. Sexual harassment is not a crime, but an act or a series of acts that can lead to large monetary awards for aggrieved employees who have sued their employers under Title VII. To win such lawsuits, plaintiffs must follow a two-step process. First, they must establish actionable harassment. Second, they must show that the employer should be held liable for this harassment.[7]

To establish actionable hostile environment harassment, plaintiffs must prove that the activity in question was unwelcome and that it constituted "a sexually objectionable environment" which was (a) objectively offensive and (b) subjectively offensive. An environment is deemed *objectively offensive* if a "reasonable person" would find it to be hostile or abusive, and it will be found *subjectively offensive* if the victim in fact perceived it to be so.

The objectively offensive inquiry is inevitably the most complex. Courts must look at

all the circumstances, including the frequency of the discriminatory conduct; its severity; whether it is physically threatening or humiliat-

---

* Adapted from Stuart Biegel, Beyond Our Control? Confronting the Limits of Our Legal System in the Age of Cyberspace, MIT Press (2001).

5. *See* Meritor Savings Bank v. Vinson, 477 U.S. 57 (1986).

6. The four cases were *Oncale v. Sundowner Offshore Services,* 523 U.S. 75 (1998), *Gebser v. Lago Vista Indep. Sch. Dist.,* 524 U.S. 274 (1998), *Faragher v. City of Boca Raton,* 524 U.S. 775 (1998), & *Ellerth v. Burlington Indus.,* 524 U.S. 951 (1998).

7. Once actionable harassment is shown, plaintiff still needs to prove that employer's actions should give rise to liability. Such proof is not necessary if there was a "tangible employment action" as a result of the events in question (such as retaliatory firing after plaintiff complained). However, if there was no tangible employment action, the employer can prevail if it can be shown that:

    1. Employer exercised reasonable care to prevent and correct promptly any sexually harassing behavior, and

    2. Plaintiff employee unreasonably failed to take advantage of any preventive or corrective opportunities provided by employer or to avoid harm otherwise. *Faragher,* 524 U.S. at 807.

ing, or a mere offensive utterance; and whether it unreasonably interferes with an employee's work performance.[8]

Increasingly, the Court has worked very hard to try to distinguish between simple teasing on the one hand and hostile environment sexual harassment on the other. "A recurring point" in recent court opinions, Justice Souter noted in *Faragher,* is that "simple teasing, offhand comments, and isolated incidents (unless extremely serious) will not amount to discriminatory changes in the terms and conditions of employment. These standards for judging hostility," he continued, "are sufficiently demanding to ensure that Title VII does not become a 'general civility code.' "[9]

A version of this framework has recently been applied by the Courts in federally funded education programs under Title IX of the Education Amendments of 1972 to the Civil Rights Act of 1964. In *Davis v. Monroe County Board of Education,* 526 U.S. 629 (1999) the Court held that educational institutions can be held liable for peer-to-peer hostile environment sexual harassment "that is so severe, pervasive, and objectively offensive that it effectively bars the victim's access to an educational opportunity or benefit." But even if plaintiff can meet the requirements of this stringent test for actionable harassment, he or she can only prevail if the education officials in charge acted "with deliberate indifference to known acts of harassment."[10]

DAVIS v. MONROE COUNTY BD. OF ED.

526 U.S. 629, 119 S.Ct. 1661 (1999)

JUSTICE O'CONNOR delivered the opinion of the Court.

Petitioner brought suit against the Monroe County Board of Education and other defendants, alleging that her fifth-grade daughter had been the victim of sexual harassment by another student in her class. Among petitioner's claims was a claim for monetary and injunctive relief under Title IX of the Education Amendments of 1972 (Title IX), 86 Stat. 373, as amended, 20 U.S.C. § 1681 *et seq.* The District Court dismissed petitioner's Title IX claim on the ground that "student-on-student," or peer, harassment provides no ground for a private cause of action under the statute. The Court of Appeals for the Eleventh Circuit, sitting en banc, affirmed. We consider here whether a private damages action may lie against the school board in cases of student-on-student harassment. We conclude that it may, but only where the funding recipient acts with deliberate indifference to known acts of harassment in its programs or activities. Moreover, we conclude that such an action will lie only for harassment that is so severe, pervasive, and objectively offensive that it effectively bars the victim's access to an educational opportunity or benefit.

---

8. *Id.* at 787–88.

9. *Id.*

10. *See* Davis v. Monroe County Board of Education, 526 U.S. 629, 633 (1999).

I

* * *

A

Petitioner's minor daughter, LaShonda, was allegedly the victim of a prolonged pattern of sexual harassment by one of her fifth-grade classmates at Hubbard Elementary School, a public school in Monroe County, Georgia. According to petitioner's complaint, the harassment began in December 1992, when the classmate, G.F., attempted to touch LaShonda's breasts and genital area and made vulgar statements such as " 'I want to get in bed with you' " and " 'I want to feel your boobs.' " Similar conduct allegedly occurred on or about January 4 and January 20, 1993. LaShonda reported each of these incidents to her mother and to her classroom teacher, Diane Fort. Petitioner, in turn, also contacted Fort, who allegedly assured petitioner that the school principal, Bill Querry, had been informed of the incidents. Petitioner contends that, notwithstanding these reports, no disciplinary action was taken against G.F.

G.F.'s conduct allegedly continued for many months. In early February, G.F. purportedly placed a door stop in his pants and proceeded to act in a sexually suggestive manner toward LaShonda during physical education class. LaShonda reported G.F.'s behavior to her physical education teacher, Whit Maples. Approximately one week later, G.F. again allegedly engaged in harassing behavior, this time while under the supervision of another classroom teacher, Joyce Pippin. Again, LaShonda allegedly reported the incident to the teacher, and again petitioner contacted the teacher to follow up.

Petitioner alleges that G.F. once more directed sexually harassing conduct toward LaShonda in physical education class in early March, and that LaShonda reported the incident to both Maples and Pippen. In mid-April 1993, G.F. allegedly rubbed his body against LaShonda in the school hallway in what LaShonda considered a sexually suggestive manner, and LaShonda again reported the matter to Fort.

The string of incidents finally ended in mid-May, when G.F. was charged with, and pleaded guilty to, sexual battery for his misconduct. The complaint alleges that LaShonda had suffered during the months of harassment, however; specifically, her previously high grades allegedly dropped as she became unable to concentrate on her studies, and, in April 1993, her father discovered that she had written a suicide note. The complaint further alleges that, at one point, LaShonda told petitioner that she " 'didn't know how much longer she could keep [G.F.] off her.' "

Nor was LaShonda G.F.'s only victim; it is alleged that other girls in the class fell prey to G.F.'s conduct. At one point, in fact, a group composed of LaShonda and other female students tried to speak with Principal Querry about G.F.'s behavior. According to the complaint, however, a teacher denied the students' request with the statement, " 'If [Querry] wants you, he'll call you.' "

Petitioner alleges that no disciplinary action was taken in response to G.F.'s behavior toward LaShonda. In addition to her conversations with Fort and Pippen, petitioner alleges that she spoke with Principal Querry in mid-May 1993. When petitioner inquired as to what action the school intended to take against G.F., Querry simply stated, " 'I guess I'll have to threaten him a little bit harder.' " Yet, petitioner alleges, at no point during the many months of his reported misconduct was G.F. disciplined for harassment. Indeed, Querry allegedly asked petitioner why LaShonda " 'was the only one complaining.' "

Nor, according to the complaint, was any effort made to separate G.F. and LaShonda. On the contrary, notwithstanding LaShonda's frequent complaints, only after more than three months of reported harassment was she even permitted to change her classroom seat so that she was no longer seated next to G.F. Moreover, petitioner alleges that, at the time of the events in question, the Monroe County Board of Education (Board) had not instructed its personnel on how to respond to peer sexual harassment and had not established a policy on the issue.

B

On May 4, 1994, petitioner filed suit in the United States District Court for the Middle District of Georgia against the Board, Charles Dumas, the school district's superintendent, and Principal Querry. The complaint alleged that the Board is a recipient of federal funding for purposes of Title IX, that "[t]he persistent sexual advances and harassment by the student G.F. upon [LaShonda] interfered with her ability to attend school and perform her studies and activities," and that "[t]he deliberate indifference by Defendants to the unwelcome sexual advances of a student upon LaShonda created an intimidating, hostile, offensive and abus[ive] school environment in violation of Title IX." The complaint sought compensatory and punitive damages, attorney's fees, and injunctive relief.

* * *

II

Title IX provides, with certain exceptions not at issue here, that

[n]o person in the United States shall, on the basis of sex, be excluded from participation in, be denied the benefits of, or be subjected to discrimination under any education program or activity receiving Federal financial assistance.

20 U.S.C. § 1681(a).

* * *

There is no dispute here that the Board is a recipient of federal education funding for Title IX purposes. Nor do respondents support an argument that student-on-student harassment cannot rise to the level of "discrimination" for purposes of Title IX. Rather, at issue here is the question whether a recipient of federal education funding may be liable for damages under Title IX under any circumstances for discrimination in the form of student-on-student sexual harassment.

A

* * * [W]e are asked to do more than define the scope of the behavior that Title IX proscribes. We must determine whether a district's failure to respond to student-on-student harassment in its schools can support a private suit for money damages. This Court has indeed recognized an implied private right of action under Title IX, and we have held that money damages are available in such suits.

* * *

Gebser * * * established that a recipient intentionally violates Title IX, and is subject to a private damages action, where the recipient is deliberately indifferent to known acts of teacher-student discrimination. Indeed, whether viewed as "discrimination" or "subject[ing]" students to discrimination, Title IX "[u]nquestionably * * * placed on [the Board] the duty not" to permit teacher-student harassment in its schools, and recipients violate Title IX's plain terms when they remain deliberately indifferent to this form of misconduct.

We consider here whether the misconduct identified in *Gebser*— deliberate indifference to known acts of harassment—amounts to an intentional violation of Title IX, capable of supporting a private damages action, when the harasser is a student rather than a teacher. We conclude that, in certain limited circumstances, it does. * * *

* * * [A] recipient's damages liability ... [is limited] ... to circumstances wherein the recipient exercises substantial control over both the harasser and the context in which the known harassment occurs. Only then can the recipient be said to "expose" its students to harassment or "cause" them to undergo it "under" the recipient's programs. * * *

Where, as here, the misconduct occurs during school hours and on school grounds—the bulk of G.F.'s misconduct, in fact, took place in the classroom—the misconduct is taking place "under" an "operation" of the funding recipient. In these circumstances, the recipient retains substantial control over the context in which the harassment occurs. More importantly, however, in this setting the Board exercises significant control over the harasser. We have observed, for example, "that the nature of [the State's] power [over public schoolchildren] is custodial and tutelary, permitting a degree of supervision and control that could not be exercised over free adults." On more than one occasion, this Court has recognized the importance of school officials' "comprehensive authority * * * consistent with fundamental constitutional safeguards, to prescribe and control conduct in the schools." *Tinker* v. *Des Moines Independent Community School Dist.*, 393 U.S. 503, 507, 89 S. Ct. 733 (1969). The common law, too, recognizes the school's disciplinary authority. We thus conclude that recipients of federal funding may be liable for "subject[ing]" their students to discrimination where the recipient is deliberately indifferent to known acts of student-on-student sexual harassment and the harasser is under the school's disciplinary authority.

* * *

We stress that our conclusion here—that recipients may be liable for their deliberate indifference to known acts of peer sexual harassment—does not mean that recipients can avoid liability only by purging their schools of actionable peer harassment or that administrators must engage in particular disciplinary action. We thus disagree with respondents' contention that, if Title IX provides a cause of action for student-on-student harassment, "nothing short of expulsion of every student accused of misconduct involving sexual overtones would protect school systems from liability or damages." Likewise, the dissent erroneously imagines that victims of peer harassment now have a Title IX right to make particular remedial demands. In fact, as we have previously noted, courts should refrain from second-guessing the disciplinary decisions made by school administrators.

School administrators will continue to enjoy the flexibility they require so long as funding recipients are deemed "deliberately indifferent" to acts of student-on-student harassment only where the recipient's response to the harassment or lack thereof is clearly unreasonable in light of the known circumstances. The dissent consistently mischaracterizes this standard to require funding recipients to "remedy" peer harassment, and to "ensur[e] that ... students conform their conduct to" certain rules. Title IX imposes no such requirements. On the contrary, the recipient must merely respond to known peer harassment in a manner that is not clearly unreasonable. This is not a mere "reasonableness" standard, as the dissent assumes. In an appropriate case, there is no reason why courts, on a motion to dismiss, for summary judgment, or for a directed verdict, could not identify a response as not "clearly unreasonable" as a matter of law.

Like the dissent, we acknowledge that school administrators shoulder substantial burdens as a result of legal constraints on their disciplinary authority. To the extent that these restrictions arise from federal statutes, Congress can review these burdens with attention to the difficult position in which such legislation may place our Nation's schools. We believe, however, that the standard set out here is sufficiently flexible to account both for the level of disciplinary authority available to the school and for the potential liability arising from certain forms of disciplinary action. A university might not, for example, be expected to exercise the same degree of control over its students that a grade school would enjoy, and it would be entirely reasonable for a school to refrain from a form of disciplinary action that would expose it to constitutional or statutory claims.

* * *

C

Applying this standard to the facts at issue here, we conclude that the Eleventh Circuit erred in dismissing petitioner's complaint. Petitioner alleges that her daughter was the victim of repeated acts of sexual harassment by G.F. over a 5–month period, and there are allegations in support of the conclusion that G.F.'s misconduct was severe, pervasive, and objectively offensive. The harassment was not only verbal; it included numerous acts of objectively offensive touching, and, indeed, G.F. ultimately pleaded guilty to criminal sexual misconduct. Moreover, the complaint alleges that there were multiple victims who were sufficiently disturbed by G.F.'s misconduct to seek an audience with the school principal. Further, petitioner contends that the harassment had a concrete, negative effect on her daughter's ability to receive an education. The complaint also suggests that petitioner may be able to show both actual knowledge and deliberate indifference on the part of the Board, which made no effort whatsoever either to investigate or to put an end to the harassment.

* * * Accordingly, the judgment of the United States Court of Appeals for the Eleventh Circuit is reversed, and the case is remanded for further proceedings consistent with this opinion.

It is so ordered.

JUSTICE KENNEDY, with whom THE CHIEF JUSTICE, JUSTICE SCALIA, and JUSTICE THOMAS join, dissenting.

II

* * * The majority * * * imposes on schools potentially crushing financial liability for student conduct that is not prohibited in clear terms by Title IX and that cannot, even after today's opinion, be identified by either schools or courts with any precision.

The law recognizes that children—particularly young children—are not fully accountable for their actions because they lack the capacity to exercise mature judgment. It should surprise no one, then, that the schools that are the primary locus of most children's social development are rife with inappropriate behavior by children who are just learning to interact with their peers. The *amici* on the front lines of our schools describe the situation best:

> Unlike adults in the workplace, juveniles have limited life experiences or familial influences upon which to establish an understanding of appropriate behavior. The real world of school discipline is a rough-and-tumble place where students practice newly learned vulgarities, erupt with anger, tease and embarrass each other, share offensive notes, flirt, push and shove in the halls, grab and offend.

No one contests that much of this "dizzying array of immature or uncontrollable behaviors by students," is inappropriate, even "objectively offensive" at times, and that parents and schools have a moral and ethical responsibility to help students learn to interact with their peers in an appropriate manner. It is doubtless the case, moreover, that much of this inappropriate behavior is directed toward members of the opposite sex, as children in the throes of adolescence struggle to express their emerging sexual identities.

It is a far different question, however, whether it is either proper or useful to label this immature, childish behavior gender discrimination. Nothing in Title IX suggests that Congress even contemplated this question, much less answered it in the affirmative in unambiguous terms.

The majority, nevertheless, has no problem labeling the conduct of fifth graders "sexual harassment" and "gender discrimination." * * *

A school faced with a peer sexual harassment complaint in the wake of the majority's decision may well be beset with litigation from every side. One student's demand for a quick response to her harassment complaint will conflict with the alleged harasser's demand for due process. Another student's demand for a harassment-free classroom will conflict with the alleged harasser's claim to a mainstream placement under the IDEA or with his state constitutional right to a continuing, free public education. On college campuses, and even in secondary schools, a student's claim that the school should remedy a sexually hostile environment will conflict with the alleged harasser's claim that his speech, even if offensive, is protected by the First Amendment. In each of these situations, the school faces the risk of suit, and maybe even multiple suits, regardless of its response.

* * *

The complaint of this fifth grader survives and the school will be compelled to answer in federal court. We can be assured that like suits will follow—suits, which in cost and number, will impose serious financial burdens on local school districts, the taxpayers who support them, and the children they serve. Federalism and our struggling school systems deserve better from this Court. I dissent.

NOTES

1. The *Davis* case was a closely fought, 5–4 decision, with the two female justices voting with the majority in favor of the plaintiff. It is important to note that *Davis* sets forth a much higher bar for plaintiffs in an education setting under Title IX than the courts have done for plaintiffs in a workplace setting under Title VII. Is such a higher bar appropriate? Why or why not?

2. The dissent's warnings regarding the likelihood of this decision opening the floodgates of litigation do not appear to have panned out ... perhaps because the bar has been set so high.

3. In *Fitzgerald v. Barnstable School Committee*, 504 F.3d 165 (1st Cir. 2007), the First Circuit applied *Davis* to rule against the plaintiff in a peer-to-peer sexual harassment case. While acknowledging the highly egregious nature of the actions perpetrated by a third grade boy against a girl who was only in kindergarten, the Court found no deliberate indifference on the part of the school officials, who investigated the allegations immediately and took additional steps to seek to address the matter. While other incidents of harassment apparently occurred after these initial steps, the Court concluded

that these "subsequent interactions [do] not render the School Committee deliberately indifferent. To avoid Title IX liability, an educational institution must act reasonably to prevent future harassment; it need not succeed in doing so." *Id.* at 175.

Plaintiff also sought to find school officials liable under Section 1983, which may generally be used to redress the deprivation of a right guaranteed by a federal statute. The Court, however, found that "those claims, as presented in this case, are precluded by Title IX's comprehensive remedial scheme." *Id.* at 176–180. In June 2008, the U.S. Supreme Court granted certiorari in this case, and oral arguments were scheduled to be heard during the 2008–2009 term. 128 S.Ct. 2903 (Mem.) (2008).

4.   Amici briefs filed on behalf of the petitioner in the *Fitzgerald* case reflected the frustration of many women's rights advocates with the persistence of sexual harassment in the education community and the difficulties faced by plaintiffs seeking to prevail in these cases under the highly rigorous requirements adopted by the *Davis* Court. For an overview of key issues in this context, *see, e.g.,* Lexie Kuznick, *Changing Social Norms? Title IX and Legal Activism,* 31 Harvard Journal of Law & Gender 367 (2008).

5.   While *Davis* is a K–12 ruling, it can be argued that its two-part test for liability is equally applicable in higher education settings, given the fact that Title IX also applies at colleges and universities. Indeed, Justice Kennedy appeared to presume its applicability at the higher education level, warning of negative consequences that could flow in that setting from this decision. *But see Benefield v. Board of Trustees,* 214 F. Supp. 2d 1212 (S.D. Ala. 2002), questioning the applicability of *Davis* in a higher education setting.

At colleges and universities, most claims of peer harassment are handled internally, through student conduct committees.

2.   LIABILITY FOR MISTREATMENT OF LESBIAN, GAY, BISEXUAL, & TRANSGENDER (LGBT) STUDENTS

There are numerous parallels that can be identified between peer-to-peer sexual harassment and peer mistreatment of LGBT students. In both instances, for example, such behavior was generally viewed as acceptable for a very long time by a very large percentage of people. In both instances, the phrase "boys will be boys" continues to be used to justify the behavior. And both types of "harassment" have often been accompanied by allegations that the victim is to blame for what happened.

For both types of behavior, it has only been in recent decades that concrete legal protection has begun to emerge, including but not limited to frameworks whereby school officials can be found liable. In the sexual harassment area, a test has evolved under Title IX. In the LGBT mistreatment area, although cases have been brought under Title IX and the OCR has developed guidelines that apply Title IX to this area, the major victories in federal court have been under the Equal Protection Clause of the Fourteenth Amendment.

Two of the most prominent opinions in this context are *Nabozny v. Podlesny* and *Flores v. Morgan Hill USD*, both of which are set forth below.

NABOZNY v. PODLESNY

92 F.3d 446 (7th Cir. 1996)

ESCHBACH, CIRCUIT JUDGE.

Jamie Nabozny was a student in the Ashland Public School District (hereinafter "the District") in Ashland, Wisconsin throughout his middle school and high school years. During that time, Nabozny was continually harassed and physically abused by fellow students because he is homosexual. Both in middle school and high school Nabozny reported the harassment to school administrators. Nabozny asked the school officials to protect him and to punish his assailants. Despite the fact that the school administrators had a policy of investigating and punishing student-on-student battery and sexual harassment, they allegedly turned a deaf ear to Nabozny's requests. Indeed, there is evidence to suggest that some of the administrators themselves mocked Nabozny's predicament. * * *

* * * Around the time that Nabozny entered the seventh grade, Nabozny realized that he is gay. Many of Nabozny's fellow classmates soon realized it too. Nabozny decided not to "closet" his sexuality, and considerable harassment from his fellow students ensued. Nabozny's classmates regularly referred to him as "faggot," and subjected him to various forms of physical abuse, including striking and spitting on him. Nabozny spoke to the school's guidance counselor, Ms. Peterson, about the abuse, informing Peterson that he is gay. Peterson took action, ordering the offending students to stop the harassment and placing two of them in detention. However, the students' abusive behavior toward Nabozny stopped only briefly. Meanwhile, Peterson was replaced as guidance counselor by Mr. Nowakowski. Nabozny similarly informed Nowakowski that he is gay, and asked for protection from the student harassment. Nowakowski, in turn, referred the matter to school Principal Mary Podlesny; Podlesny was responsible for school discipline.

Just before the 1988 Winter holiday, Nabozny met with Nowakowski and Podlesny to discuss the harassment. During the meeting, Nabozny explained the nature of the harassment and again revealed his homosexuality. Podlesny promised to protect Nabozny, but took no action. Following the holiday season, student harassment of Nabozny worsened, especially at the hands of students Jason Welty and Roy Grande. Nabozny complained to Nowakowski, and school administrators spoke to the students. The harassment, however, only intensified. A short time later, in a science classroom, Welty grabbed Nabozny and pushed him to the floor. Welty and Grande held Nabozny down and performed a mock rape on Nabozny, exclaiming that Nabozny should enjoy it. The boys carried out the mock rape as twenty other students looked on and laughed. Nabozny escaped and fled to Podlesny's office. Podlesny's alleged response is somewhat astonishing; she said that "boys will be boys" and told Nabozny that if he was "going to be so openly gay," he should "expect" such behavior from his fellow students. In the wake of Podlesny's comments, Nabozny ran home. The next day Nabozny was forced to speak with a counselor, not because he was subjected to a mock rape in a classroom, but because he left the school without obtaining the proper permission. No action was taken against the students involved. Nabozny was forced to return to his regular schedule. Understandably, Nabozny was "petrified" to attend school; he was subjected to abuse throughout the duration of the school year.

The situation hardly improved when Nabozny entered the eighth grade. Shortly after the school year began, several boys attacked Nabozny in a school bathroom, hitting him and pushing his books from his hands. This time Nabozny's parents met with Podlesny and the alleged perpetrators. The offending boys denied that the incident occurred, and no action was taken. Podlesny told both Nabozny and his parents that Nabozny should expect such incidents because he is "openly" gay. Several similar meetings between Nabozny's parents and Podlesny followed subsequent incidents involving Nabozny. Each time perpetrators were identified to Podlesny. Each time Podlesny pledged to take action. And, each time nothing was done. Toward the end of the school year, the harassment against Nabozny intensified to the point that a district attorney purportedly advised Nabozny to take time off from school. Nabozny took one and a half weeks off from school. When he returned, the harassment resumed, driving Nabozny to attempt suicide. After a stint in a hospital, Nabozny finished his eighth grade year in a Catholic school.

The Catholic school attended by Nabozny did not offer classes beyond the eighth grade. Therefore, to attend the ninth grade, Nabozny enrolled in Ashland High School. Almost immediately Nabozny's fellow students sang an all too familiar tune. Early in the year, while Nabozny was using a urinal in the restroom, Nabozny was assaulted. Student Stephen Huntley struck Nabozny in the back of the knee, forcing him to fall into the urinal. Roy Grande then urinated on Nabozny. Nabozny immediately reported the incident to the principal's office. Nabozny recounted the incident to the office secretary, who in turn relayed the story to Principal William Davis. Davis ordered Nabozny to go home and change clothes. Nabozny's parents scheduled a meeting with Davis and Assistant Principal Thomas Blauert. At the meeting, the parties discussed numerous instances of harassment against Nabozny, including the restroom incident.

Rather than taking action against the perpetrators, Davis and Blauert referred Nabozny to Mr. Reeder, a school guidance counselor. Reeder was supposed to change Nabozny's schedule so as to minimize Nabozny's exposure to the offending students. Eventually the school placed Nabozny in a special education class; Stephen Huntley and Roy Grande were special education students. Nabozny's parents continued to insist that the school take action, repeatedly meeting with Davis and Blauert among others. Nabozny's parents' efforts were futile; no action was taken. In the middle of his ninth grade year, Nabozny again attempted suicide. Following another hospital stay and a period living with relatives, Nabozny ran away to Minneapolis. His parents convinced him to return to Ashland by promising that Nabozny would not have to attend Ashland High. Because Nabozny's parents were unable to afford private schooling, however, the Department of Social Services ordered Nabozny to return to Ashland High.

In tenth grade, Nabozny fared no better. Nabozny's parents moved, forcing Nabozny to rely on the school bus to take him to school. Students on the bus regularly used epithets, such as "fag" and "queer," to refer to Nabozny. Some students even pelted Nabozny with dangerous objects such as steel nuts and bolts. When Nabozny's parents complained to the school, school officials changed Nabozny's assigned seat and moved him to the front of the bus. The harassment continued. Ms. Hanson, a school guidance counselor, lobbied the school's administration to take more aggressive action to no avail. The worst was yet to come, however. One morning when Nabozny arrived early to school, he went to the library to study. The library was not yet open, so Nabozny sat down in the hallway. Minutes later he was met by a group of eight boys led by Stephen Huntley. Huntley began kicking Nabozny in the stomach, and continued to do so for five to ten minutes while the other students looked on laughing. Nabozny reported the incident to Hanson, who referred him to the school's "police liaison" Dan Crawford. Nabozny told Crawford that he wanted to press charges, but Crawford dissuaded him. Crawford promised to speak to the offending boys instead. Meanwhile, at Crawford's behest, Nabozny reported the incident to Blauert. Blauert, the school official supposedly in charge of disciplining, laughed and told Nabozny that Nabozny deserved such treatment because he is gay. Weeks later Nabozny collapsed from internal bleeding that resulted from Huntley's beating. Nabozny's parents and counselor Hanson repeatedly urged Davis and Blauert to take action to protect Nabozny. Each time aggressive action was promised. And, each time nothing was done.

Finally, in his eleventh grade year, Nabozny withdrew from Ashland High School. Hanson told Nabozny and his parents that school administrators were unwilling to help him and that he should seek educational opportunities elsewhere. Nabozny left Ashland and moved to Minneapolis where he was diagnosed with Post Traumatic Stress Disorder. In addition to seeking medical help, Nabozny sought legal advice.

On February 6, 1995, Nabozny filed the instant suit pursuant to 42 U.S.C. § 1983...alleging, among other things, that the defendants violated his Fourteenth Amendment rights to equal protection and due process. * * *

The district court ruled in favor of the defendants. * * * Nabozny now brings this timely appeal. * * *

    * * *

Since at least 1988, in compliance with * * * state statute, the Ashland Public School District has had a policy of prohibiting discrimination against students on the basis of gender or sexual orientation. The District's policy and practice includes protecting students from student-on-student sexual harassment and battery. Nabozny maintains that the defendants denied him the equal protection of the law by denying him the protection extended to other students, based on his gender and sexual orientation.

* * *

The gravamen of equal protection lies not in the fact of deprivation of a right but in the invidious classification of persons aggrieved by the state's action. A plaintiff must demonstrate intentional or purposeful discrimination to show an equal protection violation. Discriminatory purpose, however, implies more than intent as volition or intent as awareness of consequences. It implies that a decisionmaker singled out a particular group for disparate treatment and selected his course of action at least in part for the purpose of causing its adverse effects on the identifiable group.

A showing that the defendants were negligent will not suffice. Nabozny must show that the defendants acted either intentionally or with deliberate indifference. To escape liability, the defendants either must prove that they did not discriminate against Nabozny, or at a bare minimum, the defendants' discriminatory conduct must satisfy one of two well-established standards of review: heightened scrutiny in the case of gender discrimination, or rational basis in the case of sexual orientation.

The district court found that Nabozny had proffered no evidence to support his equal protection claims. In the alternative, the court granted to the defendants qualified immunity. Considering the facts in the light most favorable to Nabozny, we respectfully disagree with the district court's conclusions.

A. Gender and Equal Protection.

The district court disposed of Nabozny's equal protection claims in two brief paragraphs. Regarding the merits of Nabozny's gender claim, the court concluded that "[t]here is absolutely nothing in the record to indicate that plaintiff was treated differently because of his gender." The district court's conclusion affords two interpretations: 1) there is no evidence that the defendants treated Nabozny differently from other students; or, 2) there is no evidence that the discriminatory treatment was based on Nabozny's gender. We will examine each in turn.

The record viewed in the light most favorable to Nabozny, combined with the defendants' own admissions, suggests that Nabozny was treated differently from other students. The defendants stipulate that they had a commendable record of enforcing their anti-harassment policies. Yet Nabozny has presented evidence that his classmates harassed and battered him for years and that school administrators failed to enforce their anti-harassment policies, despite his repeated pleas for them to do so. If the defendants otherwise enforced their anti-harassment policies, as they contend, then Nabozny's evidence strongly suggests that they made an exception to their normal practice in Nabozny's case.

Therefore, the question becomes whether Nabozny can show that he received different treatment because of his gender. Nabozny's evidence regarding the defendants' punishment of male-on-female battery and harassment is not overwhelming. Nabozny contends that a male student that struck his girlfriend was immediately expelled, that males were reprimanded for striking girls, and that when pregnant girls were called "slut" or "whore," the school took action. Nabozny's evidence does not include specific facts, such as the names and dates of the individuals involved. Nabozny does allege, however, that when he was subjected to a mock rape Podlesny responded by saying "boys will be boys," apparently dismissing the incident because both the perpetrators and the victim were males. We find it impossible to believe that a female lodging a similar complaint would have received the same response.

* * * If Nabozny's evidence is considered credible, the record taken in conjunction with the defendants' admissions demonstrates that the defendants treated male and female victims differently.

The defendants also argue that there is no evidence that they either intentionally discriminated against Nabozny, or were deliberately indifferent to his complaints. The defendants concede that they had a policy and practice of punishing perpetrators of battery and harassment. It is well settled law that departures from established practices may evince discriminatory intent. Moreover, Nabozny introduced evidence to suggest that the defendants literally laughed at Nabozny's pleas for help. The defendants' argument, considered against Nabozny's evidence, is simply indefensible.

    * * *

B. Sexual Orientation and Equal Protection.

    * * *

Our discussion of equal protection analysis thus far has revealed a well established principle: the Constitution prohibits intentional invidious discrimination between otherwise similarly situated persons based on one's membership in a definable minority, absent at least a rational basis for the discrimination. There can be little doubt that homosexuals are an identifiable minority[10] subjected to discrimination in our society. Given

---

10. The Sixth Circuit has ruled that:

[T]he reality remains that no law can successfully be drafted that is calculated to penalize, or to benefit, or to protect, an unidentifiable group or class of individuals whose identity is defined by subjective and unapparent characteristics such as innate desires, drives, and thoughts. Those persons having a homosexual "orientation" simply do not, as such, comprise an identifiable class.... Because homosexuals generally are not identifiable "on sight" ... they cannot constitute a suspect class or a quasi-suspect class....

* * * We express no opinion on whether sexual orientation is an "obvious, immutable, or distinguishing" characteristic. However, it does seem dubious to suggest that someone would

the legislation across the country both positing and prohibiting homosexual rights, that proposition was as self-evident in 1988 as it is today. In addition, the Wisconsin statute expressly prohibits discrimination on the basis of sexual orientation. Obviously that language was included because the Wisconsin legislature both recognized that homosexuals are discriminated against, and sought to prohibit such discrimination in Wisconsin schools. The defendants stipulate that they knew about the Wisconsin law, and enforced it to protect homosexuals. Therefore, it appears that the defendants concede that they knew that homosexuals are a definable minority and treated them as such.

In this case we need not consider whether homosexuals are a suspect or quasi-suspect class, which would subject the defendants' conduct to either strict or heightened scrutiny. * * * The rational basis standard is sufficient for our purposes herein.

Under rational basis review there is no constitutional violation if "there is any reasonably conceivable state of facts" that would provide a rational basis for the government's conduct. We are unable to garner any rational basis for permitting one student to assault another based on the victim's sexual orientation, and the defendants do not offer us one.

     * * *

FLORES v. MORGAN HILL UNIFIED SCH. DIST.

324 F.3d 1130 (9th Cir. 2003)

SCHROEDER, CHIEF JUDGE:

Plaintiffs are former students in the Morgan Hill Unified School District who have sued the school district, administrators, and school board members. * * *

We affirm because we find sufficient evidence for a jury to infer that defendants acted with deliberate indifference. We also hold that the law was clearly established and that the evidence would support a finding that the administrators' actions were unreasonable.

I. BACKGROUND

The plaintiffs allege that during their time as students in public schools within the Morgan Hill Unified School District ("the District"), they suffered anti-gay harassment by their classmates. The alleged harassment took place between 1991 and 1998. All of the plaintiffs were, or were perceived by other students to be, lesbian, gay, or bisexual.

The plaintiffs recount incidents in which the named defendants and their agents, subordinates, and employees allegedly responded to the plaintiffs' complaints in a discriminatory fashion. Flores and the other plaintiffs allege that teachers and administrators failed to stop name-

---

choose to be homosexual, absent some genetic predisposition, given the considerable discrimination leveled against homosexuals.

calling and anti-gay remarks, and that the administrators responded with inadequate disciplinary action to physical abuse.

The following is a sampling of incidents that the plaintiffs have described in affidavits or depositions. On several occasions, plaintiff Alana Flores found pornography and notes to the effect of "Die, dyke bitch" inside her locker. Similar messages were scrawled on the outside of her locker. When Flores showed one note to an assistant principal, defendant Delia Schizzano, and asked to be reassigned to a new locker, Schizzano allegedly replied, "Yes, sure, sure, later. You need to go back to class. Don't bring me this trash any more. This is disgusting." During the conversation, the assistant principal allegedly asked Flores, "Are you gay?" When Flores answered, "No, no. I'm not gay," she was asked, "Why are you crying, then?" Flores alleges that she continued to receive notes and pornography in her locker, and continued to bring these materials to Schizzano's attention, but that school officials took no action.

The complaint alleges that during plaintiff FF's time at Martin Murphy Middle School, he was beaten by six other students who said, "Faggot, you don't belong here." He was hospitalized and treated for "severely bruised ribs." The incident was reported to Principal Don Schaefer and Assistant Principal Frank Nucci. Schaefer and Nucci punished only one of the six students involved in the incident, and FF was transferred to another school.

Plaintiffs CL and HA, two female students, allege that other students began making anti-gay comments and sexual gestures at them when they began dating during their senior year at Live Oak High School. On one occasion, a group of boys in the school parking lot shouted anti-gay slurs and threw a plastic cup at the girls. CL and HA reported the incident to defendant Assistant Principal Maxine Bartschi. Bartschi told the girls to report the incident to a campus police officer, and did not follow-up with them or conduct her own investigation of the incident.

JD alleges that she was subjected to name-calling and food throwing. She complained to a campus monitor, with no effect. One campus monitor would not take action to stop the harassment, even when it repeatedly occurred in her presence. On one occasion, that campus monitor initiated a rumor among the students that JD and another female student were having oral sex in the bathroom. JD alleges that she also complained to a teacher that her classmates in physical education class called her "dyke" and "queer," and made comments such as "Oh, I don't want [JD] to touch me. I don't want her to look at me. I don't want to be her [weight training] partner." According to JD, the teacher failed to take action against the harassers, and instead suggested that JD change clothes away from the locker room so that her classmates would not feel uncomfortable.

The plaintiffs brought suit under 42 U.S.C. § 1983, Title IX of the Education Amendments of 1972(20 U.S.C. §§ 1681–88), the California Constitution, and California statutes. This interlocutory appeal relates only to the plaintiffs' § 1983 claim that the defendants denied the plaintiffs' Fourteenth Amendment right to equal protection on the basis of their actual or perceived sexual orientation.

* * *

III. QUALIFIED IMMUNITY

We must decide whether the defendant school administrators enjoy qualified immunity from suit for the actions they are alleged to have taken. Government officials who perform discretionary functions generally are entitled to qualified immunity from liability for civil damages "insofar as their conduct does not violate clearly established statutory or constitutional rights of which a reasonable person would have known."

A. *Constitutional Violation*

The initial inquiry is whether the defendants violated the plaintiffs' constitutional rights. To establish a § 1983 equal protection violation, the plaintiffs must show that the defendants, acting under color of state law, discriminated against them as members of an identifiable class and that the discrimination was intentional. The plaintiffs are members of an identifiable class for equal protection purposes because they allege discrimination on the basis of sexual orientation.

In their complaint, the plaintiffs alleged that the defendants failed to enforce the District's disciplinary, anti-harassment and anti-discrimination policies to prevent physical and emotional harm to the plaintiffs. * * * The record suggests that the defendants treated plaintiffs' complaints of harassment differently from other types of harassment. The record contains evidence that the defendants believed that, under District policies, harassment of any kind would not be tolerated. The plaintiffs presented evidence, however, that they were harassed for years and that the defendants failed to enforce these policies to protect them. When viewed in the context of the other evidence plaintiffs presented and their interactions with the defendants, there is sufficient evidence for a jury to reasonably find that plaintiffs were treated differently.

The record also contains sufficient evidence for a jury to find that the defendants acted with an unconstitutional motive. We agree with the other circuits that have considered similar issues that the plaintiffs must show either that the defendants intentionally discriminated or acted with deliberate indifference. * * *

1. *Defendant Bartschi*

The record contains evidence that Assistant Principal Maxine Bartschi failed to follow-up or conduct an independent investigation after two of the plaintiffs reported to her that they were assaulted by a group of students in the Live Oak High School parking lot. Bartschi's sole response was to tell the students to report the incident to a campus police officer. According to the plaintiffs, Bartschi took no action to locate or discipline the harassing students. The jury may find deliberate indifference despite Bartschi referring the girls to the campus police.

2. Defendant Davis

The record contains sufficient evidence for a jury to infer that Principal Bob Davis was deliberately indifferent in responding to plaintiff Flores' and FF's report of an incident in the quad area where a student handed them a pornographic depiction of heterosexual sex acts. Although there were several students involved in the incident, Davis disciplined only one of them. He also failed to take any further action after Flores and FF complained that the atmosphere in the school was hostile and that the student was bragging that his punishment was light. Davis' failure to take any further steps once he knew his remedial measures were inadequate supports a finding of deliberate indifference.

3. Defendant Gaston

When two students reported harassment by other students and a campus monitor to Assistant Principal Rick Gaston, he acknowledged that the students had a hard time on campus because they were gay. The extent of his response, however, was to refrain from disciplining the two students for being in the hall without a hall pass. Gaston's failure to take any steps to investigate and stop the harassment would support a finding of deliberate indifference.

4. Defendants Schaefer and Nucci

Principal Don Schaefer and Assistant Principal Frank Nucci disciplined only one of the six students who physically assaulted FF at the bus stop while he attended Martin Murphy Middle School. Although Schaefer recommended expulsion for one student, the failure to take any disciplinary action against the other five students is sufficient to infer deliberate indifference.

5. Defendant Schizzano

The record contains evidence that Schizzano took no action to stop the harassment Flores reported, including the defacing of her locker and the placing of notes and pornography inside it. Schizzano promised more than once to change Flores' locker, but failed to follow through, and instead told Flores not to bring her the pornography that she found in her locker again. Schizzano's failure to do anything about the ongoing harassment supports an inference of deliberate indifference.

6. Failure to Train

The plaintiffs have also produced sufficient evidence that the defendants failed to adequately train teachers, students, and campus monitors about the District's policies prohibiting harassment on the basis of sexual orientation. The record contains evidence that training regarding sexual harassment was limited and did not specifically deal with sexual orientation discrimination. The defendants also inadequately communicated District anti-harassment policies to students despite defendants' awareness of hostility toward homosexual students at the schools, and in some cases despite plaintiffs' requests to do so. A jury may conclude, based on this evidence, that there was an obvious need for training and that the discrimination the plaintiffs faced was a highly predictable consequence of the defendants not providing that training.

B. Clearly Established Law

Defendants are entitled to qualified immunity only if the law at the time of the alleged constitutional violation was not clearly established. * * * In order to find that the law was clearly established, however, we need not find a prior case with identical, or even "materially similar," facts.

The Seventh Circuit has expressly held that school administrators are not immune from an equal protection claim involving peer sexual orientation harassment. *Nabozny,* 92 F.3d at 460–61. * * *

The Seventh Circuit in *Nabozny,* however, went out of its way to point out that the unconstitutionality of the defendants' conduct did not turn on the existence of the statute. *Nabozny,* 92 F.3d at 457 n.11. Rather, it held that the decisional law was sufficiently established to put defendants on notice of their obligations to gay and lesbian students, regardless of the existence of the statute. Here, our 1990 decision in *High Tech Gays* established that homosexuals were a definable minority prior to the period of the alleged discrimination in this case. The absence of a state statute, therefore, does not point us to a conclusion that differs from that of the Seventh Circuit.

* * *

The defendants do not advance any reason to justify the alleged differential enforcement of District policies. Here, as in *Nabozny,* "[w]e are unable to garner any rational basis for permitting one student to assault another based on the victim's sexual orientation, and the defendants do not offer us one." *Nabozny,* 92 F.3d at 458.

CONCLUSION

For the foregoing reasons, we affirm the district court's denial of summary judgment on qualified immunity grounds. The record contains sufficient evidence for a jury to conclude that the defendants intentionally discriminated against the plaintiffs in violation of the Equal Protection Clause. At the time of the harassment, the plaintiffs' right to be free from intentional discrimination on the basis of sexual orientation was clearly established.

AFFIRMED.

NOTES

1. The Seventh Circuit's *Nabozny* decision has proven to be a significant turning point. Since 1996, LGBT students who have been mistreated in this manner have won consistent victories in court and have achieved landmark settlements. These settlements often include both money and mandatory professional development. *Flores* was ultimately settled for $1.1 million in January 2004.

2. It is particularly noteworthy that both Nabozny and Flores were victorious under rational basis review, which is the lowest level of Equal Protection Clause scrutiny and is generally very deferential to defendant school districts. In recent years, however, there are signs that courts are beginning to move toward the recognition of a higher level of scrutiny for discrimination on the basis of sexual orientation.

In *Lawrence v. Texas,* for example, Justice O'Connor recognized a heightened level of review for classifications based on "a bare desire to harm a politically unpopular group," 539 U.S. 558, 579–85 (2003) (O'Connor, J., concurring). *See generally* Nan D. Hunter, *Twenty-First Century Equal Protection: Making Law in an Interregnum,* 7 Georgetown Journal of Gender & the Law 141 (2006) (identifying a heightened rational basis that could benefit LGBT plaintiffs in future discrimination cases). Building on such reasoning, the Ninth Circuit determined that not only was the *Lawrence* ruling applicable to a former Air Force major's challenge to "Don't Ask, Don't Tell," but that "*Lawrence* requires something more than traditional rational basis review":

> We hold that when the government attempts to intrude upon the personal and private lives of homosexuals, in a manner that implicates the rights identified in *Lawrence*, the government must advance an important governmental interest, the intrusion must significantly further that interest, and the intrusion must be necessary to further that interest. Witt v. Dept. of Air Force, 527 F.3d 806, 819 (9th Cir. 2008).

Earlier in the same week in May 2008, the California Supreme Court became the first court in the land to recognize strict scrutiny for discrimination against gays and lesbians. Ruling on behalf of the plaintiffs in the marriage equality cases, Chief Justice Ronald George wrote:

> [W]e conclude that sexual orientation should be viewed as a suspect classification for purposes of the California Constitution's equal protection clause and that statutes that treat persons differently because of their sexual orientation should be subjected to strict scrutiny under this constitutional provision. In Re Marriage Cases, 43 Cal.4th 757, 840–841; 76 Cal.Rptr.3d 683, 751 (2008).

The sweeping level of strict scrutiny articulated by the California Court arguably extends to other settings in the public sector–including education– where people similarly situated are treated differently on the basis of their sexual orientation. *See generally id.,* 43 Cal.4th at 832–843, 76 Cal.Rptr.3d at 744–753.

3. Although progress has been evident in this area across a wide variety of fronts, the raw numbers continue to be shocking. LGBT runaways may comprise up to 40 percent of the entire teen homeless population in certain places, and the suicide rate for LGBT students continues to be 3–4 times higher than the numbers for their straight counterparts.

A 2003 National Mental Health Association survey found that not only had over 75 percent of all teenagers witnessed bullying of classmates who are gay or thought to be gay, but that LGBT's as a group were bullied twice as much as any other group that had been identified. In a survey of 12 to 17–year-olds asking "who gets bullied all the time," the groups ranking highest on the list were students with disabilities (6%), overweight students (11%), students "who dress differently" (12%), and students "who are gay or are thought to be gay" (24%). *See* Robert Tomsho, *Schools' Efforts to Protect Gays Face Opposition*, WALL STREET J., Feb. 20, 2003.

A 2002 Report of the National Education Association (NEA) Task Force on Sexual Orientation found that "the majority" of LGBT students "feel unsafe at school," and that this forces them "to concentrate on survival rather than on education, . . . destroy[ing] . . . [their] . . . self-esteem during a critical developmental period." NEA, REPORT OF THE NEA TASK FORCE ON SEXUAL ORIENTATION (Feb. 2002), *available at* http://www.nea.org/nr/02taskforce.html#25 (last visited Sept. 22, 2005).

The National Mental Health Association has classified LGBT students as an at-risk population. "Gay and lesbian teens are at high risk," the NMHA reports, "because 'their distress is a direct result of the hatred and prejudice that surround them,' not because of their inherently gay or lesbian identity orientation." NMHA, BULLYING IN SCHOOLS: HARASSMENT PUTS GAY YOUTH AT RISK, *at* http://www.nmha.org/pbedu/backtoschool/bullyingGayYouth.cfm (last visited Sept. 22, 2005).

4. As discussed *supra*, in Chapter 1, legal victories in an education context are often only the first step in effecting change. Given the fact that peer mistreatment continues to be a problem, what more might be done in this area as a matter of policy?

PROBLEM 21: NABOZNY AND FLORES AS HYPOTHETICALS

Assume that you have been retained to represent Jamie Nabozny and Alana Flores in their respective cases. In addition to the equal protection arguments set forth in their actual briefs, assume that you have decided to also argue that the school districts should be held liable for negligence, and that the respective student perpetrators should be held to have violated relevant laws prohibiting threats. What arguments would you set forth in this context? What result? Discuss.

CHAPTER V

THE RIGHT TO EQUAL EDUCATIONAL OPPORTUNITY

■ ■ ■

The right to equal educational opportunity has appeared in many different guises, typically in the form of judicially recognized rights or state statutory entitlements. At the K–12 level, for example, major cases have pinpointed a right to acquire knowledge, a right to a free and suitable "publicly supported education," a right of "advancement on the basis of individual merit," and a right to "direct the education of children by selecting reputable teachers and places." State and federal entitlements provide public school students and their parents with additional, specific protection against the denial of opportunity, such as the right to procedural safeguards when a student is suspended or expelled, the right to a free and appropriate public education for students with disabilities, and the right to a safe school environment.

Typical statutory guidelines also give citizens the right to an education that "meets the needs" of all pupils, within the framework of specific subject matter that the state deems essential. Many provisions spell out clear educational goals, specifying particular skills that parents have a right to expect their children to attain in a public school system.

At the higher education level, the parameters of the right may sometimes be more difficult to discern, since access to higher education is not always explicitly guaranteed. However, many statutory mandates and protections do exist, and no one doubts that equal educational opportunity principles continue to be applicable at public colleges and universities.

Contextually, it is important to note that the right to equal educational opportunity has expanded beyond issues of race and ethnicity over time. The right is now generally recognized as a broad protection for students against the denial of equal access and equal opportunity on the basis of such group delineations as gender, disability, language status, sexual orientation, gender identity, and religion. As referenced in Chapter 3, all students in public education settings are generally expected to be treated with equal respect and equal dignity, consistent with the mandate of the Fourteenth Amendment.

This chapter begins with a detailed examination of paradigmatic issues relating to admissions, placement, and race. It continues with a related inquiry into the persistence of the standardized testing controversy, and follows with an exploration of equal opportunity issues in the area of school sports. The chapter then turns to an examination of ongoing disputes relating to gender equity in education. It concludes with a brief overview of litigation relating to the rights of undocumented students.

* * *

Consider the following perspectives on the right to equal educational opportunity. What additional comments or quotes would you add to this collection today?

● **1954**

Today, education is perhaps the most important function of state and local governments. Compulsory school attendance laws and the great expenditures for education both demonstrate our recognition of the importance of education to our democratic society. * * * In these days, it is doubtful that any child may reasonably be expected to succeed in life if he is denied the opportunity of an education. Such an opportunity, where the state has undertaken to provide it, is a right which must be made available to all on equal terms.

—Chief Justice Earl Warren
for a Unanimous Supreme Court
Brown v. Board of Education
347 U.S. 483, 493, 74 S.Ct. 686 (1954)

● **1968**

* * *

[T]he present awakening of the American conscience in the matter of equal rights and equal opportunity ... is a hopeful phenomenon in our national life. Never before as a nation have we committed ourselves so directly to the hard, practical tasks of defining equality in a way that embraces millions of citizens who have heretofore been cheated in access to education, jobs, housing, medical care, and the other necessities of American life.

—Harold Howe II
U.S. Commissioner of Education

Preface to Special Issue of Harvard Educational Review

Vol. 38, Pgs. 3–4

● **1973**

It is typically American that the most significant modern attempt to achieve racial equality, *Brown v. Board of Education,* involved the schools.

Americans insist that education offered on some equitable basis will permit the economically and culturally deprived to improve their lot and to claim their fair share of society's status and income rewards. * * *

Accompanying the exalted status of education in this society is a more or less general consensus that equal educational opportunity is of paramount importance. As an abstract principle, equal educational opportunity occupies a position in the pantheon of widely share values equal to monopoly regulation, monogamy, and peace.

—Mark G. Yudof
University of Texas

Equal Educational Opportunity and the Courts
51 TEX. L. REV. 411–12 (1973)

● **1984**

Assumptions about biological difference and destiny provided the prime justification for creating a separate, inferior legal status for women. The law denied women equal opportunity for wage work and participation in public life. * * * Women were required, by law and custom, to care for men and children. * * *

Legal structures that support the dominance of men and subservience of women are fundamentally inconsistent with constitutional ideals of individual worth and equality of opportunity.

—Sylvia Law
NYU Law School
Rethinking Sex and the Constitution
132 U. Pa. L. Rev. 955

For women, then, poetry is not a luxury. It is a vital necessity of our existence. It forms the quality of the light within which we predicate our hopes and dreams toward survival and change, first made into language, then into idea, then into more tangible action. Poetry is the way we help give name to the nameless so it can be thought. The farthest horizons of our hopes and fears are cobbled by our poems, carved from the rock experiences of our daily lives.

—Audre Lorde
Poetry Is Not a Luxury
Sister Outsider: Essays & Speeches

● **1994**

It is not enough to win court rulings, as in *Brown,* or stirring legislative victories, like the Civil Rights Act of 1964. * * * Such victories, while sweet, are not ends in themselves. They are opportunities, tools to be used in the next phase of the struggle for liberty and equal opportunity.

—Bob Herbert
After Brown, What?, N.Y. TIMES, May 1994

● **2004**

Over the past fifty years we have learned and relearned that *Brown v. Board of Education* was not a victory over institutional and structural biases and racism, but one battle in a long and continuing struggle. *Brown* remains a seminal civil rights and constitutional moment. And yet, as the case recedes into the past, we can picture the promise of educational opportunities "made available to all on equal terms" on one side of a scale of justice, balancing—but not outweighing—lingering sentiments and practices of "separate and equal."

—Jeannie Oakes
UCLA Graduate School of
Education & Information Studies
Schools That Shock the Conscience
15 Berkeley La Raza L.J. 25 (2004)

Looking beyond our borders * * * we are not in the lead. The Chief Justice of the Supreme Court of Canada is a woman, as are two of that Court's eight other Justices. The Chief Justice of New Zealand is a woman. Five of the sixteen judges on Germany's Federal Constitutional Court are women, and a woman served as president of that court from 1994 until 2002. Currently, five women are members of the European Court of Justice, three as judges and two as advocates general. Women account for seven out of eighteen Judges recently placed on the International Criminal Court; two of them serve as that court's vice-presidents.

True, as Jeanne Coyne of Minnesota's Supreme Court famously said: At the end of the day, 'a wise old man and a wise old woman will reach the same decision.' But it is also true that women, like persons of different racial groups and ethnic origins, contribute what a fine jurist, the late Fifth Circuit Judge Alvin Rubin, described as 'a distinctive medley of views influenced by differences in biology, cultural impact, and life experience.' Our system of justice is surely richer for the diversity of background and experience of its judges. It was poorer, in relation to the society law exists to serve, when nearly all of its participants were cut from the same mold.

—Justice Ruth Bader Ginsburg
Remarks on Women's Progress at the Bar and on the Bench
89 Cornell L. Rev. 801

A. ADMISSIONS, PLACEMENT, AND RACE

1. THE EVOLUTION OF BASIC FOURTEENTH AMENDMENT DOCTRINE

BROWN v. BOARD OF EDUC.

347 U.S. 483, 74 S.Ct. 686 (1954)

MR. CHIEF JUSTICE WARREN delivered the opinion of the Court.

These cases come to us from the States of Kansas, South Carolina, Virginia, and Delaware. They are premised on different facts and different local conditions, but a common legal question justifies their consideration together in this consolidated opinion.

In each of the cases, minors of the Negro race, through their legal representatives, seek the aid of the courts in obtaining admission to the public schools of their community on a nonsegregated basis. In each instance, they have been denied admission to schools attended by white children under laws requiring or permitting segregation according to race. This segregation was alleged to deprive the plaintiffs of the equal protection of the laws under the Fourteenth Amendment. In each of the cases other than the Delaware case, a three-judge federal district court denied relief to the plaintiffs on the so-called "separate but equal" doctrine announced by this Court in *Plessy v. Ferguson*. Under that doctrine, equality of treatment is accorded when the races are provided substantially equal facilities, even though these facilities be separate. In the Delaware case, the Supreme Court of Delaware adhered to that doctrine, but ordered that the plaintiffs be admitted to the white schools because of their superiority to the Negro schools.

The plaintiffs contend that segregated public schools are not "equal" and cannot be made "equal," and that hence they are deprived of the equal protection of the laws. Because of the obvious importance of the question presented, the Court took jurisdiction. * * *

In the first cases in this Court construing the Fourteenth Amendment, decided shortly after its adoption, the Court interpreted it as proscribing all state-imposed discriminations against the Negro race. The doctrine of "separate but equal" did not make its appearance in this court until 1896 in the case of *Plessy v. Ferguson*, involving not education but transportation. American courts have since labored with the doctrine for over half a century. In this Court, there have been six cases involving the "separate but equal" doctrine in the field of public education. In *Cumming v. Board of Education of Richmond County* and *Gong Lum v. Rice*, the validity of the doctrine itself was not challenged. In more recent cases, all on the graduate school level, inequality was found in that specific benefits enjoyed by white students were denied to Negro students of the same educational qualifications. In none of these cases was it necessary to re-examine the doctrine to grant relief to the Negro plaintiff. And in

Sweatt v. Painter, the Court expressly reserved decision on the question whether *Plessy v. Ferguson* should be held inapplicable to public education.

In the instant cases, that question is directly presented. Here, unlike *Sweatt v. Painter*, there are findings below that the Negro and white schools involved have been equalized, or are being equalized, with respect to buildings, curricula, qualifications and salaries of teachers, and other "tangible" factors. Our decision, therefore, cannot turn on merely a comparison of these tangible factors in the Negro and white schools involved in each of the cases. We must look instead to the effect of segregation itself on public education.

In approaching this problem, we cannot turn the clock back to 1868 when the Amendment was adopted, or even to 1896 when *Plessy v. Ferguson* was written. We must consider public education in the light of its full development and its present place in American life throughout the Nation. Only in this way can it be determined if segregation in public schools deprives these plaintiffs of the equal protection of the laws.

Today, education is perhaps the most important function of state and local governments. Compulsory school attendance laws and the great expenditures for education both demonstrate our recognition of the importance of education to our democratic society. It is required in the performance of our most basic public responsibilities, even service in the armed forces. It is the very foundation of good citizenship. Today it is a principal instrument in awakening the child to cultural values, in preparing him for later professional training, and in helping him to adjust normally to his environment. In these days, it is doubtful that any child may reasonably be expected to succeed in life if he is denied the opportunity of an education. Such an opportunity, where the state has undertaken to provide it, is a right which must be made available to all on equal terms.

We come then to the question presented: Does segregation of children in public schools solely on the basis of race, even though the physical facilities and other "tangible" factors may be equal, deprive the children of the minority group of equal educational opportunities? We believe that it does.

In *Sweatt v. Painter*, in finding that a segregated law school for Negroes could not provide them equal educational opportunities, this Court relied in large part on "those qualities which are incapable of objective measurement but which make for greatness in a law school." In *McLaurin v. Oklahoma State Regents*, the Court, in requiring that a Negro admitted to a white graduate school be treated like all other students, again resorted to intangible considerations: " * * * his ability to study, to engage in discussions and exchange views with other students, and, in general, to learn his profession." Such considerations apply with added force to children in grade and high schools. To separate them from others of similar age and qualifications solely because of their race generates a feeling of inferiority as to their status in the community that may affect their hearts and minds in a way unlikely ever to be undone. The effect of this separation on their educational opportunities was well stated by a finding in the Kansas case by a court which nevertheless felt compelled to rule against the Negro plaintiffs:

> Segregation of white and colored children in public schools has a detrimental effect upon the colored children. The impact is greater when it has the sanction of the law; for the policy of separating the races is usually interpreted as denoting the inferiority of the negro group. A sense of inferiority affects the motivation of a child to learn. Segregation with the sanction of law, therefore, has a tendency to [retard] the educational and mental development of Negro children and to deprive them of some of the benefits they would receive in a racial[ly] integrated school system.

Whatever may have been the extent of psychological knowledge at the time of *Plessy v. Ferguson*, this finding is amply supported by modern authority.[11] Any language in *Plessy v. Ferguson* contrary to this finding is rejected.

We conclude that in the field of public education the doctrine of "separate but equal" has no place. Separate educational facilities are inherently unequal. Therefore, we hold that the plaintiffs and others similarly situated for whom the actions have been brought are, by reason of the segregation complained of, deprived of the equal protection of the laws guaranteed by the Fourteenth Amendment. * * *

SAN ANTONIO INDEP. SCH. DIST. v. RODRIGUEZ

411 U.S. 1, 93 S.Ct. 1278 (1973)

MR. JUSTICE POWELL delivered the opinion of the Court.

This suit attacking the Texas system of financing public education was initiated by Mexican–American parents whose children attend the elementary and secondary schools in the Edgewood Independent School District, an urban school district in San Antonio, Texas. They brought a class action on behalf of schoolchildren throughout the State who are members of minority groups or who are poor and reside in school districts having a low property tax base. * * *

I

The first Texas State Constitution, promulgated upon Texas' entry into the Union in 1845, provided for the establishment of a system of free

---

11. K. B. Clark, *Effect of Prejudice and Discrimination on Personality Development* (Midcentury White House Conference on Children and Youth, 1950); [HELEN] WITMER & [RUTH] KOTINSKY, PERSONALITY IN THE MAKING c. 6 (1952); Deutscher and Chein, *The Psychological Effects of Enforced Segregation: A Survey of Social Science Opinion*, 26 J. PSYCHOL. 259 (1948); Chein, *What are the Psychological Effects of Segregation Under Conditions of Equal Facilities?*, 3 INT. J. OPINION & ATTITUDE RES. 229 (1949); Brameld, EDUCATIONAL COSTS, IN DISCRIMINATION AND NATIONAL WELFARE 44–48 (MacIver, ed., 1949); [E. FRANKLIN] FRAZIER, THE NEGRO IN THE UNITED STATES 674–81 (1949). *See generally* [GUNNAR] MYRDAL, AN AMERICAN DILEMMA (1944).

schools. Early in its history, Texas adopted a dual approach to the financing of its schools, relying on mutual participation by the local school districts and the State. As early as 1883, the state constitution was amended to provide for the creation of local school districts empowered to levy ad valorem taxes with the consent of local taxpayers for the "erection ... of school buildings" and for the "further maintenance of public free schools." Such local funds as were raised were supplemented by funds distributed to each district from the State's Permanent and Available School Funds. * * *

Until recent times, Texas was a predominantly rural State and its population and property wealth were spread relatively evenly across the State. Sizable differences in the value of assessable property between local school districts became increasingly evident as the State became more industrialized and as rural-to-urban population shifts became more pronounced. The location of commercial and industrial property began to play a significant role in determining the amount of tax resources available to each school district. These growing disparities in population and taxable property between districts were responsible in part for increasingly notable differences in levels of local expenditure for education.

In due time it became apparent to those concerned with financing public education that contributions from the Available School Fund were not sufficient to ameliorate these disparities. * * *

The school district in which appellees reside, the Edgewood Independent School District, has been compared throughout this litigation with the Alamo Heights Independent School District. This comparison between the least and most affluent districts in the San Antonio area serves to illustrate the manner in which the dual system of finance operates and to indicate the extent to which substantial disparities exist despite the State's impressive progress in recent years. Edgewood is one of seven public school districts in the metropolitan area. Approximately 22,000 students are enrolled in its 25 elementary and secondary schools. The district is situated in the core-city sector of San Antonio in a residential neighborhood that has little commercial or industrial property. The residents are predominantly of Mexican–American descent: approximately 90% of the student population is Mexican–American and over 6% is Negro. The average assessed property value per pupil is $5,960—the lowest in the metropolitan area—and the median family income ($4,686) is also the lowest. At an equalized tax rate of $1.05 per $100 of assessed property—the highest in the metropolitan area—the district contributed $26 to the education of each child for the 1967–1968 school year above its Local Fund Assignment for the Minimum Foundation Program. The Foundation Program contributed $222 per pupil for a state-local total of $248. Federal funds added another $108 for a total of $356 per pupil.

Alamo Heights is the most affluent school district in San Antonio. Its six schools, housing approximately 5,000 students, are situated in a residential community quite unlike the Edgewood District. The school population is predominantly "Anglo," having only 18% Mexican–Americans and less than 1% Negroes. The assessed property value per pupil exceeds $49,000, and the median family income is $8,001. In 1967–1968 the local tax rate of $.85 per $100 of valuation yielded $333 per pupil over and above its contribution to the Foundation Program. Coupled with the $225 provided from that Program, the district was able to supply $558 per student. Supplemented by a $36 per-pupil grant from federal sources, Alamo Heights spent $594 per pupil.

* * *

* * * [S]ubstantial interdistrict disparities in school expenditures found by the District Court to prevail in San Antonio and in varying degrees throughout the State still exist. And it was these disparities, largely attributable to differences in the amounts of money collected through local property taxation, that led the District Court to conclude that Texas' dual system of public school financing violated the Equal Protection Clause. The District Court held that the Texas system discriminates on the basis of wealth in the manner in which education is provided for its people. Finding that wealth is a "suspect" classification and that education is a "fundamental" interest, the District Court held that the Texas system could be sustained only if the State could show that it was premised upon some compelling state interest. On this issue the court concluded that "[n]ot only are defendants unable to demonstrate compelling state interests ... they fail even to establish a reasonable basis for these classifications."

* * *

We must decide, first, whether the Texas system of financing public education operates to the disadvantage of some suspect class or impinges upon a fundamental right explicitly or implicitly protected by the Constitution, thereby requiring strict judicial scrutiny. If so, the judgment of the District Court should be affirmed. If not, the Texas scheme must still be examined to determine whether it rationally furthers some legitimate, articulated state purpose and therefore does not constitute an invidious discrimination in violation of the Equal Protection Clause of the Fourteenth Amendment.

II

The District Court's opinion does not reflect the novelty and complexity of the constitutional questions posed by appellees' challenge to Texas' system of school financing. In concluding that strict judicial scrutiny was required, that court relied on decisions dealing with the rights of indigents to equal treatment in the criminal trial and appellate processes, and on cases disapproving wealth restrictions on the right to vote. Those cases, the District Court concluded, established wealth as a suspect classification. Finding that the local property tax system discriminated on the basis of wealth, it regarded those precedents as controlling. It then reasoned, based on decisions of this Court affirming the undeniable importance of education, that there is a fundamental right to education and that, absent some compelling state justification, the Texas system could not stand.

We are unable to agree that this case, which in significant aspects is *sui generis*, may be so neatly fitted into the conventional mosaic of constitutional analysis under the Equal Protection Clause. Indeed, for the several reasons that follow, we find neither the suspect-classification not the fundamental-interest analysis persuasive.

A

The wealth discrimination discovered by the District Court in this case, and by several other courts that have recently struck down school-financing laws in other States, is quite unlike any of the forms of wealth discrimination heretofore reviewed by this Court. * * *

The case comes to us with no definitive description of the classifying facts or delineation of the disfavored class. Examination of the District Court's opinion and of appellees' complaint, briefs, and contentions at oral argument suggests, however, at least three ways in which the discrimination claimed here might be described. The Texas system of school financing might be regarded as discriminating (1) against "poor" persons whose incomes fall below some identifiable level of poverty or who might be characterized as functionally "indigent," or (2) against those who are relatively poorer than others, or (3) against all those who, irrespective of their personal incomes, happen to reside in relatively poorer school districts. Our task must be to ascertain whether, in fact, the Texas system has been shown to discriminate on any of these possible bases and, if so, whether the resulting classification may be regarded as suspect.

* * *

[The Court then found that "[In] the absence of any evidence that the financing system discriminates against any definable category of 'poor' people or that it results in the absolute deprivation of education—the disadvantaged class is not susceptible of identification in traditional terms." It discerned "no factual basis exists upon which to found a claim of comparative wealth discrimination."]

* * *

This brings us, then, to the third way in which the classification scheme might be defined—*district* wealth discrimination. * * *

However described, it is clear that appellees' suit asks this Court to extend its most exacting scrutiny to review a system that allegedly discriminates against a large, diverse, and amorphous class, unified only by the common factor of residence in districts that happen to have less taxable wealth than other districts. The system of alleged discrimination and the class it defines have none of the traditional indicia of suspectness: the class is not saddled with such disabilities, or subjected to such a history of purposeful unequal treatment, or relegated to such a position of political powerlessness as to command extraordinary protection from the majoritarian political process.

We thus conclude that the Texas system does not operate to the peculiar disadvantage of any suspect class. But in recognition of the fact that this Court has never heretofore held that wealth discrimination alone provides an adequate basis for invoking strict scrutiny, appellees have not relied solely on this contention. They also assert that the State's system impermissibly interferes with the exercise of a "fundamental" right and that accordingly the prior decisions of this Court require the application of the strict standard of judicial review. It is this question—whether education is a fundamental right, in the sense that it is among the rights and liberties protected by the Constitution—which has so consumed the attention of courts and commentators in recent years.

B

In *Brown v. Board of Education*, 347 U.S. 483, 74 S. Ct. 686 (1954), a unanimous Court recognized that "education is perhaps the most important function of state and local governments." *Id.* at 493, 74 S. Ct. at 691. What was said there in the context of racial discrimination has lost none of its vitality with the passage of time * * * .

This theme, expressing an abiding respect for the vital role of education in a free society, may be found in numerous opinions of Justices of this Court writing both before and after *Brown* was decided.

Nothing this Court holds today in any way detracts from our historic dedication to public education. We are in complete agreement with the conclusion of the three-judge panel below that "the grave significance of education both to the individual and to our society" cannot be doubted. But the importance of a service performed by the State does not determine whether it must be regarded as fundamental for purposes of examination under the Equal Protection Clause. * * *

The lesson of these cases in addressing the question now before the Court is plain. It is not the province of this Court to create substantive constitutional rights in the name of guaranteeing equal protection of the laws. Thus, the key to discovering whether education is "fundamental" is not to be found in comparisons of the relative societal significance of education as opposed to subsistence or housing. Nor is it to be found by weighing whether education is as important as the right to travel. Rather, the answer lies in assessing whether there is a right to education explicitly or implicitly guaranteed by the Constitution.

Education, of course, is not among the rights afforded explicit protection under our Federal Constitution. Nor do we find any basis for saying it is implicitly so protected. As we have said, the undisputed importance of education will not alone cause this Court to depart from the usual standard for reviewing a State's social and economic legislation. It is appellees' contention, however, that education is distinguishable from other services and benefits provided by the State because it bears a peculiarly close relationship to other rights and liberties accorded protection under the Constitution. Specifically, they insist that education is itself a fundamental personal right because it is essential to the effective exercise of First Amendment freedoms and to intelligent utilization of the right to vote. In asserting a nexus between speech and education, appellees urge that the right to speak is meaningless unless the speaker is capable of articulating his thoughts intelligently and persuasively. The "marketplace of ideas" is an empty forum for those lacking basic communicative tools. Likewise, they argue that the corollary right to receive information becomes little more than a hollow privilege when the recipient has not been taught to read, assimilate, and utilize available knowledge.

A similar line of reasoning is pursued with respect to the right to vote. Exercise of the franchise, it is contended, cannot be divorced from the educational foundation of the voter. The electoral process, if reality is to conform to the democratic ideal, depends on an informed electorate: a voter cannot cast his ballot intelligently unless his reading skills and thought processes have been adequately developed.

We need not dispute any of these propositions. The Court has long afforded zealous protection against unjustifiable governmental interference with the individual's rights to speak and to vote. Yet we have never presumed to possess either the ability or the authority to guarantee to the citizenry the most *effective* speech or the most *informed* electoral choice. That these may be desirable goals of a system of freedom of expression and of a representative form of government is not to be doubted. These are indeed goals to be pursued by a people whose thoughts and beliefs are freed from governmental interference. But they are not values to be implemented by judicial instruction into otherwise legitimate state activities.

Even if it were conceded that some identifiable quantum of education is a constitutionally protected prerequisite to the meaningful exercise of either right, we have no indication that the present levels of educational expenditures in Texas provide an education that falls short. Whatever merit appellees' argument might have if a State's financing system occasioned an absolute denial of educational opportunities to any of its children, that argument provides no basis for finding an interference with fundamental rights where only relative differences in spending levels are involved and where—as is true in the present case—no charge fairly could be made that the system fails to provide each child with an opportunity to acquire the basic minimal skills necessary for the enjoyment of the rights of speech and of full participation in the political process.

* * *

We have carefully considered each of the arguments supportive of the District Court's finding that education is a fundamental right or liberty and have found those arguments unpersuasive. In one further respect we find this a particularly inappropriate case in which to subject state action to strict judicial scrutiny. The present case, in another basic sense, is significantly different from any of the cases in which the Court has applied strict scrutiny to state or federal legislation touching upon constitutionally protected rights. Each of our prior cases involved legislation which "deprived," "infringed," or "interfered" with the free exercise of some such fundamental personal right or liberty. A critical distinction between those cases and the one now before us lies in what Texas is endeavoring to do with respect to education. * * *

* * * Every step leading to the establishment of the system Texas utilizes today—including the decisions permitting localities to tax and expend locally, and creating and continuously expanding the state aid—was implemented in an effort to extend public education and to improve its quality. Of course, every reform that benefits some more than others may be criticized for what it fails to accomplish. But we think it plain that, in substance, the thrust of the Texas system is affirmative and reformatory and, therefore, should be scrutinized under judicial principles sensitive to the nature of the State's efforts and to the rights reserved to the States under the Constitution.

C

* * *

[The Court then found that the finance system survived rational basis analysis.]

* * *

IV

* * *

* * * The consideration and initiation of fundamental reforms with respect to state taxation and education are matters reserved for the legislative processes of the various States, and we do no violence to the values of federalism and separation of powers by staying our hand. We hardly need add that this Court's action today is not to be viewed as placing its judicial imprimatur on the status quo. The need is apparent for reform in tax systems which may well have relied too long and too heavily on the local property tax. And certainly innovative thinking as to public education, its methods, and its funding is necessary to assure both a higher level of quality and greater uniformity of opportunity. These matters merit the continued attention of the scholars who already have contributed much by their challenges. But the ultimate solutions must come from the lawmakers and from the democratic pressures of those who elect them.

Reversed.

NOTES

1. Justice Marshall, writing on behalf of four justices, issued a highly influential 67-page dissent in the *Rodriguez* case, significantly longer than the majority opinion itself, and containing the most elaborate statement of Marshall's position regarding equal protection jurisprudence. Indeed, both Marshall's contention regarding the parameters of equal protection jurisprudence at the time and his articulation of the reasons behind the push to recognize education as a fundamental right arguably anticipate future directions in law and public policy. Certainly, as a matter of law, commentators have argued that the Court, in subsequent opinions, actually adopted Marshall's "sliding scale" approach, with "variations in the degree of care with which the Court will scrutinize particular classifications depending * * * on the constitutional and societal importance of the interest adversely affected and the recognized invidiousness of the basis upon which the particular classification is drawn." *Rodriguez*, 411 U.S. at 98–99 (Marshall, J., dissenting).

2. How different, if at all, might things have been in public education today had Justice Marshall been able to garner a fifth vote recognizing education as a fundamental right and wealth as a suspect classification under the Fourteenth Amendment in 1973?

3. Three years after *Rodriguez,* the Court in *Washington v. Davis* cast doubt on the continuing viability of the Fourteenth Amendment as a vehicle for the protection of individual rights in the public school setting.

Davis addressed the elements of discrimination under the Equal Protection Clause. Until 1976, it was arguably unclear whether plaintiffs in certain cases were able to trigger strict scrutiny on the basis of racial or ethnic discrimination by demonstrating a discriminatory impact alone. The *Davis* Court held that plaintiffs challenging facially neutral state action in this context must prove discriminatory purpose and cannot prevail simply by showing discriminatory effects.

The *Davis* doctrine of discriminatory purpose was particularly troubling for activists in this area. With many of the inequities in public school programs at the time occurring as a result of facially neutral practices that could not be linked to any overt discriminatory intent, commentators generally concluded that *Davis* significantly limited the ability of education plaintiffs to prevail under the traditional Fourteenth Amendment Equal Protection framework.

However, it can be argued that at least on some level concerns in many quarters regarding the impact of the *Rodriguez* and *Davis* rulings are no longer relevant, because legislatures and courts have provided—and continue to provide—so many other vehicles for addressing education-related "deprivations" that are neither purposeful nor less-than-absolute. In fact, it can be argued that in the "No Child Left Behind" Act, Congress has in fact recognized education to be a fundamental right at the federal level, without specifically using the same terminology. *See* 20 U.S.C. § 6301, which provides in pertinent part that "The purpose of [the Act] is to ensure that all children have a fair, equal, and significant opportunity to obtain a high-quality education." *See generally infra,* Chapter 6 of this casebook.

2. AFFIRMATIVE ACTION IN HIGHER EDUCATION ADMISSIONS

During the 1990s, the push to end racial preferences in the public sector—and particularly at the higher education level—resulted in significant changes. Not only had Fourteenth Amendment jurisprudence at the Supreme Court level evolved to a point where many commentators and jurists could reasonably conclude that *no* use of race as a factor in admissions decisions would be constitutional, but a growing number of states actually banned race-based affirmative action at their public colleges and universities. By 2003, when *Grutter* and *Gratz*—the University of Michigan affirmative action cases—came before the Court, the list had grown to include California (under Proposition 209), Texas (under the Fifth Circuit's *Hopwood* decision), Louisiana (under *Hopwood*), Mississippi (under *Hopwood*), Georgia (under the Eleventh Circuit's *Johnson* decision), Florida (under Governor Jeb Bush's Executive Order), and Washington (under I–200). *See generally* Patricia Gurin, Jeffrey S. Lehman, Earl Lewis, Eric L. Dey, Sylvia Hurtado, & Gerald Gurin, *Defending Diversity: Affirmative Action at the University of Michigan,* University of Michigan Press (2004).

The *Grutter* case, decided in favor of the law school by a vote of 5–4, was therefore seen as a major turning point in the battle over affirmative action. Had the plaintiffs succeeded in garnering one more vote in *Grutter,* and had the justices then explicitly banned the use of racial preferences in affirmative action programs, as they were being asked to do, the above list would have immediately grown to include all 50 states. Instead, it was pared down to only three, California, Washington, and Florida.

The controversy regarding affirmative action has not subsided in the aftermath of *Grutter,* and efforts to prohibit racial preferences via the ballot initiative process have continued to proliferate.[a] However, the parameters of the debate regarding public sector admissions programs have arguably changed. *Grutter* made it clear that under the Fourteenth Amendment, while race could be used as a factor in admissions decisions, it could not be the only factor. Indeed, this principle had been a central component of Justice Powell's opinion in *Regents of UC v. Bakke,* 25 years earlier, although no other justice had joined in. Now, a Supreme Court

---

a Three years after the University of Michigan Law School prevailed in the *Grutter* case, the Michigan voters approved Proposal 2, The Michigan Civil Rights Initiative, by a 58%–42% margin. Modeled after California Proposition 209, the new law prohibited race-based affirmative action in the public sector throughout the state.

The American Civil Rights Institute (ACRI), led by former UC Regent Ward Connerly, continues to work toward passing additional "Civil Rights Initiatives" of this type in other states. Thus far, Connerly has spearheaded victorious campaigns in California (1996), Washington (1998), Michigan (2006), and Nebraska (2008). However, Amendment 46, on the ballot in Colorado in November 2008, was defeated by that state's voters, 51% to 49%.

majority had confirmed that only multi-faceted diversity, determined pursuant to a policy that met a rigorous *narrow tailoring* test, would be constitutional. *See, e.g.,* Stephan Thernstrom, *Beyond the Color Line: New Perspectives on Race and Ethnicity,* Hoover Institution Press (2002); *see generally* Michael A. Olivas, *Law School Admissions after Grutter: Student Bodies, Pipeline Theory, and the River,* 55 Journal of Legal Education 16 (2005).

Thus the affirmative action debate in the public sector today is clearly and unequivocally about whether race can or should be employed as one of many factors—including but not limited to preferential status on the basis of bilingualism, athletic ability, unique life experiences, having overcome unique challenges generally, age, socioeconomic status, veteran status, and legacy. Colleges and universities generally can and often do grant preferential status based on most, if not all, of these other factors. The question now is whether and to what extent race can also be included in such a list. It is a very different debate than it would be if the only determining factor was race alone.

PROBLEM 22: MEGLINO V. REGENTS OF ATLANTIS STATE TEACHERS COLLEGE

The following hypothetical takes place in the fictional State of Atlantis.

Concerned about the shortage of qualified teachers in urban settings, the Atlantis state legislature approved funds for the construction of a new, unique and prestigious state teachers college devoted to training students for leadership roles in urban education. Five years later the high-tech campus—located in the heart of Capital City (a major urban center)—was finally completed. Faculty and staff were hired, an admissions committee was formed, and applications for the fall were accepted.

The following is a quote from the application bulletin:

Atlantis State Teachers College (ASTC) is an innovative institution designed to prepare students for leadership roles in urban education. The college offers an undergraduate liberal arts program, a two-year master's in urban schooling (which includes training for a K–12 teacher credential), and a doctorate in educational leadership. The college is committed to the eventual training of 1,000 urban school teachers per year, and to the dissemination of research relating to the needs of urban youth.

As per our legislative mandate, the college is designed to serve a diverse urban community, and to that end it seeks applicants from diverse backgrounds. Priority will be given to applicants who (1) have attended urban schools, (2) are fluent in Spanish, Cantonese, Mandarin, or Korean, and/or (3) can contribute to the diversity of the cohort.

To take advantage of the latest technology and to assure fairness in the application process, all applicants will initially be processed by computer. The computer will rank students based on both the traditional indicators (grades and test scores) and the priority categories.

With regard to the diversity category, the computer will be programmed to rank the applicant's potential contribution to the diversity of the cohort by employing the following objective factors: (a) socioeconomic status (SES) of the student's parents, (b) amount of work with economically disadvantaged young people (e.g. tutoring, serving as a teacher's aide, other forms of public service), and (c) race or ethnicity.

Members of the admissions committee will make final decisions regarding applicants based on computer rankings and on other relevant factors such as exceptional personal talents, unique work or service experience, leadership potential, maturity, demonstrated compassion, and a history of overcoming disadvantage.

After the first year, the computer will generate a diversity index for the entire student population at ASTC, based on the three factors identified above. Applicants will then be ranked in the diversity category based on how well they contribute to the diversity of the college's population. Thus, for example, if the college in a given year has a small number of students from a low SES background, then low SES applicants will have greater priority during that year.

The college proved very popular, and students from all over the country sought admission.

One of these applicants—Maria Meglino—sought to be admitted to the teacher education/master's program but was denied admission. Maria was an Italian American from a middle class family who had worked extensively with young people in an urban setting and was strongly committed to helping the community. However, even though she had a 3.85 undergraduate GPA and scored 1450 on the GRE, she only spoke English, and did not herself attend an urban school. Faculty gave her additional points for demonstrated compassion, but this was not enough to compensate for her lack of priority points in other areas. Bitterly disappointed, she consulted the local office of the Institute for Justice for the purpose of filing a lawsuit in federal court.

A. What arguments would Maria be expected to set forth under the Equal Protection Clause of the Fourteenth Amendment? What result in light of the Michigan decisions? Discuss.

B. If you were asked to recommend any changes in this admissions policy, would you do so? Why? If you would, what would you recommend?

GRUTTER v. BOLLINGER

539 U.S. 306, 123 S.Ct. 2325 (2003)

Justice O'Connor delivered the opinion of the Court.

This case requires us to decide whether the use of race as a factor in student admissions by the University of Michigan Law School (Law School) is unlawful.

I

A

The Law School ranks among the Nation's top law schools. It receives more than 3,500 applications each year for a class of around 350 students.

Seeking to "admit a group of students who individually and collectively are among the most capable," the Law School looks for individuals with "substantial promise for success in law school" and "a strong likelihood of succeeding in the practice of law and contributing in diverse ways to the well-being of others." More broadly, the Law School seeks "a mix of students with varying backgrounds and experiences who will respect and learn from each other." * * *

The hallmark of [the law school's admissions policy] policy is its focus on academic ability coupled with a flexible assessment of applicants' talents, experiences, and potential "to contribute to the learning of those around them." The policy requires admissions officials to evaluate each applicant based on all the information available in the file, including a personal statement, letters of recommendation, and an essay describing the ways in which the applicant will contribute to the life and diversity of the Law School. In reviewing an applicant's file, admissions officials must consider the applicant's undergraduate grade point average (GPA) and Law School Admissions Test (LSAT) score because they are important (if imperfect) predictors of academic success in law school. The policy stresses that "no applicant should be admitted unless we expect that applicant to do well enough to graduate with no serious academic problems."

The policy makes clear, however, that even the highest possible score does not guarantee admission to the Law School. Nor does a low score automatically disqualify an applicant. Rather, the policy requires admissions officials to look beyond grades and test scores to other criteria that are important to the Law School's educational objectives. So-called " 'soft' variables' such as 'the enthusiasm of recommenders, the quality of the undergraduate institution, the quality of the applicant's essay, and the areas and difficulty of undergraduate course selection" are all brought to bear in assessing an "applicant's likely contributions to the intellectual and social life of the institution."

The policy aspires to "achieve that diversity which has the potential to enrich everyone's education and thus make a law school class stronger than the sum of its parts." The policy does not restrict the types of diversity contributions eligible for "substantial weight" in the admissions process, but instead recognizes "many possible bases for diversity admissions." The policy does, however, reaffirm the Law School's longstanding commitment to "one particular type of diversity," that is, "racial and ethnic diversity with special reference to the inclusion of students from groups which have been historically discriminated against, like African–Americans, Hispanics and Native Americans, who without this commitment might not be represented in our student body in meaningful numbers." By enrolling a " 'critical mass' of [underrepresented] minority students," the Law School seeks to "ensur[e] their ability to make unique contributions to the character of the Law School."

The policy does not define diversity "solely in terms of racial and ethnic status." Nor is the policy "insensitive to the competition among all students for admission to the [L]aw [S]chool." Rather, the policy seeks to guide admissions officers in "producing classes both diverse and academically outstanding, classes made up of students who promise to continue the tradition of outstanding contribution by Michigan Graduates to the legal profession."

B

Petitioner Barbara Grutter is a white Michigan resident who applied to the Law School in 1996 with a 3.8 grade point average and 161 LSAT score. The Law School initially placed petitioner on a waiting list, but subsequently rejected her application. In December 1997, petitioner filed suit in the United States District Court * * * [, alleging] that respondents discriminated against her on the basis of race in violation of the Fourteenth Amendment; Title VI of the Civil Rights Act of 1964, 42 U. S. C. § 2000d; and 42 U. S. C. § 1981.

Petitioner further alleged that her application was rejected because the Law School uses race as a "predominant" factor, giving applicants who belong to certain minority groups "a significantly greater chance of admission than students with similar credentials from disfavored racial groups." Petitioner also alleged that respondents "had no compelling interest to justify their use of race in the admissions process." * * *

During the 15–day bench trial, the parties introduced extensive evidence concerning the Law School's use of race in the admissions process. Dennis Shields, Director of Admissions when petitioner applied to the Law School, testified that he did not direct his staff to admit a particular percentage or number of minority students, but rather to consider an applicant's race along with all other factors. Shields testified that at the height of the admissions season, he would frequently consult the so-called "daily reports" that kept track of the racial and ethnic composition of the class (along with other information such as residency status and gender). This was done, Shields testified, to ensure that a critical mass of underrepresented minority students would be reached so as to realize the educational benefits of a diverse student body. Shields stressed, however, that he did not seek to admit any particular number or percentage of underrepresented minority students.

Erica Munzel, who succeeded Shields as Director of Admissions, testified that "critical mass" means "meaningful numbers" or "meaningful representation," which she understood to mean a number that encourages underrepresented minority students to participate in the classroom and not feel isolated. Munzel stated there is no number, percentage, or range of numbers or percentages that constitute critical mass. Munzel also asserted that she must consider the race of applicants because a critical mass of underrepresented minority students could not be enrolled if admissions decisions were based primarily on undergraduate GPAs and LSAT scores.

The current Dean of the Law School, Jeffrey Lehman, also testified. Like the other Law School witnesses, Lehman did not quantify critical mass in terms of numbers or percentages. He indicated that critical mass means numbers such that underrepresented minority students do not feel isolated or like spokespersons for their race. When asked about the extent to which race is considered in admissions, Lehman testified that it varies from one applicant to another. In some cases, according to Lehman's testimony, an applicant's race may play no role, while in others it may be a "determinative" factor.

The District Court heard extensive testimony from Professor Richard Lempert, who chaired the faculty committee that drafted the 1992 policy. Lempert emphasized that the Law School seeks students with diverse interests and backgrounds to enhance classroom discussion and the educational experience both inside and outside the classroom. When asked about the policy's "commitment to racial and ethnic diversity with special reference to the inclusion of students from groups which have been historically discriminated against," Lempert explained that this language did not purport to remedy past discrimination, but rather to include students who may bring to the Law School a perspective different from that of members of groups which have not been the victims of such discrimination. Lempert acknowledged that other groups, such as Asians and Jews, have experienced discrimination, but explained they were not mentioned in the policy because individuals who are members of those groups were already being admitted to the Law School in significant numbers.

Kent Syverud was the final witness to testify about the Law School's use of race in admissions decisions. Syverud was a professor at the Law School when the 1992 admissions policy was adopted and is now Dean of Vanderbilt Law School. In addition to his testimony at trial, Syverud submitted several expert reports on the educational benefits of diversity. Syverud's testimony indicated that when a critical mass of underrepresented minority students is present, racial stereotypes lose their force because nonminority students learn there is no "minority viewpoint" but rather a variety of viewpoints among minority students.

* * *

We granted certiorari, to resolve the disagreement among the Courts of Appeals on a question of national importance: Whether diversity is a compelling interest that can justify the narrowly tailored use of race in selecting applicants for admission to public universities.

II

A

We last addressed the use of race in public higher education over 25 years ago. In the landmark *Bakke* case, we reviewed a racial set-aside program that reserved 16 out of 100 seats in a medical school class for members of certain minority groups. The decision produced six separate opinions, none of which commanded a majority of the Court. * * *

The only holding for the Court in *Bakke* was that a "State has a substantial interest that legitimately may be served by a properly devised admissions program involving the competitive consideration of race and ethnic origin." Thus, we reversed that part of the lower court's judgment that enjoined the university "from any consideration of the race of any applicant."

Since this Court's splintered decision in *Bakke*, Justice Powell's opinion announcing the judgment of the Court has served as the touchstone for constitutional analysis of race-conscious admissions policies. Public and private universities across the Nation have modeled their own admissions programs on Justice Powell's views on permissible race-conscious policies. * * *

* * * [F]or the reasons set out below, today we endorse Justice Powell's view that student body diversity is a compelling state interest that can justify the use of race in university admissions.

* * *

We first wish to dispel the notion that the Law School's argument has been foreclosed, either expressly or implicitly, by our affirmative-action cases decided since *Bakke*. It is true that some language in those opinions might be read to suggest that remedying past discrimination is the only permissible justification for race-based governmental action. But we have never held that the only governmental use of race that can survive strict scrutiny is remedying past discrimination. Nor, since *Bakke*, have we directly addressed the use of race in the context of public higher education. Today, we hold that the Law School has a compelling interest in attaining a diverse student body.

The Law School's educational judgment that such diversity is essential to its educational mission is one to which we defer. The Law School's assessment that diversity will, in fact, yield educational benefits is substantiated by respondents and their *amici*. Our scrutiny of the interest asserted by the Law School is no less strict for taking into account complex educational judgments in an area that lies primarily within the expertise of the university. Our holding today is in keeping with our tradition of giving a degree of deference to a university's academic decisions, within constitutionally prescribed limits.

We have long recognized that, given the important purpose of public education and the expansive freedoms of speech and thought associated with the university environment, universities occupy a special niche in our constitutional tradition. In announcing the principle of student body diversity as a compelling state interest, Justice Powell invoked our cases recognizing a constitutional dimension, grounded in the First Amendment, of educational autonomy: "The freedom of a university to make its own judgments as to education includes the selection of its student body."

From this premise, Justice Powell reasoned that by claiming "the right to select those students who will contribute the most to the 'robust exchange of ideas,' " a university "seek[s] to achieve a goal that is of paramount importance in the fulfillment of its mission." Our conclusion that the Law School has a compelling interest in a diverse student body is informed by our view that attaining a diverse student body is at the heart of the Law School's proper institutional mission, and that "good faith" on the part of a university is "presumed" absent "a showing to the contrary."

As part of its goal of "assembling a class that is both exceptionally academically qualified and broadly diverse," the Law School seeks to "enroll a 'critical mass' of minority students." The Law School's interest is not simply "to assure within its student body some specified percentage of a particular group merely because of its race or ethnic origin." That would amount to outright racial balancing, which is patently unconstitutional. Rather, the Law School's concept of critical mass is defined by reference to the educational benefits that diversity is designed to produce.

These benefits are substantial. As the District Court emphasized, the Law School's admissions policy promotes "cross-racial understanding," helps to break down racial stereotypes, and "enables [students] to better understand persons of different races." These benefits are "important and laudable," because "classroom discussion is livelier, more spirited, and simply more enlightening and interesting' when the students have 'the greatest possible variety of backgrounds."

The Law School's claim of a compelling interest is further bolstered by its *amici*, who point to the educational benefits that flow from student body diversity. In addition to the expert studies and reports entered into evidence at trial, numerous studies show that student body diversity promotes learning outcomes, and "better prepares students for an increasingly diverse workforce and society, and better prepares them as professionals."

These benefits are not theoretical but real, as major American businesses have made clear that the skills needed in today's increasingly global marketplace can only be developed through exposure to widely diverse people, cultures, ideas, and viewpoints. What is more, high-ranking retired officers and civilian leaders of the United States military assert that, "[b]ased on [their] decades of experience," a "highly qualified, racially diverse officer corps ... is essential to the military's ability to fulfill its principle mission to provide national security." The primary sources for the Nation's officer corps are the service academies and the Reserve Officers Training Corps (ROTC), the latter comprising students already admitted to participating colleges and universities. At present, "the military cannot achieve an officer corps that is *both* highly qualified *and* racially diverse unless the service academies and the ROTC used limited race-conscious recruiting and admissions policies." To fulfill its mission, the military "must be selective in admissions for training and education for the officer corps, *and* it must train and educate a highly qualified, racially diverse officer corps in a racially diverse setting." We agree that "[i]t requires only a small step from this analysis to conclude that our country's other most selective institutions must remain both diverse and selective."

We have repeatedly acknowledged the overriding importance of preparing students for work and citizenship, describing education as pivotal to "sustaining our political and cultural heritage" with a fundamental role in maintaining the fabric of society. *Plyler v. Doe.* This Court has long recognized that "education . . . is the very foundation of good citizenship." *Brown v. Board of Education,* 347 U. S. 483, 493 (1954). For this reason, the diffusion of knowledge and opportunity through public institutions of higher education must be accessible to all individuals regardless of race or ethnicity. The United States, as *amicus curiae,* affirms that "[e]nsuring that public institutions are open and available to all segments of American society, including people of all races and ethnicities, represents a paramount government objective." And, "[n]owhere is the importance of such openness more acute than in the context of higher education." Effective participation by members of all racial and ethnic groups in the civic life of our Nation is essential if the dream of one Nation, indivisible, is to be realized.

Moreover, universities, and in particular, law schools, represent the training ground for a large number of our Nation's leaders. Individuals with law degrees occupy roughly half the state governorships, more than half the seats in the United States Senate, and more than a third of the seats in the United States House of Representatives. The pattern is even more striking when it comes to highly selective law schools. A handful of these schools accounts for 25 of the 100 United States Senators, 74 United States Courts of Appeals judges, and nearly 200 of the more than 600 United States District Court judges.

In order to cultivate a set of leaders with legitimacy in the eyes of the citizenry, it is necessary that the path to leadership be visibly open to talented and qualified individuals of every race and ethnicity. All members of our heterogeneous society must have confidence in the openness and integrity of the educational institutions that provide this training. As we have recognized, law schools "cannot be effective in isolation from the individuals and institutions with which the law interacts." Access to legal education (and thus the legal profession) must be inclusive of talented and qualified individuals of every race and ethnicity, so that all members of our heterogeneous society may participate in the educational institutions that provide the training and education necessary to succeed in America.

The Law School does not premise its need for critical mass on "any belief that minority students always (or even consistently) express some characteristic minority viewpoint on any issue." To the contrary, diminishing the force of such stereotypes is both a crucial part of the Law School's mission, and one that it cannot accomplish with only token numbers of minority students. Just as growing up in a particular region or having particular professional experiences is likely to affect an individual's views, so too is one's own, unique experience of being a racial minority in a society, like our own, in which race unfortunately still matters. The Law School has determined, based on its experience and expertise, that a "critical mass" of underrepresented minorities is necessary to further its compelling interest in securing the educational benefits of a diverse student body.

B

Even in the limited circumstance when drawing racial distinctions is permissible to further a compelling state interest, government is still "constrained in how it may pursue that end: [T]he means chosen to accomplish the [government's] asserted purpose must be specifically and narrowly framed to accomplish that purpose." * * *

Since *Bakke*, we have had no occasion to define the contours of the narrow-tailoring inquiry with respect to race-conscious university admissions programs. That inquiry must be calibrated to fit the distinct issues raised by the use of race to achieve student body diversity in public higher education. * * *

To be narrowly tailored, a race-conscious admissions program cannot use a quota system—it cannot "insulat[e] each category of applicants with certain desired qualifications from competition with all other applicants." Instead, a university may consider race or ethnicity only as a " 'plus' in a particular applicant's file," without "insulat[ing] the individual from comparison with all other candidates for the available seats." In other words, an admissions program must be "flexible enough to consider all pertinent elements of diversity in light of the particular qualifications of each applicant, and to place them on the same footing for consideration, although not necessarily according them the same weight."

We find that the Law School's admissions program bears the hallmarks of a narrowly tailored plan. As Justice Powell made clear in *Bakke*, truly individualized consideration demands that race be used in a flexible, nonmechanical way. It follows from this mandate that universities cannot establish quotas for members of certain racial groups or put members of those groups on separate admissions tracks. Nor can universities insulate applicants who belong to certain racial or ethnic groups from the competition for admission. Universities can, however, consider race or ethnicity more flexibly as a "plus" factor in the context of individualized consideration of each and every applicant.

We are satisfied that the Law School's admissions program, like the Harvard plan described by Justice Powell, does not operate as a quota. Properly understood, a "quota" is a program in which a certain fixed number or proportion of opportunities are "reserved exclusively for certain minority groups." Quotas " 'impose a fixed number or percentage which must be attained, or which cannot be exceeded,' " and "insulate the individual from comparison with all other candidates for the available seats." In contrast, "a permissible goal ... require[s] only a good-faith effort ... to come within a range demarcated by the goal itself," and permits consideration of race as a "plus" factor in any given case while still ensuring that each candidate "compete[s] with all other qualified applicants."

Justice Powell's distinction between the medical school's rigid 16–seat quota and Harvard's flexible use of race as a "plus" factor is instructive. Harvard certainly had minimum *goals* for minority enrollment, even if it had no specific number firmly in mind. What is more, Justice Powell flatly rejected the argument that Harvard's program was "the functional equivalent of a quota" merely because it had some "plus" for race, or gave greater "weight" to race than to some other factors, in order to achieve student body diversity.

The Law School's goal of attaining a critical mass of underrepresented minority students does not transform its program into a quota. As the Harvard plan described by Justice Powell recognized, there is of course "some relationship between numbers and achieving the benefits to be derived from a diverse student body, and between numbers and providing a reasonable environment for those students admitted." "[S]ome attention to numbers," without more, does not transform a flexible admissions system into a rigid quota. * * *

That a race-conscious admissions program does not operate as a quota does not, by itself, satisfy the requirement of individualized consideration. When using race as a "plus" factor in university admissions, a university's admissions program must remain flexible enough to ensure that each applicant is evaluated as an individual and not in a way that makes an applicant's race or ethnicity the defining feature of his or her application. The importance of this individualized consideration in the context of a race-conscious admissions program is paramount.

Here, the Law School engages in a highly individualized, holistic review of each applicant's file, giving serious consideration to all the ways an applicant might contribute to a diverse educational environment. The Law School affords this individualized consideration to applicants of all races. There is no policy, either *de jure* or *de facto*, of automatic acceptance or rejection based on any single "soft" variable. Unlike the program at issue in *Gratz v. Bollinger*, the Law School awards no mechanical, predetermined diversity "bonuses" based on race or ethnicity. Like the Harvard plan, the Law School's admissions policy "is flexible enough to consider all pertinent elements of diversity in light of the particular qualifications of each applicant, and to place them on the same footing for consideration, although not necessarily according them the same weight."

We also find that, like the Harvard plan Justice Powell referenced in *Bakke*, the Law School's race-conscious admissions program adequately ensures that all factors that may contribute to student body diversity are meaningfully considered alongside race in admissions decisions. With respect to the use of race itself, all underrepresented minority students admitted by the Law School have been deemed qualified. By virtue of our Nation's struggle with racial inequality, such students are both likely to have experiences of particular importance to the Law School's mission, and less likely to be admitted in meaningful numbers on criteria that ignore those experiences.

The Law School does not, however, limit in any way the broad range of qualities and experiences that may be considered valuable contributions to student body diversity. To the contrary, the 1992 policy makes clear "[t]here are many possible bases for diversity admissions," and provides examples of admittees who have lived or traveled widely abroad, are fluent in several languages, have overcome personal adversity and family hardship, have exceptional records of extensive community service, and have had successful careers in other fields. The Law School seriously considers each "applicant's promise of making a notable contribution to the class by way of a particular strength, attainment, or characteristic—*e.g.*, an unusual intellectual achievement, employment experience, nonacademic performance, or personal background." All applicants have the opportunity to highlight their own potential diversity contributions through the submission of a personal statement, letters of recommendation, and an essay describing the ways in which the applicant will contribute to the life and diversity of the Law School.

What is more, the Law School actually gives substantial weight to diversity factors besides race. The Law School frequently accepts nonminority applicants with grades and test scores lower than underrepresented minority applicants (and other nonminority applicants) who are rejected. This shows that the Law School seriously weighs many other diversity factors besides race that can make a real and dispositive difference for nonminority applicants as well. By this flexible approach, the Law School sufficiently takes into account, in practice as well as in theory, a wide variety of characteristics besides race and ethnicity that contribute to a diverse student body. * * *

Petitioner and the United States argue that the Law School's plan is not narrowly tailored because race-neutral means exist to obtain the educational benefits of student body diversity that the Law School seeks. We disagree. Narrow tailoring does not require exhaustion of every conceivable race-neutral alternative. Nor does it require a university to choose between maintaining a reputation for excellence or fulfilling a commitment to provide educational opportunities to members of all racial groups. Narrow tailoring does, however, require serious, good faith consideration of workable race-neutral alternatives that will achieve the diversity the university seeks.

We agree with the Court of Appeals that the Law School sufficiently considered workable race-neutral alternatives. The District Court took the Law School to task for failing to consider race-neutral alternatives such as "using a lottery system" or "decreasing the emphasis for all applicants on undergraduate GPA and LSAT scores." But these alternatives would require a dramatic sacrifice of diversity, the academic quality of all admitted students, or both.

The Law School's current admissions program considers race as one factor among many, in an effort to assemble a student body that is diverse in ways broader than race. Because a lottery would make that kind of nuanced judgment impossible, it would effectively sacrifice all other educational values, not to mention every other kind of diversity. So too with the suggestion that the Law School simply lower admissions standards for all students, a drastic remedy that would require the Law School to become a much different institution and sacrifice a vital component of its educational mission. The United States advocates "percentage plans," recently adopted by public undergraduate institutions in Texas, Florida, and California to guarantee admission to all students above a certain class-rank threshold in every high school in the State. The United States does not, however, explain how such plans could work for graduate and professional schools. More-over, even assuming such plans are race-neutral, they may preclude the university from conducting the individualized assessments necessary to assemble a student body that is not just racially diverse, but diverse along all the qualities valued by the university. We are satisfied that the Law School adequately considered race-neutral alternatives currently capable of producing a critical mass without forcing the Law School to abandon the academic selectivity that is the cornerstone of its educational mission.

We acknowledge that "there are serious problems of justice connected with the idea of preference itself." Narrow tailoring, therefore, requires that a race-conscious admissions program not unduly harm members of any racial group. Even remedial race-based governmental action generally "remains subject to continuing oversight to assure that it will work the least harm possible to other innocent persons competing for the benefit." To be narrowly tailored, a race-conscious admissions program must not "unduly burden individuals who are not members of the favored racial and ethnic groups."

We are satisfied that the Law School's admissions program does not. Because the Law School considers "all pertinent elements of diversity," it can (and does) select nonminority applicants who have greater potential to enhance student body diversity over underrepresented minority applicants. As Justice Powell recognized in *Bakke*, so long as a race-conscious admissions program uses race as a "plus" factor in the context of individualized consideration, a rejected applicant "will not have been foreclosed from all consideration for that seat simply because he was not the right color or had the wrong surname.... His qualifications would have been weighed fairly and competitively, and he would have no basis to complain of unequal treatment under the Fourteenth Amendment."

We agree that, in the context of its individualized inquiry into the possible diversity contributions of all applicants, the Law School's race-conscious admissions program does not unduly harm nonminority applicants.

We are mindful, however, that "[a] core purpose of the Fourteenth Amendment was to do away with all governmentally imposed discrimination based on race." Accordingly, race-conscious admissions policies must be limited in time. This requirement reflects that racial classifications, however compelling their goals, are potentially so dangerous that they may be employed no more broadly than the interest demands. Enshrining a permanent justification for racial preferences would offend this fundamental equal protection principle. We see no reason to exempt race-conscious admissions programs from the requirement that all governmental use of race must have a logical end point. The Law School, too, concedes that all "race-conscious programs must have reasonable durational limits."

In the context of higher education, the durational requirement can be met by sunset provisions in race-conscious admissions policies and periodic reviews to determine whether racial preferences are still necessary to achieve student body diversity. Universities in California, Florida, and Washington State, where racial preferences in admissions are prohibited by state law, are currently engaged in experimenting with a wide variety of alternative approaches. Universities in other States can and should draw on the most promising aspects of these race-neutral alternatives as they develop.

The requirement that all race-conscious admissions programs have a termination point "assure[s] all citizens that the deviation from the norm of equal treatment of all racial and ethnic groups is a temporary matter, a measure taken in the service of the goal of equality itself."

We take the Law School at its word that it would "like nothing better than to find a race-neutral admissions formula" and will terminate its race-conscious admissions program as soon as practicable. It has been 25 years since Justice Powell first approved the use of race to further an interest in student body diversity in the context of public higher education. Since that time, the number of minority applicants with high grades and test scores has indeed increased. We expect that 25 years from now, the use of racial preferences will no longer be necessary to further the interest approved today.

IV

In summary, the Equal Protection Clause does not prohibit the Law School's narrowly tailored use of race in admissions decisions to further a compelling interest in obtaining the educational benefits that flow from a diverse student body. * * * The judgment of the Court of Appeals for the Sixth Circuit, accordingly, is affirmed.

It is so ordered.

* * *

JUSTICE THOMAS, with whom JUSTICE SCALIA joins as to Parts I–VII, concurring in part and dissenting in part.

Frederick Douglass, speaking to a group of abolitionists almost 140 years ago, delivered a message lost on today's majority:

> [I]n regard to the colored people, there is always more that is benevolent, I perceive, than just, manifested towards us. What I ask for the negro is not benevolence, not pity, not sympathy, but simply *justice*. The American people have always been anxious to know what they shall do with us.... I have had but one answer from the beginning. Do nothing with us! Your doing with us has already played the mischief with us. Do nothing with us! If the apples will not remain on the tree of their own strength, if they are worm-eaten at the core, if they are early ripe and disposed to fall, let them fall! ... And if the negro cannot stand on his own legs, let him fall also. All I ask is, give him a chance to stand on his own legs! Let him alone! ... [Y]our interference is doing him positive injury.

Like Douglass, I believe blacks can achieve in every avenue of American life without the meddling of university administrators. Because I wish to see all students succeed whatever their color, I share, in some respect, the sympathies of those who sponsor the type of discrimination advanced by the University of Michigan Law School (Law School). The Constitution does not, however, tolerate institutional devotion to the status quo in admissions policies when such devotion ripens into racial discrimination. Nor does the Constitution countenance the unprecedented deference the Court gives to the Law School, an approach inconsistent with the very concept of "strict scrutiny."

No one would argue that a university could set up a lower general admission standard and then impose heightened requirements only on black applicants. Similarly, a university may not maintain a high admission standard and grant exemptions to favored races. The Law School, of its own choosing, and for its own purposes, maintains an exclusionary admissions system that it knows produces racially disproportionate results. Racial discrimination is not a permissible solution to the self-inflicted wounds of this elitist admissions policy.

The majority upholds the Law School's racial discrimination not by interpreting the people's Constitution, but by responding to a faddish slogan of the cognoscenti. Nevertheless, I concur in part in the Court's opinion. First, I agree with the Court insofar as its decision, which approves of only one racial classification, confirms that further use of race in admissions remains unlawful. Second, I agree with the Court's holding that racial discrimination in higher education admissions will be illegal in 25 years. I respectfully dissent from the remainder of the Court's opinion and the judgment, however, because I believe that the Law School's current use of race violates the Equal Protection Clause and that the Constitution means the same thing today as it will in 300 months.

* * *

CHIEF JUSTICE REHNQUIST, with whom JUSTICE SCALIA, JUSTICE KENNEDY, and JUSTICE THOMAS join, dissenting.

I agree with the Court that, "in the limited circumstance when drawing racial distinctions is permissible," the government must ensure that its means are narrowly tailored to achieve a compelling state interest. I do not believe, however, that the University of Michigan Law School's (Law School) means are narrowly tailored to the interest it asserts. The Law School claims it must take the steps it does to achieve a " 'critical mass' " of underrepresented minority students. But its actual program bears no relation to this asserted goal. Stripped of its "critical mass" veil, the Law School's program is revealed as a naked effort to achieve racial balancing.

* * *

NOTES

1. In *Grutter,* the Court set forth, for the first time, a series of guidelines for determining whether the use of race in public education admissions programs was narrowly tailored to further the compelling state interest in "student body diversity." While subsequent court of appeals decisions applying these principles at the K–12 level differed slightly in their conclusions as to the number of factors to consider and which factors would be more directly applicable to desegregation programs, the following checklist is arguably an appropriate characterization of the questions that a Court should ask in determining under Fourteenth Amendment Equal Protection Clause jurisprudence whether *a university admissions policy that includes race as a factor* is in fact narrowly tailored:

I.   Was it clear that the policy did not operate as a quota (i.e. that it was not "a program in which a certain fixed number or proportion of opportunities were reserved exclusively for certain minority groups")?

II.   Did the policy satisfy the requirement of "individualized consideration"?

    A.   No mechanical, predetermined diversity "bonuses" based on race/ethnicity.

    B.   Adequate assurance that "all factors that may contribute to student body diversity are meaningfully considered alongside race."

        1.   Not limiting in any way the broad range of qualities and experiences that may be considered valuable contributions to student body diversity.

        2.   Giving substantial weight to diversity factors besides race.

        3.   Establishing "a flexible approach, taking into account, in practice as well as in theory, a wide variety of characteristics besides race and ethnicity that contribute to a diverse student body."

III. Did the university in good faith consider workable, race-neutral alternatives that would achieve the diversity it seeks?

IV. Did the race-conscious admissions program "not unduly burden individuals who are not members of the favored racial and ethnic groups"?

V. Was the admissions policy "limited in time"?

Finding that *all* the above factors were satisfied by the Michigan law school admissions policy, the Court upheld its constitutionality (*Grutter*).

Not finding that all the above factors were satisfied by the Michigan undergraduate admissions policy, the Court struck that policy down as unconstitutional (*Gratz*).

Is it reasonable to conclude that all these requirements must in fact be met for a policy to be found constitutional under *Grutter*?

2. *Grutter* and *Gratz* were companion cases, decided on the same day. In *Gratz v. Bollinger*, 539 U.S. 244, 123 S.Ct. 2411 (2003), the Court addressed an admissions policy for undergraduates that had changed several times during the course of the litigation. Beginning with the 1998 academic year, the university had set up a "selection index," on which an applicant could score a maximum of 150 points. Those scoring 100 or above were definitely admitted, and those scoring below 75 were delayed or rejected.

Each application received points based on high school grade point average, standardized test scores, academic quality of an applicant's high school, strength or weakness of high school curriculum, in-state residency, alumni relationship, personal essay, and personal achievement or leadership. Of particular significance here, under a "miscellaneous" category, an applicant was entitled to 20 points based upon his or her membership in an underrepresented racial or ethnic minority group. *Id.* at 255.

The Court found that this practice did not satisfy the individualized consideration requirement of the narrow tailoring guidelines articulated in *Grutter* that day:

The current LSA policy does not provide such individualized consideration. The LSA's policy automatically distributes 20 points to every single applicant from an "underrepresented minority" group, as defined by the University. The only consideration that accompanies this distribution of points is a factual review of an application to determine whether an individual is a member of one of these minority groups. Moreover, * * * the LSA's automatic distribution of 20 points has the effect of making "the factor of race ... decisive" for virtually every minimally qualified underrepresented minority applicant. *Id.* at 271–72.

While the admissions policy had features and nuances that made it much more complex than simply an automatic distribution of numbers, six justices found the fixed 20–point bonus to be violative of the Fourteenth Amendment.

As a result of the two decisions, Michigan—committed to an affirmative action program—adjusted its undergraduate policy to comply with the guidelines set forth by the Court. For other public colleges and universities, the law school's "critical mass" policy became an example of a plan that would meet the requirements of the Constitution, while the undergraduate numerical bonus policy became an example of a plan that should not be replicated.

3. In *Grutter,* the Court ruled that affirmative action could be implemented, and that race could be employed as a factor in admissions decision, if the policy was narrowly tailored to further the compelling interest in student body diversity. But it is important to emphasize that the Court was not requiring affirmative action. States were still free to "experiment" with race neutral programs, should they so desire. California, Washington, and Florida were therefore able to continue their respective prohibitions on affirmative action.

4. In her discussion regarding the narrow tailoring requirement that the policy be "limited in time," Justice O'Connor wrote: "We expect that 25 years from now, the use of racial preferences will no longer be necessary to further the interest approved today." This language has been the subject of much debate. Some have argued, as Justice Thomas appears to have done, that this means that any use of race in admissions programs will automatically be unconstitutional in 2028. Others have argued that this statement is dicta, or, at best, a broad goal with no legal impact and no precedential value.

Is it now time to target a specific end-date for the use of racial preferences in affirmative action programs? Would you personally support such an approach? Why or why not?

Similar questions have been asked regarding school desegregation. These questions are addressed below, in the pages that follow.

THE CALIFORNIA CIVIL RIGHTS INITIATIVE (PROPOSITION 209) (1996)

Approved by the Voters (54 percent to 46 percent)

California became the first state in the country to ban race-based affirmative action programs in admissions and hiring when the Regents of the University of California—at the urging of then-Governor Pete Wilson—approved SP–1 and SP–2. The following year, these resolutions were superseded by Proposition 209, a ballot initiative that applied statewide throughout the public sector.

The proposition also banned "preferential treatment" on the basis of "sex, color, or national origin." But it was soon clear that preferential treatment could still be granted in public education—as discussed above—based upon a myriad of other factors.[a] In addition, questions remained regarding the scope of 209. And while some of these questions were addressed by subsequent court decisions, others—such as 209's applicability at the K–12 level—remained unanswered.

Early on, many believed that the proposition was a harbinger of things to come, and that it would only be a matter of time before all states

---

a. *See generally* Eugene Volokh, *The California Civil Rights Initiative: An Interpretive Guide,* 44 UCLA L. Rev. 1335 (1997).

had similar restrictions in place. Yet by 2009 this clearly had not happened.

Of course, these issues have not gone away. Indeed, more than a decade after the initiative became law, it continued to engender great controversy and emotion, particularly on California's public college and university campuses. Many have come to view the state as "cutting edge" in this regard. For many others, however—especially after the U.S. Supreme Court ruling in *Grutter*—it made no sense for a handful of educational institutions to be prohibiting only these preferences when the overwhelming majority of colleges and universities throughout the country were able and willing to act otherwise.

Consider the text of California Proposition 209. What are the arguments today for not only keeping 209 in place, but for adding similar provisions to other state constitutions? What are the arguments for modifying or overturning 209?

Assume that you have been asked to advise a coalition of public interest groups regarding possible modifications to 209 consistent with recent federal court jurisprudence? What suggestions might you provide? How do you think the voters would react if your proposed revisions were placed on the ballot? Why?

Article I, Section 31 of the California Constitution (Proposition 209) provides:

a) The state shall not discriminate against, or grant preferential treatment to, any individual or group on the basis of race, sex, color, ethnicity, or national origin in the operation of public employment, public education, or public contracting.

b) This section shall apply only to action taken after this section's effective date.

c) Nothing in this section shall be interpreted as prohibiting bona fide qualifications based on sex which are reasonably necessary to the normal operation of public employment, public education, or public contracting.

d) Nothing in this section shall be interpreted as invalidating any court order or consent decree which is in force as of the effective date of this section.

e) Nothing in this section shall be interpreted as prohibiting action which must be taken to establish or maintain any federal program, where ineligibility would result in a loss of federal funds to the state.

f) For the purposes of this section, 'state' shall include, but not necessarily be limited to, the state itself, any city, county, city and county, public university system, including the University of California, community college district, school district, special district, or any other political subdivision or governmental instrumentality of or within the state.

g) The remedies available for violations of this section shall be the same, regardless of the injured party's race, sex, color, ethnicity, or national origin, as are otherwise available for violations of then-existing California and discrimination law.

h) This section shall be self-executing. If any part or parts of this section are found to be in conflict with federal law or the United States Constitution, the section shall be implemented to the maximum extent that federal law and the United States Constitution permit. Any provision held invalid shall be severable from the remaining portions of this section.

PROBLEM 23: THE NEW MENDOCINO PROFESSIONAL DEVELOPMENT PROGRAM

The following hypothetical takes place in the fictional state of New Mendocino.

Concerned about the quality of public education in New Mendocino, and in particular about the low test scores of language minority students, wealthy entrepreneur Manuel Rodriguez establishes a new foundation for the sole purpose of focusing on bilingual education reform issues. After consulting with a task force of educators and community leaders, Rodriguez announces an ambitious plan composed of three interrelated parts: (1) substantial grants to private schools that volunteer to "adopt" public schools with high percentages of English learners; (2) the development of model gifted programs for bilingual students; and (3) extensive professional development for bilingual teachers linked to a career ladder that would double the current salaries of bilingual educators so that the top teachers in the field would actually earn the same amount of money as first-year associates at major law firms.

The adoption process would be limited to public schools with English learner populations of 50% or greater. As envisioned, substantial interaction—both online and, if possible, in real time—would occur between and among the faculty and students of both schools. Courses would be team taught, interactive projects would bring students together, and a range of extracurricular activities would cement the bonds.

The professional development/career ladder program, also funded with substantial grant money from the Rodriguez Foundation and administered jointly by the public and private schools involved in the adoption partnerships, would be limited to teachers in the high need language areas of Spanish, Cantonese, and Vietnamese (reflecting an English learner population in New Mendocino that is approximately 35% Spanish-speaking, 20% Cantonese-speaking, and 15% Vietnamese-speaking). Teachers applying to the program would need to be fully credentialed under state law, and would need to present evidence of proficiency in one of the three high need languages. They would be admitted by language skill in direct proportion to the percentages of students in the three targeted groups. A numerical rating system for applicants would include bonus points based on the amount of work they have done with economically disadvantaged young people, their years of experience as bilingual teachers, and other relevant factors such as exceptional personal talents, unique work or service experience, and a history of overcoming disadvantage. In the event that two applicants earn the same score, those applicants who are Latino, Chinese American, or Vietnamese American (in that order) would receive priority.

The Rodriguez Foundation programs receive highly positive feedback from all relevant stakeholders, and many low performing public schools with large English learner populations are adopted by private schools throughout the state. In addition, teachers rush to participate in the professional development/career ladder program, seeing it as a unique opportunity to improve the quality of public education while at the same time increasing their salaries. By the second year, 1,934 qualified teachers had submitted applications for 500 spaces.

Assume that you are representing the defendants in the following cases arising out of the above facts, and that no state action issues will be raised.

A. A federal Equal Protection Clause lawsuit filed on behalf of two Filipino American teachers, both veteran bilingual educators who were fluent in English, Spanish, and Tagalog but were denied admission to the professional development program based on the tie-breaker process. What arguments should defendants expect plaintiffs to set forth, and how should they be countered? What result? Discuss.

B. Assume that New Mendocino has a state constitutional provision identical to CA Prop. 209, and that plaintiffs bring this action under that provision. What result? Discuss.

C. Assume instead that there is a state statute identical to Washington's I–200, and that the litigation is brought under that provision. What result?

3. SORTING OUT THE PARAMETERS OF K–12 DESEGREGATION LAW IN THE AFTERMATH OF *GRUTTER* AND *SEATTLE-LOUISVILLE*

Desegregation issues are very different during this era than they were in the decades immediately following *Brown,* but they are no less compelling.

An unresolved issue in this context, for example, is the question of what constitutes a *vestige* of "state-enforced segregation." *See, e.g.,* Ryan Tacorda, *Acknowledging Those Stubborn Facts of History: The Vestiges of Segregation,* 50 UCLA L. Rev. 1547 (2003). But the central issue at this point in time is whether and to what extent school districts can employ race-conscious remedies in circumstances where desegregation may no longer be mandated by court order or consent decree.

Indeed, as a matter of policy, the debate regarding the efficacy of desegregation programs continues in many communities. While many contend that desegregation is an outmoded strategy that "did not work," others insist that many people have benefited greatly from desegregation programs over time, particularly when these programs also addressed within-school segregation issues and were linked to carefully thought-out education plans.

This section of the chapter begins with an examination of the U.S. Supreme Court's 2007 *Seattle-Louisville* decision and its prospective implications. Building on this inquiry, it explores the prospective lessons of San Francisco unique desegregation decree (1983–2005). The materials that follow in other sections, addressing such issues as within-school segregation and standardized testing, all interrelate as well.

PROBLEM 24: THE VISTA CREEK SCHOOL DISTRICT-UNIVERSITY PARTNERSHIP

The following hypothetical takes place at public educational institutions in the fictional state of Eldorado.

For the past five years, the Vista Creek Unified School District (a large and diverse urban district) and the University of Eldorado (a large public university with seven campuses throughout the state) have jointly administered an academically advanced program for students 16 and older. In lieu of the final two years of high school, participating students enroll in the functional equivalent of the first two years of college. The program has been very popular, and over 750 students currently participate.

Some courses are taught at high school campuses, and others at the university. The program is funded in part from the district's budget, in part from the university's budget, and in part through an enrollment fee charged to participating families. Students who complete the program are guaranteed admission to the University of Eldorado should they decide to go there, although they are not necessarily guaranteed the campus of their choice. They can enter automatically with the status of juniors.

The program has been lauded as a cutting-edge example of education reform, and several other institutions have begun planning their own versions. In addition, a growing number of colleges and universities nationwide have announced that they will also award college credit for courses completed in the joint Vista–Eldorado program.

Philosophically, the program has adopted the goals of K–12 school desegregation plans that have been recognized as successful. The online brochure, explicitly referencing pre–1999 San Francisco as an example, states that these goals include "equal access, equal opportunity, increased academic achievement, multi-faceted diversity, and an end to the geographic isolation of low-income students of color." Thus the classes that are offered at K–12 sites are situated primarily at facilities located in low-income and racially isolated areas. And program officials also administer an outreach office that seeks to attract students from underrepresented racial/ethnic groups. Local businesses have contributed to the recruitment effort by funding scholarships for members of these groups.

In addition, the admissions process has been structured to help further these same desegregation-related goals. To be eligible for admission, students must earn a GPA of 3.0 or higher in their grade 6 through 10 academic subjects, and they must score at the 80th percentile or higher on each part of the PSAT.** But special priority is given to applicants who (1) have attended low-performing schools, (2) live in racially isolated, low-income areas, (3) have spent at least one summer participating in some form of community service, and/or (4) are fluent in at least two languages.

All applicants are initially processed by computer. The computer ranks students based on both the traditional indicators (grades and test scores) and the priority categories.

Members of the admissions committee then make final decisions regarding applicants based on computer rankings and on other relevant factors such as exceptional personal talents, leadership potential, maturity, demonstrated compassion, and a history of overcoming disadvantage.

* * *

A lawsuit is filed by parents whose children were denied admission to the joint program. Plaintiffs contend that the race-conscious features of the program are unconstitutional under either *Grutter* or the 2007 *Seattle-Louisville* decision. What arguments would you set forth in defense of the plan under *Grutter*? Under *Seattle-Louisville*? What result? Discuss.

PARENTS INVOLVED IN COMMUNITY SCHOOLS v. SEATTLE SCHOOL DISTRICT NO. 1

__ U.S. __, 127 S.Ct. 2738 (2007)

Chief Justice ROBERTS announced the judgment of the Court, and delivered the opinion of the Court with respect to Parts I, II, III–A, and III–C, and an opinion with respect to Parts III–B and IV, in which Justices SCALIA, THOMAS, and ALITO join.

* * *

I

Both [the Seattle and the Louisville] cases present the same underlying legal question-whether a public school that had not operated legally segregated schools or has been found to be unitary may choose to classify students by race and rely upon that classification in making school assignments. Although we examine the plans under the same legal framework, the specifics of the two plans, and the circumstances surrounding their adoption, are in some respects quite different.

A

Seattle School District No. 1 operates 10 regular public high schools. In 1998, it adopted the plan at issue in this case for assigning students to

---

** Assume that this is in fact the actual "Preliminary SAT" that is currently administered by the College Board nationwide.

these schools. The plan allows incoming ninth graders to choose from among any of the district's high schools, ranking however many schools they wish in order of preference.

Some schools are more popular than others. If too many students list the same school as their first choice, the district employs a series of "tiebreakers" to determine who will fill the open slots at the oversubscribed school. The first tiebreaker selects for admission students who have a sibling currently enrolled in the chosen school. The next tiebreaker depends upon the racial composition of the particular school and the race of the individual student. In the district's public schools approximately 41 percent of enrolled students are white; the remaining 59 percent, comprising all other racial groups, are classified by Seattle for assignment purposes as nonwhite. If an oversubscribed school is not within 10 percentage points of the district's overall white/nonwhite racial balance, it is what the district calls "integration positive," and the district employs a tiebreaker that selects for assignment students whose race "will serve to bring the school into balance." If it is still necessary to select students for the school after using the racial tiebreaker, the next tiebreaker is the geographic proximity of the school to the student's residence. * * *

B

Jefferson County Public Schools operates the public school system in metropolitan Louisville, Kentucky. In 1973 a federal court found that Jefferson County had maintained a segregated school system, and in 1975 the District Court entered a desegregation decree. Jefferson County operated under this decree until 2000, when the District Court dissolved the decree after finding that the district had achieved unitary status by eliminating "[t]o the greatest extent practicable" the vestiges of its prior policy of segregation.

In 2001, after the decree had been dissolved, Jefferson County adopted the voluntary student assignment plan at issue in this case. Approximately 34 percent of the district's 97,000 students are black; most of the remaining 66 percent are white. The plan requires all nonmagnet schools to maintain a minimum black enrollment of 15 percent, and a maximum black enrollment of 50 percent.

At the elementary school level, based on his or her address, each student is designated a "resides" school to which students within a specific geographic area are assigned; elementary resides schools are "grouped into clusters in order to facilitate integration." The district assigns students to nonmagnet schools in one of two ways: Parents of kindergartners, first-graders, and students new to the district may submit an application indicating a first and second choice among the schools within their cluster; students who do not submit such an application are assigned within the cluster by the district. "Decisions to assign students to schools within each cluster are based on available space within the schools and the racial guidelines in the District's current student assignment plan." If a school has reached the "extremes of the racial guidelines," a student whose race would contribute to the school's racial imbalance will not be assigned there. After assignment, students at all grade levels are permitted to apply to transfer between nonmagnet schools in the district. Transfers may be requested for any number of reasons, and may be denied because of lack of available space or on the basis of the racial guidelines.

* * *

III

A

It is well established that when the government distributes burdens or benefits on the basis of individual racial classifications, that action is reviewed under strict scrutiny. As the Court recently reaffirmed, " 'racial classifications are simply too pernicious to permit any but the most exact connection between justification and classification.' " *Gratz* v. *Bollinger.* In order to satisfy this searching standard of review, the school districts must demonstrate that the use of individual racial classifications in the assignment plans here under review is "narrowly tailored" to achieve a "compelling" government interest.

Without attempting in these cases to set forth all the interests a school district might assert, it suffices to note that our prior cases, in evaluating the use of racial classifications in the school context, have recognized two interests that qualify as compelling. The first is the compelling interest of remedying the effects of past intentional discrimination. Yet the Seattle public schools have not shown that they were ever segregated by law, and were not subject to court-ordered desegregation decrees. The Jefferson County public schools were previously segregated by law and were subject to a desegregation decree entered in 1975. In 2000, the District Court that entered that decree dissolved it, finding that Jefferson County had "eliminated the vestiges associated with the former policy of segregation and its pernicious effects," and thus had achieved "unitary" status. Jefferson County accordingly does not rely upon an interest in remedying the effects of past intentional discrimination in defending its present use of race in assigning students.

Nor could it. We have emphasized that the harm being remedied by mandatory desegregation plans is the harm that is traceable to segregation, and that "the Constitution is not violated by racial imbalance in the schools, without more." Once Jefferson County achieved unitary status, it had remedied the constitutional wrong that allowed race-based assignments. Any continued use of race must be justified on some other basis.

The second government interest we have recognized as compelling for purposes of strict scrutiny is the interest in diversity in higher education upheld in *Grutter.* The specific interest found compelling in *Grutter* was student body diversity "in the context of higher education." The diversity interest was not focused on race alone but encompassed "all factors that may contribute to student body diversity."

* * *

The entire gist of the analysis in *Grutter* was that the admissions program at issue there focused on each applicant as an individual, and not simply as a member of a particular racial group. The classification of applicants by race upheld in *Grutter* was only as part of a "highly individualized, holistic review." As the Court explained, "[t]he importance of this individualized consideration in the context of a race-conscious admissions program is paramount." The point of the narrow tailoring analysis in which the *Grutter* Court engaged was to ensure that the use of racial classifications was indeed part of a broader assessment of diversity, and not simply an effort to achieve racial balance, which the Court explained would be "patently unconstitutional."

In the present cases, by contrast, race is not considered as part of a broader effort to achieve "exposure to widely diverse people, cultures, ideas, and viewpoints"; race, for some students, is determinative standing alone. The districts argue that other factors, such as student preferences, affect assignment decisions under their plans, but under each plan when race comes into play, it is decisive by itself. It is not simply one factor weighed with others in reaching a decision, as in *Grutter*; it is *the* factor. Like the University of Michigan undergraduate plan struck down in *Gratz*, the plans here "do not provide for a meaningful individualized review of applicants" but instead rely on racial classifications in a "nonindividualized, mechanical" way.

Even when it comes to race, the plans here employ only a limited notion of diversity, viewing race exclusively in white/nonwhite terms in Seattle and black/"other" terms in Jefferson County. * * * [U]nder the Seattle plan, a school with 50 percent Asian–American students and 50 percent white students but no African–American, Native–American, or Latino students would qualify as balanced, while a school with 30 percent Asian–American, 25 percent African–American, 25 percent Latino, and 20 percent white students would not. It is hard to understand how a plan that could allow these results can be viewed as being concerned with achieving enrollment that is "broadly diverse."

Prior to *Grutter*, the courts of appeals rejected as unconstitutional attempts to implement race-based assignment plans-such as the plans at issue here-in primary and secondary schools. * * * After *Grutter*, however, the two Courts of Appeals in these cases, and one other, found that race-based assignments were permissible at the elementary and secondary level, largely in reliance on that case.

In upholding the admissions plan in *Grutter*, though, this Court relied upon considerations unique to institutions of higher education, noting that in light of "the expansive freedoms of speech and thought associated with the university environment, universities occupy a special niche in our constitutional tradition." * * * The Court in *Grutter* expressly articulated key limitations on its holding-defining a specific type of broad-based diversity and noting the unique context of higher education-but these limitations were largely disregarded by the lower courts in extending *Grutter* to uphold race-based assignments in elementary and secondary schools. The present cases are not governed by *Grutter*.

Ba

Perhaps recognizing that reliance on *Grutter* cannot sustain their plans, both school districts assert additional interests, distinct from the interest upheld in *Grutter*, to justify their race-based assignments. In briefing and argument before this Court, Seattle contends that its use of race helps to reduce racial concentration in schools and to ensure that racially concentrated housing patterns do not prevent nonwhite students from having access to the most desirable schools. Jefferson County has articulated a similar goal, phrasing its interest in terms of educating its students "in a racially integrated environment." Each school district argues that educational and broader socialization benefits flow from a racially diverse learning environment, and each contends that because the diversity they seek is racial diversity-not the broader diversity at issue in *Grutter*-it makes sense to promote that interest directly by relying on race alone.

The parties and their *amici* dispute whether racial diversity in schools in fact has a marked impact on test scores and other objective yardsticks or achieves intangible socialization benefits. The debate is not one we need to resolve, however, because it is clear that the racial classifications employed by the districts are not narrowly tailored to the goal of achieving the educational and social benefits asserted to flow from racial diversity. In design and operation, the plans are directed only to racial balance, pure and simple, an objective this Court has repeatedly condemned as illegitimate. * * *

Accepting racial balancing as a compelling state interest would justify the imposition of racial proportionality throughout American society, contrary to our repeated recognition that "[a]t the heart of the Constitution's guarantee of equal protection lies the simple command that the Government must treat citizens as individuals, not as simply components of a racial, religious, sexual or national class." Allowing racial balancing as a compelling end in itself would "effectively assur[e] that race will always be relevant in American life, and that the 'ultimate goal' of 'eliminating entirely from governmental decisionmaking such irrelevant factors as a human being's race' will never be achieved."

* * *

The principle that racial balancing is not permitted is one of substance, not semantics. Racial balancing is not transformed from "patently

---

a. This portion of Chief Justice Roberts' opinion constituted a plurality, representing a total of four votes.

unconstitutional" to a compelling state interest simply by relabeling it "racial diversity." * * *

Jefferson County phrases its interest as "racial integration," but integration certainly does not require the sort of racial proportionality reflected in its plan. Even in the context of mandatory desegregation, we have stressed that racial proportionality is not required, * * * and here Jefferson County has already been found to have eliminated the vestiges of its prior segregated school system.

The en banc Ninth Circuit declared that "when a racially diverse school system is the goal (or racial concentration or isolation is the problem), there is no more effective means than a consideration of race to achieve the solution." *Parents Involved VII.* For the foregoing reasons, this conclusory argument cannot sustain the plans. However closely related race-based assignments may be to achieving racial balance, that itself cannot be the goal, whether labeled "racial diversity" or anything else. To the extent the objective is sufficient diversity so that students see fellow students as individuals rather than solely as members of a racial group, using means that treat students solely as members of a racial group is fundamentally at cross-purposes with that end.

C

* * *

The districts have also failed to show that they considered methods other than explicit racial classifications to achieve their stated goals. Narrow tailoring requires "serious, good faith consideration of workable race-neutral alternatives," *Grutter,* and yet in Seattle several alternative assignment plans-many of which would not have used express racial classifications-were rejected with little or no consideration. Jefferson County has failed to present any evidence that it considered alternatives, even though the district already claims that its goals are achieved primarily through means other than the racial classifications. * * *

IV[b]

* * * [W]hen it comes to using race to assign children to schools, history will be heard. In *Brown* v. *Board of Education* (*Brown I*), we held that segregation deprived black children of equal educational opportunities regardless of whether school facilities and other tangible factors were equal, because government classification and separation on grounds of race themselves denoted inferiority. It was not the inequality of the facilities but the fact of legally separating children on the basis of race on which the Court relied to find a constitutional violation in 1954. (" 'The impact [of segregation] is greater when it has the sanction of the law' "). The next Term, we accordingly stated that "full compliance" with *Brown*

---

b. This portion of Chief Justice Roberts' opinion constituted a plurality, representing a total of four votes.

I required school districts "to achieve a system of determining admission to the public schools *on a nonracial basis.*" *Brown II* (emphasis added).

The parties and their *amici* debate which side is more faithful to the heritage of *Brown*, but the position of the plaintiffs in *Brown* was spelled out in their brief and could not have been clearer: "[T]he Fourteenth Amendment prevents states from according differential treatment to American children on the basis of their color or race." Brief for Appellants in Nos. 1, 2, and 4 and for Respondents in No. 10 on Reargument in *Brown I*, O. T. 1953, p. 15 (Summary of Argument). What do the racial classifications at issue here do, if not accord differential treatment on the basis of race? As counsel who appeared before this Court for the plaintiffs in *Brown* put it: "We have one fundamental contention which we will seek to develop in the course of this argument, and that contention is that no State has any authority under the equal-protection clause of the Fourteenth Amendment to use race as a factor in affording educational opportunities among its citizens." Tr. of Oral Arg. in *Brown I*, p. 7 (Robert L. Carter, Dec. 9, 1952). There is no ambiguity in that statement. And it was that position that prevailed in this Court, which emphasized in its remedial opinion that what was "[a]t stake is the personal interest of the plaintiffs in admission to public schools as soon as practicable *on a nondiscriminatory basis*," and what was required was "determining admission to the public schools *on a nonracial basis.*" *Brown II, supra*, at 300–301 (emphasis added). What do the racial classifications do in these cases, if not determine admission to a public school on a racial basis? Before *Brown*, schoolchildren were told where they could and could not go to school based on the color of their skin. The school districts in these cases have not carried the heavy burden of demonstrating that we should allow this once again-even for very different reasons. For schools that never segregated on the basis of race, such as Seattle, or that have removed the vestiges of past segregation, such as Jefferson County, the way "to achieve a system of determining admission to the public schools on a nonracial basis," *Brown II*, is to stop assigning students on a racial basis. The way to stop discrimination on the basis of race is to stop discriminating on the basis of race.

The judgments of the Courts of Appeals for the Sixth and Ninth Circuits are reversed, and the cases are remanded for further proceedings.

It is so ordered.

JUSTICE THOMAS, concurring.

Today, the Court holds that state entities may not experiment with race-based means to achieve ends they deem socially desirable. I wholly concur in The Chief Justice's opinion. I write separately to address several of the contentions in Justice Breyer's dissent (hereinafter the dissent). Contrary to the dissent's arguments, resegregation is not occurring in Seattle or Louisville; these school boards have no present interest in remedying past segregation; and these race-based student-assignment programs do not serve any compelling state interest. Accordingly, the plans are unconstitutional. Disfavoring a color-blind interpretation of the Constitution, the dissent would give school boards a free hand to make decisions on the basis of race-an approach reminiscent of that advocated by the segregationists in *Brown* v. *Board of Education*. This approach is just as wrong today as it was a half-century ago. The Constitution and our cases require us to be much more demanding before permitting local school boards to make decisions based on race.

I

The dissent repeatedly claims that the school districts are threatened with resegregation and that they will succumb to that threat if these plans are declared unconstitutional. It also argues that these plans can be justified as part of the school boards' attempts to "eradicat[e] earlier school segregation." Contrary to the dissent's rhetoric, neither of these school districts is threatened with resegregation, and neither is constitutionally compelled or permitted to undertake race-based remediation. Racial imbalance is not segregation, and the mere incantation of terms like resegregation and remediation cannot make up the difference.

A

Because this Court has authorized and required race-based remedial measures to address *de jure* segregation, it is important to define segregation clearly and to distinguish it from racial imbalance. In the context of public schooling, segregation is the deliberate operation of a school system to "carry out a governmental policy to separate pupils in schools solely on the basis of race." *Swann* v. *Charlotte-Mecklenburg Bd. of Ed.* * * *

Racial imbalance is the failure of a school district's individual schools to match or approximate the demographic makeup of the student population at large. Racial imbalance is not segregation. * * *

The dissent appears to pin its interpretation of the Equal Protection Clause to current societal practice and expectations, deference to local officials, likely practical consequences, and reliance on previous statements from this and other courts. Such a view was ascendant in this Court's jurisprudence for several decades. It first appeared in *Plessy,* where the Court asked whether a state law providing for segregated railway cars was "a reasonable regulation." The Court deferred to local authorities in making its determination, noting that in inquiring into reasonableness "there must necessarily be a large discretion on the part of the legislature." The Court likewise paid heed to societal practices, local expectations, and practical consequences by looking to "the established usages, customs and traditions of the people, and with a view to the promotion of their comfort, and the preservation of the public peace and good order." * * *

The segregationists in *Brown* embraced the arguments the Court endorsed in *Plessy*. Though *Brown* decisively rejected those arguments, today's dissent replicates them to a distressing extent. * * * The dissent argues that "weight [must be given] to a local school board's knowledge, expertise, and concerns," and with equal vigor, the segregationists argued for deference to local authorities. * * *

The similarities between the dissent's arguments and the segregationists' arguments do not stop there. Like the dissent, the segregationists repeatedly cautioned the Court to consider practicalities and not to embrace too theoretical a view of the Fourteenth Amendment. And just as the dissent argues that the need for these programs will lessen over time, the segregationists claimed that reliance on segregation was lessening and might eventually end.

What was wrong in 1954 cannot be right today. Whatever else the Court's rejection of the segregationists' arguments in *Brown* might have established, it certainly made clear that state and local governments cannot take from the Constitution a right to make decisions on the basis of race by adverse possession. The fact that state and local governments had been discriminating on the basis of race for a long time was irrelevant to the *Brown* Court. The fact that racial discrimination was preferable to the relevant communities was irrelevant to the *Brown* Court. And the fact that the state and local governments had relied on statements in this Court's opinions was irrelevant to the *Brown* Court. The same principles guide today's decision. None of the considerations trumpeted by the dissent is relevant to the constitutionality of the school boards' race-based plans because no contextual detail-or collection of contextual details-can "provide refuge from the principle that under our Constitution, the government may not make distinctions on the basis of race."

In place of the color-blind Constitution, the dissent would permit measures to keep the races together and proscribe measures to keep the races apart. Although no such distinction is apparent in the Fourteenth Amendment, the dissent would constitutionalize today's faddish social theories that embrace that distinction. The Constitution is not that malleable. Even if current social theories favor classroom racial engineering as necessary to "solve the problems at hand," the Constitution enshrines principles independent of social theories. * * * Indeed, if our history has taught us anything, it has taught us to beware of elites bearing racial theories.

> * * *

The plans before us base school assignment decisions on students' race. Because "[o]ur Constitution is color-blind, and neither knows nor tolerates classes among citizens," such race-based decisionmaking is unconstitutional. I concur in the Chief Justice's opinion so holding.

JUSTICE KENNEDY, concurring in part and concurring in the judgment.

The Nation's schools strive to teach that our strength comes from people of different races, creeds, and cultures uniting in commitment to the freedom of all. In these cases two school districts in different parts of the country seek to teach that principle by having classrooms that reflect the racial makeup of the surrounding community. That the school districts consider these plans to be necessary should remind us our highest aspirations are yet unfulfilled. But the solutions mandated by these school districts must themselves be lawful. To make race matter now so that it might not matter later may entrench the very prejudices we seek to overcome. In my view the state-mandated racial classifications at issue * * * are unconstitutional as the cases now come to us.

* * * My views do not allow me to join [Part III–B and Part IV] of the opinion by The Chief Justice, which [seem] to me to be inconsistent in both [their] approach and [their] implications with the history, meaning, and reach of the Equal Protection Clause. Justice Breyer's dissenting opinion, on the other hand, rests on what in my respectful submission is a misuse and mistaken interpretation of our precedents. This leads it to advance propositions that, in my view, are both erroneous and in fundamental conflict with basic equal protection principles. As a consequence, this separate opinion is necessary to set forth my conclusions in the two cases before the Court.

     * * *

II

Our Nation from the inception has sought to preserve and expand the promise of liberty and equality on which it was founded. Today we enjoy a society that is remarkable in its openness and opportunity. Yet our tradition is to go beyond present achievements, however significant, and to recognize and confront the flaws and injustices that remain. This is especially true when we seek assurance that opportunity is not denied on account of race. The enduring hope is that race should not matter; the reality is that too often it does.

This is by way of preface to my respectful submission that parts of the opinion by The Chief Justice imply an all-too-unyielding insistence that race cannot be a factor in instances when, in my view, it may be taken into account. The plurality opinion is too dismissive of the legitimate interest government has in ensuring all people have equal opportunity regardless of their race. The plurality's postulate that "[t]he way to stop discrimination on the basis of race is to stop discriminating on the basis of race," is not sufficient to decide these cases. Fifty years of experience since *Brown* v. *Board of Education* should teach us that the problem before us defies so easy a solution. School districts can seek to reach *Brown*'s objective of equal educational opportunity. The plurality opinion is at least open to the interpretation that the Constitution requires school districts to ignore the problem of *de facto* resegregation in schooling. I cannot endorse that conclusion. To the extent the plurality opinion suggests the Constitution mandates that state and local school authorities must accept the status quo of racial isolation in schools, it is, in my view, profoundly mistaken.

The statement by Justice Harlan that "[o]ur Constitution is color-blind" was most certainly justified in the context of his dissent in *Plessy v. Ferguson* (1896). The Court's decision in that case was a grievous error it took far too long to overrule. *Plessy*, of course, concerned official classification by race applicable to all persons who sought to use railway carriages. And, as an aspiration, Justice Harlan's axiom must command our assent. In the real world, it is regrettable to say, it cannot be a universal constitutional principle.

In the administration of public schools by the state and local authorities it is permissible to consider the racial makeup of schools and to adopt general policies to encourage a diverse student body, one aspect of which is its racial composition. Cf. *Grutter* v. *Bollinger*. If school authorities are concerned that the student-body compositions of certain schools interfere with the objective of offering an equal educational opportunity to all of their students, they are free to devise race-conscious measures to address the problem in a general way and without treating each student in different fashion solely on the basis of a systematic, individual typing by race.

School boards may pursue the goal of bringing together students of diverse backgrounds and races through other means, including strategic site selection of new schools; drawing attendance zones with general recognition of the demographics of neighborhoods; allocating resources for special programs; recruiting students and faculty in a targeted fashion; and tracking enrollments, performance, and other statistics by race. These mechanisms are race conscious but do not lead to different treatment based on a classification that tells each student he or she is to be defined by race, so it is unlikely any of them would demand strict scrutiny to be found permissible.[c] * * * Executive and legislative branches, which for generations now have considered these types of policies and procedures, should be permitted to employ them with candor and with confidence that a constitutional violation does not occur whenever a decisionmaker considers the impact a given approach might have on students of different races. Assigning to each student a personal designation according to a crude system of individual racial classifications is quite a different matter; and the legal analysis changes accordingly.

Each respondent has asserted that its assignment of individual students by race is permissible because there is no other way to avoid racial isolation in the school districts. Yet, as explained, each has failed to provide the support necessary for that proposition. * * * And individual racial classifications employed in this manner may be considered legitimate only if they are a last resort to achieve a compelling interest.

---

c. Justice Kennedy reproduces a quote from the 1996 redistricting case of *Bush* v. *Vera*, 517 U. S. 952 in support of this assertion:

Strict scrutiny does not apply merely because redistricting is performed with consciousness of race.... . Electoral district lines are 'facially race neutral' so a more searching inquiry is necessary before strict scrutiny can be found applicable in redistricting cases than in cases of 'classifications based explicitly on race' *Id.* at 958 (plurality opinion).

In the cases before us it is noteworthy that the number of students whose assignment depends on express racial classifications is limited. I join Part III–C of the Court's opinion because I agree that in the context of these plans, the small number of assignments affected suggests that the schools could have achieved their stated ends through different means. These include the facially race-neutral means set forth above or, if necessary, a more nuanced, individual evaluation of school needs and student characteristics that might include race as a component. The latter approach would be informed by *Grutter*, though of course the criteria relevant to student placement would differ based on the age of the students, the needs of the parents, and the role of the schools.

III

The dissent rests on the assumptions that these sweeping race-based classifications of persons are permitted by existing precedents; that its confident endorsement of race categories for each child in a large segment of the community presents no danger to individual freedom in other, prospective realms of governmental regulation; and that the racial classifications used here cause no hurt or anger of the type the Constitution prevents. Each of these premises is, in my respectful view, incorrect. * * *

C

* * * The idea that if race is the problem, race is the instrument with which to solve it cannot be accepted as an analytical leap forward. And if this is a frustrating duality of the Equal Protection Clause it simply reflects the duality of our history and our attempts to promote freedom in a world that sometimes seems set against it. Under our Constitution the individual, child or adult, can find his own identity, can define her own persona, without state intervention that classifies on the basis of his race or the color of her skin.

* * *

This Nation has a moral and ethical obligation to fulfill its historic commitment to creating an integrated society that ensures equal opportunity for all of its children. A compelling interest exists in avoiding racial isolation, an interest that a school district, in its discretion and expertise, may choose to pursue. Likewise, a district may consider it a compelling interest to achieve a diverse student population. Race may be one component of that diversity, but other demographic factors, plus special talents and needs, should also be considered. What the government is not permitted to do, absent a showing of necessity not made here, is to classify every student on the basis of race and to assign each of them to schools based on that classification. Crude measures of this sort threaten to reduce children to racial chits valued and traded according to one school's supply and another's demand.

That statement, to be sure, invites this response: A sense of stigma may already become the fate of those separated out by circumstances beyond their immediate control. But to this the replication must be: Even so, measures other than differential treatment based on racial typing of individuals first must be exhausted.

The decision today should not prevent school districts from continuing the important work of bringing together students of different racial, ethnic, and economic backgrounds. Due to a variety of factors-some influenced by government, some not-neighborhoods in our communities do not reflect the diversity of our Nation as a whole. Those entrusted with directing our public schools can bring to bear the creativity of experts, parents, administrators, and other concerned citizens to find a way to achieve the compelling interests they face without resorting to widespread governmental allocation of benefits and burdens on the basis of racial classifications.

With this explanation I concur in the judgment of the Court.

JUSTICE STEVENS, dissenting.

* * *

The Court has changed significantly since * * * 1968. It was then more faithful to *Brown* and more respectful of our precedent than it is today. It is my firm conviction that no Member of the Court that I joined in 1975 would have agreed with today's decision.

JUSTICE BREYER, with whom JUSTICE STEVENS, JUSTICE SOUTER, and JUSTICE GINSBURG join, dissenting.

These cases consider the longstanding efforts of two local school boards to integrate their public schools. The school board plans before us resemble many others adopted in the last 50 years by primary and secondary schools throughout the Nation. All of those plans represent local efforts to bring about the kind of racially integrated education that *Brown* v. *Board of Education* long ago promised-efforts that this Court has repeatedly required, permitted, and encouraged local authorities to undertake. This Court has recognized that the public interests at stake in such cases are "compelling." We have approved of "narrowly tailored" plans that are no less race-conscious than the plans before us. And we have understood that the Constitution *permits* local communities to adopt desegregation plans even where it does not *require* them to do so.

The plurality pays inadequate attention to this law, to past opinions' rationales, their language, and the contexts in which they arise. As a result, it reverses course and reaches the wrong conclusion. In doing so, it distorts precedent, it misapplies the relevant constitutional principles, it announces legal rules that will obstruct efforts by state and local governments to deal effectively with the growing resegregation of public schools, it threatens to substitute for present calm a disruptive round of race-related litigation, and it undermines *Brown*'s promise of integrated primary and secondary education that local communities have sought to make a reality. This cannot be justified in the name of the Equal Protection Clause.

* * *

III

* * *

The compelling interest at issue here * * * includes an effort to eradicate the remnants, not of general "societal discrimination," but of primary and secondary school segregation; it includes an effort to create school environments that provide better educational opportunities for all children; it includes an effort to help create citizens better prepared to know, to understand, and to work with people of all races and backgrounds, thereby furthering the kind of democratic government our Constitution foresees. If an educational interest that combines these three elements is not "compelling," what is?

* * *

VI

* * * [T]he consequences of the approach the Court takes today are serious. Yesterday, the plans under review were lawful. Today, they are not. Yesterday, the citizens of this Nation could look for guidance to this Court's unanimous pronouncements concerning desegregation. Today, they cannot. Yesterday, school boards had available to them a full range of means to combat segregated schools. Today, they do not.

The Court's decision undermines other basic institutional principles as well. What has happened to *stare decisis?* The history of the plans before us, their educational importance, their highly limited use of race-all these and more-make clear that the compelling interest here is stronger than in *Grutter.* The plans here are more narrowly tailored than the law school admissions program there at issue. Hence, applying *Grutter*'s strict test, their lawfulness follows *a fortiori.* To hold to the contrary is to transform that test from "strict" to "fatal in fact"-the very opposite of what *Grutter* said. And what has happened to *Swann?* To *McDaniel?* To *Crawford?* To *Harris?* To *School Committee of Boston?* To *Seattle School Dist. No. 1?* After decades of vibrant life, they would all, under the plurality's logic, be written out of the law.

And what of respect for democratic local decisionmaking by States and school boards? For several decades this Court has rested its public school decisions upon *Swann*'s basic view that the Constitution grants local school districts a significant degree of leeway where the inclusive use of race-conscious criteria is at issue. Now localities will have to cope with the difficult problems they face (including resegregation) deprived of one means they may find necessary.

And what of law's concern to diminish and peacefully settle conflict among the Nation's people? Instead of accommodating different good-faith visions of our country and our Constitution, today's holding upsets settled expectations, creates legal uncertainty, and threatens to produce considerable further litigation, aggravating race-related conflict.

And what of the long history and moral vision that the Fourteenth Amendment itself embodies? The plurality cites in support those who argued in *Brown* against segregation, and Justice Thomas likens the approach that I have taken to that of segregation's defenders. But segregation policies did not simply tell schoolchildren "where they could and could not go to school based on the color of their skin"; they perpetuated a caste system rooted in the institutions of slavery and 80 years of legalized subordination. The lesson of history is not that efforts to continue racial segregation are constitutionally indistinguishable from efforts to achieve racial integration. Indeed, it is a cruel distortion of history to compare Topeka, Kansas, in the 1950's to Louisville and Seattle in the modern day-to equate the plight of Linda Brown (who was ordered to attend a Jim Crow school) to the circumstances of Joshua McDonald (whose request to transfer to a school closer to home was initially declined). This is not to deny that there is a cost in applying "a state-mandated racial label." But that cost does not approach, in degree or in kind, the terrible harms of slavery, the resulting caste system, and 80 years of legal racial segregation.

* * *

Finally, what of the hope and promise of *Brown?* For much of this Nation's history, the races remained divided. It was not long ago that people of different races drank from separate fountains, rode on separate buses, and studied in separate schools. In this Court's finest hour, *Brown* v. *Board of Education* challenged this history and helped to change it. For *Brown* held out a promise. It was a promise embodied in three Amendments designed to make citizens of slaves. It was the promise of true racial equality-not as a matter of fine words on paper, but as a matter of everyday life in the Nation's cities and schools. It was about the nature of a democracy that must work for all Americans. It sought one law, one Nation, one people, not simply as a matter of legal principle but in terms of how we actually live.

Not everyone welcomed this Court's decision in *Brown*. Three years after that decision was handed down, the Governor of Arkansas ordered state militia to block the doors of a white schoolhouse so that black children could not enter. The President of the United States dispatched the 101st Airborne Division to Little Rock, Arkansas, and federal troops were needed to enforce a desegregation decree. Today, almost 50 years later, attitudes toward race in this Nation have changed dramatically. Many parents, white and black alike, want their children to attend schools with children of different races. Indeed, the very school districts that once spurned integration now strive for it. The long history of their efforts reveals the complexities and difficulties they have faced. And in light of those challenges, they have asked us not to take from their hands the instruments they have used to rid their schools of racial segregation, instruments that they believe are needed to overcome the problems of cities divided by race and poverty. The plurality would decline their modest request.

The plurality is wrong to do so. The last half-century has witnessed great strides toward racial equality, but we have not yet realized the promise of *Brown*. To invalidate the plans under review is to threaten the promise of *Brown*. The plurality's position, I fear, would break that promise. This is a decision that the Court and the Nation will come to regret.

I must dissent.

NOTES

1. The fractured set of five opinions in the *Seattle-Louisville* case reflected unresolvable differences between and among the justices. Chief Justice Roberts' opinion announcing the result garnered a bare majority for its description of the facts and its articulation of the decision, but won the agreement of only a plurality (himself and three others) for what were arguably the boldest and most far-reaching assertions. Justice Breyer, writing on behalf of four other justices, objected strongly in a lengthy and emotional dissent to the direction that the slim majority had adopted.

2. Justice Kennedy signed on only to the portions of the Chief Justice's opinion that set forth the facts, announced the ruling in favor of the plaintiffs, and addressed the applicability of *Grutter*. In his own opinion–concurring in part and concurring in the judgment–Kennedy took great issue with key components of what the plurality had said, even as he also took great issue with key components of what the dissenting justices had said. Seeking to find five votes in favor of possible guiding principles, some have sought to read the Roberts opinion along with the Kennedy opinion and identify points that they would agree upon, while others have combined the Breyer opinion with the Kennedy opinion and have identified a different set of points that five justices would agree on. Indeed, commentators have noted that five justices (Kennedy plus the plurality) found the analysis in *Grutter v. Bollinger* to be applicable only at the higher education level, while also recognizing that five justices (Kennedy plus the dissenting justices) would discern a number of compelling governmental interests that could justify race-conscious K–12 school desegregation. Given the fact that Kennedy's position garners five votes in both instances, is it appropriate to conclude that it is his opinion rather than anyone else's that will come to represent what this decision ultimately stands for?

3. Perhaps the most volatile of all the interrelated issues in this litigation was the debate regarding the applicability of *Brown v. Board of Education*. All of the justices sought to wrap themselves in the mantle of *Brown*, and their opinions exemplify the profound disagreement that has emerged in this nation about what *Brown* truly stands for.

Has *Brown* been overruled by the *Seattle-Louisville* decision? By characterizing traditional desegregation practices mandated under *Brown* as unconstitutional racial balancing, the Chief Justice and the four others who joined him arguably eviscerated much of what the landmark case had come to represent. At the same time, five votes arguably still exist for a continued right to equal educational opportunity in this context, and school districts are still obligated to act under a range of federal and state laws that often contain race-conscious mandates–including but not limited to the U.S. "No Child Left Behind" Act. *See infra,* Chapter 6.

4. In June 2008, the Seattle Times reported that "...[the] Seattle Public Schools, like many districts across the nation, has slowly, steadily resegregated," and the local school board "is weighing what, if anything, to do about the situation":

> Nearly three decades after Seattle Public Schools integrated almost all its schools through busing, that racial balance is long gone. * * *

> Seattle schools don't look exactly like they did before districtwide busing began in 1978. There are fewer nearly all-white schools. Minority students are not as concentrated as they once were in the central part of the city. * * *

> Parents Involved in Community Schools, the group that filed the lawsuit against the racial tiebreaker, argued in court that Seattle no longer needed the racial tiebreaker because the city's high schools already are racially diverse. The group looked at data from 2000–01, when only one high school—Rainier Beach—had a student body that was less than 10 percent white. The picture has changed since then. Three high schools—Rainier Beach, Cleveland and Franklin—now have white populations under 10 percent. At the elementary level, some schools have just a handful of white kids, or just a few minority ones.

> The city's north-south split is economic as well as racial. * * * Linda Shaw, *The Resegregation of Seattle's Schools,* Seattle Times, June 1, 2008.

Many cities across the country are facing similar issues and challenges. *See, e.g,* Jonathan D. Glater & Alan Finder, *Diversity Plans Based on Income Leave Some Schools Segregated,* N.Y. Times, July 15, 2007. *See also* Goodwin Liu, *Seattle and Louisville,* 95 California Law Review 277 (2007).

5. The author of this casebook served as the independent, court-appointed Consent Decree Monitor for the San Francisco school desegregation case from 1997–2005. Over this nine-year period, 15 public reports were filed with the U.S. District Court, Northern District of California, documenting both the successes and the failures of the Decree. All the reports of the Monitoring Team during this era are available at www.gseis.ucla.edu/courses/edlaw/sfrepts.htm. For an overview of San Francisco desegration issues from the perspective of the *Ho* plaintiffs, *see generally* David I. Levine, *The Chinese American Challenge to Court–Mandated Quotas in San Francisco's Public Schools: Notes from a (Partisan) Participant–Observer,* 16 Harvard BlackLetter Law Journal 39 (2000).

Consider the overview of these developments in the "San Francisco Case Study" section that follows. Do you agree that desegregation–if conceptualized as one of many reform strategies designed to equalize access, foster opportunity, accelerate educational quality, improve school climate, and increase academic achievement–can "help maximize the chances of success" for school districts in this context? Or, particularly in light of the result in the *Seattle-Louisville* litigation, is it now appropriate to view desegregation as the product of a bygone era rather than as a viable goal for the future?

4. THE SAN FRANCISCO UNIFIED SCHOOL DISTRICT CONSENT DECREE: A CASE STUDY

COURT-MANDATED EDUCATION REFORM: THE SAN FRANCISCO EXPERIENCE AND THE SHAPING OF EDUCATIONAL POLICY AFTER *SEATTLE-LOUISVILLE* AND *BRIAN HO v. SFUSD*

Stuart Biegel
4 Stanford Journal of Civil Rights & Civil Liberties 159 (2008)

* * *

[T]he San Francisco Decree was unique in that it did not rely on desegregation alone as its primary purpose. With its dual focus on both multi-faceted desegregation and increased academic achievement, and with its precise articulation of numerous interrelated strategies for achieving these two goals, the Decree ultimately stood for equal access to quality education for all students. In this manner, and particularly when it was working, it can serve as an exemplar for future efforts in this area, whether these efforts are launched through local initiatives or come about as a result of litigation or legislation.

Under the approach set forth by the Decree, desegregation (by school, program, and classroom) was designed to be a vehicle to improve educational quality and increase academic achievement. But the desegregation plan outlined in Paragraphs 12 and 13 was only one of a menu of strategies adopted for this purpose.[a] Others included

- The creation of new, high-quality schools in low-income and racially isolated areas;

- Reconstitution or closing of low-performing schools;

- A special plan for Bayview–Hunters Point (perhaps the most racially isolated of all the neighborhoods in San Francisco at the time);

---

a. Under the terms of the Decree, applicable to all children of every race/ethnicity, the District was obligated to desegregate on the basis of school, program, and classroom, and it was also expressly obligated to focus on improving academic achievement. No more than 45% of any one race/ethnicity (40% at alternative schools) coul be enrolled at any SFUSD school, and at least four of nine designated racial/ethnic groups had to be represented at each school. The designated groups were African American, Chinese American, Filipino, Korean American, Japanese American, Latino, Native American, Other Non–White, and White.

Ultimately, it was the dissatisfaction with these race-conscious desegregation mandates that led to the filing of the *Brian Ho v. SFUSD* lawsuit in 1994, the removal of race from the student assignment plan in 1999, a failed experiment with race-neutral approaches to desegregation for the next six years, and the termination of the Decree in 2005. *See* SFNAACP v. SFUSD, 413 F.Supp.2d 1051 (N.D. Cal. 2005).

- An explicit focus on ending discriminatory discipline practices;
- Diversity goals for faculty and staff;
- New requirements for both teacher and school-site administrator professional development;
- The adoption of philosophical tenets designed to raise teacher expectations for all students;
- Independent monitoring.

As conceptualized, none of these strategies were designed to operate in a vacuum. Instead, the drafters contemplated that the initiatives would work together on multiple levels, with efforts in one area fueling efforts in another, and with activities in one sector building upon the activities in other offices, neighborhoods, and school sites.

While some of these mandates were race-conscious, others were not. The Decree envisioned increased diversity, the closing of the achievement gap between and among racial/ethnic groups, and an end to the racial isolation of low-income students of color. However, its broader goals focused on overall educational quality and embodied efforts on behalf of all students.

- **The Varied Success of the Decree Over Time**

Looking back on the history of the San Francisco Unified School District from 1983 to 2005 under the terms and conditions of the Decree, it is clear from past Monitoring Team reports that progress varied significantly over time. While lasting benefits were apparent for many young people throughout the duration of the Decree, the greatest successes arguably occurred during two periods, 1983–1985 and 1993–1995.

* * *

In retrospect, [this] uneven progression * * * can be traced in part to the structural and procedural components of the Decree, and in particular to the nature of the collaboration mandated and the loopholes in the accountability mechanisms.

The collaborative nature of the Decree was both a strength and a weakness. Any changes in the Decree and even any decisions about steps that might be taken under the Decree required the agreement of all the parties. When the goals of the parties were in sync, much could be accomplished. But in practice such a structure meant that both the deliberations and many of the actual decisions were made by the attorneys representing the parties, or by the attorneys in concert with District officials. At times, the attorneys for the parties would meet with District officials to gather information and discuss initiatives. At other times, the attorneys would meet with each other, and none of the actual parties would be at the table. The parties themselves do not appear to have ever met with each other in a formal setting. Consent Decree meetings were primarily legal in nature and thus one or more steps removed from what took place at local school sites and out in the community.

As a result of this structure, the Decree was criticized for creating a system in which a team of lawyers operated as an unelected "super school board" with a level of power over the District that thwarted the democratic process. Indeed, the exclusion of teachers, principals, and members of the community from much, if not all, of the Consent Decree decision-making process led to periods of anger, discontent, and resistance that might have been avoided had these stakeholders been consulted.

The accountability mechanisms of the Decree also left much to be desired. Too often, the District and other involved parties could ignore findings in the Monitoring Team reports, no matter how egregious and no matter how much they indicated a lack of compliance. Indeed, in most cases, nothing was done to address these detailed and independent findings unless (a) the District wanted to address them, which it did from time to time, (b) negotiations were convened for the express purpose of concluding a settlement agreement, such as in 1999 and 2001, or (c) one of the attorneys filed a motion to compel the District to act, which did not happen at all during the last decade of the Decree. In practice, then, superintendents and school boards had at their disposal many ways to resist the mandates of the Decree * * * when they chose to do so. * * *

● **Consent Decree Balance Sheet**

Reflecting the developments in the intersecting cases of *SFNAACP v. SFUSD* and *Brian Ho v. SFUSD,* a balance sheet for the San Francisco Consent Decree helps document both its enduring achievements and the work that still remained to be done.[b]

1. Enduring Achievements Pursuant to the Requirements of the Decree

On the positive side, those who developed and implemented the Decree can point to the successes of the [1983–1985] Phase One reforms, the value of the philosophical tenets, and the efficacy of the Special Plan for Bayview–Hunters Point. They can highlight the achievements of noteworthy schools that had been created under the Decree, point to the turning around of key low-performing schools over time, and reference the fact that by 1997 the District had complied with the [desegregation] mandate * * * and had for all practical purposes completely desegregated school-by-school. They can also note that even during the turbulent

---

b. *See, e.g.,* SFNAACP v. SFUSD, 576 F.Supp. 34 (N.D. Cal. 1983) (setting forth the original Consent Decree). The *SFNAACP* desegregation and academic achievement lawsuit was filed in 1978 and resulted in a Consent Decree in 1983, while the *Ho* lawsuit challenging the Decree was filed in 1994 and resulted in settlements in 1999 and 2001 that ultimately led to the termination of the Decree in 2005.

The interrelated lawsuits generated a number of decisions at both the U.S. District Court level and the Ninth Circuit Court of Appeals. *See, e.g.,* Brian Ho v. SFUSD, 147 F.3d 854 (9th Cir. 1998) (setting forth substantial "guidance" for the parties and the District Court on the issues remaining for trial); SFNAACP v. SFUSD; Ho v. SFUSD, 59 F.Supp.2d 1021 (N.D. Cal. 1999) (setting forth the 1999 settlement for the interrelated lawsuits); SFNAACP v. SFUSD; Ho v. SFUSD, 2001 WL 1922333 (N.D. Cal. 2001) (setting forth the 2001 settlement for the interrelated lawsuits); and SFNAACP v. SFUSD; Ho v. SFUSD, 413 F.Supp.2d 1051 (N.D. Cal. 2005) (terminating the Decree on December 31, 2005).

unraveling of the final six years, certain schools were highly successful at closing the achievement gap.

Indeed, in late 2005, the Monitoring Team devoted considerable space to the identification of thirteen schools that–pursuant to our findings– exemplified success under the mandates of the Decree. Located in every corner of the city, they embodied wide-ranging achievements that benefited students of every race, ethnicity, and socioeconomic status.

The noteworthy schools ranged from campuses in low-income areas such as Carver Elementary (a "Phase One" school in Bayview–Hunters Point that had maintained a solid academic record over two decades), Golden Gate Elementary (a reconstituted school in the Western Addition that showed record gains for its African American population in 2003 and 2004), and Marshall Elementary (a school in a low-SES, high-crime area of the Mission that developed an enriched curriculum pursuant to high standards for all its students) to facilities in middle and upper middle class neighborhoods such as Aptos Middle School (building on its successful reconstitution by retaining its young and highly motivated faculty), Claire Lillienthal (a dynamic K–8 school known for its academic programs), and Alice Fong Yu (a unique high-performing school, guided from the beginning by Consent Decree principles and offering an innovative and inclusive Cantonese immersion program for students of every ethnicity). The list also included both traditional schools such as Galileo High (which showed great gains in the last years of the Decree) and alternative schools such as Harvey Milk Elementary (which maintained a civil rights focus that reflected both the mandates of the Decree and the work of the gay activist for whom the school is named).

Moreover, common factors can be identified that enabled schools such as these to achieve their successes. These factors include maintaining a diverse student body, awareness of the individual learning differences and personal needs of every student, a school-wide commitment to improving African American and Latino student performance, strong intervention programs, a school culture that promotes academic excellence for all students, qualified and caring faculty who understood the tenets of the Consent Decree, communication and collaboration between the administration and faculty, strong parent involvement in the school community, and effective site-based professional development programs that specifically address issues relating to the narrowing of the achievement gap.

2. Key Unresolved Issues under the Terms and Conditions of the Decree

Among the most significant unresolved issues under the Decree were the severe resegregation that emerged after the *Ho* Settlements of 1999 and 2001; the relentless within-school segregation exemplified by the disproportionate representation of African Americans in the separate special education classes; the workings of a school bus transportation system that remained impervious to change; and the persistence of the achievement gap between and among racial and ethnic groups, a gap that worsened in the final years of the Decree as the resegregation percentages increased across the city.

a. Resegregation. After the racial preferences mandated by the original Decree were removed in 1999, the District experienced immediate resegregation, particularly at the elementary school level. The race-neutral "diversity index" experiment implemented pursuant to the 2001 Settlement Agreement not only failed to halt the resegregation trends, but in certain cases may have even accelerated the pace of the resegregation.

In our final Supplemental Report, we found that the resegregation had continued unabated, and that the number of SFUSD schools severely resegregated (60% or higher) at one or more grade levels had now reached approximately 50 schools out of 115 for the first time in this era. * * *

In addition, the actual percentages of students of one race/ethnicity at these schools were higher overall than they had been at any time since the resegregation began. More than half of the resegregated schools now showed 70% or more of one race/ethnicity, and 11 of them showed 80% or more of one race/ethnicity at one or more grade levels.

* * * [W]e also found "a direct relationship between this resegregation and the disparities in academic achievement" that we had been documenting in many of our recent reports. "The effect," we explained, "is corrosive and widespread, impacting not only the quality of the education at individual school sites, but also the culture of the community."

b. Within–School Segregation and Special Education. Throughout the period from 1997 to 2005, the Monitoring Team also documented "a recurring pattern of *within-school* segregation." We consistently found that large percentages of SFUSD students were "separated out from each other within individual schools, and that this separation too often result[ed] in students of certain races being segregated from students of other races at the program and classroom levels....a separation that reflect[ed] academic performance." In particular, we reported on the disproportionate representation of African American and Latino students in special education, and on the commensurate disproportionate underrepresentation of these students in GATE and advanced placement classes and programs. * * *

The extent to which SFUSD African American students were placed in special education, classified as emotionally disturbed, and separated out into the "Special Day Classes" is very striking indeed when compared with the percentages for their counterparts in other racial/ethnic groups. This raises some very troubling questions that the Monitoring Team was not able to follow up on because the Decree sunsetted only eight months after we released these findings.

c. Transportation. In San Francisco, "busing" was a reality for less than 20% of the students, and the District typically provided transportation only for younger children and for those in special education. Older children who attended schools that were not within walking distance often took public transportation, benefiting from a relatively efficient system of buses, streetcars, and trains and from the fact that San Francisco covers a very small geographical area–only 49 square miles in its entirety. * * *

[Yet transportation issues] proved to be a "pressing concern" for both educators and parents, with "travel considerations" deemed "a barrier" to both school choice and diversity. School site administrators in all areas of the city described the logistical difficulties of travel for students in the southeast quadrant who wished to attend schools outside of their neighborhood. Principals also stated that there were not enough bus routes to allow students to access many of the schools they might wish to attend, and most reported that they did not actively seek out students from areas beyond those they had traditionally served because they knew that the students would not be able to get to their sites.

[In addition], bus routes negatively impacted "students' ability to participate in after-school programs and extracurricular activities." Students were often not able to take advantage of what in many cases were stellar programs because their buses would depart right at the close of the formal school day, and no late buses were available. * * *

d. The Persistence and Ultimate Worsening of the Achievement Gap. By 2004, the Monitoring Team had identified a substantial achievement gap between the African American and Latino students and the other students in the District. We found dramatic disparities within individual school sites, within the District as a whole, and between members of these ethnic groups in San Francisco and their counterparts in other Districts. Based on Monitoring Team reports from the earlier years of the Decree, it was clear that the achievement gap had been a persistent issue all along. But it also became clear that with the resegregation of 1999 to 2005, the gap was getting worse. Looking to data from the 1980s and 1990s, we uncovered evidence of substantial progress toward closing the gap at various points in time. We also observed the quality of the educational programs at representative school sites in the 1990s, before resegregation, and we reported on the striking differences between the positive realities that existed when the District had desegregated as compared with the realities that had developed by the end of the Decree.

* * *

• Building on the Findings of the Monitoring Team in San Francisco

The Monitoring Team is not the first group of researchers and officials to have found a link between desegregation and academic achievement. Many recognize the lasting gains realized by students in successful desegregation programs and have documented the impediments to achievement that are often found in segregated and racially isolated schools, particularly those schools comprised of low-income students of color.[123] Still, findings such as these continue to engender skepticism and criticism. Two key points are often set forth in response to this type of evidence: (1) a direct causal link between segregation and academic achievement has not been firmly established, and (2) if we put our minds to it, we can establish top quality schools even in the most racially isolated, low-income areas where the enrollment is comprised entirely of children of color of one race in deep poverty.

It is true that our findings in San Francisco did not establish a direct causal link. We did not identify resegregation as *the* direct cause or even as *a* direct cause of lower academic achievement, and neither did we identify desegregation as a direct cause of higher academic achievement. However, for low-income African American and Latino children, the evidence of a link between segregation and academic performance was both dramatic and striking. The numbers are indisputable, and they tell a story that is impossible to ignore.

In addition, it is indeed true that successful "segregated" schools have been established for racially isolated children of color in their own neighborhoods. Yet these schools are few and far between. Indeed, the effort during the final years of the Decree to establish so-called "Dream Schools" in racially isolated areas of San Francisco exemplifies the difficulties inherent in such an approach. Of the ten schools, three performed so poorly that they had to be closed, one closed before it even opened, and almost all of the others continue to be among the lowest performing schools in the District.

* * *

---

123. Research has consistently documented the persistent inequities experienced by low-income students of color in racially isolated public schools and public school classrooms. *See, e.g.,* Meredith Phillips & Tiffani Chin, *School Inequality: What Do We Know?, in* SOCIAL INEQUALITY 467–519 (Kathryn Neckerman ed., 2004); John T. Yun & Jose F. Moreno, *College Access, K–12 Concentrated Disadvantage, and the Next 25 Years of Education Research,* 35 EDUC. RESEARCHER 12 (2006). *See also* Jeannie Oakes et al., *Curriculum Differentiation: Opportunities, Outcomes, and Meanings, in* HANDBOOK OF RESEARCH ON CURRICULUM 570–608 (Philip W. Jackson ed., 1992). *See generally* Brief of 553 Social Scientists as Amici Curiae in Support of Respondents at 30–35, Parents Involved in Cmty. Sch. v. Seattle Sch. Dist. No. 1, 127 S. Ct. 2738 (2007) (Nos. 05–908, 05–915).

Recent studies in California have also found that African American and Latino students who attend segregated schools have diminished access to the University of California (UC) system. *See, e.g.,* Robert Teranishi et al., *Opportunity at the Crossroads: Racial Inequality, School Segregation, and Higher Education in California,* 106 TCHRS. C. REC. 2224, 2234 tbl.3 (2004); *see also* Isaac Martin et al., *High School Segregation and Access to the University of California,* 19 EDUC. POL'Y 308, 318, 319 tbl. 3 (2005). Other studies focusing on this area have found that segregated schools provide "inferior educational opportunities." *See* CAMILLE E. ESCH ET AL., TEACHING AND CALIFORNIA'S FUTURE: THE STATUS OF THE TEACHING PROFESSION 2005, at 70–71 (2005) (documenting the low percentages of fully credentialed teachers and the high teacher turnover rate in racially isolated schools attended by low-income students of color). *See also* JOHN ROGERS ET AL., CALIFORNIA EDUCATIONAL OPPORTUNITY REPORT 2006: ROADBLOCKS TO COLLEGE 6, 15–17 (2006) (examining "three roadblocks to college" in racially segregated schools: (a) more students per counselor than the national average, (b) more students per teacher than the national average, along with inadequate training of teachers in college prep courses, and (c) shortage of college prep courses in the curriculum). *See generally* Brief of 19 Former Chancellors of the University of California As Amici Curiae in Support of Respondents, [Parents Involved in Cmty. Sch. v. Seattle Sch. Dist. No. 1, 127 S. Ct. 2738 (2007) (Nos. 05–908, 05–915)].

The evidence is incontrovertible that desegregation by school, program, and classroom, if done right, can and does bring substantial benefits to both individual students and the larger community. Likewise, the evidence is overwhelming that segregated schools provide little if any benefit while potentially causing great harm. The San Francisco experience has shown that desegregation and neighborhood schools are not mutually exclusive, but that a creative and well-thought-out plan can have both.

* * * Despite unprecedented advances in communication and other technologies, research has shown that racially isolated schools in low-income neighborhoods are much more likely to be low-performing. During the final six years of the San Francisco Consent Decree, we consistently found a direct relationship between resegregation and a decline in educational quality, a relationship that is too strong to be ignored.

However, it is also clear that desegregation can operate most effectively if it is one of many reform strategies designed to equalize access, foster opportunity, accelerate educational quality, improve school climate, and increase academic achievement. History has shown that desegregation alone often accomplishes very little, but desegregation as part of a multifaceted approach can maximize the chances of success across the board.

* * *

5. WITHIN–SCHOOL SEGREGATION, TRACKING, & HOMOGENEOUS ABILITY GROUPING

One of the most significant unresolved issues in education from an equal opportunity perspective is within-school segregation. In the public schools today, a large percentage of students continue to be separated out from their peers either for programmatic reasons or on the basis of perceived ability. As a result of this separation, many receive a lower quality curriculum, are unable to complete the coursework required for college admission, or are otherwise disadvantaged in a variety of troubling ways.

Legal challenges to these types of practices have had mixed success. *See, e.g.,* KEVIN G. WELNER, LEGAL RIGHTS, LOCAL WRONGS: WHEN COMMUNITY CONTROL COLLIDES WITH EDUCATIONAL EQUITY, SUNY Press (2001). The 1967 case of *Hobson v. Hansen* represents a landmark victory that achieved great results, yet to the extent that this pre-*Washington v. Davis* case was decided on the basis of discriminatory effects alone, the decision may no longer be good law. On the other hand, *Hobson* remains an important touchstone in this context, since the District's approach to tracking and its justification for tracking are now, in light of almost four decades of additional research, clearly unacceptable. *See generally* JEANNIE OAKES, KEEPING TRACK: HOW SCHOOLS STRUCTURE INEQUALITY, Yale University Press (2d ed. 2005).

HOBSON v. HANSEN

269 F.Supp. 401 (D.D.C. 1967)

J. SKELLY WRIGHT, CIRCUIT JUDGE:

SUMMARY

In *Bolling v. Sharpe*, the Supreme Court held that the District of Columbia's racially segregated public school system violated the due process clause of the Fifth Amendment. The present litigation, brought in behalf of Negro as well as poor children generally in the District's public schools, tests the current compliance of those schools with the principles announced in *Bolling*, its companion case, *Brown v. Board of Education*, 347 U.S. 483, 74 S. Ct. 686 (1954), and their progeny. The basic question presented is whether the defendants, the Superintendent of Schools and the members of the Board of Education, in the operation of the public school system here, unconstitutionally deprive the District's Negro and poor public school children of their right to equal educational opportunity with the District's white and more affluent public school children. This court concludes that they do.

In support of this conclusion the court makes the following principal findings of fact:

* * *

9. The track system as used in the District's public schools is a form of ability grouping in which students are divided in separate, self-contained curricula or tracks ranging from "Basic" for the slow student to "Honors" for the gifted.

10. The aptitude tests used to assign children to the various tracks are standardized primarily on white middle class children. Since these tests do not relate to the Negro and disadvantaged child, track assignment based on such tests relegates Negro and disadvantaged children to the lower tracks from which, because of the reduced curricula and the absence of adequate remedial and compensatory education, as well as continued inappropriate testing, the chance of escape is remote.

11. Education in the lower tracks is geared to what Dr. Hansen, the creator of the track system, calls the "blue collar" student. Thus such children, so stigmatized by inappropriate aptitude testing procedures, are denied equal opportunity to obtain the white collar education available to the white and more affluent children.

* * *

In sum, all of the evidence in this case tends to show that the Washington school system is a monument to the cynicism of the power structure which governs the voteless capital of the greatest country on earth.

Remedy

To correct the racial and economic discrimination found in the operation of the District of Columbia public school system, the court has issued a decree attached to its opinion ordering: 1. An injunction against racial and economic discrimination in the public school system here. 2. Abolition of the track system. * * *

FINDINGS OF FACT

* * *

IV. THE TRACK SYSTEM

The District of Columbia school system employs a form of ability grouping commonly known as the track system, by which students at the elementary and secondary level are placed in tracks or curriculum levels according to the school's assessment of each student's ability to learn. * * *

A. *Origin.*

The track system was approved for introduction into the Washington school system by the Board of Education in 1956, just two years after the desegregation decision in *Bolling v. Sharpe.* * * * The court is persuaded that [Superintendent] Hansen personally was then and is now motivated by a desire to respond—according to his own philosophy—to an educational crisis in the District school system. On the other hand, the court cannot ignore the fact that until 1954 the District schools were by direction of law operated on a segregated basis. It cannot ignore the fact that of all the possible forms of ability grouping, the one that won acceptance in the District was the one that—with the exception of completely separate schools—involves the greatest amount of physical separation by grouping students in wholly distinct, homogeneous curriculum levels. It cannot ignore that the immediate and known effect of this separation would be to insulate the more academically developed white student from his less fortunate black schoolmate, thus minimizing the impact of integration; nor can the court ignore the fact that this same cushioning effect remains evident even today. Therefore, although the track system cannot be dismissed as nothing more than a subterfuge by which defendants are attempting to avoid the mandate of *Bolling v. Sharpe*, neither can it be said that the evidence shows racial considerations to be absolutely irrelevant to its adoption and absolutely irrelevant in its continued administration. To this extent the track system is tainted.

The court does not, however, rest its decision on a finding of intended racial discrimination. Apart from such intentional aspects, the effects of the track system must be held to be a violation of plaintiffs' constitutional rights. As the evidence in this case makes painfully clear, ability grouping as presently practiced in the District of Columbia school system is a denial of equal educational opportunity to the poor and a majority of the Negroes attending school in the nation's capital, a denial that contravenes not only the guarantees of the Fifth Amendment but also the fundamental premise of the track system itself. * * *

B. *Track Theory.*

Basic to an understanding of the conflict between the parties in this lawsuit is an appreciation of the theory that motivates the track system as it operates in the District school system. The most comprehensive statement of that theory can be found in Dr. Hansen's book, FOUR TRACK CURRICULUM FOR TODAY'S HIGH SCHOOLS, published in 1964. Although Dr. Hansen disclaims full responsibility for creating the track system, a reading of his book leaves no doubt that it was his firm guiding hand that shaped that system in its essential characteristics. Thus, as principal architect of the track system and as Superintendent of Schools, Dr. Hansen presumably can be looked to as the authoritative spokesman on the subject.

Purpose and philosophy. Dr. Hansen believes that the comprehensive high school (and the school system generally) must be systematically organized and structured to provide differing levels of education for students with widely differing levels of academic ability. This is the purpose of the track system. In expressing the track system's philosophy Dr. Hansen has said, "Every pupil in the school system must have the maximum opportunity for self-development and this can best be brought about by adjusting curriculum offerings to different levels of need and ability as the pupil moves through the stages of education and growth in our schools." And he has identified as the two objectives on which the track system is founded: "(1) The realization of the doctrine of equality of education and (2) The attainment of quality education."

Student types. Within the student body Dr. Hansen sees generally four types of students: the intellectually gifted, the above-average, the average, and the retarded. He assumes that each of these types of students has a maximum level of academic capability and, most importantly, that that level of ability can be accurately ascertained. The duty of the school is to identify these students and provide a curriculum commensurate with their respective abilities. Dr. Hansen contends that the traditional school curriculum—including the usual two-level method of ability grouping—does a disservice to those at either end of the ability spectrum.

The gifted student is not challenged, so that he becomes bored, lazy, and perhaps performs far below his academic potential; his intellectual talents are a wasted resource. The remedy lies in discovering the gifted student, placing him with others of his own kind, thereby stimulating him through this select association as well as a rigorous, demanding curriculum to develop his intellectual talent. Indeed, "the academically capable student should be required as a public necessity to take the academically challenging honors curriculum."

On the other hand, continues Dr. Hansen, the retarded or "stupid" student typically has been forced to struggle through a curriculum he cannot possibly master and only imperfectly comprehends. Typically he is slow to learn and soon falls behind in class; he repeatedly fails, sometimes repeating a grade again and again; he becomes isolated, frustrated, depressed, and—if he does not drop out before graduation—graduates with a virtually useless education. Here the remedy is seen as separating out the retarded student, directing him into a special curriculum geared to his limited abilities and designed to give him a useful "basic" education—one which makes no pretense of equalling traditionally taught curricula.

In short, Hansen views the traditional school curriculum as doing too little for some students and expecting too much of others. As for the latter type, whom Dr. Hansen characterizes as "the blue-collar student," going to school—a "white-collar occupation"—can be an artificial experience.

"Twelve years of white-collar experience is unrealistic preparation for the young man or woman who will suddenly make the change into work clothes for jobs in kitchens, stockrooms, street maintenance or building construction.

* * *

"One reason (for education's failure to meet the needs of the blue collar student) * * * is that it is at best an environment artificially created for the education of the young. From the beginning of his career in school, the child enjoys the comforts of a protected and unrealistic environment. Most of the Nation's classrooms are insulated from reality. To many students what happens in the classroom has little connection with what happens outside the classroom.

"Another reason * * * is that the school environment excludes most of the sterner discipline of the work-a-day world * * *."

Tracking. In order to tailor the educational process to the level appropriate to each student, Dr. Hansen adopted the track system. Each track is intended to be a separate and self-contained curriculum, with the educational content ranging from the very basic to the very advanced according to the track level. In the elementary and junior high schools three levels are used: Basic or Special Academic (retarded students), General (average and above-average), and Honors (gifted). In the senior high school a fourth level is added: the Regular Track, a college-preparatory track intended to accommodate the above-average student.

The significant feature of the track system in this regard is its emphasis on the ability of the student. A student's course of instruction depends upon what the school system decides he is capable of handling.
* * *

OPINION OF LAW

* * *

VI. THE TRACK SYSTEM

* * *

As the court's findings have shown, the track system is undeniably an extreme form of ability grouping. Students are early in elementary school sorted into homogeneous groups or tracks (and often into subgroups within a track), thereby being physically separated into different class-rooms. Not only is there homogeneity, in terms of supposed levels of ability—the intended result—but as a practical matter there is a distinct sameness in terms of socio-economic status as well. More importantly, each track offers a substantially different kind of education, both in pace of learning and in scope of subject matter. At the bottom there is the slow-paced, basic (and eventually almost purely low-skill vocational) Special Academic Track; at the top is the intense and challenging Honors program for the gifted student. For a student locked into one of the lower tracks, physical separation from those in other tracks is of course complete insofar as classroom relationships are concerned; and the limits on his academic progress, and ultimately the kind of life work he can hope to attain after graduation, are set by the orientation of the lower curricula. Thus those in the lower tracks are, for the most part, molded for various levels of vocational assignments; those in the upper tracks, on the other hand, are given the opportunity to prepare for the higher ranking jobs and, most significantly, for college.

In theory, since tracking is supposed to be kept flexible, relatively few students should actually ever be locked into a single track or curriculum. Yet, in violation of one of its principal tenets, the track system is not flexible at all. Not only are assignments permanent for 90% or more of the students but the vast majority do not even take courses outside their own curriculum. Moreover, another significant failure to implement track theory—and in major part responsible for the inflexibility just noted—is the lack of adequate remedial and compensatory education programs for the students assigned to or left in the lower tracks because of cultural handicaps. Although one of the express reasons for placing such students in these tracks is to facilitate remediation, little is being done to accomplish the task. Consequently, the lower track student, rather than obtaining an enriched educational experience, gets what is essentially a limited or watered-down curriculum.

These are, then, the significant features of the track system: separation of students into rigid curricula, which entails both physical segregation and a disparity of educational opportunity; and, for those consigned to the lower tracks, opportunities decidedly inferior to those available in the higher tracks.

A precipitating cause of the constitutional inquiry in this case is the fact that those who are being consigned to the lower tracks are the poor and the Negroes, whereas the upper tracks are the provinces of the more affluent and the whites. Defendants have not, and indeed could not have, denied that the pattern of grouping correlates remarkably with a student's status, although defendants would have it that the equation is to be stated in terms of income, not race. However, as discussed elsewhere, to focus solely on economics is to oversimplify the matter in the District of Columbia where so many of the poor are in fact the Negroes. And even if race could be ruled out, which it cannot, defendants surely "can no more discriminate on account of poverty than on account of religion, race, or color." As noted before, the law has a special concern for minority groups for whom the judicial branch of government is often the only hope for redressing their legitimate grievances; and a court will not treat lightly a showing that educational opportunities are being allocated according to a pattern that has unmistakable signs of invidious discrimination. Defendants, therefore, have a weighty burden of explaining why the poor and the Negro should be those who populate the lower ranks of the track system.

Since by definition the basis of the track system is to classify students according to their ability to learn, the only explanation defendants can legitimately give for the pattern of classification found in the District schools is that it does reflect students' abilities. If the discriminations being made are founded on anything other than that, then the whole premise of tracking collapses and with it any justification for relegating certain students to curricula designed for those of limited abilities. While government may classify persons and thereby effect disparities in treatment, those included within or excluded from the respective classes should be those for whom the inclusion or exclusion is appropriate; otherwise the classification risks becoming wholly irrational and thus unconstitutionally discriminatory. It is in this regard that the track system is fatally defective, because for many students placement is based on traits other than those on which the classification purports to be based.

The evidence shows that the method by which track assignments are made depends essentially on standardized aptitude tests which, although given on a system-wide basis, are completely inappropriate for use with a large segment of the student body. Because these tests are standardized primarily on and are relevant to a white middle class group of students, they produce inaccurate and misleading test scores when given to lower class and Negro students. As a result, rather than being classified according to ability to learn, these students are in reality being classified according to their socio-economic or racial status, or—more precisely—according to environmental and psychological factors which have nothing to do with innate ability.

Compounding and reinforcing the inaccuracies inherent in test measurements are a host of circumstances which further obscure the true abilities of the poor and the Negro. For example, teachers acting under false assumptions because of low test scores will treat the disadvantaged student in such a way as to make him conform to their low expectations; this acting out process—the self-fulfilling prophecy—makes it appear that the false assumptions were correct, and the student's real talent is wasted. Moreover, almost cynically, many Negro students are either denied or have limited access to the very kinds of programs the track system makes a virtual necessity: kindergartens; Honors programs for the fast-developing Negro student; and remedial and compensatory education programs that will bring the disadvantaged student back into the mainstream of education. Lacking these facilities, the student continues hampered by his cultural handicaps and continues to appear to be of lower ability than he really is. Finally, the track system as an institution cannot escape blame for the error in placements, for it is tracking that places such an emphasis on defining ability, elevating its importance to the point where the whole of a student's education and future are made to turn on his facility in demonstrating his qualifications for the higher levels of opportunity. Aside from the fact that this makes the consequences of misjudgments so much the worse, it also tends to alienate the disadvantaged student who feels unequal to the task of competing in an ethnocentric school system dominated by white middle class values; and alienated students inevitably do not reveal their true abilities—either in school or on tests.

All of these circumstances, and more, destroy the rationality of the class structure that characterizes the track system. Rather than reflecting classifications according to ability, track assignments are for many students placements based on status. Being, therefore, in violation of its own premise, the track system amounts to an unlawful discrimination against those students whose educational opportunities are being limited on the erroneous assumption that they are capable of accepting no more. * * *

CLOSING THE ACHIEVEMENT
GAP BY DETRACKING

Carol Corbett Burris & Kevin G. Welner
4/1/05 Phi Delta Kappan 594
2005 WLNR 5373631

* * *

Because African American and Hispanic students are consistently overrepresented in low-track classes, the effects of tracking greatly concern educators who are interested in closing the achievement gap. Detracking reforms are grounded in the established ideas that higher achievement follows from a more rigorous curriculum and that low-track classes with unchallenging curricula result in lower student achievement.[4] Yet, notwithstanding the wide acceptance of these ideas, we lack concrete case studies of mature detracking reforms and their effects. This article responds to that shortage, describing how the school district in which

---

4. CLIFFORD ADELMAN, ANSWERS IN THE TOOL BOX: ACADEMIC INTENSITY, ATTENDANCE PATTERNS, AND BACHELOR'S DEGREE ATTAINMENT (Washington, D.C.: Office of Educational Research, U.S. Department of Education, 1999), available on the Web at http://www.ed.gov/pubs/Toolbox; HENRY LEVIN, ACCELERATED SCHOOLS FOR AT RISK STUDENTS (New Brunswick, N.J.: Rutgers University, Center for Policy Research in Education, Report No. 142, 1988); Mano Singham, *The Achievement Gap: Myths and Realities*, PHI DELTA KAPPAN, April 2003, pp. 586 91; and JAY P. HEUBERT AND ROBERT M. HAUSER, HIGH STAKES: TESTING FOR TRACKING, PROMOTION, AND GRADUATION (Washington, D.C.: National Research Council, 1999).

Carol Burris serves as a high school principal was able to close the gap by offering its high-track curriculum to all students, in detracked classes.

    * * *

PROVIDING 'HIGH–TRACK' CURRICULUM TO ALL STUDENTS

The Rockville Centre School District is a diverse suburban school district located on Long Island. In the late 1990s, it embarked on a multiyear detracking reform that increased learning expectations for all students. The district began replacing its tracked classes with heterogeneously grouped classes in which the curriculum formerly reserved for the district's high-track students was taught.

This reform began as a response to an ambitious goal set by the * * * [District]: By the year 2000, 75% of all graduates will earn a New York State Regents diploma. At that time, the district and state rates of earning Regents diplomas were 58% and 38% respectively.

To qualify for a New York State Regents diploma, students must pass, at a minimum, eight end-of-course Regents examinations, including two in mathematics, two in laboratory sciences, two in social studies, one in English language arts, and one in a foreign language. * * *

Regents exams are linked with coursework; therefore, the district gradually eliminated low-track courses. The high school eased the transition by offering students instructional support classes and carefully monitoring the progress of struggling students. * * *

ACCELERATED MATHEMATICS IN HETEROGENEOUS CLASSES

    * * * In order to provide all students with ample opportunity to pass the needed courses and to study calculus prior to graduation, [the superintendent] decided that all students would study the accelerated math curriculum formerly reserved for the district's highest achievers. * * * [M]iddle school math teachers revised and condensed the curriculum. The new curriculum was taught to all students, in heterogeneously grouped classes. To support struggling learners, the school initiated support classes called math workshops and provided after-school help four afternoons a week.

The results were remarkable. Over 90% of incoming freshmen entered the high school having passed the first Regents math examination. The achievement gap dramatically narrowed. Between the years of 1995 and 1997, only 23% of regular education African American or Hispanic students had passed this algebra-based Regents exam before entering high school. After universally accelerating all students in heterogeneously grouped classes, the percentage more than tripled—up to 75%. The percentage of white or Asian American regular education students who passed the exam also greatly increased—from 54% to 98%.

DETRACKING THE HIGH SCHOOL

    * * *

The entire 1999 cohort also studied science in heterogeneous classes throughout middle school, and it became the first cohort to be heterogeneously grouped in ninth-grade English and social studies classes.

Ninth-grade teachers were pleased with the results. The tone, activities, and discussions in the heterogeneously grouped classes were academic, focused, and enriched. Science teachers reported that the heterogeneously grouped middle school science program prepared students well for ninth-grade biology.

Detracking at the high school level continued, paralleling the introduction of revised New York State curricula. Students in the 2000 cohort studied the state's new biology curriculum, "The Living Environment," in heterogeneously grouped classes. This combination of new curriculum and heterogeneous grouping resulted in a dramatic increase in the passing rate on the first science Regents exam, especially for minority students who were previously overrepresented in the low-track biology class. After just one year of heterogeneous grouping, the passing rate for African American and Hispanic students increased from 48% to 77%, while the passing rate for white and Asian American students increased from 85% to 94%.

The following September, the 2001 cohort became the first class to be heterogeneously grouped in all subjects in the ninth grade. The state's new multiyear "Math A" curriculum was taught to this cohort in heterogeneously grouped classes in both the eighth and ninth grades.

In 2003, some 10th-grade classes detracked. Students in the 2002 cohort became the first to study a heterogeneously grouped pre–International Baccalaureate (IB) 10th-grade curriculum in English and social studies. To help all students meet the demands of an advanced curriculum, the district provides every-other-day support classes in math, science, and English language arts. These classes are linked to the curriculum and allow teachers to pre–and post-teach topics to students needing additional reinforcement.

CLOSING THE GAP ON OTHER MEASURES THAT MATTER

New York's statewide achievement gap in the earning of Regents diplomas has persisted. In 2000, only 19.3% of all African American or Hispanic 12th–graders and 58.7% of all white or Asian American 12th–graders graduated with Regents diplomas. By 2003, while the percentage of students in both groups earning the Regents diploma increased (26.4% of African American or Hispanic students, 66.3% of white or Asian American students), the gap did not close.

In contrast, Rockville Centre has seen both an increase in students' rates of earning Regents diplomas and a decrease in the gap between groups. For those students who began South Side High School in 1996 (the graduating class of 2000), 32% of all African American or Hispanic and 88% of all white or Asian American graduates earned Regents diplomas. By the time the cohort of 1999 graduated in 2003, the gap had closed dramatically—82% of all African American or Hispanic and 97% of all white or Asian American graduates earned Regents diplomas. In fact, * * * for this 1999 cohort (the first to experience detracking in all middle school and most ninth-grade subjects), the Regents diploma rate for the district's minority students surpassed New York State's rate for white or Asian American students.

In order to ensure that the narrowing of the gap was not attributable to a changing population, we used binary logistic regression analyses to compare the probability of earning a Regents diploma before and after detracking. In addition to membership in a detracked cohort, the model included socioeconomic and special education status as covariates. Those students who were members of the 1996 and 1997 cohorts were compared with members of the 1998–2000 cohorts. We found that membership in a cohort subsequent to the detracking of middle school math was a significant contributor to earning a Regents diploma (p <.0001). In addition, low-SES students and special education students in the 2001 cohort also showed sharp improvement.

These same three cohorts (1998–2000) showed significant increases in the probability of minority students' studying advanced math courses. Controlling for prior achievement and SES, minority students' enrollment in trigonometry, precalculus, and Advanced Placement calculus all grew.[15] And as more students from those cohorts studied AP calculus, the enrollment gap decreased from 38% to 18% in five years, and the AP calculus scores significantly increased (p <.01).

Finally, detracking in the 10th grade, combined with teaching all students the pre-IB curriculum, appears to be closing the gap in the study of the IB curriculum. This year 50% of all minority students will study IB English and "History of the Americas" in the 11th grade. In the fall of 2003, only 31% chose to do so.

Achievement follows from opportunities—opportunities that tracking denies. The results of detracking in Rockville Centre are clear and compelling. When all students were taught the high-track curriculum, achievement rose for all groups of students—majority, minority, special education, low-SES, and high-SES. This evidence can now be added to the larger body of tracking research that has convinced the Carnegie Council for Adolescent Development, the National Governors' Association, and most recently the National Research Council to call for the reduction or elimination of tracking.[16] The Rockville Centre reform confirms common sense: closing the "curriculum gap" is an effective way to close the "achievement gap."

---

15. Carol Corbett Burris, Jay P. Heubert, and Henry M. Levin, MATH ACCELERATION FOR ALL, EDUCATIONAL LEADERSHIP, February 2004, pp. 68–71.

16. CARNEGIE COUNCIL ON ADOLESCENT DEVELOPMENT, TURNING POINTS: PREPARING AMERICAN YOUTH FOR THE 21ST CENTURY (New York: Carnegie Corporation, 1989); ABILITY GROUPING AND TRACKING: CURRENT ISSUES AND CONCERNS (Washington, D.C.: National Governors Association, 1993); and NATIONAL RESEARCH COUNCIL, ENGAGING SCHOOLS: FOSTERING HIGH SCHOOL STUDENTS' MOTIVATION TO LEARN (Washington, D.C.: National Academies Press, 2004).

NOTE

1. For updated research findings in this regard, *see* Carol Corbett Burris, Ed Wiley, Kevin Welner, & John Murphy, *Accountability, Rigor, and Detracking: Achievement Effects of Embracing a Challenging Curriculum As a Universal Good for All Students,* 110 Teachers College Record 571 (2008). Using a quasi-experimental cohort design to compare students' success before and after detracking, the authors find substantially better performance in the earning of the New York State Regents diploma and the diploma of the International Baccalaureate.

PROBLEM 25: TRACKING & ABILITY GROUPING

For each of these examples, as a matter of law, would the practices be upheld? As a matter of policy, should the practices be upheld? In light of the findings by the Hobson court and the recent developments documented in the Burris–Welner piece, what viable alternatives might be appropriate? Why?

A. After a court order mandating the desegregation of the Seminole County School District, students were placed in tracks based primarily on group intelligence test scores. Three tracks in elementary and junior high grades (special academic (retarded), general (average), and honors (gifted)), with a fourth track added in high school for above-average college-bound students. Movement between tracks bordered on the non-existent. Each track was provided with a different curriculum, commensurate with the students' perceived abilities. Low-income and black students were placed disproportionately in the low tracks. Key underlying assumptions, according to the district, were that each type of student had a maximum level of academic capability, and that this ability could be accurately ascertained.

B. After a court order mandating the desegregation of the Orchard School District, students in grades 4–12 were to be assigned to one of the two schools in the district on the basis of their California Achievement Test scores.

C. The Eldorado County School District set aside one of its eleven high schools as a "preferred," college-preparatory school which admitted students on the basis of past academic achievement. The percentage of students who qualified for admission was substantially disproportionate to the percentage of black, Hispanic, and low-income students in the district at large.

D. Several school districts in the State of Freedonia instituted ability grouping practices in the elementary grades, typically for reading and math only. Such practices were neither mandated nor prohibited by state law. Grouping decisions were predicated on a variety of factors, including subject-specific standardized tests and teacher evaluations. Movement between groups occurred regularly, based on continuous progress rating systems and formalized, periodic reevaluations of achievement.

B. THE PERSISTENCE OF THE STANDARDIZED TESTING CONTROVERSY

Legal challenges to standardized testing have mirrored the major public policy questions facing educators in this area today: what type of tests to use, and how to use them. Litigation has therefore focused on either the test instrument itself and/or the alleged misuse of these instruments.

Few people dispute the need for accountability measures that could help determine what is going on in the schools and how children are doing. The key questions that are raised in this context, however, focus on whether and to what extent current practices most appropriately and most effectively accomplish the task.

In this regard, it is especially important to note a basic principle of educational assessment and evaluation. Experts in the field are nearly unanimous in their findings that multiple measures yield the most precise and the most complete results. The prototypical multiple choice test only tells part of the story.

Yet multiple choice tests predominate in education today. U.S. public school students must take a very large number of these tests in the course of a given year (perhaps more than in any other country), and major life-changing decisions are often made based on the results of just one of them.

This section provides an introduction to these issues, which correlate directly with much of the material in the chapter. It focuses in particular on the *Debra P.* case, a landmark decision regarding the constitutionality of basing of such life-changing decisions on tests of questionable validity.

Issues raised in this section re-occur in Chapters 6 & 7, particularly in the educational quality inquiry, and notably under the "No Child Left Behind" Act.

DEBRA P. v. TURLINGTON

644 F.2d 397 (5th Cir. 1981)

FAY, CIRCUIT JUDGE:

The State of Florida, concerned about the quality of its public educational system, enacted statutory provisions leading to the giving of a competency examination covering certain basic skills. Many students passed the examination but a significant number failed. The failing group included a disparate number of blacks. This class action, brought on their behalf, challenges the right of the state to impose the passing of the examination as a condition precedent to the receipt of a high school diploma. The overriding legal issue of this appeal is whether the State of Florida can constitutionally deprive public school students of their high school diplomas on the basis of an examination which *may* cover matters not taught through the curriculum. We hold that the State may not constitutionally so deprive its students unless it has submitted proof of the curricular validity of the test. Accordingly, we vacate the judgment of the district court and remand for further findings of fact.

I.

* * *

We find, based upon stipulated facts, that because the state had not made any effort to make certain whether the test covered material actually studied in the classrooms of the state and because the record is insufficient in proof on that issue, the case must be remanded for further findings. If the test covers material not taught the students, it is unfair and violates the Equal Protection and Due Process clauses of the United States Constitution.

II.

At the outset, we wish to stress that neither the district court nor we are in a position to determine educational policy in the State of Florida. The state has determined that minimum standards must be met and that the quality of education must be improved. We have nothing but praise for these efforts. The state's plenary powers over education come from the powers reserved to the states through the Tenth Amendment, and usually they are defined in the state constitution. As long as it does so in a manner consistent with the mandates of the United States Constitution, a state may determine the length, manner, and content of any education it provides.

The United States courts have interfered with state educational directives only when necessary to protect freedoms and privileges guaranteed by the United States Constitution. In 1899, for example, in the case of *Cumming v. Board of Education*, the Court upheld the decision of a local board to close a black school while keeping a white school open. Finding that the decision was based on economic reasons, the Court said:

> [T]he education of the people in schools maintained by state taxation is a matter belonging to the respective States, and any interference on the part of Federal authority with the management of such schools cannot be justified except in the case of a clear and unmistakable disregard of the rights secured by the supreme law of the land.

While the outcome of the *Cumming* case might be questioned in this post *Brown* era, it must be remembered that it was not until just before the First World War that compulsory school attendance laws were in force in all states.[7] Public education was virtually unknown at the time of the adoption of the Constitution. In 1647 Colonial Massachusetts directed its towns to establish schools, and in 1749, Franklin proposed the Philadelphia academy. Until after the turn of the century, education was primarily

---

7. Brown v. Board of Education, 347 U.S. 483, 489–90 n.4, 74 S. Ct. 686, 691, n.4 (1954).

private and usually sectarian. Once part of the government, however, education became a significant governmental responsibility. As the Court noted in *Brown v. Board of Education*, 347 U.S. 483, 493, 74 S. Ct. 686, 691 (1954):

> Today, education is perhaps the most important function of State and local governments. Compulsory school attendance laws and the great expenditures for education both demonstrate our recognition of the importance of education to our democratic society.

Stating that the provision of education ranks at the apex of the functions of a state, the Court in *Wisconsin v. Yoder*, 406 U.S. 205, 92 S. Ct. 1526 (1971) was required to balance the state's need for its citizens to be educated against the citizens' hallowed right to free exercise of religion. "There is no doubt," the Court said, "as to the power of a state, having a high responsibility for education of its citizens, to impose reasonable regulations for the control and duration of basic education."

Though the state has plenary power, it cannot exercise that power without reason and without regard to the United States Constitution. Although the Court has never labeled education as a "fundamental right" automatically triggering strict scrutiny of state actions, see *San Antonio School District v. Rodriguez*, 411 U.S. 1, 93 S. Ct. 1278 (1972), it is clear that if the state does provide an educational system, it must do so in a non-discriminatory fashion. "Among other things, the State is constrained to recognize a student's legitimate entitlement to a public education as a property interest which may be protected by the Due Process Clause...."

III.

It is in the light of the foregoing discussion of the relationship between the state and federal governments that we must analyze the plaintiffs' claims that [the Florida State Assessment Test (SSAT II)] violates the equal protection and due process clauses of the Fourteenth Amendment. It is clear that in establishing a system of free public education and in making school attendance mandatory,[8] the state has created an expectation in the students. From the students' point of view, the expectation is that if a student attends school during those required years, and indeed more, and if he takes and passes the required courses, he will receive a diploma. This is a property interest as that term is used constitutionally. Although the state of Florida constitutionally may not be obligated to establish and maintain a school system, it has done so, required attendance and created a mutual expectation that the student who is successful will graduate with a diploma. This expectation can be viewed as a state-created "understanding" that secures certain benefits and that supports claims of entitlement to those benefits. As the trial court noted, "graduation is the logical extension of successful attend-

---

8. FLA.STAT.ANN. § 232.01 (West Supp. 1981) mandates that children between the ages of 6 and 16 attend school.

ance," and as appellees note in brief, before SSAT II, a student completing the necessary number of credits would graduate with a diploma.

Based upon this implied property right, we find that the trial court was correct in holding that the implementation schedule for the test violated due process of law.

* * *

The due process violation potentially goes deeper than deprivation of property rights without adequate notice. When it encroaches upon concepts of justice lying at the basis of our civil and political institutions, the state is obligated to avoid action which is arbitrary and capricious, does not achieve or even frustrates a legitimate state interest, or is fundamentally unfair. We believe that the state administered a test that was, at least on the record before us, fundamentally unfair in that it may have covered matters not taught in the schools of the state.

Testimony at trial by experts for both plaintiffs and defendants indicated that several types of studies were done before and after the administration of the test. The experts agreed that of the several types of validity studies,[10] a content validity study would be most important for a competency examination such as SSAT II. The trial court apparently found that the test had adequate content validity, but we find that holding upon the record before us to be clearly erroneous. In the field of competency testing, an important component of content validity is curricular validity, defined by defendants' expert Dr. Foster, as "things that are currently taught." This record is simply insufficient in proof that the test administered measures what was actually taught in the schools of Florida.

* * *

Dr. Thomas H. Fisher, Administrator of the Student Assessment Section, Department of Education, testified that the DOE merely assumed that things were being taught. Dr. John E. Hills, professor of Educational Research at Florida State University, testified that the test reliably and validly assessed applications of basic communications and math skills to everyday situations, but he agreed that everything on the test might not have been taught. Appellants placed into evidence some math books and communications teaching materials, but at least one teacher, Mr. Crihfield, testified that he did not cover the whole book in class.

---

10. Basic types of validity as defined by the American Psychological Association, *Standards for Educational and Psychological Tests* (1974) are as follows:

Criterion—related validity—measurements of how well the test items predict the future performance of the test takers and how well the test results correlate with other criteria which might provide the same type of information.

content validity—measurements of how well a test measures a representative sample of behaviors in the universe of situations the test is intended to represent.

construct validity—how well the test measures the construct (defined as the theoretical idea developed to explain and organize some aspects of existing knowledge) for which it was designed.

For an excellent discussion of the APA Standards as they relate to competency testing, see M.S. McClung, *Competency Testing Programs: Legal and Educational Issues*, 47 FORDHAM L. REV. 651, 683 (1979).

We acknowledge that in composing items for a test, the writer is dealing with applications of knowledge, and therefore the form of the test question would not necessarily be the same as the form of the information taught in class. We think, however, that fundamental fairness requires that the state be put to test on the issue of whether the students were tested on material they were or were not taught.

We note that in requiring the state to prove on remand that the material was covered in class, we are not substituting our judgment for that of the state legislature on a matter of state policy. We do not question the right of the state to condition the receipt of a diploma upon the passing of a test so long as it is a fair test of that which was taught. Nor do we seek to dictate what subjects are to be taught or in what manner. We do not share appellants' fear that our decision would prevent new items from being added to the curriculum. * * *

Just as a teacher in a particular class gives the final exam on what he or she has taught, so should the state give its final exam on what has been taught in its classrooms.

It follows that if the test is found to be invalid for the reason that it tests matters outside the curriculum, its continued use would violate the Equal Protection Clause. In analyzing the constitutionality of the examination under the Equal Protection Clause, the trial court stated, "[i]f the test by dividing students into two categories, passers and failers, did so without a rational relation to the purpose for which it was designed, then the Court would be compelled to find the test unconstitutional." Analyzing the test from the viewpoint of its objectives, the court found that it does have adequate construct validity, that is, it does test functional literacy as defined by the Board.[13] We accept this finding and affirm that part of the trial court's opinion holding that having a functional literacy examination bears a rational relation to a valid state interest. That finding is, however, subject to a further finding on remand that the test is a fair test of that which was taught. If the test is not fair, it cannot be said to be rationally related to a state interest.

* * *

CONCLUSION

* * * We hold * * * that the State may not deprive its high school seniors of the economic and educational benefits of a high school diploma until it has demonstrated that the SSAT II is a fair test of that which is taught in its classrooms and that the racially discriminatory impact is not due to the educational deprivation in the "dual school" years.

* * *

NOTES

1. In general, testing instruments and practices have been successfully challenged under one or more of the following theories: perpetuating racial segregation, lack of test validity, cultural/linguistic bias; and gender bias.

---

13. Functional literacy is defined as "the ability to apply basic skills in reading, writing, and arithmetic to problems and tasks of a practical nature as encountered in everyday life."

Perpetuating Segregation. Several cases have discussed the relationship between ability grouping, standardized testing, tracking, and racial segregation. In determining whether tracking and ability grouping practices are constitutional, the courts have looked at several key factors:

(1) the methods of assessment and evaluation that the schools rely upon when making placement decisions;

(2) the extent to which these placement decisions are reassessed on a regular basis;

(3) how often the students actually change groups or move into different tracks if such changes are warranted; and

(4) whether a disproportionate number of minority students are placed in the lower groups or tracks. *Georgia State Conference of Branches of NAACP v. Georgia,* 775 F.2d 1403, 1409–1412, 1417–1420 (11th Cir. 1985). *See generally* Note, *Teaching Inequality: The Problem of Public School Tracking* 102 Harv. L. Rev. 1318,1323–1326 (1989).

The critical message from tracking cases is that the courts will not allow educators to perpetuate or promote racial segregation. A disproportionate number of minority students in the lower groups is not, in and of itself, unconstitutional. However, if this disproportionate placement is the result of questionable assessment techniques, if student performance is not carefully monitored, and if movement between groups does not occur on a regular basis, educators will have difficulty justifying their actions. Assessment practices, then, must not exclude or segregate children because of race, ethnicity, or national origin.

Test Validity. A fundamental educational principle in the area of testing is that a test should measure what it is supposed to measure: i.e., that the test should be "valid." It follows, then, that tests of educational progress should be accurate measures of what a child is actually learning. Where test validity is shown to be lacking, and where the result of failing to pass the test has major implications for the student's life, the test is subject to being challenged on due process grounds. Where the test has a disproportionate impact upon a particular racial or ethnic group, the test can be challenged on equal protection grounds as well.

In *Debra P. v. Turlington,* plaintiffs successfully challenged the Florida minimum competency testing program by focusing on the validity of the test instrument itself. An injunction was issued prohibiting further use of the exam until the state could show that the schools were teaching the material that was included in the exam.

Cultural/Linguistic Bias. Latino students in many school districts in California were overrepresented in special education classes in the 1960s. This led to a class action lawsuit in 1970 by nine elementary school pupils against the State of California—*Diana v. State Board of Education.* They alleged that they had been misdiagnosed as mentally retarded on the basis of biased and invalid intelligence tests (the Stanford–Binet and Wechsler Intelligence Scale for Children–Revised [WISC–R]). These misdiagnoses, they claimed, resulted in adverse stigma and irreparable educational harm.

The bias charge was based upon two contentions. First, the tests were not administered in the children's first language (Spanish). Second, the tests were culturally biased because they did not take into account the students' Mexican, rural, and migrant background. Apparently recognizing the validity of at least a portion of these assertions, the State Board settled out of court in 1974. *Diana v. State Board of Education, et al.*, No. C–70–37.

A year later, the Education for All Handicapped Children Act, Public Law 94–142, was passed by Congress. Consistent with the *Diana* settlement, the Act provides that testing and evaluation materials must 1) be racially and culturally nondiscriminatory and 2) be "administered in the child's native language or mode of communication, unless it is clearly not feasible to do so."

In another case, *Larry P. v. Riles,* African–American students successfully challenged the use of intelligence tests for the purpose of special education placements. After concluding that these tests were indeed culturally biased, the court ruled that school districts are prohibited from administering standardized intelligence tests to African–American students with regard to special education eligibility or placement in special day classes for the educable mentally retarded (E.M.R.). See infra, Chapter 7.

In situations where students of racial and ethnic diversity are inappropriately placed or overrepresented in special education, a successful challenge to current testing practices could be based upon the *Diana* and *Larry P.* cases. Expert testimony could be used to demonstrate that a particular test was culturally biased. A court would then be asked to conclude that, under the rationale of the *Diana* settlement and *Larry P.* decision, any administration of a culturally-biased test to a racial or ethnic minority group for the purposes of educational placement would violate the law.

Gender Bias. In 1989, a federal district court in New York State found that the Scholastic Aptitude Test (SAT) was biased on the basis of gender. It held that New York may not determine the winners of its Empire & Regents Scholarship Awards by relying solely on SAT scores. "After a careful review of the evidence," the court declared in *Sharif v. N.Y. State Education Department,* "SAT scores capture a student's academic achievement no more than a student's yearbook photograph captures the full range of her experiences in high school."

Adapted from Allan H. Keown & Stuart Biegel, *General Legal Principles Involving Challenges to Standardized Tests,* Ca. State Dep't of Ed. Legal Advisory LO: 2–92 (Nov. 30, 1992).

2. A new study funded by the National Science Foundation found that by 2008 girls were performing as well as boys on standardized math tests. A key factor, according to study co-author Marcia Linn, is that girls are taking just as many advanced math courses as boys. The study was based on math scores from seven million students in 10 states who were tested pursuant to the NCLB Act:

Janet Hyde, a professor at the University of Wisconsin, Madison, who led the study, said the persistent stereotypes about girls and math had taken a toll.

"The stereotype that boys do better at math is still held widely by teachers and parents," Dr. Hyde said. "And teachers and parents guide girls, giving them advice about what courses to take, what careers to pursue. I still hear anecdotes about guidance counselors steering girls away from engineering, telling them they won't be able to do the math." *See* Tamar Lewin, *Math Scores Show No Gap for Girls, Study Finds,* N.Y. Times, July 25, 2008.

3. Inevitably, controversies regarding tests administered by the Educational Testing Service (ETS) continue to arise. For example, it was reported that the proctoring environment at an Orange County high school in the spring of 2008 led ETS to void the advanced placement (AP) exams of nearly 400 students:

> Students at Trabuco Hills High School were allowed to talk, consult study aids, send text messages to friends and leave the room in groups during the exam, the Educational Testing Service said.

> Meanwhile, an attorney representing many of the students sued ETS on Wednesday, arguing that the Princeton, N.J.-based nonprofit failed to conduct even the most cursory investigation before voiding the students' exams.

> An attorney representing ETS conceded that it was impossible to know whether students took advantage of the poor proctoring at the high school to cheat, but said it would be unfair to other AP test takers throughout the nation to allow their scores to stand. * * *

> ETS has strict rules about test-taking protocol, but at Trabuco, as 385 students sat for various subject exams, there were insufficient proctors in classrooms and inadequate monitoring of students, who were allowed to sit close together and face each other. Some proctors were seen reading or sleeping and some left the rooms, according to students. * * * Seema Mehta, *Group Explains Voiding of Tests in O.C.,* L.A. Times, July 24, 2008.

C. INTERSCHOLASTIC AND INTERCOLLEGIATE ATHLETICS GENERALLY

PROBLEM 26: SCHOOL SPORTS, TESTING, AND RELATED ACADEMIC ISSUES

Consider the following hypotheticals, all taking place at public educational institutions in the fictional state of Columbia.

A. The Marine Valley Interscholastic Federation adopts a policy whereby no student in any Marine Valley school is eligible to participate in interscholastic athletics unless he or she scores in the "basic" or above category in every subject on the Columbia Standards Test. Plaintiff, after obtaining proof that much of the material on the test is not covered in class, files a lawsuit challenging the policy under principles articulated in *Debra P. v. Turlington.*

B. The University of Catalina Ridge adopts a policy whereby no student may participate in intercollegiate athletics unless he or she scores at least 1000 on the SAT. A group of female students file a lawsuit challenging the policy under principles articulated in gender equity cases, statutes, and regulations.

C. A student athlete at the University of Vernal Falls becomes ineligible to participate after failing introductory psychology. After obtaining proof that 7 of the 100 questions on the multiple choice final tested material that was neither in the readings nor covered in class, he files a lawsuit seeking relief under a variety of legal theories.

What arguments will plaintiffs set forth? What result? Discuss.

1. EQUAL EDUCATIONAL OPPORTUNITY ISSUES IN SCHOOL SPORTS

STEFFES v. CALIFORNIA INTERSCHOLASTIC FED'N

176 Cal.App.3d 739, 222 Cal.Rptr. 355 (1986)

ARABIAN, ASSOCIATE JUSTICE.

INTRODUCTION

The principal question in this case of first impression is whether, under the California Constitution, the right to participate in interscholastic athletics is a "fundamental right."

FACTS

Plaintiff and appellant, Kent Conrad Steffes * * * appeals from an order of the trial court denying his petition for a preliminary injunction to restrain defendants * * * from enforcing a California Interscholastic Federation (CIF) rule under which Steffes was declared ineligible to participate in varsity level competition in basketball and volleyball at Palisades High School (Pali High) during the 1984–1985 academic year.

Defendant CIF is a statewide organization that was established to enact and enforce rules and regulations governing secondary school interscholastic athletics in the state of California. Defendant CIF, Los Angeles City Section, is a division of CIF with responsibility for administering interscholastic athletics in the Los Angeles City School District. * * *

Steffes spent his freshman and sophomore years at Brentwood School. During his sophomore year (the 1983–1984 academic year), Steffes participated in junior varsity cross-country and varsity basketball and volleyball. At the end of his sophomore year, Steffes' parents decided to transfer him to Pali High, the public high school for the area in which the Steffes' family home is located. Steffes was not encouraged nor recruited for athletics by any of the personnel at Pali High.

Since Steffes transferred from Brentwood School to Pali High without a change of his parents' residence, CIF rule 214 (Rule 214) rendered him ineligible to participate in varsity athletics for one calendar year after his transfer.

* * *

According to Thomas E. Byrnes, Commissioner of the CIF, the purpose of Rule 214 is to "eliminate or minimize recruiting and school shopping."

Steffes filed an "Application for Residential Eligibility Form 214" with the CIF Los Angeles City Section to obtain a waiver of his ineligibility to participate in varsity level athletics at Pali High. In the application, Steffes stated that he had not been influenced to transfer schools for recruitment reasons. Despite this fact, the principal at Brentwood, Hunter M. Temple, declined to approve unrestricted athletic eligibility for Steffes. In a letter to Jim Cheffers, the Los Angeles City Section Director of Athletics for CIF, Mr. Temple stated that he supported the Rule 214 restriction because "a coherent athletic program can only be achieved if students complete [their] program here [at Brentwood School]."

* * *

CONTENTIONS

1.   The trial court erred in applying the "rational basis" test, rather than the "strict scrutiny" test, to review Rule 214 because, under the California Constitution, the fundamental right to a public school education includes the right to participate in interscholastic athletics.

a.   Rule 214 impermissibly deprives Steffes of his fundamental right to participate in extracurricular activities offered by a public school.

* * *

DISCUSSION

* * *

II.   *The trial court did not err in applying the "rational basis" test to determine whether Rule 214 violates the equal protection guarantee of the California Constitution, because the right to participate in interscholastic athletics is not a fundamental right requiring "strict scrutiny."*

Steffes contends the trial court erred in denying his request for a preliminary injunction because it applied the "rational basis" test to determine whether Rule 214 violates the equal protection guarantee of the California Constitution. He argues the trial court should have applied the "strict scrutiny" standard of review, because the fundamental right to a public school education, which is guaranteed by the California Constitution, includes the right to participate in interscholastic athletics.

We note initially that, inasmuch as CIF is an organization with responsibility for administering interscholastic athletics in all California secondary schools the enforcement of its rules constitutes "state action" for purposes of constitutional analysis.

* * *

* * * The strict scrutiny test for which Steffes argues applies only in cases involving "suspect classifications" or touching on "fundamental rights."

The right to public education is a fundamental right under the California Constitution. In *Hartzell v. Connell*, the California Supreme Court had the opportunity to address the question whether extracurricular activities are encompassed within the *Serrano* concept of education as a fundamental right but, it did not do so.[3] Instead, the Court simply held that "all educational activities—curricular or 'extracurricular'—offered to students by school districts fall within the free school guarantee of article IX, section 5 [of the California Constitution]."

The *Hartzell* Court recognized that extracurricular activities (which would include interscholastic sports) constitute "an integral component of public education" and are " 'generally recognized as a fundamental ingredient of the educational process.' " However, the *Hartzell* majority never concluded that extracurricular activities are encompassed within the *Serrano* concept of education as a "fundamental right."

Therefore, the question of whether participation in interscholastic athletics involves a fundamental right requiring strict judicial scrutiny is an issue of first impression in California. However, other state and federal courts have recently addressed the issue.

In a number of these decisions, the courts have concluded that the right to participate in interscholastic athletics is not a fundamental right because, under the *federal constitution,* even the right to education itself is not a "fundamental right" which requires strict judicial scrutiny. (*See, e.g., San Antonio Independent School District v. Rodriguez* (1973) 411 U.S. 1, 29–39, 93 S. Ct. 1278, 1295–1300, * * *.) Other courts, based on a procedural due process analysis, have rejected the notion that participation in interscholastic athletics is a property right.

To the extent these other courts rely for their rationale on the federal constitution (or state constitutions which provide education is not a fundamental right), they are not directly in point. That is so because,

---

3. However, Chief Justice Bird, the author of the majority opinion, in a separate concurring opinion, stated: "[E]xtracurricular activities—like their credit-generating counterparts—promote the constitutionally recognized purposes of public education. Accordingly, they are encompassed within the concept of *education as a fundamental interest.*" (emphasis added).

under the California Constitution, public education is itself a fundamental right requiring strict judicial scrutiny, while public education is not a fundamental right under the federal constitution (see *San Antonio Independent School District v. Rodriguez, supra,* 411 U.S. 1, 29–39, 93 S. Ct. 1278, 1295–1300).

However, the fact that public education is a fundamental right under the California Constitution does not compel a finding that in California the right to participate in interscholastic athletics is also a fundamental right entitled to the highest degree of constitutional protection. Therefore, we hold that an equal protection challenge involving that right is properly tested by the rational basis standard, rather than by the strict scrutiny standard of judicial review.

* * *

CONCLUSION

The rules, regulations and procedures discussed herein, as they relate to the interscholastic athletic transfer rule, are prophylactic in nature, reasonable in scope and rationally based. As such, they neither trammel upon fundamental rights nor occasion unnecessary burdens.

Curtailment or reduction of the abuses and transgressions which threaten to undermine student athletics are salutory goals which preserve equity between schools and protect the integrity of extracurricular programs.

DISPOSITION

The order of the trial court denying the preliminary injunction is affirmed.

Note

1. In *Young v. Montgomery County Board of Education,* 922 F.Supp. 544 (M.D. Ala. 1996), plaintiffs challenged a 1995 policy requiring student athletes to sit out a year of eligibility if they transfer to "a school for which they are not otherwise zoned" under a special "Majority-to-Minority Transfer Program." Plaintiffs, all of whom were black students negatively impacted by the policy, argued that they were discriminated against under both the Fourteenth Amendment Equal Protection Clause and Title VI of the Civil Rights Act of 1964. While the court acknowledged that the school board members knew that the policy "would disparately impact black student athletes, their knowledge of the disparate impact is not enough to prove that they intended to discriminate based on race, especially in light of their clear intent to benefit the predominantly black schools of W. Montgomery." The court held for the defendants.

WASHINGTON v. INDIANA HIGH SCH. ATHLETIC ASS'N, INC.

181 F.3d 840 (7th Cir. 1999)

RIPPLE, CIRCUIT JUDGE.

Eric Washington and Central Catholic High School obtained a preliminary injunction in the district court enjoining the Indiana High School Athletic Association ("IHSAA") from denying Mr. Washington athletic eligibility for the second semester of the 1998–99 school year. The IHSAA appeals. We affirm the district court's decision to grant the preliminary injunction.

I

BACKGROUND

A. Facts

Mr. Washington is a learning disabled student at Central Catholic High School ("Central Catholic") in Lafayette, Indiana. Throughout elementary school, he had been allowed to advance to the next grade despite academic insufficiency. He was held back, however, in the eighth grade. During the first semester of the 1994–95 academic year, while he was repeating the eighth grade, he continued to receive failing grades. School officials then decided that he might do better if he stayed with his class, and they therefore advanced him to the ninth grade at Lafayette Jefferson High School at the beginning of the second semester during the 1994–95 academic year. In this new environment, Mr. Washington continued to fail during that semester and throughout the following academic year. Early in the 1996–97 academic year, a school counselor suggested that Mr. Washington drop out of high school. Mr. Washington took that advice.

In the summer of 1997, Mr. Washington * * * met the coach of the Central Catholic basketball team, Chad Dunwoody * * * and decided to attend Central Catholic * * * and play basketball. Mr. Dunwoody, who also became Mr. Washington's academic mentor at Central Catholic, suggested that Mr. Washington be tested for learning disabilities. Although Mr. Washington had previously been tested and found not to be learning disabled, a January 1998 test indicated that he was in fact learning disabled.

The IHSAA has a rule that limits a student's athletic eligibility to the first eight semesters following the student's commencement of the ninth grade ("the eight semester rule"). The purposes of that rule, according to the IHSAA, include discouraging redshirting, promoting competitive equality, protecting students' safety, creating opportunities for younger students and promoting the idea that academics are more important than athletics. Under the rule in question, because Mr. Washington entered the ninth grade during the second semester of the 1994–95 academic year, he would no longer be eligible to play basketball in the second semester of the 1998–99 year (nine semesters after he began the ninth grade).

Central Catholic applied for a waiver of the eight semester rule for Mr. Washington. It requested that the IHSAA not count the semesters that he was not enrolled in any high school for purposes of eligibility under the eight semester rule. It requested a waiver under IHSAA Rule C12–3, which allows an exemption "if a student is injured which necessitates the student's complete withdrawal from the school or prohibits enrollment in the school for that semester, and the student does not receive any academic credit for that semester." Central Catholic also requested a waiver under IHSAA Rule 17–8, referred to by the parties as "the hardship rule." That rule allows the IHSAA not to enforce a rule if strict enforcement in the particular case would not serve to accomplish the purpose of the rule, the spirit of the rule would not be violated, and there is a showing of undue hardship in the particular case. Even though it had granted waivers for physical injuries in the past, the IHSAA denied Mr. Washington's application. Mr. Washington appealed the denial to the IHSAA Executive Committee, which denied the appeal.

* * * [Our] focus is exclusively on the eight semester rule; it is challenged on the ground that failure to grant a waiver of the eight semester rule in this case violates Title II of the Americans with Disabilities Act, 42 U.S.C. § 12132.

* * *

II

DISCUSSION

* * *

To receive protection under Title II of the ADA, the plaintiffs must establish that the IHSAA rendered Mr. Washington ineligible to play "by reason of" his disability.[8] The IHSAA contends that Mr. Washington has not presented any evidence that the IHSAA discriminated intentionally on the basis of disability. It further submits that Mr. Washington's ineligibility stems not from his disability but from the application of a facially neutral eight semester rule and the passage of time. In reply, the plaintiffs contend that they need not prove intentional discrimination. They further submit that they must show only that, but for Mr. Washington's disability, he would be eligible.

We cannot accept the suggestion that liability under Title II of the Discrimination Act must be premised on an intent to discriminate on the basis of disability. This court previously has recognized that a plaintiff making a claim under the Rehabilitation Act need not prove an impermissible intent. As we have noted, this and other circuits interpret § 504 of

---

8. Title II of the ADA provides: Subject to the provisions of this subchapter, no qualified individual with a disability shall, by reason of such disability, be excluded from participation in or be denied the benefits of the services, programs, or activities of a public entity, or be subjected to discrimination by any such entity. 42 U.S.C. § 12132 (1999).

the Rehabilitation Act and Title II of the ADA as coextensive, except for differences not relevant here. Although the Supreme Court has not held squarely that a plaintiff need not prove discriminatory intent, it has implied that requiring such proof would be contrary to the intent of Congress. In *Choate,* the Court indicated that there is strong support in the legislative history for the proposition that the Rehabilitation Act was not intended to prohibit solely intentional discrimination. "Discrimination against the handicapped was perceived by Congress to be most often the product, not of invidious animus, but rather of thoughtlessness and indifference—of benign neglect." The Court also noted that "much of the conduct that Congress sought to alter in passing the Rehabilitation Act would be difficult if not impossible to reach were the Act construed to proscribe only conduct fueled by a discriminatory intent." Moreover, the other circuits that have considered the issue have taken the view that a plaintiff need not prove an impermissible intent under § 504 of the Rehabilitation Act and Title II of the ADA.

* * *

The approach the Sixth Circuit has taken, and the approach we take, does not completely do away with a discrimination requirement. We simply hold that it is possible to demonstrate discrimination on the basis of disability by a defendant's refusal to make a reasonable accommodation. Therefore, we conclude that the plaintiffs need not prove that the IHSAA intended to discriminate on the basis of disability. The statute simply requires that the plaintiffs establish that the defendant's refusal to grant Mr. Washington a waiver was a failure to make a reasonable accommodation. * * *

We believe * * * that Mr. Washington has met the causation requirement for his claims. The "by reason of" language merely indicates that he must establish that, but for his learning disability, he would have been eligible to play sports in his junior year. Simply stated, Mr. Washington claims that his disability caused him to drop out of school; otherwise he would have been able to play high school basketball. In the absence of his disability, the passage of time would not have made him ineligible. There is ample record evidence to support Mr. Washington's claim. Mark Zello, a school psychologist, testified at the preliminary injunction hearing. He stated that Mr. Washington's learning disability caused him to fail at school, and that students with learning disabilities like Mr. Washington's have a high drop-out rate. Moreover, Zello testified that Mr. Washington has above average intelligence and, without the learning disability, would be fully capable of performing in high school. Under these circumstances, the district court was justified in concluding that, but for Mr. Washington's learning disability, he would not have dropped out of school.

* * *

* * * [W]aiver of the rule in Mr. Washington's case does not indicate that athletics is valued over education. Indeed, waiver of the rule in Mr. Washington's case has promoted his education. Mr. Washington has reentered school because of basketball, has improved his grades in part due to the influence of basketball and his coach, and is even considering going to college.

* * *

[W]e affirm the judgment of the district court.

PROBLEM 27: COOPER V. CLARION UNIFIED SCHOOL DISTRICT (CUSD)

The following events take place in the fictional state of Valhalla.

By the time he was in kindergarten, it was apparent to all who knew him that Kevin Cooper would be a gifted athlete. Basketball soon became his favorite sport, particularly since he was always so much taller than most of his peers.

Kevin, an African–American student, grew up in the city of Clarion, which was served by a large urban public school district. All the CUSD secondary schools grouped students by ability in two subject areas: English and Mathematics.

Throughout his elementary and junior high years, Kevin was encouraged by the educators in his life to build his athletic skills. Basketball was seen as his future livelihood, his "ticket out of the ghetto." Thus, although Kevin was a bright young man, he put very little effort into his academic subjects.

Indeed, at Clarion High, the coaching staff had identified a "preferred program" for top student athletes. With the help of school counselors and administrators, many athletes were typically kept in the "remedial" English and math classes. For social studies and science, these same athletes were channeled into classes that were either taught by coaches or by teachers who were "supporters" of the athletic program and would help the students "get by."

Kevin had been placed in the remedial English and math classes when he entered middle school, and remained there until he graduated from Clarion High. He continued to receive passing grades in all his classes, typically by expending very little effort. On the basketball court, as a muscular power forward, Kevin started for the varsity team three years in a row. In his senior year, having grown to an agile 6–10, he led the school to the state championship . . . averaging 31 points and 17 rebounds a game. He was rated the top high school basketball player in the entire state of Valhalla.

Three weeks after graduation, however, Kevin was badly injured in a tragic automobile accident. His left knee was crushed, and although a series of miraculous operations enabled him to walk (albeit with a bad limp), his basketball career had ended.

Kevin enrolled in a junior college, but found that even the basic subjects were too difficult for him, and soon dropped out. With few job prospects, he faced a future that was uncertain at best.

* * *

One day, while attending a local college basketball game, Kevin happened to be sitting next to an attorney who recognized him and remembered reading about his high school exploits. Kevin told the attorney that he was only working on an irregular basis, and spoke bitterly about his lack of preparation for junior college. During the conversation, it became apparent that Kevin knew of many other former black athletes who had pursued a similar "academic program" in the Clarion schools and had graduated with a similar level of skills.

Eventually, a class action suit was filed against the district in federal court. Not only did the former black athletes seek a mandatory injunction for themselves (i.e. additional training in basic skills), but they sought wide-ranging injunctive and declaratory relief for current black athletes in the Clarion School District.

What legal theories, identified in this chapter, might be employed on behalf of the plaintiffs? What additional facts might need to be identified before plaintiffs might have a chance of prevailing? What changes in existing law might be necessary before they could, in fact, prevail?

2. TITLE IX ISSUES IN SCHOOL SPORTS

NEAL v. BOARD OF TRUSTEES OF THE CAL. STATE UNIVS.

198 F.3d 763 (9th Cir. 1999)

CYNTHIA HOLCOMB HALL, CIRCUIT JUDGE:

The instant case requires us to consider whether Title IX prevents a university in which male students occupy a disproportionately high percentage of athletic roster spots from making gender-conscious decisions to reduce the proportion of roster spots assigned to men. We hold that Title IX does not bar such remedial actions.

* * * Neal's suit alleged that the decision of California State University, Bakersfield ("CSUB") to reduce the number of spots on its men's wrestling team, undertaken as part of a university-wide program to achieve "substantial proportionality" between each gender's participation in varsity sports and its composition in the campus's student body, violated Title IX and the Equal Protection Clause of the United States Constitution. * * *

I.

Defendant/Appellant CSUB is a large public university where female students outnumbered male students by roughly 64% to 36% in 1996. The composition of CSUB's varsity athletic rosters, however, was quite different. In the 1992–93 academic year, male students took 61% of the university's spots on athletic rosters and received 68% of CSUB's available athletic scholarship money.

This imbalance helped prompt a lawsuit by the California chapter of the National Organization for Women, alleging that the California State University system was violating a state law that is similar to the federal government's Title IX. That lawsuit eventually settled, resulting in a consent decree mandating, inter alia, that each Cal State campus have a proportion of female athletes that was within five percentage points of the proportion of female undergraduate students at that school. This portion of the consent decree was patterned after the first part of the three-part Title IX compliance test promulgated by the Department of Education's Office for Civil Rights ("OCR").

When the university agreed to the consent decree, * * * CSUB administrators were seriously constrained in what they could spend on athletic programs. The university chose to adopt squad size targets, which would encourage the expansion of the women's teams while limiting the size of the men's teams. In order to comply with the consent decree, CSUB opted for smaller men's teams across the board, rejecting the alternative of eliminating some men's teams entirely. CSUB's plan was designed to bring it into compliance with the consent decree by the 1997–98 academic year, meaning that female students would fill at least 55% of the spaces on the school's athletic teams.[1]

As part of this across-the-board reduction in the number of slots available to men's athletic teams, the size of the men's wrestling team was capped at 27. Although the reduction was protested vigorously by wrestling coach Terry Kerr, and team captain Stephen Neal expressed concerns that a smaller squad would prove less competitive, the smaller CSUB team performed exceptionally well, winning the Pac–10 Conference title and finishing third in the nation in 1996. In 1996–97, the men's wrestling roster was capped at 25, and four of these spots went unused. Nevertheless, in response to the rumored elimination of the men's wrestling team, on January 10, 1997, the team filed the instant lawsuit, alleging that the university's policy capping the size of the men's team constituted discrimination on the basis of gender in violation of Title IX and the Equal Protection Clause of the Federal Constitution.

     * * *

III.

This case has its origins in Congress's passage of Title IX in 1972. Title IX was Congress's response to significant concerns about discrimination against women in education. In the words of the legislation's primary sponsor, Senator Birch Bayh, Title IX was enacted to "provide for the women of America something that is rightfully theirs—an equal chance to attend the schools of their choice, to develop the skills they want, and to apply those skills with the knowledge that they will have a fair chance to secure the jobs of their choice with equal pay for equal work."

The regulations promulgated pursuant to Title IX require schools receiving federal funding to "provide equal athletic opportunity for members of both sexes." In evaluating schools' compliance with that provision, one factor that will be considered is "whether the selection of sports and levels of competition effectively accommodate the interests and abilities of

---

1.   This figure assumed 60% female enrollment for that year.

members of both sexes." At the same time, "it would require blinders to ignore that the motivation for promulgation of the regulation on athletics was the historic emphasis on boys' athletic programs to the exclusion of girls' athletic programs in . . . colleges." The drafters of these regulations recognized a situation that Congress well understood: Male athletes had been given an enormous head start in the race against their female counterparts for athletic resources, and Title IX would prompt universities to level the proverbial playing field.

Appellees recognize that, given this backdrop, it would be imprudent to argue that Title IX prohibits the use of all gender-conscious remedies. Appellees therefore suggest that gender-conscious remedies are appropriate only when necessary to ensure that schools provide opportunities to males and females in proportion to their relative levels of interest in sports participation. By contrast, Appellants contend that schools may make gender-conscious decisions about sports-funding levels to correct for an imbalance between the composition of the undergraduate student body and the composition of the undergraduate student athletic participants pool. This disagreement has real significance: Men's expressed interest in participating in varsity sports is apparently higher than women's at the present time—although the "interest gap" continues to narrow—so permitting gender-conscious remedies until the proportions of students and athletes are roughly proportional gives universities more remedial freedom than permitting remedies only until expressed interest and varsity roster spots correspond.

Appellees' argument that equal opportunity is achieved when each gender's athletic participation roughly matches its interest in participating is hardly novel. Several courts of appeals have considered and rejected Appellees' approach as fundamentally inconsistent with the purpose of Title IX.

Cohen v. Brown University ("*Cohen I*")[2], was the first case to rule on the issues raised in the instant appeal. In *Cohen I,* female members of Brown's volleyball and gymnastics teams brought suit under Title IX after the university eliminated their teams. Women comprised 48% of the school's student body, but less than 37% of the athletes on campus.

The *Cohen I* court interpreted Title IX's requirements in light of the three-part test set forth in the Policy Interpretation promulgated by the Department of Health, Education, and Welfare in 1979.[3] That test is used to assess whether a school's athletic program is in compliance with Title IX. A university's athletics program is Title IX-compliant if it satisfies *one* of the following conditions:

> (1) . . . [I]ntercollegiate level participation opportunities for male and female students are provided in numbers substantially proportionate to their respective enrollments; or

---

2. The First Circuit numbers the *Cohen* decisions differently. Because we discuss only two opinions, we refer to them as *Cohen I* and *Cohen II.*

3. The OCR later was authorized by Congress to issue Title IX's regulations with respect to athletic opportunities.

(2) Where the members of one sex have been and are underrepresented among intercollegiate athletes, . . . the institution can show a history and continuing practice of program expansion which is demonstrably responsive to the developing interest and abilities of the members of that sex; or

(3) Where the members of one sex are underrepresented among intercollegiate athletes, and the institution cannot show a continuing practice of program expansion such as that cited above, . . . it can be demonstrated that the interests and abilities of the members of that sex have been fully and effectively accommodated by the present program.

Appellees attack only the first part of this test, which declares a university Title IX-compliant if participation levels for each gender are "substantially proportionate" to their representation in the student body.

The *Cohen I* court explicitly rejected Brown's argument that, because male athletes were more interested in athletics, the school could bring itself into Title IX compliance by providing females with fewer athletic roster spots "as long as the school's response is in direct proportion to the comparative levels of interest." In *Cohen II*, the rejection of Brown's argument was even more emphatic: "Brown's relative interests approach cannot withstand scrutiny on either legal or policy grounds, because it disadvantages women and undermines the remedial purposes of Title IX by limiting required program expansion for the underrepresented sex to the status quo level of relative interests."

Under *Cohen I,* if a university wanted to comply with the first part of the three-part test, it had to provide "athletics opportunities in proportion to the gender composition of the student body," not in proportion to the expressed interests of men and women.

* * *

Title IX is a dynamic statute, not a static one. It envisions continuing progress toward the goal of equal opportunity for all athletes and recognizes that, where society has conditioned women to expect less than their fair share of the athletic opportunities, women's interest in participating in sports will not rise to a par with men's overnight. The percentage of college athletes who are women rose from 15% in 1972 to 37% in 1998, and Title IX is at least partially responsible for this trend of increased participation by women. Title IX has altered women's preferences, making them more interested in sports, and more likely to become student athletes. Adopting Appellees' interest-based test for Title IX compliance would hinder, and quite possibly reverse, the steady increases in women's participation and interest in sports that have followed Title IX's enactment.

A number of courts of appeals have addressed another potentially dispositive issue in this appeal—namely, whether Title IX permits a university to diminish athletic opportunities available to men so as to bring them into line with the lower athletic opportunities available to women. Every court, in construing the Policy Interpretation and the text of Title IX, has held that a university may bring itself into Title IX compliance by increasing athletic opportunities for the underrepresented gender (women in this case) *or* by decreasing athletic opportunities for the overrepresented gender (men in this case). An extensive survey of Title IX's legislative history and the regulations promulgated to apply its provisions to college athletics concluded that boosters of male sports argued vociferously before Congress that the proposed regulations would require schools to shift resources from men's programs to women's programs, but that Congress nevertheless sided "with women's advocates" by deciding not to repeal the HEW's athletics-related Title IX regulations. Congress thus appears to have believed that Title IX would result in funding reductions to male athletic programs. If a university wishes to comply with Title IX by leveling down programs instead of ratcheting them up, as Appellant has done here, Title IX is not offended.

* * *

Finally, the district court below rejected the interpretation of Title IX advocated by the OCR and Appellants on the ground that such a reading of the statute might violate the Constitution. * * *

The First and Seventh Circuits both have considered at length the constitutionality of the first prong of the OCR's test. In *Cohen I; Cohen II;* and *Kelley,* the courts emphatically rejected the claim that the Policy Interpretation was unconstitutional under the Fourteenth Amendment. The separate reasoning in the two *Cohen* opinions is particularly well-developed. It applied intermediate scrutiny, which we would also do were we addressing the constitutional merits. *Cohen II* noted that the Policy Interpretation furthered the "clearly important" objectives of "avoid[ing] the use of federal resources to support discriminatory practices, and provid[ing] individual citizens effective protection against those practices." Moreover, it found that "judicial enforcement of federal anti-discrimination statutes is at least an important governmental objective." And *Cohen II* held that the district court's relief, which was essentially identical to what the OCR Policy Interpretation calls for, was "clearly substantially related" to these objectives. Along the same lines, the Seventh Circuit has held that "the remedial scheme established by Title IX and the applicable regulation and policy interpretation are clearly substantially related to" the objective of prohibiting "educational institutions from discriminating on the basis of sex." We adopt the reasoning of *Cohen I, Cohen II,* and *Kelley,* and hold that the constitutional analysis contained therein persuasively disposes of any serious constitutional concerns that might be raised in relation to the OCR Policy Interpretation. The district court's final basis for rejecting the OCR's interpretation of Title IX was therefore erroneous.

IV.

This past summer, 90,185 enthusiastic fans crowded into Pasadena's historic Rose Bowl for the finals of the Women's World Cup soccer match.

An estimated 40 million television viewers also tuned in to watch a thrilling battle between the American and Chinese teams. The match ended when American defender Brandi Chastain fired the ball past Chinese goalkeeper Gao Hong, breaking a 4–4 shootout tie. The victory sparked a national celebration and a realization by many that women's sports could be just as exciting, competitive, and lucrative as men's sports. And the victorious athletes understood as well as anyone the connection between a 27-year-old statute and tangible progress in women's athletics. Title IX has enhanced, and will continue to enhance, women's opportunities to enjoy the thrill of victory, the agony of defeat, and the many tangible benefits that flow from just being given a chance to participate in intercollegiate athletics. Today we join our sister circuits in holding that Title IX does not bar universities from taking steps to ensure that women are approximately as well represented in sports programs as they are in student bodies. We REVERSE, and VACATE the preliminary injunction.

D. GENDER EQUITY IN THE EDUCATION PROCESS

As documented in the rich body of literature addressing women's issues over the past fifty years, great progress has been achieved in this area. This progress has been due, in no small part, to the tireless efforts of many members of the education community.

Yet many gender-related concerns still remain unresolved, both within educational institutions and in society as a whole.

Gender equity issues arise in many places throughout this casebook, including but not limited to the campus safety and privacy chapter, the peer harassment and mistreatment section, earlier portions of this chapter, and the religion, morality and values materials that follow in Chapters 8 and 9.

This section highlights the range of controversies in this area that relate directly to the education process. It begins with an examination of disputes regarding the separation of students on the basis of gender, focusing in particular on the landmark decision in the 1996 VMI case, *U.S. v. Virginia.* It continues by highlighting research documenting differential treatment of boys and girls in day-to-day K–12 settings, and identifying what might be done to change these realities. The section concludes by addressing transgender issues in a gender equity context.

1. SEPARATING STUDENTS ON THE BASIS OF GENDER

PROBLEM 28: ADMISSIONS AND GENDER

Assume that the following practices have taken place in public educational institutions, and that lawsuits are filed challenging these practices. For each hypothetical, please address two questions: (a) In general, should plaintiffs prevail? and (b) If plaintiffs allege gender discrimination under the Equal Protection Clause, would plaintiffs prevail?

A.   The Eldorado County School District sets aside one of its eleven high schools as a "preferred," college-preparatory school which admits students on the basis of past academic achievement. However, female applicants are subject to more stringent admission requirements. The district argues that this practice is necessary to maintain equal numbers of boys and girls in the special school. A lawsuit is filed on behalf of female applicants who have been denied admission.

B.   The Emerald City Board of Education establishes three new male academies designed to meet the special needs of the city's African American boys. These academies are designed to include an enriched educational setting, an African-centered curriculum, a "rites of passage" program to emphasize male responsibility, the use of mentors, a Saturday program, school uniforms, and special counseling. The board's decision is heavily influenced by the writings of Spencer H. Holland, director of the Center for Educating African American Males at Morgan State University in Baltimore. Mr. Holland is an originator of the concept of separate classes for minority boys taught by a man who can serve as a role model. A lawsuit is filed on behalf of two women who want to enroll their daughters in the all male academies.

C.   Responding to the concerns of community members regarding the quality of education in their public schools, the Eldorado School District turns all of the district's twenty high schools into "schools of choice." Major portions of three schools, including eighteen out of fifty-four classrooms at Susan B. Anthony High, are set aside for girls only. The decision to establish these "schools within schools" is informed by recent research. No classes are set aside for boys only, however, because similar research has revealed that although single sex high school classes benefit girls, they are not particularly advantageous for boys. Mr. and Mrs. Saticoy file a lawsuit seeking to have their two teenage sons placed in the all girls "school within a school" at Susan B. Anthony High. Among other things, the parents claim (and the district stipulates) that (a) their sons' best friends are in these classes, (b) the two boys do better in school when placed in classes with students that are primarily female, and (c) most of Anthony High's most popular teachers are now teaching in the "school within a school."

D.   In the aftermath of Proposition 209, the faculty admissions committee for the Graduate School of Computer Sciences at UC San Joaquin sets forth a revised policy for reviewing applicants. The policy focuses on only three objective indicators: GRE scores in math, undergraduate GPA in math and science courses, and overall undergraduate GPA. Plaintiffs seeking to modify the new policy contend that such an undue and inappropriate emphasis on math and science performance inevitably favors male applicants.

UNITED STATES v. VIRGINIA

518 U.S. 515, 116 S.Ct. 2264 (1996)

JUSTICE GINSBURG delivered the opinion of the Court.

Virginia's public institutions of higher learning include an incomparable military college, Virginia Military Institute (VMI). The United States maintains that the Constitution's equal protection guarantee precludes Virginia from reserving exclusively to men the unique educational opportunities VMI affords. We agree.

I

Founded in 1839, VMI is today the sole single-sex school among Virginia's 15 public institutions of higher learning. VMI's distinctive mission is to produce "citizen-soldiers," men prepared for leadership in civilian life and in military service. VMI pursues this mission through pervasive training of a kind not available anywhere else in Virginia. Assigning prime place to character development, VMI uses an "adversative method" modeled on English public schools and once characteristic of military instruction. VMI constantly endeavors to instill physical and mental discipline in its cadets and impart to them a strong moral code. The school's graduates leave VMI with heightened comprehension of their capacity to deal with duress and stress, and a large sense of accomplishment for completing the hazardous course.

VMI has notably succeeded in its mission to produce leaders; among its alumni are military generals, Members of Congress, and business executives. The school's alumni overwhelmingly perceive that their VMI training helped them to realize their personal goals. VMI's endowment reflects the loyalty of its graduates; VMI has the largest per-student endowment of all public undergraduate institutions in the Nation.

Neither the goal of producing citizen-soldiers nor VMI's implementing methodology is inherently unsuitable to women. And the school's impressive record in producing leaders has made admission desirable to some women. Nevertheless, Virginia has elected to preserve exclusively for men the advantages and opportunities a VMI education affords.

II

* * *2

VMI attracts some applicants because of its reputation as an extraordinarily challenging military school, and "because its alumni are exceptionally close to the school." "[W]omen have no opportunity anywhere to gain the benefits of [the system of education at VMI]."

B

In 1990, prompted by a complaint filed with the Attorney General by a female high-school student seeking admission to VMI, the United States sued the Commonwealth of Virginia and VMI, alleging that VMI's exclusively male admission policy violated the Equal Protection Clause of the Fourteenth Amendment. * * *

The District Court ruled in favor of VMI, however, and rejected the equal protection challenge pressed by the United States. That court

---

2. Historically, most of Virginia's public colleges and universities were single sex; by the mid–1970's, however, all except VMI had become coeducational.

correctly recognized that *Mississippi Univ. for Women v. Hogan* was the closest guide. There, this Court underscored that a party seeking to uphold government action based on sex must establish an "exceedingly persuasive justification" for the classification. To succeed, the defender of the challenged action must show "at least that the classification serves important governmental objectives and that the discriminatory means employed are substantially related to the achievement of those objectives."

The District Court reasoned that education in "a single-gender environment, be it male or female," yields substantial benefits. VMI's school for men brought diversity to an otherwise coeducational Virginia system, and that diversity was "enhanced by VMI's unique method of instruction." If single-gender education for males ranks as an important governmental objective, it becomes obvious, the District Court concluded, that the *only* means of achieving the objective "is to exclude women from the all-male institution—VMI."

* * *

The Court of Appeals for the Fourth Circuit disagreed and vacated the District Court's judgment. The appellate court held: "The Commonwealth of Virginia has not ... advanced any state policy by which it can justify its determination, under an announced policy of diversity, to afford VMI's unique type of program to men and not to women."

* * *

* * * The Court of Appeals, however, accepted the District Court's finding that "at least these three aspects of VMI's program—physical training, the absence of privacy, and the adversative approach—would be materially affected by coeducation." Remanding the case, the appeals court assigned to Virginia, in the first instance, responsibility for selecting a remedial course. The court suggested these options for the Commonwealth: Admit women to VMI; establish parallel institutions or programs; or abandon state support, leaving VMI free to pursue its policies as a private institution.

C

In response to the Fourth Circuit's ruling, Virginia proposed a parallel program for women: Virginia Women's Institute for Leadership (VWIL). The 4–year, state-sponsored undergraduate program would be located at Mary Baldwin College, a private liberal arts school for women, and would be open, initially, to about 25 to 30 students. Although VWIL would share VMI's mission—to produce "citizen-soldiers"—the VWIL program would differ, as does Mary Baldwin College, from VMI in academic offerings, methods of education, and financial resources.

The average combined SAT score of entrants at Mary Baldwin is about 100 points lower than the score for VMI freshmen. Mary Baldwin's faculty holds "significantly fewer Ph.D.'s than the faculty at VMI," and receives significantly lower salaries. While VMI offers degrees in liberal arts, the sciences, and engineering, Mary Baldwin, at the time of trial, offered only bachelor of arts degrees. A VWIL student seeking to earn an engineering degree could gain one, without public support, by attending Washington University in St. Louis, Missouri, for two years, paying the required private tuition.

Experts in educating women at the college level composed the Task Force charged with designing the VWIL program; Task Force members were drawn from Mary Baldwin's own faculty and staff. Training its attention on methods of instruction appropriate for "most women," the Task Force determined that a military model would be "wholly inappropriate" for VWIL.

VWIL students would participate in ROTC programs and a newly established, "largely ceremonial" Virginia Corps of Cadets, but the VWIL House would not have a military format, and VWIL would not require its students to eat meals together or to wear uniforms during the schoolday. In lieu of VMI's adversative method, the VWIL Task Force favored "a cooperative method which reinforces self-esteem." In addition to the standard bachelor of arts program offered at Mary Baldwin, VWIL students would take courses in leadership, complete an off-campus leadership externship, participate in community service projects, and assist in arranging a speaker series.

* * *

D

Virginia returned to the District Court seeking approval of its proposed remedial plan, and the court decided the plan met the requirements of the Equal Protection Clause. The District Court again acknowledged evidentiary support for these determinations: "[T]he VMI methodology could be used to educate women and, in fact, some women . . . may prefer the VMI methodology to the VWIL methodology." But the "controlling legal principles," the District Court decided, "do not require the Commonwealth to provide a mirror image VMI for women." The court anticipated that the two schools would "achieve substantially similar outcomes." It concluded: "If VMI marches to the beat of a drum, then Mary Baldwin marches to the melody of a fife and when the march is over, both will have arrived at the same destination."

A divided Court of Appeals affirmed the District Court's judgment.
* * *

III

The cross-petitions in this suit present two ultimate issues. First, does Virginia's exclusion of women from the educational opportunities provided by VMI—extraordinary opportunities for military training and civilian leadership development—deny to women "capable of all of the individual activities required of VMI cadets," the equal protection of the laws guaranteed by the Fourteenth Amendment? Second, if VMI's "unique" situation,—as Virginia's sole single-sex public institution of higher education—offends the Constitution's equal protection principle, what is the remedial requirement?

IV

We note, once again, the core instruction of this Court's pathmarking decisions in *J.E.B. v. Alabama ex rel. T. B.* and *Mississippi Univ. for Women*: Parties who seek to defend gender-based government action must demonstrate an "exceedingly persuasive justification" for that action.

Today's skeptical scrutiny of official action denying rights or opportunities based on sex responds to volumes of history. As a plurality of this Court acknowledged a generation ago, "our Nation has had a long and unfortunate history of sex discrimination." Through a century plus three decades and more of that history, women did not count among voters composing "We the People"; not until 1920 did women gain a constitutional right to the franchise. And for a half century thereafter, it remained the prevailing doctrine that government, both federal and state, could withhold from women opportunities accorded men so long as any "basis in reason" could be conceived for the discrimination. * * *

In 1971, for the first time in our Nation's history, this Court ruled in favor of a woman who complained that her State had denied her the equal protection of its laws. Since *Reed,* the Court has repeatedly recognized that neither federal nor state government acts compatibly with the equal protection principle when a law or official policy denies to women, simply because they are women, full citizenship stature—equal opportunity to aspire, achieve, participate in and contribute to society based on their individual talents and capacities.

Without equating gender classifications, for all purposes, to classifications based on race or national origin, the Court, in post-*Reed* decisions, has carefully inspected official action that closes a door or denies opportunity to women (or to men). To summarize the Court's current directions for cases of official classification based on gender: Focusing on the differential treatment or denial of opportunity for which relief is sought, the reviewing court must determine whether the proffered justification is "exceedingly persuasive." The burden of justification is demanding and it rests entirely on the State. The State must show "at least that the [challenged] classification serves 'important governmental objectives and that the discriminatory means employed' are 'substantially related to the achievement of those objectives.' " The justification must be genuine, not hypothesized or invented *post hoc* in response to litigation. And it must not rely on overbroad generalizations about the different talents, capacities, or preferences of males and females.

The heightened review standard our precedent establishes does not make sex a proscribed classification. Supposed "inherent differences" are no longer accepted as a ground for race or national origin classifications. Physical differences between men and women, however, are enduring:

"[T]he two sexes are not fungible; a community made up exclusively of one [sex] is different from a community composed of both."

"Inherent differences" between men and women, we have come to appreciate, remain cause for celebration, but not for denigration of the members of either sex or for artificial constraints on an individual's opportunity. Sex classifications may be used to compensate women "for particular economic disabilities [they have] suffered," to "promot[e] equal employment opportunity," to advance full development of the talent and capacities of our Nation's people.[7] But such classifications may not be used, as they once were, to create or perpetuate the legal, social, and economic inferiority of women.

Measuring the record in this case against the review standard just described, we conclude that Virginia has shown no "exceedingly persuasive justification" for excluding all women from the citizen-soldier training afforded by VMI. We therefore affirm the Fourth Circuit's initial judgment, which held that Virginia had violated the Fourteenth Amendment's Equal Protection Clause. Because the remedy proffered by Virginia—the Mary Baldwin VWIL program—does not cure the constitutional violation, *i.e.,* it does not provide equal opportunity, we reverse the Fourth Circuit's final judgment in this case.

* * *

2. DIFFERENTIAL TREATMENT IN K–12 SETTINGS

GENDER EQUITY IN THE CLASSROOM

Lynn Kepford
NCSC News, Vol. 1, No. 6 (2002),
http://www.ncsc.info/newsletter/June_2002/gender.htm

* * * Gender bias, built upon unconscious acceptance of stereotypes and gender role expectations, is still evident in today's classrooms. Sadker & Sadker in *Failing at Fairness* assert "girls enter school at a higher achievement level and leave it with a lower achievement level" [than their male counterparts]. Girls appear to be the ideal students in elementary school. They seem to be doing well. They receive better grades and are disciplined less frequently. The unfortunate result is that girls receive less—time, attention, help, encouragement, challenges, and feedback.

---

7. Several *amici* have urged that diversity in educational opportunities is an altogether appropriate governmental pursuit and that single-sex schools can contribute importantly to such diversity. Indeed, it is the mission of some single-sex schools "to dissipate, rather than perpetuate, traditional gender classifications." We do not question the Commonwealth's prerogative evenhandedly to support diverse educational opportunities. We address specifically and only an educational opportunity recognized by the District Court and the Court of Appeals as "unique," an opportunity available only at Virginia's premier military institute, the Commonwealth's sole single-sex public university or college. *Cf. Mississippi Univ. for Women v. Hogan* ("Mississippi maintains no other single-sex public university or college. Thus, we are not faced with the question of whether States can provide 'separate but equal' undergraduate institutions for males and females.").

"When female students are offered the leftovers of teacher time and attention ... they achieve less ... girls and women learn to speak softly or not at all; to submerge honest feelings, withhold opinions, and defer to boys; to avoid math and science as male domains; to value neatness and quiet more than assertiveness and creativity; to emphasize appearance and hide intelligence ... they are turned into educational spectators instead of players; but education is not a spectator sport" (Sadker & Sadker). As a result, their self-esteem, independence, motivation and academic opportunities suffer.

THE DISPARITIES

Teacher Attention

AAUW studies indicate that girls are less assertive in the classroom. They need more time to think when responding to questions. Sadly, they receive less time. Boys, on the other hand, call out 8 times more frequently than girls and are more often called upon to respond. Boys are allowed to call out answers while girls must raise their hands and be recognized before speaking. Accordingly, boys participate more in class and secure more teacher attention and feedback than their female counterparts. This need not occur. Research conducted by the AAUW and the WEEA indicates that girls become almost as assertive as boys in class when teachers receive training in gender equity.

Differential Feedback

When providing feedback educators are more likely to praise, correct, help, and criticize boys—all of which foster achievement. Boys are more likely to receive comments on the content of their work and suggestions for improvement. Conversely, girls receive more superficial communication, frequently focusing on the appearance rather than the academic content of their work. The message portrayed is that a higher level of performance is possible and expected of boys than girls. Accordingly, girls receive less valuable feedback impeding their ability to correct mistakes and leaving them unprepared for future real-life situations.

Classroom Assistance

A difference also exists when students request assistance. Boys are led through the exercise and given suggestions. They are encouraged to work through problems and finish projects. When girls need help, teachers are likely to tell them the answer or complete the project for them depriving them of active learning experiences. Teacher interaction of this type fosters dependence in girls and independence in boys. As a consequence, girls get less practice at problem solving skills than boys.

Belief Systems

Girls attribute the cause of academic failure to an internal locus of control. In other words, their failure is due to internal factors such as lack of ability or intelligence. Boys, on the other hand attribute academic failure to an external locus of control-teacher bias, illness, poor instruction, etc. When children internalize success and externalize failure (the male approach), they are able to tackle new and challenging tasks with a mastery orientation, one that perseveres in the face of difficulty and leads to future achievement. Children who attribute success to effort and failure to lack of ability (the female approach) exhibit "learned helplessness." Girls frequently downplay academic achievement or attribute it to luck. Boys take credit. Sadly, many teachers unconsciously support these erroneous beliefs.

Predictions for Success

A positive correlation exists between professional position, economic success, and success in math, science, and technology. Although males and females enter junior high school on equal footing in these areas, boys' performance begins to surpass that of their female classmates at this stage. This outcome appears to be largely a result of attitude and expectation, rather than of innate ability and can be attributed to:

- Expectations of parents and teachers.
- Science and math teachers are primarily male.
- Few women role models are furnished.
- Boys have higher expectations for themselves.

Most devastating of all is the fact that teachers are unaware of this inadvertent discrimination. They try to and honestly believe that they do treat all of their students equally regardless of sex. Research however indicates an entirely different reality. Incidents of discrimination are so subtle, that frequently, girls themselves cannot pinpoint it. The result is that females feel less intelligent and less valued and receive an inferior education than that of their male counterparts.

Solutions

Although this problem is sociologically based, the structures are already in place to implement solutions within the educational system. Teacher training is an ideal place to begin as research indicates that educators teach the way they were taught and they most strongly model the styles of their most recent instructors.

- Wait a few seconds after asking a question before calling on students. Girls, more than boys formulate their response prior to raising their hands.
- Assign more team projects as girls learn better through collaboration.
- Facilitate a cooperative, rather than a competitive environment, by conducting some classes with students sitting in a circle. (Girls will be more comfortable and learn better in this type of setting.)
- Provide coaching to develop problem-solving skills.

- Incorporate interdisciplinary teaching using real-world problems and hands-on projects to demonstrate the value of the learning being acquired.
- Create an environment that reduces stereotyping and helps students relate to each other as individuals.
- Praise students equally for achievement, creativity and effort.
- Attribute cause for poor performance accurately.
- Attend equally to the misbehavior of both sexes.
- Provide numerous opportunities for girls to experience science, math, and technology.
- Examine the rules (both implicit and explicit) set for girls and the underlying assumptions.
- Provide girls with more opportunities to be leaders.
- Create an environment that is safe for mistakes, not safe from mistakes.
- Encourage more outdoor and physical opportunities for girls.
- Teach girls how to assess the risk and how to insure their own safety. Offer more access to machinery and equipment.
- Let girls know that they are capable of learning math, science, and technology; and encourage them to choose these courses in high school.
- Expect females to pursue higher education.
- Select curriculum materials that equally and realistically represent both sexes.

REFERENCES

AMERICAN ASS'N OF UNIVERSITY WOMEN, BEYOND THE "GENDER WARS": A CONVERSATION ABOUT GIRLS, BOYS, AND EDUCATION (Washington, D.C. 2001).

AMERICAN ASS'N OF UNIVERSITY WOMEN, SHORTCHANGING GIRLS, SHORT-CHANGING AMERICA: EXECUTIVE SUMMARY (Washington, D.C., 2d ed. 1994).

MYRA & DAVID SADKER, FAILING AT FAIRNESS 1–135, 251–80 (1994).

WEEA EQUITY RESOURCE CENTER, RESOURCES TO INFUSE EQUITY, http://www.edc.org/WomensEquity/equity.htm (last visited Oct. 2002).

3. LEGAL AND POLICY PERSPECTIVES ON TRANSGENDER ISSUES

Transgender persons may be among the most misunderstood of any identifiable group in existence today. *See, e.g.,* Dean Spade, *Compliance Is Gendered: Struggling for Gender Self–Determination in a Hostile Economy,* in Paisley Currah, Richard Juang, and Shannon Minter, *Transgender Rights,* University of Minnesota Press (2006). *See generally* Dylan Vade,

Expanding Gender and Expanding the Law: Toward a Social and Legal Conceptualization of Gender That Is More Inclusive of Transgender People, 11 Michigan Journal of Gender and Law 253 (2005).

Given this misunderstanding, which can be greatly exacerbated by the discomfort that many have with people who do not adhere to conventional gender norms, it is not surprising that transgender youth face additional challenges above and beyond those faced by other members of traditionally disenfranchised groups. But the actual numbers in this area go far beyond what most people might contemplate. The percentages of transgender youth involved in substance abuse, runaway/homeless situations, and prostitution are significantly higher than those of their peers. And transgender persons in general are not only faced with pandemic employment discrimination at all levels of society, but are much more likely than other recognizable groups to be victims of violent assaults, including rape and murder. *See, e.g.,* Gwendolyn Ann Smith and Ethan St. Pierre, *Trans Murder Statistics: 1970 to 2004*, available at http://www.gender.org/resources/dge/gea02002.pdf (last accessed May 3, 2007).

Transgender persons are distinguished by their gender identities, which are typically different from the ones they were assigned at birth. According to members of the legal community who work in this area, "*gender identity* refers to a person's internal, deeply felt sense of being male or female (or both or neither). It is a person's psychological identification as masculine or feminine."[1]

The word *transgender* is often viewed as an umbrella term that may include FTMs (female-to-male), MTFs (male-to-female), transsexuals, cross dressers, androgynous persons, and those who identify as genderqueer. The definitions for these terms can vary, with different people defining them in different ways, often without any apparent consensus.[2]

Contrary to popular perception, while many transgender persons choose to have at least some type of gender reassignment surgery, many others do not ... or simply cannot afford it. The most common transgender health care is hormone therapy, and a good number not only take

---

1. *See, e.g.,* Jody Marksamer & Dean Spade, *Serving Transgender & Gender Non–Conforming Youth: A Guide for Juvenile Halls, Group Homes, and Other Congregate Care Facilities* (2007) (on file with the author).

Transgender persons typically confront issues relating to both their sexual orientation and their gender identity. With regard to the former, transgender persons may, of course, also identify as gay, lesbian, bisexual, or heterosexual. With regard to the latter, they may see their gender identity as conforming to the traditional binary model of male or female, or they may identify as perhaps more male than female or more female than male, but not exclusively one or the other. *See id.*

2. Among the more contested definitions are those for the words *transsexual and genderqueer.* For example, *transsexual* is often used as a synonym for a transgender person who has had at least one surgical intervention that may be classified as gender reassignment surgery. But others define the term more broadly. And *genderqueer* is typically employed to characterize someone who at least at certain times identifies as not entirely male and not entirely female, but somewhere in between or apart from those binaries. But others view the term as contextually different from that characterization. *See, e.g.,* Shannon Minter, *Do Transsexuals Dream of Gay Rights?* in Paisley Currah, Richard M. Juang, and Shannon Minter, eds., *Transgender Rights*, University of Minnesota Press (2006). *See generally* Brett Beemyn, *Transgender Terminology*, Gay, Lesbian, Bisexual, and Transgender Student Services, Ohio State University.

estrogen or testosterone on a regular basis, but plan to continue doing so indefinitely; others use these hormones occasionally or not at all.

The right to be out can prove to be quite different for transgender persons than for others who may seek to convey fundamental aspects of identity and personhood. Many, for example, may want to be out only as male or female, and they may see "transgender" as not necessarily the equivalent of an identity at all, but instead as the description of a process that they went through and have now completed. For others, transgender may be seen primarily or perhaps even entirely as the equivalent of a medical condition.[3] Still others view transgender as central to their very persona, and it is highly important for these persons to be able to identify openly.

The term *gender non-conforming* may be employed by some as a synonym for transgender, although many view *gender non-conforming* as a broader term that may include, but is not limited to, transgender persons. It may be appropriate in this context to differentiate between two separate but interrelated categories of gender non-conforming youth. One category would include those who have already begun transitioning or have already transitioned, and now identify as a gender other than the one they were assigned at birth.[4] The other category would include those who may view themselves and/or may be viewed by others as not conforming to the so-called traditional or accepted gender norms. Some in this latter group may one day come out as transgender, but they do not currently identify under the trans umbrella. Others may never be transgender, but may still be subject to a great deal of ongoing mistreatment and abuse–especially in education settings–because of how much they vary from perceived norms without even trying to do so.

For purposes of addressing the needs of transgender youth at the K–12 level, it is important to recognize that it is not typically possible to pursue a gender transition without coming out as transgender. Once they begin presenting differently as part of their transition process, they are immediately and abruptly out to those who knew them previously. Many cannot or will not do this, and instead transfer to a different school. Some, of course, even leave home.[5]

---

3. The medical term that has been employed to describe transgender identity is 'Gender Identity Disorder,' which is included in the American Psychiatric Association's revised 1994 version of its Diagnostic and Statistical Manual (DSM–IV).

While some have advocated pursuing equal rights for transgender persons through a "disability civil rights law framework," many others have rejected the notion for a wide variety of reasons. For an example of the argument in favor of taking advantage of state disability law in this manner, *see, e.g.,* Jennifer L. Levi & Bennett H. Klein, *Pursuing Protection for Transgender People through Disability Laws*; and for an articulation of some of the pitfalls of this approach, *see, e.g.,* Judith Butler, *Undiagnosing Gender,* both pieces in Currah, Juang & Minter, *Transgender Rights. See also* Dean Spade, Resisting Medicine/Remodeling Gender, 18 Berkeley Women's Law Journal 15 (2003) (arguing against the use of disability law claims in trans cases).

4. *See, e.g., The Transsexual Road Map,* www.tsroadmap.com (last accessed May 10, 2007), a comprehensive resource for those in the process of transitioning, with materials ranging from a "transition timetable" to a listing of the standards of care any health care provider must follow.

5. *See, e.g.,* Patricia Gagne et al., *Coming Out and Crossing Over: Identity Formation and Proclamation in a Transgender Community,* 11 Gender and Society 478 (1997). *See also* Alan B.

Thus the typical transgender student who is transitioning has either recently changed schools or is making a statement at the current school that flies in the face of traditionally accepted gender norms and often leads to dramatic changes in day-to-day interaction. In either case, the experience is invariably unsettling, even with the unconditional support of family, friends, and/or the school community.

More often than not, transgender persons who come out in a K–12 setting today will be presenting primarily as one gender but will have the physical and biological characteristics of the other. Not only will those who desire gender reassignment surgery of any kind not generally be able to afford it at this stage of their lives, but doctors will not typically perform such surgeries on people that young. This reality is central, and cannot be ignored.

A second key aspect of this territory is that many transgender youth may seek to obtain hormones, even as medical doctors may refrain from prescribing them to persons that young. While hormones taken in a controlled environment can prove very beneficial even for younger trans persons, experts have warned of the possible damage that high doses of estrogen or testosterone can cause for those who are still going through puberty.[6] Still, many gender non-conforming youth work very hard to obtain such hormones, often illegally. And not only are they at-risk during the process of obtaining these items, since attempts to both find the hormones and pay for them can sometimes lead to dangerous circumstances, but they may subsequently be at-risk medically . . . particularly if they are making ad hoc determinations as to the quantity and strength of the hormones they are taking.[7]

At the same time, privacy concerns are among the most significant challenges faced by transgender persons, since many people still do not believe that someone who is identifying as a different gender than the one assigned at birth should be entitled to keep that to themselves. Those who adopt such a position view transgender persons as engaged in "deceit," a deceit that can have negative consequences for all concerned.

The tragic case of transgender teenager Gwen Araujo exemplifies the continued prevalence of the "deceit" mindset. Upon learning at a party

---

Goldberg and Joneil Adriano, " 'I'm a Girl'–Understanding Transgender Children," ABC News, http://abcnews.go.com2020/story?ibid=3088298 & page=1 (last accessed May 10, 2007).

6. The World Professional Association for Transgender Health's *Standards of Care for Gender Identity Disorders* takes the position that adolescents can begin reversible hormone therapy intervention as soon as puberty begins, but that irreversible surgical intervention should take place only after the age of 18 and only after two years of real-life experience living full-time in the gender identity that the patient identifies with. See *The Harry Benjamin International Gender Dysphoria Association's Standards of Care for Gender Identity Disorders, Sixth Version* (2001), http://wpath.org/Documents2/socv6.pdf (last accessed May 14, 2008).

7. The availability of hormones on the street and the inability of minors to get hormones legally can be a dangerous combination, as seeing their friends progress can fuel desires to start hormone therapy, or even to "catch up" by taking greater doses. *See* Reyhan Harmanci, *They Didn't Wait Until Middle Age to Question Their Birth Sex*, San Francisco Chronicle, September 15, 2005. *See generally* Chris Beam, *Transparent: Love, Family, and Living the T with Transgender Teenagers*, Harcourt (2007).

that Gwen was biologically male, three men who had previously engaged in sexual activity with her attacked her brutally and beat her to death. At their trial, the men claimed to have "panicked" at the idea that they might be gay after realizing they had sex with a biologically male person.[8]

In recent years, there has been growing criticism of the deception argument, and a significant body of scholarly literature and personal narrative is now available. Many have argued that both legally and as a matter of policy, there is no justification—other than fear or misunderstanding—for requiring members of this particular group to disclose what may be highly personal aspects of such things as their past, their medical condition, or their anatomy. Such a level of blanket disclosure on a day-to-day level is arguably not required or expected of any other group.[9]

DOE v. YUNITS

2000 WL 33162199 (Mass. Super. Ct. 2000)

Plaintiff Pat Doe ("plaintiff"), a fifteen-year-old student, has brought this action by her next friend, Jane Doe, requesting that this court prohibit defendants from excluding the plaintiff from South Junior High School ("South Junior High"), Brockton, Massachusetts, on the basis of the plaintiff's sex, disability, or gender identity and expression. Plaintiff has been diagnosed with gender identity disorder, which means that, although plaintiff was born biologically male, she has a female gender identity.[4] Plaintiff seeks to attend school wearing clothes and fashion accouterments that are consistent with her gender identity. Defendants have informed plaintiff that she could not enroll in school this academic year if she wore girls' clothes or accessories. After a hearing, and for the reasons stated below, plaintiff's motion for preliminary injunction is *ALLOWED.*

BACKGROUND

Plaintiff began attending South Junior High, a Brockton public school, in September 1998, as a 7th grader. In early 1999, plaintiff first began to express her female gender identity by wearing girls' make-up,

---

8. *See, e.g.,* Wyatt Buchanan, *'Gay Panic' Defense Tactic Under Scrutiny at Conference,* San Francisco Chronicle, July 19, 2006; Kamala Harris, *United Against Violence,* Bay Area Reporter, July 20, 2006. The jury in the first trial remained deadlocked on a first degree murder conviction, and a mistrial was declared. A second trial was held, with two defendants ultimately convicted of second degree murder and a third of manslaughter.

9. See, e.g., Martha C. Nussbaum, *Hiding from Humanity: Disgust, Shame, & the Law,* Princeton University Press (2004). In late 2006, California adopted a new law designed to limit the use of "gay panic" or "transgender panic" defenses in its courts. AB 1160, the "Gwen Araujo Justice for Victims Act," directed the Office of Emergency Services to create training materials for district attorneys on best practices to address the use of bias-motivated defense strategies in criminal trials. The bill also required the Judicial Council to adopt a jury instruction that tells jurors not to consider bias against people because of sexual orientation, gender identity or other characteristics in rendering a verdict.

4. This court will use female pronouns to refer to plaintiff: a practice which is consistent with the plaintiff's gender identity and which is common among mental health and other professionals who work with transgender clients.

shirts, and fashion accessories to school. South Junior High has a dress code which prohibits, among other things, "clothing which could be disruptive or distractive to the educational process or which could affect the safety of students." In early 1999, the principal, Kenneth Cardone ("Cardone"), would often send the plaintiff home to change if she arrived at school wearing girls' apparel. On some occasions, plaintiff would change and return to school; other times, she would remain home, too upset to return. In June 1999, after being referred to a therapist by the South Junior High, plaintiff was diagnosed with gender identity disorder. Plaintiff's treating therapist, Judith Havens ("Havens"), determined that it was medically and clinically necessary for plaintiff to wear clothing consistent with the female gender and that failure to do so could cause harm to plaintiff's mental health.

Plaintiff returned to school in September 1999, as an 8th grader, and was instructed by Cardone to come to his office every day so that he could approve the plaintiff's appearance. Some days the plaintiff would be sent home to change, sometimes returning to school dressed differently and sometimes remaining home. During the 1999–2000 school year, plaintiff stopped attending school, citing the hostile environment created by Cardone. Because of plaintiff's many absences during the 1999–2000 school year, plaintiff was required to repeat the 8th grade this year.

Over the course of the 1998–1999 and 1999–2000 school years, plaintiff sometimes arrived at school wearing such items as skirts and dresses, wigs, high-heeled shoes, and padded bras with tight shirts. The school faculty and administration became concerned because the plaintiff was experiencing trouble with some of her classmates. Defendants cite one occasion when the school adjustment counselor had to restrain a male student because he was threatening to punch the plaintiff for allegedly spreading rumors that the two had engaged in oral sex. Defendants also point to an instance when a school official had to break up a confrontation between the plaintiff and a male student to whom plaintiff persistently blew kisses. At another time, plaintiff grabbed the buttock of a male student in the school cafeteria. Plaintiff also has been known to primp, pose, apply make up, and flirt with other students in class. Defendants also advance that the plaintiff sometimes called attention to herself by yelling and dancing in the halls. Plaintiff has been suspended at least three times for using the ladies' restroom after being warned not to.

On Friday, September 1, 2000, Cardone and Dr. Kenneth Sennett ("Sennett"), Senior Director for Pupil Personnel Services, met with the plaintiff relative to repeating the 8th grade. At that meeting, Cardone and Sennett informed the plaintiff that she would not be allowed to attend South Junior High if she were to wear any outfits disruptive to the educational process, specifically padded bras, skirts or dresses, or wigs. On September 21, 2000, plaintiff's grandmother tried to enroll plaintiff in school and was told by Cardone and Sennett that plaintiff would not be permitted to enroll if she wore any girls' clothing or accessories. Defendants allege that they have not barred the plaintiff from school but have merely provided limits on the type of dress the plaintiff may wear. Defendants claim it is the plaintiff's own choice not to attend school because of the guidelines they have placed on her attire. Plaintiff is not currently attending school, but the school has provided a home tutor for her to allow her to keep pace with her classmates.

On September 26, 2000, the plaintiff filed a complaint in this court claiming a denial of her right to freedom of expression in the public schools * * *.

* * * According to federal analysis, this court must first determine whether the plaintiff's symbolic acts constitute expressive speech which is protected, in this case, by Article VXI of the Massachusetts Declaration of Rights. If the speech is expressive, the court must next determine if the defendants' conduct was impermissible because it was meant to suppress that speech. If the defendants' conduct is not related to the suppression of speech, furthers an important or substantial governmental interest, and is within the constitutional powers of the government, and if the incidental restriction on speech is no greater than necessary, the government's conduct is permissible. In addition, because this case involves public school students, suppression of speech that "materially and substantially interferes with the work of the school" is permissible.

1.   The Plaintiff's Conduct is Expressive Speech Which is Understood by Those Perceiving It

Symbolic acts constitute expression if the actor's intent to convey a particularized message is likely to be understood by those perceiving the message.

Plaintiff in this case is likely to establish that, by dressing in clothing and accessories traditionally associated with the female gender, she is expressing her identification with that gender. In addition, plaintiff's ability to express herself and her gender identity through dress is important to her health and well-being, as attested to by her treating therapist. Therefore, plaintiff's expression is not merely a personal preference but a necessary symbol of her very identity. Contrast *Olesen v. Board of Education of School District No. 228* (school's anti-gang policy of prohibiting males from wearing earrings, passed for safety reasons, was upheld because plaintiff's desire to wear an earring as an expression of his individuality and attractiveness to girls was a message not within the scope of the First Amendment).

This court must next determine if the plaintiff's message was understood by those perceiving it, i.e., the school faculty and plaintiff's fellow students. * * * [P]laintiff is likely to establish, through testimony, that her fellow students are well aware of the fact that she is a biological male more comfortable wearing traditionally "female"-type clothing because of her identification with that gender.

2.   The Defendants' Conduct Was a Suppression of the Plaintiff's Speech

Plaintiff also will probably prevail on the merits of the second prong of the *Texas v. Johnson* test, that is, the defendants' conduct was meant to suppress plaintiff's speech. Defendants in this case have prohibited the plaintiff from wearing items of clothing that are traditionally labeled girls' clothing, such as dresses and skirts, padded bras, and wigs. This constitutes direct suppression of speech because biological females who wear items such as tight skirts to school are unlikely to be disciplined by school officials, as admitted by defendants' counsel at oral argument. * * *

3.   Plaintiff's Conduct is not Disruptive

This court also must consider if the plaintiff's speech "materially and substantially interferes with the work of the school." *Tinker v. Des Moines Community School Dist.* Defendants argue that they are merely preventing disruptive conduct on the part of the plaintiff by restricting her attire at school. Their argument is unpersuasive. Given the state of the record thus far, the plaintiff has demonstrated a likelihood of proving that defendants, rather than attempting to restrict plaintiff's wearing of distracting items of clothing, are seeking to ban her from donning apparel that can be labeled "girls' clothes" and to encourage more conventional, male-oriented attire. Defendants argue that any other student who came to school dressed in distracting clothing would be disciplined as the plaintiff was. However, defendants overlook the fact that, if a female student came to school in a frilly dress or blouse, make-up, or padded bra, she would go, and presumably has gone, unnoticed by school officials. Defendants do not find plaintiff's clothing distracting *per se*, but, essentially, distracting simply because plaintiff is a biological male.

In addition to the expression of her female gender identity through dress, however, plaintiff has engaged in behavior in class and towards other students that can be seen as detrimental to the learning process. This deportment, however, is separate from plaintiff's dress. Defendants vaguely cite instances when the principal became aware of threats by students to beat up the "boy who dressed like a girl" to support the notion that plaintiff's dress alone is disruptive. To rule in defendants' favor in this regard, however, would grant those contentious students a "heckler's veto." The majority of defendants' evidence of plaintiff's disruption is based on plaintiff's actions as distinct from her mode of dress. Some of these acts may be a further expression of gender identity, such as applying make-up in class; but many are instances of misconduct for which any student would be punished. Regardless of plaintiff's gender identity, any student should be punished for engaging in harassing behavior towards classmates. Plaintiff is not immune from such punishment but, by the same token, should not be punished on the basis of dress alone.

        * * *

III.   The Balance of the Equities

The balance of the equities tips in favor of plaintiff in his case. * * * [T]he harm to the school in readmitting plaintiff is minimal. On the other hand, if plaintiff is barred from school, the potential harm to plaintiff's sense of self-worth and social development is irreparable. Defendants cite cases that stand for the proposition that a school's interest in disciplining students by barring them from school outweigh the harm to the student. In this case, however, the school is not disciplining the plaintiff for certain conduct. The school is barring her from school on account of the expression of her very identity. Defendants maintain that plaintiff is free to enroll in school as long as she complies with the stated dress code. This is not entirely true because the defendants have placed specific restrictions on plaintiff's dress that may not be placed on other female students. This court does take note of the fact that defendants made efforts to accommodate the plaintiff's desire to dress in girl's clothes for over a year. However, their proscription of the items of clothing that can be worn by plaintiff is likely to be impermissible. Therefore, the harm to plaintiff by the actions of the defendants outweigh the harm to the defendants in granting this injunction.

IV.   The Harm to the Public Interest

Defendants have not made a showing that the granting of this injunction will harm the public interest. Although defendants contend that plaintiff's dress is disruptive to the learning process, the workings of the school will not be disrupted if they are permitted to discipline plaintiff according to normal procedures for truly disruptive attire and inappropriate behavior. Furthermore, this court trusts that exposing children to diversity at an early age serves the important social goals of increasing their ability to tolerate such differences and teaching them respect for everyone's unique personal experience in that "Brave New World" out there.

* * *

For all the foregoing reasons, plaintiff's motion for preliminary injunction is *ALLOWED* * * *.

NOTES

1.   In May 2001, the plaintiff in the *Yunits* case reached a settlement agreement with the school department which would allow her to wear "girls clothing" to school the following fall. Brockton, Massachusetts Mayor John Yunits was quoted as saying that "I think in the end there was a certain realization that the continued litigation wasn't in the student's best interests." Associated Press, *School, Transgender Student Reach Agreement,* May 17, 2001.

2.   California law requires that all public school districts develop and implement policies to protect transgender youth. The San Francisco Unified School District, in early 2004, became the first District in the state to comply.

Consider the parameters of the San Francisco policy, set forth below. What additional steps might be taken at the individual school site level to maximize its effectiveness? What changes in the policy, if any, might you suggest?

The SFUSD Policy on Transgender Youth (2004)

ARTICLE 5: STUDENTS

SECTION: Non–Discrimination for Students and Employees

This regulation is meant to advise school site staff and administration regarding transgender and gender non-conforming student concerns in order to create a safe learning environment for all students, and to ensure that every student has equal access to all components of their educational program.

California Law Prohibits Gender–Based Discrimination in Public Schools

The California Education Code states that "all pupils have the right to participate fully in the educational process, free from discrimination and harassment." Cal. Ed. Code § 201(a). Section 220 of the Education Code provides that no person shall be subject to discrimination on the basis of gender in any program or activity conducted by an educational institution that receives or benefits from state financial assistance. The Code further provides that public schools have an affirmative obligation to combat sexism and other forms of bias, and a responsibility to provide equal educational opportunity to all pupils. Cal. Ed. Code § 201(b).

The California Code of Regulations similarly provides that "No person shall be excluded from participation in or denied the benefits of any local agency's program or activity on the basis of sex, sexual orientation, gender, ethnic group identification, race, ancestry, national origin, religion, color, or mental or physical disability in any program or activity conducted by an 'educational institution' or any other 'local agency' ... that receives or benefits from any state financial assistance." 5 CCR § 4900(a).

The California Code of Regulations defines "gender" as: "a person's actual sex or perceived sex and includes a person's perceived identity, appearance or behavior, whether or not that identity, appearance, or behavior is different from that traditionally associated with a person's sex at birth." 5 CCR § 4910(k).

SFUSD Board Policy Prohibits Gender–Based Harassment

SFUSD Board Policy 5163 requires that "All educational programs, activities and employment practices shall be conducted without discrimination based on ... sex, sexual orientation, [or] gender identity...." Board Policy 5162 requires that "students should treat all persons equally and respectfully and refrain from the willful or negligent use of slurs against any person" based on sex or sexual orientation.

Therefore, transgender and gender non-conforming students must be protected from discrimination and harassment in the public school system. Staff must respond appropriately to ensure that schools are free from any such discrimination or harassment.

Names/Pronouns

Students shall have the right to be addressed by a name and pronoun corresponding to their gender identity that is exclusively and consistently asserted at school. Students are not required to obtain a court ordered name and/or gender change or to change their official records as a prerequisite to being addressed by the name and pronoun that corresponds to their gender identity. This directive does not prohibit inadvertent slips or honest mistakes, but it does apply to an intentional and persistent refusal to respect a student's gender identity. The requested name shall be included in the SIS system in addition to the student's legal name, in order to inform teachers of the name and pronoun to use when addressing the student.

Official Records

The District is required to maintain a mandatory permanent pupil record which includes the legal name of the pupil, as well as the pupil's gender. 5 Cal. Code Reg. 432(b)(1)(A), (D). The District shall change a student's official records to reflect a change in legal name or gender upon receipt of documentation that such legal name and/or gender have been changed pursuant to California legal requirements.

Restroom Accessibility

Students shall have access to the restroom that corresponds to their gender identity exclusively and consistently asserted at school. Where available, a single stall bathroom may be used by any student who desires increased privacy, regardless of the underlying reason. The use of such a single stall bathroom shall be a matter of choice for a student, and no student shall be compelled to use such bathroom.

Locker Room Accessibility

Transgender students shall not be forced to use the locker room corresponding to their gender assigned at birth. In locker rooms that involve undressing in front of others, transgender students who want to use the locker room corresponding to their gender identity exclusively and consistently asserted at school will be provided with the available accommodation that best meets the needs and privacy concerns of all students involved. Based on availability and appropriateness to address privacy concerns, such accommodations could include, but are not limited to:

- Use of a private area in the public area (i.e., a bathroom stall with a door, an area separated by a curtain, a PE instructor's office in the locker room);

- A separate changing schedule (either utilizing the locker room before or after the other students); or

- Use of a nearby private area (i.e., a nearby restroom, a nurse's office).

Sports and Gym Class

Transgender students shall not be denied the opportunity to participate in physical education, nor shall they be forced to have physical education outside of the assigned class time. Generally, students should be permitted to participate in gender-segregated recreational gym class activities and sports in accordance with the student's gender identity that is exclusively and consistently asserted at school. Participation in competitive athletic activities and contact sports will be resolved on a case by case basis.

Dress Codes

School sites can enforce dress codes that are adopted pursuant to Education Code 35291. Students shall have the right to dress in accordance with their gender identity that is exclusively and consistently asserted at school, within the constraints of the dress codes adopted at their school site. This regulation does not limit a student's right to dress in accordance with the Dress/Appearance standards articulated in the Student and Parent/Guardian Handbook, page 23.

Gender Segregation in Other Areas

As a general rule, in any other circumstances where students are separated by gender in school activities (i.e., class discussions, field trips), students shall be permitted to participate in accordance with their gender identity exclusively and consistently asserted at school. Activities that may involve the need for accommodations to address student privacy concerns will be addressed on a case by case basis. In such circumstances, staff shall make a reasonable effort to provide an available accommodation that can address any such concerns.

E.   THE RIGHTS OF UNDOCUMENTED STUDENTS

PLYLER v. DOE

457 U.S. 202, 102 S.Ct. 2382 (1982)

JUSTICE BRENNAN delivered the opinion of the Court

The question presented by these cases is whether, consistent with the Equal Protection Clause of the Fourteenth Amendment, Texas may deny to undocumented school-age children the free public education that it provides to children who are citizens of the United States or legally admitted aliens.

I

* * *

In May 1975, the Texas Legislature revised its education laws to withhold from local school districts any state funds for the education of children who were not "legally admitted" into the United States. The 1975 revision also authorized local school districts to deny enrollment in their public schools to children not "legally admitted" to the country. These cases involve constitutional challenges to those provisions.

* * *

This is a class action, filed in the United States District Court for the Eastern District of Texas in September 1977, on behalf of certain school-age children of Mexican origin residing in Smith County, Tex., who could not establish that they had been legally admitted into the United States. * * *

* * *

II

* * *

The Fourteenth Amendment to the Constitution is not confined to the protection of citizens. It says: "Nor shall any state deprive any person of life, liberty, or property without due process of law; nor deny to any person within its jurisdiction the equal protection of the laws." *These provisions are universal in their application, to all persons within the territorial jurisdiction*, without regard to any differences of race, of color, or of nationality; and the protection of the laws is a pledge of the protection of equal laws.

* * *

Our conclusion that the illegal aliens who are plaintiffs in these cases may claim the benefit of the Fourteenth Amendment's guarantee of equal protection only begins the inquiry. The more difficult question is whether the Equal Protection Clause has been violated by the refusal of the State of Texas to reimburse local school boards for the education of children who cannot demonstrate that their presence within the United States is lawful, or by the imposition by those school boards of the burden of tuition on those children. It is to this question that we now turn.

III

* * *

Public education is not a "right" granted to individuals by the Constitution. *San Antonio Independent School Dist. v. Rodriguez*, 411 U.S. 1, 35, 93 S. Ct. 1278 (1973). But neither is it merely some governmental "benefit" indistinguishable from other forms of social welfare legislation. Both the importance of education in maintaining our basic institutions, and the lasting impact of its deprivation on the life of the child, mark the distinction. The "American people have always regarded education and [the] acquisition of knowledge as matters of supreme importance." We have recognized "the public schools as a most vital civic institution for the preservation of a democratic system of government," and as the primary vehicle for transmitting "the values on which our society rests." "[A]s ...

pointed out early in our history, . . . some degree of education is necessary to prepare citizens to participate effectively and intelligently in our open political system if we are to preserve freedom and independence." And these historic "perceptions of the public schools as inculcating fundamental values necessary to the maintenance of a democratic political system have been confirmed by the observations of social scientists." In addition, education provides the basic tools by which individuals might lead economically productive lives to the benefit of us all. In sum, education has a fundamental role in maintaining the fabric of our society. We cannot ignore the significant social costs borne by our Nation when select groups are denied the means to absorb the values and skills upon which our social order rests.

In addition to the pivotal role of education in sustaining our political and cultural heritage, denial of education to some isolated group of children poses an affront to one of the goals of the Equal Protection Clause: the abolition of governmental barriers presenting unreasonable obstacles to advancement on the basis of individual merit. Paradoxically, by depriving the children of any disfavored group of an education, we foreclose the means by which that group might raise the level of esteem in which it is held by the majority. But more directly, "education prepares individuals to be self-reliant and self-sufficient participants in society." Illiteracy is an enduring disability. The inability to read and write will handicap the individual deprived of a basic education each and every day of his life. The inestimable toll of that deprivation on the social economic, intellectual, and psychological well-being of the individual, and the obstacle it poses to individual achievement, make it most difficult to reconcile the cost or the principle of a status-based denial of basic education with the framework of equality embodied in the Equal Protection Clause. What we said 28 years ago in *Brown v. Board of Education*, 347 U.S. 483, 74 S. Ct. 686 (1954), still holds true:

> Today, education is perhaps the most important function of state and local governments. Compulsory school attendance laws and the great expenditures for education both demonstrate our recognition of the importance of education to our democratic society. It is required in the performance of our most basic public responsibilities, even service in the armed forces. It is the very foundation of good citizenship. Today it is a principal instrument in awakening the child to cultural values, in preparing him for later professional training, and in helping him to adjust normally to his environment. In these days, it is doubtful that any child may reasonably be expected to succeed in life if he is denied the opportunity of an education. Such an opportunity, where the state has undertaken to provide it, is a right which must be made available to all on equal terms. *Id.*, at 493, 74 S. Ct., at 691.

B

These well-settled principles allow us to determine the proper level of deference to be afforded § 21.031. Undocumented aliens cannot be treated as a suspect class because their presence in this country in violation of federal law is not a "constitutional irrelevancy." Nor is education a fundamental right; a State need not justify by compelling necessity every variation in the manner in which education is provided to its population. See *San Antonio Independent School Dist. v. Rodriguez, supra,* at 28–39, 93 S. Ct., at 1293–1300. But more is involved in these cases than the abstract question whether § 21.031 discriminates against a suspect class, or whether education is a fundamental right. Section 21.031 imposes a lifetime hardship on a discrete class of children not accountable for their disabling status. The stigma of illiteracy will mark them for the rest of their lives. By denying these children a basic education, we deny them the ability to live within the structure of our civic institutions, and foreclose any realistic possibility that they will contribute in even the smallest way to the progress of our Nation. In determining the rationality of § 21.031, we may appropriately take into account its costs to the Nation and to the innocent children who are its victims. In light of these countervailing costs, the discrimination contained in § 21.031 can hardly be considered rational unless it furthers some substantial goal of the State.

IV

It is the State's principal argument, and apparently the view of the dissenting Justices, that the undocumented status of these children *vel non* establishes a sufficient rational basis for denying them benefits that a State might choose to afford other residents. The State notes that while other aliens are admitted "on an equality of legal privileges with all citizens under non-discriminatory laws," the asserted right of these children to an education can claim no implicit congressional imprimatur. Indeed, in the State's view, Congress' apparent disapproval of the presence of these children within the United States, and the evasion of the federal regulatory program that is the mark of undocumented status, provides authority for its decision to impose upon them special disabilities. Faced with an equal protection challenge respecting the treatment of aliens, we agree that the courts must be attentive to congressional policy; the exercise of congressional power might well affect the State's prerogatives to afford differential treatment to a particular class of aliens. But we are unable to find in the congressional immigration scheme any statement of policy that might weigh significantly in arriving at an equal protection balance concerning the State's authority to deprive these children of an education.

    * * *

VI

If the State is to deny a discrete group of innocent children the free public education that it offers to other children residing within its borders, that denial must be justified by a showing that it furthers some substantial state interest. No such showing was made here. Accordingly, the judgment of the Court of Appeals in each of these cases is

Affirmed.

JUSTICE MARSHALL, concurring.

While I join the Court's opinion, I do so without in any way retreating from my opinion in *San Antonio Independent School District v. Rodriguez,* 411 U.S. 1, 70–133, 93 S. Ct. 1278, 1315–48 (1973) (dissenting opinion). I continue to believe that an individual's interest in education is fundamental, and that this view is amply supported "by the unique status accorded public education by our society, and by the close relationship between education and some of our most basic constitutional values." *Id.* at 111, 93 S. Ct. at 1336. Furthermore, I believe that the facts of these cases demonstrate the wisdom of rejecting a rigidified approach to equal protection analysis, and of employing an approach that allows for varying levels of scrutiny depending upon "the constitutional and societal importance of the interest adversely affected and the recognized invidiousness of the basis upon which the particular classification is drawn." *Id.* at 99, 93 S. Ct. at 1330. It continues to be my view that a class-based denial of public education is utterly incompatible with the Equal Protection Clause of the Fourteenth Amendment.

* * *

CHIEF JUSTICE BURGER, with whom JUSTICE WHITE, JUSTICE REHNQUIST, and JUSTICE O'CONNOR join, dissenting.

Were it our business to set the Nation's social policy, I would agree without hesitation that it is senseless for an enlightened society to deprive any children—including illegal aliens—of an elementary education. I fully agree that it would be folly—and wrong—to tolerate creation of a segment of society made up of illiterate persons, many having a limited or no command of our language. However, the Constitution does not constitute us as "Platonic Guardians" nor does it vest in this Court the authority to strike down laws because they do not meet our standards of desirable social policy, "wisdom," or "common sense." We trespass on the assigned function of the political branches under our structure of limited and separated powers when we assume a policymaking role as the Court does today.

The Court makes no attempt to disguise that it is acting to make up for Congress' lack of "effective leadership" in dealing with the serious national problems caused by the influx of uncountable millions of illegal aliens across our borders. The failure of enforcement of the immigration laws over more than a decade and the inherent difficulty and expense of sealing our vast borders have combined to create a grave socioeconomic dilemma. It is a dilemma that has not yet even been fully assessed, let alone addressed. However, it is not the function of the Judiciary to provide "effective leadership" simply because the political branches of government fail to do so.

The Court's holding today manifests the justly criticized judicial tendency to attempt speedy and wholesale formulation of "remedies" for the failures—or simply the laggard pace—of the political processes of our system of government. The Court employs, and in my view abuses, the Fourteenth Amendment in an effort to become an omnipotent and omniscient problem solver. That the motives for doing so are noble and compassionate does not alter the fact that the Court distorts our constitutional function to make amends for the defaults of others.

I

In a sense, the Court's opinion rests on such a unique confluence of theories and rationales that it will likely stand for little beyond the results in these particular cases. Yet the extent to which the Court departs from principled constitutional adjudication is nonetheless disturbing.

* * *

LEAGUE OF UNITED LATIN AM. CITIZENS v. WILSON

908 F.Supp. 755 (C.D. Cal. 1995)

PFAELZER, DISTRICT JUDGE

Proposition 187 is an initiative measure which was submitted to the voters of the State of California in the November 8, 1994 general election. It was passed by a vote of 59% to 41% and became effective the following day. The stated purpose of Proposition 187 is to "provide for cooperation between [the] agencies of state and local government with the federal government, and to establish a system of required notification by and between such agencies to prevent illegal aliens in the United States from receiving benefits or public services in the State of California." The initiative's provisions require law enforcement, social services, health care and public education personnel to (i) verify the immigration status of persons with whom they come in contact; (ii) notify certain defined persons of their immigration status; (iii) report those persons to state and federal officials; and (iv) deny those persons social services, health care, and education.

After the initiative was passed, several actions challenging the constitutionality of Proposition 187 were commenced in state and federal courts in California. Ultimately, five actions filed in the United States District Court were consolidated in this Court for purposes of motions, hearings, petitions and trial (collectively, the "consolidated actions").

The plaintiffs in the consolidated actions have brought suit for declaratory and injunctive relief seeking to bar California Governor Pete Wilson ("Wilson"), Attorney General Dan Lungren ("Lungren"), and other state actors (collectively, defendants) from enforcing the provisions of Proposition 187.

On November 16, 1994, the Court entered a temporary restraining order enjoining the implementation of sections 4, 5, 6, 7 and 9 of the initiative. On December 14, 1995, the Court granted plaintiffs' motions for preliminary injunction, enjoining the implementation and enforcement of those sections.

* * *

III. *Whether Proposition 187 is Preempted Under Federal Law*

The question of whether provisions of Proposition 187 are preempted by federal law is governed by the Supreme Court's decision in *De Canas v. Bica* (California statute prohibiting an employer from knowingly employing an alien who is not entitled to lawful residence in the United States held not preempted under federal law). In *De Canas,* the Supreme Court set forth three tests to be used in determining whether a state statute related to immigration is preempted. Pursuant to *De Canas,* if a statute fails any one of the three tests, it is preempted by federal law.

Under the first test, the Court must determine whether a state statute is a "regulation of immigration." * * * Under the second test, even if the state law is not an impermissible regulation of immigration, it may still be preempted * * * where Congress intended to "occupy the field" which the statute attempts to regulate. * * * Under the third test, a state law is preempted if it * * * conflicts with federal law making compliance with both state and federal law impossible.

A. *Whether Proposition 187 Constitutes an Impermissible Regulation of Immigration.*

The federal government possesses the exclusive power to regulate immigration. That power derives from the Constitution's grant to the federal government of the power to "establish a uniform Rule of Naturalization," and to "regulate Commerce with foreign Nations." In addition, the Supreme Court has held that the federal government's power to control immigration is inherent in the nation's sovereignty.

* * *

3. Section 7

Section 7 is entitled "Exclusion of Illegal Aliens From Public Elementary and Secondary Schools." Like sections 5 and 6, section 7 contains classification, notification and cooperation/reporting requirements that, taken together, serve only to further the scheme to regulate immigration and are unnecessary to the denial of public education.

In section 7, subsections (a) through (c) require schools to verify the immigration status of children for the purposes of denying access to public elementary and secondary education. Subsection (d) requires verification of the immigration status of *parents* of school children. Subsection (e) requires school districts to report the "illegal" status of any parent, guardian, enrollee or pupil to state agencies and the INS. Subsection (f) requires school districts to "fully cooperate" in "accomplish[ing] an orderly transition to a school in the child's country of origin."

Subsections (a), (b) and (c), together, assure that undocumented children will be denied access to public education. Subsection (d) is wholly unnecessary to implementing the denial of education mandated by section 7, because the state has no need to know the immigration status of *parents* in order to deny benefits to *children*. * * * [T]he only purpose and effect of subsections (d), (e), and (f) is to ensure that persons determined by the state to be in the United States unlawfully are "transitioned" to the "country of their origin." Subsections (d), (e) and (f) are part of an impermissible scheme to regulate immigration and are therefore preempted under the first *De Canas* test.

In any event, an analysis of section 7 under the rigors of the first *De Canas* test is not necessary to sustain the Court's ruling on these motions. In light of the United States Supreme Court's decision in *Plyler v. Doe*, 457 U.S. 202, 102 S. Ct. 2382 (1982), in which the Court held that the Equal Protection Clause of the Fourteenth Amendment prohibits states from excluding undocumented alien children from public schools, section 7 in its entirety conflicts with and is therefore preempted by federal law.

    * * *

IV. *Conclusion*

The California voters' overwhelming approval of Proposition 187 reflects their justifiable frustration with the federal government's inability to enforce the immigration laws effectively. No matter how serious the problem may be, however, the authority to regulate immigration belongs exclusively to the federal government and state agencies are not permitted to assume that authority. The State is powerless to enact its own scheme to regulate immigration or to devise immigration regulations which run parallel to or purport to supplement the federal immigration laws.

The classification, notification and cooperation/reporting provisions in sections 4 through 9 of the initiative, taken together, constitute a regulatory scheme (1) to detect persons present in California in violation of state-created categories of lawful immigration status; (2) to notify state and federal officials of their purportedly unlawful status; and (3) to effect their removal from the United States. These provisions create an impermissible state scheme to regulate immigration and are preempted under the first and second *De Canas* tests. Plaintiffs' motions for summary judgment are granted with respect to these provisions.

The benefits denial provisions of the initiative—if implemented by state regulations which would require verification of immigration status by reference to federal determinations of status—have only an incidental impact on immigration and thus do not violate the first *De Canas* test. Nor do those provisions violate the second *De Canas* test. Plaintiffs have failed to direct the Court to any authority for the proposition that Congress intended to completely oust state authority to legislate in the area of benefits denial. Consequently, the Court must conclude that those provisions are preempted only if their operation conflicts with or impedes the objectives of federal laws.

Section 7's denial of primary and secondary education conflicts with federal law as announced by the Supreme Court in *Plyler v. Doe* and is therefore preempted. Section 8's denial of postsecondary education does not appear to conflict with any federal law and thus is not preempted. * * *

The preliminary injunction entered by the Court on December 14, 1994, shall remain in effect until further order of the Court.

NOTES

1. In a related matter, California Assembly 540 was signed into law by the governor in 2001. The bill allowed all students (including undocumented students)–who attended a high school in California for at least three years and graduated or attained the equivalent of a high school diploma–to pay the significantly lower nonresident tuition at the state's public colleges and universities. Undocumented students, however, were still barred from federal or state financial aid. Since the passage of the legislation, comparable bills were also adopted in nine other states. *See* Leisy Abrego, *Legitimacy, Social Identity, and the Mobilization of Law: The Effects of Assembly Bill 540 on Undocumented Students in California,* 33 Law & Social Inquiry 709 (2008).

Abrego explains the thinking behind AB 540:

Undocumented migratory status has important legal and social implications in people's lives. Barred from most legal resources, undocumented immigrants often live in the shadows of society. With limited access to jobs, education, and social services, undocumented immigrants are also restricted in their efforts for socioeconomic mobility and community development. However, while the law renders undocumented immigrants "criminals, fugitives, and illicit", migrants inhabit legitimate spaces through practices that include work, paying for legal services, and sending remittances. In these ways, undocumented migrants are agents in the creation of legitimate actions and spaces. * * *

The case of undocumented students is arguably even more contradictory than that of adult undocumented immigrants. Because many arrived in the United States as young children, they were able to learn the language, absorb the customs, and make the culture their own in ways that are not available to those who migrate as adults. For example, whereas working-class adults signal to others through their clothing and language practices that they are outsiders, undocumented students dress and speak English in ways that make them largely indistinguishable from their U.S.-born peers. Thus, undocumented students can manipulate social assumptions to avoid questions about their legal status. In this sense, undocumented students are simultaneously included and excluded from U.S. society.

Undocumented youth also have legal access to public education through high school. * * *

California Assembly Bill 540 aimed to improve undocumented youth's prospects for higher education. The potential effects are noteworthy because California is the most popular U.S. destination for undocumented immigrants. It is estimated that between 5,800 and 7,450 undocumented students per year are eligible to benefit from AB 540. To qualify, a student must have attended and graduated from a California high school (or obtained a GED), she must enroll in an accredited institution of higher education in California, and must declare, through an affidavit, that she is in the process of legalizing her immigration status or will seek to do so as soon as she becomes eligible. Students who meet each of the bill's requirements are exempt from nonresident tuition. * * * *See generally id.*

2.   In 2005, the Immigration Reform Law Institute (IRLI), the legal arm of the Federation for American Immigration Reform, filed a lawsuit in California state court challenging the validity of AB 540. The lawsuit was filed on behalf of U.S. citizens from outside the state who wished to pay the same in-state tuition at California's public postsecondary institutions as the undocumented immigrants who were attending these schools. Plaintiffs contended that undocumented students unjustly received a tuition discount that they were not eligible to receive.

The California Court of Appeal, in September 2008, reversed the lower court decision in this case and ruled in favor of the plaintiffs. An appeal was expected. *See Martinez v. Regents of University of California,* 166 Cal.App.4th 1121, 83 Cal.Rptr.3d 518 (Cal. App. 3 Dist. 2008).

3.   At the federal level, various versions of the Development, Relief and Education for Alien Minors Act (also known as "The DREAM Act") have been introduced continually in both houses of Congress for some time. The Act would allow undocumented students paths to achieve legal status.

CHAPTER VI

EDUCATIONAL QUALITY AND THE LAW

■ ■ ■

This chapter focuses on the education process and examines attempts to use the legal system to improve the quality of education in the public schools. At this point in time, there is a relatively limited amount of case law in this area, with legal issues and strands of relevant law still in relatively early stages of development. Indeed, few cases focusing primarily on educational quality have reached the highest courts. But quality-related issues are appearing increasingly in education cases over the past twenty years, and foundational principles are beginning to emerge.

Policy context is particularly important in this area, since the issues that arise not only require an understanding of educational systems themselves, but also call for an assessment of the complex interaction between and among educators, students, parents, the community, and the political process.

For many years, when litigators and legislators looked at the education process and related matters, issues of equality—as referenced in Chapter 5—were a natural starting point. But by the 1980s it had become clear to many people that victories in those cases were not going to be enough to turn things around for many of the country's students.

A major impetus for this gradual change in thinking was the Education Reform Movement, which "officially" began in 1983 with *A Nation at Risk,* a report by the National Commission on Excellence in Education. The report documented in great detail the extensive "mediocrity" that existed in America's public schools, and played a primary role in leading many to conclude that the status quo in our educational system was no longer acceptable. Educators and elected officials on both sides of the political spectrum sought to forge a consensus, united in a new "commitment to excellence," even as they continued to disagree on the relative importance and inherent workability of the various reform proposals.

In the late 1980s and throughout the 1990s, a school choice movement emerged, and many began pushing for vouchers that could be used by parents at either public schools or private schools. In response, many school districts, cities, and states began offering parents much more choice than they had before. The charter school movement also emerged within this context, and the growing popularity of these creative alternatives added to the options that had become available.

At the same time, a new round of school finance litigation was being brought in state courts under state constitutional law, focusing less on equity-related issues and more on educational "adequacy." In retrospect, the combination of the school choice movement and the new wave of school finance litigation had the effect of putting many educational quality issues on the table in courtrooms, state legislatures, and public policy settings. By the turn of the century, the U.S. Congress was heavily involved in these debates, and the "No Child Left Behind" Act emerged as a major bipartisan statement by the federal government in this area.

At the earlier stages of the Education Reform Movement, there was much discussion about the alleged tension between "equity" and "excellence," with many arguing that schools needed to choose between one or the other, but could not have both. A classic example in this regard was the issue of tracking and homogeneous ability grouping. Some argued that a focus on equity should be primary, and that heterogeneous grouping should be employed to keep students from being locked into low level classes that condemned generations of young people to a second rate education. Others argued that ability grouping was necessary to maximize excellence and enable students who were already achieving to move farther and faster and accomplish even more.

By the end of the 1990s, however, it became clear to most people that education reform need not focus on *either* equity or excellence, but that there can and should be a focus on *both*. Indeed, an examination of the anti-tracking movement, the educational finance litigation of that era, the school choice movement, the "No Child Left Behind" Act, and recent efforts to improve the quality of programs for English learners and students with disabilities reveals that all these efforts embody attempts to both maximize equal educational opportunities and improve educational quality for all students.

This chapter begins with an examination of how litigators, legislators, jurists, and commentators have sought to define and identify educational quality. It then turns to the "No Child Left Behind" Act, focusing in particular on the controversial accountability provisions and on interrelated issues of equity and excellence under the Act's mandate. Finally, it explores issues and trends relating to school choice, under the law and as a matter of policy.

A. DEFINING AND IDENTIFYING QUALITY EDUCATION

Members of the legal and public policy communities have wrestled with issues of educational quality in different ways, and in so doing have begun to set forth relevant definitions and guiding principles. Examples of these developments include "educational malpractice" lawsuits, efforts to raise issues of quality in desegregation and school finance contexts, and attempts to construe educational quality under an individual state's fundamental right to an education.

1. EDUCATIONAL MALPRACTICE LITIGATION

In the 1970s, an era when additional new torts were being recognized by many state courts, litigators sought to bring lawsuits under an educational malpractice theory. The *Peter W.* case is a prime example of this litigation, which proved unsuccessful throughout the country.

Consider the scope of the arguments and the parameters of the legal theories raised in *Peter W.* What might be learned about educational quality and the law from this litigation, and from the arguments that were set forth?

PETER W. v. SAN FRANCISCO UNIFIED SCH. DIST.

60 Cal.App.3d 814, 131 Cal.Rptr. 854 (1976)

RATTIGAN, JUDGE

The novel—and troublesome—question on this appeal is whether a person who claims to have been inadequately educated, while a student in a public school system, may state a cause of action in tort against the public authorities who operate and administer the system.

* * * The [complaint's] first count, which is the prototype of the others (each of which incorporates all of its allegations by reference), sounds in negligence. Its opening allegations may be summarized, and quoted in part, as follows:

> XI. Defendant school district, its agents and employees, negligently and carelessly failed to provide plaintiff with adequate instruction, guidance, counseling and/or supervision in basic academic skills such as reading and writing, although said school district had the authority, responsibility and ability [to do so]. Defendant school district, its agents and employees, negligently failed to use reasonable care in the discharge of its duties to provide plaintiff with adequate instruction * * * in basic academic skills[,] and failed to exercise that degree of professional skill required of an ordinary prudent educator under the same circumstances[,] as exemplified, but not limited to[,] the following acts:

In five enumerated subsections which follow in the same paragraph ("XI."), plaintiff alleges that the school district and its agents and employees, "negligently and carelessly" in each instance, (1) failed to apprehend his reading disabilities, (2) assigned him to classes in which he could not read "the books and other materials," (3) allowed him "to pass and advance from a course or grade level" with knowledge that he had not achieved either its completion or the skills "necessary for him to succeed or benefit from subsequent courses" (4) assigned him to classes in which the instructors were unqualified or which were not "geared" to his reading level, and (5) permitted him to graduate from high school although he was "unable to read above the eighth grade level, as required by Education Code section 8573, ... thereby depriving him of additional instruction in reading and other academic skills."

The first count continues with allegations of proximate cause and injury:

> XII. * * * [As] a direct and proximate result of the negligent acts and omissions by the defendant school district, its agents and employees, plaintiff graduated from high school with a reading ability of only the fifth grade [sic]. As a further proximate result [thereof], plaintiff has suffered a loss of earning capacity by his limited ability to read and write and is unqualified for any employment other than * * * labor which requires little or no ability to read or write. * * *

In the closing paragraphs of the first count, plaintiff alleges general damages based upon his "permanent disability and inability to gain meaningful employment"; special damages incurred as the cost of compensatory tutoring allegedly required by reason of the "negligence, acts and omissions of defendants"; that he had presented to the school district an appropriate and timely claim for such damages; and that the claim had been rejected in its entirety.

We proceed to assess the first count for the cause of action in negligence which it purports to plead; the others are separately treated below. * * *

According to the familiar California formula, the allegations requisite to a cause of action for negligence are (1) facts showing a duty of care in the defendant, (2) negligence constituting a breach of the duty, and (3) injury to the plaintiff as a proximate result. The present parties do not debate the adequacy of plaintiff's first count with respect to the elements of negligence, proximate cause, and injury; they focus exclusively upon the issue (which we find dispositive, as will appear) of whether it alleges facts sufficient to show that defendants owed him a "duty of care."

The facts which it shows in this respect—or not—appear in its allegations that he had been a student undergoing academic instruction in the public school system operated and administered by defendants. He argues that these facts alone show the requisite "duty of care." * * * Of course, no reasonable observer would be heard to say that these facts did not impose upon defendants a "duty of care" within any common meaning of the term; given the commanding importance of public education in society, we state a truism in remarking that the public authorities who are duty-bound to educate are also bound to do it with "care." But the truism does not answer the present inquiry, in which "duty of care" is not a term of common parlance; it is instead a legalistic concept of "duty" which will sustain liability for negligence in its breach, and it must be analyzed in that light. * * *

On occasions when the Supreme Court has opened or sanctioned new areas of tort liability, it has noted that the wrongs and injuries involved were both comprehensible and assessable within the existing judicial framework. This is simply not true of wrongful conduct and injuries allegedly involved in educational malfeasance. Unlike the activity of the highway or the marketplace, classroom methodology affords no readily acceptable standards of care, or cause, or injury. The science of pedagogy itself is fraught with different and conflicting theories of how or what a child should be taught, and any layman might—and commonly does—have his own emphatic views on the subject. The "injury" claimed here is plaintiff's inability to read and write. Substantial professional authority attests that the achievement of literacy in the schools, or its failure, are influenced by a host of factors which affect the pupil subjectively, from outside the formal teaching process, and beyond the control of its ministers. They may be physical, neurological, emotional, cultural, environmental; they may be present but not perceived, recognized but not identified.

We find in this situation no conceivable "workability of a rule of care" against which defendants; alleged conduct may be measured, no reasonable "degree of certainty that ... plaintiff suffered injury" within the meaning of the law of negligence, and no such perceptible "connection between the defendant's conduct and the injury suffered," as alleged, which would establish a causal link between them within the same meaning.

These recognized policy considerations alone negate an actionable "duty of care" in persons and agencies who administer the academic phases of the public educational process. Others, which are even more important in practical terms, command the same result. Few of our institutions, if any, have aroused the controversies, or incurred the public dissatisfaction, which have attended the operation of the public schools during the last few decades. Rightly or wrongly, but widely, they are charged with outright failure in the achievement of their educational objectives; according to some critics, they bear responsibility for many of the social and moral problems of our society at large. Their public plight in these respects is attested in the daily media, in bitter governing board elections, in wholesale rejections of school bond proposals, and in survey upon survey. To hold them to an actionable "duty of care," in the discharge of their academic functions, would expose them to the tort claims—real or imagined—of disaffected students and parents in countless numbers. They are already beset by social and financial problems which have gone to major litigation, but for which no permanent solution has yet appeared. The ultimate consequences, in terms of public time and money, would burden them—and society—beyond calculation. * * *

The judgment of dismissal is affirmed.

NOTE

1. The *SFNAACP v. SFUSD* litigation that led to a high-profile, widely publicized 1983 Consent Decree was filed only two years after the *Peter W.* decision. It can be argued that the *SFNAACP* litigation represents an alternative approach to addressing the same range of issues that were raised by the plaintiffs in the *Peter W.* case. *See SFNAACP v. SFUSD*, 576 F.Supp. 34 (N.D. Cal. 1983) (opinion and order setting forth the Consent Decree).

While the *SFNAACP* case never went to trial, it resulted in a unique and long-lasting Decree that focused explicitly on both desegregation and educational quality, and led to significant progress on both fronts for a very large number of students. *See* The SFUSD Consent Decree: A Case Study, *supra*, Ch. 5. *See generally* Independent Reports of the SF Consent Decree Monitoring Team, submitted to the U.S. District Court, Northern District of California (1997–2005), *at* http://www.gseis.ucla.edu/courses/ edlaw/sfrepts.htm (last visited January 7, 2009).

2. Twenty-five years after the decision in *Peter W. v. SFUSD*, the Independent Consent Decree Monitoring Team, in its annual report for the federal court on the District's progress under the mandates of the Decree, identified forty-eight factors that it considered in assessing educational quality.

Which of the following forty-eight factors, in your view, are the most important? Why? What additions, deletions, or modifications might you suggest?

REPORT 18:
THE ANNUAL REPORT OF THE SAN FRANCISCO CONSENT DECREE MONITORING TEAM

(July 2001)

Our monitoring team has compiled a checklist of both traditional objective indicators and supplementary objective and subjective indicators of educational quality in K–12 schools. We employ these 48 indicators to assess the quality of a school as part of our systematic monitoring efforts.

Traditional objective indicators of educational quality include the following items:[1]

1. Test scores (on a range of tests)
2. Average GPA's (secondary level)
3. Average SAT scores (high school)

---

1. We note that these 48 factors can be divided into those factors which the school site has the primary ability to change and those which the district's central office has the primary ability to change.

Also, it should be noted that research has shown a direct correlation between the "performance" of a school and the "poverty factor"—how low the socioeconomic status level of the students might be. However, these 48 factors only address what district administrators and school site educators can do to improve a school, whatever the poverty level of the student population might be.

4. Attendance

5. Drop-out rate (secondary level)

6. AP courses offered, and number of students taking AP exams (high school)

7. AP exam passage rate (high school)

8. Percentage of students graduating "UC eligible"

9. Percentage of students going on to college

Other objective and subjective indicators of educational quality include:

1. The direction the school is heading generally (history, trends, patterns, etc.)

2. Level of engagement between educators and students

3. Level of engagement of students generally

4. Enthusiasm level of students

5. Energy and enthusiasm level of teachers & school site administrators

6. Quality of student work

7. Organization & management of school site programs, activities, and day-to-day affairs

8. Leadership skills of school site administrators

9. Pedagogical skills of teachers

10. Stability of faculty and administration

11. Percentage of credentialed teachers

12. School culture (includes mood, degree to which people get along, respect for differences, motivation, pride, vision)

13. Awards to educators

14. Awards to students

15. Awards to school

16. Record in inter-district and intra-district competitions

17. Condition of physical plant

18. Classroom environment

19. Availability of instructional materials

20. Availability of research tools

21. Quality of instructional materials & research tools

22. Quality of computer technology generally

23. Extent to which computer technology has been integrated into the instructional program

24. Degree to which school is meeting the needs of its students (can include special programs)

25. Level of teacher and school site administrator expectations

26. Quality and relevance of on-site staff development

27. Richness of the curriculum generally

28. Extent to which curriculum challenges the students

29. Curriculum for LEP students

30. Curriculum for Special Education students

31. Curriculum for low achieving students

32. Curriculum for high achieving students

33. Discipline practices generally

34. Suspension and expulsion rates

35. Diversity or lack thereof

36. Within school desegregation

37. Redesignation practices

38. Mainstreaming practices

39. School-family-community partnerships

2. FEDERAL COURT EFFORTS TO DEFINE EDUCATIONAL QUALITY IN A DESEGREGATION CONTEXT

Consider the language in the opinions that follow regarding the interface between desegregation and "educational quality." What lessons can be learned from the respective courts' efforts to wrestle with these interrelated concepts?

Freeman is one of the few examples of a decision where a federal judge in a desegregation case mentions educational quality directly. Indeed, it might be argued that the federal courts in the language below have identified a number of factors that might together comprise educational quality under the law—both in desegregation cases and in future lawsuits addressing educational quality in other contexts. (These factors have been highlighted in bold.)

from **PITTS v. FREEMAN**, 887 F.2d 1438 (11th Cir. 1989)

* * * The district court considered six factors set forth in *Green v. County Sch. Bd. of New Kent County, Va.*: student assignment, **faculty, staff,** transportation, **extracurricular activities,** and **facilities.**[8] *See,*

---

8. The district court also considered a seventh factor: "quality of education." We conclude that the Green Court intended quality of education to be considered in conjunction with each of its six enumerated factors. See Green, 391 U.S. at 435, 88 S.Ct. at 1692 (describing the six factors as comprising "every facet of school operations"). In this case, the district court should consider

391 U.S. at 435, 88 S.Ct. at 1692. A review of these six factors constitutes the best approach for determining whether a school system has eliminated the vestiges of a dual system. Therefore, we hold that district courts should review the six Green factors to determine whether a school system has achieved unitary status. If the school system fulfills all six factors at the same time for several years, the court should declare that the school system has achieved unitary status. If the school system fails to fulfill all six factors at the same time for several years, the district court should retain jurisdiction.

from FREEMAN v. PITTS, 503 U.S. 467, 112 S.Ct. 1430 (1992)

[In this excerpt from the U.S. Supreme Court opinion, Justice Kennedy—in referencing the district court findings—is attempting to justify a finding of unitary status and thus an end to mandatory desegregation.]

* * * The District Court approached the question whether DCSS had achieved unitary status by asking whether DCSS was unitary with respect to each of the factors identified in Green. The court considered an additional factor that is not named in Green: the quality of education being offered to the white and black student populations. * * *

* * * Addressing the more ineffable category of quality of education, the District Court rejected most of respondents' contentions that there was racial disparity in the **provision of certain educational resources (e.g., teachers with advanced degrees, teachers with more experience, library books)**, contentions made to show that black students were not being given equal educational opportunity. The District Court went further, however, and examined the **evidence concerning achievement** of black students in DCSS. It cited expert testimony praising the overall educational program in the district, as well as objective evidence of black achievement: Black students at DCSS made greater gains on the Iowa Tests of Basic Skills than white students, and black students at DCSS are more successful than black students nationwide on the Scholastic Aptitude Test. It made the following finding:

> While there will always be something more that the DCSS can do to improve the chances for black students to achieve academic success, the court cannot find, as plaintiffs urge, that the DCSS has been negligent in its duties to implement programs to assist black students. The DCSS is a very **innovative** school system. It has implemented a number of **programs to enrich the lives and enhance the academic potential of all students**, both blacks and whites. Many **remedial programs** are targeted in the majority black schools. Programs have been implemented to **involve the parents** and **offset negative socio-economic factors**. If the DCSS has failed in any way in this regard, it is not because the school system has been negligent in its duties.

---

the distribution of educational resources in relation to the area in which the school system applies the resource.

* * * Despite its finding that there was no intentional violation, the District Court found that DCSS had not achieved unitary status with respect to quality of education because teachers in schools with disproportionately high percentages of white students tended to be better educated and have more experience than their counterparts in schools with disproportionately high percentages of black students, and because per-pupil expenditures in majority white schools exceeded per-pupil expenditures in majority black schools. From these findings, the District Court ordered DCSS to equalize spending and remedy the other problems. * * *

In contrast to the circumstances in [other cases] the District Court in this case stated that throughout the period of judicial supervision it has been impressed by the **successes** DCSS has achieved and its **dedication to providing a quality education** for all students, and that DCSS "has travelled the often long road to unitary status almost to its end." [emphasis added].

3. CONCEPTUALIZING EDUCATIONAL QUALITY IN A SCHOOL FINANCE CONTEXT

EDUCATIONAL ADEQUACY: A THEORY AND ITS REMEDIES

William H. Clune
28 U. MICH. J.L. REF. 481 (1995)

* * * School finance litigation typically has been based on one of two theories: equity or adequacy. "Equity" in school finance means equal resources across a state; for example, equal spending per pupil or equal taxable resources. "Adequacy" refers to resources that are sufficient (or adequate) to achieve some educational result, such as a minimum passing grade on a state achievement test. The two theories are not always clearly distinguishable in practice. Adequacy theory may be used as the legal basis for reaching equity when courts have rejected traditional equity theories, such as equal protection. Conversely, equity litigation may produce adequacy as a by-product. State legislatures that are required to equalize school funding often allocate large amounts of minimum-level funding in order to achieve equality without excessive budget cutting.

In at least three circumstances, adequacy may dictate results or remedies that are different from those required by equity: (1) where practically all schools in a state are inadequate and the remedy must guarantee new resources for education; (2) where certain groups of students, schools, or districts need extra resources to meet minimum achievement standards, and the remedy must include some kind of compensatory aid, such as for children in poverty; and (3) where reaching minimum achievement levels requires schools to become more effective and efficient, forcing the remedy to include elements of educational reform and accountability. * * *

II.   Judicial Remedies in School Finance Litigation

* * * At its heart, adequacy refers to a shift in the emphasis of school finance from inputs to outcomes, e.g. from dollars to student achievement as measured by standardized tests and avoidance of dropping out. Courts deciding school finance litigation cases are beginning to mirror the rest of society by seeing the present time as the age of information and efficiency. * * * [E]arlier cases viewed the "opportunity" in "equality of educational opportunity" as referring to equal access to educational resources for all students—or for their school districts. The central problem confronting courts and school finance plaintiffs was large variations in property tax bases and spending per pupil among districts within a state. Questions of how effectively and efficiently resources were used were left for local communities and educational experts to resolve. Courts deemed consideration of educational outcomes as "unmanageable," a virtual kiss of death for any case that required it. In contrast, dollar equality of tax base or spending offered a measurable standard.

The United States Supreme Court expressed early concern about outcomes in *San Antonio Independent School District v. Rodriguez.* Under the Equal Protection Clause of the United States Constitution, a guarantee of any level of resources would be possible only if tied to a fundamental right. This right would have to be a right to some minimum level of adequate education or, in other words, a right to minimum outcomes. * * * [S]chool finance litigation then shifted to the states, because the "common school ideal" was reflected through both state equal protection requirements and so-called "education clauses" in state constitutions. Some cases continued to find a guarantee of equal resources under state constitutions. Many more recent cases, however, remarkably have invoked all types of clauses and constitutional language to speak—and speak at length—of a student's right to function fully in society.

* * *

The most common and critical facet [in this area] is a method of measuring student achievement against minimum state standards. In Kentucky, despite the availability of existing standardized tests, the legislature was asked to create a new test to meet a new vision of education. In other words, "adequate" might refer to minimum achievement either on an old-style test of educational basics or on a cutting-edge test aimed at world-class standards. * * *

Accountability policies also typically include some kind of state monitoring and sanctions in the form of rewards and punishments for districts and schools that make acceptable or unacceptable progress. In other words, the state test is likely to be high stakes in some sense—potentially leading to important consequences for either the student's graduation, the school's independence, or the school's eligibility for cash rewards.

The combination of state testing, with its implied guidance of curriculum in every school, and high-stakes monitoring means that adequacy litigation assumes a strong central role for government. This strong accountability contrasts with the old equality-based litigation, which was indifferent to the ways in which extra resources were spent and thus tolerated unmonitored local control.

* * *

[A]dequacy remedies explicitly or implicitly assume a protracted period of educational change. While equal resources, especially money, can be made available in a short period of time, improved student achievement assumes a learning process for teachers and students. For example, in a full cycle, students will need to begin and sustain higher levels of achievement from the early grades. Teachers must learn such skills as teaching new subjects and providing accelerated education for disadvantaged students. * * *

STATE EDUCATION ARTICLES

Virtually every state constitution contains provisions guaranteeing some form of public education for its residents. While education is not mentioned at all in the U.S. Constitution, it has traditionally been viewed as an integral component of state constitutional law. *See, e.g.,* Allen W. Hubsch, *Education and Self–Government: The Right to Education Under State Constitutional Law,* 18 J.L. & EDUC. 93, 134–40 (1989). Some of these education provisions contain broad general language setting forth the minimum requirements of a school system. Others include specific guarantees of "thoroughness," "efficiency," or both. *See* William E. Thro, *To Render Them Safe: The Analysis of State Constitutional Provisions in Public School Finance Reform Litigation,* 75 VA. L. REV. 1639, 1661–63 (1989).

The following are selected examples of education articles from state constitutions.

California
Article IX, Section 1

A general diffusion of knowledge and intelligence being essential to the preservation of the rights and liberties of the people, the Legislature shall encourage by all suitable means the promotion of intellectual, scientific, moral, and agricultural improvement.

Kentucky
Section 183

The General Assembly shall, by appropriate legislation, provide for an efficient system of common schools throughout the State.

Maryland
Article VIII, Section 1

The General Assembly, at its First Session after the adoption of this Constitution, shall by Law establish throughout the State a thorough and efficient System of Free Public Schools; and shall provide by taxation, or otherwise, for their maintenance.

Massachusetts

Chapter V, Section 2

Wisdom, and knowledge, as well as virtue, diffused generally among the body of the people, being necessary for the preservation of their rights and liberties; and as these depend on spreading the opportunities and advantages of education in the various parts of the country, and among the different orders of the people, it shall be the duty of legislatures and magistrates, in all future periods of this commonwealth, to cherish the interests of literature and the sciences, and all seminaries of them; especially the university at Cambridge, public schools and grammar schools in the towns; to encourage private societies and public institutions, rewards and immunities, for the promotion of agriculture, arts, sciences, commerce, trades, manufactures, and a natural history of the country; to countenance and inculcate the principles of humanity and general benevolence, public and private charity, industry and frugality, honesty and punctuality in their dealings; sincerity, good humor, and all social affections, and generous sentiments among the people.

Litigants in the area of school finance have relied upon key words in state education articles to win major victories. Plaintiffs in the *Rose* case, *infra,* for example, focused entirely on the word *efficient* in the Kentucky Constitution. And in an unprecedented ruling, the *Rose* Court determined not only that the Kentucky school finance system was inefficient, but found the entire state school system unconstitutional. Significant education reforms were implemented as a result, and many things changed for the better.

In *McDuffy v. Secretary of the Executive Office of Educ.,* 615 N.E.2d 516, 527 (Mass. 1993), Massachusetts plaintiffs won a similar victory. The Supreme Judicial Court based its decision to overturn school funding laws solely on the constitutional duty of "legislatures and magistrates" to "cherish ... the public schools." Parallel lawsuits in Alabama and Maryland resulted in remedial orders and settlement agreements mandating changes both in funding structures and in the education process.

State constitutional provisions have become increasingly more important for litigants over the past two decades. *See* Stanley Mosk, *State Constitutionalism: Both Liberal and Conservative,* 63 TEX. L. REV. 1081, 1081 (1985) (noting that "state constitutionalism has something to offer both liberals and conservatives"). Under these provisions, states can provide greater protection for individual rights than the federal government has provided. The protections provided by Congress and the federal courts typically constitute a baseline. State legislatures and state courts may not fall below this baseline, but they can, and often do, go much further. *See generally* William J. Brennan, Jr., *State Constitutions and the Protection of Individual Rights,* 90 HARV. L. REV. 489, 495 (1977) (noting that "of late * * * more and more state courts are construing state constitutional counterparts of provisions of the Bill of Rights as guaranteeing citizens of their states even more protection than the federal provisions, even those identically phrased."). In addition, state courts typically feel more comfortable with broad interpretations of state constitutional provisions because these documents, unlike the federal constitution, are relatively easy to amend. Many states actually allow their constitutions to be amended by ballot initiative. *See* Julian N. Eule, *Judicial Review of Direct Democracy*, 99 YALE L.J. 1503, 1509 n.22 (1990).

ROSE v. COUNCIL FOR BETTER ED., INC.

790 S.W.2d 186 (Ky.1989)

STEPHENS, CHIEF JUSTICE

The issue we decide on this appeal is whether the Kentucky General Assembly has complied with its constitutional mandate to "provide an efficient system of common schools throughout the state." * * *

In a word, the present system of common schools in Kentucky is not an "efficient" one in our view of the clear mandate of Section 183. The common school system in Kentucky is constitutionally deficient.

In reaching this decision, we are ever mindful of the immeasurable worth of education to our state and its citizens, especially to its young people. The framers of our constitution intended that each and every child in this state should receive a proper and an adequate education, *to be provided for by the General Assembly.* This opinion dutifully applies the constitutional test of Section 183 to the existing system of common schools. We do no more, nor may we do any less.

The goal of the framers of our constitution, and the polestar of this opinion, is eloquently and movingly stated in the landmark case of *Brown v. Board of Education:* "education is perhaps the most important function of state and local governments.... Such an opportunity, where the state has undertaken to provide it, is a right which must be made available to all on equal terms."

These thoughts were as applicable in 1891 when Section 183 was adopted as they are today and the goals they express reflect the goals set out by the framers of our Kentucky Constitution.

* * *

If one were to summarize the history of school funding in Kentucky, one might well say that every forward step taken to provide funds to local districts and to equalize money spent for the poor districts has been countered by one backward step. * * *

The overall effect of appellants' evidence is a virtual concession that Kentucky's system of common schools is underfunded and inadequate; is fraught with inequalities and inequities throughout the 177 local school districts; is ranked nationally in the lower 20–25% in virtually every category that is used to evaluate educational performance; and is not uniform among the districts in educational opportunities. * * *

In a few simple, but direct words, the framers of our present Constitution, set forth the will of the people with regard to the importance of providing public education in the Commonwealth. "General Assembly to provide for school system—The General Assembly shall, by appropriate legislation, provide for an efficient system of common schools throughout the State." Ky. Const. Sec. 183.

* * * A brief sojourn into the Constitutional debates will give some idea—a contemporaneous view—of the depth of the delegates' intention when Section 183 was drafted. * * * It will provide a background for our definition of "efficient."

* * * Delegates Beckner and Moore told their fellow delegates and have told us, what this section means.

— The providing of public education through a system of common schools by the General Assembly is the most "vital question" presented to them.

— Education of children must not be minimized to the "slightest degree."

— Education must be provided to the children of the rich and poor alike.

— Education of children is essential to the prosperity of our state.

— Education of children should be supervised by the State.

— There must be a constant and continuing effort to make our schools more efficient.

— We must not finance our schools in a *de minimis* fashion.

— All schools and children stand upon one level in their entitlement to equal state support.

This Court, in defining efficiency must, at least in part, be guided by these clearly expressed purposes. The framers of Section 183 emphasized that education is essential to the welfare of the citizens of the Commonwealth. By this animus to Section 183, we recognize that education is a fundamental right in Kentucky. * * *

In our sister and adjoining state of West Virginia, the state Constitution requires that "The legislature shall provide, by general law, for a thorough and efficient system of free schools." W.Va. Const, Art. XII, Sec. 1.

In the landmark case of *Pauley v. Kelly,* 162 W.Va. 672, 255 S.E.2d 859 (1979), the West Virginia Supreme Court faced a lawsuit similar to the one before us. * * * The Court engaged in extensive historical analysis, in which it carefully interpreted other states' constitutional mandates with regard to public education. The Court rejected the contention that legislative discretion in public school system matters is determinative. * * *

In turning to the definition of "efficient" the Court, began with definition which was "lexically" founded. "(T)he mandate ... becomes a command that the education system be absolutely complete, attentive to every detail, extending beyond ordinary parameters, and further, it must produce results without waste."

Following an analysis of the admitted plethora of legal precedent, the West Virginia Supreme Court adopted a definition of "thorough and efficient." "We may now define a thorough and efficient system of schools: It develops, as best the state of education expertise allows, the minds, bodies and social morality of its charges to prepare them for useful and happy occupations, recreation and citizenship, and does so economically."

The court continued by recognizing areas in which each child educated in the system should develop to full capacity: 1) literacy; 2) mathematical ability; 3) knowledge of government sufficient to equip the individual to make informed choices as a citizen; 4) self-knowledge sufficient to intelligently choose life work; 5) vocational or advanced academic training; 6) recreational pursuits; 7) creative interests; 8) social ethics. Support services, such as good physical facilities and instructional resources, and state and local monitoring for waste and incompetency were considered to be implicit in the definition of "a thorough and efficient system."

We cite *Pauley,* and quote from it at some length to show that Courts may, should and have involved themselves in defining the standards of a constitutionally mandated educational system. * * *

We consider foreign cases, along with our constitutional debates, Kentucky precedents and the opinion of experts in formulating the definition of "efficient" as it appears in our Constitution.

OPINIONS OF EXPERTS

Numerous well-qualified experts testified in this case. They were all well educated, experienced teachers, educators, or administrators; and all were familiar with the Kentucky system of common schools and with other states' and national school issues.

Dr. Richard Salmon testified that the concept of efficiency was a three part concept. First, the system should impose no financial hardship or advantage on any group of citizens. Further, local school districts must make comparable tax efforts. Second, resources provided by the system must be adequate and uniform throughout the state. Third, the system must not waste resources.

Dr. Kern Alexander opined that an efficient system is one which is unitary. It is one in which there is uniformity throughout the state. It is one in which equality is a hallmark and one in which students must be given equal educational opportunities, regardless of economic status, or place of residence. He also testified that "efficient" involves pay and training of teachers, school buildings, other teaching staff, materials, and adequacy of all educational resources. Moreover, he, like Dr. Salmon, believed that "efficient" also applies to the quality of management of schools. Summarizing Dr. Alexander's opinion, an efficient system is unitary, uniform, adequate and properly managed.

The definitions of "efficient" were documented and supported by numerous national and local studies, prepared and authorized by many of the giants of the education profession.

The primary expert for the appellees was a local school superintendent who felt that an efficient system is one which is operated as best as can be with the money that was provided. We reject such a definition which could result in a system of common schools, efficient only in the uniformly deplorable conditions it provides throughout the state.

In summary the experts in this case believed that an "efficient" system of common schools should have several elements:

1. The system is the sole responsibility of the General Assembly.

2. The tax effort should be evenly spread.

3. The system must provide the necessary resources throughout the state—they must be uniform.

4. The system must provide an adequate education.

5. The system must be properly managed.

DEFINITION OF "EFFICIENT"

We now hone in on the heart of this litigation. In defining "efficient," we use all the tools that are made available to us. In spite of any protestations to the contrary, we do not engage in judicial legislating. We do not make policy. We do not substitute our judgment for that of the General Assembly. We simply take the plain directive of the Constitution, and, armed with its purpose, we decide what our General Assembly must achieve in complying with its solemn constitutional duty.

Any system of common schools must be created and maintained with the premise that education is absolutely vital to the present and to the future of our Commonwealth.

The General Assembly must not only establish the system, but it must monitor it on a continuing basis so that it will always be maintained in a constitutional manner. The General Assembly must carefully supervise it, so that there is no waste, no duplication, no mismanagement, at any level.

The system of common schools must be adequately funded to achieve its goals. The system of common schools must be substantially uniform throughout the state. Each child, *every child,* in this Commonwealth must be provided with an equal opportunity to have an adequate education. Equality is the key word here. The children of the poor and the children of the rich, the children who live in the poor districts and the children who live in the rich districts must be given the same opportunity and access to an adequate education. This obligation cannot be shifted to local counties and local school districts. * * *

We do not instruct the General Assembly to enact any specific legislation. We do not direct the members of the General Assembly to raise taxes. It is their decision how best to achieve efficiency. We only decide the nature of the constitutional mandate. We only determine the intent of the framers. Carrying-out that intent is the duty of the General Assembly.

A child's right to an adequate education is a fundamental one under our Constitution. The General Assembly must protect and advance that right. We concur with the trial court that an efficient system of education must have as its goal to provide each and every child with at least the seven following capacities: (i) sufficient oral and written communication skills to enable students to function in a complex and rapidly changing civilization; (ii) sufficient knowledge of economic, social, and political systems to enable the student to make informed choices; (iii) sufficient understanding of governmental processes to enable the student to understand the issues that affect his or her community, state, and nation; (iv) sufficient self-knowledge and knowledge of his or her mental and physical wellness; (v) sufficient grounding in the arts to enable each student to appreciate his or her cultural and historical heritage; (vi) sufficient training or preparation for advanced training in either academic or vocational fields so as to enable each child to choose and pursue life work intelligently; and (vii) sufficient levels of academic or vocational skills to enable public school students to compete favorably with their counterparts in surrounding states, in academics or in the job market.[22]

The essential, and minimal, characteristics of an "efficient" system of common schools, may be summarized as follows:

1. The establishment, maintenance and funding of common schools in Kentucky is the sole responsibility of the General Assembly.

2. Common schools shall be free to all.

3. Common schools shall be available to all Kentucky children.

4. Common schools shall be substantially uniform throughout the state.

5. Common schools shall provide equal educational opportunities to all Kentucky children, regardless of place of residence or economic circumstances.

6. Common schools shall be monitored by the General Assembly to assure that they are operated with no waste, no duplication, no mismanagement, and with no political influence.

---

22. In recreating and redesigning the Kentucky system of common schools, these seven characteristics should be considered as *minimum* goals in providing an adequate education. Certainly, there is no prohibition against higher goals—whether such are implemented statewide by the General Assembly or through the efforts of any local education entities that the General Assembly may establish—so long as the General Assembly meets the standards set out in this Opinion.

7. The premise for the existence of common schools is that all children in Kentucky have a constitutional right to an adequate education.

8. The General Assembly shall provide funding which is sufficient to provide each child in Kentucky an adequate education.

9. An adequate education is one which has as its goal the development of the seven capacities recited previously.

* * *

SUMMARY/CONCLUSION

We have decided this case solely on the basis of our Kentucky Constitution, Section 183. We find it unnecessary to inject any issues raised under the United States Constitution or the United States Bill of Rights in this matter. We decline to issue any injunctions, restraining orders, writs of prohibition or writs of mandamus.

We have decided one legal issue—and one legal issue only—viz., that the General Assembly of the Commonwealth has failed to establish an efficient system of common schools throughout the Commonwealth.

Lest there be any doubt, the result of our decision is that Kentucky's *entire system* of common schools is unconstitutional. There is no allegation that only part of the common school system is invalid, and we find no such circumstance. This decision applies to the entire sweep of the system—all its parts and parcels. * * *

Since we have, by this decision, declared the system of common schools in Kentucky to be unconstitutional, Section 183 places an absolute duty on the General Assembly to re-create, re-establish a new system of common schools in the Commonwealth. As we have said, the premise of this opinion is that education is a basic, fundamental constitutional right that is available to all children within this Commonwealth.

The General Assembly must provide adequate funding for the system. How they do this is their decision. * * *

This decision has not been reached without much thought and consideration. We do not take our responsibilities lightly, and we have decided this case based on our perception and interpretation of the Kentucky Constitution. We intend no criticism of any person, persons or institutions. We view this decision as an opportunity for the General Assembly to launch the Commonwealth into a new era of educational opportunity which will ensure a strong economic, cultural and political future.

NOTES

1. Education-related lawsuits in this area have relied upon state education articles, state equal protection guarantees, or some combination thereof. Noteworthy school finance lawsuits brought under the state's education articles include: *Rose v. Council for Better Educ., Inc.*, 790 S.W.2d 186 (Ky.

1989); *McDuffy v. Secretary of the Executive Office of Educ.*, 415 Mass. 545, 615 N.E.2d 516 (1993); *Helena Elementary Sch. Dist. Number One v. State*, 236 Mont. 44, 769 P.2d 684 (1989); *Edgewood Indep. Sch. Dist. v. Kirby*, 777 S.W.2d 391 (Tex. 1989). Lawsuits relying on state equal protection guarantees include *Serrano v. Priest*, 18 Cal.3d 728, 135 Cal.Rptr. 345, 557 P.2d 929 (1976), *cert. denied*, 432 U.S. 907, 97 S.Ct. 2951 (1977); *Horton v. Meskill*, 172 Conn. 615, 376 A.2d 359 (1977); and *Washakie County Sch. Dist. Number One v. Herschler*, 606 P.2d 310 (Wyo. 1980), *cert. denied*, 449 U.S. 824, 101 S.Ct. 86 (1980). Lawsuits relying on both the education clauses and the equal protection provisions include *Robinson v. Cahill*, 62 N.J. 473, 303 A.2d 273 (1973), *cert. denied*, 414 U.S. 976, 94 S.Ct. 292 (1973); *Pauley v. Kelly*, 162 W.Va. 672, 255 S.E.2d 859 (1979).

2.   Plaintiffs in the Education Articles cases of the past 25 years have prevailed within the context of school finance. What are the prospects for applying the principles and the reasoning of these cases to a wider range of educational quality issues? Consider the following framework for prospective litigation under a broader "right to an education." The framework contemplates an extension of this framework beyond school finance, and could be employed to either seek relief for a violation of the right to an education in specific situations, or to mandate quality education generally under the right. Might plaintiffs be successful employing such an approach? What types of fact patterns might lead to greater chances of success?

Alternatively, or in addition, might such a framework interface successfully with the requirements and mandates of the "No Child Left Behind" Act, *infra*?

a.   Planning the Litigation

Step 1—Identify relevant words in the state's education articles.

Step 2—Identify lists of *quality standards, guidelines, or requirements* from published education articles cases, other court orders, relevant consent decrees, expert testimony, and/or relevant literature.

Step 3—Determine whether to seek relief for a violation of the right to an education in specific situations, or to mandate quality education generally under the right. (Other approaches may be available as well.)

b.   If Seeking Declaratory and/or Injunctive Relief for a Violation of the Right to an Education in Specific Situations

Step 1—Attempt to establish a consensus on what constitutes a "Right to an Education" in a particular situation. This consensus may include excerpts from the lists of *quality standards, guidelines, or requirements*.

Step 2—Argue that a school district's actions in particular instances constitute a violation of this right under the state's education articles as reflected in key words (such as "efficient") because they run counter to the standards, guidelines, or requirements that have been identified.

c.   If Seeking a Court Order to Mandate Quality Education Generally

Step 1—In the complaint, set forth quality standards, guidelines, requirements, etc.

Step 2—Argue that these standards should be implemented to give effect to the language in the education articles.

PROBLEM 29: THE PETER W. EDUCATION ARTICLES LAWSUIT

Assume facts virtually identical to those set forth in the *Peter W.* case, *supra,* for several plaintiffs in a hypothetical school district today. Assume, also, that the district is located in the State of Maryland. If plaintiffs seek to bring a lawsuit under the prospective framework outlined in the above note, what arguments might they set forth? What result? Discuss.

ACHIEVING "ADEQUACY" IN THE CLASSROOM
William S. Koski
27 B.C. THIRD WORLD L.J. 13 (2007)

* * * The full recognition of a right to an education is still a work in progress. In the last twenty years, two strands of educational law and policy—adequacy litigation and standards-based reform and accountability—have worked separately and, in a few instances, together to develop and refine the educational resources and educational outcomes that we should expect from our school systems. * * * Even if this nascent effort to define the inputs required for all children to achieve at high levels is sustained, [however,] one still should not assume complacently that those resources and conditions will actually be delivered. Policymakers and school systems must be held accountable to children, parents, and communities for providing those educational necessities. * * *

Yet most standards-based accountability systems have fallen short of ensuring that schools have the capacity to reform themselves. Granted, many accountability schemes provide to failing schools modest infusions of cash, some technical assistance, and even a period of time to design and implement school improvement plans. Equally common, however, are policies that do nothing to build the capacity of failing schools, but rather permit students in those schools to avoid the policies altogether. But, as * * * Richard Elmore and his colleagues found in a recent study of accountability in high schools, "there isn't much evidence ... of major external investments in new knowledge and skill in schools." So long as state accountability policies are based on the theory that external pressure for performance can mobilize existing capacity rather than create new capacity, "it is possible that the long-term effect of accountability policies ... could be to increase the gap in performance between high and low capacity schools."[82] An educational policy that endeavors to ensure that schools produce proficient learners will not succeed without the capacity to produce those learners.

---

82. [Richard Elmore, *Accountability and Capacity, in* THE NEW ACCOUNTABILITY: HIGH SCHOOLS AND HIGH-STAKES TESTING 195, 206–208 (Martin Carnoy et al. eds., 2003).]

The marriage of standards-based accountability and adequacy litigation, however, provides the possibility that opportunities to learn can be achieved through litigation. Indeed, whether at the point of identifying the substantive elements of an adequate education or designing the appropriate remedial interventions, courts are beginning to compel policymakers to flesh-out the substantive entitlement to educational resources and conditions based on the state's own expected educational outcomes.

While this sounds hopeful, two major caveats remain. First, even in those courts that have entered the school reform fracas, judges have just barely begun to look to standards-based accountability schemes as guidance for determining whether states have offered a constitutionally adequate education to their children. Even fewer have relied upon output standards in crafting or approving remedial finance schemes or school reform remedies.[83] Second, and the subject to which I now turn, is the difficulty of relying on the judicial system as the primary enforcement mechanism to ensure that necessary resources and conditions will be delivered at the classroom level. As a consequence, the future of adequacy litigation should seek to secure and implement meaningful, user-friendly monitoring and enforcement schemes.

C. *Enforcing Educational Rights Through Monitoring and Reciprocal Accountability*

* * * While schools and districts are held accountable to the public for student performance through public reporting, the tools available to families and communities to pressure schools to improve are, in my view, ill-defined and not well-suited to the communities who need them most. For instance, requiring schools and districts to publish their students' academic performance disaggregated by race and ethnicity, ELL status, and disability could provide a useful accountability tool to communities and families. But this assumes several conditions that are not necessarily present in low-income communities with low-performing schools. First, data must be published in a clear, accessible way so that all may understand its meaning. Yet a recent study in California suggests that the state's mandated "school accountability report cards" (SARCs), which provide information on schools' and districts' student performance, facilities, and teacher qualifications, are too complex for most Californians to decipher.[84] Next, disadvantaged communities must have the capacity to

---

83. There are other possible risks for this advocacy strategy. As James E. Ryan recently cautioned at the *Rethinking* Rodriguez: *Education as a Fundamental Right* Symposium at the Boalt Hall School of Law (Apr. 27–28, 2006), holding states accountable for providing resources to achieve at high standards may have the perverse effects of (1) encouraging states to lower their standards for proficiency; (2) encouraging schools and teachers to narrow their curriculum to only those items that will be tested; and (3) providing states with an opportunity to demonstrate that schools are doing "good enough" on standards-based tests so that courts will find them in compliance with state constitutions, despite dramatic inequality in educational resources among schools and districts. That said, each of these three criticisms could be equally directed at test-based accountability schemes, like the NCLB, even without court involvement.

84. GABRIEL BACA ET AL., GRADING THE REPORT CARD: A REPORT ON THE READABILITY OF THE SCHOOL ACCOUNTABILITY REPORT CARD (SARC) 4 (2005), *available at* http://www.idea.gseis.ucla.edu/publications/sarc/pdf/GradingSARCff–1.pdf. * * *

act meaningfully on this information. "Voting with their feet" is simply not an option for low-income families who cannot afford to move to higher performing school districts and schools.

This leaves only the "voice" option—political mobilization. * * * For many families in low-income communities, [however,] group political mobilization is not a viable option. * * *

Virtually none of the modern accountability systems formally and systematically hold policymakers and states accountable for what they can provide—the conditions and resources (i.e., the capacity) necessary to reach proficiency targets. In other words, such systems lack meaningful reciprocal accountability. Such an accountability system would provide, in the words of Jeannie Oakes, Gary Blasi, and John Rogers, at least two missing components: (1) "[c]lear standards or benchmarks against which actors in the system can be measured.... [including] both learning outcomes students are expected to achieve *and the resources and conditions necessary to support teachers and students to ... produce those outcomes*" and (2) "[l]egitimate roles for local communities, parents, and students in holding the system accountable."[88]

What would such a meaningful reciprocal accountability system look like on the ground level? Some flexibility for local conditions is warranted here, but I would identify two major components. First, in the same way that a state's department of education is often charged with the monitoring of data from and periodic inspection of local school districts in areas such as the implementation of special education programs under the Individuals with Disabilities Education Act[89] or federal programs like free and reduced lunch programs, state departments of education should supplement their obligation to monitor student performance data with the monitoring of data regarding opportunities to learn, and follow up with on-the-ground inspections to verify those data. Since the meeting of the "Chicago Group" (a group of experts in state monitoring systems for special education convened to lay out a blue print for a new system of special education monitoring in Texas), such a system of monitoring key performance or outcome indicators followed by heightened verification reviews and focused inspections that are tailored to local conditions has been the direction in which special education monitoring has been headed in a few states, including Texas and California. These monitoring and inspection mechanisms could easily be adapted to monitoring performance, inputs, and processes for all students.

Second, an accessible and user-friendly system of complaints management should be available to students, parents, communities, and even teachers who believe that schools do not have the resources and conditions

88. [Jeannie Oakes et al., *Accountability for Adequate and Equitable Opportunities to Learn, in* HOLDING ACCOUNTABILITY ACCOUNTABLE: WHAT OUGHT TO MATTER IN PUBLIC EDUCATION 92–94 (Kenneth A. Sirotnik ed., 2004) (emphasis added).]

89. *See* NAT'L COUNCIL ON DISABILITY, BACK TO SCHOOL ON CIVIL RIGHTS 37 (2000), *available at* http:// www.ncd.gov/newsroom/publications/2000/pdf/backtoschool.pdf [hereinafter BACK TO SCHOOL].

deemed necessary to reach proficiency targets. Whatever resources and conditions are deemed—through adequacy litigation, legislation, or otherwise—necessary for children to enjoy an adequate education must be widely publicized both in and outside of school. Schools must also publicize that individual students, parents, teachers, and, perhaps, site administrators may file a complaint with a state oversight agency when such resources and conditions are not provided at the desk level. Such a complaint must be promptly investigated, findings issued, and a corrective action ordered. Already, similar systems are commonplace in special education. The goal, of course, is that with an order of noncompliance and corrective action in hand, the relevant provider—the state or local school district—will ensure that the child receives the necessary educational resources.

Tying this discussion together, modern adequacy litigation and standards-based accountability policies are beginning to work in tandem to not only monitor and hold schools accountable for student performance, but also to specify the conditions and resources that provide the opportunity for all students, based on their needs, to reach proficiency. The final link in this chain of reciprocal accountability is a system of monitoring and complaints management that ensures meaningful opportunities for students, families, and communities, to hold policymakers, the state, and schools accountable for providing opportunities to learn.

4. CONSTRUING EDUCATIONAL QUALITY UNDER AN INDIVIDUAL STATE'S FUNDAMENTAL RIGHT TO AN EDUCATION

T. K. BUTT v. CALIFORNIA

4 Cal.4th 668, 15 Cal.Rptr.2d 480, 842 P.2d 1240 (1992)

BAXTER, JUDGE.

In late April 1991, after a period of mounting deficits, the Richmond Unified School District (District) announced it lacked funds to complete the final six weeks of its 1990–1991 school term. The District proposed to close its doors on May 1, 1991. The Superior Court of Contra Costa County issued a preliminary injunction directing the State of California (State), its Controller, and its Superintendent of Public Instruction (SPI) to ensure that the District's students would receive a full school term or its equivalent. The court approved the SPI's plan for an emergency State loan, and for appointment by the SPI of an administrator to take temporary charge of the District's operation.

We declined to stay implementation of the plan pending the State's appeal. However, we transferred the appeal here in order to decide an important issue of first impression: Whether the State has a constitutional duty, aside from the equal allocation of educational funds, to prevent the budgetary problems of a particular school district from depriving its students of ''basic'' educational equality.

We affirm the trial court's determination that such a duty exists under the California Constitution. Further, the court did not err in concluding, on the basis of the plaintiffs' preliminary showing, that the particular circumstances of this case demanded immediate State intervention. However, the court exceeded its judicial powers by approving the diversion of emergency loan funds from appropriations clearly intended by the Legislature for other purposes.

FACTS AND PROCEDURAL HISTORY

On April 17, 1991, Thomas K. Butt and other named District parents filed a class action for temporary and permanent injunctive relief against the State and the District's board of education (Board). The complaint alleged as follows: The State is responsible for educating all California children, and the Board is the State's agent for carrying out this responsibility in the District. The scheduled final day of the District's 1990–1991 school term was June 14, 1991, but the District had announced that its 44 elementary, secondary, and adult schools would close on May 1, 1991. The resulting loss of six weeks of instruction would cause serious, irreparable harm to the District's 31,500 students and would deny them their "fundamental right to an effective public education" under the California Constitution. Moreover, as an unjustified discrimination against District students compared to those elsewhere in California, the closure would violate equal protection guarantees of the California and United States Constitutions. Therefore, defendants should be enjoined from closing the District's schools before the scheduled end of the scholastic term.

* * * Plaintiffs' motion papers also included declarations by District teachers, academicians in the field of education, and members of the Contra Costa County board of education. These statements detailed the serious disruptive effect the proposed closure would have upon the educational process in the District and upon the quality of education afforded its students. * * * The motion was heard on April 29, 1991. The Attorney General represented the State in opposition.

The trial court ruled orally that under the California Constitution, the State itself is responsible for the "fundamental" educational rights of California students and must remedy a local district's inability to provide its students an education "basically equivalent" to that provided elsewhere in the State. The State and its agents were directed to act "as ... appropriate" to ensure District students, within the school year ending June 30, 1991, an education "equivalent basically" to that provided elsewhere in California for a full school term.

    * * *

2. Merits of Plaintiffs' Claims

* * * At the outset, the State does not claim it lacks any and all constitutional role in local educational affairs. Instead, its reasoning proceeds as follows: The State fulfills its financial responsibility for

educational equality by subjecting all local districts, rich and poor, to an equalized statewide revenue base.[11] Unless a district fails to provide the minimum six-month school term set forth in the "free school" clause,[12] the State has no duty to ensure prudent use of the equalized funds by local administrators. Even if local mismanagement causes one district's services to fall seriously below prevailing statewide standards, the resulting educational inequality is not grounded in district wealth, nor does it involve a "suspect classification" such as race. Thus, "strict scrutiny" of the disparity is not required, and the State's refusal to intervene must be upheld as rationally related to its policy of local control and accountability. Even if strict scrutiny is appropriate, the local-control policy is "compelling" enough to justify the State's inaction.

Under the unprecedented circumstances of this case, we cannot accept the State's contentions. We set forth our reasons in detail.

Since its admission to the Union, California has assumed specific responsibility for a statewide public education system open on equal terms to all. The Constitution of 1849 directed the Legislature to "provide for a system of common schools, by which a school shall be kept up and supported in each district...." That constitutional command, with the additional proviso that the school maintained by each district be "free," has persisted to the present day.

* * * [T]he State itself has broad responsibility to ensure basic educational equality under the California Constitution. Because access to a public education is a uniquely fundamental personal interest in California, our courts have consistently found that the State charter accords broader rights against State-maintained educational discrimination than does federal law. Despite contrary federal authority, California constitutional principles require State assistance to correct basic "interdistrict" disparities in the system of common schools, even when the discriminatory effect was not produced by the purposeful conduct of the State or its agents.

In *Serrano v. Priest* (1971) 5 Cal.3d 584 (*Serrano I*), this court struck down the existing State public school financing scheme, which caused the amount of basic revenues per pupil to vary substantially among the respective districts depending on their taxable property values. *Serrano I* concluded at length that such a scheme violated both state and federal

---

11. The funding scheme for public education is complex, but no party disputes the summary description provided in the State's brief: "The Legislature has attempted to equalize school district funding ... by the use of a 'base revenue limit' for each district. Each district is classified by size and type. Based upon this classification scheme, each district has a 'base revenue limit' per unit of average daily attendance. The base revenue limit for any district includes the amount of property tax revenues a district can raise, with other specific local revenues, coupled with an equalization payment by the State, thus bringing each district into a rough equivalency of revenues. Because the student population is so diverse, the Legislature had to supplement the base revenue limit with specific augmentations targeted for categories of children with needs that require special attention. These supplements are designated as 'categorical' aid...."

12. Article IX, section 5 provides: "The Legislature shall provide for a system of common schools by which a free school shall be kept up and supported in each district at least six months in every year, after the first year in which a school has been established."

equal protection guaranties because it discriminated against a fundamental interest—education—on the basis of a suspect classification—district wealth—and could not be justified by a compelling state interest under the strict scrutiny test thus applicable. As the court concluded, "where fundamental rights or suspect classifications are at stake, a state's general freedom to discriminate on a geographical basis will be significantly curtailed by the equal protection clause."

Among other things, *Serrano I* rejected a claim that the wealth-based financing scheme was immune from challenge because the interdistrict revenue disparities it produced were not de jure, but merely de facto. Our opinion detailed the purposeful state legislative action which had produced the geographically based wealth classifications. It also made clear, however, that under California principles developed in cases involving school racial segregation, the absence of purposeful conduct by the State would not prevent a finding that the State system for funding public education had produced unconstitutional results.

Serrano I also discussed two groups of federal cases suggesting that place of residence was an impermissible basis for State discrimination in the quality of education.

In *San Antonio School District v. Rodriguez* 411 U.S. 1 (1973), decided after S*errano I,* the United States Supreme Court declined to subject Texas's similar local-property-tax based school financing scheme to heightened scrutiny under the Fourteenth Amendment. The *Rodriguez* majority concluded that a school finance scheme dependent on district tax values does not discriminate against the poor as a distinct class; in any event, the majority observed, wealth alone had never been deemed a suspect classification for federal purposes. Moreover, the majority reasoned, education is not a fundamental interest protected by the federal Constitution. Therefore finding the strict scrutiny standard of review inapplicable, the majority upheld Texas's system as rationally related to that state's policy of local control of schools.

Nonetheless, in *Serrano v. Priest* (1976) 18 Cal.3d 728, this court reaffirmed the reasoning and result of *Serrano I* as required by the separate equal protection guaranties of the California Constitution. Among other things, *Serrano II* reiterated that for California purposes, education remains a fundamental interest "which [lies] at the core of our free and representative form of government...."

Hence, *Serrano II* declared, "[i]n applying our state constitutional provisions guaranteeing equal protection of the laws we shall continue to apply strict and searching judicial scrutiny" to claims of discriminatory educational classifications.

* * * It therefore appears well settled that the California Constitution makes public education uniquely a fundamental concern of the State and prohibits maintenance and operation of the common public school system in a way which denies basic educational equality to the students of particular districts. The State itself bears the ultimate authority and

responsibility to ensure that its district-based system of common schools provides basic equality of educational opportunity.

Both federal and California decisions make clear that heightened scrutiny applies to State-maintained discrimination whenever the disfavored class is suspect or the disparate treatment has a real and appreciable impact on a fundamental right or interest. As we have seen, education is such a fundamental interest for purposes of equal protection analysis under the California Constitution.

The State suggests there was no showing that the impact of the threatened closure on District students' fundamental right to basic educational equality was real and appreciable. Of course, the Constitution does not prohibit all disparities in educational quality or service. Despite extensive State regulation and standardization, the experience offered by our vast and diverse public school system undoubtedly differs to a considerable degree among districts, schools, and individual students. These distinctions arise from inevitable variances in local programs, philosophies, and conditions. "[A] requirement that [the State] provide [strictly] 'equal' educational opportunities would thus seem to present an entirely unworkable standard requiring impossible measurements and comparisons. . . ." Moreover, principles of equal protection have never required the State to remedy all ills or eliminate all variances in service.

Accordingly, the California Constitution does not guarantee uniformity of term length for its own sake. While the current statutory system for allocating State educational funds strongly encourages a term of at least 175 days, that system is not constitutionally based and is subject to change. In an uncertain future, local districts, faced with mounting fiscal pressures, may be forced to seek creative ways to gain maximum educational benefit from limited resources. In such circumstances, a planned reduction of overall term length might be compensated by other means, such as extended daily hours, more intensive lesson plans, summer sessions, volunteer programs, and the like. An individual district's efforts in this regard are entitled to considerable deference.

Even unplanned truncation of the intended school term will not necessarily constitute a denial of "basic" educational equality. A finding of constitutional disparity depends on the individual facts. Unless the actual quality of the district's program, viewed as a whole, falls fundamentally below prevailing statewide standards, no constitutional violation occurs.

Here, however, plaintiffs' preliminary showing suggested that closure of the District's schools on May 1, 1991, would cause an extreme and unprecedented disparity in educational service and progress. District students faced the sudden loss of the final six weeks, or almost one-fifth, of the standard school term originally intended by the District and provided everywhere else in California. The record indicates that the decision to close early was a desperate, unplanned response to the District's impending insolvency and the impasse in negotiations for further emergency State aid. Several District teachers declared that they were operating on standard-term lesson schedules made at the beginning of the school year. These declarants outlined in detail how the proposed early closure would prevent them from completing instruction and grading essential for academic promotion, high school graduation, and college entrance. Faced with evidence of such extensive educational disruption, the trial court did not abuse its discretion by concluding that the proposed closure would have a real and appreciable impact on the affected students' fundamental California right to basic educational equality.

* * * Nothing in the *Serrano* cases themselves, or in other California decisions, supports the State's argument. On the contrary, the cases suggest that the State's responsibility for basic equality in its system of common schools extends beyond the detached role of fair funder or fair legislator. In extreme circumstances at least, the State "has a duty to intervene to prevent unconstitutional discrimination" at the local level.

CONCLUSION AND DISPOSITION

The District's financial inability to complete the final six weeks of its 1990–1991 school term threatened to deprive District students of their California constitutional right to basic educational equality with other public school students in this State. As the court further concluded, discrimination of this nature against education, a fundamental interest, could only be justified as necessary to serve a compelling interest. The State itself, as the entity with plenary constitutional responsibility for operation of the common school system, had a duty to protect District students against loss of their right to basic educational equality. Local control of public schools was not a compelling interest which would justify the State's failure to intervene.

The trial court thus properly ordered the State and its officials to protect the students' rights. The court also acted within its remedial powers by authorizing the SPI to assume control of the District's affairs, relieve the Board of its duties, and supervise the District's financial recovery. However, the court invaded the exclusive legislative power of appropriation by approving the diversion of appropriations for GAIN and the OUSD to an emergency loan for the District.

Accordingly, we reverse the trial court's remedial order of May 2, 1991, insofar as it approves funding of an emergency loan to the District from appropriations for the Oakland Unified School District and the Greater Avenues for Independence program. In all other respects, the court's orders of April 29 and May 2, 1991, are affirmed. The Court of Appeal is directed to remand the cause to the trial court for such further proceedings as may be appropriate under the views expressed in this opinion.

NOTE

1. Recall the references to the *T. K. Butt* decision and the inclusion of relevant quotes in the Chapter 1 introductory section on the right to an

education, *supra. T. K. Butt* is arguably a watershed case that clarifies and expands this right under state constitutional law.

2. State constitutions contain a variety of equal protection guarantees ranging from explicit equal protection clauses to provisions that attempt to guarantee equality in certain specific instances. *See* Robert F. Williams, *Equality Guarantees in State Constitutional Law,* 63 TEX. L. REV. 1195, 1196–97 (1985). When asked to interpret these provisions, some state courts follow federal constitutional jurisprudence without deviation. *Id.* at 1219–20. Other courts employ the federal equal protection framework but reserve the right to make their own decisions as to what constitutes a fundamental right or a suspect classification. For example, in *Serrano v. Priest,* 18 Cal.3d 728, 135 Cal.Rptr. 345, 557 P.2d 929, 950–51 (1976) (*Serrano II*), the California Supreme Court rejected the U.S. Supreme Court's approach to Fourteenth Amendment jurisprudence as set forth in *San Antonio Independent School District v. Rodriguez,* 411 U.S. 1, 93 S.Ct. 1278 (1973). The California court declared that, under California's independent jurisprudence, education would indeed be recognized as a fundamental right and wealth would be added to the list of suspect classifications triggering strict scrutiny. *Serrano,* 557 P.2d at 950–52.

A small number of state courts reject the federal approach entirely and seek to develop their own independent jurisprudence.

WILLIAMS v. STATE

Cal. Super. Ct. No. 312236
Filed May 2000
Settled August 2004

One of the highest profile cases of its era, garnering national attention and generating substantial ongoing inquiry at both the political level and within the legal and education communities, *Williams* was an example of litigation in this area that was able to have an impact even though it never went to trial.

In this regard, *Williams* exemplifies the principle that—particularly in cases focusing on the education process and seeking to maximize equal opportunity and improve educational quality—a lawsuit need not lead to a written opinion to achieve results. The *SFNAACP v. SFUSD* litigation referenced above is another example of this type of approach.

Settlement agreements in these cases may vary in both form and content. Some include consent decrees, and are accompanied by judicial supervision and independent monitoring. In the case of *Williams,* the agreement led to state legislation, and to the explicit adoption of basic principles in California law regarding student rights of equal access to a quality education.

I. The Legal Complaint

The *Williams* complaint relied to a great extent on the holding in *T.K. Butt, supra,* regarding the parameters of the fundamental right to an education under state constitutional law. It also sought to fill in the gaps remaining from the *Serrano* litigation of the 1960s and 1970s, which had resulted in the equalization of per-pupil expenditures from the general fund across all school districts, but had not addressed inequities in school facilities, instructional materials, and teacher quality.

The following is a representative excerpt from the complaint, filed in May 2000:

1. Tens of thousands of children attending public schools located throughout the State of California are being deprived of basic educational opportunities available to more privileged children attending the majority of the State's public schools. State law requires students to attend school. Yet all too many California school children must go to school without trained teachers, necessary educational supplies, classrooms, or seats in classrooms. Students attempt to learn in schools that lack functioning heating or air conditioning systems, that lack sufficient numbers of functioning toilets, and that are infested with vermin, including rats, mice, and cockroaches. These appalling conditions in California public schools have persisted for years and have worsened over time. The Plaintiffs bring this suit in an effort to ensure that their schools meet basic minimal educational standards.

2. The schools at which these manifestly substandard conditions exist are overwhelmingly populated by low-income and nonwhite students and students who are still learning the English language. In all but three of the schools the Plaintiffs attend, more than half the student body is eligible for free or reduced-price meals at school. Nearly all the Plaintiffs in this action are black, Latino or Latina, or Asian Pacific American, and in each of the schools the Plaintiffs attend, nonwhite students constitute far more than half the student body. In all but one of the schools, nonwhite students constitute more than 90 percent of the student body. And in all but four of the schools, more than 30 percent of the students are still learning the English language.

5. State officials charged with carrying out the State's critical education obligations have failed to develop or implement appropriate procedures to identify and correct the substandard conditions at the schools the Plaintiffs attend. Although the State has established academic standards that students must meet, the State has failed to meet its responsibility to ensure that schools provide teachers who are adequately trained to prepare students to satisfy those standards, has failed to provide sufficient materials to enable students to have a reasonable chance to pass tests that measure their performance, and has failed to provide facilities in which students can safely learn the materials they need to meet the State-mandated standards. In other words, the State has established a system for education but has abdicated its responsibility to oversee and superintend that system to ensure it functions. This lawsuit seeks to require the State and State officials charged with affording basic educational opportunity to fulfill their obligation to all California public school children.

Without relief, these children will continue to be denied their constitutional right to a free, common, and equal public school education.

II. Supporting Evidence from Expert's Reports

The *Williams* plaintiffs were able to generate substantial expert testimony in support of the complaint. The following excerpt summarizes a synthesis of expert reports, prepared by Education Professor Jeannie Oakes.

The following findings stand out:

- Qualified teachers, relevant instructional materials that students may use in school and at home, and clean, safe, and educationally appropriate facilities are fundamentally important to students' education. They enable students to learn the knowledge and skills that the state has specified as important. They promote students' chances to compete for good jobs and economic security. They provide students with the tools to engage in civic life as adults. The consequences of not having access to such teachers, materials, and facilities are particularly harsh in California's current high-stakes, standards-based education system.

- Actions (and inaction) by the State have either contributed to or failed to prevent students' lack of access to qualified teachers, appropriate instructional materials, and adequate school facilities. These actions include a) the failure to specify and/or enforce standards for adequate and equitable resources and conditions that could prevent inadequacies and inequities; b) the failure to build the capacity of districts and schools to provide these resources and conditions; c) the failure to collect and/or analyze data in ways that would permit the State to know the extent of needs and problems regarding basic educational necessities; and d) insufficient interventions and assistance to address inadequacies and disparities when they occur.

- The inadequacies and disparities in access to teachers, instructional materials, and facilities are symptomatic of deeper, systemic flaws in California's education system. These flaws include a) a fragmented and incoherent approach to state policymaking; b) a system of school finance constructed in the absence of an overall plan for providing equitable and adequate resources and conditions, let alone ensuring education of the highest quality to all students; and c) a reluctance to invest in ways that ensure an equitable distribution of adequate resources and conditions; d) the delegation of responsibility for providing adequate and equitable education to local districts in the absence of State will or capacity to prevent the occurrence of serious inadequacies and disparities or to detect and correct them, should they arise. These flaws grow out of California's peculiar education policy history since the 1960s, and they have been exacerbated by the State's recent decision to rely on test-based accountability to drive educational improvement.

In many ways, this paper goes to great lengths to demonstrate what is patently obvious to great numbers of California school children and their parents as well as uncontested by nearly all observers of California's education system. For children to be educated, they require basic educational tools—teachers, books, and safe, healthy, and uncrowded schools. Teachers, books, and adequate school buildings are the staples of American teaching and learning. They are not usually thought of as educational resources or conditions whose availability varies significantly among schools, or whose centrality to education requires examination, documentation, and defense. The state has failed to provide these basic educational tools to many, many school children. Most often these are children who are poor, non-English speaking, African American, and Latino. It is unacceptable that the educational system would deprive any California child of these basics. It is reprehensible that those children most deprived educationally are also those who society neglects most in other ways.

Jeannie Oakes, *Education Inadequacy, Inequality, and Failed State Policy: A Synthesis of Expert Reports Prepared for* Williams v. State of California, *at* http://www.idea.gseis.ucla.edu/publications/williams/reports/wws16.html (Aug. 2002).

III. The Settlement Agreement

The following excerpt is from an overview of the *Williams* settlement agreement, available at http://www.decentschools.org, the Web site that has been established as a guide to the *Williams* implementation process:

The *Williams* settlement requires that all students have instructional materials and that their schools be clean and safe. It also takes steps toward assuring they have qualified teachers. The settlement holds schools accountable for delivering these fundamental elements, and provides nearly $1 billion to accomplish these goals. * * *

The parties announced a settlement agreement on August 13, 2004, and approximately six weeks later, on September 29, 2004, five bills implementing the legislative proposals set forth in the Settlement Agreement were signed into law by Governor Schwarzenegger. The Court approved the Settlement Agreement at a hearing on March 23, 2005.

The five bills implementing the Settlement Agreement were:

● **SB 550 & AB 2727** (establishing minimum standards regarding school facilities, teacher quality, and instructional materials and accountability systems to enforce these standards);

● **AB 1550** (phasing out the use of the Concept 6 [limited number of school days] calendar by July 1, 2012, and setting benchmarks for districts to reach this goal);

● **AB 3001** (encouraging placement of qualified teachers in low performing schools; enhancing an existing oversight mechanism to ensure that teachers are qualified to teach the subject matter to which they have been assigned and to ensure that teachers of English learners are properly trained; and streamlining the process for highly qualified teachers from out-of-state to teach in California schools); and

- **SB 6** (providing up to $800 million beginning in the 2005–06 fiscal year for districts to repair facility conditions that threaten health and safety and approximately $25 million in 2004–05 for a one-time comprehensive facilities needs assessment of schools ranked in the bottom 3 deciles under the 2003 statewide Academic Performance Index (API)).

IV. Legal Benchmarks: "a floor, rather than a ceiling, and a beginning, not an end"

Consider the following language, included in Section 25 of SB 550 as a result of the *Williams* litigation. What additional steps, above and beyond what has been documented above, are contemplated by this language? What additional steps would maximize the prospective effectiveness of the agreement?

How might this language be employed in future, education-related litigation that could become necessary?

> The Legislature finds and the Governor agrees that these minimum thresholds [for teacher quality, instructional materials, and school facilities] are essential in order to ensure that all of California's public school pupils have access to the basic elements of a quality public education. However, these minimum thresholds in no way reflect the full extent of the Legislature's and the Governor's expectations of what California's public schools are capable of achieving. Instead, these thresholds for teacher quality, instructional materials, and school facilities are intended by the Legislature and by the Governor to be a floor, rather than a ceiling, and a beginning, not an end, to the State of California's commitment and effort to ensure that all California school pupils have access to the basic elements of a quality public education.

> It is the intent of the Legislature and of the Governor that teachers, school administrators, trustees and staff, parents, and pupils all recommit themselves to the pursuit of academic excellence in California public schools.

PROBLEM 30: AMENDING THE U.S. CONSTITUTION

Consider the text of the following proposed amendment to the U.S. Constitution, set forth in House Joint Resolution 29 (2003). If such an amendment were actually to pass, how if at all might things change?

HOUSE JOINT RESOLUTION 29 (JACKSON)

The Right to a Public Education of Equal High Quality
2003 CONG US HJ 29 (March 2003)

H.J. RES. 29

Proposing an amendment to the Constitution of the United States regarding the right of all citizens of the United States to a public education of equal high quality.

JOINT RESOLUTION

Proposing an amendment to the Constitution of the United States regarding the right of all citizens of the United States to a public education of equal high quality.

Resolved by the Senate and House of Representatives of the United States of America in Congress assembled (two-thirds of each House concurring therein), That the following article is proposed as an amendment to the Constitution of the United States, which shall be valid to all intents and purposes as part of the Constitution when ratified by the legislatures of three-fourths of the several States:

> SECTION 1. All citizens of the United States shall enjoy the right to a public education of equal high quality.

> SECTION 2. The Congress shall have power to implement this article by appropriate legislation.

PROBLEM 31: EDUCATIONAL QUALITY ISSUES IN THE STATE OF OCEAN WAVE

The following hypothetical takes place in the State of Ocean Wave, and focuses in particular on the fictional public school district of Shell Beach Unified, where approximately one third of the students are "English learners" (EL).

April 2009: In a shocking decision, the Shell Beach Unified school board voted unanimously (and with no prior warning) to reconstitute its three lowest performing schools. All adults working at the school were told that their positions were being terminated, that they could reapply for their former jobs should they choose to do so, but that no positions would be guaranteed. Tenured teachers were guaranteed a job in the District, but not necessarily at a school of their choice.

While reconstitution continued to spread across the country, and indeed was included as a potential "corrective action" under the U.S. "No Child Left Behind" Act, this was the first time it had been used in Ocean Wave.

At a press conference, School Board President Alicia Johnson declared: "We can no longer afford to operate schools where the average scores on tests of basic skills continue to be in the lowest quartile. Neither can we afford the luxury of placing schools in one or two-year "reconstitution-eligible" programs, as San Francisco did in the 1990s. We must take action now."

In addition to the reconstitution bombshell, the Board announced that it would immediately end the district policy of offering instruction in a student's primary language to the extent possible under the law. "We have informed all the bilingual aides in the District that their services will no longer be needed," Johnson explained. "Our education of English learners will be in English only. Students will be grouped together in a heterogeneous manner, with no instruction in a student's primary language. Special assistance, however, will be provided to EL students. This special assistance will include volunteer tutors from the local colleges and universities, and special after-school programs for interested families, taught by volunteer parents."

June 2011: New norm-referenced test scores for all students in the District were released. The District scored, overall, at the 46th percentile in reading (compared with the 46th percentile in 2003 and the 45th in 2004) and at the 51st percentile in math (compared with the 49th percentile in 2003 and the 53rd percentile in 2004), based on national norms. Students at the three reconstituted schools (which had been scoring in the bottom quartile in both reading and math) showed no overall improvement, and in fact the eleventh grade students at one of the three schools scored lower in both reading and math than they had during the previous year. The EL students tested in Spanish and Cantonese District-wide showed no overall improvement either. While EL students at some schools did better, EL students at other schools did worse. At the reconstituted schools, which had hired a large percentage of new and "partially credentialed" teachers, the EL student test scores actually dropped slightly.

A.   In late June 2011, a lawsuit was filed by a group of concerned parents determined to stop the District from reconstituting any more schools, and seeking additional assistance to "clean up the mess" that they argue had been made at the three reconstituted schools. What arguments might plaintiffs set forth under state constitutional law? Under other viable legal frameworks? What result? Discuss.

B.   Assume that, pursuant to House Joint Resolution 29, the U.S. Constitution was amended, and now includes the following language: "All citizens of the United States shall enjoy the right to a public education of equal high quality." If a group of parents of English learners in Shell Beach Unified file a lawsuit under this provision, seeking declaratory and injunctive relief, what arguments might they set forth? What result?

B.   THE U.S. "NO CHILD LEFT BEHIND" ACT

The "No Child Left Behind" Act (NCLB) represents a giant shift in the role of federal officials with regard to K–12 education governance. While individual states retain substantial autonomy and significant decision-making authority, they no longer have the final say in shaping educational policy across the board.

As referenced above, NCLB is a wide-ranging, bipartisan statutory framework with requirements that extend across a broad spectrum. Indeed, most of the K–12 issues addressed in this casebook are touched on in some fashion by provisions of this Act.

While many of these provisions are controversial, none have generated more emotion than those relating to accountability. Critics have focused in particular on the heavy price that teachers, administrators, individual schools, and in fact entire districts might have to pay if certain benchmarks are not reached. People can lose their jobs, schools can be closed, and entire districts can be dis-established.

Many who question the structure and content of the accountability provisions do not typically quarrel with the importance of accountability, but wonder instead how so many important decisions can be made based on test scores alone. They also wonder how loosely defined phrases such as "relevant to the failure to make adequate yearly progress" can be applied on a day-to-day level in the real world of public schooling.

As the years passed and education officials were required to implement "corrective action" and "alternative governance" arrangements when schools were not meeting designated adequate yearly progress (AYP) targets,[1] criticisms of the accountability mechanisms increased in both quantity and scope. Many deplored a structure that enabled individual states to set different cut-off points for what constituted "proficiency." Practitioners chafed at the fact that some high-performing schools were being penalized because the AYP requirements did not take into account the level of performance a school had already achieved when NCLB took effect. Others focused on the way in which student scores were disaggregated by race/ethnicity, taking the government to task for decisions such as the one to group all Asian Americans together in one broad category. And commentators bemoaned the apparent negative impact on the curriculum in many locations, with courses in the arts, humanities, and social sciences being cut back so that schools could spend more time on areas that were actually tested under NCLB.

At the same time, school districts were criticized for not doing enough to communicate to parents, at schools that failed to make AYP for two or more years, that their children had the right to transfer to higher-performing schools or that they might be eligible for free tutoring.[2]

Against the backdrop of these ongoing controversies, reflected in several lawsuits that focused on a range of procedural issues, an anticipated reauthorization of NCLB in 2007 was put on hold until after the presidential election of 2008. In the meantime, however, Secretary of

---

1. Under NCLB, to qualify for Title I funding, each state was required to develop and submit a plan demonstrating that it had adopted "challenging academic content standards and challenging student academic achievement standards." The standards had to be uniformly applicable to students in all the state's public schools, and they had to cover at least reading, math, and science skills. States were then required to develop and administer assessments which would determine levels of student achievement under these standards. *See generally* 20 U.S.C. § 6311. Schools and school districts were responsible for making "adequate yearly progress" ("AYP") on these assessments, such that a minimum percentage of students, both overall and in each designated subgroup, attained proficiency in a given year. *See* 34 C.F.R. § 200.20(a)(1).

2. *See, e.g.,* the NCLB "School Choice" Provisions, *infra,* this chapter. *See also* U.S. Dept. of Education, *Supplemental Educational Services Brochure,* www.ed.gov (2008):

> The term "supplemental educational services" refers to extra help in academic subjects, such as reading, language arts and mathematics, provided free-of-charge to certain students. These services are provided outside the regular school day—before or after school, on weekends or in the summer. * * * Generally, students who are eligible for free or reduced-price lunch and are enrolled in Title I schools that have been placed on the state's "in need of improvement" list for two or more years are eligible to receive free supplemental educational services. * * * Your school district will notify you if your child is eligible for supplemental educational services.

Education Margaret Spellings sought to develop and implement a series of administrative adjustments at the U.S. Department of Education level to address some of the many criticisms by school officials, researchers, and political leaders.[3]

Two lawsuits, in particular, continued to move forward in the courts. In *Connecticut v. Spellings,* the state challenged the Secretary of Education's interpretation of several key elements of NCLB. In separate decisions over a period of years, the U.S. District Court ruled against Connecticut, and in April 2008 it upheld the Secretary's rejection of the state's efforts to provide alternative ways to test English learners and students with disabilities.[4] An appeal to the Second Circuit was pending.

In *School District of the City of Pontiac v. Secretary of the U.S. Department of Education,* the National Education Association (NEA) filed a lawsuit on behalf of nine school districts in Michigan, Texas, and Vermont, focusing in particular on funding issues. The Sixth Circuit in May 2008 agreed to rehear the case *en banc* after a panel had originally ruled on behalf of the plaintiffs.[5]

The legal terrain in this context remains unsettled, with an ongoing effort in many parts of the country to push for changes in the statutory and regulatory requirements. And it is possible that as more "corrective action" provisions are applied, substantive challenges will be brought contesting the sanctions themselves.

Yet it must be emphasized that many people from all walks of life and every spot on the political spectrum favor the type of aggressive approach that NCLB exemplifies. Not only do people see great value in the higher standards and the more ambitious goals, but few would disagree with the

---

3. *See* David J. Hoff, *NCLB Plan Would Add New Rules: Spellings Proposes Changes on Testing, Tutoring, Data,* Education Week, April 30, 2008.

4. *See* Connecticut v. Spellings, 549 F.Supp.2d 161, 172 (D. Conn. 2008):

* * * [T]he Court wishes to emphasize that it is not faced with the issue of the wisdom of the Secretary's decisions or whether they will hinder, or advance, the educational achievement of Connecticut's LEP students or special education students. While the Court is certainly not an expert on educational policy, one could presumably make a decent argument that testing students who are newly arrived from foreign lands in English, when they are not at all proficient in English, may not be a particularly sensible way to determine the level of the students' academic achievement or knowledge. One might mount a similar argument for testing special education students at grade level, rather than instructional level. But those are not the issues before this Court. The only question is whether the Secretary's denials of the State's requests on the ground that they were contrary to the statute was [sic] arbitrary and capricious. For the reasons set forth below, the Court concludes that it was not.

5. Based on the "Unfunded Mandates Provision," which provides that "[n]othing in this Act shall be construed to . . . mandate a State or any subdivision thereof to spend any funds or incur any costs not paid for under this Act," 20 U.S.C. § 7907(a), Plaintiffs sought, "among other relief, a judgment declaring that they need not comply with the Act's requirements where federal funds do not cover the increased costs of compliance." The Sixth Circuit panel initially determined that under the rule that "statutes enacted under the Spending Clause of the United States Constitution must provide clear notice to the States of their liabilities should they decide to accept federal funding under those statutes," the "NCLB fails to provide clear notice as to who bears the additional costs of compliance." School Dist. of the City of Pontiac v. Secretary of the U.S. Dept. of Educ., 512 F.3d 252, 254 (6th Cir. 2008) (rehearing *en banc* granted, opinion vacated May 1, 2008).

efforts to close the dramatic achievement gap on the basis of race that still exists in this country.

Finally, as referenced above, legal activists continue to focus on possible ways that NCLB could be employed by private litigants to address the disparities in educational quality that persist. From the earliest days of the Act, for example, many in the "civil rights" community sought to identify legal strategies for actually employing the explicit mandates of NCLB to challenge a range of questionable policies and practices that arguably have a negative impact on student rights of equal access to a quality education.[6] In addition, as time has passed, commentators have put forth the proposition that by enacting NCLB, Congress has in fact recognized education to be a fundamental right at the federal level, without actually using the same terminology.[7] And by the end of 2007, two major advocacy groups had called for changes in the Act that would expressly provide aggrieved plaintiffs in certain circumstances with a private cause of action.[8]

---

6. *See, e.g.,* James S. Leibman & Charles F. Sabel, *The Federal No Child Left Behind Act and the Post–Desegregation Civil Rights Agenda,* 81 N.C. L. Rev. 1703 (2003).

7. *See* 20 U.S.C. § 6301, which provides in pertinent part that "The purpose of [the Act] is to ensure that all children have a fair, equal, and significant opportunity to obtain a high-quality education."

8. *See, e.g.,* Josh Dunn and Martha Derthick, *The Enforcers: Parents May Gain Right to Sue over NCLB,* Education Next (Hoover Institution), Vol. 7, No. 4, www.hoover.org/publications/ednext (Fall 2007):

One proposal comes from the Education Trust, which has a 17–year track record of commitment to school reform. The Ed Trust proposes that parents of children in Title I schools, those that have a disadvantaged population and are the main recipients of federal funds, be vested with a private right of action "to enforce their rights under the law." The rights that the Trust names are of two kinds. One is for access to data on funding patterns, teacher distributions, and high school graduation rates. The other is for participation in school-level decisions about allocation of supplemental educational services funds, for example, whether to use them for tutoring or expanded in-school instruction.

See also The Commission on No Child Left Behind, Tommy G. Thompson & Roy E. Barnes, Co-Chairs, *Beyond NCLB: Fulfilling the Promise to Our Nation's Children,* The Aspen Institute, www.aspeninstitute.org (2007) at 75–76:

* * * [W]e recommend that parents and other concerned parties have the right to hold districts, states and the U.S. Department of Education (DOE) accountable for faithfully implementing the requirements of NCLB through enhanced enforcement options with the state and the U.S. DOE. Under our recommendation, the state would establish a procedure to allow individuals or groups of citizens to bring their complaints against the district or state to the state. If the agency rejects the claim, citizens would be able to file an appeal with the U.S. DOE, which would be permitted to select the complaints worthy of response or needing clarifying rulings. If the U.S. DOE chooses to hear the appeal, it can order the state to comply when necessary. If the U.S. DOE does not do so, the citizen(s) can file suit in state court. In any case, the only available remedy would be an order to enforce the law; there would be no financial or other penalties assessed. A court could not issue an injunction to prohibit the flow of federal funds to the state or the continued implementation of any other provision of the law while the case is pending. An analogous procedure would be established for individuals who have complaints with the U.S. DOE's implementation of the statute. * * *

CHALLENGING RACIAL DISPARITIES: THE PROMISE AND PITFALLS OF THE NO CHILD LEFT BEHIND ACT'S RACE–CONSCIOUS ACCOUNTABILITY

Daniel J. Losen
47 HOWARD L.J. 243 (2004)

INTRODUCTION

* * * One new step toward fulfilling Brown's promise might be found in the principle of race-conscious accountability embedded within the No Child Left Behind Act of 2001 (NCLB). The No Child Left Behind Act is the short title for the reauthorization of the Elementary and Secondary Education Act (ESEA), which first passed in 1965. Title I of NCLB provides the largest single source of federal education funding targeted to help the states meet the needs of socioeconomically disadvantaged students.[9] Each state is required to use Title I funds to supplement its own educational spending and is prohibited from supplanting its expenditures.[10] Nearly every school district in the nation receives some of the approximately $10 billion appropriated each year. To achieve its goal, however, Title I also contains numerous monitoring and enforcement requirements that accompany state, district and school level spending.

In passing NCLB, a bipartisan Congress added explicitly race-conscious accountability requirements to Title I in order to redress severe racial disparities in educational achievement. The Act's Statement of Purpose includes the following, "[c]losing the achievement gap between high and low-performing children, especially the achievement gaps between minority and nonminority students, and between disadvantaged and their more advantaged peers...." The new accountability system includes technical assistance, and increasingly severe sanctions at the school and district level. The emphasis is on improving the academic proficiency of all students with an additional layer of subgroup accountability to prevent glossing over disparities in achievement that might be hidden when achievement data is analyzed in the aggregate. Therefore, the persistent failure of any major racial or ethnic group; of students with disabilities; of socio-economically disadvantaged students; or of students

---

9. Title I accounts for more than $12 billion of federal education spending each year. *See* 20 U.S.C.A. § 6302 (West 2000 & Supp. 2003). More than $18 billion dollars is scheduled for budget year 2004 and funding is scheduled to rise to $25 billion by fiscal year 2007. *Id.* The authorized amount, however, is expected to fall short of what the President approved in an appropriations bill before Congress. *See, e.g.,* TITLE I REPORT, EDUCATION SPENDING BILLS ADVANCE 13 (2003) [hereinafter TITLE I REPORT] (reporting "Democrats continued to criticize the administration for not providing enough funding to help states and school districts meet the mandates in the No Child Left Behind Act, noting that the law authorizes far more spending"). Moreover, under Title I, Part A, the Bush administration proposed a budget of $12.35 billion, which was more than $6 billion less than what the Act authorized when President Bush signed it into law. *Id.*

10. Early in Title I's history, investigations by advocacy groups revealed hundreds of schools spending the money inappropriately. *See* UNITED STATES COMM'N ON CIVIL RIGHTS, EQUAL EDUCATIONAL OPPORTUNITY PROJECT SERIES VOLUME I 218 (1996) [hereinafter EQUAL EDUCATIONAL OPPORTUNITY]. As recently as 1999, the Citizens' Commission on Civil Rights criticized Alabama for supplanting rather than supplementing state education funds with federal dollars. *See* CITIZENS' COMM'N ON CIVIL RIGHTS, TITLE I IN ALABAMA: THE STRUGGLE TO MEET BASIC NEEDS 46–47 (Corrine M. Yu & William L. Taylor eds., 1999), *available at* http://www.civilrights.org/issues/education/action.cfm? CurrentPage=3&content_type_id=6&selected_issues=5_ALL&action=search. The report concluded that federal money is being used in place of state and local funds to employ non-Title I teachers, make renovations, and provide basic operating expenses. *Id.*

with limited English proficiency, at the school or district level, can trigger intervention and possibly sanctions.[16]

Despite serious shortcomings with its implementation, and what many educators argue is an inappropriately test-driven accountability design,[18] Title I's new accountability system is among the most race-conscious legislative remedies to racial inequity in K–12 education since Title VI of the Civil Rights Act of 1964 (Title VI).

Pursuant to Title VI, the Department of Education promulgated regulations that, similar to NCLB, result in intervening in public schools on the basis of trends in racial and ethnic data that are regarded as unacceptable. Neither the Title VI regulations nor NCLB requires proof that intentional discrimination caused the unacceptable trends as a prerequisite for intervention. One of the most significant differences may be that Title VI interventions are designed to protect minority students from policies or practices that have an unjustifiable racially disparate and negative impact—regarded as a form of unintentional discrimination. NCLB interventions, on the other hand, never raise the possibility of unlawful discrimination, but instead seek to ensure that all students meet state standards of proficiency. * * *

II. BACKGROUND OF NCLB AND RACE-BASED ACCOUNTABILITY

* * * As its name suggests, the No Child Left Behind Act of 2001 has accountability provisions intended to at least ensure racially equitable outcomes at a basic level of educational achievement. As noted earlier, the law requires that all major racial and ethnic groups achieve 100% proficiency in reading and math in twelve years while meeting specified benchmarks of "adequate yearly progress" along the way. Failure by any racial or ethnic group to meet the benchmarks (over two or more consecutive years) mandates increasingly harsh interventions. These actions can include firing staff, taking over school boards, or closing schools completely.

A. The General Accountability Scheme

The broader accountability principle in NCLB is based on the concept of ensuring adequacy, for both progress and educational outcomes, over time. This broader scheme was made part of the ESEA in 1994. Thus far,

---

16. 20 U.S.C.A. § 6311(b)(2)(C)(v)(II) (West Supp. 2003). Each subgroup is held to the same standards for accountability purposes and no matter what percent are proficient in reading and math, each group must reach 100% proficiency in these areas over the next twelve years to avoid intervention. *Id.* at (b)(1).

18. *See, e.g.,* Tamar Levin, *City to Track Why Students Leave School,* N.Y. Times, Sept. 15, 2003, at B1 (describing how school officials are intending to crack down on "push outs" by school personnel). It is critically important that readers distinguish the concept of setting outcome goals for accountability using racially disaggregated data from the specific mechanisms, sanctions and incentive structures as set forth in NCLB. This Article is highly critical of many of the specific mechanisms and details how some of the more promising requirements are not being properly implemented. *See infra* Parts III and IV. This Article should not be construed as endorsing or supporting the NCLB.

proficiency in reading and mathematics as indicated by scores on state-wide achievement tests has been the yardstick for adequacy. This test-driven accountability system was maintained and modified when NCLB Title I provisions were drafted.

Under NCLB, the federal government oversees the state educational agencies (SEA), the states oversee the local educational agencies (LEA) and the LEA oversee the individual schools. Accountability in this context consists of monitoring, enforcement, and due process. States are obligated to create a plan to ensure that all students meet the state's "challenging academic . . . achievement standards." Each plan must have benchmarks to determine whether each school and district that received Title I funding is making "adequate yearly progress" (AYP). NCLB is notable in that it requires that all (100%) students be proficient in reading and math by the 2013–2014 school year.

Each state sets its own benchmarks for "proficiency." Under the Act's AYP provisions, each state must calibrate the acceptable yearly rate of progress necessary to meet the ultimate twelve-year goal of 100% proficiency. The state then annually assesses all schools and districts for their progress toward this goal under the rubric developed by that state. Schools and districts whose students persistently fail to fulfill AYP's progress benchmarks are flagged for technical assistance and labeled as "needing improvement."

If a school or district consistently fails to make adequate yearly progress, and cannot improve by utilizing technical assistance provided by the overseeing agency, that agency must intervene. NCLB provides for a wide range of choices, from closing schools, withdrawing federal funds, and firing staff at the harsh end, to requiring the school or district to hire a consultant and submit a school improvement plan at the gentler end. This flexibility with regard to interventions must be considered in under-standing what passes for accountability under NCLB. Decisions about interventions are made by the agency responsible for oversight. While the public receives information and can apply pressure, it is unlikely that parents or advocates have standing to bring a private action in court pursuant to NCLB.

Since 1994, the ESEA has required districts and states to publicly report disaggregated test scores and other accountability data by race, ethnicity, gender, migrant status, disability, LEP status, and socioeconomic status. Public reporting is designed to trigger local pressure and involvement from parents and community members at the school and district level. To effectuate this parental involvement goal, the statute requires an extensive system of school district and state report cards that are widely disseminated to the public as well as distributed to every family. There are also requirements that school improvement plans be created with the input from parents, and that governance of schools needing improvement or interested in school-wide reforms using Title I funds include parents as part of the school governance structure.

B. Race–Conscious Accountability Under NCLB

It is important to know that racially disaggregated data collection and reporting were required under the ESEA at least as far back as 1994, but the requirements were never enforced in the face of widespread noncompliance. It is also true, however, that under the ESEA before NCLB, if a school or district's aggregate test scores met the state's standards, that entity could make adequate yearly progress and no further information was required. It is reasonable to assume that without pressure from the federal government to report racially disaggregated data to the public, as required, and with no requirement that technical assistance or sanctions follow persistent failure of a given racial group, the lack of enforced requirements contributed to the lax attention to lower performing minority groups.

Additional components to NCLB's race-conscious provisions allow a school or district to escape the consequences of its failure to generate adequate yearly progress for one particular subgroup. The "safe harbor" provision in the Act stays otherwise required intervention for a school or district if the subgroup in question reduced it's failure rate significantly (by 10%) and improved on at least one other academic measure, such as graduation rates.

NCLB modified the ESEA further to require that students attending a school "needing improvement" be provided with an opportunity to transfer to another public school within the district.[109] A specified percentage of Title I funds may be used to transport these children to adequately performing schools. If a school has failed for three consecutive years, all the "eligible" students in that school must also be offered supplemental educational services.

In addition to the accountability scheme for adequate yearly progress, NCLB also added a requirement that state plans include a system to ensure that poor and minority students are not taught at higher rates by unqualified teachers and that states publicly report their progress toward this goal each year. While some regard the public reporting of specific data and its progress as a form of accountability, there are no other federal interventions or sanctions triggered by non-compliance. Unlike the other accountability provisions of the Act, the teacher quality provisions concern resource "inputs" more directly than achievement outcomes. It is well established, however, that teacher quality is a leading predictor of academic success, including for minority and low-income students.

* * * [T]he Department of Education did make explicit in the regulations that all state plans must address how the state will ensure poor and minority students' equitable access to highly qualified teachers. If successfully implemented, this provision could be among the most effective in the

---

109. In regulations, the Department of Education added language requiring transfers be made available, even if there was no existing capacity to receive the transfers in adequately performing schools within the district. *See* 20 U.S.C.A. § 6316(E) (West 2000 & Supp. 2003). "An LEA may not use lack of capacity to deny students the option to transfer under paragraph (a)(1) of this section." *Id.*

entire Act. Yet the required student access to highly qualified teachers has no real statutory enforcement consequences for non-compliance and pales in comparison to the test-based accountability under the adequate yearly progress provisions.

A closer look at the statute, however, reveals that the relatively concrete accountability requirements for AYP actually have a great deal of flexibility built into them. For example, each state is expected to create its own standards for proficiency. Despite the appearance that the new requirement of 100% proficiency for each major racial and ethnic sub-group in twelve-years creates a clear federal standard, the law only requires that standards be "high," with no definition of the term. NCLB also requires that the statewide achievement tests that are used for determining AYP must be "aligned" with the state's high standards and that the curriculum and instruction are aligned as well. While the standards, tests and benchmarks a state selects must pass review of the U.S. Secretary of Education, the approval process is not a rigorous one. As a result, what passes for high standards from one state to the next varies considerably.

States with higher "world class" standards have changed what they deem to be proficient depending on the consequences that flow with the label. Specifically, between 2001–2003, Louisiana, Colorado, and Connecticut each lowered their required score for "proficient" in response to new NCLB requirements.

One promising development is that NCLB added graduation rates and other academic indicators to the definition of adequate yearly progress. While AYP must be based primarily on test scores, failure on other academic indicators selected by the state can also send a school or district into "school improvement status." Given that Black and Latino minority youth are failing to earn diplomas at rates often exceeding 50% of their projected enrollment, accountability for graduation rates could prove critically important for driving more effective education reforms. In a controversial decision, however, Secretary Paige, in issuing regulations, decided that in the first analysis, graduation rates did not have to be disaggregated by minority subgroups for accountability purposes unless the "safe harbor" provision is being used. Therefore, given the limitations created by the U.S. Department of Education, the only thing that could be considered part of accountability is that districts' graduation rates must be "adequate," for all students, in the aggregate. Thus, based on the Department's disputed interpretation of the statute, graduation rates, unlike test scores, could be very low for any given racial sub-group without triggering any accountability interventions.

One critical aspect of NCLB's race-based accountability is the race-neutrality of the required enforcement actions triggered by the failure of any major racial or ethnic group within a school or district to meet the achievement standards. To correct a failing school or district, the overseeing authority chooses at least one intervention among those required.

However, even if a school or district is driven into "needs improvement status" based on the lackluster performance of a single racial or ethnic group, the proscribed interventions make no explicit reference to even a possibility that racial discrimination, via stereotypes or racial or ethnic bias, contributed to the academic failure of the subgroup in question. In other words, education authorities will look at racial equality and opportunity pursuant to NCLB only where a racial or ethnic subgroup is not performing at a level the state has defined as "proficient." So long as these "proficiency" benchmarks are met, and are the same ostensibly "high" standards for all children, NCLB's requirements are satisfied.

KEY STATUTORY PROVISIONS: THE "NO CHILD LEFT BEHIND" ACT

20 U.S.C. § 6301—Statement of purpose

The purpose of this subchapter is to ensure that all children have a fair, equal, and significant opportunity to obtain a high-quality education and reach, at a minimum, proficiency on challenging state academic achievement standards and state academic assessments. This purpose can be accomplished by—

(1) ensuring that high-quality academic assessments, accountability systems, teacher preparation and training, curriculum, and instructional materials are aligned with challenging State academic standards so that students, teachers, parents, and administrators can measure progress against common expectations for student academic achievement;

(2) meeting the educational needs of low-achieving children in our Nation's highest-poverty schools, limited English proficient children, migratory children, children with disabilities, Indian children, neglected or delinquent children, and young children in need of reading assistance;

(3) closing the achievement gap between high and low-performing children, especially the achievement gaps between minority and nonminority students, and between disadvantaged children and their more advantaged peers;

(4) holding schools, local educational agencies, and States accountable for improving the academic achievement of all students, and identifying and turning around low-performing schools that have failed to provide a high-quality education to their students, while providing alternatives to students in such schools to enable the students to receive a high-quality education;

(5) distributing and targeting resources sufficiently to make a difference to local educational agencies and schools where needs are greatest;

(6) improving and strengthening accountability, teaching, and learning by using State assessment systems designed to ensure that students are meeting challenging State academic achievement and content standards and increasing achievement overall, but especially for the disadvantaged;

(7) providing greater decisionmaking authority and flexibility to schools and teachers in exchange for greater responsibility for student performance;

(8) providing children an enriched and accelerated educational program, including the use of schoolwide programs or additional services that increase the amount and quality of instructional time;

(9) promoting schoolwide reform and ensuring the access of children to effective, scientifically based instructional strategies and challenging academic content;

(10) significantly elevating the quality of instruction by providing staff in participating schools with substantial opportunities for professional development;

(11) coordinating services under all parts of this title with each other, with other educational services, and, to the extent feasible, with other agencies providing services to youth, children, and families; and

(12) affording parents substantial and meaningful opportunities to participate in the education of their children.

Basic SCHOOL Accountability Provisions Under the "No Child Left Behind" Act

20 U.S.C. § 6316(b)—School improvement[a]

(1) General requirements

(A) Identification

* * * a local educational agency shall identify for school improvement any elementary school or secondary school served under this part that fails, for 2 consecutive years, to make adequate yearly progress as defined in the State's plan under section 6311(b)(2) of this title * * *

(7) Corrective action

(A) In general

In this subsection, the term "corrective action" means action, consistent with State law, that—

(i) substantially and directly responds to—

(I) the consistent academic failure of a school that caused the local educational agency to take such action; and

---

a. *See also* 34 C.F.R. §§ 200.30, 200.31, 200.32, 200.36–200.38.

(II) any underlying staffing, curriculum, or other problems in the school; and

(ii) is designed to increase substantially the likelihood that each group of students described in 6311(b)(2)(C) of this title[b] enrolled in the school identified for corrective action will meet or exceed the State's proficient levels of achievement on the State academic assessments described in section 6311(b)(3) of this title.

(B) System

In order to help students served under this part meet challenging State student academic achievement standards, each local educational agency shall implement a system of corrective action in accordance with subparagraphs (C) through (E).

(C) Role of local educational agency

In the case of any school served by a local educational agency under this part that fails to make adequate yearly progress, as defined by the State under section 6311(b)(2) of this title, by the end of the second full school year after the identification under paragraph (1), the local educational agency shall—

---

b. 20 U.S.C. 6311(b)(2)(C) provides:

"Adequate yearly progress" shall be defined by the State in a manner that—

(i) applies the same high standards of academic achievement to all public elementary school and secondary school students in the State;

(ii) is statistically valid and reliable;

(iii) results in continuous and substantial academic improvement for all students;

(iv) measures the progress of public elementary schools, secondary schools and local educational agencies and the State based primarily on the academic assessments described in paragraph (3);

(v) includes separate measurable annual objectives for continuous and substantial improvement for each of the following:

  (I) The achievement of all public elementary school and secondary school students.

  (II) The achievement of—

    (aa) economically disadvantaged students;

    (bb) students from major racial and ethnic groups;

    (cc) students with disabilities; and

    (dd) students with limited English proficiency;

except that disaggregation of data under subclause (II) shall not be required in a case in which the number of students in a category is insufficient to yield statistically reliable information or the results would reveal personally identifiable information about an individual student;

(vi) in accordance with subparagraph (D), includes graduation rates for public secondary school students (defined as the percentage of students who graduate from secondary school with a regular diploma in the standard number of years) and at least one other academic indicator, as determined by the State for all public elementary school students; and

(vii) in accordance with subparagraph (D), at the State's discretion, may also include other academic indicators, as determined by the State for all public school students, measured separately for each group described in clause (v), such as achievement on additional State or locally administered assessments, decreases in grade-to-grade retention rates, attendance rates, and changes in the percentages of students completing gifted and talented, advanced placement, and college preparatory courses.

    (i) continue to provide all students enrolled in the school with the option to transfer to another public school served by the local educational agency, in accordance with paragraph (1)(E) and (F);

    (ii) continue to provide technical assistance consistent with paragraph (4) while instituting any corrective action under clause (iv);

    (iii) continue to make supplemental educational services available, in accordance with subsection (e) of this section, to children who remain in the school; and

    (iv) identify the school for corrective action and take at least one of the following corrective actions:

        (I) Replace the school staff who are relevant to the failure to make adequate yearly progress.

        (II) Institute and fully implement a new curriculum, including providing appropriate professional development for all relevant staff, that is based on scientifically based research and offers substantial promise of improving educational achievement for low-achieving students and enabling the school to make adequate yearly progress.

        (III) Significantly decrease management authority at the school level.

        (IV) Appoint an outside expert to advise the school on its progress toward making adequate yearly progress, based on its school plan under paragraph (3).

        (V) Extend the school year or school day for the school.

        (VI) Restructure the internal organizational structure of the school.

(D) Delay

Notwithstanding any other provision of this paragraph, the local educational agency may delay, for a period not to exceed 1 year, implementation of the requirements under paragraph (5), corrective action under this paragraph, or restructuring under paragraph (8) if the school makes adequate yearly progress for 1 year or if its failure to make adequate yearly progress is due to exceptional or uncontrollable circumstances, such as a natural disaster or a precipitous and unforeseen decline in the financial resources of the local educational agency or school. No such period shall be taken into account in determining the number of consecutive years of failure to make adequate yearly progress.

(E) Publication and dissemination

The local educational agency shall publish and disseminate information regarding any corrective action the local educational agency takes under this paragraph at a school—

    (i) to the public and to the parents of each student enrolled in the school subject to corrective action;

(ii) in an understandable and uniform format and, to the extent practicable, provided in a language that the parents can understand; and

(iii) through such means as the Internet, the media, and public agencies.

(8) Restructuring

(A) Failure to make adequate yearly progress

If, after 1 full school year of corrective action under paragraph (7), a school subject to such corrective action continues to fail to make adequate yearly progress, then the local educational agency shall—

(i) continue to provide all students enrolled in the school with the option to transfer to another public school served by the local educational agency, in accordance with paragraph (1)(E) and (F);

(ii) continue to make supplemental educational services available, in accordance with subsection (e) of this section, to children who remain in the school; and

(iii) prepare a plan and make necessary arrangements to carry out subparagraph (B).

(B) Alternative governance

Not later than the beginning of the school year following the year in which the local educational agency implements subparagraph (A), the local educational agency shall implement one of the following alternative governance arrangements for the school consistent with State law:

(i) Reopening the school as a public charter school.

(ii) Replacing all or most of the school staff (which may include the principal) who are relevant to the failure to make adequate yearly progress.

(iii) Entering into a contract with an entity, such as a private management company, with a demonstrated record of effectiveness, to operate the public school.

(iv) Turning the operation of the school over to the State educational agency, if permitted under State law and agreed to by the State.

(v) Any other major restructuring of the school's governance arrangement that makes fundamental reforms, such as significant changes in the school's staffing and governance, to improve student academic achievement in the school and that has substantial promise of enabling the school to make adequate yearly progress as defined in the State plan under section 6311(b)(2) of this title. In the case of a rural local educational agency with a total of less than 600 students in average daily attendance at the schools that are served by the agency and all of whose schools have a School Locale Code of 7 or 8, as determined by the Secretary, the

Secretary shall, at such agency's request, provide technical assistance to such agency for the purpose of implementing this clause.

(C) Prompt notice

The local educational agency shall—

(i) provide prompt notice to teachers and parents whenever subparagraph (A) or (B) applies; and

(ii) provide the teachers and parents with an adequate opportunity to—

(I) comment before taking any action under those subparagraphs; and

(II) participate in developing any plan under subparagraph (A)(iii).

* * *

(12) Duration

If any school identified for school improvement, corrective action, or restructuring makes adequate yearly progress for two consecutive school years, the local educational agency shall no longer subject the school to the requirements of school improvement, corrective action, or restructuring or identify the school for school improvement for the succeeding school year.

Basic SCHOOL DISTRICT Accountability Provisions Under the "No Child Left Behind" Act

20 U.S.C. § 6316(c)—State review and local educational agency improvement

* * *

(3) Identification of local educational agency for improvement

A State shall identify for improvement any local educational agency that, for 2 consecutive years, including the period immediately prior to January 8, 2002, failed to make adequate yearly progress as defined in the State's plan under section 6311(b)(2) of this title.

* * *

(10) Corrective action

In order to help students served under this part meet challenging State student academic achievement standards, each State shall implement a system of corrective action in accordance with the following:

(A) Definition

As used in this paragraph, the term "corrective action" means action, consistent with State law, that—

(i) substantially and directly responds to the consistent academic failure that caused the State to take such action and to any underlying staffing, curricular, or other problems in the agency; and

(ii) is designed to meet the goal of having all students served under this part achieve at the proficient and advanced student academic achievement levels.

(B) General requirements

After providing technical assistance under paragraph (9) and subject to subparagraph (E), the State—

(i) may take corrective action at any time with respect to a local educational agency that has been identified under paragraph (3);

(ii) shall take corrective action with respect to any local educational agency that fails to make adequate yearly progress, as defined by the State, by the end of the second full school year after the identification of the agency under paragraph (3); and

(iii) shall continue to provide technical assistance while instituting any corrective action under clause (i) or (ii).

(C) Certain corrective actions required

In the case of a local educational agency identified for corrective action, the State educational agency shall take at least one of the following corrective actions:

(i) Deferring programmatic funds or reducing administrative funds.

(ii) Instituting and fully implementing a new curriculum that is based on State and local academic content and achievement standards, including providing appropriate professional development based on scientifically based research for all relevant staff, that offers substantial promise of improving educational achievement for low-achieving students.

(iii) Replacing the local educational agency personnel who are relevant to the failure to make adequate yearly progress.

(iv) Removing particular schools from the jurisdiction of the local educational agency and establishing alternative arrangements for public governance and supervision of such schools.

(v) Appointing, through the State educational agency, a receiver or trustee to administer the affairs of the local educational agency in place of the superintendent and school board.

(vi) Abolishing or restructuring the local educational agency.

(vii) Authorizing students to transfer from a school operated by the local educational agency to a higher-performing public school operated by another local educational agency in accordance with subsections (b)(1)(E) and (F) of this section, and providing to such students transportation (or the costs of transportation) to such schools consistent with subsection (b)(9) of this section, in conjunction with carrying out not less than one additional action described under this subparagraph.

(D) Hearing

Prior to implementing any corrective action under this paragraph, the State educational agency shall provide notice and a hearing to the affected local educational agency, if State law provides for such notice and hearing. The hearing shall take place not later than 45 days following the decision to implement corrective action.

(E) Notice to parents

The State educational agency shall publish, and disseminate to parents and the public, information on any corrective action the State educational agency takes under this paragraph through such means as the Internet, the media, and public agencies.

(F) Delay

Notwithstanding subparagraph (B)(ii), a State educational agency may delay, for a period not to exceed 1 year, implementation of corrective action under this paragraph if the local educational agency makes adequate yearly progress for 1 year or its failure to make adequate yearly progress is due to exceptional or uncontrollable circumstances, such as a natural disaster or a precipitous and unforeseen decline in the financial resources of the local educational agency. No such period shall be taken into account in determining the number of consecutive years of failure to make adequate yearly progress.

PROBLEM 32: CHALLENGING THE IMPLEMENTATION OF THE NCLB IN OCEAN WAVE

Assume the same set of facts set forth in Problem 31, *supra*. Assume, also, that the Shell Beach schools continue their pattern of lackluster performance on standardized tests, and that the District therefore fails to meet its designated Adequate Yearly Progress goals as required under the terms of the NCLB. Assume that the State, acting pursuant to 20 U.S.C. Section 6316 (c), chooses the "corrective action" of "[d]eferring programmatic funds or reducing administrative funds" for the entire District. Assume that you have been consulted by a group of angry parents for the purpose of filing a challenge to the implementation of NCLB in this regard. In particular, the parents are prepared to argue that school funding decisions based on only one of many possible indicators of educational quality violate the rights of the students under federal and state law. What legal theories might be set forth on their behalf? What result? Discuss.

QUALIFICATIONS FOR EDUCATORS UNDER THE "NO CHILD LEFT BEHIND" ACT

20 U.S.C. Section 6319(a)

(a) Teacher qualifications and measurable objectives

(1) In general

Beginning with the first day of the first school year after January 8, 2002, each local educational agency receiving assistance under this part shall ensure that all teachers hired after such day and teaching in a program supported with funds under this part are highly qualified.

(2) State plan

As part of the plan described in section 6311 of this title, each State educational agency receiving assistance under this part shall develop a plan to ensure that all teachers teaching in core academic subjects within the State are highly qualified not later than the end of the 2005–2006 school year. Such plan shall establish annual measurable objectives for each local educational agency and school that, at a minimum—

(A) shall include an annual increase in the percentage of highly qualified teachers at each local educational agency and school, to ensure that all teachers teaching in core academic subjects in each public elementary school and secondary school are highly qualified not later than the end of the 2005–2006 school year;

(B) shall include an annual increase in the percentage of teachers who are receiving high-quality professional development to enable such teachers to become highly qualified and successful classroom teachers; and

(C) may include such other measures as the State educational agency determines to be appropriate to increase teacher qualifications.

(3) Local plan

As part of the plan described in section 6312 of this title, each local educational agency receiving assistance under this part shall develop a plan to ensure that all teachers teaching within the school district served by the local educational agency are highly qualified not later than the end of the 2005–2006 school year.

from 34 **C.F.R. §§ 200.55–.57**

§ 200.55   Qualifications of teachers.

(a) Newly hired teachers in Title I programs.

(1) An LEA must ensure that all teachers hired after the first day of the 2002–2003 school year who teach core academic subjects in a program supported with funds under subpart A of this part are highly qualified as defined in § 200.56.

(2) For the purpose of paragraph (a)(1) of this section, a teacher teaching in a program supported with funds under subpart A of this part is—

(i) A teacher in a targeted assisted school who is paid with funds under subpart A of this part;

(ii) A teacher in a schoolwide program school; or

(iii) A teacher employed by an LEA with funds under subpart A of this part to provide services to eligible private school students under § 200.62.

(b) All teachers of core academic subjects.

(1) Not later than the end of the 2005–2006 school year, each State that receives funds under subpart A of this part, and each LEA in that State, must ensure that all public elementary and secondary school teachers in the State who teach core academic subjects, including teachers employed by an LEA to provide services to eligible private school students under § 200.62, are highly qualified as defined in § 200.56.

(2) A teacher who does not teach a core academic subject—such as some vocational education teachers—is not required to meet the requirements in § 200.56.

(c) Definition. The term "core academic subjects" means English, reading or language arts, mathematics, science, foreign languages, civics and government, economics, arts, history, and geography.

(d) Private school teachers. The requirements in this section do not apply to teachers hired by private elementary and secondary schools.

§ 200.56 Definition of "highly qualified teacher."

To be a "highly qualified teacher," a teacher covered under § 200.55 must meet the requirements in paragraph (a) and either paragraph (b) or (c) of this section.

(a) In general.

(1) Except as provided in paragraph (a)(3) of this section, a teacher covered under § 200.55 must—

(i) Have obtained full State certification as a teacher, which may include certification obtained through alternative routes to certification; or

(ii)(A) Have passed the State teacher licensing examination; and

(B) Hold a license to teach in the State.

(2) A teacher meets the requirement in paragraph (a)(1) of this section if the teacher—

(i) Has fulfilled the State's certification and licensure requirements applicable to the years of experience the teacher possesses; or

(ii) Is participating in an alternative route to certification program under which—

(A) The teacher—

(1) Receives high-quality professional development that is sustained, intensive, and classroom-focused in or-

der to have a positive and lasting impact on classroom instruction, before and while teaching;

(2) Participates in a program of intensive supervision that consists of structured guidance and regular ongoing support for teachers or a teacher mentoring program;

(3) Assumes functions as a teacher only for a specified period of time not to exceed three years; and

(4) Demonstrates satisfactory progress toward full certification as prescribed by the State; and

(B) The State ensures, through its certification and licensure process, that the provisions in paragraph (a)(2)(ii) of this section are met.

(3) A teacher teaching in a public charter school in a State must meet the certification and licensure requirements, if any, contained in the State's charter school law.

(4) If a teacher has had certification or licensure requirements waived on an emergency, temporary, or provisional basis, the teacher is not highly qualified.

(b) *Teachers new to the profession.* A teacher covered under § 200.55 who is new to the profession also must—

(1) Hold at least a bachelor's degree; and

(2) At the public elementary school level, demonstrate, by passing a rigorous State test (which may consist of passing a State certification or licensing test), subject knowledge and teaching skills in reading/language arts, writing, mathematics, and other areas of the basic elementary school curriculum; or

(3) At the public middle and high school levels, demonstrate a high level of competency by—

(i) Passing a rigorous State test in each academic subject in which the teacher teaches (which may consist of passing a State certification or licensing test in each of these subjects); or

(ii) Successfully completing in each academic subject in which the teacher teaches—

(A) An undergraduate major;

(B) A graduate degree;

(C) Coursework equivalent to an undergraduate major; or

(D) Advanced certification or credentialing.

(c) *Teachers not new to the profession.* A teacher covered under § 200.55 who is not new to the profession also must—

(1) Hold at least a bachelor's degree; and

(2)(i) Meet the applicable requirements in paragraph (b)(2) or (3) of this section; or

(ii) Based on a high, objective, uniform State standard of evaluation in accordance with section 9101(23)(C)(ii) of the ESEA, demonstrate competency in each academic subject in which the teacher teaches.

§ 200.57 Plans to increase teacher quality.

(a) State plan.

(1) A State that receives funds under subpart A of this part must develop, as part of its State plan under section 1111 of the ESEA, a plan to ensure that all public elementary and secondary school teachers in the State who teach core academic subjects are highly qualified not later than the end of the 2005–2006 school year.

(2) The State's plan must—

(i) Establish annual measurable objectives for each LEA and school that include, at a minimum, an annual increase in the percentage of—

(A) Highly qualified teachers at each LEA and school; and

(B) Teachers who are receiving high-quality professional development to enable them to become highly qualified and effective classroom teachers;

(ii) Describe the strategies the State will use to—

(A) Help LEAs and schools meet the requirements in paragraph (a)(1) of this section; and

(B) Monitor the progress of LEAs and schools in meeting these requirements; and

(iii) Until the SEA fully complies with paragraph (a)(1) of this section, describe the specific steps the SEA will take to—

(A) Ensure that Title I schools provide instruction by highly qualified teachers, including steps that the SEA will take to ensure that minority children and children from low-income families are not taught at higher rates than other children by inexperienced, unqualified, or out-of-field teachers; and

(B) Evaluate and publicly report the progress of the SEA with respect to these steps.

(3) The State's plan may include other measures that the State determines are appropriate to increase teacher qualifications.

(b) Local plan. An LEA that receives funds under subpart A of this part must develop, as part of its local plan under section 1112 of the ESEA, a plan to ensure that—

(1) All public elementary and secondary school teachers in the LEA who teach core academic subjects, including teachers employed by the LEA to provide services to eligible private school students under § 200.62, are highly qualified not later than the end of the 2005–2006 school year; and

(2) Through incentives for voluntary transfers, professional development, recruitment programs, or other effective strategies, minority students and students from low-income families are not taught at higher rates than other students by unqualified, out-of-field, or inexperienced teachers.

NOTE

1.   Inevitably, given how fast events have been moving in this area, there have been developments subsequent to the publication of this volume that could alter the nature and extent of the inquiry. In your view, what have been the most significant recent changes in this area, legally and as a matter of policy? What do these developments tell you about where the accountability movement might be headed in the U.S.?

C. SCHOOL CHOICE, VOUCHERS, AND PRIVATIZATION

PROBLEM 33: CHOICE FOR LITERACY IN THE 21ST CENTURY

The following hypothetical takes place in the State of Columbia in 2006.

Concerned about the lack of viable educational alternatives for language minority students, the Columbia legislature approved a bill establishing an innovative school choice program for English learners. The passage of this "Choice for Literacy in the Twenty-first Century" Act reflected a highly unusual alliance between prominent Republicans and prominent Democrats statewide.

Under the Act, families of students identified as "English learners" would be given vouchers which could then be redeemed at any public or private school in the state. These vouchers, which would be equivalent to the average per-pupil expenditure in Columbia *plus* the average expenditure per EL student in 2005, would guarantee families of EL students a free education. Private schools would not be required to accept these vouchers, but if they did, they would be precluded from charging the families any additional money.

Publicity surrounding the passage of the Act was highly positive, and the governor did not hesitate to sign it immediately. Leaders from business, education, and politics hailed the public interest nature of this choice program and the importance of addressing language acquisition issues in a free-market context. Trustees of most major private schools in the state announced that they would be establishing programs for language minority students to further the public good.

All schools accepting vouchers would be required to submit a curriculum plan to the State Department of English Language Instruction, a new agency established by the Act. No one approach to language acquisition would be required. However, the Act specified that *private* schools would be free to provide as much primary language instruction as they desired.

To guarantee a uniform system of measurement and accountability, the Educational Testing Service (ETS) was commissioned to set up tests (entry-level and exit-level) which would measure English Language Proficiency. All students entering a California public or private school for the first time would be required to take the entry-level test, and only students whose test results identified them as EL would be eligible for vouchers. At the end of every subsequent year, these same students would be required to take the exit-level test to ascertain continued eligibility. A three-year limit, however, was placed on the acquisition of vouchers under this program.

In the Winter of 2007, you are consulted by a group of parents who seek to block the implementation of this statutory scheme. The prospective plaintiffs would like to challenge the Act under principles of equity and educational quality. What legal and policy arguments might you set forth in such a case? What result? Discuss.

1. SCHOOL CHOICE GENERALLY

REFORMING SCHOOL REFORM

Martha Minow
68 FORDHAM L. REV. 257 (1999)

* * * American public schools are commonly described as "in crisis," or failing to generate adequate levels of achievement. Another persistent charge addresses the disparate quality of educational opportunities between cities and suburbs, between public and private, and across other familiar social divisions. The contemporary push for reforms thus mirrors longstanding, potentially conflicting aspirations for American schooling: quality and equality. Universally available inadequate schooling would offer a tragic sort of equality; thus far, however, society has had far more success generating individual schools of high quality rather than widespread high quality schooling.

* * *[R]eforms [in the mid to late 1990s have gathered] under the banner of "choice." Rather than assigning students to public schools based on the location of their residence or some other characteristic, choice proposals would let parents and guardians select a school. In so doing, they seek to generate competitive pressures to promote higher quality schooling overall. In addition, choice proposals are said to afford some measure of equality. Voucher plans are meant to grant to poor and low-income families some of the latitude for selecting schools already enjoyed by families with enough resources to move to high quality subur-

ban districts or to opt for private schools. Charter plans, offering resources to entrepreneurial groups interested in running innovative public schools, are intended to offer high quality options within the public system.

Vouchers and charters also risk perpetuating inequality by excluding and segregating children with special needs, skimming from public schools those families motivated enough to take advantage of voucher and charter programs, and diverting resources from the project of improving the entire public school system.

In some respects, choice reforms try to redress failures of the last wave of school reform, the law-driven equality movement. Starting with racial desegregation, the push for equality expanded to gender equity, education rights for children with disabilities, bilingual and bi-cultural programs for English-language-learners, school finance reform, and even equal access for religious as well as non-religious student activities in public school settings. Each of these efforts reflects an underlying impetus to ensure equal opportunities for individual students, regardless of their race, gender, disability, linguistic and national background, economic class, or religion. Another way to perceive these reforms is to see them as extensions into our schools of the deep social struggles over group status and equality that pervade other sectors of the society. Under either formulation, these equality-based reforms absorbed enormous energy and dramatically reshaped schools and school practices around the country— with results both admirable and less than admirable.

Specific critiques of versions of school desegregation, special education for children with disabilities, school finance plans, bilingual education, and other equality reforms repeatedly appear in contemporary debates over reform. Yet the choice movement most immediately affects the equality reforms by rejecting their central features: centralized student assignment and bureaucratic compliance mechanisms. It may be coincidence, but the choice movement urges greater parental and guardian control over where and with whom each child will be educated after decades of desegregation orders and following more recent efforts to include children with disabilities in mainstream classrooms. Voucher and charter programs do not focus on either specific equality initiatives or their categorical approaches. Racial desegregation, school finance litigation, special education, and bilingual education may be once proud names of prior school reforms, but now they often are blamed, directly or indirectly, for the bureaucratization, fragmentation, and misallocation that needs redress.

Will today's reforms themselves generate the pressing need for future reforms twenty or thirty years hence? I worry that the choice movement will accelerate the already zany tendency noted by Linda Darling–Hammond, a wise observer of schools, who commented, "[s]chools chew up and spit out undigested reforms on a regular basis. This creates a sense within schools that whatever the innovation, 'this too will pass'—and that it probably should." Often it is difficult to evaluate education reforms because they come fast and furiously, with teachers and administrators sometimes participating and sometimes resisting. Schools are littered with the carcasses of partially or wholly abandoned school reforms. We have had school-based budgeting, computer-based learning, whole language reading, and back-to-basics. More recently, the standards movement has called for high expectations and the frequent use of standardized evaluations. It oversimplifies matters to suggest that new school reforms simply react to old ones. Yet the new reforms both implicitly and explicitly reject the older methods. In simple terms, the new reforms emphasize competition and standards, choice and incentives. The older efforts, framed by rights and remedies, focused on equality and fairness. The new reforms include valuable strategies but also faulty assumptions and dangers. The old reforms generated cumbersome bureaucracies and sometimes counterproductive court orders, but also provided fundamental values and protections.

Can we construct reform not by reacting against a prior wave, but instead by building upon it? Can we challenge what it means to reform schools by reforming reform? The very phrase, "reforming reform," is gaining currency. It appears in contemporary efforts to fix what seems to have gone wrong with campaign finance reforms, Eastern European democratization, welfare reform, juvenile justice reform, bankruptcy reform, as well as school reform. Yet to be more than just another round of change, reformed reforms must anticipate what are usually the unanticipated consequences of the fresh turn of reforms. This can be done without waiting until current initiatives prompt still another demand for starting anew. It means starting with a sober evaluation of the claims and assumptions of the new reform movement. At the very least, this will reduce a new round of false promises and disappointments. It also means resisting the temptation to neglect goals that remain important because of the underrealization of other goals. Reforming reform involves learning to build constructively on the past while putting in place the capacity to learn from new initiatives.

For school reform, the relationship between equality and quality deserves sustained and simultaneous attention. Equality reforms hit the barriers of reaction, such as "white flight" in the face of desegregation orders and English-only referenda that have halted bilingual education in some communities. In trying to create remedies for unequal education along the lines of race, gender, language, disability, and financial inputs, the equality reforms also confronted the basic difficulties in elevating the quality of instruction and educational experiences. It makes sense, therefore, for current reforms to embrace the goal of quality through a combination of competition through choice mechanisms, and high expectations through standards. Yet the new reforms expose children to new risks of inequality by leaving some students in dismal existing schools and by making crucial to the selection of children's schools the parents' and guardians' motivation and knowledge—qualities that are most certainly not equally distributed.

In hopes of preventing yet another reform movement's demise and facile replacement by a similar successor, I here explore the limitations of both the choice and equality reforms. I identify potential common ground and synergies of present and past school improvement struggles. I will end by suggesting ways that legislators and other public bodies can craft choice reforms that sustain the commitments to both equality and quality.

I. THE CHOICE MOVEMENT

School choice is a broad phrase which can encompass many kinds of proposals and programs, some of which are quite inconsistent with one another. One cluster of programs works exclusively within the public system. Here, choice could refer to modest opportunities for parents and guardians to seek to enroll a child in one of a handful of specialized, or "magnet," schools within a public school system. It could refer to more ambitious efforts to de-link residence from school assignment, such as the system-wide controlled choice plan of Cambridge, Massachusetts. In this approach, parents rank desired schools throughout the system, and a complex algorithm produces school assignments by combining private preferences with targets for racial and gender mixing, along with special weights for families seeking to keep siblings in the same school or seeking to enroll in the neighborhood school. Choice within public school systems also might involve limited cross-district enrollments, such as the Metco Program offered in Boston to enable inner city residents to enroll in participating suburban schools on a limited basis.

The newest element of choice within the public system is the charter school idea. Established by a chartering agency, such as a legislature or municipality, these independent schools are intended to operate with public funds but outside the regulations of the public system. Actually, authorizing legislation in different jurisdictions varies considerably in the degree of autonomy charter schools are granted. Some governmental units exempt these schools from otherwise prevailing collective bargaining agreements, curricular requirements, and spending requirements, while others impose some or all of these obligations. Typically awarded on a competitive basis to entrepreneurial groups, charters for such schools usually have a limited term before which they must be either renewed or else terminated by the authorizing authority. Charter school arrangements also vary in the degree to which they specify how school admissions are to be governed. Some authorizing legislation does not address whether charter schools may select among applicants and, if so, on what bases.

A different set of choice initiatives cross the border between public and private systems. Typically using the device of vouchers, these initiatives offer public monetary payments to enable families to enroll their children in private schools. One kind of program extends only to secular, non-parochial private schools. Another, considerably more controversial kind allows the vouchers to be used in any approved private school, including parochial schools. More than 3700 students in Cleveland—about five percent of the public school enrollment—use public vouchers to pay for private schooling. The vast majority of these students attend religious schools. However, the usual amount set for a voucher is insufficient to cover the costs of the most elite, selective private schools. Instead, the voucher total approximates the tuition level set by parochial schools, a tuition level that reflects subsidies from other sources. Some parents, of course, gladly choose parochial schools precisely for the instruction in religion and values, or because they hope that the school will offer discipline and social mobility. But for others, the religious schools are simply the one available option to get out of failing public schools. Voucher programs could vary the degree to which they target low-income families as recipients as opposed to all families.

The movement for educational choice may seem modest or almost marginal because it often involves small-scale experiments. Yet actually, the choice movement involves a radical challenge to the common school ideal that generated public schools and compulsory schooling from the nineteenth through the early part of the twentieth century. As Seymour Sarason recently observed, "charter schools rest on a devastating critique of the present system because it implies that for a school meaningfully to innovate to achieve more desirable outcomes, it must be free of the usual rules, regulations, and traditions of a school system." If real innovation and desirable results are possible only for schools that diverge from the public school system, then the system itself is the problem. The choice movement thus represents a dramatic departure from almost all prior school reforms. Rather than aspiring to create the "one best system" of public schooling that is run by experts for all children, charter, magnet, and voucher-based education proposals seek to multiply options, promote competition, and concentrate the mechanisms for evaluation and accountability in the hands of individual parents. In theory, some measure of comparability and public accountability would then be sought through general, even legislated, standards to set expectations and methods for assessment. * * *

Aside from predictable start-up problems, most of the other fundamental assumptions behind choice proposals also are at best problematic. For example, the assumption that competition will produce accountability is flawed. Competition may produce schools that offer superficial attractions but little actual accountability. * * *

Further, there are key analytic problems with the claim that successful schools and programs will expand and that failing ones will shut down or change. Growth, or scaling up, of successful schools or schooling methods is the single most notable gap in prior effective school reforms. There is abundant knowledge about how to build one good school, yet we have poor or at best mixed results in spreading that knowledge to other school buildings. Schools do not operate with the kind of economies of scale that generate expansion in the private sector. Schooling is a retail, not wholesale business. For-profit schools are inclined to expand without waiting for demonstrated success or developing a sensible strategy precisely because short-term expansion may look like success.

Market-style failures may significantly injure children caught in schools that shut down. * * *

One of the most emphatic claims by advocates for choice is the benefit of bypassing central bureaucracies. Whether through charters or vouchers, or simply as adopted within existing public schools, school-based management offenders bypass some features of centralized bureaucracy, but sometimes at the cost of fraud. Arizona, for example, adopted vouchers to bypass public school bureaucracies and ended up with a full-fledged fraud scandal, requiring the state to shut down schools mid-term. In addition, new inefficiencies are likely to emerge as each school has to make expenditure and managerial decisions. There are also obvious risks of misallocation of funds into public relations and marketing rather than programming. And there is the loss of economies of scale in the provision of specialized services, such as education for students with disabilities. Each individual school will have more difficulty spreading the costs of educating students with particular disabilities than the entire system would and thus, each individual school will have strong incentives to exclude students with disabilities.

Independent of academic quality, at least in theory, choice programs enhance pluralism. Absent some external regulation, having unregulated pluralism in the educational world may produce its own problems. Rather than generating a desirable pluralism of methods and values, vouchers and charters could instead produce self-segregation that exacerbates inter-group misunderstandings along the familiar fault-lines of race, class, gender, religion, disability, and national origin.

The most basic assumption behind the choice programs is that competition mechanisms are at least sufficiently suited to the educational task to warrant their use. It seems difficult to disagree that some degree of competition and some additional efforts to promote accountability could improve school systems that notoriously have been plagued by laborious top-down managerial bureaucracies. Yet, a full-fledged market approach to schooling seems a mismatch between means and ends. Schooling has crucial features that depart from privately consumed goods and services. The fit between market models and schooling is awkward and partial. The choosers are parents and guardians, who are not themselves the consumers, or children, who are not usually empowered to make crucial choices about such important matters. The consequences of these choices are not the same as the consequences of choices about what kind of bicycle or dishwasher to buy.

Education has dimensions of a public good, with crucial externalities affecting the entire population. Ensuring a good education for members of the next generation is important to the entire society; to our economic, cultural, and political well-being, as well as to the life prospects for the individual students involved. Cultivating capacities to act as informed and responsible citizens and as productive workers matters to everyone else. Our political fortunes, retirement benefits, and tax dollars are all at stake.

In addition, public education has distinct purposes in a democratic society. Philosophers and pundits have debated the purposes of education through the centuries. Historians still dispute the core motivations behind America's public school movement. But a basic statement of public school purposes would include forging commonality, promoting civic engagement in a diverse and democratic nation, and offering quality opportunities on an equal basis.

Further, the capacity of schools to reach all children pose special public concerns because so many children risk remaining in or falling into poverty, failing to obtain needed skills, never getting connected to the political process, and drifting into crime, drugs, and violence. Students with disabilities who do not learn well may become dependent on the state for support. The assumptions at work in market competition to produce better products for private consumption are not mirrored in the school context. Although the particular taxpayer may not see the direct benefits of public education today, failure to invest and to provide universal education will affect national economic, political, and social conditions for decades. Have we become so captivated by free market rhetoric that it is our answer to everything? It is often said that everything looks like a nail if you only have a hammer. But who will be helped, and who will be hammered, if market mechanisms pervade schooling? The classic economic rationales for regulation—inadequacy of information, large externalities, collective action problem—are particularly acute in the educational context.

The final assumption behind current choice proposals is that radical change is necessary because prior reform efforts have failed to remedy chronic school crises. This assumption is overstated, yet, in my view, it is the most compelling of the entire set. It is overstated in part because measuring the success and failure of past educational reforms is complex and highly politicized. * * *

[H]owever, there are [still] real signs of failure. * * *

III.   EQUALITY AND QUALITY: PRIVATE CHOICE AND PUBLIC COMMITMENTS

Choice reforms, notably vouchers and charters, could undermine equality goals unless there are direct efforts to maintain and enforce them. Offering vouchers and creating charters would exacerbate existing problems for the most disadvantaged students. Either there will be only a limited number of exit tickets or, if there are universally available vouchers and charter school places, they will not offer quality instruction for everyone. Not enough slots exist in demonstrably good schools, not enough is known about how to start up quality programs quickly and effectively, and there are not enough qualified and competent teachers.

African–American and Latino students in impoverished areas disproportionately attend inadequate schools that will lose out in any real competition. Anyone able to move or afford transportation would select other schools. Those unable to move or pay for transportation "will be trapped in inferior institutions providing inferior educations. . . . '' The loss of motivated students and families from those inferior institutions will cause them to decline further.

Indeed, the most vulnerable children are those who are not only poor and members of historically disadvantaged groups, but who also have parents lacking the skills, motivation, or ability to be engaged advocates for their children. Taking advantage of a choice system requires knowledge and initiative, which not all parents have. Children have no choice about who their parents are. A system that makes the content and form of schooling turn on parental choice makes the differences in parents matter even more than they already do in shaping educational opportunities. A choice system will make the inequalities among parents directly cost the children currently enrolled in public schools.

Inequalities along these fault-lines already deeply affect children's chances, to be sure. Wealthier, more educated, and more motivated parents already choose to live in districts with better schools, to pay for private schools, or to press for scholarships or slots in magnet schools, Metco programs, or a particularly effective teacher's classroom. Expanding choice options through vouchers and charter schools initially may seem to advance equality by opening up more options for more children. In practice, however, at least for a considerable time to come, such choice schemes will also put the most vulnerable children at an even greater disadvantage by simply abandoning them to failing schools. * * *

What is or should be the mission of public education? The equality reformers fundamentally pursued the public missions of forging commonality, promoting civic engagement in a diverse and democratic nation, and offering quality opportunities on an equal basis. Such goals may seem lost at times in the conflicts and disappointments surrounding racial desegregation, bilingual education, gender equity struggles, school finance fights, and special education reform. Yet, the equality focus articulates the understanding that the entire society is affected by the educational opportunities and achievements of each new generation, and that no one can be wasted. * * *

* * *

Judicial decisions are too remote and indirect for addressing the policy judgments today about how much should public dollars for schooling also entail public norms and obligations. Rather than pursue the arguments that could be mounted through litigation surrounding state-action issues or legal restrictions on private school conduct, those concerned with the direct consequences for equality of choice proposals should work to ensure that the governing legislation includes appropriate restrictions and guidelines.

These are the most obvious, basic questions that must be tackled:

(1) Can a participating charter or voucher school exclude students on the basis of race, class, or religion?

(2) Can a participating school reserve places for students of one race or gender in order to produce a desired balance or mix?

(3) Under what, if any, conditions can a participating school restrict enrollment to students of one gender, or students with or without particular disabilities, or students with or without English language proficiency?

(4) Can participating schools mitigate the tendency toward segregation along the many lines of difference among students by joining in system-wide programs or activities?

(5) How will participating schools be evaluated and how can analysis be generated to permit parents, school administrators, governmental and non-governmental leaders, as well as other community members, to assess choice experiments seriously as well as to assess particular schools?

More crucial than my own answers is the basic proposition that authorizing legislation, backed by enforcement possibilities, address each of these issues with specificity.

I offer my own initial responses simply to begin to sketch possible legislative guidelines. First, no school receiving public dollars through charter or voucher programs should be permitted to exclude applicants on the basis of race, class, or religion; but schools should be allowed to seek racial and gender balance by reserving spots until a brief period (such as one month) before each fall starting date, at which time unreserved spots should open on a random basis. Second, no school should be allowed to accept a voucher and then demand additional tuition payments from the family; the voucher should cover the entire tuition expense. Third, no school should be allowed to exclude persons of one sex, persons with (or without) particular disabilities, or persons based on their degree of English proficiency unless the school is part of a cooperative plan with other school(s) or systems ensuring comparable opportunities for those excluded from that school. If an all-boy charter school is permitted, for example, there must be comparable educational programs available in all-girl settings and also in co-ed settings. If students with mental retardation are excluded from a school, there must be integrated educational programs designed for those students available elsewhere. Fourth, segregation that occurs either by design or through patterns of self-selection must be mitigated by requiring each school to participate in city or region-wide programs to mix students enrolled in different schools and programs in joint projects such as journalism, drama, music, and sports (on cross-school teams). Only such programs have been shown to have success in reducing stereotypes and mistrust among students across group lines. Finally, participating schools must join in gathering data with uniform guidelines to permit evaluations of each school; the data should include standardized tests, but also richer measures of school programming, implementation, and results.

These recommendations balance the current law governing public schools with respect for innovation and experimentation that choice initiatives can bring. They also embody cautions about choice initiatives, cautions anchored in the hopes and the disappointments of the equality reforms of the recent past. * * *

NOTES

1. As discussed below in Chapter 8, the U.S. Supreme Court ruled in 2002 that public money could in fact be used to fund private sectarian education, at least within the context of a menu of options that sought to increase the educational opportunities of low-income children attending failing schools. *Zelman v. Simmons–Harris,* 536 U.S. 639, 122 S.Ct. 2460 (2002). At the same time, however, other voucher programs have been struck down under the constitutions of individual states. *See, e.g., Bush v. Holmes,* 919 So.2d 392 (Fla. 2006). *See also Cain v. Horne,* 218 Ariz. 301, 183 P.3d 1269 (Ariz.App. 2008).

2. While only a relatively small number of actual voucher programs have been implemented nationwide as of 2009, school choice has become an integral component of the education reform landscape on many levels, from desegregation to charter schools to NCLB. Thus the analysis set forth by Martha Minow remains relevant not only for its historical value and its policy context generally, but also for its articulation of principles that might inform future choice programs in this regard.

2. THE SCHOOL CHOICE PROVISIONS OF NCLB

School choice, as referenced above, is a key component of the 2001 U.S. "No Child Left Behind" Act. Under the legislation, parents have gained the right to choose additional educational options for their children if—among other things—their child's current school either fails to meet "performance" requirements or is deemed "persistently dangerous." Indeed, both proponents and critics of NCLB have alluded to the fact that this Act continues the push toward more school choice that has been a central policy imperative for many who favor a free-market approach and greater privatization in the nation's educational system.

In addition to the choice options built into other provisions, the Act includes a separate section that directly addresses school choice.

School Choice Provisions Under the "No Child Left Behind" Act and Relevant Federal Regulations

20 U.S.C. § 6316(b)—School improvement * * *

(9) Transportation

In any case described in paragraph (1)(E) for schools described in paragraphs (1)(A), (5), (7)(C)(i), and (8)(A), and subsection (c)(10)(C)(vii) of this section, the local educational agency shall provide, or shall pay for the provision of, transportation for the student to the public school the student attends. * * *

(13) Special rule

A local educational agency shall permit a child who transferred to another school under this subsection to remain in that school until the child has completed the highest grade in that school. The obligation of the local educational agency to provide, or to provide for, transportation for the child ends at the end of a school year if the local educational agency determines that the school from which the child transferred is no longer identified for school improvement or subject to corrective action or restructuring.

from 34 C.F.R. § 200.44 Public school choice

(a) Requirements.

(1) In the case of a school identified for school improvement under § 200.32, for corrective action under § 200.33, or for restructuring under § 200.34, the LEA must provide all students enrolled in the school with the option to transfer to another public school served by the LEA.

(2) The LEA must offer this option not later than the first day of the school year following the year in which the LEA administered the assessments that resulted in its identification of the school for improvement, corrective action, or restructuring.

(3) The schools to which students may transfer under paragraph (a)(1) of this section—

　(i) May not include schools that—

　　(A) The LEA has identified for improvement under § 200.32, corrective action under § 200.33, or restructuring under § 200.34; or

　　(B) Are persistently dangerous as determined by the State; and

　(ii) May include one or more public charter schools.

(4) If more than one school meets the requirements of paragraph (a)(3) of this section, the LEA must—

　(i) Provide to parents of students eligible to transfer under paragraph (a)(1) of this section a choice of more than one such school; and

　(ii) Take into account the parents' preferences among the choices offered under paragraph (a)(4)(i) of this section.

(5) The LEA must offer the option to transfer described in this section unless it is prohibited by State law in accordance with paragraph (b) of this section.

(6) Except as described in §§ 200.32(d) and 200.33(c), if a school was in school improvement or subject to corrective action before January 8, 2002, the State must ensure that the LEA provides a public school choice option in accordance with paragraph (a)(1) of this section not later than the first day of the 2002–2003 school year.

(b) Limitation on State law prohibition. An LEA may invoke the State law prohibition on choice described in paragraph (a)(5) of this section only if the State law prohibits choice through restrictions on public school assignments or the transfer of students from one public school to another public school.

(c) Desegregation plans.

(1) If an LEA is subject to a desegregation plan, whether that plan is voluntary, court-ordered, or required by a Federal or State administrative agency, the LEA is not exempt from the requirement in paragraph (a)(1) of this section.

(2) In determining how to provide students with the option to transfer to another school, the LEA may take into account the requirements of the desegregation plan.

(3) If the desegregation plan forbids the LEA from offering the transfer option required under paragraph (a)(1) of this section, the LEA must secure appropriate changes to the plan to permit compliance with paragraph (a)(1) of this section.

(d) Capacity. An LEA may not use lack of capacity to deny students the option to transfer under paragraph (a)(1) of this section.

(e) Priority.

(1) In providing students the option to transfer to another public school in accordance with paragraph (a)(1) of this section, the LEA must give priority to the lowest-achieving students from low-income families.

(2) The LEA must determine family income on the same basis that the LEA uses to make allocations to schools under subpart A of this part.

(f) Status. Any public school to which a student transfers under paragraph (a)(1) of this section must ensure that the student is enrolled in classes and other activities in the school in the same manner as all other students in the school.

(g) Duration of transfer.

(1) If a student exercises the option under paragraph (a)(1) of this section to transfer to another public school, the LEA must permit the student to remain in that school until the student has completed the highest grade in the school.

(2) The LEA's obligation to provide transportation for the student may be limited under the circumstances described in paragraph (i) of this section and in § 200.48.

(h) No eligible schools within an LEA. If all public schools to which a student may transfer within an LEA are identified for school improvement, corrective action, or restructuring, the LEA—

(1) Must, to the extent practicable, establish a cooperative agreement for a transfer with one or more other LEAs in the area; and

(2) May offer supplemental educational services to eligible students under § 200.45 in schools in their first year of school improvement under § 200.39.

(i) Transportation.

(1) If a student exercises the option under paragraph (a)(1) of this section to transfer to another public school, the LEA must, consistent with § 200.48, provide or pay for the student's transportation to the school.

(2) The limitation on funding in § 200.48 applies only to the provision of choice-related transportation, and does not affect in any way the basic obligation to provide an option to transfer as required by paragraph (a) of this section.

(3) The LEA's obligation to provide transportation for the student ends at the end of the school year in which the school from which the student transferred is no longer identified by the LEA for school improvement, corrective action, or restructuring.

(j) Students with disabilities and students covered under Section 504 of the Rehabilitation Act of 1973 (Section 504). For students with disabilities under the IDEA and students covered under Section 504, the public school choice option must provide a free appropriate public education as that term is defined in section 602(8) of the IDEA or 34 CFR 104.33, respectively.

3. OBLIGATIONS OF PRIVATE INSTITUTIONS UNDER PUBLIC LAW IF THEY ACCEPT PUBLIC FUNDING

Would private schools that accept vouchers be subject to greater regulation as a result? Some have argued that school choice may actually result in a larger and more unwieldy educational bureaucracy than currently exists.

Consider the following quotation from Frank R. Kemerer, *The Constitutionality of School Vouchers*, 101 ED. L. REP. 17 n.51 (1995):

Government regulation of private schools creates problems for institutional autonomy. In an important but often overlooked passage, Justice McReynolds noted in *Pierce v. Society of Sisters*, that "No question is raised concerning the power of the State reasonably to regulate all schools, to inspect, supervise and examine them, their teachers and pupils; to require that all children of proper age attend some school, that teachers shall be of good moral character and patriotic disposition, that certain studies plainly essential to good citizenship must be taught, and that nothing be taught which is manifestly inimical to the public welfare." In the years since Pierce, there have many challenges to state regulation of private schools. For the most part, these challenges have been unsuccessful.

State regulation at issue in most of the decisions has been relatively limited and has occurred in the absence of any substantial flow of public funds to private schools. The case for regulation of private schools is enhanced under a publicly-funded voucher program because of the potential increase in the number of students educated in the private sector, the state's traditional role in overseeing its educational system, and the need to assure accountability for the expenditure of public money. The types of regulation public policymakers are likely to consider are multifarious, ranging from the constitutional and statutory rights of students and teachers to teacher qualifications, curriculum, student admissions, health and safety, tuition and fees, and information and transportation. Many of these regulatory features will have cost implications.

The more regulation, the greater the threat to institutional autonomy. At the extreme, substantial regulation could conceivably convert some private action to state action, thus requiring institutional adherence to Fourteenth Amendment liberty and property rights.

NOTE

1. For an earlier discussion of state regulation of private schools and how a state funded voucher program encompassing sectarian private schools might affect such regulation, see Frank R. Kemerer, et al., *Vouchers and Private School Autonomy,* 21 J.L. & EDUC. 601 (1992). *See also* ARNOLD FEGE, *Private School Vouchers: Separate and Unequal, in* WHY WE STILL NEED PUBLIC SCHOOLS 233, (Art Must, Jr. ed., 1992) (asserting that if vouchers were implemented, private schools "would come under mounting pressure for public regulation.").

2. In 1995, Republican presidential candidate Patrick Buchanan argued that vouchers were " 'wolves in sheep's clothing' that could open the way to federal control of private and religious education." Ralph Z. Hallow, *Buchanan Hits School Vouchers*, WASH. TIMES, Sept. 14, 1995, at A4.

3. In light of recent developments and the current state of the law, what are the chances that private schools voluntarily choosing to accept publicly funded vouchers would be subject to increasing regulation under current federal and state laws impacting public education? As a matter of policy, what should be the parameters of the regulatory approach in this context? Does the charter school model offer any guidance here?

D. CHARTER SCHOOLS

THE POLITICS OF CHARTER SCHOOLS

Sandra Vergari
21 Educational Policy 15 (2007)

Charter schools, and other market-based reforms such as school vouchers and the student tutoring provision of the No Child Left Behind Act of 2001, are steeped in politics largely because they challenge the legitimacy of traditional power and funding arrangements in public education. These reforms are blurring conventional distinctions between "public" and "private" in education. The first charter school law was adopted by Minnesota in 1991. Fifteen years and 40 additional charter school laws later, the charter school reform remains the subject of substantial controversy in both the political and the scholarly arenas.

Charter schools are publicly funded entities that operate free from some or most of the regulations that apply to traditional public schools. The degree of regulatory freedom varies across the 41 charter school laws and the individual school charters. As originally conceived, charter schools are legally and fiscally autonomous entities that operate under contracts or charters. Negotiated between founders and authorizers, the charters address matters such as finance, governance, personnel, curriculum, and performance measures. The authorizers are public entities such as local and state school boards, university boards, the city of Milwaukee, the Indianapolis mayor's office, and statutorily created charter school authorizer boards in Arizona and the District of Columbia. The authorizers monitor compliance with the charter and applicable state and local rules.

The decision to send a child to a charter school is made by a parent or guardian, not by a government entity. Charter schools may not charge tuition, and admissions processes must be nondiscriminatory. However, unlike traditional public schools, charter schools may cap enrollment. In return for regulatory relief, charter schools are supposed to be held accountable for their performance by their respective authorizers and by parental choice in the education marketplace.[3]

* * * Most charter schools enjoy the freedom to contract with private entities for any number of services, including academic instruction and overall school operations. This private contracting is often beyond the control of school districts and teachers unions, thus provoking political controversy. * * *

Privatization in Education

Privatization is a broad concept. In the discourse on public education, *privatization* typically refers to reforms that shift delivery of education

---

3. There are various processes by which charter schools can be held accountable, such as placing a school on probation. Moreover, charter school authorizers can threaten and implement mandatory school closure in cases of poorly performing charter schools. Extant research indicates that charter school accountability processes and outcomes vary across states and charter school authorizers (e.g., SRI International, 2004). Finally, charter schools that fail to attract and maintain enrollment may be forced to close because of lack of per-pupil funding. * * *

from the public sector to private providers. Education not only serves private interests but also yields substantial public benefits, and it is costly. Therefore, the polity has an interest in requiring some amount of education for all constituents and in funding education so that all have access. Privatization advocates propose that policy makers continue public funding of education while turning over delivery of education to private entities. * * *

Questions regarding how much and what types of education regulation are appropriate are at the heart of charter school politics. Charter school advocates claim that charter schools are overregulated, whereas opponents assert that they are underregulated. Charter schools that are subject to substantial regulation might not be viewed as genuine charter schools. * * *

The National Education Association and the American Federation of Teachers maintain that charter schools should be required to secure approval from school districts. Similarly, the Republican chair of the New York State Senate Education Committee, Steve Saland, has stated, "I have little or no problem with the concept of charter schools.... I have a problem with how they're funded.... If local government decides to fund a [charter] school in their district, that's fine. But it shouldn't be imposed on them". Requiring school district approval of charter schools was a part of the early idea of charter schooling advanced by Ray Budde and Albert Shanker. In contrast, the concept developed subsequently by [Ted Kolderie and Joe Nathan] emphasizes that charter schools herald the end of the "exclusive franchise" in public education long enjoyed by school districts.

Opponents of introducing the profit motive to the core technology of schooling question the wisdom of laws that permit charter schools to contract with for-profit management companies. They suggest that private contracting arrangements may require charter school governing boards to delegate an inappropriate degree of decision-making power to management companies, thereby undermining the "autonomy, flexibility, and site-based decisionmaking ... at the core of the charter school concept". Private contracting advocates, on the other hand, maintain that as long as profit-seeking entities can produce satisfactory student outcomes, they should be permitted to receive public funds and operate public schools. Thus, political debates on charter schools reflect divergent opinions about acceptable degrees of privatization in education. * * *

Charter Schools

Charter schools are less controversial than school vouchers in large part because the charter school reform reflects fewer degrees of privatization than voucher plans. However, as a school choice reform, the charter school concept is much more controversial than intra-or interdistrict school choice programs that offer some decision-making power to parents but remain controlled by the traditional public school system.

In terms of delivery, charter schools are founded by individuals or groups based in the public or private sectors. In most states, a charter school governing board can hire a for-profit entity to operate the school, but the charter itself cannot be awarded to the for-profit company. A few states permit charters to be awarded to for-profit entities, and a few states prohibit for-profit entities from managing or operating charter schools.[8]

On the matter of finance, charter schools may not charge tuition or levy taxes. They receive public funding from school districts and states and grants from the federal government. Charter schools may also seek and receive funding from for-profit entities, nonprofit organizations, and philanthropists.

Charter school governance is supposed to be genuine site-based decision making rather than government by school district boards. Charter school governing boards are not elected by the general public but are bound by open-meetings laws. Some charter school laws regulate board membership with provisions such as those that prohibit charter school employees and members of school district boards from serving on charter school boards and requirements that charter school boards include parents.

As publicly funded entities, charter schools are typically bound by state rules pertaining to academic standards and testing. Accordingly, the academic purposes and outcomes of a charter school are supposed to be aligned with those public requirements. On the other hand, charter school curricula and pedagogy may diverge from those of traditional public schools—in concert with the private preferences and interests of both school founders and families sending students to the school. Thus, the charter school landscape includes a diverse array of curricula and instructional approaches. For example, some charter schools emphasize training in foreign language, others emphasize the arts, some emphasize vocational education, and others emphasize college preparation.

* * *

In a provocative volume entitled *The Emancipatory Promise of Charter Schools*, [Eric Rofes & Lisa Stulberg]—self-described "progressives" with a hopeful and positive view of charter schooling—levy several charges against the institutionalized Left. They argue that its members display a status quo approach to education policy, a double standard by publicly opposing school choice for low-income families while simultaneously using choice themselves, and laziness in their lack of consideration of different types of charter schooling and diverse constituencies supporting the concept. They aim to promote "a new voice on the Left, the beginning of a progressive response to school choice" with a focus on charter schools. The diversity and dynamism of charter school politics make it an especially intriguing area for political analysts.

---

8. Charter school laws in Hawaii, Iowa, Mississippi, and Tennessee prohibit for-profit entities from managing or operating charter schools (Center for Education Reform, 2006a).

* * * As a result of political compromises, charter school laws in several states diverge significantly from the charter concept promoted by advocates. Therefore, charter school politics differ across state and local settings, in concert with differences across state laws and local political cultures. * * *

NOTES

1. In a key portion of her article, Professor Vergari emphasizes that "[a]t the core of the charter school concept is genuine site-based management whereby key decisions about budget, human resources, and curriculum and pedagogy are determined at the building level." She goes on to explain that "[s]ome charter schools have delegated a significant portion of their decision-making authority to for-profit management companies by hiring them to operate their schools..."

2. Ground-breaking studies conducted by Amy Stuart Wells in the mid to late 1990s examined charter schools from both an equity perspective and an educational quality perspective. *See, e.g.,* Amy Stuart Wells, Alejandra Lopez, Janelle Scott & Jennifer Jellison Holme, *Charter Schools as Postmodern Paradox: Rethinking Social Stratification in an Age of Deregulated School Choice,* 69 Harvard Ed. Rev. (Summer 1999). *See generally* Amy Stuart Wells, ed., *Where Charter School Policy Fails: The Problems of Accountability and Equity,* Teachers College Press (2002).

3. Vergari cites with approval *The Emancipatory Promise of Charter Schools: Toward a Progressive Politics of School Choice,* by Eric Rofes and Lisa Stulberg, eds., SUNY Press (2004). The editors of the volume argue that progressives can and should embrace charter schools as a powerful tool for reviving public participation in education. Indeed, Professor Rofes asserts that charters can expand opportunities for progressive methods in the classroom and can generate new energy for community-based, community-controlled school initiatives.

4. During the first decade of the charter school movement, challenges to the existence and/or the practices of these schools were brought in both federal and state courts, but the lawsuits were generally unsuccessful. *See, e.g.,* Robert J. Martin, *Charting the Court Challenges to Charter Schools,* 109 Penn St. L. Rev. 43 (2004). At the federal court level, Martin found that judges typically ruled against plaintiffs who attempted to establish that state charter school programs violated constitutional provisions or other federal laws. At the state court level, Martin documented a pattern in which judges rejected challenges by school boards and other "adversaries" against the opening or continued operation of charter schools, with most of the cases involving the interpretation of state constitutional provisions and the application of statewide enabling acts. As a general rule, reported decisions in this area at that time came primarily at the lower courts. *Id.* at 65–101.

In light of this trend, Martin concluded that "the charter school movement successfully survived the initial legal challenges to its right of operation and continued expansion during the first decade of its existence":

The legal battles, however, may be far from over. To the extent that the movement continues to grow and leads to the creation of still more charter schools, especially in districts with high concentrations of historically disadvantaged students, the concern regarding the movement's fiscal impact on traditional public schools will probably increase in significance. This may likely produce further court challenges, regarding fundamental issues of public school financing that the courts up to now have tended to avoid. Failure on the part of individual charter schools to comply with federal laws specifically designed to assist historically disadvantaged students may also lead to additional court challenges, especially [with regard to] students with disabilities. *Id.* at 102–103.

5. A recent study by David R. Garcia examined the extent to which parental choice affects the degree of segregation in Arizona's charter schools. The study relied on the ability to track the student attendance patterns of nearly all Arizona students in grades 2 to 9, and it found that when evidence of segregation did exist, it varied significantly depending on the type of charter school. Traditional and Montessori charter schools, for example, enrolled a more academically and racially integrated population than district schools. However, college-preparatory and "back-to-basics" charter schools proved to be more racially segregated than the other schools in the districts. *See* David R. Garcia, *Academic and Racial Segregation in Charter Schools: Do Parents Sort Students into Specialized Charter Schools?* 40 Education and Urban Society 590 (2008).

6. In 2008, attorneys representing local charter schools in Southern California sought to identify major ongoing areas of controversy in this context. In particular, they highlighted funding issues and disputes regarding rights, responsibilities, and prospective revocation. *See* Michael M. Amir, Mary T. Glarum, & Hemmy So, *Charter Fights: The Competing Rights of Charter Schools and Local School Districts Are Triggering Myriad Legal Disputes,* L.A. Lawyer, July–August 2008.

In light of emerging patterns and recent developments, how might educational quality lawsuits focusing on charter schools play out in the future? What types of scenarios are more likely to generate litigation? How might such litigation differ from other education-related lawsuits brought against school districts and state officials generally?

7. From a policy perspective, Richard Kahlenberg is one of a growing number of scholars in this area who have focused on the apparent tension between charter school leaders and teachers unions, and on the prevailing view among many union activists that charter schools are anti-union. Noting that, in 1988, it was American Federation of Teachers President Albert Shanker who "first proposed the creation of 'charter schools,'" Kahlenberg has argued that a reasonable middle ground might be possible here, with charter school leaders and teachers unions working together for the common good. *See* Richard D. Kahlenberg, *The Charter School Idea Turns 20: A History of Evolution and Role Reversals,* Education Week, March 26, 2008.

8. For additional commentary and analysis in this area, *see, e.g.,* John Morley, *For-Profit and Nonprofit Charter Schools: An Agency Costs Approach,* 115 Yale Law Journal 1782 (2006); Martin H. Malin & Charles Taylor

Kerchner, *Charter Schools and Collective Bargaining: Compatible Marriage or Illegitimate Relationship?* 30 Harvard Journal of Law & Public Policy 885 (2007); Rebekah Gleason, *Charter Schools and Special Education: Part of the Solution or Part of the Problem?* 9 U. D.C. L. Rev. 145 (2007).

PROBLEM 34: LITIGATING EDUCATIONAL QUALITY AT GLEN PARK CHARTER HIGH SCHOOL

This question is based on the following hypothetical, which takes place at a fictional high school in San Francisco, California.

In an effort to turn around low-performing Glen Park High School pursuant to the "No Child Left Behind" Act, the San Francisco Unified School District (SFUSD) not only reconstitutes the school but also turns it into a new public charter school with an emphasis on science and technology for the digital age.

As envisioned, the school would not only be built on a strong foundation of requisite basic skills, but it would also serve as a model for the integration of smartphone technology into the daily education program. Every student would be required to own a smartphone with certain minimum technical features and to bring it to school every day, for use as a centerpiece in an Internet-based curriculum that emphasizes analysis, synthesis, and creative problem solving.

Yet once the school is open it is not only plagued by inconsistent cell phone and Wi–Fi connections, but teachers find that there is a significant difference between and among the phones that the students possess. Some have the latest version of the iPhone or similar products recently released by Apple's competitors, while others must use relatively outdated phones such as earlier-generation Blackberries and Treos that have been donated to the school for use by students who cannot afford their own equipment. In addition, school officials are constantly in the process of trying to repair some of the older and more unreliable phones.

At the end of the first year, the school's overall test scores on the California Standards Test show a definite increase over the previous year, but complaints abound and dissatisfaction is prevalent on a wide variety of fronts. The school board commissions an independent review by an outside evaluator, to be conducted during the Fall Semester of the second year. The following are among the key findings of the independent review:

- School spirit is high. The athletic teams and the debate teams are among the strongest in the city, the drama program continues to win awards, and in general students are proud to attend Glen Park.

- Teacher morale is questionable. A noteworthy feature of the school's charter is that teachers are evaluated in part on their classes' test scores, and bonuses are given to teachers with the higher scores. Teachers knew this when they applied to teach at the reconstituted school, but many tell the evaluator that little or no camaraderie exists between and among faculty members. Instead, they find that a negative spirit of competitiveness is highly prevalent, and that teachers often complain about the students that are assigned to their classes.

- The school's attendance figures have not improved since reconstitution, and they remain among the very lowest in the district.

- The evaluator visited 6–8 classrooms over the course of the semester, and found that:

  "...[a]t best the teaching practices were mediocre, and at worst they were downright unacceptable. AP English students were sitting and reading silently, when they should have been actively engaged with each other and with their teacher. A veteran ESL teacher complained about the students, and showed me the detention corner of her room, complete with rules that students who were excluded from the group were expected to follow...Even worse were two classrooms where no teaching at all was taking place. In a science class, taught by a veteran teacher, the students were spending inordinate amounts of time on a binder check, even though most of the students did not have their binder ... and thus nothing to check. Students were just sitting there doing nothing. In another class, the lights were off (on a dark, cloudy day)—ostensibly, according to the teacher, to calm the students. And the students were all on their cell phones, playing games, texting each other, listening to music, or watching videos on YouTube ..."

- Several students whom the evaluator met with "laughed when they were asked if they felt challenged by the curriculum. They told me that they felt the teachers did not care about them, that they were not pushed, and that they were hardly assigned any homework." Yet other students, particularly those in drama, music, art, debate, and athletic programs, expressed great satisfaction with their teachers and with the school, and indicated that they "loved the creative activities based on the smartphone technology."

- The evaluator found "a significant difference in energy and enthusiasm" between students who attended the school before reconstitution and those who either subsequently entered as ninth graders or transferred in from other schools. The new students showed a much higher level of enthusiasm for Glen Park High.

- During more than half of the evaluator's visits, the library was closed. Apparently the school does not have a certificated librarian, and the library is open only intermittently.

* * *

At the end of the second year, Glen Park High's test scores continued to show improvement. The school's overall Academic Performance Index (API)–based on a state ranking of test score results generally, on a scale of 1 (lowest) to 10 (highest)–had improved over two years from a "1" to a "3." Its *similar schools* ranking (also on a scale of 1–10)–based on a statewide comparison of factors designed to compare a particular school to others like it in the state–had improved over two years from a "2" to a "6."*

However, a group of parents, infuriated by many of the findings in the independent evaluator's report, by test scores that continue to be at the lower end of all the high schools in the city, by ongoing complaints from their sons and daughters, and in general by what they perceive to be a second rate education for the students, consult you for the purpose of filing a lawsuit on the grounds that their children's *right to an education* has been violated.

What arguments might you consider setting forth under emerging *educational quality law* generally at both the federal and state levels? Under California state constitutional law in particular? What remedies would you seek under the circumstances? In the end, which party do you think would prevail? Discuss.

---

* The state computes the *similar schools* rankings using a complicated formula that weighs 14 characteristics (mostly demographic in nature), including parental education level, percentage of students receiving free or reduced lunch, percentage of students in gifted programs, percentage of English learners, percentage of students with disabilities, ethnicity, level of turnover in the school population, and the percentage of teachers who hold full credentials. Other characteristics, such as funding levels and the number of special programs, are not factored in. *See generally* CA Department of Education explanatory documents, http://www.cde.ca.gov/ta/ac/ap/documents/tdgreport0708.pdf.

CHAPTER VII

THE RIGHTS OF STUDENTS WITH PARTICULAR NEEDS: ENGLISH LEARNERS & STUDENTS WITH DISABILITIES

■ ■ ■

Issues relating to English learners and students with disabilities come up often in both an equal opportunity context and an educational quality context. This chapter turns to a detailed examination of these issues, focusing on efforts to secure legal rights for students with particular needs and on attempts to translate those rights into positive change on a day-to-day level.

Effecting such change at the individual school sites is often the most difficult challenge. At the K-12 level, for example, many see bilingual education and special education as highly specialized areas, appropriately delegated to *other* people and appropriately relegated to *separate* offices, *separate* inquiries, and *separate* programs. In many instances, it is assumed by educators that once students are identified as participating in such programs, they no longer need to be the focus of the basic educational planning that takes place in the central office and at local school sites, since they are under the purview of a separate program office. Such a mindset too often results in the marginalizing of these students.

Indeed, in many K-12 settings, very few discussions regarding educational policy even appear to acknowledge the fact that in many urban districts—particularly at the elementary grades and especially in states such as California, Illinois, New York, and Texas—at least 50 percent of all the students are either English learners and/or students with disabilities. And it can be argued that a failure to improve educational outcomes in such settings can be traced directly to the inability of education leaders to place the needs of these students at the forefront of reform efforts and strategies for change.

At the postsecondary level, college and university officials are increasingly recognizing the prevalence of disability rights issues and the importance of addressing the problems that remain. While great progress has been made regarding physical access, for example, controversies regarding different types of accommodations—including but not limited to timed testing—continue to represent major challenges for both students and educators alike.

In recent years, programs and practices in all of these areas are being reexamined, and renewed efforts by advocates are focusing on what might be done to build on the legal successes of the recent past while addressing the many unresolved issues that still remain.

A. BILINGUAL EDUCATION AND OTHER PROGRAMS FOR ENGLISH LEARNERS

The legal and policy debates regarding appropriate curricular and pedagogical approaches for educating students who are in the process of learning English have raised issues that continue to reverberate throughout the nation. At the heart of the debate has been the question of whether and to what extent instruction should be delivered, if possible, in the student's primary language.

A range of "bilingual" models have been identified, and they include *transitional* programs that begin with instruction and materials almost entirely in a student's primary language, gradually introducing English into the classroom until the instruction and materials are almost entirely in English. Transitional programs may also include "maintenance" of proficiency in the primary language, and indeed many programs seek to build strength in both languages with the stated goal that the students will exit the program or graduate from the K–12 schools completely bilingual.

Another model of bilingual education that has grown in popularity in many places over time is dual immersion. Under that model, English learners are grouped together in the same classroom with English speakers whose parents want them to become proficient in a language other than English. Thus, for example, a class may be comprised of English learners whose primary language is Spanish, and English speakers whose parents want them to learn Spanish. Students may remain together in this configuration for their entire elementary school careers, with instruction and materials in both English and Spanish. The stated goal is that all the students will exit the program completely fluent in both.

Other research-based models contemplate instruction that is primarily if not exclusively in English from the beginning. These include, but are not limited to, English as a Second Language (ESL), English Language Development (ELD), and Specially Designed Academic Instruction in English (SDAIE). Often such programs are necessary, particularly if no teacher is fluent in the child's primary language, and/or if only a small number of students speak a particular language.

While conflicting studies abound, there is a broad consensus within the education community that bilingual education, if done right, is the most effective approach to maximizing equal access to a quality education for English learners.

Literature in this field consistently emphasizes that language proficiency is not just a matter of conversational fluency. It ranges across four interrelated areas: reading, writing, speaking, and listening. And it cannot easily be picked up in a short period of time. In this respect, some scholars distinguish between Basic Interpersonal Conversation Skill (BICS) and Cognitive Academic Language Proficiency (CALP). BICS is necessary to communicate in everyday settings, while CALP is needed to perform academic tasks successfully. Conversational skills have been found to approach native-like levels within two years of exposure to English, but 5–12 years may be required to match native speakers in academic English. *See* LYNNE T. DÍAZ-RICO & KATHRYN Z. WEED, THE CROSSCULTURAL, LANGUAGE, AND ACADEMIC DEVELOPMENT (CLAD) HANDBOOK 29 (1995).

A highly acclaimed study by Stanford University scholars in January 2000 found that even in schools that are considered the most successful in teaching English to EL students, oral proficiency takes 3 to 5 years to develop, and academic English proficiency can take 4 to 7 years. The study, by UC Merced Professor Kenji Hakuta, reveals a continuing and widening gap between EL and native English speakers, and concludes:

> The gap illustrates the daunting task facing these students, who not only have to acquire oral and academic English, but also have to keep pace with native English speakers, who continue to develop their language skills. It may simply not be possible, within the constraints of the time available in regular formal school hours, to offer efficient instruction that would enable the EL students to catch up with the rest. Alternatives such as special summer and after-school programs may be needed. The results suggest that policies that assume rapid acquisition of English * * * are wildly unrealistic. A much more sensible policy would be one that sets aside the entire spectrum of the elementary grades as the realistic range within which English acquisition is accomplished, and plans a balanced curriculum that pays attention not just to English, but to the full array of academic needs of the students. Kenji Hakuta et al., *How Long Does it Take English Learners to Attain Proficiency?* 1 (The University of California Linguistic Minority Research Institute Policy Report, January 2000).

This section of the casebook provides an overview of the legal and public policy issues that have arisen in this area over the past 40–50 years. It begins with *Lau v. Nichols,* the one U.S. Supreme Court case that addresses bilingual education issues and in so doing sets forth foundational federal guidelines. It also highlights the portion of the U.S. Equal Educational Opportunity Act that codified *Lau,* and the Fifth Circuit's test for compliance with the Act that is generally accepted as the law of the land.

The section then turns to state issues, focusing in particular on California, which has the largest number of English learners in the country and has been the site of so many high profile disputes in this context. The state has seen a pendulum shift with regard to these issues, requiring bilingual education in the public schools from 1976–1987 but then seeking to end bilingual education instruction in the 1990s.

In conclusion, the section examines the complex inquiry regarding within-school segregation in this context, seeking to address the needs of all concerned.

PROBLEM 35: THE COMMUNITY LANGUAGE ACADEMY

The following hypothetical takes place in the fictional state of Eldorado.

Assume for the purposes of this hypothetical that you have been retained by the founders and directors of a new charter school—the Community Language Academy—to advise them on their policies with regard to language programs for the forthcoming academic year. Charter schools, by definition, are generally exempt from state education code requirements, and pursuant to a recent legal advisory issued by the Eldorado State Department of Education, charter schools have been notified that they only need to comply with basic *federal* law in this area.

The Community Language Academy has been formed by educators who believe that English learners have been subjected to a "dumbed-down" curriculum in too many classrooms throughout the state for too long a period of time. One of the founders' stated goals is "to provide innovative learning opportunities for English learners," and 50 percent of the slots at the school will be reserved for students who have been identified EL. The directors anticipate, however, that the percentage of English learners at the school may very well be much higher than 50 percent.

Your consulting contract specifies that you will be asked to focus on four questions:

A. What basic legal principles should the founders and directors of the Community Language Academy have at their fingertips and keep in mind as they put together programs and plan curriculum for this charter school?

B. What educational methods and models of instruction do you recommend for the students of this school? Why? Could these methods and models vary depending on the language background and proficiency of the students enrolled?

C. What specific curricular programs would you put in place to ensure that English learners at this school do not receive a "dumbed-down" curriculum?

D. How would your recommended methods, models, and programs be consistent with current legal requirements outside of the state's education code? What legal challenges might be anticipated, and how might you recommend responding?

1. BASIC FEDERAL DOCTRINE

LAU v. NICHOLS

414 U.S. 563, 94 S.Ct. 786 (1974)

MR. JUSTICE DOUGLAS delivered the opinion of the Court.

The San Francisco, California, school system was integrated in 1971 as a result of a federal court decree. The District Court found that there are 2,856 students of Chinese ancestry in the school system who do not speak English. Of those who have that language deficiency, about 1,000 are given supplemental courses in the English language.[1] About 1,800, however, do not receive that instruction.

This class suit brought by non-English-speaking Chinese students against officials responsible for the operation of the San Francisco Unified School District seeks relief against the unequal educational opportunities, which are alleged to violate, inter alia, the Fourteenth Amendment. No specific remedy is urged upon us. Teaching English to the students of Chinese ancestry who do not speak the language is one choice. Giving instructions to this group in Chinese is another. There may be others. Petitioners ask only that the Board of Education be directed to apply its expertise to the problem and rectify the situation.

The District Court denied relief. The Court of Appeals affirmed, holding that there was no violation of the Equal Protection Clause of the Fourteenth Amendment or of § 601 of the Civil Rights Act of 1964, which excludes from participation in federal financial assistance, recipients of aid which discriminate against racial groups. One judge dissented. A hearing en banc was denied, two judges dissenting.

We granted the petition for certiorari because of the public importance of the question presented.

The Court of Appeals reasoned that "[e]very student brings to the starting line of his educational career different advantages and disadvantages caused in part by social, economic and cultural background, created and continued completely apart from any contribution by the school system." Yet in our view the case may not be so easily decided. This is a public school system of California and § 71 of the California Education Code states that "English shall be the basic language of instruction in all schools." That section permits a school district to determine "when and under what circumstances instruction may be given bilingually." That section also states as "the policy of the state" to insure "the mastery of English by all pupils in the schools." And bilingual instruction is author-

---

1. A report adopted by the Human Rights Commission of San Francisco and submitted to the Court by respondents after oral argument shows that, as of April 1973, there were 3,457 Chinese students in the school system who spoke little or no English. The document further showed 2,136 students enrolled in Chinese special instruction classes, but at least 429 of the enrollees were not Chinese but were included for ethnic balance. Thus, as of April 1973, no more than 1,707 of the 3,457 Chinese students needing special English instruction were receiving it.

ized "to the extent that it does not interfere with the systematic, sequential, and regular instruction of all pupils in the English language."

Moreover, § 8573 of the Education Code provides that no pupil shall receive a diploma of graduation from grade 12 who has not met the standards of proficiency in English, as well as other prescribed subjects. Moreover, by § 12101 of the Education Code (Supp. 1973) children between the ages of six and 16 years are (with exceptions not material here) "subject to compulsory full-time education."

Under these state-imposed standards there is no equality of treatment merely by providing students with the same facilities, textbooks, teachers, and curriculum; for students who do not understand English are effectively foreclosed from any meaningful education.

Basic English skills are at the very core of what these public schools teach. Imposition of a requirement that, before a child can effectively participate in the educational program, he must already have acquired those basic skills is to make a mockery of public education. We know that those who do not understand English are certain to find their classroom experiences wholly incomprehensible and in no way meaningful.

We do not reach the Equal Protection Clause argument which has been advanced but rely solely on § 601 of the Civil Rights Act of 1964, to reverse the Court of Appeals.

That section bans discrimination based "on the ground of race, color, or national origin," in "any program or activity receiving Federal financial assistance." The school district involved in this litigation receives large amounts of federal financial assistance. The Department of Health, Education, and Welfare (HEW), which has authority to promulgate regulations prohibiting discrimination in federally assisted school systems in 1968 issued one guideline that "[s]chool systems are responsible for assuring that students of a particular race, color, or national origin are not denied the opportunity to obtain the education generally obtained by other students in the system." In 1970 HEW made the guidelines more specific, requiring school districts that were federally funded "to rectify the language deficiency in order to open" the instruction to students who had "linguistic deficiencies."

By § 602 of the Act HEW is authorized to issue rules, regulations, and orders[2] to make sure that recipients of federal aid under its jurisdiction conduct any federally financed projects consistently with § 601. HEW's regulations specify that the recipients may not

---

2. Section 602 provides:

Each Federal department and agency which is empowered to extend Federal financial assistance to any program or activity, by way of grant, loan, or contract other than a contract of insurance or guaranty, is authorized and directed to effectuate the provisions of section 2000d of this title with respect to such program or activity by issuing rules, regulations, or orders of general applicability which shall be consistent with achievement of the objectives of the statute authorizing the financial assistance in connection with which the action is taken....

42 U.S.C. § 2000d–1.

(ii) Provide any service, financial aid, or other benefit to an individual which is different, or is provided in a different manner, from that provided to others under the program;

* * *

(iv) Restrict an individual in any way in the enjoyment of any advantage or privilege enjoyed by others receiving any service, financial aid, or other benefit under the program.

Discrimination among students on account of race or national origin that is prohibited includes "discrimination . . . in the availability or use of any academic . . . or other facilities of the grantee or other recipient."

Discrimination is barred which has that *effect* even though no purposeful design is present: a recipient "may not . . . utilize criteria or methods of administration which have the effect of subjecting individuals to discrimination" or have "the effect of defeating or substantially impairing accomplishment of the objectives of the program as respect individuals of a particular race, color, or national origin."

It seems obvious that the Chinese-speaking minority receive fewer benefits than the English-speaking majority from respondents' school system which denies them a meaningful opportunity to participate in the educational program—all earmarks of the discrimination banned by the regulations. In 1970 HEW issued clarifying guidelines, which include the following:

"Where inability to speak and understand the English language excludes national origin—minority group children from effective participation in the educational program offered by a school district, the district must take affirmative steps to rectify the language deficiency in order to open its instructional program to these students."

"Any ability grouping or tracking system employed by the school system to deal with the special language skill needs of national origin-minority group children must be designed to meet such language skill needs as soon as possible and must not operate as an educational dead end or permanent track."

Respondent school district contractually agreed to "comply with title VI of the Civil Rights Act of 1964 . . . and all requirements imposed by or pursuant to the Regulation" of HEW which are "issued pursuant to that title . . ." and also immediately to "take any measures necessary to effectuate this agreement." The Federal Government has power to fix the terms on which its money allotments to the States shall be disbursed. Whatever may be the limits of that power, they have not been reached here. Senator Humphrey, during the floor debates on the Civil Rights Act of 1964, said:

"Simple justice requires that public funds, to which all taxpayers of all races contribute, not be spent in any fashion which encourages, entrenches, subsidizes, or results in racial discrimination."

We accordingly reverse the judgment of the Court of Appeals and remand the case for the fashioning of appropriate relief.

Reversed and remanded.

* * *

MR. JUSTICE BLACKMUN, with whom THE CHIEF JUSTICE joins, concurring in the result.

I join Mr. Justice STEWART'S opinion and thus I, too, concur in the result. Against the possibility that the Court's judgment may be interpreted too broadly, I stress the fact that the children with whom we are concerned here number about 1,800. This is a very substantial group that is being deprived of any meaningful schooling because the children cannot understand the language of the classroom. We may only guess as to why they have had no exposure to English in their preschool years. Earlier generations of American ethnic groups have overcome the language barrier by earnest parental endeavor or by the hard fact of being pushed out of the family or community nest and into the realities of broader experience.

I merely wish to make plain that when, in another case, we are concerned with a very few youngsters, or with just a single child who speaks only German or Polish or Spanish or any language other than English, I would not regard today's decision, or the separate concurrence, as conclusive upon the issue whether the statute and the guidelines require the funded school district to provide special instruction. For me, numbers are at the heart of this case and my concurrence is to be understood accordingly.

NOTES

1. The Court's 1974 *Lau* opinion reversed the Ninth Circuit's decision in favor of the school officials. Judge Shirley Hufstedler, dissenting from the denial of hearing *en banc* by the appellate panel, had emphasized that "[t]he majority's characterization of the relief sought as 'bilingual education' is misleading. The children do not seek to have their classes taught in both English and Chinese. All they ask is that they receive instruction in the English language. Access to education offered by the public schools is completely foreclosed to these children who cannot comprehend any of it."

Hufstedler also contextualized the barrier that the Chinese American children in San Francisco were facing:

[T]he language barrier, which the state helps to maintain, insulates the children from their classmates as effectively as any physical bulwarks. Indeed, these children are more isolated from equal educational opportunity than were those physically segregated blacks in *Brown*; these children cannot communicate at all with their classmates or their teachers. Lau v. Nichols, 483 F.2d 791, 805–06 (9th Cir. 1973) (Hufstedler, J., dissenting).

2. In late 1974, Congress passed the Equal Educational Opportunity Act (EEOA), which included a key provision that appears to have explicitly

adopted the *Lau* court's approach. *See* Rachel F. Moran, *Bilingual Education as a Status Conflict,* 75 California Law Review 321, 329 (1987).

Section 204 of the Act provides:

No State shall deny equal educational opportunity to an individual on account of his or her race, color, sex, or national origin, by ... (f) the failure by an educational agency to take appropriate action to overcome language barriers that impede equal participation by its students in the instructional programs. 20 U.S.C. Section 1703 (f).

The broad, general mandate of the EEOA triggered many questions of statutory interpretation, including an inquiry into what groups are covered, what kinds of programs are called for, and whether "equal participation" is synonymous with "effective participation." While the U.S. Department of Health, Education & Welfare (HEW) attempted to answer many of these questions in its *"Lau* Guidelines," it was the Fifth Circuit in *Castaneda v. Pickard,* 648 F.2d 989 (5th Cir. 1981), that ultimately determined the Act's applicability and scope. For a comprehensive overview of the history and development of programs for English learners in this context, *See generally* Mark G. Yudof et al., *Educational Policy and the Law* 637–670 (4th Ed. 2002).

3. In *Castaneda*, a group of Mexican–American children and their parents challenged the practices of a Texas school district that allegedly resulted in a deprivation of equal educational opportunity. Among plaintiffs' allegations was the charge that the district failed "to implement adequate bilingual education to overcome the linguistic barriers that impede the plaintiffs' equal participation in the educational program of the district." 648 F.2d at 992. Applying the EEOA, the court decided in favor of the plaintiffs. Judge Randall, however, considered the meaning of "appropriate action" in the Act and concluded that the phrase was not intended to be synonymous with "bilingual education":

Congress ... did not specify that a state must provide a program of bilingual education.... We think Congress' use of the less specific term, "appropriate action," rather than "bilingual education," indicates that Congress intended to leave state and local educational authorities a substantial amount of latitude in choosing the programs and techniques they would use to meet their obligations under the EEOA. *Id.* at 1009.

In the end, *Castaneda* set forth a three-prong analysis that federal courts continue to follow when evaluating a school district's language remediation program. The cases that follow are notable recent examples of how the *Castaneda* test has been applied.

FLORES v. ARIZONA

516 F.3d 1140 (9th Cir. 2008)

BERZON, CIRCUIT JUDGE:

[English language learner (ELL)] students and parents in Nogales (we refer to them as "Flores," after class representative Miriam Flores), were faced with serious inadequacies in ELL instruction and sued to correct them. The suit proceeded as a class action, with the class defined as "all minority 'at risk' and limited English proficient children now or hereafter, enrolled in Nogales Unified School District ..., as well as their parents and guardians."

Flores' second amended complaint, filed November 29, 1996, primarily alleged that the "State has failed to provide financial and other resources necessary for adequate implementation of mandatory [ELL] programs by public school districts in Arizona," because "[t]he cost of [ELL] instruction complying with federally prescribed state mandates far exceeds the only financial assistance the State theoretically provides school districts for such purposes." As a result, Flores contended, Arizona, the state Superintendent, and the state Board of Education violated the EEOA.

The relevant portion of the EEOA provides:

No State shall deny equal educational opportunity to an individual on account of his or her race, color, sex, or national origin, by—

... (f) the failure by an educational agency to take appropriate action to overcome language barriers that impede equal participation by its students in its instructional programs.

20 U.S.C. § 1703. This provision of the EEOA was intended to remedy the linguistic discrimination identified by *Lau v. Nichols,* in which the Supreme Court held that failing to provide for the needs of non-English speaking students "is to make a mockery of public education," rendering classroom experiences for these children "wholly incomprehensible and in no way meaningful." *See also Castaneda v. Pickard,* 648 F.2d 989, 1008 (5th Cir.1981) (noting that the EEOA codifies the "essential holding of *Lau, i.e.,* that schools are not free to ignore the need of limited English speaking children for language assistance to enable them to participate in the instructional program of the district.").[2]

Flores alleged that such needs were not being met in Arizona. She charged Arizona with "administer[ing] a school finance scheme that is just sufficient to let less distressed, predominantly Anglo districts impart State-mandated essential skills to their mainstream student bodies ... but that does not and will not enable NUSD or similarly situated districts to impart the same State-mandated essential skills to decisively minority enrollments requiring expanded compensatory programs, smaller class sizes and further efforts of like nature in order to acquire them."

Flores' complaint was premised on the EEOA analytic framework provided by the Fifth Circuit in *Castaneda.* The *Castaneda* framework is three-fold: First, courts must be satisfied that the "school system is purs[uing] a program informed by an educational theory recognized as sound by some experts in the field or, at least, deemed a legitimate experimental strategy." Second, "the programs and practices actually

---

2. The EEOA contains an express private right of action, 20 U.S.C. § 1706, under which this suit proceeds. * * * We have held that § 1706 abrogates state sovereign immunity. Arizona does not contend otherwise.

used by a school system [must be] reasonably calculated to implement effectively the educational theory adopted by the school." There must, in other words, be sufficient "practices, resources and personnel ... to transform the theory into reality." Third, even if theory is sound and resources are adequate, the program must be borne out by practical results. Flores alleged, consistent with *Castaneda* step two, that Arizona had "failed to provide financial and other resources necessary for adequate implementation" of its ELL programs.

B. The Declaratory Judgment and Arizona's School Funding System

After lengthy pre-trial proceedings and a bench trial, the district court on January 24, 2000, held that Arizona was in violation of the EEOA and granted declaratory judgment in Flores' favor. Of the many issues raised in Flores' complaint, only one EEOA issue was decided by the court: "[W]hether or not Defendants' [sic] adequately fund and oversee the *Lau* program in NUSD...."[4] The rest of the EEOA violations originally alleged, including failures adequately to evaluate and monitor ELL students, to provide tutoring and other forms of compensatory instruction, and to design successful ELL programming, were covered by a consent decree approved by the district court on July 31, 2000.

* * *

The core assumption of Arizona's funding formula * * * is that ELL students impose *incremental* costs on a district, above the base level funding allocation. So, while all of the funding [in this regard] is allocated to the district as a block grant, a district that spends more on ELL incremental costs than allocated is necessarily spending less on basic educational needs per pupil.

* * * [T]he district court in its 2000 declaratory judgment opinion inquired whether Arizona's funding specifically for ELL students * * * actually covered the incremental costs of ELL programming. The court found that it did not.

* * * That this support was inadequate to live up to Arizona's EEOA obligations to its school districts and their students was supported by several examples of resource-linked ELL program deficiencies in NUSD, including:

1) too many students in a class room,

2) not enough class rooms,

3) not enough qualified teachers, including teachers to teach [English as a Second Language] and bilingual teachers to teach content area studies,

4) not enough teacher aides,

---

4. Because 20 U.S.C. § 1703(f) codifies the central holding of *Lau*, ELL programs are sometimes referred to as "*Lau* programs."

5) an inadequate tutoring program, and

6) insufficient teaching materials for both [English as a Second Language] and content area courses.

In short, Arizona's "minimum base level for funding *Lau* programs [was] arbitrary and capricious and [bore] no relation to the actual funding needed to ensure that [ELL] students in NUSD are achieving mastery of its specified 'essential skills.' " In particular, the court held, the ELL * * * appropriation was "not reasonably calculated to effectively implement" the ELL programs, and Arizona had, therefore, "failed to follow through with . . . resources . . . necessary to transform theory into reality," as the *Castaneda* framework requires.

C. Post–Judgment Relief and Arizona's ELL Programs

The lower court's decision on behalf of the plaintiffs was not appealed. Nonetheless, Arizona did not take action to eliminate the violations found in the Declaratory Judgment. * * * On December 15, 2005, deploring the fact that "[t]housands of children who have now been impacted by the State's inadequate funding of ELL programs had yet to begin school when Plaintiffs filed this case," the court held that Arizona was in civil contempt. It set a deadline of fifteen days after the start of the 2006 legislative session for compliance with its order, and imposed a schedule of fines that would begin to accrue if Arizona did not act and that were to be distributed to Arizona schools to support ELL students.

Arizona did not enact compliant legislation and accrued over $20 million in fines. Eventually, in the spring of 2006, Arizona Governor Janet Napolitano allowed HB 2064, the legislature's effort to create a permanent compliant funding system, to become law without her signature.

HB 2064 * * * includes some additional ELL funds designed to cover incremental costs * * *, although there are no guaranteed appropriations for these funds. Along with this funding structure, the statute provides for further statewide standardization of ELL programs, presumably in part to make it possible for the state more easily to monitor and assess the impact and use of allocated funds and the need for additional funds. * * *

HB 2064 was for the most part immediately effective. School districts and charter schools, however, could not adopt the models until they were developed * * *. Most importantly, the provisions associated with the [funding increase for ELL students] require court approval. * * *

The district court * * * [ruled] on April 25, 2006, that HB 2064 does not comply with its orders or with the Declaratory Judgment because the "Act does not [bear] any rational relationship to the cost of providing an ELL program . . . and it has added new hurdles to the mix." The court held the * * * [monetary] increase insufficient, and the two-year cut-off on most funds irrational. * * * The Superintendent and Legislative Intervenors appealed both that order and the December 2005 contempt order.

On August 23, 2006, in an unpublished memorandum disposition, this court vacated both orders as well as the obligation to pay fines. The court noted that "the landscape of educational funding has changed significantly" since 2000 and remanded for the district court to hold "an evidentiary hearing ... regarding whether changed circumstances required modification of the original court order or otherwise had a bearing on the appropriate remedy." *Id.* at 582. The court made clear that it reached none of the other issues in the case. After the evidentiary hearing at which the facts concerning the current status of ELL students and ELL funding were presented, the district court again denied relief from judgment.* * * [It] concluded that, without a rational funding system for ELL incremental costs, Arizona remains out of compliance * * *

II. ANALYSIS

* * *

a. Changes in Fact

* * * There was no clear error in the district court's factual findings and no abuse of discretion in its legal conclusion that the landscape was not so radically changed as to justify relief from judgment without compliance.

b. Changes in Law

The Superintendent and Legislative Intervenors also offer a legal change argument as to why the premises of the Declaratory Judgment have been so undermined as to justify relief from judgment despite noncompliance. They maintain that the passage of NCLB-and, in particular its Title III, which focuses on ELL students-has in some fashion altered their obligations by making the *Castaneda v. Pickard* framework "obsolete," urging two points: First, that state compliance with NCLB benchmarks should be enough to satisfy the EEOA, and hence the judgment and, second, that NCLB obviates any need to do a state-wide cost study of ELL program incremental costs.

We are unpersuaded by the first, more important point. The Superintendent and Legislative Intervenors fail to appreciate the distinct purposes of the EEOA and NCLB: The first is an equality-based civil rights statute, while the second is a program for overall, gradual school improvement. Compliance with the latter may well not satisfy the former.[42]

Title III of NCLB sets out to "help ensure that children who are limited English proficient ... attain English proficiency ... and meet the same challenging State academic content and student achievement standards as all children are expected to meet." 20 U.S.C. § 6812(1). To aid in

---

42. We also note that NCLB became law on January 8, 2002, prior to the district court's compliance rulings on HB 2010, prior to the parties' previous appearance before this court in 2006, and more than five years prior to this appeal. It is now more than a little late to argue that NCLB effectively repeals the EEOA, and so justifies relief from the district court's judgment and orders. Any such change occurred well before the most recent orders were entered.

this goal, it provides grants to states with federal government-approved plans to benefit ELL students. *See* 20 U.S.C. §§ 6821–26. To retain grant eligibility, grantees must meet "annual measurable achievement objectives ... includ[ing] ... making adequate yearly progress for limited English proficient children." *See* 20 U.S.C. § 6842.

* * * Importantly, this very gradual improvement plan does not set as an objective immediate equalization of educational opportunities for each such student.

NCLB, in other words, packages federal grants with discrete, incremental achievement standards as part of a general plan gradually to improve overall performance. It does not deal in the immediate, rights-based framework inherent in civil rights law, although it is intended to ameliorate over the longer haul the conditions that lead to civil rights violations. Perhaps recognizing as much, Title III of NCLB explicitly provides that "[n]othing in this part shall be construed in a manner inconsistent with any Federal law guaranteeing a civil right." 20 U.S.C. § 6847.

The EEOA is just such a rights-enforcing law. It requires states "to ensure that needs of students with limited English language proficiency are addressed," *Idaho Migrant Council v. Bd. of Educ.*, 647 F.2d 69, 71 (9th Cir. 1981), by requiring them to remove barriers to equal participation in educational programs now rather than later, and it provides students with a right of action to enable them to enforce their rights, *see* 20 U.S.C. § 1706; *Los Angeles NAACP v. Los Angeles Unified Sch. Dist.*, 714 F.2d 946, 950–51 (9th Cir. 1983). The EEOA's concerns, in other words, lie fundamentally with the current rights of individual students, while NCLB seeks gradually to improve their schools. An individual student whose needs are not being met under the EEOA need not wait for help just because, year after year, his school as a whole makes "adequate yearly progress" towards improving academic achievement overall, including for ELL students.

The position pressed by the Superintendent and the Legislative Intervenors-that state compliance with NCLB necessarily satisfies the EEOA[45] —cannot be squared with this understanding of the two statutes. In their view, NCLB now defines "appropriate action" under the EEOA, such that NCLB compliance is dispositive of EEOA compliance, regardless of whether incremental ELL funding is currently adequate to provide equal educational access to ELL students. But such an interpretation would, first, produce strange results: If a state happened to meet adequate yearly progress under NCLB one year, no suits could proceed under the EEOA, even if fundamental linguistic inequalities persisted in some or all of its schools, even if ELL financial resources were entirely inadequate, and even if the particular students bringing suit had not received adequate ELL assistance nor made any progress towards English language profi-

---

45. We note that even if the state as a whole complies with NCLB, that does not mean that the individual district is in compliance.

ciency. Any meaningful ability to use the right of action under the EEOA would thus wink in and out of existence based upon the year-to-year vagaries of overall school test scores. The EEOA does not tolerate such ephemeral compliance. *See Castaneda*, 648 F.2d at 1010 (holding that a state violates the EEOA if even an adequately-funded program "fails, after being employed for a period of time sufficient to give the plan a legitimate trial"). The district court so held in the Declaratory Judgment.

Our point, boiled down, is that the Superintendent's and Legislative Intervenors' view, if adopted, would effectively repeal the EEOA by replacing its equality-based framework with the gradual remedial framework of NCLB. Such a result is simply not consistent with the text of either the EEOA or NCLB. There is certainly no express repeal provision in NCLB. Quite to the contrary, NCLB contains a savings clause with regard to civil rights statutes.

Nor did NCLB repeal the EEOA by implication. * * * The goals of the two statutes are complementary * * *

In sum, just as no changes in fact have eliminated the premises of the Declaratory Judgment, no changes in law have done so either. * * *

III. CONCLUSION

Arizona did not appeal the original judgment and has not complied with the Declaratory Judgment or with the bulk of the post-judgment relief orders. For all the reasons we have given, it is not inequitable to continue to require compliance. We therefore affirm the district court.

AFFIRMED.

UNITED STATES v. TEXAS

572 F.Supp.2d 726 (E.D.Tex. 2008)

MEMORANDUM OPINION

WILLIAM WAYNE JUSTICE, SENIOR DISTRICT JUDGE.

* * * The complex factual and procedural background of this case begins thirty-seven years ago, with a suit filed in the United States District Court for the Eastern District of Texas. That action involved nine all-black school districts located in northeastern Texas and resulted in a comprehensive order directed to the Texas Education Agency ("TEA"), concerning its responsibilities with regard to all Texas school districts. The Court entered a permanent injunctive order and retained jurisdiction over TEA and thereby, indirectly, over the Texas public education system.

The Court crafted the injunctive order to ensure that "no child w[ould] be effectively denied equal educational opportunities on account of race, color or national origin." The original injunctive order was modified by this Court, and later by the United States Court of Appeals for the Fifth Circuit, *United States v. Texas*, 447 F.2d 441 (5th Cir.1971). The original injunctive order as modified will be referred to herein as the "Modified Order." * * *

On February 9, 2006, [League of United Latin American Citizens (LULAC)] and GI–Forum filed a Motion for * * * Relief under the Modified Order. The instant action is a successive motion in Intervenors' original 1981 intervention, lineally descending from the Fifth Circuit's remand * * *. Intervenors assert that TEA's actions deny [limited English proficient ("LEP")] students equal educational opportunity and therefore violate section 1703(f) of the [Equal Educational Opportunity Act (EEOA)] and the Modified Order. Intervenors claim (1) that TEA has abandoned monitoring, enforcing, and supervising school districts to ensure compliance with Texas's bilingual education program and (2) that TEA has failed to provide equal educational opportunity to LEP students above the elementary level. On February 28, 2006, the United States intervened in a limited capacity.

[The Court then proceeded to engage in a lengthy examination of data, including a comparative analysis of academic achievement, retention rates, and drop-out rates.]

* * *

III. Conclusions of Law

* * *

B. Equal Education Opportunity Act

The remaining issue is whether Defendants' administration of the state's chosen program for educating LEP students violates the Equal Education Opportunity Act, 20 U.S.C. § 1703(f) (2006). Identical to their argument under the Modified Order, Intervenors' first argue that Defendants fail to adequately monitor the components of the LEP program, as required by the EEOA. *See Castaneda,* 648 F.2d at 1010 (holding that in examining a violation of § 1703(f) of the EEOA, courts must determine "whether the programs and practices actually used by a school system are reasonably calculated to implement effectively the educational theory adopted by the school"). They argue that Defendants monitoring fails because TEA does not conduct onsite monitoring and because [the Performance Based Monitoring Analysis System ("PBMAS")][a] is so structurally flawed that it does not fulfill Defendants' monitoring obligations. In their second argument, Intervenors contend that the poor performance of LEP students in secondary schools demonstrates that Defendants' LEP education policy, though appropriate when adopted, has been unsuccessful in practice. *See Castaneda,* 648 F.2d at 1010 (holding that in examining a violation of § 1703(f) of the EEOA, court's also must examine, after an appropriate time period, if "a legitimate educational theory[,] . . . implemented through the use of adequate techniques, fails . . . to produce

---

a. In 2003, TEA replaced the District Effectiveness Compliance Monitoring System ("DEC") with the Performance Based Monitoring Analysis System ("PBMAS"). Unlike DEC, PBMAS does not use onsite visits as the primary monitoring tool to evaluate compliance. Instead, PBMAS is "essentially a result and data-driven system that evaluates performance in four program areas: bilingual education and ESL, career and technology education, No Child Left Behind, and special education." *See* U.S. v. Texas, 572 F.Supp.2d at 737.

results indicating that the language barriers confronting students are actually being overcome . . .'").

The United States also asserts that Defendants have violated section 1703(f) of the EEOA. The United States contends that Defendants' monitoring efforts are deficient in two respects. First, Defendants do not intervene in low-performing individual campuses that are located within otherwise satisfactory school districts. Second, the United States asserts that because Defendants have abandoned * * * cyclical onsite visits, Defendants have no mechanism to ensure compliance with state standards for LEP programs.

1. EEOA Statutory Text and Legislative History

* * * The EEOA was a floor amendment, and therefore, it has almost no legislative history. In light of this scarcity of evidence of congressional intent, the Fifth Circuit has held that courts should "adhere closely to the ordinary meaning of the [statute's] language." * * *

3. *Castaneda* Three Prong Test

The seminal case on section 1703(f) is *Castaneda v. Pickard,* 648 F.2d 989 (5th Cir.1981). The plaintiffs in *Castaneda,* Mexican–American school children and their parents, argued that the bilingual-ESL program in the Raymondville, Texas school district violated the EEOA by failing to take "appropriate action to overcome language barriers." *Id.* at 1006.The plaintiffs contended "that in three areas essential to the adequacy of a bilingual program[,] curriculum, staff and testing[,] Raymondville [fell] short."

While acknowledging that Congress had provided little direction for courts interpreting the statute, the court reasoned that by requiring educational agencies to take "*appropriate action* to overcome language barriers"—rather than "bilingual education" or some other prescriptive measure to overcome the barriers-that Congress intended to leave state and local educational authorities "a substantial amount of latitude in choosing the programs and techniques they would use to meet their obligations under the EEOA." However, reasoning that because Congress obligated school systems to overcome language barriers and provided a private right of action in 20 U.S.C. § 1706, the court found that the latitude afforded state and local agencies was circumscribed by Congress's intent "to [ensure] that schools made a genuine and good faith effort, consistent with local circumstances and resources, to remedy language deficiencies of their students. . . ."

The court also reasoned that because the language of 1703(f) did not include the words "intent" or "discrimination," Congress deliberately excluded an intent requirement from 1703(f). Accordingly, the court concluded that "the failure of an educational agency to undertake appropriate efforts to remedy language deficiencies of its students, regardless of whether such a failure is motivated by intent to discriminate against those students, would violate § 1703(f). . . ."

In accord with these precepts, the court articulated a three prong test to determine the "appropriateness of a particular school system's language remediation program" under 1703(f). Courts must inquire if (1) the language remediation program is based upon sound educational theory; (2) whether the school system is making reasonable efforts to implement that theory; and (3) whether, after a legitimate trial period, that implementation has achieved results in overcoming language barriers. *Id.* at 1009–10.

a.   * * * *Flores v. Arizona,* 516 F.3d 1140 (9th Cir.2008)

* * * Persuaded by the [Ninth Circuit's February 2008 decision in *Flores*], this Court adopts conclusions of law from [its] holdings. * * *

In a ruling particularly relevant to the instant action, the Ninth Circuit concluded that, as a matter of fact, [English Language Learner ("ELL," the equivalent of LEP)] students achievement had not changed to the degree necessary to eliminate the need for additional ELL funding. The court recognized that it did not "have data that conclusively demonstrate[d] whether ELL programs ultimately succeed-that is, whether children pass through [ELL programs] rapidly and ultimately perform as well as non-ELL students." * * * Despite this and other caveats, the court found, based upon the achievement test scores of ELL students, that the superintendent and legislative intervenors had not met their burden of establishing changed circumstances. * * *

In its factual analysis of the evidentiary hearing, the Ninth Circuit thoroughly explicated the failures of ELL students statewide and in the district at issue. In terms of statewide test scores, the court noted that though Arizona students passed the state standardized test at rates between sixty and seventy percent in math and reading, ELL students lagged far behind. For ELL third graders statewide in 2005, only 50% passed the math exam and only 40% passed the reading exam. As in Texas, the court found that "the situation grows worse in higher grades"; in 2005, only 33% of ELL tenth graders passed the math exam, only 20% in 2006, and in reading, only 30% passed in 2005, and barely more than 10% passed in 2006.[b]

* * *

b.   Prong One: Sound Educational Theory

Courts must first determine if the language remediation program is based upon sound educational theory: whether a school "is pursuing a program informed by an educational theory recognized as sound by some experts in the field or, at least, deemed a legitimate experimental strategy." There is no dispute that Defendants bilingual and ESL programs are sound in theory.

---

b. The Texas Court noted here that the Ninth Circuit in *Flores* had acknowledged that "[s]tandardized test scores do not ... provide a full measure of a school's successes and failures.... But test scores do provide us with at least a rough sense of relative performance, and so are useful here". 515 F.3d at 1155, n. 21.

c.   Prong Two: Implementation

Courts next must inquire if the school system is making a reasonable effort to implement that theory: whether "the programs and practices actually used . . . are reasonably calculated to implement effectively the educational theory adopted by the school"; that is, whether "the [school] system follows through with practices, resources, and personnel necessary to transform the theory into reality."

* * * Intervenors argue that Defendants fail the implementation prong because TEA does not conduct onsite monitoring and because the [Performance Based Monitoring Analysis System (PBMAS)] system is so structurally flawed that it does not fulfill Defendants' monitoring obligations. The United States asserts that Defendants fail the implementation prong because TEA does not perform cyclical onsite visits and because TEA does not intervene in low-performing individual campuses that are located within otherwise satisfactory school districts. * * *

i.   Onsite monitoring is not required by the EEOA

The EEOA, like the Modified Order, does not require onsite monitoring. Nothing in the language of the EEOA or in *Castaneda* requires periodic onsite monitoring. * * * However, once failure on the local level is evident, because of its state mandated enforcement powers and responsibilities to administer, evaluate, and monitor LEP programs, TEA must take further appropriate action. Under the PBMAS system adopted by the state, this action will most likely be onsite intervention to correct failures in implementation.

ii.   The PBMAS system is flawed

* * * Effective implementation includes effective monitoring of the progress of LEP students and ultimately of the program itself. Since at least 1995, TEA has failed to conduct appropriate monitoring of the state's LEP program. From 1995 to 2003, the DEC cyclical onsite monitoring system repeatedly failed to review LEP programs in numerous school districts. In 2003, PBMAS replaced DEC, and although a data based monitoring system could constitute appropriate action, PBMAS, in its current form, is fatally flawed in its data collection, data analysis, and intervention systems. PBMAS under-identifies LEP students; the achievement standards used for intervention are arbitrary and not based upon equal education opportunity; monitors are not qualified; the failing achievement of higher grades is masked by passing scores of lower grades; and the failure of individual school campuses is masked by only analyzing data on the larger district level. In a monitoring system such as PBMAS, the reliability of the data on which the system is based should be paramount. Actions at every level of PBMAS are based upon data; if the data is seriously flawed then the actions at every level will also be seriously flawed. Even data that is collected accurately can be distorted if it is analyzed in a manner that overextends its explanatory breadth or if the data's explanatory power is compromised by unreasonable aggregation. Because PBMAS is based upon this data and because the totality of the data is seriously flawed, PBMAS, in its present form, does not constitute appropriate action to transform the educational theory into reality. * * *

iii. Other monitoring systems and PBMAS's nascent development do not remedy its shortcomings under the EEOA

Other TEA monitoring-through PBMAS, NCLB, and Texas accountability rating system-that incidentally monitor the achievement of LEP students does not compensate for the flaws of PBMAS. These other monitoring programs are not based upon providing equal education opportunities and do not initiate intervention based upon failure to provide equal education opportunities.

d. Prong Three: Results

i. Results based inquiry and limitations of standardized tests

Under the third prong, a court must determine whether the program has achieved results: if the program, after a legitimate period of implementation, "fails ... to produce results indicating that the language barriers confronting students are actually being overcome, that program may, at that point no longer constitute appropriate action...." * * *

The *Castaneda* court warns * * * that test scores are often difficult to interpret and that differing performance on standardized test scores could have multiple causes. Other courts have been similarly wary of judging the success or failure of a program based upon achievement scores, but, constrained in part by a scarcity of other data, courts usually rely upon achievement scores despite their limitations. * * *

As the *Castaneda* court indicated, there are a multitude of indicators, other than achievement scores, of a program's success or failure. For instance, in dicta, one district court noted that "two very significant indictors of failure in achieving the objective of equal educational opportunity for LEP children" were increased drop-out rates after students exited LEP status and the school system's use of simplified English handouts for LEP students instead of more robust English language text books.*Keyes v. School District No. 1, Denver, Colo.,* 576 F.Supp. 1503, 1519 (D.C.Colo. 1983). In the instant action, in addition to achievement scores, the Court has data on drop-out rates, retention rates, achievement scores of students after they have exited LEP programs, and data on the length of time LEP students remain in language programs.

ii. [Causation]

* * * [T]he Court will not attempt to broadly define the standard of causation, if any, for failures of LEP programs under prong three of *Castaneda.* Instead, the Court holds, consistent with precedent, that sufficient evidence of student failure sufficiently proves program failure. But as discussed *infra,* the evidence of prolonged failure of secondary LEP students is so overwhelming on a multitude of indicators that it narrows potential causes of student failure to the educational program's failure. Based upon the same evaluative tools used by TEA, the clear failure of secondary LEP students unquestionably demonstrates that, despite its

efforts, TEA has not met its obligation to remedy the language deficiencies of Texas students.

iii. The marginal success of primary LEP students in bilingual programs

* * * The performance of primary LEP students in bilingual education programs is not overwhelming. LEP students in the primary grades are not advancing on pace with their peers: LEP students are retained at significantly higher rates than their all-student peers, and the disparity in retention rates has gradually increased since 1994. Encouragingly, primary LEP students have started to narrow the margin with all students on the [Texas Assessment of Knowledge and Skills ("TAKS")]. Former LEP students also have had remarkable success two years after exiting the program, though the data may be distorted by a few high achievers. These mixed results are diminished by the fact that TEA enacted the current program a quarter of a century ago. In that light, the fact that, in 2006, the margin between sixth grade LEP students taking the test in Spanish and all students remains at 28% in the all-tests category and that only 50% of sixth grade LEP students passed all the tests is not an endorsement of the program's success. Nevertheless, because of the bilingual program's recent success in decreasing the margin of performance, the Court will defer to the state for the time being. However, the Court recognizes that it has perhaps set the bar unreasonably low in order to defer to the state; if the upward trend, narrowing the performance margin, does not continue, the Court may be inclined to revisit its ruling upon a party's motion.

iv. The Failure of Secondary LEP Students in ESL Programs

LEP secondary students drop-out of school at a rate at least twice that of the all-students category. In 2003–2004, for students in grades seven through twelve, LEP students dropped out at an annual rate of 2.0% twice the rate for all students, 0.9%. For students who would have graduated with the class of 2004, 16.3% of LEP students dropped out of school statewide compared with 3.9% of all students. For what would have been the class of 2005, only 55.2% of LEP students graduated with their class whereas 84% of all students graduated with their class.

For grades seven through twelve, the margin between non-LEP and LEP student retention rates were consistently disparate, beginning at a margin of 6.2% in 1998–1999 and ending at a rate of 7.5% in 2003–2004. By 2003–2004, LEP students were retained at a rate, 13.8%, more than double that of other students, 6.3%. * * *

v. Exclusion From Advanced Academic Achievement

Contrary to the EEOA, LEP students complete dual enrollment, advanced placement, and international baccalaureates at much lower rates than all students. The EEOA prohibits TEA from denying equal educational opportunity through "failure ... to take appropriate action to overcome language barriers that impede equal participation by its students in its instructional programs."20 U.S.C. § 1703(f). The plain language of the statute, which in light of the scarcity of evidence of congressional intent the Court must closely follow, indicates that TEA must take appropriate action in regard to its instructional programs. The advanced academic courses are part of TEA's instructional programs and therefore, TEA must take appropriate action to overcome language barriers in those programs. * * *

vi.   The Totality of Data Establishes Causation

The court holds that sufficient evidence of student failure can establish that educational agencies have not met their obligation to overcome language barriers. The failure of secondary LEP students under every metric clearly and convincingly demonstrates student failure, and accordingly, the failure of the ESL secondary program in Texas. * * *

IV.   Conclusion

Recognizing the stagnation of LEP secondary students in comparison to their non-LEP counterparts, Defendants note that "Plaintiffs have not suggested that English proficient students should be held back so that LEP students can catch up." The EEOA is a civil rights based statute, with the goal of equality. Defendants are correct; it would be unjust to require non-LEP students to be held back in order to achieve equality. However, Defendants' statement demonstrates what they have failed to consider after a quarter century: under the EEOA, it is equally unjust to perpetually fail to provide the resources and LEP programs necessary to ensure LEP students "catch up." The palpable injustice is equivalent whether it comes from depriving non-LEP students or from depriving LEP students.

The PBMAS system does not fulfill TEA'S requirement to effectively implement the LEP program. This failure does not excuse failing results on the secondary level. After a quarter century of sputtering implementation. Defendants have failed to achieve results that demonstrate they are overcoming language barriers for secondary LEP students. Failed implementation cannot prolong the existence of a failed program in perpetuity.

Defendants must soon rectify the monitoring failures and begin implementing a new language program for secondary LEP students. As a nonbinding option, the secondary LEP program could consist of a variation of the current ESL program with substantially enhanced remedial education. The Court recognizes the difficult position of Defendants and the ongoing nature of this task. The Court will defer to Defendants and their course of action as much as possible, but the Court must ensure the rights of LEP students under the EEOA. With this in mind, demonstrations of good faith by Defendants will be looked upon favorably.

2.   CALIFORNIA PROPOSITION 227

Perhaps the most volatile turning point in the recent history of bilingual education has been California Proposition 227, approved overwhelmingly by the voters in 1998. This ballot initiative generated tremendous emotion, and reverberated throughout the country, particularly in states with substantial numbers of English learners.

California had long been perceived as being in the forefront of efforts to maximize the educational opportunities of English learners by providing at least some instruction to these students in their primary language, to the extent possible. Indeed, in the aftermath of *Lau*, the California Legislature passed the Chacon–Moscone Bilingual–Bicultural Education Act of 1976, an aggressive and far-reaching statute that mandated bilingual education in the state's public schools. *See, e.g.,* Stuart Biegel, *The Parameters of the Bilingual Education Debate in California Twenty Years After Lau v. Nichols,* 14 Chicano–Latino Law Review 48 (1994). Yet in 1998 the same state took the lead in seeking to ban bilingual education across the board.

Proposition 227 significantly limited the type of instruction that could be offered to English learners in the public schools. It must be emphasized, however, that the new law did not succeed in ending bilingual education in California, and the aftermath of that campaign is still playing out in interesting and unpredictable ways.

The situation nationwide remains very fluid. Other states have since considered legislation similar to Proposition 227, adopting a parallel approach in some instances but rejecting such an approach in others. And there has been a renewed interest in identifying innovative new directions that build on well-settled principles regarding curriculum and pedagogy identified by educators in this area.

Consider the following excerpts from 227 in light of these developments. What opportunities are available under the statutory scheme for those who seek greater flexibility in providing at least some instruction in a student's primary language?

CALIFORNIA EDUCATION CODE, TITLE 1, DIVISION 1, PART 1, CHAPTER 3

(as approved by the voters in 1998, 61 percent to 39 percent)

305: Subject to the exceptions provided in Article 3 (commencing with section 310), all children in California public schools shall be taught English by being taught in English. In particular, this shall require that all children be placed in English language classrooms. Children who are English learners shall be educated through sheltered English immersion during a temporary transition period not normally intended to exceed one year. Local schools shall be permitted to place in the same classroom English learners of different ages but whose degree of English proficiency is similar. Local schools shall be encouraged to mix together in the same classroom English learners from different native-language groups but with the same degree of English fluency. Once English learners have acquired a good working knowledge of English, they shall be transferred to English language mainstream classrooms. As much as possible, current supplemental funding for English learners shall be maintained, subject to possible modification under Article 8 (commencing with section 335) below.

306: The definitions of the terms used in this article and in Article 3 (commencing with section 310) are as follows: (a) "**English learner**" means a child who does not speak English or whose native language is not English and who is not currently able to perform ordinary classroom work in English, also known as a Limited English Proficiency or LEP child; (b) "**English language classroom**" means a classroom in which the language of instruction used by the teaching personnel is overwhelmingly the English language, and in which such teaching personnel possess a good knowledge of the English language; (c) "**English language mainstream classroom**" means a classroom in which the pupils either are native English language speakers or already have acquired reasonable fluency in English; (d) "**Sheltered English immersion**" or "structured English immersion" means an English language acquisition process for young children in which nearly all classroom instruction is in English but with the curriculum and presentation designed for children who are learning the language; (e) "**Bilingual education/native language instruction**" means a language acquisition process for pupils in which much or all instruction, textbooks, and teaching materials are in the child's native language.

310: The requirements of section 305 may be waived with the prior written informed consent, to be provided annually, of the child's parents or legal guardian under the circumstances specified below and in section 311. Such informed consent shall require that said parents or legal guardian personally visit the school to apply for the waiver and that they there be provided a full description of the educational materials to be used in the different educational program choices and all the educational opportunities available to the child. Under such parental waiver conditions, children may be transferred to classes where they are taught English and other subjects through bilingual education techniques or other generally recognized educational methodologies permitted by law. Individual schools in which 20 pupils or more of a given grade level receive a waiver shall be required to offer such a class; otherwise, they must allow the pupils to transfer to a public school in which such a class is offered.

311: The circumstances in which a parental exception waiver may be granted under section 310 are as follows:

(a) Children who already know English: the child already possesses good English language skills, as measured by standardized tests of English vocabulary comprehension, reading, and writing, in which the child scores at or above the state average for his or her grade level or at or above the 5th grade average, whichever is lower; or

(b) Older children: the child is age 10 years or older, and it is the informed belief of the school principal and educational staff that an alternate course of educational study would be better suited to the child's rapid acquisition of basic English language skills; or

(c) Children with special needs: the child already has been placed for a period of not less than thirty days during that school year in an English language classroom and it is subsequently the informed belief of the school principal and educational staff that the child has such special physical, emotional, psychological, or educational needs that an alternate course of educational study would be better suited to the child's overall educational development. A written description of these special needs must be provided and any such decision is to be made subject to the examination and approval of the local school superintendent, under guidelines established by and subject to the review of the local Board of Education and ultimately the State Board of Education. The existence of such special needs shall not compel issuance of a waiver, and the parents shall be fully informed of their right to refuse to agree to a waiver.

320: As detailed in Article 2 (commencing with section 305) and Article 3 (commencing with section 310), all California school children have the right to be provided with an English language public education. If a California school child has been denied the option of an English language instructional curriculum in public school, the child's parent or legal guardian shall have legal standing to sue for enforcement of the provisions of this statute, and if successful shall be awarded normal and customary attorney's fees and actual damages, but not punitive or consequential damages. Any school board member or other elected official or public school teacher or administrator who willfully and repeatedly refuses to implement the terms of this statute by providing such an English language educational option at an available public school to a California school child may be held personally liable for fees and actual damages by the child's parents or legal guardian.

Notes

1.   A Fourteenth Amendment lawsuit challenging the constitutionality of Proposition 227 after its passage was defeated in U.S. District Court, and the decision was upheld by the Ninth Circuit. In *Valeria v. Davis*, 307 F.3d 1036, 1042 (9th Cir. 2002), the Court stated:

Given Proposition 227's facial neutrality, and the lack of evidence that it was motivated by racial considerations, we hold that Proposition 227's reallocation of political authority over bilingual education does not offend the Equal Protection Clause.

But note Judge Pregerson's dissent from the denial of rehearing *en banc*, Valeria v. Davis, 320 F.3d 1014, 1018–20 (9th Cir. 2003):

Proposition 227 generates the type of restructuring of the political process that runs afoul of the equal protection guarantees of the Fourteenth Amendment. Proposition 227 siphons power away from those minorities who are directly affected by bilingual education policy and transfers the power to influence that area of educational policy to the general electorate. While public school students and parents could influence policy at the local level before the passage of Proposition 227, they must now launch a successful statewide ballot initiative to bring about any meaningful change. Requiring the affected minority to navigate this remote and amorphous level of governmental decision-making to effect any change in bilingual education policy undoubtedly "mak[es] it more difficult for certain racial ... minorities ... to achieve legislation that is in their interest." * * * Proposition 227 creates a political structure that has the consequence of making it substantially more difficult to effect change with respect to an issue with a racial focus. Therefore, because Proposition 227: (1) restructures the political process and (2) only with respect to an area of educational policy that has a racial focus, the statute violates the Equal Protection Clause * * *.

2. The *Valeria* Court ruled against the plaintiffs in a facial challenge to the constitutionality of the statutory scheme, but might there be a set of circumstances that could lead to an "as applied" challenge? Would plaintiffs stand a chance of prevailing in such a challenge? Under what arguments?

3. At the district court level, in addition to the Fourteenth Amendment, plaintiffs alleged violations under the First Amendment, the Equal Educational Opportunity Act (EEOA), the Supremacy Clause, and international charters. With regard to the EEOA, the Court appeared to suggest that a challenge under the third prong of *Castaneda* might become relevant over time.

PROBLEM 36: THE NEW MENDOCINO EDUCATION CODE LITIGATION

The following hypothetical takes place in the fictional state of New Mendocino.

Concerned about the quality of public education in New Mendocino, and in particular about the low test scores of language minority students years after they enter the school system with limited proficiency in English, wealthy entrepreneur Manuel Rodriguez establishes a new foundation for the sole purpose of focusing on bilingual education reform issues. After consulting with a task force of educators and community leaders, Rodriguez announces an ambitious plan composed of three interrelated parts: (1) substantial grants to private schools that volunteer to "adopt" public schools with high percentages of English learners; (2) the development of model gifted programs for bilingual students; and (3) extensive professional development for bilingual teachers linked to a career ladder that would double the current salaries of bilingual educators so that the top teachers in the field would actually earn the same amount of money as first-year associates at major law firms.

The adoption process would be limited to public schools with English Learner populations of 50 percent or greater. As envisioned, substantial interaction—both online and, if possible, in real time—would occur between and among the faculty and students of both schools. Courses would be team taught, interactive projects would bring students together, and a range of extracurricular activities would cement the bonds.

The Rodriguez Foundation programs receive highly positive feedback from all relevant stakeholders, and many low performing public schools with large English Learner populations are adopted by private schools throughout the state. In addition, teachers rush to participate in the professional development/career ladder program, seeing it as a unique opportunity to improve the quality of public education while at the same time increasing their salaries.

Assume that a lawsuit brought by the New Mendocino English First Coalition. The group is prepared to argue that a separate gifted program for English learners violates the requirements set forth in New Mendocino Education Code § 305. (Assume that New Mendocino has adopted an exact version of CA Prop. 227, and that their Education Codes in this area are identical.) What arguments should defendants expect plaintiffs to set forth, and how should they be countered? What result? Discuss.

DEFINING AN ADEQUATE EDUCATION FOR ENGLISH LEARNERS

Patricia Gándara & Russell W. Rumberger
3 EDUC. FINANCE & POLICY 130 (2008)

1. INTRODUCTION

In order to meet the same challenging standards and to have the opportunity to achieve the same educational outcomes, some students need more support and resources than others. Students who come from households where a language other than English is spoken are in one such category. Although some arrive at school already proficient in English, most linguistic minority (LM) students are not yet proficient in English when they start school. These students, referred to as English learners (EL),[1] require additional resources and support in order to acquire English proficiency and to be successful in school. School districts differ substantially in the criteria they use to redesignate EL students to the status of fluent English speaker (FEP), so many students who are considered fluent English speakers in one district are considered EL in another (Parrish et al., 2006). Moreover, many students who ostensibly speak English sufficiently well to converse at a superficial level lack the academic English that is so critical for school success. Thus, English fluency is best conceptualized as a continuum, rather than a dichotomy in which a student either is or is not fluent in English. Seen in this way, linguistic minority students are arrayed at all points on this continuum and need correspondingly different kinds of services and academic support. As such, we do not always draw clear distinctions between LM and EL students. We argue

---

1. Terms used to label students who are not fluent English speakers vary widely from region to region. "Limited English Proficient" (LEP) remains in many legislative documents, though it is no longer widely used by practitioners. English Language Learner (ELL) has replaced LEP in many places, but for ease of expression the term English Learner or "EL" has gained popularity, especially in the West, and we choose to use the term and its acronym "EL" for reasons of simplicity.

that the literature has overly simplified these categories and thus has failed to acknowledge the ongoing needs of students who come from linguistically different circumstances. We also note that students from English dialect communities may be considered as linguistic minorities for pedagogical and policy purposes * * *.

This article explores what it might mean to provide an "adequate" education for linguistic minority students in California, and attempts to distinguish this from the components of an adequate education for low-income students who are native English speakers. * * * Although most low-income students need some additional educational support to compensate for the limited socio-economic and educational resources in their homes and communities, the needs of linguistic minority students differ to some extent from the needs of other disadvantaged populations; they also need language support. Moreover, the needs of these students differ from each other depending on their linguistic, social, and academic backgrounds and the age at which they enter the US school system. California, the state with the highest percentage of EL students in its K–12 population, faces particular challenges in meeting the needs of these students.

2.   CALIFORNIA'S LINGUISTIC MINORITY POPULATION

According to data from the U.S. Census, there were 3 million children, ages 5–17, living in California in 2005 who spoke a language other than English, representing 44 percent of the school-age population (Rumberger, 2006). This is a much larger percentage than the rest of the country where linguistic minority children represent 16 percent of the population. Overall, 29 percent of all school-age linguistic minority children in the U.S. reside in California; 85 percent of all students categorized as English Learners speak Spanish.

Over the last 25 years, the linguistic minority population has exploded relative to the English only population, both in California and in the rest of the U.S. In California, the linguistic minority population increased 187 percent, while the English only population increased by only 8 percent. Elsewhere in the U.S., the linguistic minority population increased by 113 percent, while the English only population actually declined by 2.2 percent. Demographers project that these percentages will continue to grow.

Using the definition of eligibility for free or reduced lunch, which is the primary way in which government entities categorize low income within school settings, about 85 percent of EL students in California are economically disadvantaged (California Legislative Analysts Office, 2007, p. E–123). As such, these students usually face a double disadvantage–language difference and poverty.

School performance

Linguistic minority children, particularly those who are not yet proficient in English, lag far behind children from English only backgrounds. * * * Over the grade span, the achievement gap between English only students and current/former EL students remains essentially unchanged.

Conditions for Learning

Linguistic minority students also face poorer conditions for learning in school. Drawing on data from a variety of sources (Gándara, et al., 2003; Rumberger & Gándara, 2004) identified seven inequitable conditions that affect these students' opportunities to learn in California, and which are linked to resources:[3]

(1) *Inequitable access to appropriately trained teachers.* English Learners are more likely than any other group of students to be taught by a teacher who lacks appropriate teaching credentials. For example, Rumberger (2003) found that while 14 percent of teachers statewide were not fully credentialed, 25 percent of teachers of English Learners lacked a teaching credential. Although the percent of teachers lacking credentials has continued to decline each year (in part due to a redefinition of the term "credentialed"), EL's continue to be disproportionately taught by under-qualified teachers. In 2005, less than half (48%) of teachers of EL students had an appropriate EL authorization to teach them (Esch et al., 2005).

(2) *Inadequate professional development opportunities to help teachers address their instructional needs.* In a recent survey of 5300 teachers of English Learners in California, Gándara, Maxwell–Jolly and Driscoll (2005) found that more than half of teachers with 26–50% of their students designated EL had no more than one professional development session devoted to the instruction of EL students over a period of five years. Moreover, about one third of respondents complained that sessions were of low quality and limited utility.

(3) *Inequitable access to appropriate assessment to measure their achievement, gauge their learning needs, and hold the system accountable for their progress.* Because the state's accountability system consists of standards-based tests developed for English speakers, and makes no accommodation for the fact that EL students are, by definition, not proficient in English, these tests are neither valid nor reliable indicators of what these students know and can do (AERA/APA/NCME, 1999).

(4) *Inadequate instructional time to accomplish learning goals.* Across the state, English Learners are provided no additional classroom instructional time even though they have additional learning tasks–acquiring English as well as learning a new culture and its demands. One way that schools can effectively provide more instructional time is by providing additional instructors within the same time. That is, more one on one instruction within the confines of the same number of hours. However, classrooms in California with large numbers of EL students have fewer adult assistants in them to help provide individual attention for students—an average of 7 hours assistance weekly for

---

3. Although this analysis focused primarily on the English learners, the conditions would generally apply to all linguistic minority students.

classrooms with more than 50% EL students versus 11 hours for those with no ELs (Gándara et al., 2003).

(5) *Inequitable access to instructional materials and curriculum.* A 2002 survey of 829 California teachers found that among classrooms with over 30 percent EL students, 29 percent of teachers reported not having adequate materials in English for their students, while only 19 percent of teachers with fewer than 30 percent EL students reported this same shortage (cited in Gándara et al., 2003).

(6) *Inequitable access to adequate facilities.* In the same survey of California teachers cited above, 43 percent of teachers in schools with more than one-fourth EL students reported their physical facilities were only fair or poor. Among teachers with less than one-fourth EL students in their school, only 26 percent reported similarly dismal conditions on their campus.

(7) *Intense segregation into schools and classrooms that place them at particularly high risk for educational failure.* In 2005, more than half of California's elementary English learners attended schools where they comprised more than 50 percent of the student body, which limited their exposure to native English speakers who serve as language models (Rumberger, Gándara, & Merino, 2006).

These conditions contribute to the lack of progress in narrowing the sizeable achievement gap between English only and linguistic minority students.

3. GOALS OF INSTRUCTION

In a recent article critiquing the methodologies used in "costing out" studies,[4] Rebell (2007) notes that one of the weaknesses of such studies is their failure to identify the premises behind their outcome standards. In order to address this legitimate concern we outline four possible standards for an adequate education of linguistic minorities, which would have implications for different types and levels of expenditures, as well as quite different outcomes for students: (1) reclassification to FEP only; (2) reclassification and maintenance of academic proficiency; (3) reclassification with biliteracy. (4) reclassification and closing of achievement gaps.

(1) *Reclassification to FEP only.* The first standard is a basic, minimal standard, much like that which is tacitly in place today (and which probably contributes to the exceptionally low performance of EL students in the schools). The goals for this standard are to pass an English proficiency test[5] and an English Language Arts standards test *at some minimal level and at one point in time,* in order to be reclassified as Fluent English Proficient. This standard does not speak to the students' overall

---

4. Rebell here refers to studies that have used a variety of methods to determine the actual costs of providing some agreed upon level of education for public school students. These studies are usually motivated by an attempt to define an "adequate" or an "equal" education for educationally disadvantaged students.

5. The California English Language Development Test (CELDT) is currently used for this purpose.

academic proficiency, nor does it consider the skills that students need to maintain the level of academic proficiency attained at the point of reclassification. Once classified as FEP all additional supportive services typically end. This standard focuses almost exclusively on attainment of sufficient English to be mainstreamed into the regular curriculum. Although it represents current practice, it is a lower standard for adequacy than that set for English speakers who are expected to meet standards at a level of "proficient" at EVERY subsequent grade level. Therefore, the state might choose to define an adequate education for EL students at a somewhat higher level.

(2) *Reclassification and maintenance of academic proficiency.* The second level standard would provide for students to become reclassified as FEP *and* sustain a level of proficient in English Language Arts and other tested areas of the curriculum (e.g., mathematics and science). This would align more closely with the definition of an adequate education for all students, certainly as specified by NCLB. Given that English Learners, by definition, come to school with greater needs than their peers who already have a command of English, the implications for this definition are that ongoing resources would be needed for schools to bring linguistic minority students to this level, and to maintain them there. This is akin to what happens for low-income students—resources are continuous no matter what level of achievement they attain.

(3) *Reclassification, maintenance of academic proficiency, and biliteracy.* The third standard is achievement of reclassification to English proficiency, proficiency in academic subjects, and biliteracy. This goal also incorporates an inherent compensating advantage for EL students. The one area in which these students have a decided advantage over their English speaking, native born peers is that they have the immediate potential of becoming fully bilingual and biliterate, with all of the attendant economic and occupational advantages that may accrue to those competencies (Saiz & Zoido, 2005). This third definition of an adequate education for linguistic minority students could include providing a socioeconomically compensating skill (on an optional basis) for LM students—biliteracy—in addition to meeting the basic educational adequacy definition for all students. The goal of attaining biliteracy would necessarily have to be optional, or voluntary, on the part of students and families (and could be extended to all students in California), as it would entail not only additional resources (and benefits) on the part of the state, but also additional effort on the part of the students.

(4) *Reclassification, maintenance of academic proficiency, and closing of achievement gaps.* This fourth goal implies a focus on achievement across the performance continuum, raising the achievement of high performers as well as lower performers so that the end result is something like parity with native English speaking peers. We suggest that this standard deserves particular consideration since many school reform efforts purport to be dedicated to this goal, without specifying exactly how this would happen and the additional resources that would be required

beyond those to reach the previous goals. The research on second language acquisition suggests that the closing of achievement gaps is most likely to occur in the context of a biliteracy curriculum (August & Shanahan, 2006; Genesee et al, 2006; Slavin & Cheung, 2004). However, there are many who argue that it is impossibl'e to reach such a standard given U.S. social policy and the paradigm of public schooling (see, for example, Rothstein, 2004).

Language of Instruction

With the exception of the 3rd standard—biliteracy—we have been agnostic about the linguistic strategies for achieving these goals. However, the language(s) used for instruction may, in fact, imply a different level of resources because (1) a different configuration of personnel may be required if a student is educated using the primary language; and (2) it may take more or less time to achieve proficiency in academic subjects, and to sustain that learning, depending on the linguistic strategy used. So, for each of these goals, we posit that a separate calculation should be considered for English only and bilingual strategies. It is not evident, however, that the cost differentials would always vary in the same ways. For example, the existing research on the costs of teachers for EL students has found that, all things being equal, using bilingual teachers is a more cost effective strategy than using monolingual teachers and then having to supplement the classroom instruction by bringing in aides and other support personnel (Parrish, 1994; Carpenter–Huffman & Samulon, 1981). On the other hand, if no supplemental teaching staff are used in the English only classroom, it MAY require that teachers have smaller classes in order to achieve the same results. In California today, most EL students who have not yet been mainstreamed receive some kind of supplemental instruction if they are not in a bilingual program with a bilingual teacher, although this varies in unknown ways.

California's Language Policy Environment and Its Impact on Classroom Instruction

In spite of laws passed in the 1970's and 1980's in California that expressly mandated bilingual education for most English Learners, the state has never provided primary language instruction for the majority of its EL students. Prior to the 1998 passage of Proposition 227—the ballot initiative that aimed to dismantle bilingual education in the state—only 29 percent of eligible students were enrolled in a bilingual program (California Department of Education, 2007). The reasons for the relatively low penetration of bilingual education are many, but most fundamentally the state lacked sufficient numbers of appropriately credentialed teachers to adequately staff bilingual classrooms. Parents, too, could opt their children out of such classes, and the ongoing political controversy over the efficacy of bilingual education coupled with a natural immigrant desire to learn English as quickly as possible also dampened the demand for bilingual instruction in some communities. Thus, in spite of the fact that about 40 percent of school age students in 1998 were linguistic minorities and had been exposed to another language in their own homes (Rumberger, 2006), policies to stimulate the production of bilingual teachers in the state were never seriously pursued. Today, only a little more than 5 percent of students receive academic instruction in their primary language, and many bilingual teachers have either dispersed to different positions or left the field. Hence, books and materials that supported primary language instruction have been packed away or disposed of. California currently has a limited infrastructure for providing primary language instruction. * * *

REFERENCES

AERA/APA/NCME (American Educational Research Association/American Psychological Association/National Council for Measurement in Education (1999)). *Standards for Educational and Psychological Testing.* Washington DC: American Educational Research Association.

August, D. & Shanahan, T. (Eds.). (2006). *Developing literacy in second language learners: Report of the National Literacy Panel on Language Minority Children and Youth.* New York: Lawrence Erlbaum Associates. * * *

California Department of Education. (2007). *Dataquest.* Retrieved July 29, 2007, from http://data1.cde.ca.gov/dataquest/

Carpenter–Huffman, P. & Samulon, M. (1981). *Case Studies of Delivery and Cost of Bilingual Education.* Santa Monica: Rand Corporation. N–1684–ED. * * *

Esch, C. E., Chang–Ross, C. M., Guha, R., Humphrey, D. C., Shields, P. M., Tiffany–Morales, J. D., Wechsler, M. E., and Woodworth, K. R. (2005). *The status of the teaching profession 2005.* Santa Cruz, CA: The Center for the Future of Teaching and Learning.

Gándara, P. & Merino, B. (1993). Measuring the outcomes of LEP programs: Test scores, exit rates, and other mythological data. *Educational Evaluation and Policy Analysis, 15,* 320–338.

Gándara, P., Maxwell–Jolly, J., Driscoll, A. (2005). *Listening to Teachers of English Learners.* Santa Cruz, CA: Center for the Future of Teaching and Learning.

Gándara, P., Rumberger, R.W., Maxwell–Jolly, J., & Callahan, R. (2003). English Learners in California schools: Unequal resources, unequal outcomes. *Educational Policy Analysis Archives, 11.* Retrieved October 21, 2006 from http://epaa.asu.edu/epaa/v11n36/

Genesee, F., Lindholm–Leary, K., Saunders, W., & Christian, D. (2006). *Educating English Language Learners. A Synthesis of Evidence.* New York: Cambridge University Press. * * *

Parrish, T. (1994). A cost analysis of alternative instructional models for Limited English Proficient Students in California. *Journal of Education Finance, 19,* 256–78.

Rebell, M. (2007). Professional rigor, public engagement, and judicial review: A proposal for enhancing the validity of education adequacy studies, *Teachers College Record*. 109. 1303–1373. 41 Rothstein, R. (2004). *Class and Schools*. Washington DC: Economic Policy Institute.

Rumberger, R.W. (2006). The growth of the linguistic minority population in the U.S. and California, 1980–2005. *UC LMRI EL Facts, 8*. Retrieved July 13, 2007 from http://lmri.ucsb.edu/publications/elfacts–8 corrected.pdf

Rumberger, R.W. (2003). One quarter of California's teachers for English Learners not fully certified. *UC LMRI EL Facts, 3*. Retrieved July 26, 2003 from http://lmri.ucsb.edu/publications/elfacts–3.pdf

Rumberger, R.W. & Gándara, P. (2004). Seeking equity in the education of California's English learners. *Teachers College Record, 106*, 2032–2056.

Rumberger, R.W., Gándara, P., & Merino, B. (2006). Where California's English Learners attend school and why it matters. *UC LMRI Newsletter, 15 (2)*, 1–2.

Saiz, A. & Zoido, E. (2005). Listening to what the world says: Bilingualism and earnings in the United States. *Review of Economics and Statistics, 87*, 523–538. * * *

3. ENGLISH LEARNERS AND WITHIN-SCHOOL SEGREGATION ISSUES

BILINGUAL EDUCATION AND RESEGREGATION: RECONCILING THE APPARENT PARADOX BETWEEN BILINGUAL EDUCATION PROGRAMS AND DESEGREGATION GOALS

Edward W. Lew
7 ASIAN PAC. AM. L.J. 88 (2001)

INTRODUCTION

During the last half of the twentieth century, racial minorities have won significant legal battles in the context of primary and secondary public education. On more than one occasion, the federal courts have rendered decisions that have increased both the accessibility and quality of public education for people of color. In 1954, the Supreme Court held in *Brown v. Board of Education* that a state could not permit or require the segregation of white and black students in public schools solely on the basis of race. Nearly twenty years after *Brown*, the Court added that a state school system must also take affirmative steps to provide students who could not speak English with a meaningful opportunity to participate in public education. In *Lau v. Nichols*, the Court held that a state school system's failure to take such affirmative steps violated federal statutory law prohibiting discrimination based on race, color, or national origin.

While the two decisions are generally considered to be victories for the rights of racial minorities, a dilemma arises as to how a state school system can simultaneously achieve both goals. A paradox appears to exist in trying to promote certain types of bilingual education programs while maintaining racially-integrated classrooms. The maintenance of certain bilingual education programs has often resulted in the classroom segregation of minority students in school classrooms.

Generally, the term "bilingual education" describes a wide range of programs designed to provide a meaningful education for non-English and limited-English speaking students. Bilingual education programs include basic bilingual classes, also called English-as-a-second language ("ESL") classes, and bilingual-bicultural classes. The primary purpose of ESL classes is to teach non-English proficient ("NEP") and limited-English proficient ("LEP") students the English language by using English language instruction. In contrast, bilingual-bicultural classes have multiple purposes. Bilingual classes are designed to teach students to be "bilingual and bi-literate, in English and at least one other language." Bilingualism and bi-literacy are usually achieved by teaching students core subjects in their native languages.

Of the two bilingual education programs, bilingual-bicultural classes have been more controversial. Bilingual-bicultural classes have often undermined the process of racial integration. Students in bilingual-bicultural classes are typically placed in classrooms with other students of the same race or ethnicity, where they spend their entire school day. Students often remain in bilingual-bicultural classes for several years and in some cases, will remain in bilingual-bicultural classes indefinitely. Many of these students never develop the English-language proficiency required to transfer from the bilingual-bicultural classes. As a result, students in bilingual-bicultural classes often lack any exposure to students outside of their particular programs.

In this Comment, I [set forth] * * * a framework to reconcile the apparent paradox between bilingual education programs and desegregation goals. I conclude that bilingual education programs do not inherently contradict the principles of desegregation. * * * [And] I suggest modifications to the existing bilingual education programs in each school that may help reduce the harms created by segregation.

I. ESTABLISHED LEGAL PRINCIPLES REGARDING DESEGREGATION AND LANGUAGE RIGHTS IN EDUCATION

A. *Paving the Road for Desegregation—Brown v. Board of Education*

In *Brown v. Board of Education*, the Supreme Court rejected the doctrine of "separate but equal" in public education and held that the segregation of students in separate educational facilities solely on the basis of race violated the Equal Protection Clause of the Fourteenth Amendment. The Court announced its unanimous decision in response to four cases from different jurisdictions that asked for resolution of the same legal question. In each case, black children were "denied admission to schools attended by white children under laws requiring or permitting segregation according to race."

The Court dismissed the relevance of findings that the black and white schools were equalized "with respect to buildings, curricula, qualifications and salaries of teachers, and other 'tangible' factors." Instead, the Court was more concerned with "the effect of segregation itself on public education." Based on the intangible effects of segregation, the Court expressly rejected the 1896 "separate but equal" doctrine from *Plessy v. Ferguson*:

> Segregation of white and colored children in public schools has a detrimental effect upon the colored children. The impact is greater when it has the sanction of the law; for the policy of separating the races is usually interpreted as denoting the inferiority of the Negro group. A sense of inferiority affects the motivation of a child to learn. Segregation with the sanction of law, therefore, has a tendency to [retard] the educational and mental development of Negro children and to deprive them of some of the benefits they would receive in a racial[ly] integrated society.... We conclude that in the field of public education the doctrine of "separate but equal" has no place. Separate educational facilities are inherently unequal.

Although the school districts were allowed to fashion their own desegregation plans, the Court clearly announced that state-sanctioned segregation no longer comported with contemporary equal protection jurisprudence.

B. Providing Language Minorities with a Meaningful Education—Lau v. Nichols

In *Lau v. Nichols*, the Supreme Court held that a school district that received federal funds was required to "take affirmative steps" to ensure that non-English speaking students could effectively participate in the school system's educational program. In *Lau*, students brought a class action suit against the SFUSD for failing to provide any type of English language instruction to nearly 1,800 of the 2,856 non-English speaking Chinese American students in violation of the Equal Protection Clause of the Fourteenth Amendment. The Court did not reach the equal protection claim but held for the students under section 601 of the Federal Civil Rights Act of 1964. Section 601 "excludes from participation in federal financial assistance, recipients of aid which discriminate against racial groups."

The Court relied on two federal guidelines promulgated by the Department of Health, Education, and Welfare ("HEW") to hold that SFUSD's failure to provide English language instruction to non-English speaking students constituted impermissible discrimination based on race, color, or national origin. The first HEW guideline was issued in 1968 and required that "school systems are responsible for assuring that students of a particular race, color, or national origin are not denied the opportunity to obtain the education generally obtained by other students in the system." In 1970, HEW elaborated on the first guideline by issuing a second guideline that required federally-funded school districts "to rectify the language deficiency in order to open the instruction to students who had 'linguistic' deficiencies."

The Court reasoned that the students of Chinese ancestry who could not speak English were "effectively foreclosed from any meaningful education." The Court found it "obvious" that these non-English speaking students would receive "fewer benefits [from SFUSD] than the English speaking majority." Thus, the Court held that SFUSD's failure to provide English language instruction constituted either a form of "discrimination" or at least had "the effect of defeating or substantially impairing accomplishment of the objectives of the [educational] program [with respect to] individuals of a particular race, color, or national origin." Because either result violated federal regulations, the Court held, "Where inability to speak and understand the English language excludes national origin-minority group children from effective participation in the educational program offered by a school district, the district must take affirmative steps to rectify the language deficiency in order to open its instructional program to these."

Although the Court did not specify what types of programs should be implemented to satisfy the "affirmative step requirement," it became clear that schools districts had to do something to comply with the federal mandate to create a meaningful opportunity for linguistic minorities to participate in the public educational system.

C.   The Apparent Paradox Between Bilingual Education and Desegregation

In *Brown*, the Court held that racially-segregated schools are unconstitutional under the Equal Protection Clause. In *Lau*, the Court held that federally-funded school districts are required under section 601 of the Civil Rights Act of 1964 to take affirmative steps to provide non-English speaking students with a meaningful education. To date, the Court has not spoken directly as to which of the two goals should take precedence when they conflict. Two federal circuit courts, however, have addressed the issue in the cases of *Keyes v. School District Number 1*, and *Bradley v. Milliken*. Although the circuit court decisions arose in distinct contexts, the analytical frameworks contained within them help explain the contours of the debate.

1.   *Keyes v. School District Number 1*

Keyes culminated in a long battle against racial segregation in the Denver School District. In 1969, plaintiffs raised a claim in federal court that the school board had intentionally created racially segregated schools within the district throughout the decade. The district court considered evidence that the board had purposefully contained racial minority students within particular schools and prevented their movement into predominantly white schools through three mechanisms: 1) manipulating school boundaries to contain racial minority students; 2) establishing a new school with conscious knowledge that it would be a one-race school; and 3) increasing the number of classrooms in a one-race minority school with the intent of preventing overflow into predominantly white schools.

The court held for the plaintiffs, finding that the board's intentional acts of segregation created a "dual school system." To execute a remedy, the court ordered the parties to submit desegregation plans. After considering each of the plans during a separate trial and determining that each one was inadequate, the court then conducted its own independent study and adopted the desegregation plan submitted by the court consultant, Dr. John A. Finger, which led to the creation of the "Finger Plan."

Under the "Finger Plan," five elementary schools were each left with Latino enrollments between seventy-seven and eighty-eight percent. The court justified the continued segregation of students in four of the schools partially on grounds of "the institution of bilingual-bicultural programs." The Tenth Circuit subsequently reviewed the court's desegregation order and considered whether it was permissible to leave certain schools predominantly one-race. The Tenth Circuit applied the rule from *Swann v. Charlotte–Mecklenburg Board of Education* and prescribed a strict limitation on when the school district would be able to maintain segregated schools: "In a system with a history of segregation the need for remedial criteria of sufficient specificity to assure a school authority's compliance with its constitutional duty warrants a presumption against schools that are substantially disproportionate in their racial composition."

Given the Denver School District's history of segregation, the Tenth Circuit held that continued segregation would only be allowable: 1) "where practical or legitimate considerations render[ed] desegregation unwise," or 2) "on the basis of proof that the racial compositions of [the] schools [was] not the result of past discriminatory action on the part of the Board." In keeping with the heavy presumption against the school district, the Tenth Circuit held that bilingual education was insufficient to justify the continued segregation: "Bilingual education . . . is not a substitute for desegregation. Although bilingual instruction may be required to prevent isolation of minority students in a predominantly Anglo school system, such instruction must be subordinate to a plan of desegregation." The court then remanded the case to the district judge with instructions to "make every effort to achieve the greatest possible degree of actual desegregation and . . . necessarily be concerned with the elimination of one-race schools."

2. *Bradley v. Milliken*

In *Bradley v. Milliken*, the Sixth Circuit again confronted the conflict between bilingual education and segregation while reviewing a desegregation plan. The district court had adopted the plan, on remand from the Supreme Court, under the order to promptly formulate "a decree to eliminat[e] the segregation found to exist in Detroit city schools. . . ." The district court had found at trial that the defendants, the state of Michigan and the Detroit school board, had created acts and policies that resulted in impermissible de jure segregation. The state and the school board did not challenge these findings.

The district court's plan to desegregate included the reassignment of Latinos between school district Region 2, where they were heavily concentrated in bilingual education programs, and district Region 1, where Latino representation was lacking. The school board challenged that part of the plan by arguing that the reassignment would "disrupt state required bilingual educational programs while achieving only token integration." Specifically, "the Director of the Bilingual Education for the School Board testified that reassigning Spanish speaking students . . . enrolled in Region 2 bilingual programs would impede the Board's ability to develop a model program and train bilingual teachers; produce fear and anxiety for students; limit community participation and interest in the schools; produce shortages of qualified bilingual teachers and necessary resource materials; and require the Board to adopt less efficient and effective methods of instruction."

The Sixth Circuit rejected the school board's challenge and agreed "with the district court that when the choice is between maintaining optimal conditions in a bilingual education program and desegregating all-black schools, desegregation must prevail." However, the Sixth Circuit's decision was subject to many caveats. Prior to the holding, the court observed that "[c]ircumstances permitting, we might well agree that the desegregative benefits would not justify the disruption created by reassigning Spanish-dominant students. Circumstances, however, do not so permit." Moreover, the district court's finding that "desegregation must prevail," was followed by a supplemental order to the school board "to develop a plan for reassigning pupils between Regions 1 and 2 which would provide for bilingual education in receiving schools."

II. RECONCILING THE APPARENT PARADOX BETWEEN BILINGUAL EDUCATION AND DESEGREGATION

A. *The Difference Between Effects of Segregation Resulting from Bilingual Education Programs and Effects Prohibited by the Supreme Court in Brown v. Board of Education*

Segregation resulting from bilingual education programs differs in purpose and effect from the segregation that the Court expressly rejected in *Brown*. In *Brown*, the Court held for the black children in order to protect them from the "detrimental effects" that resulted from state-imposed segregation. The Court's holding thus focused on two problematic aspects of the segregation: 1) the segregation had detrimental effects on the black students, and 2) the segregation was state-imposed.

With respect to the purpose analysis, the Court challenged the constitutional validity of any legislation that was unfriendly to racial minorities because they were racial minorities, finding no other reason to explain the reason for segregation than prejudice and discrimination. The Court viewed such legislation as being repugnant to the Equal Protection Clause of the Fourteenth Amendment, which declared "that the law in the States shall be the same for the black as for the white; that all persons, whether colored or white, shall stand equal before the laws of the States...." It recognized that the Equal Protection Clause was primarily designed to prohibit states from discriminating against racial minorities because of their color and to provide a positive immunity for them from such discriminatory laws. Moreover, the Court found the Equal Protection Clause to be grounded in the belief that legal discrimination "impl[ied] inferiority in civil society, lessen[ed] the security of their enjoyment of the rights which others enjoy, and ... are steps towards reducing them to the condition of a subject race."

With respect to the effects analysis, the Court was concerned about the social, psychological, and educational harms resulting from the "segregation of white and colored children in public schools." The Court cited to social science studies and literature that discussed these detrimental effects. It found a nexus between the prejudice and discrimination underlying the state sanction of segregation in public schools and the resulting detrimental effects of the sanction. Observing that "the policy of separating the races is usually interpreted as denoting the inferiority of the [N]egro group," the Court reasoned state-imposed segregation affected "the motivation of a child to learn."

The Court held that "[s]egregation, with the sanction of law, therefore, has a tendency to [retard] the educational and mental development of Negro children and to deprive them of the benefits they would receive in a racial[ly] integrated school system." This holding clearly indicates the Court's foremost concern with the diminished educational and learning opportunities for segregated black students that resulted from a state policy of segregation. Thus, the Court took great care to emphasize the importance of education.

> Today, education is perhaps the most important function of state and local governments. [Education is important] to our democratic society. It is required in the performance of our most basic public responsibilities.... It is the very foundation of good citizenship.... Today, it is a principal instrument in awakening the child to cultural values, in preparing him for later professional training, and in helping him to adjust normally to his environment. In these days, it is doubtful that any child may reasonably be expected to succeed in life if he is denied the opportunity of an education. Such an opportunity, where the state has undertaken to provide it, is a right which must be made available to all on equal terms.

The Court had decided an earlier case, *McLaurin v. Oklahoma State Regents*, based on similar "intangible considerations." In *McLaurin*, the Court required that a black student admitted to a white graduate school be treated like all other students in his ability to study, engage in discussions, exchange views with other students, and in general, learn his profession. The Court in *Brown* found the *McLaurin* reasoning to be even more compelling when dealing with elementary and high school children, where "[t]o separate [children] from others of similar age and qualifications solely because of their race generates a feeling of inferiority as to their status in the community that may affect their hearts and minds in a way unlikely to ever be undone." The appropriate remedy to address the constitutional violation in Brown, therefore, was to end segregation.

Any segregation that arises from bilingual education programs are distinguishable in purpose and effect from the segregation that was rejected in *Brown*. With respect to purpose, bilingual education programs differ from the *Brown*-type segregation because they do not invidiously discriminate against children based on race. Bilingual education programs serve a distinct educational purpose and are not grounded on prejudice and discrimination. Although students in bilingual education programs may ultimately be grouped with others of the same race, such segregation is not based on racial classifications. The students' native language and proficiency with English, are the factors which determine their placement.

The bilingual education programs do not result in the detrimental effects prohibited by *Brown*. In fact, it appears that bilingual education helps to achieve the results that *Brown* championed. The Court in *Brown* argued that state-imposed segregation violated the Equal Protection Clause because it denied racial minorities an education equal to that which was available to white students. Bilingual education programs are designed to allow non-and limited-English speaking students meaningful participation in the school's educational program. In the absence of programs implemented to affirmatively rectify language deficiencies, these students would otherwise receive "fewer benefits ... than the English-speaking majority."

B. The Difference Between Segregated Bilingual Classrooms and Segregated Schools

The form of segregation that results from bilingual education programs is predominantly within-school, as opposed to within-district. Schools create bilingual education classrooms by grouping LEP and NEP students together according to native languages. Because a student's native language is usually related to his race or ethnicity, bilingual education classrooms each assume an identifiable racial or ethnic character. For example, Spanish bilingual classrooms are usually comprised entirely of Latino students, while Cantonese bilingual classrooms are usually comprised entirely of Cantonese students.

The courts in *Keyes* and *Bradley* were concerned with the elimination of one-race schools and not one-race classrooms. Moreover, the circuit courts found no inherent problems with bilingual education programs. Although both the Tenth and Sixth Circuits chose desegregation goals over bilingual education, their holdings were limited by the following factors: 1) both the Denver and Detroit school systems had histories of de jure segregation resulting in one-race schools, and 2) desegregation goals were undermined by bilingual education programs when bilingual education goals were being used to justify the continuation of one-race schools. The Sixth Circuit defended the goal of bilingual education and noted that "[t]he Board's concern for the continued viability of its bilingual educational programs is commendable. Circumstances permitting, we might well agree that the desegregative benefits would not justify the disruption created by reassigning Spanish-dominant students. Circumstances, however, do not so permit." Moreover, the Sixth Circuit did not indicate that there was any question of the legality of the district court's supplemental order requiring the Board to "provide for bilingual education in receiving schools." The Tenth Circuit also spoke in defense of bilingual education when it noted that "bilingual instruction may be required to prevent the isolation of minority students...." One-race classrooms resulting from bilingual education under normal circumstances, therefore, seemingly do not contradict the decisions nor reasoning from *Keyes* and *Bradley*.

Nevertheless, many critics contend that the one-race classroom is equally as harmful as one-race schools. One-race classrooms resulting from bilingual education programs are defensible, however, because bilingual education programs: are intended to separate students only temporarily, and do not foreclose the opportunity to meaningfully interact with students of other races and ethnicities.

With respect to the ephemerality of bilingual education programs, Lau requires schools that adopt bilingual education programs as a method to rectify language deficiencies to tailor the programs to be educational and transitory. "Any ability grouping or tracking system employed by the school system to deal with the special language skill needs of national origin-minority children must be designed to meet such language skill needs as soon as possible and must not operate as an educational dead-end or permanent track." In defense of ephemeral segregation, therefore, bilingual education is premised on the notion that students should and will eventually integrate with students of other races. This differs from the case of one-race schools, where ultimate integration is not even possible. Where bilingual education has been criticized as resulting in a "dead-end or permanent track," the problem of segregation lies in the execution of the particular bilingual education program and not in the concept of bilingual education per se.

Moreover, students are not foreclosed from integrating with students of other races even during the time that they are enrolled in bilingual education programs. Such integration can occur both informally and formally. Informally, integration can occur on the playground, in extracurricular activities, and during all the various social activities that occur in schools on a daily basis. Formally, integration can result by mixing bilingual education students with other students during classes such as art and physical education, and during school-sponsored activities such as assemblies.

When students are racially segregated by school, however, the students within the segregated school are foreclosed from any integration with students of other races. They are unable to mix with students of different races because the school lacks racial diversity among the student body.

* * *

B. Principles for School Districts to Minimize the Detrimental Effects of Segregation Resulting from Bilingual Education Programs

With a better understanding of the legal and policy considerations that establish the parameters of the conflict between desegregation and bilingual education, I now offer three strategies to minimize concerns that segregation resulting from bilingual education programs creates detrimental effects: 1) maximizing and monitoring integration time; 2) involving students in the integration process; and 3) making an ideological commitment to both desegregation and bilingual education. Throughout this section, I incorporate observations from my visits at Starr King, Golden Gate, Sherman, and Commodore Stockton elementary schools in San Francisco.

1. Maximizing and Monitoring Integration Time

The most practical solution to the problem of segregation arising from bilingual education programs is to integrate the students. While full classroom integration during the entire day will likely undermine the effectiveness of most bilingual pedagogical approaches, bilingual education students should be integrated with non-bilingual students in a controlled learning environment for at least some substantial portion of the day. Principal Chin of Commodore Stockton seems to think that the twenty-percent standard is a good minimum to balance the goal of desegregation with bilingual education.

Moreover, a school should try to integrate students in substantive courses, beyond simply art, drama, music, and physical education. Often, those courses do not require any verbal participation. A primary purpose of integrated classes should be to encourage discourse in topics such as culture or poetry. The purpose of integration should thus extend beyond encouraging mere facial recognition of students of other races. A dual immersion program that emphasizes the acquisition of two languages could also succeed in completely integrating students.

A school must also monitor the success of integration efforts. Although Superintendent Rojas indicated that the district is keeping abreast of within-school segregation, Sherman was the only school I visited that suggested they had a structured system to evaluate how well students were integrating. Sherman surveys its students using a standard form. Nevertheless, the survey merely touches upon the students' comfort levels with one another while addressing a wide range of other issues. Schools should be required to prepare formal integration plans to administrators and to compile detailed reports specifying the time and substance of integration time.

2. Student Involvement in the Integration Process

A school should also encourage students to integrate with students outside of the classroom. A school could form a student council, for example, comprised of student leaders who initiate activities including bilingual education students and non-bilingual education students. The student council at Commodore Stockton succeeds in integrating students that actually serve on the council but does not do much to facilitate integration among its peers.

The student council should include at least one student from every classroom in the school, including bilingual education classrooms. This group of student leaders could also help to monitor integration efforts. They could serve as members of focus groups, expressing views on behalf of their peers as to feelings about race, culture, and integration.

A school cannot rely on the expectation that students will naturally integrate with one another under informal conditions, such as recess or lunchtime. For example, although Golden Gate has implemented "Friday Funtime," in hopes of encouraging student interaction, I witnessed that most students only interacted with other students whom they already knew. A reporter from the *San Francisco Examiner* made a similar observation when she wrote that "on a recent visit, it was clear that at recess students rarely ventured beyond their classroom cliques." A school must be aware of the fact that students may be shy or influenced by the same cultural prejudices that permeate throughout our society. To the extent that schools can promote tolerance and acceptance early in life, they should certainly do so.

3. Ideological Commitment to Both Bilingual Education and Integration

An overarching principle to my previous suggestions is that administrators and teachers should maintain an ideological commitment to both bilingual education and integration. The mutual goal underlying both bilingual education and desegregation is the notion that discrete and insular minorities should be afforded some special scrutiny under law and policy. Most of society shares the common desire to eliminate unfair barriers to the enjoyment of life to which we are all fundamentally entitled. The most revealing part of my visit was speaking to Principal Cleveland at Golden Gate and hearing about the overt racism that existed among the pre-reconstruction faculty. Those faculty members seemed to be oblivious to the inherent contradiction of supporting either desegregation or bilingual education, but not both. In order to move forward in finding a solution to the apparent paradox between desegregation and bilingual education, we must be able to comprehend and internalize the ideals that they embody and the promise they can offer to our society. Without such comprehension and internalization, our efforts to resolve the paradox will be in vain.

* * *

B. SPECIAL EDUCATION AND OTHER PROGRAMS FOR STUDENTS WITH DISABILITIES

Over the past 30–40 years, major federal statutes have dramatically expanded the rights of persons with disabilities and in so doing have literally transformed the educational landscape for students in this area. Section 504 of the Rehabilitation Act of 1973, amounting to nothing less than a federal civil rights act for persons with disabilities in the public sector, provided broad protection for students of all ages in all public educational settings. The Individuals with Disabilities Education Act (IDEA)—formerly Pub. Law No. 94–142, the 1975 Education of All Handicapped Children Act—created a structure whereby K–12 students with special needs could have an Individualized Education Plan (IEP) prepared that would qualify them for a wide range of support services under the umbrella of special education. And the Americans with Disabilities Act (ADA) of 1990 not only extended Section 504 rights to the private sector, but added additional protections for persons with disabilities in the public sphere.

This section focuses primarily on K–12 issues, but also provides an overview of key legal principles applicable to students with disabilities in higher education. As a general rule, progress under these statutes has been more consistent at colleges and universities. At the K–12 level, many students have benefited greatly from changes in the law and the accompanying efforts of dedicated educators in this context, but many others have arguably been deprived of equal access to quality education under the unwieldy principles and inconsistent practices of special education. Indeed, commentators are increasingly voicing concerns with regard to both educational quality (under the "free appropriate public education" requirement of the IDEA) and equal educational opportunity (under the "least restrictive environment" component of the Act).

Analyzing the quality of special education curriculum and pedagogy, some have looked back at *Board of Education v. Rowley,* 458 U.S. 176, 102 S.Ct. 3034 (1982), the first U.S. Supreme Court decision to address special education, and have argued that the decision should now be reassessed. The *Rowley* Court concluded that schools were not required to maximize potential for students with disabilities, but only to provide a basic floor of opportunity. Arguably, in light of related developments in the law in the years since *Rowley,* this holding is no longer consistent with either federal or state mandates.

With regard to the "least restrictive environment" requirement of the law, commentators have noted that a range of options and organizational structures exist, including but not limited to inclusion (where students are generally placed in heterogeneous settings but are provided with additional support in those settings) and resource specialist programs (RSP, where students are grouped together with everyone else for part of the time, and in separate settings with additional support for the remainder of the time). But reports documenting special education practices nationwide have found that too often, arguably in violation of express provisions of the IDEA—which require that students with disabilities be segregated "only when the nature or severity of the disability of a child is such that education in regular classes with the use of supplementary aids and services cannot be achieved satisfactorily"—many students are separated out into "special day classes" (SDC) for the entire day and often for their entire public school careers. Compounding the problem, many schools group students with a wide range of disabilities together in one classroom.

Perhaps the most volatile of all the issues in this context is the disproportionate representation of African American students, not only in the separate special education classes, but also in the highly subjective categories of "emotionally disturbed" (ED) and "learning disabled," (LD). These two categories are the most controversial of all the special education classifications.

While no one doubts the importance of providing additional support services for students with special needs, researchers and policy makers nationwide have highlighted problematic aspects of these categories, both in theory and in practice. A review of relevant literature reveals that (a) these categories, unlike other "disabilities" such as physical impairments, are often very imprecise, and classification by its very nature can be quite subjective, (b) they are based on school identification rather than some organicity, (c) the nebulous criteria that may be employed to identify students in this area have been compared in recent studies with substantially discredited categories of the past, such as "educable mentally retarded" (EMR), (d) red flags have been raised with regard to the fact that it is in these categories that students who may be viewed as "discipline problems" or "low performing" end up being placed, when it may be that a more adept classroom teacher can effectively work with these students in a non-special education setting, and (e) in this context, educators have been taken to task for placing a disproportionate percentage of students of color in separate classes as a result of classifying them as ED or LD. *See, e.g.,* Matthew Ladner & Christopher Hammons, *Special But Unequal: Race and Special Education, in* Rethinking Special Education for a New Century (Chester E. Finn, Jr. et al. eds., 2001); Nat'l Research Council, Minority Students in Special and Gifted Education (2002). *See generally* Daniel J. Losen & Gary Orfield, Racial Inequity in Special Education (2002).

This section begins with an overview of special education law as it relates to K–12 education. It then focuses on the "appropriateness" of the education, analyzing the *Rowley* decision and its aftermath. Within-school segregation issues are then addressed, followed by ongoing issues relating to standardized testing. The chapter concludes with an examination of how these issues are playing out at the higher education level.

1. FEDERAL SPECIAL EDUCATION LAW GENERALLY

THE INDIVIDUALS WITH DISABILITIES EDUCATION ACT: WHY CONSIDERING INDIVIDUALS ONE AT A TIME CREATES UNTENABLESITUATIONS FOR STUDENTS AND EDUCATORS

Megan Roberts
55 UCLA L. Rev. 1041 (2008)

* * *

I. The History and Predecessors of the IDEA and IDEIA[19]

A. The IDEA and Congressional Intent

From its creation of the Education of All Handicapped Children Act (EAHCA) in 1975 through its 2004 amendments to the Individuals with Disabilities Education Act, Congress has affirmed and reaffirmed the importance it places on educating all of America's children. When it passed the EAHCA, Congress sought to rectify the great injustice suffered by students with disabilities: 1.75 million were excluded from schools entirely and 2.2 million languished in classrooms without help or curriculum adapted to their needs.[20] These students were essentially denied any meaningful access to learning in schools. The original intent of the EAHCA—to provide an educational opportunity to all children—has been preserved through later amendments * * *. [In addition,] [s]chools today are expected to provide students with meaningful educational opportunities and the tools with which to gain from those opportunities.[22] Additionally, schools are expected to provide these meaningful educational opportunities in the "least restrictive environment" appropriate.[23]

1. The Education for the Handicapped Act of 1970 and the Education of All Handicapped Children Act of 1975

---

19. Because the Act is commonly known as the "IDEA," and because cases and articles discussed in this comment refer to the Act as the "IDEA," I will use "IDEA" and "IDEIA" interchangeably after Part I's discussion of their differences.

20. See Mark C. Weber, Reflections on the New Individuals With Disabilities Education Improvement Act, 58 Fla. L. Rev. 7, 10 (2006).

22. See Cynthia L. Kelly, Individuals With Disabilities Education Act—The Right "IDEA" for All Childrens' Education, 75 J. Kan. Bus. Ass'n 24, 26 (Mar. 2006) (referencing Pub. L. No. 105–17, 111 Stat. 88 (1997), and Pub. L. No. 108–446, 118 Stat. 2715 (2004), and noting that the IDEA's "[f]ocus [has] shifted from access to educational opportunities to improvement of performance and educational achievement").

23. 20 U.S.C. § 1412(5) (2000).

Congress's passage of the Education of the Handicapped Act[24] (EHA) of 1970 marked the beginning of significant efforts by the federal government to include children with disabilities in public schools. * * * [However,] significant court decisions,[26] [along with evidence that the EHA had not achieved its goals,] motivated Congress to seek to rectify the lack of adequate educational opportunities for students with disabilities by passing the Education for All Handicapped Children Act (EAHCA).[27]

This groundbreaking legislation mandated that all states receiving federal funding for education ensure that students not be denied an education as a result of their handicaps.[29] School districts were thus required to provide the special education and related services necessary for students to benefit from the educational experience. To achieve this goal, the EAHCA included certain key provisions that have remained consistent throughout the many later versions of the Act; three fundamental and continuing requirements of the EAHCA are (1) that children with disabilities receive Individualized Education Programs (IEPs);[31] (2) that schools provide to students with disabilities a free and appropriate public education (FAPE); and (3) that this education occur in the least restrictive environment (LRE) appropriate.[32] Just as these provisions have remained constant since the Act's inception, so too has disagreement over what constitutes a FAPE and how to determine the appropriate placement for a given child under the LRE requirement.

2.   The Individuals With Disabilities Education Act

In 1990, the EAHCA was renamed the Individuals with Disabilities Education Act.[34] (IDEA). With the new name came a few significant

---

24. Pub. L. No. 91–230, §§ 601–685, 84 Stat. 175 (1970) (codified as amended at 20 U.S.C. §§ 1400–1485 (2000 & Supp. 2005)).

26. The decisions in two class action suits brought on behalf of students with disabilities who were denied meaningful opportunities to learn demonstrated a need for legislation in the area of educating students with disabilities. See Pa. Ass'n for Retarded Children (PARC) v. Pennsylvania, 334 F. Supp. 1257 (E.D. Pa. 1971), 343 F. Supp. 279 (E.D. Pa. 1972); Mills v. Bd. of Educ., 348 F. Supp. 866 (D.D.C. 1972); see also Weber, supra note 20, at 10 (noting that the decisions in Pennsylvania Ass'n for Retarded Children v. Pennsylvania and Mills v. Board of Education established "entitlements to education" for students with disabilities before Congress took action).

27. Pub. L. No. 94–142, 89 Stat. 773 (1975) (codified as amended at 20 U.S.C. §§ 1400–1485 (2000 & Supp. 2005)).

29. See 89 Stat. at 780–83.

31. A child is eligible for an IEP when the child's educational progress is adversely affected by his or her disability such that special services or accommodations are needed. See 20 U.S.C. § 1414(d)(1)(A)(i). The child's parents (and the child, if old enough) join a team of school officials (a regular education teacher, an administrator or other school official knowledgeable about district resources, a special education teacher, and a psychologist or other person qualified to interpret the student's testing results) to design an IEP. See 20 U.S.C. § 1414(d)(1)(B). The IEP will take into account the child's current academic performance, how the child's disabilities affect his or her learning, and any special services or accommodations that the child needs in order to meet measurable performance goals set by the team. See 20 U.S.C. § 1414(d)(1)(A). Parents and the school team must agree on the services the school will provide and the manner in which these services will be provided. See 20 U.S.C. § 1414(d)(2)(b)(ii). Each IEP is created on a child-by-child basis, without reliance on other students' placements and IEPs. See 20 U.S.C. § 1414(d)(3).

32. See 20 U.S.C. § 1412.

34. Individuals with Disabilities Education Act of 1990, Pub. L. No. 101–476, § 901, 104 Stat. 1103, 1141–42 (1990) (codified as amended 20 U.S.C. §§ 1400–85).

amendments. For one, autism and traumatic brain injury were included as categories of disabilities recognized by the Act.[35] Additionally, the amendment stated that schools must provide assistive technology aids and services to students with disabilities.[36] The 1990 IDEA also required school districts to provide students with transition services to assist them upon their exit from the public school system.[37] * * *

3. The 1997 and 2004 Amendments to the IDEA

Later amendments to the 1990 IDEA have not significantly altered the original Act. A few of the changes are noteworthy, however, because they raise questions about what constitutes the least restrictive environment and how a school district can ensure that it is procedurally and substantively fulfilling this requirement for each child. Unfortunately, the amendments do not fully answer these questions.

a. The 1997 Amendments to the IDEA

Some of the changes to the IDEA in 1997 made clear that with regard to the least restrictive environment requirement, Congress preferred "mainstreaming"—the practice of including students with disabilities with their nondisabled peers.[38] One important change, for instance, was to explicitly recognize a presumption that placing the child with disabilities in the regular education classroom is appropriate.[39] Having found that students with disabilities benefited from being in the regular education classroom with supplemental aids and services,[40] Congress amended the Act to provide that before a school removes a student from the regular educational setting, the school must include in the student's IEP an explanation for this removal.[41]

Because the determination of whether a setting is the appropriate one for a particular child necessarily requires individualized consideration, it would be difficult to define the LRE requirement in a way that could apply uniformly to all children with disabilities. In its 1997 amendments, Congress did not explain the substance of appropriate placement but rather focused on procedural aspects of determining this placement, starting with a presumption that every child belongs in a regular class-

---

35. See id.; see also Stanley S. Herr, Special Education Law and Children With Reading and Other Disabilities, 28 J.L. & Educ. 337, 345–46 (1999). By broadening the types of disabilities covered by the law, Congress increased the number of students who would qualify for services.

36. See 104 Stat. 1103.

37. See id.

38. See, e.g., 20 U.S.C. § 1401(c)(5)(D) (1994 & Supp. 1999); § 1414(d)(1)(A).

39. See S. Rep. No. 105–17, at 21 (1997) (stating that "the law and this bill contain a presumption that children with disabilities are to be educated in regular classes").

40. See § 1401(c)(5)(D).

41. See § 1414(d)(1)(A) (requiring "an explanation of the extent, if any, to which the child will not participate with nondisabled children in the regular class"). Thus, Congress clearly intended for schools to place a student with disabilities in regular educational settings with appropriate aids and services before determining that a more restrictive environment would be appropriate for the student. In contrast, the previous version of the IDEA required schools to include in a child's IEP an explanation of "the extent" to which "[the] child will be able to participate in regular educational programs." H.R. Rep. No. 105–95, at 149 (1997); 34 C.F.R. § 300.346(a)(3) (2006).

room.[42] Thus, apart from establishing that it favored a presumption of inclusion, Congress's 1997 amendment to the IDEA did little to alleviate the confusion that continues to swirl around the LRE determination.

> b. The 2004 Amendments to the IDEA—The Individuals With Disabilities Education Improvement Act

In 2004, the IDEA was amended and renamed the Individuals with Disabilities Education Improvement Act[43] (IDEIA). Despite its new name, the IDEIA did not significantly change the IDEA. Regarding LRE and litigation, however, the IDEIA did bring two important changes to the realm of special education.

One important change involves the prevailing party's right to recover attorney fees.[45] Previously, under the IDEA, only parents could recover attorney fees when they prevailed.[46] The IDEIA, however, enables school districts to recover attorney fees when parents bring suit to harass the school district or when the suit is frivolous or unreasonable.[47] Some worry that this change will have a chilling effect on parents who might have legitimate reasons for bringing suit.[48] But this provision may also lead to fewer illegitimate suits, reducing the time and money schools are forced to spend on litigation, even if some legitimate suits might be stayed in the process.

Another important change that the IDEIA brings is some alignment with the No Child Left Behind Act[49] (NCLB). Both acts require schools to fully educate their students with disabilities and hold schools accountable for the students' success. While the IDEA is often interpreted to require consideration of both the social and academic benefits of including students with disabilities in regular classrooms, however, the NCLB focuses strictly on student performance and achievement.[51] Even with more alignment of the two Acts, it will be difficult for schools to comply with both because for some students the goals conflict.

The changes in the IDEA over time have done nothing to address the serious problem schools face trying to accommodate students with conflict-

---

42. Pub. L. No. 105–17, § 101 (1997). Some have argued that the wording of the LRE section indicates that "the provision describing LRE begins with 'to the maximum extent appropriate[,]' ... [so s]ubstance (the IEP) comes before setting (LRE)." Julie F. Mead, Expressions of Congressional Intent: Examining the 1997 Amendments to the IDEA, 127 West's Educ. L. Rep. 511, 517 (1998).

43. See Pub. L. No. 108–446, 118 Stat. 2647 (2004) (codified as amended at 20 U.S.C. § 1415 (Supp. 2005)).

45. Compare 20 U.S.C. § 1415(i)(3)(B) (2000), with 20 U.S.C. § 1415(i)(3)(B) (Supp. 2005).

46. See 20 U.S.C. § 1415(i)(3)(B) (Supp. 2005).

47. See id.

48. See, e.g., Eileen M. Blackwood, Special Education: Will the "Improvements" Decrease Protections for Parents and Students?, 32 Vt. B.J. & L. Dig. 52, 54 (2006).

49. Pub. L. No. 107–110, 115 Stat. 1425 (2002); see Weber, supra note 20, at 16–17 (noting that both the IDEA and NCLB require that special education teachers be highly qualified). The NCLB also requires that students with disabilities take the same standardized tests as their nondisabled peers, holding schools accountable for educating their disabled students as the IDEIA likewise seeks to do. Id. at 19–21.

51. Id. At 16–21.

ing or competing needs. As more students with disabilities are placed in regular classrooms, a teacher's ability to meet the needs of all students may be compromised, and one student's needs may directly interfere with another's. Thus, even while disputes in some areas decrease, the potential for legal and educational conflict concerning incompatible learning environments will likely increase.

B.   Explanation of FAPE

With the EHA and IDEA came the requirement that all students receive a free and appropriate public education (FAPE).[52] While seemingly uncontroversial, the FAPE concept has led to thousands of lawsuits over what constitutes "appropriate" and "free."

1.   What Must Be Covered to Constitute an Appropriate Education?

There is no way to define "appropriate" both generally and precisely in the educational context, because what is appropriate varies from student to student. A student's Individualized Education Program (IEP) is meant to set out a program that, when followed, will provide the child with an appropriate education.[54] Thus, the IEP has become the cornerstone for the education of students with disabilities, as it allows a school to consider each child's unique needs and goals within the educational context. The IEP allows educators and parents to work together to develop a plan aimed at providing the child with a FAPE in the least restrictive environment. Thus, "appropriateness" is determined primarily by those involved in creating the IEP. When they disagree about what is appropriate, however, legal disputes may arise.

When determining whether a child has received a FAPE, courts generally consider whether procedural requirements for the IEP have been met, and if so, they often give deference to the school district.[57] An IEP is found to be in compliance with the IDEA's requirements when the IDEA's procedures have been followed and when the IEP has been designed to provide the child with some educational benefits.[58] Courts generally find that the student has been provided with an appropriate education when the child has been provided with: an IEP that sets forth attainable and reasonable goals with the necessary supplemental aids and services, classroom opportunities commensurate with the IEP, and the inclusion of the child's parents in meetings in which their views were considered in forming the IEP.[59]

2.   What Must Be Covered to Constitute a Free Education?

---

52.   20 U.S.C. § 1400.

54.   20 U.S.C. § 1414.

57.   See, e.g., Cerra v. Pawling Cent. Sch. Dist., 427 F.3d 186, 193 (2d Cir. 2005) (finding that because parents had an opportunity to participate in designing the IEP, procedural requirements were not violated). But see M.L. v. Fed. Way Sch. Dist., 394 F.3d 634, 646 (9th Cir. 2005) (noting that the lack of a regular education teacher on the IEP team was significant and violated the IDEA procedural requirements).

58.   See Bd. of Educ. v. Rowley, 458 U.S. 176, 206–07 (1982).

59.   See, e.g., Cerra, 427 F.3d 186.

What constitutes a "free" education has been somewhat more easily categorized. For controversies regarding whether a school district must pay for certain services, the overwhelming consensus among courts has been that a service need not be the best available, but rather that a school must provide adequate services reasonably calculated to allow the student to receive meaningful benefits from the educational setting.[60] There have also been controversies over whether [and to what extent] parents may recover tuition costs for placing their children in private or parochial schools.[61] * * *

C.   The "Least Restrictive Environment Appropriate" Requirement

Much of the litigation involving students with disabilities arises over what the "least restrictive environment" is.[63] Because each student with disabilities is uniquely situated, the least restrictive environment (LRE) has no blanket definition. The law, however, requires that "[t]o the maximum extent appropriate, children with disabilities . . . are educated with children who are not disabled, and . . . removal of children with disabilities from the regular educational environment occurs only when the nature or severity of the disability of a child is such that education in regular classes with the use of supplementary aids and services cannot be achieved satisfactorily."[64]

Thus, fundamentally the LRE is meant to be the environment in which a student, with essential supplemental aids and services, can benefit from academic and social opportunities.[65] Because the statute refers to the least restrictive environment "appropriate",[66] however, there is much room for disagreement between parents and educators as to what constitutes the appropriate environment for the child.[67] Although the U.S. Supreme Court in * * * Rowley did not have the LRE issue before it, its determination that a FAPE requires that the IEP be "reasonably calculated to enable the child to receive educational benefits" has sometimes been used as a starting point for determining whether a school district has provided the FAPE in the LRE.[70]

The reality is that what parents believe is least restrictive is often different from what educators on the school site level believe is appropri-

---

60. See. id.

61. See, e.g., Jacobsen v. District of Columbia Bd. of Educ., 564 F. Supp. 166 (D.D.C. 1983); Christen G. v. Lower Merion Sch. Dist., 919 F. Supp. 793 (E.D. Pa. 1996).

63. See [See James R. Newcomer & Perry A. Zirkel, An Analysis of Judicial Outcomes of Special Education Cases, 65 Exceptional Child. 469, 478, note 13 (1999)].

64. 20 U.S.C. § 1412(a)(5) (quoting from the section headed, "Least Restrictive Environment").

65. See id.

66. Id. (emphasis added).

67. It is important to note that the appropriateness of the setting selected for the child is judged prospectively, so the setting need not result in the sought-after results in order for the school district to be in compliance with LRE requirements. Carlisle Area Sch. Dist. v. Scott P., 62 F.3d 520, 530 (3d Cir. 1995) (noting that "appropriateness is judged prospectively so that any lack of progress under a particular IEP . . . does not render that IEP inappropriate").

70. See, e.g., Daniel R.R. v. State Bd. of Educ., 874 F.2d 1036 (5th Cir. 1989).

ate.[71] There are some who believe the social benefits of inclusion justify all students' inclusion in all classes, regardless of ability or capacity to learn the material. Others believe that full inclusion would interfere with regular classroom activities and would recreate the pre-EHA model of education in which millions of students with disabilities languished in classrooms with programs they could not access. The potential for conflicts between students' needs in a single class, like the debate over placements, will only grow with NCLB's focus on academic outcomes as the number of students qualifying under the IDEA increases.

D.   The No Child Left Behind Act's Requirements for All Children and for Those With Special Needs Specifically

With the passage of the NCLB in 2001, Congress began to align the requirements of the IDEA with those of the NCLB. The NCLB requires schools to show progress toward meeting state standards for each of its subgroups, and students with disabilities are no exception.[74] This alignment ensures that schools cannot ignore students with disabilities, lest the schools come under corrective sanctions.[75] While the NCLB does not dramatically alter the landscape of special education, it does increase the pressure on schools to ensure that each special education student receives whatever he or she needs to succeed and to improve on standards-based standardized tests alongside his or her peers without disabilities.[76] It is a difficult balance required of schools to provide students with disabilities a FAPE in the LRE, but the increased pressure on schools to maximize the potential of every student under the NCLB may tip this balance. If schools are required to ensure that each student progress toward achieving the standards, then the emphasis that some courts have placed on mainstreaming students even when academic benefits are marginal will have to be cast aside in favor of whatever environment will most likely result in an improved, maximized academic product. Not only will schools have to consider where their various students with disabilities will learn best, but they will also have to weigh into their placement decisions "the effect the student with disabilities will have on the rest of the classroom" in

---

71.   Many of the famous cases in which circuit courts present a test for determining whether a student is being educated in the least restrictive environment originated because the parents wanted their children in less restrictive environments. See, e.g., Beth B. v. Van Clay, 282 F.3d 493 (7th Cir. 2002); Sacramento City Unified Sch. Dist. v. Rachel H., 14 F.3d 1398 (9th Cir. 1994); Daniel R.R., 874 F.2d 1036; Roncker v. Walter, 700 F.2d 1058 (6th Cir. 1983). However, the majority of cases brought regarding placement involve parents seeking a more restrictive environment for their children with disabilities. Newcomer & Zirkel, supra note [63], at 478.

74.   [As of 2004, for example,] [o]ver 90 percent of students with disabilities identified under the IDEA [were required to] take the standardized tests with accommodations, while those whom the school districts find to have the "most significant cognitive disabilities" [could] take an alternate form of assessment. U.S. Education Department Allows Alternate Testing of Some Students With Disabilities, Andrews Disability Litig. Rep., Jan. 2004, at 13.

75.   See 34 C.F.R. § 200.13(c)(1) (2007).

76.   The NCLB includes students with disabilities as one of the four disaggregated groups, making the improvement and success of this group paramount to a school's overall progress and success. See Perry A. Zirkel, Initial Implications of the NCLB for Section 504, 191 West's Educ. L. Rep. 541, 542 (2004) (acknowledging that the pressure on schools to maintain passing scores of the disaggregated group of students with disabilities might lead to schools manipulating data); see also Weber, supra note 20, at 20–21.

selecting a placement, as the progress and success of all students will depend on making the most of every learning environment.

E. Section 504 of the Rehabilitation Act: Increasing the Complexity of Meeting the Needs of All Students in a Single Classroom

In addition to those students who qualify for services under the IDEA, there are many students who qualify for accommodations only under Section 504 of the Rehabilitation Act (Section 504) and the Americans with Disabilities Act (ADA).[77] A student can qualify for special accommodations under Section 504 when he or she has a disability that creates a "substantial limitation on a major or life activity."[78] A student who qualifies for a Section 504 program can receive specialized services, modifications to the regular education curriculum, or accommodations necessary to provide the student with a FAPE in the LRE (which is generally the regular classroom).[79] All students who qualify under the IDEA are covered by Section 504 and the ADA, but not all students who qualify under Section 504 and the ADA qualify for services under the IDEA.[80] Additionally, parents may find that their children do not qualify under the IDEA because there is not a significant difference in measured ability and performance or because their children's disabilities do not fall into one of the categories recognized by the IDEA.[81] For these groups of parents, Section 504 provides an alternative avenue for their children to receive support.[82]

Although a student who qualifies for an individualized program under Section 504 may not qualify under the IDEA, the student still must have special accommodations in the regular education classroom. Over six and a half million students qualify for some sort of accommodation under the IDEA and Section 504. * * *

PROBLEM 37: JOHNSON V. SUTTER SPRINGS UNIFIED SCHOOL DISTRICT

This hypothetical focuses on Sutter Springs Unified, a large and diverse urban district located in the fictional state of Eldorado.

A coalition of civil rights organizations, determined to establish case precedent that would "blow the top off of the many abuses" that they believe are taking place within the special education system in the public schools, files a highly publicized lawsuit against the Sutter Springs Unified School District (SSUSD).

---

77. See 20 U.S.C. § 1401(3)(a) (Supp. 2005).

78. Tom E.C. Smith, Section 504, the ADA, and Public Schools, LD Online, 2001, http://www.ldonline.org/article/6108 (indicating that major life activities include, for example, "caring for oneself, performing manual tasks, walking, seeing, hearing, speaking, breathing, learning, and working").

79. Id.

80. See 20 U.S.C. § 1401(3)(a) (explaining that only those students whose disabilities necessitate their receiving special education and related services qualify for such under the IDEA).

81. See Smith, supra note 78.

82. See id.

The lawsuit is filed on behalf of African American, Cambodian, Filipino, Latino, and Samoan families. All plaintiff families have annual incomes significantly below the poverty line, and all have children in the District who have been identified "emotionally disturbed" or "learning disabled" by their local school sites pursuant to the provisions of the IDEA. In addition, all these children have been placed in separate "special day classes," many of which include students with diverse disabilities ... ranging from students who are hearing impaired and visually impaired to paraplegics, quadriplegics, students who are autistic, and students with Down Syndrome.

All the children of the plaintiff families score "below basic" or "far below basic" on every section of the Eldorado Standards Test. And over 50 percent of their teachers in this setting have either been long-term substitutes and/or persons who have not completed the requirements necessary to be fully credentialed by the State.

Plaintiffs allege in their complaint that "the District has misused the special education system," citing to reports of an independent reviewer that document "a widespread pattern of classroom activities amounting to babysitting rather than education." They declare that "not only are the low-income students from these five racial/ethnic groups often incorrectly identified as eligible for special education, but once they are identified and placed, they are often relegated to a separate and unequal education that locks them into third-rate programs, prevents them from meeting the basic requirements for admission to the state universities, and generally serves to limit their life chances in significant ways."

In further support of these allegations, plaintiffs plan to rely in particular on the following data available to the public on the Eldorado Department of Education Web site:

- Low-income SSUSD students from these five racial/ethnic groups together comprise 23% of the District's overall student population, yet they comprise over 80% of all the students in District special education programs.

- 79 percent of all the low-income students from these racial/ethnic groups who are in SSUSD special education programs are classified as either "emotionally disturbed" or as having a "specific learning disability." This compares with 43 percent of the low-SES Whites, 32 percent of the low-income Chinese Americans, and 24 percent of the low-income Korean Americans who are in SSUSD special education programs.

At a press conference held in response to plaintiffs' filing, the Superintendent declares that the District is complying fully with the IDEA and that it is not discriminating against any of these children, but is doing all that is practicable to provide the level of education and support that is due under relevant federal and state law. With regard to the identification issues, she emphasizes that all children labeled "emotionally disturbed" or "learning disabled" have been identified pursuant to the recommendations of teachers and school site administrators, as well as the evaluations of licensed school psychologists.

What arguments should the plaintiffs set forth under the IDEA as interpreted by the federal courts? Under state constitutional law? How might provisions of the U.S. "No Child Left Behind" Act be employed to provide additional support for plaintiff's arguments? What result? Discuss.

2.   "APPROPRIATENESS" OF THE SPECIAL EDUCATION: AN INCREASING FOCUS ON EDUCATIONAL QUALITY

BOARD OF EDUCATION v. ROWLEY
458 U.S. 176, 102 S.Ct. 3034 (1982)

Justice Rehnquist delivered the opinion of the Court.

This case presents a question of statutory interpretation. Petitioners contend that the Court of Appeals and the District Court misconstrued the requirements imposed by Congress upon States which receive federal funds under the Education of the Handicapped Act. We agree and reverse the judgment of the Court of Appeals.

I

The Education of the Handicapped Act (Act), 84 Stat. 175, as amended, 20 U.S.C. § 1401 *et seq.* (1976 ed. and Supp. IV), provides federal money to assist state and local agencies in educating handicapped children, and conditions such funding upon a State's compliance with extensive goals and procedures. The Act represents an ambitious federal effort to promote the education of handicapped children, and was passed in response to Congress' perception that a majority of handicapped children in the United States "were either totally excluded from schools or [were] sitting idly in regular classrooms awaiting the time when they were old enough to 'drop out.' " * * *

In order to qualify for federal financial assistance under the Act, a State must demonstrate that it "has in effect a policy that assures all handicapped children the right to a free appropriate public education." That policy must be reflected in a state plan submitted to and approved by the Secretary of Education, § 1413, which describes in detail the goals, programs, and timetables under which the State intends to educate handicapped children within its borders. States receiving money under the Act must provide education to the handicapped by priority, first "to handicapped children who are not receiving an education" and second "to handicapped children ... with the most severe handicaps who are receiving an inadequate education," § 1412(3), and "to the maximum extent appropriate" must educate handicapped children "with children who are not handicapped." The Act broadly defines "handicapped children" to include "mentally retarded, hard of hearing, deaf, speech impaired, visually handicapped, seriously emotionally disturbed, orthopedically impaired,

[and] other health impaired children, [and] children with specific learning disabilities."[5]

The "free appropriate public education" required by the Act is tailored to the unique needs of the handicapped child by means of an "individualized educational program" (IEP)[,] * * * which is prepared at a meeting between a qualified representative of the local educational agency, the child's teacher, the child's parents or guardian, and, where appropriate, the child[.] * * *

In addition to the state plan and the IEP already described, the Act imposes extensive procedural requirements upon States receiving federal funds under its provisions.

* * *

II

This case arose in connection with the education of Amy Rowley, a deaf student at the Furnace Woods School in the Hendrick Hudson Central School District, Peekskill, N.Y. Amy has minimal residual hearing and is an excellent lipreader. During the year before she began attending Furnace Woods, a meeting between her parents and school administrators resulted in a decision to place her in a regular kindergarten class in order to determine what supplemental services would be necessary to her education. Several members of the school administration prepared for Amy's arrival by attending a course in sign-language interpretation, and a teletype machine was installed in the principal's office to facilitate communication with her parents who are also deaf. At the end of the trial period it was determined that Amy should remain in the kindergarten class, but that she should be provided with an FM hearing aid which would amplify words spoken into a wireless receiver by the teacher or fellow students during certain classroom activities. Amy successfully completed her kindergarten year.

As required by the Act, an IEP was prepared for Amy during the fall of her first-grade year. The IEP provided that Amy should be educated in a regular classroom at Furnace Woods, should continue to use the FM hearing aid, and should receive instruction from a tutor for the deaf for one hour each day and from a speech therapist for three hours each week. The Rowleys agreed with parts of the IEP, but insisted that Amy also be provided a qualified sign-language interpreter in all her academic classes in lieu of the assistance proposed in other parts of the IEP. Such an interpreter had been placed in Amy's kindergarten class for a 2–week experimental period, but the interpreter had reported that Amy did not need his services at that time. The school administrators likewise concluded that Amy did not need such an interpreter in her first-grade classroom. They reached this conclusion after consulting the school district's Com-

---

5. In addition to covering a wide variety of handicapping conditions, the Act requires special educational services for children "regardless of the severity of their handicap." §§ 1412(2)(C), 1414(a)(1)(A).

mittee on the Handicapped, which had received expert evidence from
Amy's parents on the importance of a sign-language interpreter, received
testimony from Amy's teacher and other persons familiar with her academic and social progress, and visited a class for the deaf.

When their request for an interpreter was denied, the Rowleys demanded and received a hearing before an independent examiner. After
receiving evidence from both sides, the examiner agreed with the administrators' determination that an interpreter was not necessary because
"Amy was achieving educationally, academically, and socially" without
such assistance. The examiner's decision was affirmed on appeal by the
New York Commissioner of Education on the basis of substantial evidence
in the record. Pursuant to the Act's provision for judicial review, the
Rowleys then brought an action in the United States District Court for the
Southern District of New York, claiming that the administrators' denial of
the sign-language interpreter constituted a denial of the "free appropriate
public education" guaranteed by the Act.

The District Court found that Amy "is a remarkably well-adjusted
child" who interacts and communicates well with her classmates and has
"developed an extraordinary rapport" with her teachers. It also found
that "she performs better than the average child in her class and is
advancing easily from grade to grade," but "that she understands considerably less of what goes on in class than she could if she were not deaf"
and thus "is not learning as much, or performing as well academically, as
she would without her handicap." This disparity between Amy's achievement and her potential led the court to decide that she was not receiving a
"free appropriate public education," which the court defined as "an
opportunity to achieve [her] full potential commensurate with the opportunity provided to other children." According to the District Court, such a
standard "requires that the potential of the handicapped child be measured and compared to his or her performance, and that the resulting
differential or 'shortfall' be compared to the shortfall experienced by
nonhandicapped children." The District Court's definition arose from its
assumption that the responsibility for "giv[ing] content to the requirement of an 'appropriate education'" had "been left entirely to the
[federal] courts and the hearing officers."

A divided panel of the United States Court of Appeals for the Second
Circuit affirmed. The Court of Appeals "agree[d] with the [D]istrict
[C]ourt's conclusions of law," and held that its "findings of fact [were] not
clearly erroneous."

We granted certiorari to review the lower courts' interpretation of the
Act. * * *

III

A

This is the first case in which this Court has been called upon to
interpret any provision of the Act. As noted previously, the District Court

and the Court of Appeals concluded that "[t]he Act itself does not define 'appropriate education,'" but leaves "to the courts and the hearing officers" the responsibility of "giv[ing] content to the requirement of an 'appropriate education.'" Petitioners contend that the definition of the phrase "free appropriate public education" used by the courts below overlooks the definition of that phrase actually found in the Act. Respondents agree that the Act defines "free appropriate public education," but contend that the statutory definition is not "functional" and thus "offers judges no guidance in their consideration of controversies involving 'the identification, evaluation, or educational placement of the child or the provision of a free appropriate public education.'" The United States, appearing as *amicus curiae* on behalf of respondents, states that "[all-though the Act includes definitions of a 'free appropriate public education' and other related terms, the statutory definitions do not adequately explain what is meant by 'appropriate.'"

We are loath to conclude that Congress failed to offer any assistance in defining the meaning of the principal substantive phrase used in the Act. It is beyond dispute that, contrary to the conclusions of the courts below, the Act does expressly define "free appropriate public education":

> The term 'free appropriate public education' means *special education* and *related services* which (A) have been provided at public expense, under public supervision and direction, and without charge, (B) meet the standards of the State educational agency, (C) include an appropriate preschool, elementary, or secondary school education in the State involved, and (D) are provided in conformity with the individualized education program required under section 1414(a)(5) of this title.

"Special education," as referred to in this definition, means "specially designed instruction, at no cost to parents or guardians, to meet the unique needs of a handicapped child, including classroom instruction, instruction in physical education, home instruction, and instruction in hospitals and institutions." "Related services" are defined as "transportation, and such developmental, corrective, and other supportive services ... as may be required to assist a handicapped child to benefit from special education."[10]

Like many statutory definitions, this one tends toward the cryptic rather than the comprehensive, but that is scarcely a reason for abandoning the quest for legislative intent. Whether or not the definition is a "functional" one, as respondents contend it is not, it is the principal tool which Congress has given us for parsing the critical phrase of the Act. We think more must be made of it than either respondents or the United States seems willing to admit.

---

10. Examples of "related services" identified in the Act are "speech pathology and audiology, psychological services, physical and occupational therapy, recreation, and medical and counseling services, except that such medical services shall be for diagnostic and evaluation purposes only." § 1401(17).

According to the definitions contained in the Act, a "free appropriate public education" consists of educational instruction specially designed to meet the unique needs of the handicapped child, supported by such services as are necessary to permit the child "to benefit" from the instruction. Almost as a checklist for adequacy under the Act, the definition also requires that such instruction and services be provided at public expense and under public supervision, meet the State's educational standards, approximate the grade levels used in the State's regular education, and comport with the child's IEP. Thus, if personalized instruction is being provided with sufficient supportive services to permit the child to benefit from the instruction, and the other items on the definitional checklist are satisfied, the child is receiving a "free appropriate public education" as defined by the Act.

Other portions of the statute also shed light upon congressional intent. Congress found that of the roughly eight million handicapped children in the United States at the time of enactment, one million were "excluded entirely from the public school system" and more than half were receiving an inappropriate education. In addition, as mentioned in Part I, the Act requires States to extend educational services first to those children who are receiving no education and second to those children who are receiving an "inadequate education." When these express statutory findings and priorities are read together with the Act's extensive procedural requirements and its definition of "free appropriate public education," the face of the statute evinces a congressional intent to bring previously excluded handicapped children into the public education systems of the States and to require the States to adopt *procedures* which would result in individualized consideration of and instruction for each child.

Noticeably absent from the language of the statute is any substantive standard prescribing the level of education to be accorded handicapped children. Certainly the language of the statute contains no requirement like the one imposed by the lower courts—that States maximize the potential of handicapped children "commensurate with the opportunity provided to other children."

* * *

By passing the Act, Congress sought primarily to make public education available to handicapped children. But in seeking to provide such access to public education, Congress did not impose upon the States any greater substantive educational standard than would be necessary to make such access meaningful.

* * *

That the Act imposes no clear obligation upon recipient States beyond the requirement that handicapped children receive some form of specialized education is perhaps best demonstrated by the fact that Congress, in explaining the need for the Act, equated an "appropriate education" to the receipt of some specialized educational services. * * *

(ii)

Respondents contend that "the goal of the Act is to provide each handicapped child with an equal educational opportunity." We think, however, that the requirement that a State provide specialized educational services to handicapped children generates no additional requirement that the services so provided be sufficient to maximize each child's potential "commensurate with the opportunity provided other children." Respondents and the United States correctly note that Congress sought "to provide assistance to the States in carrying out their responsibilities under . . . the Constitution of the United States to provide equal protection of the laws." But we do not think that such statements imply a congressional intent to achieve strict equality of opportunity or services.

The educational opportunities provided by our public school systems undoubtedly differ from student to student, depending upon a myriad of factors that might affect a particular student's ability to assimilate information presented in the classroom. The requirement that States provide "equal" educational opportunities would thus seem to present an entirely unworkable standard requiring impossible measurements and comparisons. Similarly, furnishing handicapped children with only such services as are available to nonhandicapped children would in all probability fall short of the statutory requirement of "free appropriate public education"; to require, on the other hand, the furnishing of every special service necessary to maximize each handicapped child's potential is, we think, further than Congress intended to go. Thus to speak in terms of "equal" services in one instance gives less than what is required by the Act and in another instance more. The theme of the Act is "free appropriate public education," a phrase which is too complex to be captured by the word "equal" whether one is speaking of opportunities or services.

The legislative conception of the requirements of equal protection was undoubtedly informed by the two District Court decisions referred to above. But cases such as *Mills* and *PARC* held simply that handicapped children may not be excluded entirely from public education. * * *

The District Court and the Court of Appeals thus erred when they held that the Act requires New York to maximize the potential of each handicapped child commensurate with the opportunity provided nonhandicapped children. Desirable though that goal might be, it is not the standard that Congress imposed upon States which receive funding under the Act. Rather, Congress sought primarily to identify and evaluate handicapped children, and to provide them with access to a free public education.

(iii)

Implicit in the congressional purpose of providing access to a "free appropriate public education" is the requirement that the education to which access is provided be sufficient to confer some educational benefit upon the handicapped child. It would do little good for Congress to spend millions of dollars in providing access to a public education only to have the handicapped child receive no benefit from that education. The statutory definition of "free appropriate public education," in addition to requiring that States provide each child with "specially designed instruction," expressly requires the provision of "such ... supportive services ... as may be required to assist a handicapped child *to benefit* from special education." We therefore conclude that the "basic floor of opportunity" provided by the Act consists of access to specialized instruction and related services which are individually designed to provide educational benefit to the handicapped child.

The determination of when handicapped children are receiving sufficient educational benefits to satisfy the requirements of the Act presents a more difficult problem. The Act requires participating States to educate a wide spectrum of handicapped children, from the marginally hearing-impaired to the profoundly retarded and palsied. It is clear that the benefits obtainable by children at one end of the spectrum will differ dramatically from those obtainable by children at the other end, with infinite variations in between. One child may have little difficulty competing successfully in an academic setting with nonhandicapped children while another child may encounter great difficulty in acquiring even the most basic of self-maintenance skills. We do not attempt today to establish any one test for determining the adequacy of educational benefits conferred upon all children covered by the Act. Because in this case we are presented with a handicapped child who is receiving substantial specialized instruction and related services, and who is performing above average in the regular classrooms of a public school system, we confine our analysis to that situation.

The Act requires participating States to educate handicapped children with nonhandicapped children whenever possible.[24] When that "mainstreaming" preference of the Act has been met and a child is being educated in the regular classrooms of a public school system, the system itself monitors the educational progress of the child. Regular examinations are administered, grades are awarded, and yearly advancement to higher grade levels is permitted for those children who attain an adequate knowledge of the course material. The grading and advancement system thus constitutes an important factor in determining educational benefit. Children who graduate from our public school systems are considered by our society to have been "educated" at least to the grade level they have completed, and access to an "education" for handicapped children is precisely what Congress sought to provide in the Act.[25]

---

24. Title 20, U.S.C. § 1412(5) requires that participating States establish "procedures to assure that, to the maximum extent appropriate, handicapped children, including children in public or private institutions or other care facilities, are educated with children who are not handicapped, and that special classes, separate schooling, or other removal of handicapped children from the regular educational environment occurs only when the nature or severity of the handicap is such that education in regular classes with the use of supplementary aids and services cannot be achieved satisfactorily."

25. We do not hold today that every handicapped child who is advancing from grade to grade in a regular public school system is automatically receiving a "free appropriate public education."

C

When the language of the Act and its legislative history are considered together, the requirements imposed by Congress become tolerably clear. Insofar as a State is required to provide a handicapped child with a "free appropriate public education," we hold that it satisfies this requirement by providing personalized instruction with sufficient support services to permit the child to benefit educationally from that instruction. Such instruction and services must be provided at public expense, must meet the State's educational standards, must approximate the grade levels used in the State's regular education, and must comport with the child's IEP. In addition, the IEP, and therefore the personalized instruction, should be formulated in accordance with the requirements of the Act and, if the child is being educated in the regular classrooms of the public education system, should be reasonably calculated to enable the child to achieve passing marks and advance from grade to grade.

IV

* * * [A] court's inquiry in suits brought under § 1415(e)(2) is twofold. First, has the State complied with the procedures set forth in the Act? And second, is the individualized educational program developed through the Act's procedures reasonably calculated to enable the child to receive educational benefits? If these requirements are met, the State has complied with the obligations imposed by Congress and the courts can require no more.

B

In assuring that the requirements of the Act have been met, courts must be careful to avoid imposing their view of preferable educational methods upon the States. The primary responsibility for formulating the education to be accorded a handicapped child, and for choosing the educational method most suitable to the child's needs, was left by the Act to state and local educational agencies in cooperation with the parents or guardian of the child. The Act expressly charges States with the responsibility of "acquiring and disseminating to teachers and administrators of programs for handicapped children significant information derived from educational research, demonstration, and similar projects, and [of] adopting, where appropriate, promising educational practices and materials." In the face of such a clear statutory directive, it seems highly unlikely that Congress intended courts to overturn a State's choice of appropriate educational theories in a proceeding conducted pursuant to § 1415(e)(2).

We previously have cautioned that courts lack the "specialized knowledge and experience" necessary to resolve "persistent and difficult questions of educational policy." We think that Congress shared that view when it passed the Act. As already demonstrated, Congress's intention

---

In this case, however, we find Amy's academic progress, when considered with the special services and professional consideration accorded by the Furnace Woods school administrators, to be dispositive.

was not that the Act displace the primacy of States in the field of education, but that States receive funds to assist them in extending their educational systems to the handicapped. Therefore, once a court determines that the requirements of the Act have been met, questions of methodology are for resolution by the States.

* * *

VI

Applying these principles to the facts of this case, we conclude that the Court of Appeals erred in affirming the decision of the District Court. Neither the District Court nor the Court of Appeals found that petitioners had failed to comply with the procedures of the Act, and the findings of neither court would support a conclusion that Amy's educational program failed to comply with the substantive requirements of the Act. On the contrary, the District Court found that the "evidence firmly establishes that Amy is receiving an 'adequate' education, since she performs better than the average child in her class and is advancing easily from grade to grade." In light of this finding, and of the fact that Amy was receiving personalized instruction and related services calculated by the Furnace Woods school administrators to meet her educational needs, the lower courts should not have concluded that the Act requires the provision of a sign-language interpreter. Accordingly, the decision of the Court of Appeals is reversed, and the case is remanded for further proceedings consistent with this opinion.

So ordered.

JUSTICE BLACKMUN, concurring in the judgment.

Although I reach the same result as the Court does today, I read the legislative history and goals of the Education of the Handicapped Act differently. Congress unambiguously stated that it intended to "take a more active role under its responsibility for equal protection of the laws to guarantee that handicapped children are provided *equal educational opportunity.*"

As I have observed before, "[i]t seems plain to me that Congress, in enacting [this statute], intended to do more than merely set out politically self-serving but essentially meaningless language about what the [handicapped] deserve at the hands of state ... authorities." The clarity of the legislative intent convinces me that the relevant question here is not, as the Court says, whether Amy Rowley's individualized education program was "reasonably calculated to enable [her] to receive educational benefits," measured in part by whether or not she "achieve[s] passing marks and advance[s] from grade to grade." Rather, the question is whether Amy's program, *viewed as a whole*, offered her an opportunity to understand and participate in the classroom that was substantially equal to that given her nonhandicapped classmates. This is a standard predicated on equal educational opportunity and equal access to the educational process, rather than upon Amy's achievement of any particular educational outcome.

In answering this question, I believe that the District Court and the Court of Appeals should have given greater deference than they did to the findings of the School District's impartial hearing officer and the State's Commissioner of Education, both of whom sustained petitioners' refusal to add a sign-language interpreter to Amy's individualized education program. I would suggest further that those courts focused too narrowly on the presence or absence of a particular service—a sign-language interpreter—rather than on the total package of services furnished to Amy by the School Board.

As the Court demonstrates, petitioner Board has provided Amy Rowley considerably more than "a teacher with a loud voice." By concentrating on whether Amy was "learning as much, or performing as well academically, as she would without her handicap," the District Court and the Court of Appeals paid too little attention to whether, on the entire record, respondent's individualized education program offered her an educational opportunity substantially equal to that provided her nonhandicapped classmates. Because I believe that standard has been satisfied here, I agree that the judgment of the Court of Appeals should be reversed.

JUSTICE WHITE, with whom JUSTICE BRENNAN and JUSTICE MARSHALL join, dissenting.

In order to reach its result in this case, the majority opinion contradicts itself, the language of the statute, and the legislative history. Both the majority's standard for a "free appropriate education" and its standard for judicial review disregard congressional intent.

* * *

The majority reads [the] statutory language as establishing a congressional intent limited to bringing "previously excluded handicapped children into the public education systems of the States and [requiring] the States to adopt *procedures* which would result in individualized consideration of and instruction for each child." In its attempt to constrict the definition of "appropriate" and the thrust of the Act, the majority opinion states: "Noticeably absent from the language of the statute is any substantive standard prescribing the level of education to be accorded handicapped children. Certainly the language of the statute contains no requirement like the one imposed by the lower courts—that States maximize the potential of handicapped children 'commensurate with the opportunity provided to other children.' "

I agree that the language of the Act does not contain a substantive standard beyond requiring that the education offered must be "appropriate." However, if there are limits not evident from the face of the statute on what may be considered an "appropriate education," they must be found in the purpose of the statute or its legislative history. The Act itself announces it will provide a *"full* educational opportunity to all handicapped children." This goal is repeated throughout the legislative history, in statements too frequent to be " 'passing references and isolated phrases.' " These statements elucidate the meaning of "appropriate." According to the Senate Report, for example, the Act does "guarantee that handicapped children are provided *equal* educational opportunity." This promise appears throughout the legislative history. Indeed, at times the purpose of the Act was described as tailoring each handicapped child's educational plan to enable the child "to achieve his or her maximum potential." Senator Stafford, one of the sponsors of the Act, declared: "We can all agree that education [given a handicapped child] should be equivalent, at least, to the one those children who are not handicapped receive." The legislative history thus directly supports the conclusion that the Act intends to give handicapped children an educational opportunity commensurate with that given other children.

The majority opinion announces a different substantive standard, that "Congress did not impose upon the States any greater substantive educational standard than would be necessary to make such access meaningful." While "meaningful" is no more enlightening than "appropriate," the Court purports to clarify itself. Because Amy was provided with *some* specialized instruction from which she obtained *some* benefit and because she passed from grade to grade, she was receiving a meaningful and therefore appropriate education.

This falls far short of what the Act intended. The Act details as specifically as possible the kind of specialized education each handicapped child must receive. It would apparently satisfy the Court's standard of "access to specialized instruction and related services which are individually designed to provide educational benefit to the handicapped child," for a deaf child such as Amy to be given a teacher with a loud voice, for she would benefit from that service. The Act requires more. It defines "special education" to mean "specifically designed instruction, at no cost to parents or guardians, to *meet the unique needs* of a handicapped child...."[3] Providing a teacher with a loud voice would not meet Amy's needs and would not satisfy the Act. The basic floor of opportunity is instead, as the courts below recognized, intended to eliminate the effects of the handicap, at least to the extent that the child will be given an equal opportunity to learn if that is reasonably possible. Amy Rowley, without a sign-language interpreter, comprehends less than half of what is said in the classroom—less than half of what normal children comprehend. This is hardly an equal opportunity to learn, even if Amy makes passing grades.

Despite its reliance on the use of "appropriate" in the definition of the Act, the majority opinion speculates that "Congress used the word as much to describe the settings in which handicapped children should be educated as to prescribe the substantive content or supportive services of their education." Of course, the word "appropriate" can be applied in

---

3. "Related services" are "transportation, and such developmental, corrective, and other supportive services ... as may be required to assist a handicapped child to benefit from special education." § 1401(17).

many ways; at times in the Act, Congress used it to recommend main-streaming handicapped children; at other points, it used the word to refer to the content of the individualized education. The issue before us is what standard the word "appropriate" incorporates when it is used to modify "education." The answer given by the Court is not a satisfactory one.

II

The Court's discussion of the standard for judicial review is as flawed as its discussion of a "free appropriate public education." According to the Court, a court can ask only whether the State has "complied with the procedures set forth in the Act" and whether the individualized education program is "reasonably calculated to enable the child to receive educational benefits." Both the language of the Act and the legislative history, however, demonstrate that Congress intended the courts to conduct a far more searching inquiry.

* * *

NOTES

1. As discussed above, in the introduction to Chapter 7, many in the legal and education communities have been reassessing the *Rowley* decision and its implications. *See, e.g.,* Daniel J. Losen & Kevin G. Welner, *Disabling Discrimination in Our Public Schools: Comprehensive Legal Challenges to Inappropriate and Inadequate Special Education Services for Minority Children,* 36 HARV. C.R.-C.L. L. REV. 407 (2001).

2. Jane K. Babin explained in 2000 that "[t]he Rowley decision has been widely criticized as a setback" for students with disabilities:

> Scholars who had read great promise of bountiful rewards into the EAHCA were left with only the minimal expectation of "some benefit." Despite admonitions by the Court that Rowley should be read narrowly, it was feared that the decision would permit states to receive EAHCA funds yet provide only de minimis services.

> Indeed, many courts have relied on Rowley to deny services * * * Recent attempts to require schools to demonstrate that a child has actually benefitted from his or her education have been largely unsuccessful. Courts have interpreted the FAPE requirement as prospective, requiring that school districts devise educational plans calculated to provide some benefit rather than provide education that actually benefits the child in a meaningful way. * * *

> In a small number of cases, however, courts have departed from the general trend by applying Rowley narrowly. Such courts have either interpreted Rowley to require additional services because the disputed IEP offered no benefit or have distinguished the facts of a case to avoid applying Rowley. Babin, *supra,* 37 SAN DIEGO L. REV. 211, 227–229 (2000).

3. In 2003, Scott F. Johnson identified some of the arguments in support of the growing effort to rethink *Rowley*:

> Three important events occurred after the Rowley decision, all of which impact the validity of the "some educational benefit" standard and change the nature of educational services that schools must provide students who receive special education services under the IDEA. The first

significant post-Rowley event is state litigation over the constitutional requirements of providing an "adequate" education to students * * * under state constitutional law. * * * The second event is the education standards movement that created high expectations for all students, including students with disabilities, by creating generally applicable content and proficiency standards. * * * The third event is the reauthorization of IDEA in 1997. * * * These three changes require a reevaluation of what the standard for FAPE and Rowley mean today. * * *

Reexamining Rowley is no small undertaking. It has provided the basic framework for special education services for the last 20 years. However, the 1997 amendments to the IDEA make clear that the foundation underlying Rowley's reasoning is no longer present. That is, the IDEA is no longer intended to simply provide students with access to educational services that provide some benefit. The IDEA is intended to go beyond that to ensure that students with disabilities receive educational services based upon the high expectations in state educational standards and in state court cases regarding an adequate education. Once these elements are incorporated into the analysis, much of Rowley seems inapplicable to questions about the contours of a free and appropriate public education. * * *

Scott F. Johnson, *Reexamining* Rowley*: A New Focus in Special Education Law,* 2003 B.Y.U. EDUC. & L.J. 561, 567, 584–585.

4.   In another FAPE-related dispute, the U.S. Supreme Court in January 2009 granted certiorari in *Forest Grove Sch. Dist. v. T.A.,* 129 S.Ct. 987 (2009) in order to address a circuit split regarding the parameters of the IDEA's tuition reimbursement requirement.[a] Although he had not previously received *special education and related services,* plaintiff was still able to win a reimbursement award to fund his private school tuition.

3.   WITHIN–SCHOOL SEGREGATION ISSUES IN SPECIAL EDUCATION

A.   DISPUTES REGARDING INCLUSION, MAINSTREAMING, AND THE LEAST RESTRICTIVE ENVIRONMENT GENERALLY

SACRAMENTO CITY UNIFIED SCH. DIST. v. RACHEL H.

14 F.3d 1398 (9th Cir. 1994)

SNEED, CIRCUIT JUDGE:

The Sacramento Unified School District ("the District") timely appeals the district court's judgment in favor of Rachel Holland ("Rachel") and the California State Department of Education. The court found that the appropriate placement for Rachel under the Individuals with Disabilities Act ("IDEA") was full-time in a regular second grade classroom with some supplemental services. The District contends that the appropriate

---

a.   20 U.S.C. § 1412(a)(10)(C) provides, in pertinent part, that "If the parents of a child with a disability, who previously received special education and related services under the authority of a public agency, enroll the child in [a private school] without the consent of or referral by the public agency, a court * * * may require the agency to reimburse the parents for the cost of that

placement for Rachel is half-time in special education classes and half-time in a regular class. We affirm the judgment of the district court.

I.

FACTS AND PRIOR PROCEEDINGS

Rachel Holland is now 11 years old and is mentally retarded. She was tested with an I.Q. of 44. She attended a variety of special education programs in the District from 1985–89. Her parents sought to increase the time Rachel spent in a regular classroom, and in the fall of 1989, they requested that Rachel be placed full-time in a regular classroom for the 1989–90 school year. The District rejected their request and proposed a placement that would have divided Rachel's time between a special education class for academic subjects and a regular class for non-academic activities such as art, music, lunch, and recess. The district court found that this plan would have required moving Rachel at least six times each day between the two classrooms. The Hollands instead enrolled Rachel in a regular kindergarten class at the Shalom School, a private school. Rachel remained at the Shalom School in regular classes and at the time the district court rendered its opinion was in the second grade.

The Hollands and the District were able to agree on an Individualized Education Program ("IEP") for Rachel. Although the IEP is required to be reviewed annually, because of the dispute between the parties, Rachel's IEP has not been reviewed since January 1990.[3]

The Hollands appealed the District's placement decision to a state hearing officer pursuant to 20 U.S.C. § 1415(b)(2). They maintained that Rachel best learned social and academic skills in a regular classroom and would not benefit from being in a special education class. The District contended Rachel was too severely disabled to benefit from full-time placement in a regular class. The hearing officer concluded that the District had failed to make an adequate effort to educate Rachel in a regular class pursuant to the IDEA. The officer found that (1) Rachel had benefited from her regular kindergarten class—that she was motivated to learn and learned by imitation and modeling; (2) Rachel was not disruptive in a regular classroom; and (3) the District had overstated the cost of putting Rachel in regular education—that the cost would not be so great that it weighed against placing her in a regular classroom. The hearing officer ordered the District to place Rachel in a regular classroom with support services, including a special education consultant and a part-time aide.

The District appealed this determination to the district court. Pursuant to 20 U.S.C. § 1415(e)(2), the parties presented additional evidence at an evidentiary hearing. The court affirmed the decision of the hearing officer that Rachel should be placed full-time in a regular classroom.

---

enrollment if [it is found] that the agency had not made a free appropriate public education available to the child in a timely manner prior to that enrollment."

3. The 1990 IEP objectives include: speaking in 4–or 5–word sentences; repeating instructions of complex tasks; initiating and terminating conversations; stating her name, address and phone number; participating in a safety program with classmates; developing a 24–word sight vocabulary; counting to 25; printing her first and last names and the alphabet; playing cooperatively; participating in lunch without supervision; and identifying upper and lower case letters and the sounds associated with them.

In considering whether the District proposed an appropriate placement for Rachel, the district court examined the following factors: (1) the educational benefits available to Rachel in a regular classroom, supplemented with appropriate aids and services, as compared with the educational benefits of a special education classroom; (2) the non-academic benefits of interaction with children who were not disabled; (3) the effect of Rachel's presence on the teacher and other children in the classroom; and (4) the cost of mainstreaming Rachel in a regular classroom.

1. Educational Benefits

The district court found the first factor, educational benefits to Rachel, weighed in favor of placing her in a regular classroom. Each side presented expert testimony which is summarized in the margin. The court noted that the District's evidence focused on Rachel's limitations but did not establish that the educational opportunities available through special education were better or equal to those available in a regular classroom. Moreover, the court found that the testimony of the Hollands' experts was more credible because they had more background in evaluating children with disabilities placed in regular classrooms and that they had a greater opportunity to observe Rachel over an extended period of time in normal circumstances. The district court also gave great weight to the testimony of Rachel's current teacher, Nina Crone, whom the court found to be an experienced, skillful teacher. Ms. Crone stated that Rachel was a full member of the class and participated in all activities. Ms. Crone testified that Rachel was making progress on her IEP goals: She was learning one-to-one correspondence in counting, was able to recite the English and Hebrew alphabets, and was improving her communication abilities and sentence lengths.

The district court found that Rachel received substantial benefits in regular education and that all of her IEP goals could be implemented in a regular classroom with some modification to the curriculum and with the assistance of a part-time aide.

2. Non-academic Benefits

The district court next found that the second factor, non-academic benefits to Rachel, also weighed in favor of placing her in a regular classroom. The court noted that the Hollands' evidence indicated that Rachel had developed her social and communications skills as well as her self-confidence from placement in a regular class, while the District's evidence tended to show that Rachel was not learning from exposure to other children and that she was isolated from her classmates. The court concluded that the differing evaluations in large part reflected the predisposition of the evaluators. The court found the testimony of Rachel's mother and her current teacher to be the most credible. These witnesses testified regarding Rachel's excitement about school, learning, and her new friendships and Rachel's improved self-confidence.

3. Effect on the Teacher and Children in the Regular Class

The district court next addressed the issue of whether Rachel had a detrimental effect on others in her regular classroom. The court looked at two aspects: (1) whether there was detriment because the child was disruptive, distracting or unruly, and (2) whether the child would take up so much of the teacher's time that the other students would suffer from lack of attention. The witnesses of both parties agreed that Rachel followed directions and was well-behaved and not a distraction in class. The court found the most germane evidence on the second aspect came from Rachel's second grade teacher, Nina Crone, who testified that Rachel did not interfere with her ability to teach the other children and in the future would require only a part-time aide. Accordingly, the district court determined that the third factor, the effect of Rachel's presence on the teacher and other children in the classroom weighed in favor of placing her in a regular classroom.

4. Cost

Finally, the district court found that the District had not offered any persuasive or credible evidence to support its claim that educating Rachel in a regular classroom with appropriate services would be significantly more expensive than educating her in the District's proposed setting.

The District contended that it would cost $109,000 to educate Rachel full-time in a regular classroom. This figure was based on the cost of providing a full-time aide for Rachel plus an estimated $80,000 for school-wide sensitivity training. The court found that the District did not establish that such training was necessary. Further, the court noted that even if such training were necessary, there was evidence from the California Department of Education that the training could be had at no cost. Moreover, the court found it would be inappropriate to assign the total cost of the training to Rachel when other children with disabilities would benefit. In addition, the court concluded that the evidence did not suggest that Rachel required a full-time aide.

In addition, the court found that the District should have compared the cost of placing Rachel in a special class of approximately 12 students with a full-time special education teacher and two full-time aides and the cost of placing her in a regular class with a part-time aide. The District provided no evidence of this cost comparison.

The court also was not persuaded by the District's argument that it would lose significant funding if Rachel did not spend at least 51% of her time in a special education class. The court noted that a witness from the California Department of Education testified that waivers were available if a school district sought to adopt a program that did not fit neatly within the funding guidelines. The District had not applied for a waiver.

By inflating the cost estimates and failing to address the true comparison, the District did not meet its burden of proving that regular placement would burden the District's funds or adversely affect services available to other children. Therefore, the court found that the cost factor did not weigh against mainstreaming Rachel.

The district court concluded that the appropriate placement for Rachel was full-time in a regular second grade classroom with some supplemental services and affirmed the decision of the hearing officer.

* * *

III.

STANDARDS OF REVIEW

The appropriateness of a special education placement under the IDEA is reviewed de novo. The district court's findings of fact are reviewed for clear error. The clearly erroneous standard applies to the district court's factual determinations regarding (1) whether Rachel was receiving academic and non-academic benefits in the regular classroom; (2) whether her presence was a detriment to others in the classroom; and (3) whether the District demonstrated that the cost of placing her in a regular classroom would be significantly more expensive. * * *

IV.

DISCUSSION

* * *

B.   *Mainstreaming Requirements of the IDEA*

1.   *The Statute*

The IDEA provides that each state must establish:

[P]rocedures to assure that, to the maximum extent appropriate, children with disabilities ... are educated with children who are not disabled, and that special classes, separate schooling, or other removal of children with disabilities from the regular educational environment occurs only when the nature or severity of the disability is such that education in regular classes with the use of supplementary aids and services cannot be achieved satisfactorily.... 20 U.S.C. § 1412(5)(B).

This provision sets forth Congress's preference for educating children with disabilities in regular classrooms with their peers.

2.   *Burden of Proof*

* * * [T]he District * * * [has] the burden of demonstrating in the district court that its proposed placement provided mainstreaming to "the maximum extent appropriate."

3.   *Test for Determining Compliance with the IDEA's Mainstreaming Requirement*

We have not adopted or devised a standard for determining the presence of compliance with 20 U.S.C. § 1412(5)(B). The Third, Fifth and

Eleventh Circuits use what is known as the *Daniel R.R.* test.[5] The Fourth, Sixth and Eighth Circuits apply the *Roncker* test.[6]

Although the district court relied principally on *Daniel R.R.* and *Greer,* it did not specifically adopt the *Daniel R.R.* test over the *Roncker* test. Rather, it employed factors found in both lines of cases in its analysis. The result was a four-factor balancing test in which the court considered (1) the educational benefits of placement full-time in a regular class; (2) the non-academic benefits of such placement; (3) the effect Rachel had on the teacher and children in the regular class; and (4) the costs of mainstreaming Rachel. This analysis directly addresses the issue of the appropriate placement for a child with disabilities under the requirements of 20 U.S.C. § 1412(5)(B). Accordingly, we approve and adopt the test employed by the district court.

4. The District's Contentions on Appeal

The District strenuously disagrees with the district court's findings that Rachel was receiving academic and non-academic benefits in a regular class and did not have a detrimental effect on the teacher or other students. It argues that the court's findings were contrary to the evidence of the state Diagnostic Center and that the court should not have been persuaded by the testimony of Rachel's teacher, particularly her testimony that Rachel would need only a part-time aide in the future. The district court, however, conducted a full evidentiary hearing and made a thorough analysis. The court found the Hollands' evidence to be more persuasive. Moreover, the court asked Rachel's teacher extensive questions regarding Rachel's need for a part-time aide. We will not disturb the findings of the district court.

---

5. First, the court must determine "whether education in the regular classroom, with the use of supplemental aids and services, can be achieved satisfactorily...." *Daniel R.R.,* 874 F.2d at 1048. If the court finds that education cannot be achieved satisfactorily in the regular classroom, then it must decide "whether the school has mainstreamed the child to the maximum extent appropriate." *Id.*

Factors the courts consider in applying the first prong of this test are (1) the steps the school district has taken to accommodate the child in a regular classroom; (2) whether the child will receive an educational benefit from regular education; (3) the child's overall educational experience in regular education; and (4) the effect the disabled child's presence has on the regular classroom. *Daniel R.R.,* 874 F.2d at 1048–49. In *Greer* the court added the factor of cost, stating that "if the cost of educating a handicapped child in a regular classroom is so great that it would significantly impact upon the education of other children in the district, then education in a regular classroom is not appropriate." 950 F.2d at 697.

Regarding the second factor, the *Oberti* and *Greer* courts compared the educational benefits received in a regular classroom with the benefits received in a special education class. *Oberti,* 995 F.2d at 1216; *Greer,* 950 F.2d at 697.

6. According to the court in *Roncker* [*v. Walter,* 700 F.2d 1058, 1063 (6th Cir. 1983)], "[W]here the segregated facility is considered superior, the court should determine whether the services which make that placement superior could be feasibly provided in a non-segregated setting. If they can, the placement in the segregated school would be inappropriate under the Act."

Courts are to (1) compare the benefits the child would receive in special education with those she would receive in regular education; (2) consider whether the child would be disruptive in the non-segregated setting; and (3) consider the cost of mainstreaming. *Id.*

The District is also not persuasive on the issue of cost. The District now claims that it will lose up to $190,764 in state special education funding if Rachel is not enrolled in a special education class at least 51% of the day. However, the District has not sought a waiver pursuant to California Education Code § 56101. This section provides that (1) any school district may request a waiver of any provision of the Education Code if the waiver is necessary or beneficial to the student's IEP, and (2) the Board may grant the waiver when failure to do so would hinder compliance with federal mandates for a free appropriate education for children with disabilities.

Finally, the District, citing *Wilson v. Marana Unified Sch. Dist.,* 735 F.2d 1178 (9th Cir.1984), argues that Rachel must receive her academic and functional curriculum in special education from a specially credentialed teacher. *Wilson* does not stand for this proposition. Rather, the court in *Wilson* stated:

> The school district argues that under state law a child who qualifies for special education *must* be taught by a teacher who is certificated in that child's particular area of disability. We do not agree and do not reach a decision on that broad assertion. We hold only, under our standard of review, that the school district's decision was a reasonable one under the circumstances of this case.

735 F.2d at 1180 (emphasis in original). More importantly, the District's proposition that Rachel must be taught by a special education teacher runs directly counter to the congressional preference that children with disabilities be educated in regular classes with children who are not disabled.

We affirm the judgment of the district court. While we cannot determine what the appropriate placement is for Rachel at the present time, we hold that the determination of the present and future appropriate placement for Rachel should be based on the principles set forth in this opinion and the opinion of the district court.

AFFIRMED.

BETH B. v. VAN CLAY

282 F.3d 493 (7th Cir. 2002)

FLAUM, CHIEF JUDGE.

Thirteen-year-old Beth B. and her parents appeal the district court's grant of summary judgment to the Lake Bluff School District, affirming an administrative decision that upheld the school district's recommendation to place Beth in a special education classroom. Beth is severely mentally and physically challenged. Her parents have long been fighting a battle to keep her in the regular education classroom[.] * * * For the reasons stated herein, we affirm the decision of the district court.

I. BACKGROUND

Beth has Rett Syndrome, a neurological disorder that almost exclusively affects girls. It results in severe disabilities, both cognitive and physical. Beth is nonverbal; she uses an instrument called an eye gaze, a board with various pictures and symbols that she singles out with eye contact, to communicate her wants and needs, as well as other communication devices that allow her to choose among symbols or to hear messages recorded by others. She relies on a wheelchair for mobility. She, like nearly all Rett sufferers, has an extreme lack of control over body movement. Although her mental capacity is difficult to assess precisely, due to her extreme communicative and motor impairments, some experts contend that she has the cognitive ability of a twelve-to-eighteen-month old infant. Others estimate that she has the ability of a four-to-six-year old. She is unable to read or recognize numbers.

Beth has been educated in regular classrooms at her neighborhood public school for seven years. She is currently in the seventh grade at Lake Bluff Middle School with other thirteen-year-old children. Students in the seventh grade attend six 42–minute classes a day. They have three-minute passing periods between class. Beth's aides help her travel from room to room during the passing periods, although it is extremely difficult for her to do so in such a short time frame. Since the first grade, Beth has worked with a one-on-one aide at all times and has used an individualized curriculum tied in subject matter, as much as possible, to that of the other students in the class. Beth's current curriculum is geared toward someone at a preschool level. When her peers worked on mathematics, she was exposed to various numbers. When the class studied meteorology and weather patterns, she looked at pictures of clouds. Beth cannot participate in class discussions or lectures.

The school district held an annual conference with Beth's parents, teachers, and district administrators to review Beth's individualized education program ("IEP"). After her second grade year, the school district recommended at her IEP meeting that Beth be placed in an ELS setting. No appropriate special education environment exists in the Lake Bluff District; Beth would have to attend school in a neighboring school district. The ELS program recommended by the district would be located in a public school building and would serve students between the ages of six and twenty one with mild, moderate, or severe handicaps. Generally, six to eight students comprise one ELS classroom, and the student-teacher ratio is one-to-one. ELS students in the program are mainstreamed into regular education classrooms during music, library, art, computer, and certain social studies and science classes, and join other students at the school during lunch, recess, assemblies, and field trips. Additionally, reverse mainstreaming is employed; that is, regular education students come into the ELS classroom to allow for interaction between ELS and non ELS students.

Beth's parents disagreed with Beth's placement in an ELS program, requested a due process review under the IDEA, and invoked the Act's stay-put provision, which has allowed Beth to remain in the regular classroom at her neighborhood school pending the resolution of this litigation.

II. Discussion

Beth's parents argue that the school district's placement of Beth in an ELS classroom violates the IDEA. The district court erred, they contend, in upholding the administrative decision finding otherwise. Although we review the school board's ultimate decision *de novo* because it is a mixed question of law and fact, we will reverse only if the district court's findings were clearly erroneous, absent a mistake of law.

* * *

B. *The IDEA*

The IDEA, enacted in 1975 as The Education of All Handicapped Children's Act, entitles all children with disabilities to access to public education. It conditions federal funding for educating disabled children on a state's compliance with certain conditions. A school district must provide such children with a free appropriate public education ("FAPE"), together, to the maximum extent appropriate, with nondisabled children ("least restrictive environment" or "LRE"). The FAPE provision and LRE provision are two sides of the same IEP coin. The first requirement is absolute and focuses on the school district's proposed placement—here, the ELS program; the second is relative and concentrates on other placement options—here, keeping Beth in the regular classroom. The LRE requirement shows Congress's strong preference in favor of mainstreaming, but does not require, or even suggest, doing so when the regular classroom setting provides an unsatisfactory education. 34 C.F.R. § 300.550(b)(2) ("[S]pecial classes, separate schooling or other removal of children with disabilities from the regular educational environment occurs only if the nature or severity of the disability is such that education in regular classes with the use of supplementary aids and services cannot be achieved satisfactorily.").

1. *FAPE*

We agree with the district court and the hearing officer, and find that the district's recommendation to place Beth in an ELS classroom satisfies the FAPE requirement. In determining whether the district's placement of Beth meets the standard, we must ask: "First, has the State complied with the procedures set forth in the Act? And second, is the individualized educational program developed through the Act's procedures reasonably calculated to enable the child to receive educational benefits?" No one contests that the program recommended during Beth's IEP review passes muster under this test; the FAPE mandate is, therefore, not at issue. Its discussion is required, however, because of the confusion that ensues when language from the FAPE requirement and analysis is misapplied to the LRE inquiry.

Beth's parents confuse the FAPE side of the coin with the LRE side. They contend that Beth's current placement satisfies the *Rowley* standard because she received an educational benefit at Lake Bluff Middle School. So long as the regular classroom confers "some educational benefit" to Beth, they argue, the school district cannot remove her from that setting. This language is misplaced. The *Rowley* holding applies only to the school district's responsibility to provide a FAPE—a requirement that analyzes the appropriateness of the district's placement—not the appropriateness of the ELS alternatives, including the regular education classroom. As the district court properly noted, the FAPE determination is at the threshold of the placement inquiry. Only with the subsequent LRE analysis does the question of the educational benefit to Beth in the regular classroom arise; in that context, the *Rowley* language does not apply.

2. LRE

The core of this dispute involves whether the school district's decision to place Beth in an ELS classroom violates the LRE provision of the IDEA. Under this clause, the district must mainstream Beth—that is, provide her an education with her nondisabled peers—to the "greatest extent appropriate." Again, Congress used the modifier "appropriate" in stating the requirements of the Act, limiting its mainstreaming mandate. The regular class room would be a less restrictive environment than the ELS classroom. That point is not at issue, however, because the Lake Bluff school district is not required to educate Beth in such an environment unless doing so would be appropriate. The Supreme Court, although it has not yet interpreted the language of the LRE provision, has stated that "[t]he Act's use of the word 'appropriate' thus seems to reflect Congress' recognition that some settings simply are not suitable environments for the participation of some handicapped children." This case turns, then, on whether educating Beth in the regular classroom (or, more appropriately in the middle school setting, classrooms) would be appropriate.

The relevant IDEA regulation provides that children may not be removed from the regular classroom unless their education there, with the use of supplementary aids and services, cannot be achieved satisfactorily. This preference for mainstreaming demands a hard look and a careful analysis of the education Beth was receiving at Lake Bluff Middle School. Beth's parents rely on misplaced language from *Rowley* to argue that so long as she was receiving *any* benefit—improvement in eye contact, or progress in responding to a request to "look" or "touch"—her removal would violate the LRE requirement. We cannot agree with this definition of satisfactory education.

Rowley requires, in its analysis of the FAPE provision, "that the education to which access is provided be sufficient to confer some educational benefit upon the handicapped child." The Court's rationale behind using this standard was "to leave the selection of educational policy and methods where they traditionally have resided—with state and local school officials." The standard is intended to give school districts "flexibility in educational planning." By applying it to the LRE directive and arguing that the school district cannot remove Beth from the regular classroom if she receives *any* benefit there, Beth's parents turn the "some educational benefit" language on its head. Instead of granting flexibility to educators and school officials, it places an extreme restriction on their policymaking authority and the deference they are owed; it essentially vitiates school districts' authority to place any disabled children in separate special education environments. Neither Congress nor the Supreme Court intended such a result. *Rowley,* 458 U.S. at 181, 102 S.Ct. 3034, fn. 4 ("Congress recognized that regular classrooms simply would not be a suitable setting for the education of many handicapped children.").

Each student's educational situation is unique. We find it unnecessary at this point in time to adopt a formal test for district courts uniformly to apply when deciding LRE cases. The Act itself provides enough of a framework for our discussion; if Beth's education at Lake Bluff Middle School was satisfactory, the school district would be in violation of the Act by removing her. If not, if its recommended placement will mainstream her to the maximum appropriate extent, no violation occurs. In this case we can say with confidence that the Lake Bluff school district's decision to remove Beth from her regular school did not violate the IDEA's mandate to mainstream disabled children to the maximum extent appropriate. Beth was in class for about fifty percent of each day. Her academic progress was virtually nonexistent and her developmental progress was limited. Although the school district provided her with aides, communication devices, computerized books, and an individual curriculum, she was receiving very little benefit from her time there.

We agree with the school district's decision that a modicum of developmental achievement does not constitute a satisfactory education. The ELS classroom, so long as it includes reverse mainstreaming opportunities, as well as time spent with nondisabled peers in nonacademic classes, during special projects, lunch, and the like, is at an acceptable point along the "continuum of services" between total integration and complete segregation, and satisfies the requirement that Beth be mainstreamed to the maximum extent appropriate. The school officials' decision about how to best educate Beth is based on expertise that we cannot match. They relied on years of evidence that Beth was not receiving a satisfactory education in the regular classroom. The placement shows a concern both for her development and for keeping her mainstreamed, to an appropriate extent, with her nondisabled peers. We cannot hold that the Lake Bluff School District has failed to provide her with the free, appropriate public education where she is mainstreamed to the maximum extent appropriate, to which she is entitled under the IDEA. Although we respect the input Beth's parents have given regarding her placement and the their continued participation in IEP decisionmaking, educators "have the power to provide handicapped children with an education they consider more appropriate than that proposed by the parents." We find that the district's proposed IEP, which includes reverse mainstreaming and provides that Beth will take part in certain regular-education classes, does not violate the statutory LRE mandate.

III. CONCLUSION

For the reasons stated herein, we find that the school district's recommendation to place Beth in an ELS classroom does not violate the IDEA. We AFFIRM the decision of the district court.

B. DISPROPORTIONATE REPRESENTATION OF MINORITY STUDENTS IN SEPARATE SPECIAL EDUCATION CLASSROOMS

LARRY P. v. RILES

343 F.Supp. 1306 (N.D. Cal. 1972)

PECKHAM, DISTRICT JUDGE.

Plaintiffs in this case have asked the Court to issue a preliminary injunction restraining the San Francisco Unified School District from administering I.Q. tests for purposes of determining whether to place black students in classes for the educable mentally retarded. Named plaintiffs, who remain anonymous for their own protection, are black San Francisco elementary school children who have been placed in EMR (Educable Mentally Retarded) classes because, *inter alia,* they scored below 75 on the defendant School District's I.Q. tests. They claim that they are not mentally retarded, and that they have been placed in EMR classes on the basis of tests which are biased against the culture and experience of black children as a class, in violation of their fourteenth amendment rights. In fact, plaintiffs have presented evidence, in the form of affidavits from certain black psychologists, that when they were given the same I.Q. tests but with special attempts by the psychologists to establish rapport with the test takers, to overcome plaintiffs' defeatism and easy distraction, to reword items in terms more consistent with plaintiffs' cultural background, and to give credit for non-standard answers which nevertheless showed an intelligent approach to problems in the context of that background, plaintiffs scored significantly above the cutting-off point of 75.

Irreparable injury is alleged to flow from plaintiffs' placement in EMR classes because the curriculum is so minimal academically, teacher expectations are so low, and because other students subject EMR students to ridicule on account of their status. Furthermore, EMR students allegedly acquire severe feelings of inferiority. To add to this alleged irreparable harm, the fact of placement in EMR classes is noted on a student's permanent school record, for colleges, prospective employers, and the armed forces to see. Plaintiffs charge that the harm is especially great because under state law placement in EMR classes is reevaluated only once every three years; this law was recently changed, however, to require reevaluation yearly.

Defendants justify the EMR program by noting that the curriculum, pace, and increased attention available in its classes are designed to be beneficial to retarded students, and that in San Francisco the classes are labeled "ungraded" or "adjustment" in order to minimize any stigma. However, defendants do not seem to controvert plaintiffs' assertion that a student who does not belong in an EMR class is harmed by being placed there. Rather, defendants claim that since students are permitted to achieve their way out of EMR classes on the basis of yearly evaluations, plaintiffs can be suffering only negligible harm as a result of their placement in such classes, even if it is true that they are not mentally retarded. The Court finds this contention to be specious. For even if a student remains in an EMR class for only one month, that placement is noted on his permanent record, his education is retarded to some degree, and he is subjected to whatever humiliation students are exposed to for being separated into classes for the educable mentally retarded.

This Court is thus of the view that for those students who are wrongfully placed in EMR classes, irreparable harm ensues. * * *

The fact of racial imbalance is demonstrated by plaintiffs' undisputed statistics, which indicate that while blacks constitute 28.5 per cent of all students in the San Francisco Unified School District, 66 per cent of all students in San Francisco's EMR program are black. Statewide, the disproportion is similar. Blacks comprise 9.1 per cent of all school children in California, but 27.5 per cent of all school children in EMR classes. Certainly these statistics indicate that there is a significant disproportion of blacks in EMR classes in San Francisco and in California. * * *

4. STANDARDIZED TESTING AND K-12 STUDENTS WITH DISABILITIES

LARRY P. v. RILES

793 F.2d 969 (9th Cir. 1984)

POOLE, CIRCUIT JUDGE:

The State Superintendent of Public Instruction appeals a decision holding that IQ tests used by the California school system to place children into special classes for the educable mentally retarded (E.M.R.) violated federal statutes and the equal protection clauses of the United States and California Constitutions. The district court enjoined the use of non-validated IQ tests, and ordered the state to develop plans to eliminate the disproportionate enrollment of black children in E.M.R. classes. We affirm on the statutory grounds and reverse on the federal and state constitutional issues.

I. PROCEDURE BELOW

The initial complaint for declaratory and injunctive relief was filed in 1971, with six black elementary schoolchildren in the San Francisco

Unified School District as named plaintiffs. Appellees challenged as unconstitutional the use of standardized intelligence tests for placement of black children in E.M.R. classes in San Francisco. The defendants were the city and state superintendents, the members of the State Board of Public Instruction and the members of the City Board of Education. The district court certified the plaintiff class as consisting "of all black San Francisco schoolchildren who have been classified as mentally retarded on the bases of IQ test results" and granted appellees' motion for a preliminary injunction.

* * * In December 1974 the district court expanded the class to include "all Black California school children who have been or may in the future be classified as mentally retarded on the basis of I.Q. tests." The terms of the preliminary injunction were correspondingly expanded. * * *

Trial began on October 11, 1977 and concluded on March 15, 1978. On October 16, 1979 the district court entered judgment for the appellees. The district court held that the plaintiffs were adequate representatives of the class of black children who had been or in the future would be wrongly placed and maintained in special classes for the educable mentally retarded. The court held that the use of IQ tests for placement of black children in E.M.R. classes violated Title VI of the Civil Rights Act of 1964, 42 U.S.C. § 2000d et seq., the Rehabilitation Act of 1973, 29 U.S.C. § 794, and the Education For All Handicapped Children Act of 1975, 20 U.S.C. §§ 1401–1461, and the equal protection clauses of the federal and state constitutions. * * *

The district court permanently enjoined the defendants from utilizing any standardized IQ test for the identification of black E.M.R. children or their placement into E.M.R. classes, without securing prior approval of the court. The court ordered the defendants to direct each school district to reevaluate every black child currently identified as an E.M.R. pupil without using standardized intelligence tests.

Further, the defendants were "ordered to monitor and eliminate disproportionate placement of black children in California's E.M.R. classes." The district court specifically ordered the defendants to obtain an annual report from each school district on the racial proportions of E.M.R. classes, to prepare a statewide report, and to direct each school district with a black E.M.R. pupil enrollment one standard deviation above the district rate of white E.M.R. pupil enrollment to prepare a plan to correct the imbalance. The defendants were ordered to bring to the attention of the court any district imbalance if the disparity in excess of one standard deviation existed after three years.

Wilson Riles, California Superintendent of Public Instruction, filed a timely notice of appeal. The other defendants did not appeal.

II. FACTS

In the mid–60's California created programs for several categories of students with educational problems. The "educable mentally retarded"

(E.M.R.) program was for schoolchildren of retarded intellectual development who are considered incapable of being educated through the regular educational program, but who could benefit from special educational facilities to make them economically useful and socially adjusted. The "trainable mentally retarded" (T.M.R.) category was for children with more severe retardation than educable mentally retarded. In addition, there were two categories for students who, with help, could be returned to a regular school program. These were the programs for "culturally disadvantaged minors," children with cultural or economic disadvantages, but with potential for successfully completing a regular educational program, and for "educationally handicapped minors" (E.H.), students with marked learning or behavioral disorders, capable of returning to a regular school program but who cannot presently benefit from the regular program.

The E.M.R. classes are for children who are considered "incapable of learning in the regular classes," and the E.M.R. curriculum "is not designed to help students learn the skills necessary to return to the regular instructional program." The E.M.R. classes are designed only to teach social adjustment and economic usefulness.

"The [E.M.R.] classes are conceived of as 'dead-end classes,'" and a misplacement in E.M.R. causes a stigma and irreparable injury to the student.

From 1968 until trial in 1977, black children have been significantly overrepresented in E.M.R. classes. For example, in 1968–69, black children were about 9% of the state school population, yet accounted for 27% of the E.M.R. population.

"These apparent overenrollments could not be the result of chance. For example, there is less than a one in a million chance that the overenrollment of black children and the underenrollment of non-black children in the E.M.R. classes in 1976–77 would have resulted under a color-blind system." *Id.* at 944. To explain this overenrollment, the defendants proffered a theory that there is a higher incidence of mental retardation among the black population. The district court found that this theory fails to account for the problem, because even "if it is assumed that black children have a 50 percent greater incidence of this type of mental retardation, there is still less than a one in 100,000 chance that the enrollment could be so skewed towards black children.... [Further,] the disproportionate E.M.R. enrollment of black children is not duplicated in the classes for the so-called 'trainable mentally retarded' children."

Since 1967 complaints and concern had been mounting about the use of IQ tests and the placement of minorities in E.M.R. classes. In 1969 the state legislature enacted a resolution calling for a study by the State Board of Education of the overenrollment of minorities in E.M.R. classes. Litigation began in 1969 that raised many of these same issues on the behalf of children from Spanish-speaking backgrounds.[2]

* * *

On the average, black children score fifteen points, or one standard deviation, below white children on standardized intelligence tests. Thus, utilizing the premoratorium criteria used by California for E.M.R. placement, "approximately two percent of the total population fall below the two standard deviation cut-off, while about 15 percent of black children fall below that level."

The court found that "the tests were never designed to eliminate cultural biases against black children; it was assumed in effect that black children were less 'intelligent' than whites.... The tests were standardized and developed on an all-white population, and naturally their scientific validity is questionable for culturally different groups." Since the 1920's it has been generally known that black persons perform less well than white persons on the standardized intelligence tests. IQ tests had been standardized so that they yielded no bias because of sex. For example, when sample tests yielded different scores for boys and girls, the testing experts assumed such differences were unacceptable and modified the tests so that the curve in the standardization sample for boys and girls was identical. No such modifications on racial grounds has ever been tried by the testing companies. The district court noted that "the experts have from the beginning been willing to tolerate or even encourage tests that portray minorities, especially blacks, as intellectually inferior."

The district court analyzed and rejected the defendants' arguments advanced at trial that would explain the test score differences, which theorized that the lower scores for blacks were the result of actual, relevant differences between black and white children. The first argument is the genetic argument, which states that natural selection has resulted in black persons having a "gene pool" with lower intelligence than whites. The district court found the assumptions underlying the genetic argument highly suspect, and in any event that the defendants "were unwilling to admit any reliance on [this theory] for policy-making purposes."

The second theory is the socioeconomic argument, which theorizes that because of blacks' lower socioeconomic status, they are at a greater risk for all kinds of diseases due to malnutrition and poor medical attention. The district court found that the facts did not support this theory, since it did not explain why more severe mental retardation, *e.g.* that consistent with placement into classes for the trainable mentally

---

2. [Diana v. Board of Education, No. C–70–37 RFP (N.D. Cal.)] *Diana* made essentially the same claims as *Larry P.* with respect to Hispanic children, and also involved the issue of linguistic discrimination. The issues of that case were resolved through a stipulated settlement approved by the court on June 18, 1973. Under the terms of the settlement, the State Board of Education agreed to inquire into any school district in which there was a "significant variance" between the expected and actual percentage of Mexican–Americans in E.M.R. classes, to collect relevant data and to develop a plan to eliminate any such variances or disproportionate enrollments.

retarded children, does not occur in greater proportions among blacks and poorer sections of the population.

The district court found that the appellants failed to show that the IQ tests were validated for blacks with respect to the characteristics consistent with E.M.R. status and placement in E.M.R. classes, *i.e.*, that the defendants failed to establish that the IQ tests were accurate predictors that black elementary schoolchildren who scored less than 70 were indeed mentally retarded.

The district court found that alternatives to IQ testing for E.M.R. placement have been in effect since the state moratorium on IQ testing in 1975. These procedures, in which schools take more time and care with their assessments for E.M.R. classification and rely more on observational data, are less discriminatory than under the IQ-centered standard.

The district court found that defendants were guilty of intentional discrimination in the use of the IQ tests for E.M.R. placement. The court based this determination on the facts that the historical background of the IQ tests shows cultural bias; the adoption of the mandatory IQ testing requirement in 1969 was riddled with procedural and substantive irregularities, in which no outside sources were consulted by the State Board and the question of bias was never considered, even though the officials were well aware of the bias and disproportionate placement problems caused by the IQ tests (this problem having been addressed in a legislative resolution); the defendants' "complete failure to ascertain or attempt to ascertain the validity of the tests for minority children;" and the failure of the state to investigate and act on legal requirements to report significant variances in racial and ethnic composition in E.M.R. classes. The court noted that "the SDE's actions revealed a complacent acceptance of those disproportions, and that complacency was evidently built on easy but unsubstantiated assumptions about the incidence of retardation or at least low intelligence among black children."

The court found that the named plaintiffs' assignments to E.M.R. classes were based on their scores on IQ tests, and that these plaintiffs were either in E.M.R. classes or subject to reassignment at the time the class was certified. Further, the court found that "the only relevant evidence on their cases indicated that they were not retarded."

* * *

VI. REHABILITATION ACT

The Rehabilitation Act of 1973 provides *inter alia*:

No otherwise qualified handicapped individual in the United States, as defined in section 706(7) of this Title, shall, solely by reason of his handicap, be excluded from the participation in, be denied the benefits of, or be subjected to discrimination under any program or activity receiving Federal financial assistance. 29 U.S.C. § 794.[5]

---

5. Even though the named plaintiffs claim not to be handicapped (retarded), they are still protected by this Act. The Rehabilitation Act provides that it covers persons who are "regarded" as handicapped. 29 U.S.C. § 706(7)(B); 29 C.F.R. § 32.3.

The Education For All Handicapped Children Act ("EAHCA"), provides that a state qualifying for federal assistance under the Act must establish:

> procedures to assure that testing and evaluation materials and procedures utilized for the purposes of evaluation and placement of handicapped children will be selected and administered so as not to be racially or culturally discriminatory ... [N]o single procedure shall be the sole criterion for determining an appropriate educational program for a child. 20 U.S.C. § 1412(5)(C).

Congress was clearly concerned with the misclassification of students as retarded. The Senate Report for the Rehabilitation Act states that "racial and ethnic factors may contribute to misclassification as mentally retarded." The Senate Report for the Education For All Handicapped Children Act states that "[t]he [Labor and Public Welfare] Committee is deeply concerned about practices and procedures which result in classifying children as having handicapping conditions when, in fact, they do not have such conditions."

The Department of Education adopted almost identical regulations under both of these acts. These regulations require that recipients of federal funds under the acts ensure that:

> [t]ests and other evaluation materials have been validated for the specific purpose for which they are used ... [and] assess specific areas of educational need and not merely those which are designed to provide a single general intelligence quotient. 34 C.F.R. § 104.35(b)(1), (2) and 34 C.F.R. § 300.532(a)(2), (b), originally adopted as 45 C.F.R. § 121a.532(a)(2), (b).

The regulations further provide that evaluation and placement be based on "a variety of sources, including aptitude and achievement tests, teacher recommendations, physical conditions, social or cultural background, and adaptive behavior."

In summary, the Education For All Handicapped Children Act specifically requires that tests and evaluation procedures be free of racial and cultural bias. Both the EAHCA and the Rehabilitation Act require that the tests used for evaluation be validated for the specific purpose for which they are used, and that placement not be based upon a single criterion but on a variety of sources. It is undisputed that California receives substantial federal assistance under these acts, and thus is required to conform to these procedures and regulations. The regulations place the burden on the recipient to show it has complied with the requirements.

Appellant argues that the IQ tests were validated for the specific purposes for which they are used. Appellant analogizes to Title VII cases, notably *Washington v. Davis*, 426 U.S. 229, 96 S. Ct. 2040 (1976), for the proposition that tests that are valid predictors of future performance can be utilized even if they have a discriminatory impact. There are two problems with appellant's proposition. First, the employment context is quite different from the educational situation. As the district court stated, "[i]f tests can predict that a person is going to be a poor employee, the employer can legitimately deny that person a job, but if tests suggest that a young child is probably going to be a poor student, the school cannot on that basis alone deny that child the opportunity to improve and develop the academic skills necessary to success in our society." Assigning a student to an E.M.R. class denies that child the opportunity to develop the necessary academic skills, since E.M.R. classes do not teach academic subjects and are essentially a dead-end academic track. Second, and more important, the question for predictive validity in schools is not whether the standardized intelligence tests predict future school performance generally, as appellant argues, but whether the tests predict specifically that black elementary schoolchildren (as opposed to white elementary schoolchildren) who score at or below 70 on the IQ tests are mentally retarded and incapable of learning the regular school curriculum. In this case, the appellant would have to have shown that the tests are a proven tool to determine which students have characteristics consistent with E.M.R. status and placement in E.M.R. classes, *i.e.*, "whose mental capabilities make it impossible for them to profit from the regular educational programs" even with remedial instruction. The regulations place the burden of showing such validation on the defendants.

The district court found that defendants failed to show that the tests were validated for placing black students with scores of 70 or less in E.M.R. classes. The district court noted that very few studies had examined the difference of IQ predictability for black as compared to white populations, and that those studies which had examined this problem found the tests much less valid for blacks than for whites. Further, the district court found that, even assuming the tests were validated for placement of white schoolchildren in E.M.R. classes, such validation for blacks had been generally assumed but not established. For example, the tests had been adjusted to eliminate differences in the average scores between the sexes, but such adjustment was never made to adjust the scores to be equal for black and white children. The court found that the reason for this was a basic assumption of a lower level of intelligence in blacks than in whites. The fact that early test developers indeed made this assumption is borne out by the literature and testimony at trial. In addition, no studies have been made, either by the defendants or the testing companies, to investigate the reasons for the one standard deviation difference in test scores between the races or to determine whether test redesign could eliminate any bias. There was expert testimony that a much larger percentage of black than white children had been misplaced in E.M.R. classes. Based on the evidence in the record, the district court finding that the appellant had not established validation of the test is not clearly erroneous.

The district court also found that the appellant did not utilize the variety of information required by statute and regulation to make E.M.R. placements, but relied primarily on the IQ test. This finding also is not clearly erroneous. Testimony showed that school records lacked sufficient evidence of educational history, adaptive behavior, social and cultural background or health history for these factors to have been utilized in placement.

Since the appellant has not shown that these findings are clearly erroneous, we affirm the district court's holding that the defendants violated the provisions of the Rehabilitation Act and the Education For All Handicapped Children Act (1) by not insuring that the tests were validated for the specific purpose for which they are used, and (2) by not using the variety of statutorily mandated evaluation tools.

* * *

CONNECTICUT v. SPELLINGS

549 F.Supp.2d 161 (D. Conn. 2008)

MEMORANDUM OF DECISION

MARK R. KRAVITZ, DISTRICT JUDGE.

* * *

I.

The dispute in this case arises under the No Child Left Behind Act of 2001, 20 U.S.C. §§ 6301–7941 (2006) (the "Act"). * * *

A. Relevant Requirements of the No Child Left Behind Act

In 2001, pursuant to its power under the Spending Clause of the United States Constitution, Art. I, § 8, cl. 1, Congress passed the No Child Left Behind Act, the overriding goal of which, the parties agree, is to ensure high-quality education for all our Nation's children. *See* 20 U.S.C. § 6301. Congress provided that in return for federal educational funds under the Act, States must adhere to a comprehensive set of educational assessments and accountability measures. * * *

As is relevant to the pending motions, the Act [requires] * * * that [1.] "[t]he academic standards ... shall be the same academic standards that the State applies to all schools and children in the State"[;] * * * [2.] [s]tates must define annual yearly progress in a manner that "applies the same high standards of academic achievement to all ... students in the State; ... is statistically valid and reliable; [and] includes separate measurable annual objectives for continuous and substantial improvement for ... the achievement of ... students with disabilities [and] students with limited English proficiency"[;] * * * [and 3.] "the same academic assessments [must be] used to measure the achievement of all children." In assessing the academic progress of students, the Act reiterates that a state must provide for "the participation in such assessments of all students." The Act also requires States to provide for "the reasonable adaptations and accommodations for students with disabilities ... necessary to measure the academic achievement of such students relative to ... State student academic achievement standards," and "the inclusion of [LEP] students, who shall be assessed in a valid and reliable manner and provided reasonable accommodations on assessments administered . . . under this paragraph. . . . " LEP students must be tested in English after attending schools in the United States for three years, though case-by-case exceptions can be made.

The Act gives the Secretary "the authority to disapprove a State plan for not meeting the requirements" of the Act, but adds that she "shall not have the authority to require a State, as a condition of approval of the State plan, to include in, or delete from, such plan one or more specific elements of the State's academic content standards or to use specific academic assessment instruments or items." The Act also anticipates the possibility that a State may wish to modify its plan after initial approval. In such cases, the Act provides that "[i]f significant changes are made to a State's plan, such as the adoption of . . . new academic assessments . . . such information shall be submitted to the Secretary." * * *

B. Relevant Regulations Under the Act

* * * On July 5, 2002, former Secretary of Education Rod Paige issued final regulations implementing the Act. *See* Improving the Academic Achievement of the Disadvantaged, 67 Fed.Reg. 45038, 45041–42 (July 5, 2002); 34 C.F.R. §§ 200.2, 200.6. These regulations emphasize that the Act requires States to test special education students (a specific subset of "students with disabilities") and LEP students at grade-level standards; in other words, the regulations do not permit out-of-level testing for these students. *See* 67 Fed.Reg. at 45038, 45040–42; 34 C.F.R. §§ 200.2(b), 200.6(a)(1).

* * * [Secretary Paige] issued [a proposed exception to these regulations] on March 20, 2003, suggesting that students with the "most significant cognitive disabilities," estimated to be only approximately one percent of the entire student population, be tested using alternate assessments. * * * In December 2003, the Secretary issued regulations adopting the one percent exemption from testing. *See* Improving the Academic Achievement of the Disadvantaged, 68 Fed.Reg. 68698,68700–01 (Dec. 9,2003); 34 C.F.R. §§ 200.1(d), 200.6(a)(2).[6] * * *

Following publication of the final regulations, on December 3, 2004, Congress passed legislation—the Individuals with Disabilities Act (the "IDEA"), 20 U.S.C. § 1412 (2006)—that statutorily adopted the one percent exemption that was contained in the Secretary's final regulations. The IDEA specifically allows local educational agencies to "measure the achievement of children with disabilities" against "alternative academic achievement standards permitted under the regulations promulgated to carry out section 6311(b)(1)" of the Act. 20 U.S.C. § 1412(a)(16)(C)(ii)(II).

---

6. The alternate achievement standards and assessments for this population must meet certain criteria set forth in 34 C.F.R. § 200.1(d).

In a policy letter issued on May 10, 2005, Secretary Spellings discussed the one percent exemption, stating:

> [I]n the past, [students with disabilities] have often been held to lower standards and assessed in ways that failed to accommodate their disabilities and demonstrate what they know. As a result, I support emphatically the requirements that are the cornerstone of [the Act]: that **all** students, including students with disabilities, be held to challenging content and achievement standards; that their progress be measured annually by high-quality assessments aligned with those high standards; and that school districts be held accountable for achieving results.

* * *

C. Connecticut's Proposed Plan Amendment

On March 31, 2005, following the submission of Connecticut's plans and correspondence discussing the requirements for LEP and special education students, the State submitted two proposed plan amendments regarding the timing and method of assessment for LEP and special education students. The proposed plan amendments sought: (1) to assess special education students at instructional, rather than grade, level, when deemed "most appropriate"; and (2) to exempt recently arrived LEP students from testing for three years. Specifically, the proposed plan amendment regarding special education students stated: "We request that we be allowed to return to our practice of testing special education students at their instructional level when their planning and placement teams determine that this is *most appropriate*." (emphasis added). As to LEP students, the proposed plan amendment read: "Connecticut ... proposes a reasonable length of time, *three years,* for [LEP] students to be in our schools before we test them in reading, math and science." (emphasis added).

After the State's requests had been submitted but before the Secretary had responded to them, the Secretary announced that she would be more flexible in implementing the Act and publicly stated that up to two percent of the student population might have "academic disabilities" and thus may be more appropriately tested using alternative assessment instruments. The State then submitted additional letters reiterating its previous request that it be allowed to return to its previous testing practices and welcoming the expected two percent student exemption, but noting some concern with the Secretary's intention to link the alternate assessments of these students to grade-level testing. On May 27, 2005, Connecticut submitted an updated plan amendment and waiver request letter. Under the "amendment" section, the State's letter reiterated its March 31, 2005 LEP proposed plan amendment, and under the "waiver" section, sought to exempt special education students when deemed most appropriate, which it apparently calculated would occur with up to two percent of the special education students.

On June 20, 2005, the Secretary denied the State's proposed plan amendments regarding LEP and special education students, because they did "not comply with the statute and regulations." Under a heading labeled "Amendments that are not fully aligned with the statute and regulations," the Secretary reiterated that the proposed plan amendments "do not comply with the statute and regulations." As to the request to test special education students at grade level, the Secretary wrote:

> Connecticut requests to assess students with disabilities at instructional levels when deemed most appropriate. The statute and regulations do not allow for students with disabilities to be tested at instructional levels. The only exception to grade-level achievement standards is the authority in the regulations to hold students with the most significant cognitive disabilities to alternate achievement standards.

> Regarding the LEP request, the Secretary stated, "Connecticut requests to exempt recently arrived LEP students for three years from mathematics, reading, and writing assessments. Current policy on this issue allows recently arrived LEP students one year before taking the reading assessment."

II.

The State now appeals from the Secretary's denials of these proposed plan amendments. * * *

B. Review Under the Arbitrary and Capricious Standard

* * * [T]he Secretary has agreed that its decisions to reject the State's proposed plan amendments are reviewable under the [Administrative Procedure Act (the "APA")] and that they can be set aside if "arbitrary, capricious, an abuse of discretion, or otherwise not in accordance with law," 5 U.S.C. § 706(2)(A). * * * Consistent with [her June 20, 2005] letter, the Secretary has repeatedly represented to the Court that her decision to reject the State's proposed amendments was based solely on statutory requirements and not on considerations of educational policy. * * *

Therefore, the Court wishes to emphasize that it is not faced with the issue of the wisdom of the Secretary's decisions or whether they will hinder, or advance, the educational achievement of Connecticut's LEP students or special education students. While the Court is certainly not an expert on educational policy, one could presumably make a decent argument that testing students who are newly arrived from foreign lands in English, when they are not at all proficient in English, may not be a particularly sensible way to determine the level of the students' academic achievement or knowledge. One might mount a similar argument for testing special education students at grade level, rather than instructional level. But those are not the issues before this Court. The only question is whether the Secretary's denials of the State's requests on the ground that they were contrary to the statute was arbitrary and capricious. For the reasons set forth below, the Court concludes that it was not.

1. Standard of Review

The State bears a heavy burden on this appeal since it must show that the Secretary's decision was "arbitrary, capricious, an abuse of discretion, or otherwise not in accordance with law...." 5 U.S.C. § 706(2)(A). "Agency action is arbitrary and capricious 'if the agency has relied on factors which Congress has not intended it to consider, entirely failed to consider an important aspect of the problem, offered an explanation for its decision that runs counter to the evidence before the agency, or is so implausible that it could not be ascribed to a difference in view or the product of agency expertise.' " A court's authority to review agency action under the APA standard is narrow, and the court must ensure that it does not substitute its own judgment for that of the agency. * * *

2. Special Education Students

The State's argument with respect to the provisions of the Act regarding special education students (and for that matter, LEP students) is quite straightforward. According to the State, even the Secretary must agree that the Act permits instructional-level testing for at least some special education students because the Secretary's 2003 regulations exempted from testing one percent of special education students. * * * The State does not challenge the validity of that decision but instead argues that the Secretary's regulations show that the Act has flexibility and the only issue is what best achieves its goals-which is a decision grounded in educational policy, not the statute. According to Connecticut, the flexibility provided in the Act is demonstrated because the Act "requires 'all' student participation on one hand, and then sets forth separate statutory directives for special education student assessments, on the other. Although the Act provides for 'reasonable adaptations and accommodations' for students with disabilities, it is silent on the issue of alternative assessments." In short, the State argues that the Secretary acted arbitrarily, capriciously, and contrary to law because she cannot explain why the State's proposed plan amendment for special education students violates the Act, while the Secretary's one percent exemption does not.

The Secretary responds that the State's special education amendments "violated the statutory requirement that the same academic standards apply to all students in the state." And, she notes, the State "recognized this statutory requirement when it initially sought a waiver" from that requirement. * * * The Act * * * does require States to assist students with disabilities in taking these assessments by providing "reasonable adaptations and accommodations ... necessary to measure the academic achievement of such students relative to State academic content and State student academic achievement standards." Further, she adds, the Act requires States to define the annual yearly progress in a way that separately measures the achievement of students with disabilities. However, there is no exception from the Act's directive that States develop grade-level assessments and that they "shall be the same academic standards that the State applies to all schools and children in the State."

The Secretary also disputes the relevance of her December 2003 regulations and in any event argues that the one percent exemption was embraced by Congress in the IDEA and that the exemption is much narrower than what the State sought in its plan amendment. The Secretary notes that the State's approach (even if capped at two percent of all students as suggested in its May 27, 2005 waiver request) exceeds the scope of the Secretary's 2003 regulations, which were subsequently affirmed by Congress in the IDEA of 2004. Thus, the Secretary argues that her "regulations are narrowly tailored to address a particular issue with respect to very small segments of the ... students with disabilities populations; in contrast, the State's proposed plan amendment would eliminate Congress's requirement of annual grade-level testing of these students." Sec'y's Reply Brief [doc. #151], at 5.

[5] The Secretary did not act arbitrarily, capriciously, or contrary to law in concluding that the State's proposed plan amendments were contrary to the dictates of the Act. * * * The very clear message of Congress in the text of the Act was that States should apply the same academic standards to all students-including special education students, who were a particular focus of congressional interest. The Act could not be clearer and nothing about the structure of its provisions suggests otherwise.

* * *

3. LEP Students

* * *

[T]he Act does have special provisions for LEP (and special education) students and does require States to accommodate those students, but not by exempting them entirely from testing for three years (or in the case of special education students, testing them at instructional, rather than grade, level). LEP (and special education) students require reasonable accommodations, not no tests (or different tests).

* * *

III.

For the reasons detailed above, * * * [t]he Clerk should enter a final judgment in favor of the Secretary and the NAACP and against the State on all counts * * * and close this file.

IT IS SO ORDERED.

C. HIGHER EDUCATION AND DISABILITY RIGHTS

While most of the controversies regarding students with disabilities at the K–12 level tend to arise within the context of the special education system, the range of legal and public policy debates at the higher education level arguably mirrors more directly the broad range of issues faced by persons with disabilities in society as a whole.

Models of historical treatment. It is useful in this context to highlight the changes in the way persons with disabilities have been treated over time. Six different models of historical treatment have generally been identified by scholars. In chronological order, they include the following:

- The "Morally Deficient" Model—In ancient times, people with disabilities were often considered cursed, or viewed as sinners who were being punished. Descriptions of lepers and the way they were treated at the time are perhaps the classic example of this thinking. People were segregated and even killed pursuant to this model.

- The Imperial/Colonial Model—Rooted in concepts of Darwinism and "survival of the fittest," people with disabilities were often seen as inferior beings who would not and/or should not survive. The Nazis, pursuant to this model, removed people with disabilities from their jobs, placed them in camps, and even executed them.

- The Charity Model—As time passed, persons with disabilities began to be seen as "charity cases." Their disabilities were viewed as their individual misfortune, but pursuant to this model others felt badly about it and saw them as a cause to be supported with charitable contributions. Disability in this context was defined as an inability to work, and the model often led to abuse and to low expectations.

- The Medical Model—Under this model, persons with disabilities are viewed as "patients." In addition, society is seen as having a duty to protect the non-disabled from the disabled through such strategies as eugenics, sterilization, and isolation (by medical communities, the government and/or the family). Persons with disabilities are only fully accepted into society if they have been "cured."

- The Rights–Based Independence Model—An emerging and often-favored model among the disability rights community today, it contemplates enabling people with disabilities live as independently as possible. A guiding principle is that impairments are individual, but become disabilities under social constructs. Movement activism is geared toward the recognition and attainment of civil rights.

- The Disability Culture Model—This model contemplates the identification and fostering of a culture of disability, with a primary goal being the valuing of disability as contributing to society. It is perhaps most fully realized in the growth and development of deaf culture.

The concept of reasonable accommodation. It is at the higher education level that the concept of reasonable accommodation arguably becomes central. Indeed, the concept is recognized in both Section 504 of the Rehabilitation Act of 1973 and the Americans with Disabilities Act (ADA) of 1990 as being at the very heart of the focus of disability rights law and policy. Under the ADA, as a general rule, failure to provide reasonable accommodations is considered to be discrimination against persons with disabilities.

Basic definitions. A person is protected under ADA if she or he has an actual disability, has a record of a disability; or is regarded or treated as if she or he has a disability. "Disability" is defined as a physical or mental impairment that substantially limits one or more of the major life activities of such an individual.

Key areas of controversy at the college and university level. In addition to issues regarding reasonable accommodations generally, controversies continue to arise with regard to physical access generally, including but not limited to architectural barriers and restrooms. Communication issues, including access to technology, have moved to the forefront, with technological advances increasingly holding out the promise of independent living for persons with disabilities at a level previously not thought to be possible. In addition, the legal and public policy implications of timed testing rules and regulations often become a central area of inquiry during this era, reflecting concerns regarding access to professions across the board.

Representative cases that follow in this section embody many of these controversies as educational institutions seek to move forward to a better future.

SOUTHEASTERN CMTY. COLL. v. DAVIS
442 U.S. 397, 99 S.Ct. 2361 (1979)

MR. JUSTICE POWELL delivered the opinion of the Court.

This case presents a matter of first impression for this Court: Whether § 504 of the Rehabilitation Act of 1973, which prohibits discrimination against an "otherwise qualified handicapped individual" in federally funded programs "solely by reason of his handicap," forbids professional schools from imposing physical qualifications for admission to their clinical training programs.

I

Respondent, who suffers from a serious hearing disability, seeks to be trained as a registered nurse. During the 1973–1974 academic year she was enrolled in the College Parallel program of Southeastern Community College, a state institution that receives federal funds. Respondent hoped to progress to Southeastern's Associate Degree Nursing program, completion of which would make her eligible for state certification as a registered nurse. In the course of her application to the nursing program, she was interviewed by a member of the nursing faculty. It became apparent that respondent had difficulty understanding questions asked, and on inquiry she acknowledged a history of hearing problems and dependence on a hearing aid. She was advised to consult an audiologist.

On the basis of an examination at Duke University Medical Center, respondent was diagnosed as having a "bilateral, sensori-neural hearing loss." A change in her hearing aid was recommended, as a result of which it was expected that she would be able to detect sounds "almost as well as a person would who has normal hearing." But this improvement would not mean that she could discriminate among sounds sufficiently to understand normal spoken speech. Her lipreading skills would remain necessary for effective communication: "While wearing the hearing aid, she is well aware of gross sounds occurring in the listening environment. However, she can only be responsible for speech spoken to her, when the talker gets her attention and allows her to look directly at the talker."

Southeastern next consulted Mary McRee, Executive Director of the North Carolina Board of Nursing. On the basis of the audiologist's report, McRee recommended that respondent not be admitted to the nursing program. In McRee's view, respondent's hearing disability made it unsafe for her to practice as a nurse. In addition, it would be impossible for respondent to participate safely in the normal clinical training program, and those modifications that would be necessary to enable safe participation would prevent her from realizing the benefits of the program: "To adjust patient learning experiences in keeping with [respondent's] hearing limitations could, in fact, be the same as denying her full learning to meet the objectives of your nursing programs."

After respondent was notified that she was not qualified for nursing study because of her hearing disability, she requested reconsideration of the decision. The entire nursing staff of Southeastern was assembled, and McRee again was consulted. McRee repeated her conclusion that on the basis of the available evidence, respondent "has hearing limitations which could interfere with her safely caring for patients." Upon further deliberation, the staff voted to deny respondent admission.

Respondent then filed suit in the United States District Court for the Eastern District of North Carolina, alleging both a violation of § 504 of the Rehabilitation Act of 1973, 87 Stat. 394, as amended, 29 U.S.C. § 794 (1976 ed., Supp. II),[2] and a denial of equal protection and due process. After a bench trial, the District Court entered judgment in favor of Southeastern. It confirmed the findings of the audiologist that even with a hearing aid respondent cannot understand speech directed to her except through lipreading, and further found:

> [I]n many situations such as an operation room intensive care unit, or post-natal care unit, all doctors and nurses wear surgical masks which would make lip reading impossible. Additionally, in many situations a Registered Nurse would be required to instantly follow the physician's instructions concerning procurement of various types of instruments

---

2. The statute, as set forth in 29 U.S.C. § 794 (1976 ed., Supp. II), provides in full:

No otherwise qualified handicapped individual in the United States, as defined in section 706(7) of this title, shall, solely by reason of his handicap, be excluded from the participation in, be denied the benefits of, or be subjected to discrimination under any program or activity receiving Federal financial assistance * * *

and drugs where the physician would be unable to get the nurse's attention by other than vocal means.

Accordingly, the court concluded:

> [Respondent's] handicap actually prevents her from safely performing in both her training program and her proposed profession. The trial testimony indicated numerous situations where [respondent's] particular disability would render her unable to function properly. Of particular concern to the court in this case is the potential of danger to future patients in such situations.

Based on these findings, the District Court concluded that respondent was not an "otherwise qualified handicapped individual" protected against discrimination by § 504. In its view, "[o]therwise qualified, can only be read to mean otherwise able to function sufficiently in the position sought in spite of the handicap, if proper training and facilities are suitable and available." Because respondent's disability would prevent her from functioning "sufficiently" in Southeastern's nursing program, the court held that the decision to exclude her was not discriminatory within the meaning of § 504.[3]

On appeal, the Court of Appeals for the Fourth Circuit reversed. It did not dispute the District Court's findings of fact, but held that the court had misconstrued § 504. In light of administrative regulations that had been promulgated while the appeal was pending, the appellate court believed that § 504 required Southeastern to "reconsider plaintiff's application for admission to the nursing program without regard to her hearing ability." It concluded that the District Court had erred in taking respondent's handicap into account in determining whether she was "otherwise qualified" for the program, rather than confining its inquiry to her "academic and technical qualifications." The Court of Appeals also suggested that § 504 required "affirmative conduct" on the part of Southeastern to modify its program to accommodate the disabilities of applicants, "even when such modifications become expensive."

Because of the importance of this issue to the many institutions covered by § 504, we granted certiorari. We now reverse.

II

As previously noted, this is the first case in which this Court has been called upon to interpret § 504. It is elementary that "[t]he starting point in every case involving construction of a statute is the language itself." Section 504 by its terms does not compel educational institutions to disregard the disabilities of handicapped individuals or to make substantial modifications in their programs to allow disabled persons to participate. Instead, it requires only that an "otherwise qualified handicapped individual" not be excluded from participation in a federally funded program "solely by reason of his handicap," indicating only that mere

---

3. The District Court also dismissed respondent's constitutional claims. The Court of Appeals affirmed that portion of the order, and respondent has not sought review of this ruling.

possession of a handicap is not a permissible ground for assuming an inability to function in a particular context.[6]

* * * We think the understanding of the District Court is closer to the plain meaning of the statutory language. An otherwise qualified person is one who is able to meet all of a program's requirements in spite of his handicap.

The regulations promulgated by the Department of HEW to interpret § 504 reinforce, rather than contradict, this conclusion. * * *

III

The remaining question is whether the physical qualifications Southeastern demanded of respondent might not be necessary for participation in its nursing program. It is not open to dispute that, as Southeastern's Associate Degree Nursing program currently is constituted, the ability to understand speech without reliance on lipreading is necessary for patient safety during the clinical phase of the program. As the District Court found, this ability also is indispensable for many of the functions that a registered nurse performs.

Respondent contends nevertheless that § 504, properly interpreted, compels Southeastern to undertake affirmative action that would dispense with the need for effective oral communication. First, it is suggested that respondent can be given individual supervision by faculty members whenever she attends patients directly. Moreover, certain required courses might be dispensed with altogether for respondent. It is not necessary, she argues, that Southeastern train her to undertake all the tasks a registered nurse is licensed to perform. Rather, it is sufficient to make § 504 applicable if respondent might be able to perform satisfactorily some of the duties of a registered nurse or to hold some of the positions available to a registered nurse.[8]

---

6. The Act defines "handicapped individual" as follows:

The term "handicapped individual" means any individual who (A) has a physical or mental disability which for such individual constitutes or results in a substantial handicap to employment and (B) can reasonably be expected to benefit in terms of employability from vocational rehabilitation services provided pursuant to subchapters I and III of this chapter. For the purposes of subchapters IV and V of this chapter, such term means any person who (A) has a physical or mental impairment which substantially limits one or more of such person's major life activities, (B) has a record of such an impairment, or (C) is regarded as having such an impairment.

§ 7(6) of the Rehabilitation Act of 1973, 87 Stat. 361, *as amended*, 88 Stat. 1619, 89 Stat. 2–5, 29 U.S.C. § 706(6). This definition comports with our understanding of § 504. A person who has a record of, or is regarded as having, an impairment may at present have no actual incapacity at all. Such a person would be exactly the kind of individual who could be "otherwise qualified" to participate in covered programs. And a person who suffers from a limiting physical or mental impairment still may possess other abilities that permit him to meet the requirements of various programs. Thus, it is clear that Congress included among the class of "handicapped" persons covered by § 504 a range of individuals who could be "otherwise qualified." *See* S. REP. No. 93–1297, at 38–39 (1974); U.S.CODE CONG. & ADMIN.NEWS, at 6373.

8. The court below adopted a portion of this argument:

[Respondent's] ability to read lips aids her in overcoming her hearing disability; however, it was argued that in certain situations such as in an operating room environment where surgical masks are used, this ability would be unavailing to her.

Respondent finds support for this argument in portions of the HEW regulations discussed above. In particular, a provision applicable to post-secondary educational programs requires covered institutions to make "modifications" in their programs to accommodate handicapped persons, and to provide "auxiliary aids" such as sign-language interpreters. Respondent argues that this regulation imposes an obligation to ensure full participation in covered programs by handicapped individuals and, in particular, requires Southeastern to make the kind of adjustments that would be necessary to permit her safe participation in the nursing program.

We note first that on the present record it appears unlikely respondent could benefit from any affirmative action that the regulation reasonably could be interpreted as requiring. Section 84.44(d)(2), for example, explicitly excludes "devices or services of a personal nature" from the kinds of auxiliary aids a school must provide a handicapped individual. Yet the only evidence in the record indicates that nothing less than close, individual attention by a nursing instructor would be sufficient to ensure patient safety if respondent took part in the clinical phase of the nursing program. Furthermore, it also is reasonably clear that § 84.44(a) does not encompass the kind of curricular changes that would be necessary to accommodate respondent in the nursing program. In light of respondent's inability to function in clinical courses without close supervision, Southeastern, with prudence, could allow her to take only academic classes. Whatever benefits respondent might realize from such a course of study, she would not receive even a rough equivalent of the training a nursing program normally gives. Such a fundamental alteration in the nature of a program is far more than the "modification" the regulation requires.

Moreover, an interpretation of the regulations that required the extensive modifications necessary to include respondent in the nursing program would raise grave doubts about their validity. If these regulations were to require substantial adjustments in existing programs beyond those necessary to eliminate discrimination against otherwise qualified individuals, they would do more than clarify the meaning of § 504. Instead, they would constitute an unauthorized extension of the obligations imposed by that statute.

The language and structure of the Rehabilitation Act of 1973 reflect a recognition by Congress of the distinction between the evenhanded treatment of qualified handicapped persons and affirmative efforts to overcome the disabilities caused by handicaps. Section 501(b), governing the employ-

---

Be that as it may, in the medical community, there does appear to be a number of settings in which the plaintiff could perform satisfactorily as an RN, such as in industry or perhaps a physician's office. Certainly [respondent] could be viewed as possessing extraordinary insight into the medical and emotional needs of those with hearing disabilities.

If [respondent] meets all the other criteria for admission in the pursuit of her RN career, under the relevant North Carolina statutes, it should not be foreclosed to her simply because she may not be able to function effectively in all the roles which registered nurses may choose for their careers.

574 F.2d 1158, 1161 n.6 (1978).

ment of handicapped individuals by the Federal Government, requires each federal agency to submit "an affirmative action program plan for the hiring, placement, and advancement of handicapped individuals...." These plans "shall include a description of the extent to which and methods whereby the special needs of handicapped employees are being met." Similarly, § 503(a), governing hiring by federal contractors, requires employers to "take affirmative action to employ and advance in employment qualified handicapped individuals...." The President is required to promulgate regulations to enforce this section.

Under § 501(c) of the Act, by contrast, state agencies such as Southeastern are only "encourage[d] ... to adopt and implement such policies and procedures." Section 504 does not refer at all to affirmative action, and except as it applies to federal employers it does not provide for implementation by administrative action. A comparison of these provisions demonstrates that Congress understood accommodation of the needs of handicapped individuals may require affirmative action and knew how to provide for it in those instances where it wished to do so.

Although an agency's interpretation of the statute under which it operates is entitled to some deference, "this deference is constrained by our obligation to honor the clear meaning of a statute, as revealed by its language, purpose, and history." Here, neither the language, purpose, nor history of § 504 reveals an intent to impose an affirmative-action obligation on all recipients of federal funds. Accordingly, we hold that even if HEW has attempted to create such an obligation itself, it lacks the authority to do so.

IV

We do not suggest that the line between a lawful refusal to extend affirmative action and illegal discrimination against handicapped persons always will be clear. It is possible to envision situations where an insistence on continuing past requirements and practices might arbitrarily deprive genuinely qualified handicapped persons of the opportunity to participate in a covered program. Technological advances can be expected to enhance opportunities to rehabilitate the handicapped or otherwise to qualify them for some useful employment. Such advances also may enable attainment of these goals without imposing undue financial and administrative burdens upon a State. Thus, situations may arise where a refusal to modify an existing program might become unreasonable and discriminatory. Identification of those instances where a refusal to accommodate the needs of a disabled person amounts to discrimination against the handicapped continues to be an important responsibility of HEW.

In this case, however, it is clear that Southeastern's unwillingness to make major adjustments in its nursing program does not constitute such discrimination. The uncontroverted testimony of several members of Southeastern's staff and faculty established that the purpose of its program was to train persons who could serve the nursing profession in all customary ways. This type of purpose, far from reflecting any animus against handicapped individuals is shared by many if not most of the institutions that train persons to render professional service. It is undisputed that respondent could not participate in Southeastern's nursing program unless the standards were substantially lowered. Section 504 imposes no requirement upon an educational institution to lower or to effect substantial modifications of standards to accommodate a handicapped person.

One may admire respondent's desire and determination to overcome her handicap, and there well may be various other types of service for which she can qualify. In this case, however, we hold that there was no violation of § 504 when Southeastern concluded that respondent did not qualify for admission to its program. Nothing in the language or history of § 504 reflects an intention to limit the freedom of an educational institution to require reasonable physical qualifications for admission to a clinical training program. Nor has there been any showing in this case that any action short of a substantial change in Southeastern's program would render unreasonable the qualifications it imposed.

V

Accordingly, we reverse the judgment of the court below, and remand for proceedings consistent with this opinion.

So ordered.

ZUKLE v. REGENTS OF THE UNIV. OF CAL.

166 F.3d 1041 (9th Cir. 1999)

O'SCANNLAIN, CIRCUIT JUDGE:

We must decide whether a medical school violated the Americans with Disabilities Act or the Rehabilitation Act when it dismissed a learning disabled student for failure to meet the school's academic standards.

I

Sherrie Lynn Zukle entered the University of California, Davis School of Medicine ("Medical School") in the fall of 1991 for a four year course of study. The first two years comprise the "basic science" or "pre-clinical" curriculum, consisting of courses in the function, design and processes of the human body. The final two years comprise the "clinical curriculum." In the third year, students take six consecutive eight-week clinical clerkships. During the fourth year, students complete clerkships of varying lengths in more advanced areas. Most clerkships involve treating patients in hospitals or clinics, and oral and written exams.

From the beginning, Zukle experienced academic difficulty. During her first quarter, she received "Y" grades in Anatomy and Biochemistry.[1]

1. The Medical School assigns letter grades of A, B, C, D, F, I and Y to measure academic performance. A "Y" grade in a pre-clinical course is provisional; it means that a student has earned a failing grade but will be or has been permitted to retake the exam. However, a "Y"

Upon reexamination, her Biochemistry grade was converted to a "D." She did not convert her Anatomy grade at that time. In her second quarter, she received a "Y" grade in Human Physiology, which she converted to a "D" upon reexamination.

In April 1992, the Medical School referred Zukle to the Student Evaluation Committee ("SEC"). Although subject to dismissal pursuant to the Medical School's bylaws, Zukle was allowed to remain in school. The SEC (1) placed Zukle on academic probation, (2) required her to retake Anatomy and Biochemistry, (3) required her to be tested for a learning disability, and (4) placed her on a "split curriculum," meaning that she was given three years to complete the pre-clinical program, instead of the usual two years. Zukle continued to experience academic difficulty. For the spring quarter of 1992 (while on academic probation) she received a "Y" grade in Neurobiology. In the fall, she received a "Y" grade in Medical Microbiology and in the winter she received a "Y" in Principles of Pharmacology. In total, Zukle received eight "Y" grades during the pre-clinical portion of her studies. Five were converted to "C" after reexamination, two to "D" and one to "F."

In November 1992, Zukle was tested for a learning disability. The results received in January 1993, revealed that Zukle suffered from a reading disability which "affects visual processing as it relates to reading comprehension and rate when under timed constraints." In short, it takes Zukle longer to read and to absorb information than the average person.[5] Zukle asked Christine O'Dell, Coordinator of the University's Learning Disability Resource Center, to inform the Medical School of her test results in mid-July 1993. O'Dell informed Gail Currie of the Office of Student Affairs in a letter dated July 21, 1993. O'Dell recommended that the Medical School make various accommodations for Zukle's disability and recommended various techniques for Zukle to try to increase her reading comprehension. The Medical School offered all of these accommodations to Zukle.

After completing the pre-clinical portion of Medical School, Zukle took the United States Medical Licensing Exam, Part I ("USMLE") in June 1994. Shortly thereafter, she began her first clinical clerkship, OB–GYN. During this clerkship, Zukle learned that she had failed the USLME.[6] The Medical School allowed Zukle to interrupt her OB–GYN clerkship to take a six-week review course to prepare to retake the USMLE, for which the Medical School paid.

Before leaving school to take the USMLE review course offered in southern California, Zukle asked Donal A. Walsh, the Associate Dean of Curricular Affairs, if she could rearrange her clerkship schedule. At this point, Zukle had completed the first half of her OB–GYN clerkship. She

---

grade in a clinical clerkship indicates unsatisfactory performance in a major portion of that clerkship and may not be converted until the student repeats that portion of the clerkship.

5. Under timed conditions, Zukle's reading comprehension is in the 2nd percentile, whereas when untimed her comprehension is in the 83rd percentile.

6. Zukle's score placed her in the 5th percentile nationally.

asked Dean Walsh if, instead of completing the second half of her OB–GYN clerkship upon return from retaking the USMLE, she could start the first half of a Family Practice Clerkship, and then repeat the OB–GYN clerkship in its entirety at a later date. Zukle testified that she made this request because she was concerned about how far behind she would be when she returned from the USMLE review course. She further asserted that she thought that if she started the Family Practice clerkship (which apparently requires less reading than the OB–GYN clerkship), she would be able to read for her upcoming Medicine clerkship at night. Zukle testified that Dean Walsh, and several other faculty members, including the Instructor of Record for Family Practice and the Instructor of Record for OB–GYN, initially approved her request. Later, however, Dean Walsh denied Zukle's request and informed her that she had to complete the OB–GYN clerkship before beginning another clerkship.

In September 1994, Zukle took and passed the USMLE on her second attempt.[7] She returned to the Medical School and finished her OB–GYN clerkship. Without requesting any accommodations, she began her Medicine clerkship. During this clerkship, she learned that she had earned a "Y" grade in her OB–GYN clerkship. Because of this grade, Zukle was automatically placed back on academic probation.[8]

Two weeks before the Medicine written exam, Zukle contacted her advisor, Dr. Joseph Silva, and expressed concern that she had not completed the required reading. Dr. Silva offered to speak with Dr. Ruth Lawrence, the Medicine Instructor of Record, on Zukle's behalf. According to Zukle, she then spoke with Dr. Lawrence in person and requested time off from the clerkship to prepare for the exam. Dr. Lawrence denied Zukle's request. Zukle passed the written exam, but failed the Medicine clerkship because of unsatisfactory clinical performance. On Zukle's grade sheet, Dr. Lawrence rated Zukle as unsatisfactory in clinical problem solving skills; data acquisition, organization and recording; and skill/ability at oral presentations. Dr. Lawrence also reported negative comments from the people who worked with Zukle during the clerkship. Because Zukle had earned a failing grade while on academic probation, she was again subject to dismissal pursuant to the Medical School's bylaws.

On January 13, 1995, Zukle appeared before the SEC. The SEC recommended that Zukle (1) drop her current clerkship, Pediatrics; (2) start reviewing for the OB–GYN exam, and retake it; (3) repeat the Medicine clerkship in its entirety; (4) obtain the approval of the SEC before enrolling in any more clerkships; and (5) remain on academic probation for the rest of her medical school career.

On January 17, 1995, the Promotions Board met to consider Zukle's case. The Promotions Board voted to dismiss Zukle from the Medical

---

7. Zukle's score placed her in the 9th percentile nationally.

8. The Promotions Board had voted to remove Zukle from academic probation in October 1994. At that time, it was unaware of her OB–GYN clerkship grade. The Medical School's bylaws provide that a student who receives a "Y" grade in her third or fourth years is automatically placed on academic probation at the time of receipt of the grade.

School for "failure to meet the academic standards of the School of Medicine." According to Dr. Lewis, who was a member of the Promotions Board and was present when it reached its decision, "the Promotions Board considered Plaintiff's academic performance throughout her tenure at the medical school and determined that it demonstrated an incapacity to develop or use the skills and knowledge required to competently practice medicine."

The Board on Student Dismissal voted unanimously to uphold the Promotions Board's decision of dismissal.

On January 22, 1996, Zukle filed a complaint in federal district court for damages and injunctive relief against the Regents of the University of California ("Regents"). The complaint alleged discrimination based on disability, sex and race, and sexual harassment. On June 6, 1997, the Regents filed a motion for summary judgment. The district court entered its Memorandum of Opinion and Order on August 7, 1997, granting summary judgment to The Regents on all of Zukle's claims. The court found that Zukle's "race, sex, and sexual harassment claims are unsupported by the record and do not merit discussion." On Zukle's Americans with Disabilities Act ("ADA") and Rehabilitation Act claims, the district court found that "[b]ecause the evidence before the court shows that Zukle could not meet the minimum standards of the UCD School of Medicine with reasonable accommodation, she is not an otherwise qualified individual with a disability under the Rehabilitation Act or the ADA."

Zukle timely appeals from the district court's grant of summary judgment on her ADA and Rehabilitation Act claims.

II

Zukle claims that she was dismissed from the Medical School in violation of Title II of the ADA and section 504 of the Rehabilitation Act. Title II of the ADA provides, in relevant part:

> no qualified individual with a disability shall, by reason of such disability, be excluded from participation in or be denied the benefits of the services, programs, or activities of a public entity, or be subjected to discrimination by any such entity. 42 U.S.C. § 12132.

Title II prohibits discrimination by state and local agencies, which includes publicly funded institutions of higher education.

Title II of the ADA was expressly modeled after Section 504 of the Rehabilitation Act, which provides:

> No otherwise qualified individual with a disability ... shall, solely by reason of her or his disability, be excluded from the participation in, be denied the benefits of, or be subjected to discrimination under any program or activity receiving Federal financial assistance.... 29 U.S.C. § 794.

To make out a prima facie case under either the ADA or Rehabilitation Act Zukle must show that (1) she is disabled under the Act; (2) she is "otherwise qualified" to remain a student at the Medical School, i.e., she can meet the essential eligibility requirements of the school, with or without reasonable accommodation; (3) she was dismissed solely because of her disability; and (4) the Medical School receives federal financial assistance (for the Rehabilitation Act claim), or is a public entity (for the ADA claim).[11]

The Regents do not dispute that Zukle is disabled and that the Medical School receives federal financial assistance and is a public entity. The Regents argue, however, that Zukle was not "otherwise qualified" to remain at the Medical School. Zukle responds that she *was* "otherwise qualified" with the aid of reasonable accommodations and that the Medical School failed reasonably to accommodate her.

A

The ADA defines a "qualified individual with a disability" as one who "meets the essential eligibility requirements ... for participation in [a given] program[ ] provided by a public entity" "*with or without reasonable modifications* to rules, policies, or practices...." 42 U.S.C. § 12131(2) (emphasis added); *accord* Southeastern Community College v. Davis, 442 U.S. 397, 406, 99 S. Ct. 2361 (1979) (holding that under the Rehabilitation Act, an otherwise qualified individual is "one who is able to meet all of a program's requirements in spite of his handicap"). In the school context, the implementing regulations of the Rehabilitation Act define an otherwise qualified individual as an individual who, although disabled, "meets the academic and technical standards requisite to admission or participation in the [school's] education program or activity."

However, under Rehabilitation Act regulations, educational institutions are required to provide a disabled student with reasonable accommodations to ensure that the institution's requirements do not discriminate on the basis of the student's disability. Similarly, the ADA's implementing regulations require a public entity to "make reasonable modifications in policies, practices, or procedures when the modifications are necessary to avoid discrimination on the basis of disability, unless the public entity can demonstrate that making the modifications would fundamentally alter the nature of the services, program, or activity." The Supreme Court has made clear that an educational institution is not required to make fundamental or substantial modifications to its program or standards; it need only make reasonable ones.

* * *

C

* * *

We agree with the First, Second and Fifth circuits that an educational institution's academic decisions are entitled to deference. Thus, while we

---

11. There is no significant difference in analysis of the rights and obligations created by the ADA and the Rehabilitation Act. *See* 42 U.S.C. § 12133 ("The remedies, procedures, and rights set forth in [the Rehabilitation Act] shall be the remedies, procedures, and rights [applicable to ADA claims].") * * *

recognize that the ultimate determination of whether an individual is otherwise qualified must be made by the court, we will extend judicial deference "to the evaluation made by the institution itself, absent proof that its standards and its application of them serve no purpose other than to deny an education to handicapped persons."

Deference is also appropriately accorded an educational institution's determination that a reasonable accommodation is not available. Therefore, we agree with the First Circuit that "a court's duty is to first find the basic facts, giving due deference to the school, and then to evaluate whether those facts add up to a professional, academic judgment that reasonable accommodation is not available."

We recognize that extending deference to educational institutions must not impede our obligation to enforce the ADA and the Rehabilitation Act. Thus, we must be careful not to allow academic decisions to disguise truly discriminatory requirements. The educational institution has a "real obligation ... to seek suitable means of reasonably accommodating a handicapped person and to submit a factual record indicating that it conscientiously carried out this statutory obligation." Once the educational institution has fulfilled this obligation, however, we will defer to its academic decisions.

III

* * * [W]e now turn to the ultimate question—did Zukle establish a prima facie case of discrimination under the ADA or the Rehabilitation Act? As noted before, only the "otherwise qualified" prong of the prima facie case requirements is disputed by the parties. Zukle argues that she was otherwise qualified to remain at the Medical School, with the aid of the three accommodations she requested. The Medical School argues that Zukle's requested accommodations were not reasonable because they would have required a fundamental or substantial modification of its program.

Zukle bears the burden of pointing to the existence of a reasonable accommodation that would enable her to meet the Medical School's essential eligibility requirements. Once she meets this burden, the Medical School must show that Zukle's requested accommodation would fundamentally alter the nature of the school's program. We must determine, viewing the evidence in the light most favorable to Zukle, if there are any genuine issues of material fact with regard to the reasonableness of Zukle's requested accommodations.

We note at this stage that "[r]easonableness is not a constant. To the contrary, what is reasonable in a particular situation may not be reasonable in a different situation-even if the situational differences are relatively slight." Thus, we must evaluate Zukle's requests in light of the totality of her circumstances.

The evidence is undisputed that the Medical School offered Zukle all of the accommodations that it normally offers learning disabled students. When the Medical School first learned of Zukle's disability she was offered double time on exams, notetaking services and textbooks on audio cassettes. Further, Zukle was allowed to retake courses, proceed on a decelerated schedule and remain at the Medical School despite being subject to dismissal under the Medical School's bylaws.

Even with these accommodations, Zukle consistently failed to achieve passing grades in her courses. Though Zukle was on a decelerated schedule, she continued to receive "Y" grades in her pre-clinical years and failed the USMLE on her first attempt. Further, although she was able to remedy some of her failing grades in her pre-clinical years, she was only able to do so by retaking exams. Moreover, she received a "Y" grade in her first clinical clerkship, automatically placing her on academic probation, and an "F" in her second. Because Zukle received a failing grade while on academic probation, she was subject to dismissal pursuant to the Medical School's bylaws. Clearly, Zukle could not meet the Medical School's essential eligibility requirements without the additional accommodations she requested.

The issue, then, is whether the ADA and Rehabilitation Act required the Medical School to provide Zukle with those additional accommodations. As noted above, the Medical School was only required to provide Zukle with *reasonable* accommodations. Accordingly, we examine the reasonableness of Zukle's requested accommodations.

A

Zukle claims that the Medical School should have granted her request to modify her schedule by beginning the first half of the Family Practice Clerkship instead of finishing the second half of her OB–GYN clerkship when she returned from retaking the USMLE. She proposed that she would then begin the Medicine clerkship, and finish Family Practice and OB–GYN at a later time.

The Regents presented evidence that granting this request would require a substantial modification of its curriculum.

    * * *

The facts are undisputed that no student had been allowed to rearrange their clerkship schedule as Zukle requested. Indeed, Zukle admitted in the district court that "no student has been permitted to finish an interrupted course in the fashion [she] requested because it would require substantial curricular alteration." We defer to the Medical School's academic decision to require students to complete courses once they are begun and conclude, therefore, that this requested accommodation was not reasonable.

B

Two weeks before the scheduled written exam in her Medicine clerkship, Zukle asked Dr. Silva, her advisor, if she could have more time to prepare for the exam because she was behind in the readings. Zukle testified that she specifically requested to leave the hospital early every day so that she could spend more time preparing for the written exam in Medicine. Dr. Silva and Zukle spoke with the Instructor of Record in Zukle's Medicine clerkship, Dr. Lawrence. Dr. Lawrence told Zukle that she could not excuse her from the in-hospital part of the clerkship. Dr. Lawrence testified that she denied this request because she thought that it would be unfair to the other students.

The Medical School presented uncontradicted evidence that giving Zukle reduced clinical time would have fundamentally altered the nature of the Medical School curriculum.

* * *

We defer to the Medical School's academic decision that the in-hospital portion of a clerkship is a vital part of medical education and that allowing a student to be excused from this requirement would sacrifice the integrity of its program. Thus, we conclude that neither the ADA nor the Rehabilitation Act require the Medical School to make this accommodation.

In any event, the evidence shows that Zukle was not prejudiced by the Medical School's failure to grant this accommodation because she in fact passed the Medicine written exam. Zukle's low score on the exam did not help her Medicine grade, but Zukle failed the clerkship because of her inadequate clinical performance. Indeed, as the district court stated, because Zukle was doing so poorly in the clinical portion of the clerkship, "[g]iving [her] time off from the clinical portion to study for the test[ ] could not have helped, but could only have further damaged, her already marginal clinical skills." Thus, Zukle did not establish that she would have been able to meet the Medical School's requirements with the requested accommodation.

C

Finally, after she was dismissed, Zukle requested that the *ad hoc* Board place her on a decelerated schedule during the clinical portion of her studies. Specifically, Zukle sought eight weeks off before each clerkship to read the assigned text for that clerkship in its entirety.

Zukle presented evidence that the Medical School regularly allowed students to proceed on a decelerated schedule. Indeed, Zukle herself was allowed an extra year to complete the pre-clinical curriculum. However, no student had been provided the specific accommodation that Zukle requested, *i.e.*, taking eight weeks off between clerkships. Furthermore, simply because the Medical School had granted other students' requests to proceed on a decelerated schedule, does not mean that Zukle's request was reasonable. The reasonableness of Zukle's request must be evaluated in light of Zukle's particular circumstances.

We agree with the district court that the Board's denial of Zukle's request to proceed on a decelerated schedule was a "rationally justifiable conclusion." The Board noted that, even on a decelerated schedule during the pre-clinical phase, Zukle experienced severe academic difficulties: Zukle earned deficient grades in five courses and failed the USMLE exam on her first attempt even though she had taken several pre-clinical courses twice. The Board noted that there is "a fair amount of overlap on written exams of material from second-year courses and that the clinical work overlaps with the written." In sum, the evidence makes clear that the decelerated schedule would not have aided Zukle in meeting the Medical School's academic standards. Given Zukle's unenviable academic record, allowing her to remain in Medical School on a decelerated schedule would have lowered the Medical School's academic standards, which it was not required to do to accommodate Zukle.

IV

In conclusion, we are persuaded that Zukle failed to establish that she could meet the essential eligibility requirements of the Medical School with the aid of reasonable accommodations. Accordingly, she failed to establish a prima facie case of disability discrimination under the ADA or the Rehabilitation Act.

AFFIRMED.

STEERE v. GEORGE WASHINGTON UNIVERSITY SCHOOL OF MEDICINE AND HEALTH SCIENCES

439 F.Supp.2d 17 (D.D.C. 2006)

FINDINGS OF FACT AND CONCLUSIONS OF LAW

LAMBERTH, DISTRICT JUDGE.

This case arises from a dispute between plaintiff Eric Steere, and the medical school that dismissed him from its program, defendant the George Washington University School of Medicine and Health Sciences ("G.W").

* * * Based on all of the evidence presented, the Court makes the following findings of fact and conclusions of law and will, consistent with them, enter judgment in favor of defendant and against plaintiff.

FINDINGS OF FACT

1. Mr. Steere's educational history reveals many academic achievements, along with some instances of poor performance and some indications of difficulty focusing. * * *

(f) Upon entering a graduate program in physical therapy, plaintiff reports that he repeatedly failed his tests until his professors enabled him to take his exams in an oral format.

(g) Mr. Steere also reports that he was easily distracted when he studied on his own in a place where others were present, but that studying as part of an interactive group improved his concentration greatly, as did studying alone in a completely silent environment.

(h) Tests sometimes posed a problem for Mr. Steere. After approximately an hour, he found his mind drifting. He attempted to ameliorate this problem by taking short breaks during which he would eat and drink. On time-pressured tests, however, this practice left him without sufficient time to read and answer each question on the test. When he noticed that time was running low, he would complete the remaining answers randomly. Accordingly, his performance suffered.

2.   Mr. Steere reports that he had difficulty remaining attentive in non-academic environments. * * *

3.   Mr. Steere was a student at GW in the regular four-year doctor of medicine program from the fall of 2000 until the spring of 2003. * * *

6.   Mr. Steere struggled academically at GW. * * *

7.   Throughout his struggles in medical school, Mr. Steere consulted with numerous sources in an effort to improve his performance. First, he visited the University's counseling center in December 2000 for test anxiety and insomnia, but he did not complete the recommended treatment. Second, he met with psychiatrist Dr. Garro in the spring of 2001, complaining of the same symptoms. Dr. Garro wanted to continue seeing plaintiff, but Mr. Steere discontinued treatment after a few visits. Third, plaintiff visited the University's Disability Support Services Center in January 2003.

8.   After being called before the Medical Student Evaluation Committee ("MSEC") in January 2003, Mr. Steere visited with Dr. Dorothy Kaplan and was tested for a learning disability.

(a) Dr. Kaplan is a clinical psychologist. While the bulk of her experience is in the area of brain injury rehabilitation, she has some experience in diagnosing and treating young adults with learning disorders. Currently, Dr. Kaplan is in private practice, where she conducts, each week, approximately three assessments for learning disabilities.

(b) After interviewing and testing plaintiff, Dr. Kaplan issued a written evaluation in which she concluded that Mr. Steere suffered from two learning disabilities: attention deficit hyperactivity disorder ("ADHD"), inattentive type; and a math learning disorder.

(c) Based on the learning disabilities Dr. Kaplan identified, she made several recommendations to accommodate plaintiff, including that he receive time and a half to complete his examinations.

9.   Dean Williams received Dr. Kaplan's report prior to his meeting with Mr. Steere in April 2003. Dean Williams concedes that, while he did read Dr. Kaplan's report, it had no effect on his decision to dismiss plaintiff for academic reasons.

10.   While the dean's ordinary practice is to notify students by mail of their dismissal from the program for academic reasons, he did not do so in this case. Dean Williams attributes the failure to send a letter to an administrative oversight by his office.

11.   After his dismissal from GW, plaintiff enrolled in the doctor of medicine program at the American University of the Caribbean, an unaccredited program. Plaintiff has been achieving passing grades in that program.

CONCLUSIONS OF LAW

I. Legal Standard

Plaintiff claims that GW's failure to offer reasonable accommodations before dismissing him constitutes discrimination in violation of 12182(a) of the ADA. That section provides:

> No individual shall be discriminated against on the basis of disability in the full and equal enjoyment of the goods, services, facilities, privileges, advantages, or accommodations of any place of public accommodation by any person who owns, leases (or leases to), or operates a place of public accommodation.

42 U.S.C. 12182(a).

As this Court noted in *Steere,* 368 F.Supp.2d at 55, plaintiff must establish a violation of this provision by demonstrating "1) that he has a disability; (2) that he is otherwise qualified for the benefit in question; and (3) that he was excluded from the benefit due to discrimination because of the disability." This Court shall consider, under a preponderance standard, each element in turn.

As to the first element, to prove that he has a disability under the ADA, plaintiff must demonstrate that (1) he has an impairment (2) that is related to a major life activity (3) and that substantially limits that major life activity. *Haynes v. Williams,* 392 F.3d 478, 481–82 (D.C.Cir.2004) (citing 12102(2)(A) of the ADA and construing its language that a protected disability is "a physical or mental impairment that substantially limits one or more of the major life activities of [an] individual").

II. Analysis

A. Impairment

Based on the evidence presented at trial, this Court does not find that plaintiff has a disability as defined by the ADA and case law. Plaintiff has submitted insufficient evidence that his academic struggles at GW are due to a learning disability. Specifically, this Court finds that plaintiff has failed to prove by a preponderance that his symptoms satisfy the elements required before one can be diagnosed with ADHD.

Expert testimony indicated that a key factor in diagnosing ADHD is early developmental onset.[2] What evidence plaintiff provides for this element is scant and anecdotal: he claims to have had difficulty learning math, poor handwriting and problems paying attention. He contends that his difficulties continued into middle and high school, and offers as proof

---

2.   Although, as noted *infra,* a diagnosis is not sufficient to prove a disability under the ADA, this Court finds that it is necessary.

the fact that he was a known daydreamer and sometimes fell asleep in class, in church or while driving. This Court finds this evidence to be insufficient. Vague memories of falling asleep, or even of having trouble focusing, do not necessarily establish that one suffers from a disability. To the contrary, in this Court's opinion, very few children would not resemble plaintiff's description at some point in their youthful lives. The factors he describes are characteristically childish: anyone who has been around children knows that they often have trouble paying attention. These scraps of vague memories cannot sufficiently establish that plaintiff satisfies the early onset requirement.

The additional evidence provided by plaintiff also fails to satisfy the standard necessary for him to prevail. The record reveals that plaintiff enjoyed a great deal of academic success throughout his life, including his strength from a young age in areas that require an ability to concentrate and pay attention. Had he the disability that he claims to have, this Court might expect his achievement to have been more consistently impaired. Instead, plaintiff's educational career demonstrates strong academic achievement and ability—his test performance several times resulted in advanced placement, he attended numerous colleges and graduate degree programs, amassing a strong academic record despite personal struggles—and performed extremely well in many subjects. Indeed, to be accepted into the regular doctor of medicine program at GW, one must have a demonstrated record of achievement.

Although this Court accepts that ADHD could certainly affect plaintiff's ability to complete time-pressured multiple choice exams, it does not find that such a diagnosis is consistent with his success on various other academic tasks—undoubtedly some of them requiring concentration—on which he has repeatedly excelled. In any event, it is not consistent with a determination that any impairment substantially affects a major life activity. To the contrary, plaintiff appears quite able to succeed in the major life activity of learning, including test-taking in general.

Similarly, this Court is unconvinced that plaintiff's relatively recent academic difficulty is more likely than not due to ADHD. In his testimony, plaintiff seized upon his claimed learning disorder to explain why he was unable to convey on tests the material he knew that he had learned, but this Court finds, first, that such a discrepancy is not necessarily so unusual in competitive educational environments that it requires some external explanation; and second, that it could be explained by many other factors. Test anxiety, personal struggles, lack of attention to detail, poor studying habits, lack of motivation, poor health, insufficient time devoted to studying—any or all of these factors might explain plaintiff's poor performance at GW and in the physical therapy program. That his poor performance has been a relatively recent phenomenon further supports the conclusion that the cause is due to temporary circumstances rather than a lifelong disability that has impaired, and continues to impair, his ability to perform in academic environments. Indeed, plaintiff's recent struggles are uncharacteristic in light of his academic record, and may simply reflect his inability to successfully adjust to new, more competitive tests. It is possible, even likely, that plaintiff either did not encounter such difficulties in prior, less competitive academic environments, or simply that, in the past, he was better able to compensate for them.

While the preponderance standard does not require plaintiff to rule out every other possible explanation, he must demonstrate that his explanation is more likely than not true. Since this Court finds, however, that many other explanations remain plausible, this Court is not persuaded that plaintiff suffers from a disability as defined by the ADA that has substantially limited his academic performance. The report and testimony of Dr. Kaplan, on which plaintiff heavily relies, is insufficient to convince the Court for two reasons.

First, this Court does not find Dr. Kaplan's testimony and report to be sufficient, in light of the relatively sparse corroborating evidence, to establish plaintiff's claim that he suffers from ADHD. Dr. Kaplan appeared to this Court as generally competent, but she failed to demonstrate that she based her diagnosis of plaintiff on valid and reliable sources. This Court has already discussed the paucity of evidence that plaintiff's symptoms manifested themselves at a young age. Dr. Kaplan also chose to rely upon a questionnaire completed by plaintiff's mother, even though she noted that plaintiff had not lived with his parents for many years and that the questionnaire would ideally have been completed by a person who has been able to "closely observe" the patient.

Additionally, it is not clear that Dr. Kaplan sufficiently ruled out the effect that plaintiff's other conditions might have had on the test results. For example, plaintiff states that he suffers from shade degradation, a condition which prevents him from distinguishing different color hues and contrasts. Dr. Kaplan, however, largely based her diagnosis on a test that required plaintiff to distinguish between different colors. Similarly, Dr. Kaplan employed a test that requires motor dexterity even though she knew that plaintiff suffered from an impairment in that area. More generally, Dr. Kaplan considered several subjective, anecdotal and self-reported factors in arriving at her diagnosis. While clinical observations may be useful to corroborate reliable test results, Dr. Kaplan's reliance upon them as diagnostic tools in the context of potentially unreliable test results may raise questions as to the validity of her diagnosis. In light of all these considerations, this Court finds that Dr. Kaplan's testimony and report failed to persuade this Court that plaintiff's difficulties are due to ADHD.

Second, the Supreme Court has held that a mere diagnosis is not sufficient to establish a disability under the ADA. Rather, plaintiff must offer "evidence that the extent of the limitation in terms of their own experience ... is substantial." *Id.* As discussed in the next section, it is this Court's determination that plaintiff has not demonstrated that the extent of his ADHD is substantial in terms of his own experience.

B. *Substantial Limitation of Major Life Activity*

Plaintiff's own experience is replete with academic successes. He performed very well in a number of educational environments before he reached graduate school. Plaintiff contends that his ADHD impairs his ability to learn in the following manner: it inhibits his ability to absorb material taught during lectures; it makes it difficult for him to study the material after the lecture; and it impairs his ability to correctly complete test questions in the allotted time. This Court is unpersuaded, however, that his academic record is consistent with such a pattern. Plaintiff's evidence is largely anecdotal and based solely on his memory and his interpretation of events that occurred many years prior. Mr. Steere does not offer sufficient data to establish a consistent pattern of performance over the years of his formal education.

For example, Mr. Steere describes struggling in the physical therapy graduate program. He explains that he was able to bring his failing performance to a passing performance merely by changing the testing format. If he suffers from a disability that impairs him at each step of the learning process, this Court fails to understand how merely changing the testing format would solve the problem. It fails to explain, for example, how he overcame the effects of his claimed impairment in listening to the lectures and in studying the material. Rather, a more likely explanation might be that the test format enabled plaintiff to compensate for whatever non-disability reason accounted for his problems. It is entirely possible that plaintiff was motivated to study harder when he knew that he was facing a panel of professors for an oral exam, rather than multiple choice test. Indeed, a similar pattern appears in plaintiff's medical school experience: after receiving two inadequate grades in his first semester, and taking a leave of absence during his second semester, plaintiff appears to have returned to school with a renewed resolve to succeed. He describes aggressively amassing a study group and devoting a great deal of time to his studies. Not surprisingly, he passed all of his courses that semester.

If one accepts the disability hypothesis, these experiences are difficult to explain. It is unclear to this Court how plaintiff could, at times, overcome his claimed disability by varying his habits and, at other times, find himself utterly defeated by it. It is more likely, in this Court's opinion, that plaintiff's inconsistent performance results from motivational problems or other personal problems that might be expected to manifest differently at different times—and in different environments—in plaintiff's life. Another possibility is that either the material taught, or the type of knowledge sought by the tests, simply varied greatly from a physical therapy program at a local university to a top national medical school program. Plaintiff explains, for example, that the oral exams in the physical therapy program gave him an opportunity to repeat back to his teachers what they had been telling him in class. It may well be that in a competitive medical school environment, simple regurgitation would not have been sufficient to achieve passing grades, regardless of whether it was elicited in written or oral format. Additionally, it goes without saying that medical school, and the skills taught therein, cover a far broader range of complex material, and that successful doctors must be able to synthesize a great deal of material and view a patient in the context of innumerable factors. Physical therapy, while undoubtedly a challenging and complex subject, is nonetheless a narrower subject. That plaintiff might succeed in physical therapy while failing in medical school is not a discrepancy that is most likely explained by ADHD.

More generally, if plaintiff has an impairment that substantially interferes with learning in such broad areas as listening, studying and test-taking, this Court would expect such interference to consistently appear throughout similar academic environments. Indeed, as compared to someone who took a more traditional path of attending one college and one medical school, plaintiff's attendance in numerous college and graduate programs[8] should provide ample sources in which to locate such a pattern. His recent failures in medical school, and relatively poor performance on some tests prior to medical school, have not been shown to be the result of his claimed impairment.

It should also be noted that defendant's expert witness, Dr. Rick Ostrander, has extensive experience in the field of assessing learning disabilities. He testified that, in his professional opinion, plaintiff's achievement in medical school was not necessarily inconsistent with his abilities. Dr. Ostrander noted that Dr. Kaplan's tests may have been affected by plaintiff's other conditions, such as color blindness and lack of manual dexterity. Finally, Dr. Ostrander also called into question the reliability of the tests Dr. Kaplan chose to administer: it is his professional opinion that low scores on the tests have not been proven to correlate with the presence of disabilities. That is, the tests do a poor job of "discriminat[ing] between normals and ADHD." This Court finds Dr. Ostrander's testimony, on the whole, to be credible and persuasive.

In light of all the evidence, this Court finds that there are many other factors that could have impaired plaintiff's ability to perform well on tests-some of which were the result of plaintiff's own choices and study habits. Plaintiff has failed to demonstrate that his low scores on certain tests were the result of ADHD. Thus, those low scores are not sufficient to convince this Court that he has a disability as defined by the ADA. Similarly, considering all of the evidence plaintiff offered, taken together, and in light of defendant's evidence, this Court finds that plaintiff fails to establish by a preponderance that he suffers from a learning disability cognizable under the ADA. Accordingly, he is not entitled to accommodations and defendant cannot be held to have violated the ADA by failure to provide him with accommodations. In light of this finding, this Court need not address the remaining elements of an ADA claim; namely, whether plaintiff was otherwise qualified or whether he was discriminated on the basis of a claimed disability.

---

8. The record indicates that plaintiff attended no fewer than seven institutions of higher education over a ten-year period, in which he took a great deal of courses, including all of the pre-medical coursework, language classes, and two-year physical therapy Master's degree program.

As a final note, the Court would like to caution defendant that, as an educational institution, it is obligated to provide reasonable accommodations to students who demonstrate that they are entitled to them under the ADA. Defendant's practice of dismissing a student after receiving documentation of the student's disability—and without even considering whether the disability exists—is imprudent given the possibility that the student actually does suffer from a disability under the ADA. If the request for reasonable accommodations is received prior to the official dismissal, as it was in this case, defendant must consider it before issuing its final decision whether to dismiss the student. This is necessary not only so that defendant can avoid being held liable in a lawsuit where a plaintiff prevails, but also because defendant ought to be concerned about whether students truly have learning disabilities. A well-regarded institution of higher learning, such as George Washington University, should be committed to the success of all its students, and surely that entails a sincere evaluation of their abilities and needs before issuing a decision to dismiss them.

CONCLUSION

For the foregoing reasons, judgment consistent with these findings of fact and conclusions of law shall be entered for defendant. * * *

NOTES

1. People with disabilities continue to face major hurdles on every level when they seek accommodations in testing situations. With regard to legal education and related matters, for example, the LSAT and the bar exam appear to pose the greatest hurdles of all, with applicants who seek accommodations often reporting that they are treated by the Law School Admissions Council (LSAC) and Committees of Bar Examiners as if the presumption is that they are lying. For additional perspectives on testing issues in this context, *see, e.g.,* Helia Garrido Hull, *Equal Access to Post–Secondary Education: The Sisyphean Impact of Flagging Test Scores of Persons with Disabilities,* 55 Cleveland State Law Review 15 (2007); Dylan Gallagher, *Wong v. Regents of the University of California: The ADA, Learning Disabled Students, and the Spirit of Icarus,* 16 George Mason University Civil Rights Law Journal 153 (2005).

2. In Turner v. Association of American Medical Colleges (AAMC), 167 Cal.App.4th 1401, 85 Cal.Rptr.3d 94 (1 Dist. 2008), the Court considered the question of "whether persons taking standardized tests in California are entitled to additional accommodations under the state's Unruh Civil Rights Act (Unruh Act) and Disabled Persons Act (DPA)." Plaintiffs were applicants to medical school with reading-related learning disabilities and/or ADHD who applied to take the MCAT and requested more time and/or a private room. After the AAMC denied their request, they filed a class action lawsuit, joined by two national disability rights organizations. Their complaint alleged that their requests for accommodations "should have been considered under these state laws, which define 'disability' more broadly than the Americans with

Disabilities Act (ADA) to include a mental, psychological or physical condition that 'limits a major life activity,' i.e., that 'makes the achievement of the major life activity difficult.' " The Court found in favor of the defendants:

> Individuals with learning and reading-related disabilities affecting their ability to rapidly process written information are entitled to reasonable accommodations when taking the MCAT, assuming they suffer from an impairment that "substantially limits" the major life activities of reading and/or test-taking within the meaning of the ADA. AAMC is not required to utilize the more inclusive standard for assessing disabilities under the Unruh Act and DPA. * * *

> We emphasize that our holding today is a narrow one-that the Unruh Act and DPA do not, by their own terms, require performance-related accommodations (additional time, private rooms) for MCAT applicants with learning or reading-related disabilities. There was no allegation by plaintiffs that MCAT applicants with purely physical disabilities had been denied reasonable accommodations for those disabilities, and we have no occasion to consider whether the Unruh Act or DPA would apply in such a situation. We also emphasize that plaintiffs asserted no cause of action based on a violation of the ADA, and that the issue of whether AAMC has properly applied ADA standards to accommodation requests is not before us.

3. In a related matter, it is important to note that advances in technology are increasingly enabling persons with disabilities to complete tasks in an education setting that may not have been possible in the past. Disputes over access to such technologies have generated additional issues under the law and as a matter of policy. For example, in 2008, a highly publicized lawsuit challenging the refusal of Target to make the minor changes that would enable visually impaired persons to have access to the company Web sites was settled. The lawsuit, *National Federation of the Blind v. Target Corporation,* No. C 06–01802 MHP, was seen as bellweather case for disability rights advocates across the board. *See generally* Evan Hill, *Settlement Over Target's Web Site Marks a Win for ADA Plaintiffs,* The Recorder, August 28, 2008:

> * * * Target Corp. will pay out $6 million in damages and make its Web site fully accessible to blind customers as part of a class action settlement filed on Wednesday.

> The National Federation of the Blind, which sued the Minneapolis-based corporation in 2006 in San Francisco federal court for maintaining a site that blind people said they couldn't use, will also be paid to oversee the changes and train the coders responsible for reprogramming the site.

> The case will "send a message to the entire Internet industry that access for people with disabilities is not only good business sense but an absolutely legal civil right; it's mandatory," said Laurence Paradis, a lawyer at Berkeley, Calif.-based Disability Rights Advocates who worked on the case.

> Target released a statement saying it was "pleased to have resolved the matter" and has made changes to its Web site "to improve the experience for guests who require assistive technology." * * *

Blind people can use specialized keyboards as well as software that converts Web sites and documents into speech or Braille. But such technology won't work if a site is improperly coded, as the plaintiffs alleged about Target.com. The case pressed the legal question of whether the protections of the federal Americans with Disabilities Act could be extended to businesses' Web sites.

Paradis said Target fought the suit "tooth and nail" and that settlement negotiations broke down twice, first because the company wouldn't agree to fix the problems and second because the two sides couldn't agree on damages. Only after Northern District of California Judge Marilyn Hall Patel certified a state and national class in November 2007 was a settlement possible, he said. * * *

Patel's rulings that the federal ADA and state Unruh Civil Rights Act both apply to businesses' Web sites were particularly crucial, Paradis said. * * *

Daniel Goldstein, a Baltimore-based attorney at Brown, Goldstein & Levy who has represented the Federation for 20 years and worked on the case, said the Target suit is a "bellwether case in that it announces loud and clear to those who have Web sites that they need to be accessible to everyone."

"The cost of making a Web site accessible, if it's done at the beginning, is fairly nominal," he said, "and the increase in market share is always going to be greater than the cost." * * *

CHAPTER VIII

RELIGION AND PUBLIC EDUCATION: DETERMINING THE SHIFTING CONTOURS OF ESTABLISHMENT CLAUSE JURISPRUDENCE

■ ■ ■

This chapter provides an introduction to the interplay between religion and public education, as reflected in the development of First Amendment Establishment Clause jurisprudence. In general, public education is expected to be secular in nature, with parents having the right to send their children to private sectarian schools if they wish to provide them with an education that is religious in nature. But cases and statutes recognize numerous instances where religion-related expression and activities can in fact take place in a public educational setting. And there is an ongoing battle over boundaries in this regard.

A basic principle that appears often in both Establishment Clause and Free Exercise Clause cases over time is that the nature and extent of the religion that can be included by public officials in public sector activities is not dependent on what percentage of people may be members of a particular religion, practitioners of a particular sect or denomination, or affiliated with organized religion at all. Justice O'Connor described this principle in her analysis of the issues in the 2005 Kentucky Ten Commandments case:

> * * * The First Amendment expresses our Nation's fundamental commitment to religious liberty by means of two provisions—one protecting the free exercise of religion, the other barring establishment of religion. They were written by the descendents of people who had come to this land precisely so that they could practice their religion freely. Together with the other First Amendment guarantees—of free speech, a free press, and the rights to assemble and petition—the Religion Clauses were designed to safeguard the freedom of conscience and belief that those immigrants had sought. They embody an idea that was once considered radical: Free people are

622

entitled to free and diverse thoughts, which government ought neither to constrain nor to direct.

Reasonable minds can disagree about how to apply the Religion Clauses in a given case. But the goal of the Clauses is clear: to carry out the Founders' plan of preserving religious liberty to the fullest extent possible in a pluralistic society. By enforcing the Clauses, we have kept religion a matter for the individual conscience, not for the prosecutor or bureaucrat. * * *

Our guiding principle has been James Madison's—that "[t]he Religion . . . of every man must be left to the conviction and conscience of every man." To that end, we have held that the guarantees of religious freedom protect citizens from religious incursions by the States as well as by the Federal Government. Government may not coerce a person into worshiping against her will, nor prohibit her from worshiping according to it. It may not prefer one religion over another or promote religion over nonbelief. It may not entangle itself with religion. And government may not, by "endorsing religion or a religious practice," "mak[e] adherence to religion relevant to a person's standing in the political community."

When we enforce these restrictions, we do so for the same reason that guided the Framers—respect for religion's special role in society. Our Founders conceived of a Republic receptive to voluntary religious expression, and provided for the possibility of judicial intervention when government action threatens or impedes such expression. Voluntary religious belief and expression may be as threatened when government takes the mantle of religion upon itself as when government directly interferes with private religious practices. When the government associates one set of religious beliefs with the state and identifies nonadherents as outsiders, it encroaches upon the individual's decision about whether and how to worship. In the marketplace of ideas, the government has vast resources and special status. Government religious expression therefore risks crowding out private observance and distorting the natural interplay between competing beliefs. Allowing government to be a potential mouthpiece for competing religious ideas risks the sort of division that might easily spill over into suppression of rival beliefs. Tying secular and religious authority together poses risks to both. * * *

It is true that many Americans find the Commandments in accord with their personal beliefs. But we do not count heads before enforcing the First Amendment. * * * Nor can we accept the theory that Americans who do not accept the Commandments' validity are outside the First Amendment's protections. There is no list of approved and disapproved beliefs appended to the First Amendment—and the Amendment's broad terms ("free exercise," "establishment," "religion") do not admit of such a cramped reading. It is true that the Framers lived at a time when our national religious diversity was neither as robust nor as well recognized as it is now. They may not have foreseen the variety of religions for which this Nation would eventually provide a home. They surely could not have predicted new religions, some of them born in this country. But they did know that line-drawing between religions is an enterprise that, once begun, has no logical stopping point. They worried that "the same authority which can establish Christianity, in exclusion of all other Religions, may establish with the same ease any particular sect of Christians, in exclusion of all other Sects." The Religion Clauses, as a result, protect adherents of all religions, as well as those who believe in no religion at all. * * * McCreary County v. ACLU, 125 S.Ct. 2722, 2746–47 (2005) (O'Connor, J., concurring).

A significant percentage of the U.S. Supreme Court's Establishment Clause cases over the past 35 years have focused on the public schools, and the seminal case of *Lemon v. Kurtzman* was itself an education-related dispute. In *Lemon,* the Court considered the constitutionality of public aid to private sectarian schools in Pennsylvania and Rhode Island, and in so doing set forth a three-part test. Under this test, a statute or policy would be violative of the Establishment Clause if any one of the following could be proven: (1) its purpose is not secular, (2) its principal/ primary effect either advances or inhibits religion, or (3) it fosters an excessive entanglement with religion.

While the inquiry in *Lemon* was limited to the constitutionality of public funding for private religious education, subsequent cases began to apply the tripartite test in virtually every Establishment Clause dispute that arose. Over time, however, many came to believe that this approach was inappropriately "hostile to religion." Not only was the *Lemon* test itself ultimately modified, but additional Establishment Clause frameworks were developed, with the justices struggling to identify guidelines that would help determine which principles and frameworks to apply in what types of situations.

The broad, general framework for all Establishment Clause disputes continues to reflect a foundational inquiry into *purpose* and *effects.* This chapter thus begins with an examination of key cases, both before *Lemon* and subsequent to *Lemon,* which show the Court wrestling with this inquiry. The chapter then goes on to document the emergence of additional inquiries focusing on endorsement, coercion, and perhaps on neutrality alone. While some commentators and jurists have viewed these as components of the broader inquiry into purpose and effects, others have insisted that they stand alone as separate and independent tests.

Establishment Clause jurisprudence remains relatively unsettled, with lower courts—unsure of which frameworks and principles to apply— sometimes taking the time to conduct as many as 3–4 separate analytical inquiries in a single case decision. But multiple inquiries are not generally found in the individual opinions at the Supreme Court level. And recognizable patterns are in fact beginning to emerge. In a school setting, for example, endorsement is typically found to be an appropriate test for displays and programs. A coercion test is applied within the context of school prayer. And neutrality is arguably a central principle underlying the inquiry into public funding for private religious education.

PROBLEM 38: UNITED PARENTS OF NEWMAN COUNTY v. NCUSD

Every semester, from time to time, Ms. Mayberry reads Bible stories to her second graders. These stories are children's versions of events described in the Holy Bible. To the best of anyone's recollection, this pattern has continued for at least ten years.

The Newman County Unified School District agrees to provide each classroom teacher with a check for $1,000, which "may be used at the teacher's individual discretion to provide additional resources to his or her classroom." As a condition of receiving this money, teachers are required to complete a simple form, documenting their expenditures and attaching receipts. An administrator at each school site is appointed to review these forms, and this review is generally *pro forma*.

Many teachers use the funds to pay for the duplication of materials that were once paid for out of their own pockets. Others use the funds for supplies. Ms. Mayberry decides to use a portion of the funds to purchase new editions of books with children's versions of Bible stories.

Every year, Ms. Mayberry turns her room into a "World's Fair" as a culminating activity for her World Religions and Culture Unit. She decides to use a portion of her funds to purchase primary religious texts, religious objects, and religious paintings to enhance the World's Fair Pavilions depicting the world's major religions.

After failing in their informal attempts to restrict Ms. Mayberry's activities and expenditures in this context, a coalition of Newman County parents files a lawsuit against the District, contending that the First Amendment has been violated. What arguments might be set forth under Establishment Clause jurisprudence? What result? Discuss.

A. THE EVOLVING INQUIRY INTO PURPOSE & EFFECTS

The three cases in this section show the evolution of the Court's Establishment Clause jurisprudence in particularly stark terms. In *Engel v. Vitale,* nine years before *Lemon,* one has to look very hard to discern what may be an implicit focus on purpose and effects. In *Wallace v. Jaffree,* fourteen years after *Lemon,* an arguably splintered majority appears to feel obligated to follow the rigid strictures of the traditional *Lemon* test but is also struggling to move away from its seeming rigidity. In *Agostini v. Felton,* twelve more years down the road, the Court takes the step of explicitly modifying *Lemon,* overruling two *Lemon*-era precedents on the grounds that the jurisprudence has changed, and establishing a more forgiving inquiry.

Consider the opinions of the respective justices in this context. What lessons might be discerned regarding the parameters and viability of the inquiry into purpose and effects today?

ENGEL v. VITALE

370 U.S. 421, 82 S.Ct. 1261 (1962)

MR. JUSTICE BLACK delivered the opinion of the Court.

The respondent Board of Education of Union Free School District No. 9, New Hyde Park, New York, acting in its official capacity under state law, directed the School District's principal to cause the following prayer to be said aloud by each class in the presence of a teacher at the beginning of each school day:

> Almighty God, we acknowledge our dependence upon Thee, and we beg Thy blessings upon us, our parents, our teachers and our Country.

This daily procedure was adopted on the recommendation of the State Board of Regents, a governmental agency created by the State Constitution to which the New York Legislature has granted broad supervisory, executive, and legislative powers over the State's public school system. These state officials composed the prayer which they recommended and published as a part of their "Statement on Moral and Spiritual Training in the Schools," saying: "We believe that this Statement will be subscribed to by all men and women of good will, and we call upon all of them to aid in giving life to our program."

Shortly after the practice of reciting the Regents' prayer was adopted by the School District, the parents of ten pupils brought this action in a New York State Court insisting that use of this official prayer in the public schools was contrary to the beliefs, religions, or religious practices of both themselves and their children. Among other things, these parents challenged the constitutionality of both the state law authorizing the School District to direct the use of prayer in public schools and the School District's regulation ordering the recitation of this particular prayer on the ground that these actions of official governmental agencies violate that part of the First Amendment of the Federal Constitution which commands that "Congress shall make no law respecting an establishment of religion"—a command which was "made applicable to the State of New York by the Fourteenth Amendment of the said Constitution." The New York Court of Appeals, over the dissents of Judges Dye and Fuld, sustained an order of the lower state courts which had upheld the power of New York to use the Regents' prayer as a part of the daily procedures of its public schools so long as the schools did not compel any pupil to join in the prayer over his or his parents' objection. We granted certiorari to review this important decision involving rights protected by the First and Fourteenth Amendments.

We think that by using its public school system to encourage recitation of the Regents' prayer, the State of New York has adopted a practice wholly inconsistent with the Establishment Clause. There can, of course, be no doubt that New York's program of daily classroom invocation of God's blessings as prescribed in the Regents' prayer is a religious activity. It is a solemn avowal of divine faith and supplication for the blessings of the Almighty. The nature of such a prayer has always been religious, none of the respondents has denied this and the trial court expressly so found:

> The religious nature of prayer was recognized by Jefferson and has been concurred in by theological writers, the United States Supreme Court and state courts and administrative officials, including New York's Commissioner of Education. A committee of the New York Legislature has agreed.

> The Board of Regents as amicus curiae, the respondents and intervenors all concede the religious nature of prayer, but seek to distinguish this prayer because it is based on our spiritual heritage. * * *

The petitioners contend among other things that the state laws requiring or permitting use of the Regents' prayer must be struck down as a violation of the Establishment Clause because that prayer was composed by governmental officials as a part of a governmental program to further religious beliefs. For this reason, petitioners argue, the State's use of the Regents' prayer in its public school system breaches the constitutional wall of separation between Church and State. We agree with that contention since we think that the constitutional prohibition against laws respecting an establishment of religion must at least mean that in this country it is no part of the business of government to compose official prayers for any group of the American people to recite as a part of a religious program carried on by government.

 * * *

There can be no doubt that New York's state prayer program officially establishes the religious beliefs embodied in the Regents' prayer. The respondents' argument to the contrary, which is largely based upon the contention that the Regents' prayer is "nondenominational" and the fact that the program, as modified and approved by state courts, does not require all pupils to recite the prayer but permits those who wish to do so to remain silent or be excused from the room, ignores the essential nature of the program's constitutional defects. Neither the fact that the prayer may be denominationally neutral nor the fact that its observance on the part of the students is voluntary can serve to free it from the limitations of the Establishment Clause, as it might from the Free Exercise Clause, of the First Amendment, both of which are operative against the States by virtue of the Fourteenth Amendment. Although these two clauses may in certain instances overlap, they forbid two quite different kinds of governmental encroachment upon religious freedom. The Establishment Clause, unlike the Free Exercise Clause, does not depend upon any showing of direct governmental compulsion and is violated by the enactment of laws

which establish an official religion whether those laws operate directly to coerce nonobserving individuals or not. This is not to say, of course, that laws officially prescribing a particular form of religious worship do not involve coercion of such individuals. When the power, prestige and financial support of government is placed behind a particular religious belief, the indirect coercive pressure upon religious minorities to conform to the prevailing officially approved religion is plain. But the purposes underlying the Establishment Clause go much further than that. Its first and most immediate purpose rested on the belief that a union of government and religion tends to destroy government and to degrade religion. The history of governmentally established religion, both in England and in this country, showed that whenever government had allied itself with one particular form of religion, the inevitable result had been that it had incurred the hatred, disrespect and even contempt of those who held contrary beliefs. That same history showed that many people had lost their respect for any religion that had relied upon the support for government to spread its faith. The Establishment Clause thus stands as an expression of principle on the part of the Founders of our Constitution that religion is too personal, too sacred, too holy, to permit its "unhallowed perversion" by a civil magistrate. Another purpose of the Establishment Clause rested upon an awareness of the historical fact that governmentally established religions and religious persecutions go hand in hand.
* * *

It has been argued that to apply the Constitution in such a way as to prohibit state laws respecting an establishment of religious services in public schools is to indicate a hostility toward religion or toward prayer. Nothing, or course, could be more wrong. The history of man is inseparable from the history of religion. And perhaps it is not too much to say that since the beginning of that history many people have devoutly believed that "More things are wrought by prayer than this world dreams of." It was doubtless largely due to men who believed this that there grew up a sentiment that caused men to leave the cross-currents of officially established state religions and religious persecution in Europe and come to this country filled with the hope that they could find a place in which they could pray when they pleased to the God of their faith in the language they chose. And there were men of this same faith in the power of prayer who led the fight for adoption of our Constitution and also for our Bill of Rights with the very guarantees of religious freedom that forbid the sort of governmental activity which New York has attempted here. These men knew that the First Amendment, which tried to put an end to governmental control of religion and of prayer, was not written to destroy either. They knew rather that it was written to quiet well-justified fears which nearly all of them felt arising out of an awareness that governments of the past had shackled men's tongues to make them speak only the religious thoughts that government wanted them to speak and to pray only to the God that government wanted them to pray to. It is neither sacrilegious nor antireligious to say that each separate government in this country should stay out of the business of writing or sanctioning official prayers and leave that purely religious function to the people themselves and to those the people choose to look to for religious guidance.[21]

* * *

The judgment of the Court of Appeals of New York is reversed and the cause remanded for further proceedings not inconsistent with this opinion.

Reversed and remanded.

MR. JUSTICE DOUGLAS, concurring.

* * * First, a word as to what this case does not involve.

Plainly, our Bill of Rights would not permit a State or the Federal Government to adopt an official prayer and penalize anyone who would not utter it. This, however, is not that case, for there is no element of compulsion or coercion in New York's regulation requiring that public schools be opened each day with the following prayer:

> Almighty God, we acknowledge our dependence upon Thee, and we beg Thy blessings upon us, our parents, our teachers and our Country.

The prayer is said upon the commencement of the school day, immediately following the pledge of allegiance to the flag. The prayer is said aloud in the presence of a teacher, who either leads the recitation or selects a student to do so. No student, however, is compelled to take part. The respondents have adopted a regulation which provides that "Neither teachers nor any school authority shall comment on participation or nonparticipation * * * nor suggest or request that any posture or language be used or dress be worn or be not used or not worn." Provision is also made for excusing children, upon written request of a parent or guardian, from the saying of the prayer or from the room in which the prayer is said. A letter implementing and explaining this regulation has been sent to each taxpayer and parent in the school district. As I read this regulation, a child is free to stand or not stand, to recite or not recite, without fear of reprisal or even comment by the teacher or any other school official.

In short, the only one who need utter the prayer is the teacher; and no teacher is complaining of it. Students can stand mute or even leave the classroom, if they desire.

* * *

---

21. There is of course nothing in the decision reached here that is inconsistent with the fact that school children and others are officially encouraged to express love for our country by reciting historical documents such as the Declaration of Independence which contain references to the Deity or by singing officially espoused anthems which include the composer's professions of faith in a Supreme Being, or with the fact that there are many manifestations in our public life of belief in God. Such patriotic or ceremonial occasions bear no true resemblance to the unquestioned religious exercise that the State of New York has sponsored in this instance.

The question presented by this case is therefore an extremely narrow one. It is whether New York oversteps the bounds when it finances a religious exercise.

What New York does on the opening of its public schools is what we do when we open court. Our Crier has from the beginning announced the convening of the Court and then added "God save the United States and this Honorable Court." That utterance is a supplication, a prayer in which we, the judges, are free to join, but which we need not recite any more than the students need recite the New York prayer.

* * *

[I] cannot say that to authorize this prayer is to establish a religion in the strictly historic meaning of those words. A religion is not established in the usual sense merely by letting those who choose to do so say the prayer that the public school teacher leads. Yet once government finances a religious exercise it inserts a divisive influence into our communities. The New York Court said that the prayer given does not conform to all of the tenets of the Jewish, Unitarian, and Ethical Culture groups. One of the petitioners is an agnostic.

"We are a religious people whose institutions presuppose a Supreme Being." Under our Bill of Rights free play is given for making religion an active force in our lives.[9] But "if a religious leaven is to be worked into the affairs of our people, it is to be done by individuals and groups, not by the Government." By reason of the First Amendment government is commanded "to have no interest in theology or ritual," for on those matters "government must be neutral." The First Amendment leaves the Government in a position not of hostility to religion but of neutrality. The philosophy is that the atheist or agnostic—the nonbeliever—is entitled to go his own way. The philosophy is that if government interferes in matters spiritual, it will be a divisive force. The First Amendment teaches that a government neutral in the field of religion better serves all religious interests.

* * *

NOTES

1. What evidence can be found in both Justice Black's majority opinion and Justice Douglas' concurrence that an analysis based on purpose and effects may in fact have been conducted?

2. It is also important to note the explicit reliance in this decision on core Establishment Clause principles prohibiting coercion and requiring neutrality.

3. One year later, the Court decided the related case of *School District of Abington Township v. Schempp,* finding unconstitutional the requirement

---

9. Religion was once deemed to be a function of the public school system. The Northwest Ordinance, which antedated the First Amendment, provided in Article III that "Religion, morality, and knowledge being necessary to good government and the happiness of mankind, schools and the means of education shall forever be encouraged."

that schools in Pennsylvania and Maryland begin each day with readings from the Bible. It is interesting to note just how united the Court was in these two cases, with Justice Stewart casting the lone dissenting vote in each.

4.   Twenty-two years later, however, the Court was anything but united when it considered the constitutionality of Alabama's "moment of silence" laws in Wallace v. Jaffree, which follows.

WALLACE v. JAFFREE

472 U.S. 38, 105 S.Ct. 2479 (1985)

JUSTICE STEVENS delivered the opinion of the Court.

[The primary focus of this dispute is the constitutionality of § 16–1–20.1, enacted in 1981, which authorized a period of silence "for meditation or voluntary prayer" in Alabama.[a]

The statute was actually the second of three passed in Alabama between 1978 and 1982. § 16–1–20 (1978) had authorized a 1–minute period of silence in all public schools "for meditation", but § 16–1–20.1 (1981) authorized a period of silence "for meditation or voluntary prayer." Plaintiffs apparently conceded that the 1978 law was constitutional, and the dispute among the justices centered primarily on the second statute that includes "voluntary prayer" as a permitted purpose.]

* * *

III

When the Court has been called upon to construe the breadth of the Establishment Clause, it has examined the criteria developed over a period of many years. Thus, in *Lemon v. Kurtzman,* we wrote:

> Every analysis in this area must begin with consideration of the cumulative criteria developed by the Court over many years. Three such tests may be gleaned from our cases. First, the statute must have a secular legislative purpose; second, its principal or primary effect must be one that neither advances nor inhibits religion; finally, the statute must not foster "an excessive government entanglement with religion."

It is the first of these three criteria that is most plainly implicated by this case. As the District Court correctly recognized, no consideration of the second or third criteria is necessary if a statute does not have a clearly secular purpose. For even though a statute that is motivated in part by a religious purpose may satisfy the first criterion, the First Amendment

---

a.   Alabama Code § 16–1–20.1 (Supp.1984) provides:

At the commencement of the first class of each day in all grades in all public schools the teacher in charge of the room in which each class is held may announce that a period of silence not to exceed one minute in duration shall be observed for meditation or voluntary prayer, and during any such period no other activities shall be engaged in.

Also at issue in the lower courts was § 16–1–20.2, enacted in 1982, which authorized teachers to lead "willing students" in a prescribed prayer to "Almighty God ... the Creator and Supreme Judge of the world."

requires that a statute must be invalidated if it is entirely motivated by a purpose to advance religion.

In applying the purpose test, it is appropriate to ask "whether government's actual purpose is to endorse or disapprove of religion."[42] In this case, the answer to that question is dispositive. For the record not only provides us with an unambiguous affirmative answer, but it also reveals that the enactment of § 16–1–20.1 was not motivated by any clearly secular purpose—indeed, the statute had *no* secular purpose.

IV

The sponsor of the bill that became § 16–1–20.1, Senator Donald Holmes, inserted into the legislative record—apparently without dissent— a statement indicating that the legislation was an "effort to return voluntary prayer" to the public schools. Later Senator Holmes confirmed this purpose before the District Court. In response to the question whether he had any purpose for the legislation other than returning voluntary prayer to public schools, he stated: "No, I did not have no other purpose in mind."[44] The State did not present evidence of *any* secular purpose.

     * * *

The legislative intent to return prayer to the public schools is, of course, quite different from merely protecting every student's right to engage in voluntary prayer during an appropriate moment of silence during the school day. The 1978 statute already protected that right, containing nothing that prevented any student from engaging in voluntary prayer during a silent minute of meditation.[47] Appellants have not identi- fied any secular purpose that was not fully served by § 16–1–20 before the enactment of § 16–1–20.1. Thus, only two conclusions are consistent with the text of § 16–1–20.1: (1) the statute was enacted to convey a message of state endorsement and promotion of prayer; or (2) the statute was enacted for no purpose. No one suggests that the statute was nothing but a meaningless or irrational act.[48]

We must, therefore, conclude that the Alabama Legislature intended to change existing law and that it was motivated by the same purpose that the Governor's answer to the second amended complaint expressly admit- ted; that the statement inserted in the legislative history revealed; and

---

42. *Lynch v. Donnelly,* 465 U.S. at 690, 104 S.Ct. at 1368 (O'CONNOR, J., concurring) ("The purpose prong of the *Lemon* test asks whether government's actual purpose is to endorse or disapprove of religion. The effect prong asks whether, irrespective of government's actual purpose, the practice under review in fact conveys a message of endorsement or disapproval. An affirmative answer to either question should render the challenged practice invalid").

44. The District Court and the Court of Appeals agreed that the purpose of § 16–1–20.1 was "an effort on the part of the State of Alabama to encourage a religious activity." * * *

47. Indeed, for some persons meditation itself may be a form of prayer.

48. If the conclusion that the statute had no purpose were tenable, it would remain true that no purpose is not a secular purpose. But such a conclusion is inconsistent with the common sense presumption that statutes are usually enacted to change existing law. Appellants do not even suggest that the State had no purpose in enacting § 16–1–20.1.

that Senator Holmes' testimony frankly described. The legislature enacted § 16–1–20.1, despite the existence of § 16–1–20 for the sole purpose of expressing the State's endorsement of prayer activities for one minute at the beginning of each school day. The addition of "or voluntary prayer" indicates that the State intended to characterize prayer as a favored practice. Such an endorsement is not consistent with the established principle that the government must pursue a course of complete neutrality toward religion.

The importance of that principle does not permit us to treat this as an inconsequential case involving nothing more than a few words of symbolic speech on behalf of the political majority. For whenever the State itself speaks on a religious subject, one of the questions that we must ask is "whether the government intends to convey a message of endorsement or disapproval of religion." The well-supported concurrent findings of the District Court and the Court of Appeals—that § 16–1–20.1 was intended to convey a message of state approval of prayer activities in the public schools—make it unnecessary, and indeed inappropriate, to evaluate the practical significance of the addition of the words "or voluntary prayer" to the statute. Keeping in mind, as we must, "both the fundamental place held by the Establishment Clause in our constitutional scheme and the myriad, subtle ways in which Establishment Clause values can be eroded," we conclude that § 16–1–20.1 violates the First Amendment.

The judgment of the Court of Appeals is affirmed.

It is so ordered.

JUSTICE POWELL, concurring.

I concur in the Court's opinion and judgment that Alabama Code § 16–1–20.1 violates the Establishment Clause of the First Amendment. My concurrence is prompted by Alabama's persistence in attempting to institute state-sponsored prayer in the public schools by enacting three successive statutes. I agree fully with Justice O'CONNOR's assertion that some moment-of-silence statutes may be constitutional, a suggestion set forth in the Court's opinion as well.

I write separately to express additional views and to respond to criticism of the three-pronged *Lemon* test. *Lemon v. Kurtzman* identifies standards that have proved useful in analyzing case after case both in our decisions and in those of other courts. It is the only coherent test a majority of the Court has ever adopted. Only once since our decision in *Lemon, supra,* have we addressed an Establishment Clause issue without resort to its three-pronged test. *Lemon* has not been overruled or its test modified. Yet, continued criticism of it could encourage other courts to feel free to decide Establishment Clause cases on an ad hoc basis.

The first inquiry under *Lemon* is whether the challenged statute has a "secular legislative purpose." As Justice O'CONNOR recognizes, this secular purpose must be "sincere"; a law will not pass constitutional muster if the secular purpose articulated by the legislature is merely a "sham." In *Stone v. Graham* for example, we held that a statute requiring the posting of the Ten Commandments in public schools violated the Establishment Clause, even though the Kentucky Legislature asserted that its goal was educational. We have not interpreted the first prong of *Lemon,* however, as requiring that a statute have "exclusively secular" objectives.[6] If such a requirement existed, much conduct and legislation approved by this Court in the past would have been invalidated.

The record before us, however, makes clear that Alabama's purpose was solely religious in character. Senator Donald Holmes, the sponsor of the bill that became Alabama Code § 16–1–20.1, freely acknowledged that the purpose of this statute was "to return voluntary prayer" to the public schools. I agree with Justice O'CONNOR that a single legislator's statement, particularly if made following enactment, is not necessarily sufficient to establish purpose. But, as noted in the Court's opinion, the religious purpose of § 16–1–20.1 is manifested in other evidence, including the sequence and history of the three Alabama statutes.

I also consider it of critical importance that neither the District Court nor the Court of Appeals found a secular purpose, while both agreed that the purpose was to advance religion. In its first opinion (enjoining the enforcement of § 16–1–20.1 pending a hearing on the merits), the District Court said that the statute did "not reflect a clearly secular purpose." Instead, the District Court found that the enactment of the statute was an "effort on the part of the State of Alabama to encourage a religious activity." The Court of Appeals likewise applied the *Lemon* test and found "a lack of secular purpose on the part of the Alabama Legislature." It held that the objective of § 16–1–20.1 was the "advancement of religion." When both courts below are unable to discern an arguably valid secular purpose, this Court normally should hesitate to find one.

I would vote to uphold the Alabama statute if it also had a clear secular purpose. Nothing in the record before us, however, identifies a clear secular purpose, and the State also has failed to identify any nonreligious reason for the statute's enactment. Under these circumstances, the Court is required by our precedents to hold that the statute fails the first prong of the *Lemon* test and therefore violates the Establishment Clause.

Although we do not reach the other two prongs of the *Lemon* test, I note that the "effect" of a straightforward moment-of-silence statute is unlikely to "advanc[e] or inhibi[t] religion." Nor would such a statute "foster 'an excessive government entanglement with religion.'" *Lemon v. Kurtzman.*

I join the opinion and judgment of the Court.

NOTES

1. What evidence can be discerned in this decision that although the Court explicitly invoked the tripartite *Lemon* test, the *Wallace* case might

---

6. The Court's opinion recognizes that "a statute that is motivated in part by a religious purpose may satisfy the first criterion." The Court simply holds that "a statute must be invalidated if it is *entirely motivated* by a purpose to advance religion."

have actually been decided under an *endorsement* inquiry? Four years later, in *Allegheny,* a non-education-related case addressing the constitutionality of a holiday display, Justice Blackmun explicitly recognized the endorsement analysis as a method of determining whether the effects prong of *Lemon* has been violated. *County of Allegheny v. ACLU,* 492 U.S. 573, 109 S.Ct. 3086 (1989).

2.   A "moment of silence" in the public schools, by itself...and absent additional facts, is generally deemed to be constitutional. *See, e.g., Bown v. Gwinnett County Sch. Dist.,* 112 F.3d 1464 (11th Cir. 1997).

AGOSTINI v. FELTON

521 U.S. 203, 117 S.Ct. 1997 (1997)

JUSTICE O'CONNOR delivered the opinion of the Court.

In *Aguilar v. Felton,* this Court held that the Establishment Clause of the First Amendment barred the city of New York from sending public school teachers into parochial schools to provide remedial education to disadvantaged children pursuant to a congressionally mandated program. On remand, the District Court for the Eastern District of New York entered a permanent injunction reflecting our ruling. Twelve years later, petitioners—the parties bound by that injunction—seek relief from its operation. Petitioners maintain that *Aguilar* cannot be squared with our intervening Establishment Clause jurisprudence and ask that we explicitly recognize what our more recent cases already dictate: *Aguilar* is no longer good law. We agree with petitioners that *Aguilar* is not consistent with our subsequent Establishment Clause decisions and further conclude that, on the facts presented here, petitioners are entitled * * * to relief from the operation of the District Court's prospective injunction.

       * * *

III

       * * *

B

Our more recent cases have undermined the assumptions upon which [previous decisions of this Court] relied. To be sure, the general principles we use to evaluate whether government aid violates the Establishment Clause have not changed since *Aguilar* was decided. For example, we continue to ask whether the government acted with the purpose of advancing or inhibiting religion, and the nature of that inquiry has remained largely unchanged. * * * Likewise, we continue to explore whether the aid has the "effect" of advancing or inhibiting religion. What has changed * * * is our understanding of the criteria used to assess whether aid to religion has an impermissible effect.

1

As we have repeatedly recognized, government inculcation of religious beliefs has the impermissible effect of advancing religion. Our cases subsequent to *Aguilar* have, however, modified in two significant respects the approach we use to assess indoctrination. First, we have abandoned the presumption erected in [previous decisions] that the placement of public employees on parochial school grounds inevitably results in the impermissible effect of state-sponsored indoctrination or constitutes a symbolic union between government and religion. * * *

Second, we have departed from the rule * * * that all government aid that directly assists the educational function of religious schools is invalid. * * * [U]nder current law, * * * New York City's Title I program in *Aguilar* will not, as a matter of law, be deemed to have the effect of advancing religion through indoctrination. Indeed, each of the premises upon which we relied in [past decisions] to reach a contrary conclusion is no longer valid. First, there is no reason to presume that, simply because she enters a parochial school classroom, a full-time public employee such as a Title I teacher will depart from her assigned duties and instructions and embark on religious indoctrination * * *. Certainly, no evidence has ever shown that any New York City Title I instructor teaching on parochial school premises attempted to inculcate religion in students. Thus, both our precedent and our experience require us to reject respondents' remarkable argument that we must presume Title I instructors to be "uncontrollable and sometimes very unprofessional."

[Recent decisions] * * * also repudiate * * * [prior] assumption[s] that the presence of Title I teachers in parochial school classrooms will, without more, create the impression of a "symbolic union" between church and state.

* * *

3

* * *

The * * * Title I program does not result in an "excessive" entanglement that advances or inhibits religion. As discussed previously, the Court's finding of "excessive" entanglement in *Aguilar* rested on three grounds: (i) the program would require "pervasive monitoring by public authorities" to ensure that Title I employees did not inculcate religion; (ii) the program required "administrative cooperation" between the Board and parochial schools; and (iii) the program might increase the dangers of "political divisiveness." Under our current understanding of the Establishment Clause, the last two considerations are insufficient by themselves to create an "excessive" entanglement. They are present no matter where Title I services are offered, and no court has held that Title I services cannot be offered off campus. * * * Further, the assumption underlying the first consideration has been undermined. In *Aguilar,* the Court presumed that full-time public employees on parochial school grounds would be tempted to inculcate religion, despite the ethical standards they were required to uphold. Because of this risk *pervasive* monitoring would be required. But * * * we no longer presume that public employees will inculcate religion simply because they happen to be in a sectarian environment. Since we have abandoned the assumption that properly instructed public employees will fail to discharge their duties faithfully, we must also discard the assumption that *pervasive* monitoring of Title I teachers is required. There is no suggestion in the record before us that unannounced monthly visits of public supervisors are insufficient to prevent or to detect inculcation of religion by public employees. Moreover, we have not found excessive entanglement in cases in which States imposed far more onerous burdens on religious institutions than the monitoring system at issue here.

To summarize, New York City's Title I program does not run afoul of any of three primary criteria we currently use to evaluate whether government aid has the effect of advancing religion: It does not result in governmental indoctrination; define its recipients by reference to religion; or create an excessive entanglement. We therefore hold that a federally funded program providing supplemental, remedial instruction to disadvantaged children on a neutral basis is not invalid under the Establishment Clause when such instruction is given on the premises of sectarian schools by government employees pursuant to a program containing safeguards such as those present here. The same considerations that justify this holding require us to conclude that this carefully constrained program also cannot reasonably be viewed as an endorsement of religion. * * * Accordingly, we must acknowledge that *Aguilar* * * * [is] no longer good law.

        * * *

IV

We therefore conclude that our Establishment Clause law has "signif-icant[ly] change[d]" since we decided *Aguilar*. * * *

[W]e reverse the judgment of the Court of Appeals and remand the cases to the District Court with instructions to vacate its September 26, 1985, order.

It is so ordered.

B. THE ENDORSEMENT INQUIRY

In the 1980s, Justice O'Connor became the leading proponent of an argument that a separate and independent endorsement framework could be discerned as emerging under Establishment Clause jurisprudence. Declaring that a central tenet of Establishment Clause doctrine was the principle that the State must not make "adherence to a religion relevant in any way to a person's standing in the community," O'Connor asserted that "the government violates this prohibition if it endorses or disapproves of religion." Such endorsement or disapproval, she explained, sent a message of exclusion to "nonadherents that they are outsiders ... and an accompanying message to adherents that they are insiders." Lynch v. Donnelly, 465 U.S. 668, 687–88, 104 S.Ct. 1355 (1984) (O'Connor, J., concurring)

In *County of Allegheny v. ACLU,* 492 U.S. 573, 109 S.Ct. 3086 (1989), four justices joined the portion of Justice Blackmun's opinion of the Court that recognized the validity of an endorsement inquiry:

> Our * * * decisions [after *Lemon*] have refined the definition of governmental action that unconstitutionally advances religion. In recent years, we have paid particularly close attention to whether the challenged governmental practice either has the purpose or effect of "endorsing" religion, a concern that has long had a place in our Establishment Clause jurisprudence. See *Engel v. Vitale,* 370 U.S. 421, 436, 82 S.Ct. 1261, 1270 (1962). Thus, in *Wallace v. Jaffree,* 472 U.S. at 60, 105 S.Ct. at 2491, the Court held unconstitutional Alabama's moment-of-silence statute because it was "enacted ... for the sole purpose of expressing the State's endorsement of prayer activities." The Court similarly invalidated Louisiana's "Creationism Act" because it "endorses religion" in its purpose. *Edwards v. Aguillard,* [*infra,* Chapter 9]. * * *

> Of course, the word "endorsement" is not self-defining. Rather, it derives its meaning from other words that this Court has found useful over the years in interpreting the Establishment Clause. Thus, it has been noted that the prohibition against governmental endorsement of religion "preclude[s] government from conveying or attempting to convey a message that religion or a particular religious belief is *favored* or *preferred.*" *Wallace v. Jaffree,* 472 U.S. at 70, 105 S.Ct. at 2497 (O'CONNOR, J., concurring in judgment) (emphasis added). Accord, * * * *Edwards v. Aguillard* ("preference" for particular religious beliefs constitutes an endorsement of religion). Moreover, the term "endorsement" is closely linked to the term "promotion," * * * and this Court long since has held that government "may not ... promote one religion or religious theory against another or even against the militant opposite." *See also Wallace v. Jaffree,* 472 U.S. at 59–60, 105 S.Ct. at 2491 (using the concepts of endorsement, promotion, and favoritism interchangeably). * * * County of Allegheny v. ACLU, 492 U.S. 573, 592–93 (1989).

Justice O'Connor, concurring in that same case, reaffirmed the principle that the endorsement test should be conducted from the point of view of a reasonable observer. In addition, she emphasized the importance of historical context:

> Under the endorsement test, * * * *the "history and ubiquity" of a practice is relevant because it provides part of the context in which a reasonable observer evaluates whether a challenged governmental practice conveys a message of endorsement of religion.* It is the combination of the longstanding existence of practices such as open-

ing legislative sessions with legislative prayers or opening Court sessions with "God save the United States and this honorable Court," as well as their nonsectarian nature, that leads me to the conclusion that those particular practices, despite their religious roots, do not convey a message of endorsement of particular religious beliefs. *Id.* at 630–31 (emphasis added).

As referenced in the introductory material to this chapter, federal judges at the district court and appellate levels are often unable to determine from the Supreme Court's Establishment Clause cases exactly which inquiry to conduct in what circumstances. They do sometimes apply an endorsement test in education-related religion disputes, but often as one of several interrelated inquiries. The 1995 *Duncanville* decision, which follows, is an example of such an approach.

DOE v. DUNCANVILLE INDEP. SCH. DIST.

70 F.3d 402 (5th Cir. 1995)

W. Eugene Davis, Circuit Judge:

Defendants (collectively, the Duncanville Independent School District or DISD) appeal the district court's permanent injunction forbidding certain religious practices in curricular and extracurricular activities at their schools as violations of the Establishment Clause of the First Amendment of the United States Constitution. * * *

I. FACTS

Plaintiffs in this case are Jane Doe, a student in the Duncanville Independent School District, and John Doe, her father.

* * *

Jane Doe * * * joined the choir program at DISD. Students in this program also receive academic credit for their participation. In the seventh and eighth grade choruses, Doe was required to sing the choir theme song *Go Ye Now in Peace,* which is based on Christian text. Upon progressing to the high school choirs, Doe was required to sing another Christian theme song, *The Lord Bless You and Keep You.* David McCullar, the director for the ninth through twelfth grade choirs, testified that *The Lord Bless You and Keep You* had been the choirs' theme song for at least 20 years; he did not know how it had originally been chosen. The choirs learn this song as part of their overall repertoire, sing it at the end of class on Fridays, at the end of some performances and during choral competitions. They also sing this song on the bus on the way home from performances. The parties stipulated that the choir's theme song is a "Christian religious song."

* * *

II. ANALYSIS

As we noted in *Doe I,* modern Establishment Clause jurisprudence is rife with confusion. This Court attempted to bring some order to the organization and application of the existing precedents * * * by identifying three tests that the Supreme Court has used to determine whether a government action or policy constitutes an establishment of religion. First, we identified the Establishment Clause test of longest lineage: the *Lemon* test. * * * We then recognized that the Court has also analyzed school-sponsored religious activity in terms of the coercive effect that the activity has on students. * * * Lastly, we found that the Court has disapproved of governmental practices that appear to endorse religion.

* * *

B. DISD Choirs' Theme Song

DISD contends that the district court erred by enjoining DISD from permitting DISD choirs to sing songs with religious content as their theme songs. The district court enjoined DISD, its employees and agents from:

> 2. initiating, leading, authorizing, encouraging, or condoning the recitation or singing of religious songs as a theme song of the Duncanville school choirs. Religious songs may be sung, however, for their artistic and historic qualities if presented objectively as part of a secular program of education.

The district court made only two findings specific to this issue: (1) that "Jane Doe is a member of the DISD choir and receives academic credit for her participation in the choir"; and (2) that "[a]s a DISD choir member, Jane Doe was required to sing a religious Christian song entitled, *The Lord Bless You and Keep You.* This song is sung at each DISD choir performance and has been adopted by school personnel and students as the choir's theme song."

All parties recognize that the Establishment Clause does not prohibit DISD choirs from singing religious songs as part of a secular music program. * * * Thus, the Does essentially contend that the act of treating *The Lord Bless You and Keep You* as the theme song, rather than as simply one song in the repertoire, transforms the permissible practice of singing this song into an endorsement of religion. The record reveals that two practical effects flow from designating this as the theme song: it is sung often and it is carried over from year to year.

Legitimate secular reasons exist for maintaining *The Lord Bless You and Keep You* as the theme song. As the choir director, David McCullar, testified, this song is particularly useful to teach students to sight read and to sing *a capella*. In Mr. McCullar's words, it is also "a good piece of music . . . by a reputable composer."

Neither does utilizing *The Lord Bless You and Keep You* as a theme song advance or endorse religion. The Does do not argue that the choir sings the theme song as a religious exercise per se[7] so we do not accept the notion that repeated singing of a particular religious song amounts to an

---

7. * * * The fact that singing these songs is not a religious exercise also means that maintaining them as theme songs does not impermissibly entangle government with religion or coerce students into participating in a religious activity.

endorsement of religion. At trial, Mr. McCullar estimated that 60–75 percent of serious choral music is based on sacred themes or text. Given the dominance of religious music in this field, DISD can hardly be presumed to be advancing or endorsing religion by allowing its choirs to sing a religious theme song. As a matter of statistical probability, the song best suited to be the theme is more likely to be religious than not. Indeed, to forbid DISD from having a theme song that is religious would force DISD to disqualify the majority of appropriate choral music simply because it is religious. Within the world of choral music, such a restriction would require hostility, not neutrality, toward religion.

A position of neutrality towards religion must allow choir directors to recognize the fact that most choral music is religious. Limiting the number of times a religious piece of music can be sung is tantamount to censorship and does not send students a message of neutrality. Where, as here, singing the theme song is not a religious exercise, we will not find an endorsement of religion exists merely because a religious song with widely recognized musical value is sung more often than other songs. Such animosity towards religion is not required or condoned by the Constitution.

We conclude that the district court erred by enjoining DISD from using songs with religious content as theme songs for its choirs.

* * *

MAHON, DISTRICT JUDGE, dissenting in part:

* * * I respectfully disagree with my colleagues that DISD's choice of religious theme songs for its choirs is consistent with the First Amendment. Viewed as a whole, the facts in this case fully support the district court's prohibition of DISD's participation, in any form, in the use by its choirs of religious theme songs. Accordingly, I dissent from the majority's decision to reverse the district court's ruling on this issue.

Although the majority opinion sets forth many of the facts in the case, it will help to recount here those facts which demonstrate the similarity between the DISD's choice of a religious theme song and its other religious practices, which the majority agree are unconstitutional.

It is undisputed that for some twenty years, DISD, through the actions of its teachers and other employees, permitted, encouraged and even sponsored the recitation of prayers during curricular and extracurricular activities. Prayers were recited during classes. Many events were begun and closed with a prayer. Sports teams recited prayers before games in the locker rooms, after games on the field and in the buses returning to school. At award ceremonies, prayers were recited and DISD teachers distributed pamphlets of religious songs for participants to sing. The prayers and songs were always Christian.

During the same twenty year period, DISD choir teachers treated as the theme song for the ninth grade and high school choirs what the parties have stipulated is a Christian religious song entitled *The Lord*

Bless You and Keep You. The song is in the form of a prayer seeking God's blessings on behalf of a third party.[1] The theme song was sung at the end of each performance except when circumstances made it inappropriate, such as when members of the choir performed as a barbershop quartet. In addition, the choir sang the song on the bus on the way home from performances and at the end of class each Friday. The students were not given an opportunity to choose a new theme song each year or to determine whether to have a theme song at all. Rather, the song was passed on as an established tradition to incoming choir teachers, who in turn taught it to each new group of students. Although there apparently was no formal, written designation of the theme song, choir teachers and students were aware that the specified song was the theme song and treated it accordingly.

DISD's intermediate school choir had a different theme song, which was also a Christian religious song. Although the record is less developed as to this song, *Go Ye Now in Peace,* the evidence shows that it also was sung at the end of each performance.

* * *

The district court did not err in viewing DISD's choice of religious theme songs as an inseparable part of its historical pattern of encouraging and endorsing Christian religious beliefs through the activities of its teachers. This is not a case where the choice of theme songs was the only arguably religious practice involved, but one where expression of religious belief was permitted and approved at almost every level of school life. In virtually the same way that prayers were recited during classes, sports and other events, the choirs' theme songs were used to mark the close of performances and the week, and to unify participants in a common outlook. Viewed in this context, the theme songs served as yet another vehicle for inculcating a Christian attitude, and their singing constituted a religious exercise.

The majority does not disagree with the legal principles applied by the district court. Instead, by ignoring the role and effect of theme songs in general, and the connection between DISD's theme songs and its other religious practices in particular, the majority reaches the conclusion that DISD's religious theme songs had a secular purpose and did not have the effect of advancing or endorsing religion. An analysis of the majority's reasoning shows it to be faulty in several respects.

* * *

As with the question of purpose, the majority's narrow findings regarding the effects of designating a religious theme song—that the song

---

1. The words of the song are:

The Lord bless you and keep you, the Lord lift His countenance upon you; and give you peace, and give you peace, the Lord make his face to shine upon you, and be gracious unto you, be gracious, the Lord be gracious, gracious unto you. Amen, Amen, Amen, Amen, Amen.

This text, taken from the Old Testament, Numbers VI, 24 26, would be better characterized as Judeo–Christian.

was sung often and was carried over from year to year—disregard the characteristic role and resulting effects of a theme song. In common understanding, a theme song is a song used by a group to represent or identify itself. By choosing a particular song, the group expresses a shared emotion, experience or outlook. The theme song is played at each of the group's meetings or performances and has special significance for the group and for others who identify the group by its song.

DISD intended its choirs' religious theme songs to play this role. Though the theme songs were singled out from the overall music program by their continual singing throughout the year, thereby achieving a prominence not enjoyed by other songs, this was not the sole effect of their designation. More importantly, the theme songs were given special emphasis by their placement at the close of performances and, in the case of the high school choirs' song, its use to end class on Fridays, treatment that served to highlight the songs' sacred character.[4] Choir members were informed that the song was their theme song and a tradition at the school, thereby being directed, in effect, to at least superficially identify themselves with it. Indeed, the choir teacher testified that the theme song was supposed to give the students a sense of unity, camaraderie, belonging, and something to identify with. Since any student, upon learning that a particular song is his or her group's theme song, would look to the words of the song as an important part of its special meaning, the school's designation of a theme song that consists entirely of calls for God's blessing could not help but reinforce existing religious belief and convey the impression to believers and nonbelievers alike that the school favored religion. In fact, Jane Doe indicated she felt the choirs' theme songs reflected and embodied DISD's favor for Christian beliefs. The district court did not err in determining that DISD's choice of religious theme songs had the primary effect of advancing and endorsing religion.

Adopting DISD's reasoning, the majority attempts to minimize the significance of the choice of a religious theme song by pointing to the choir teacher's estimate that 60–75 percent of serious choral music is based on sacred themes or text. Considering these figures, it suggests, statistical probability would predict that a religious song would be best suited to serve as the theme song. This apparent logic obscures the real questions at issue—the purpose and effects of DISD choosing religious theme songs. This is not a case where the students, or even the teachers, have picked a theme song each year and statistics would predict the choice of a religious song some percentage of the time. Nor has DISD directly claimed that it chose its particular theme songs because they were better suited to that purpose than any secular songs. Thus, there is no basis to conclude that the relative percentages of religious and secular music have had any bearing on DISD's purpose in choosing a religious theme song. Similarly,

---

4. The evidence suggests that DISD choir performances were carefully arranged to give religious songs, including the theme songs, the role that prayers played in other DISD events. For example, during the time that Jane Doe was in the intermediate school choir, one performance began with the song *Before Our Lord and King* and ended with the theme song. The rest of the songs in the performance were secular in nature.

that religious songs may constitute the majority of serious choral music does not minimize the religious effects, discussed above, of DISD designating a religious theme song.

* * *

Because the record supports the injunction against any school involvement in the choice or use of a religious theme song, I would affirm the district court on this issue.

PROBLEM 39: RE-LITIGATING DOE V. DUNCANVILLE TODAY

Assume the same set of facts as those set forth in *Doe v. Duncanville*, except that the case is being litigated today, and the Supreme Court ultimately agrees to hear the case.

In light of developments in the law since 1995, and particularly in light of the Court's decision in the 2005 Kentucky Ten Commandments case, how might plaintiffs case be strengthened? Would plaintiffs have a better chance of prevailing today? Why or why not?

Might the implicit *respect principle,* arguably emerging in education cases across all areas of the law, provide additional support for plaintiffs? Or would such a principle provide equal support for defendants?

As a matter of policy, what approach should schools be taking in this context, and in this era? Why?

BORDEN v. SCH. DIST. OF THE TOWNSHIP OF EAST BRUNSWICK

523 F.3d 153 (3d Cir. 2008)

OPINION OF THE COURT

FISHER, Circuit Judge.

Marcus Borden, the head football coach at East Brunswick High School, would like to engage in the silent acts of bowing his head during his team's pre-meal grace and taking a knee with his team during a locker-room prayer. He brought suit seeking a declaratory judgment that the East Brunswick School District's policy prohibiting faculty participation in student-initiated prayer was unconstitutionally overbroad and vague, and violated his federal and state constitutional rights to freedom of speech, academic freedom, freedom of association, and due process. On cross-motions for summary judgment, the District Court for the District of New Jersey declared the policy unconstitutional on all grounds, and it additionally held that Borden's silent acts would not violate the Establishment Clause of the First Amendment. However, we hold that the policy is not unconstitutional on its face or as applied to Borden. Additionally, we hold that Borden's silent acts violate the Establishment Clause because, when viewing the acts in light of Borden's twenty-three years of prior prayer activities with the East Brunswick High School football team during which he organized, participated in, and even led prayer activities with his team, a reasonable observer would conclude that Borden was endorsing religion when he engaged in these acts. Therefore, and for the reasons set forth in further detail below, we will reverse the District Court's order.

I.

A. Factual History

1. 1983–2005 (Pre-litigation)

Marcus Borden is the head football coach at East Brunswick High School ("EBHS"), and he has held that position since 1983.[1] During his tenure at EBHS, Borden engaged in two pre-game prayer activities that occurred (1) at the team dinner; and (2) while taking a knee in the locker room.

As part of the pre-game activities for the EBHS football team, the team ate a pasta dinner together at approximately 3:00 p.m. on game day in the high school cafeteria. In addition to the team, parents and other guests, including the cheerleading squad, were present. Prior to the time Borden coached the team to 1997, a local minister, Reverend Smith, said a pre-meal prayer. However, in 1997, the athletic director told Borden that Reverend Smith could not continue to say the prayer. Instead, Reverend Smith wrote a prayer that the students took turns reading. Then, in 2003, Reverend Smith retired, and Borden did not continue to have the students read Reverend Smith's prayer. Borden instead began a new tradition: he said the prayer prior to the first pre-game dinner of the 2003, 2004, and 2005 seasons. For the subsequent weeks of those seasons, Borden asked those attending the dinner to "please stand," and chose a senior player to say a prayer.

In addition to the prayer before the team dinner, Borden led his team in a prayer immediately before the game. Prior to taking the field, Borden and his assistant coaches asked the players to take a knee in the locker room. The team gathered in front of the chalkboard or dry erase board on one knee, and at that time, Borden discussed the tactics and strategy for that particular game. Following that discussion, Borden led the team in a prayer. Borden described an example of the prayer he said as follows:

> "[D]ear lord, please guide us today in our quest in our game, our championship. Give us the courage and determination that we would need to come out successful. Please let us represent our families and our community well. Lastly, please guide our players and opponents so that they can come out of this game unscathed, [and] no one is hurt."

The team participated in this tradition for twenty-three seasons, beginning when Borden became the coach of the EBHS football team in 1983 and continuing until the 2005 football season.

---

1. Borden is also a tenured teacher of Spanish at EBHS.

On September 26, 2005, Jo Ann Magistro, the Superintendent of the East Brunswick School District ("School District"), received a complaint from a parent about the prayer at the team dinner. The parent told Magistro that she thought it was inappropriate that Borden requested that everyone stand for the prayer and that he bowed his head during the prayer. Over the course of that week, two other parents complained to Magistro about the prayer. One of the complaining parents had a son on the team, and the parent told Magistro that her son felt uncomfortable during the prayer and feared that the coach would select him to say the prayer.

Although Magistro did not contact Borden herself, the EBHS principal and athletic director contacted Borden about these complaints. They told him not to lead the team in prayer, and he responded that he did not lead them in prayer. At the team dinner on September 30, 2005, he continued the prayer traditions in the manner described above. It was alleged that he told the students that if they felt uncomfortable during the prayer, they could wait in the restroom until it was over. Following that game, Magistro received several more complaints.

On October 6, 2005, the School District's counsel, Martin Pachman, advised Magistro and the East Brunswick Board of Education ("Board") regarding Borden's conduct, stating that a coach for the school could not lead, encourage, or participate in student prayer. Magistro met with Borden the next day, October 7, 2005, and told him that all prayer needed to be student initiated, including the selection of which student would recite the prayer. * * * At the end of the conversation, Magistro asked Pachman to provide clear guidelines on faculty participation in student prayer.

Later that day, Magistro sent Borden a memorandum and attached the guidelines provided by Pachman. Magistro stated that she recognized Borden's disappointment, but she expected him to comply with the guidelines, and "[n]ot to comply will be viewed as insubordination." The attached guidelines, which stated that they were not "exhaustive or final," were as follows:

"1. Students have a constitutional right to engage in prayer on school property, at school events, and even during the course of the school day, provided that:

A. The activity is truly student initiated; and

B. The prayer activity does not interfere with the normal operations of the school district. * * *

2. Neither the school district nor any representative of the school district (teacher, coach, administrator, board member, etc.) may constitutionally encourage, lead, initiate, mandate, or otherwise coerce, directly or indirectly, student prayer at any time in any school-sponsored setting, including classes, practices, pep rallies, team meetings, or athletic events.

3. Representatives of the school district, as referenced above, cannot participate in student-initiated prayer. * * *

That same evening, Borden resigned, effective immediately, and he did not attend the football game scheduled for that evening. However, on October 17, 2005, Borden withdrew his resignation and agreed to abide by the School District's policy for the remainder of the 2005 season.[a]

* * *

Following the issuance of the October 7 guidelines and [a school board statement reinforcing these guidelines] on October 20, Borden conducted himself in accordance with the School District's new policy for the balance of the school year, notwithstanding the litigation he instituted on November 21, 2005.

2.   2006–Present

Prior to the 2006 football season, Borden sent an email to Sergio Garcia and Randall Nixon, the co-captains of the team for the 2006 season, requesting that they ask the players whether they would like to continue the tradition of praying at the team dinner and prior to the game. In his email request, he told the co-captains that "[w]hatever the players decide to do is fine with me." He asked the captains to pass on the players' response and to ensure him that they spoke with all of the players on the team. Nixon's response indicated that the players voted to continue both the pre-meal and pre-game prayer. Following the grant of summary judgment in his favor in this case, Borden stood and bowed his head during the prayer before the meal, and remained on one knee during the pre-game prayer.

* * *

III.

* * *

C. The School District Had a Right to Adopt the Guidelines Because It Was Concerned About Establishment Clause Violations.

* * *

The School District has a legitimate educational interest in avoiding Establishment Clause violations, and the guidelines are reasonably related to that interest. The Supreme Court has stated that "compliance with the Establishment Clause is a state interest sufficiently compelling to justify content-based restrictions on speech." If compliance with the Establishment Clause can rise to a compelling state interest, surely it is a legitimate educational interest. * * * In fact, based on the history and context of Borden's conduct in coaching the EBHS football team over the past

---

a. According to the Court, "[f]ollowing the media hype created by this case, EBHS student internet message boards were bombarded with posts, several of which included derogatory comments based on religion and race."

twenty-three years, Borden is in violation of the Establishment Clause when he bows his head and takes a knee while his team prays.

Under the Establishment Clause of the First Amendment, "Congress shall make no law respecting an establishment of religion." U.S. Const. amend. I. This provision applies equally to the states, including public school systems, through the Fourteenth Amendment. The Supreme Court has set forth three tests for determining whether governmental action violates the Establishment Clause: the coercion test, the *Lemon* test, and the endorsement test. We do not address whether Borden's conduct violates the Establishment Clause under the coercion and *Lemon* tests because we find that Borden's behavior violates the Establishment Clause under the endorsement test.

The endorsement test applies "[i]n cases involving state participation in a religious activity." * * * [The test] is applicable here because these facts involve a state employee engaging in the religious activity of students in some fashion.

The relevant question under the endorsement test is "whether a reasonable observer familiar with the history and context of the display would perceive the display as a government endorsement of religion." The test does not focus on the government's subjective purpose when behaving in a particular manner, but instead focuses on the perceptions of the reasonable observer.

The history and context of Borden's prayer activities with the team, if challenged, could have been Establishment Clause violations. In a case that is similar to the facts of the present case prior to the School District's enactment of the policy, the Court of Appeals for the Fifth Circuit found that a basketball coach's involvement in prayer "signal[ed] an unconstitutional endorsement of religion." * * *

For twenty-three years, Borden led the team in a pre-game prayer in the locker room. During that same period of time, Borden orchestrated a pre-meal grace for his team. He originally had a chaplain conduct the pre-meal grace. This practice changed only after school officials asked him to stop; then he had the chaplain write the grace and he selected seniors on the team to recite it. Additionally, during at least three seasons, Borden led the team in the first prayer of the season. Both of these activities, the locker room preparations and the pre-game meals, were school-sponsored events. As in [the Fifth Circuit case], Borden's involvement in prayer at these two activities—as a participant, an organizer, and a leader—would lead a reasonable observer to conclude that he was endorsing religion.

In analyzing Borden's request to engage in silent acts with his teams, we must consider all of his prior prayer activities with his team as the Supreme Court did in [*Santa Fe Independent School District v. Doe,* 530 U.S. 290, 120 S.Ct. 2266 (2000)]. * * *

[A]s discussed above, the current controversy is built upon a significant history of pre-game prayers that involved Borden. Borden organized prayers for the pre-meal grace at the team dinner; he had a chaplain say a prayer and then selected seniors to say the prayer. But even more importantly, Borden led prayers himself—on at least three occasions for the pre-meal grace, and before each game for twenty-three years for the locker room prayer. Additionally, when EBHS officials asked Borden to discontinue this conduct, he initially resigned from his position as coach of the team rather than continue as coach without engaging in the prayer activities. This history of Borden's prayers with the football team leads to a reasonable inference that his current requested conduct is meant "to preserve a popular 'state-sponsored religious practice' " of praying with his team prior to games. *Santa Fe*, 530 U.S. at 309.

Borden has stated that his intention in taking a knee and bowing during prayer is to show signs of respect to his team, not endorse religion.[20] Borden attempts to support this argument by pointing to language in [the Fifth Circuit case] which states that "neither the Establishment Clause nor the district court's order prevent [school district] employees from treating students' religious beliefs and practices with deference and respect; indeed, the constitution requires this. Nothing compels [school district] employees to make their non-participation vehemently obvious or to leave the room when students pray...."[21]

However, we find Borden's argument to be unavailing. [T]he inquiry is not whether Borden intends to endorse religion, but whether a reasonable observer, with knowledge of the history and context of the display, would conclude that he is endorsing religion. * * *

We find that, based on the history of Borden's conduct with the team's prayers, his acts cross the line and constitute an unconstitutional endorsement of religion. Although Borden believes that he must continue to engage in these actions to demonstrate solidarity with his team, which is perhaps good for a football team's unity, we must consider whether a reasonable observer would perceive his actions as endorsing religion, not whether Borden intends to endorse religion. A reasonable observer would have knowledge of Borden's extensive involvement with the team's prayers over the past twenty-three years during which he organized, partici-

---

20. As an employee of the School District as both a coach and tenured teacher, Borden's actions can be imputed to the School District. For this reason, Borden's claim that the School District could remove any Establishment Clause violation by writing a disclaimer saying that Borden's speech does not represent the ideals of the School District is simply wrong. Although the Supreme Court has previously suggested disclaimers as a way to demonstrate that a school district is not endorsing religion, *see Bd. of Educ. v. Mergens*, 496 U.S. 226, 251, 110 S.Ct. 2356 (1990), that was only applicable in the context of permitting student clubs of a religious nature to meet on school grounds. The Court reasoned that "there is little if any risk of official state endorsement or coercion where no formal classroom activities are involved and no school officials actively participate." *Id.* The circumstances are different where, as here, a school official could reasonably be perceived as engaging in the students' prayer activities. Therefore, a disclaimer by the School District would not remove the Establishment Clause violation.

21. Borden also invokes the football greats, like Bear Bryant, to indicate that taking a knee is merely a gesture in the land of football. However, although taking a knee in a huddle to discuss strategy is a gesture well known to football gurus as being part of the game, Borden said a prayer while taking a knee with his team for over twenty-three years. Based on this undisputed history, a reasonable EBHS player would conclude that Borden is endorsing religion if he continues to take a knee while his team prays.

pated in, and led prayer. Based on this history, we hold that a reasonable observer would conclude that Borden is showing not merely respect when he bows his head and takes a knee with his teams and is instead endorsing religion.

* * *

IV.

For all of the above reasons, we conclude that the guidelines * * * were not unconstitutional on their face, were not unconstitutional as applied to Borden, and in fact, were necessary for the School District in order to avoid Establishment Clause violations. Therefore, we will reverse the District Court's order.

McKEE, Circuit Judge, concurring.

I join Judge Fisher's lead opinion, but write separately to clarify a few points, and express a few concerns. At the outset, I emphasize that we today hold only that (i) the School District's policy is not overbroad and vague; (ii) the policy did not violate Borden's constitutional rights to free speech, freedom of association, academic freedom, or due process; and (iii) under the circumstances here, Borden's practice of bowing his head and "taking a knee" as his team prays violates the Establishment Clause.

However, I do not join my colleagues' suggestion that we might reach a different result here absent Borden's 23–year history of promoting team prayer. That question is not before us, and I believe that Borden's "respectful display," might well violate the Establishment Clause even absent his 23–year history. Similarly, I can not agree that the football team's pregame ritual can accurately be characterized as "student-initiated" prayer.

I.

* * * "[E]very Establishment Clause challenge requires a fact-specific, case-by-case analysis." As discussed in the lead opinion, our Establishment Clause inquiry here turns on whether an objective observer would interpret Borden's proposed actions as a state endorsement of religion. I believe such an observer could interpret Borden's proposed actions as an endorsement of religion even absent the coach's history of promoting team prayer.

* * * [I]f Coach Borden silently bows his head and takes a knee as he requests, even without knowledge of Borden's 23–year history of involvement with pregame prayer, any such observer who peered into East Brunswick's locker room before a game would probably observe something very much like [the picture submitted in the School District's Reply Brief.] * * * It would be neither surprising nor unreasonable if that observer were to conclude that the coach is praying with his team-perhaps even that he is leading the team in prayer. Such a conclusion would certainly be buttressed by knowledge of Coach Borden's history of involvement in team prayer, but the absence of that history would not necessarily yield a different result.

II.

Another troubling consideration (which I amplify below) is that a non-religious student or one who adheres to a minority religion might feel subtle (albeit unintentional) coercion to participate in the ritual despite disagreement or discomfort with it. That raises a serious Establishment Clause issue under the Supreme Court's "coercion" test.[28]

The district court accepted the argument that the prayer that occurred after October 7, 2005, was "student-initiated." It clearly was not. I have no doubt that Coach Borden is a sincere and remarkably dedicated individual who cares deeply for his players. He is also a very successful coach. Unfortunately, in an apparent desire to do what he thought was best for his players, he lost sight of his role as a teacher in a public school.

After initiating this litigation, and prior to the start of the 2006 season, Coach Borden directed the captains to poll the football team and ask each player whether or not he wanted to "follow the same practices as last year" regarding prayer at the pregame meals and in the locker room before the games. The captains then personally phoned every member of the football team. Not surprisingly, given the non-anonymous nature of the poll, no player objected. Given the uproar this issue visited on the community, the players must have known how important prayer was to their coach-and no high school athlete would want to disappoint the coach, or (as I shall explain) risk incurring the communal wrath that had been visited on the unfortunate cheerleaders the year before.[29]

I am not suggesting that Coach Borden intentionally pressured his players into voting for pregame prayer ceremonies or that he wanted to manipulate the outcome. Nevertheless, these players were put in the untenable position of either compromising any opposing beliefs they may have had or going on record (at the very least with their captains) as opposing their coach and perhaps a majority of their teammates.

Although the coach thought that the prayers would foster team unity, and even though the captains reported that all players wanted to continue the tradition, the record suggests that the reality was quite different. In the fall of 2005, Superintendent Magistro received a phone call from a "crying and overwrought" woman who identified herself as the mother of an East Brunswick football player. The mother complained that her son "was extremely upset at Mr. Borden's fostering and participating in prayer amongst the football players." When Magistro asked why her son

---

28. The Supreme Court has applied the "coercion" test as well as the "endorsement" test in determining whether state action violates the Establishment Clause in the public school context. *See Santa Fe Indep. Sch. Dist. v. Doe* (applying endorsement test and coercion test) * * *.

29. Moreover, the Supreme Court has held on more than one occasion that "fundamental rights may not be submitted to vote; they depend on the outcome of no elections." *West Virginia Bd. of Ed. v. Barnette, quoted in Santa Fe.* "The whole theory of viewpoint neutrality is that minority views are treated with the same respect as are majority views."

participated in the team prayers despite his discomfort, the mother responded that he "was fearful that if he did not go along with what was obviously the coach's desire, he would not get playing time." The call was one of the factors that led to the School District policy Borden challenges.

Unfortunately, the coach appears not to have considered the possibility that the tradition he wanted to foster could be troubling for some players and possibly deter others from playing football at all. * * *

Regrettably, Coach Borden as a teacher (and therefore as a state actor for purposes of the First and Fourteenth Amendments) failed to appreciate that others may not agree with his beliefs or that the religious beliefs that he held dear might be in tension with contrary (but equally valid) beliefs of some of his players. Any player who held opposing beliefs should not have had to "go along to get along" by silently participating in religious observances he disagreed with.

> For, "the government may no more use social pressure to enforce orthodoxy than it may use more direct means." ... "[W]hat to most believers may seem nothing more than a reasonable request that the nonbeliever respect their religious practices, in a school context may appear to the nonbeliever or dissenter to be an attempt to employ the machinery of the State to enforce a religious orthodoxy." ... The constitutional command will not permit the District "to exact religious conformity from a student as the price" of joining [his] classmates at a varsity football game. *Santa Fe,* 530 U.S. at 312.

Indeed, "it is quite possible that parents of some [students] chose public education precisely so that their children would not be compelled to follow the religious beliefs of others." * * *

This does not, of course, mean that students have no right to pray; they clearly do. Whatever else it may be, prayer is a form of speech and deserves no less protection than secular speech.[30] The policy the School District developed in response to the complaints about pregame prayers was an effort to protect the First Amendment liberties of *everyone* in the school community.

III.

The Supreme Court has observed that "[w]e are a religious people whose institutions presuppose a Supreme Being." Yet, the Court also reminds us that "[i]t is neither sacrilegious nor anti-religious to say that each separate government in this country should stay out of the business of [religion] ... and leave ... purely religious function[s] to the people themselves and to those the people choose to look to for religious guidance."

Coach Borden's dedication to instilling in his players values such as respect and team unity is certainly praiseworthy. However, as we have explained, the laudable intentions of state actors do not control an

---

30. Such prayer does not, however, have to occur in the locker room.

analysis under the First Amendment. "For just as religion throughout history has provided spiritual comfort, guidance, and inspiration to many, it can also serve powerfully to divide societies and to exclude those whose beliefs are not in accord with particular religions or sects that have from time to time achieved dominance." This record contains powerful evidence of such division.

Superintendent Magistro testified that she received telephone calls in September 2005 from some parents of cheerleaders. They complained that their daughters were "uncomfortable" when Borden initiated a prayer at a pregame dinner. Students apparently learned of these complaints, and blamed two Jewish cheerleaders. Thereafter, those cheerleaders were publicly ridiculed by other students at athletic events, and the cheerleading squad was taunted, bullied, and booed. The cheerleaders were even harassed and threatened on a student internet "blog." In the days following Coach Borden's resignation, several internet posts appeared under the heading, "Jewish Cheerleaders who suck!!!." The following are a few examples of the disgusting comments that were posted:

- "First they crucify Jesus, then they got Borden fired. . . . Jews gotta learn to stop ruining everything cool."

- "The jew is wrong. Borden is right. Let us pray."

- "d**n jews . . . then you wonder why hitler did what he did back in the day."

- "MAYBE if [Borden] held a gun to the jjjjewwws head and was like b*tch get on ur knees and pray to jesus!! then that might be breaking the law . . . ehhh maybe not! . . . just suck it up if u don't fu*king like whats going on in america then GO THE FU*K BACK TO YOUR COUNTRY AND STAY THERE AND PRAY. . . ."

- "Heil Hitla! ! ! sieg heill."

These exchanges illustrate the continuing relevance of Justice O'Connor's admonition that "[e]ndorsement sends a message to nonadherents that they are outsiders, not full members of the political community, and an accompanying message to adherents that they are insiders, favored members of the political community." The School District attempted to address these concerns by adopting the policy that the district court struck down in the face of Coach Borden's challenge. In reversing the district court, we help to ensure the continued vitality of the Establishment Clause as well as the rights of all to worship as they please.

BARRY, CIRCUIT JUDGE, concurring.

There was no question, and the parties clearly understood, that there was one predominant issue before the District Court: whether the actions in which Borden wished to engage would violate the Establishment Clause of the First Amendment, not whether the conduct in which he had engaged would pass constitutional muster. Put in specific terms, the parties and the District Court focused their attention on how this public high school football coach could react, consistent with the Establishment

Clause, when members of his team decide to initiate voluntary prayers at a pre-game meal attended only by players, staff, players' parents, and invited guests, and in the locker room before a game where only players and coaches are present. * * *

Suffice it to say that when they were before the District Court, the parties were in good faith trying to avoid an Establishment Clause problem, with defendants explicitly agreeing to abide by the District Court's decision. But defendants did not do so. Rather, now armed with new counsel, they filed an appeal, creating before us a legal landscape that bears little or no resemblance to what went on before the District Court and surely causing the temperature of this litigation to soar.

Given my druthers, I would hold defendants to their word and would not entertain, as my distinguished colleagues have so generously entertained, the new issues and arguments raised on this appeal. I will not, however, tarry to push the proverbial waiver rock uphill as to all of those issues and arguments because I cannot disagree, nor does Judge McKee, with the bottom-line conclusions of Judge Fisher's superb lead opinion * * *.

I write separately, however, to express my view that whether or not Borden's past prayer activities with the team signaled an unconstitutional endorsement of religion-and I have little doubt that they did-a reasonable observer would not conclude that the "respectful display" he proposes would violate the Establishment Clause. * * *

This is a difficult and close case, complicated by the fact that, unlike the vast majority of Establishment Clause cases which are brought by plaintiffs complaining of a state's actions, this case was brought by an employee of a state complaining about pre-emptive action taken by the state in its attempt to avoid an Establishment Clause problem. With this litigation hopefully nearing its end, one also hopes that those involved will move forward as a team for the benefit of the young people who look to them for guidance and support.

C. THE COERCION INQUIRY

In the *Allegheny* case, *supra,* Justice Kennedy argued against the endorsement inquiry as set forth by Justices Blackmun and O'Connor. He contended that a coercion inquiry would be the more appropriate approach for deciding the dispute, and explained that it would also permit government "some latitude in recognizing and accommodating the central role religion plays in our society."

Joined by Chief Justice Rehnquist, Justice White, and Justice Scalia, Kennedy declared:

Our cases disclose two limiting principles: government may not coerce anyone to support or participate in any religion or its exercise; and it may not, in the guise of avoiding hostility or callous indifference, give direct benefits to religion in such a degree that it in fact "establishes a [state] religion or religious faith, or tends to do so." County of Allegheny v. ACLU, 492 U.S. 573, 659 (Kennedy, J., concurring in the judgment and dissenting in part).

According to Kennedy, such an approach was a more correct characterization of Establishment Clause principles and case law than either the *Lemon* test or the endorsement test. He pointed out that James Madison, who proposed the First Amendment in Congress, "apprehended the meaning of the [Religion Clauses] to be, that Congress should not establish a religion, and *enforce* the legal observation of it by law, nor *compel* men to worship God in any manner contrary to their conscience." *See generally* Michael W. McConnell, *Coercion: the Lost Element of Establishment,* 27 WILLIAM & MARY L. REV. 933 (1986).

Three years later, Kennedy was able to apply this very coercion test to the facts of *Lee v. Weisman.* However, in a somewhat ironic turn of events, the test was not employed to justify state action, but to strike down as unconstitutional the actions of a school district in a dispute over graduation invocations and benedictions.

LEE v. WEISMAN
505 U.S. 577, 112 S.Ct. 2649 (1992)

JUSTICE KENNEDY delivered the opinion of the Court.

School principals in the public school system of the city of Providence, Rhode Island, are permitted to invite members of the clergy to offer invocation and benediction prayers as part of the formal graduation ceremonies for middle schools and for high schools. The question before us is whether including clerical members who offer prayers as part of the official school graduation ceremony is consistent with the Religion Clauses of the First Amendment, provisions the Fourteenth Amendment makes applicable with full force to the States and their school districts.

I

A

Deborah Weisman graduated from Nathan Bishop Middle School, a public school in Providence, at a formal ceremony in June 1989. She was about 14 years old. For many years it has been the policy of the Providence School Committee and the Superintendent of Schools to permit principals to invite members of the clergy to give invocations and benedictions at middle school and high school graduations. Many, but not all, of the principals elected to include prayers as part of the graduation ceremonies. Acting for himself and his daughter, Deborah's father, Daniel Weisman, objected to any prayers at Deborah's middle school graduation, but to no avail. The school principal, petitioner Robert E. Lee, invited a rabbi to deliver prayers at the graduation exercises for Deborah's class. Rabbi Leslie Gutterman, of the Temple Beth El in Providence, accepted.

It has been the custom of Providence school officials to provide invited clergy with a pamphlet entitled "Guidelines for Civic Occasions," prepared by the National Conference of Christians and Jews. The Guidelines recommend that public prayers at nonsectarian civic ceremonies be composed with "inclusiveness and sensitivity," though they acknowledge that "[p]rayer of any kind may be inappropriate on some civic occasions." The principal gave Rabbi Gutterman the pamphlet before the graduation and advised him the invocation and benediction should be nonsectarian.

Rabbi Gutterman's prayers were as follows:

INVOCATION

God of the Free, Hope of the Brave:

For the legacy of America where diversity is celebrated and the rights of minorities are protected, we thank You. May these young men and women grow up to enrich it.

For the liberty of America, we thank You. May these new graduates grow up to guard it.

For the political process of America in which all its citizens may participate, for its court system where all may seek justice we thank You. May those we honor this morning always turn to it in trust.

For the destiny of America we thank You. May the graduates of Nathan Bishop Middle School so live that they might help to share it.

May our aspirations for our country and for these young people, who are our hope for the future, be richly fulfilled.

AMEN

BENEDICTION

O God, we are grateful to You for having endowed us with the capacity for learning which we have celebrated on this joyous commencement.

Happy families give thanks for seeing their children achieve an important milestone. Send Your blessings upon the teachers and administrators who helped prepare them.

The graduates now need strength and guidance for the future, help them to understand that we are not complete with academic knowledge alone. We must each strive to fulfill what You require of us all: To do justly, to love mercy, to walk humbly.

We give thanks to You, Lord, for keeping us alive, sustaining us and allowing us to reach this special, happy occasion.

AMEN

* * *

The school board (and the United States, which supports it as *amicus curiae*) argued that these short prayers and others like them at graduation exercises are of profound meaning to many students and parents throughout this country who consider that due respect and acknowledgment for divine guidance and for the deepest spiritual aspirations of our people ought to be expressed at an event as important in life as a graduation. We assume this to be so in addressing the difficult case now before us, for the significance of the prayers lies also at the heart of Daniel and Deborah Weisman's case.

    * * *

II

These dominant facts mark and control the confines of our decision: State officials direct the performance of a formal religious exercise at promotional and graduation ceremonies for secondary schools. Even for those students who object to the religious exercise, their attendance and participation in the state-sponsored religious activity are in a fair and real sense obligatory, though the school district does not require attendance as a condition for receipt of the diploma.

This case does not require us to revisit the difficult questions dividing us in recent cases, questions of the definition and full scope of the principles governing the extent of permitted accommodation by the State for the religious beliefs and practices of many of its citizens. For without reference to those principles in other contexts, the controlling precedents as they relate to prayer and religious exercise in primary and secondary public schools compel the holding here that the policy of the city of Providence is an unconstitutional one. We can decide the case without reconsidering the general constitutional framework by which public schools' efforts to accommodate religion are measured. Thus we do not accept the invitation of petitioners and *amicus* the United States to reconsider our decision in *Lemon v. Kurtzman*. The government involvement with religious activity in this case is pervasive, to the point of creating a state-sponsored and state-directed religious exercise in a public school. Conducting this formal religious observance conflicts with settled rules pertaining to prayer exercises for students, and that suffices to determine the question before us.

The principle that government may accommodate the free exercise of religion does not supersede the fundamental limitations imposed by the Establishment Clause. It is beyond dispute that, at a minimum, the Constitution guarantees that government may not coerce anyone to support or participate in religion or its exercise, or otherwise act in a way which "establishes a [state] religion or religious faith, or tends to do so." The State's involvement in the school prayers challenged today violates these central principles.

That involvement is as troubling as it is undenied. A school official, the principal, decided that an invocation and a benediction should be given; this is a choice attributable to the State, and from a constitutional perspective it is as if a state statute decreed that the prayers must occur.

The principal chose the religious participant, here a rabbi, and that choice is also attributable to the State. The reason for the choice of a rabbi is not disclosed by the record, but the potential for divisiveness over the choice of a particular member of the clergy to conduct the ceremony is apparent.

Divisiveness, of course, can attend any state decision respecting religions, and neither its existence nor its potential necessarily invalidates the State's attempts to accommodate religion in all cases. The potential for divisiveness is of particular relevance here though, because it centers around an overt religious exercise in a secondary school environment where, as we discuss below, subtle coercive pressures exist and where the student had no real alternative which would have allowed her to avoid the fact or appearance of participation.

* * *

We are asked to recognize the existence of a practice of nonsectarian prayer, prayer within the embrace of what is known as the Judeo–Christian tradition, prayer which is more acceptable than one which, for example, makes explicit references to the God of Israel, or to Jesus Christ, or to a patron saint. There may be some support, as an empirical observation, to the statement of the Court of Appeals for the Sixth Circuit, picked up by Judge Campbell's dissent in the Court of Appeals in this case, that there has emerged in this country a civic religion, one which is tolerated when sectarian exercises are not. If common ground can be defined which permits once conflicting faiths to express the shared conviction that there is an ethic and a morality which transcend human invention, the sense of community and purpose sought by all decent societies might be advanced. But though the First Amendment does not allow the government to stifle prayers which aspire to these ends, neither does it permit the government to undertake that task for itself.

The First Amendment's Religion Clauses mean that religious beliefs and religious expression are too precious to be either proscribed or prescribed by the State. The design of the Constitution is that preservation and transmission of religious beliefs and worship is a responsibility and a choice committed to the private sphere, which itself is promised freedom to pursue that mission. It must not be forgotten then, that while concern must be given to define the protection granted to an objector or a dissenting nonbeliever, these same Clauses exist to protect religion from government interference. James Madison, the principal author of the Bill of Rights, did not rest his opposition to a religious establishment on the sole ground of its effect on the minority. A principal ground for his view was: "[E]xperience witnesseth that ecclesiastical establishments, instead of maintaining the purity and efficacy of Religion, have had a contrary operation."

These concerns have particular application in the case of school officials, whose effort to monitor prayer will be perceived by the students as inducing a participation they might otherwise reject. Though the efforts of the school officials in this case to find common ground appear to have been a good-faith attempt to recognize the common aspects of religions and not the divisive ones, our precedents do not permit school officials to assist in composing prayers as an incident to a formal exercise for their students. *Engel v. Vitale*. And these same precedents caution us to measure the idea of a civic religion against the central meaning of the Religion Clauses of the First Amendment, which is that all creeds must be tolerated and none favored. The suggestion that government may establish an official or civic religion as a means of avoiding the establishment of a religion with more specific creeds strikes us as a contradiction that cannot be accepted.

The degree of school involvement here made it clear that the graduation prayers bore the imprint of the State and thus put school-age children who objected in an untenable position. We turn our attention now to consider the position of the students, both those who desired the prayer and she who did not.

To endure the speech of false ideas or offensive content and then to counter it is part of learning how to live in a pluralistic society, a society which insists upon open discourse towards the end of a tolerant citizenry. And tolerance presupposes some mutuality of obligation. It is argued that our constitutional vision of a free society requires confidence in our own ability to accept or reject ideas of which we do not approve, and that prayer at a high school graduation does nothing more than offer a choice. By the time they are seniors, high school students no doubt have been required to attend classes and assemblies and to complete assignments exposing them to ideas they find distasteful or immoral or absurd or all of these. Against this background, students may consider it an odd measure of justice to be subjected during the course of their educations to ideas deemed offensive and irreligious, but to be denied a brief, formal prayer ceremony that the school offers in return. This argument cannot prevail, however. It overlooks a fundamental dynamic of the Constitution.

The First Amendment protects speech and religion by quite different mechanisms. Speech is protected by ensuring its full expression even when the government participates, for the very object of some of our most important speech is to persuade the government to adopt an idea as its own. The method for protecting freedom of worship and freedom of conscience in religious matters is quite the reverse. In religious debate or expression the government is not a prime participant, for the Framers deemed religious establishment antithetical to the freedom of all. The Free Exercise Clause embraces a freedom of conscience and worship that has close parallels in the speech provisions of the First Amendment, but the Establishment Clause is a specific prohibition on forms of state intervention in religious affairs with no precise counterpart in the speech provisions. The explanation lies in the lesson of history that was and is the inspiration for the Establishment Clause, the lesson that in the hands of government what might begin as a tolerant expression of religious views may end in a policy to indoctrinate and coerce. A state-created orthodoxy puts at grave risk that freedom of belief and conscience which are the sole assurance that religious faith is real, not imposed.

The lessons of the First Amendment are as urgent in the modern world as in the 18th century when it was written. One timeless lesson is that if citizens are subjected to state-sponsored religious exercises, the State disavows its own duty to guard and respect that sphere of inviolable conscience and belief which is the mark of a free people. To compromise that principle today would be to deny our own tradition and forfeit our standing to urge others to secure the protections of that tradition for themselves.

As we have observed before, there are heightened concerns with protecting freedom of conscience from subtle coercive pressure in the elementary and secondary public schools. * * * Our decisions in *Engel v. Vitale*, 370 U.S. 421, 82 S.Ct. 1261 (1962), and *School Dist. of Abington* recognize, among other things, that prayer exercises in public schools carry a particular risk of indirect coercion. The concern may not be limited to the context of schools, but it is most pronounced there. What to most believers may seem nothing more than a reasonable request that the nonbeliever respect their religious practices, in a school context may appear to the nonbeliever or dissenter to be an attempt to employ the machinery of the State to enforce a religious orthodoxy.

We need not look beyond the circumstances of this case to see the phenomenon at work. The undeniable fact is that the school district's supervision and control of a high school graduation ceremony places public pressure, as well as peer pressure, on attending students to stand as a group or, at least, maintain respectful silence during the invocation and benediction. This pressure, though subtle and indirect, can be as real as any overt compulsion. Of course, in our culture standing or remaining silent can signify adherence to a view or simple respect for the views of others. And no doubt some persons who have no desire to join a prayer have little objection to standing as a sign of respect for those who do. But for the dissenter of high school age, who has a reasonable perception that she is being forced by the State to pray in a manner her conscience will not allow, the injury is no less real. There can be no doubt that for many, if not most, of the students at the graduation, the act of standing or remaining silent was an expression of participation in the rabbi's prayer. That was the very point of the religious exercise. It is of little comfort to a dissenter, then, to be told that for her the act of standing or remaining in silence signifies mere respect, rather than participation. What matters is that, given our social conventions, a reasonable dissenter in this milieu could believe that the group exercise signified her own participation or approval of it.

Finding no violation under these circumstances would place objectors in the dilemma of participating, with all that implies, or protesting. We do not address whether that choice is acceptable if the affected citizens are mature adults, but we think the State may not, consistent with the

Establishment Clause, place primary and secondary school children in this position. Research in psychology supports the common assumption that adolescents are often susceptible to pressure from their peers towards conformity, and that the influence is strongest in matters of social convention. To recognize that the choice imposed by the State constitutes an unacceptable constraint only acknowledges that the government may no more use social pressure to enforce orthodoxy than it may use more direct means.

The injury caused by the government's action, and the reason why Daniel and Deborah Weisman object to it, is that the State, in a school setting, in effect required participation in a religious exercise. It is, we concede, a brief exercise during which the individual can concentrate on joining its message, meditate on her own religion, or let her mind wander. But the embarrassment and the intrusion of the religious exercise cannot be refuted by arguing that these prayers, and similar ones to be said in the future, are of a *de minimis* character. To do so would be an affront to the rabbi who offered them and to all those for whom the prayers were an essential and profound recognition of divine authority. * * *

Attendance may not be required by official decree, yet it is apparent that a student is not free to absent herself from the graduation exercise in any real sense of the term "voluntary," for absence would require forfeiture of those intangible benefits which have motivated the student through youth and all her high school years. Graduation is a time for family and those closest to the student to celebrate success and express mutual wishes of gratitude and respect, all to the end of impressing upon the young person the role that it is his or her right and duty to assume in the community and all of its diverse parts.

* * *

The Government's argument gives insufficient recognition to the real conflict of conscience faced by the young student. The essence of the Government's position is that with regard to a civic, social occasion of this importance it is the objector, not the majority, who must take unilateral and private action to avoid compromising religious scruples, hereby electing to miss the graduation exercise. This turns conventional First Amendment analysis on its head. It is a tenet of the First Amendment that the State cannot require one of its citizens to forfeit his or her rights and benefits as the price of resisting conformance to state-sponsored religious practice. To say that a student must remain apart from the ceremony at the opening invocation and closing benediction is to risk compelling conformity in an environment analogous to the classroom setting, where we have said the risk of compulsion is especially high. Just as in *Engel v. Vitale,* 370 U.S. at 430, 82 S.Ct. at 1266, where we found that provisions within the challenged legislation permitting a student to be voluntarily excused from attendance or participation in the daily prayers did not shield those practices from invalidation, the fact that attendance at the graduation ceremonies is voluntary in a legal sense does not save the religious exercise.

* * *

Our society would be less than true to its heritage if it lacked abiding concern for the values of its young people, and we acknowledge the profound belief of adherents to many faiths that there must be a place in the student's life for precepts of a morality higher even than the law we today enforce. We express no hostility to those aspirations, nor would our oath permit us to do so. A relentless and all-pervasive attempt to exclude religion from every aspect of public life could itself become inconsistent with the Constitution. We recognize that, at graduation time and throughout the course of the educational process, there will be instances when religious values, religious practices, and religious persons will have some interaction with the public schools and their students. But these matters, often questions of accommodation of religion, are not before us. The sole question presented is whether a religious exercise may be conducted at a graduation ceremony in circumstances where, as we have found, young graduates who object are induced to conform. No holding by this Court suggests that a school can persuade or compel a student to participate in a religious exercise. That is being done here, and it is forbidden by the Establishment Clause of the First Amendment.

For the reasons we have stated, the judgment of the Court of Appeals is

Affirmed.

NOTE

1. *Weisman* was a closely fought, 5–4 decision. Eight years later, in *Santa Fe Independent School District v. Doe,* 530 U.S. 290, 120 S.Ct. 2266 (2000), the Court, by a vote of 6–3, applied the coercion test set forth in *Weisman* to find that a student-led prayer delivered over the public address system before each varsity football game for the entire season violated the Establishment Clause:

> Even if we regard every high school student's decision to attend a home football game as purely voluntary, we are nevertheless persuaded that the delivery of a pregame prayer has the improper effect of coercing those present to participate in an act of religious worship. For "the government may no more use social pressure to enforce orthodoxy than it may use more direct means." As in *Lee,* "[w]hat to most believers may seem nothing more than a reasonable request that the nonbeliever respect their religious practices, in a school context may appear to the nonbeliever or dissenter to be an attempt to employ the machinery of the State to enforce a religious orthodoxy." The constitutional command will not permit the District "to exact religious conformity from a student as the price" of joining her classmates at a varsity football game. Santa Fe Indep. Sch. Dist. v. Doe, 530 U.S. 290, 313 (2000).

The Court also rejected the *percentages* argument cited above in the introductory materials to this Chapter. The District had authorized an election to determine whether "invocations" should be delivered at the football games, and also to select the spokesperson to deliver them, and its attorneys argued that this election served to justify its subsequent practices. But the Court found that "while Santa Fe's majoritarian election might ensure that *most* of the students are represented, it does nothing to protect the minority; indeed, it likely serves to intensify their offense."

SCHOOL PRAYER
UNDER THE "NO CHILD LEFT BEHIND" ACT

Much to the surprise of many educators, the "No Child Left Behind" Act included specific provisions addressing school prayer. 20 U.S.C § 7904 provides:

(a) Guidance. The Secretary shall provide and revise guidance, not later than September 1, 2002, and of every second year thereafter, to State educational agencies, local educational agencies, and the public on constitutionally protected prayer in public elementary schools and secondary schools, including making the guidance available on the Internet. The guidance shall be reviewed, prior to distribution, by the Office of Legal Counsel of the Department of Justice for verification that the guidance represents the current state of the law concerning constitutionally protected prayer in public elementary schools and secondary schools.

(b) Certification. As a condition of receiving funds under this Act [*20 USCS §§ 6301* et seq.], a local educational agency shall certify in writing to the State educational agency involved that no policy of the local educational agency prevents, or otherwise denies participation in, constitutionally protected prayer in public elementary schools and secondary schools, as detailed in the guidance required under subsection (a). The certification shall be provided by October 1 of each year. The State educational agency shall report to the Secretary by November 1 of each year a list of those local educational agencies that have not filed the certification or against which complaints have been made to the State educational agency that the local educational agencies are not in compliance with this section.

(c) Enforcement. The Secretary is authorized and directed to effectuate subsection (b) by issuing, and securing compliance with, rules or orders with respect to a local educational agency that fails to certify, or is found to have certified in bad faith, that no policy of the local educational agency prevents, or otherwise denies participation in, constitutionally protected prayer in public elementary schools and secondary schools.

The provisions, and the subsequent "guidance" issued by the U.S. Department of Education, proved to be the subject of considerable debate . . . with some members of the legal and education communities declaring that the posted document contained misleading and in some cases questionable assertions regarding the current state of Establishment Clause law.

MELLEN v. BUNTING

327 F.3d 355 (4th Cir. 2003)

KING, CIRCUIT JUDGE:

General Josiah Bunting, III, the former Superintendent of the Virginia Military Institute ("VMI"), appeals the district court's award of declaratory and injunctive relief, prohibiting VMI from sponsoring a daily "supper prayer." * * *

I.

* * *

B.

All members of VMI's Corps of Cadets (the student body) are required to pay a room and board fee. This fee covers all of a cadet's meals, which are served in the Post mess hall. Although VMI serves supper to the Corps twice each evening in the mess hall, nearly all cadets attend the first seating; only those who participate in athletics or have other special circumstances can obtain authorization to attend the second seating.

The first seating begins with the "supper roll call" (the "SRC"), initiated by a bugle call summoning the Corps into formation in front of the Barracks. * * * [T]he Corps is called to attention, and the Regimental Commander—the senior cadet officer—presents the Corps to the TAC Officer. Salutes are then exchanged, and the command "REST" is given. While standing at rest, a cadet may move to a limited extent, leaving his or her right foot in place. The daily announcements are made, and the Cadet Chaplain then reads the supper prayer to the assembled Corps.[5]

The SRC ceremony is conducted every day except Saturday, and the Post Chaplain, Colonel James S. Park, has composed a separate supper prayer for each day. Depending on the day, the prayer begins with "Almighty God," "O God," "Father God," "Heavenly Father," or "Sovereign God." As the district court recognized, "[e]ach day's prayer is dedicated to giving thanks or asking for God's blessing." The court also observed that "a prayer may thank God for the Institute, ask for God's blessing on the Corps, or give thanks for the love and support of family and friends," and that "each day's prayer ends with the following invocation: 'Now O God, we receive this food and share this meal together with thanksgiving. Amen.'" The Corps must remain standing and silent while

---

5. In the past, VMI sponsored a similar meal-time prayer, but the school's administration discontinued this practice in 1990 as a result of a decision to replace family-style dining with cafeteria-style dining. In 1995, General Bunting assumed control of VMI. Seeking to bring a stronger sense of unity to the Corps, he decided to return the Corps to a traditional SRC formation and family-style dining, including the supper prayer. Although now retired, General Bunting possessed the authority during his tenure at VMI over all VMI activities, including the supper prayer.

the supper prayer is read, but cadets are not obliged to recite the prayer, close their eyes, or bow their heads.

C.

On January 23, 2001, the Plaintiffs submitted a Permit Form to VMI's administration, requesting that cadets "be allowed to go about their business in the Mess Hall during the supper prayer (in a sense of not acknowledging that the prayer is occurring)." After their request was denied, the Plaintiffs wrote to General Bunting, asserting that the supper prayer was unconstitutional. The General promptly rejected this contention, advising them that "[t]he Constitution does not prohibit our saying grace before supper. And we shall continue to do so." General Bunting also informed the Plaintiffs that the supper prayer "is a precious link to our heritage and an admirable practice for a school of our provenience and culture," and that it would continue.

On May 9, 2001, Plaintiffs filed their complaint in the Western District of Virginia, seeking declaratory and injunctive relief, along with nominal damages, costs, and attorney's fees. They alleged that the supper prayer violated the Establishment Clause of the First Amendment; Article I, § 16 of the Virginia Constitution; and the Virginia Act for Religious Freedom, Va. Code Ann. § 57–1.

* * *

IV.

* * *

A.

* * *

As [the K–12 school prayer] decisions reflect, the Court has been unwavering in its position that the Establishment Clause prohibits public schools from sponsoring an official prayer. The Court has not, however, directly addressed whether, or to what extent, a state may sponsor prayer at an institution of higher education. Because VMI is such an institution, we briefly consider how our sister circuits have dealt with the issue of state-sponsored prayer in public colleges and universities.

B.

In a situation closely analogous to that presented here, the Court of Appeals for the District of Columbia, in *Anderson v. Laird*, addressed a federal regulation that required all cadets and midshipmen at the military academies to attend "Protestant, Catholic or Jewish chapel services on Sundays." In *Anderson,* the court ruled that this chapel attendance requirement violated the Establishment Clause. In its lead opinion, the court concluded that the "government may not require an individual to engage in religious practices or be present at religious exercises." Significantly, the court held that the regulation violated the Constitution even though: (1) attendance at the military academies was voluntary; and (2) cadets and midshipmen could be excused from the chapel attendance requirement.

More recently, in *Tanford v. Brand*, the Seventh Circuit considered whether a state university could include a religious invocation as part of its graduation ceremony. In upholding the practice, the court suggested that the invocation was not coercive, in that students were not required to attend and attendees did not feel compelled to participate in the invocation—in fact, students and their guests frequently came in and out (or remained seated) while the invocation was delivered. The court characterized the invocation as "simply a tolerable acknowledgment of beliefs widely held among the people of this country."

In *Chaudhuri v. Tennessee*, the Sixth Circuit also declined to enjoin a state university's practice of including prayer in its graduation ceremony. Evaluating the practice under the *Lemon* test, the court first held that such prayers had a secular purpose in that they "solemniz[ed] public occasions, express[ed] confidence in the future, and encourag[ed] the recognition of what is worthy of appreciation in society." Moving to *Lemon*'s second prong, the court decided that "an audience of college-educated adults could [not] be influenced unduly by prayers of the sort in question here." On *Lemon*'s final criterion, the court concluded: "[i]t does not seem to us that the practice of including nonsectarian prayers or moments of silence at [school] events creates any church-state entanglement at all."

V.

General Bunting * * * suggests that we should apply the standard employed by the Supreme Court in *Marsh v. Chambers*, where the Court—based on the unique history of the practice—upheld Nebraska's practice of opening its legislative sessions with a prayer. In support of his position, the General insists that prayer during military ceremonies and before meals is part of the fabric of our society, and that the drafters of the First Amendment did not intend to prohibit prayer before meals at a military school.[8] Independently, General Bunting maintains that, even if the traditional Establishment Clause analysis applies, the supper prayer should be upheld because the prohibition on state-sponsored prayer does not apply to a military college.

The Plaintiffs, by contrast, contend that the supper prayer is no different than the government-sponsored prayers struck down by the Supreme Court in *Engel, Schempp, Lee,* and *Santa Fe*. They emphasize that the supper prayer is composed by a state official (the VMI Post

---

8. General Bunting also suggests that VMI has a First Amendment interest that must be weighed in the Establishment Clause analysis. Contrary to this contention, VMI has no First Amendment interests that it can wield against the constitutional rights of its cadets. *See Hopwood v. Texas* ("Saying that a [state] university has a First Amendment interest in this context is somewhat troubling.... The First Amendment generally protects citizens from the actions of government, not government from its citizens.").

Chaplain) and that it is delivered on a daily basis at mealtime, when the Corps is assembled as a "family." Furthermore, the prayer is delivered as part of an official VMI function, entirely controlled by the school. The supper prayer, according to the Plaintiffs, bears the strong imprimatur of the state: VMI's cadets are marched in uniform and in formation to the mess hall before the state-composed prayer is delivered.

A.

We must begin our resolution of these competing positions by identifying the standard that should guide our analysis of the constitutionality of VMI's supper prayer. General Bunting first suggests that we should view the prayer as a uniquely historical practice, in an approach similar to that employed by the Supreme Court in *Marsh*. In *Marsh*, though, the Court was specifically influenced by the fact that, in September of 1789, members of the first Congress voted to submit the First Amendment to the states in the same week that they voted "to appoint and to pay a Chaplain for each House" of Congress. In upholding the Nebraska practice, Chief Justice Burger reasoned: "[t]his unique history leads us to accept the interpretation of the First Amendment draftsmen who saw no real threat to the Establishment Clause arising from a practice of prayer similar to that now challenged."

The Supreme Court has since emphasized that *Marsh* is applicable only in narrow circumstances. In *County of Allegheny v. ACLU Greater Pittsburgh Chapter*, the Court recognized that the *Marsh* decision "relied specifically on the fact that Congress authorized legislative prayer at the same time that it produced the Bill of Rights." The Court expressly declined to interpret *Marsh* to mean that "all accepted practices 200 years old and their equivalents are constitutional today." Likewise, in *North Carolina Civil Liberties Union Legal Foundation v. Constangy*, we emphasized, in invalidating a judge's practice of opening court with a prayer, that *Marsh* was "predicated on the particular historical circumstances presented in that case."

Put simply, the supper prayer does not share *Marsh*'s "unique history." In fact, public universities and military colleges, such as VMI, did not exist when the Bill of Rights was adopted. We are therefore unable to apply *Marsh*'s reasoning to the evaluation of the constitutionality of the supper prayer. *See Edwards v. Aguillard*, 482 U.S. 578, 583 n.4, 107 S.Ct. 2573 (1987) (emphasizing that the *Marsh* analysis "is not useful in determining the proper roles of church and state in public schools, since free public education was virtually nonexistent at the time the Constitution was adopted").

B.

In rejecting the *Marsh* analysis, we are left to choose among the three traditional tests that the Supreme Court has used to evaluate Establishment Clause challenges. The test most often employed is that enunciated by the Court in *Lemon*. A second test, known as the "endorsement test," was first articulated by Justice O'Connor in her concurrence in *Lynch v. Donnelly*, and later adopted by a majority of the Court in *County of Allegheny*. Under the endorsement test, the government may not engage in a practice that suggests to the reasonable, informed observer that it is endorsing religion. Finally, in *Lee,* the Court formulated its "coercion test," under which "government may not coerce anyone to support or participate in religion or its exercise." 505 U.S. 577, 587, 112 S.Ct. 2649 (1992).

While the *Lemon* test dominates Establishment Clause jurisprudence, coercion has emerged as a prevailing consideration in the school prayer context. Because the Court has applied a variety of tests (in various combinations) in school prayer cases, federal appellate courts have also followed an inconsistent approach. * * *

During the past decade, we have emphasized that the *Lemon* test guides our analysis of Establishment Clause challenges. In the context of school prayer, though, we must give special consideration, under the principles discussed in *Lee* and *Santa Fe,* to whether a state has coerced religious worship. In the analysis that follows, we therefore assess the supper prayer against the principles announced in *Lee* and *Santa Fe,* and we then apply the *Lemon* criteria, treating the endorsement test as a refinement of *Lemon*'s second prong.

VI.

A.

Under the Supreme Court's decisions in *Lee* and *Santa Fe,* school officials may not, consistent with the Establishment Clause, compel students to participate in a religious activity. As the Court emphasized in *Lee,* "our precedents do not permit school officials to assist in composing prayers as an incident to a formal exercise for their students." 505 U.S. at 590, 112 S.Ct. 2649. The efforts of school officials "to monitor prayer will be perceived by the students as inducing a participation they might otherwise reject." *Id.* In defending the constitutionality of the supper prayer, General Bunting gives two reasons why the prayer should be upheld. First, he insists that VMI's cadets are mature adults, who will not feel coerced to participate in the supper prayer. Alternatively, he suggests that the members of the Corps (other than the rats) may avoid the prayer by falling out of the SRC formation before the Corps enters the mess hall.

It is undoubtedly true that grade school children are particularly "susceptible to pressure from their peers towards conformity." *Id.* at 593, 112 S.Ct. 2649. Recognizing a difference between such children and college students, certain of our sister circuits have approved the decisions of public universities to offer an invocation at graduation ceremonies. For example, in *Tanford,* the Seventh Circuit found that an invocation at a university commencement was not coercive. Similarly, in *Chaudhuri,* the Sixth Circuit allowed a state university to include a prayer at its graduation ceremonies, concluding that "here there was no coercion—real or otherwise—to participate in the nonsectarian prayers," because "an audience of college-educated adults could [not] be influenced unduly by prayers of the sort in question here."

Although VMI's cadets are not children, in VMI's educational system they are uniquely susceptible to coercion. VMI's adversative method of education emphasizes the detailed regulation of conduct and the indoctrination of a strict moral code. Entering students are exposed to the "rat line," in which upperclassmen torment and berate new students, bonding "new cadets to their fellow sufferers and, when they have completed the 7–month experience, to their former tormentors." *United States v. Virginia*, 518 U.S. 515, 522, 116 S.Ct. 2264 (1996). At VMI, even upperclassmen must submit to mandatory and ritualized activities, as obedience and conformity remain central tenets of the school's educational philosophy. In this atmosphere, General Bunting reinstituted the supper prayer in 1995 to build solidarity and bring the Corps together as a family. In this context, VMI's cadets are plainly coerced into participating in a religious exercise. Because of VMI's coercive atmosphere, the Establishment Clause precludes school officials from sponsoring an official prayer, even for mature adults.

The technical "voluntariness" of the supper prayer does not save it from its constitutional infirmities. At all relevant times, VMI's upperclass cadets could avoid the mess hall in order to shield themselves from the prayer. Nevertheless, the communal dining experience, like other official activities, is undoubtedly experienced as obligatory.[9] Through the hazing rituals that dominate a cadet's first year, members of the Corps are trained to participate in VMI's official activities. With this atmosphere as a background, VMI cannot avoid Establishment Clause problems by simply asserting that a cadet's attendance at supper and his or her participation in the supper prayer are "voluntary." In the words of the Supreme Court, " 'the government may no more use social pressure to enforce orthodoxy than it may use more direct means.' " *Santa Fe Indep. School Dist. v. Doe*, 530 U.S. 290, 312, 120 S.Ct. 2266 (2000) (quoting *Lee*, 505 U.S. at 594, 112 S.Ct. 2649). Put simply, VMI's supper prayer exacts an unconstitutional toll on the consciences of religious objectors. While the First Amendment does not in any way prohibit VMI's cadets from praying before, during, or after supper, the Establishment Clause prohibits VMI from sponsoring such a religious activity.

B.

We are compelled to reach the same conclusion when the supper prayer is measured against the three-part *Lemon* test. Under *Lemon*, a prayer must have a secular purpose; the primary effect of the prayer must be one that neither advances nor inhibits religion; and finally, the prayer must not foster an excessive government entanglement with religion. If we

---

9. Even if dining in the mess hall was truly voluntary, the First Amendment prohibits General Bunting from requiring religious objectors to alienate themselves from the VMI community in order to avoid a religious practice. *Lee*, 505 U.S. at 596, 112 S.Ct. 2649.

accept General Bunting's asserted purposes, the supper prayer may satisfy *Lemon*'s "secular purpose" prong. Nevertheless, in sponsoring an official prayer, VMI has plainly violated *Lemon*'s second and third prongs.

1.

The first prong of *Lemon* contemplates an inquiry into the subjective intentions of the government. "In applying the purpose test, it is appropriate to ask 'whether government's actual purpose is to endorse or disapprove of religion.'" *Wallace v. Jaffree,* 472 U.S. 38, 56, 105 S.Ct. 2479 (1985) (quoting *Lynch,* 465 U.S. at 690, 104 S.Ct. 1355 (O'Connor, J., concurring)). The secular purpose requirement presents "a fairly low hurdle" for the state, and a state-sponsored practice violates this prong of *Lemon* only "if it is *entirely* motivated by a purpose to advance religion." *Wallace,* 472 U.S. at 56, 105 S.Ct. 2479 (emphasis added). Nevertheless, a state may disingenuously profess a secular purpose for what is, in fact, a religious practice. While the state's characterization of its purpose is entitled to deference, it is our obligation to distinguish "a sham secular purpose from a sincere one." *Santa Fe,* 530 U.S. at 308, 120 S.Ct. 2266 (internal quotation marks omitted).

General Bunting has proffered several purposes (purportedly secular) for the supper prayer. First, he maintains that the prayer serves "an academic function by aiding VMI's mission of developing cadets into military and civilian leaders." Toward this end, the supper prayer supposedly promotes religious tolerance, educates cadets about religion, and gets "students to engage with their own beliefs." According to General Bunting, the supper prayer encourages "cadets to reflect on and develop their own spiritual dimension." The prayer, in the General's words, also serves an expressive and institutional function by "providing an occasion for American's tradition of expressing thanksgiving and requesting divine guidance." Finally, General Bunting contends that the prayer "accommodate[s] the spiritual needs and free exercise rights of cadets, whose opportunities to meet those needs and exercise those rights are limited by the demands of barracks life and the highly structured nature of the VMI program."

In assessing General Bunting's asserted purposes for the supper prayer, we are concerned that he seeks to obscure the difference between educating VMI's cadets about religion, on the one hand, and forcing them to practice it, on the other. When a state-sponsored activity has an overtly religious character, courts have consistently rejected efforts to assert a secular purpose for that activity. Indeed, we have emphasized that "an act so intrinsically religious as prayer cannot meet, or at least would have difficulty meeting, the secular purpose prong of the *Lemon* test." And we have also recognized the obvious, that recitation of a prayer "is undeniably religious and has, by its nature, both a religious purpose and effect."

In an analogous situation, the Court of Appeals for the District of Columbia rejected the government's contention that a federal regulation requiring chapel attendance had a secular purpose. The federal government maintained (as VMI does here) that chapel services accommodated the free exercise rights of cadets and midshipmen, as well as sensitizing them to the religious beliefs of the soldiers and sailors they would someday lead. Rejecting the contention that these purposes justified the chapel attendance requirement, the court found that the regulation lacked a secular purpose. *See also Edwards,* 482 U.S. at 581, 586, 107 S.Ct. 2573 (concluding that statute violated *Lemon*'s secular purpose prong by prohibiting "the teaching of the theory of evolution in public schools unless accompanied by instruction in 'creation science' ").

Similarly, in *Stone v. Graham,* the Supreme Court found no secular purpose for a statute that required the Ten Commandments be posted on the walls of all of a state's public schools. In that situation, the legislature of Kentucky had required that each copy of the Ten Commandments be printed with the words: "[t]he secular application of the Ten Commandments is clearly seen in its adoption as the fundamental legal code of Western Civilization and the Common Law of the United States." The Supreme Court rejected this characterization, concluding that:

> [t]he pre-eminent purpose for posting the Ten Commandments on schoolroom walls is plainly religious in nature. The Ten Commandments are undeniably a sacred text in the Jewish and Christian faiths, and no legislative recitation of a supposed secular purpose can blind us to that fact.

In invalidating the statute, the Court refused to ignore the religious purpose of this overtly religious text.

We are inclined to agree that the purpose of an official school prayer "is plainly religious in nature."[11] In evaluating the constitutionality of the supper prayer, however, we will accord General Bunting the benefit of all doubt and credit his explanation of the prayer's purposes. Assuming the supper prayer to be motivated by secular goals, we turn to the second and third prongs of *Lemon*.

2.

Regardless of the purposes motivating it, the supper prayer fails *Lemon*'s second prong. This "primary effect" prong must be assessed objectively, in order to measure whether the principal effect of government action "is to suggest government preference for a particular religious view or for religion in general." Put differently, "[t]he effect prong asks whether, irrespective of government's actual purpose, the practice under review in fact conveys a message of endorsement or disapproval [of religion]." *Wallace,* 472 U.S. at 56 n.42, 105 S.Ct. 2479 (internal quotation marks omitted).

The supper prayer has the primary effect of promoting religion, in that it sends the unequivocal message that VMI, as an institution,

---

11. Indeed, the district court found that the supper prayer lacked a secular purpose, stating that "[t]he only logical conclusion that can be drawn from [the asserted purposes] is that part of the Institute's educational mission, in the eyes of General Bunting, is religious indoctrination."

endorses the religious expressions embodied in the prayer. *See Engel v. Vitale,* 370 U.S. 421, 430, 82 S.Ct. 1261 (1962) ("There can be no doubt that New York's state prayer program officially establishes the religious beliefs embodied in the ... prayer."). The supper prayer is "delivered to a large audience assembled as part of a regularly scheduled, school-sponsored function conducted on school property." *Santa Fe,* 530 U.S. at 307, 120 S.Ct. 2266. In this context, "an objective observer, acquainted with the [supper prayer] would perceive it as a state endorsement of prayer in public schools." *Id.* at 308, 120 S.Ct. 2266 (internal quotation marks omitted).

As the Court has observed, "[s]uch an endorsement is not consistent with the established principle that the government must pursue a course of complete neutrality toward religion." *Wallace,* 472 U.S. at 60, 105 S.Ct. 2479. Even though VMI intended the supper prayer to be both inclusive and nondenominational, the Establishment Clause prohibits a state from promoting religion by authoring and promoting prayer for its citizens. In the words of the Court, "[t]he First Amendment was added to the Constitution to stand as a guarantee that neither the power nor the prestige of the Federal Government would be used to control, support or influence the kinds of prayer the American people can say." *Engel,* 370 U.S. at 429, 82 S.Ct. 1261. In establishing its supper prayer, VMI has done precisely what the First Amendment forbids.

In numerous other cases, courts have struck down similar practices under *Lemon*'s "primary effect" prong. *See, e.g., Doe v. Duncanville Indep. Sch. Dist.,* 70 F.3d 402, 406 (5th Cir.1995) (striking down policy requiring participation of basketball coach in prayer after games).

With these decisions as a jurisprudential background, we are constrained to conclude that the supper prayer conflicts with *Lemon*'s second prong. Although we recognize and respect a cadet's individual desire to say grace before supper, the Establishment Clause prohibits VMI from sponsoring this religious practice.

3.

While *Lemon*'s second prong could dispose of the constitutional issue, VMI's sponsorship of the supper prayer also brings the school into conflict with *Lemon*'s third prong, excessively entangling it with religious activity. As the Eleventh Circuit recently stated, "[t]he ability to regulate the content of speech is a hallmark of state involvement." Here, VMI has composed, mandated, and monitored a daily prayer for its cadets. In this way, VMI has taken a position on what constitutes appropriate religious worship—an entanglement with religious activity that is forbidden by the Establishment Clause.

C.

Our decision today does not reflect any "hostility toward religion or toward prayer."[13] *Engel*, 370 U.S. at 434, 82 S.Ct. 1261. As we have recognized, our " 'Nation's history has not been one of entirely sanitized separation between Church and State,' and it 'has never been thought either possible or desirable to enforce a regime of total separation.' " Indeed, the Establishment Clause protects religious expression from governmental interference. "The Establishment Clause thus stands as an expression of principle on the part of the Founders of our Constitution that religion is too personal, too sacred, too holy, to permit its 'unhallowed perversion' " by government. *Engel*, 370 U.S. at 431–32, 82 S.Ct. 1261 (quoting *Memorial and Remonstrance against Religious Assessments*, II WRITINGS OF JAMES MADISON 183, 187).

While General Bunting may have instituted the supper prayer with the best of intentions, in so doing he has placed VMI at odds with the Establishment Clause. The Founding Fathers "led the fight for adoption of our Constitution and also for our Bill of Rights with the very guarantees of religious freedom that forbid [this] sort of governmental activity." *Engel*, 370 U.S. at 435, 82 S.Ct. 1261. Indeed, "one of the greatest dangers to the freedom of the individual to worship in his own way [lies] in the Government's placing its official stamp of approval upon one particular kind of prayer." *Id.* at 429, 82 S.Ct. 1261.

VII.

Having decided that VMI's supper prayer conflicts with First Amendment principles, we turn to whether General Bunting is nevertheless entitled to qualified immunity. As a state official, General Bunting is immune from damages unless he violated "clearly established statutory or constitutional rights of which a reasonable person would have known." In this regard, a principle of constitutional law may be "clearly established" even though the precise factual situation has never been presented to a court. Accordingly, "officials can still be on notice that their conduct violates established law even in novel factual circumstances."

Although the Establishment Clause plainly forbids public schools from sponsoring an official prayer for young children, the Supreme Court has never addressed the constitutionality of state-sponsored prayer in any university setting, much less in a military college. Indeed, some of our sister circuits have approved prayer at certain university functions. In addition, the Court has not had the occasion to consider whether, or to what extent, the military may incorporate religious practices in its ceremonies. In these circumstances, General Bunting could reasonably have believed that the supper prayer was constitutional, and we must affirm the district court's decision to award him qualified immunity.

VIII.

For the foregoing reasons, we vacate the district court's judgment awarding Plaintiffs declaratory and injunctive relief. We affirm the court's

---

13. We also note that we are not called upon to address whether, or to what extent, the military may incorporate religious practices into its ceremonies. The Virginia General Assembly, not the Department of Defense, controls VMI.

decision that the Plaintiffs have alleged a violation of their rights under the Establishment Clause, but that General Bunting is nevertheless entitled to qualified immunity.

AFFIRMED IN PART AND VACATED IN PART.

D. APPLYING THE NEUTRALITY PRINCIPLE: PUBLIC FUNDING FOR PRIVATE RELIGIOUS EDUCATION

As mentioned above, neutrality has been an explicit component of Establishment Clause jurisprudence for a very long time. The question, though, has always been whether and to what extent neutrality amounts to an actual legal requirement. Can neutrality actually constitute a separate legal framework, or perhaps a test, similar in form and substance to other Establishment Clause tests? Is it a guiding principle or at least a relevant inquiry that can play a major role in the legal analysis, even if it is not actually a test? Is it, in reality, little more than a policy imperative that can assist judges in determining the contours of the debate in complex legal disputes? Does the impact of the neutrality question vary depending on the type of dispute at issue?

In the area of public funding for private religious education, recent decisions of the U.S. Supreme Court arguably give credence to the argument that—within this context—neutrality is at least a guiding principle. And for more than just 1–2 justices, it may actually amount to a framework for deciding a case itself.

Consider the treatment of the neutrality question in the *Zobrest* and *Simmons-Harris* cases, which follow? At this point in time, is there a separate and independent test for public funding of private religious education based at least in part, if not entirely, on a neutrality requirement?

PROBLEM 40: THE ELDORADO TEACHER EDUCATION INSTITUTE

The following hypothetical takes place in the fictional state of Eldorado.

Concerned about the ongoing shortage of applicants for public school teaching positions in high-need areas, the Eldorado Department of Education and the Eldorado State University system establish a highly publicized partnership for the purpose of identifying innovative methods of teacher recruitment and training. The statewide Eldorado Teacher Education Institute (ETI) is formed, jointly administered by the partnership and funded by a combination of public and private money. An unprecedented program with no actual campus, the ETI will not only have a site-based component leading to a teacher credential, but is also expected to generate new research in this area.

The ETI will offer an alternative approach for those wishing to begin careers in K–12 education. Student teaching requirements will be expanded to comprise the equivalent of a half-time teaching position for two full years, under the supervision of trained professionals.[a] In addition, the student teachers admitted to the ETI will all receive stipends of $75,000 per year. One-half of the stipend will be in the form of a check payable to the student teacher, and this check will in essence comprise a full-time salary for the half-time teaching position. The second half of the stipend will be in the form of a voucher that the student teacher will then turn over to the participating training site to fund the on-site supervision required.

Under the terms of the ETI's policies, these training sites can be public or private, religious or sectarian. Student teachers complete a formal request sheet, specifying their preferred type of student teaching assignment and listing up to five choices of training sites. These training sites are chosen, generally, from a list of eligible schools provided by the ETI, but may also include sites where the student teacher has established personal contacts. While ETI personnel consult with the student teachers and seek to collaborate with them on the choice of assignment, in the end the final decision regarding the training sites is necessarily made by the ETI professionals.

Admission to the ETI is limited to applicants interested in becoming special education teachers for students of any language background, or those interested in becoming bilingual teachers in the high-need language areas of Spanish, Cantonese, and Vietnamese.

Volatile data regarding the first cohort, however, leads to widespread debate throughout the state regarding the efficacy of the program and its prospective implications. An independent evaluation of the ETI program had in fact revealed that approximately 40 percent of the student teachers in the first cohort used their stipends to student teach at traditional religious schools, while another 25 percent used their stipends to teach at schools with a religious affiliation but with programs that are primarily secular in nature.[b]

A lawsuit is ultimately filed by members of the Eldorado branch of Parents United for the Separation of Church and State. Plaintiffs plan to argue that both the student teacher salary provision of the stipend program and the voucher provision of the stipend program violate the Establishment Clause. They are not only prepared to argue under principles articulated by Chief Justice Rehnquist in *Zobrest* and *Simmons-Harris,* but also under the principles articulated by Justice Souter in the latter case.

---

a. Student teaching, or "practice teaching"—as it is sometimes called—is an integral component of teacher credential programs. Students enrolled in these programs are given student teaching assignments in actual classrooms, typically at local public schools, where they teach lessons under the supervision of experienced classroom teachers who are legally responsible for the class. In the typical assignment, students eventually take over the class for a specific portion of the day (at the elementary level) or for an entire period (at the secondary level), grade papers, assign grades, etc. Each state specifies, by statute and/or regulation, the requisite number of "student teaching" hours required before the teacher education student is eligible to receive a credential. Alternate avenues of credentialing are often available as well.

b. "Traditional" religious schools can be defined as those with required religious instruction delivered by members of the clergy, as well as required participation in religious ceremonies and observances on campus. The more secular institutions are those with some religious affiliation but relatively limited religious activity. Harvard–Westlake in Los Angeles, for example, is listed in the Episcopal diocese, but describes itself as "a nondenominational independent institution" that includes "a Rabbi and Episcopal Chaplain on the faculty who are available to students. Both lead religious activities for interested students and faculty."

What arguments will be set forth by the plaintiffs under the respective Rehnquist opinions? Under the Souter opinion in *Simmons-Harris?* What result? Discuss.

ZOBREST v. CATALINA FOOTHILLS SCH. DIST.
509 U.S. 1, 113 S.Ct. 2462 (1993)

CHIEF JUSTICE REHNQUIST delivered the opinion of the Court.

Petitioner James Zobrest, who has been deaf since birth, asked respondent school district to provide a sign-language interpreter to accompany him to classes at a Roman Catholic high school in Tucson, Arizona, pursuant to the Individuals with Disabilities Education Act (IDEA) and its Arizona counterpart. The United States Court of Appeals for the Ninth Circuit decided, however, that provision of such a publicly employed interpreter would violate the Establishment Clause of the First Amendment. We hold that the Establishment Clause does not bar the school district from providing the requested interpreter.

James Zobrest attended grades one through five in a school for the deaf, and grades six through eight in a public school operated by respondent. While he attended public school, respondent furnished him with a sign-language interpreter. For religious reasons, James' parents (also petitioners here) enrolled him for the ninth grade in Salpointe Catholic High School, a sectarian institution.[1] When petitioners requested that respondent supply James with an interpreter at Salpointe, respondent referred the matter to the county attorney, who concluded that providing an interpreter on the school's premises would violate the United States Constitution. Pursuant to Ariz. Rev. Stat. Ann. § 15–253(B) (1991), the question next was referred to the Arizona attorney general, who concurred in the county attorney's opinion. Respondent accordingly declined to provide the requested interpreter.

* * *

We have never said that "religious institutions are disabled by the First Amendment from participating in publicly sponsored social welfare programs." For if the Establishment Clause did bar religious groups from receiving general government benefits, then "a church could not be protected by the police and fire departments, or have its public sidewalk kept in repair." *Widmar v. Vincent,* 454 U.S. 263, 274–75, 102 S.Ct. 269, 277 (1981) (internal quotation marks omitted). Given that a contrary rule would lead to such absurd results, we have consistently held that government programs that neutrally provide benefits to a broad class of citizens defined without reference to religion are not readily subject to an Establishment Clause challenge just because sectarian institutions may also receive an attenuated financial benefit. Nowhere have we stated this principle more clearly than in *Mueller v. Allen,* and *Witters v. Washington*

---

1. The parties have stipulated: "The two functions of secular education and advancement of religious values or beliefs are inextricably intertwined throughout the operations of Salpointe."

Dept. of Services for Blind, two cases dealing specifically with government programs offering general educational assistance.

In *Mueller*, we rejected an Establishment Clause challenge to a Minnesota law allowing taxpayers to deduct certain educational expenses in computing their state income tax, even though the vast majority of those deductions (perhaps over 90%) went to parents whose children attended sectarian schools. Two factors, aside from States' traditionally broad taxing authority, informed our decision. We noted that the law "permits *all* parents—whether their children attend public school or private—to deduct their children's educational expenses." See *Widmar, supra,* 454 U.S. at 274, 102 S.Ct. at 277 ("The provision of benefits to so broad a spectrum of groups is an important index of secular effect"); *Board of Ed. of Westside Community Schools (Dist. 66) v. Mergens,* 496 U.S. 226, 248, 110 S.Ct. 2356, 2371 (1990) (plurality opinion) (same). We also pointed out that under Minnesota's scheme, public funds become available to sectarian schools "only as a result of numerous private choices of individual parents of school-age children," thus distinguishing *Mueller* from our other cases involving "the direct transmission of assistance from the State to the schools themselves."

Witters was premised on virtually identical reasoning. In that case, we upheld against an Establishment Clause challenge the State of Washington's extension of vocational assistance, as part of a general state program, to a blind person studying at a private Christian college to become a pastor, missionary, or youth director. Looking at the statute as a whole, we observed that "[a]ny aid provided under Washington's program that ultimately flows to religious institutions does so only as a result of the genuinely independent and private choices of aid recipients." The program, we said, "creates no financial incentive for students to undertake sectarian education." We also remarked that, much like the law in *Mueller,* "Washington's program is 'made available generally without regard to the sectarian-nonsectarian, or public-nonpublic nature of the institution benefited.'" In light of these factors, we held that Washington's program—even as applied to a student who sought state assistance so that he could become a pastor—would not advance religion in a manner inconsistent with the Establishment Clause.

That same reasoning applies with equal force here. The service at issue in this case is part of a general government program that distributes benefits neutrally to any child qualifying as "disabled" under the IDEA, without regard to the "sectarian-nonsectarian, or public-nonpublic nature" of the school the child attends. By according parents freedom to select a school of their choice, the statute ensures that a government-paid interpreter will be present in a sectarian school only as a result of the private decision of individual parents. In other words, because the IDEA creates no financial incentive for parents to choose a sectarian school, an interpreter's presence there cannot be attributed to state decisionmaking. Viewed against the backdrop of *Mueller* and *Witters,* then, the Court of Appeals erred in its decision. When the government offers a neutral service on the premises of a sectarian school as part of a general program that "is in no way skewed towards religion," it follows under our prior decisions that provision of that service does not offend the Establishment Clause. Indeed, this is an even easier case than *Mueller* and *Witters* in the sense that, under the IDEA, no funds traceable to the government ever find their way into sectarian schools' coffers. The only indirect economic benefit a sectarian school might receive by dint of the IDEA is the disabled child's tuition—and that is, of course, assuming that the school makes a profit on each student; that, without an IDEA interpreter, the child would have gone to school elsewhere; and that the school, then, would have been unable to fill that child's spot.

* * *

The IDEA creates a neutral government program dispensing aid not to schools but to individual handicapped children. If a handicapped child chooses to enroll in a sectarian school, we hold that the Establishment Clause does not prevent the school district from furnishing him with a sign-language interpreter there in order to facilitate his education. The judgment of the Court of Appeals is therefore

Reversed.

ZELMAN v. SIMMONS–HARRIS

536 U.S. 639, 122 S.Ct. 2460 (2002)

CHIEF JUSTICE REHNQUIST delivered the opinion of the Court.

The State of Ohio has established a pilot program designed to provide educational choices to families with children who reside in the Cleveland City School District. The question presented is whether this program offends the Establishment Clause of the United States Constitution. We hold that it does not.

There are more than 75,000 children enrolled in the Cleveland City School District. The majority of these children are from low-income and minority families. Few of these families enjoy the means to send their children to any school other than an inner-city public school. For more than a generation, however, Cleveland's public schools have been among the worst performing public schools in the Nation. In 1995, a Federal District Court declared a "crisis of magnitude" and placed the entire Cleveland school district under state control. Shortly thereafter, the state auditor found that Cleveland's public schools were in the midst of a "crisis that is perhaps unprecedented in the history of American education." The district had failed to meet any of the 18 state standards for minimal acceptable performance. Only 1 in 10 ninth graders could pass a basic proficiency examination, and students at all levels performed at a dismal rate compared with students in other Ohio public schools. More than two-thirds of high school students either dropped or failed out before gradua-tion. Of those students who managed to reach their senior year, one of every four still failed to graduate. Of those students who did graduate, few could read, write, or compute at levels comparable to their counterparts in other cities.

It is against this backdrop that Ohio enacted, among other initiatives, its Pilot Project Scholarship Program. The program provides financial assistance to families in any Ohio school district that is or has been "under federal court order requiring supervision and operational management of the district by the state superintendent." Cleveland is the only Ohio school district to fall within that category.

The program provides two basic kinds of assistance to parents of children in a covered district. First, the program provides tuition aid for students in kindergarten through third grade, expanding each year through eighth grade, to attend a participating public or private school of their parent's choosing. Second, the program provides tutorial aid for students who choose to remain enrolled in public school.

The tuition aid portion of the program is designed to provide educational choices to parents who reside in a covered district. Any private school, whether religious or nonreligious, may participate in the program and accept program students so long as the school is located within the boundaries of a covered district and meets statewide educational standards. Participating private schools must agree not to discriminate on the basis of race, religion, or ethnic background, or to "advocate or foster unlawful behavior or teach hatred of any person or group on the basis of race, ethnicity, national origin, or religion." Any public school located in a school district adjacent to the covered district may also participate in the program. Adjacent public schools are eligible to receive a $2,250 tuition grant for each program student accepted in addition to the full amount of per-pupil state funding attributable to each additional student. All participating schools, whether public or private, are required to accept students in accordance with rules and procedures established by the state superintendent.

Tuition aid is distributed to parents according to financial need. Families with incomes below 200% of the poverty line are given priority and are eligible to receive 90% of private school tuition up to $2,250. For these lowest income families, participating private schools may not charge a parental copayment greater than $250. For all other families, the program pays 75% of tuition costs, up to $1,875, with no copayment cap. These families receive tuition aid only if the number of available scholarships exceeds the number of low-income children who choose to participate.[2] Where tuition aid is spent depends solely upon where parents who receive tuition aid choose to enroll their child. If parents choose a private school, checks are made payable to the parents who then endorse the checks over to the chosen school.

* * *

---

2. The number of available scholarships per covered district is determined annually by the Ohio Superintendent for Public Instruction.

The program has been in operation within the Cleveland City School District since the 1996–1997 school year. In the 1999–2000 school year, 56 private schools participated in the program, 46 (or 82%) of which had a religious affiliation. None of the public schools in districts adjacent to Cleveland have elected to participate. More than 3,700 students participated in the scholarship program, most of whom (96%) enrolled in religiously affiliated schools. Sixty percent of these students were from families at or below the poverty line. In the 1998–1999 school year, approximately 1,400 Cleveland public school students received tutorial aid. This number was expected to double during the 1999–2000 school year.

The program is part of a broader undertaking by the State to enhance the educational options of Cleveland's schoolchildren in response to the 1995 takeover. That undertaking includes programs governing community and magnet schools.

* * *

In July 1999, respondents filed this action in United States District Court, seeking to enjoin the reenacted program on the ground that it violated the Establishment Clause of the United States Constitution. In August 1999, the District Court issued a preliminary injunction barring further implementation of the program, which we stayed pending review by the Court of Appeals. In December 1999, the District Court granted summary judgment for respondents. In December 2000, a divided panel of the Court of Appeals affirmed the judgment of the District Court, finding that the program had the "primary effect" of advancing religion in violation of the Establishment Clause. The Court of Appeals stayed its mandate pending disposition in this Court. We granted certiorari and now reverse the Court of Appeals.

The Establishment Clause of the First Amendment, applied to the States through the Fourteenth Amendment, prevents a State from enacting laws that have the "purpose" or "effect" of advancing or inhibiting religion. *Agostini v. Felton,* 521 U.S. 203, 222–23, 117 S.Ct. 1997 (1997) ("[W]e continue to ask whether the government acted with the purpose of advancing or inhibiting religion [and] whether the aid has the 'effect' of advancing or inhibiting religion"). There is no dispute that the program challenged here was enacted for the valid secular purpose of providing educational assistance to poor children in a demonstrably failing public school system. Thus, the question presented is whether the Ohio program nonetheless has the forbidden "effect" of advancing or inhibiting religion.

To answer that question, our decisions have drawn a consistent distinction between government programs that provide aid directly to religious schools, *Mitchell v. Helms,* 530 U.S. 793, 810–14, 120 S.Ct. 2530 (2000) (plurality opinion); *id.* at 841–44, 120 S.Ct. 2530 (O'CONNOR, J., concurring in judgment); *Agostini, supra,* at 225–27, 117 S.Ct. 1997; *Rosenberger v. Rector and Visitors of Univ. of Va.,* 515 U.S. 819, 842, 115 S.Ct. 2510 (1995) (collecting cases), and programs of true private choice, in which government aid reaches religious schools only as a result of the genuine and independent choices of private individuals, *Zobrest v. Catalina Foothills School Dist.*, 509 U.S. 1, 113 S.Ct. 2462 (1993). While our jurisprudence with respect to the constitutionality of direct aid programs has "changed significantly" over the past two decades, *Agostini, supra,* at 236, 117 S.Ct. 1997, our jurisprudence with respect to true private choice programs has remained consistent and unbroken. Three times we have confronted Establishment Clause challenges to neutral government programs that provide aid directly to a broad class of individuals, who, in turn, direct the aid to religious schools or institutions of their own choosing. Three times we have rejected such challenges.

[The Court then discusses *Mueller, Witters,* and *Zobrest* at some length.]

    * * *

Mueller, Witters, and *Zobrest* * * * make clear that where a government aid program is neutral with respect to religion, and provides assistance directly to a broad class of citizens who, in turn, direct government aid to religious schools wholly as a result of their own genuine and independent private choice, the program is not readily subject to challenge under the Establishment Clause. A program that shares these features permits government aid to reach religious institutions only by way of the deliberate choices of numerous individual recipients. The incidental advancement of a religious mission, or the perceived endorsement of a religious message, is reasonably attributable to the individual recipient, not to the government, whose role ends with the disbursement of benefits. * * *

[W]e have never found a program of true private choice to offend the Establishment Clause.

We believe that the program challenged here is a program of true private choice, consistent with *Mueller, Witters,* and *Zobrest,* and thus constitutional. As was true in those cases, the Ohio program is neutral in all respects toward religion. It is part of a general and multifaceted undertaking by the State of Ohio to provide educational opportunities to the children of a failed school district. It confers educational assistance directly to a broad class of individuals defined without reference to religion, *i.e.,* any parent of a school-age child who resides in the Cleveland City School District. The program permits the participation of *all* schools within the district, religious or nonreligious. Adjacent public schools also may participate and have a financial incentive to do so. Program benefits are available to participating families on neutral terms, with no reference to religion. The only preference stated anywhere in the program is a preference for low-income families, who receive greater assistance and are given priority for admission at participating schools.

There are no "financial incentive[s]" that "ske[w]" the program toward religious schools. Such incentives "[are] not present . . . where the aid is allocated on the basis of neutral, secular criteria that neither favor nor disfavor religion, and is made available to both religious and secular beneficiaries on a nondiscriminatory basis." *Agostini, supra,* at 231, 117 S.Ct. 1997. The program here in fact creates financial *dis*incentives for religious schools, with private schools receiving only half the government assistance given to community schools and one-third the assistance given to magnet schools. Adjacent public schools, should any choose to accept program students, are also eligible to receive two to three times the state funding of a private religious school. Families too have a financial disincentive to choose a private religious school over other schools. Parents that choose to participate in the scholarship program and then to enroll their children in a private school (religious or nonreligious) must copay a portion of the school's tuition. Families that choose a community school, magnet school, or traditional public school pay nothing. Although such features of the program are not necessary to its constitutionality, they clearly dispel the claim that the program "creates ... financial incentive[s] for parents to choose a sectarian school." *Zobrest,* 509 U.S. at 10, 113 S.Ct. at 2462.

Respondents suggest that even without a financial incentive for parents to choose a religious school, the program creates a "public perception that the State is endorsing religious practices and beliefs." But we have repeatedly recognized that no reasonable observer would think a neutral program of private choice, where state aid reaches religious schools solely as a result of the numerous independent decisions of private individuals, carries with it the *imprimatur* of government endorsement. *Zobrest, supra,* at 10–11, 113 S.Ct. 2462; *e.g., Mitchell, supra,* at 842–43, 120 S.Ct. 2530 (O'CONNOR, J., concurring in judgment) ("In terms of public perception, a government program of direct aid to religious schools ... differs meaningfully from the government distributing aid directly to individual students who, in turn, decide to use the aid at the same religious schools"). The argument is particularly misplaced here since "the reasonable observer in the endorsement inquiry must be deemed aware" of the "history and context" underlying a challenged program. *Good News Club v. Milford Central School,* 533 U.S. 98, 119, 121 S.Ct. 2093 (2001) (internal quotation marks omitted). Any objective observer familiar with the full history and context of the Ohio program would reasonably view it as one aspect of a broader undertaking to assist poor children in failed schools, not as an endorsement of religious schooling in general.

There also is no evidence that the program fails to provide genuine opportunities for Cleveland parents to select secular educational options for their school-age children. Cleveland schoolchildren enjoy a range of educational choices: They may remain in public school as before, remain in public school with publicly funded tutoring aid, obtain a scholarship and choose a religious school, obtain a scholarship and choose a nonreligious private school, enroll in a community school, or enroll in a magnet school. That 46 of the 56 private schools now participating in the program are religious schools does not condemn it as a violation of the Establishment Clause. The Establishment Clause question is whether Ohio is coercing parents into sending their children to religious schools, and that question must be answered by evaluating *all* options Ohio provides Cleveland schoolchildren, only one of which is to obtain a program scholarship and then choose a religious school.

JUSTICE SOUTER speculates that because more private religious schools currently participate in the program, the program itself must somehow discourage the participation of private nonreligious schools. But Cleveland's preponderance of religiously affiliated private schools certainly did not arise as a result of the program; it is a phenomenon common to many American cities. * * *

Respondents and JUSTICE SOUTER claim that even if we do not focus on the number of participating schools that are religious schools, we should attach constitutional significance to the fact that 96% of scholarship recipients have enrolled in religious schools. They claim that this alone proves parents lack genuine choice, even if no parent has ever said so. We need not consider this argument in detail, since it was flatly rejected in *Mueller,* where we found it irrelevant that 96% of parents taking deductions for tuition expenses paid tuition at religious schools. Indeed, we have recently found it irrelevant even to the constitutionality of a direct aid program that a vast majority of program benefits went to religious schools. See *Agostini,* 521 U.S. at 229, 117 S.Ct. 1997 ("Nor are we willing to conclude that the constitutionality of an aid program depends on the number of sectarian school students who happen to receive the otherwise neutral aid" (citing *Mueller,* 463 U.S. at 401, 103 S.Ct. 3062)); see also *Mitchell,* 530 U.S. at 812 n.6, 120 S.Ct. 2530 (plurality opinion) ("[*Agostini*] held that the proportion of aid benefiting students at religious schools pursuant to a neutral program involving private choices was irrelevant to the constitutional inquiry"); *id.,* at 848, 120 S.Ct. 2530 (O'CONNOR, J., concurring in judgment) (same) (quoting *Agostini, supra,* at 229, 117 S.Ct. 1997). The constitutionality of a neutral educational aid program simply does not turn on whether and why, in a particular area, at a particular time, most private schools are run by religious organizations, or most recipients choose to use the aid at a religious school. As we said in *Mueller,* "[s]uch an approach would scarcely provide the certainty that this field stands in need of, nor can we perceive principled standards by which such statistical evidence might be evaluated." 463 U.S. at 401, 103 S.Ct. 3062.

This point is aptly illustrated here. The 96% figure upon which respondents and JUSTICE SOUTER rely discounts entirely (1) the more than 1,900 Cleveland children enrolled in alternative community schools, (2) the more than 13,000 children enrolled in alternative magnet schools, and (3) the more than 1,400 children enrolled in traditional public schools with tutorial assistance. Including some or all of these children in the denominator of children enrolled in nontraditional schools during the 1999–2000 school year drops the percentage enrolled in religious schools from 96% to under 20%. The 96% figure also represents but a snapshot of one particular school year. In the 1997–1998 school year, by contrast, only 78% of scholarship recipients attended religious schools. The difference was attributable to two private nonreligious schools that had accepted 15% of all scholarship students electing instead to register as community schools, in light of larger per-pupil funding for community schools and the uncertain future of the scholarship program generated by this litigation. Many of the students enrolled in these schools as scholarship students remained enrolled as community school students, thus demonstrating the arbitrariness of counting one type of school but not the other to assess primary effect. In spite of repeated questioning from the Court at oral argument, respondents offered no convincing justification for their approach, which relies entirely on such arbitrary classifications.

* * *

In sum, the Ohio program is entirely neutral with respect to religion. It provides benefits directly to a wide spectrum of individuals, defined only by financial need and residence in a particular school district. It permits such individuals to exercise genuine choice among options public and private, secular and religious. The program is therefore a program of true private choice. In keeping with an unbroken line of decisions rejecting challenges to similar programs, we hold that the program does not offend the Establishment Clause.

The judgment of the Court of Appeals is reversed.

It is so ordered.

JUSTICE O'CONNOR, concurring.

* * * While I join the Court's opinion, I write separately for two reasons. First, although the Court takes an important step, I do not believe that today's decision, when considered in light of other longstanding government programs that impact religious organizations and our prior Establishment Clause jurisprudence, marks a dramatic break from the past. Second, given the emphasis the Court places on verifying that parents of voucher students in religious schools have exercised "true private choice," I think it is worth elaborating on the Court's conclusion that this inquiry should consider all reasonable educational alternatives to religious schools that are available to parents. To do otherwise is to ignore how the educational system in Cleveland actually functions.

I

These cases are different from prior indirect aid cases in part because a significant portion of the funds appropriated for the voucher program reach religious schools without restrictions on the use of these funds. The share of public resources that reach religious schools is not, however, as significant as respondents suggest. Data from the 1999–2000 school year indicate that 82 percent of schools participating in the voucher program were religious and that 96 percent of participating students enrolled in religious schools, but these data are incomplete. These statistics do not take into account all of the reasonable educational choices that may be available to students in Cleveland public schools. When one considers the option to attend community schools, the percentage of students enrolled in religious schools falls to 62.1 percent. If magnet schools are included in the mix, this percentage falls to 16.5 percent.

* * *

II

Nor does today's decision signal a major departure from this Court's prior Establishment Clause jurisprudence. A central tool in our analysis of cases in this area has been the *Lemon* test. As originally formulated, a statute passed this test only if it had "a secular legislative purpose," if its "principal or primary effect" was one that "neither advance[d] nor inhibit[ed] religion," and if it did "not foster an excessive government entanglement with religion." In *Agostini v. Felton,* 521 U.S. 203, 218, 232–233, 117 S.Ct. 1997 (1997), we folded the entanglement inquiry into the primary effect inquiry. This made sense because both inquiries rely on the same evidence, and the degree of entanglement has implications for whether a statute advances or inhibits religion. The test today is basically the same as that set forth in *School Dist. of Abington Township v. Schempp*, over 40 years ago.

The Court's opinion in these cases focuses on a narrow question related to the *Lemon* test: how to apply the primary effects prong in indirect aid cases? Specifically, it clarifies the basic inquiry when trying to determine whether a program that distributes aid to beneficiaries, rather than directly to service providers, has the primary effect of advancing or inhibiting religion, or, as I have put it, of "endors[ing] or disapprov[ing] . . . religion." Courts are instructed to consider two factors: first, whether the program administers aid in a neutral fashion, without differentiation based on the religious status of beneficiaries or providers of services; second, and more importantly, whether beneficiaries of indirect aid have a genuine choice among religious and nonreligious organizations when determining the organization to which they will direct that aid. If the answer to either query is "no," the program should be struck down under the Establishment Clause.

* * *

III

There is little question in my mind that the Cleveland voucher program is neutral as between religious schools and nonreligious schools. Justice SOUTER rejects the Court's notion of neutrality, proposing that the neutrality of a program should be gauged not by the opportunities it presents but rather by its effects. In particular, a "neutrality test . . . [should] focus on a category of aid that may be directed to religious as well as secular schools, and ask whether the scheme favors a religious direction." Justice SOUTER doubts that the Cleveland program is neutral under this view. He surmises that the cap on tuition that voucher schools may charge low-income students encourages these students to attend religious rather than nonreligious private voucher schools. But Justice SOUTER's notion of neutrality is inconsistent with that in our case law. As we put it in *Agostini,* government aid must be "made available to both religious and secular beneficiaries on a nondiscriminatory basis." 521 U.S. at 231, 117 S.Ct. 1997.

     * * *

In my view the more significant finding in these cases is that Cleveland parents who use vouchers to send their children to religious private schools do so as a result of true private choice. * * *

JUSTICE SOUTER, with whom JUSTICE STEVENS, JUSTICE GINSBURG, and JUSTICE BREYER join, dissenting.

The Court's majority holds that the Establishment Clause is no bar to Ohio's payment of tuition at private religious elementary and middle schools under a scheme that systematically provides tax money to support the schools' religious missions. The occasion for the legislation thus upheld is the condition of public education in the city of Cleveland. The record indicates that the schools are failing to serve their objective, and the vouchers in issue here are said to be needed to provide adequate alternatives to them. If there were an excuse for giving short shrift to the Establishment Clause, it would probably apply here. But there is no excuse. Constitutional limitations are placed on government to preserve constitutional values in hard cases, like these. "[C]onstitutional lines have to be drawn, and on one side of every one of them is an otherwise sympathetic case that provokes impatience with the Constitution and with the line. But constitutional lines are the price of constitutional government." *Agostini v. Felton,* 521 U.S. 203, 254, 117 S.Ct. 1997 (1997) (SOUTER, J., dissenting). I therefore respectfully dissent.

The applicability of the Establishment Clause to public funding of benefits to religious schools was settled in *Everson v. Board of Ed. of Ewing*, which inaugurated the modern era of establishment doctrine. The Court stated the principle in words from which there was no dissent:

> No tax in any amount, large or small, can be levied to support any religious activities or institutions, whatever they may be called, or whatever form they may adopt to teach or practice religion.

The Court has never in so many words repudiated this statement, let alone, in so many words, overruled *Everson.*

Today, however, the majority holds that the Establishment Clause is not offended by Ohio's Pilot Project Scholarship Program, under which students may be eligible to receive as much as $2,250 in the form of tuition vouchers transferable to religious schools. In the city of Cleveland the overwhelming proportion of large appropriations for voucher money must be spent on religious schools if it is to be spent at all, and will be spent in amounts that cover almost all of tuition. The money will thus pay for eligible students' instruction not only in secular subjects but in religion as well, in schools that can fairly be characterized as founded to teach religious doctrine and to imbue teaching in all subjects with a religious dimension. Public tax money will pay at a systemic level for teaching the covenant with Israel and Mosaic law in Jewish schools, the primacy of the Apostle Peter and the Papacy in Catholic schools, the truth of reformed Christianity in Protestant schools, and the revelation to the Prophet in Muslim schools, to speak only of major religious groupings in the Republic.

How can a Court consistently leave *Everson* on the books and approve the Ohio vouchers? The answer is that it cannot. It is only by ignoring *Everson* that the majority can claim to rest on traditional law in its invocation of neutral aid provisions and private choice to sanction the Ohio law. It is, moreover, only by ignoring the meaning of neutrality and private choice themselves that the majority can even pretend to rest today's decision on those criteria.

I

The majority's statements of Establishment Clause doctrine cannot be appreciated without some historical perspective on the Court's announced limitations on government aid to religious education, and its repeated repudiation of limits previously set. My object here is not to give any nuanced exposition of the cases, which I tried to classify in some detail in an earlier opinion, see *Mitchell v. Helms,* 530 U.S. 793, 873–99, 120 S.Ct. 2530 (2000) (dissenting opinion), but to set out the broad doctrinal stages covered in the modern era, and to show that doctrinal bankruptcy has been reached today.

Viewed with the necessary generality, the cases can be categorized in three groups. In the period from 1947 to 1968, the basic principle of no aid to religion through school benefits was unquestioned. Thereafter for some 15 years, the Court termed its efforts as attempts to draw a line against aid that would be divertible to support the religious, as distinct from the secular, activity of an institutional beneficiary. Then, starting in 1983, concern with divertibility was gradually lost in favor of approving aid in amounts unlikely to afford substantial benefits to religious schools, when offered evenhandedly without regard to a recipient's religious character, and when channeled to a religious institution only by the genuinely free choice of some private individual. Now, the three stages are succeeded by a fourth, in which the substantial character of government aid is held to have no constitutional significance, and the espoused criteria of neutrality in offering aid, and private choice in directing it, are shown to be nothing but examples of verbal formalism. * * *

II

Although it has taken half a century since *Everson* to reach the majority's twin standards of neutrality and free choice, the facts show that, in the majority's hands, even these criteria cannot convincingly legitimize the Ohio scheme.

A

Consider first the criterion of neutrality. As recently as two Terms ago, a majority of the Court recognized that neutrality conceived of as evenhandedness toward aid recipients had never been treated as alone sufficient to satisfy the Establishment Clause, *Mitchell,* 530 U.S. at 838–39, 120 S.Ct. 2530 (O'CONNOR, J., concurring in judgment); *id.* at 884, 120 S.Ct. 2530 (SOUTER, J., dissenting). But at least in its limited significance, formal neutrality seemed to serve some purpose. Today, however, the majority employs the neutrality criterion in a way that renders it impossible to understand.

Neutrality in this sense refers, of course, to evenhandedness in setting eligibility as between potential religious and secular recipients of public money. *Id.* at 809–10, 120 S.Ct. 2530 (plurality opinion); *id.* at 878–84, 120 S.Ct. 2530 (SOUTER, J., dissenting) (three senses of "neutrality"). Thus, for example, the aid scheme in *Witters* provided an eligible recipient with a scholarship to be used at any institution within a practically unlimited universe of schools; it did not tend to provide more or less aid depending on which one the scholarship recipient chose, and there was no indication that the maximum scholarship amount would be insufficient at secular schools. Neither did any condition of Zobrest's interpreter's subsidy favor religious education.

In order to apply the neutrality test, then, it makes sense to focus on a category of aid that may be directed to religious as well as secular schools, and ask whether the scheme favors a religious direction. Here, one would ask whether the voucher provisions, allowing for as much as $2,250 toward private school tuition (or a grant to a public school in an adjacent district), were written in a way that skewed the scheme toward benefiting religious schools.

This, however, is not what the majority asks. The majority looks not to the provisions for tuition vouchers, but to every provision for educational opportunity: "The program permits the participation of *all* schools within the district, [as well as public schools in adjacent districts], religious or nonreligious." The majority then finds confirmation that "participation of *all* schools" satisfies neutrality by noting that the better part of total state educational expenditure goes to public schools, thus showing there is no favor of religion.

The illogic is patent. If regular, public schools (which can get no voucher payments) "participate" in a voucher scheme with schools that can, and public expenditure is still predominantly on public schools, then the majority's reasoning would find neutrality in a scheme of vouchers available for private tuition in districts with no secular private schools at all. "Neutrality" as the majority employs the term is, literally, verbal and nothing more. This, indeed, is the only way the majority can gloss over the very nonneutral feature of the total scheme covering "*all* schools": public tutors may receive from the State no more than $324 per child to support extra tutoring (that is, the State's 90% of a total amount of $360), whereas the tuition voucher schools (which turn out to be mostly religious) can receive up to $2,250.

Why the majority does not simply accept the fact that the challenge here is to the more generous voucher scheme and judge its neutrality in relation to religious use of voucher money seems very odd. It seems odd, that is, until one recognizes that comparable schools for applying the criterion of neutrality are also the comparable schools for applying the other majority criterion, whether the immediate recipients of voucher aid have a genuinely free choice of religious and secular schools to receive the voucher money. And in applying this second criterion, the consideration of "*all* schools" is ostensibly helpful to the majority position.

B

The majority addresses the issue of choice the same way it addresses neutrality, by asking whether recipients or potential recipients of voucher aid have a choice of public schools among secular alternatives to religious schools. Again, however, the majority asks the wrong question and misapplies the criterion. The majority has confused choice in spending scholarships with choice from the entire menu of possible educational placements, most of them open to anyone willing to attend a public school. I say "confused" because the majority's new use of the choice criterion, which it frames negatively as "whether Ohio is coercing parents into sending their children to religious schools," ignores the reason for having a private choice enquiry in the first place. Cases since *Mueller* have found private choice relevant under a rule that aid to religious schools can be permissible so long as it first passes through the hands of students or parents. The majority's view that all educational choices are comparable for purposes of choice thus ignores the whole point of the choice test: it is a criterion for deciding whether indirect aid to a religious school is legitimate because it passes through private hands that can spend or use the aid in a secular school. The question is whether the private hand is genuinely free to send the money in either a secular direction or a religious one. The majority now has transformed this question about private choice in channeling aid into a question about selecting from examples of state spending (on education) including direct spending on magnet and community public schools that goes through no private hands and could never reach a religious school under any circumstance. When the choice test is transformed from where to spend the money to where to go to school, it is cut loose from its very purpose.

* * *

If, contrary to the majority, we ask the right question about genuine choice to use the vouchers, the answer shows that something is influencing choices in a way that aims the money in a religious direction: of 56 private schools in the district participating in the voucher program (only 53 of which accepted voucher students in 1999–2000), 46 of them are religious; 96.6% of all voucher recipients go to religious schools, only 3.4% to nonreligious ones. Unfortunately for the majority position, there is no explanation for this that suggests the religious direction results simply from free choices by parents. One answer to these statistics, for example, which would be consistent with the genuine choice claimed to be operating, might be that 96.6% of families choosing to avail themselves of vouchers choose to educate their children in schools of their own religion. This would not, in my view, render the scheme constitutional, but it would speak to the majority's choice criterion. Evidence shows, however, that almost two out of three families using vouchers to send their children to religious schools did not embrace the religion of those schools. The families made it clear they had not chosen the schools because they wished their children to be proselytized in a religion not their own, or in any religion, but because of educational opportunity. * * *

There is, in any case, no way to interpret the 96.6% of current voucher money going to religious schools as reflecting a free and genuine choice by the families that apply for vouchers. The 96.6% reflects, instead, the fact that too few nonreligious school desks are available and few but religious schools can afford to accept more than a handful of voucher students. And contrary to the majority's assertion, public schools in adjacent districts hardly have a financial incentive to participate in the Ohio voucher program, and none has. For the overwhelming number of children in the voucher scheme, the only alternative to the public schools is religious. And it is entirely irrelevant that the State did not deliberately design the network of private schools for the sake of channeling money into religious institutions. The criterion is one of genuinely free choice on the part of the private individuals who choose, and a Hobson's choice is not a choice, whatever the reason for being Hobsonian.

III

* * *

If the divisiveness permitted by today's majority is to be avoided in the short term, it will be avoided only by action of the political branches at the state and national levels. Legislatures not driven to desperation by the problems of public education may be able to see the threat in vouchers negotiable in sectarian schools. Perhaps even cities with problems like Cleveland's will perceive the danger, now that they know a federal court will not save them from it.

My own course as a judge on the Court cannot, however, simply be to hope that the political branches will save us from the consequences of the majority's decision. *Everson's* statement is still the touchstone of sound law, even though the reality is that in the matter of educational aid the Establishment Clause has largely been read away. True, the majority has not approved vouchers for religious schools alone, or aid earmarked for religious instruction. But no scheme so clumsy will ever get before us, and in the cases that we may see, like these, the Establishment Clause is largely silenced. I do not have the option to leave it silent, and I hope that a future Court will reconsider today's dramatic departure from basic Establishment Clause principle.

NOTES

1. *Simmons-Harris* was a long-awaited opinion by both proponents and opponents of school voucher programs. The 5–4 decision ended at least one component of the debate: channeling public funds through parents for the funding of private religious education was not a blanket violation of the Establishment Clause. What is the scope of the *Simmons–Harris* decision? Is it limited to the type of voucher program at issue in the Ohio case, or are all voucher programs now going to be constitutional under Establishment Clause jurisprudence? How important was it to Chief Justice Rehnquist and Justice O'Connor that this was a particular type of program, geared toward helping low socioeconomic status (SES) children who had been attending the lowest performing schools in a District that was clearly in crisis? How important was it that the program was part of an entire menu of options that had been made available to these students under the rubric of equal educational opportunity? How central to the legal analysis were these facts? How applicable would this decision be in determining the constitutionality of a voucher program that provided equally for all students in a given city or state, despite differences in such factors as SES and individual school performance?

2. Church-state issues continue to play either a direct or an indirect role in current and prospective legal challenges to voucher program under state constitutional law. At least ten state constitutions, in fact, appear to provide for a greater level of separation between church and state than the federal baseline. *See, e.g., Bush v. Holmes*, 919 So.2d 392, 416 (Fla.2006). In *Holmes*, the Florida Supreme Court held by a vote of 5–2 that the Florida voucher program–the only statewide program of its kind in the country at the time– violated its own state constitution. However, it did so under a provision that was found to indirectly bar public money for private sectarian education in this manner. Excerpts from this recent decision follow.

BUSH v. HOLMES

919 So.2d 392 (Fla. 2006)

PARIENTE, C.J.

* * * The issue we decide is whether the State of Florida is prohibited by the Florida Constitution from expending public funds to allow students to obtain a private school education in kindergarten through grade twelve, as an alternative to a public school education. The law in question, now codified at section 1002.38, Florida Statutes (2005), authorizes a system of school vouchers and is known as the Opportunity Scholarship Program (OSP).

Under the OSP, a student from a public school that fails to meet certain minimum state standards has two options. The first is to move to another public school with a satisfactory record under the state standards. The second option is to receive funds from the public treasury, which would otherwise have gone to the student's school district, to pay the student's tuition at a private school. The narrow question we address is whether the second option violates a part of the Florida Constitution requiring the state to both provide for "the education of all children residing within its borders" and provide "by law for a uniform, efficient, safe, secure, and high quality system of free public schools that allows students to obtain a high quality education." Art. IX, § 1(a), Fla. Const.

As a general rule, courts may not reweigh the competing policy concerns underlying a legislative enactment. The arguments of public policy supporting both sides in this dispute have obvious merit, and the Legislature with the Governor's assent has resolved the ensuing debate in favor of the proponents of the program. In most cases, that would be the end of the matter. However, as is equally self-evident, the usual deference given to the Legislature's resolution of public policy issues is at all times circumscribed by the Constitution. Acting within its constitutional limits, the Legislature's power to resolve issues of civic debate receives great deference. Beyond those limits, the Constitution must prevail over any enactment contrary to it.

Thus, in reviewing the issue before us, the justices emphatically are not examining whether the public policy decision made by the other branches is wise or unwise, desirable or undesirable. Nor are we examining whether the Legislature intended to supplant or replace the public school system to any greater or lesser extent. Indeed, we acknowledge, as does the dissent, that the statute at issue here is limited in the number of students it affects. * * *

Our inquiry begins with the plain language of the second and third sentences of article IX, section 1(a) of the Constitution. The relevant words are these: "It is ... a paramount duty of the state to make adequate provision for the education of all children residing within its borders." Using the same term, "adequate provision," article IX, section 1(a) further states: "Adequate provision shall be made by law for a uniform, efficient, safe, secure, and high quality system of free public schools." For reasons expressed more fully below, we find that the OSP violates this language. It diverts public dollars into separate private systems parallel to and in competition with the free public schools that are the sole means set out in the Constitution for the state to provide for the education of Florida's children. This diversion not only reduces money available to the free schools, but also funds private schools that are not "uniform" when compared with each other or the public system. Many standards imposed by law on the public schools are inapplicable to the private schools receiving public monies. * * * [T]hrough the OSP the state is fostering plural, nonuniform systems of education in direct violation of the constitutional mandate for a uniform system of free public schools.

* * *

In sum, article IX, section 1(a) provides for the manner in which the state is to fulfill its mandate to make adequate provision for the education of Florida's children—through a system of public education. The OSP contravenes this constitutional provision because it allows some children to receive a publicly funded education through an alternative system of private schools that are not subject to the uniformity requirements of the public school system. The diversion of money not only reduces public funds for a public education but also uses public funds to provide an alternative education in private schools that are not subject to the "uniformity" requirements for public schools. Thus, in two significant respects, the OSP violates the mandate set forth in article IX, section 1(a).

We do not question the basic right of parents to educate their children as they see fit. We recognize that the proponents of vouchers have a strongly held view that students should have choices. Our decision does not deny parents recourse to either public or private school alternatives to a failing school. Only when the private school option depends upon public funding is choice limited. This limit is necessitated by the constitutional mandate in article IX, section 1(a), which sets out the state's responsibilities in a manner that does not allow the use of state monies to fund a private school education. * * *

WELLS, ANSTEAD, LEWIS, and QUINCE, concur.

BELL, J., dissents with an opinion, in which CANTERO, J., concurs.

BELL, J., dissenting.

"[N]othing in article IX, section 1 clearly prohibits the Legislature from allowing the well-delineated use of public funds for private school education, particularly in circumstances where the Legislature finds such use is necessary." *Bush v. Holmes,* 767 So.2d 668, 675 (Fla. 1st DCA 2000). This conclusion, written by Judge Charles Kahn for a unanimous panel of the First District Court of Appeal, is the only answer this Court is empowered to give to the constitutional question the majority has decided to answer. Therefore, I dissent.

* * *

The majority's reading of article IX, section 1 is flawed. * * * [The] mandate is to make adequate provision *for* a public school system. The text does not provide that the government's provision for education shall be "by" or "through" a system of free public schools. Without language of exclusion or preclusion, there is no support for the majority's finding that public schools are the exclusive means by or through which the government may fulfill its duty to make adequate provision for the education of every child in Florida.

As the ultimate sovereign, if the people of Florida had wanted to mandate this exclusivity, they could have very easily written article IX to include such a proscription. Ten other states have constitutional provisions that expressly prohibit the allocation of public education funds to private schools. *Compare* art. IX, Fla. Const., *with, e.g.,* Miss. Const. art. 8, § 208 ("[N]or shall any funds be appropriated toward the support of any sectarian school, or to any school that at the time of receiving such appropriation is not conducted as a free school."), *and* S.C. Const. art. XI,

§ 4 ("No money shall be paid from public funds nor shall the credit of the State or any of its political subdivisions be used for the direct benefit of any religious or other private educational institution."). However, the people of Florida have not included such a proscription in article IX, section 1 of the Florida Constitution. Therefore, without any express or necessarily implied proscription in article IX, section 1 of Florida's Constitution, this Court has no authority to declare the OSP unconstitutional as violative of article IX, section 1.

* * *

Our position as justices vests us with the right and the responsibility to declare a legislative enactment invalid—but only when such a declaration is an "imperative and unavoidable necessity." *State ex rel. Crim,* 159 So. at 664. No such necessity is evident in this case. Nothing in the plain language or history of article IX requires a finding that the Opportunity Scholarship Program is unconstitutional. The clear purpose behind article IX is to ensure that every child in Florida has the opportunity to receive a high-quality education and to ensure access to such an education by requiring the Legislature to make adequate provision for a uniform system of free public schools. There is absolutely no evidence before this Court that this mandate is not being fulfilled. * * *

CHAPTER IX

MORALITY, VALUES, AND EDUCATIONAL POLICY

■ ■ ■

This chapter focuses on recent controversies that exemplify competing visions of "morality" and "values." Underlying many of the debates in this area is the question of whether and to what extent morality and values should be reflected in the requirements of public education. Related inquiries include volatile questions of who gets to define *morality* and *which values* might appropriately inform the day-to-day decisions and practices of educators.

Controversies in this area are often based implicitly or explicitly on religion, and they may be even more emotional than the ones addressed in the previous chapter. Indeed, not only are there continuing examples in these materials of disagreements regarding the extent to which religion should be reflected in the legal mandates, but the efficacy of religious doctrine itself may be questioned.

The U.S. is a pluralistic society, and its residents often hold widely differing views on the place of religion in the public sector. Many Americans, for example, insist that religious doctrine is the necessary basis for any decision regarding morality and values in the schools. Many other Americans hold to the view that not only does religion not necessarily equal morality, but that religious doctrine as determined by certain religious leaders and denominations may sometimes be immoral.

The disputes in this chapter often epitomize these differences of opinion. Arguably, however, the cases together reflect the emergence of a broad middle ground. Religion must be respected in the public sector, but it is not automatically viewed as synonymous with morality. And religious "values"—depending on how the term is defined—may have a place in the public schools, but religious "teachings" may be violative of the First Amendment.

Consider the materials that follow in light of these conflicting strands of thought. To what extent have the courts succeeded in reconciling the range of perspectives that Americans express on these issues? To what extent have the courts shown little or no interest in reconciling perspectives, given the requirements of U.S. law? What conclusions might be drawn regarding future directions in this context?

A. THE RIGHT TO ALTERNATIVE MODELS OF EDUCATION

WISCONSIN v. YODER

406 U.S. 205, 92 S.Ct. 1526 (1972)

MR. CHIEF JUSTICE BURGER delivered the opinion of the Court.

[In this case, the Court reviews the decision of the Wisconsin Supreme Court in favor of Amish families. The families contend that their rights under the Free Exercise Clause of the First Amendment were violated because the State—pursuant to compulsory school-attendance laws—required them to send their children to formal high school until the age of 16.]

* * *

In support of their position, [the Amish families] presented as expert witnesses scholars on religion and education whose testimony is uncontradicted. They expressed their opinions on the relationship of the Amish belief concerning school attendance to the more general tenets of their religion, and described the impact that compulsory high school attendance could have on the continued survival of Amish communities as they exist in the United States today. The history of the Amish sect was given in some detail, beginning with the Swiss Anabaptists of the 16th century who rejected institutionalized churches and sought to return to the early, simple, Christian life de-emphasizing material success, rejecting the competitive spirit, and seeking to insulate themselves from the modern world. As a result of their common heritage, Old Order Amish communities today are characterized by a fundamental belief that salvation requires life in a church community separate and apart from the world and worldly influence. This concept of life aloof from the world and its values is central to their faith.

A related feature of Old Order Amish communities is their devotion to a life in harmony with nature and the soil, as exemplified by the simple life of the early Christian era that continued in America during much of our early national life. Amish beliefs require members of the community to make their living by farming or closely related activities. Broadly speaking, the Old Order Amish religion pervades and determines the entire mode of life of its adherents. Their conduct is regulated in great detail by the Ordnung, or rules, of the church community. Adult baptism, which occurs in late adolescence, is the time at which Amish young people voluntarily undertake heavy obligations, not unlike the Bar Mitzvah of the Jews, to abide by the rules of the church community.

Amish objection to formal education beyond the eighth grade is firmly grounded in these central religious concepts. They object to the high school, and higher education generally, because the values they teach are in marked variance with Amish values and the Amish way of life; they view secondary school education as an impermissible exposure of their children to a "worldly" influence in conflict with their beliefs. The high school tends to emphasize intellectual and scientific accomplishments, self-distinction, competitiveness, worldly success, and social life with other students. Amish society emphasizes informal learning-through-doing; a life of "goodness," rather than a life of intellect; wisdom, rather than technical knowledge, community welfare, rather than competition; and separation from, rather than integration with, contemporary worldly society.

* * * Dr. John Hostetler, one of the experts on Amish society, testified that the modern high school is not equipped, in curriculum or social environment, to impart the values promoted by Amish society.

The Amish do not object to elementary education through the first eight grades as a general proposition because they agree that their children must have basic skills in the "three R's" in order to read the Bible, to be good farmers and citizens, and to be able to deal with non-Amish people when necessary in the course of daily affairs. They view such a basic education as acceptable because it does not significantly expose their children to worldly values or interfere with their development in the Amish community during the crucial adolescent period. * * *

On the basis of such considerations, Dr. Hostetler testified that compulsory high school attendance could not only result in great psychological harm to Amish children, because of the conflicts it would produce, but would also, in his opinion, ultimately result in the destruction of the Old Order Amish church community as it exists in the United States today. The testimony of Dr. Donald A. Erickson, an expert witness on education, also showed that the Amish succeed in preparing their high school age children to be productive members of the Amish community. He described their system of learning through doing the skills directly relevant to their adult roles in the Amish community as "ideal" and perhaps superior to ordinary high school education. The evidence also showed that the Amish have an excellent record as law-abiding and generally self-sufficient members of society.

* * *

I

There is no doubt as to the power of a State, having a high responsibility for education of its citizens, to impose reasonable regulations for the control and duration of basic education. Providing public schools ranks at the very apex of the function of a State. Yet even this paramount responsibility was, in *Pierce*, made to yield to the right of parents to provide an equivalent education in a privately operated system. There the Court held that Oregon's statute compelling attendance in a public school from age eight to age 16 unreasonably interfered with the interest of parents in directing the rearing of their off-spring, including their education in church-operated schools. As that case suggests, the values of parental direction of the religious upbringing and education of their children in their early and formative years have a high place in our society. Thus, a State's interest in universal education, however highly we rank it, is not totally free from a balancing process when it impinges on fundamental rights and interests, such as those specifically protected by the Free Exercise Clause of the First Amendment, and the traditional interest of parents with respect to the religious upbringing of their children so long as they, in the words of Pierce, "prepare (them) for additional obligations."

It follows that in order for Wisconsin to compel school attendance beyond the eighth grade against a claim that such attendance interferes with the practice of a legitimate religious belief, it must appear either that the State does not deny the free exercise of religious belief by its requirement, or that there is a state interest of sufficient magnitude to override the interest claiming protection under the Free Exercise Clause. Long before there was general acknowledgment of the need for universal formal education, the Religion Clauses had specifically and firmly fixed the right to free exercise of religious beliefs, and buttressing this fundamental right was an equally firm, even if less explicit, prohibition against the establishment of any religion by government. The values underlying these two provisions relating to religion have been zealously protected, sometimes even at the expense of other interests of admittedly high social importance.

> * * *

The essence of all that has been said and written on the subject is that only those interests of the highest order and those not otherwise served can overbalance legitimate claims to the free exercise of religion. We can accept it as settled, therefore, that, however strong the State's interest in universal compulsory education, it is by no means absolute to the exclusion or subordination of all other interests.

II

* * * In evaluating [plaintiffs' claims] we must be careful to determine whether the Amish religious faith and their mode of life are, as they claim, inseparable and interdependent. A way of life, however virtuous and admirable, may not be interposed as a barrier to reasonable state regulation of education if it is based on purely secular considerations; to have the protection of the Religion Clauses, the claims must be rooted in religious belief.

> * * *

[T]he record in this case abundantly supports the claim that the traditional way of life of the Amish is not merely a matter of personal preference, but one of deep religious conviction, shared by an organized group, and intimately related to daily living.

* * *

In sum, the unchallenged testimony of acknowledged experts in education and religious history, almost 300 years of consistent practice, and strong evidence of a sustained faith pervading and regulating respondents' entire mode of life support the claim that enforcement of the State's requirement of compulsory formal education after the eighth grade would gravely endanger if not destroy the free exercise of respondents' religious beliefs.

III

Neither the findings of the trial court nor the Amish claims as to the nature of their faith are challenged in this Court by the State of Wisconsin. Its position is that the State's interest in universal compulsory formal secondary education to age 16 is so great that it is paramount to the undisputed claims of respondents that their mode of preparing their youth for Amish life, after the traditional elementary education, is an essential part of their religious belief and practice. * * *

* * *

We turn, then, to the State's broader contention that its interest in its system of compulsory education is so compelling that even the established religious practices of the Amish must give way. * * *

The State advances two primary arguments in support of its system of compulsory education. It notes, as Thomas Jefferson pointed out early in our history, that some degree of education is necessary to prepare citizens to participate effectively and intelligently in our open political system if we are to preserve freedom and independence. Further, education prepares individuals to be self-reliant and self-sufficient participants in society. We accept these propositions.

However, the evidence adduced by the Amish in this case is persuasively to the effect that an additional one or two years of formal high school for Amish children in place of their long-established program of informal vocational education would do little to serve those interests.

* * *

The requirement for compulsory education beyond the eighth grade is a relatively recent development in our history. Less than 60 years ago, the educational requirements of almost all of the States were satisfied by completion of the elementary grades, at least where the child was regularly and lawfully employed. The independence and successful social functioning of the Amish community for a period approaching almost three centuries and more than 200 years in this country are strong evidence that there is at best a speculative gain, in terms of meeting the duties of citizenship, from an additional one or two years of compulsory formal education. Against this background it would require a more particularized showing from the State on this point to justify the severe interference with religious freedom such additional compulsory attendance would entail.

* * *

IV

Finally, the State * * * argues that a decision exempting Amish children from the State's requirement fails to recognize the substantive right of the Amish child to a secondary education, and fails to give due regard to the power of the State as *parens patriae* to extend the benefit of secondary education to children regardless of the wishes of their parents.

* * *

Contrary to the suggestion of the dissenting opinion of Mr. Justice DOUGLAS, our holding today in no degree depends on the assertion of the religious interest of the child as contrasted with that of the parents. It is the parents who are subject to prosecution here for failing to cause their children to attend school, and it is their right of free exercise, not that of their children, that must determine Wisconsin's power to impose criminal penalties on the parent.

* * *

[T]his case involves the fundamental interest of parents, as contrasted with that of the State, to guide the religious future and education of their children. The history and culture of Western civilization reflect a strong tradition of parental concern for the nurture and upbringing of their children. This primary role of the parents in the upbringing of their children is now established beyond debate as an enduring American tradition. If not the first, perhaps the most significant statements of the Court in this area are found in *Pierce v. Society of Sisters*, in which the Court observed:

> 'Under the doctrine of *Meyer v. Nebraska*, we think it entirely plain that the Act of 1922 unreasonably interferes with the liberty of parents and guardians to direct the upbringing and education of children under their control. * * * The fundamental theory of liberty upon which all governments in this Union repose excludes any general power of the State to standardize its children by forcing them to accept instruction from public teachers only. The child is not the mere creature of the State; those who nurture him and direct his destiny have the right, coupled with the high duty, to recognize and prepare him for additional obligations.'

The duty to prepare the child for 'additional obligations,' referred to by the Court, must be read to include the inculcation of moral standards, religious beliefs, and elements of good citizenship. * * *

[T]he Court's holding in Pierce stands as a charter of the rights of parents to direct the religious upbringing of their children. And, when the interests of parenthood are combined with a free exercise claim of the nature revealed by this record, more than merely a "reasonable relation to some purpose within the competency of the State" is required to sustain the validity of the State's requirement under the First Amendment. To be sure, the power of the parent, even when linked to a free exercise claim, may be subject to limitation * * * if it appears that parental decisions will jeopardize the health or safety of the child, or have a potential for significant social burdens. But in this case, the Amish have introduced persuasive evidence undermining the arguments the State has advanced to support its claims in terms of the welfare of the child and society as a whole. The record strongly indicates that accommodating the religious objections of the Amish by forgoing one, or at most two, additional years of compulsory education will not impair the physical or mental health of the child, or result in an inability to be self-supporting or to discharge the duties and responsibilities of citizenship, or in any other way materially detract from the welfare of society.

* * *

V

For the reasons stated we hold, with the Supreme Court of Wisconsin, that the First and Fourteenth Amendments prevent the State from compelling respondents to cause their children to attend formal high school to age 16.

* * *

MR. JUSTICE DOUGLAS, dissenting in part.

I

I agree with the Court that the religious scruples of the Amish are opposed to the education of their children beyond the grade schools, yet I disagree with the Court's conclusion that the matter is within the dispensation of parents alone. The Court's analysis assumes that the only interests at stake in the case are those of the Amish parents on the one hand, and those of the State on the other. The difficulty with this approach is that, despite the Court's claim, the parents are seeking to vindicate not only their own free exercise claims, but also those of their high-school-age children.

It is argued that the right of the Amish children to religious freedom is not presented by the facts of the case, as the issue before the Court involves only the Amish parents' religious freedom to defy a state criminal statute imposing upon them an affirmative duty to cause their children to attend high school. * * *

[However,] no analysis of religious-liberty claims can take place in a vacuum. If the parents in this case are allowed a religious exemption, the inevitable effect is to impose the parents' notions of religious duty upon their children. Where the child is mature enough to express potentially conflicting desires, it would be an invasion of the child's rights to permit such an imposition without canvassing his views. * * * And, if an Amish child desires to attend high school, and is mature enough to have that desire respected, the State may well be able to override the parents' religiously motivated objections.

* * *

II

This issue has never been squarely presented before today. Our opinions are full of talk about the power of the parents over the child's education. And we have in the past analyzed similar conflicts between parent and State with little regard for the views of the child. Recent cases, however, have clearly held that the children themselves have constitutionally protectible interests.

* * *

In *Tinker v. Des Moines Independent Community School District*, we dealt with 13–year-old, 15–year-old, and 16–year-old students who wore armbands to public schools and were disciplined for doing so. We gave them relief, saying that their First Amendment rights had been abridged. * * *

In *West Virginia State Board of Education v. Barnette*, we held that school-children, whose religious beliefs collided with a school rule requiring them to salute the flag, could not be required to do so. * * *

It is the future of the student, not the future of the parents, that is imperiled by today's decision. If a parent keeps his child out of school beyond the grade school, then the child will be forever barred from entry into the new and amazing world of diversity that we have today. The child may decide that that is the preferred course, or he may rebel. It is the student's judgment, not his parents', that is essential if we are to give full meaning to what we have said about the Bill of Rights and of the right of students to be masters of their own destiny.[3] If he is harnessed to the Amish way of life by those in authority over him and if his education is truncated, his entire life may be stunted and deformed. The child, therefore, should be given an opportunity to be heard before the State gives the exemption which we honor today.

The views of the two children in question were not canvassed by the Wisconsin courts. The matter should be explicitly reserved so that new hearings can be held on remand of the case.[4]

* * *

---

3. The court below brushed aside the students' interests with the offhand comment that '(w)hen a child reaches the age of judgment, he can choose for himself his religion.' But there is nothing in this record to indicate that the moral and intellectual judgment demanded of the student by the question in this case is beyond his capacity. Children far younger than the 14 and 15 year olds involved here are regularly permitted to testify in custody and other proceedings. Indeed, the failure to call the affected child in a custody hearing is often reversible error. Moreover, there is substantial agreement among child psychologists and sociologists that the moral and intellectual maturity of the 14 year old approaches that of the adult. The maturity of Amish youth, who identify with and assume adult roles from early childhood, is certainly not less than that of children in the general population.

4. Canvassing the views of all school age Amish children in the State of Wisconsin would not present insurmountable difficulties. A 1968 survey indicated that there were at that time only 256 such children in the entire State.

NOTES

1. *Pierce v. Society of Sisters*, referenced in the *Yoder* decision, is generally viewed as a paradigmatic case in the development of the law relating to parental rights in the public sector. Indeed, *Pierce* and *Yoder* together stand for a broad parental right to direct the upbringing of children. How far the right extends, however, is the subject of ongoing controversy.

2. Issues of conflicting values are at the heart of the controversy in *Yoder,* and it is important to note that the word *values* appears in the opinions many times. In this regard, how applicable might the *Yoder* decision be to the range of controversies that are discussed throughout this chapter? Does *Yoder* provide a workable rule whereby courts can determine who prevails when values are in conflict, or is it—in the end—a very narrow and fact-specific decision?

3. Consider the Court's language to the effect that "the activities of individuals, even when religiously based, are often subject to regulation by the States in the exercise of their undoubted power to promote the health, safety, and general welfare." Indeed, the Court emphasizes that "the power of the parent, even when linked to a free exercise claim, may be subject to limitation . . . if it appears that parental decisions will jeopardize the health or safety of the child, or have a potential for significant social burdens." Under this language, might a public school district be able to restrict parental ability to "opt out" of HIV-related education on the grounds that the policy imperative of seeking to eradicate the disease would outweigh any competing religious claims under the Free Exercise Clause? *See infra,* Section E of this chapter.

4. The area of home schooling is directly relevant to the inquiry in this sub-section. *See, e.g.,* Brad Colwell & Brian D. Schwartz, *Implications for Public Schools: Legal Aspects of Home Schools,* 173 ED. LAW REP. 381 (2003); *see also* David W. Fuller, Note, *Public School Access: The Constitutional Right of Home–Schoolers to "Opt In" to Public Education on a Part–Time Basis,* 82 MINN. L. REV. 1599 (1998).

5. In California, a highly publicized dispute arose in 2007 when a state appellate court construed the Education Code provisions in a manner that appeared to require unexpectedly challenging procedural barriers for parents seeking to home school their children. Upon rehearing in 2008, the Court engaged in extensive statutory interpretation, including an analysis of legislative history. It ultimately scaled back the earlier decision, to the great relief of those within the home-schooling community. See *Jonathan L. v. Superior Court,* 165 Cal.App.4th 1074, 81 Cal.Rptr.3d 571 (2008):

> We * * * conclude that: (1) California statutes permit home schooling as a species of private school education; and (2) the statutory permission to home school may constitutionally be overridden in order to protect the safety of a child who has been declared dependent. * * * 165 Cal.App.4th at 1082, 81 Cal.Rptr.3d at 577 (2008).

> In this case, we sought amicus briefing from the Superintendent of Public Instruction and the Department of Education. In their letter brief, they expressed their opinion that, "it is legally permissible for [parents] to

qualify as a private school and teach their children in their own home." Both the Governor and Attorney General agree with this interpretation, as does the Los Angeles Unified School District (LAUSD). * * * It is estimated that there are 166,000 children being home schooled in California. It is a growing practice across the nation. The Legislature is aware that home schooling parents file affidavits as private schools, and has passed laws based on that awareness. The Department of Education has not challenged the practice, and the LAUSD has not asserted that the children of such parents are truant. * * * 165 Cal.App.4th at 1100, 81 Cal.Rptr.3d at 591.

In conclusion, however, after examining the way other states regulate home schooling, the Court called for more clarity in the law:

We close with an observation that the fact that home schooling is permitted in California as the result of implicit legislative recognition rather than explicit legislative action has resulted in a near absence of objective criteria and oversight for home schooling. In this regard, while we do not attempt a comprehensive review of other states' requirements, we note some of the methods used by other states to guarantee that their home schooled children are receiving an adequate education.

In some states, discretion to approve home schooling is granted to state, county or district officials. See, e.g., Fla. Stat., § 1003.26, subd. (1)(f) [approval by a "home education review committee," which reviews the student's portfolio every 30 days until it deems the program satisfactory]; La. Rev. Stat. Ann., § 17:236.1; N.M. Stat. Ann., § 22–2–2, subd. (H); Ohio Admin. Code, 3301:34–03, subd. (c); 24 Pa. Stat., § 13–1327.1, subds. (h)-(m); Vt. Stat. Ann., tit. 16, § 166b. * * * In several states, capable teaching is assured by requiring the parent to possess a certain minimum level of education in order to home school, generally a high school diploma or its equivalent. See, e.g., Ga. Code Ann., § 20–2–690, subd. (c)(3); N.M. Stat. Ann., § 22–1–2.1, subd. (C); N.C. Gen. Stat., § 115C–564; 24 Pa. Stat., § 13–1327.1, subd. (a); S.C. Code Ann., § 59–65–40, subd. (A)(1); Tenn. Code Ann., § 49–6–3050, subd. (b) (high school diploma sufficient to home school through 8th grade; further education required to home school at high school level). Ohio permits a parent without a high school diploma to home school only if supervised. (Ohio Admin. Code, 3301:34–03, subd. (A)(9).) North Dakota requires a baccalaureate degree to home school, and will permit a high school graduate to home school only if monitored. (N.D. Cent. Code §§ 15.1–23–03, 15.1–23–06.) Various states require home schooling parents to regularly submit documents-either reports or samples of the children's work-to authorities, in order to ensure the child is being educated. E.g., Iowa Code, § 299A.4; Minn. Stat., § 120A.24; Md. Code Regs. § 13A.10.01.01(D)(3); Ohio Admin. Code, 3301:34–04; 24 Pa. Stat., § 13–1327.1, subd. (e); S.C. Code Ann., § 59–65–40, subd. (A)(4); Vt. Stat. Ann., tit. 16, § 166b, subd. (d); Va. Code Ann., § 22.1–254.1, subd. (C); *Combs v. Homer Center School Dist.* (W.D. Pa.2006) 468 F. Supp. 2d 738, 745–746, 778 (upholding such a requirement against a constitutional challenge). A few states measure home schooling students' progress by means of standardized testing, although alternative means of evaluation are often permitted. E.g., Ark. Code Ann., § 6–15–504; Colo. Rev. Stat., § 22–33–104.5, subd. (3)(f); Fla.

Stat., § 1002.41, subd. (1)(c); Ga. Code Ann., § 20–2–690, subd. (c)(7); Haw. Code R. § 8–12–18, subd. (a); Minn.Stat., § 120A.22, subd. (11). In several states, if a child fails to demonstrate sufficient progress, the home schooling of that child is placed on probation, or terminated altogether. E.g., Colo. Rev. Stat., § 22–33–104.5, subd. (5)(a)(I); Fla. Stat., § 1002.41, subd. (2); Md. Code Regs., § 13A.10.01.03, subd. (B). A number of states require home visits, although there is some dispute among the courts which have considered the issue whether requiring home visits is a constitutional limitation on parental rights.

A few states have comprehensive regulations imposing several different requirements. For example, New York has promulgated regulations which require: (1) the parent to send an individualized home instruction plan for each student to the school district each year; (2) quarterly reports; (3) an annual assessment including a standardized achievement test (or alternative means of review); (4) a plan of remediation if the student falls below the 33rd percentile on a standardized test; and (5) possible termination of home schooling if the remediation objectives are not met within two years. (N.Y. Comp.Codes R. & Regs. tit. 8, § 100.10.)

In contrast, California impliedly allows parents to home school as a private school, but has provided no enforcement mechanism. As long as the local school district verifies that a private school affidavit has been filed, there is no provision for further oversight of a home school. It appears that the propriety of any parent's home schooling will arise only in dependency (or family law) proceedings, as in this case, or in a prosecution for failing to comply with the compulsory education law. * * *

Given the state's compelling interest in educating all of its children (Cal. Const., art. IX, § 1), and the absence of an express statutory and regulatory framework for home schooling in California, additional clarity in this area of the law would be helpful. 165 Cal. App. 4th at 1105–1106, 81 Cal. Rptr. 3d at 595–596.

B. PATRIOTISM, RELIGION, AND FREEDOM OF EXPRESSION: THE FLAG SALUTE CONTROVERSIES

WEST VIRGINIA STATE BD. OF EDUC. v. BARNETTE

319 U.S. 624, 63 S.Ct. 1178 (1943)

Mr. Justice Jackson delivered the opinion of the Court.

* * *

The Board of Education on January 9, 1942, adopted a resolution ... ordering that the salute to the flag become "a regular part of the program of activities in the public schools," that all teachers and pupils "shall be required to participate in the salute honoring the Nation represented by the Flag; provided, however, that refusal to salute the Flag be regarded as an Act of insubordination, and shall be dealt with accordingly."

The resolution originally required the "commonly accepted salute to the Flag" which it defined. Objections to the salute as "being too much like Hitler's" were raised by the Parent and Teachers Association, the Boy and Girl Scouts, the Red Cross, and the Federation of Women's Clubs. Some modification appears to have been made in deference to these objections, but no concession was made to Jehovah's Witnesses.[4] What is now required is the "stiff-arm" salute, the saluter to keep the right hand raised with palm turned up while the following is repeated: "I pledge allegiance to the Flag of the United States of America and to the Republic for which it stands; one Nation, indivisible, with liberty and justice for all."

Failure to conform is "insubordination" dealt with by expulsion. Readmission is denied by statute until compliance. Meanwhile the expelled child is "unlawfully absent" and may be proceeded against as a delinquent. His parents or guardians are liable to prosecution, and if convicted are subject to fine not exceeding $50 and jail term not exceeding thirty days.

Appellees, citizens of the United States and of West Virginia, brought suit in the United States District Court for themselves and others similarly situated asking its injunction to restrain enforcement of these laws and regulations against Jehovah's Witnesses. The Witnesses are an unincorporated body teaching that the obligation imposed by law of God is superior to that of laws enacted by temporal government. Their religious beliefs include a literal version of Exodus, Chapter 20, verses 4 and 5, which says: "Thou shalt not make unto thee any graven image, or any likeness of anything that is in heaven above, or that is in the earth beneath, or that is in the water under the earth; thou shalt not bow down thyself to them nor serve them." They consider that the flag is an "image" within this command. For this reason they refuse to salute it.

Children of this faith have been expelled from school and are threatened with exclusion for no other cause. Officials threaten to send them to reformatories maintained for criminally inclined juveniles. Parents of such children have been prosecuted and are threatened with prosecutions for causing delinquency.

* * *

---

4. They have offered in lieu of participating in the flag salute ceremony "periodically and publicly" to give the following pledge:

I have pledged my unqualified allegiance and devotion to Jehovah, the Almighty God, and to His Kingdom, for which Jesus commands all Christians to pray.

I respect the flag of the United States and acknowledge it as a symbol of freedom and justice to all.

I pledge allegiance and obedience to all the laws of the United States that are consistent with God's law, as set forth in the Bible.

[T]he refusal of these persons to participate in the ceremony does not interfere with or deny rights of others to do so. Nor is there any question in this case that their behavior is peaceable and orderly. The sole conflict is between authority and rights of the individual. The State asserts power to condition access to public education on making a prescribed sign and profession and at the same time to coerce attendance by punishing both parent and child. The latter stand on a right of self-determination in matters that touch individual opinion and personal attitude.

* * *

There is no doubt that, in connection with the pledges, the flag salute is a form of utterance. Symbolism is a primitive but effective way of communicating ideas. The use of an emblem or flag to symbolize some system, idea, institution, or personality, is a short cut from mind to mind. Causes and nations, political parties, lodges and ecclesiastical groups seek to knit the loyalty of their followings to a flag or banner, a color or design. The State announces rank, function, and authority through crowns and maces, uniforms and black robes; the church speaks through the Cross, the Crucifix, the altar and shrine, and clerical reiment. Symbols of State often convey political ideas just as religious symbols come to convey theological ones. Associated with many of these symbols are appropriate gestures of acceptance or respect: a salute, a bowed or bared head, a bended knee. A person gets from a symbol the meaning he puts into it, and what is one man's comfort and inspiration is another's jest and scorn.

* * *

Whether the First Amendment to the Constitution will permit officials to order observance of ritual of this nature does not depend upon whether as a voluntary exercise we would think it to be good, bad or merely innocuous. Any credo of nationalism is likely to include what some disapprove or to omit what others think essential, and to give off different overtones as it takes on different accents or interpretations. If official power exists to coerce acceptance of any patriotic creed, what it shall contain cannot be decided by courts, but must be largely discretionary with the ordaining authority, whose power to prescribe would no doubt include power to amend. Hence validity of the asserted power to force an American citizen publicly to profess any statement of belief or to engage in any ceremony of assent to one presents questions of power that must be considered independently of any idea we may have as to the utility of the ceremony in question.

Nor does the issue as we see it turn on one's possession of particular religious views or the sincerity with which they are held. While religion supplies appellees' motive for enduring the discomforts of making the issue in this case, many citizens who do not share these religious views hold such a compulsory rite to infringe constitutional liberty of the individual. It is not necessary to inquire whether non-conformist beliefs will exempt from the duty to salute unless we first find power to make the salute a legal duty.

* * *

The Fourteenth Amendment, as now applied to the States, protects the citizen against the State itself and all of its creatures—Boards of Education not excepted. These have, of course, important, delicate, and highly discretionary functions, but none that they may not perform within the limits of the Bill of Rights. That they are educating the young for citizenship is reason for scrupulous protection of Constitutional freedoms of the individual, if we are not to strangle the free mind at its source and teach youth to discount important principles of our government as mere platitudes.

* * *

Struggles to coerce uniformity of sentiment in support of some end thought essential to their time and country have been waged by many good as well as by evil men. Nationalism is a relatively recent phenomenon but at other times and places the ends have been racial or territorial security, support of a dynasty or regime, and particular plans for saving souls. As first and moderate methods to attain unity have failed, those bent on its accomplishment must resort to an ever-increasing severity. As governmental pressure toward unity becomes greater, so strife becomes more bitter as to whose unity it shall be. Probably no deeper division of our people could proceed from any provocation than from finding it necessary to choose what doctrine and whose program public educational officials shall compel youth to unite in embracing. Ultimate futility of such attempts to compel coherence is the lesson of every such effort from the Roman drive to stamp out Christianity as a disturber of its pagan unity, the Inquisition, as a means to religious and dynastic unity, the Siberian exiles as a means to Russian unity, down to the fast failing efforts of our present totalitarian enemies. Those who begin coercive elimination of dissent soon find themselves exterminating dissenters. Compulsory unification of opinion achieves only the unanimity of the graveyard.

It seems trite but necessary to say that the First Amendment to our Constitution was designed to avoid these ends by avoiding these beginnings. There is no mysticism in the American concept of the State or of the nature or origin of its authority. We set up government by consent of the governed, and the Bill of Rights denies those in power any legal opportunity to coerce that consent. Authority here is to be controlled by public opinion, not public opinion by authority.

The case is made difficult not because the principles of its decision are obscure but because the flag involved is our own. Nevertheless, we apply the limitations of the Constitution with no fear that freedom to be intellectually and spiritually diverse or even contrary will disintegrate the social organization. To believe that patriotism will not flourish if patriotic ceremonies are voluntary and spontaneous instead of a compulsory routine is to make an unflattering estimate of the appeal of our institutions to free minds. We can have intellectual individualism and the rich cultural diversities that we owe to exceptional minds only at the price of occasional eccentricity and abnormal attitudes. When they are so harmless to others or to the State as those we deal with here, the price is not too great. But freedom to differ is not limited to things that do not matter much. That would be a mere shadow of freedom. The test of its substance is the right to differ as to things that touch the heart of the existing order.

If there is any fixed star in our constitutional constellation, it is that no official, high or petty, can prescribe what shall be orthodox in politics, nationalism, religion, or other matters of opinion or force citizens to confess by word or act their faith therein. If there are any circumstances which permit an exception, they do not now occur to us.

We think the action of the local authorities in compelling the flag salute and pledge transcends constitutional limitations on their power and invades the sphere of intellect and spirit which it is the purpose of the First Amendment to our Constitution to reserve from all official control.

* * *

Affirmed.

PROBLEM 41: DECIDING NEWDOW UNDER THE ESTABLISHMENT CLAUSE

On June 14, 2004, the U.S. Supreme Court decided *Elk Grove Unified School District v. Newdow*. In that case, Michael Newdow had challenged the constitutionality of the school district's requirement that the pledge of allegiance be recited every day in all its elementary school classes. Newdow contended that because the Pledge contains the words "under God," the policy amounted to a religious indoctrination of his child in violation of the First Amendment.

A divided Ninth Circuit panel agreed with Newdow. In a 5–4 decision, the U.S. Supreme Court reversed, but the majority did not reach the Establishment Clause question, ruling instead that Newdow did not have standing because he did not have legal custody of his biological child.

Pushing ahead with further legal action, Newdow essentially re-filed the same lawsuit, this time joining with a group of parents who indeed had legal custody of their children. In 2005, the U.S. District Court, Eastern District of California, ruled in favor of the plaintiffs on Establishment Clause grounds. The school district appealed yet again, and oral argument was heard in the Ninth Circuit in December 2007. As of the date of publication of this volume, a decision had yet to be released.

Consider the following excerpts and overviews from various selected opinions at both the Ninth Circuit and the Supreme Court level. Were the Supreme Court to hear this case again, and should the justices reach the Establishment Clause question, how would the case be decided? Why?

ELK GROVE UNIFIED SCHOOL DIST. v. NEWDOW

542 U.S. 1, 124 S.Ct. 2301 (2004)

STEVENS, J., delivered the opinion of the Court, in which KENNEDY, SOUTER, GINSBURG, and BREYER, JJ., joined. REHNQUIST, C.J., filed an opinion concurring in the judgment, in which O'CONNOR, J., joined, and in which THOMAS, J., joined as to Part I. O'CONNOR, J., and THOMAS, J., filed opinions concurring in the judgment. SCALIA, J., took no part in the consideration or decision of the case.

● Facts of the Case (from the majority opinion by Justice Stevens)

Each day elementary school teachers in the Elk Grove Unified School District (School District) lead their classes in a group recitation of the Pledge of Allegiance. Respondent, Michael A. Newdow, is an atheist whose daughter participates in that daily exercise. Because the Pledge contains the words "under God," he views the School District's policy as a religious indoctrination of his child that violates the First Amendment. A divided panel of the Court of Appeals for the Ninth Circuit agreed with Newdow. In light of the obvious importance of that decision, we granted certiorari to review the First Amendment issue and, preliminarily, the question whether Newdow has standing to invoke the jurisdiction of the federal courts. We conclude that Newdow lacks standing and therefore reverse the Court of Appeals' decision.

I

"The very purpose of a national flag is to serve as a symbol of our country," and of its proud traditions "of freedom, of equal opportunity, of religious tolerance, and of good will for other peoples who share our aspirations." As its history illustrates, the Pledge of Allegiance evolved as a common public acknowledgement of the ideals that our flag symbolizes. Its recitation is a patriotic exercise designed to foster national unity and pride in those principles.

The Pledge of Allegiance was initially conceived more than a century ago. As part of the nationwide interest in commemorating the 400th anniversary of Christopher Columbus' discovery of America, a widely circulated national magazine for youth proposed in 1892 that pupils recite the following affirmation: 'I pledge allegiance to my Flag and the Republic for which it stands: one Nation indivisible, with Liberty and Justice for all.' In the 1920's, the National Flag Conferences replaced the phrase 'my Flag' with 'the flag of the United States of America.'

In 1942, in the midst of World War II, Congress adopted, and the President signed, a Joint Resolution codifying a detailed set of "rules and customs pertaining to the display and use of the flag of the United States of America." Section 7 of this codification provided in full:

That the pledge of allegiance to the flag, "I pledge allegiance to the flag of the United States of America and to the Republic for which it stands, one Nation indivisible, with liberty and justice for all", be rendered by standing with the right hand over the heart; extending the right hand, palm upward, toward the flag at the words "to the flag" and holding this position until the end, when the hand drops to the side. However, civilians will always show full respect to the flag when the pledge is given by merely standing at attention, men removing the headdress. Persons in uniform shall render the military salute.

This resolution, which marked the first appearance of the Pledge of Allegiance in positive law, confirmed the importance of the flag as a symbol of our Nation's indivisibility and commitment to the concept of liberty.

Congress revisited the Pledge of Allegiance 12 years later when it amended the text to add the words "under God." The House Report that accompanied the legislation observed that, "[f]rom the time of our earliest history our peoples and our institutions have reflected the traditional concept that our Nation was founded on a fundamental belief in God." The resulting text is the Pledge as we know it today: "I pledge allegiance to the Flag of the United States of America, and to the Republic for which it stands, one Nation under God, indivisible, with liberty and justice for all."

II

Under California law, "every public elementary school" must begin each day with "appropriate patriotic exercises." The statute provides that "[t]he giving of the Pledge of Allegiance to the Flag of the United States of America shall satisfy" this requirement. The Elk Grove Unified School District has implemented the state law by requiring that "[e]ach elementary school class recite the pledge of allegiance to the flag once each day." Consistent with our case law, the School District permits students who object on religious grounds to abstain from the recitation. See *West Virginia Bd. of Ed. v. Barnette*, 319 U.S. 624 (1943).

In March 2000, Newdow filed suit in the United States District Court for the Eastern District of California against the United States Congress, the President of the United States, the State of California, and the Elk Grove Unified School District and its superintendent. At the time of filing, Newdow's daughter was enrolled in kindergarten in the Elk Grove Unified School District and participated in the daily recitation of the Pledge.... [T]he complaint explains that Newdow is an atheist who was ordained more than 20 years ago in a ministry that "espouses the religious philosophy that the true and eternal bonds of righteousness and virtue stem from reason rather than mythology." The complaint seeks a declaration that the 1954 Act's addition of the words "under God" violated the Establishment and Free Exercise Clauses of the United States Constitution, as well as an injunction against the School District's policy requiring daily recitation of the Pledge. It alleges that Newdow has standing to sue on his own behalf and on behalf of his daughter as "next friend."

... We granted the School District's petition for a writ of certiorari to consider two questions: (1) whether Newdow has standing as a noncustodial parent to challenge the School District's policy, and (2) if so, whether the policy offends the First Amendment.

* * *

● Highlights of the Various Opinions at the Supreme Court Level

1. It was the "liberal" wing, plus Justice Kennedy, that held that Newdow did not have "standing."

2. The conservative wing (minus Justice Scalia, who had recused himself), plus Justice O'Connor, held that Newdow *did* have standing.

3. Both Chief Justice Rehnquist and Justice O'Connor wrote separately to argue that under Establishment Clause principles, as they saw them, the pledge as it stood *was* constitutional.

4. Justice O'Connor asserted that under an endorsement analysis, history, character, and context prevent certain instances of "ceremonial deism" from being constitutional violations. She argued that this was the case here, relying on four key points: history and ubiquity, absence of worship or prayer, absence of reference to particular religion, and minimal religious content. No one else joined her opinion, in the end.

5. Justice Thomas wrote separately to say: "I conclude that, as a matter of our precedent, the Pledge policy is unconstitutional." He therefore wrote that "I would take this opportunity to begin the process of rethinking the Establishment Clause."

* * *

● Excerpts from the Amended Majority Opinion by Judge Goodwin, 328 F.3d 466 (9th Cir. 2003)

The Establishment Clause of the First Amendment states that "Congress shall make no law respecting an establishment of religion," U.S. CONST. amend. I, a provision that "the Fourteenth Amendment makes applicable with full force to the States and their school districts." * * *

[W]e conclude that the school district policy impermissibly coerces a religious act and accordingly hold the policy unconstitutional....

In the context of the Pledge, the statement that the United States is a nation "under God" is a profession of a religious belief, namely, a belief in monotheism. The recitation that ours is a nation "under God" is not a mere acknowledgment that many Americans believe in a deity. Nor is it merely descriptive of the undeniable historical significance of religion in the founding of the Republic. Rather, the phrase "one nation under God" in the context of the Pledge is normative. To recite the Pledge is not to describe the United States; instead, it is to swear allegiance to the values for which the flag stands: unity, indivisibility, liberty, justice, and—since 1954—monotheism. A profession that we are a nation "under God" is identical, for Establishment Clause purposes, to a profession that we are a nation "under Jesus," a nation "under Vishnu," a nation "under Zeus," or a nation "under no god," because none of these professions can be neutral with respect to religion. The school district's practice of teacher-led recitation of the Pledge aims to inculcate in students a respect for the ideals set forth in the Pledge, including the religious values it incorporates.

The Supreme Court recognized the normative and ideological nature of the Pledge in *Barnette*, 319 U.S. 624, 63 S.Ct. 1178. There, the Court held unconstitutional a school district's wartime policy of punishing students who refused to recite the Pledge and salute the flag. *Id.* at 642, 63 S.Ct. 1178. The Court noted that the school district was compelling the students "to declare a belief," *id.* at 631, 63 S.Ct. 1178, and "requir[ing] the individual to communicate by word and sign his acceptance of the political ideas [the flag] . . . bespeaks," *id.* at 633, 63 S.Ct. 1178. "[T]he compulsory flag salute and pledge requires affirmation of a belief and an attitude of mind." *Id.* The Court emphasized that the political concepts articulated in the Pledge[4] were idealistic, not descriptive: " '[L]iberty and justice for all,' if it must be accepted as descriptive of the present order rather than an ideal, might to some seem an overstatement." *Id.* at 634 n. 14, 63 S.Ct. 1178. The Court concluded that: "If there is any fixed star in our constitutional constellation, it is that no official, high or petty, can prescribe what shall be orthodox in politics, nationalism, religion, or other matters of opinion or force citizens to confess by word or act their faith therein." *Id.* at 642, 63 S.Ct. 1178.

The school district's policy here, like the school's action in *Lee v. Weisman,* places students in the untenable position of choosing between participating in an exercise with religious content or protesting. The defendants argue that the religious content of "one nation under God" is minimal. To an atheist or a believer in non-Judeo–Christian religions or philosophies, however, this phrase may reasonably appear to be an attempt to enforce a "religious orthodoxy" of monotheism, and is therefore impermissible. As the Court observed with respect to the graduation prayer in *Lee:* "What to most believers may seem nothing more than a reasonable request that the nonbeliever respect their religious practices, in a school context may appear to the nonbeliever or dissenter to be an attempt to employ the machinery of the State to enforce a religious orthodoxy." *Lee,* 505 U.S. at 592, 112 S.Ct. 2649.

The coercive effect of the policy here is particularly pronounced in the school setting given the age and impressionability of schoolchildren, and their understanding that they are required to adhere to the norms set by their school, their teacher and their fellow students.[5] Furthermore, under

---

4. *Barnette* was decided before "under God" was added, and thus the Court's discussion was limited to the political ideals contained in the Pledge.

5. The "subtle and indirect" social pressure which permeates the classroom also renders more acute the message sent to non-believing school-children that they are outsiders. *See Lee,* 505 U.S. at 592–93, 112 S.Ct. 2649 (stating that "the risk of indirect coercion" from prayer exercises is

Lee, non-compulsory participation is no basis for distinguishing *Barnette* from the case at bar because, even without a recitation requirement for each child, the mere presence in the classroom every day as peers recite the statement "one nation under God" has a coercive effect.[6] The coercive effect of the Pledge is also made even more apparent when we consider the legislative history of the Act that introduced the phrase "under God." These words were designed to be recited daily in school classrooms. President Eisenhower, during the Act's signing ceremony, stated: "From this day forward, the millions of our school children will daily proclaim in every city and town, every village and rural schoolhouse, the dedication of our Nation and our people to the Almighty."[7] All in all, there can be little doubt that under the controlling Supreme Court cases the school district's policy fails the coercion test.

● **Excerpts from the opinion of Justice O'Connor, who would have found the District policy constitutional.**

JUSTICE O'CONNOR

* * * As I have said before, the Establishment Clause "cannot easily be reduced to a single test. There are different categories of Establishment Clause cases, which may call for different approaches." When a court confronts a challenge to government-sponsored speech or displays, I continue to believe that the endorsement test "captures the essential command of the Establishment Clause, namely, that government must not make a person's religious beliefs relevant to his or her standing in the political community by conveying a message 'that religion or a particular religious belief is favored or preferred.' " In that context, I repeatedly have applied the endorsement test, *Wallace* [*v. Jaffree,* 472 U.S. 38, 69 (1985)] (statute authorizing a meditative moment of silence in classrooms), and I would do so again here.

Endorsement, I have explained, "sends a message to nonadherents that they are outsiders, not full members of the political community, and an accompanying message to adherents that they are insiders, favored members of the political community." In order to decide whether endorsement has occurred, a reviewing court must keep in mind two crucial and related principles.

---

particularly "pronounced" in elementary and secondary public school because students are subjected to peer pressure and public pressure which is "as real as any overt compulsion").

6. The objection to the Pledge in *Barnette,* like in the case at bar, was based upon a religious ground. The Pledge in the classroom context imposes upon schoolchildren the constitutionally unacceptable choice between participating and protesting. Recognizing the severity of the effect of this form of coercion on children, the Supreme Court in *Lee* stated, "the State may not, consistent with the Establishment Clause, place primary and secondary school children in this position." 505 U.S. at 593, 112 S.Ct. 2649.

7. In addition, the legislative history of the 1954 Act makes it plain that the sponsors of the amendment knew about and capitalized on the state laws and school district rules that mandate recitation of the Pledge. The legislation's House sponsor, Representative Louis C. Rabaut, testified at the Congressional hearing that "the children of our land, in the daily recitation of the pledge in school, will be daily impressed with a true understanding of our way of life and its origins." This statement was incorporated into the report of the House Judiciary Committee.

First, because the endorsement test seeks "to identify those situations in which government makes adherence to a religion relevant ... to a person's standing in the political community," it assumes the viewpoint of a reasonable observer. Given the dizzying religious heterogeneity of our Nation, adopting a subjective approach would reduce the test to an absurdity. Nearly any government action could be overturned as a violation of the Establishment Clause if a "heckler's veto" sufficed to show that its message was one of endorsement. Second, because the "reasonable observer" must embody a community ideal of social judgment, as well as rational judgment, the test does not evaluate a practice in isolation from its origins and context. Instead, the reasonable observer must be deemed aware of the history of the conduct in question, and must understand its place in our Nation's cultural landscape.

The Court has permitted government, in some instances, to refer to or commemorate religion in public life. While the Court's explicit rationales have varied, my own has been consistent; I believe that although these references speak in the language of religious belief, they are more properly understood as employing the idiom for essentially secular purposes. One such purpose is to commemorate the role of religion in our history. In my view, some references to religion in public life and government are the inevitable consequence of our Nation's origins. Just as the Court has refused to ignore changes in the religious composition of our Nation in explaining the modern scope of the Religion Clauses, *see, e.g., Wallace, supra,* at 52–54 (even if the Religion Clauses were originally meant only to forestall intolerance between Christian sects, they now encompass all forms of religious conscience), it should not deny that our history has left its mark on our national traditions. It is unsurprising that a Nation founded by religious refugees and dedicated to religious freedom should find references to divinity in its symbols, songs, mottoes, and oaths. Eradicating such references would sever ties to a history that sustains this Nation even today.

Facially religious references can serve other valuable purposes in public life as well. Twenty years ago, I wrote that such references "serve, in the only ways reasonably possible in our culture, the legitimate secular purposes of solemnizing public occasions, expressing confidence in the future, and encouraging the recognition of what is worthy of appreciation in society." For centuries, we have marked important occasions or pronouncements with references to God and invocations of divine assistance. Such references can serve to solemnize an occasion instead of to invoke divine provenance. The reasonable observer discussed above, fully aware of our national history and the origins of such practices, would not perceive these acknowledgments as signifying a government endorsement of any specific religion, or even of religion over non-religion.

There are no *de minimis* violations of the Constitution—no constitutional harms so slight that the courts are obliged to ignore them. Given the values that the Establishment Clause was meant to serve, however, I believe that government can, in a discrete category of cases, acknowledge or refer to the divine without offending the Constitution. This category of "ceremonial deism" most clearly encompasses such things as the national motto ("In God We Trust"), religious references in traditional patriotic songs such as the Star–Spangled Banner, and the words with which the Marshal of this Court opens each of its sessions ("God save the United States and this honorable Court"). These references are not minor trespasses upon the Establishment Clause to which I turn a blind eye. Instead, their history, character, and context prevent them from being constitutional violations at all.

This case requires us to determine whether the appearance of the phrase "under God" in the Pledge of Allegiance constitutes an instance of such ceremonial deism. Although it is a close question, I conclude that it does, based on my evaluation of the following four factors.

History and Ubiquity

The constitutional value of ceremonial deism turns on a shared understanding of its legitimate nonreligious purposes. That sort of understanding can exist only when a given practice has been in place for a significant portion of the Nation's history, and when it is observed by enough persons that it can fairly be called ubiquitous. By contrast, novel or uncommon references to religion can more easily be perceived as government endorsements because the reasonable observer cannot be presumed to be fully familiar with their origins. As a result, in examining whether a given practice constitutes an instance of ceremonial deism, its 'history and ubiquity' will be of great importance. As I explained in *Allegheny*:

> Under the endorsement test, the "history and ubiquity" of a practice is relevant not because it creates an "artificial exception" from that test. On the contrary, the "history and ubiquity" of a practice is relevant because it provides part of the context in which a reasonable observer evaluates whether a challenged governmental practice conveys a message of endorsement of religion.

Fifty years have passed since the words "under God" were added, a span of time that is not inconsiderable given the relative youth of our Nation. In that time, the Pledge has become, alongside the singing of the Star–Spangled Banner, our most routine ceremonial act of patriotism; countless schoolchildren recite it daily, and their religious heterogeneity reflects that of the Nation as a whole. As a result, the Pledge and the context in which it is employed are familiar and nearly inseparable in the public mind. No reasonable observer could have been surprised to learn the words of the Pledge, or that petitioner school district has a policy of leading its students in daily recitation of the Pledge.

It cannot be doubted that "no one acquires a vested or protected right in violation of the Constitution by long use, even when that span of time covers our entire national existence and indeed predates it. Yet an unbroken practice . . . is not something to be lightly cast aside." And the history of a given practice is all the more relevant when the practice has been employed pervasively without engendering significant controversy. In *Lynch*, where we evaluated the constitutionality of a town Christmas display that included a crèche, we found relevant to the endorsement question the fact that the display had "apparently caused no political divisiveness prior to the filing of this lawsuit" despite its use for over 40 years. Similarly, in the 50 years that the Pledge has been recited as it is now, by millions of children, this was, at the time of its filing, only the third reported case of which I am aware to challenge it as an impermissible establishment of religion. The citizens of this Nation have been neither timid nor unimaginative in challenging government practices as forbidden "establishments" of religion. Given the vigor and creativity of such challenges, I find it telling that so little ire has been directed at the Pledge.

Absence of worship or prayer

"[O]ne of the greatest dangers to the freedom of the individual to worship in his own way [lies] in the Government's placing its official stamp of approval upon one particular kind of prayer or one particular form of religious services." *Engel v. Vitale*, 370 U.S. 421, 429 (1962). Because of this principle, only in the most extraordinary circumstances could actual worship or prayer be defended as ceremonial deism. We have upheld only one such prayer against Establishment Clause challenge, and it was supported by an extremely long and unambiguous history. Any statement that has as its purpose placing the speaker or listener in a penitent state of mind, or that is intended to create a spiritual communion or invoke divine aid, strays from the legitimate secular purposes of solemnizing an event and recognizing a shared religious history. *Santa Fe Independent School Dist. v. Doe*, 530 U.S. 290, 309 (2000) ("[T]he use of an invocation to foster ... solemnity is impermissible when, in actuality, it constitutes [state-sponsored] prayer").

Of course, any statement *can* be imbued by a speaker or listener with the qualities of prayer. But, as I have explained, the relevant viewpoint is that of a reasonable observer, fully cognizant of the history, ubiquity, and context of the practice in question. Such an observer could not conclude that reciting the Pledge, including the phrase "under God," constitutes an instance of worship. I know of no religion that incorporates the Pledge into its canon, nor one that would count the Pledge as a meaningful expression of religious faith. Even if taken literally, the phrase is merely descriptive; it purports only to identify the United States as a Nation subject to divine authority. That cannot be seen as a serious invocation of God or as an expression of individual submission to divine authority. *Cf. Engel, supra*, at 424 (describing prayer as "a solemn avowal of faith and supplication for the blessing of the Almighty"). A reasonable observer would note that petitioner school district's policy of Pledge recitation appears under the heading of "Patriotic Observances," and the California law which it implements refers to "appropriate patriotic exercises." Petitioner school district also employs teachers, not chaplains or religious instructors, to lead its students' exercise; this serves as a further indication that it does not treat the Pledge as a prayer. *Cf. Lee v. Weisman*, 505 U.S. 577, 594 (1992) (reasoning that a graduation benediction could not be construed as a *de minimis* religious exercise without offending the rabbi who offered it).

It is true that some of the legislators who voted to add the phrase "under God" to the Pledge may have done so in an attempt to attach to it an overtly religious message. But their intentions cannot, on their own, decide our inquiry. First of all, those legislators also had permissible secular objectives in mind—they meant, for example, to acknowledge the religious origins of our Nation's belief in the "individuality and the dignity of the human being." Second—and more critically—the *subsequent* social and cultural history of the Pledge shows that its original secular character was not transformed by its amendment. In *School Dist. of Abington Township v. Schempp*, we explained that a government may initiate a practice "for the impermissible purpose of supporting religion" but nevertheless "retai[n] the la[w] for the permissible purpose of furthering overwhelmingly secular ends." Whatever the sectarian ends its authors may have had in mind, our continued repetition of the reference to "one Nation under God" in an exclusively patriotic context has shaped the cultural significance of that phrase to conform to that context. Any religious freight the words may have been meant to carry originally has long since been lost. See *Lynch* (Brennan, J., dissenting) (suggesting that the reference to God in the Pledge might be permissible because it has "lost through rote repetition any significant religious content").

Absence of reference to particular religion

"The clearest command of the Establishment Clause is that one religious denomination cannot be officially preferred over another." While general acknowledgments of religion need not be viewed by reasonable observers as denigrating the nonreligious, the same cannot be said of instances "where the endorsement is sectarian, in the sense of specifying details upon which men and women who believe in a benevolent, omnipotent Creator and Ruler of the world are known to differ." *Weisman, supra,* at 641 (SCALIA, J., dissenting). As a result, no religious acknowledgment could claim to be an instance of ceremonial deism if it explicitly favored one particular religious belief system over another.

The Pledge complies with this requirement. It does not refer to a nation "under Jesus" or "under Vishnu," but instead acknowledges religion in a general way: a simple reference to a generic "God." Of course, some religions—Buddhism, for instance—are not based upon a belief in a separate Supreme Being. But one would be hard pressed to imagine a brief solemnizing reference to religion that would adequately encompass every religious belief expressed by any citizen of this Nation. The phrase "under God," conceived and added at a time when our national religious diversity was neither as robust nor as well recognized as it is now, represents a tolerable attempt to acknowledge religion and to invoke its solemnizing power without favoring any individual religious sect or belief system.

Minimal religious content

A final factor that makes the Pledge an instance of ceremonial deism, in my view, is its highly circumscribed reference to God. In most of the cases in which we have struck down government speech or displays under the Establishment Clause, the offending religious content has been much more pervasive. *See, e.g., Weisman, supra,* at 581–582 (prayers involving repeated thanks to God and requests for blessings). Of course, a ceremony cannot avoid Establishment Clause scrutiny simply by avoiding an explicit mention of God. See *Wallace v. Jaffree,* 472 U.S. 38 (1985) (invalidating Alabama statute providing moment of silence for meditation or voluntary prayer). But the brevity of a reference to religion or to God in a ceremonial exercise can be important for several reasons. First, it tends to confirm that the reference is being used to acknowledge religion or to solemnize an event rather than to endorse religion in any way. Second, it makes it easier for those participants who wish to "opt out" of language they find offensive to do so without having to reject the ceremony entirely. And third, it tends to limit the ability of government to express a preference for one religious sect over another.

The reference to "God" in the Pledge of Allegiance qualifies as a minimal reference to religion; respondent's challenge focuses on only two of the Pledge's 31 words. Moreover, the presence of those words is not absolutely essential to the Pledge, as demonstrated by the fact that it existed without them for over 50 years. As a result, students who wish to avoid saying the words 'under God' still can consider themselves meaningful participants in the exercise if they join in reciting the remainder of the Pledge.

I have framed my inquiry as a specific application of the endorsement test by examining whether the ceremony or representation would convey a message to a reasonable observer, familiar with its history, origins, and context, that those who do not adhere to its literal message are political outsiders. But consideration of these factors would lead me to the same result even if I were to apply the 'coercion' test that has featured in several opinions of this Court. *Santa Fe Independent School Dist. v. Doe,* 530 U.S. 290 (2000); *Lee v. Weisman,* 505 U.S. 577 (1992).

The coercion test provides that, "at a minimum ... government may not coerce anyone to support or participate in religion or its exercise, or otherwise act in a way which 'establishes a [state] religion or religious faith, or tends to do so.'" Any coercion that persuades an onlooker to participate in an act of ceremonial deism is inconsequential, as an Establishment Clause matter, because such acts are simply not religious in character. As a result, symbolic references to religion that qualify as instances of ceremonial deism will pass the coercion test as well as the endorsement test. This is not to say, however, that government could *overtly* coerce a person to participate in an act of ceremonial deism. Our cardinal freedom is one of belief; leaders in this Nation cannot force us to proclaim our allegiance to *any* creed, whether it be religious, philosophic, or political. That principle found eloquent expression in a case involving the Pledge itself, even before it contained the words to which respondent now objects. See *West Virginia Bd. of Ed. v. Barnette*, 319 U.S. 624, 642 (1943) (Jackson, J.). The compulsion of which Justice Jackson was concerned, however, was of the direct sort—the Constitution does not guarantee citizens a right entirely to avoid ideas with which they disagree. It would betray its own principles if it did; no robust democracy insulates its citizens from views that they might find novel or even inflammatory.

* * *

Michael Newdow's challenge to petitioner school district's policy is a well-intentioned one, but his distaste for the reference to "one Nation under God," however sincere, cannot be the yardstick of our Establishment Clause inquiry. Certain ceremonial references to God and religion in our Nation are the inevitable consequence of the religious history that gave birth to our founding principles of liberty. It would be ironic indeed if this Court were to wield our constitutional commitment to religious freedom so as to sever our ties to the traditions developed to honor it.

C. DISPUTED ACCESS TO CAMPUS FORUMS AND FACILITIES

1. ACCESS TO FORUMS

ROSENBERGER v. RECTOR & VISITORS OF UNIV. OF VA.

515 U.S. 819, 115 S.Ct. 2510 (1995)

[The facts of this case are set forth in Chapter 3, *supra,* where the Free Speech Clause aspects of the opinion are included.

Plaintiffs had relied upon the First Amendment in challenging the university's denial of funds to a registered student group, Wide Awake Productions. The group had requested money from the Student Activities Fund to help cover the cost of publication for an on-campus newspaper with "a Christian perspective on both personal and community issues." But the request was denied by a student committee on the grounds that the newspaper "promote[d] or manifest[ed] a particular belie[f] in or about a deity or an ultimate reality."

Analyzing the Free Speech Clause issue under the viewpoint discrimination doctrine, the Court ruled in favor of the students.[a] The Court then turned to the Establishment Clause component of the case.]

---

a. *See* 515 U.S. at 829: "Once it has opened a limited forum, . . . the State must respect the lawful boundaries it has itself set. The State may not exclude speech where its distinction is not "reasonable in light of the purpose served by the forum," nor may it discriminate against speech on the basis of its viewpoint. . . . The SAF is a forum more in a metaphysical than in a spatial or geographic sense, but the same principles are applicable."

KENNEDY, J.

* * *

III

Before its brief on the merits in this Court, the University had argued at all stages of the litigation that inclusion of WAP's contractors in SAF funding authorization would violate the Establishment Clause.

* * *

The Court of Appeals ruled that withholding SAF support from Wide Awake contravened the Speech Clause of the First Amendment, but proceeded to hold that the University's action was justified by the necessity of avoiding a violation of the Establishment Clause, an interest it found compelling.

* * *

If there is to be assurance that the Establishment Clause retains its force in guarding against those governmental actions it was intended to prohibit, we must in each case inquire first into the purpose and object of the governmental action in question and then into the practical details of the program's operation. Before turning to these matters, however, we can set forth certain general principles that must bear upon our determination.

A central lesson of our decisions is that a significant factor in upholding governmental programs in the face of Establishment Clause attack is their neutrality towards religion.... We have held that the guarantee of neutrality is respected, not offended, when the government, following neutral criteria and evenhanded policies, extends benefits to recipients whose ideologies and viewpoints, including religious ones, are broad and diverse. More than once have we rejected the position that the Establishment Clause even justifies, much less requires, a refusal to extend free speech rights to religious speakers who participate in broad-reaching government programs neutral in design.

The governmental program here is neutral toward religion. There is no suggestion that the University created it to advance religion or adopted some ingenious device with the purpose of aiding a religious cause. The object of the SAF is to open a forum for speech and to support various student enterprises, including the publication of newspapers, in recognition of the diversity and creativity of student life. The University's SAF Guidelines have a separate classification for, and do not make third-party payments on behalf of, "religious organizations," which are those "whose purpose is to practice a devotion to an acknowledged ultimate reality or deity." The category of support here is for "student news, information,

---

While on its most basic level the free speech component of *Rosenberger* stands for the proposition that regulating religious speech on campus constitutes viewpoint discrimination, the language of the decision is very broad and sweeping. Commentators have thus viewed the case as not only strengthening the viewpoint discrimination doctrine in general, but as significantly expanding its scope.

opinion, entertainment, or academic communications media groups," of which Wide Awake was 1 of 15 in the 1990 school year. WAP did not seek a subsidy because of its Christian editorial viewpoint; it sought funding as a student journal, which it was.

The neutrality of the program distinguishes the student fees from a tax levied for the direct support of a church or group of churches. A tax of that sort, of course, would run contrary to Establishment Clause concerns dating from the earliest days of the Republic. The apprehensions of our predecessors involved the levying of taxes upon the public for the sole and exclusive purpose of establishing and supporting specific sects. The exaction here, by contrast, is a student activity fee designed to reflect the reality that student life in its many dimensions includes the necessity of wide-ranging speech and inquiry and that student expression is an integral part of the University's educational mission. The fee is mandatory, and we do not have before us the question whether an objecting student has the First Amendment right to demand a pro rata return to the extent the fee is expended for speech to which he or she does not subscribe. We must treat it, then, as an exaction upon the students. But the $14 paid each semester by the students is not a general tax designed to raise revenue for the University. The SAF cannot be used for unlimited purposes, much less the illegitimate purpose of supporting one religion. * * * [T]he money goes to a special fund from which any group of students with CIO status can draw for purposes consistent with the University's educational mission; and to the extent the student is interested in speech, withdrawal is permitted to cover the whole spectrum of speech, whether it manifests a religious view, an antireligious view, or neither. Our decision, then, cannot be read as addressing an expenditure from a general tax fund. Here, the disbursements from the fund go to private contractors for the cost of printing that which is protected under the Speech Clause of the First Amendment. This is a far cry from a general public assessment designed and effected to provide financial support for a church.

Government neutrality is apparent in the State's overall scheme in a further meaningful respect. The program respects the critical difference "between *government* speech endorsing religion, which the Establishment Clause forbids, and *private* speech endorsing religion, which the Free Speech and Free Exercise Clauses protect."

* * *

It does not violate the Establishment Clause for a public university to grant access to its facilities on a religion-neutral basis to a wide spectrum of student groups, including groups that use meeting rooms for sectarian activities, accompanied by some devotional exercises. See *Widmar*, 454 U.S. at 269, 102 S.Ct. at 274; *Mergens*, 496 U.S. at 252, 110 S.Ct. at 2373. This is so even where the upkeep, maintenance, and repair of the facilities attributed to those uses are paid from a student activities fund to which students are required to contribute.

* * *

By paying outside printers, the University in fact attains a further degree of separation from the student publication, for it avoids the duties of supervision, escapes the costs of upkeep, repair, and replacement attributable to student use, and has a clear record of costs. As a result, and as in *Widmar,* the University can charge the SAF, and not the taxpayers as a whole, for the discrete activity in question. It would be formalistic for us to say that the University must forfeit these advantages and provide the services itself in order to comply with the Establishment Clause. It is, of course, true that if the State pays a church's bills it is subsidizing it, and we must guard against this abuse. That is not a danger here, based on the considerations we have advanced and for the additional reason that the student publication is not a religious institution, at least in the usual sense of that term as used in our case law, and it is not a religious organization as used in the University's own regulations. It is instead a publication involved in a pure forum for the expression of ideas, ideas that would be both incomplete and chilled were the Constitution to be interpreted to require that state officials and courts scan the publication to ferret out views that principally manifest a belief in a divine being.

* * *

To obey the Establishment Clause, it was not necessary for the University to deny eligibility to student publications because of their viewpoint. The neutrality commanded of the State by the separate Clauses of the First Amendment was compromised by the University's course of action. The viewpoint discrimination inherent in the University's regulation required public officials to scan and interpret student publications to discern their underlying philosophic assumptions respecting religious theory and belief. That course of action was a denial of the right of free speech and would risk fostering a pervasive bias or hostility to religion, which could undermine the very neutrality the Establishment Clause requires. There is no Establishment Clause violation in the University's honoring its duties under the Free Speech Clause.

The judgment of the Court of Appeals must be, and is, reversed.

It is so ordered.

NOTE

1. In *Christian Legal Society (CLS) v. Walker,* 453 F.3d 853 (7th Cir. 2006), the appellate panel, by a 2–1 vote, ruled against Southern Illinois University (SIU). The dean of the SIU School of Law "had revoked the official student organization status of the [CLS] chapter at SIU because he concluded that CLS's membership policies, which preclude membership to those who engage in or affirm homosexual conduct, violate SIU's nondiscrimination policies." CLS sought injunctive relief under the First and Fourteenth Amendments. *Id.* at 857.

In deciding on behalf of the CLS, the panel majority noted, among other things, that the policy in question actually applied to both gay and straight students:

CLS is a nationwide association of legal professionals and law students who share (broadly speaking) a common faith-Christianity. Members are expected to subscribe to a statement of faith and agree to live by certain moral principles. One of those principles, the one that has caused the dispute in this case, is that sexual activity outside of a traditional (one man, one woman) marriage is forbidden. That means, in addition to fornication and adultery, CLS disapproves [of] active homosexuality. CLS welcomes anyone to its meetings, but voting members and officers of the organization must subscribe to the statement of faith, meaning, among other things, that they must not engage in or approve of fornication, adultery, or homosexual conduct; or, having done so, must repent of that conduct. *Id.* at 857–858.

Relying in great part on principles set forth in *Rosenberger* and in *Healy v. James, supra,* Chapter 3, Judge Diane S. Sykes found that while the SIU policy "is viewpoint neutral on its face, * * * there is strong evidence that the policy has not been applied in a viewpoint neutral way." [According to the evidence presented,] CLS is the only student group that has been stripped of its recognized status on the basis that it discriminates on a ground prohibited by [the] * * * policy. CLS alleged that other recognized student organizations discriminate in their membership requirements on grounds prohibited by SIU's policy. They referenced the fact that "the Muslim Students' Association, for example, limits membership to Muslims," and that "membership in the Adventist Campus Ministries is limited to those 'professing the Seventh Day Adventist Faith, and all other students who are interested in studying the Holy Bible and applying its principles.'" They also noted that "[m]embership in the Young Women's Coalition is for women only, though regardless of their race, color, creed, religion, ethnicity, sexual orientation, or physical ability." *Id.* at 866.

Judge Diane P. Wood dissented, noting that the majority had conceded that the evidence presented thus far was "spartan," and in fact that SIU had not yet submitted any evidence at all to the Court. She would have dissolved the injunction and proceeded with a trial on the merits. In particular, she questioned the attempt by the majority to distinguish between orientation and conduct:

> The majority attempts to [draw] a distinction between discrimination on the basis of sexual *orientation* and discrimination on the basis of sexual *conduct.* The record contains absolutely no evidence, however, either supporting or refuting the notion that CLS actively bans from membership or leadership positions heterosexual students who may be sexually active outside the boundaries of marriage. Likewise, the record is thoroughly devoid of evidence indicating that a gay or lesbian who has chosen not to be sexually active has been permitted to be a member or leader of CLS. * * *

PECK v. BALDWINSVILLE CENTRAL SCH. DIST.

426 F.3d 617 (2nd Cir. 2005)

CALABRESI, CIRCUIT JUDGE.

This case invites us to cut a path through the thorniest of constitutional thickets—among the tangled vines of public school curricula and student freedom of expression.

* * * The Pecks [allege] that officials at Antonio's elementary school had censored one of his school assignments to exclude religious content, and had thereby violated both the Establishment Clause and Antonio's First Amendment right to free speech. * * * We now affirm the district court's determination that no Establishment Clause violation attended The District's actions, but vacate and remand the court's disposition of the Pecks' free speech claims.

I. Background

* * *

THE POSTER ASSIGNMENT AND THE SCHOOL RESPONSE

During the 1999–2000 school year Antonio was a kindergarten student at the Catherine McNamara Elementary School, enrolled in a class taught by Susan Weichert ("Weichert"). Part of the kindergarten curriculum taught by Weichert was a two-month environmental unit that * * * focused on "simple ways to save the environment, such as preserving trees and animals, using water and other natural resources sparingly and wisely, [and] keeping the environment clean * * *." The unit culminated, near the end of the school year, in an assignment in which students in the class were instructed to create a poster showing what they had learned about the environment[, and an environmental assembly that] * * * consisted of students planting a tree and singing environmentally-themed songs. In addition, the kindergartners' posters would be displayed at the assembly.

[Weichert sent two notes home to the parents of her kindergartners describing the assignment and the assembly.] * * *

JoAnne Peck * * * stated that she and Antonio sat down together one night to do the poster, and she told Antonio that the school wanted him to do a poster on how to save the environment. Antonio responded, according to Peck, that the only way to save the world was through Jesus. Peck then provided Antonio with art materials and some magazines, and Antonio selected pictures, cut them out, and, with his mother's assistance, arranged them on a piece of paper. Antonio (who could not read) told his mother what he wanted the poster to say, and Peck wrote out what Antonio said so that he could include the words on to the poster.

This poster, which was turned in to Weichert, was comprised of the following images: a robed figure (who is described by both parties as "Jesus") kneeling and raising his hands to the sky, two children on a rock bearing the word "Savior," and the Ten Commandments. Written on the poster were the phrases, "the only way to save our world," "prayer changes things," "Jesus loves children," "God keeps his promises," and "God's love is higher than the heavens."

Upon receiving Antonio's poster Weichert took it to the school principal, Robert Creme ("Creme"). Creme told Weichert that Antonio should be instructed to do another poster. Creme also contacted Superintendent Theodore Gilkey ("Gilkey") to tell him of the situation and of how Creme had decided to handle it. Gilkey agreed with the decision to have Antonio prepare a second poster.

Some time after Antonio turned in his first poster, JoAnne Peck attended an art show at the elementary school. At the show she saw Weichert, who told her, for the first time, that Antonio's poster would not be displayed at the environmental assembly. According to Peck, Weichert stated that "she legally didn't think she could hang the poster for religious reasons," and also that the poster didn't demonstrate Antonio's learning of the environmental lessons. Peck subsequently contacted Creme, who told her that Antonio could make a new poster with "a little bit of religious content and more showing the recycling, kids throwing trash. . . . [or] kids holding hands around the world."[2]

Soon thereafter, Antonio and his mother sat down together to do a second poster. According to Peck's deposition testimony, she again assisted Antonio in selecting images (from the computer and from a religiously-themed coloring book), and in arranging pictures on the poster. The second poster depicted, on its left side, the same robed, praying figure pictured in the first poster. It also showed, in the center, a church with a cross. To the right of the church were pictures of people picking up trash and placing it in a recycling can, of children holding hands encircling the globe, and of clouds, trees, a squirrel, and grass.

After receiving the second poster Weichert again took it to Creme, who, according to Weichert, stated "[t]hat there were portions of the poster . . . that clearly showed an understanding of some of the things that I had been teaching in the environmental unit [and] there was a portion that didn't relate to what . . . had been t[aught]." Creme then told Weichert "that we should hang the poster [at the environmental program] with the kneeling figure folded under."

Notwithstanding Creme's determination that Antonio's second poster was partly unacceptable, Antonio was allowed to "show and tell" his poster to his own kindergarten class. According to Weichert, when Antonio presented his poster she asked him "to explain the poster to the class and how he could help the earth. . . . He said you could pick up trash and help keep the earth clean." Antonio did not mention the robed figure or the church, or make any reference to God or religion, in his explanation. Weichert never asked Antonio—either during his presentation, or privately—to explain the significance of the robed figure.

Antonio's poster was displayed at the June 11 environmental assembly, alongside those of approximately eighty other kindergartners, on the wall of the school cafeteria. Pursuant to Creme's instructions, however,

---

2. The Pecks do not, at this stage of the litigation, base any of their claims on The District's conduct in relation to the first poster.

Weichert asked the parent volunteer who was hanging the posters to place Antonio's on the wall with the robed figure (the left-hand side of the poster) folded under. Apparently because of a mistake made by the parent volunteer, a greater portion of the poster than Weichert had intended was concealed: the poster was ultimately displayed with both the robed figure and half of the church folded under. Only the right half of the church (including the cross) was visible, along with the above-described images of recycling, children holding hands, and the nature-related pictures. Antonio's poster, folded as thus described, was smaller than some of the other students' projects, but was the same size as others. * * *

B. Free Speech Claim

* * * The Pecks contend a) that the court erroneously analyzed The District's actions under the rubric set forth by the Supreme Court in *Hazelwood School District v. Kuhlmeier* rather than under the more speech-protective standard of *Tinker* and b) that, even under the standards enunciated in *Hazelwood,* disputed issues of material fact had been raised with respect to the reasonableness and viewpoint neutrality of The District's actions. Although we agree with the district court that *Hazelwood,* rather then *Tinker,* provides the applicable framework for our analysis of the speech restrictions at issue in this case, we think that the Pecks have raised genuine issues of material fact under that standard, and therefore agree with the Pecks that summary judgment should not have been granted as to the free speech claim.

1. Applicable Level of Constitutional Scrutiny

* * * Garnering the lowest level of scrutiny along the forum analysis spectrum is the "non-public forum," which is neither traditionally open to public expression nor designated for such expression by the State. "Restrictions on speech in a nonpublic forum need only be reasonable and viewpoint neutral." "Although a speaker may be excluded from a nonpublic forum if he wishes to address a topic not encompassed within the purpose of the forum, or if he is not a member of the class of speakers for whose especial benefit the forum was created, the government violates the First Amendment when it denies access to a speaker solely to suppress the point of view he espouses on an otherwise includible subject."

[The parties apparently agree that Antonio's classroom, the school cafeteria, and "any other aspect" of the Catherine McNamara Elementary School were non-public fora.]. * * * Hence, there is no dispute that The District was entitled, in the non-public fora at issue in this case, at least to regulate the content of Antonio's poster in a reasonable manner.

* * * The speech at issue [in *Hazelwood*] consisted of two articles that were written by students in a high school journalism class and that were to appear in a school newspaper published as part of the class's curriculum. [The principal prohibited the paper from printing either one.]

In assessing the Hazelwood School District's actions, the Court deemed *Tinker* inapposite to the context of student expression that the court characterized as curricular and, hence, "school-sponsored"[.] * * * *Tinker's* * * * standard was, in the Court's view, insufficiently deferential to the prerogative of educators to "assure that participants learn whatever lessons the activity is designed to teach, that readers or listeners are not exposed to material that may be inappropriate for their level of maturity, and that the views of the individual speaker are not erroneously attributed to the school." Accordingly, *Hazelwood* held, "educators do not offend the First Amendment by exercising editorial control over the style and content of student speech in school-sponsored expressive activities so long as their actions are *reasonably related to legitimate pedagogical concerns.*" (emphasis added).

[W]e think it clear that the facts in the record bring Antonio's poster, the vehicle of his censored expression, within *Hazelwood's* framework. It is undisputed that the poster was prepared by Antonio pursuant to a class assignment, and one that was given under highly specific parameters: to "depict[ ] ways to save our environment" and to reflect what had been taught in the kindergarten environmental unit. Additionally, the posters were to be displayed at a school-sponsored assembly, to take place in the school cafeteria, to which parents of the kindergartners were invited. Aside from the students' posters, the environmental assembly included songs and other presentations that were prepared as part of the kindergarten curriculum.

These undisputed facts demonstrate that the poster assignment and the environmental assembly at which the posters were hung—perhaps even more starkly than in the context of the newspaper articles at issue in *Hazelwood*—were indisputably "part of the school curriculum. . . . supervised by faculty members and designed to impart particular knowledge or skills to student participants and audiences."[a]

Accordingly, we find the case before us to fall within the core of *Hazelwood's* framework. And, the district court correctly concluded that the *Hazelwood* "reasonable relation to legitimate pedagogical concerns" test provides the appropriate lens through which to examine The District's censorship of Antonio's poster.

2. Application of *Hazelwood*

a) Was there a fact question as to viewpoint discrimination?

We must ask, then, whether the record demonstrates triable issues as to whether The District's reasons for censoring Antonio's poster are, in

---

a. Judge Calabresi quoted *Fleming v. Jefferson County Sch. Dist. R–1,* 298 F.3d 918, 924 (10th Cir.2002) ("Few activities bear a school's 'imprimatur' and 'involve pedagogical interests' more significantly than speech that occurs within a classroom setting as part of a school's curriculum."). It then cited *Bannon v. School Dist. of Palm Beach County,* 387 F.3d 1208, 1214 (11th Cir.2004) (finding that a student's murals constituted school-sponsored expression because they were located in prominent school locations where members of the public might reasonably believe that they bore the imprimatur of the school). It also cited *Settle v. Dickson County Sch. Bd.,* 53 F.3d 152, 155–56 (6th Cir.1995) ("Where learning is the focus, as in the classroom, student speech may be even more circumscribed than in the school newspaper or other open forum.").

the language of *Hazelwood,* "reasonably related to legitimate pedagogical concerns." * * * We reject some of the Pecks' arguments concerning The District's treatment of Antonio's poster[.] * * * The *Hazelwood* standard does not require that the guidelines be the *most* reasonable or the *only* reasonable limitations, only that they be reasonable." * * * Just as *Hazelwood* requires only that the school's employed method of censorship be reasonable, we similarly conclude that the predicate factual determinations made by the school in triggering the censorship need only be reasonable. * * *

Other fact questions to which the Pecks point, however, implicate a more troubling concern: the viewpoint neutrality of The District's decision with respect to Antonio's poster. In our judgment, the district court overlooked evidence that, if construed in the light most favorable to Pecks, suggested that Antonio's poster was censored *not* because it was unresponsive to the assignment, and not because Weichert and Creme believed that JoAnne Peck rather than Antonio was responsible for the poster's content, but because it offered a religious perspective on the topic of how to save the environment.

We recognize at the outset that drawing a precise line of demarcation between content discrimination, which is permissible in a non-public forum, and viewpoint discrimination, which traditionally has been prohibited *even* in non-public fora, is, to say the least, a problematic endeavor. * * *

Nevertheless, we think that there are at least disputed factual questions, which may not be resolved on summary judgment, as to whether Antonio's poster offered a "religious viewpoint," and whether, if the poster had depicted a purely secular image that was equally outside the scope of Weichert's environmental lessons, it would similarly have been censored. Weichert testified that there were a number of potential images that Antonio could have placed on his poster, such as specific endangered species, the Sierra Club logo, and atoms, all of which would have been non-responsive to the assignment to the extent that such topics were not specifically covered in class. The District's actions might well amount to viewpoint discrimination.

b) Does *Hazelwood* permit viewpoint discrimination "reasonably related to legitimate pedagogical concerns"?

The District counters that, even assuming there to be evidence that its decision was based on the *viewpoint* rather than the *content* of Antonio's poster, the district court's dismissal of the free speech claim would still have been proper because *Hazelwood* permits schools to discriminate on the basis of viewpoint—so long as such discrimination is, itself, reasonably related to a legitimate pedagogical interest. Whether *Hazelwood* represents a departure from the long-held requirement of viewpoint neutrality in any and all government restriction of private speech, *see, e.g., Rosenberger* ("Viewpoint discrimination is . . . an egregious form of content discrimination. The government must abstain from regulating speech when the specific motivating ideology or the opinion or perspective of the speaker is the rationale for the restriction."), is an issue that has been the subject of much debate among Circuit Courts, which have reached conflicting conclusions.[9]

As the varying approaches of other courts suggest, the proper answer to the question of whether *Hazelwood* contemplates "reasonable" viewpoint discrimination by school administrators in the context of school-sponsored speech is anything but clear.

[The Court proceeds to analyze in some detail the arguments for the respective positions on this issue.]

* * *

[W]e decline The District's invitation to depart, without clear direction from the Supreme Court, from what has, to date, remained a core facet of First Amendment protection.[b] Thus, on the facts and the legal arguments as they are currently developed before us, we conclude that a manifestly viewpoint discriminatory restriction on school-sponsored speech is, prima facie, unconstitutional, *even if* reasonably related to legitimate pedagogical interests.

In remanding the free speech claim to the district court for further consideration of the viewpoint neutrality issue, however, we do not *foreclose* the possibility that certain aspects of the record might be developed in such a manner as to disclose a state interest so overriding as to justify, under the First Amendment, The District's potentially viewpoint discriminatory censorship. For example, The District has proffered its interest in avoiding the perception of religious *endorsement* as a rationale for not including Antonio's full poster in the environmental assembly. On the facts before us we cannot say, at this time, as a matter of law that The District's concern in this regard would justify viewpoint discrimination.

* * *

---

9. The First and Tenth Circuits have expressly held that educators may make viewpoint-based decisions about school-sponsored speech. *See Ward v. Hickey*, 996 F.2d 448, 452 (1st Cir.1993); *Fleming v. Jefferson County Sch. Dist. R–1*, 298 F.3d 918, 926–28 (10th Cir.2002). The Ninth Circuit and Eleventh Circuits have, instead, decided that *Hazelwood* did not alter the general requirement of viewpoint neutrality in non-public fora. *See Planned Parenthood of S. Nevada, Inc. v. Clark County Sch. Dist.*, 941 F.2d 817, 829 (9th Cir.1991) (en banc) (applying, without discussion, *Cornelius* viewpoint neutrality standard to a nonpublic school forum); *Searcey v. Harris*, 888 F.2d 1314, 1319 n. 7 (11th Cir.1989); *see also Downs v. Los Angeles Unified Sch. Dist.*, 228 F.3d 1003, 1010–11 (9th Cir.2000) (noting that "despite the absence of express 'viewpoint neutrality' discussion anywhere in *Hazelwood,* the *Planned Parenthood* court incorporated 'viewpoint neutrality' analysis into nonpublic forum, school-sponsored speech cases in our Circuit," but deciding, ultimately, that *Hazelwood* did not supply the appropriate standard for the issue before it). A panel of the Third Circuit held that a viewpoint restriction "may reasonably be related to legitimate pedagogical concerns" and therefore constitutional, but on a rehearing en banc, the circuit was equally-divided on the question. *See C.H. ex rel. Z.H. v. Oliva*, 195 F.3d 167, 172 (3d Cir.1999), *vacated and reh'g en banc granted by* 197 F.3d 63 (3d Cir.1999), *on reh'g en banc* 226 F.3d 198 (3d Cir.2000) (affirming the district court judgment regarding one expressive act without explication and deciding the remaining expressive issue on procedural grounds, thereby obviating the need to reach the viewpoint neutrality question).

b. The Court cites here to Searcey v. Harris, 888 F.2d 1314, 1325 (11th Cir. 1989): "Without more explicit direction, we will continue to require school officials to make decisions relating to speech which are viewpoint neutral.".

We think it prudent to leave it to the district court * * * to ascertain whether The District's actions were necessary to avoid an Establishment Clause violation, and if so, whether avoidance of that violation was a sufficiently compelling state interest as to justify viewpoint discrimination by The District.

C. Establishment Clause Claim

The Pecks also appeal the district court's dismissal of their Establishment Clause claim against The District. They argue that triable issues exist on the question of whether The District's censorship of Antonio's poster had the primary effect of inhibiting Antonio's religious expression, exhibiting hostility toward Christianity, and resulting in The District's excessive religious entanglement.

In this Circuit, as the parties appear to agree, the Supreme Court's *Lemon* test continues to govern our analysis of Establishment Clause claims. * * *

Applying the above factors to the undisputed facts, we conclude that the district court properly dismissed the Pecks' Establishment Clause claim. We see nothing in the record to suggest that The District acted, as the Pecks contend, with the purpose of inhibiting religion. As discussed above, two of the three rationales given by the district court for not displaying Antonio's full poster—the concern that the poster was both not responsive to the assignment and that it was not Antonio's work—were wholly secular. While the third stated reason, avoidance of the perception of religious endorsement, is no doubt involved with religion, such a goal does not bespeak an intent to inhibit religion itself. We note as well that the partial censorship of Antonio's poster, resulting in the concealment of the robed figure but the display of a church with a cross, strongly cuts against the Pecks' bare allegation that The District's actions were intended to demonstrate hostility toward religion. In short, no triable issue exists on this score.

As to the "primary effect" inquiry, * * * [we] reject the suggestion by the Pecks that, because Antonio was prevented from expressing his religious perspective in the context of the kindergarten poster project, The District's decision had the impermissible "effect" of inhibiting religion. * * *

For all of the foregoing reasons, we concur with the judgment of the district court that no triable issues exist with respect to The District's alleged Establishment Clause violation. Accordingly, that claim was properly dismissed.

III. Conclusion

The district court's dismissal of the Pecks' free speech claim is VACATED, and its dismissal of the Establishment Clause claim is AFFIRMED. The case is REMANDED for further proceedings consistent with this opinion.

2. ACCESS TO CAMPUS FACILITIES

GOOD NEWS CLUB v. MILFORD CENTRAL SCH.

533 U.S. 98, 121 S.Ct. 2093 (2001)

JUSTICE THOMAS delivered the opinion of the Court.

This case presents two questions. The first question is whether Milford Central School violated the free speech rights of the Good News Club when it excluded the Club from meeting after hours at the school. The second question is whether any such violation is justified by Milford's concern that permitting the Club's activities would violate the Establishment Clause. We conclude that Milford's restriction violates the Club's free speech rights and that no Establishment Clause concern justifies that violation.

I.

* * * Stephen and Darleen Fournier reside within Milford's district and therefore are eligible [under school district policy] to use the school's facilities as long as their proposed use is approved by the school. Together they are sponsors of the local Good News Club, a private Christian organization for children ages 6 to 12. Pursuant to Milford's policy, in September 1996 the Fourniers submitted a request to Dr. Robert McGruder, interim superintendent of the district, in which they sought permission to hold the Club's weekly afterschool meetings in the school cafeteria. * * * The next month, McGruder formally denied the Fourniers' request on the ground that the proposed use—to have "a fun time of singing songs, hearing a Bible lesson and memorizing scripture,"—was "the equivalent of religious worship." According to McGruder, the community use policy, which prohibits use "by any individual or organization for religious purposes," foreclosed the Club's activities.

In response to a letter submitted by the Club's counsel, Milford's attorney requested information to clarify the nature of the Club's activities. The Club sent a set of materials used or distributed at the meetings and the following description of its meeting:

> The Club opens its session with Ms. Fournier taking attendance. As she calls a child's name, if the child recites a Bible verse the child receives a treat. After attendance, the Club sings songs. Next Club members engage in games that involve, *inter alia,* learning Bible verses. Ms. Fournier then relates a Bible story and explains how it applies to Club members' lives. The Club closes with prayer. Finally, Ms. Fournier distributes treats and the Bible verses for memorization.

McGruder and Milford's attorney reviewed the materials and concluded that "the kinds of activities proposed to be engaged in by the Good News Club were not a discussion of secular subjects such as child rearing, development of character and development of morals from a religious perspective, but were in fact the equivalent of religious instruction itself." In February 1997, the Milford Board of Education adopted a resolution rejecting the Club's request to use Milford's facilities "for the purpose of conducting religious instruction and Bible study."

In March 1997, petitioners * * * filed an action under Rev. Stat. § 1979, 42 U.S.C. § 1983, against Milford in the United States District Court for the Northern District of New York. The Club alleged that Milford's denial of its application violated its free speech rights under the First and Fourteenth Amendments, its right to equal protection under the Fourteenth Amendment, and its right to religious freedom under the Religious Freedom Restoration Act of 1993. * * *

II.

The standards that we apply to determine whether a State has unconstitutionally excluded a private speaker from use of a public forum depend on the nature of the forum. If the forum is a traditional or open public forum, the State's restrictions on speech are subject to stricter scrutiny than are restrictions in a limited public forum. We have previously declined to decide whether a school district's opening of its facilities pursuant to N.Y. Educ. Law § 414 creates a limited or a traditional public forum. See *Lamb's Chapel, supra,* at 391–392, 113 S.Ct. 2141. Because the parties have agreed that Milford created a limited public forum when it opened its facilities in 1992 * * * we need not resolve the issue here. Instead, we simply will assume that Milford operates a limited public forum.

When the State establishes a limited public forum, the State is not required to and does not allow persons to engage in every type of speech. The State may be justified "in reserving [its forum] for certain groups or for the discussion of certain topics." *Rosenberger v. Rector and Visitors of Univ. of Va.,* 515 U.S. 819 (1995). The State's power to restrict speech, however, is not without limits. The restriction must not discriminate against speech on the basis of viewpoint, *Rosenberger,* and the restriction must be "reasonable in light of the purpose served by the forum."

III.

Applying this test, we first address whether the exclusion constituted viewpoint discrimination. We are guided in our analysis by two of our prior opinions, *Lamb's Chapel* and *Rosenberger.* In *Lamb's Chapel,* we held that a school district violated the Free Speech Clause of the First Amendment when it excluded a private group from presenting films at the school based solely on the films' discussions of family values from a religious perspective. Likewise, in *Rosenberger,* we held that a university's refusal to fund a student publication because the publication addressed issues from a religious perspective violated the Free Speech Clause. Concluding that Milford's exclusion of the Good News Club based on its religious nature is indistinguishable from the exclusions in these cases, we hold that the exclusion constitutes viewpoint discrimination. Because the restriction is viewpoint discriminatory, we need not decide whether it is unreasonable in light of the purposes served by the forum. * * *

Just as there is no question that teaching morals and character development to children is a permissible purpose under Milford's policy, it is clear that the Club teaches morals and character development to children. For example, no one disputes that the Club instructs children to overcome feelings of jealousy, to treat others well regardless of how they treat the children, and to be obedient, even if it does so in a nonsecular way. * * *

Applying *Lamb's Chapel*, we find it quite clear that Milford engaged in viewpoint discrimination when it excluded the Club from the after-school forum. In *Lamb's Chapel,* the local New York school district similarly had … prohibited use "by any group for religious purposes." Citing this prohibition, the school district excluded a church that wanted to present films teaching family values from a Christian perspective. We held that, because the films "no doubt dealt with a subject otherwise permissible" under the rule, the teaching of family values, the district's exclusion of the church was unconstitutional viewpoint discrimination.

Like the church in *Lamb's Chapel,* the Club seeks to address a subject otherwise permitted under the rule, the teaching of morals and character, from a religious standpoint. Certainly, one could have characterized the film presentations in *Lamb's Chapel* as a religious use, as the Court of Appeals did. And one easily could conclude that the films' purpose to instruct that "society's slide toward humanism … can only be counter-balanced by a loving home where Christian values are instilled from an early age," was "quintessentially religious." The only apparent difference between the activity of Lamb's Chapel and the activities of the Good News Club is that the Club chooses to teach moral lessons from a Christian perspective through live storytelling and prayer, whereas Lamb's Chapel taught lessons through films. This distinction is inconsequential. Both modes of speech use a religious viewpoint. Thus, the exclusion of the Good News Club's activities, like the exclusion of Lamb's Chapel's films, consti-tutes unconstitutional viewpoint discrimination.

Our opinion in *Rosenberger* also is dispositive. In *Rosenberger,* a student organization at the University of Virginia was denied funding for printing expenses because its publication, *Wide Awake*, offered a Christian viewpoint. Just as the Club emphasizes the role of Christianity in stu-dents' morals and character, *Wide Awake* "challenge[d] Christians to live, in word and deed, according to the faith they proclaim and … encour-age[d] students to consider what a personal relationship with Jesus Christ means." Because the university "select[ed] for disfavored treatment those student journalistic efforts with religious editorial viewpoints," we held that the denial of funding was unconstitutional. Although in *Rosenberger* there was no prohibition on religion as a subject matter, our holding did not rely on this factor. Instead, we concluded simply that the university's denial of funding to print *Wide Awake* was viewpoint discrimination, just as the school district's refusal to allow Lamb's Chapel to show its films was viewpoint discrimination. Given the obvious religious content of *Wide Awake*, we cannot say that the Club's activities are any more "religious" or deserve any less First Amendment protection than did the publication of *Wide Awake* in *Rosenberger.*

Despite our holdings in *Lamb's Chapel* and *Rosenberger,* the Court of Appeals, like *Milford*, believed that its characterization of the Club's activities as religious in nature warranted treating the Club's activities as different in kind from the other activities permitted by the school. The "Christian viewpoint" is unique, according to the court, because it contains an "additional layer" that other kinds of viewpoints do not. That is, the Club "is focused on teaching children how to cultivate their relationship with God through Jesus Christ," which it characterized as "quintessentially religious." With these observations, the court concluded that, because the Club's activities "fall outside the bounds of pure 'moral and character development,' " the exclusion did not constitute viewpoint discrimination.

We disagree that something that is "quintessentially religious" or "decidedly religious in nature" cannot also be characterized properly as the teaching of morals and character development from a particular viewpoint. What matters for purposes of the Free Speech Clause is that we can see no logical difference in kind between the invocation of Christianity by the Club and the invocation of teamwork, loyalty, or patriotism by other associations to provide a foundation for their lessons. It is apparent that the unstated principle of the Court of Appeals' reasoning is its conclusion that any time religious instruction and prayer are used to discuss morals and character, the discussion is simply not a "pure" discussion of those issues. According to the Court of Appeals, reliance on Christian principles taints moral and character instruction in a way that other foundations for thought or viewpoints do not. We, however, have never reached such a conclusion. Instead, we reaffirm our holdings in *Lamb's Chapel* and *Rosenberger* that speech discussing otherwise permissible subjects cannot be excluded from a limited public forum on the ground that the subject is discussed from a religious viewpoint. Thus, we conclude that Milford's exclusion of the Club from use of the school, pursuant to its community use policy, constitutes impermissible viewpoint discrimination. * * *

V.

When Milford denied the Good News Club access to the school's limited public forum on the ground that the Club was religious in nature, it discriminated against the Club because of its religious viewpoint in violation of the Free Speech Clause of the First Amendment. Because Milford has not raised a valid Establishment Clause claim, we do not address the question whether such a claim could excuse Milford's viewpoint discrimination. * * *

The judgment of the Court of Appeals is reversed, and the case is remanded for further proceedings consistent with this opinion.

It is so ordered.

JUSTICE STEVENS, dissenting.

The Milford Central School has invited the public to use its facilities for educational and recreational purposes, but not for "religious purposes." Speech for "religious purposes" may reasonably be understood to encompass three different categories. First, there is religious speech that is simply speech about a particular topic from a religious point of view. The film in *Lamb's Chapel v. Center Moriches Union Free School District* illustrates this category. Second, there is religious speech that amounts to worship, or its equivalent. Our decision in *Widmar v. Vincent* concerned such speech. Third, there is an intermediate category that is aimed principally at proselytizing or inculcating belief in a particular religious faith.

A public entity may not generally exclude even religious worship from an open public forum. Similarly, a public entity that creates a limited public forum for the discussion of certain specified topics may not exclude a speaker simply because she approaches those topics from a religious point of view. Thus, in *Lamb's Chapel* we held that a public school that permitted its facilities to be used for the discussion of family issues and child rearing could not deny access to speakers presenting a religious point of view on those issues.

But, while a public entity may not censor speech about an authorized topic based on the point of view expressed by the speaker, it has broad discretion to "preserve the property under its control for the use to which it is lawfully dedicated." * * * Accordingly, "control over access to a nonpublic forum can be based on subject matter and speaker identity so long as the distinctions drawn are reasonable in light of the purpose served by the forum and are viewpoint neutral." The novel question that this case presents concerns the constitutionality of a public school's attempt to limit the scope of a public forum it has created. More specifically, the question is whether a school can, consistently with the First Amendment, create a limited public forum that admits the first type of religious speech without allowing the other two.

Distinguishing speech from a religious viewpoint, on the one hand, from religious proselytizing, on the other, is comparable to distinguishing meetings to discuss political issues from meetings whose principal purpose is to recruit new members to join a political organization. If a school decides to authorize after-school discussions of current events in its classrooms, it may not exclude people from expressing their views simply because it dislikes their particular political opinions. But must it therefore allow organized political groups—for example, the Democratic Party, the Libertarian Party, or the Ku Klux Klan—to hold meetings, the principal purpose of which is not to discuss the current-events topic from their own unique point of view but rather to recruit others to join their respective groups? I think not. Such recruiting meetings may introduce divisiveness and tend to separate young children into cliques that undermine the school's educational mission. * * *

This case is undoubtedly close. Nonetheless, regardless of whether the Good News Club's activities amount to "worship," it does seem clear, based on the facts in the record, that the school district correctly classified those activities as falling within the third category of religious speech and therefore beyond the scope of the school's limited public forum. In short, I am persuaded that the school district could (and did) permissibly exclude from its limited public forum proselytizing religious speech that does not rise to the level of actual worship. I would therefore affirm the judgment of the Court of Appeals.

Accordingly, I respectfully dissent.

JUSTICE SOUTER, with whom JUSTICE GINSBURG joins, dissenting.

* * * It is beyond question that Good News intends to use the public school premises not for the mere discussion of a subject from a particular, Christian point of view, but for an evangelical service of worship calling children to commit themselves in an act of Christian conversion. The majority avoids this reality only by resorting to the bland and general characterization of Good News's activity as "teaching of morals and character, from a religious standpoint." If the majority's statement ignores reality, as it surely does, then today's holding may be understood only in equally generic terms. Otherwise, indeed, this case would stand for the remarkable proposition that any public school opened for civic meetings must be opened for use as a church, synagogue, or mosque, * * *

NOTES

1. While the *Milford* dispute concerned only access to campus facilities after school, how applicable might the decision be in subsequent disputes regarding what might be allowable in the public school classroom on school time? Assume, for example, that students in an eleventh grade English class are assigned to write essays on a hero or heroine of their choice, but that when a student indicates that she wishes to write about Jesus, she is told by her teacher that she must keep to secular figures. If the student challenges the decision as violative of her First Amendment rights, can the *Milford* decision be the basis of a successful argument? How might such an argument be structured?

2. In *Child Evangelism Fellowship of New Jersey v. Stafford*, 386 F.3d 514 (3d Cir. 2004), the Third Circuit provided the fellowship, which sponsors Good News Clubs, with another victory in a disputed access case. The decision applied *Milford* to uphold the legality of the organization's posting and distribution of religious materials and its participation in so-called "Back-to-School" nights.

EQUAL ACCESS TO PUBLIC SCHOOL FACILITIES UNDER THE "NO CHILD LEFT BEHIND" ACT

20 U.S.C. § 7905 (2005)

(a) Short title

This section may be cited as the "Boy Scouts of America Equal Access Act".

(b) In general

(1) Equal access

Notwithstanding any other provision of law, no public elementary school, public secondary school, local educational agency, or State educational agency that has a designated open forum or a limited public forum and that receives funds made available through the Department shall deny equal access or a fair opportunity to meet to, or discriminate against, any group officially affiliated with the Boy Scouts of America, or any other youth group listed in Title 36 of the United States Code (as a patriotic society), that wishes to conduct a meeting within that designated open forum or limited public forum, including denying such access or opportunity or discriminating for reasons based on the membership or leadership criteria or oath of allegiance to God and country of the Boy Scouts of America or of the youth group listed in Title 36 of the United States Code (as a patriotic society).

(d) Definition and rule

(1) Definition

In this section, the term "youth group" means any group or organization intended to serve young people under the age of 21.

(2) Rule

For the purpose of this section, an elementary school or secondary school has a limited public forum whenever the school involved grants an offering to, or opportunity for, one or more outside youth or community groups to meet on school premises or in school facilities before or after the hours during which attendance at the school is compulsory.

ACCESS OF THE MILITARY TO EDUCATIONAL INSTITUTIONS

Two federal statutes providing the military with access to students for purposes of recruiting have been the subject of considerable debate in recent years. At the K–12 level, the U.S. "No Child Left Behind" Act, 20 U.S.C. Section 7908, provides military recruiters with "access to students and student recruiting information." At the higher education level, the Solomon Amendment, 10 U.S.C. Section 983, requires the U.S. Department of Defense to deny federal funding to institutions that prohibit military representatives access to and assistance for recruiting purposes.

By 2006, the NCLB provision had generated extensive debate, with widespread accusations of alleged improprieties by military recruiters being set forth. At the same time, the constitutionality of the Solomon Amendment was being challenged in *Rumsfeld v. FAIR,* a case that reached the U.S. Supreme Court in December 2005.

Armed Forces Recruiter Access to Students and Student Recruiting Information

Under the U.S. "No Child Left Behind" Act

20 U.S.C. § 7908 provides, in pertinent part:

(a) Policy

(1) Access to student recruiting information

* * * [E]ach local educational agency receiving assistance under this chapter shall provide, on a request made by military recruiters or an institution of higher education, access to secondary school students names, addresses, and telephone listings.

(2) Consent

A secondary school student or the parent of the student may request that the student's name, address, and telephone listing described in paragraph (1) not be released without prior written parental consent, and the local educational agency or private school shall notify parents of the option to make a request and shall comply with any request.

(3) Same access to students

Each local educational agency receiving assistance under this chapter shall provide military recruiters the same access to secondary school students as is provided generally to post secondary educational institutions or to prospective employers of those students.

* * *

The Solomon Amendment and "Don't Ask, Don't Tell"

Unlike other areas of the public sector, and in contrast to the policies of our strongest military allies, gays and lesbians in the U.S. military have no legal right to be out. As recently as 2009, if they did reveal their sexual orientation, they were subject to immediate and dishonorable discharge. Indeed, over 11,000 gays and lesbians have been removed from the military since the inception of the "Don't Ask, Don't Tell" mandate in 1993.[a]

---

a. In a 1993 compromise reached between President Bill Clinton—who sought to end the formal ban on gays and lesbians serving in the U.S. armed forces—and a coalition of military leaders and members of Congress on both sides of the aisle who opposed the lifting of the ban, gays and lesbians would be officially allowed to serve, but only if they kept their identities to themselves. *See* 10 U.S.C. § 654(b). The new federal mandate, which became known as "Don't Ask, Don't Tell," has been the subject of several unsuccessful challenges in the federal courts. *See, e.g.,* Able v. U.S., 155 F.3d 628 (2d Cir. 1998); Holmes v. California Army Nat'l Guard, 124

U.S. law schools "have long maintained formal policies of nondiscrimination that withhold career placement services from employers who exclude employees and applicants based on such factors as race, gender, and religion. In the 1970s law schools began expanding these policies to prohibit discrimination based on sexual orientation as well." 390 F.3d 219, 224 (3d Cir. 2004). As described by the Third Circuit, "[i]n response to this trend the American Association of Law Schools ("AALS") voted unanimously in 1990 to include sexual orientation as a protected category. As a result, virtually every law school now has a comprehensive policy like the following:

> [The] School of Law is committed to a policy of equal opportunity for all students and graduates. The Career Services facilities of this school shall not be available to those employers who discriminate on the grounds of race, color, religion, national origin, sex, handicap or disability, age, or sexual orientation. . . . Before using any of the Career Services interviewing facilities of this school, an employer shall be required to submit a signed statement certifying that its practices conform to this policy." *Id.* at 224–225.

As early as the 1980s, some law schools, citing their nondiscrimination policies, refused to provide access and assistance to military recruiters. By 1994, in the aftermath of the highly publicized debate regarding the passage of the "Don't Ask, Don't Tell" mandate, Representative Gerald Solomon of New York sponsored an amendment to the annual defense appropriation bill that "proposed to withhold DOD funding from any educational institution with a policy of denying or effectively preventing the military from obtaining entry to campuses (or access to students on campuses) for recruiting purposes." In the summer of 2003, "Congress amended the Solomon Amendment to codify the DOD's informal policy. Under the terms of the statute itself, law schools and their parent institutions [were] penalized for preventing military representatives from gaining entry to campuses for the purpose of military recruiting 'in a manner that is at least equal in quality and scope to the [degree of] access to campuses and to students that is provided to any other employer.' " See 10 U.S.C. Section 983. *See generally* 390 F.3d at 225–228.

F.3d 1126 (9th Cir. 1997); Richenberg v. Perry, 97 F.3d 256 (8th Cir. 1996); and Thomasson v. Perry, 80 F.3d 915 (4th Cir. 1996) (en banc).

Many of our strongest allies—including but not limited to Israel and the United Kingdom—now allow gays and lesbians to serve openly. The UK lifted its ban on gays in the military after the European Court of Human Rights ruled unanimously in favor of four LGBT soldiers who had been discharged in the mid–1990's. In ruling against the British government, the court found that the UK ban violated the fundamental human right to privacy, as set out in the European Convention on Human Rights. Soon afterward, in 2000, the UK joined Canada, France, Germany and most other NATO countries that already allowed gays and lesbians to serve openly. *See, e.g.,* Sarah Lyall, *Gays in the British Military: Ask, Tell and Then Move On,* N.Y. Times, February 10, 2001.

It should be noted that transgender persons in the U.S. are prohibited from serving, whether or not they keep their identities to themselves. The military considers transgender to be a disqualifying psychiatric condition both for those wishing to enlist and for those already serving who wish to transition from male to female or from female to male.

Law schools were now faced with the loss of large amounts of federal money if they continued to restrict the access of military recruiters. A lawsuit was filed, challenging the constitutionality of the Solomon Amendment. But the U.S. Supreme Court, by a vote of 8–0, ruled against the law schools. *Rumsfeld v. Forum for Academic and Institutional Rights (FAIR),* 547 U.S. 47, 126 S.Ct. 1297 (2006):

> * * * [The Solomon Amendment] specifies that if any part of an institution of higher education denies military recruiters access equal to that provided other recruiters, the entire institution would lose certain federal funds. * * * [Respondent Forum for Academic and Institutional Rights, Inc. (FAIR), an association of law schools and law faculties, brought a lawsuit] alleging that the Solomon Amendment infringed their First Amendment freedoms of speech and association. * * *
>
> The Solomon Amendment neither limits what law schools may say nor requires them to say anything. Law schools remain free under the statute to express whatever views they may have on the military's congressionally mandated employment policy, all the while retaining eligibility for federal funds. See Tr. of Oral Arg. 25 (Solicitor General acknowledging that law schools "could put signs on the bulletin board next to the door, they could engage in speech, they could help organize student protests"). As a general matter, the Solomon Amendment regulates conduct, not speech. It affects what law schools must *do*—afford equal access to military recruiters—not what they may or may not *say*. * * *
>
> In this case, FAIR has attempted to stretch a number of First Amendment doctrines well beyond the sort of activities these doctrines protect. The law schools object to having to treat military recruiters like other recruiters, but that regulation of conduct does not violate the First Amendment. To the extent that the Solomon Amendment incidentally affects expression, the law schools' effort to cast themselves as just like the schoolchildren in *Barnette,* the parade organizers in *Hurley,* and the Boy Scouts in *Dale* plainly overstates the expressive nature of their activity and the impact of the Solomon Amendment on it, while exaggerating the reach of our First Amendment precedents.
>
> Because Congress could require law schools to provide equal access to military recruiters without violating the schools' freedoms of speech or association, the Court of Appeals erred in holding that the Solomon Amendment likely violates the First Amendment. We therefore reverse the judgment of the Third Circuit and remand the case for further proceedings consistent with this opinion.

GILLES v. BLANCHARD

477 F.3d 466 (7th Cir. 2007)

POSNER, CIRCUIT JUDGE.

Vincennes University, the oldest institution of higher education in Indiana (founded in 1806 by future President William Henry Harrison before Indiana was admitted to statehood)-[has been] a public institution since its inception * * * .

James Gilles ("Brother Jim") (home page http://www.thecampus ministry.org/, visited Feb. 2, 2007) is a traveling evangelist—the latest in a line of Christian itinerant preachers stretching back to Saint Paul and prominent in Methodism in nineteenth-century America. * * * There is no reason to doubt either his bona fides or that the content of his religious advocacy is protected by the First Amendment. The question is whether the protection extends to a particular site on the university campus.

Vincennes University and Brother Jim first intersected in 2001, when he entered the campus uninvited and walked to a lawn in the middle of the campus, next to the university library. He preached from the lawn and a disturbance ensued, the nature of which is not revealed by the record, although the university's dean of students stated in his deposition that "when I went there, he [Brother Jim] was in the grassy area in front of the library. He had had—he was speaking to a number of students there. There was some—a disturbance, and at one point the campus police felt like he was in danger. And they asked him to leave, and he did." From another case we learn that "when preaching, [Brother Jim] uses a confrontational style that includes calling people in the crowd names, such as whoremonger and drunkard, once the individuals have answered certain questions that he poses to them. He has been arrested on numerous occasions in the past." Brother Jim denied that his preaching at Vincennes in 2001 had caused a disturbance, and in the procedural posture of the case we must credit his denial.

In reaction to the incident—whatever exactly it was—the university for the first time adopted a formal policy governing access to the campus by outsiders to the university community. Entitled "Sales and/or Solicitation Policy," the policy requires prior approval by the dean of students of all sales on campus. In addition, and more to the point of this case, the policy also requires the dean's prior approval of all "solicitations" on campus. Solicitation is defined as "the act of seeking to obtain by persuasion; to entice a person to action; or the recruiting of possible sales." Solicitors, if approved, are limited to soliciting in the brick walkway directly in front of the student union. * * *

Brother Jim returned to the campus the following year, proceeded to the lawn, was turned back and told he could preach only on the brick walkway. He tried to preach there, but the fact that the walkway is adjacent to a street makes it a noisy locale for a speech. Unable to attract an audience, he broke off and left, and filed this suit against the responsible university officials, contending that the solicitation policy infringes his right of free speech. The district court granted summary judgment for the defendants.

Brother Jim argues that since the lawn is public property and is suitable for speechifying, he can no more be forbidden to preach there than he could be forbidden to preach in a public park. That is incorrect. * * * [T]he First Amendment does not require the department to make the auditorium available for that purpose even when it is not being used for departmental business. Public property is property, and the law of trespass protects public property, as it protects private property, from uninvited guests. Since public and private universities compete with each other, courts hesitate to impose in the name of the Constitution extravagant burdens on public universities that private universities do not bear.

It is not as if requiring a public university to throw open its grounds to itinerant speakers would merely redress the advantage that a public university has over a private one because it has taxpayer support; the requirement would deny the university control over its facilities. The courts reject the proposition "that a campus must make all of its facilities equally available to students and nonstudents alike, or that a university must grant free access to all of its grounds or buildings." * * *

No matter how wonderfully suited the library lawn is to religious and other advocacy, Vincennes University could if it wanted bar access to the lawn to any outsider who wanted to use it for any purpose, just as it could bar outsiders from its classrooms, libraries, dining halls, and dormitories. It wouldn't have to prove that allowing them in would disrupt its educational mission. * * *

What is true is that a university that decided to permit its open spaces to be used by some outsiders could not exclude others just because it disapproved of their message. E.g., *Rosenberger v. Rector & Visitors of University of Virginia*, 515 U.S. 819, 828–30, 115 S.Ct. 2510, 132 L.Ed.2d 700 (1995). But it could use neutral criteria for access, such as that an outsider must be invited to speak on campus by a faculty member or a student group. * * *

The application of the university's solicitation policy to Brother Jim brings him to the verge of victory. The policy as interpreted by the defendants to cover preaching the Gospel is hopelessly vague and thus a supple weapon for excluding from the university lawn those outsiders whose message the university disapproves of. But Brother Jim falls just short of prevailing because he has failed to show that *any* uninvited outsider has ever been permitted to use the lawn for any purpose. No doubt outsiders wander in from time to time. The campus is not fenced, and outsiders are not forbidden to visit. They are classic licensees. But we are given no instance of an outsider's being permitted to do more than stroll on the lawn—no instance of an outsider's being permitted to give a speech, to play the bongo drums, to pitch a tent, to beg, to sunbathe, to play frisbee, or to engage in solicitation—without an invitation, whether from the university or from a faculty member or a student group.

This has long been a norm, and not just a practice: strangers to the university community are not to use the library lawn for purposes other than those unobtrusive, implicitly authorized uses of land (generally as a shortcut or other pathway) that distinguish a licensee from a trespasser. So unlikely is it that a university or any other landowner would, as Brother Jim contends Vincennes University does, give strangers a right to roam the campus speechifying, begging, buttonholing, skateboarding, drag racing, etc., that he had to produce *some* evidence of that unlikely authorization in order to create a genuine issue of material fact—some evidence that would allow a reasonable jury to find that the university has such a permissive policy and merely denies Brother Jim the benefit of it lest his incendiary preaching ignite another disturbance.

Brother Jim does point to numerous expressive activities that have taken place on the library lawn, including religious activities—preaching by a couple named Duncan and the annual distribution of free Bibles by the Gideon Society. But of all the expressive activities that have taken place on the lawn, the record discloses only one that was not by invitation. The Duncans had not been invited. They had preached on the lawn in 1998, three years before Brother Jim's first visit, and the circumstances of their visit are hazy. One unauthorized use of the lawn would not come close to establishing the absence of a policy against use of the lawn by uninvited speakers. Maybe no one complained, and as a result the violation did not come to the attention of the university authorities-indeed, the dean of students attested that he had never learned of the matter. Perfect past compliance with a rule is not a precondition to being allowed to continue enforcing the rule. Otherwise few rules could be enforced, and universities would have to fence their open areas in order to limit access.

Brother Jim lists the following speakers or events that have taken place on the library lawn, in addition to the Duncans' preaching and the Gideons' handing out Bibles: Women of Essence; Black Male Initiative; Indiana National Guard; Kernan and Davis for Indiana campaign; Rebekka Armstrong (an HIV-positive former Playboy Playmate); Mark Sterner (speaker on drunk driving); Mentalist Craig Karges; TB Re–Screening; Student Part Time Job Fair; The Man Without a Face (an oral cancer survivor * * *); Health Screening; Ariana Huffington; Dr. Peter DeBenedittis (speaker on how the media manipulate consumers); Manufacturing Job Fair; Amanda Persinger (pharmaceutical representative); Prentis Hall Sales Representative; Tupperware Multihost Bingo/Party; Kevin Riggins (speaker against athletic doping); Kelly Craig (speaker against drunk driving); and the Red Cross Blood Drive. This bewildering miscellany refutes an inference of discrimination against disfavored points of view, or of a university administration fearful of controversy and of the disturbances that might ensue. As far as appears, any student group can invite any speaker to speak on the library lawn. The diversity of speakers mirrors the diversity of the university community.

Of course there would be even greater diversity of viewpoints if *anyone,* invited or uninvited, could use the lawn for expressive activity; for apparently no one in the Vincennes University community wants to invite Brother Jim to speak. He wants to turn the lawn into an American version of Speakers' Corner in London's Hyde Park, where anyone can speak on any subject other than the Royal family or the overthrow of the British government. The limits that Vincennes University has placed on the use of the library lawn are consistent with limiting university facilities to activities that further the interests of the university community. The limits are constitutional. * * *

D. THE PARAMETERS OF THE RIGHT TO RECEIVE INFORMATION & IDEAS

PROBLEM 42: MONTOYA V. GOLD COAST UNIFIED SCHOOL DISTRICT

The following problem takes place in the fictional city of Gold Coast, Eldorado. Gold Coast Unified is a large urban public school district with over 250,000 pupils.

As a result of the June elections, the political and philosophical makeup of the Gold Coast school board changed dramatically. Two new members with ties to the Millennium Institute were elected, and they immediately joined together with two other members to enact a series of curricular and structural reforms.

The Millennium Institute, formed in 1999, includes members of all the world's major religions and is "committed to peace and understanding through the promotion of good will between and among all nations, cultures, and religions."

One of the key reforms enacted by the new school board majority was the establishment of three new magnet schools focusing on "philosophy and culture." In Gold Coast, as in other urban districts nationwide, magnet schools had long been the most popular method of desegregating students via parental choice. The magnet schools provide distinct educational programs designed to attract students of different races or ethnic backgrounds. As Professor Amy Stuart Wells explains, "The idea is to create schools that offer an enhanced and engaging educational program that parents of all races prefer to their neighborhood school." *See* AMY STUART WELLS, TIME TO CHOOSE: AMERICA AT THE CROSSROADS OF SCHOOL CHOICE POLICY (1993).

The curriculum mandated by the school board for the new philosophy and culture magnets included the following controversial requirements:

A. An intensive twenty-week focus on the Book of Genesis. Students will attempt to make sense out of the book's recurring patterns: the violent conflicts between siblings, the eventual victory—against all custom—of latter-born sons, the fragility of inheritance. They will address the question of how covenants such as the one set forth in Genesis can continue in a world ruled by covetousness, murder, lust and disorder.

B. A twenty-week exploration into the nature of Zen, as reflected in such diverse sources as the writings of Lao Tzu, the formulas of Chinese herbalists, the teachings of the Dalai Lama, and the "beat" literature of 20th Century America. Students will learn a value system based on Zen's way of looking at the world: where the best moment is now, where things *are* what they seem to be, where we see with the refreshing directness of a child, and not through eyes grown stale from routine.

In addition, the following books were among those added to the school library as resources:

1. Bill Moyers, *Genesis: A Living Conversation* (based on the PBS series)

2. Karen Armstrong, *In the Beginning: A New Interpretation of Genesis*

3. A.G. Zornberg, *The Beginning of Desire: Reflections on Genesis*

4. Alan Watts, *The Way of Zen*

5. *Tao Te Ching* (writings of Lao Tzu)

6. *The City Lights Pocket Poets Anthology* (edited by Lawrence Ferlinghetti)

* * *

A group of angry Gold Coast parents consults you for the purpose of filing a wide-ranging lawsuit against the district. In their conversations with you, it becomes clear that they oppose the recent actions of the school board for three basic reasons: (1) the new magnet schools were formed without any input from parent groups, and they feel that accountability to the community seems to be lacking; (2) religious teachings have been introduced into the public school curriculum; and (3) they believe that the value-laden education mandated by the new curriculum is completely inappropriate in a public school setting.

What arguments might you set forth on behalf of the plaintiffs? What result? Discuss.

* * *

Assume, instead, that you are counsel for the school district, and that you were consulted before all these changes were made. Would you have advised the district to do anything differently from a legal perspective? From a policy perspective? Explain.

PROBLEM 43: THE COLUMBIA EDUCATION INITIATIVES

This question is based on the following hypothetical, which takes place in the fictional State of Columbia.

In order to pursue the goals set forth by the U.S. "No Child Left Behind" Act, the Columbia State Board of Education adopts a new statewide curriculum geared to basic skills. However, consistent with the perceived will of the people as reflected in the election of political leaders who openly espouse religious values, the curriculum also contains values-based lessons on the importance of spirituality. These lessons include instruction based on primary religious texts (or edited children's versions, as appropriate). Each semester, students are expected to spend two weeks reading from a different primary religious text, until they have been exposed to the holy books of Judaism, Christianity, Islam, Hinduism and Buddhism.

Consistent with this new curriculum, the State Board encourages local boards of education to remove from their school libraries all books containing rock music lyrics and to replace them with at least 25 copies of primary religious texts per library. Most school boards follow this advice within the next three months.

* * *

As a result of these events, the following legal action takes place:

A. An Establishment Clause challenge to the new curriculum. Plaintiffs, the United Coalition for Religious Freedom, are prepared to argue that whether the court analyzes this curriculum under purpose and effects, endorsement, coercion, or even a neutrality inquiry as applied in *Simmons-Harris,* the curriculum will ultimately be found unconstitutional.

B. A "right not to receive information & ideas" lawsuit, filed by parents who do not want their children exposed to primary texts of religions other than their own.

C. A lawsuit challenging the removal of the library books under the "right to receive information & ideas" set forth in *Pico.*

What arguments will be set forth by plaintiffs? What result? Discuss.

1. THE RIGHT TO RECEIVE INFORMATION

BOARD OF EDUC., ISLAND TREES UNION FREE SCH. DIST. NO. 26 v. PICO

457 U.S. 853, 102 S.Ct. 2799 (1982)

JUSTICE BRENNAN announced the judgment of the Court and delivered an opinion, in which JUSTICE MARSHALL and JUSTICE STEVENS joined, and in which JUSTICE BLACKMUN joined except for Part II–A–(1).

The principal question presented is whether the First Amendment imposes limitations upon the exercise by a local school board of its discretion to remove library books from high school and junior high school libraries.

I

Petitioners are [current and former members of] the Board of Education of the Island Trees Union Free School District No. 26, in New York.... The Board is a state agency charged with responsibility for the operation and administration of the public schools within the Island Trees School District, including the Island Trees High School and Island Trees

Memorial Junior High School. Respondents are [former students of the District's junior and senior high schools].

In September 1975, [three school board members] attended a conference sponsored by Parents of New York United (PONYU), a politically conservative organization of parents concerned about education legislation in the State of New York. At the conference these petitioners obtained lists of books described by [Board President] Ahrens as "objectionable," and by [Board Vice–President] Martin as "improper fare for school students."[2] It was later determined that the High School library contained nine of the listed books, and that another listed book was in the Junior High School library.[3] In February 1976, at a meeting with the Superintendent of Schools and the Principals of the High School and Junior High School, the Board gave an "unofficial direction" that the listed books be removed from the library shelves and delivered to the Board's offices, so that Board members could read them.[4] When this directive was carried out, it became publicized, and the Board issued a press release justifying its action. It characterized the removed books as "anti-American, anti-Christian, anti-Sem[i]tic, and just plain filthy," and concluded that "[i]t is our duty, our moral obligation, to protect the children in our schools from this moral danger as surely as from physical and medical dangers."

A short time later, the Board appointed a "Book Review Committee," consisting of four Island Trees parents and four members of the Island Trees schools staff, to read the listed books and to recommend to the Board whether the books should be retained, taking into account the books' "educational suitability," "good taste," "relevance," and "appropriateness to age and grade level." In July, the Committee made its final report to the Board, recommending that five of the listed books be retained and that two others be removed from the school libraries. As for the remaining four books, the Committee could not agree on two, took no position on one, and recommended that the last book be made available to students only with parental approval. The Board substantially rejected the Committee's report later that month, deciding that only one book should

---

2. The District Court noted, however, that petitioners "concede that the books are not obscene."

3. The nine books in the High School library were: Slaughter House Five, by Kurt Vonnegut, Jr.; The Naked Ape, by Desmond Morris; Down These Mean Streets, by Piri Thomas; Best Short Stories of Negro Writers, edited by Langston Hughes; Go Ask Alice, of anonymous authorship; Laughing Boy, by Oliver LaFarge; Black Boy, by Richard Wright; A Hero Ain't Nothin' But A Sandwich, by Alice Childress; and Soul On Ice, by Eldridge Cleaver. The book in the Junior High School library was A Reader for Writers, edited by Jerome Archer. Still another listed book, The Fixer, by Bernard Malamud, was found to be included in the curriculum of a twelfth-grade literature course.

4. The Superintendent of Schools objected to the Board's informal directive, noting:

[W]e already have a policy ... designed expressly to handle such problems. It calls for the Superintendent, upon receiving an objection to a book or books, to appoint a committee to study them and make recommendations. I feel it is a good policy—and it is Board policy—and that it should be followed in this instance. Furthermore, I think it can be followed quietly and in such a way as to reduce, perhaps avoid, the public furor which has always attended such issues in the past.

The Board responded to the Superintendent's objection by repeating its directive "that *all copies* of the library books in question be removed from the libraries to the Board's office."

be returned to the High School library without restriction, that another should be made available subject to parental approval, but that the remaining nine books should "be removed from elementary and secondary libraries and [from] use in the curriculum."[12] The Board gave no reasons for rejecting the recommendations of the Committee that it had appointed.

Respondents reacted to the Board's decision by bringing the present action under 42 U.S.C. § 1983 in the United States District Court for the Eastern District of New York. They alleged that petitioners had

> ordered the removal of the books from school libraries and proscribed their use in the curriculum because particular passages in the books offended their social, political and moral tastes and not because the books, taken as a whole, were lacking in educational value.

Respondents claimed that the Board's actions denied them their rights under the First Amendment. They asked the court for a declaration that the Board's actions were unconstitutional, and for preliminary and permanent injunctive relief ordering the Board to return the nine books to the school libraries and to refrain from interfering with the use of those books in the schools' curricula.

> * * *

II

We emphasize at the outset the limited nature of the substantive question presented by the case before us. Our precedents have long recognized certain constitutional limits upon the power of the State to control even the curriculum and classroom. For example, *Meyer v. Nebraska* struck down a state law that forbade the teaching of modern foreign languages in public and private schools, and *Epperson v. Arkansas* declared unconstitutional a state law that prohibited the teaching of the Darwinian theory of evolution in any state-supported school. But the current action does not require us to re-enter this difficult terrain, which *Meyer* and *Epperson* traversed without apparent misgiving. For as this case is presented to us, it does not involve textbooks, or indeed any books that Island Trees students would be required to read. Respondents do not seek in this Court to impose limitations upon their school Board's discretion to prescribe the curricula of the Island Trees schools. On the contrary, the only books at issue in this case are *library* books, books that by their nature are optional rather than required reading. Our adjudication of the present case thus does not intrude into the classroom, or into the compulsory courses taught there. Furthermore, even as to library books, the action before us does not involve the *acquisition* of books. Respondents have not sought to compel their school Board to add to the school library shelves any books that students desire to read. Rather, the only action challenged in this case is the *removal* from school libraries of

---

12. As a result, the nine removed books could not be assigned or suggested to students in connection with school work. However, teachers were not instructed to refrain from discussing the removed books or the ideas and positions expressed in them.

books originally placed there by the school authorities, or without objection from them.

* * *

[D]oes the First Amendment impose *any* limitations upon the discretion of petitioners to remove library books from the Island Trees High School and Junior High School?

* * *

A

(1)

The Court has long recognized that local school boards have broad discretion in the management of school affairs. *Epperson v. Arkansas* reaffirmed that, by and large, "public education in our Nation is committed to the control of state and local authorities," and that federal courts should not ordinarily "intervene in the resolution of conflicts which arise in the daily operation of school systems." *Tinker v. Des Moines School Dist.*, 393 U.S. 503, 507, 89 S.Ct. 733, 736 (1969), noted that we have "repeatedly emphasized ... the comprehensive authority of the States and of school officials ... to prescribe and control conduct in the schools." We have also acknowledged that public schools are vitally important "in the preparation of individuals for participation as citizens," and as vehicles for "inculcating fundamental values necessary to the maintenance of a democratic political system." We are therefore in full agreement with petitioners that local school boards must be permitted "to establish and apply their curriculum in such a way as to transmit community values," and that "there is a legitimate and substantial community interest in promoting respect for authority and traditional values be they social, moral, or political."

At the same time, however, we have necessarily recognized that the discretion of the States and local school boards in matters of education must be exercised in a manner that comports with the transcendent imperatives of the First Amendment. In *West Virginia Board of Education v. Barnette*, 319 U.S. 624, 63 S.Ct. 1178 (1943), we held that under the First Amendment a student in a public school could not be compelled to salute the flag. We reasoned:

> Boards of Education ... have, of course, important, delicate, and highly discretionary functions, but none that they may not perform within the limits of the Bill of Rights. That they are educating the young for citizenship is reason for scrupulous protection of Constitutional freedoms of the individual, if we are not to strangle the free mind at its source and teach youth to discount important principles of our government as mere platitudes. *Id.* at 637, 63 S.Ct. at 1185.

Later cases have consistently followed this rationale. Thus *Epperson v. Arkansas*, invalidated a State's anti-evolution statute as violative of the Establishment Clause, and reaffirmed the duty of federal courts "to apply the First Amendment's mandate in our educational system where essential to safeguard the fundamental values of freedom of speech and inquiry." And *Tinker v. Des Moines School Dist., supra*, held that a local school board had infringed the free speech rights of high school and junior high school students by suspending them from school for wearing black armbands in class as a protest against the Government's policy in Vietnam; we stated there that the "comprehensive authority . . . of school officials" must be exercised "consistent with fundamental constitutional safeguards." 393 U.S. at 507, 89 S.Ct. at 736. In sum, students do not "shed their constitutional rights to freedom of speech or expression at the schoolhouse gate," *id.* at 506, 89 S.Ct. at 736, and therefore local school boards must discharge their "important, delicate, and highly discretionary functions" within the limits and constraints of the First Amendment.

The nature of students' First Amendment rights in the context of this case requires further examination. *West Virginia Board of Education v. Barnette, supra*, is instructive. There the Court held that students' liberty of conscience could not be infringed in the name of "national unity" or "patriotism." 319 U.S. at 640–41, 63 S.Ct. at 1186. We explained that

> the action of the local authorities in compelling the flag salute and pledge transcends constitutional limitations on their power and invades the sphere of intellect and spirit which it is the purpose of the First Amendment to our Constitution to reserve from all official control. *Id.* at 642, 63 S.Ct. at 1187.

Similarly, *Tinker v. Des Moines School Dist.*, held that students' rights to freedom of expression of their political views could not be abridged by reliance upon an "undifferentiated fear or apprehension of disturbance" arising from such expression:

> Any departure from absolute regimentation may cause trouble. Any variation from the majority's opinion may inspire fear. Any word spoken, in class, in the lunchroom, or on the campus, that deviates from the views of another person may start an argument or cause a disturbance. But our Constitution says we must take this risk, and our history says that it is this sort of hazardous freedom—this kind of openness—that is the basis of our national strength and of the independence and vigor of Americans who grow up and live in this . . . often disputatious society. 393 U.S. at 508–09, 89 S.Ct. at 737.

In short, "First Amendment rights, applied in light of the special characteristics of the school environment, are available to . . . students." *Id.* at 506, 89 S.Ct. at 736.

Of course, courts should not "intervene in the resolution of conflicts which arise in the daily operation of school systems" unless "basic constitutional values" are "directly and sharply implicate[d]" in those conflicts. But we think that the First Amendment rights of students may be directly and sharply implicated by the removal of books from the shelves of a school library. Our precedents have focused "not only on the role of the First Amendment in fostering individual self-expression but also on its role in affording the public access to discussion, debate, and the dissemination of information and ideas." And we have recognized that "the State may not, consistently with the spirit of the First Amendment, contract the spectrum of available knowledge." In keeping with this principle, we have held that in a variety of contexts "the Constitution protects the right to receive information and ideas." This right is an inherent corollary of the rights of free speech and press that are explicitly guaranteed by the Constitution, in two senses. First, the right to receive ideas follows ineluctably from the *sender's* First Amendment right to send them: "The right of freedom of speech and press ... embraces the right to distribute literature, and necessarily protects the right to receive it." "The dissemination of ideas can accomplish nothing if otherwise willing addressees are not free to receive and consider them. It would be a barren marketplace of ideas that had only sellers and no buyers."

More importantly, the right to receive ideas is a necessary predicate to the *recipient's* meaningful exercise of his own rights of speech, press, and political freedom. Madison admonished us:

> A popular Government, without popular information, or the means of acquiring it, is but a Prologue to a Farce or a Tragedy; or, perhaps both. Knowledge will forever govern ignorance: And a people who mean to be their own Governors, must arm themselves with the power which knowledge gives.[20]

As we recognized in *Tinker*, students too are beneficiaries of this principle:

> In our system, students may not be regarded as closed-circuit recipients of only that which the State chooses to communicate.... [S]chool officials cannot suppress "expressions of feeling with which they do not wish to contend." 393 U.S. at 511, 89 S.Ct. at 739 (quoting *Burnside v. Byars*, 363 F.2d 744, 749 (5th Cir. 1966)).

In sum, just as access to ideas makes it possible for citizens generally to exercise their rights of free speech and press in a meaningful manner, such access prepares students for active and effective participation in the pluralistic, often contentious society in which they will soon be adult members. Of course all First Amendment rights accorded to students must be construed "in light of the special characteristics of the school environment." *Tinker v. Des Moines School Dist.*, 393 U.S. at 506, 89 S.Ct. at 736. But the special characteristics of the school *library* make that

---

20. For a modern version of this observation, see A. MEIKLEJOHN, FREE SPEECH AND ITS RELATION TO SELF-GOVERNMENT 26 (1948):

Just so far as ... the citizens who are to decide an issue are denied acquaintance with information or opinion or doubt or disbelief or criticism which is relevant to that issue, just so far the result must be ill-considered, ill-balanced planning, for the general good.

See also Butler v. Michigan; Procunier v. Martinez; Houchins v. KQED, Inc. (STEVENS, J., dissenting) ("[T]he First Amendment protects not only the dissemination but also the receipt of information and ideas"); *Saxbe v. Washington Post Co.* (POWELL, J., dissenting) ("[P]ublic debate must not only be unfettered; it must be informed. For that reason this Court has repeatedly stated that First Amendment concerns encompass the receipt of information and ideas as well as the right of free expression").

environment especially appropriate for the recognition of the First Amendment rights of students.

A school library, no less than any other public library, is "a place dedicated to quiet, to knowledge, and to beauty." *Keyishian v. Board of Regents* observed that " 'students must always remain free to inquire, to study and to evaluate, to gain new maturity and understanding.' " The school library is the principal locus of such freedom. As one District Court has well put it, in the school library

> a student can literally explore the unknown, and discover areas of interest and thought not covered by the prescribed curriculum.... Th[e] student learns that a library is a place to test or expand upon ideas presented to him, in or out of the classroom.

Petitioners emphasize the inculcative function of secondary education, and argue that they must be allowed *unfettered* discretion to "transmit community values" through the Island Trees schools. But that sweeping claim overlooks the unique role of the school library. It appears from the record that use of the Island Trees school libraries is completely voluntary on the part of students. Their selection of books from these libraries is entirely a matter of free choice; the libraries afford them an opportunity at self-education and individual enrichment that is wholly optional. Petitioners might well defend their claim of absolute discretion in matters of *curriculum* by reliance upon their duty to inculcate community values. But we think that petitioners' reliance upon that duty is misplaced where, as here, they attempt to extend their claim of absolute discretion beyond the compulsory environment of the classroom, into the school library and the regime of voluntary inquiry that there holds sway.

(2)

In rejecting petitioners' claim of absolute discretion to remove books from their school libraries, we do not deny that local school boards have a substantial legitimate role to play in the determination of school library content. We thus must turn to the question of the extent to which the First Amendment places limitations upon the discretion of petitioners to remove books from their libraries. In this inquiry we enjoy the guidance of several precedents. *West Virginia Board of Education v. Barnette*, stated:

> If there is any fixed star in our constitutional constellation, it is that no official, high or petty, can prescribe what shall be orthodox in politics, nationalism, religion, or other matters of opinion.... If there are any circumstances which permit an exception, they do not now occur to us. 319 U.S. at 642, 63 S.Ct. at 1187.

This doctrine has been reaffirmed in later cases involving education. For example, *Keyishian v. Board of Regents* noted that "the First Amendment ... does not tolerate laws that cast a pall of orthodoxy over the classroom." And *Mt. Healthy City Board of Ed. v. Doyle* recognized First Amendment limitations upon the discretion of a local school board to refuse to rehire a nontenured teacher. The school board in *Mt. Healthy* had declined to renew respondent Doyle's employment contract, in part because he had exercised his First Amendment rights. Although Doyle did not have tenure, and thus "could have been discharged for no reason whatever," *Mt. Healthy* held that he could "nonetheless establish a claim to reinstatement if the decision not to rehire him was made by reason of his exercise of constitutionally protected First Amendment freedoms." We held further that once Doyle had shown "that his conduct was constitutionally protected, and that this conduct was a 'substantial factor' . . . in the Board's decision not to rehire him," the school board was obliged to show "by a preponderance of the evidence that it would have reached the same decision as to respondent's reemployment even in the absence of the protected conduct."

With respect to the present case, the message of these precedents is clear. Petitioners rightly possess significant discretion to determine the content of their school libraries. But that discretion may not be exercised in a narrowly partisan or political manner. If a Democratic school board, motivated by party affiliation, ordered the removal of all books written by or in favor of Republicans, few would doubt that the order violated the constitutional rights of the students denied access to those books. The same conclusion would surely apply if an all-white school board, motivated by racial animus, decided to remove all books authored by blacks or advocating racial equality and integration. Our Constitution does not permit the official suppression of *ideas*. Thus whether petitioners' removal of books from their school libraries denied respondents their First Amendment rights depends upon the motivation behind petitioners' actions. If petitioners *intended* by their removal decision to deny respondents access to ideas with which petitioners disagreed, and if this intent was the decisive factor in petitioners' decision,[22] then petitioners have exercised their discretion in violation of the Constitution. To permit such intentions to control official actions would be to encourage the precise sort of officially prescribed orthodoxy unequivocally condemned in *Barnette*. On the other hand, respondents implicitly concede that an unconstitutional motivation would *not* be demonstrated if it were shown that petitioners had decided to remove the books at issue because those books were pervasively vulgar. And again, respondents concede that if it were demonstrated that the removal decision was based solely upon the "educational suitability" of the books in question, then their removal would be "perfectly permissible." In other words, in respondents' view such motivations, if decisive of petitioners' actions, would not carry the danger of an official suppression of ideas, and thus would not violate respondents' First Amendment rights.

As noted earlier, nothing in our decision today affects in any way the discretion of a local school board to choose books to *add* to the libraries of their schools. Because we are concerned in this case with the suppression of ideas, our holding today affects only the discretion to *remove* books. In

---

22. By "decisive factor" we mean a "substantial factor" in the absence of which the opposite decision would have been reached.

brief, we hold that local school boards may not remove books from school library shelves simply because they dislike the ideas contained in those books and seek by their removal to "prescribe what shall be orthodox in politics, nationalism, religion, or other matters of opinion." *West Virginia Board of Education v. Barnette*, 319 U.S. at 642, 63 S.Ct. at 1187. Such purposes stand inescapably condemned by our precedents.

* * *

Affirmed.

EDWARDS v. AGUILLARD

482 U.S. 578, 107 S.Ct. 2573 (1987)

JUSTICE BRENNAN delivered the opinion of the Court.

The question for decision is whether Louisiana's "Balanced Treatment for Creation–Science and Evolution–Science in Public School Instruction" Act (Creationism Act) is facially invalid as violative of the Establishment Clause of the First Amendment.

I

The Creationism Act forbids the teaching of the theory of evolution in public schools unless accompanied by instruction in "creation science." No school is required to teach evolution or creation science. If either is taught, however, the other must also be taught. The theories of evolution and creation science are statutorily defined as "the scientific evidences for [creation or evolution] and inferences from those scientific evidences."

Appellees, who include parents of children attending Louisiana public schools, Louisiana teachers, and religious leaders, challenged the constitutionality of the Act in District Court, seeking an injunction and declaratory relief.

* * *

II

The Establishment Clause forbids the enactment of any law "respecting an establishment of religion." The Court has applied a three-pronged test to determine whether legislation comports with the Establishment Clause. First, the legislature must have adopted the law with a secular purpose. Second, the statute's principal or primary effect must be one that neither advances nor inhibits religion. Third, the statute must not result in an excessive entanglement of government with religion. *Lemon v. Kurtzman.*[4] State action violates the Establishment Clause if it fails to satisfy any of these prongs.

* * *

---

4. The *Lemon* test has been applied in all cases since its adoption in 1971, except in *Marsh v. Chambers*, where the Court held that the Nebraska Legislature's practice of opening a session with a prayer by a chaplain paid by the State did not violate the Establishment Clause. The Court based its conclusion in that case on the historical acceptance of the practice. Such a historical

The Court has been particularly vigilant in monitoring compliance with the Establishment Clause in elementary and secondary schools.[5] Families entrust public schools with the education of their children, but condition their trust on the understanding that the classroom will not purposely be used to advance religious views that may conflict with the private beliefs of the student and his or her family. Students in such institutions are impressionable and their attendance is involuntary.... Furthermore, "[t]he public school is at once the symbol of our democracy and the most pervasive means for promoting our common destiny. In no activity of the State is it more vital to keep out divisive forces than in its schools...."

* * *

III

Lemon's first prong focuses on the purpose that animated adoption of the Act. "The purpose prong of the *Lemon* test asks whether government's actual purpose is to endorse or disapprove of religion." A governmental intention to promote religion is clear when the State enacts a law to serve a religious purpose. This intention may be evidenced by promotion of religion in general, see *Wallace v. Jaffree*, 472 U.S. [38,] 52–53, 105 S.Ct. [2479,] 2487 [(1985)] (Establishment Clause protects individual freedom of conscience "to select any religious faith or none at all"), or by advancement of a particular religious belief, *e.g., Stone v. Graham* (invalidating requirement to post Ten Commandments, which are "undeniably a sacred text in the Jewish and Christian faiths"); *Epperson v. Arkansas* (holding that banning the teaching of evolution in public schools violates the First Amendment since "teaching and learning" must not "be tailored to the principles or prohibitions of any religious sect or dogma"). If the law was enacted for the purpose of endorsing religion, "no consideration of the second or third criteria [of *Lemon*] is necessary." *Wallace v. Jaffree, supra,* 472 U.S. at 56, 105 S.Ct. at 2489. In this case, appellants have identified no clear secular purpose for the Louisiana Act.

True, the Act's stated purpose is to protect academic freedom. This phrase might, in common parlance, be understood as referring to enhancing the freedom of teachers to teach what they will. The Court of Appeals, however, correctly concluded that the Act was not designed to further that goal. We find no merit in the State's argument that the "legislature may not [have] use[d] the terms 'academic freedom' in the correct legal sense. They might have [had] in mind, instead, a basic concept of fairness; teaching all of the evidence." Even if "academic freedom" is read to mean

---

approach is not useful in determining the proper roles of church and state in public schools, since free public education was virtually nonexistent at the time the Constitution was adopted. * * *

5. The potential for undue influence is far less significant with regard to college students who voluntarily enroll in courses. "This distinction warrants a difference in constitutional results." *Abington School Dist. v. Schempp* (BRENNAN, J., concurring). Thus, for instance, the Court has not questioned the authority of state colleges and universities to offer courses on religion or theology. See *Widmar v. Vincent,* 454 U.S. 263, 271, 102 S.Ct. 269, 275; *id.,* at 281, 102 S.Ct., at 280 (STEVENS, J., concurring in judgment). (*footnote moved*)

"teaching all of the evidence" with respect to the origin of human beings, the Act does not further this purpose. The goal of providing a more comprehensive science curriculum is not furthered either by outlawing the teaching of evolution or by requiring the teaching of creation science.

A

While the Court is normally deferential to a State's articulation of a secular purpose, it is required that the statement of such purpose be sincere and not a sham. See *Wallace v. Jaffree,* 472 U.S. at 64, 105 S.Ct. at 2494 (POWELL, J., concurring); *id.* at 75, 105 S.Ct. at 2499 (O'CONNOR, J., concurring in judgment); *Abington School Dist. v. Schempp,* 374 U.S. at 223–24, 83 S.Ct. at 1572–73. As JUSTICE O'CONNOR stated in *Wallace:* "It is not a trivial matter, however, to require that the legislature manifest a secular purpose and omit all sectarian endorsements from its laws. That requirement is precisely tailored to the Establishment Clause's purpose of assuring that Government not intentionally endorse religion or a religious practice." 472 U.S. at 75, 105 S.Ct. at 2499–500 (concurring in judgment).

It is clear from the legislative history that the purpose of the legislative sponsor, Senator Bill Keith, was to narrow the science curriculum. During the legislative hearings, Senator Keith stated: "My preference would be that neither [creationism nor evolution] be taught." Such a ban on teaching does not promote—indeed, it undermines—the provision of a comprehensive scientific education.

It is equally clear that requiring schools to teach creation science with evolution does not advance academic freedom. The Act does not grant teachers a flexibility that they did not already possess to supplant the present science curriculum with the presentation of theories, besides evolution, about the origin of life. Indeed, the Court of Appeals found that no law prohibited Louisiana public school teachers from teaching any scientific theory. As the president of the Louisiana Science Teachers Association testified, "[a]ny scientific concept that's based on established fact can be included in our curriculum already, and no legislation allowing this is necessary." The Act provides Louisiana school teachers with no new authority. Thus the stated purpose is not furthered by it.

The Alabama statute held unconstitutional in *Wallace v. Jaffree* is analogous. In *Wallace,* the State characterized its new law as one designed to provide a 1–minute period for meditation. We rejected that stated purpose as insufficient, because a previously adopted Alabama law already provided for such a 1–minute period. Thus, in this case, as in *Wallace,* "[a]ppellants have not identified any secular purpose that was not fully served by [existing state law] before the enactment of [the statute in question]." 472 U.S. at 59, 105 S.Ct. at 2491.

Furthermore, the goal of basic "fairness" is hardly furthered by the Act's discriminatory preference for the teaching of creation science and against the teaching of evolution. While requiring that curriculum guides be developed for creation science, the Act says nothing of comparable guides for evolution. Similarly, resource services are supplied for creation science but not for evolution. Only "creation scientists" can serve on the panel that supplies the resource services. The Act forbids school boards to discriminate against anyone who "chooses to be a creation-scientist" or to teach "creationism," but fails to protect those who choose to teach evolution or any other non-creation science theory, or who refuse to teach creation science.

If the Louisiana Legislature's purpose was solely to maximize the comprehensiveness and effectiveness of science instruction, it would have encouraged the teaching of all scientific theories about the origins of humankind. But under the Act's requirements, teachers who were once free to teach any and all facets of this subject are now unable to do so. Moreover, the Act fails even to ensure that creation science will be taught, but instead requires the teaching of this theory only when the theory of evolution is taught. Thus we agree with the Court of Appeals' conclusion that the Act does not serve to protect academic freedom, but has the distinctly different purpose of discrediting "evolution by counterbalancing its teaching at every turn with the teaching of creationism...."

* * *

In this case, the purpose of the Creationism Act was to restructure the science curriculum to conform with a particular religious viewpoint. Out of many possible science subjects taught in the public schools, the legislature chose to affect the teaching of the one scientific theory that historically has been opposed by certain religious sects. As in *Epperson,* the legislature passed the Act to give preference to those religious groups which have as one of their tenets the creation of humankind by a divine creator. The "overriding fact" that confronted the Court in *Epperson* was "that Arkansas' law selects from the body of knowledge a particular segment which it proscribes for the sole reason that it is deemed to conflict with ... a particular interpretation of the Book of Genesis by a particular religious group." Similarly, the Creationism Act is designed *either* to promote the theory of creation science which embodies a particular religious tenet by requiring that creation science be taught whenever evolution is taught *or* to prohibit the teaching of a scientific theory disfavored by certain religious sects by forbidding the teaching of evolution when creation science is not also taught. The Establishment Clause, however, "forbids *alike* the preference of a religious doctrine *or* the prohibition of theory which is deemed antagonistic to a particular dogma." Because the primary purpose of the Creationism Act is to advance a particular religious belief, the Act endorses religion in violation of the First Amendment.

We do not imply that a legislature could never require that scientific critiques of prevailing scientific theories be taught. Indeed, the Court acknowledged in *Stone* that its decision forbidding the posting of the Ten Commandments did not mean that no use could ever be made of the Ten Commandments, or that the Ten Commandments played an exclusively religious role in the history of Western Civilization. In a similar way, teaching a variety of scientific theories about the origins of humankind to schoolchildren might be validly done with the clear secular intent of enhancing the effectiveness of science instruction. But because the primary purpose of the Creationism Act is to endorse a particular religious doctrine, the Act furthers religion in violation of the Establishment Clause.

* * *

NOTES

1. In August 2005, the *New York Times* reported the results of a recent national poll, which found that "nearly two-thirds of Americans say that creationism should be taught alongside evolution in public schools.":

> The poll found that 42 percent of respondents held strict creationist views, agreeing that "living things have existed in their present form since the beginning of time."

> In contrast, 48 percent said they believed that humans had evolved over time. But of those, 18 percent said that evolution was "guided by a supreme being," and 26 percent said that evolution occurred through natural selection. In all, 64 percent said they were open to the idea of teaching creationism in addition to evolution, while 38 percent favored replacing evolution with creationism.

> The poll was conducted July 7–17 by the Pew Forum on Religion and Public Life and the Pew Research Center for the People and the Press. The questions about evolution were asked of 2,000 people. The margin of error was 2.5 percentage points. Laurie Goodstein, *Teaching of Creationism Is Endorsed in New Survey*, N.Y. TIMES, Aug. 31, 2005.

2. In September 2005, the U.S. District Court held a bench trial in the case of *Kitzmiller v. Dover Area Sch. Dist.*, 2005 WL 3465563 (M.D. Pa. 2005). In *Kitzmiller,* parents challenged the constitutionality of a decision by the Dover Area School Board to require science teachers—in addition to teaching evolution—to read the following statement to their students:

> The Pennsylvania Academic Standards require students to learn about Darwin's theory of evolution and eventually to take a standardized test of which evolution is a part.

> Because Darwin's theory is a theory, it continues to be tested as new evidence is discovered. The theory is not a fact. Gaps in the theory exist for which there is no evidence. A theory is defined as a well-tested explanation that unifies a broad range of observations.

> Intelligent design is an explanation of the origin of life that differs from Darwin's view. The reference book, "Of Pandas and People," is available for students who might be interested in gaining an understanding of what intelligent design actually involves.

> With respect to any theory, students are encouraged to keep an open mind. The school leaves the discussion of the origins of life to individual

students and their families. As a standards-driven district, class instruction focuses upon preparing students to achieve proficiency on standards-based assessments.

Applying Establishment Clause principles as reflected primarily in the endorsement inquiry, the Court ruled in favor of the plaintiffs:

First, we will consider "the message conveyed by the disclaimer to the students who are its intended audience," from the perspective of an objective Dover Area High School student. At a minimum, the pertinent inquiry is whether an "objective observer" in the position of a student of the relevant age would "perceive official school support" for the religious activity in question. * * *

A "hypothetical reasonable observer," adult or child, who is "aware of the history and context of the community and forum" is also presumed to know that [intelligent design (ID)] is a form of creationism. The evidence at trial demonstrates that ID is nothing less than the progeny of creationism. What is likely the strongest evidence supporting the finding of ID's creationist nature is the history and historical pedigree of the book to which students in Dover's ninth grade biology class are referred, *Pandas.* *Pandas* is published by an organization called FTE, as noted, whose articles of incorporation and filings with the Internal Revenue Service describe it as a religious, Christian organization. *Pandas* was written by Dean Kenyon and Percival Davis, both acknowledged creationists, and Nancy Pearcey, a Young Earth Creationist, contributed to the work.

As Plaintiffs meticulously and effectively presented to the Court, *Pandas* went through many drafts, several of which were completed prior to and some after the Supreme Court's decision in *Edwards,* which held that the Constitution forbids teaching creationism as science. By comparing the pre and post *Edwards* drafts of *Pandas,* three astonishing points emerge: (1) the definition for creation science in early drafts is identical to the definition of ID; (2) cognates of the word creation (creationism and creationist), which appeared approximately 150 times were deliberately and systematically replaced with the phrase ID; and (3) the changes occurred shortly after the Supreme Court held that creation science is religious and cannot be taught in public school science classes in *Edwards.* This word substitution is telling, significant, and reveals that a purposeful change of *words* was effected without any corresponding change in *content,* which directly refutes FTE's argument that by merely disregarding the words "creation" and "creationism," FTE expressly rejected creationism in *Pandas.* * * *

This compelling evidence strongly supports Plaintiffs' assertion that ID is creationism re-labeled. Importantly, the objective observer, whether adult or child, would conclude from the fact that *Pandas* posits a master intellect that the intelligent designer is God. * * *

After a careful review of the record, we find that an objective student would view the [four-paragraph statement] as a strong official endorsement of religion. * * *

In summary, the disclaimer singles out the theory of evolution for special treatment, misrepresents its status in the scientific community, causes students to doubt its validity without scientific justification, presents students with a religious alternative masquerading as a scientific theory, directs them to consult a creationist text as though it were a science resource, and instructs students to forego scientific inquiry in the public school classroom and instead to seek out religious instruction elsewhere.
* * *

As a result of the foregoing analysis, we conclude that an informed, objective adult member of the Dover community aware of the social context in which the ID Policy arose would view [also] Defendants' conduct and the challenged Policy to be a strong endorsement of a religious view.

* * *

After a searching review of the record and applicable case law, we find that while ID arguments may be true, a proposition on which the Court takes no position, ID is not science. We find that ID fails on three different levels, any one of which is sufficient to preclude a determination that ID is science. They are: (1) ID violates the centuries-old ground rules of science by invoking and permitting supernatural causation; (2) the argument of irreducible complexity, central to ID, employs the same flawed and illogical contrived dualism that doomed creation science in the 1980's; and (3) ID's negative attacks on evolution have been refuted by the scientific community. [I]t is additionally important to note that ID has failed to gain acceptance in the scientific community, it has not generated peer-reviewed publications, nor has it been the subject of testing and research.

* * *

Although Defendants attempt to persuade this Court that each Board member who voted for the biology curriculum change did so for the secular purpose of improving science education and to exercise critical thinking skills, their contentions are simply irreconcilable with the record evidence. Their asserted purposes are a sham, and they are accordingly unavailing.

* * *

To briefly reiterate, we first note that since ID is not science, the conclusion is inescapable that the only real effect of the ID Policy is the advancement of religion. Second, the disclaimer read to students "has the effect of implicitly bolstering alternative religious theories of origin by suggesting that evolution is a problematic theory even in the field of science." Third, reading the disclaimer not only disavows endorsement of educational materials but also "juxtaposes that disavowal with an urging to contemplate alternative religious concepts implies School Board approval of religious principles."

The effect of Defendants' actions in adopting the curriculum change was to impose a religious view of biological origins into the biology course, in violation of the Establishment Clause. * * *

Before the decision was handed down, the school board majority that had introduced intelligent design into the science curriculum was voted out of office. After the decision, the new majority announced that it would not appeal. *See Board Rescinds 'Intelligent Design Policy,* AP Online, January 4, 2006.

If a school board decided to introduce the same four-paragraph statement into a history class, pursuant to an effort to comply with a state law that mandates the teaching of values, and this decision were challenged under the Establishment Clause, would the result be the same? Should the result be the same?

3. In *The Bible & Public Schools: A First Amendment Guide* (1999), the National Bible Association and the First Amendment Center posted a widely acclaimed roadmap online for those wishing to ascertain the parameters of a public school district's ability to include the Bible in its curriculum and instructional materials. A wide array of secular and religious organizations endorsed the positions set forth in the Guide, which arguably constitute a reasonable middle ground in this area.

According to the Guide, "[m]any Americans continue to hold the mistaken view that the Supreme Court decisions in the 1960s concerning prayer and devotional Bible-reading prohibited students from expressing their faith in a public school. Actually, the Court did not eliminate prayer or the Bible from public schools; it barred state-sponsored religious practices, including devotional use of the Bible by public-school officials."

In a particularly noteworthy portion of the Guide, issues relating to goals, objectives, and approaches were addressed:

> If teachers are to understand clearly how to teach *about* the Bible—and to feel safe doing so—then local school boards should adopt policies on the role of study about religion in the curriculum. The policy should reflect constitutional principles and current law, and should be developed with the full involvement of parents and other community members. Parents need to be assured that the goals of the school in teaching about religion, including teaching about the Bible, are academic and not devotional, and that academic teaching about the Bible is not intended to either undermine or reinforce the beliefs of those who accept the Bible as sacred scripture or of those who do not. Faith formation is the responsibility of parents and religious communities, not the public schools.

In recent years, a consensus has emerged among many religious and educational groups about the appropriate role for religion in the public-school curriculum. In 1989, a coalition of 17 religious and educational organizations issued the following statements to distinguish between teaching *about* religion in public schools and religious indoctrination:

- The school's approach to religion is *academic*, not *devotional*.
- The school may strive for student *awareness* of religions, but should not press for student *acceptance* of any religion.

- The school may sponsor *study* about religion, but may not sponsor the *practice* of religion.

- The school may *expose* students to a diversity of religious views, but may not *impose, discourage, or encourage* any particular view.

- The school may *educate* about all religions, but may not *promote or denigrate* any religion.

The school may *inform* the student about various beliefs, but should not seek to *conform* him or her to any particular belief. www.first amendment center.org/PDF/bible_guide_graphics.PDF (last accessed January 3, 2009).

CALIFORNIA EDUCATION CODE SECTION 233.5
(Values Instruction)

(a) Each teacher shall endeavor to impress upon the minds of the pupils the principles of morality, truth, justice, patriotism, and a true comprehension of the rights, duties, and dignity of American citizenship, and the meaning of equality and human dignity, including the promotion of harmonious relations, kindness toward domestic pets and the humane treatment of living creatures, to teach them to avoid idleness, profanity, and falsehood, and to instruct them in manners and morals and the principles of a free government.

(b) Each teacher is also encouraged to create and foster an environment that encourages pupils to realize their full potential and that is free from discriminatory attitudes, practices, events, or activities, in order to prevent acts of hate violence, as defined in subdivision (e) of Section 233.

2. THE RIGHT NOT TO RECEIVE INFORMATION

MOZERT v. HAWKINS COUNTY BD. OF EDUC.
827 F.2d 1058 (6th Cir. 1987)

LIVELY, CHIEF JUDGE.

This case arose under the Free Exercise Clause of the First Amendment, made applicable to the states by the Fourteenth Amendment. * * *

I.

A.

Early in 1983 the Hawkins County, Tennessee Board of Education adopted the Holt, Rinehart and Winston basic reading series (the Holt series) for use in grades 1–8 of the public schools of the county. In grades 1–4, reading is not taught as a separate subject at a designated time in the school day. Instead, the teachers in these grades use the reading texts throughout the day in conjunction with other subjects. In grades 5–8, reading is taught as a separate subject at a designated time in each class. However, the schools maintain an integrated curriculum which requires that ideas appearing in the reading programs reoccur in other courses. By statute public schools in Tennessee are required to include "character education" in their curricula. The purpose of this requirement is "to help each student develop positive values and to improve student conduct as students learn to act in harmony with their positive values and learn to become good citizens in their school, community, and society."

Like many school systems, Hawkins County schools teach "critical reading" as opposed to reading exercises that teach only word and sound recognition. "Critical reading" requires the development of higher order cognitive skills that enable students to evaluate the material they read, to contrast the ideas presented, and to understand complex characters that appear in reading material. Plaintiffs do not dispute that critical reading is an essential skill which their children must develop in order to succeed in other subjects and to function as effective participants in modern society. Nor do the defendants dispute the fact that any reading book will do more than teach a child how to read, since reading is instrumental in a child's total development as an educated person.

The plaintiff Vicki Frost is the mother of four children, three of whom were students in Hawkins County public schools in 1983. At the beginning of the 1983–84 school year Mrs. Frost read a story in a daughter's sixth grade reader that involved mental telepathy. Mrs. Frost, who describes herself as a "born again Christian," has a religious objection to any teaching about mental telepathy. Reading further, she found additional themes in the reader to which she had religious objections. After discussing her objections with other parents, Mrs. Frost talked with the principal of Church Hill Middle School and obtained an agreement for an alternative reading program for students whose parents objected to the assigned Holt reader. The students who elected the alternative program left their classrooms during the reading sessions and worked on assignments from an older textbook series in available office or library areas. Other students in two elementary schools were excused from reading the Holt books.

B.

In November 1983 the Hawkins County School Board voted unanimously to eliminate all alternative reading programs and require every student in the public schools to attend classes using the Holt series. Thereafter the plaintiff students refused to read the Holt series or attend reading classes where the series was being used. The children of several of the plaintiffs were suspended for brief periods for this refusal. Most of the plaintiff students were ultimately taught at home, or attended religious schools, or transferred to public schools outside Hawkins County. One student returned to school because his family was unable to afford alternate schooling. Even after the board's order, two students were allowed some accommodation, in that the teacher either excused them from reading the Holt stories, or specifically noted on worksheets that the student was not required to believe the stories.

On December 2, 1983, the plaintiffs, consisting of seven families—14 parents and 17 children—filed this action pursuant to 42 U.S.C. § 1983. In their complaint the plaintiffs asserted that they have sincere religious beliefs which are contrary to the values taught or inculcated by the reading textbooks and that it is a violation of the religious beliefs and convictions of the plaintiff students to be required to read the books and a violation of the religious beliefs of the plaintiff parents to permit their children to read the books. The plaintiffs sought to hold the defendants liable because "forcing the student-plaintiffs to read school books which teach or inculcate values in violation of their religious beliefs and convictions is a clear violation of their rights to the free exercise of religion protected by the First and Fourteenth Amendments to the United States Constitution."

* * *

B.

[At trial,] Vicki Frost ... presented the most complete explanation of the plaintiffs' position. The plaintiffs do not belong to a single church or denomination, but all consider themselves born again Christians. Mrs. Frost testified that the word of God as found in the Christian Bible "is the totality of my beliefs." There was evidence that other members of their churches, and even their pastors, do not agree with their position in this case.

Mrs. Frost testified that she had spent more than 200 hours reviewing the Holt series and had found numerous passages that offended her religious beliefs. She stated that the offending materials fell into seventeen categories which she listed. These ranged from such familiar concerns of fundamentalist Christians as evolution and "secular humanism" to less familiar themes such as "futuristic supernaturalism," pacifism, magic and false views of death.

In her lengthy testimony Mrs. Frost identified passages from stories and poems used in the Holt series that fell into each category. Illustrative is her first category, futuristic supernaturalism, which she defined as teaching "Man As God." Passages that she found offensive described Leonardo da Vinci as the human with a creative mind that "came closest to the divine touch." Similarly, she felt that a passage entitled "Seeing Beneath the Surface" related to an occult theme, by describing the use of imagination as a vehicle for seeing things not discernible through our physical eyes. She interpreted a poem, "Look at Anything," as presenting the idea that by using imagination a child can become part of anything and thus understand it better. Mrs. Frost testified that it is an "occult practice" for children to use imagination beyond the limitation of scriptural authority. She testified that the story that alerted her to the problem with the reading series fell into the category of futuristic supernaturalism. Entitled "A Visit to Mars," the story portrays thought transfer and telepathy in such a way that "it could be considered a scientific concept," according to this witness. This theme appears in the testimony of several witnesses, *i.e.,* the materials objected to "could" be interpreted in a manner repugnant to their religious beliefs.

Mrs. Frost described objectionable passages from other categories in much the same way. Describing evolution as a teaching that there is no God, she identified 24 passages that she considered to have evolution as a theme. She admitted that the textbooks contained a disclaimer that evolution is a theory, not a proven scientific fact. Nevertheless, she felt that references to evolution were so pervasive and presented in such a factual manner as to render the disclaimer meaningless. After describing her objection to passages that encourage children to make moral judgments about whether it is right or wrong to kill animals, the witness stated, "I thought they would be learning to read, to have good English and grammar, and to be able to do other subject work." * * *

Another witness for the plaintiffs was Bob Mozert, father of a middle school and an elementary school student in the Hawkins County system.... He also found objectionable passages in the readers that dealt with magic, role reversal or role elimination, particularly biographical material about women who have been recognized for achievements outside their homes, and emphasis on one world or a planetary society. Both witnesses testified under cross-examination that the plaintiff parents objected to passages that expose their children to other forms of religion and to the feelings, attitudes and values of other students that contradict the plaintiffs' religious views without a statement that the other views are incorrect and that the plaintiffs' views are the correct ones.

C.

The district court held that the plaintiffs' free exercise rights have been burdened[.]

    * * *

The court entered an injunction prohibiting the defendants "from requiring the student-plaintiffs to read from the Holt series," and ordering the defendants to excuse the student plaintiffs from their classrooms "[d]uring the normal reading period" and to provide them with suitable space in the library or elsewhere for a study hall. * * *

III.

A.

The first question to be decided is whether a governmental requirement that a person be exposed to ideas he or she finds objectionable on religious grounds constitutes a burden on the free exercise of that person's religion as forbidden by the First Amendment. This is precisely the way the superintendent of the Hawkins County schools framed the issue in an affidavit filed early in this litigation. In his affidavit the superintendent set forth the school system's interest in a uniformity of reading texts. The affidavit also countered the claims of the plaintiffs that the schools were inculcating values and religious doctrines contrary to their religious beliefs, stating: "Without expressing an opinion as to the plaintiffs' religious beliefs, I am of the opinion that plaintiffs misunderstand the fact that exposure to something does not constitute teaching, indoctrination, opposition or promotion of the things exposed. While it is true that these textbooks expose the student to varying values and religious backgrounds, neither the textbooks nor the teachers teach, indoctrinate, oppose or promote any particular value or religion." That the district court accepted the issue as thus framed is clear from its reference to "exposure to the Holt series."

It is also clear that exposure to objectionable material is what the plaintiffs objected to albeit they emphasize the repeated nature of the exposure. The complaint mentioned only the textbooks that the students were required to read. It did not seek relief from any method of teaching the material and did not mention the teachers' editions. The plaintiffs did not produce a single student or teacher to testify that any student was ever required to affirm his or her belief or disbelief in any idea or practice mentioned in the various stories and passages contained in the Holt series. However, the plaintiffs appeared to assume that materials clearly presented as poetry, fiction and even "make-believe" in the Holt series were presented as facts which the students were required to believe. Nothing in the record supports this assumption.

At numerous places in her testimony Vicki Frost referred to various exercises and suggestions in the teachers' manuals as support for her view that objectionable ideas were being inculcated as truth rather than being offered as examples of the variety of approaches possible to a particular question. However, the students were not required to read the teachers' materials. While these materials suggested various ways of presenting the lessons, including "acting out" and round table discussions, there was no proof that any plaintiff student was ever called upon to say or do anything that required the student to affirm or deny a religious belief or to engage or refrain from engaging in any act either required or forbidden by the student's religious convictions. Mrs. Frost seemed to assume that each teacher used every suggested exercise or teaching tool in the teachers' editions. There was evidence that reading aloud and acting out the themes encountered in school lessons help young people learn. One of the teachers stated that students read some of the stories aloud. Proof that an objecting student was *required* to participate beyond reading and discussing assigned materials, or was disciplined for disputing assigned materials, might well implicate the Free Exercise Clause because the element of compulsion would then be present. But this was not the case either as pled or proved. The record leaves no doubt that the district court correctly viewed this case as one involving exposure to repugnant ideas and themes as presented by the Holt series.

* * *

The only way to avoid conflict with the plaintiffs' beliefs in these sensitive areas would be to eliminate all references to the subjects so identified. However, the Supreme Court has clearly held that it violates the Establishment Clause to tailor a public school's curriculum to satisfy the principles or prohibitions of any religion.

* * *

C.

* * * [P]laintiffs, in this court, have relied particularly upon [certain] Supreme Court decisions. We find them all distinguishable.

* * *

Board of Education v. Barnette, 319 U.S. 624, 63 S.Ct. 1178 (1943), grew out of a school board rule that required all schools to make a salute to the flag and a pledge of allegiance a regular part of their daily program. All teachers and students were required to participate in the exercise and refusal to engage in the salute was considered an act of insubordination which could lead to expulsion and possible delinquency charges for being unlawfully absent. The plaintiff was a Jehovah's Witness who considered the flag an "image" which the Bible forbids worshiping in any way. Justice Jackson, writing for the Court, stated:

> Here, . . . we are dealing with a compulsion of students to declare a belief. They are not merely made acquainted with the flag salute so that they may be informed as to what it is or even what it means.
>
> * * *

It is abundantly clear that the exposure to materials in the Holt series did not compel the plaintiffs to "declare a belief," "communicate by word and sign [their] acceptance" of the ideas presented, or make an "affirmation of a belief and an attitude of mind." In *Barnette* the unconstitutional burden consisted of compulsion either to do an act that violated the plaintiff's religious convictions or communicate an acceptance of a particular idea or affirm a belief. No similar compulsion exists in the present case.

It is clear that governmental compulsion either to do or refrain from doing an act forbidden or required by one's religion, or to affirm or disavow a belief forbidden or required by one's religion, is the evil prohibited by the Free Exercise Clause. * * *

The plaintiffs appear to contend that the element of compulsion was supplied by the requirement of class participation in the reading exercises. As we have pointed out earlier, there is no proof in the record that any plaintiff student was required to engage in role play, make up magic chants, read aloud or engage in the activity of haggling. In fact, the Director of Education for the State of Tennessee testified that most teachers do not adhere to the suggestions in the teachers' manuals and a teacher for 11 years in the Hawkins County system stated that she looks at the lesson plans in the teachers' editions, but "does her own thing." Being exposed to other students performing these acts might be offensive to the plaintiffs, but it does not constitute the compulsion described in the

Supreme Court cases, where the objector was required to affirm or deny a religious belief or engage or refrain from engaging in a practice contrary to sincerely held religious beliefs.

D.

The third Supreme Court decision relied upon by the plaintiffs is the only one that might be read to support the proposition that requiring mere exposure to materials that offend one's religious beliefs creates an unconstitutional burden on the free exercise of religion. *Wisconsin v. Yoder,* 406 U.S. 205, 92 S.Ct. 1526 (1972). However, *Yoder* rested on such a singular set of facts that we do not believe it can be held to announce a general rule that exposure without compulsion to act, believe, affirm or deny creates an unconstitutional burden. The plaintiff parents in *Yoder* were Old Order Amish and members of the Conservative Amish Mennonite Church, who objected to their children being required to attend either public or private schools beyond the eighth grade. Wisconsin school attendance law required them to cause their children to attend school until they reached the age of 16. Unlike the plaintiffs in the present case, the parents in *Yoder* did not want their children to attend any high school or be exposed to any part of a high school curriculum. The Old Order Amish and the Conservative Amish Mennonites separate themselves from the world and avoid assimilation into society, and attempt to shield their children from all worldly influences. The Supreme Court found from the record that—

> [C]ompulsory school attendance to age 16 for Amish children carries with it a very real threat to undermining the Amish community and religious practice as they exist today; they must either abandon belief and be assimilated into society at large, or be forced to migrate to some other and more tolerant region. *Id.* at 218, 92 S.Ct. at 1534 (footnote omitted).

As if to emphasize the narrowness of its holding because of the unique 300 year history of the Old Amish Order, the Court wrote:

> It is one thing to say that compulsory education for a year or two beyond the eighth grade may be necessary when its goal is the preparation of the child for life in modern society as the majority live, but it is quite another if the goal of education be viewed as the preparation of the child for life in the separated agrarian community that is the keystone of the Amish faith. *Id.* at 222, 92 S.Ct. at 1536 (citation omitted).

This statement points up dramatically the difference between *Yoder* and the present case. The parents in *Yoder* were required to send their children to some school that prepared them for life in the outside world, or face official sanctions. The parents in the present case want their children to acquire all the skills required to live in modern society. They also want to have them excused from exposure to some ideas they find offensive. Tennessee offers two options to accommodate this latter desire. The plaintiff parents can either send their children to church schools or private schools, as many of them have done, or teach them at home. Tennessee law prohibits any state interference in the education process of church schools:

> The state board of education and local boards of education are prohibited from regulating the selection of faculty or textbooks or the establishment of a curriculum in church-related schools.

Similarly the statute permitting home schooling by parents or other teachers prescribes nothing with respect to curriculum or the content of class work.

Yoder was decided in large part on the impossibility of reconciling the goals of public education with the religious requirement of the Amish that their children be prepared for life in a separated community. As the Court noted, the requirement of school attendance to age 16 posed a "very real threat of undermining the Amish community and religious practice as they exist today...." 406 U.S. at 218, 92 S.Ct. at 1534. No such threat exists in the present case, and Tennessee's school attendance laws offer several options to those parents who want their children to have the benefit of an education which prepares for life in the modern world without being exposed to ideas which offend their religious beliefs.

E.

At oral argument plaintiffs' counsel identified [a concurring opinion in] *Grove v. Mead School Dist. No. 354* as [one] which strongly supports the plaintiffs' position.... [But] the plaintiffs failed to note other ... statements in the same concurring opinion that, while addressing a different issue, are at odds with their theories:

> Were the free exercise clause violated whenever governmental activity is offensive to or at variance with sincerely held religious precepts, virtually no governmental program would be constitutionally possible. *Id.* at 1542.

> The lesson is clear: governmental actions that merely offend or cast doubt on religious beliefs do not on that account violate free exercise. An actual burden on the profession or exercise of religion is required.

> In short, distinctions must be drawn between those governmental actions that actually interfere with the exercise of religion, and those that merely require or result in exposure to attitudes and outlooks at odds with perspectives prompted by religion. *Id.* at 1543 (citation omitted).

These statements echo similar ones in the majority opinion, *e.g.,*

> To establish a violation of that clause [Free Exercise], a litigant must show that challenged state action has a coercive effect that operates against a litigant's *practice* of his or her religion. *Id.* at 1533 (emphasis added).

IV.

A.

The Supreme Court has recently affirmed that public schools serve the purpose of teaching fundamental values "essential to a democratic society." These values "include tolerance of divergent political and religious views" while taking into account "consideration of the sensibilities of others." *Bethel School Dist. No. 403 v. Fraser,* 478 U.S. 675, 106 S.Ct. 3159, 3164 (1986). The Court has noted with apparent approval the view of some educators who see public schools as an "assimilative force" that brings together "diverse and conflicting elements" in our society "on a broad but common ground." The critical reading approach furthers these goals. Mrs. Frost stated specifically that she objected to stories that develop "a religious tolerance that all religions are merely different roads to God." Stating that the plaintiffs reject this concept, presented as a recipe for an ideal world citizen, Mrs. Frost said, "We cannot be tolerant in that we accept other religious views on an equal basis with ours." While probably not an uncommon view of true believers in any religion, this statement graphically illustrates what is lacking in the plaintiffs' case.

The "tolerance of divergent ... religious views" referred to by the Supreme Court is a civil tolerance, not a religious one. It does not require a person to accept any other religion as the equal of the one to which that person adheres. It merely requires a recognition that in a pluralistic society we must "live and let live." If the Hawkins County schools had required the plaintiff students either to believe or say they believe that "all religions are merely different roads to God," this would be a different case. No instrument of government can, consistent with the Free Exercise Clause, require such a belief or affirmation. However, there was absolutely no showing that the defendant school board sought to do this; indeed, the school board agreed at oral argument that it could not constitutionally do so. Instead, the record in this case discloses an effort by the school board to offer a reading curriculum designed to acquaint students with a multitude of ideas and concepts, though not in proportions the plaintiffs would like. While many of the passages deal with ethical issues, on the surface at least, they appear to us to contain no religious or anti-religious messages. Because the plaintiffs perceive every teaching that goes beyond the "three Rs" as inculcating religious ideas, they admit that any value-laden reading curriculum that did not affirm the truth of their beliefs would offend their religious convictions.

Although it is not clear that the plaintiffs object to all critical reading, Mrs. Frost did testify that she did not want her children to make critical judgments and exercise choices in areas where the Bible provides the answer. There is no evidence that any child in the Hawkins County schools was required to make such judgments. It was a goal of the school system to encourage this exercise, but nowhere was it shown that it was required. When asked to comment on a reading assignment, a student would be free to give the Biblical interpretation of the material or to interpret it from a different value base. The only conduct compelled by the defendants was reading and discussing the material in the Holt series, and hearing other students' interpretations of those materials. This is the exposure to which the plaintiffs objected. What is absent from this case is the critical element of compulsion to affirm or deny a religious belief or to engage or refrain from engaging in a practice forbidden or required in the exercise of a plaintiff's religion.

B.

* * *

Since we have found none of the prohibited forms of governmental compulsion in this case, we conclude that the plaintiffs failed to establish the existence of an unconstitutional burden. * * *

The judgment of the district court granting injunctive relief and damages is reversed, and the case is remanded with directions to dismiss the complaint. * * *

PARKER v. HURLEY

514 F.3d 87 (1st Cir. 2008)

LYNCH, CIRCUIT JUDGE.

Two sets of parents, whose religious beliefs are offended by gay marriage and homosexuality, sued the Lexington, Massachusetts school district in which their young children are enrolled. They assert that they must be given prior notice by the school and the opportunity to exempt their young children from exposure to books they find religiously repugnant. Plaintiffs assert violations of their own and their children's rights under the Free Exercise Clause and their substantive parental and privacy due process rights under the U.S. Constitution.

The Parkers object to their child being presented in kindergarten and first grade with two books that portray diverse families, including families in which both parents are of the same gender. The Wirthlins object to a second-grade teacher's reading to their son's class a book that depicts and celebrates a gay marriage. The parents do not challenge the use of these books as part of a nondiscrimination curriculum in the public schools, but challenge the school district's refusal to provide them with prior notice and to allow for exemption from such instruction. They ask for relief until their children are in seventh grade.

Massachusetts does have a statute that requires parents be given notice and the opportunity to exempt their children from curriculum which primarily involves human sexual education or human sexuality issues. Mass. Gen. Laws ch. 71, § 32A. The school system has declined to apply this statutory exemption to these plaintiffs on the basis that the materials do not primarily involve human sexual education or human sexuality issues.

The U.S. District Court dismissed plaintiffs' complaint for failure to state a federal constitutional claim upon which relief could be granted. Plaintiffs appeal.

I.

* * * In addition to the complaint, we consider the three books plaintiffs find objectionable. We also take notice of the statewide curricular standards of the Commonwealth of Massachusetts and start with those to put this dispute in context.

A. *Massachusetts Statewide Curricular Standards*

The Commonwealth of Massachusetts enacted a comprehensive education reform bill in 1993, requiring the State Board of Education (SBE) to establish academic standards for core subjects. Mass. Gen. Laws ch. 69, § 1D. The statute mandates that the standards "be designed to inculcate respect for the cultural, ethnic and racial diversity of the commonwealth." *Id.* Further, "[a]cademic standards shall be designed to avoid perpetuating gender, cultural, ethnic or racial stereotypes." *Id.* * * * The statute does not specify sexual orientation in these lists.

The SBE established such standards, including a Comprehensive Health Curriculum Framework in 1999. That Framework establishes Learning Standards, which set different measurable goals for students in pre-kindergarten through grade 5, grades 6–8, and grades 9–12. The Health Framework also specifically notes that "public schools must notify parents before implementing curriculum that involves human sexuality."

Within the Framework are Strands, and Strands have different components. Under the Social and Emotional Health Strand, there is a Family Life component, which states:

> Students will gain knowledge about the significance of the family on individuals and society, and will learn skills to support the family, balance work and family life, be an effective parent, and nurture the development of children.

The Learning Standard for elementary school grades under the Family Life component states that children should be able to "[d]escribe different types of families."

In addition, the Social and Emotional Health Strand includes an Interpersonal Relationships component. That component provides:

> Students will learn that relationships with others are an integral part of the human life experience and the factors that contribute to healthy interpersonal relationships, and will acquire skills to enhance and make many of these relationships more fulfilling through commitment and communication.

The associated Learning Standard for pre-kindergarten through grade 5 recommends that children be able to "[d]escribe the concepts of prejudice and discrimination."

It is not until grades 6–8 that the Learning Standards under this component address "the detrimental effect of prejudice (such as prejudice on the basis of race, gender, sexual orientation, class, or religion) on individual relationships and society as a whole."

There is also a Reproduction/Sexuality component under the Physical Health Strand. Within that component, the Learning Standards provide that by grade 5, students should be able to "[d]efine sexual orientation using the correct terminology (such as heterosexual, and gay and lesbian)."

These statewide academic standards do not purport to select particular instructional materials, but only to be a guide to assist others in that selection. Mass. Gen. Laws ch. 69, § 1E. Thus, there is no statewide regulation or policy providing for the use of the particular texts in dispute here.

By statute, the actual selection of books is the responsibility of a school's principal, with the approval of the superintendent of schools. Mass. Gen. Laws ch. 71, § 48. We assume these books were chosen locally subject to the terms of that statute. * * *

On November 18, 2003, a divided Supreme Judicial Court of Massachusetts held, in *Goodridge v. Department of Public Health*, 440 Mass. 309, 798 N.E.2d 941 (2003), that the state constitution mandates the recognition of same-sex marriage. A later effort to reverse this decision through the mechanism of a constitutional convention and a popular vote failed.

B. *The Parkers*

David and Tonia Parker's sons, Jacob and Joshua Parker, and Joseph and Robin Wirthlin's son, Joseph Robert Wirthlin, Jr., are students at Estabrook Elementary School in Lexington, Massachusetts. Both families assert that they are devout Judeo–Christians and that a core belief of their religion is that homosexual behavior and gay marriage are immoral and violate God's law.

In January 2005, when Jacob Parker ("Jacob") was in kindergarten, he brought home a "Diversity Book Bag." This included a picture book, *Who's in a Family?*, which depicted different families, including single-parent families, an extended family, interracial families, animal families, a family without children, and—to the concern of the Parkers—a family with two dads and a family with two moms. The book concludes by answering the question, "Who's in a family?": "The people who love you the most!" The book says nothing about marriage.

The Parkers were concerned that this book was part of an effort by the public schools "to indoctrinate young children into the concept that homosexuality and homosexual relationships or marriage are moral and acceptable behavior." Such an effort, they feared, would require their sons to affirm a belief inconsistent with their religion. On January 21, 2005, they met with Estabrook's principal, Joni Jay ("Jay"), to request that

Jacob not be exposed to any further discussions of homosexuality. Principal Jay disagreed that the school had any obligation under section 32A to notify parents in advance of such class discussions. In March 2005, the Parkers repeated their request that "no teacher or adult expose [Jacob] to any materials or discussions featuring sexual orientation, same-sex unions, or homosexuality without notification to the Parkers and the right to 'opt out,'" this time including in their communication the then-Superintendent of Lexington's schools, William Hurley ("Hurley"), and two other district-wide administrators. This request was met with the same response. A further meeting to discuss these issues was held at Estabrook on April 27, 2005, which resulted in Mr. Parker's arrest when he refused to leave the school until his demands were met.

As the 2005–2006 school year began, Paul Ash ("Ash"), the current Superintendent, released a public statement explaining the school district's position that it would not provide parental notification for "discussions, activities, or materials that simply reference same-gender parents or that otherwise recognize the existence of differences in sexual orientation." When Jacob entered first grade that fall, his classroom's book collection included *Who's in a Family?* as well as *Molly's Family,* a picture book about a girl who is at first made to feel embarrassed by a classmate because she has both a mommy and a mama but then learns that families can come in many different varieties. In December 2005, the Parkers repeated their request for advance notice, which Superintendent Ash again denied.

C. *The Wirthlins*

We turn to the other plaintiff family.

In March 2006, an Estabrook teacher read aloud *King and King* to her second grade class, which included Joseph Robert Wirthlin, Jr. ("Joey"). This picture book tells the story of a prince, ordered by his mother to get married, who first rejects several princesses only to fall in love with another prince. A wedding scene between the two princes is depicted. The last page of the book shows the two princes kissing, but with a red heart superimposed over their mouths. There is no allegation in the complaint that the teacher further discussed the book with the class. That evening, Joey told his parents about the book; his parents described him as "agitated" and remembered him calling the book "so silly." Eventually the Wirthlins were able to secure a meeting with the teacher and Jay on April 6, 2006, to object to what they considered to be indoctrination of their son about gay marriage in contravention of their religious beliefs. Jay reiterated the school district's position that no prior notice or exemption would be given.

D. *Procedural History*

* * * The complaint alleges that the public schools are systematically indoctrinating the Parkers' and the Wirthlins' young children contrary to the parents' religious beliefs and that the defendants held "a specific intention to denigrate the [families'] sincere and deeply-held faith." They

claim, under 42 U.S.C. § 1983, violations of their and their children's First Amendment right to the free exercise of religion and of their Fourteenth Amendment due process right to parental autonomy in the upbringing of their children, as well as of their concomitant state rights. They also assert a violation of the Massachusetts "opt out" statute, Mass. Gen. Laws ch. 71, § 32A.

The plaintiffs argue that their ability to influence their young children toward their family religious views has been undercut in several respects. First, they believe their children are too young to be introduced to the topic of gay marriage. They also point to the important influence teachers have on this age group. They fear their own inability as parents to counter the school's approval of gay marriage, particularly if parents are given no notice that such curricular materials are in use. As for the children, the parents fear that they are "essentially" required "to affirm a belief inconsistent with and prohibited by their religion." The parents assert it is ironic, and unconstitutional under the Free Exercise Clause, for a public school system to show such intolerance towards their own religious beliefs in the name of tolerance.

For relief, the plaintiffs seek a declaration of their constitutional rights; damages; and an injunction requiring the school (1) to provide an opportunity to exempt their children from "classroom presentations or discussions the intent of which is to have children accept the validity of, embrace, affirm, or celebrate views of human sexuality, gender identity, and marriage constructs," (2) to allow the parents to observe any such classroom discussions, and (3) to not present any "materials graphically depicting homosexual physical contact" to students before the seventh grade. * * *

II.

Our review of the district court's order of dismissal is de novo. * * * We affirm the order of dismissal, albeit on grounds different from the district court's reasoning.

There are several ways to approach the parents' claim depending upon how this case is categorized. * * * [W]e approach the parents' claims as the Court did in *Yoder.* In that case, the Court did not analyze separately the due process and free exercise interests of the parent-plaintiffs, but rather considered the two claims interdependently, given that those two sets of interests inform one other. * * * [T]he level of justification the government must demonstrate-a rational basis, a compelling interest, or something in between-is irrelevant in this case. While we accept as true plaintiffs' assertion that their sincerely held religious beliefs were deeply offended, we find that they have not described a constitutional burden on their rights, or on those of their children.

* * * [T]he standard constitutional threshold question * * * is "whether the plaintiff's free exercise is interfered with at all." * * *

In *Yoder,* the Court found unconstitutional Wisconsin's application of its compulsory school attendance law to Amish parents who believed that any education beyond eighth grade undermined their entire, religiously focused way of life. The heart of the *Yoder* opinion is a lengthy consideration of "the interrelationship of belief with [the Amish] mode of life, the vital role that belief and daily conduct play in the continued survival of Old Order Amish communities and their religious organization," and how as a result compulsory high school education would "substantially inter-fer[e] with the religious development of the Amish child and his integration into the way of life of the Amish faith community." The Court thus found Wisconsin's compulsory attendance law to be flatly incompatible with the plaintiffs' free exercise rights and parental liberty interests, which it considered in tandem. That is, compulsory attendance at *any* school—whether public, private, or home-based—prevented these Amish parents from making *fundamental* decisions regarding their children's religious upbringing and effectively overrode their ability to pass their religion on to their children, as their faith required. Further, the parents in *Yoder* were able to demonstrate that their alternative informal vocational training of their older children still met the state's professed interest behind its compulsory attendance requirement.

To the extent that *Yoder* embodies judicial protection for social and religious "sub-groups from the public cultivation of liberal tolerance," plaintiffs are correct to rely on it. But there are substantial differences between the plaintiffs' claims in *Yoder* and the claims raised in this case. One ground of distinction is that the plaintiffs have chosen to place their children in public schools and do not live, as the Amish do, in a largely separate culture. There are others. While plaintiffs do invoke *Yoder's* language that the state is threatening their very "way of life," they use this language to refer to the centrality of these beliefs to their faith, in contrast to its use in *Yoder* to refer to a distinct community and life style. Exposure to the materials in dispute here will not automatically and irreversibly prevent the parents from raising Jacob and Joey in the religious belief that gay marriage is immoral. Nor is there a criminal statute involved, or any other punishment imposed on the parents if they choose to educate their children in other ways. They retain options, unlike the parents in *Yoder.* Tellingly, *Yoder* emphasized that its holding was essentially sui generis, as few sects could make a similar showing of a unique and demanding religious way of life that is fundamentally incompatible with *any* schooling system. Plaintiffs' case is not *Yoder.*

Despite defendants' contention, plaintiffs' case is also not *Brown.* *Brown* concerned a federal constitutional challenge to a one-time failure by a Massachusetts high school to comply with the notice and exemption procedures required by Mass. Gen. Laws ch. 71, § 32A, for a student's attendance at a discrete sex education assembly. *Brown* is factually and legally distinct. Most significantly, *Brown* involved the education of high school students, not the education of kindergarten through second-grade students. Educators treat this age differential as significant. The statewide curricular standards themselves, including those related to sexual orientation, distinguish between elementary and high school students. Further, as the plaintiffs sensibly point out, high school students are less responsive to what adults say than are very young elementary school children.

The impressionability of young school children has been noted as a relevant factor in the Establishment Clause context. * * * The relevance of the age of school children has been noted in a free speech case involving religious expression. The age of the student has also been identified as relevant in the context of parental due process rights. * * *

We see no principled reason why the age of students should be irrelevant in Free Exercise Clause cases. * * * Based on this distinction alone, *Brown* does not control this case.

We turn afresh to plaintiffs' complementary due process and free exercise claims. * * * In sum, the substantive due process clause by itself, either in its parental control or its privacy focus, does not give plaintiffs the degree of control over their children's education that their requested relief seeks. We turn then to whether the combination of substantive due process and free exercise interests give the parents a cause of action.

* * * The Free Exercise Clause, importantly, is not a general protection of religion or religious belief. It has a more limited reach of protecting the *free exercise* of religion.

* * *

Generally, the fundamental parental control/free exercise claims regarding public schools have fallen into several types of situations: claims that failure to provide benefits given to public school students violates free exercise rights, claims that plaintiffs should not be subjected to compulsory education, demands for removal of offensive material from the curriculum, and, as here, claims that there is a constitutional right to exemption from religiously offensive material.

* * *

In *Mozert v. Hawkins County Board of Education,* which is * * * factually similar to this case, the Sixth Circuit rejected a broader claim for an exemption from a school district's use of an entire series of texts. The parents in that case asserted that the books in question taught values contrary to their religious beliefs and that, as a result, the school violated the parents' religious beliefs by allowing their children to read the books and violated their children's religious beliefs by requiring the children to read them. The court, however, found that exposure to ideas through the required reading of books did not constitute a constitutionally significant burden on the plaintiffs' free exercise of religion. In so holding, the court emphasized that "the evil prohibited by the Free Exercise Clause" is "governmental compulsion either to do or refrain from doing an act forbidden or required by one's religion, or to affirm or disavow a belief forbidden or required by one's religion," and reading or even discussing the books did not compel such action or affirmation.

In the present case, the plaintiffs claim that the exposure of their children, at these young ages and in this setting, to ways of life contrary to the parents' religious beliefs violates their ability to direct the religious upbringing of their children. We try to identify the categories of harms alleged. The parents do not allege coercion in the form of a direct interference with their religious beliefs, nor of compulsion in the form of punishment for their beliefs, as in *Yoder.* Nor do they allege the denial of benefits. Further, plaintiffs do not allege that the mere listening to a book being read violated any religious duty on the part of the child. There is no claim that as a condition of attendance at the public schools, the defendants have forced plaintiffs—either the parents or the children—to violate their religious beliefs. In sum there is no claim of direct coercion.

The heart of the plaintiffs' free exercise claim is a claim of "indoctrination": that the state has put pressure on their children to endorse an affirmative view of gay marriage and has thus undercut the parents' efforts to inculcate their children with their own opposing religious views. The Supreme Court, we believe, has never utilized an indoctrination test under the Free Exercise Clause, much less in the public school context. The closest it has come is *Barnette,* a free speech case that implicated free exercise interests * * *. In *Barnette,* the Court held that the state could not coerce acquiescence through compelled statements of belief, such as the mandatory recital of the pledge of allegiance in public schools. It did not hold that the state could not attempt to inculcate values by instruction, and in fact carefully distinguished the two approaches. We do not address whether or not an indoctrination theory under the Free Exercise Clause is sound. Plaintiffs' pleadings do not establish a viable case of indoctrination, even assuming that extreme indoctrination can be a form of coercion.

First, as to the parents' free exercise rights, the mere fact that a child is exposed on occasion in public school to a concept offensive to a parent's religious belief does not inhibit the parent from instructing the child differently. A parent whose "child is exposed to sensitive topics or information [at school] remains free to discuss these matters and to place them in the family's moral or religious context, or to supplement the information with more appropriate materials." * * * The parents here did in fact have notice, if not prior notice, of the books and of the school's overall intent to promote toleration of same-sex marriage, and they retained their ability to discuss the material and subject matter with their children. Our outcome does not turn, however, on whether the parents had notice.

Turning to the children's free exercise rights, we cannot see how Jacob's free exercise right was burdened at all: two books were made available to him, but he was never required to read them or have them read to him. Further, these books do not endorse gay marriage or homosexuality, or even address these topics explicitly, but merely describe how other children might come from families that look different from one's own. There is no free exercise right to be free from any reference in public elementary schools to the existence of families in which the parents are of different gender combinations.

Joey has a more significant claim, both because he was required to sit through a classroom reading of *King and King* and because that book affirmatively endorses homosexuality and gay marriage. It is a fair inference that the reading of *King and King* was precisely *intended* to influence the listening children toward tolerance of gay marriage. That was the point of why that book was chosen and used. Even assuming there is a continuum along which an intent to influence could become an attempt to indoctrinate, however, this case is firmly on the influence-toward-tolerance end. There is no evidence of systemic indoctrination. There is no allegation that Joey was asked to affirm gay marriage. Requiring a student to read a particular book is generally not coercive of free exercise rights.

Public schools are not obliged to shield individual students from ideas which potentially are religiously offensive, particularly when the school imposes no requirement that the student agree with or affirm those ideas, or even participate in discussions about them. *Mozert.* * * * The reading of *King and King* was not instruction in religion or religious beliefs.

On the facts, there is no viable claim of "indoctrination" here. Without suggesting that such showings would suffice to establish a claim of indoctrination, we note the plaintiffs' children were not forced to read the books on pain of suspension. Nor were they subject to a constant stream of like materials. There is no allegation here of a formalized curriculum requiring students to read many books affirming gay marriage. * * * The reading by a teacher of one book, or even three, and even if to a young and impressionable child, does not constitute "indoctrination."

Because plaintiffs do not allege facts that give rise to claims of constitutional magnitude, the district court did not err in granting defendants' motion to dismiss the claims under the U.S. Constitution.

III.

Public schools often walk a tightrope between the many competing constitutional demands made by parents, students, teachers, and the schools' other constituents. * * * The balance the school struck here does not offend the Free Exercise or Due Process Clauses of the U.S. Constitution.

We do not suggest that the school's choice of books for young students has not deeply offended the plaintiffs' sincerely held religious beliefs. If the school system has been insufficiently sensitive to such religious beliefs, the plaintiffs may seek recourse to the normal political processes for change in the town and state. They are not entitled to a federal judicial remedy under the U.S. Constitution. * * *

Affirmed.

NOTES

1. In *Downs v. LAUSD,* 228 F.3d 1003 (9th Cir. 2000), a high school teacher objected to the Los Angeles Unified School District's decision to establish June as "Gay and Lesbian Awareness Month," and to the accompanying materials that were distributed and displayed. Across the hall from one such display, Downs had put up a competing bulletin board, which included statements condemning homosexual relations and opposing both the adoption of children by same-sex couples and the idea of gay marriage generally. After being asked to take the material down, he filed a lawsuit in federal court, arguing that his *freedom of expression* rights under the First Amendment had been violated.

Upholding the lower court's ruling in favor of the school district, the U.S. Court of Appeals for the Ninth Circuit in 2000 found the District's acts to be the equivalent of "government speech," and determined that under the First Amendment not only did a District have the right to engage in such speech, but that District employees could not then engage in speech on school grounds that ran counter to the memorandum setting forth the parameters of the awareness month. The Court explained that as "an arm of local government,"

> [a] school board "may decide not only to talk about gay and lesbian awareness and tolerance in general, but also to advocate such tolerance if it so decides, and restrict the contrary speech of one of its representatives."*Id.* at 1014.

The Court cited approvingly the language from the lower court opinion that emphasized that "[j]ust as a school could prohibit a teacher from posting racist material on a bulletin board designated for Black History Month, [LAUSD] may prohibit [Downs] from posting intolerant materials during 'Gay and Lesbian Awareness Month.' " *Id.* at 1016.

Finally, the Court also noted that the ruling did not prohibit Downs from "propounding his own opinion on the morality of homosexuality": "Subject to any applicable forum analysis, he may do so on the sidewalks, in the parks, through the chat-rooms, at his dinner table and in countless other locations. He may not do so, however, when he is speaking as the government, unless the government allows him to be its voice." *Id.*

2. In the Fall 2008 election campaign, proponents of California Proposition 8—which sought to reverse the state supreme court's decision recognizing a right to marry for same-sex couples—put the issue of curriculum, religion, morality, and values at the forefront of their campaign. A central tenet of the *Yes on 8* campaign, emphasized in advertisements throughout the election season, was the contention that a *no* vote would result in schools being required to "teach gay marriage" to children in the primary grades. Signs in pro-Proposition 8 rallies repeatedly equated a *yes* vote with a vote for "parental rights." And television ads actually cited *Parker v. Hurley,* decided earlier that same year, in support of these arguments.

State curriculum frameworks do not typically require schools to teach about marriage per se, other than in health education and sex education programs that are usually implemented at the secondary level and allow parents to opt out. Most states, however, include a unit in the primary grades on "The Family," such as the one at the heart of the *Parker v. Hurley* controversy.

In California, the Content Standards and State Curricular Frameworks mandate a study of "People Who Make A Difference" in Grade Two. During the course of this study, students are expected to focus on their individual family members and report this information to their class.

Problem 44: Curriculum Disputes in Moss Grove

Assume the same facts and circumstances that were originally set forth in Problem 12, Chapter III, where a simmering controversy regarding conflicting values had erupted between residents of Moss Grove and the neighboring collective in the fictional state of New Tuolumne. Assume that in addition to the T–Shirt controversies, a dispute had arisen regarding a teacher who read to her students from a book she had written.

Ms. Mayberry, a member of the collective and a tenured teacher in the Moss Grove Unified School District (MGUSD), always reads stories to her second graders from time to time. Pursuant to the state's curricular frameworks, she makes sure that the stories relate to the social studies unit she is currently teaching. In the fall of 2009, after launching the state-mandated unit on "the family," Mayberry–who also writes children's books–chooses to read from her recently published book on the Moss Grove collective. The story she reads includes a detailed explanation of how the members of the collective reject marriage and how the children are raised by everyone as communal resources.

Every year, Ms. Mayberry and the other second grade teachers put on a "Family Diversity Fair," celebrating the many different types of families that exist in New Tuolumne. Students prepare reports and displays on their families, which include pictures, drawings, and a variety of audio and video presentations. Members of the school community are always invited to attend. Pursuant to the state curricular standards, the overarching theme of the fair is that in a pluralistic society and a public setting everyone's family and everyone's family traditions must be equally valued.

After hearing about the plans for the upcoming fair and after learning from their pastor in an angry sermon that Ms. Mayberry read her new book aloud to the class, the parents of a child in the class meet with school officials and demand that their child be allowed to opt out of the Fair and all activities and assignments relating to it. Their demands are rejected. The angry parents then bring a lawsuit against MGUSD, arguing that both their right to direct the upbringing of their child and their rights under the Free Exercise Clause have been violated. What arguments should the District expect the elementary school parents to set forth? What arguments should the District be prepared to make in response? What result? Discuss.

PROBLEM 45: THE CHANGING NATURE OF THE FAMILY AND ITS IMPACT ON THE CURRICULUM

Children in the U.S. are now growing up in a highly diverse and wide-ranging variety of family scenarios. They are being raised in single-parent households, by their aunts or uncles, by their grandparents, or by foster parents or adoptive parents, and often in bi-racial or multi-racial settings. In addition, many children are being raised by one or both parents in circumstances that have never included marriage. Finally, a substantial number of children are being raised by openly gay and lesbian parents, some single, but many others in long-term relationships. A growing number are biological parents, while many others have chosen to adopt children locally or overseas.

At the same time, the first decade of the Twenty-first century has seen dramatic changes in the legal recognition of same-sex couples. Gay marriage has become legal in at least six countries (Belgium, Canada, the Netherlands, Norway, South Africa, and Spain) and in at least two states (Connecticut and Massachusetts). Other jurisdictions, while not allowing same-sex couples to marry, will recognize such marriages if performed in other places. These include New York, France, and Israel. Many other jurisdictions have recognized some form of domestic partnership or civil union, including 10 states in the U.S. and a significant number of other countries across the globe. And gay relations between consenting adults in the privacy of their own home are now legal in all 50 states.

As a matter of policy, in light of all these changes, and given the conflicting values in this context, is it wise to eliminate units on *the family* from the elementary school curriculum? Would you support the removal of these units at this time?

Alternatively, assuming that such units continue to be part of the curriculum frameworks in your state, how might you approach the teaching of such material? At what age would you recommend introducing this content? In particular, given the emotion surrounding these issues, how would you recommend approaching the topic of families headed by one or more gay parents? Is it possible to design a unit on the family that would respect what may be very divergent views in our pluralistic society during this difficult time of transition?

E.   SEX EDUCATION

PROBLEM 46: THE RIVERVIEW LAWSUITS

The following hypothetical takes place in the fictional state of Riverview.

The state legislature, determined to bring religion, morality, and values back into public education, revises its sex education statutes and implementing regulations. As now set forth, the following key guidelines apply:

1. Public school campuses shall forbid any discussion of sexual activity and birth control other than abstinence.

2. The words *abortion* and *condom* shall not appear in any of the instructional materials, nor are they to be used in any classroom lesson.

* * *

A. A group of angry Riverview parents file a lawsuit challenging the new instructional framework. What arguments might be set forth under the right to an education generally? Under the right to receive information and ideas? What result? Discuss.

B. Assume that, some time during the second year of implementation, an eleventh grader at Riverview High is diagnosed as HIV positive. It soon becomes clear that this student had been infected by a fellow student after the two had engaged in consensual sexual activity over a period of several months in a variety of secluded locations on the way home from school. If the parents of the student who had become infected seek to file a negligence lawsuit against the school district, what arguments might be set forth under the duty to supervise/protect? Under the duty to warn? What result? Discuss.

C. Assume, instead, that the state legislature—under a different leadership—adopts an exact version of California Senate Bill 71. A group of parents, infuriated with the new law, file a lawsuit under the right not to receive information and ideas, and are prepared to contend that the statutory scheme is not only *not* educationally suitable (under *Pico*), but is violative of the Free Exercise Clause. What arguments will be set forth? What result? Discuss.

D. Same facts as C, except that the opt-out provisions of SB 71 have been deleted. Under this new version of SB 71, which supersedes any inconsistent policies established by individual school districts, no family may opt out of the mandatory instruction. What arguments might then be set forth by the parents under the First Amendment? Under the Fourteenth Amendment right to direct the upbringing of their children? What result? Discuss.

Curriculum-Related Controversies
in the Area of Sex Education

In general, the U.S. courts have upheld as legal the good faith efforts of school districts and state legislatures to develop and implement sex education programs, even when the programs offend the religious sensibilities of particular parents. *See Brown v. Hot, Sexy and Safer Productions, Inc.,* 68 F.3d 525 (1st Cir. 1995), where the Court found that a highly questionable sex education assembly for high school students that included arguably inappropriate humor and overly explicit commentary did not amount to a constitutional violation under any of the theories set forth by the plaintiffs.

Several courts have considered challenges to the distribution of condoms by school districts on school grounds. *See, e.g., Parents United for*

Better Schools, Inc. v. School Dist. of Philadelphia Bd. of Ed., 148 F.3d 260 (3rd Cir. 1998), ruling in favor of the District. *But see* the U.S. "No Child Left Behind" Act, 20 U.S.C. Section 7906, which provides, in pertinent part:

None of the funds authorized under this chapter shall be used—

(1) to develop or distribute materials, or operate programs or courses of instruction directed at youth, that are designed to promote or encourage sexual activity;

* * *

(3) to provide sex education or HIV-prevention education in schools unless that instruction is age appropriate and includes the health benefits of abstinence; or

(4) to operate a program of contraceptive distribution in schools.

In *Leebaert v. Harrington,* 332 F.3d 134 (2d Cir. 2003), the Court considered the question of whether a school district was obligated to excuse a child—upon the request of the parent—from attending health education classes. Finding in favor of the District, the Court ruled that the parental right to direct the upbringing and education of a child does not require the District to comply with such a request.

In *Fields v. Palmdale Sch. Dist.,* 427 F.3d 1197 (9th Cir. 2005), the Court found that the administration of a psychological questionnaire to elementary school students—containing some questions involving sexual topics and with the announced goal "of establishing a community baseline measure of children's exposure to early trauma"—was neither a violation of "the due process right to control a child's upbringing" nor nor a violation of "the constitutional right to privacy." The Court declared that "there is no fundamental right of parents to be the exclusive provider of information regarding sexual matters to their children, either independent of their right to direct the upbringing and education of their children or encompassed by it." It also found "that parents have no due process or privacy right to override the determination of public schools as to the information to which their children will be exposed while enrolled as students."

Consider the following excerpts from the 2003 California Sex Education Statutes, which are generally viewed as among the most progressive of the era. What changes might you recommend, as a matter of policy, in light of recent and ongoing developments in this area?

THE CALIFORNIA SEX EDUCATION STATUTES

California Education Code
From SB 71 (Kuehl) (2003)

CHAPTER 5.6. CALIFORNIA COMPREHENSIVE SEXUAL HEALTH AND HIV/AIDS PREVENTION EDUCATION ACT

Article 1. General Provisions

51930.   (a) This chapter shall be known and may be cited as the California Comprehensive Sexual Health and HIV/AIDS Prevention Education Act.

(b) The purposes of this chapter are as follows:

(1) To provide a pupil with the knowledge and skills necessary to protect his or her sexual and reproductive health from unintended pregnancy and sexually transmitted diseases.

(2) To encourage a pupil to develop healthy attitudes concerning adolescent growth and development, body image, gender roles, sexual orientation, dating, marriage, and family.

51931.   For the purposes of this chapter, the following definitions apply:

(a) "Age appropriate" refers to topics, messages, and teaching methods suitable to particular ages or age groups of children and adolescents, based on developing cognitive, emotional, and behavioral capacity typical for the age or age group.

(b) "Comprehensive sexual health education" means education regarding human development and sexuality, including education on pregnancy, family planning, and sexually transmitted diseases.

* * *

(d) "HIV/AIDS prevention education" means instruction on the nature of HIV/AIDS, methods of transmission, strategies to reduce the risk of human immunodeficiency virus (HIV) infection, and social and public health issues related to HIV/AIDS. For the purposes of this chapter, "HIV/AIDS prevention education" is not comprehensive sexual health education.

(e) "Instructors trained in the appropriate courses" means instructors with knowledge of the most recent medically accurate research on human sexuality, pregnancy, and sexually transmitted diseases.

(f) "Medically accurate" means verified or supported by research conducted in compliance with scientific methods and published in peer-reviewed journals, where appropriate, and recognized as accurate and objective by professional organizations and agencies with expertise in the relevant field, such as the federal Centers for Disease Control and Prevention, the American Public Health Association, the American Academy of Pediatrics, and the American College of Obstetricians and Gynecologists.

* * *

51932.   (a) This chapter does not apply to description or illustration of human reproductive organs that may appear in a textbook, adopted pursuant to law, on physiology, biology, zoology, general science, personal hygiene, or health.

(b) This chapter does not apply to instruction or materials that discuss gender, sexual orientation, or family life and do not discuss human reproductive organs and their functions.

Article 2. Authorized Comprehensive Sexual Health Education

51933.   (a) School districts may provide comprehensive sexual health education, consisting of age-appropriate instruction, in any kindergarten to grade 12, inclusive, using instructors trained in the appropriate courses.

(b) A school district that elects to offer comprehensive sexual health education pursuant to subdivision (a), whether taught by school district personnel or outside consultants, shall satisfy all of the following criteria:

(1) Instruction and materials shall be age appropriate.

(2) All factual information presented shall be medically accurate and objective.

(3) Instruction shall be made available on an equal basis to a pupil who is an English learner, consistent with the existing curriculum and alternative options for an English learner pupil as otherwise provided in this code.

(4) Instruction and materials shall be appropriate for use with pupils of all races, genders, sexual orientations, ethnic and cultural backgrounds, and pupils with disabilities.

(5) Instruction and materials shall be accessible to pupils with disabilities, including, but not limited to, the provision of a modified curriculum, materials and instruction in alternative formats, and auxiliary aids.

(6) Instruction and materials shall encourage a pupil to communicate with his or her parents or guardians about human sexuality.

(7) Instruction and materials shall teach respect for marriage and committed relationships.[2]

(8) Commencing in grade 7, instruction and materials shall teach that abstinence from sexual intercourse is the only certain way to prevent unintended pregnancy, teach that abstinence from sexual activity is the only certain way to prevent sexually transmitted diseases, and provide information about the value of abstinence while also providing medically accurate information on other methods of preventing pregnancy and sexually transmitted diseases.

(9) Commencing in grade 7, instruction and materials shall provide information about sexually transmitted diseases. This instruction shall include how sexually transmitted diseases are and are not transmitted, the effectiveness and safety of all federal Food and Drug Administration (FDA) approved methods of reducing the risk of contracting sexually transmitted diseases, and information on local resources for testing and medical care for sexually transmitted diseases.

(10) Commencing in grade 7, instruction and materials shall provide information about the effectiveness and safety of all FDA-approved contraceptive methods in preventing pregnancy, including, but not limited to, emergency contraception.

(11) Commencing in grade 7, instruction and materials shall provide pupils with skills for making and implementing responsible decisions about sexuality.

(12) Commencing in grade 7, instruction and materials shall provide pupils with information on the law on surrendering physical custody of a minor child 72 hours or younger, pursuant to Section 1255.7 of the Health and Safety Code and Section 271.5 of the Penal Code.

(c) A school district that elects to offer comprehensive sexual health education pursuant to subdivision (a) earlier than grade 7 may provide age appropriate and medically accurate information on any of the general topics contained in paragraphs (8) to (12), inclusive, of subdivision (b).

(d) If a school district elects to offer comprehensive sexual health education pursuant to subdivision (a), whether taught by school district personnel or outside consultants, the school district shall comply with the following:

---

2. This language replaced the following language in former Cal. Educ. Code Section 51553: "(6) Course material and instruction shall teach honor and respect for monogamous heterosexual marriage."

      (1) Instruction and materials may not teach or promote religious doctrine.

      (2) Instruction and materials may not reflect or promote bias against any person on the basis of any category protected by Section 220.

Article 3. Required HIV/AIDS Prevention Education

51934.   (a) A school district shall ensure that all pupils in grades 7 to 12, inclusive, receive HIV/AIDS prevention education from instructors trained in the appropriate courses. Each pupil shall receive this instruction at least once in junior high or middle school and at least once in high school.

      (b) HIV/AIDS prevention education, whether taught by school district personnel or outside consultants, shall satisfy all of the criteria set forth in paragraphs (1) to (6), inclusive, of subdivision (b) and paragraphs (1) and (2) of subdivision (d) of Section 51933, shall accurately reflect the latest information and recommendations from the United States Surgeon General, the federal Centers for Disease Control and Prevention, and the National Academy of Sciences, and shall include the following:

      (1) Information on the nature of HIV/AIDS and its effects on the human body.

      (2) Information on the manner in which HIV is and is not transmitted, including information on activities that present the highest risk of HIV infection.

      (3) Discussion of methods to reduce the risk of HIV infection. This instruction shall emphasize that sexual abstinence, monogamy, the avoidance of multiple sexual partners, and abstinence from intravenous drug use are the most effective means for HIV/AIDS prevention, but shall also include statistics based upon the latest medical information citing the success and failure rates of condoms and other contraceptives in preventing sexually transmitted HIV infection, as well as information on other methods that may reduce the risk of HIV transmission from intravenous drug use.

      (4) Discussion of the public health issues associated with HIV/AIDS.

      (5) Information on local resources for HIV testing and medical care.

      (6) Development of refusal skills to assist pupils in overcoming peer pressure and using effective decisionmaking skills to avoid high-risk activities.

(7) Discussion about societal views on HIV/AIDS, including stereotypes and myths regarding persons with HIV/AIDS. This instruction shall emphasize compassion for persons living with HIV/AIDS.

* * *

Article 5. Notice and Parental Excuse

51937. It is the intent of the Legislature to encourage pupils to communicate with their parents or guardians about human sexuality and HIV/AIDS and to respect the rights of parents or guardians to supervise their children's education on these subjects. The Legislature intends to create a streamlined process to make it easier for parents and guardians to review materials and evaluation tools related to comprehensive sexual health education and HIV/AIDS prevention education, and, if they wish, to excuse their children from participation in all or part of that instruction or evaluation.

The Legislature recognizes that while parents and guardians overwhelmingly support medically accurate, comprehensive sex education, parents and guardians have the ultimate responsibility for imparting values regarding human sexuality to their children.

51938. A parent or guardian of a pupil has the right to excuse their child from all or part of comprehensive sexual health education, HIV/AIDS prevention education, and assessments related to that education, as follows:

(a) At the beginning of each school year, or, for a pupil who enrolls in a school after the beginning of the school year, at the time of that pupil's enrollment, each school district shall notify the parent or guardian of each pupil about instruction in comprehensive sexual health education and HIV/AIDS prevention education and research on pupil health behaviors and risks planned for the coming year. The notice shall include all of the following:

(1) Advise the parent or guardian that written and audio visual educational materials used in comprehensive sexual health education and HIV/AIDS prevention education are available for inspection.

(2) Advise the parent or guardian whether the comprehensive sexual health education or HIV/AIDS prevention education will be taught by school district personnel or by outside consultants.

(3) Information explaining the parent's or guardian's right to request a copy of this chapter.

(4) Advise the parent or guardian that the parent or guardian may request in writing that his or her child not receive comprehensive sexual health education or HIV/AIDS prevention education.

* * *

F. INTERNET FILTERING AND THE SAFETY OF CHILDREN IN CYBERSPACE

JUST HOW DIFFERENT IS CYBERSPACE?

From Beyond Our Control? Confronting the Limits
of Our Legal System in the Age of Cyberspace
Stuart Biegel
MIT Press (2001)

For those who seek to regulate cyberspace, the question of how different it is becomes a central component of the inquiry. If the Internet is simply another high-tech method of sending and receiving information, then arguably the same legal and policy principles that apply to other forms of communication are applicable here. If the differences are only a matter of degree, then minor adjustments can be made in the law and the task still remains relatively straightforward. But if the online world is different enough to be distinguishable from the offline world in significant ways—and noted commentators have argued as much—then the task of would-be regulators becomes much more complicated indeed.

At the most basic level, everyone agrees. The 1990s version of the Internet has become a new, widely used form of communication with three distinguishing features. It has provided the means for instantaneous global transmission of written messages, which may also be accompanied by graphic and audio-visual material. It has expanded the ability of individuals to communicate easily with large numbers of people. And it has emerged as a vehicle for unprecedented access to information. While fax machines and various other forms of telephone, radio, and satellite transmission may provide many similar benefits, the scope of Internet communication via e-mail, newsgroups, and the World Wide Web—combined with the relatively low cost for those who already have the hardware—makes it at least somewhat different from anything that has come before.

For the majority of people, however, the Internet is more than just a bit different. Most would concede that it is different enough to merit a level of attention that very few other modes of communication have received. And many see the Internet as something more than simply another communication tool, although just how one might classify this new medium has been the subject of debate at the highest levels of government and industry.

The controversy regarding the correct classification—or perhaps the most appropriate analogy—for the Internet came to the forefront during the *Reno v. ACLU* litigation of 1996–1997.[3] At the oral arguments for the first Internet-related case to reach the U.S. Supreme Court, both the attorneys and the justices focused extensively on the nature of cyberspace and sought to identify the most relevant analogy.

Deputy Solicitor General Seth P. Waxman, representing the government, argued that the Internet might be viewed as analogous to a library. Building on the fact that many people do indeed use the Internet as a research tool, he argued that the Communications Decency Act (CDA) simply required that certain indecent material be put in "a different room" of this library.[4] Plaintiffs also liked the library analogy, but for different reasons. Judith Krug of the American Library Association noted with pleasure that during the oral arguments in the *Reno* case "the justices paid special attention to the threat that the CDA would pose to libraries around the country seeking to use the Internet to provide greater public access to information."[5]

Justice Stephen Breyer wondered aloud at the oral argument whether the Internet might simply be more like a telephone. With a great percentage of online users at the time communicating via modems over telephone lines, the analogy seemed quite appropriate. Breyer asked whether a group of high school students discussing their sexual experiences online might appropriately be characterized as simply teenagers talking on the telephone, and he appeared genuinely concerned about the prospect of criminalizing such behavior.[6]

Justices Sandra Day O'Connor and Anthony Kennedy suggested in their questions to Mr. Waxman that the Internet might be considered analogous to "a street corner or a park," raising the question of whether the online world could be viewed as a traditional public forum for purposes of First Amendment analysis.[7] Commentators have wrestled extensively with this issue, seeking to determine whether the Internet might best be characterized as a public street corner or more akin to a private shopping mall.[8]

The government, however, appeared at other times to prefer that the Internet be viewed as more akin to broadcast media. The Justice Department's brief in *Reno* relied heavily on *FCC v. Pacifica*,[9] the case that

---

3. 521 U.S. 844 (1997).

4. See Oral Argument of Seth P. Waxman, Esq. On Behalf of the Appellants, *Cyber-Liberties: American Civil Liberties Union*, *at* http://www.aclu.org/issues/cyber/trial/sctran.html#waxman (last visited May 17, 2000) [hereinafter *Reno v. ACLU Oral Argument*].

5. Stuart Biegel, Reno v. ACLU in the Supreme Court: Justices Hear Oral Argument in Communication Decency Act Case, *UCLA Online Institute for Cyberspace Law and Policy*, March 27, 1997, *at* http://www.gseis.ucla.edu/iclp/mar97.html (last visited August 28, 2000).

6. *See Reno v. ACLU Oral Argument, supra* note 2.

7. *See id.*

8. *See, e.g., PruneYard Shopping Center v. Robins*, 447 U.S. 74 (1980).

9. 438 U.S. 726 (1978).

considered the complaints of a father who heard the broadcast of George Carlin's "Seven Dirty Words" monologue with his young son. In *Pacifica,* the Court found that "broadcasting . . . has received the most limited First Amendment protection" . . . both because of its pervasiveness and because of child accessibility.[10] Building on *Pacifica* in its brief, the government argued that it should be able to regulate online speech because there is a "danger of inadvertent exposure to indecent material on the Internet as well."[11] Plaintiffs countered, however, with the argument that if the Internet is analogous to any form of media, the most appropriate analogy would be newspapers and magazines—which are afforded much greater First Amendment protection under constitutional law.[12]

While in the end the Court found that the Internet—at least for purposes of deciding the *Reno* case—is more analogous to both a library *and* a shopping mall, it can be argued that every one of the analogies raised in the oral arguments might apply at some point depending on the circumstances. Indeed, at the turn of the century, the Internet can probably be viewed as all of the above, and more: a library, a telephone, a public park, a local bar, a shopping mall, a broadcast medium, a print medium, a medical clinic, a private living room, and a public educational institution. No previous mode of communication in the history of mankind has served so many purposes all at once.

* * *

In cyberspace, one can achieve a level of anonymity that is generally just not possible in our day-to-day affairs. While on some level there is less privacy in cyberspace, on another level a person can change his/her age, gender, race, and/or socioeconomic status and present a completely different persona to others in online chat rooms and discussion forums. People become less inhibited and feel more free to act in ways that they might not think of acting in the actual physical presence of others. Countless stories have emerged of people with minimal social skills who have raised havoc in cyberspace, relying implicitly or explicitly on the apparent lack of accountability for ones actions that has often become part of this picture. A certain level of anarchy has in fact been tolerated in many parts of the online world, reflecting a libertarian Net culture that insists on freedom of expression at all times and in all contexts.

* * * [The] level of openness that has emerged as a result of both the nature of the online world and the still-prevalent Net culture can also lead to some very extreme and unsettling experiences. Laws are broken with impunity, unsubstantiated rumors take on an inappropriate level of credibility, young people have unprecedented access to adult information, and people witness things they may not have chosen to witness.

* * *

---

10. *Id.* at 748.

11. *See Reno v. ACLU Oral Argument, supra* note 2.

12. *See* Biegel, *supra* note 3.

[In this context,] most people are concerned on at least some level that young people may encounter obscenity years before they have the emotional maturity to sort out the relevant issues that may be involved. As the Internet becomes a central component of innovative education programs, more and more young people have been accessing the online world. When they do, they can easily find some of the most extreme pornography ever available to the average person of any age.

* * *

[T]he only viable option for the average online user who [does] not want to encounter obscenity in cyberspace [is] to try [an] architectural solution of some sort. Internet filtering, for example, ... proliferated in the aftermath of the U.S. Supreme Court's Reno decision, bolstered by the majority opinion's clear suggestion that the control of obscenity would be up to individual users.

Filtering software [has] improved significantly, and many [see] it as a viable option. But typical filtering systems [continue] to block many sites that could be important to access depending on the nature of one's online use.

PROBLEM 47: THE MARBURY STUDENT COUNCIL COMMUNITY WEB SITE

Over a twenty-year period, Marbury Middle School—a fictional urban campus located in Southern California—developed a unique relationship with the Fred Korematsu Public Library. Both the school's main office & classroom facility and the public library were situated in the same complex, and when a combination of overcrowding and budget cutbacks led to the dismantling and closing down of the school's own library collection, a close working arrangement was established between the two separate institutions. Under this informal arrangement, all Marbury students received automatic borrowing privileges, later expanded to include free and unlimited use of the fifteen computer terminals. Teachers brought their classes to the library on a regular basis pursuant to a schedule worked out by Korematsu librarians. And when the library installed unrestricted Internet access on all the terminals, students were able to benefit from this additional service as well.

Several years later, the Marbury Student Council voted to set up several "community service" subcommittees, with the express goal of identifying key problems in the community and investigating possible solutions. One day in late February, while visiting the American College Health Association Web site via a Korematsu library terminal, s.t.d./teen pregnancy subcommittee member Bill Jones discovered a page entitled "Making Sex Safer." The page contained an overview of various sexually transmitted diseases, and discussed explicit ways that men and women could protect themselves. It concluded by classifying fifteen different sexual "acts" into four categories: safe, less risky, risky, and dangerous. Believing that the entire school community could benefit from this information, Bill decided to include a link to the page on the new Student Council Community Service Web Site.

A. Assume that the Student Council goes ahead with these plans, and that Principal Janet Morrison receives several complaints from parents regarding the link. Morrison subsequently appears at the next student council meeting, and informs the students that under no circumstances are they to be conducting their own sex education program at Marbury Middle School. The entire Web site is taken down, and a new Student Council Faculty Advisor is appointed. The students, represented by the ACLU, file a lawsuit, arguing that their rights have been violated. What arguments might the respective parties set forth? What result? Discuss.

B. Assume instead that no parents complain, but that a major controversy develops regarding the unrestricted access to the Internet that had been available to Marbury students in the Fred Korematsu library. In response, the school district and the library announce at a joint press conference that because some Internet content is not "educationally suitable," they have arranged with familyclick.com to implement server-based content filtering on all library computers. And while familyclick.com enables adults with proper passwords to override the filtering system, passwords would not be distributed to patrons here because so many young students walked around the library throughout the day and could conceivably view unsuitable material as they passed by computer screens.

After the content filtering system is finally installed, Albert Hall, Editor of *The Marbury Street Sheet* (a newspaper published by the city's homeless population), files a lawsuit challenging the new system as violative of his right to receive information and ideas. What arguments would Hall set forth under *Pico* and *Loudoun*? What result? Discuss.

C. Assume that instead of agreeing to install a content filtering system, the library breaks with the school district and refuses to make any changes. Assume that a lawsuit is then filed by a group of Marbury families who are highly religious and object to the unfiltered Internet access at the library. According to the families' religious precepts, mere exposure to graphic pictorial sexual content is considered an abomination. What arguments might the parents set forth? What result? Discuss.

MAINSTREAM LOUDOUN v. BOARD OF TRUSTEES OF THE LOUDOUN COUNTY LIBRARY

2 F.Supp.2d 783 (E.D. Va. 1998)

BRINKEMA, DISTRICT JUDGE.

Before the Court ... [is] a case of first impression, involving the applicability of the First Amendment's free speech clause to public libraries' content-based restrictions on Internet access.

I. Background

The plaintiffs in this case are an association, Mainstream Loudoun, and ten individual plaintiffs, all of whom are both members of Mainstream Loudoun and adult patrons of Loudoun County public libraries. * * *

On October 20, 1997, the Library Board voted to adopt a "Policy on Internet Sexual Harassment" (the "Policy"), which requires that "[s]ite-blocking software . . . be installed on all [library] computers" so as to: "a. block child pornography and obscene material (hard core pornography)"; and "b. block material deemed Harmful to Juveniles under applicable Virginia statutes and legal precedents (soft core pornography)." To implement the Policy, the Library Board chose "X–Stop," a commercial software product intended to limit access to sites deemed to violate the Policy.

Plaintiffs allege that the Policy impermissibly blocks their access to protected speech such as the Quaker Home Page, the Zero Population Growth Web site, and the site for the American Association of University Women–Maryland. They also claim that there are no clear criteria for blocking decisions and that defendants maintain an unblocking policy that unconstitutionally chills plaintiffs' receipt of constitutionally protected materials.

* * *

IV. Plaintiffs' First Amendment Claim

* * *

[D]efendants concede that the Policy prohibits access to speech on the basis of its content. However, defendants argue that the "First Amendment does not in any way limit the decisions of a public library on whether to provide access to information on the Internet." . . . Thus, the central question before this Court is whether a public library may, without violating the First Amendment, enforce content-based restrictions on access to Internet speech.

No cases directly address this issue. However, the parties agree that the most analogous authority on this issue is *Board of Education v. Pico,* 457 U.S. 853, 102 S.Ct. 2799 (1982), in which the Supreme Court reviewed the decision of a local board of education to remove certain books from a high school library based on the board's belief that the books were "anti-American, anti-Christian, anti-Sem[i]tic, and just plain filthy." *Id.* 457 U.S. at 856. . . . A sharply-divided Court voted to affirm the Court of Appeal's decision to remand the case for a determination of the school board's motives. However, the Court did not render a majority opinion. Justice Brennan, joined by three Justices, wrote what is commonly referred to as the "plurality" opinion. Justice Brennan held that the First Amendment necessarily limits the government's right to remove materials on the basis of their content from a high school library. *See id.* at 864–69 (plurality op.). Justice Brennan reasoned that the right to receive information is inherent in the right to speak and that "the State may not, consistently with the spirit of the First Amendment, contract the spectrum of available knowledge." [*S*]*ee also Stanley v. Georgia*, 394 U.S. 557, 564, 89 S.Ct. 1243 (1969)("the Constitution protects the right to receive information and ideas"). Justice Brennan explained that this principle was particularly important given the special role of the school's library as a locus for free and independent inquiry. *See* [*Pico*] 457 U.S. at 869. At the same time, Justice Brennan recognized that public high schools play a crucial inculcative role in "the preparation of individuals for participation as citizens" and are therefore entitled to great discretion "to establish and apply their curriculum in such a way as to transmit community values." *Id.* at 863–64. Accordingly, Justice Brennan held that the school board members could not remove books "simply because they dislike the ideas contained [in them]," thereby "prescrib[ing] what shall be orthodox in politics, nationalism, religion, or other matters of opinion," but that the board might remove books for reasons of educational suitability, for example pervasive vulgarity.

* * *

Defendants contend that the *Pico* plurality opinion has no application to this case because it addressed only decisions to remove materials from libraries and specifically declined to address library decisions to acquire materials. *See id.* at 861–63, 871–72 (plurality op.). Defendants liken the Internet to a vast Interlibrary Loan system, and contend that restricting Internet access to selected materials is merely a decision not to acquire such materials rather than a decision to remove them from a library's collection. As such, defendants argue, the instant case is outside the scope of the *Pico* plurality.

In response, plaintiffs argue that, unlike a library's collection of individual books, the Internet is a "single, integrated system." As plaintiffs explain, "[t]hough information on the Web is contained in individual computers, the fact that each of these computers is connected to the Internet through [World Wide Web] protocols allows all of the information to become part of a single body of knowledge." Accordingly, plaintiffs analogize the Internet to a set of encyclopedias, and the Library Board's enactment of the Policy to a decision to "black out" selected articles considered inappropriate for adult and juvenile patrons.

After considering both arguments, we conclude that defendants have misconstrued the nature of the Internet. By purchasing Internet access, each Loudoun library has made all Internet publications instantly accessible to its patrons. Unlike an Interlibrary loan or outright book purchase, no appreciable expenditure of library time or resources is required to make a particular Internet publication available to a library patron. In contrast, a library must actually expend resources to restrict Internet access to a publication that is otherwise immediately available. In effect, by purchasing one such publication, the library has purchased them all. The Internet therefore more closely resembles plaintiffs' analogy of a collection of encyclopedias from which defendants have laboriously redacted portions deemed unfit for library patrons. As such, the Library Board's action is more appropriately characterized as a removal decision. We therefore conclude that the principles discussed in the *Pico* plurality are relevant and apply to the Library Board's decision to promulgate and enforce the Policy.

* * *

To the extent that *Pico* applies to this case, we conclude that it stands for the proposition that the First Amendment applies to, and limits, the discretion of a public library to place content-based restrictions on access to constitutionally protected materials within its collection. Consistent with the mandate of the First Amendment, a public library, "like other enterprises operated by the State, may not be run in such a manner as to 'prescribe what shall be orthodox in politics, nationalism, religion, or other matters of opinion.'" *Id.* at 876 (Blackmun, J., concurring) (quoting *Barnette*, 319 U.S. at 642).

Furthermore, the factors which justified giving high school libraries broad discretion to remove materials in *Pico* are not present in this case. The plaintiffs in this case are adults rather than children. Children, whose minds and values are still developing, have traditionally been afforded less First Amendment protection, particularly within the context of public high schools. *See Tinker v. Des Moines Sch. Dist.*, 393 U.S. 503, 506, 89 S.Ct. 733 (1969). In contrast, adults are deemed to have acquired the maturity needed to participate fully in a democratic society, and their right to speak and receive speech is entitled to full First Amendment protection. Accordingly, adults are entitled to receive categories of speech, for example "pervasively vulgar" speech, which may be inappropriate for children. *See Reno v. ACLU*, 521 U.S. 844, 117 S.Ct. 2329, 2346 (1997).

More importantly, the tension Justice Blackmun recognized between the inculcative role of high schools and the First Amendment's prohibition on content-based regulation of speech does not exist here. *See Pico*, 457 U.S. at 876–80 (Blackmun, J., concurring). Public libraries lack the inculcative mission that is the guiding purpose of public high schools. Instead, public libraries are places of freewheeling and independent inquiry. *See id.* at 914 (Rehnquist, J., dissenting). Adult library patrons are presumed to have acquired already the "fundamental values" needed to act as citizens, and have come to the library to pursue their personal intellectual interests rather than the curriculum of a high school classroom. As such, no curricular motive justifies a public library's decision to restrict access to Internet materials on the basis of their content.

Finally, the unique advantages of Internet speech eliminate any resource-related rationale libraries might otherwise have for engaging in content-based discrimination. The Supreme Court has analogized the Internet to a "vast library including millions of readily available and indexed publications," the content of which "is as diverse as human thought." *Reno*, 117 S.Ct. at 2335. Unlike more traditional libraries, however, there is no marginal cost associated with acquiring Internet publications. Instead, all, or nearly all, Internet publications are jointly available for a single price. Indeed, it costs a library more to restrict the content of its collection by means of blocking software than it does for the library to offer unrestricted access to all Internet publications. Nor do Internet publications, which exist only in "cyberspace," take up shelf space or require physical maintenance of any kind. Accordingly, considerations of cost or physical resources cannot justify a public library's decision to restrict access to Internet materials. *Cf. Pico,* 457 U.S. at 909 (Rehnquist, J., dissenting) (budgetary considerations force schools to choose some books over others); 879 n. 1 (Blackmun, J., concurring)(same).

In sum, there is "no basis for qualifying the level of First Amendment scrutiny" that must be applied to a public library's decision to restrict access to Internet publications. *Reno,* 117 S.Ct. at 2344. We are therefore left with the First Amendment's central tenet that content-based restrictions on speech must be justified by a compelling governmental interest and must be narrowly tailored to achieve that end. This principle was recently affirmed within the context of Internet speech. *See Reno,* 117 S.Ct. at 2343–48. Accordingly, we hold that the Library Board may not adopt and enforce content-based restrictions on access to protected Internet speech absent a compelling state interest and means narrowly drawn to achieve that end.

This holding does not obligate defendants to act as unwilling conduits of information, because the Library Board need not provide access to the Internet at all. Having chosen to provide access, however, the Library Board may not thereafter selectively restrict certain categories of Internet speech because it disfavors their content. * * *

A. *Obscenity, Child Pornography, and Speech "Harmful to Juveniles"*

Having determined that a public library must satisfy strict scrutiny before it may engage in content-based regulation of protected speech, we now consider the speech regulated by the Policy. The Policy prohibits access to three types of speech: obscenity, child pornography, and materials deemed "[h]armful to [j]uveniles." Obscenity and child pornography are not entitled to the protections of the First Amendment, and the government may legitimately restrict access to such materials. *See New York v. Ferber* (child pornography); *Miller v. California* (obscenity). Indeed, "[t]ransmitting obscenity and child pornography, whether via the Internet or other means, is already illegal under federal law for both adults and juveniles." *Reno,* 117 S.Ct. at 2348 n.44. In the instant case, however, plaintiffs allege that the X–Stop filtering software chosen by defendants restricts many publications which are not obscene or pornographic, including materials unrelated to sex altogether, such as the Quaker's Web site. Moreover, plaintiffs allege that X–Stop fails to block access to pornographic materials arguably covered by the Policy. Most importantly, plaintiffs allege that the decision as to which materials to block is made by a California corporation based on secret criteria not disclosed even to defendants, criteria which may or may not bear any relation to legal definitions of obscenity or child pornography. As such, plaintiffs argue that the means called for by the Policy are not narrowly tailored to any legitimate interest defendants may have in regulating obscenity and child pornography.

The Policy also prohibits access to materials which are "deemed Harmful to Juveniles under applicable Virginia statutes and legal precedents." ... Plaintiffs allege that the Policy improperly limits adult Internet speech to what is fit for children. In support, plaintiffs cite *Reno*, 117 S.Ct. at 2329. In *Reno,* the Supreme Court held that a content-based Internet regulation intended to prevent the transmission of material harmful to minors was unconstitutional because it suppressed speech adults were constitutionally entitled to send and receive. The Court stated:

> It is true that we have repeatedly recognized the governmental interest in protecting children from harmful materials. But that interest does not justify an unnecessarily broad suppression of speech addressed to adults. As we have explained, the Government may not "reduc[e] the adult population ... to ... only what is fit for children."

> * * *

As plaintiffs point out, even when government regulation of content is undertaken for a legitimate purpose, whether it be to prevent the communication of obscene speech or materials harmful to children, the means it uses must be a "reasonable response to the threat" which will alleviate the harm "in a direct and material way." Plaintiffs have adequately alleged a lack of such reasonable means here. As such, plaintiffs have stated a valid First Amendment claim which may go forward.

B. *The Unblocking Policy*

Defendants contend that, even if the First Amendment limits the Library Board's discretion to remove materials, the unblocking procedure ensures the constitutionality of the Policy because it allows library staff to make certain that only constitutionally unprotected materials are blocked. Under the unblocking policy, library patrons who have been denied access to a site may submit a written request which must include their name, telephone number, and a detailed explanation of why they desire access to the blocked site. The library staff then "decide[s] whether the request should be granted."

Plaintiffs argue that the unblocking procedure constitutes an unconstitutional burden on the right of library patrons to access protected speech, citing *Lamont*. The statute at issue in *Lamont* directed the Postmaster General not to deliver "communist propaganda" to postal patrons unless they first returned to the Post Office a card bearing their names and addresses and specifically requesting that such materials be sent to them. The Supreme Court held the statute to be "unconstitutional because it require[d] an official act (viz., returning the reply card) as a limitation on the unfettered exercise of the addressees' First Amendment rights." In particular, the Court noted the severe chilling effect of forcing citizens to publicly petition the Government for access to speech it clearly disfavored.

Here, as in *Lamont,* the unblocking policy forces adult patrons to petition the Government for access to otherwise protected speech, for example speech "Harmful to Juveniles." Indeed, the Loudoun County unblocking policy appears more chilling than the restriction at issue in *Lamont,* because it grants library staff standardless discretion to refuse access to protected speech, whereas the statute at issue in *Lamont* required postal employees to grant access requests automatically. As such, defendants' alleged unblocking procedure does not in any way undercut plaintiffs' First Amendment claim.

NOTES

1. Neither *Loudoun* nor the *U.S. v. ALA* case that follows are school-related per se, but of course public libraries provide a very important educative function to many members of the community ... and particularly to those with fewer economic resources at their disposal.

2. In November 1998, Judge Brinkema issued a new decision in this case following a trial on the merits. While somewhat different in its focus, the ultimate result was consistent with the earlier determination by the Court that the filtering policy violated the First Amendment. *See* Mainstream Loudoun v. Board of Trustees of the Loudoun County Public Library, 24 F.Supp.2d 552 (E.D. Va. 1998).

UNITED STATES v. AMERICAN LIBRARY ASS'N, INC.

539 U.S. 194, 123 S.Ct. 2297 (2003)

Chief JUSTICE REHNQUIST announced the judgment of the Court.

To address the problems associated with the availability of Internet pornography in public libraries, Congress enacted the Children's Internet Protection Act (CIPA). Under CIPA, a public library may not receive federal assistance to provide Internet access unless it installs software to block images that constitute obscenity or child pornography, and to prevent minors from obtaining access to material that is harmful to them. The District Court held these provisions facially invalid on the ground that they induce public libraries to violate patrons' First Amendment rights. We now reverse.

To help public libraries provide their patrons with Internet access, Congress offers two forms of federal assistance. First, the E-rate program established by the Telecommunications Act of 1996 entitles qualifying libraries to buy Internet access at a discount. In the year ending June 30, 2002, libraries received $58.5 million in such discounts. Second, pursuant to the Library Services and Technology Act (LSTA), the Institute of

Museum and Library Services makes grants to state library administrative agencies to "electronically lin[k] libraries with educational, social, or information services," "assis[t] libraries in accessing information through electronic networks," and "pa[y] costs for libraries to acquire or share computer systems and telecommunications technologies." In fiscal year 2002, Congress appropriated more than $149 million in LSTA grants. These programs have succeeded greatly in bringing Internet access to public libraries: By 2000, 95% of the Nation's libraries provided public Internet access.

          * * *

By connecting to the Internet, public libraries provide patrons with a vast amount of valuable information. But there is also an enormous amount of pornography on the Internet, much of which is easily obtained. The accessibility of this material has created serious problems for libraries, which have found that patrons of all ages, including minors, regularly search for online pornography. Some patrons also expose others to pornographic images by leaving them displayed on Internet terminals or printed at library printers.

Upon discovering these problems, Congress became concerned that the E-rate and LSTA programs were facilitating access to illegal and harmful pornography. Congress learned that adults "us[e] library computers to access pornography that is then exposed to staff, passersby, and children," and that "minors acces[s] child and adult pornography in libraries."

But Congress also learned that filtering software that blocks access to pornographic Web sites could provide a reasonably effective way to prevent such uses of library resources. By 2000, before Congress enacted CIPA, almost 17% of public libraries used such software on at least some of their Internet terminals, and 7% had filters on all of them. A library can set such software to block categories of material, such as "Pornography" or "Violence." When a patron tries to view a site that falls within such a category, a screen appears indicating that the site is blocked. But a filter set to block pornography may sometimes block other sites that present neither obscene nor pornographic material, but that nevertheless trigger the filter. To minimize this problem, a library can set its software to prevent the blocking of material that falls into categories like "Education," "History," and "Medical." A library may also add or delete specific sites from a blocking category, and anyone can ask companies that furnish filtering software to unblock particular sites.

Responding to this information, Congress enacted CIPA. It provides that a library may not receive E-rate or LSTA assistance unless it has "a policy of Internet safety for minors that includes the operation of a technology protection measure . . . that protects against access" by all persons to "visual depictions" that constitute "obscen[ity]" or "child pornography," and that protects against access by minors to "visual depictions" that are "harmful to minors." The statute defines a "[t]echnology protection measure" as "a specific technology that blocks or filters Internet access to material covered by" CIPA. CIPA also permits the library to "disable" the filter "to enable access for bona fide research or other lawful purposes." 20 U.S.C. § 9134(f)(3); 47 U.S.C. § 254(h)(6)(D). Under the E-rate program, disabling is permitted "during use by an adult." Under the LSTA program, disabling is permitted during use by any person.

Appellees are a group of libraries, library associations, library patrons, and Web site publishers, including the American Library Association (ALA) and the Multnomah County Public Library in Portland, Oregon (Multnomah). They sued the United States and the Government agencies and officials responsible for administering the E-rate and LSTA programs in District Court, challenging the constitutionality of CIPA's filtering provisions. A three-judge District Court convened pursuant to § 1741(a) of CIPA.

* * *

Congress has wide latitude to attach conditions to the receipt of federal assistance in order to further its policy objectives. But Congress may not "induce" the recipient "to engage in activities that would themselves be unconstitutional." To determine whether libraries would violate the First Amendment by employing the filtering software that CIPA requires, we must first examine the role of libraries in our society.

Public libraries pursue the worthy missions of facilitating learning and cultural enrichment. Appellee ALA's Library Bill of Rights states that libraries should provide "[b]ooks and other ... resources ... for the interest, information, and enlightenment of all people of the community the library serves." To fulfill their traditional missions, public libraries must have broad discretion to decide what material to provide to their patrons. Although they seek to provide a wide array of information, their goal has never been to provide "universal coverage." Instead, public libraries seek to provide materials "that would be of the greatest direct benefit or interest to the community." To this end, libraries collect only those materials deemed to have "requisite and appropriate quality." See W. Katz, Collection Development: The Selection of Materials for Libraries ("The librarian's responsibility ... is to separate out the gold from the garbage, not to preserve everything"); F. Drury, Book Selection xi ("[I]t is the aim of the selector to give the public, not everything it wants, but the best that it will read or use to advantage"); Rebuttal Expert Report of Donald G. Davis, Jr. ("A hypothetical collection of everything that has been produced is not only of dubious value, but actually detrimental to users trying to find what they want to find and really need").

We have held in two analogous contexts that the government has broad discretion to make content-based judgments in deciding what private speech to make available to the public. In *Arkansas Ed. Television Comm'n v. Forbes*, we held that public forum principles do not generally apply to a public television station's editorial judgments regarding the private speech it presents to its viewers. "[B]road rights of access for outside speakers would be antithetical, as a general rule, to the discretion that stations and their editorial staff must exercise to fulfill their journalistic purpose and statutory obligations." Recognizing a broad right of public access "would [also] risk implicating the courts in judgments that should be left to the exercise of journalistic discretion."

Similarly, in *National Endowment for Arts v. Finley*, we upheld an art funding program that required the National Endowment for the Arts (NEA) to use content-based criteria in making funding decisions. We explained that "[a]ny content-based considerations that may be taken into account in the grant-making process are a consequence of the nature of arts funding." In particular, "[t]he very assumption of the NEA is that grants will be awarded according to the 'artistic worth of competing applicants,' and absolute neutrality is simply inconceivable." We expressly declined to apply forum analysis, reasoning that it would conflict with "NEA's mandate ... to make esthetic judgments, and the inherently content-based 'excellence' threshold for NEA support."

The principles underlying *Forbes* and *Finley* also apply to a public library's exercise of judgment in selecting the material it provides to its patrons. Just as forum analysis and heightened judicial scrutiny are incompatible with the role of public television stations and the role of the NEA, they are also incompatible with the discretion that public libraries must have to fulfill their traditional missions. Public library staffs necessarily consider content in making collection decisions and enjoy broad discretion in making them.

The public forum principles on which the District Court relied are out of place in the context of this case. Internet access in public libraries is neither a "traditional" nor a "designated" public forum. First, this resource—which did not exist until quite recently—has not "immemorially been held in trust for the use of the public and, time out of mind, ... been used for purposes of assembly, communication of thoughts between citizens, and discussing public questions." We have "rejected the view that traditional public forum status extends beyond its historic confines." The doctrines surrounding traditional public forums may not be extended to situations where such history is lacking.

Nor does Internet access in a public library satisfy our definition of a "designated public forum." To create such a forum, the government must make an affirmative choice to open up its property for use as a public forum. "The government does not create a public forum by inaction or by permitting limited discourse, but only by intentionally opening a non-traditional forum for public discourse." The District Court likened public libraries' Internet terminals to the forum at issue in *Rosenberger v. Rector and Visitors of Univ. of Va.,* 515 U.S. 819, 115 S.Ct. 2510 (1995). In *Rosenberger,* we considered the "Student Activity Fund" established by the University of Virginia that subsidized all manner of student publications except those based on religion. We held that the fund had created a limited public forum by giving public money to student groups who wished to publish, and therefore could not discriminate on the basis of viewpoint.

The situation here is very different. A public library does not acquire Internet terminals in order to create a public forum for Web publishers to express themselves, any more than it collects books in order to provide a public forum for the authors of books to speak. It provides Internet access, not to "encourage a diversity of views from private speakers," *Rosenberger*, 515 U.S. at 834, 115 S.Ct. 2510, but for the same reasons it offers other library resources: to facilitate research, learning, and recreational pursuits by furnishing materials of requisite and appropriate quality. As Congress recognized, "[t]he Internet is simply another method for making information available in a school or library." It is "no more than a technological extension of the book stack."

* * *

Because public libraries' use of Internet filtering software does not violate their patrons' First Amendment rights, CIPA does not induce libraries to violate the Constitution, and is a valid exercise of Congress' spending power. Nor does CIPA impose an unconstitutional condition on public libraries. Therefore, the judgment of the District Court for the Eastern District of Pennsylvania is

Reversed.

JUSTICE KENNEDY, concurring in the judgment.

If, on the request of an adult user, a librarian will unblock filtered material or disable the Internet software filter without significant delay, there is little to this case.

* * *

There are, of course, substantial Government interests at stake here. The interest in protecting young library users from material inappropriate for minors is legitimate, and even compelling, as all Members of the Court appear to agree. Given this interest, and the failure to show that the ability of adult library users to have access to the material is burdened in any significant degree, the statute is not unconstitutional on its face. For these reasons, I concur in the judgment of the Court.

JUSTICE BREYER, concurring in the judgment.

The Children's Internet Protection Act (Act) sets conditions for the receipt of certain Government subsidies by public libraries. Those conditions require the libraries to install on their Internet-accessible computers technology, say, filtering software, that will help prevent computer users from gaining Internet access to child pornography, obscenity, or material comparably harmful to minors. The technology, in its current form, does not function perfectly, for to some extent it also screens out constitutionally protected materials that fall outside the scope of the statute (*i.e.,* "overblocks") and fails to prevent access to some materials that the statute deems harmful (*i.e.,* "underblocks"). In determining whether the statute's conditions consequently violate the First Amendment, the plurality first finds the "public forum" doctrine inapplicable, and then holds that the statutory provisions are constitutional. I agree with both determinations. But I reach the plurality's ultimate conclusion in a different way.

In ascertaining whether the statutory provisions are constitutional, I would apply a form of heightened scrutiny, examining the statutory requirements in question with special care. The Act directly restricts the public's receipt of information. And it does so through limitations imposed by outside bodies (here Congress) upon two critically important sources of information—the Internet as accessed via public libraries. See *Board of Ed., Island Trees Union Free School Dist. No. 26 v. Pico,* 457 U.S. 853, 915, 102 S.Ct. 2799 (1982) (REHNQUIST, J., dissenting)(describing public libraries as places "designed for freewheeling inquiry"). For that reason, we should not examine the statute's constitutionality as if it raised no special First Amendment concern—as if, like tax or economic regulation, the First Amendment demanded only a "rational basis" for imposing a restriction. Nor should we accept the Government's suggestion that a presumption in favor of the statute's constitutionality applies.

* * *

In [heightened scrutiny] cases the Court has asked whether the harm to speech-related interests is disproportionate in light of both the justifications and the potential alternatives. It has considered the legitimacy of the statute's objective, the extent to which the statute will tend to achieve that objective, whether there are other, less restrictive ways of achieving that objective, and ultimately whether the statute works speech-related harm that, in relation to that objective, is out of proportion. * * *

The Act's restrictions satisfy these constitutional demands. The Act seeks to restrict access to obscenity, child pornography, and, in respect to access by minors, material that is comparably harmful. These objectives are "legitimate," and indeed often "compelling." . . . As the District Court found, software filters "provide a relatively cheap and effective" means of furthering these goals. Due to present technological limitations, however, the software filters both "overblock," screening out some perfectly legitimate material, and "underblock," allowing some obscene material to escape detection by the filter. But no one has presented any clearly superior or better fitting alternatives.

At the same time, the Act contains an important exception that limits the speech-related harm that "overblocking" might cause. As the plurality points out, the Act allows libraries to permit any adult patron access to an "overblocked" Web site; the adult patron need only ask a librarian to unblock the specific Web site or, alternatively, ask the librarian, "Please disable the entire filter."

The Act does impose upon the patron the burden of making this request. But it is difficult to see how that burden (or any delay associated with compliance) could prove more onerous than traditional library practices associated with segregating library materials in, say, closed stacks, or with interlibrary lending practices that require patrons to make requests that are not anonymous and to wait while the librarian obtains the desired materials from elsewhere. Perhaps local library rules or practices could further restrict the ability of patrons to obtain "overblocked" Internet material.... But we are not now considering any such local practices. We here consider only a facial challenge to the Act itself.

Given the comparatively small burden that the Act imposes upon the library patron seeking legitimate Internet materials, I cannot say that any speech-related harm that the Act may cause is disproportionate when considered in relation to the Act's legitimate objectives. I therefore agree with the plurality that the statute does not violate the First Amendment, and I concur in the judgment.

JUSTICE STEVENS, dissenting.

"To fulfill their traditional missions, public libraries must have broad discretion to decide what material to provide their patrons." Accordingly, I agree with the plurality that it is neither inappropriate nor unconstitutional for a local library to experiment with filtering software as a means of curtailing children's access to Internet Web sites displaying sexually explicit images. I also agree with the plurality that the 7% of public libraries that decided to use such software on *all* of their Internet terminals in 2000 did not act unlawfully. Whether it is constitutional for the Congress of the United States to impose that requirement on the other 93%, however, raises a vastly different question. Rather than allowing local decisionmakers to tailor their responses to local problems, the Children's Internet Protection Act (CIPA) operates as a blunt nationwide restraint on adult access to "an enormous amount of valuable information" that individual librarians cannot possibly review. Most of that information is constitutionally protected speech. In my view, this restraint is unconstitutional.

NOTES

1. The Children's Internet Protection Act (CIPA) is one of four major pieces of federal legislation passed during the years that the Internet emerged as a central feature of daily life for most Americans. All were designed to "protect our children" in cyberspace, and all faced major challenges in court. In the end, the "decency provisions" of the Communications Decency Act (CDA) were struck down by the U.S. Supreme Court in Reno v. ACLU, 521 U.S. 844, 117 S.Ct. 2329 (1997), the Child Online Protection Act (COPA) was held up in the courts for many years (*cf.* Ashcroft v. ACLU, 542 U.S. 656, 124 S.Ct. 2783 (2004)), and portions of the Child Pornography Prevention Act (CPPA) were struck down in *Ashcroft v. The Free Speech Coalition*, 535 U.S. 234, 122 S.Ct. 1389 (2002). Only the CIPA appears to have withstood a legal challenge. But even so, in upholding the constitutionality of the CIPA, the justices could muster only a plurality opinion.

2. Note that CIPA also applied to public schools, but that school districts did not ultimately contest it.

3. Is *Loudoun* no longer good law after *U.S. v. ALA*, or are the two decisions reconcilable? Why?

Problem 48: Cleaning Up the Inconsistencies in Current Age Requirements

Many contend that our legal system has done a very poor job identifying appropriate age requirements. Indeed, inconsistencies abound in this area. Consider the following examples of circumstances where age requirements exist. In your view, what would be the ideal age requirement in each case? Alternatively, would you support one age requirement in every case? If so, what would that age be?

1. Able to enter into a legally binding contract
2. Capable of committing a crime
3. Capable of being found liable for negligence
4. Able to purchase real property
5. Able to purchase alcohol
6. Able to purchase tobacco
7. Able to purchase any magazine or video
8. Able to attend any film without being accompanied by an adult
9. Able to purchase weapons, firearms, etc.
10. Age of majority (where parents are no longer responsible)
11. Able to obtain a driver's license
12. Eligible to vote
13. Eligible to serve in the military
14. Age at which persons would no longer be required to attend school
15. Able to make own decisions as to which school/what type of school to attend
16. Able to make own decisions regarding course selection & content, including sex education
17. Able to make own decisions regarding religion/religious affiliation or lack thereof
18. Able to make own decisions regarding sexual and/or gender identity
19. Eligible to be suspended or expelled for being a sexual harasser
20. Age at which one's appearance in sexually explicit material is no longer child porn
21. Age of consent for sexual relations between consenting persons
22. Age of consent for abortions (without parental notification)
23. Able to marry
24. Eligible to be admitted to the bar
25. Able to access unfiltered Internet without adult permission or supervision

CHAPTER X

COPYRIGHT ISSUES IN EDUCATION

■ ■ ■

This chapter provides an overview of intellectual property issues in the area of copyright that have confronted educators and educational institutions. Intellectual property law is comprised primarily of copyright, trademark, and patent; and while issues arise in education settings under all three of these areas, copyright disputes are far-and-away the most prominent and the most complex. These disputes include, but are not limited to, litigation addressing fair use and disagreements over the applicability of traditional principles to Internet-related activities.

Controversies regarding intellectual property have emerged at all levels of the educational system, but it is at colleges and universities that the issues are particularly compelling. With most research taking place primarily in a digital environment, traditional questions regarding protection for academic work have become more intricate. In addition, major efforts by the entertainment industry to limit online copyright infringement have led to increased pressure on the higher education community to intervene, both legally and as a matter of a policy.

It is important to note, at the outset, the basic distinctions between copyright, trademark, and patent. Copyright law only protects the expression of ideas; a person's ideas themselves are protected by patent law. And copyright law does not generally protect names, titles, or short phrases. Such protection is relegated to trademark law, which has been designed to provide rights in distinctive words, phrases, logos, symbols, slogans and any other devices used to identify and distinguish products or services in the marketplace.

While copyright issues predominate in education, trademark questions involving the unauthorized use of university names and symbols have been widespread, and the changing nature of patent law has led to novel issues in recent years. Most trademark disputes are not education specific, and very few trademark cases are actually situated in education settings. Patent-related questions, however, are being raised with much greater frequency at the higher education level, and it is anticipated that this area of intellectual property will expand over time.[a]

---

a. In 1980, the federal government passed two laws allowing universities to patent ideas that resulted from government-funded research. *See* Bayh–Dole Act, 96 Pub. L. No. 517, 94 Stat. 3015

The chapter begins by providing an overview of basic copyright law principles. It then addresses copyright ownership disputes, the parameters of the fair use doctrine and its applicability, the "No Electronic Theft" Act, and the Digital Millennium Copyright Act. It concludes by highlighting ongoing issues regarding peer-to-peer file sharing.

A. BASIC PRINCIPLES OF U.S. COPYRIGHT LAW

U.S. copyright law grants certain exclusive rights to the creator of an original work that has been "fixed in a tangible medium of expression." As a general rule, the protection is automatic, and creators do not typically need to register a copyright or even indicate on the work itself that it has been "copyrighted" as of a particular date. The basic term of copyright protection for works completed on or after January 1, 1978 is "the life of the author plus 70 years."

Most copyright disputes are pursued in civil proceedings, but certain egregious copyright violations may also be considered crimes. Persons and entities who are not themselves infringers can be held responsible for violations of copyright law if they help facilitate the infringement under either a contributory copyright infringement theory or a vicarious liability theory.

The five exclusive rights of the copyright owner include (1) the reproduction right, (2) the modification right, (3) the distribution right, (4) the public performance right, and (5) the public display right. Each of these rights embody complex rules and various exceptions, but the basic principle is that a creator is granted a "monopoly" interest in his or her work. The creator may, of course, convey an interest in these rights to others. In addition, persons may be entitled to share these rights through implied licenses that may emerge over time.

(1980) (codified as amended in scattered sections of 35 U.S.C.); Stevenson–Wydler Technology Innovation Act of 1980, 96 Pub. L. No. 480, 94 Stat. 2311 (codified as amended in 15 U.S.C. §§ 3710–3714). That same year, the Supreme Court stated that "anything under the sun that is made by man" is patentable. *Diamond v. Chakrabarty*, 447 U.S. 303, 309, 100 S.Ct. 2204 (1980).

University technology transfer offices sprang into existence to take advantage of this newfound source of possible wealth. But, while universities were able to negotiate profitable deals, there were costs as well. The requirement that patents not be issued for ideas that have been "described in a printed publication ... more than one year prior to the date of the application for patent" (35 U.S.C.A. § 102(b) (2005)) has resulted in a trend of less peer review and more secrecy among university scientists. Consequently, many ideas are not shared until they are in their final stages and virtually ready for publication. This has several deleterious effects, influencing everything from the overall spirit of collegiality and collaboration to the requirement of "publish or perish." For a fuller discussion of the problems, see Jeremy M. Grushcow, *Measuring Secrecy: A Cost of the Patent System Revealed*, 33 J. LEGAL STUD. 59 (2004).

Additionally, with "anything under the sun" being patentable, research in new and exciting fields is stagnating under the weight of a "patent anticommons." For example, because the law requires permission to use a patented idea even for experimental or research purposes (as long as the proposed research has any possible commercial implication), university scientists may find it increasingly difficult to conduct any nanotechnology-related research at all. For a greater overview of the problem of a patent anticommons, see Terry Tullis, *Application of the Government License Defense to Federally Funded Nanotechnology Research: The Case for a Limited Patent Compulsory Licensing Regime*, 53 UCLA L. REV. 279 (2005).

Several explicit exceptions to the five exclusive rights have been included in the specific text of the law. The First Sale Doctrine, for example, allows a person who has legally obtained a copy to sell or dispose of it without authorization from the copyright holder. Under section 109 of the U.S. Copyright Act, once a copy of a work is sold, the owner has no further right to control the distribution of *that particular copy*. Thus an individual, a library, or another entity is free to give away, lend, rent, or sell its copies of books and many other materials. But the distribution of "phonorecords" and computer programs is subject to certain detailed restrictions.

There is no copyright protection for works that are in the public domain. Some works, such as government documents, are automatically in the public domain. Others move into the public domain when their term of protection has expired. As a general rule, for example, the basic texts of the bible and Shakespeare are both in the public domain. Works in the public domain may be freely copied and distributed by anyone at any time.

In addition, even if a work is protected under one or more of the five exclusive rights, it may be copied, modified, distributed, performed, or displayed without permission if the fair use doctrine applies. Particularly with the advent of the Internet, many believe that the fair use doctrine has become the single most important set of legal principles under U.S. copyright law. This doctrine exemplifies the balance of interests contemplated by Article I, Section 8, Clause 8 of the U.S. Constitution, which states that Congress shall have the power

> To promote the Progress of Science and useful Arts, by securing for limited Times to Authors and Inventors the exclusive Right to their respective Writings and Discoveries.

Indeed, the U.S. Supreme Court has repeatedly emphasized that the copyright protections granted to creators constitute a "monopoly privilege," and it has explained that this privilege is "neither unlimited nor primarily designed to provide a special private benefit." It is, the Court determined, "a means by which an important public purpose may be achieved." Thus, unlike the laws of many other countries, copyright law in the U.S. is not—as many people incorrectly believe—an absolute protection of the creator's work. In fact, the law "makes reward to the owner a secondary consideration," and the "granting of such exclusive rights" to the creator has been viewed as conferring "a benefit upon the public that outweighs the evils of the temporary monopoly." *Sony Corp. v. Universal City Studios, Inc.*, 464 U.S. 417, 429, 104 S.Ct. 774 (1984) (quoting H.R. Rep. No. 2222, 60th Cong., 2d Sess. 7 (1909)).

Copyright law thus embodies a tension between the interests of an individual creator and the interests of the public as a whole. Creators may have individual property rights in their works, but only for the ultimate purpose of benefiting the public by encouraging the creation of more works. And these principles are particularly compelling in an education setting, since the entire enterprise of education is geared toward the public good.

The following sections highlight the range of copyright disputes that arise in such settings.

B. OWNERSHIP OF COPYRIGHT AND RELATED MATTERS

WILLIAMS v. WEISSER

273 Cal.App.2d 726, 78 Cal.Rptr. 542 (1969)

KAUS, P. J.

Defendant Weisser, who does business under the fictitious name of Class Notes, appeals from a judgment which enjoins him from copying, publishing and selling notes of lectures delivered by plaintiff in his capacity as an Assistant Professor of Anthropology at the University of California at Los Angeles ("UCLA"). The judgment also awards plaintiff $1,000 in compensatory and $500 in exemplary damages.

A joint pretrial statement described the nature of the case as follows: "Plaintiff is Assistant Professor at UCLA in the Anthropology Department. Defendant does business in Westwood, California as Class Notes selling outlines for various courses given at UCLA. In 1965, defendant paid Karen Allen, a UCLA student, to attend plaintiff's class in Anthropology 1 to take notes from the lectures, and to type up the notes. Allen delivered the typed notes to defendant and defendant placed a copyright notice thereon in defendant's name, reproduced the typed notes, and sold and offered them for sale. Plaintiff objected. Defendant did not cease these activities until served with summons, complaint and temporary restraining order. Plaintiff seeks a permanent injunction, general damages, and punitive damages."

At the pretrial it was agreed that: "Defendant has used plaintiff's name in selling the publications here in question."

The judgment in plaintiff's favor was based on two grounds: 1. defendant infringed plaintiff's common law copyright in his lectures; and 2. defendant invaded plaintiff's privacy by the use of plaintiff's name.

* * *

1. The product of the mind in which the plaintiff claims a copyright consists of the extensive notes which he had compiled before the beginning of the course, together with the oral expression at the time of delivery of the lectures, based on the notes, which delivery included charts and diagrams placed on the classroom blackboard. This is, therefore, not a case where the concrete expression of the "composition" consists solely of an intangible oral presentation. As far as this litigation is concerned, the chief importance of the oral presentation is that it provided defendant

with access to plaintiff's work and with an argument that there had been a divestive publication.

* * *

Ownership of Copyright

Plaintiff became employed by UCLA starting in July 1965. Defendant's relations with the university started in 1948 when he began to publish and sell to students what purported to be notes of various courses. In 1963 defendant and the university authorities agreed on certain ground rules as a condition to advertising in the Daily Bruin, the student newspaper. Friction arose between defendant and the administration. The matter culminated in a memorandum dated November 19, 1964, addressed to all members of the faculty.

* * *

We are * * * convinced that in the absence of evidence the teacher, rather than the university, owns the common law copyright to his lectures. [T]here was no evidence that plaintiff had assigned his copyright to the university[.] * * *

Defendant claims that the opposite is the law. His sole statutory authority is section 2860 of the Labor Code which reads as follows: "Everything which an employee acquires by virtue of his employment, except the compensation which is due to him from his employer, belongs to the employer, whether acquired lawfully or unlawfully, or during or after the expiration of the term of his employment."

It is obvious that a literal application of that section does not cover the present situation. The code speaks of things which the employee "acquires," not matters which he creates. * * * [And] the section has been applied principally, though not exclusively, to unfair competition carried on by former employees with the use of trade secrets and the like. Even so it has been narrowly employed. We do not believe it applies here.

Defendant also claims that plaintiff is in the position of an employee for hire whose employment calls for the creation of a copyrightable work or, perhaps, of an independent contractor who has been so commissioned. In such cases it is usually presumed that, unless a different intention is shown, the employer or commissioner is the owner of the copyright.

This contention calls for some understanding of the purpose for which a university hires a professor and what rights it may reasonably expect to retain after the services have been rendered. A university's obligation to its students is to make the subject matter covered by a course available for study by various methods, including classroom presentation. It is not obligated to present the subject by means of any particular expression. As far as the teacher is concerned, neither the record in this case nor any custom known to us suggests that the university can prescribe his way of expressing the ideas he puts before his students. Yet expression is what this lawsuit is all about. No reason has been suggested why a university would want to retain the ownership in a professor's expression. Such retention would be useless except possibly for making a little profit from a publication and for making it difficult for the teacher to give the same lectures, should he change jobs.

Indeed the undesirable consequences which would follow from a holding that a university owns the copyright to the lectures of its professors are such as to compel a holding that it does not. Professors are a peripatetic lot, moving from campus to campus. The courses they teach begin to take shape at one institution and are developed and embellished at another. That, as a matter of fact, was the case here. Plaintiff testified that the notes on which his lectures were based were derived from a similar course which he had given at another university. If defendant is correct, there must be some rights of that school which were infringed at UCLA. Further, should plaintiff leave UCLA and give a substantially similar course at his next post, UCLA would be able to enjoin him from using the material which, according to defendant, it owns.

No one but defendant, an outsider as far as the relationship between plaintiff and UCLA is concerned, suggests that such a state of the law is desirable.

Another strange consequence which would follow from equating university lectures with other products of the mind which an employee is hired to create, is, that in order to determine just what it is getting, the university would have to find out the precise extent to which a professor's lectures have taken concrete shape when he first comes to work. Not even defendant suggests that a contract for employment implies an assignment to the university of any common law copyright which the professor already owns.

The many cases cited by defendant for the general rule probably reach desirable results that are in accord with common understanding in their respective areas, but a rule of law developed in one context should not be blindly applied in another where it violates the intention of the parties and creates undesirable consequences. (8) University lectures are *sui generis*. Absent compulsion by statute or precedent, they should not be blindly thrown into the same legal hopper with valve designs, motion picture background music, commercial drawings, mosaics designed for the Congressional Library in Washington, D.C., high school murals, song stylings, radio scripts, commercial jingles, lists of courses taught by a correspondence school, and treatises on the use of ozone or on larceny and homicide.

* * *

[N]o authority supports the argument that the copyright to plaintiff's notes is in the university. The indications from the authorities are the other way and so is common sense.

* * *

Taking the evidence as a whole, the trial court was amply justified in concluding that defendant was not an innocent layman, caught in the complexities of the law, but a businessman who, for personal profit, was determined to pursue a certain course of action even if it meant riding roughshod over the rights of others.

The judgment is affirmed.

WEINSTEIN v. UNIVERSITY OF ILLINOIS

811 F.2d 1091 (7th Cir. 1987)

EASTERBROOK, CIRCUIT JUDGE.

[This dispute] ... is about the order in which the names of an article's authors will be listed. The article is D.J. Belsheim, R.A. Hutchinson & M.M. Weinstein, *The Design and Evaluation of a Clinical Clerkship for Hospital Pharmacists,* 50 Am. J. Pharmaceutical Education 139–45 (1986). Weinstein believes that it should have been published as M.M. Weinstein, D.J. Belsheim & R.A. Hutchinson, *Etc.* According to Weinstein, the publication of the article with the names in the wrong order violated the due process clause of the fourteenth amendment.

I

Weinstein was an Assistant Professor of Pharmacy Administration in the College of Pharmacy of the University of Illinois at Chicago. According to his complaint, from which we take these facts, he proposed a clinical program for practicing pharmacists, who would operate for two weeks in a "clerkship" under the guidance of professors. * * * Although Weinstein asserts that he supplied most of the ideas and did most of the work, he concedes that the three [professors] agreed to write jointly on the results. Weinstein believes that he had an agreement with Belsheim under which Weinstein would be the first-listed author of a paper describing the clerkship and the data obtained from questionnaires, while Belsheim would be lead author of a paper to be called "Teaching Problem Solving in a Post–Graduate Clinical Pharmacy Clerkship."

In January 1984 Weinstein gave Belsheim a draft. Belsheim was dissatisfied. The two disagreed about the subjects to be covered and the conclusions to be drawn. By January 1985 Weinstein had completed another draft. One day he found the draft in Belsheim's wastebasket, with many editorial marks and sections snipped out. Belsheim denied doing more than making "notes" but shortly produced a new draft, revising both the text and the order of listing of authors. Weinstein did not like either the new order or the new text. * * * [O]n July 19, 1985, Belsheim submitted the article to the American Journal of Pharmaceutical Education. It was published in the Journal's Summer 1986 issue. * * * [Weinstein's lawsuit contends that the others] mutilated his work and stole the credit, denying him due process of law. * * *

Weinstein says that the listing of names is no small matter. He is seeking a topic on which to write a dissertation and believes that the clerkship program would have been suitable, but that Belsheim's being listed as first author precludes it. * * * He also believes that because the principal author is listed first, the appearance of his name in third place will diminish his accomplishments in the eyes of other professors—a significant problem because, as we discuss below, he is looking for a job. His attorney adds the point that academic departments sometimes use the number of citations to a scholar's work as one indication of the importance of that work in the profession. The principal citation services list articles by first author only, so that any citations to the Belsheim, Hutchinson & Weinstein article would be collected under Belsheim's name.

We shall assume, given the posture of the case, that Weinstein could make good his claims of injury-in-fact. We shall also assume that the acts of Belsheim, an employee of a state university, were taken "under color of state law".... None of these assumptions assists Weinstein unless the acts to which he objects have deprived him of "property", for the due process clause applies only to deprivations of "life, liberty or property", and Weinstein does not invoke the first two.

II

The district court concluded that the article was the University's property rather than Weinstein's because it was a "work for hire". The copyright law gives an employer the full rights in an employee's "work for hire", 17 U.S.C. § 201(b), unless a contract provides otherwise. The statute is general enough to make every academic article a "work for hire" and therefore vest exclusive control in universities rather than scholars. The University of Illinois, like many other academic institutions, responded to the 1978 revision of the copyright laws by adopting a policy defining "work for hire" for purposes of its employees, including its professors. According to the policy, which is a part of each professor's contract with the University, a professor retains the copyright unless the work falls into one of three categories:

(1) The terms of a University agreement with an external party require the University to hold or transfer ownership in the copyrightable work, or

(2) Works expressly commissioned in writing by the University, or

(3) Works created as a specific requirement of employment or as an assigned University duty. Such requirements or duties may be contained in a job description or an employment agreement which designates the content of the employee's University work. If such requirements or duties are not so specified, such works will be those for which the topic or content is determined by the author's employment duties and/or which are prepared at the University's

     instance and expense, that is, when the University is the motivating factor in the preparation of the work.

The district court held that Weinstein's work is covered by paragraph (3) because the University funded the clerkship program and because, as a clinical professor, Weinstein was required to conduct and write about clinical programs.

This interpretation of the University's policy collides with the role of the three categories as exceptions to a rule that faculty members own the copyrights in their academic work. A university "requires" all of its scholars to write. Its demands—especially the demands of departments deciding whether to award tenure—will be "the motivating factor in the preparation of" many a scholarly work. When Dean Manasse told Weinstein to publish or perish, he was not simultaneously claiming for the University a copyright on the ground that the work had become a "requirement or duty" within the meaning of paragraph (3). The University concedes in this court that a professor of mathematics who proves a new theorem in the course of his employment will own the copyright to his article containing that proof. This has been the academic tradition since copyright law began, a tradition the University's policy purports to retain. The tradition covers scholarly articles and other intellectual property. When Saul Bellow, a professor at the University of Chicago, writes a novel, he may keep the royalties.

The University's copyright policy reads more naturally when applied to administrative duties. Perhaps the University forms a committee to study the appropriate use of small computers and conscripts professors as members. The committee may publish a report, in which the University will claim copyright. We do not say that a broader reading is impossible, but such a reading should be established by evidence about the deliberations underlying the policy and the course of practice—material that is neither in the record nor an appropriate basis on which to dismiss the complaint for failure to state a claim. We would be surprised if any member of the faculty of the College of Pharmacy treats his academic work as the property of the University. Dean Manasse, for example, has not submitted an affidavit stating that the faculty regularly obtains consent (or a transfer of copyright) from the University before publishing articles. The record does not contain the contracts between the American Journal of Pharmaceutical Education and Professors Belsheim, Hutchinson, and Weinstein, but we venture a guess that each represented to the Journal that he owned the copyright and was empowered to transfer the copyright to the Journal. (The article as published carries the Journal's copyright notice rather than that of the authors or the University of Illinois.) Dean Manasse told Weinstein to *publish* the article, not to ask the University for permission to publish—permission that would have been essential if the University owned the copyright.

If the members of the University's faculty own the copyright interest in their scholarly articles, Weinstein has some "property". But did the

University "deprive" him of this property without "due process"? Both "deprivation" and "due process" are problematic. If the University does not own the copyright, the article is covered by 17 U.S.C. § 201(a), which states that "[t]he authors of a joint work are coowners of copyright in the work." This provision applies to all works of joint authorship, and Weinstein concedes that the article in question is (and was supposed to be) a jointly written work. Each coowner of a copyright may revise the work (that is, make a derivative work) and publish the original or the revision. So far as copyright law is concerned, Belsheim was entitled to do what he did. Belsheim is answerable to Weinstein for Weinstein's share of any royalties, but Weinstein does not claim that Belsheim made off with the profits. Belsheim did not diminish any of Weinstein's property rights; neither did the University. The University did not make Belsheim's acts possible. It therefore did not "deprive" Weinstein of any property interest. Indeed it could not have done so. No amount of academic deliberation or hearings before the College Executive Committee could have diminished Belsheim's entitlement to revise the article. Perhaps the University could have threatened Belsheim with sanctions, such as a duty to teach boring subjects, to induce him to desist, but the due process clause does not require a state to impose penalties on those who exercise legal entitlements.

Perhaps Weinstein, Belsheim, and the University could have agreed by contract to give the University the power to make binding decisions concerning disputes over academic papers, but Weinstein does not identify any such agreement. The University therefore had no more power over this manuscript than it did over the title to Belsheim's car or Weinstein's family heirlooms. The potential use of contracts does identify the essence of this dispute, however. It is really a contract dispute between Belsheim and Weinstein about their contributions to the article. Authors may make contracts as they please about their endeavors. These derive their force from private agreement, and disputes about them arise under state law rather than copyright law.

The courts of Illinois are open to Weinstein if he claims that the state "deprived" him of any rights established by contract with Belsheim. Contractual rights are a kind of property. * * *

III

If war is the extension of diplomacy by other means, this suit—like other litigation a form of warfare—is the extension of academic politics by other means. Weinstein and Belsheim were unable to compromise, and Weinstein has dragged his fellow scholars and the University into the contest. His willingness, even eagerness, to sue his colleagues may be explained by the fact that the University has fired him.

　　　* * *

Weinstein is litigating a defunct claim. He hasn't a chance; he never did; but he has put the University to some expense. This is frivolous litigation. * * * The defendants are entitled to attorneys' fees for the time necessary to reply to Weinstein's attack in this court on his discharge. They have 15 days to file an appropriate statement with the clerk of this court.

AFFIRMED.

CUDAHY, CIRCUIT JUDGE, concurring in part and dissenting in part.

I agree that Weinstein must lose in all branches of his case, although I believe that the majority inaccurately diminishes Weinstein's complaint by saying that it involves only the order of authors' names. Weinstein also alleges that the procedure employed by the university to evaluate him for a tenured position denied him due process, that the publication of his article in a revised form denied him his property interest in the writing without due process and that the university violated his first amendment rights. Although Weinstein does not win on any of these claims, his suit is not as meritless as the majority's brief description of the dispute implies.

* * *

SHAUL v. CHERRY VALLEY–SPRINGFIELD CENT. SCH. DIST.

218 F.Supp.2d 266 (N.D.N.Y. 2002)

HURD, DISTRICT JUDGE.

I. *INTRODUCTION*

On May 8, 2000, plaintiff William R. Shaul ("Shaul" or "plaintiff") commenced the instant action, pursuant to 42 U.S.C. § 1983 alleging that the defendants violated his Fourth Amendment rights. * * *

II. *FACTS*

Shaul was and is a tenured teacher at the School District, since 1969. In a 1990 administrative hearing, he was found guilty of having an inappropriate relationship with a female student. In November of 1998, as a result of an investigation performed by the School District into alleged improprieties toward another young female student, plaintiff was suspended with pay on January 15, 1999 to March 10, 2000, and ordered to remain off school property.

* * *

Plaintiff * * * claims that Principals Strange and Culbert conducted an unconstitutional search of his assigned room, and during this search unconstitutionally seized property belonging to him in violation of his Fourth Amendment rights. * * *

As to the plaintiff's illegal search claim, the defendants assert that Shaul did not have an expectation of privacy in anything within his assigned classroom and accordingly there was no illegal search. With respect to the illegal seizure claim, the defendants contend that plaintiff abandoned his property, and in the alternative, the School District owned the educational materials found in plaintiff's former classroom under the work for hire doctrine in copyright law.

* * *

2. *The Illegal Seizure Claim*

* * *

The defendants' second argument claims that the tests, quizzes, and other educational material found in plaintiff's former classroom belong to the School District under the work for hire doctrine found in the Copyright Act of 1976. Copyright ownership usually "vests initially in the author or authors of the work." However, "work made for hire" is defined as "a work prepared by an employee within the scope of his or her employment."[2] "In the case of work made for hire, the employer ... is considered the author ... and, unless the parties have expressly agreed otherwise in a written instrument signed by them, owns all the rights comprised in the copyright."

In determining whether copyrighted work is work made for hire, the hired party that created the work has to be an employee under the common law of agency. The Supreme Court has identified thirteen factors to consider in determining if one is an employee.[3] It is well established that tenured public teachers are employees who have a constitutionally protected property interest in their employment. Accordingly, the work made for hire doctrine applies in this case to Shaul's tests, quizzes, and other educational materials produced in furtherance of his employment duties as a public teacher.

Plaintiff's illegal seizure claim fails. A seizure of property "occurs when 'there is some meaningful interference with an individual's possessory interests in that property.'" Shaul does not have a possessory

---

2. There is a second definition under "work made for hire" stating that the author retains ownership when,

> a work [is] specially ordered or commissioned for use as a contribution to a collective work, as a part of a motion picture or other audiovisual work, as a translation, as a supplementary work, as a compilation, as an instructional text, as a test, as answer material for a test, or as an atlas, if the parties expressly agree in a written instrument signed by them that the work shall be considered a work made for hire.

17 U.S.C.A. § 101 (West Supp. 2002). This second definition is not applicable to this case because there has been no express written agreement between the parties designating plaintiff's work product as work made for hire and plaintiff's work was not specially ordered or commissioned.

3. The factors are,

> the hiring party's right to control the manner and means by which the product is accomplished ... the skill required; the source of the instrumentalities and tools; the location of the work; the duration of the relationship between the parties; whether the hiring party has the right to assign additional projects to the hired party; the extent of the hired party's discretion over when and how long to work; the method of payment; the hired party's role in hiring and paying assistants; whether the work is part of the regular business of the hiring party; whether the hiring party is in business; the provision of employee benefits; and the tax treatment of the hired party.

interest in the educational materials he used to teach his students, which makes up the bulk of his illegal seizure complaint.

* * *

Accordingly, the defendants are entitled to summary judgment as to plaintiff's first claim, because no reasonable jury could return a verdict for the plaintiff.

* * *

IV. *CONCLUSION*

There is no genuine issue for trial on the issue of an illegal search and seizure of the contents in plaintiff's former classroom. Thus, no award for punitive damages can be granted. Shaul's cause of action against the municipality fails to state a claim.

NOTE

1.   In *Foraste v. Brown University,* 290 F.Supp.2d 234 (D. R.I. 2003), the Court noted—in finding against the plaintiff (a former photographer for the university)—that:

> the traditional "faculty exception" to the work made for hire doctrine, "whereby academic writing [is] presumed not to be work made for hire," is inapposite here. That exception is meant to protect the "scholarly articles and other intellectual property" created by university professors while in the employ of an academic institution. *Weinstein v. University of Illinois,* 811 F.2d 1091, 1094 (7th Cir.1987). Various equitable considerations often mandate that a scholar retain the copyrights in his work, notwithstanding the work made for hire doctrine. *See, e.g., id.* at 1094–95 (for example, the requirement that a scholar "publish or perish"). These equitable policy concepts do not apply here because Foraste was not working under an implicit or explicit "publish or perish" directive, and because he was usually directed by Brown officials to photograph specific scenes.

C.   **THE PARAMETERS OF THE FAIR USE DOCTRINE**

The language of the fair use doctrine can be found in Section 107 of the U.S. Copyright Act. The statute begins with an introduction, which establishes the scope of the doctrine and has set the tone for its application by courts of law. Indeed, many judges have quoted from this introduction when faced with difficult questions of interpretation in this area:

> the fair use of a copyrighted work ... for purposes such as criticism, comment, news reporting, teaching (including multiple copies for classroom use), scholarship, or research, is not an infringement of copyright.

While the use of copyrighted materials without permission for these specified purposes is not automatically a "fair use," it is clear from numerous subsequent court decisions as well as from the discussions in Congress that copying for purposes of criticism, comment, news reporting, teaching, scholarship, or research has achieved favored status under the law.

No matter what the use, however, the four "statutory factors" described in Section 107 must be considered when an alleged copyright infringer raises the fair use defense:

> In determining whether the use made of a work in any particular case is a fair use the factors to be considered shall include—
>
> (1) the purpose and character of the use, including whether such use is of a commercial nature or is for nonprofit educational purposes;
>
> (2) the nature of the copyrighted work;
>
> (3) the amount and substantiality of the portion used in relation to the copyrighted work as a whole; and
>
> (4) the effect of the use upon the potential market for or value of the copyrighted work.

No one formula exists for weighing the four factors. Thus it may be the case that only one of the factors may be decided in favor of a defendant, but that this one factor—under the circumstances—may be sufficient to decide the case ... even if the other three factors tilt the other way.

In addition, it must be noted that a court's analysis is not limited to the four statutory factors, but can also include additional factors relevant to the particular case.

Fair use disputes engender great emotion. Copyright owners, for example, chafe at the possibility that their work can be freely copied, at times, without permission. In the education community, professors may become very upset when persons in charge of copying in their department tell them that their copy requests cannot be fulfilled because of written or unwritten policy guidelines. And K–12 teachers can become incredulous when they are told that they may not show an educational video that they themselves may have recorded at home.

Online issues have brought the debate over the parameters of fair use to the forefront. Copyright disputes are consistently viewed as reflecting the most unique aspects of cyberspace ... including speed, scale, and the ability to make perfect digital copies. The PC is a versatile copy machine, and so much of what the typical online user does from day to day constitutes copying under traditional legal doctrine. A new reality has thus emerged that simply did not exist before. Although there were copyright enforcement problems in the offline world before the 1990s, and although many parallels to the current situation can be discerned in some of the issues raised by the introduction of xerox machines, audiotaping, and videotaping, the speed, scale, and perfect quality of the digital reproduction has generated a set of circumstances that can truly be described as unique. Further complicating the debate is the extent to which some form of reproduction, distribution, or modification of copyrighted material actually occurs online from day-to-day.

The dramatic power and easy availability of digital technology, combined with the libertarian online culture of the early and mid 1990s that encouraged the widespread sharing of information, led to intensive efforts by content owners to strengthen copyright laws at the federal level. Three major statutes were passed by Congress and signed into law as a result of these efforts: the "No Electronic Theft" (NET) Act, the Digital Millennium Copyright Act (DMCA), and the Sonny Bono Copyright Term Extension Act. Many who opposed these statutes argued that the balance of interests contemplated by the U.S. Constitution had been disrupted by the changes. But perhaps the most vehement criticism was reserved for the drafters of the DMCA, which arguably represented a significant departure from federal copyright law in that it foreclosed the possibility of a fair use defense for a violation of its terms. Indeed, commentators and activists continue to raise questions regarding the future of the fair use doctrine, focusing in particular on education.

Consider the opinions in the diverse range of fair use cases that follow. What consistent principles can be discerned that would be applicable to future education-related disputes in this context?

MARCUS v. ROWLEY

695 F.2d 1171 (9th Cir. 1983)

PFAELZER, DISTRICT JUDGE:

This is an appeal from a dismissal on the merits of a suit for copyright infringement brought by a public school teacher who is the owner of a registered copyright to a booklet on cake decorating. The defendant, also a public school teacher, incorporated a substantial portion of the copyrighted work into a booklet which she prepared for use in her classes. * * * The district court * * * dismissed the action on the merits on the ground that defendant's copying of plaintiff's material constituted fair use. We reverse.

I. FACTUAL BACKGROUND

From September 1972 to June 1974, plaintiff, Eloise Toby Marcus was employed by the defendant, San Diego Unified School District ("District") as a teacher of home economics. Plaintiff resigned from the District's employ in 1974 and taught adult education classes intermittently from 1975 to 1980. Shortly after leaving her teaching position with the District, she wrote a booklet entitled "Cake Decorating Made Easy". Plaintiff's booklet consisted of thirty-five pages of which twenty-nine were her original creation. The remaining six pages consisted of material incorporated with the permission of the authors of the materials for which the authors were given appropriate credit.

Plaintiff properly registered the copyright for "Cake Decorating Made Easy" with the Register of Copyrights, and one hundred and twenty-five copies of the booklet were published in the spring of 1975. All of the copies of plaintiff's booklet contained a designation of copyright as evidenced by an encircled "c" followed by "1975 Eloise Marcus." This designation appeared on the table of contents page, the first page, and the page following the cover-title sheet.

Plaintiff sold all but six of the copies of her booklet for $2.00 each to the students in the adult education cake decorating classes which she taught. Plaintiff's profit was $1.00 on the sale of each booklet. Copies of plaintiff's booklet were never distributed to or sold by a bookstore or other outlet. Plaintiff never authorized anyone to copy or reproduce her booklet or any part of it.

Defendant, Shirley Rowley ("Rowley"), teaches food service career classes in the District. In the spring of 1975, she enrolled in one of plaintiff's cake decorating classes and purchased a copy of plaintiff's book. During the following summer, Rowley prepared a booklet entitled "Cake Decorating Learning Activity Package" ("LAP") for use in her food service career classes. The LAP consisted of twenty-four pages and was designed to be used by students who wished to study an optional section of her course devoted to cake decorating. Defendant had fifteen copies of the LAP made and put them in a file so that they would be available to her students. She used the LAP during the 1975, 1976 and 1977 school years. The trial court found that sixty of Rowley's two hundred twenty-five students elected to study cake decorating. The trial court further found that neither Rowley nor the District derived any profit from the LAP.

Rowley admits copying eleven of the twenty-four pages in her LAP from plaintiff's booklet. The eleven pages copied consisted of the supply list, icing recipes, three sheets dealing with color flow and mixing colors, four pages showing how to make and use a decorating bag, and two pages explaining how to make flowers and sugar molds. * * * Twenty pages of plaintiff's booklet were not included in Rowley's LAP. Rowley did not give plaintiff credit for the eleven pages she copied, nor did she acknowledge plaintiff as the owner of a copyright with respect to those pages.

Plaintiff learned of Rowley's LAP in the summer of 1977 when a student in plaintiff's adult education class refused to purchase plaintiff's book. The student's son had obtained a copy of the LAP from Rowley's class. After examining Rowley's booklet, the student accused plaintiff of plagiarizing Rowley's work. Following these events, plaintiff made a claim of infringement against Rowley and the District. Both denied infringement and the plaintiff filed suit.

* * * The trial court * * * dismissed the case on the merits. The ground for dismissal was that the defendant's copying of the plaintiff's material for nonprofit educational purposes constituted fair use.

II. THE APPLICABLE COPYRIGHT ACT

* * * [T]he outcome of this case * * * turns entirely on the application of the doctrine of fair use[,] * * * a judicially articulated concept until Congress recognized its importance and incorporated it into section 107 of the revised Copyright Act. The legislative history states that "section 107 is a restatement of this judicially developed doctrine—it neither enlarges nor changes it in any way." Section 107 codifies the factors developed under the prior case law.

III. THE DOCTRINE OF FAIR USE

Fair use is most often defined as the "privilege in others than the owner of a copyright to use the copyrighted material in a reasonable manner without his consent, notwithstanding the monopoly granted to the owner...." This doctrine was judicially created to "avoid rigid application" of the copyright laws when that application would defeat the law's original purpose which was the fostering of creativity. Because the doctrine was developed with a view to the introduction of flexibility and equity into the copyright laws, it has evolved in such a manner as to elude precise definition. It is clear, however, that "assuming the applicable criteria are met, fair use can extend to the reproduction of copyrighted material for purposes of classroom teaching." * * *

A. *The Purpose and Character of the Use*

The first factor to be considered in determining the applicability of the doctrine of fair use is the purpose and character of the use, and specifically whether the use is of a commercial nature or is for a nonprofit educational purpose. It is uncontroverted that Rowley's use of the LAP was for a nonprofit educational purpose and that the LAP was distributed to students at no charge. These facts necessarily weigh in Rowley's favor. Nevertheless, a finding of a nonprofit educational purpose does not automatically compel a finding of fair use.

This court has often articulated the principle that a finding that the alleged infringers copied the material to use it for the same intrinsic purpose for which the copyright owner intended it to be used is strong indicia of no fair use.

In this case, both plaintiff's and defendant's booklets were prepared for the purpose of teaching cake decorating, a fact which weighs against a finding of fair use.[6]

Because fair use presupposes that the defendant has acted fairly and in good faith, the propriety of the defendant's conduct should also be weighed in analyzing the purpose and character of the use.

---

6. Of course, this finding is not decisive on the issue of fair use. The fact that both works were used for the same intrinsic purpose carries less weight in a case such as this, because plainly the doctrine of fair use permits some copying of educational materials for classroom use. The critical issues here are the nature and the extent of defendant's copying.

Here, there was no attempt by defendant to secure plaintiff's permission to copy the contents of her booklet or to credit plaintiff for the use of her material even though Rowley's copying was for the most part verbatim.[8] Rowley's conduct in this respect weighs against a finding of fair use.

B.   *The Nature of the Copyrighted Work*

The second factor to be weighed is the nature of the copyrighted work. * * * [T]his court stated that analysis of this factor requires consideration of whether the work is "informational" or "creative." The court stated that "the scope of fair use is greater when informational type works, as opposed to more creative products, are involved." Here, plaintiff's booklet involved both informational and creative aspects. Some pages in her booklet undoubtedly contained information available in other cake decorating books or in recipe books. Other parts of her booklet contained creative hints she derived from her own experiences or ideas; certainly the manner in which plaintiff assembled her book represented a creative expression. Thus, on balance, it does not appear that analysis of this factor is of any real assistance in reaching a conclusion as to applicability of fair use.

C.   *The Amount and Substantiality of the Portion Used*

The third factor to be considered is the amount and substantiality of the portion used in relation to the copyrighted work as a whole. Any conclusion with respect to this factor requires analysis of both the quantity and quality of the alleged infringement.

With respect to this factor, this court has long maintained the view that wholesale copying of copyrighted material precludes application of the fair use doctrine. Other courts are in accord with this principle, and two courts have specifically addressed the issue in relation to copying for educational purposes.

Wihtol v. Crow involved alleged infringement by the defendant, a school teacher and church choir director, of a hymn entitled "My God and I". The defendant Crow incorporated plaintiff's original piano and solo voice composition into an arrangement for his choirs. He made forty-eight copies of his arrangement and had the piece performed on two occasions: once by the high school choir at the school chapel, and once in church on Sunday. The music was identified as "arranged Nelson E. Crow", but no reference was made to plaintiff as the original composer. The Eighth Circuit affirmed the trial court's finding that Crow had infringed plaintiff's copyright and in addressing the issue of whether Crow's copying constituted fair use, the court stated that "whatever may be the breadth of the doctrine of 'fair use', it is not conceivable to us that the copying of all, or substantially all, of a copyrighted song can be held to be a 'fair use' merely because the infringer had no intent to infringe."

---

8. Attribution is, of course, but one factor. Moreover, acknowledgment of a source does not excuse infringement when the other factors listed in section 107 are present.

The court in *Encyclopaedia Britannica Educational Corp. v. Crooks* also considered the issue of fair use in the educational context. In that case, three corporations which produced educational motion picture films sued the Board of Cooperative Educational Services of Erie County ("BOCES") for videotaping several of plaintiffs' copyrighted films without permission. BOCES distributed the copied films to schools for delayed student viewing. Defendants' fair use defense was rejected on the ground that although defendants were involved in non-commercial copying to promote science and education, the taping of entire copyrighted films was too excessive for the fair use defense to apply.[9]

In this case, almost 50% of defendant's LAP was a verbatim copy of plaintiff's booklet and that 50% contained virtually all of the substance of defendant's book. Defendant copied the explanations of how to make the decorating bag, how to mix colors, and how to make various decorations as well as the icing recipes. In fact, the only substantive pages of plaintiff's booklet which defendant did not put into her booklet were hints on how to ice a cake and an explanation of how to make leaves. Defendant argues that it was fair to copy plaintiff's booklet because the booklet contained only facts which were in the public domain. Even if it were true that plaintiff's book contained only facts, this argument fails because defendant engaged in virtually verbatim copying. Defendant's LAP could have been a photocopy of plaintiff's booklet but for the fact that defendant retyped plaintiff's material. This case presents a clear example of both substantial quantitative and qualitative copying.

D. *The Effect of the Use Upon the Potential Market for or Value of the Copyrighted Work*

The final factor to be considered with respect to the fair use defense is the effect which the allegedly infringing use had on the potential market for or value of the copyrighted work. * * * Here, despite the fact that at least one of plaintiff's students refused to purchase her booklet as a result of defendant's copying, the trial court found that it was unable to conclude that the defendant's copying had any effect on the market for the plaintiff's booklet. Even assuming that the trial court's finding was not erroneous, and that that finding must be accepted and weighed in Rowley's favor, it does not alter our conclusion. The mere absence of measurable pecuniary damage does not require a finding of fair use. Fair use is to be determined by a consideration of all of the evidence in the case. Thus, despite the trial court's finding, we conclude that the factors analyzed weigh decisively in favor of the conclusion of no fair use. This conclusion is [also] in harmony with the Congressional guidelines[.]

* * *

---

9. *Contra, Williams & Wilkins Co. v. United States*, 487 F.2d 1345, 1352–54 (Ct. Cl. 1973), aff'd, 420 U.S. 376, 95 S. Ct. 1344 (1975) (the existence of verbatim copying was not dispositive when the conduct encouraged scientific progress and did not cause plaintiff substantial monetary harm).

We conclude that the fair use doctrine does not apply to these facts[.] * * * Rowley's LAP work, which was used for the same purpose as plaintiff's booklet, was quantitatively and qualitatively a substantial copy of plaintiff's booklet with no credit given to plaintiff. Under these circumstances, neither the fact that the defendant used the plaintiff's booklet for nonprofit educational purposes nor the fact that plaintiff suffered no pecuniary damage as a result of Rowley's copying supports a finding of fair use.

The order of the district court is reversed, summary judgment is entered for the plaintiff, and the case is remanded for a determination of damages pursuant to the provisions of the Copyright Act.

PROBLEM 49: CADILLAC UNIVERSITY

After some deliberation, the President of Cadillac University (CU)—a small, private, liberal arts college in the fictional state of Eldorado—decides to create a new, updated, and glitzy high-tech web site to replace the school's old plain vanilla Internet presence. There are many motivating factors behind this decision, but the three main reasons are as follows: (1) to provide additional resources for its students; (2) to attract additional corporate funding; and (3) because every other college and university seems to be doing the same thing. A Web site committee is set up, chaired by Maria Orneles, an adjunct professor and a local librarian. Maria is particularly interested in putting together a library of resources for the Cadillac students, and she becomes actively involved in this portion of the project.

In the process of putting together the online library, the following events transpire:

A. Maria wishes to post several recent newspaper and magazine articles about Cadillac University. She obtains electronic copies of these from the Fleetwood Times Web site. However, because she is told by a member of the committee that she does not need permission to post these on CU's site, she does not contact any of these publications.

B. Coming across an elaborate spread on the history of automobiles on the General Motors Web site, Maria believes that this would be perfect for the CU students. At first she thinks it would be appropriate to simply set up a link to the GM site, but then she realizes that this particular display would not stay on the Internet forever. She then copies the entire article along with all the accompanying pictures and prepares to post the entire spread on CU's Web site. Since she believes she is doing this for educational purposes only, she does not seek permission.

C. One of Maria's favorite books is *Cadillac University: A Memoir* by Charles Osgood III, a famous graduate of CU. Believing this would be a perfect book to place on the site, she has the entire volume scanned, and she directs her administrative assistant to contact Osgood and obtain permission to post the book on the new CU site. However, the administrative assistant is unsuccessful in tracking down either Osgood or any members of his family. As the time grows closer to the day the new site will be launched, Maria decides to post three chapters (95 pages) of the five-chapter book.

Soon after the new CU site is posted on the Internet, both The Fleetwood Times and GM file copyright infringement lawsuits against the university. And Dr. Osgood—who had been out of the country for some time but returned soon after the Web site was posted—also chooses to file a lawsuit. What legal and policy arguments would CU set forth under the Federal Copyright Act generally? Under the Fair Use Doctrine of Section 107? What result?

PROBLEM 50: ETS v. WONG

Betty Wong, a student activist at Golden Valley High and op-ed editor of her student newspaper, is so offended by a new standardized testing program which requires all 10th graders to take a 10th grade version of the SAT (the TSAT) that she decides to organize a boycott of the test. In a scathing op-ed piece, she denounces the governor and the state legislature, and calls for a student boycott. She urges all the tenth graders at Golden Valley High to either stay home on the day the test is administered or to come in and refuse to take it. As a back-up position, for students who fear retribution from the administration or faculty, she calls on the tenth graders to fill in answer D for each question.

Betty is suspended for ten days to make sure that she is not anywhere near the classrooms on the day of the test, and she is also removed from her position as editor. But she decides to continue her activism online, and creates a Web site via her off-campus Comcast account that is devoted to criticism of ETS, standardized testing, and the TSAT. Taking advantage of the fact that her older brother—who recently took the regular SAT—has a remarkable memory, she asks him to type up the exact wording of 15 actual questions from the test and then posts them on the site ... along with a caption that derides the usefulness of such questions in a 21st century educational setting.

ETS files a lawsuit against Betty, and is prepared to argue that her posting of test questions without permission constitutes copyright infringement and is not fair use. What arguments will be set forth? What result? Discuss.

EDUCATIONAL TESTING SERVS. v. KATZMAN

739 F.2d 533 (3d Cir. 1986)

SLOVITER, CIRCUIT JUDGE:

Educational Testing Service (ETS), a non-profit educational organization that prepares and administers numerous standardized tests, sought and was granted a preliminary injunction that enjoined defendants Princeton Review and John Katzman, its sole shareholder and president (collectively referred to as Review unless otherwise noted), from a wide range of activities involving ETS' tests and information therefrom. * * *

I. INTRODUCTORY FACTS

ETS develops and administers testing programs, among them the Scholastic Aptitude Test (SAT) and Achievement Tests in specific subjects, which are both multiple-choice tests given to high school students for college admission purposes. ETS regards the tests as secret until they have been released by it and attempts to maintain strict secrecy with respect to these tests. It registers them for copyright under "secure test" registration. It makes the tests that it has "retired" available to the public.

Review is a company which charges a fee for preparing students to take the SAT and Achievement Tests offered by ETS. * * *

The present dispute has its genesis in events occurring a number of years ago. In 1982, ETS learned that Review had given to its enrollees copies of a "Math Level I" and of an "English Composition" Achievement test that ETS subsequently administered on November 6, 1982. Although this test was stolen from ETS, ETS does not allege that Katzman or his agents were responsible for the theft. ETS cancelled the scores of those Review students who had been given access to the stolen test.

Following these events, ETS, Katzman, and an associate not involved in this litigation entered into a written agreement in 1983 under which Katzman and his associate promised to return all copies of the purloined tests, to refrain from copying or distributing any ETS copyrighted or copyrightable materials or registering for or attending any test administered by ETS unless it was for bona fide purposes, and to notify ETS if any unlawfully obtained ETS tests came into their possession and provide ETS with information as to their source.

In its complaint in this action, ETS claims that in May 1985 (1) Katzman distributed to Review enrollees a "facsimile" "Math Level I" practice test which was "copied or paraphrased" from the same stolen test book that Review had given its students prior to the November 1982 test, and that Katzman had promised to return, which forced ETS to provide another examination for a June 1985 exam and to retire the exam in question from use; (2) Review handed out a "facsimile" English Composition Achievement Test that contained 53 questions "obviously . . . adapted directly" from the test booklet Katzman supposedly had returned earlier, forcing ETS to make a last minute substitution for an English Composition Test scheduled to be administered on June 2, 1985; and (3) Katzman and Review distributed "facsimile" SATs that contained "verbatim or nearly verbatim" SAT questions, forcing ETS to retire numerous SAT questions. ETS suggests that Review obtained these questions by having its employees register and take the SAT in violation of the 1983 agreement. ETS contends in its brief that defendants' actions have compelled it to retire from use in "secure" testing at least 289 questions, consisting of 51 Math Achievement questions, 90 English Composition Achievement Test questions, and 148 SAT questions.

ETS contends that defendants' actions constituted infringement of ETS' copyrights, breach of the 1983 agreement, and interference with "ETS' common law right to preserve the integrity of its testing program and the confidentiality of its secure tests and secure test questions." * * *

[The Court then discussed various procedural issues, as well as other copyright issues, finding that they cut in favor of ETS.]

    * * *

We are also unpersuaded by defendants' argument that the teaching instruction offered by Review makes "fair use" of ETS' questions. The Copyright Act protects "fair use ... for purposes such as criticism, comment, news reporting, teaching (including multiple copies for classroom use), scholarship, or research...." * * *

In *Association of American Medical Colleges v. Mikaelian*, Judge Broderick rejected the argument that the defendant, who operated a course very much like Review's, fit into the category of teaching for purposes of the fair use defense. The court reasoned:

> To be sure, Mikaelian and Multiprep give test preparation courses, and provide instruction in test preparation as part of these courses. However, Multiprep students do not receive a degree, do not become qualified or certified in anything after taking the course, and may not use the course as a prerequisite for further education and training in any educational or vocational endeavor.

Even assuming that Review's courses qualify as teaching within the meaning of the statute, after consideration of the statutory factors, we cannot find that its showing on the issue of fair use in this record is so strong as to require us to overturn the trial court's finding of likelihood of success on the merits. The first factor of "the purpose and character of the use" is intended to favor noncommercial and productive uses. Review's use is highly commercial.

With respect to the second factor, "the nature of the copyrighted work", the unique nature of secure tests means that any use is destructive of ETS's rights. As stated in *Mikaelian*, "The very purpose of copyrighting the ... questions is to prevent their use as teaching aids, since such use would confer an unfair advantage to those taking a test preparation course."

In its interpretation of the third factor, "the amount and substantiality of the portion used," the Supreme Court in *Harper & Row* upheld the district court's finding that copying of 300 words from a book-length manuscript was substantial because defendant copied "the heart" of the book. While the copying shown on the record to date in this case cannot be so characterized, neither can we regard it as insubstantial.

Finally, the fourth factor, "effect * * * upon the potential market," seems dispositively in favor of ETS. Although Review asserts that it is not in competition with ETS, use of ETS' materials by Review renders the materials worthless to ETS.

Thus * * * we believe that the record before us is sufficient for the purpose of concluding that there was some copying by defendants of ETS' copyrighted material, and that defendants have not shown that such copying was permissible under the doctrines they invoke. We will not disturb the district court's finding that there was a likelihood of success on the merits in the copyright infringement claim.

* * *

CHICAGO BD. OF EDUC. v. SUBSTANCE, INC.

354 F.3d 624 (7th Cir. 2003)

POSNER, CIRCUIT JUDGE:

In 1999 the Chicago Board of Education brought this suit for copyright infringement against a Chicago public school teacher named Schmidt and a corporation that owns a local newspaper called Substance, aimed at such teachers, which Schmidt edits.

* * *

The following facts are either undisputed or indisputable. At some considerable expense (more than $1 million, according to Schmidt, though the actual figure is not in the record), the school board created and copyrighted a series of standardized tests that it called the "Chicago Academic Standards Exams" (CASE). These were, in copyright lingo, "secure tests." "A secure test is a nonmarketed test administered under supervision at specified centers on specific dates, all copies of which are accounted for and either destroyed or returned to restricted locked storage following each administration. For these purposes a test is not marketed if copies are not sold but it is distributed and used in such a manner that ownership and control of copies remain with the test sponsor or publisher." To maintain secrecy, the Library of Congress does not retain a copy of such a test.

The first step in making the CASE tests was to create a pool of questions—the record does not indicate how many—that would be drawn on to create the individual exams, each consisting of between three and 30 questions. The teachers who administered the exams were instructed not to make copies of them and to collect the test papers at the end of each exam so that the tests could be reused. Reuse of questions in standardized testing is not a sign of laziness but a way of validating a test, since if performance on the same questions is inconsistent from year to year this may indicate that the questions are not well designed and are therefore eliciting random answers. Such validation is of particular importance for a new battery of standardized tests, such as CASE, the subject of a three-year pilot program. And publication of standardized tests would not only prevent validation by precluding reuse of any of the questions in them, but also require the school board to create many new questions, at additional expense; and they might not be as good as the original questions, in which event there would be diminished quality as well as added cost. Hence the copyright category "secure tests."

It may seem paradoxical to allow copyright to be obtained in secret documents, but it is not. For one thing, the tests are not secret from the students taking them. For another, federal copyright is now available for unpublished works that the author intends never to see the light of day. Most important, tests are expressive works that are not costlessly created, and the costs are greater and so the incentive to create the tests diminished if the tests cannot be reused. There is no analytical difference between destroying the market for a copyrighted work by producing and selling cheap copies and destroying the subsequent years' market for a standardized test by blowing its cover.

In the newspaper that he edits, Schmidt published six of the tests given in January 1999. He did this because he thought them bad tests and that he could best demonstrate this by publishing them in full. His answer to the school board's complaint asserted that the unauthorized copying and publication of the tests were a fair use and therefore not a copyright infringement. The district court dismissed the fair use defense * * *.

Each side of this case has a one-sided view of the law. The school board contends that the case is governed by *Harper & Row Publishers, Inc. v. Nation Enterprises*, a case in which a magazine published unauthorized excerpts from Gerald Ford's copyrighted memoirs before the memoirs were published, thus jumping the gun and by doing so reducing the value of the copyright. The school board points out that Schmidt impaired the value of the exams by publishing them prematurely. (Presumably the school board will not complain if they are published * * * a century from now.) But the board overlooks the fact that the *Nation* was not publishing the excerpts from Ford's memoirs in order to be able to criticize Ford, or anyone or anything else, and the further fact that Schmidt was not trying to steal the school board's market, because unlike Harper & Row the school board did not intend ever to publish the copyrighted work that the alleged infringer published first. The second point has little force, as we'll see; but the first is important. As Schmidt points out, one office of the fair use defense is to facilitate criticism of copyrighted works by enabling the critic to quote enough of the criticized work to make his criticisms intelligible. Copyright should not be a means by which criticism is stifled with the backing of the courts. And since doubts that fair use could ever be a defense to infringement of a copyright on an unpublished work have now been stilled, the fact that the CASE tests were quasi-secret does not exclude the possibility of a fair use defense.

But Schmidt overreads our decision in *Ty, Inc. v. Publications Int'l Ltd.* to hold that a purpose of criticizing creates a privilege of unlimited copying regardless of the harm to the copyright owner's legitimate interests. Ty was trying to enjoin the publication of Beanie Babies collectors' guides that contained criticisms of some of the Beanie Babies, with accompanying photographs that constituted derivative works of the soft-sculpture Beanie Babies and hence prima facie infringements of Ty's copyrights. There was no danger that if Ty failed to enjoin the publication of the collectors' guides the value of its copyrights would be impaired, because collectors' guides are not substitutes for the Beanie Babies themselves. More precisely, the only harm that could come to Ty from the unauthorized publication of the guides would be caused by the criticisms of particular Beanie Babies, whereas a harm to the school board from Schmidt's copying and publication that is independent of any criticisms is the cost of creating substitutes for the questions that Schmidt published and of extending the period of the pilot program because his publishing the six tests prevented the board from asking any of the questions in those tests in subsequent years.

The board thus is correct that Schmidt did it harm going beyond the force of his criticisms. Yet he was entitled to criticize the tests and to do that effectively he had to be able to quote from them, just as a parodist has to be able to quote, sometimes very extensively, from the parodied work in order to make the criticism of it that is implicit in parodying it comprehensible. Indeed, there is no per se rule against copying in the name of fair use an entire copyrighted work if necessary. This would be obvious if the school board had copyrighted each question separately, as it might well have done, since it wants to reuse questions without necessarily reusing an entire test.

So where to draw the line? The question cannot be answered precisely. The fair use defense defies codification. As we said in *Ty*, the four factors that Congress listed when it wrote a fair use defense (a judicial creation) into the *Copyright Act in 1976* are not exhaustive and do not constitute an algorithm that enables decisions to be ground out mechanically. The general standard, however, is clear enough: the fair use copier must copy no more than is reasonably necessary (not strictly necessary— room must be allowed for judgment, and judges must not police criticism with a heavy hand) to enable him to pursue an aim that the law recognizes as proper, in this case the aim of criticizing the copyrighted work effectively.

The burden of proof is on the copier because fair use is an affirmative defense and Schmidt has presented no evidence sufficient to withstand summary judgment. He insists that he had to copy six tests out of the 22 to 44 tests given in January 1999 (it is unclear from the record which number is correct, so we will give Schmidt the benefit of the doubt and assume that it is the higher number) in order to drive his criticisms home. * * * Granted that he had to quote some of the test questions in order to substantiate his criticisms, why entire tests? Does he think all the questions in all six tests bad? * * * What purpose is served by quoting the good questions?

                    * * *

[Schmidt] argues that the school board does not intend to sell the tests, and so Schmidt isn't eating into their market by publishing the tests. This is true, but irrelevant, because he is destroying the value of the tests and the fact that it's not a *market* value has no significance once the right to copyright unpublished works is conceded, as it must be. [Schmidt] argues that expert testimony would establish that there is no educational value in publishing the exact same exam year after year. No one supposes there is; the argument rather is that *some* questions must be carried over to future years in order to validate the exam. [Schmidt] argues that if [he] quoted only a few of the questions, the school board would respond that he was cherry-picking the worst. But if the board did that without a solid grounding, it would open the door for him to quote additional questions; it would be a pro tanto waiver of confidentiality. [Schmidt]'s remaining argument is that expert witnesses can be found to testify that the CASE tests are "dramatically inadequate." No doubt. But in so arguing [Schmidt] misunderstands the fair use privilege of criticism. It is not a privilege to criticize just bad works, and there is no right to copy copyrighted works promiscuously merely upon a showing that they are bad.

There is more than a suspicion that Schmidt simply does not like standardized tests. That is his right. But he does not have the right, as he believes he does (he claims a right to copy any test that an expert will testify is no good), to destroy the tests by publishing them indiscriminately, any more than a person who dislikes Michelangelo's statue of David has a right to take a sledgehammer to it. From the amicus curiae briefs filed in this case, moreover, it is apparent that many other teachers share Schmidt's unfavorable opinion of standardized tests. (A cynic might say that this is because such tests can make teachers look bad if their students don't do well on them.) So if Schmidt can publish six tests, other dissenters can each publish six other tests, and in no time all 44 will be published. The board will never be able to use the same question twice, and after a few years of Schmidtian tactics there will be such difficulty in inventing new questions without restructuring the curriculum that the board will have to abandon standardized testing. Which is Schmidt's goal.

If ever a "floodgates" argument had persuasive force, therefore, it is in this case. And this suggests another fair use factor that supports the school board: the aspect of academic freedom that consists of the autonomy of educational institutions, including their authority here gravely threatened to employ standardized tests in support of their conception of their educational mission. If Schmidt wins this case, it is goodbye to standardized tests in the Chicago public school system; Schmidt, his allies, and the federal courts will have wrested control of educational policy from the Chicago public school authorities.

* * *

PRINCETON UNIV. PRESS v. MICHIGAN DOCUMENT SERVS.

99 F.3d 1381 (6th Cir. 1996)

DAVID A. NELSON, CIRCUIT JUDGE:

This is a copyright infringement case. The corporate defendant, Michigan Document Services, Inc., is a commercial copyshop that reproduced substantial segments of copyrighted works of scholarship, bound the copies into "coursepacks," and sold the coursepacks to students for use in fulfilling reading assignments given by professors at the University of Michigan. The copyshop acted without permission from the copyright holders, and the main question presented is whether the "fair use" doctrine codified at *17 U.S.C. § 107* obviated the need to obtain such permission.

Answering this question "no," and finding the infringement willful, the district court entered a summary judgment order in which the copyright holders were granted equitable relief and were awarded damages that may have been enhanced for willfulness. A three-judge panel of this court reversed the judgment on appeal, but a majority of the active judges of the court subsequently voted to rehear the case *en banc*. The appeal has now been argued before the full court.

We agree with the district court that the defendants' commercial exploitation of the copyrighted materials did not constitute fair use, and we shall affirm that branch of the district court's judgment. We believe that the district court erred in its finding of willfulness, however, and we shall vacate the damages award because of its possible linkage to that finding.

I.

* * *

The plaintiffs allege infringement of the copyrights on six different works that were excerpted without permission. The works in question, and the statistics on the magnitude of the excerpts, are as follows: Nancy J. Weiss, *Farewell to the Party of Lincoln: Black Politics in the Age of FDR* (95 pages copied, representing 30 percent of the entire book); Walter Lippmann, *Public Opinion* (45 pages copied, representing 18 percent of the whole); Robert E. Layne, *Political Ideology: Why the American Common Man Believes What He Does* (78 pages, 16 percent); Roger Brown, *Social Psychology* (52 pages, 8 percent); Milton Rokeach, *The Nature of Human Values* (77 pages, 18 percent); James S. Olson and Randy Roberts, *Where the Domino Fell, America and Vietnam, 1945–1950* (17 pages, 5 percent). The extent of the copying is undisputed, and the questions presented by the case appear to be purely legal in nature.

II.

* * *

[The fair use doctrine] does not provide blanket immunity for "multiple copies for classroom use." Rather, "whether a use referred to in the first sentence of Section 107 is a fair use in a particular case ... depends upon the application of the determinative factors."

The four statutory factors may not have been created equal. In determining whether a use is "fair," the Supreme Court has said that the most important factor is the fourth, the one contained in *17 U.S.C. § 107*(4). We take it that this factor, "the effect of the use upon the potential market for or value of the copyrighted work," is at least *primus inter pares*, figuratively speaking, and we shall turn to it first.

The burden of proof as to market effect rests with the copyright holder if the challenged use is of a "noncommercial" nature. The alleged infringer has the burden, on the other hand, if the challenged use is "commercial" in nature. In the case at bar the defendants argue that the burden of proof rests with the publishers because the use being challenged is "noncommercial." We disagree.

It is true that the use to which the materials are put by the students who purchase the coursepacks is noncommercial in nature. But the use of the materials by the students is not the use that the publishers are challenging. What the publishers are challenging is the duplication of copyrighted materials for sale by a for-profit corporation that has decided to maximize its profits—and give itself a competitive edge over other copyshops—by declining to pay the royalties requested by the holders of the copyrights.[2]

The defendants' use of excerpts from the books at issue here was no less commercial in character than was *The Nation* magazine's use of copyrighted material in *Harper & Row*, where publication of a short article containing excerpts from the still unpublished manuscript of a book by President Ford was held to be an unfair use. Like the students who purchased unauthorized coursepacks, the purchasers of *The Nation* did not put the contents of the magazine to commercial use—but that did not stop the Supreme Court from characterizing the defendant's use of the excerpts as "a publication [that] was commercial as opposed to nonprofit...." And like the use that is being challenged in the case now before us, the use challenged in *Harper & Row* was "presumptively an unfair exploitation of the monopoly privilege that belongs to the owner of the copyright."

　　* * *

---

2. Two of the dissents suggest that a copyshop merely stands in the shoes of its customers and makes no "use" of copyrighted materials that differs materially from the use to which the copies are put by the ultimate consumer. But subject to the fair use exception, *17 U.S.C. § 106* gives the copyright owner the "exclusive" right "to reproduce the copyrighted work in copies...." And if the fairness of making copies depends on what the ultimate consumer does with the copies, it is hard to see how the manufacture of pirated editions of any copyrighted work of scholarship could ever be an unfair use. As discussed in Part III A, infra, the dissenters' suggestion—which proposes no limiting principle—runs counter to the legislative history of the Copyright Act and has properly been rejected by the courts.

If we are wrong about the existence of the presumption—if the challenged use is not commercial, in other words, and if the plaintiff publishers have the burden of proving an adverse effect upon either the potential market for the copyrighted work or the potential value of the work—we believe that the publishers have carried the burden of proving a diminution in potential market value.

One test for determining market harm—a test endorsed by the Supreme Court in *Sony, Harper & Row*, and *Campbell*—is evocative of Kant's categorical imperative. "To negate fair use," the Supreme Court has said, "one need only show that *if the challenged use 'should become widespread, it would adversely affect the potential market* for the copyrighted work.'*" Harper & Row* (emphasis supplied in part). Under this test, we believe, it is reasonably clear that the plaintiff publishers have succeeded in negating fair use.

As noted above, most of the copyshops that compete with MDS in the sale of coursepacks pay permission fees for the privilege of duplicating and selling excerpts from copyrighted works. The three plaintiffs together have been collecting permission fees at a rate approaching $500,000 a year. If copyshops across the nation were to start doing what the defendants have been doing here, this revenue stream would shrivel and the potential value of the copyrighted works of scholarship published by the plaintiffs would be diminished accordingly.

* * *

The potential uses of the copyrighted works at issue in the case before us clearly include the selling of permission to reproduce portions of the works for inclusion in coursepacks—and the likelihood that publishers actually will license such reproduction is a demonstrated fact.

* * *

III.

In the context of nontransformative uses, at least, and except insofar as they touch on the fourth factor, the other statutory factors seem considerably less important. We shall deal with them relatively briefly.

A.

As to "the purpose and character of the use, including whether such use is of a commercial nature or is for nonprofit educational purposes," we have already explained our reasons for concluding that the challenged use is of a commercial nature.

The defendants argue that the copying at issue here would be considered "nonprofit educational" if done by the students or professors themselves. The defendants also note that they can profitably produce multiple copies for less than it would cost the professors or the students to make the same number of copies. Most of the copyshops with which the defendants compete have been paying permission fees, however, and we assume that these shops too can perform the copying on a more cost-effective basis than the professors or students can. This strikes us as a more significant datum than the ability of a black market copyshop to beat the do-it-yourself cost.

As to the proposition that it would be fair use for the students or professors to make their own copies, the issue is by no means free from doubt. We need not decide this question, however, for the fact is that the copying complained of here was performed on a profit-making basis by a commercial enterprise. And "the courts have ... properly rejected attempts by for-profit users to stand in the shoes of their customers making nonprofit or noncommercial uses." As the House Judiciary Committee stated in its report on the 1976 legislation,

> It would not be possible for a non-profit institution, by means of contractual arrangements with a commercial copying enterprise, to authorize the enterprise to carry out copying and distribution functions that would be exempt if conducted by the non-profit institution itself.

It should be noted, finally, that the degree to which the challenged use has transformed the original copyrighted works—another element in the first statutory factor—is virtually indiscernible. If you make verbatim copies of 95 pages of a 316–page book, you have not transformed the 95 pages very much—even if you juxtapose them to excerpts from other works and package everything conveniently. This kind of mechanical "transformation" bears little resemblance to the creative metamorphosis accomplished by the parodists in the *Campbell* case.

B.

The second statutory factor, "the nature of the copyrighted work," is not in dispute here. The defendants acknowledge that the excerpts copied for the coursepacks contained creative material, or "expression;" it was certainly not telephone book listings that the defendants were reproducing. This factor too cuts against a finding of fair use.

C.

The third statutory factor requires us to assess "the amount and substantiality of the portion used in relation to the copyrighted work as a whole." Generally speaking, at least, "the larger the volume (or the greater the importance) of what is taken, the greater the affront to the interests of the copyright owner, and the less likely that a taking will qualify as a fair use."

The amounts used in the case at bar—8,000 words in the shortest excerpt—far exceed the 1,000–word safe harbor that we shall discuss in the next part of this opinion. The defendants were using as much as 30 percent of one copyrighted work, and in no case did they use less than 5 percent of the copyrighted work as a whole. These percentages are not insubstantial. And to the extent that the third factor requires some type of assessment of the "value" of the excerpted material in relation to the entire work, the fact that the professors thought the excerpts sufficiently important to make them required reading strikes us as fairly convincing "evidence of the qualitative value of the copied material." We have no reason to suppose that in choosing the excerpts to be copied, the professors passed over material that was more representative of the major ideas of the work as a whole in preference to material that was less representative.

The third factor may have more significance for the 95–page excerpt from the black politics book than for the 17–page excerpt from the Vietnam book. In each instance, however, the defendants have failed to carry their burden of proof with respect to "amount and substantiality."[5]

IV.

We turn now to the pertinent legislative history. The general revision of the copyright law enacted in 1976 was developed through a somewhat unusual process. Congress and the Register of Copyrights initiated and supervised negotiations among interested groups—groups that included authors, publishers, and educators—over specific legislative language. Most of the language that emerged was enacted into law or was made a part of the committee reports. The statutory fair use provisions are a direct result of this process. So too is the "Agreement on Guidelines for Classroom Copying in Not-for-Profit Educational Institutions With Respect to Books and Periodicals"—commonly called the "Classroom Guidelines"—set out in H.R. Rep. No. 1476 at 68–71, 94th Cong., 2d Sess. (1976). The House and Senate conferees explicitly accepted the Classroom Guidelines "as part of their understanding of fair use," and the Second Circuit has characterized the guidelines as "persuasive authority...."

There are strong reasons to consider this legislative history. The statutory factors are not models of clarity, and the fair use issue has long been a particularly troublesome one. Not surprisingly, courts have often turned to the legislative history when considering fair use questions.

Although the Classroom Guidelines purport to "state the minimum and not the maximum standards of educational fair use," they do evoke a general idea, at least, of the type of educational copying Congress had in mind. The guidelines allow multiple copies for classroom use provided that (1) the copying meets the test of brevity (1,000 words, in the present context); (2) the copying meets the test of spontaneity, under which "the inspiration and decision to use the work and the moment of its use for maximum teaching effectiveness [must be] so close in time that it would be unreasonable to expect a timely reply to a request for permission;" (3) no more than nine instances of multiple copying take place during a term, and only a limited number of copies are made from the works of any one author or from any one collective work; (4) each copy contains a notice of copyright; (5) the copying does not substitute for the purchase of "books,

---

5. "Fair use serves as an affirmative defense to a claim of copyright infringement, and thus the party claiming that its secondary use of the original copyrighted work constitutes a fair use typically carries the burden of proof as to all issues in the dispute."

publishers' reprints or periodicals;" and (6) the student is not charged any more than the actual cost of copying. The Classroom Guidelines also make clear that unauthorized copying to create "anthologies, compilations or collective works" is prohibited.

In its systematic and premeditated character, its magnitude, its anthological content, and its commercial motivation, the copying done by MDS goes well beyond anything envisioned by the Congress that chose to incorporate the guidelines in the legislative history. Although the guidelines do not purport to be a complete and definitive statement of fair use law for educational copying, and although they do not have the force of law, they do provide us general guidance. The fact that the MDS copying is light years away from the safe harbor of the guidelines weighs against a finding of fair use.

Although the Congress that passed the Copyright Act in 1976 would pretty clearly have thought it unfair for a commercial copyshop to appropriate as much as 30 percent of a copyrighted work without paying the license fee demanded by the copyright holder, the changes in technology and teaching practices that have occurred over the last two decades might conceivably make Congress more sympathetic to the defendants' position today. If the law on this point is to be changed, however, we think the change should be made by Congress and not by the courts.

* * *

VIII.

The grant of summary judgment on the fair use issue is **AFFIRMED**.
* * *

BOYCE F. MARTIN, JR., CHIEF JUDGE, dissenting:

This case presents for me one of the more obvious examples of how laudable societal objectives, recognized by both the Constitution and statute, have been thwarted by a decided lack of judicial prudence. Copyright protection as embodied in the Copyright Act of 1976 is intended as a public service to both the creator and the consumer of published works. Although the Act grants to individuals limited control over their original works, it was drafted to stimulate the production of those original works for the benefit of the whole nation. The fair use doctrine, which requires unlimited public access to published works in educational settings, is one of the essential checks on the otherwise exclusive property rights given to copyright holders under the Copyright Act.

Ironically, the majority's rigid statutory construction of the Copyright Act grants publishers the kind of power that Article I, Section 8 of the Constitution is designed to guard against. The Copyright Clause grants Congress the power to create copyright interests that are *limited* in scope. Consequently, the Copyright Act adopted the fair use doctrine to protect society's vested interest in the sharing of ideas and information against pursuits of illegitimate or excessive private proprietary claims. While it may seem unjust that publishers must share, in certain situations, their work-product with others, free of charge, that is not some "unforeseen byproduct of a statutory scheme;" rather, it is the "essence of copyright" and a "constitutional requirement."

Michigan Document Services provided a service to the University of Michigan that promoted scholarship and higher education. Michigan Document Services was paid for its services; however, that fact does not obviate a fair use claim under these facts. Requiring Michigan Document Services to pay permission fees in this instance is inconsistent with the primary mission of the Copyright Act. The individual rights granted by the Act are subservient to the Act's primary objective, which is the promotion of creativity generally. We must therefore consider the fair use provision of Section 107 of the Act in light of the sum total of public benefits intended by copyright law. In this instance, there is no adverse economic impact on Princeton University Press that can outweigh the benefits provided by Michigan Document Services. Indeed, to presume adverse economic impact, as has the majority, is to presume that the $50,000 in fees currently earned by plaintiff is mandated by the Act in every instance—something I hesitate to presume.

That the majority lends significance to the identity of the person operating the photocopier is a profound indication that its approach is misguided. Given the focus of the Copyright Act, the only practical difference between this case and that of a student making his or her own copies is that commercial photocopying is faster and more cost-effective. Censuring incidental private sector profit reflects little of the essence of copyright law. Would the majority require permission fees of the Professor's teaching assistant who at times must copy, at the Professor's behest, copyrighted materials for dissemination to a class, merely because such assistant is paid an hourly wage by the Professor for this work?

The majority's strict reading of the fair use doctrine promises to hinder scholastic progress nationwide. By charging permission fees on this kind of job, publishers will pass on expenses to colleges and universities that will, of course, pass such fees on to students. Students may also be harmed if added expenses and delays cause professors to opt against creating such specialized anthologies for their courses. Even if professors attempt to reproduce the benefits of such a customized education, the added textbook cost to students is likely to be prohibitive.

The Copyright Act does not suggest such a result. Rather, the fair use doctrine contemplates the creation and free flow of information; the unhindered flow of such information through, among other things, education in turn spawns the creation and free flow of new information.

In limiting the right to copy published works in the Copyright Act, Congress created an exception for cases like the one before us. When I was in school, you bought your books and you went to the library for supplemental information. To record this supplemental information, in order to learn and benefit from it, you wrote it out long-hand or typed out what you needed—not easy, but effective. Today, with the help of free enterprise and technology, this fundamental means of obtaining information for study has been made easier. Students may now routinely acquire inexpensive copies of the information they need without all of the hassle. The trend of an instructor giving information to a copying service to make a single set of copies for each student for a small fee is just a modern approach to the classic process of education. To otherwise enforce this statute is nonsensical. I therefore dissent.

MERRITT, CIRCUIT JUDGE, dissenting.

The copying done in this case is permissible under the plain language of the copyright statute that allows "multiple copies for classroom use:" "The fair use of a copyrighted work . . . for purposes such as . . . teaching (*including multiple copies for classroom use*), . . . is not an infringement of copyright." (emphasis added). * * *

I.

This is a case of first impression with broad consequences. Neither the Supreme Court nor any other court of appeals has interpreted the exception allowing "multiple copies for classroom use" found in § 107 of the copyright statute. There is no legal precedent and no legal history that supports our Court's reading of this phrase in a way that outlaws the widespread practice of copying for classroom use by teachers and students.

For academic institutions, the practical consequences of the Court's decision in this case are highly unsatisfactory, to say the least. Anyone who makes multiple copies for classroom use for a fee is guilty of copyright infringement unless the portion copied is just a few paragraphs long. Chapters from a book or articles from a journal are verboten. No longer may Kinko's and other corner copyshops, or school bookstores, libraries and student-run booths and kiosks copy anything for a fee except a small passage. I do not see why we should so construe plain statutory language that on its face permits "multiple copies for classroom use." The custom of making copies for classroom use for a fee began during my college and law school days forty years ago and is now well-established. I see no justification for overturning this long-established practice.

I disagree with the Court's method of analyzing and explaining the statutory language of § 107 providing a fair use exception.[1] Except for "teaching," the statute is cast in general, abstract language that allows fair use for "criticism," "comment," "news reporting" and "research." The scope or extent of copying allowed for these uses is left undefined. Not so for "teaching." This purpose, and this purpose alone, is immediately

---

1. Both the majority opinion and Judge Ryan's dissent approach the determination of whether the use at issue here is infringing solely by use of the four statutory factors set out in § 107. Neither the plain language of the statute nor the case law requires that determination to be made solely on the narrow grounds of those four factors. Because the plain language of the statute is clear concerning "multiple copies for classroom use" and because determinations of infringement are to be made on a case-by-case basis taking into consideration the reasonableness of the copying from an equitable perspective, I do not believe that the four factors are controlling. The specific plain language should be given much more weight in this case than the four abstract considerations of little relevance to copying for classroom use.

followed by a definition. The definition allows "multiple copies for classroom use" of copyrighted material. The four factors to be considered, *e.g.*, market effect and the portion of the work used, are of limited assistance when the teaching use at issue fits squarely within the specific language of the statute, *i.e.*, "multiple copies for classroom use." In the present case that is all we have—"multiple copies for classroom use."

There is nothing in the statute that distinguishes between copies made for students by a third person who charges a fee for their labor and copies made by students themselves who pay a fee only for use of the copy machine. Our political economy generally encourages the division and specialization of labor. There is no reason why in this instance the law should discourage high schools, colleges, students and professors from hiring the labor of others to make their copies any more than there is a reason to discourage lawyers from hiring paralegals to make copies for clients and courts. The Court's distinction in this case based on the division of labor—who does the copying—is short sighted and unsound economically.

Our Court cites no authority for the proposition that the intervention of the copyshop changes the outcome of the case. The Court errs by focusing on the "use" of the materials made by the copyshop in making the copies rather than upon the real user of the materials—the students. Neither the District Court nor our Court provides a rationale as to why the copyshops cannot "stand in the shoes" of their customers in making copies for noncommercial, educational purposes where the copying would be fair use if undertaken by the professor or the student personally.

Rights of copyright owners are tempered by the rights of the public. The copyright owner has never been accorded complete control over all possible uses of a work. Generally, "the monopoly privileges [of copyright] that Congress may authorize are neither unlimited nor primarily designed to provide a special private benefit," a statement the Court more fully explained as follows:

The limited scope of the copyright holder's statutory monopoly, like the limited copyright duration required by the Constitution, reflects a balance of competing claims upon the public interest: Creative work is to be encouraged and rewarded, but private motivation must ultimately serve the cause of promoting broad public availability of literature, music, and the other arts.... When technological change has rendered its literal terms ambiguous, the Copyright Act must be construed in light of its basic purpose.

The public has the right to make fair use of a copyrighted work and to exercise that right without requesting permission from, or paying any fee to, the copyright holder. The essence of copyright is the promotion of learning—not the enrichment of publishers.

* * *

RYAN, CIRCUIT JUDGE, dissenting:

It is clear from the application of the four fair use factors of *17 U.S.C. § 107* that MDS's copying of the publishers' copyrighted works in this case is fair use and, thus, no infringement of the publishers' rights. Indeed, it is a use which is merely an aspect of the professors' and students' classroom use, and, only in the narrowest and most technical sense, a use of a separate genre under section 107. And, so, I must dissent from the majority's contrary view and, in expressing my understanding of the matter, I shall identify three important subissues on which I think my colleagues' analysis has led them to mistakenly conclude that MDS's activity is not a fair use of the publishers' materials.

In my judgment, my colleagues have erred in

1. focusing on the loss of permission fees in evaluating "market effect" under section 107(4);

2. finding that the evidence supports the conclusion that permission fees provide an important incentive to authors to create new works or to publishers to publish new works; and

3. using legislative history, specifically the "Classroom Guidelines," to decide the issue of classroom use.

* * *

[After a lengthy analysis of the first two items on the above list, Judge Ryan turned to the third, focusing on the "Classroom Guidelines."]

Finally, a word about the majority's argument that the unenacted legislative history of the Copyright Act instructs us that the MDS's copying function is not a fair use under the enacted provisions of sections 106 and 107.

The majority opinion stresses the fact that Congress "initiated and supervised negotiations among interested groups—groups that included authors, publishers, and educators—over specific legislative language [and that m]ost of the language that emerged was enacted into law or was made a part of the committee reports." However, what were not "enacted into law," but only made a part of the conference committee reports, are the Classroom Guidelines upon which the majority so heavily relies to decide how the language enacted into law applies. Indisputably, the Classroom Guidelines assure educators that nonprofit copying for educational purposes of "not more than 1,000 words" is fair use when "the inspiration and decision to use the work and the moment of its use for maximum teaching effectiveness are so close in time that it would be unreasonable to expect a timely reply to a request for permission." The Classroom Guidelines "prohibit[] ... copying ... used to create ... anthologies, compilations or collective works." But, as the majority opinion acknowledges, that language did not survive congressional debate and was not enacted into law.

Despite the well-settled rule that legislative history is irrelevant and inappropriate to consider except to clarify an ambiguity in the text of a statute, the majority relies upon the legislative history without identifying any ambiguity in the statute, but only because "the statutory factors are not models of clarity, ... the fair use issue has long been a particularly troublesome one ..., [and other] courts have often turned to the legislative history when considering fair use questions." I wish to emphasize in the strongest terms that it is entirely inappropriate to rely on the Copyright Act's legislative history at all.

* * * The Classroom Guidelines do not become more authoritative by their adoption into a Committee Report. "It is the statute, and not the Committee Report, which is the authoritative expression of the law." We may not permit the statutory text enacted by both Houses of Congress and signed by the President "to be expanded or contracted by the statements of individual legislators or committees during the course of the enactment process." That the Classroom Guidelines are not law should be reason enough for this court to refrain from using them to find infringement, but this is not the only reason to reject out of hand arguments based on legislative history. Committee Reports are unreliable "as a genuine indicator of congressional intent" *and* "as a safe predictor of judicial construction." Committee Reports do not accurately indicate congressional intent because they do not "necessarily say anything about what Congress as a whole thought," *even if* all the members of the Committee "actually adverted to the interpretive point at issue ... [and] were in unanimous agreement on the point." The members of Congress who voted for the statutory language of section 107 could have had any variety of understandings about the application of the fair use factors; all we know for certain is that the full House, the full Senate, and the President, pursuant to the procedures prescribed by the Constitution, enacted into law the text of section 107, and did not enact the standards of the Classroom Guidelines. Committee Reports do not reliably further consistent judicial construction. I subscribe wholeheartedly to Judge Harold Leventhal's observation that "the use of legislative history [is] the equivalent of entering a crowded cocktail party and looking over the heads of the guests for one's friends." "We use [Committee Reports] when it is convenient, and ignore them when it is not."

The statutory language of section 107, like most statutory language, may not be a "model of clarity," and the fair use issue, like many issues of law we face, may be a difficult or "troublesome" one, but neither of these inconveniences is a substitute for the requisite ambiguity that, alone, justifies recourse to legislative history.

Our duty in this case, as in all cases that require application of a statute, is to apply the broad dictates of the statute to the unique factual situations presented by the evidence. The fact that the Supreme Court has indulged in explanatory side-references to the Classroom Guidelines does not diminish in any measure the *rule* that legislative history is not a proper source of authority for this court when the language of the statute is not analogous. It is particularly inappropriate to rely on the specific language of the Classroom Guidelines as an interpretive tool when we know that members of Congress actually considered the language and rejected it in favor of the very language now claimed to lack clarity. The majority substitutes language contained only in pre-enactment political maneuvering of Congress for our obligation to rely, as we are required to do, on the rich body of case law that properly guides our application of the statutory factors to the specific facts of a case. In *Campbell*, the Court noted that "the task is not to be simplified with bright-line rules, for the statute, like the doctrine it recognizes, calls for case-by-case analysis."

The case for copyright infringement is very weak indeed if the court must rely on the unenacted theater of Committee Reports to find infringement. The fact that Congress saw fit, very likely in the interests of political expediency, to pay unusual deference to the "agreement" of interested parties about what *they* would like the law to be, even to the point of declaring (but not in the statute) that the parties' agreement was part of the committee's "understanding" of fair use, does not affect the rule of construction that binds this court.

In sum, even if the four statutory factors of section 107 are not "models of clarity" and their application to the facts of this case is "troublesome"—a challenge of the kind federal appellate judges are paid to face every day—the four factors are not ambiguous. Therefore, we may not properly resort to legislative history. I am satisfied to rely exclusively upon the evidence and lack of evidence on the record before us and the plain language of the Copyright Act and its construction in the case law; and they lead me to conclude that MDS's compilation into coursepacks of excerpts selected by professors is a "fair use" of the copyrighted materials.

IV.

For all the foregoing reasons, I conclude that MDS did not infringe upon the copyrights of the publishers.

NOTE

1. Taking advantage of ongoing improvements in digital technology, a growing number of academics are working to develop new ways of packaging and distributing course materials. Some have focused only on their own courses for their own students, but others have participated in high-profile projects—funded by sizable grants—that seek to create innovative models which can then be used in other places. Many of these models contemplate the online publishing of extensive sets of course materials—such as syllabi, lecture notes, and quizzes—which could then be used freely by anyone. Some have also developed state-of-the-art software that can facilitate both the dissemination of materials and student interaction around these materials.

One such effort is MIT's Open Courseware. As the *Chronicle of Higher Education* reported in March 2005:

> * * * MIT officials are spending $6–million per year on the project, much of which is coming from grants from the William and Flora Hewlett Foundation and the Andrew W. Mellon Foundation. The project, which has already published more than 900 of MIT's 1,800 courses, is being

touted as a success, as it has drawn downloaders from around the world who are using the materials as models for their own teaching or to learn on their own.

Proponents say the main beneficiaries are in the developing world, where students cannot afford textbooks and universities are looking for help setting up courses. MIT officials say that the materials are also inspiring more people to apply to the institute, as well as helping students at MIT decide which courses to sign up for.

Though many professors at other colleges already create course Web sites, the majority do so haphazardly, or in a way that is designed to be used only by their students. Open courseware seeks to make sure each course's materials are far more complete, and are presented in a way that makes them easy for others to use.

The growth of these giveaways marks a major philosophical shift from the mid–1990s, when many colleges and professors thought they could rake in profits selling course materials online. * * *

Of course, copyright issues inevitably arise in this context. As *The Chronicle* reported * * *

Copyright is another challenge in running open-courseware projects * * *[.] Many professors regularly use charts, graphs, or other illustrations they've culled from textbooks or other copyrighted works in slide presentations or handouts. Although using those illustrations in a classroom is allowed under fair-use provisions of copyright law, universities must get permission before putting the same materials online where anyone can see them. That can take time and money because officials must track down who owns the copyright and often must pay a fee to post the materials. One college decided not to convert a popular course to an open format because it included so many copyrighted items that it would have been unmanageable. Jeffrey R. Young, *'Open Courseware' Idea Spreads,* CHRONICLE OF HIGHER ED., Mar. 4, 2005.

A.V. v. iPARADIGMS

544 F. Supp. 2d 473 (E.D. Va. 2008)

MEMORANDUM OPINION

CLAUDE M. HILTON, District Judge.

* * * Plaintiffs, four minor high school students, have filed a complaint against Defendant iParadigms, LLC alleging copyright infringement based on iParadigms' digital archiving of Plaintiffs' copyrighted materials. * * * iParadigms owns and operates Turnitin, a proprietary technology system that evaluates the originality of written works in order to prevent plagiarism. Educational institutions contract with iParadigms and require their students to submit their written works via Turnitin. When the student work is submitted to Turnitin, the system compares the work electronically to content available on the internet, student works previously submitted to Turnitin and commercial databases of journal articles and

periodicals. Turnitin then produces an Originality Report for each submitted work, which indicates whether a student's paper is not original. The teacher then evaluates the Originality Report and decides whether to address any issues with the student. Upon request to Turnitin, the teacher can obtain, for comparison purposes, copies of archived works which appear to be plagiarized by the student.

Turnitin also has the ability to archive a student's work upon its submission to Turnitin. This allows Turnitin's database to grow with each student work submitted. However, this feature must be specifically authorized by the school district in order to allow Turnitin to archive the student-submitted works. Over 7,000 educational institutions worldwide use Turnitin, resulting in the daily submission of over 100,000 works to Turnitin.

In order to submit a paper to Turnitin, a student must first register by creating a profile on the Turnitin web site. The final step in the profile creation process requires that the student click "I Agree" to the terms of the "user agreement" (also referred to as the "Clickwrap Agreement") which is displayed directly above the "I agree" link that the student must click. The Clickwrap Agreement states: "Turnitin and its services are maintained by iParadigms, LLC ['Licensor'], and are offered to you, the user ['User'], *conditioned on your acceptance without modification* of the terms, conditions, and notices contained herein." (emphasis added). The Clickwrap Agreement also contains a limitation of liability clause:

In no event shall iParadigms, LLC and/or its suppliers be liable for any direct, indirect, punitive, incidental, special, or consequential damages *arising out of or in any way connected with the use of this web site* or with the delay or inability to use this web site, or for any information, software, products, and services obtained through this web site, or *otherwise arising out of the use of this web site,* whether based in contract, tort, strict liability or otherwise, even if iParadigms, Inc. or any of its suppliers has been advised of the possibility of damages. (emphasis added).

At the time of the filing of the complaint, Plaintiffs attended high school in Virginia, in the Fairfax County Public Schools ("FCPS") system, and in Arizona, in the Tucson Unified School District ("TUSD"). Both school systems contracted with iParadigms to utilize iParadigms' Turnitin technology system and both authorized Turnitin to archive student-submitted work. According to school administrators, plagiarism had become a major problem in each school district and Turnitin was employed in an effort to decrease plagiarism in their schools. Both school districts required their students to use Turnitin to submit their written works. If a student chose not to submit his or her work via Turnitin, that student would receive a zero on the assignment.

Each of the Plaintiffs read and clicked "I agree" to the terms of the Clickwrap Agreement and each used Turnitin to submit their written works. However, in an attempt to prevent Turnitin from archiving their written works, Plaintiffs included a disclaimer on the face of their works indicating that they did not consent to the archiving of their works by Turnitin. iParadigms continued to archive all student-submitted works, including all the works submitted by Plaintiffs. Plaintiffs claim iParadigms' continued archiving of their works constitutes copyright infringement.

* * *

The Court finds that the parties entered into a valid contractual agreement when Plaintiffs clicked "I Agree" to acknowledge their acceptance of the terms of the Clickwrap Agreement. * * * The existence of disclaimers on the written works indicating that Plaintiffs did not consent to the archiving of their works does not modify the Agreement or render it unenforceable. The Clickwrap Agreement itself provides that the terms of the Agreement are not modifiable. Plaintiffs had the option to "Agree" or "Disagree;" no third option was available to allow Plaintiffs to modify the Agreement. * * *

iParadigms claims that even if the Clickwrap Agreement does not preclude liability in this case, iParadigms' use of the written works is a fair use under 17 U.S.C. § 107 and, as such, does not constitute copyright infringement. * * * In assessing [the first fair use factor,] "the purpose and character of the use," the fact that the new work, produced by the defendant, is "transformative" or "adds something new, with a further purpose or different character" is strong evidence that the use is a fair use. In fact, "the more transformative the new work, the less will be the significance of the other factors, like commercialism, that may weigh against a finding of fair use." In *Perfect 10, Inc. v. Google, Inc.,* 487 F.3d 701 (9th Cir.2007), the Ninth Circuit recently addressed the use of works in a computer database and found the defendant's use to be transformative. Plaintiff Perfect 10 sued Google for infringement based on Google's display of thumbnail-sized images from Perfect 10's web site, which were displayed by Google in response to a user search. The court held that Google's reproduction of the images was "highly transformative" because "[a]lthough an image may have been created originally to serve an entertainment . . . or informative function, a search engine transforms the image . . . [and] provides a social benefit by incorporating an original work into a new work, namely, an electronic reference tool." *Perfect 10,* 487 F.3d at 721.

This Court finds the "purpose and character" of iParadigms' use of Plaintiffs' written works to be highly transformative. Plaintiffs originally created and produced their works for the purpose of education and creative expression. iParadigms, through Turnitin, uses the papers for an entirely different purpose, namely, to prevent plagiarism and protect the students' written works from plagiarism. iParadigms achieves this by archiving the students' works as digital code and makes no use of any work's particular expressive or creative content beyond the limited use of comparison with other works. Though iParadigms makes a profit in providing this service to educational institutions, its use of the student works adds "a further purpose or different character" to the works, and provides a substantial public benefit through the network of educational institutions using Turnitin. Thus, in this case, the first factor favors a finding of fair use.

The second factor to be considered is "the nature of the copyrighted work". This factor "focuses attention on the extent to which a work falls at the core of creative expression," and, in particular, whether "the incentive for creativity has been diminished." In this case, this factor is of lesser import because the allegedly infringing use makes no use of any creative aspect of the student works. Rather, iParadigms' use relates solely to the comparative value of the works. Nevertheless, iParadigms' use in no way diminishes the incentive for creativity on the part of students. On the contrary, iParadigms' use protects the creativity and originality of student works by detecting any efforts at plagiarism by other students. Thus, the second factor either favors neither party or favors a finding of fair use.

The third factor to be considered is "the amount and substantiality of the portion used." The Supreme Court and the Fourth Circuit have indicated that a new work's complete and entire use of the original work does not automatically preclude a finding of fair use. For example, in *Perfect 10,* the fact that Google displayed the entire Perfect 10 image in its search engine results did not make the use impermissible because the use was also highly transformative.

In this case, it is clear that iParadigms uses the entirety of the original works. In order to be successful in its plagiarism detection services, it must. However, the use of the original works is limited in purpose and scope. The student works are stored digitally and reviewed electronically by Turnitin for comparison purposes only. The only circumstance in which a student work can be produced for viewing is when another student's submission triggers an Originality Report that indicates the possibility of plagiarism. If this occurs, the teacher can request to view the document which produced the plagiarism alert in order to compare the two works. This use is, as discussed above, highly transformative and highly beneficial to the public through educational institutions using Turnitin. Thus, this factor either favors neither party or favors a finding of fair use.

The fourth factor to be considered is "the effect of the use upon the potential market for or value of the copyrighted work." * * * This factor requires courts to consider both the extent of the market harm caused by the defendant and whether the conduct of the sort engaged in by the defendant "would result in a substantially adverse impact on the potential market for the original." A "key element" in this analysis is "whether the allegedly infringing work is a market substitute for the copyrighted work."

Here, it is clear that iParadigms' use of Plaintiffs' works has caused no harm to the market value of those works. Plaintiffs have failed to present any evidence of harm. In fact, when asked in deposition whether iParadigms' use of their works impinged on the marketability of their works or interfered with their use of the works, each Plaintiff answered in the negative. Furthermore, iParadigms' use of Plaintiffs' works will not have a "substantially adverse impact on the potential market" for high school papers. Clearly, iParadigms' use does not amount to a "market substitute" for Plaintiffs' works. iParadigms stores its archived papers digitally and they are not publicly accessible or disseminated in any way. In fact, iParadigms' use of Plaintiffs' works has a protective effect, preventing others from using Plaintiffs' works as their own and protecting the future marketability of Plaintiffs' works.

Plaintiffs point to a potential harm that could arise if a future recipient of Plaintiffs' work, such as a literary magazine or a college admissions counselor, checks the originality of the work using Turnitin. Plaintiffs argue that Turnitin would return a plagiarism alert because of the presence of the original work archived in the Turnitin system. According to Plaintiffs, this could falsely indicate to the recipient that Plaintiffs are plagiarists, thereby harming the marketability of their works or their chances of college admission.

This argument is unpersuasive. First, this type of harm is entirely speculative as there is no evidence indicating that Plaintiffs, or anyone else, have been harmed in this manner. Second, this type of harm is highly unlikely based on the manner in which the Turnitin system operates. After Turnitin compares the submitted work to its database of archived works, it produces an Originality Report which identifies the percentage of the work that is not original. Importantly, if the Report indicates that the work is not original, the Report identifies the original archived work and the educational institution in which it was first turned in. Anyone who is reasonably familiar with Turnitin's operation will be able to recognize that the identical match is not the result of plagiarism, but simply the result of Plaintiff's earlier submission. Individuals familiar with Turnitin, such as those in the field of education, would be expecting the works submitted to have been previously submitted. Because Plaintiffs have presented no evidence of harm and the potential harm alleged is both speculative and highly unlikely, the fourth factor strongly favors a finding of fair use.

Considering all four factors, the Court finds that iParadigms' use of Plaintiffs' written works constitutes fair use under 17 U.S.C. § 107. * * *

D. PROSECUTIONS UNDER THE "NO ELECTRONIC THEFT" ACT

PROBLEM 51: FIGHTING "ELECTRONIC THEFT"

Assume that Al and Joanne maintain a Web site on the server of a commercial ISP as part of an independent study project for their History of American Film class. On this site, they have been able to post excerpts of classic films and complete versions of *The Godfather* Saga in fifteen minute segments for easier access/viewing. In a separate section on DVD technology, they post links to sites where software and other resources are available for working with DVD files, including but not limited to file-sharing guides and technologies.

Under pressure from the entertainment industry to make examples of college students who may be violating the law, the U.S. Attorneys Office prosecutes Al and Joanne under the 'No Electronic Theft' (NET) Act.

    A.   What arguments might Al & Joanne set forth in support of their assertion that they have not violated the terms of the Act? What result?

    B.   Might there be a law that could address this sort of activity in a better way?

    C.   Consider the efficacy of the following relevant legislation. In light of your analysis of the regulatory design and whether the plan is likely to achieve its purpose, would you recommend passage of such a bill? Why? Alternatively, could you support a modified version of this bill? If so, what modifications might be appropriate?

(a)(1) Any person or entity that sells, offers for sale, advertises, distributes, disseminates, provides, or otherwise makes available peer-to-peer file sharing software that enables its user to electronically disseminate commercial recordings or audiovisual works via the Internet or any other digital network, and who fails to incorporate available filtering technology into that software to prevent use of that software to commit an unlawful act with respect to a commercial recording or audiovisual work * * * is punishable, in addition to any other penalty or fine imposed, by a fine not exceeding two thousand five hundred dollars ($2,500), imprisonment in a county jail for a period not to exceed one year, or by both that fine and imprisonment.

    (2) This section shall not apply to the following:

        (A) Computer operating system or Internet browser software.

        (B) An electronic mail service or Internet service provider.

        (C) Transmissions via a personal network or local area network (LAN).

  (b) As used in this section, 'peer-to-peer file sharing software' means software that contains a sequence of instructions written in any programming language that is executed on a computer the primary purpose of which, once installed and launched, is to enable the user to connect his or her computer to a network of other computers on which the users of these computers have made available recordings or audiovisual works for electronic dissemination to other users who are connected to the network. When a transaction is complete, the user has an identical copy of the file on his or her computer and may also then disseminate the file to other users connected to the network. * * *

A ROAD TO NO WAREZ: THE NO ELECTRONIC THEFT ACT AND CRIMINAL COPYRIGHT INFRINGEMENT

Eric Goldman

82 Or. L. Rev. 369 (2003)

The [No Electronic Theft] Act represents a significant change to copyright law because it subtly shifts the paradigm underlying criminal copyright infringement. For 100 years, criminal infringement punished infringers who derived a commercial benefit based on someone else's copyrighted work. However, through the Act, Congress adopted a paradigm that criminal copyright infringement is like physical-space theft, specifically shoplifting. As a result, the Act significantly extends the boundaries of criminal copyright infringement.

* * *

I.

Development of the Act.

Prior to the Act, criminal copyright infringement required willful infringement committed for commercial advantage or private financial gain. A case involving David LaMacchia highlighted the limits of this statute.

David LaMacchia was a twenty-one-year-old student at the Massachusetts Institute of Technology ("MIT"). From late 1993 to early 1994, he used MIT's equipment to operate Cynosure, a bulletin board system ("BBS") that allowed users to upload and download infringing software applications and videogames. LaMacchia was not accused of uploading or downloading any infringing programs himself. However, prosecutors asserted that he maintained the BBS (including deleting files and transferring files between servers) and asked BBS users to upload specific software programs. Judge Stearns described LaMacchia's behavior as, at best, "heedlessly irresponsible, and at worst as nihilistic, self-indulgent, and lacking in any fundamental sense of values." Although the term was not widely used at the time, LaMacchia was an early warez trader.

Like a typical warez trader, LaMacchia operated the BBS for fun and without any commercial advantage or private financial gain. Therefore, prosecutors could not charge him with criminal copyright infringement. Instead, prosecutors charged him with one count of conspiracy to commit wire fraud. Judge Stearns applied the U.S. Supreme Court case of Dowling v. United States, which had ruled that intangible intellectual property was not capable of being stolen, converted or taken by fraud. That case, he concluded, "precludes LaMacchia's prosecution for criminal copyright infringement under the wire fraud statute," and he dismissed the indictment.

Despite the dismissal, Judge Stearns issued a challenge to Congress:

Criminal as well as civil penalties should probably attach to willful, multiple infringements of copyrighted software even absent a commercial motive on the part of the infringer. One can envision ways that the copyright law could be modified to permit such prosecution. But, it is the legislature, not the Court, which is to define a crime, and ordain its punishment.

B.   A Legislative Response to LaMacchia

Copyright owners seized upon Judge Stearns's challenge and lobbied Congress for just such a law. * * * [T]he NET Act * * * was enacted in 1997.

The Act effected six principal changes to criminal copyright law. First, the NET Act expanded the Copyright Act's definition of "financial gain" to include the receipt (or expectation of receipt) of anything of value, including other copyrighted works. Second, in addition to willful infringement for commercial advantage or private financial gain, the Act criminalized the reproduction or distribution, in any 180 day period, of copyrighted works with a total retail value of more than $1,000. Third, the Act said that evidence of reproducing and distributing copyrighted works does not, by itself, establish willfulness. Fourth, the Act changed the punishments for criminal infringement. For infringements of more than $1,000, the punishment includes imprisonment of up to one year and a fine. For infringements of $2,500 or more, the punishment includes imprisonment of up to three years and a fine. For second or subsequent offenses involving commercial advantage or private financial gain, the punishment includes imprisonment of up to six years. Fifth, the Act permits copyright infringement victims to submit victim impact statements. Finally, the Act instructed the United States Sentencing Commission (the "Sentencing Commission") to adjust the United States Sentencing Guidelines (the "Sentencing Guidelines") for criminal copyright infringement to make the punishments sufficiently stringent to deter the crimes and to reflect the infringed items' retail value and quantity.

C.   The Act's Goals

Because the LaMacchia case directly instigated the Act, the law is often characterized as being intended to close the LaMacchia loophole. Indeed, the House Report said it desired to "reverse the practical consequences of" the LaMacchia case, and several legislators reiterated this goal. However, accepting these statements on their face still leaves open a central question: Exactly what aspects of LaMacchia did Congress intend to reverse?

Some legislators specifically targeted LaMacchia's warez trading, referencing targets such as "commercial scale" piracy and self-aggrandizing infringers.

LaMacchia's BBS primarily traded software (as opposed to other copyrighted works), and the legislative history also extensively discussed software piracy. As the House Report says, "copyright piracy flourishes in the software world" despite existing sanctions. The report cited industry estimates that software counterfeiting and piracy cost copyright owners $11 billion in 1996, resulting in "130,000 lost U.S. jobs, $5.6 billion in corresponding lost wages, $1 billion in lower tax revenue, and higher prices for honest purchasers of copyrighted software." Individual legislators also expressed a desire to target software pirates and to protect the software industry.

Finally, even though the Act criminalizes infringements regardless of distribution media, several legislators specifically targeted Internet-based piracy. Of course, the Act's title ("No Electronic Theft," with the acronym "NET") reinforces that objective.

Therefore, the legislative history suggests Congress targeted LaMacchia's use of the Internet to distribute infringing software on a commercial scale but without a profit motive. In other words, Congress specifically targeted warez trading.

* * *

II

Developments After the Act's Enactment

A.   Congressional Oversight of Implementation and Use

No convictions under the Act were announced in the first eighteen months following the Act's passage. This perceived lack of action prompted Rep. Howard Coble, one of the Act's co-sponsors, to convene hearings of the House Judiciary Committee's Subcommittee on Courts and Intellectual Property in May 1999 (the "Oversight Hearings"). * * *

Kevin DiGregory of the United States Department of Justice (the "DOJ") responded by enumerating several general challenges to prosecuting digital piracy, including: (1) Internet pirates do not have sizable or easily-located manufacturing operations; (2) calculating damages and losses is difficult because it is hard to count the number of illegitimate copies made over the Internet; (3) no government agency has primary responsibility for enforcing Internet-based crimes, and prosecutions often cut across prosecutors' territories; and (4) Internet-savvy law enforcement officials are hard to retain and often asked to help with other computer crime enforcements.

Mr. DiGregory also identified specific difficulties with enforcing the Act against pirate Web site operators: (1) for-profit criminals are a higher priority; (2) operators are often juveniles; (3) Web sites move overseas, complicating investigation and enforcement; (4) establishing an operator's identity can be challenging; (5) prosecutors cannot prove willfulness; (6) young not-for-profit operators are sympathetic defendants; (7) the Sentencing Commission had not established the mandated changes to the Sentencing Guidelines; and (8) the Sentencing Guideline's computation of retail value leads to low penalties. He concluded that "although there are many Web sites on the Internet offering illegal software and other copyrighted materials, investigating and prosecuting the offenders is hardly shooting fish in a barrel."

Despite the dozen challenges mentioned by Mr. DiGregory, the DOJ also quickly responded to the Oversight Hearings, delivering the first criminal conviction under the Act just three months later. Since then, the prosecution machine has ramped up significantly, and nearly eighty defendants have been convicted under the Act.

* * *

C.   Prosecutions under the Act

As mentioned above, nearly eighty defendants have been convicted under the Act. This subsection discusses some of the publicized convictions.

* * *

In August 1999, Jeffrey Levy, a twenty-two-year old University of Oregon senior, became the first individual convicted under the Act. He operated a Web site that allowed third parties to download thousands of software and game programs, songs, and movies, at least some of which Levy uploaded himself. After Levy was arrested and an information was filed against him, he was given a choice: he could remain in prison six months while the FBI analyzed his computers to determine the value of the infringing works, or he could plead guilty. Levy chose the latter and pleaded guilty to distributing software with a retail value of at least $5,000 (although a "conservative[] estimate" of the actual retail value was $70,000). He was sentenced to two years probation.

* * *

Eric Thornton, a twenty-four-year old Navy avionics technician, operated a Web site called "No Patience" permitting users to download software such as Adobe Premiere and Adobe Illustrator. In one specific instance, a third party downloaded twenty software programs with a retail value of $9,638. Thornton used the third party software to attract traffic to his Web site. However, when his Internet access provider noticed the traffic spike, his provider shut down the Web site and notified the FBI.

In December 1999, Thornton pleaded guilty to a misdemeanor violation of the Act. He received five years probation and had to pay restitution of $9,600. In addition, for eighteen months Thornton's Web site described his arrest and conviction.

* * *

In October 2000, twenty-one-year-old Brian Baltutat pleaded guilty to violating the Act. He operated a Web site called "Hacker Hurricane," visited by 65,000 people, that offered 142 software programs for downloading. Baltutat received three years probation, 180 days home confinement (including a tether), restitution, and forty hours of community service.

* * *

Pirates With Attitude (PWA) was [a] major warez group, characterized as "the 'oldest and most sophisticated' band of software pirates in Internet history." PWA operated thirteen FTP servers for software uploading and downloading. Its flagship site was Sentinel, located at the University of Sherbrooke in Quebec, which operated from late 1995 to January 2000. Sentinel users obtained the right to download software by uploading pirated software or by performing other services to the group. During Sentinel's operation, over 30,000 software programs (including games, MP3 files, operating systems, utilities, and applications from vendors such as Microsoft, Adobe, Norton, Oracle, IBM, Lotus, and Novell, some of which were pre-release versions) were uploaded to Sentinel and downloaded by more than 100 individuals. The FBI cracked the case when a confidential informant helped them gain access to Sentinel. PWA members claimed their activities were "for fun and entertainment, not to try to make ourselves rich."

Seventeen defendants were indicted in 2000. Twelve defendants were PWA members, and five were Intel Corporation employees who provided computer hardware to PWA for access rights to the warez library.

Following the indictments, many defendants negotiated plea agreements. After the plea agreements were entered into, the government contended that the infringements had a retail value over $10 million. A group of defendants jointly moved to limit the retail value based on expectations defendants formed while negotiating their plea agreements. The judge denied the motion but permitted defendants to rescind their plea agreements (and thus withdraw their guilty pleas) if they wanted. None chose to rescind.

A group of defendants then petitioned the court for a lower retail value, and the court agreed, setting the retail value at $1,424,640. With the retail value set, individual defendants were sentenced.

Robin Rothberg, the PWA leader, entered a blind guilty plea but requested downward departure from the Sentencing Guidelines. The court granted him some relief, and he was sentenced to eighteen months in prison.

Another PWA member, Christian Morley, did not negotiate a plea agreement and instead took his case to trial. A jury found him guilty, and he received two years in prison. Two other defendants, Jason Slater and Justin Robbins, received jail sentences of eight months and seven months, respectively. Nine defendants received five years probation (and most of these defendants also received a $5,000 fine), and two defendants, Thomas Oliver and Steven Ahnen, each received three years probation. Two defendants, Mark Veerboken and Kaj Bjorlin, are fugitives. In November 2003, two defendants, Jason Slater and Christian Morley, appealed the case to the Seventh Circuit Court of Appeals. The Seventh Circuit upheld the district court's refusal to instruct the jury on fair use and its calculation of retail value.

* * *

IV.

What Exactly Does the Act Criminalize?

A.   Criminalization of Everyday Activities

* * *

The everyday activities potentially covered by the Act are breathtaking in scope and ubiquity. Our digital society requires us to make copies—lots of copies—to function productively, and all of those copies infringe if they involve third-party copyrighted works. Thus, the Act makes every file uploaded to the Internet or email forwarded to a friend the potential basis of criminal prosecution. The process of committing little acts of infringement is endemic in our lives, and all of those are, in theory, subject to scrutiny should we ever be prosecuted.

But perhaps the most problematic everyday infringing activity is P2P file-sharing. * * * [F]ifty-seven million Americans use P2P file-sharing services, and the P2P file-sharing software programs KaZaA and Morpheus—the market leaders after Napster's shutdown—have collectively been downloaded over 360 million times.

Yet, P2P file-sharers likely violate the Act. Some users download enough files to clear the Act's financial thresholds. But even lower-activity users automatically store files in a shared directory where other users can download the files, and some users altruistically choose to share infringing files. In either of those cases, any actual downloads made could also count toward the financial threshold. If enough files are uploaded or downloaded, the user may clear the criminal financial thresholds.

Alternatively, irrespective of a user's quantity of downloads or uploads, every file-sharer may be criminally infringing due to the expanded definition of "financial gain," which could apply to the sharer's receipt of other copyrighted works through the file-sharing system.

There is little debate that P2P file-sharing could be criminal, and Congress certainly has made it clear that it wants P2P file-sharing prosecuted. In Summer 2002, nineteen members of Congress, led by Sen. Joseph Biden, wrote to U.S. Attorney General John Ashcroft requesting that the DOJ make a priority of using criminal copyright laws to curtail infringement via P2P networks. The letter specifically requested that the DOJ prosecute P2P network operators "who intentionally facilitate mass piracy" and individuals who "intentionally allow mass copying from their computer" over P2P networks. In response, the DOJ pledged to bring criminal prosecutions against individual file-sharers, but no timetable has been set.

* * *

Despite Congress's exhortations, no P2P file-sharer has been prosecuted yet. More generally, there are a number of reasons why prosecutors may choose not to prosecute average Americans for everyday and common activities: the activity could be fair use, the activity may not clear the financial thresholds, evidence may be too difficult to collect, or the infringement may not be committed "willfully."

Specifically, the willfulness standard plays a critical role in distinguishing between legal and criminal activity and thus warrants more discussion. The U.S. Supreme Court has characterized willfulness as " 'a word of many meanings' whose construction is often dependent on the context in which it appears." Yet, Congress did not define willfulness in the Act.

This omission was not an oversight. The word's definition was discussed extensively in the legislative history, and some legislators wanted to define it explicitly.

* * *

[T]he House Report says merely that the Act "will not change the current interpretation of the word as developed by case law and as applied by the Department of Justice." In floor debates, Sen. Leahy repeated those words and continued, "nor does [the Act] change the definition of 'willful' as it is used elsewhere in the Copyright Act."

Accepting these statements at face value, this legislative history still does not clarify matters because, as discussed below, the existing case law was inconsistent. Further, where the legislators did explain their views on the word, the articulations were also inconsistent and suggest a split of opinion between the House and Senate.

In the Senate discussions, Sen. Hatch articulated a traditional definition of willfulness as "the intent to violate a known legal duty." In contrast, in the House discussions, Rep. Coble articulated a more lax definition of willfulness:

> It should be emphasized that proof of the defendant's state of mind is not required. The Government should not be required to prove that the defendant was familiar with the criminal copyright statute or violated it intentionally. Particularly in cases of clear infringement, the willfulness standard should be satisfied if there is adequate proof that the defendant acted with reckless disregard of the rights of the copyright holder. In such circumstances, a proclaimed ignorance of the law should not allow the infringer to escape conviction. Willfulness is often established by circumstantial evidence, and may be inferred from the facts and circumstances of each case.

The willfulness definition has not gotten any clearer since the Act's passage. The academic commentary remains confused about the implications of the willfulness standard, and while many cases have interpreted the term willfulness in a civil infringement context, relatively few cases have done so in criminal copyright cases. As a consequence, the case law continues to create "uncertainty in an area already filled with vagueness, gray areas, and doctrines with no bright line rules."

* * * The majority view is that willfulness requires the government to prove that the defendant specifically intended to infringe such that the infringement was a voluntary, intentional violation of a known legal duty. The minority view is that willfulness requires the government to prove only that the defendant had the intent to copy.

For purposes of understanding how the Act impacts our everyday activities, the difference between the views is critical. Under the majority view, defenses to willfulness include the infringer's ignorance of the law, an infringer's subjective good-faith belief that the use was fair, and the infringer's subjective good-faith belief that the infringing work was not actually infringing, because the new work was not substantially similar to the preexisting work or a defense such as the First Sale doctrine applied.

If ignorance of the law is a defense, then many otherwise infringing activities would escape punishment. Only in rare cases can prosecutors overcome that defense. Similarly, a defense that the infringer had a good faith belief that the use was fair would significantly narrow the Act's scope. With the fair use defense's inherent unpredictability and inconsistency, defendants can legitimately believe that most de minimis infringements committed during everyday activity constitute fair use. However, case law has already said that P2P file-sharing and warez trading are not fair use, so defendants may lack a good faith belief in those situations.

Thus, under the majority view, the Act only criminalizes commercial-scale infringers who have no hope of claiming ignorance of the law or fair use. Indeed, some commentators criticize the majority view for this very reason. However, whether one agrees or disagrees with the policy implications of the majority view, there is some chance that the majority view will not apply in a particular case. In those cases, the minority view should apply, and defenses like ignorance of the law and a good faith but erroneous belief in fair use may not be available.

* * *

B. Criminalization of Facilitators

The Act's coverage also leaves open the degree to which "facilitation" is criminalized. This ambiguity can be traced to the Act's inception, because arguably LaMacchia did not commit copyright infringement at all. While LaMacchia created and maintained Cynosure, which others used to commit copyright infringement, the government did not allege that LaMacchia uploaded or downloaded any copyrighted material himself. While the Act should apply easily to Cynosure users for the files those users personally uploaded and downloaded, it is less clear why LaMacchia's facilitation role should be criminalized.

Unfortunately, Congress did not specifically address why LaMacchia's actions were criminal or how the statute distinguishes between infringers and facilitators. As with the willfulness definition, when this issue was raised to Congress, a number of legislators made strong remarks that they did not want the Act to cover Internet access providers, and Nimmer even proposed language to correct this deficiency.

However, Congress ultimately acknowledged this issue only through the weak clarifying language regarding willfulness discussed above. How does this language distinguish Internet access providers from LaMacchia? In other words, exactly what did LaMacchia do beyond operating a Web site that reproduced and distributed copyrighted works?

Two facts might distinguish LaMacchia from Internet access providers. First, LaMacchia encouraged infringement because he allegedly requested his users to upload specific software to Cynosure, and second, he knew Cynosure users would exchange pirated software and wanted them to do so. While superficially these differences may distinguish LaMacchia from an Internet access provider who passively transmits packets across its network, these factors do little to distinguish other types of online service providers like web hosts that host infringing content or directories or search engines that link to infringing content.

Indeed, any individual or entity who commits contributory civil infringement probably has criminal willfulness under either the majority or minority view. Contributory civil copyright infringement occurs when an individual with "knowledge of the infringing activity, induces, causes or materially contributes to the infringing conduct of another." Certainly anyone who meets this standard will satisfy the minority view, but the combination of scienter and involvement should satisfy the majority view as well. In the DMCA, Congress putatively provided some facilitators a safe harbor from civil liability for user-caused infringement, but this safe harbor has proved largely illusory because it does not appear to apply when an online service provider meets the standard for contributory copyright liability. So, anyone who contributes to civil copyright infringement may also be a criminal infringer (assuming, if applicable, the financial thresholds are met).

Specifically, to the extent the provider otherwise meets the definition of contributory infringement, any of the following activities could lead to criminal prosecution: allowing artists to upload MP3 files for others to enjoy, providing access to USENET newsgroups where some postings contain infringing content, establishing web links to infringing content (either directly or by allowing a user to do so), operating P2P file-sharing services, allowing users to conduct auctions of infringing items, operating swap meets, and operating a marketing network for web sites that host infringing content.

* * *

NOTES

1. In order to obtain a felony conviction under the "No Electronic Theft" Act, 17 U.S.C. § 506(a) and 18 U.S.C. § 2319, the government must demonstrate that the defendant infringed at least ten copies of one or more copyrighted works with a total retail value of more than $2,500 within a 180–day period. [For a misdemeanor,] the government must demonstrate that the

infringement was done either (a) for purposes of commercial advantage or private financial gain, or (b) by reproduction or distribution of one or more copyrighted works with a total retail value of more than $1,000 within a 180–day period. U.S. DEP'T OF JUSTICE, PROSECUTING INTELLECTUAL PROPERTY CRIMES (2001), http://www.usdoj.gov/criminal/cybercrime/ipmanual/03ipma.htm.

2.   As referenced above in the Goldman piece, the Court in *United States v. Rothberg*, 2002 WL 171963 (N.D. Ill. 2002), addressed the question of how to determine value of infringing items under the NET Act. In *Rothberg*, at issue were 3,947 software titles found to be on a File Transfer Protocol (FTP) site called Sentinel.

> * * * The government obtained the retail prices for 2,200 of the 3,947 software titles found to be on the site at the time of the seizure. After some revisions and corrections, it derived an average price of $384 per program. * * * [W]e are satisfied that the estimate is reasonably accurate such that we can rely upon it for purposes of the Sentencing Guidelines calculation.

> Defendants argue that because [Pirates with Attitude (PWA)] did not sell the infringing software, the value for Guidelines purposes is zero. The Court disagrees. First of all, the Guideline does not direct the Court to determine the retail *price*; rather it requires us to determine the retail *value*. * * * [T]he pirated software had value, even if those who down-loaded it were not charged a fee.

> The question, however, is what the value is. We cannot simply adopt the retail price of the legitimate software items without considering other factors; the 1998 version of Guideline § 2B5.3 and Application Note 1 clearly do not permit this. * * *

> In this case we lack any solid evidence of the value of the infringing items other than the retail price of the genuine articles. Defendants have offered evidence garnered from reports of other cases in which counterfeit software was sold on the black market. But even assuming some figure, or range of figures, from those cases properly could be applied in this one, black market pricing is not always a proper surrogate for actual value. In this case the programs were fully-functioning versions of the products sold at retail, and they were mass-distributed, or at least made available for mass distribution, by PWA. The only significant differences between PWA's programs and the genuine articles were the unavailability of a manual, technical support, and a warranty. There is no basis to believe, however, that these affected the value of the programs to PWA's down-loaders, particularly in view of the availability of "help" files on the programs themselves.

> The law is clear that when there is an absence of other reliable evidence concerning the value of the infringing item, and the item is materially indistinguishable from the genuine article, the Court may adopt the retail price of the genuine item as the value of the infringing item. That is the case here. For these reasons, the Court will use the $384 average price determined by the government for the 2,200 programs that it reviewed as the average price for the full set of the infringing items. We therefore find

that the value of the infringing items for purposes of Guideline § 2B5.3 is $1,424,640 (3,710 times $384). *Id.* at *4.

E. ASSESSING THE PARAMETERS OF THE DIGITAL MILLENNIUM COPYRIGHT ACT

PROBLEM 52: FIGHTING "ELECTRONIC BURGLARY"

Al and Joanne (the main characters in Problem 46) continue to maintain their Web site on Earthlink as part of an independent study project for their History of American Film class. On this site, they have been able to post excerpts of classic films and complete versions of *The Godfather* Saga in fifteen minute segments for easier access/viewing. In a separate section on DVD technology, they post links to sites where software and other resources are available for working with DVD files, including but not limited to file-sharing FAQ's and DeCSS guides.[1]

Assume that the U.S. Attorneys office prosecutes Al and Joanne under the Anti–Circumvention Provisions of the Digital Millennium Copyright Act (DMCA), 17 U.S.C. §§ 1201(a)(1)-(2), (b), 1202(a)-(b). The relevant provisions of the Act prohibit circumvention of both access controls and copy controls in copy protection systems.[2] Also prohibited is "trafficking" in technologies that are primarily designed for the circumvention of technological measures. Any person who violates Section 1201 or 1202 willfully and for purposes of commercial advantage or private financial gain faces a maximum of 5 years' imprisonment and a $500,000 fine (first offense).

A. What arguments might Al & Joanne set forth in support of their assertion that they have not violated the terms of the Act? What additional facts might need to be identified before the result can be predicted? What might be the likely result, in the end?

B. Might there be laws that could address this type of activity in a better way?

C. Alternatively, might there be another way for educational institutions to address this area as a matter of policy?

THE DIGITAL MILLENNIUM COPYRIGHT ACT: PROVISIONS ON CIRCUMVENTING PROTECTION SYSTEMS AND LIMITING LIABILITY OF SERVICE PROVIDERS

Francisco Castro
4 J. INTELL. PROP. 3 (2004)

* * * [O]n October 28, 1998, Congress passed the Digital Millennium Copyright Act (DMCA). This comprehensive piece of legislation was in-

---

1. DeCSS is a decryption computer program designed to circumvent "CSS," the encryption technology that studios place on DVDs to prevent unauthorized viewing and copying.

2. Access controls prevent usage, not copying. Copy controls can be thought of as measures which actually prevent copying. Examples of access controls include encryption, passwords, usage restrictions. Examples of copy controls include serial copy protection for digital works and old floppy protection schemes.

tended to implement the [World Intellectual Property Organization (WIPO)] treaties and to respond to a variety of pressing copyright issues affecting the entertainment industry, especially the increased ease of music and video piracy on the Internet. * * *

Among the vast number of issues addressed by the DMCA, two key sets of provisions have particular importance in the protection and access to artistic material on the Internet: the prohibition of unauthorized access to copyrighted works by technologies that circumvent protection systems and the limitation of copyright infringement liability of online service providers.

I. CIRCUMVENTION OF COPYRIGHT PROTECTION SYSTEMS

* * * Under the DMCA, protection is given to technological measures used to limit access of copyrighted works by prohibiting the use and distribution of techniques, tools, or devices that can circumvent security controls in order to gain access to copyrighted material. It is a federal offense to bypass security measures even when done as a part of a research project or in order to use copyrighted work in a manner permitted by law.

The following paragraphs provide a brief summary of the most important prohibitions, rights, limitations, defenses, and exemptions described in Section 1201:

A. *Prohibition of Technologies to Circumvent Access Controls*

The basic prohibition of circumvention states that no person shall circumvent a technological measure that effectively controls access to copyrighted material. The law does not impose any standards or requirements on the manner or purpose of technical measures used to control access. *17 U.S.C. § 1201*(a)(1)(A).

B. *Prohibition of Use or Distribution of Technologies to Circumvent Access Controls*

The manufacture, import, or traffic of any technology, service, or device for the purpose of circumventing access controls to copyrighted works is prohibited. This provision limits access to permitted copyrighted material if a device is needed to get around access controls. *17 U.S.C. § 1201*(a)(2).

C. *Prohibition of Use or Distribution of Technologies to Circumvent Protection of Copyrighted Works*

There are additional prohibitions on the use or distribution of technologies, products, services, or devices primarily intended to circumvent measures that protect the rights of a copyright owner. This section pertains to the copyrighted works or materials themselves rather than access controls. *17 U.S.C. § 1201*(b).

D. Rights, Limitations, and Defenses

* * * [D]efenses to copyright violations do not serve as defenses to violations of Section 1201. *17 U.S.C. § 1201*(c).

E. Recognized Exemptions

Congress provided for a number of exceptions since it recognized that there are several legitimate reasons for circumventing technical measures used to control access to copyrighted works. [These exceptions include * * *]

(a) Nonprofit Libraries, Archives, and Educational Institutions. Nonprofit libraries, archives, or educational institutions are allowed to gain access to a commercially exploited copyrighted work to decide whether to purchase it for a legal purpose. This exception is only available when a copy of an identical work cannot be obtained by other means and does not preclude restrictions to circumventing access controls previously discussed. In order [for] libraries or archives to qualify for this exemption, their collections must be available to the public and also to persons doing research in the field covered by the protected work. *17 U.S.C. § 1201*(d).

(b) Law Enforcement and Intelligence Activities. * * * *17 U.S.C. § 1201*(e).

(c) Reverse Engineering. * * * *17 U.S.C. § 1201*(f).

(d) Encryption Research. * * * *17 U.S.C. § 1201*(g) [and]

(e) Exception Regarding Minors. Parents would not be in violation of the DMCA when attempting to protect their children from harmful material on the Internet. This section permits a component or part to be incorporated in a technology, product, service or device which has the sole purpose to prevent the access of minors to material on the Internet. *17 U.S.C. § 1201*(h).

* * *

II. LIMITATIONS ON LIABILITY RELATING TO ONLINE MATERIALS

Title II of the DMCA limits monetary liability of online service providers (OSPs) for copyright infringement in the event that others place infringing material on web sites hosted by the OSP or in the case that the OSP provides a link or networking connection to a web site containing infringing material. These new provisions were implemented in *17 U.S.C. § 512* and provide legal protection to an OSP as long as it follows certain guidelines. These guidelines define various "safe harbors" or exemptions based upon the type of OSP activity. The exemptions offered by the DMCA are in addition to any defense that an OSP might have under copyright law or any other applicable law.

* * *

The following paragraphs provide a brief summary of the requirements for eligibility, definitions of a service provider, safe harbor requirements, and limitations described in Section 1201:

A. Requirements for Eligibility

The OSP must establish several requirements in order to qualify for the exemptions provided by the DMCA.

(a) Termination Policy. An OSP must adopt, reasonably implement, and inform its subscribers and account holders of the service provider's system or network of, a policy that provides for the termination of those who are repeat infringers. *17 U.S.C. § 512* (i)(1)(A).

(b) Accommodation of Technical Measures. An OSP cannot interfere with standard technical measures. "Standard technical measures" is defined in Section 512(i)(2) as measures used by copyright owners to protect and identify copyrighted works. * * * *17 U.S.C. § 512*(i)(1)(B).

(c) Monitoring or Access. For an OSP to qualify for the exemptions offered by the DMCA, it is not required to monitor its service or affirmatively search for facts that show infringing activity. Moreover, the OSP does not have to gain access, remove, or disable access to material in cases where such actions are prohibited by law. *17 U.S.C. § 512*(m).

B. Definition of Service Provider

[In most cases,] * * * "Service Provider" is defined as a provider of online services or network access, or the operator of facilities therefor. *17 U.S.C. § 512*(k).

C. Safe Harbor When OSP Acts as a Transitory Digital Network * * * *17 U.S.C. § 512*(a). * * *

D. Safe Harbor When OSP Temporarily Stores Material * * * *17 U.S.C. § 512*(b). * * *

E. Safe Harbor When Information Resides on System at Direction of Users

An OSP is not liable for monetary relief, and it is subject to only injunctive or equitable relief, for infringing by reason of the storage at the direction of a user of material that resides on a system or network controlled or operated by the OSP. *17 U.S.C. § 512*(c)(1). To qualify for this exemption the OSP must:

(i) not have knowledge that the material is infringing;

(ii) not be aware of facts or circumstances from which infringing activity is apparent;

(iii) upon obtaining knowledge or awareness, acts expeditiously to remove or disable access to the material; and

(iv) does not receive financial benefit directly attributable to any infringing activity, if it has the right and ability to control such activity.

Under Section 512(c)(2), the limitation on liability established by this safe harbor applies only if the OSP has designated an agent to receive notifications of claimed infringement. The OSP must make this agent available through its service, including on its Web site in a location accessible to the public, and by providing the Copyright Office with the person's name, address, phone number, electronic mail address, and any other contact information that the Register of Copyrights may deem appropriate.

Elements of proper notification of infringement are specified in Section 5129(c)(3) and include identification of the copyrighted work, identification of the infringing material in sufficient detail to allow the OSP to locate it, complaining party contact information, a statement signed electronically or physically by the complaining party which shows it has the authority to enforce the rights that are claimed to be infringed, and a good faith belief that the use of the material in the manner complained of is not authorized by the copyright owner, its agent, or the law. If a notice complies with at least the first three elements of proper notification, the OSP is required to promptly contact the complaining party in order to take advantage of the safe harbor provisions of the DMCA.

F. Safe Harbor When OSP Provides Information Location Tools * * * *17 U.S.C. § 512*(d).

G. Limitation on Liability of Nonprofit Educational Institutions

Section 512(e) contains an additional liability limitation for public or other institutions of higher education that act as an OSP. This Section provides that online infringement activities by faculty members or graduate students that take place when performing teaching or research functions will not be attributed to the institution if:

(i) the infringing activities do not involve the provision of online access to instructional material that are or were required or recommended within the preceding three-year period, for a course taught at the institution by a faculty member or graduate student;

(ii) the institution has not, within the three-year period, received more than two notifications of claimed infringement by such faculty member or graduate student; and

(iii) the institution provides all users of its system with informational materials that accurately describe and promote compliance with, the laws of the United States relating to copyright.

NOTE

1. In *Universal v. Reimerdes,* 111 F.Supp.2d 294 (S.D.N.Y. 2000), Judge Kaplan construed the DMCA as mandating "a limited prohibition against linking to web sites containing DeCSS. He required clear and convincing evidence that those responsible for the link (a) know at the relevant time that the offending material is on the linked-to site, (b) know that it is circumven-

tion technology that may not lawfully be offered, and (c) create or maintain the link for the purpose of disseminating that technology." *Universal v. Corley,* 273 F.3d 429, 456 (2d Cir. 2001).

> The anti-trafficking provision of the DMCA is implicated where one presents, holds out or makes a circumvention technology or device available, knowing its nature, for the purpose of allowing others to acquire it.

> To the extent that defendants have linked to sites that automatically commence the process of downloading DeCSS upon a user being transferred by defendants' hyperlinks, there can be no serious question. Defendants are engaged in the functional equivalent of transferring the DeCSS code to the user themselves.

> Substantially the same is true of defendants' hyperlinks to web pages that display nothing more than the DeCSS code or present the user only with the choice of commencing a download of DeCSS and no other content. The only distinction is that the entity extending to the user the option of downloading the program is the transferee site rather than defendants, a distinction without a difference.

> Potentially more troublesome might be links to pages that offer a good deal of content other than DeCSS but that offer a hyperlink for downloading, or transferring to a page for downloading, DeCSS. If one assumed, for the purposes of argument, that the *Los Angeles Times* web site somewhere contained the DeCSS code, it would be wrong to say that anyone who linked to the *Los Angeles Times* web site, regardless of purpose or the manner in which the link was described, thereby offered, provided or otherwise trafficked in DeCSS merely because DeCSS happened to be available on a site to which one linked. *Id.* at 325.

2. Pursuant to the rulemaking authority set forth in the DMCA, the Librarian of Congress, on the recommendation of the Register of Copyrights, announced that persons making noninfringing uses of six particular classes of works would not be subject to the DMCA's prohibition against circumventing access controls (17 U.S.C. § 1201(a)(1)) for the next three years. These works included audiovisual works "in the educational library of a college or university's film or media studies department, when circumvention is accomplished for the purpose of making compilations of portions of those works for educational use in the classroom by media studies or film professors." See U.S. Copyright Office: Anticircumvention Rulemaking, www.copyright.gov/1201/2006/index.html (last accessed November 9, 2008).

3. During the lead-up to the November 2008 elections, Internet law scholar Lawrence Lessig highlighted new copyright issues that were arising within the context of YouTube. In so doing, he joined a growing number of commentators who are arguing for changes in the DMCA:

> Throughout this election season, Americans have used the extraordinary capacity of digital technologies to capture and respond to arguments with which they disagree. YouTube has become the channel of choice for following who is saying what, from the presidential campaign to races for city council.

But this explosion in citizen-generated political speech has been met with a troubling response: the increasing use of copyright laws as tools for censorship.

A perfect example is a recent dispute in a race for the New York State Assembly between Mark Blanchfield, a Democrat, and the Republican incumbent, George Amedore.

Last month, Blanchfield released advertisements that included a clip from a video interview with The Albany Business Review in which Assemblyman Amedore said, "I don't look at the Assembly position as a job."

Amedore complained that the ads took his remark out of context, and the newspaper's lawyers sent Blanchfield letters calling the ads "an infringement of our client's exclusive copyright rights" (redundancy in the original), and threatening Blanchfield if he didn't cease using the material. Never mind that Blanchfield's use couldn't possibly have harmed the financial interest of The Albany Business Review. Whatever the newspaper's motive, the result is the censorship of Blanchfield's campaign.

This problem isn't limited to New York Assembly races. It has directly affected the presidential campaigns. Last year, Fox News ordered John McCain to stop using a clip of himself at a Fox News-moderated debate. Last month, Warner Music Group demanded YouTube remove an amateur video attacking Barack Obama that included its music, while NBC asked the Obama campaign to pull an ad that included some NBC News video with Tom Brokaw and Keith Olbermann.

No doubt, these corporations are simply trying to avoid controversy or embarrassment, but by claiming infringement, they are effectively censoring political speech. * * *

Copyright law has become a political weapon because of a statute passed a decade ago: the Digital Millennium Copyright Act. That law tells carriers like YouTube that unless they quickly remove material posted by users that is alleged to infringe copyright, they themselves could be liable for the infringement. Understandably, YouTube and others have become quite vigilant in removing allegedly infringing content. Indeed, the Web site has gone beyond the requirements of the law and has begun to shut down the accounts of people alleged to have violated copyright just three times.

The digital copyright act gives the alleged infringer an opportunity to demand that the content be restored. But in the height of a political campaign, even a few hours of downtime can be the difference between effective and ineffective. The law thus creates a perfect mechanism to censor political speech during the only time it could matter.

The answer to this problem is not to abolish or ignore copyright.

Instead, the law should be revised, bringing focus to the contexts in which its important economic incentives are needed, and removing it from contexts where it isn't. * * *

What content owners need to recognize is that in the long run, it's unwise to ask for a definition of "fair use" in the middle of a presidential campaign. Judges are very unlikely to find copyright infringement in a political ad, and a law of "fair use" expanded to allow such uses could well weaken the legitimate claims of musicians and Hollywood studios.

It would be far better if copyright law were narrowed to those contexts in which it serves its essential creative function—encouraging innovation and ensuring that artists get paid for their work—and left alone the battles of what criticisms candidates for office, and their supporters, are allowed to make. Lawrence Lessig, *Copyright and Politics: YouCensor,* International Herald–Tribune, October 22, 2008.

For examples of related arguments that have been put forth by those urging major changes in the DMCA ten years after it was originally signed into law, *see, e.g.,* Jerome H. Reichman, *A Reverse Notice and Takedown Regime to Enable Public Interest Uses of Technically Protected Copyright Works,* 22 Berkeley Tech. L.J. 981 (2007); Note, *Harmonizing Copyright's Internationalization with Domestic Constitutional Constraints,* 121 Harv. L. Rev. 1798 (2008); Rebecca Tushnet, *Power without Responsibility: Intermediaries and the First Amendment,* 76 Geo. Wash. L. Rev. 986 (2008).

PROBLEM 53: LINKING AND RELATED ACTIVITIES AT EDUCATIONAL INSTITUTIONS

Assume that all of the protagonists in the following hypotheticals are either employees or students at public educational institutions. Assume, also, that the activities take place on the institutions' servers. Under current legal doctrine and emerging trends, would any of the following activities be illegal? Why?

A.   Cyberspace commentator, visiting scholar, and ultimate libertarian John Perry Barlow—noted for his view that copyright law is irrelevant on the Net and that all information should be free—links to an overseas site that features and encourages the dissemination of DeCSS code.

B.   Adjunct Professor Delaine McGriff, herself an outspoken cyberspace libertarian, writes an overview of John Perry Barlow's legal troubles as a result of his linking activities and posts it on her course Web page. In the document, she includes a link to the same overseas site that features and encourages the dissemination of DeCSS code.

C.   Professor Valdez requires all students in her Technology and the Law class to present online examples that reflect the class readings for the day, and posts an updated list of links to these examples for the students on the law school course page. After a student presents a Web site that features downloads of pirated software, Valdez updates the list of links on the course page by adding a link to that site.

D.   Professor Tran, during a class presentation, goes to the blog of an Idaho militia member who is dedicated to bringing the U.S. government down. On the blog is a link to a hacker site that features instructions for hacking into the Pentagon Web site. In response to a student request, Tran e-mails a link to the blog to the whole class.

E. Law student Ryan LaFleur, in his *Journal of Law & Technology* article on the First Amendment, includes a link to an undergraduate student's blog that contains examples of alleged online obscenity. The journal publishes the article and also posts it online.

F. PEER-TO-PEER FILE SHARING AND OTHER INTERNET– RELATED DISPUTES

The longstanding tension between the content industries and the large number of persons who download and share digital copies of multimedia files without permission has impacted colleges and universities legally and as a matter of policy. While no one disputes the fact that peer-to-peer technology can and does have many legitimate uses in the higher education community, it is also true that a significant percentage of those who use this technology regularly are students who have done so primarily for the sole purpose of obtaining free music, software, and other copyright protected products. And many have taken advantage of free high-speed connections on campus to facilitate these activities.

From the earliest days of this controversy, a central question as a matter of law has been whether and to what extent educational institutions can be held liable for copyright infringement taking place on their watch. If direct copyright infringement can be shown, one or more of two theories may be invoked, criminal copyright infringement and vicarious liability for infringement.

Major court decisions addressing file sharing have strengthened these doctrines. In *A&M Records v. Napster,* 239 F.3d 1004 (9th Cir. 2001), the Court found the highly popular service liable under both contributory infringement and vicarious liability for infringement, and the ruling eventually put the company out of business. In *MGM v. Grokster,* 545 U.S. 913, 125 S.Ct. 2764 (2005), the U.S. Supreme Court bolstered the ability of plaintiffs to prevail under a contributory copyright theory by finding that if a company distributed file sharing software pursuant to a business model that relied on *inducement,* such activity could result in liability as well.

Educational institutions, however, can take advantage of the aforementioned Digital Millennium Copyright Act (DMCA) to insulate themselves from liability. Section 512 provides a safe harbor, as long as its terms and conditions are satisfied. Yet the DMCA is far from the end of the story. Many have criticized the statutory scheme, both for its apparent sublimation of fair use principles and for its "guilty until proven innocent" take-down provisions. And as a matter of policy colleges and universities are still faced with the dilemma of how to address prospective illegal activity on the part of members of the campus community every day.

Thus, even in spite of major victories by the content industries in the nation's highest courts, the problem has not gone away. Indeed, peer-to-peer technology is only becoming stronger and more efficient.

Consider these issues in light of the *Grokster* decision and its aftermath. What should the role of colleges and universities be in this context? Is an aggressive, interventionist stance warranted, or is a laissez-faire approach—albeit accompanied by compliance with the DMCA—the one that still makes the most sense under the circumstances?

What predictions would you make regarding how these issues might play out over the next 5–10 years?

METRO–GOLDWYN–MAYER STUDIOS v. GROKSTER

545 U.S. 913, 125 S.Ct. 2764 (2005)

Souter, J., delivered the opinion for a unanimous Court.

The question is under what circumstances the distributor of a product capable of both lawful and unlawful use is liable for acts of copyright infringement by third parties using the product. We hold that one who distributes a device with the object of promoting its use to infringe copyright, as shown by clear expression or other affirmative steps taken to foster infringement, is liable for the resulting acts of infringement by third parties.

I

A

Respondents, Grokster, Ltd., and StreamCast Networks, Inc., defendants in the trial court, distribute free software products that allow computer users to share electronic files through peer-to-peer networks, so called because users' computers communicate directly with each other, not through central servers. The advantage of peer-to-peer networks over information networks of other types shows up in their substantial and growing popularity. Because they need no central computer server to mediate the exchange of information or files among users, the high-bandwidth communications capacity for a server may be dispensed with, and the need for costly server storage space is eliminated. Since copies of a file (particularly a popular one) are available on many users' computers, file requests and retrievals may be faster than on other types of networks, and since file exchanges do not travel through a server, communications can take place between any computers that remain connected to the network without risk that a glitch in the server will disable the network in its entirety. Given these benefits in security, cost, and efficiency, peer-to-peer networks are employed to store and distribute electronic files by universities, government agencies, corporations, and libraries, among others.

Other users of peer-to-peer networks include individual recipients of Grokster's and StreamCast's software, and although the networks that they enjoy through using the software can be used to share any type of digital file, they have prominently employed those networks in sharing copyrighted music and video files without authorization. A group of copyright holders (MGM for short, but including motion picture studios, recording companies, songwriters, and music publishers) sued Grokster and StreamCast for their users' copyright infringements, alleging that they knowingly and intentionally distributed their software to enable users to reproduce and distribute the copyrighted works in violation of the Copyright Act, MGM sought damages and an injunction.

     * * *

In addition to * * * evidence of express promotion, marketing, and intent to promote further, the business models employed by Grokster and StreamCast confirm that their principal object was use of their software to download copyrighted works. Grokster and StreamCast receive no revenue from users, who obtain the software itself for nothing. Instead, both companies generate income by selling advertising space, and they stream the advertising to Grokster and Morpheus users while they are employing the programs. As the number of users of each program increases, advertising opportunities become worth more. While there is doubtless some demand for free Shakespeare, the evidence shows that substantive volume is a function of free access to copyrighted work. Users seeking Top 40 songs, for example, or the latest release by Modest Mouse, are certain to be far more numerous than those seeking a free Decameron, and Grokster and StreamCast translated that demand into dollars.

Finally, there is no evidence that either company made an effort to filter copyrighted material from users' downloads or otherwise impede the sharing of copyrighted files. Although Grokster appears to have sent e-mails warning users about infringing content when it received threatening notice from the copyright holders, it never blocked anyone from continuing to use its software to share copyrighted files. StreamCast not only rejected another company's offer of help to monitor infringement, but blocked the Internet Protocol addresses of entities it believed were trying to engage in such monitoring on its networks.

     * * *

The Court of Appeals affirmed [the U.S. District Court's ruling in favor of Grokster]. In the court's analysis, a defendant was liable as a contributory infringer when it had knowledge of direct infringement and materially contributed to the infringement. But the court read *Sony Corp. of America v. Universal City Studios, Inc.,* 464 U.S. 417, 104 S. Ct. 774 (1984), as holding that distribution of a commercial product capable of substantial noninfringing uses could not give rise to contributory liability for infringement unless the distributor had actual knowledge of specific instances of infringement and failed to act on that knowledge. The fact that the software was capable of substantial noninfringing uses in the Ninth Circuit's view meant that Grokster and StreamCast were not liable, because they had no such actual knowledge, owing to the decentralized architecture of their software. The court also held that Grokster and StreamCast did not materially contribute to their users' infringement because it was the users themselves who searched for, retrieved, and stored the infringing files, with no involvement by the defendants beyond providing the software in the first place.

The Ninth Circuit also considered whether Grokster and StreamCast could be liable under a theory of vicarious infringement. The court held against liability because the defendants did not monitor or control the use of the software, had no agreed-upon right or current ability to supervise its use, and had no independent duty to police infringement. We granted certiorari.

II

A

MGM and many of the *amici* fault the Court of Appeals's holding for upsetting a sound balance between the respective values of supporting creative pursuits through copyright protection and promoting innovation in new communication technologies by limiting the incidence of liability for copyright infringement. The more artistic protection is favored, the more technological innovation may be discouraged; the administration of copyright law is an exercise in managing the trade-off.

The tension between the two values is the subject of this case, with its claim that digital distribution of copyrighted material threatens copyright holders as never before, because every copy is identical to the original, copying is easy, and many people (especially the young) use file-sharing software to download copyrighted works. This very breadth of the software's use may well draw the public directly into the debate over copyright policy, and the indications are that the ease of copying songs or movies using software like Grokster's and Napster's is fostering disdain for copyright protection. As the case has been presented to us, these fears are said to be offset by the different concern that imposing liability, not only on infringers but on distributors of software based on its potential for unlawful use, could limit further development of beneficial technologies.[8]

The argument for imposing indirect liability in this case is, however, a powerful one, given the number of infringing downloads that occur every day using StreamCast's and Grokster's software. When a widely shared service or product is used to commit infringement, it may be impossible to enforce rights in the protected work effectively against all direct infring-

---

8. The mutual exclusivity of these values should not be overstated, however. On the one hand technological innovators, including those writing file-sharing computer programs, may wish for effective copyright protections for their work. *See, e.g.,* Tim Wu, *When Code Isn't Law,* 89 VA. L. REV. 679, 750 (2003). (StreamCast itself was urged by an associate to "get [its] technology written down and [its intellectual property] protected."). On the other hand the widespread distribution of creative works through improved technologies may enable the synthesis of new works or generate audiences for emerging artists. *See Eldred v. Ashcroft,* 537 U.S. 186, 223–26, 537 U.S. 186, 123 S. Ct. 769 (2003) (STEVENS, J., dissenting); Molly Van Houweling, *Distributive Values in Copyright,* 83 TEXAS L. REV. 1535, 1539–40, 1562–64 (2005); Brief for Sovereign Artists et al. as Amici Curiae 11.

ers, the only practical alternative being to go against the distributor of the copying device for secondary liability on a theory of contributory or vicarious infringement.

One infringes contributorily by intentionally inducing or encouraging direct infringement, and infringes vicariously by profiting from direct infringement while declining to exercise a right to stop or limit it.[9] Although "[t]he Copyright Act does not expressly render anyone liable for infringement committed by another," these doctrines of secondary liability emerged from common law principles and are well established in the law.

B

Despite the currency of these principles of secondary liability, this Court has dealt with secondary copyright infringement in only one recent case, and because MGM has tailored its principal claim to our opinion there, a look at our earlier holding is in order. In *Sony Corp. v. Universal City Studios,* this Court addressed a claim that secondary liability for infringement can arise from the very distribution of a commercial product. There, the product, novel at the time, was what we know today as the videocassette recorder or VCR. Copyright holders sued Sony as the manufacturer, claiming it was contributorily liable for infringement that occurred when VCR owners taped copyrighted programs because it supplied the means used to infringe, and it had constructive knowledge that infringement would occur. At the trial on the merits, the evidence showed that the principal use of the VCR was for "time-shifting," or taping a program for later viewing at a more convenient time, which the Court found to be a fair, not an infringing, use. There was no evidence that Sony had expressed an object of bringing about taping in violation of copyright or had taken active steps to increase its profits from unlawful taping. Although Sony's advertisements urged consumers to buy the VCR to "record favorite shows" or "build a library" of recorded programs, neither of these uses was necessarily infringing.

On those facts, with no evidence of stated or indicated intent to promote infringing uses, the only conceivable basis for imposing liability was on a theory of contributory infringement arising from its sale of VCRs to consumers with knowledge that some would use them to infringe. But because the VCR was "capable of commercially significant noninfringing

9. We stated in *Sony Corp. of America v. Universal City Studios, Inc.,* 464 U.S. 417, 104 S. Ct. 774 (1984), that " 'the lines between direct infringement, contributory infringement and vicarious liability are not clearly drawn'.... [R]easoned analysis of [the Sony plaintiffs' contributory infringement claim] necessarily entails consideration of arguments and case law which may also be forwarded under the other labels, and indeed the parties ... rely upon such arguments and authority in support of their respective positions on the issue of contributory infringement," *id.* at 435 n.17, 104 S. Ct. 774 (quoting Universal City Studios, Inc. v. Sony Corp., 480 F.Supp. 429, 457–58 (C.D.Cal. 1979)). In the present case MGM has argued a vicarious liability theory, which allows imposition of liability when the defendant profits directly from the infringement and has a right and ability to supervise the direct infringer, even if the defendant initially lacks knowledge of the infringement. *See, e.g.,* Shapiro, Bernstein & Co. v. H.L. Green Co., 316 F.2d 304, 308 (2d Cir. 1963); Dreamland Ball Room, Inc. v. Shapiro, Bernstein & Co., 36 F.2d 354, 355 (7th Cir. 1929). Because we resolve the case based on an inducement theory, there is no need to analyze separately MGM's vicarious liability theory.

uses," we held the manufacturer could not be faulted solely on the basis of its distribution.

* * *

In sum, where an article is "good for nothing else" but infringement, there is no legitimate public interest in its unlicensed availability, and there is no injustice in presuming or imputing an intent to infringe. Conversely, the doctrine absolves the equivocal conduct of selling an item with substantial lawful as well as unlawful uses, and limits liability to instances of more acute fault than the mere understanding that some of one's products will be misused. It leaves breathing room for innovation and a vigorous commerce.

* * *

We agree with MGM that the Court of Appeals misapplied *Sony,* which it read as limiting secondary liability quite beyond the circumstances to which the case applied. * * * The Ninth Circuit has read *Sony's* limitation to mean that whenever a product is capable of substantial lawful use, the producer can never be held contributorily liable for third parties' infringing use of it; it read the rule as being this broad, even when an actual purpose to cause infringing use is shown by evidence independent of design and distribution of the product, unless the distributors had "specific knowledge of infringement at a time at which they contributed to the infringement, and failed to act upon that information." Because the Circuit found the StreamCast and Grokster software capable of substantial lawful use, it concluded on the basis of its reading of *Sony* that neither company could be held liable, since there was no showing that their software, being without any central server, afforded them knowledge of specific unlawful uses.

This view of *Sony,* however, was error.

* * *

C

Sony's rule limits imputing culpable intent as a matter of law from the characteristics or uses of a distributed product. But nothing in *Sony* requires courts to ignore evidence of intent if there is such evidence, and the case was never meant to foreclose rules of fault-based liability derived from the common law. * * * Thus, where evidence goes beyond a product's characteristics or the knowledge that it may be put to infringing uses, and shows statements or actions directed to promoting infringement, *Sony's* staple-article rule will not preclude liability.

The classic case of direct evidence of unlawful purpose occurs when one induces commission of infringement by another, or "entic[es] or persuad[es] another" to infringe, as by advertising. Thus at common law a copyright or patent defendant who "not only expected but invoked [infringing use] by advertisement" was liable for infringement "on principles recognized in every part of the law." * * *

The rule on inducement of infringement as developed in the early cases is no different today. Evidence of "active steps ... taken to encourage direct infringement," such as advertising an infringing use or instructing how to engage in an infringing use, show an affirmative intent that the product be used to infringe, and a showing that infringement was encouraged overcomes the law's reluctance to find liability when a defendant merely sells a commercial product suitable for some lawful use[.]
* * *

For the same reasons that *Sony* took the staple-article doctrine of patent law as a model for its copyright safe-harbor rule, the inducement rule, too, is a sensible one for copyright. We adopt it here, holding that one who distributes a device with the object of promoting its use to infringe copyright, as shown by clear expression or other affirmative steps taken to foster infringement, is liable for the resulting acts of infringement by third parties. We are, of course, mindful of the need to keep from trenching on regular commerce or discouraging the development of technologies with lawful and unlawful potential. Accordingly, just as *Sony* did not find intentional inducement despite the knowledge of the VCR manufacturer that its device could be used to infringe, mere knowledge of infringing potential or of actual infringing uses would not be enough here to subject a distributor to liability. Nor would ordinary acts incident to product distribution, such as offering customers technical support or product updates, support liability in themselves. The inducement rule, instead, premises liability on purposeful, culpable expression and conduct, and thus does nothing to compromise legitimate commerce or discourage innovation having a lawful promise.

* * *

In sum, this case is significantly different from *Sony* and reliance on that case to rule in favor of StreamCast and Grokster was error. *Sony* dealt with a claim of liability based solely on distributing a product with alternative lawful and unlawful uses, with knowledge that some users would follow the unlawful course. The case struck a balance between the interests of protection and innovation by holding that the product's capability of substantial lawful employment should bar the imputation of fault and consequent secondary liability for the unlawful acts of others.

MGM's evidence in this case most obviously addresses a different basis of liability for distributing a product open to alternative uses. Here, evidence of the distributors' words and deeds going beyond distribution as such shows a purpose to cause and profit from third-party acts of copyright infringement. If liability for inducing infringement is ultimately found, it will not be on the basis of presuming or imputing fault, but from inferring a patently illegal objective from statements and actions showing what that objective was.

There is substantial evidence in MGM's favor on all elements of inducement, and summary judgment in favor of Grokster and StreamCast was error. On remand, reconsideration of MGM's motion for summary judgment will be in order.

The judgment of the Court of Appeals is vacated, and the case is remanded for further proceedings consistent with this opinion.

It is so ordered.

NOTE

1. Intellectual property scholars Mark Lemley and Anthony Reese have put forth a principled alternative for addressing peer-to-peer copyright disputes. Under their approach, copyright owners could conceivably pursue a rapid, low-cost dispute resolution process against direct infringers, rather than suing "facilitating innovators." *See* Mark A. Lemley & R. Anthony Reese, *A Quick and Inexpensive System for Resolving Peer-to-Peer Copyright Disputes,* 23 Cardozo Arts and Entertainment Law Journal 1 (2005).

Consider the following overview of the proposed process. Would you support amending the U.S. Copyright Act to provide for such a process? Why? Alternatively, might you support it with modifications?

> We suggest that Congress amend the copyright statute to provide that in a certain category of cases of copyright infringement over p2p networks, a copyright owner would have the option to enforce her copyrights either by pursuing a civil copyright infringement claim in federal court or by pursuing a claim in an administrative dispute resolution proceeding before an administrative law judge in the Copyright Office.

> * * * [T]he administrative proceeding would be available only for relatively straightforward claims of copyright infringement. To start, the process should be available only against those alleged to have uploaded copyrighted works to a p2p network, thus making them available for downloading by others. Making a copyrighted work available for other people to copy is much more likely to constitute copyright infringement than is any individual instance of downloading, where the downloader's act of reproduction might well be excused as fair use or by some other defense. The potential for justifiable instances of downloading means that keeping the dispute resolution procedure streamlined would require a focus on much less defensible acts of uploading. * * *

> In order to restrict the dispute resolution process to conduct that is fairly clearly infringing, the process should be available only when a copyright owner's evidence shows that the person targeted has uploaded at least fifty copyrighted works during any thirty-day period.

> A copyright owner whose claim comes within the scope of the administrative procedure would have to put forth a prima facie case of copyright infringement. The complaining party would need to show that it had registered claims of copyright in the works in question and provide a sworn statement that it still owns the copyright (or the relevant exclusive rights) in the works identified. Next, the complainant would have to provide evidence that the works complained of were available for downloading from a particular IP address at a particular date and time. Such

evidence could consist of, for example, screen shots showing the availability of files and a sworn statement that the copyright owner determined that the titles listed were actually available and were actually copies of the copyrighted works. * * *

The dispute resolution process we propose depends on copyright owners being able to identify the individuals engaged in high-volume uploading. * * * Once the copyright owner has established this prima facie claim of infringement and identified the uploader, the uploader would have the opportunity to rebut or defend against the claim. * * *

In order to make the results of the administrative proceedings as consistent and fair as possible, initial decisions should be subject to an administrative appeal to a panel of administrative judges. This would allow for an additional layer of review, but in a somewhat streamlined format. Any party that was dissatisfied with the outcome of a complaint on appeal would then have the option of bringing the dispute to a district court for review. In order to discourage groundless appeals, a party that brings an unsuccessful appeal could be required to pay the costs of the appeal.

The administrative dispute resolution procedure we propose would provide a quicker, lower-cost alternative for copyright owners to enforce their rights against individual infringers on p2p networks. To be effective, the process must be streamlined. Both parties should have an opportunity to present evidence and argument online, but there should not be face-to-face argument or discovery of the sort that exists in civil litigation. The decisionmaker's job should be relatively straightforward: rejecting claims that do not fit within the system's requirements or that involve plausible disputes of law or fact that are better resolved in court, and determining whether the plaintiff has proved its charges of infringement. The judges should be obliged to issue a short written decision within two months after the case is submitted. * * *

Making the procedure attractive to copyright owners as an alternative to criminal or civil infringement suits against p2p uploaders and to suits seeking to impose secondary liability against facilitators of p2p networks will also require that the process provide an adequate remedy. We suggest that it provide two types of remedies: monetary relief and the official designation of an unsuccessful defendant as an infringer.

Monetary penalties should be sufficiently large that the possibility of having uploading challenged in the administrative procedure serves to deter others from engaging in large-scale uploading. The existing maximum penalties available in civil actions under the statutory damage regime seem likely to provide far in excess of the penalties needed to have a deterrent effect. It seems likely that in cases involving the uploading of fifty or more works, a penalty in the magnitude of $250 per work infringed would have a strong deterrent effect. Someone who uploaded 1000 songs—the threshold used by the Recording Industry of America (RIAA) in its initial lawsuits—would face $250,000 in liability. * * *

While an uploader must have uploaded at least fifty works in order to be subject to the dispute resolution procedure, any actual monetary award imposed on the uploader would, of course, only include those works

Cary Sherman, president of the RIAA, says the industry is not banking on a slippery-slope strategy like the one Mr. Nesson describes and disputes accusations of bullying.

"I think that some universities feel like if they're cooperative, then we shouldn't send them so many notices because that's a burden," Mr. Sherman said. "But when our vendors detect infringement, we send out notices. That's not intending to be punitive. We really do appreciate and value the cooperation we're getting from universities, even if it hasn't been uniform across universities." * * *

Catherine Rampell, *Antipiracy Campaign Exasperates Colleges,* Chronicle of Higher Education, August 15, 2008.

THE U.S. HIGHER EDUCATION OPPORTUNITY ACT

HR 4137 (2008)

In 2008, Congress passed HR 4137, a wide-ranging statutory scheme that reauthorized the U.S. Higher Education Act and included both extensive federal oversight generally and major reporting requirements for colleges and universities.

In particular, the Act included two new provisions addressing peer-to-peer file sharing on campus networks. Commentators have noted that the provisions are arguably ambiguous in a variety of ways, and it will fall to those promulgating regulations to provide the necessary guidance for the implementation of these provisions.

Three basic requirements are included in the file sharing provisions of the Act. First, institutions must inform students on an annual basis that the illegal distribution of copyrighted materials may subject them to criminal and civil penalties, and the institutions must describe the steps they are taking to detect and punish such illegal distribution. Second, institutions will be required to certify to the U.S. Department of Education that they have developed plans to "effectively combat" the unauthorized distribution of copyrighted material. In this regard, institutions are required to consider the use of "technology-based deterrents." Finally, "to the extent practicable," institutions will be required to offer alternatives to illegal file sharing.

The 2008 Higher Education Opportunity Act provides, in pertinent part:

SEC. 488. INSTITUTIONAL AND FINANCIAL ASSISTANCE INFORMATION FOR STUDENTS.

(a) INFORMATION DISSEMINATION ACTIVITIES.—Section 485(a) (20 U.S.C. 1092(a)) is amended—

    (1) in paragraph (1)—

        (E) by adding at the end the following:

            "(P) institutional policies and sanctions related to copy-right infringement, including—

"(i) an annual disclosure that explicitly informs students that unauthorized distribution of copyrighted material, including unauthorized peer-to-peer file sharing, may subject the students to civil and criminal liabilities;

"(ii) a summary of the penalties for violation of Federal copyright laws; and

"(iii) a description of the institution's policies with respect to unauthorized peer-to-peer file sharing, including disciplinary actions that are taken against students who engage in unauthorized distribution of copyrighted materials using the institution's information technology system;

SEC. 493. PROGRAM PARTICIPATION AGREEMENTS.

(a) PROGRAM PARTICIPATION AGREEMENT REQUIREMENTS.—

(1) VOTER REGISTRATION; 90–10 RULE; CODE OF CONDUCT; DISCIPLINARY PROCEEDINGS; PREFERRED LENDER LISTS; PRIVATE EDUCATION LOAN CERTIFICATION; COPYRIGHTED MATERIAL.—

(A) AMENDMENT.—Section 487(a) (20 U.S.C. 1094(a)) is amended—

(i) in paragraph (23)—

(II) by adding at the end the following:

"(D) The institution shall be considered in compliance with the requirements of subparagraph (A) for each student to whom the institution electronically transmits a message containing a voter registration form acceptable for use in the State in which the institution is located, or an Internet address where such a form can be downloaded, if such information is in an electronic message devoted exclusively to voter registration."; and (ii) by adding at the end the following:

"(29) The institution certifies that the institution—

"(A) has developed plans to effectively combat the unauthorized distribution of copyrighted material, including through the use of a variety of technology-based deterrents; and

"(B) will, to the extent practicable, offer alternatives to illegal downloading or peer-to-peer distribution of intellectual property, as determined by the institution in consultation with the chief technology officer or other designated officer of the institution.".

Chapter XI

The Rights of Educators

■ ■ ■

This chapter highlights the range of issues that may arise in disputes between educators and their employers. Part A begins with a broad overview of perspectives on labor relations in public education. Part B addresses the right to acquire and retain tenure, and Part C follows by examining the related area of dismissal. Part D focuses on freedom of expression, first exploring the scope of constitutional protection generally and then turning to the surprisingly complex topic of academic freedom. Part E concludes by documenting the types of employment discrimination cases that have been litigated in the education community over time.

A. PERSPECTIVES ON LABOR RELATIONS IN PUBLIC EDUCATION

1. COLLECTIVE BARGAINING AND THE EDUCATION PROCESS

From **4 UCLA Journal of Education (1990)
Special Symposium Edition**

● **Craig Becker,** *Governing the Schools: Teachers' Unions and Public Education*, **4 UCLA J. Ed. 49 (1990)**

Teachers' unions are an enigma. Although less than a fifth of workers in all industries were organized in 1988, over four fifths of public school teachers now carry union cards. In the last decade, membership in public employee unions has grown dramatically: thirty six percent of all government workers are now organized. Even so, the proportion of union members in schools is more than double this figure. And while just over a tenth of female employees are organized, in the teaching profession—one long dominated by women—two unions, the National Education Association (NEA) and American Federation of Teachers (AFT), together comprise a membership of over two and one-half million.

Not only have teachers organized, they have vigorously asserted their collective right to join in setting the terms and conditions of their employment. Teachers make up roughly a third of the nation's public employees; however, they call some two thirds of the strikes among government workers. And even after agreement is reached, teachers are more likely than other public employees to press grievances to arbitration.

The new tenacity of teachers in organizing and adopting traditional trade union practices has provoked a rising tide of reaction. Critics of teachers' unions typically contrast the alleged selfishness of organized labor to the selflessness deemed essential in schools. A century ago the *Chicago Times–Herald* decried the formation of the Chicago Federation of Teachers, the predecessor of the AFT, charging that the union sprang from "a spirit not creditable to the high standards of professional ethics" Recently, a school superintendent echoed this critique, declaring: "Teachers have lost their image as being public servants and are relegating themselves to being comparable to the dinner bucket, hard-hat union member." * * *

The ideal of the teacher implied in the term "public servant" has been held up to schoolmarms since the early nineteenth century. Since the Civil War, in fact, most teachers have been women. Until the advances brought by the contemporary feminist movement, there were few other secure or relatively high status occupations open to women. In 1963, the National Opinion Research Center ranked teaching thirty fifth in its scale of all occupations by social status, but first among jobs dominated by women. As late as 1981, over two thirds of all teachers were women, yet virtually all were supervised by male principals who reported to school boards composed almost entirely of men. Traditionally, too, teaching has figured as an act of dedication—even self sacrifice—on women's part. The figures of the mother and teacher have appeared as one. As Catharine Beecher, one of the earliest advocates of teaching as a female profession, affirmed in 1829, "It is to *mothers*, and to *teachers*, that the world is to look for the character which is be enstamped on each succeeding generation." "What is *the profession of a Woman*," Beecher asked. "Is it not to form immortal minds?"

Yet teaching often proved difficult for women to reconcile with their family roles. Through the first third of this century, many schools fired women who married. And until 1974, when the United States Supreme Court struck down the policy, school boards routinely kept pregnant women out of the classroom: requiring them to go on unpaid maternity leave several months before giving birth and to remain out for several months thereafter. These constraints reflected a culture that consecrated the female role of motherhood, but which, ironically, taught women teachers that students were the only proper object of their supposedly innate maternal instincts.

For generations, custom, policy, and economic circumstances combined to channel women into teaching, but also to confine them in the classroom and inhibit union organization. However, the past two decades have witnessed striking parallel transformations both in the teaching profession itself and in legal and cultural constructions of women's status: the dynamic growth of teachers' unions is systematically linked to the dismantling of occupational sex segregation and other discriminatory policies against women.

In part, the attack on teachers' unions rests on socially constructed gender categories, the image of the nurturing female teacher—an image shattered by her audacious agency in organizing collectively, like men in industrial trades. Early efforts to organize teachers evoked especially vehement opposition precisely because they were undertaken by women. In 1915, a member of the Chicago Board of Education successfully promoted a rule prohibiting teachers from joining unions, condemning the Chicago Federation of Teachers as a "curse to the school system." He went on to explain, "in a large municipality ... there is no need for lady labor sluggers. All labor sluggers are bad but I maintain that the female of the species is more deadly than the male." In the early NEA, Nicholas Murray Butler, the president of Columbia University, denounced Margaret Haley, an elementary school teacher and the president of the Chicago Teachers, as "a fiend in petticoats."

But today's attack on teachers' unions goes far beyond nostalgia for the spinster school teacher who, with few other options, devoted herself to teaching and adopted her pupils as children. Some critics go so far as to contend that unions are at the root of all the problems in public education. * * *

● **Lisa Mendel,** *Collective Bargaining in California Under the Rodda Act,* **4 UCLA J. ED. 3 (1990)**

* * * The Rodda Act of 1975, [CAL. GOV'T CODE § 3540 (West 1988)] introduced by State Senator Albert Rodda, [sought] "to promote the improvement of personnel management and employer-employee relations within the public school systems" in California by recognizing the employees' right to exclusive representation by the organization of their choice and affording them a voice in the formulation of school policy. The Act limits the scope of negotiations to "matters relating to wages, hours of employment, and other terms and conditions of employment." Parties are required to negotiate in good faith, but the Act does not require them to reach an agreement. Other significant provisions of this Act provide for exclusive representation of employees, impasse resolution procedures, and the establishment of the Public Employee Relations Board.

The Rodda Act provides for exclusive representation for all teachers within a bargaining unit. Certification of an organization as representative is granted after submission of support by a majority of all teachers within a bargaining unit. This section grants teachers the power to negotiate and enter into a written agreement with the school district through a single group representing the teachers.

The Act also mandates impasse resolution procedures to break deadlocks between negotiating parties. If either party declares an impasse, a mediator is appointed within five days. If the mediator, after attempting to resolve the problem, agrees with the requesting party that fact-finding is needed, the issue is submitted to a three-person fact-finding panel. The fact finders' recommendations must be made public, but are only advisory to the school board.

Finally, the Rodda Act established the Public Employees Relations Board (PERB) to govern all public labor relations. The duties of PERB include the conducting of representational elections, the appointment of mediators and the resolution of unfair labor practice charges filed with the board. When an unfair labor practice is committed by a school district or an employee organization, PERB may investigate, hold hearings, and prescribe appropriate remedial action. Examples of unfair labor practices include refusal to meet and negotiate in good faith, and breach of duty of fair representation.

The Effect of the Rodda Act on Teacher Strikes

Arguably, the most obvious indication to the public of whether the Rodda Act has served its purpose by improving the quality of employment relations is the absence or occurrence of teacher strikes. One would hope that the requirement that parties attempt to negotiate in good faith and the classification of refusal to negotiate as a punishable unfair labor practice would discourage such disruptions. Yet, as early as 1977, a study suggested that the Rodda Act had been ineffective in preventing strikes. In a period of fourteen months, beginning late 1987, there were major strikes in Los Angeles, Beverly Hills, Sacramento, Stockton and Santa Maria. This continuing large number of strikes since the passage of the Act indicates deterioration rather than improvement of labor relations.

In May 1989, for example, anger and frustration led to a nine-day strike in Los Angeles, the nation's second largest school district. Throughout the strike, the number of teachers on the picket line never dropped below 20,000. Although the district and teachers finally settled, the benefits to each side are inconclusive and many issues remained unsolved. The district agreed to give the teachers a 24% raise, but this was only 2.5% above what was offered before the strike; and teachers who struck for nine days lost 4.5% of that year's salary. The strike cost the United Teachers–Los Angeles (UTLA) $750,000, and the new contract will require a cut of at least $120,000 from existing programs. The agreement did mandate a restructuring of the district to provide for more community control of the schools, but it is not clear whether community school councils can make better administrative decisions than current administrators. Also, many union demands were postponed, and other issues remained unsettled.

Further complicating the debate over whether strikes are valuable is the controversy regarding the legality of strikes under the Rodda Act. The California Labor Code expressly allows concerted activities by employees against employers. The Rodda Act—while specifically granting a right to organize, choose representatives, and be free from employer interference—

does not expressly allow or prohibit concerted activities. However, according to some commentators, judicial precedent indicates that strikes are illegal. Former Senator Rodda also contends that he did not intend the statute to grant teachers the right to strike.

* * *

● **Kelvin Lee, *Collective Bargaining and Faculty Governance at the Higher Education Level: Lessons for the K–12 Community?*, 4 UCLA J. ED. (1990)**

* * * [W]hen examining possible reforms in labor relations within the K–12 educational system, it may be instructive to turn to the higher education model of collective bargaining and faculty governance. The higher education model appears to offer a number of advantages over the K–12 system. Not only are there fewer labor disputes at the college level, college faculty have greater control over their work circumstances and more autonomy in the classroom. Furthermore, college faculty enjoy greater professional recognition and higher salaries than K–12 teachers.

However, differences between the higher education and K–12 systems will undoubtedly limit both the implementation and effectiveness of higher education models of collective bargaining and faculty governance in the K–12 system. The higher education model also has drawbacks of its own, such as a relative lack of job security for instructors, large inequities in both pay and recognition among faculty members, and methods of evaluating teacher performance which are often criticized as arbitrary, unfair and ineffectual. Thus while it is certainly instructive to compare the higher education and K–12 models, adoption of higher education "reforms" in the primary and secondary school levels should certainly be approached with caution.

Comparisons Between Higher Education and K–12 Models of Collective Bargaining and Faculty Governance

Compared to K–12 teachers, higher education instructors generally have much greater control over their work circumstances. There exist several different higher education models of faculty governance, including those employed in the University of California (UC), California State University (CSU) and community college systems; however, all allow greater autonomy and freedom to faculty members than K–12 educators enjoy.

The UC model involves faculty in many areas of governance, particularly those involving personnel matters, which include the hiring of new instructors and decisions regarding tenure. The Higher Education Act places UC employees in four different categories: (1) Academic Senate, (2) Researchers, (3) Lecturers, (4) Librarians. The Higher Education Act mandates that tenure-track faculty be placed in a separate unit[.] [T]herefore, within the UC system, lecturers and librarians are covered by collective bargaining agreements. * * *

While there is only minimal unionization among faculty in the UC system, working conditions and the general environment of the faculty in the CSU system have led to significant collective bargaining among faculty members. The CSU's make fewer distinctions between full-time and part-time faculty within their system, and the CSU administration has created a large pool of part-time faculty, largely because of a great need for flexibility in staffing within their system. In the CSU system, part-time and full-time instructors are placed in the same collective bargaining unit. Therefore long term employment is often extended to part-time CSU instructors.

Many California community colleges began as small adjuncts to public secondary schools, and their organizational forms resembled the K–12 level, with a largely credential-oriented system. During the early 1970's, the Legislature enacted AB 1725, which purported to be a comprehensive reform of the community college system designed to move it closer to models of governance in four-year institutions. AB 1725 thus allowed each of the 71 different community colleges in California to define their own requirements for faculty in different academic and service areas. Furthermore, faculty unions at the community college level are organized around each individual community college district, as opposed to faculty unions in the UC and CSU system, which operate on a systemwide basis. * * *

While higher education may be broadly described to employ a "merit-based" system in hiring and retention of instructors, primary and secondary education may be said to employ "credential-based" systems of faculty governance. In contrast to the higher education model, entry and advancement within the K–12 system still involves obtaining an initial credential and then advancing through the system by obtaining additional credentials through continuing education and accumulating seniority. K–12 instructors are initially placed in a probationary status for a number of years; however, the vast majority of teachers (85–95%) eventually advance to become licensed, certificated staff. In fact, most of those instructors who do not complete this step leave the teaching profession for personal or other reasons, rather than because of non-advancement.

Introduction of a "merit-based" rather than "credential" or "seniority-based" model in the K–12 system would certainly face considerable resistance. For a number of reasons, K–12 educators feel strongly about maintaining the current system. The principle of advancement based on seniority is firmly entrenched within the K–12 system, and there is a strong and pervasive feeling that those teachers who "last through the process" of credentialing, licensing, and classroom teaching over a number of years are entitled to claim professional advancement and pay increases based on seniority. In addition, teachers hesitate to base promotions, which are currently obtained through relatively well-defined criteria, on the more subjective evaluation procedure that a merit system would inevitably entail.

The Role of Student and Peer Teaching Evaluations in Instructor Performance Assessment

One prominent feature of the higher education model is that periodic assessments of an instructor's performance occur through student and peer evaluations. These evaluations are also employed to distinguish competent from incompetent instructors. However, student and peer teaching evaluations are only partially effective at achieving their objectives, and create several problems. In the university system, student evaluations often undermine the effectiveness of part-time and/or new instructors, who may soften their demands on students for fear of provoking poor teaching evaluations from the students. On the other hand, student evaluations are often meaningless with respect to tenured professors. While negative evaluations may affect a professor's ego and personal emotions, they usually provide professors with little constructive input, and the fact remains that few tenured professors are removed for being poor classroom instructors. Within the UC and CSU systems, there are provisions in theory for the removal of the more incompetent professors, but they are rarely, if ever, employed.

The universities also have extensive peer review concerning the merit of colleagues. In both the UC and CSU systems, faculty committees regularly review the work of faculty members at both the departmental and university wide level. Although faculty recommendations on personnel decisions are generally accepted by the administration, administrators may overrule the faculty, and in exceptional cases the chancellor or university president may make the ultimate decision.

While community colleges are striving to implement more procedures allowing peer and student evaluation of faculty members, their efforts have been largely ineffectual. Community colleges were previously based on a credential-oriented system, and teaching contracts reflect this structure. Once community college instructors enter the system, their advancement continues according to a pre-determined schedule. Only an exceptionally strong offense such as a felony conviction or serious moral turpitude may slow the promotion of a community college instructor through the system, and an even more serious offense must be found to justify firing a faculty member.

In keeping with an effort to move closer toward the higher education model of faculty governance, community colleges attempted to widen the use of peer review and student evaluations. Yet both are relatively impotent in influencing personnel decisions. Instructors who receive negative evaluations may immediately "appeal to their contracts," which give them many job rights. Those who seek to remove an instructor have the burden of proof, and therefore community college administrators only take action against faculty in the most extreme cases.

By contrast, teacher performance evaluations have a much less important role in the K–12 system. No student evaluations are conducted in the

K–12 system; the nearly unanimous consensus is that students in these grade levels lack the maturity to answer such questionnaires responsibly. There are also few situations in the K–12 system where teachers have the responsibility to evaluate each other as in the higher education system. Resistance to such evaluations exists for two major reasons. First, K–12 teachers, who have more contact with each other than higher education instructors, often are hesitant to evaluate their peers. Second, teachers are quite concerned that assessments of teaching performance, particularly those of administrators, could be affected by the biases of the evaluators. Presently, more outside pressure is being brought to bear to create a more "merit-based" system, and some suggest that unless K–12 teachers allow for more serious peer evaluation, their efforts towards achieving greater professional status will be forestalled.

* * *

Greater professional status and recognition attach to teaching positions in higher education, and college faculty have greater flexibility and control over their working conditions than K–12 teachers do. Although college faculty generally receive greater pay than K–12 teachers, salary inequities exist in higher education to a much greater extent than in the K–12 system. * * *

[On the other hand,] [t]he K–12 system has * * * historically faced a exodus of quality classroom instructors as many of the best teachers become administrators. This trend has slowed in recent years as administrator's higher salaries and greater professional status are offset by longer work hours and responsibilities. Nonetheless, many of the best classroom teachers are left performing bureaucratic work, shuffling papers and dealing with red tape, while a shortage of qualified classroom teachers persists.

* * *

Three prominent aspects of the higher education model of faculty governance may potentially be adopted in the K–12 system: (1) more extensive peer review, (2) differentiated teaching levels, and (3) merit pay based on teaching evaluations. However, each of these mechanisms employed in the higher education system also create a number of disadvantages, and barriers exist to their implementation in the K–12 system.

While the K–12 system continues to search for much-needed reforms, adopting the features of the higher education model will not be a panacea. The K–12 and higher education systems will most likely retain their largely separate identities in the area of faculty governance. Nonetheless it is instructive to compare the models, and see how the successes of the higher education model in various areas of labor relations may be translated into meaningful reforms within the K–12 system.

PUBLIC EMPLOYEES' RIGHT TO STRIKE:
LAW AND EXPERIENCE

Martin H. Malin
26 U. MICH. J.L. REFORM 313 (1993)

* * *

I. PUBLIC POLICY AND PUBLIC EMPLOYEE STRIKES

Although arguments have been made to the contrary, this Article begins with the assumption that public policy favors collective bargaining by public employees when a majority of employees in an appropriate bargaining unit opt for union representation. Impasses in collective bargaining are inevitable. Accordingly, jurisdictions that provide for public employee collective bargaining have developed three approaches to resolving such impasses. The first approach relies on the threat or actual use of economic weapons, primarily the strike or lockout, to motivate the parties to reach agreement. The second approach prohibits strikes, but provides for fact-finding in the event of impasse. Under this approach, the parties present their positions to a neutral fact finder who makes findings and recommends a settlement, which the parties are free to accept or reject as they see fit. The third approach provides that the parties submit unresolved impasses to binding arbitration.

* * *

II. THE LAW OF STRIKES WHERE STRIKES ARE LEGAL

Although it may be trite to speak of the states as laboratories experimenting with different approaches to problems, that characterization aptly applies to public sector impasse resolution. Not only are the states divided over which impasse resolution device (strike, fact-finding, or interest arbitration) should be provided, but they also display considerable diversity of approach to each device. Those states which recognize a right to strike in public employment vary considerably in how they implement that right.

Illinois, Ohio, Oregon, and Pennsylvania provide a manageable sample of the different approaches to legalizing the public employee strike. These jurisdictions differ with respect to the type of prestrike impasse resolution procedures that they mandate. Illinois requires only mediation. Ohio and Oregon mandate prestrike fact-finding, while Pennsylvania, until a recent amendment governing teacher strikes, gave its labor board discretion to require prestrike fact-finding.

The laws of these jurisdictions also differ with respect to the standards that courts must employ when deciding whether to enjoin a lawful strike. Illinois and Ohio limit the issuance of injunctions to strikes that pose a clear and present danger to public health and safety. Oregon and Pennsylvania provide for the enjoining of strikes which pose a clear and present danger to the public welfare.

* * *

III.   THE LESSONS OF EXPERIENCE

State legislatures that legalize strikes by public employees do not intend to encourage work stoppages. Rather, they believe that once strikes are legal, they can be regulated and procedures can be required which will reduce the incidence of strikes and shorten those strikes that do occur. * * *

2.   THE PERCEIVED TENSION BETWEEN REFORM EFFORTS AND THE RIGHTS OF EDUCATORS

FROM THE STATEHOUSE TO THE SCHOOLHOUSE: HOW LEGISLATURES AND COURTS SHAPED LABOR RELATIONS FOR PUBLIC EDUCATION EMPLOYEES DURING THE LAST DECADE

David J. Strom, Stephanie S. Baxter
30 J.L. & EDUC. 275 (2001)

I.   INTRODUCTION

During the last decade, * * * courts and legislatures across the country increasingly have turned to more drastic measures under the guise of education reform. Regardless of one's opinion on the "reform" in question, it is clear that these measures are having a substantial impact on the rights of public school employees. Moreover, several trends are evident throughout the varied approaches states and localities have taken in the name of reform. * * * While there have been some victories on behalf of education employees in the last decade, many have lost rights and even more have had to wage a battle to retain the rights most believed were well settled.

In this paper, we examine six areas that have shaped the rights of education employees. In section two, we discuss the labor ramifications of disestablishing local schools through reconstitution and school takeovers. In section three, we assess the movement toward privatizing education through the use of voucher and tuition tax credit programs. In section four, we examine the charter school movement and the question of whether teachers have retained their bargaining rights. In section five, we recount various measures across the country to restrict the scope of bargaining for public sector employees, and in section six we discuss various attacks on teacher tenure. Last, we examine the trend to challenge the means by which unions and their members participate in the political system.

II.   DISESTABLISHING LOCAL SCHOOLS: SCHOOL TAKEOVERS AND RECONSTITUTION

In the past decade, there has been an increase in the use of existing law, as well as a proliferation of new laws on the state and local level to "takeover" or "reconstitute" schools that repeatedly failed to properly educate students. * * *

The legal authority that allows for school takeovers or reconstitution varies. In some instances, the authority derives from a court order or consent decree in ongoing desegregation litigation. Alternatively, federal, state, or local laws may provide for intervention. In other situations, the power to reconstitute schools may arise from negotiations between school and union officials. Although the words "reconstitution" and "takeover" are often used interchangeably, they describe different situations in both a legal and labor relations context. However, as described below, reconstitution and its concomitant effects may closely follow the takeover of a district.

Generally, in a state takeover situation, either the state board of education, the state legislature, or a federal court chooses a designated entity, such as the mayor or the state department of education, to manage the affairs of a local school district for a limited period of time. State takeovers are generally triggered when a school amasses a history of problems in various prescribed areas, which differ depending on the law in question. State takeover decisions may be based on a variety of factors, including inadequate student performance, low test scores, high dropout rates, fiscal mismanagement, failing infrastructure, or indications of poor administration and management. States often put school districts on a "watch" list as a warning that in the absence of improvement, a state takeover is likely. At least 23 states have some form of legislation to allow for the takeover of deficient districts. During the last decade, various states used these laws, although the extent to which the local school board was divested of control varied. The extent to which the takeovers adversely affected staff and/or labor relations in general further varied from state-to-state.

School takeovers differ from reconstitution in several respects, not the least of which is the greater impact reconstitution generally has on staff. Reconstitution is a process by which some or all of the school staff, including administrators, teachers, custodial and cafeteria workers are replaced by new personnel. In some instances, staff may reapply for their old jobs, while in other situations, staff simply have the option to apply for positions elsewhere in the district. Reconstitution is usually the last step in a process designed to improve schools. Generally, a school will first be warned that it is eligible for reconstitution because it has been identified as a low performing school. Usually there is a second step in which a school is put on notice that it must improve or it will face reconstitution. If the school shows little or no improvement, reconstitution is the step of last resort. From a labor relations perspective, reconstitution often yields unfair outcomes.

School Takeovers

In New Jersey, school takeovers took hold in the 1980s and continued in the 1990s. At least two urban districts, Paterson and Newark, were taken over in 1992 and 1995 respectively. The New Jersey Department of Education found that students in both cities were not receiving the minimum education and had histories of poor performance on state reviews and assessments. According to New Jersey law, if the state determines that it should take over a district, local school board members and high-ranking administrators are replaced with new managers. Importantly, in the context of takeovers, the New Jersey statute requires that "collective bargaining agreements entered into by the school district shall remain in force" and "all teaching staff members and other employees of a State-operated district shall retain and continue to acquire all rights and privileges accorded by Title 18A of the New Jersey Statutes."

Connecticut also ventured into the arena of school takeovers in 1997, when the state Legislature enacted a law to abolish the locally elected school board in the city of Hartford. The school board was replaced by a board of trustees appointed by the governor in conjunction with House and Senate majority and minority leadership. With regard to labor relations, the Act provides: "All contracts and agreements, including collective bargaining agreements, made in the name of the Hartford Board of Education shall be assigned to the State Board of Trustees for the Hartford Public Schools which shall be deemed the successor party in interest and deemed to be in privity of contract for all lawful purposes." The Act also provides various procedures to reopen negotiations, negotiate, and arbitrate with the exclusive representative of the employees. Interestingly, the new law also changes the criteria that interest arbitrators are to apply in resolving a dispute between the parties. Arbitrators shall not apply any presumption in favor of prior contract terms or arbitrator awards, but rather should give the highest priority to the educational interests of the students. Thus, while the Hartford law maintains collective bargaining, it adds an interesting new twist to the relationship of the parties by placing the needs of the students above the needs of labor and management.

A similar bill was passed in Michigan; it transferred the powers of the Detroit school board to the mayor. The mayor is empowered to appoint a reform board, which ultimately will control the Detroit public schools. This bill allows elected school board members to continue to serve in an advisory capacity without compensation or staff support until their terms expire. The Michigan law permits the reform board to terminate any contract entered into by the elected school board, except for collective bargaining agreements. Individual employment contracts, however, may be terminated. Interestingly, the law provides that five years after the appointment of the reform board, the question of whether to retain the board will be placed on the ballot in the district.

Reconstitution

Perhaps the first school district to experience reconstitution, the San Francisco Unified School District (SFUSD), has reconstituted more than 10 schools since 1984. The legal authority for reconstitution in San

Francisco was * * * a consent decree entered into between the parties to the [SFNAACP v. SFUSD] lawsuit. * * * Local union affiliates of the American Federation of Teachers and the National Education Association petitioned the court to be recognized as interested parties so that they would be able to participate in the discussions of school improvement, but their petitions were denied. * * *

[During the 1990s,] the original parties to the lawsuit entered into another [agreement] when it became apparent that the schools identified as "needing help" were not achieving the same levels of academic excellence as those schools that had been reconstituted.

San Francisco created a Comprehensive School Improvement Program (CSIP) to identify low-performing schools. CSIP schools receive a central office administrator to help create and implement a school improvement plan, additional resources, and increased budget flexibility. The program also includes a management consultation process. Participating schools are periodically assessed using such factors as, student grades and writing samples, average daily attendance rates, student suspension and dropout rates, and the effective implementation of the school's improvement plan.

San Francisco teachers and their representatives were barred from participating in discussions at the critical stages of reconstitution policy development. For more than ten years, the union's only role in the process was an attempt to negotiate transfer policies for the staff that were affected by reconstitution. However, the union finally negotiated an agreement with the SFUSD on a new school improvement process in 1997. The agreement declared the mutual commitment of the district and the union to "improving teaching and learning in the schools of San Francisco and to creating alternatives which are intended to lead to the elimination of the need for reconstitution." * * *

New York City handled reconstitution in a wholly different manner. Reconstitution procedures were negotiated with the teachers union, the United Federation of Teachers. When the state determines that a school is unacceptable, it may be subject to the school redesign process. Under the process, at least half of the positions in the redesigned school can be reserved for existing qualified staff. A personnel committee, which includes two union representatives, chooses the staff for the redesigned school. Teachers that leave the school are given "priority transfers," which provide them with the first choice of other available positions in the district for which they are qualified.

Hybrid Takeover and Reconstitution Examples

In 1994, a court-enforced desegregation consent decree granted the Cleveland (Ohio) school district the power to reconstitute schools. In 1995, a United States federal judge mandated that the state take over the Cleveland public school system. Two years later, control of the school system was transferred to the mayor. The Ohio Legislature followed suit by passing legislation to identify and correct educationally deficient schools. The legislation provides for the use of corrective action plans at deficient schools, monitoring programs, and the use of experts to assist in plan implementation. It is important to note that the legislation also provides that no action taken under the statute may abrogate any term of a collective bargaining agreement and requires that where a union is in place, the union must consent to the corrective action plan in writing.

Despite the fact that the law protects collective bargaining agreements, Cleveland's early reconstitution efforts did not take union contracts into consideration. Instead, the school district took the position that it could circumvent the collective bargaining agreements based on the 1994 desegregation order. The Cleveland Teachers Union filed unfair labor practice charges and grievances claiming that the reconstitution violated transfer and reassignment provisions of the collective bargaining agreement. The district and the union ultimately reached a contractual agreement governing the transformation of the city's schools. The agreement provides that bargaining unit members receive adequate notice of reconstitution and a list of other available positions in the district, the ability to return a list of preferences, and a statement that reconstituted staff will not experience reprisals.

Similarly, the Illinois Legislature shifted control of the Chicago Public Schools to the mayor, who was charged with the power to appoint the school board and the district's chief executive officer. The chief executive officer, in turn, was empowered to fill a variety of high-ranking positions, such as chief fiscal officer, chief educational officer, and chief purchasing officer. Beyond takeover, the Legislature provided procedures for school reconstitution.

In an apparent effort to ease school reform, the Illinois Legislature also determined that a variety of traditionally accepted subjects of bargaining would be prohibited subjects of bargaining. This change left employees with little say in the process and only limited ability to negotiate regarding subjects integral to teachers employment in the system. The statute prohibits bargaining on decision-making and the impact of decisions: (1) to layoff employees or reduce staff; (2) determinations regarding class size, class staffing, assignments, scheduling, academic calendars, and pupil assignment; (3) relating to the use of technology and pilot programs; and (4) decisions regarding charter schools or the use of third-party providers.

In Illinois, reconstitution is the last step after other reform processes have failed. Once it is determined that a school will be reconstituted, the principal is generally removed and all staff members must reapply for their jobs. Staff who are not rehired at the reconstituted school can apply for other employment in the district and will receive full pay for 10 months while they attempt to find another placement. Displaced teachers are expected to substitute teach during this 10 month period. However, teachers who do not find a placement within this time frame may be dismissed.

Maryland also has experience with both takeovers and reconstitution. In 1997, the state and the city of Baltimore forged a partnership to run the Baltimore City Schools. A new nine member school board was created, with members appointed jointly by the mayor and the governor. In 1997, the Legislature also enacted a law and promulgated regulations to provide for reconstitution when a school continually fails to meet academic standards.

In January 2000, the Maryland Board of Education announced that three schools of the original 40 placed on the state's list as being eligible for reconstitution in 1994 will indeed be reconstituted. However, in an unprecedented move, the state entered into a contract with a for-profit company, Edison, Inc., to operate these schools. Unlike other reconstitutions, employees who apply for positions at the newly reconstituted schools will be employed by the private contractor, not the school system. The schools no longer will be subject to union contracts and employees no longer will be able to participate in the Teachers' Retirement System or state health plans. Teachers will also lose the tenure protections provided to public school teachers.

The Baltimore Teachers Union filed a lawsuit in Baltimore Circuit Court seeking a declaration that the city and state may not delegate their authority under various statutes to a private business. Further, the suit requests that the court void the contract with Edison and order Edison to refund any monies it was paid under the contract. On July 20, 2000, Circuit Judge Stuart Berger held that the Maryland State Board of Education acted within its statutory power when it contracted with Edison, Inc. to operate three failing schools. This case is currently on appeal before the Maryland Court of Appeals.

While both school takeovers and reconstitution inevitably effect employees in a variety of ways, from a labor relations perspective, employees enjoyed greater protection in takeover situations in the last decade. Takeover legislation generally recognized and left intact the collective bargaining relationship, which at the very least, allows the employees to retain the rights provided by contract. On the other hand, reconstitution efforts yielded varied results for the affected employees. In some instances, the union was simply ignored in the process. In others, the legislature eased reconstitution by altering the subjects over which employees are able to bargain. In Maryland, reconstitution is now being employed as a bridge to privatization. Thus, while takeovers shook up the top levels of power, reconstitution seemed to more directly affect the day to day lives of educational employees.

* * *

IV. CHARTER SCHOOLS

* * * Although the specifics of the laws vary, the general theory behind charter school legislation is to allow individuals or companies to create schools that are public, but which operate outside the traditional public school scheme. * * *

State statutes generally provide two avenues for chartering schools: (1) an existing public school converts to a charter school; or (2) an individual or group applies to charter a new school. In either case, from a labor relations perspective it is very important how employees will be treated with regard to unionization and bargaining.

Charter school laws vary in the extent to which they deal, if at all, with employee relations issues. In Alaska, Connecticut, Hawaii, Michigan, Nevada, and Wisconsin public charter school employees enjoy the same rights to organize and bargain collectively as other public employees in the respective states. These states automatically consider charter school employees a part of the existing district bargaining unit and subject to the current collective bargaining agreement. In Louisiana, charter school employees are subject to terms of existing collective bargaining agreements, unless otherwise specified in the charter.

In some states, such as Delaware, Florida, Idaho, Illinois, New Hampshire, Pennsylvania, and the District of Columbia, employees have the right to bargain, but the law requires the charter school to be a separate bargaining unit. In Minnesota, charter school employees can bargain as part of a separate unit, unless all parties agree that the employees should be part of the district unit. Interestingly, charter school employees in Oklahoma may bargain as separate units, subject to the rules of the National Labor Relations Board, as opposed to a state labor relations board.

Other states draw bargaining lines depending on how the charter school began. For instance, in New Jersey, when a public school converts to a charter school, the charter school employees must remain part of the district bargaining unit. However, start-up charter schools in New Jersey "may choose whether or not to offer the terms of any collective bargaining already established by the school district for its employees, but the board shall adopt any health and safety provisions of the agreement." Similarly, in Ohio, conversion school staff remain part of the district bargaining unit unless they vote to form a separate unit. In Rhode Island employees in district charter schools remain part of the district bargaining unit, but if the charter school is started by an outside group, the employees must secure recognition as a separate unit. In Michigan and Kansas, employees may remain in the district unit if they work in a school chartered by the district.

In New York, employees of a conversion charter school are included in the school district bargaining unit and are subject to the same collective bargaining agreement. However, a majority of members within a charter school may modify the collective bargaining agreement, with the approval of the charter school trustees, to address an issue specific to charter school employment. The New York also provides that employees of a newly created charter school, with at least 250 students, "shall be deemed to be represented in a separate negotiating unit at the charter school by the same employee organization, if any, that represents like employees in the school district in which the charter is located."

Ten states do not allow charter school employees to bargain, however, these states generally do not allow bargaining for public sector employees. These states are Arizona, Arkansas, Georgia, Mississippi, North Carolina, South Carolina, Texas, Utah, Virginia, and Wyoming.

V.   LEGISLATIVE EFFORTS TO RESTRICT THE SCOPE OF BARGAINING FOR PUBLIC SECTOR EDUCATION EMPLOYEES

In a number of states with mature public sector collective bargaining statutes, legislatures have enacted new laws that restrict the scope of bargaining for education employees. This legislation is notable for at least two reasons. First, it singles out education employees for different treatment under the state's public sector collective bargaining law. Second, the legislation does not track similar developments in the private sector under the National Labor Relations Act. Indeed, in circumstances where the parties have a well-developed collective bargaining relationship, the tradition has been to expand the scope of bargaining, even if that is accomplished informally.

* * *

Overall, the 1990s redefined collective bargaining for education employees in the public sector as a fragile right that can be threatened by an unfriendly state legislature and/or governor. Once public education employees have gained collective bargaining rights through law there are no guarantees that these rights cannot be taken away, as was the case in New Mexico, or severely eroded, as in Illinois and Michigan. * * *

VI.   ATTACKS ON TEACHER TENURE

In the last several years, there has been a growing wave of criticism about teacher tenure laws. Critics claim that schools are full of incompetent or ineffectual teachers who cannot be fired because of tenure laws. Although these critics misunderstand the purposes and rights granted by most tenure systems, states and localities have responded to these attacks in a variety of ways. Some states have repealed tenure and several states have eliminated the term "tenure," while maintaining the system's basic due process components. Other states have responded by streamlining procedural aspects of the tenure system in an effort to speed the process of dismissing a teacher. In one state, tenure policies became a collective bargaining matter to be negotiated at the local level. Further, without changing the law, some school districts attempted to circumvent the state tenure system by offering jobs contingent upon applicants waiving their rights under the tenure system.

Although tenure requirements and protections vary widely from state to state, tenure is generally achieved after a teacher successfully completes a multi-year probationary period. Tenure does not mean that a teacher cannot lose his or her job, rather, tenure provides due process when teachers are threatened with dismissal. The general purpose of tenure laws is to protect competent teachers from arbitrary employment actions, including dismissal based on personal or political beliefs, school board politics, anti-union animus, or nepotism.

In 1997, Oregon radically changed its teacher tenure law. The Oregon Fair Dismissal Law eliminated the tenure system, which had provided that employees who passed a three-year probation became permanent employees who could only be removed for several specified reasons. Although new law provides for two-year renewable contracts, it retains a variety of protections that teachers enjoyed under the previous law. Even though the new law was touted as a means to dismiss poor teachers more quickly and efficiently, it emphasizes teacher rehabilitation as opposed to dismissal by requiring districts to work with a teacher for at least one year after a teacher's contract is not renewed. Further, once the law went into effect, districts generally retained the same percentage of teachers, even though it would have been easier to dismiss poor teachers.

Colorado, Florida, Massachusetts, New Mexico, and South Dakota are among the state that have eliminated the term "tenure," replacing it with terms such as "nonrenewal of contract" and "continuing contract." However, these states generally retained the protections that were previously available for teachers, including an entitlement to re-employment based on good performance and conduct and due process provisions in the context of discipline and dismissal.

Other states, such as Connecticut, Michigan, and New York, have simply streamlined the time lines within due process procedures in an attempt to ensure a timely outcome. Interestingly, in streamlining the process teachers may benefit from the fact that changes often result in a hearing before an impartial hearing officer at an earlier time, rather than having to go multiple levels of hearings, often before bodies and individuals who may not be truly impartial. Moreover, although there is not much data available on outcomes at this stage, assuming the process is fair, a shorter process also benefits the teacher who is wrongfully terminated by returning him/her to work more quickly.

In 1995, Wisconsin also passed radical changes, eliminating the tenure system as part of state law, but allowing parties to negotiate tenure type systems pursuant to collective bargaining agreements. Although teachers in large cities and counties who obtained tenure prior to Dec. 1995, retain tenure protections, contract renewal and due process issues for all other teachers are based on the applicable collective bargaining agreement.

Several New York school districts attempted to get around the state's tenure scheme by passing resolutions requiring new teachers to waive the tenure protections provided by Section 3012 of the Education Law. Teachers in these districts were expected to work outside the tenure scheme pursuant to contracts that were renewable annually. Fortunately, at least two New York courts held that the school boards in question exceeded their authority and contravened public policy by attempting to eliminate the tenure system.

* * *

VIII.   A PEEK AT THE FUTURE

Teachers and school employees are among the most highly organized groups in the country. In the 1960's and 1970's education employees gained enormous power in the labor relations context as over 30 states passed laws that allowed collective bargaining. In the 1980's wages and employment benefits continued to improve for education employees. The 1990's, however, proved to be a challenging decade for educational labor relations.

As we look ahead * * *, it appears probable that the climate for education reform will continue and this * * * will have a definite impact on education employees. * * *

NOTES

1.   Consider the accountability provisions of the "No Child Left Behind" (NCLB) Act in light of the materials in this section. Will it be possible to harmonize the NCLB mandates with legal and policy imperatives of collective bargaining law? Once corrective action must be taken, can conflict be avoided? Or is conflict inevitable?

2.   The history of reconstitution in San Francisco provides an important case study in this context. As referenced above, reconstitution began in 1983 pursuant to the requirements of the *SFNAACP* Consent Decree, and was included in the "No Child Left Behind" Act as one of the options for corrective action under the accountability provisions. Pursuant to the San Francisco Decree, all the adults at persistently low performing schools were removed, and a new group of adults were brought in. People could reapply for their former jobs if they were willing to commit to a different operating structure, but they were not guaranteed reappointment. However, those with tenure or other types of job protection were guaranteed positions somewhere in the District

By 2005, over twenty SFUSD schools had been reconstituted, albeit in very different ways. One set of schools was reconstituted in 1983, pursuant to "Phase One" reforms mandated by the Decree. A second group was reconstituted from 1993–1997, under the highly structured Comprehensive School Improvement Program (CSIP). A third group, designated as "Dream Schools," was reconstituted from 2003–2005 in the shadow of the "No Child Left Behind" Act, with both the methods of reconstitution and the mandated reforms varying greatly from campus to campus. The United Educators of San Francisco (UESF) consistently attempted to resist reconstitution, seeking instead to implement a more collaborative process. *See generally* Kelly C.

Rozmus, *Education Reform and Education Quality: Is Reconstitution the Answer?*, 1998 BYU EDUC. & L.J. 103.

The jury is still out on the efficacy of reconstitution as a viable education reform. In certain instances, in San Francisco, there was clear evidence that reconstitution had worked. In other instances, reconstituted schools improved, but it was not clear how much the improvement had to do with reconstitution itself and how much it had to do with other factors, such as the additional resources and restructured programs that sometimes accompanied the changes. In other cases, reconstitution clearly did not work. One thing is certain, reconstitution by itself was never sufficient. For the strategy to work, it necessarily had to be accompanied by a vision and a detailed education plan.

For an overview and analysis of reconstitution in San Francisco, see generally The Independent Reports of the Consent Decree Monitoring Team (1997–2005), http://www.gseis.ucla.edu/courses/edlaw/sfrepts.htm (last visited Feb. 9, 2009). In particular, see Report #14 (September 1997) at pages 90–107 and Report #16 (July 1999) at pages 140–170, both available on that site.

Finally, it is important to note that even schools that had turned around under this Consent Decree were not always able to sustain their gains. As the independent Monitoring Team found:

> [T]here is no magic formula in the world of education reform. No one silver bullet has yet been found in this context. Research has shown that turning around a low performing school requires—among other things— the right combination of people, interpersonal communication, programs, funding, and relationships. It requires a great deal of hard, day-to-day work over time ... establishing partnerships between and among the District's educators, the school's students, and the local community. Such efforts—even if successful—do not continue automatically. People change, students change, circumstances change, and new relationships must be built. Turning around a low performing school is thus an ongoing process, not a one-time operation that can then be expected to last indefinitely. *See* Report #17 at page 172 (July 2000).

B. THE RIGHT TO ACQUIRE & RETAIN TENURE

At the K–12 level, most states have enacted legislation granting tenure protection for teachers. At the higher education level, tenure is sometimes governed by statute, sometimes by campus policy, and sometimes by a combination of the two.

While debates regarding the efficacy of prospective tenure reform continue unabated, legal disputes in this area do not generally focus on changes in tenure structures. Instead, the controversies often reflect bitter disagreements over denial of tenure, dismissal of tenured employees, and related matters.

One of the most unique and arguably far-reaching cases in this context is *Perry v. Sindermann,* where the U.S. Supreme Court considered the question of when de facto tenure might arise.

PERRY v. SINDERMANN

408 U.S. 593, 92 S.Ct. 2694 (1972)

MR. JUSTICE STEWART delivered the opinion of the Court.

From 1959 to 1969 the respondent, Robert Sindermann, was a teacher in the state college system of the State of Texas. After teaching for two years at the University of Texas and for four years at San Antonio Junior College, he became a professor of Government and Social Science at Odessa Junior College in 1965. He was employed at the college for four successive years, under a series of one-year contracts. He was successful enough to be appointed, for a time, the cochairman of his department.

During the 1968–1969 academic year, however, controversy arose between the respondent and the college administration. The respondent was elected president of the Texas Junior College Teachers Association. In this capacity, he left his teaching duties on several occasions to testify before committees of the Texas Legislature, and he became involved in public disagreements with the policies of the college's Board of Regents. In particular, he aligned himself with a group advocating the elevation of the college to four-year status—a change opposed by the Regents. And, on one occasion, a newspaper advertisement appeared over his name that was highly critical of the Regents.

Finally, in May 1969, the respondent's one-year employment contract terminated and the Board of Regents voted not to offer him a new contract for the next academic year. The Regents issued a press release setting forth allegations of the respondent's insubordination. But they provided him no official statement of the reasons for the nonrenewal of his contract. And they allowed him no opportunity for a hearing to challenge the basis of the nonrenewal.

The respondent then brought this action in Federal District Court. He alleged primarily that the Regents' decision not to rehire him was based on his public criticism of the policies of the college administration and thus infringed his right to freedom of speech. He also alleged that their failure to provide him an opportunity for a hearing violated the Fourteenth Amendment's guarantee of procedural due process. The petitioners—members of the Board of Regents and the president of the college—denied that their decision was made in retaliation for the respondent's public criticism and argued that they had no obligation to provide a hearing. * * * We granted a writ of certiorari and we have considered this case along with *Board of Regents v. Roth.*

I

The first question presented is whether the respondent's lack of a contractual or tenure right to re-employment, taken alone, defeats his claim that the nonrenewal of his contract violated the First and Fourteenth Amendments. We hold that it does not.

For at least a quarter-century, this Court has made clear that even though a person has no "right" to a valuable governmental benefit and even though the government may deny him the benefit for any number of reasons, there are some reasons upon which the government may not rely. It may not deny a benefit to a person on a basis that infringes his constitutionally protected interests—especially, his interest in freedom of speech. For if the government could deny a benefit to a person because of his constitutionally protected speech or associations, his exercise of those freedoms would in effect be penalized and inhibited. This would allow the government to "produce a result which (it) could not command directly." Such interference with constitutional rights is impermissible.

We have applied this general principle to denials of tax exemptions, unemployment benefits, and welfare payments. But, most often, we have applied the principle to denials of public employment. We have applied the principle regardless of the public employee's contractual or other claim to a job. * * *

Thus, the respondent's lack of a contractual or tenure "right" to re-employment for the 1969–1970 academic year is immaterial to his free speech claim. Indeed, twice before, this Court has specifically held that the nonrenewal of a nontenured public school teacher's one-year contract may not be predicated on his exercise of First and Fourteenth Amendment rights.

　　　* * *

[W]e hold that the grant of summary judgment against the respondent, without full exploration of this issue, was improper.

II

The respondent's lack of formal contractual or tenure security in continued employment at Odessa Junior College, though irrelevant to his free speech claim, is highly relevant to his procedural due process claim. But it may not be entirely dispositive.

We have held today in *Board of Regents v. Roth* that the Constitution does not require opportunity for a hearing before the nonrenewal of a nontenured teacher's contract, unless he can show that the decision not to rehire him somehow deprived him of an interest in "liberty" or that he had a "property" interest in continued employment, despite the lack of tenure or a formal contract. In *Roth* the teacher had not made a showing on either point to justify summary judgment in his favor.

Similarly, the respondent here has yet to show that he has been deprived of an interest that could invoke procedural due process protection. As in *Roth*, the mere showing that he was not rehired in one particular job, without more, did not amount to a showing of a loss of liberty. Nor did it amount to a showing of a loss of property.

But the respondent's allegations—which we must construe most favorably to the respondent at this stage of the litigation—do raise a genuine issue as to his interest in continued employment at Odessa Junior College. He alleged that this interest, though not secured by a formal contractual tenure provision, was secured by a no less binding understanding fostered by the college administration. In particular, the respondent alleged that the college had a de facto tenure program, and that he had tenure under that program. He claimed that he and others legitimately relied upon an unusual provision that had been in the college's official Faculty Guide for many years:

> "Teacher Tenure: Odessa College has no tenure system. The Administration of the College wishes the faculty member to feel that he has permanent tenure as long as his teaching services are satisfactory and as long as he displays a cooperative attitude toward his co-workers and his superiors, and as long as he is happy in his work."

Moreover, the respondent claimed legitimate reliance upon guidelines promulgated by the Coordinating Board of the Texas College and University System that provided that a person, like himself, who had been employed as a teacher in the state college and university system for seven years or more has some form of job tenure.[6] Thus, the respondent offered to prove that a teacher with his long period of service at this particular State College had no less a "property" interest in continued employment than a formally tenured teacher at other colleges, and had no less a procedural due process right to a statement of reasons and a hearing before college officials upon their decision not to retain him.

We have made clear in Roth that "property" interests subject to procedural due process protection are not limited by a few rigid, technical forms. Rather, "property" denotes a broad range of interests that are secured by "existing rules or understandings." A person's interest in a benefit is a "property" interest for due process purposes if there are such

---

6. The relevant portion of the guidelines, adopted as "Policy Paper 1" by the Coordinating Board on October 16, 1967, reads:

"A. Tenure

"Tenure means assurance to an experienced faculty member that he may expect to continue in his academic position unless adequate cause for dismissal is demonstrated in a fair hearing, following established procedures of due process.

"A specific system of faculty tenure undergirds the integrity of each academic institution. In the Texas public colleges and universities, this tenure system should have these components:

"(1) Beginning with appointment to the rank of full-time instructor or a higher rank, the probationary period for a faculty member shall not exceed seven years, including within this period appropriate full-time service in all institutions of higher education. This is subject to the provision that when, after a term of probationary service of more than three years in one or more institutions, a faculty member is employed by another institution, it may be agreed in writing that his new appointment is for a probationary period of not more than four years (even though thereby the person's total probationary period in the academic profession is extended beyond the normal maximum of seven years).

* * *

"(3) Adequate cause for dismissal for a faculty member with tenure may be established by demonstrating professional incompetence, moral turpitude, or gross neglect of professional responsibilities." The respondent alleges that, because he has been employed as a "full-time instructor" or professor within the Texas College and University System for 10 years, he should have 'tenure' under these provisions.

rules or mutually explicit understandings that support his claim of entitlement to the benefit and that he may invoke at a hearing.

A written contract with an explicit tenure provision clearly is evidence of a formal understanding that supports a teacher's claim of entitlement to continued employment unless sufficient "cause" is shown. Yet absence of such an explicit contractual provision may not always foreclose the possibility that a teacher has a "property" interest in reemployment. For example, the law of contracts in most, if not all, jurisdictions long has employed a process by which agreements, though not formalized in writing, may be "implied." Explicit contractual provisions may be supplemented by other agreements implied from "the promisor's words and conduct in the light of the surrounding circumstances." And, "(t)he meaning of (the promisor's) words and acts is found by relating them to the usage of the past."

A teacher, like the respondent, who has held his position for a number of years, might be able to show from the circumstances of this service— and from other relevant facts—that he has a legitimate claim of entitlement to job tenure. Just as this Court has found there to be a "common law of a particular industry or of a particular plant" that may supplement a collective-bargaining agreement, so there may be an unwritten "common law" in a particular university that certain employees shall have the equivalent of tenure. This is particularly likely in a college or university, like Odessa Junior College, that has no explicit tenure system even for senior members of its faculty, but that nonetheless may have created such a system in practice.[7]

In this case, the respondent has alleged the existence of rules and understandings, promulgated and fostered by state officials, that may justify his legitimate claim of entitlement to continued employment absent "sufficient cause." We disagree with the Court of Appeals insofar as it held that a mere subjective "expectancy" is protected by procedural due process, but we agree that the respondent must be given an opportunity to prove the legitimacy of his claim of such entitlement in light of "the policies and practices of the institution." Proof of such a property interest would not, of course, entitle him to reinstatement. But such proof would obligate college officials to grant a hearing at his request, where he could be informed of the grounds for his nonretention and challenge their sufficiency.

Therefore, while we do not wholly agree with the opinion of the Court of Appeals, its judgment remanding this case to the District Court is affirmed.

Affirmed.

---

7. We do not now hold that the respondent has any such legitimate claim of entitlement to job tenure. For "(p)roperty interests . . . are not created by the Constitution. Rather, they are created and their dimensions are defined by existing rules or understandings that stem from an independent source such as state law. . . ." If it is the law of Texas that a teacher in the respondent's position has no contractual or other claim to job tenure, the respondent's claim would be defeated.

C. DISPUTES REGARDING THE DISMISSAL PROCESS GENERALLY

This section examines two representative K–12 dismissal cases, one involving a teacher and the other involving a principal. It is important to note that dismissal controversies often involve most, if not all, of the areas addressed in this chapter. Indeed, many landmark decisions in the areas of tenure, freedom of expression, and employment discrimination often stem from disputes regarding dismissal. Problem 54 highlights some of the issues that may arise in this context.

PROBLEM 54: TEACHER DISMISSAL AT THE K–12 LEVEL

The following hypothetical takes place in the Topanga Creek Unified School District.

Sal Marcos was a longtime Filipino community activist, Green Party member, faculty sponsor of the school's large and vibrant Filipino Student Association, and outspoken union rep at Oakridge Road High School. A superior teacher and debate coach whose students "swore by him," Marcos' ten years in the District had been marred by several disputes with administrators and fellow faculty members. Finally, at the end of his tenth year, Marcos was suspended from his teaching position, and District officials began dismissal proceedings.

Four specific incidents during the most recent school year were specified by the District in these proceedings:

A. *Statements Regarding District Issues and Personnel*—Marcos occasionally debated members of his team who were in his social studies classes, during class time, in order to strengthen their debating skills. (There was no separate class for debate.) On one occasion, in late April, a debate was held on a resolution recently passed by the Topanga Creek School Board in support of the Bush administration's war effort in Iraq. Marcos' words were recorded on tape by one of the students, and included the following declaration: "All of us ultimately lose in this battle. If only the school board members realized this . . . if only we all opened our eyes we could see how evil this war effort is. . . we need to fight it at every level, starting with this campus, this principal, and this faculty."

B. *Film (shown without permission)*—In the fall, during a unit on the years 1865–1900 in his eleventh grade U.S. History class, Marcos showed a film that members of the school's Filipino Student Association had put together under his supervision. The film presented in vivid detail the argument that the U.S. not only caused significant damage to the Philippines and its inhabitants over time, but that discrimination and disparate treatment continue in this country today.

C. *Events Occurring During Student Visits to Teacher's Home*—Members of the debate team, and their friends, often visited Marcos' home. On one occasion in December, Marcos' wife recruited several of the students to help plan an anti-war demonstration.

D. *Comments Regarding Controversial Topics*—In May, during another recorded practice debate (this one on the draft), Marcos said the following: "If this administration reinstituted the draft, and I was of draft age, I would leave the country before I would become part of this madness."

It was after this last incident that Mr. Marcos was suspended. He admits that these four incidents occurred exactly as described above.

Mr. Sal Marcos, upon his dismissal, sued for reinstatement. What legal and policy arguments would the plaintiff be likely to advance? How should the court rule? Why?

Assume that Marcos was also the baseball coach, that he was 53–years-old, that he had recently been in an accident which required the use of a wheelchair from time to time, and that the baseball coach who replaced him was 16 years younger. In addition, assume that the principal was quoted by the school newspaper as saying that she felt it was important for a baseball coach to be able to demonstrate certain skills such as batting, pitching, and fielding, and that she was happy that the new coach would be able to do that. What additional arguments might the teacher set forth? What result?

* * *

Assume instead that Mr. Marcos was a middle school teacher. How much of an impact, if any, would this change in grade level have on the outcome of the case? How much of an impact, if any, should it have? Why?

* * *

Relevant provisions of the State Education Code provide, in pertinent part:

(a) No permanent employee shall be dismissed except for one or more of the following causes:

(1) Immoral or unprofessional conduct.

* * *

(3) Dishonesty.

(4) Unsatisfactory performance.

(5) Evident unfitness for service.

(6) Physical or mental condition unfitting him or her to instruct or associate with children.

(7) Persistent violation of or refusal to obey the school laws of the state or reasonable regulations prescribed for the government of the public schools by the State Board of Education or by the governing board of the school district employing him or her.

(8) Conviction of a felony or of any crime involving moral turpitude.

* * *

(10) Knowing membership by the employee in the Communist Party.

(11) Alcoholism or other drug abuse which makes the employee unfit to instruct or associate with children.

MORRISON v. STATE BD. OF EDUC.

1 Cal.3d 214, 461 P.2d 375, 82 Cal.Rptr. 175 (1969)

TOBRINER, JUSTICE.

For a number of years prior to 1965 petitioner held a General Secondary Life Diploma and a Life Diploma to Teach Exceptional Children, issued by the State Board of Education, which qualified petitioner for employment as a teacher in the public secondary schools of California. On August 5, 1965, an accusation was filed with the State Board of Education charging that petitioner's life diplomas should be revoked for cause. On March 11, 1966, following a hearing, and pursuant to the recommendations of a hearing examiner, the board revoked petitioner's life diplomas because of immoral and unprofessional conduct and acts involving moral turpitude as authorized by section 13202 of the Education Code.[1] This revocation rendered petitioner ineligible for employment as a teacher in any public school in the state. On February 14, 1967, petitioner sought a writ of mandate from the Superior Court of Los Angeles County to compel the board to set aside its decision and restore his life diplomas. After a hearing the superior court denied the writ, and this appeal followed.

For the reasons hereinafter set forth we conclude (a) that section 13202 authorizes disciplinary measures only for conduct indicating unfitness to teach, (b) that properly interpreted to this effect section 13202 is constitutional on its face and as here applied, and (c) that the record contains no evidence to support the conclusion that petitioner's conduct indicated his unfitness to teach. The judgment of the superior court must therefore be reversed.

I. *The Facts*

For a number of years prior to 1964 petitioner worked as a teacher for the Lowell Joint School District. During this period, so far as appears from the record, no one complained about, or so much as criticized, his performance as a teacher. Moreover, with the exception of a single incident, no one suggested that his conduct outside the classroom was other than beyond reproach.

---

1. Section 13202 provides: "The State Board of Education shall revoke or suspend for immoral or unprofessional conduct, or for persistent defiance of, and refusal to obey, the laws regulating the duties of persons serving in the Public School System, or for any cause which would have warranted the denial of an application for a certification document or the renewal thereof, or for evident unfitness for service, life diplomas, documents, or credentials issued pursuant to this code." Among the causes warranting denial of such documents is the commission of "any act involving moral turpitude."

Sometime before the spring of 1963 petitioner became friends with Mr. and Mrs. Fred Schneringer. Mr. Schneringer also worked as a teacher in the public school system. To the Schneringers, who were involved in grave marital and financial difficulties at the time, petitioner gave counsel and advice. In the course of such counseling Mr. Schneringer frequently visited petitioner's apartment to discuss his problems. For a one-week period in April, during which petitioner and Mr. Schneringer experienced severe emotional stress, the two men engaged in a limited, non-criminal[4] physical relationship which petitioner described as being of a homosexual nature. Petitioner has never been accused or convicted of any criminal activity whatever, and the record contains no evidence of any abnormal activities or desires by petitioner since the Schneringer incident some six years in the past. Petitioner and Schneringer met on numerous occasions in the spring and summer after the incident and nothing untoward occurred. When Schneringer later obtained a separation from his wife, petitioner suggested a number of women whom Schneringer might consider dating.

Approximately one year after the April 1963 incident, Schneringer reported it to the Superintendent of the Lowell Joint School District. As a result of that report petitioner resigned his teaching position on May 4, 1964.

Some 19 months after the incident became known to the superintendent, the State Board of Education conducted a hearing concerning possible revocation of petitioner's life diplomas. * * * Mr. Cavalier, an investigator testifying for the board, stated that the Schneringer incident "was the only time that [petitioner] ever engaged in a homosexual act with anyone." No evidence was presented that petitioner had ever committed any act of misconduct whatsoever while teaching.

The Board of Education finally revoked petitioner's life diplomas some three years after the Schneringer incident. The board concluded that that incident constituted immoral and unprofessional conduct, and an act involving moral turpitude, all of which warrant revocation of life diplomas under section 13202 of the Education Code.

II. *Petitioner's actions cannot constitute immoral or unprofessional conduct or conduct involving moral turpitude within the meaning of section 13202 unless those actions indicate his unfitness to teach.*

Section 13202 of the Education Code authorizes revocation of life diplomas for "immoral conduct," "unprofessional conduct," and "acts

---

4. Neither sodomy (Pen. Code, § 286), oral copulation (Pen. Code, § 288a), public solicitation of lewd acts (Pen. Code § 647, subd. (a)), loitering near public toilets (Pen. Code, § 647, subd. (d)), nor exhibitionism (Pen. Code, § 314) were involved.

Conviction of such offenses would have resulted in the mandatory revocation of all diplomas and life certificates issued by the State Board of Education.

The Education Code thus draws an important distinction between different types of sexual indiscretions by teachers, dealing with such conduct in two different parts of the code. Conviction of certain sex crimes entails automatic dismissal. But other sexual misconduct results in discipline only if it is "immoral," "unprofessional" or involves "moral turpitude." * * *

involving moral turpitude." Legislation authorizing disciplinary action against the holders of a variety of certificates, licenses and government jobs other than teaching also contain these rather general terms. This court has not attempted to formulate explicit definitions of those terms which would apply to all the statutes in which they are used. Rather, we have given those terms more precise meaning by referring in each case to the particular profession or the specific governmental position to which they were applicable.

In *Hallinan v. Committee of Bar Examiners* for example, we considered the meaning of "acts of moral turpitude" as applied to an applicant for admission to practice law. In that case the applicant had been arrested and convicted of a number of minor offenses in connection with peace demonstrations and civil rights "sit ins"; he had likewise been involved in a number of fistfights. We held that the applicant could not be denied admission to the bar. The nature of these acts, we ruled, "does not bear a direct relationship to petitioner's fitness to practice law. Virtually all of the admission and disciplinary cases in which we have upheld decisions of the State Bar to refuse to admit applicants or to disbar, suspend, or otherwise censure members of the bar have involved acts which bear upon the individual's manifest dishonesty and thereby provide a reasonable basis for the conclusion that the applicant or attorney cannot be relied upon to fulfill the moral obligations incumbent upon members of the legal profession. * * * Although petitioner's past behavior may not be praiseworthy it does not reflect upon his honesty and veracity *nor does it show him unfit for the proper discharge of the duties of an attorney.*" (Italics added.)

In *Yakov v. Board of Medical Examiners*, we were also concerned with moral turpitude. In that case a doctor had been convicted of nine counts of violation of section 4227 of the Business and Professions Code (furnishing dangerous drugs without prescription), and the Board of Medical Examiners had revoked his medical certificate. The superior court reversed the board's action; we upheld that court's disposition of the matter, stating, inter alia, "The purpose of an action seeking revocation of a doctor's certificate is not to punish the doctor but rather to protect the public. * * * While revocation of a certificate certainly works an unavoidable punitive effect, the board can seek to achieve a legitimate punitive purpose only through criminal prosecution. *Thus, in this proceeding the inquiry must be limited to the effect of Dr. Yakov's actions upon the quality of his service to his patients.*" (Italics added.)

Board of Education v. Swan and *Board of Trustees v. Owens* dealt with the term "unprofessional conduct" as applied to teachers. In *Swan* we stressed: "One employed in public service does not have a constitutional right to such employment and is subject to reasonable supervision and restriction by the authorized governmental body or officer *to the end that proper discipline may be maintained, and that activities among the employees may not be allowed to disrupt or impair the public service.*" (Italics added.) In *Owens* the Court of Appeal held that in deciding whether certain conduct by a teacher constituted unprofessional conduct which warranted discipline, a trial court must inquire whether that conduct had produced "any disruption or impairment of discipline or the teaching process * * * ."

In *Orloff v. Los Angeles Turf Club, Inc.*, we dealt with a statute authorizing the exclusion from theaters, museums, and race courses of persons of "immoral character." We reasoned that the objective of the statute was "the protection of others on the premises." Accordingly we held that a person might be excluded if, for example, he committed a lewd act or an act inimical to the public safety or welfare after gaining admittance to the place of entertainment. But we stressed that no sweeping inquiry could be made into the background and reputation of each person seeking admission. "[T]he private business, the personal relations with others, the past conduct not on the premises, of a person applying for or admitted to the [race] course, whether or not relevant to indicate his character, are immaterial in the application of the statutory standards. * * *"

In *Jarvella v. Willoughby–Eastlake City School Dist.*, the court faced the issue of whether a teacher could be dismissed for "immorality" merely because he had written a private letter to a friend containing language which some adults might find vulgar and offensive. The court held that Ohio Revised Code Section 3319.16, authorizing dismissal for "immorality," did not cover the teacher's actions, and that he could not therefore be dismissed. The court explained, "Whatever else the term 'Immorality' may mean to many, it is clear that when used in a statute it is inseparable from 'conduct' * * * But it is not 'immoral conduct' considered in the abstract. It must be considered in the context in which the Legislature considered it, as conduct which is hostile to the welfare of the general public; more specifically in this case, conduct which is hostile to the welfare of the school community. * * * In providing standards to guide school boards in placing restraints on conduct of teachers, the Legislature is concerned with the welfare of the school community. Its objective is the protection of students from corruption. This is a proper exercise of the power of a state to abridge personal liberty and to protect larger interests. But reasonableness must be the governing criterion. * * * The private conduct of a man, who is also a teacher, is a proper concern to those who employ him only to the extent it mars him as a teacher * * * . Where his professional achievement is unaffected, where the school community is placed in no jeopardy, his private acts are his own business and may not be the basis of discipline."

By interpreting these broad terms to apply to the employee's performance on the job, the decisions in *Hallinan, Yakov, Swan, Owens, Orloff* and *Jarvella* give content to language which otherwise would be too sweeping to be meaningful. Terms such as "immoral or unprofessional conduct" or "moral turpitude" stretch over so wide a range that they embrace an unlimited area of conduct. In using them the Legislature surely did not mean to endow the employing agency with the power to dismiss any employee whose personal, private conduct incurred its disapproval. Hence the courts have consistently related the terms to the issue of whether, when applied to the performance of the employee on the job, the employee has disqualified himself.

In the instant case the terms denote immoral or unprofessional conduct or moral turpitude of the teacher which indicates unfitness to teach. Without such a reasonable interpretation the terms would be susceptible to so broad an application as possibly to subject to discipline virtually every teacher in the state.[15] In the opinion of many people laziness, gluttony, vanity, selfishness, avarice, and cowardice constitute immoral conduct. A recent study by the State Assembly reported that educators differed among themselves as to whether "unprofessional conduct" might include "imbibing alcoholic beverages, use of tobacco, signing petitions, revealing contents of school documents to legislative committees, appealing directly to one's legislative representative, and opposing majority opinions * * * ." We cannot believe that the Legislature intended to compel disciplinary measures against teachers who committed such peccadillos if such passing conduct did not affect students or fellow teachers. Surely incidents of extramarital heterosexual conduct against a background of years of satisfactory teaching would not constitute "immoral conduct" sufficient justify revocation of a life diploma without any showing of an adverse effect on fitness to teach.

Nor is it likely that the Legislature intended by section 13202 to establish a standard for the conduct of teachers that might vary widely with time, location, and the popular mood. One could expect a reasonably stable consensus within the teaching profession as to what conduct adversely affects students and fellow teachers. No such consensus can be presumed about "morality." "Today's morals may be tomorrow's ancient and absurd customs." And conversely, conduct socially acceptable today may be anathema tomorrow. Local boards of education, moreover, are authorized to revoke their own certificates and dismiss permanent teachers for immoral and unprofessional conduct; an overly broad interpretation of that authorization could result in disciplinary action in one county for conduct treated as permissible in another. A more, constricted inter-

---

15. A sweeping provision purporting to penalize or sanction so large a group of people as to be incapable of effective enforcement against all or even most of them necessarily might offend due process. Such a statute, unless narrowed by clear and well-known standards, affords too great a potential for arbitrary and discriminatory application and administration. (See United States v. Reese ("It would certainly be dangerous if the Legislature could set a net large enough to catch all possible offenders, and leave it to the courts to step inside and say who could be rightfully detained, and who should be set at large.")) In *Norton v. Macy*, the United States Civil Service Commission defined "immorality" as a violation of "the prevailing mores of our society." The court commented, "So construed, 'immorality' covers a multitude of sins. Indeed, it may be doubted whether there are in the entire Civil Service many persons so saintly as never to have done any act disapproved by the 'prevailing mores of our society.'" With regard to the feasibility of a ban on all persons with any sort of homosexual background, the court argued, "The most widely accepted study of American sexual practices estimates that 'at least 37 per cent' of the American male population have at least one homosexual experience during their lifetime. If this is so, a policy excluding all persons who have engaged in homosexual conduct from government employ would disqualify for public service over one-third of the male population. This result would be both inherently absurd and devastating to the public service."

pretation of "immoral," "unprofessional," and "moral turpitude" avoids these difficulties, enabling the State Board of Education to utilize its expertise in educational matters rather than having to act "as the prophet to which is revealed the state of morals of the people or the common conscience."[19]

That the meaning of "immoral," "unprofessional," and "moral turpitude" must depend upon, and thus relate to, the occupation involved finds further confirmation in the fact that those terms are used in a wide variety of contexts. Along with public school teachers, all state college employees, all state civil service workers, and all barbers can be disciplined for "immoral conduct." The prohibition against "acts involving moral turpitude" applies to attorneys and to technicians, bioanalysts and trainees employed in clinical laboratories, as well as to teachers. The ban on "unprofessional conduct" is particularly common, covering not only teachers, but also dentists, physicians, vocational nurses, optometrists, pharmacists, psychiatric technicians, employment agency officials, state college employees, certified shorthand reporters, and funeral directors and embalmers. Surely the Legislature did not intend that identical standards of probity should apply to more than half a million professionals and government employees in widely varying fields without regard to their differing duties, responsibilities, and degree of contact with the public.

We therefore conclude that the Board of Education cannot abstractly characterize the conduct in this case as "immoral," "unprofessional," or "involving moral turpitude" within the meaning of section 13202 of the Education Code unless that conduct indicates that the petitioner is unfit to teach. In determining whether the teacher's conduct thus indicates unfitness to teach the board may consider such matters as the likelihood that the conduct may have adversely affected students or fellow teachers, the degree of such adversity anticipated, the proximity or remoteness in time of the conduct, the type of teaching certificate held by the party involved, the extenuating or aggravating circumstances, if any, surrounding the conduct, the praiseworthiness or blameworthiness of the motives resulting in the conduct, the likelihood of the recurrence of the questioned conduct, and the extent to which disciplinary action may inflict an adverse impact or chilling effect upon the constitutional rights of the teacher involved or other teachers. These factors are relevant to the extent that they assist the board in determining whether the teacher's fitness to teach, i.e., in determining whether the teacher's future classroom performance and overall impact on his students are likely to meet the board's standards.

* * *

---

19. The problem of ascertaining the appropriate standard of "morality" was aptly put in Robert N. Harris, Jr., *Private Consensual Adult Behavior: The Requirement of Harm to Others in the Enforcement of Morality*, 14 UCLA L. REV. 581, 582 & n.4. "[I]n a secular society—America today—there may be a plurality of moralities. Whose morals shall be enforced? * * * There is a tendency to say that public morals should be enforced. But that just begs the question. Whose morals are the public morals?"

IV. *The record contains no evidence that petitioner's conduct indicated his unfitness to teach.*

As we have stated above, the statutes, properly interpreted, provide that the State Board of Education can revoke a life diploma or other document of certification and thus prohibit local school officials from hiring a particular teacher only if that individual has in some manner indicated that he is unfit to teach. Thus an individual can be removed from the teaching profession only upon a showing that his retention in the profession poses a significant danger of harm to either students, school employees, or others who might be affected by his actions as a teacher. * * * Petitioner's conduct in this case is not disputed. Accordingly, we must inquire whether any adverse inferences can be drawn from that past conduct as to petitioner's teaching ability, or as to the possibility that publicity surrounding past conduct may in and of itself substantially impair his function as a teacher.

As to this crucial issue, the record before the board and before this court contains no evidence whatsoever. The board called no medical, psychological, or psychiatric experts to testify as to whether a man who had had a single, isolated, and limited homosexual contact would be likely to repeat such conduct in the future. The board offered no evidence that a man of petitioner's background was any more likely than the average adult male to engage in any untoward conduct with a student. The board produced no testimony from school officials or others to indicate whether a man such as petitioner might publicly advocate improper conduct. The board did not attempt to invoke the provisions of the Government Code authorizing official notice of matters within the special competence of the board.

This lack of evidence is particularly significant because the board failed to show that petitioner's conduct in any manner affected his performance as a teacher. There was not the slightest suggestion that petitioner had ever attempted, sought, or even considered any form of physical or otherwise improper relationship with any student. There was no evidence that petitioner had failed to impress upon the minds of his pupils the principles of morality as required by section 13556.5 of the Education Code. There is no reason to believe that the Schneringer incident affected petitioner's apparently satisfactory relationship with his co-workers.

The board revoked petitioner's license three years after the Schneringer incident; that incident has now receded six years into the past. Petitioner's motives at the time of the incident involved neither dishonesty nor viciousness, and the emotional pressures on both petitioner and Schneringer suggest the presence of extenuating circumstances. Finally, the record contains no evidence that the events of April 1963 have become so notorious as to impair petitioner's ability to command the respect and confidence of students and fellow teachers in schools within or without the Lowell Joint School District.

Before the board can conclude that a teacher's continued retention in the profession presents a significant danger of harm to students or fellow teachers, essential factual premises in its reasoning should be supported by evidence or official notice. In this case, despite the quantity and quality of information available about human sexual behaviour, the record contains no such evidence as to the significance and implications of the Schneringer incident. Neither this court nor the superior court is authorized to rectify this failure by uninformed speculation or conjecture as to petitioner's future conduct.

* * *

V. *Conclusion*

In deciding this case we are not unmindful of the public interest in the elimination of unfit elementary and secondary school teachers. But petitioner is entitled to a careful and reasoned inquiry into his fitness to teach by the Board of Education before he is deprived of his right to pursue his profession. "The right to practice one's profession is sufficiently precious to surround it with a panoply of legal protection" and terms such as "immoral," "unprofessional," and "moral turpitude" constitute only lingual abstractions until applied to a specific occupation and given content by reference to fitness for the performance of that vocation.

The power of the state to regulate professions and conditions of government employment must not arbitrarily impair the right of the individual to live his private life, apart from his job, as he deems fit. Moreover, since modern hiring practices purport to rest on scientific judgments of fitness for the job involved, a government decision clothed in such terms can seriously inhibit the possibility of the dismissed employee thereafter successfully seeking non-government positions. That danger becomes especially acute under circumstances such as the present case in which loss of certification will impose upon petitioner "a 'badge of infamy,' * * * fixing upon him the stigma of an official defamation of character."

* * *

The judgment of the superior court denying the writ of mandate is reversed, and the cause is remanded to the superior court for proceedings consistent with this opinion.

HEAD v. CHICAGO SCH. REFORM BD. OF TRUSTEES
225 F.3d 794 (7th Cir. 2000)

WILLIAMS, CIRCUIT JUDGE.

* * *

I

In March of 1994, the Chicago Board of Education, acting through the Local School Council, hired Head as the principal for Nathaniel Pope

Elementary School ("Pope Elementary") and gave him a four-year contract ending June 30, 1998. By its own terms, the contract could be terminated only on certain limited grounds.[2] Similarly, under the Illinois School Code, Head could be discharged during the term of his contract only for cause following an extensive and detailed notice and hearing process.

Beginning in 1995, the Board, aided by newly enacted state laws granting it greater powers, began to step up its efforts to remedy deficient performance in Chicago's public schools. Pursuant to these efforts, in October 1996, Pope Elementary was identified as a poorly performing school and was placed on probation. A school on probation is subject to greater Board oversight and must take certain steps to improve performance. In particular, Head, as Pope Elementary's principal, had primary responsibility for implementing a Corrective Action Plan to raise student test scores.

During the 1996–97 school year, the Board came to the conclusion that Head was not fulfilling his responsibility in this regard. Therefore, in early June of 1997, Hazel Stewart, the Education Officer for the region encompassing Pope Elementary, advised Head that the Board would seek to remove him as Pope Elementary's principal at the end of that school year. A letter signed by Chicago Public Schools CEO Paul Vallas and dated July 2, notified Head that pursuant to 105 Ill. Comp. Stat. 5/34–8.3(d), which governs schools under probation, a principal removal hearing would be scheduled for Pope Elementary. Head received a second letter signed by Vallas, dated July 3, scheduling the removal hearing for July 14 and detailing the criteria the Board used in deciding to seek his removal.[3] A

---

2. The contract provides:

This Agreement may be terminated for any one of the following reasons or by any one of the following methods:

    (a) written agreement of the Local School Council, Board of Education and the Principal;

    (b) discharge of the Principal for cause pursuant to Ill.Rev.Stat. Ch. 122, sec. 34–85;

    (c) closure of the attendance center;

    (d) death, resignation or retirement of the Principal;

    (e) misrepresentation referred to in section IX of this Agreement [which requires certain truthful representations to be made].

3. Specifically, the criteria detailed were:

    A. Failure of the Principal to effectively and/or sufficiently implement the Corrective Action Plan, which has resulted in deficiencies in any of the following:

      * School leadership;

      * Parent/community partnerships;

      * Student centered learning climate;

      * Professional development and collaboration;

      * Quality instruction plan; and

      * School management.

    B. Failure of the school to show sufficient increase in student scores on the TAP achievement test.

    C. Failure of the Principal to effectively and/or sufficiently follow the recommendation(s) of the Probation Manager.

    D. Failure to improve student attendance and/or drop-out rate in the school.

separate letter also notified the school community of the principal removal hearing.

Margaret Fitzpatrick presided over the July 14 hearing. During the hearing, eight witnesses presented evidence supporting Head's removal while seven witnesses testified on Head's behalf. After the hearing, Head, through his attorney, submitted a brief arguing against his removal. About a week after the hearing, Fitzpatrick issued a written decision recommending that Head be removed as principal of Pope Elementary. That same week, a Chicago Public Schools official, Phillip Hansen, criticized Head's performance on a cable access program. Then, on July 28, the Board adopted Fitzpatrick's recommendation and removed Head as principal of Pope Elementary.

* * *

Eventually, Head filed suit against the Board based on the Board's actions in removing him as principal of Pope Elementary. He raised essentially four claims: (1) that, without due process, the Board had deprived him of a liberty interest in pursuing his occupation; (2) that, without due process, the Board had deprived him of a property interest in employment beyond the term of his contract; (3) that, without due process, the Board had deprived him of a property interest in employment through the end of his contract; and (4) that the Board had breached its contract with him.

* * *

III

A. Claims Resolved in Motion to Dismiss Decision

We consider first the two claims the district court dismissed under Rule 12(b)(6)—that, without due process, the Board deprived Head of a liberty interest in pursuing the occupation of his choice and that, without due process, the Board deprived Head of a property interest in employment beyond the term of his contract. We review such dismissals *de novo*, taking a plaintiff's factual allegations as true and drawing all reasonable inferences in his or her favor. * * *

1. Liberty Interest Claim

In setting out the basis for his due process liberty interest claim in his complaint, Head alleged that the Board (or at least certain persons associated with the Board) deprived him of a liberty interest in pursuing the occupation of his choice by disseminating false allegations regarding his performance as Pope Elementary's principal. * * *

A claim that a government employer has infringed an employee's liberty to pursue the occupation of his or her choice requires that (1) the employee be stigmatized by the employer's actions; (2) the stigmatizing information be publicly disclosed; and (3) the employee suffer a tangible loss of other employment opportunities as a result of the public disclosure. However, simply labeling an employee as being incompetent or otherwise unable to meet an employer's expectations does not infringe the employee's liberty. The employee's good name, reputation, honor, or integrity must be called into question in such a way as to make it virtually impossible for the employee to find new employment in his chosen field.

    * * *

[However,] [s]imple charges of professional incompetence do not impose the sort of stigma that actually infringes an employee's liberty to pursue an occupation. Only if the circumstances of an employee's discharge so sully the employee's reputation or character that the employee will essentially be blacklisted in his or her chosen profession will it be possible to pursue a due process liberty interest claim. *Lashbrook* [*v. Oerkfitz*] (listing charges of immorality, dishonesty, alcoholism, disloyalty, Communism, or subversive acts as the sort of charges that infringe an employee's liberty); *Ratliff v. City of Milwaukee* (concluding that charges of untruthfulness, neglect of duty, and insubordination against a police officer impose sufficient stigma). As Head's allegations of stigma fall short of this threshold, he has failed to state a due process liberty interest claim.

    2. Property Interest Claim

Head claims that a requirement, found both in his contract and in a 1996 Board publication, that he be given notice five months before the end of the contract term regarding whether his contract would be renewed, grants him a property interest in employment beyond the term of his contract, which the Board could not deprive him of without due process. After reviewing Head's entire contract (which Head attached to his complaint), the district court concluded that Head had no property interest in future employment with the Board and therefore could not state a due process claim. We agree.

Property interests are enforceable entitlements to a benefit or right. They can arise directly from state or federal law (as with a statute granting a benefit) or indirectly through the operation of state or federal law on certain conduct (as with a contract). A mere opportunity to acquire property, however, does not itself qualify as a property interest protected by the Constitution.

Head's contract with the Board makes it plain that Head has no enforceable entitlement to employment beyond the term of the contract. It provides, "This Agreement, including and not withstanding the procedures set forth herein, shall expire at the end of its stated term and shall not grant or create any contractual rights or other expectancy of continued employment beyond the term of this Agreement." This provision conclusively dispels any confusion regarding the possibility of a property interest in future employment created by the requirement that Head be given five months notice of whether his contract would be renewed. And, there is nothing in the Illinois School Code that overrides (or is even inconsistent with) this aspect of the contract. Accordingly, the district court properly dismissed Head's claim that the Board unconstitutionally deprived him of a protected property interest in employment beyond the term of his contract.

B. Claims Resolved in Summary Judgment Decision

We turn next to the two claims on which the district court granted summary judgment—that, without due process, the Board deprived Head of a property interest in remaining the principal of Pope Elementary through the end of his contractual term of employment, and that the Board breached its contract with him. * * *

1. Due Process Claim

In support of his remaining due process claim, Head contends that by removing him from his position as principal of Pope Elementary before the end of his contract, the Board deprived him of a property interest in continuing in that position for the term of his contract. There can be no doubt that, as a public employee who by contract and statute could be removed only on limited grounds, Head had a property interest in completing his contract in accordance with the terms of his contract, one of which specifically made him principal of Pope Elementary. The question the Board raises, which the district court never adequately addressed, is whether the deprivation Head suffered is more than *de minimis*, as it must be to be actionable.

The Board suggests that because Head received the same salary and benefits after his removal that he did when he was principal, he, at most, suffered a *de minimis* deprivation of property. The Board's suggestion is flawed, however. To begin with, the relevant question is whether Head received all the salary and benefits he would have received if he had remained Pope Elementary's principal. Head opposed the Board's summary judgment motion on the ground that he did not receive all he would have been due. If he is right, he suffered an injury that is plainly more than *de minimis*. See *Swick* [*v. City of Chicago*] (pecuniary losses qualify as actionable deprivations of property). Moreover, even if Head did receive all he would have been due had he remained Pope Elementary's principal, he might still have had a constitutionally protected property interest in remaining in that position. We have recognized that a loss of position that impedes future job opportunities or has other indirect effects on future income can inflict an actionable deprivation of property. We need not definitively answer whether Head has adequately established that he possessed a protected property interest in remaining Pope Elementary's principal through the end of his contract, however, since we agree with the district court that Head's challenges to the adequacy of the procedures afforded him prior to his removal are without merit.

A public employer who removes an employee from a job in which the employee has a constitutionally protected interest must provide certain limited pre-termination procedures, including, at a minimum: (1) oral or written notice of the charges; (2) an explanation of the employer's evidence; and (3) an opportunity for the employee to tell his or her side of the story. Also, the chosen decisionmaker must be impartial. Head contends that the procedures he was afforded did not satisfy these minimum requirements in two respects.

Head first complains that he did not receive adequate notice of the charges that led to his removal. We cannot accept this argument, however. Notice is constitutionally adequate if it is reasonably calculated to apprise interested parties of the proceeding and afford them an opportunity to present their objections. In a pair of letters sent over one week prior to the removal hearing, the Board informed Head that a principal removal hearing had been scheduled for Pope Elementary and detailed four particular grounds on which his removal was being sought. Clearly, Head was apprised of the removal proceedings, and, while the charges against him may not have been as specific as Head would have liked, they were certainly sufficient to allow him to defend himself. In any event, Head admits that he was fully apprised of the charges at the hearing and that afterwards he was able to submit a brief in response to the evidence presented at the hearing. For both of these reasons, we find it impossible to conclude that Head did not receive adequate notice of the charges that led to his removal.

Head also complains that Margaret Fitzpatrick, the hearing officer who presided over his removal hearing, was not an impartial decisionmaker. Specifically, Head contends that Fitzpatrick cannot be considered an impartial decisionmaker because she was employed by the Board, he had no input on her selection, she had previously represented him and the Board, and she had on a prior occasion presented evidence regarding an earlier controversy at Pope Elementary. Those serving as adjudicators are presumed to act in good faith, honestly, and with integrity. To overcome this presumption, a plaintiff must come forward with substantial evidence of actual or potential bias, such as evidence of a pecuniary interest in the proceeding, personal animosity toward the plaintiff, or actual prejudgment of the plaintiff's case. Evidence of prior familiarity with the plaintiff or his or her situation, or even of involvement in the particular matter under consideration, is not adequate by itself to overcome the presumption. Viewed in the light most favorable to Head, the evidence he relies on amounts to nothing more than evidence of Fitzpatrick's prior familiarity with him and Pope Elementary. As such, it does not overcome the presumption of good faith that is afforded adjudicators. Accordingly, Head's claim that Fitzpatrick was biased must fail.

As there appears to be no reason to doubt that the Board afforded Head constitutionally adequate procedures before removing him as principal of Pope Elementary, the Board was entitled to summary judgment on Head's due process property interest claim relating to his removal before the end of his contractual term of employment.

2.   Breach of Contract Claim

Head claims that by removing him from his position as principal of Pope Elementary before the end of his four-year contractual term of employment, the Board breached its contract with him. The district court concluded that no breach occurred because the Illinois School Code governs Head's contract and, in removing Head, the Board complied with the provisions of the Illinois School Code regarding the removal of a principal from a school on probation (specifically 105 Ill. Comp. Stat. 5/34–8.3(d)). Head argues that the district court misinterpreted the contract. We agree.

As the contract between Head and the Board specifically makes Head principal of Pope Elementary, there can be no doubt that the Board terminated the contract by removing Head from that position. The question is whether it had grounds for terminating the contract. As noted above, the contract provides five grounds for termination. Removal of the principal pursuant to 105 Ill. Comp. Stat. 5/34–8.3(d) is not one of them, nor has the Board ever suggested that any of the grounds for termination has been satisfied. The only ground with any connection to the reasons for Head's removal is, "discharge of the Principal for cause pursuant to Ill.Rev.Stat. Ch. 122, sec. 34–85." But, the Board concedes that it did not follow the procedures or afford Head the rights provided by § 34–85.

The district court did not consider whether the Board had established any of the contractual grounds for terminating its contract with Head. Instead, the court concluded that the contract is governed by, and therefore apparently incorporates, the Illinois School Code, and that if Head was properly removed under any provision of the Illinois School Code, there could not be a breach of the contract. This interpretation reads too much into the contract. The contract does provide that Head must fulfill the obligations placed on him by the Illinois School Code, but the contract says nothing about incorporating, wholesale, the various provisions of the Illinois School Code relating to the removal of a principal. There is, for instance, no term allowing for termination of the contract upon "discharge of the principal pursuant to the Illinois School Code." To the contrary, the contract specifically identifies a single provision, § 34–85, that must be used in discharging a principal for cause. As we read the Board's contract with Head, the contract may be terminated only if one of the five contractual grounds for termination is satisfied.

Whether by mistake or design, Head's contract grants him greater rights than the Illinois School Code appears to grant him. The Board was obligated to honor those contractual rights by satisfying one of the five contractual grounds for termination of the contract. It did not do so. Accordingly, we conclude that the district court erred in ruling that the Board did not breach its contract with Head.

IV

For the foregoing reasons, we conclude that there is no merit to Head's due process claims, but that his breach of contract claim should have survived summary judgment. Accordingly, we AFFIRM in part and REVERSE in part the judgment of the district court, and we REMAND the case for further proceedings.

D. FIRST AMENDMENT RIGHTS OF EDUCATORS

Freedom of expression for educators is a surprisingly complex area of inquiry. At the K–12 level, for example, educators may actually have fewer rights than students. And interpretations of First Amendment principles in this context not only vary from jurisdiction to jurisdiction, but sometimes prove quite difficult to pinpoint with any great degree of certainty.

At the higher education level, there are ongoing disputes over the parameters of academic freedom. Many people assume the existence of academic freedom as a matter of course, but in reality the courts have recognized some fairly substantial limitations.

Notable recent scholarship has pinpointed the depth and breadth of the complexities in this area. *See, e.g.,* Ailsa W. Chang, *Resuscitating the Constitutional "Theory" of Academic Freedom: A Search for a Standard Beyond Pickering and Connick,* 53 STAN. L. REV. 915 (2001); R. Weston Donehower, *Boring Lessons: Defining the Limits of a Teacher's First Amendment Right to Speak Through the Curriculum,* 102 MICH. L. REV. 517 (2003); Kevin G. Welner, *Locking Up the Marketplace of Ideas and Locking Out School Reform: Courts' Imprudent Treatment of Controversial Teaching in America's Public Schools,* 50 UCLA L. REV. 959 (2003).

This section begins with *Pickering* and *Connick,* the two U.S. Supreme Court cases that together comprise foundational doctrine in the area. It then follows with representative academic freedom disputes at both the K–12 and the higher education levels. Taken together, do these decisions reflect any discernible trend, or are the courts left with conflicting strands and little apparent consistency? How might current realities shift in the future? What types of controversies might engender such a shift?

A. U.S. SUPREME COURT DOCTRINE GENERALLY

PICKERING v. BOARD OF EDUC. OF TOWNSHIP HIGH SCH. DIST. 205

391 U.S. 563, 88 S.Ct. 1731 (1968)

MR. JUSTICE MARSHALL delivered the opinion of the Court.

Appellant Marvin L. Pickering, a teacher in Township High School District 205, Will County, Illinois, was dismissed from his position by the appellee Board of Education for sending a letter to a local newspaper in connection with a recently proposed tax increase that was critical of the way in which the Board and the district superintendent of schools had handled past proposals to raise new revenue for the schools. Appellant's dismissal resulted from a determination by the Board, after a full hearing, that the publication of the letter was "detrimental to the efficient operation and administration of the schools of the district" and hence, under the relevant Illinois statute, that "interests of the schools require(d) (his dismissal)."

* * *

I.

* * *

[Pickering's] letter constituted, basically, an attack on the School Board's handling of the 1961 bond issue proposals and its subsequent allocation of financial resources between the schools' educational and athletic programs. It also charged the superintendent of schools with attempting to prevent teachers in the district from opposing or criticizing the proposed bond issue.

The Board dismissed Pickering for writing and publishing the letter. Pursuant to Illinois law, the Board was then required to hold a hearing on the dismissal. At the hearing the Board charged that numerous statements in the letter were false and that the publication of the statements unjustifiably impugned the "motives, honesty, integrity, truthfulness, responsibility and competence" of both the Board and the school administration. The Board also charged that the false statements damaged the professional reputations of its members and of the school administrators, would be disruptive of faculty discipline, and would tend to foment "controversy, conflict and dissension" among teachers, administrators, the Board of Education, and the residents of the district. * * * The Board found the statements to be false as charged. No evidence was introduced at any point in the proceedings as to the effect of the publication of the letter on the community as a whole or on the administration of the school system in particular, and no specific findings along these lines were made.

* * *

III.

The Board contends that "the teacher by virtue of his public employment has a duty of loyalty to support his superiors in attaining the generally accepted goals of education and that, if he must speak out publicly, he should do so factually and accurately, commensurate with his education and experience." Appellant, on the other hand, argues that the test applicable to defamatory statements directed against public officials by persons having no occupational relationship with them, namely, that statements to be legally actionable must be made "with knowledge that [they were] * * * false or with reckless disregard of whether [they were] * * * false or not," should also be applied to public statements made by teachers. Because of the enormous variety of fact situations in which critical statements by teachers and other public employees may be thought by their superiors, against whom the statements are directed to furnish grounds for dismissal, we do not deem it either appropriate or feasible to attempt to lay down a general standard against which all such statements may be judged. However, in the course of evaluating the conflicting claims

misapplied our decision in *Pickering* and consequently, in our view, erred in striking the balance for respondent.

A

The District Court got off on the wrong foot in this case by initially finding that, "[t]aken as a whole, the issues presented in the questionnaire relate to the effective functioning of the District Attorney's Office and are matters of public importance and concern." Connick contends at the outset that no balancing of interests is required in this case because Myers' questionnaire concerned only internal office matters and that such speech is not upon a matter of "public concern," as the term was used in *Pickering*. Although we do not agree that Myers' communication in this case was wholly without First Amendment protection, there is much force to Connick's submission. The repeated emphasis in *Pickering* on the right of a public employee "as a citizen, in commenting upon matters of public concern," was not accidental. This language, reiterated in all of *Pickering's* progeny, reflects both the historical evolvement of the rights of public employees, and the common sense realization that government offices could not function if every employment decision became a constitutional matter.

For most of this century, the unchallenged dogma was that a public employee had no right to object to conditions placed upon the terms of employment—including those which restricted the exercise of constitutional rights. The classic formulation of this position was Justice Holmes', who, when sitting on the Supreme Judicial Court of Massachusetts, observed: "A policeman may have a constitutional right to talk politics, but he has no constitutional right to be a policeman." For many years, Holmes' epigram expressed this Court's law.

The Court cast new light on the matter in a series of cases arising from the widespread efforts in the 1950s and early 1960s to require public employees, particularly teachers, to swear oaths of loyalty to the state and reveal the groups with which they associated. * * * [By 1963,] it was already "too late in the day to doubt that the liberties of religion and expression may be infringed by the denial of or placing of conditions upon a benefit or privilege." It was therefore no surprise when in *Keyishian v. Board of Regents*, the Court invalidated New York statutes barring employment on the basis of membership in "subversive" organizations, observing that the theory that public employment which may be denied altogether may be subjected to any conditions, regardless of how unreasonable, had been uniformly rejected.

In all of these cases, the precedents in which *Pickering* is rooted, the invalidated statutes and actions sought to suppress the rights of public employees to participate in public affairs. The issue was whether government employees could be prevented or "chilled" by the fear of discharge from joining political parties and other associations that certain public officials might find "subversive." The explanation for the Constitution's special concern with threats to the right of citizens to participate in political affairs is no mystery. The First Amendment "was fashioned to assure unfettered interchange of ideas for the bringing about of political and social changes desired by the people." "[S]peech concerning public affairs is more than self-expression; it is the essence of self-government." Accordingly, the Court has frequently reaffirmed that speech on public issues occupies the "highest rung of the hierarchy of First Amendment values," and is entitled to special protection.

* * *

Our cases following *Pickering* also involved safeguarding speech on matters of public concern. The controversy in *Perry v. Sindermann,* 408 U.S. 593, 92 S. Ct. 2694 (1972), arose from the failure to rehire a teacher in the state college system who had testified before committees of the Texas legislature and had become involved in public disagreement over whether the college should be elevated to four-year status—a change opposed by the Regents. In *Mt. Healthy City Board of Ed. v. Doyle,* a public school teacher was not rehired because, allegedly, he had relayed to a radio station the substance of a memorandum relating to teacher dress and appearance that the school principal had circulated to various teachers. The memorandum was apparently prompted by the view of some in the administration that there was a relationship between teacher appearance and public support for bond issues, and indeed, the radio station promptly announced the adoption of the dress code as a news item. Most recently, in *Givhan v. Western Line Consolidated School District,* we held that First Amendment protection applies when a public employee arranges to communicate privately with his employer rather than to express his views publicly. Although the subject-matter of Mrs. Givhan's statements were not the issue before the Court, it is clear that her statements concerning the school district's allegedly racially discriminatory policies involved a matter of public concern.

Pickering, its antecedents and progeny, lead us to conclude that if Myers' questionnaire cannot be fairly characterized as constituting speech on a matter of public concern, it is unnecessary for us to scrutinize the reasons for her discharge. When employee expression cannot be fairly considered as relating to any matter of political, social, or other concern to the community, government officials should enjoy wide latitude in managing their offices, without intrusive oversight by the judiciary in the name of the First Amendment. Perhaps the government employer's dismissal of the worker may not be fair, but ordinary dismissals from government service which violate no fixed tenure or applicable statute or regulation are not subject to judicial review even if the reasons for the dismissal are alleged to be mistaken or unreasonable.

We do not suggest, however, that Myers' speech, even if not touching upon a matter of public concern, is totally beyond the protection of the First Amendment. "The First Amendment does not protect speech and assembly only to the extent it can be characterized as political. 'Great secular causes, with smaller ones, are guarded.'" We in no sense suggest that speech on private matters falls into one of the narrow and well-defined classes of expression which carries so little social value, such as obscenity, that the State can prohibit and punish such expression by all persons in its jurisdiction. For example, an employee's false criticism of his employer on grounds not of public concern may be cause for his discharge but would be entitled to the same protection in a libel action accorded an identical statement made by a man on the street. We hold only that when a public employee speaks not as a citizen upon matters of public concern, but instead as an employee upon matters only of personal interest, absent the most unusual circumstances, a federal court is not the appropriate forum in which to review the wisdom of a personnel decision taken by a public agency allegedly in reaction to the employee's behavior. Our responsibility is to ensure that citizens are not deprived of fundamental rights by virtue of working for the government; this does not require a grant of immunity for employee grievances not afforded by the First Amendment to those who do not work for the state.

Whether an employee's speech addresses a matter of public concern must be determined by the content, form, and context of a given statement, as revealed by the whole record. In this case, with but one exception, the questions posed by Myers to her coworkers do not fall under the rubric of matters of "public concern." We view the questions pertaining to the confidence and trust that Myers' coworkers possess in various supervisors, the level of office morale, and the need for a grievance committee as mere extensions of Myers' dispute over her transfer to another section of the criminal court.

　　　* * *

One question in Myers' questionnaire, however, does touch upon a matter of public concern. Question 11 inquires if assistant district attorneys "ever feel pressured to work in political campaigns on behalf of office supported candidates." * * *

B

Because one of the questions in Myers' survey touched upon a matter of public concern, and contributed to her discharge we must determine whether Connick was justified in discharging Myers. Here the District Court again erred in imposing an unduly onerous burden on the state to justify Myers' discharge. The District Court viewed the issue of whether Myers' speech was upon a matter of "public concern" as a threshold inquiry, after which it became the government's burden to "clearly demonstrate" that the speech involved "substantially interfered" with official responsibilities. Yet *Pickering* unmistakably states, and respondent agrees, that the state's burden in justifying a particular discharge varies depending upon the nature of the employee's expression. Although such particularized balancing is difficult, the courts must reach the most appropriate possible balance of the competing interests.

C

The *Pickering* balance requires full consideration of the government's interest in the effective and efficient fulfillment of its responsibilities to the public.

* * *

Also relevant is the manner, time, and place in which the questionnaire was distributed. As noted in *Givhan v. Western Line Consolidated School Dist.*, "Private expression . . . may in some situations bring additional factors to the *Pickering* calculus. When a government employee personally confronts his immediate superior, the employing agency's institutional efficiency may be threatened not only by the content of the employee's message but also by the manner, time, and place in which it is delivered." Here the questionnaire was prepared, and distributed at the office; the manner of distribution required not only Myers to leave her work but for others to do the same in order that the questionnaire be completed. Although some latitude in when official work is performed is to be allowed when professional employees are involved, and Myers did not violate announced office policy, the fact that Myers, unlike Pickering, exercised her rights to speech at the office supports Connick's fears that the functioning of his office was endangered.

Finally, the context in which the dispute arose is also significant. This is not a case where an employee, out of purely academic interest, circulated a questionnaire so as to obtain useful research. Myers acknowledges that it is no coincidence that the questionnaire followed upon the heels of the transfer notice. When employee speech concerning office policy arises from an employment dispute concerning the very application of that policy to the speaker, additional weight must be given to the supervisor's view that the employee has threatened the authority of the employer to run the office. * * *

III

Myers' questionnaire touched upon matters of public concern in only a most limited sense; her survey, in our view, is most accurately characterized as an employee grievance concerning internal office policy. The limited First Amendment interest involved here does not require that Connick tolerate action which he reasonably believed would disrupt the office, undermine his authority, and destroy close working relationships. Myers' discharge therefore did not offend the First Amendment. We reiterate, however, the caveat we expressed in *Pickering, supra* at 569, 88 S. Ct. at 1735: "Because of the enormous variety of fact situations in which critical statements by . . . public employees may be thought by their superiors . . . to furnish grounds for dismissal, we do not deem it either appropriate or feasible to lay down a general standard against which all such statements may be judged."

Our holding today is grounded in our long-standing recognition that the First Amendment's primary aim is the full protection of speech upon issues of public concern, as well as the practical realities involved in the administration of a government office. Although today the balance is struck for the government, this is no defeat for the First Amendment. For it would indeed be a Pyrrhic victory for the great principles of free expression if the Amendment's safeguarding of a public employee's right, as a citizen, to participate in discussions concerning public affairs were confused with the attempt to constitutionalize the employee grievance that we see presented here. The judgment of the Court of Appeals is

Reversed.

JUSTICE BRENNAN, with whom JUSTICE MARSHALL, JUSTICE BLACKMUN, and JUSTICE STEVENS join, dissenting.

Sheila Myers was discharged for circulating a questionnaire to her fellow Assistant District Attorneys seeking information about the effect of petitioner's personnel policies on employee morale and the overall work performance of the District Attorney's Office. The Court concludes that her dismissal does not violate the First Amendment, primarily because the questionnaire addresses matters that, in the Court's view, are not of public concern. It is hornbook law, however, that speech about "the manner in which government is operated or should be operated" is an essential part of the communications necessary for self-governance the protection of which was a central purpose of the First Amendment. Because the questionnaire addressed such matters and its distribution did not adversely affect the operations of the District Attorney's Office or interfere with Myers' working relationship with her fellow employees, I dissent.

I

The Court correctly reaffirms the long established principle that the government may not constitutionally compel persons to relinquish their First Amendment rights as a condition of public employment. *Pickering* held that the First Amendment protects the rights of public employees "as citizens to comment on matters of public interest" in connection with the operation of the government agencies for which they work. 391 U.S. at 568, 88 S. Ct. at 1734. We recognized, however, that the government has legitimate interests in regulating the speech of its employees that differ significantly from its interests in regulating the speech of people generally. *Ibid.* We therefore held that the scope of public employees' First Amendment rights must be determined by balancing "the interests of the [employee], as a citizen, in commenting upon matters of public concern and the interest of the State, as an employer, in promoting the efficiency of the public services it performs through its employees." *Ibid.*

The balancing test articulated in *Pickering* comes into play only when a public employee's speech implicates the government's interests as an employer. When public employees engage in expression unrelated to their employment while away from the work place, their First Amendment rights are, of course, no different from those of the general public. See *id,* at 574, 88 S. Ct. at 1737. Thus, whether a public employee's speech addresses a matter of public concern is relevant to the constitutional inquiry only when the statements at issue—by virtue of their content or the context in which they were made—may have an adverse impact on the government's ability to perform its duties efficiently.[1]

The Court's decision today is flawed in three respects. First, the Court distorts the balancing analysis required under *Pickering* by suggesting that one factor, the context in which a statement is made, is to be weighed *twice*—first in determining whether an employee's speech addresses a matter of public concern and then in deciding whether the statement adversely affected the government's interest as an employer. Second, in concluding that the effect of respondent's personnel policies on employee morale and the work performance of the District Attorney's Office is not a matter of public concern, the Court impermissibly narrows the class of subjects on which public employees may speak out without fear of retaliatory dismissal. Third, the Court misapplies the *Pickering* balancing test in holding that Myers could constitutionally be dismissed for circulating a questionnaire addressed to at least one subject that *was* "a matter of interest to the community," in the absence of evidence that her conduct disrupted the efficient functioning of the District Attorney's Office.

II

* * *

We have long recognized that one of the central purposes of the First Amendment's guarantee of freedom of expression is to protect the dissemination of information on the basis of which members of our society may make reasoned decisions about the government.

* * *

The constitutionally protected right to speak out on governmental affairs would be meaningless if it did not extend to statements expressing criticism of governmental officials.

* * *

In *Pickering* we held that the First Amendment affords similar protection to critical statements by a public school teacher directed at the Board of Education for whom he worked. 391 U.S. at 574, 88 S. Ct. at 1737. In so doing, we recognized that "free and open debate" about the operation of public schools "is vital to informed decision-making by the

---

1. Although the Court's opinion states that "if Myers' questionnaire cannot be fairly characterized as constituting speech on a matter of public concern, it is unnecessary for us to scrutinize the reasons for her discharge," I do not understand it to imply that a governmental employee's First Amendment rights outside the employment context are limited to speech on matters of public concern. To the extent that the Court's opinion may be read to suggest that the dismissal of a public employee for speech unrelated to a subject of public interest does not implicate First Amendment interests, I disagree, because our cases establish that public employees enjoy the full range of First Amendment rights guaranteed to members of the general public. Under the balancing test articulated in *Pickering*, however, the government's burden to justify such a dismissal may be lighter.

electorate." *Id.* at 571–572, 88 S. Ct. at 1736. We also acknowledged the importance of allowing teachers to speak out on school matters.

* * *

Applying these principles, I would hold that Myers' questionnaire addressed matters of public concern because it discussed subjects that could reasonably be expected to be of interest to persons seeking to develop informed opinions about the manner in which the Orleans Parish District Attorney, an elected official charged with managing a vital governmental agency, discharges his responsibilities. The questionnaire sought primarily to obtain information about the impact of the recent transfers on morale in the District Attorney's Office. It is beyond doubt that personnel decisions that adversely affect discipline and morale may ultimately impair an agency's efficient performance of its duties. Because I believe the First Amendment protects the right of public employees to discuss such matters so that the public may be better informed about how their elected officials fulfill their responsibilities, I would affirm the District Court's conclusion that the questionnaire related to matters of public importance and concern.

The Court's adoption of a far narrower conception of what subjects are of public concern seems prompted by its fears that a broader view "would mean that virtually every remark—and certainly every criticism directed at a public official—would plant the seed of a constitutional case." Obviously, not every remark directed at a public official by a public employee is protected by the First Amendment. But deciding whether a particular matter is of public concern is an inquiry that, by its very nature, is a sensitive one for judges charged with interpreting a constitutional provision intended to put "the decision as to what views shall be voiced largely into the hands of each of us...." The Court recognized the sensitive nature of this determination in *Gertz v. Robert Welch, Inc.*, which held that the scope of the constitutional privilege in defamation cases turns on whether or not the plaintiff is a public figure, not on whether the statements at issue address a subject of public concern. In so doing, the Court referred to the "difficulty of forcing state and federal judges to decide on an *ad hoc* basis which publications address issues of 'general or public interest' and which do not," and expressed "doubt [about] the wisdom of committing this task to the conscience of judges." In making such a delicate inquiry, we must bear in mind that "the citizenry is the final judge of the proper conduct of public business."

The Court's decision ignores these precepts. Based on its own narrow conception of which matters are of public concern, the Court implicitly determines that information concerning employee morale at an important government office will not inform public debate. To the contrary, the First Amendment protects the dissemination of such information so that the people, not the courts, may evaluate its usefulness. The proper means to ensure that the courts are not swamped with routine employee grievances mischaracterized as First Amendment cases is not to restrict artificially the concept of "public concern," but to require that adequate weight be given to the public's important interests in the efficient performance of governmental functions and in preserving employee discipline and harmony sufficient to achieve that end.

III

* * *

Pickering recognized the difficulty of articulating "a general standard against which all ... statements may be judged," 391 U.S. at 569, 88 S. Ct. at 1735; it did, however, identify a number of factors that may affect the balance in particular cases. Those relevant here are whether the statements are directed to persons with whom the speaker "would normally be in contact in the course of his daily work"; whether they had an adverse effect on "discipline by intermediate supervisors or harmony among coworkers"; whether the employment relationship in question is "the kind ... for which it can persuasively be claimed that personal loyalty and confidence are necessary to their proper functioning"; and whether the statements "have in any way impeded [the employee's] proper performance of his daily duties ... or ... interfered with the regular operations of the [office]." *Id.* at 568–573, 88 S. Ct. at 1734–1737. In addition, in *Givhan,* we recognized that when the statements in question are made in private to an employee's immediate supervisor, "the employing agency's institutional efficiency may be threatened not only by the content of the ... message but also by the manner, time, and place in which it is delivered."

The District Court weighed all of the relevant factors identified by our cases. It found that petitioner failed to establish that Myers violated either a duty of confidentiality or an office policy. Noting that most of the questionnaires were distributed during lunch, it rejected the contention that the distribution of the questionnaire impeded Myers' performance of her duties, and it concluded that "Connick has not shown *any* evidence to indicate that the plaintiff's work performance was adversely affected by her expression."

The Court accepts all of these findings. It concludes, however, that the District Court failed to give adequate weight to the context in which the questionnaires were distributed and to the need to maintain close working relationships in the District Attorney's Office.

* * *

Such extreme deference to the employer's judgment is not appropriate when public employees voice critical views concerning the operations of the agency for which they work. * * *

In this regard, our decision in *Tinker v. Des Moines Independent Community School District,* 393 U.S. 503, 89 S. Ct. 733 (1969), is controlling. *Tinker* arose in a public school, a context similar to the one in which the present case arose in that the determination of the scope of the Constitution's guarantee of freedom of speech required consideration of the "special characteristics of the ... environment" in which the expression took place. See *id.* at 506, 89 S. Ct. at 736. At issue was whether public high school students could constitutionally be prohibited from wearing black armbands in school to express their opposition to the Vietnam conflict. The District Court had ruled that such a ban "was reasonable because it was based on [school officials'] fear of a disturbance from the wearing of armbands." *Id.* at 508, 89 S.Ct. at 737. We found that justification inadequate, because "in our system, undifferentiated fear or apprehension of a disturbance is not enough to overcome the right to freedom of expression." *Ibid.* We concluded:

> "In order for the State ... to justify prohibition of a particular expression of opinion, it must be able to show that its action was caused by something more than a mere desire to avoid the discomfort and unpleasantness that always accompany an unpopular viewpoint. *Certainly where there is no finding and no showing that engaging in the forbidden conduct would "materially and substantially interfere with the requirements of appropriate discipline in the operation of the school,"* the prohibition cannot be sustained." *Id.* at 509, 89 S.Ct. at 738 (emphasis supplied).

Because the speech at issue addressed matters of public importance, a similar standard should be applied here. After reviewing the evidence, the District Court found that "it cannot be said that the defendant's interest in promoting the efficiency of the public services performed through his employees was either adversely affected or substantially impeded by plaintiff's distribution of the questionnaire." Based on these findings the District Court concluded that the circulation of the questionnaire was protected by the First Amendment. The District Court applied the proper legal standard and reached an acceptable accommodation between the competing interests. I would affirm its decision and the judgment of the Court of Appeals.

IV

The Court's decision today inevitably will deter public employees from making critical statements about the manner in which government agencies are operated for fear that doing so will provoke their dismissal. As a result, the public will be deprived of valuable information with which to evaluate the performance of elected officials. Because protecting the dissemination of such information is an essential function of the First Amendment, I dissent.

B.   "ACADEMIC FREEDOM" AT THE K–12 LEVEL

COCKREL v. SHELBY COUNTY SCH. DIST.
270 F.3d 1036 (6th Cir. 2001)

Moore, Circuit Judge.

* * *

I.   BACKGROUND

Plaintiff Donna Cockrel, a tenured fifth-grade teacher at Simpsonville Elementary School in the Shelby County, Kentucky School District was terminated on July 15, 1997 by the District's superintendent, Dr. Leon Mooneyhan. The School District's proffered grounds for Cockrel's termination were insubordination, conduct unbecoming a teacher, inefficiency, incompetency, and neglect of duty. As the basis for these charges, the School District detailed seventeen specific instances of misconduct engaged in by Cockrel, including: failing to teach and disparaging the school's "Just Think" curriculum; calling Principal Harry Slate names in front of staff members and students; and failing to cooperate with the Title I program and the Title I aides in her class, as well as with other faculty members and staff of Simpsonville Elementary School.

While the School District alleged numerous reasons for its decision to terminate Cockrel, she claims that the District fired her due to her decision to invite Woody Harrelson, the television and film actor most famous for his role as "Woody" on the network television show "Cheers," and others to her classroom to give presentations on the environmental benefits of industrial hemp. Hemp, an illegal substance in Kentucky, is a plant from which both marijuana and a valuable fiber can be harvested. There are two varieties of the hemp plant. One is the marijuana plant itself, with approximately four to seven percent of its weight comprised of tetrahydrocannabinol ("THC"), the active chemical in the marijuana drug; the other is industrial hemp, a plant which grows in stalks and from which fibers can be taken to make various goods such as paper and clothes. Unlike marijuana, the industrial hemp plant is only comprised of between 0.1 and 0.4 percent THC, an insufficient amount to have any narcotic effect. Nevertheless, Kentucky law prohibits possession of both varieties of the hemp plant, including "its seeds or resin or any compound, mixture, or preparation which contains any quantity of these substances."

Cockrel claims that on at least three occasions during her seven-year tenure at Simpsonville Elementary she organized outside speakers to come to her class to speak about industrial hemp. Cockrel further claims that both Principal Slate and Superintendent Mooneyhan knew that she organized industrial hemp presentations. While Principal Slate alleges that he never knew industrial hemp was being discussed in Cockrel's class, he does admit that Cockrel's lesson plans, on at least one occasion, specifically mentioned that hemp was to be discussed.

On or about April 9, 1996, following Cockrel's decision to end the 1995–96 school year with a project entitled "Saving the Trees," in which the use of industrial hemp fibers as a possible alternative to wood pulp was to be discussed, Cockrel was contacted by a representative of the Cable News Network ("CNN") and asked if she would permit CNN's cameras to film her class presentation for use in a larger program on tree conservation. Cockrel claims that she then immediately informed Slate of

CNN's potential visit to their school, though Slate does not recall this conversation.

In early May 1996, Joe Hickey, president of the Kentucky Hemp Growers Association, informed Cockrel that Woody Harrelson might visit Kentucky with CNN, and that Harrelson might also visit her classroom. Cockrel claims that she was given no specific information as to when Harrelson might visit her classroom, and that it was not until the morning of May 30, 1996, the last day of the school year, that she was notified that Harrelson would be visiting Simpsonville Elementary School that day. Cockrel informed Principal Slate of the impending visit, and he agreed to allow it, though Slate claims that he was only told that the presentation to be given was about agriculture.

Harrelson arrived at the school later that morning with an "entourage, including representatives of the Kentucky Hemp Museum and Kentucky Hemp Growers Cooperative Association, several hemp growers from foreign countries, CNN, and various Kentucky news media representatives." As stated in Cockrel's complaint, Harrelson spoke with the children about his opposition to marijuana use, yet he distinguished marijuana from industrial hemp and advocated the use of industrial hemp as an alternative to increased logging efforts. As part of the presentation, products made from hemp were shown to the children, as were hemp seeds, a banned substance in the state of Kentucky. Harrelson's visit received both local and national media attention. One student who did not have parental permission to be videotaped or photographed by the news media was included by the press in a class photograph with Harrelson.

Following Harrelson's visit and the media attention it garnered, parents and teachers wrote numerous letters to members of the Shelby County School District voicing their concern and dismay regarding the industrial hemp presentation. Several of the letters noted the mixed message the school was sending on drug use as Harrelson's presentation occurred on the same day that many Simpsonville Elementary School students were graduating from the Drug Abuse Resistance Education ("D.A.R.E.") program offered in the school.

Based on the complaints expressed in the letters, Superintendent Mooneyhan decided to initiate an investigation into Cockrel's conduct. Following the investigation, Mooneyhan advised the Kentucky Education Professional Standards Board ("EPSB") that Cockrel had allowed hemp seeds, an illegal substance, to be passed around to students in her class during Harrelson's class visit. The Standards Board, after investigating the matter, ultimately dismissed Mooneyhan's complaint without prejudice, stating that there was an "insufficient basis to warrant [a] certificate revocation action."

In the months following Harrelson's visit, Simpsonville Elementary School adopted a new visitors policy for "controversial" topics that required advance approval by school administration and written consent by students' parents. This policy was put to use when, during the next school year, Cockrel informed Slate that Harrelson would be making a second visit to her classroom to discuss industrial hemp. Cockrel met all of the requirements of the new visitors policy, including providing the requisite advance notice to Principal Slate and obtaining permission from the parents of her students for their children to attend the presentation.[2] Slate did not attempt to discourage Cockrel from having another class presentation on industrial hemp, nor did he tell her that Harrelson should not be invited back to the school. According to Cockrel, however, Superintendent Mooneyhan did tell her earlier in the school year that it would not be in her best interests if Harrelson made any more visits to her class. While Harrelson was unable to attend on the day of his scheduled visit, a small group of parents, unaware that Harrelson was not coming, went to the school and "loudly voiced their objections" to Slate about his permitting Harrelson to visit the school a second time.

Harrelson rescheduled the visit for the following week, January 29, 1997, and Cockrel again fully complied with the school's visitors policy. Principal Slate again approved Harrelson's visit. This time Harrelson did make an appearance. Harrelson was met by a group of parents outside the school who were protesting his visit. Due to school scheduling problems, Harrelson was only able to speak to the students for a few minutes before the students had to leave for lunch. Harrelson's visit again garnered national media attention from CNN.

* * *

The termination letter informing Cockrel of her discharge detailed numerous instances of misconduct, all of which allegedly served as the basis for her discharge. Several of these charges detailed misconduct that occurred well before Harrelson made his initial visit to Simpsonville Elementary. There is no evidence in the record, however, that Cockrel had been reprimanded for such activity prior to Harrelson's visits to her classroom.

* * *

On June 4, 1998, Cockrel filed suit in the United States District Court for the Eastern District of Kentucky. Cockrel brought a claim pursuant to 42 U.S.C. § 1983 in which she alleged that she was terminated in retaliation for exercising her First Amendment right of free speech when discussing the potential environmental benefits of industrial hemp. * * *

II. ANALYSIS

* * *

C. Cockrel's First Amendment Retaliation Claim

* * *

2. The Elements of a First Amendment Retaliation Claim

---

2. All but one of her students was given permission to attend the Harrelson presentation.

Donna Cockrel, a teacher in the Shelby County Public School District, is a public employee. For a public employee to establish a claim of First Amendment retaliation, this court has held that she must demonstrate:

(1) that [she] was engaged in a constitutionally protected activity; (2) that the defendant's adverse action caused [her] to suffer an injury that would likely chill a person of ordinary firmness from continuing to engage in that activity; and (3) that the adverse action was motivated at least in part as a response to the exercise of [her] constitutional rights.

To demonstrate that she was engaging in constitutionally protected speech, Cockrel must show that her speech touched on matters of public concern, and that her "interest in commenting upon matters of public concern ... outweigh[s] the interest of the State, as an employer, in promoting the efficiency of the public services it performs through its employees." If the plaintiff can establish the three elements of her First Amendment retaliation claim, the burden of persuasion then shifts to the defendants, who must show, by a preponderance of the evidence, that they "would have taken the same action even in the absence of the protected conduct."

a.   Was This Speech?

Before deciding whether Cockrel's speech was constitutionally protected, this court must first address the question of whether Cockrel's activity can be considered speech at all. The district court's decision disposing of Cockrel's First Amendment claims appears to be based on two separate theories that the court uses interchangeably. First, the district court stated that Cockrel's decision to bring in a speaker who would give a presentation on industrial hemp should not be considered speech. The district court further held that a teacher's decisions regarding the content of the curriculum she will teach to her class, even if considered speech, is still not protected by the First Amendment. We put the second holding aside for a moment and turn to the first.

The district court held that, because Cockrel simply chose to bring in speakers who would talk about industrial hemp, rather than speaking on the matter herself, "[h]er free speech claim is based solely on conduct." Also influential in the district court's decision was its notion that, in staging an industrial hemp presentation, Cockrel was not intending to convey a "particularized message," nor was she advocating or speaking against hemp's use as an environmental alternative to cutting down trees.

Regardless of the reasoning upon which it relied, the district court erred in holding Cockrel's conduct not to be speech. First, to the extent the district court was persuaded that Cockrel's actions did not constitute speech because Woody Harrelson, rather than Cockrel, was doing the speaking, this was error. As the Supreme Court stated in *Hurley v. Irish–American Gay, Lesbian & Bisexual Group*, to receive First Amendment protection, a speaker does not have "to generate, as an original matter, each item featured in the communication.'' For example, cable operators, even though they only broadcast material written, spoken, and produced by others, are still considered to be engaged in protected speech. The same First Amendment protections exist for newspapers, which in their opinion pages simply collect and present the speech of others. We see no reason, nor have the defendants explained to this court, why a teacher's selection of a speaker for an in-class presentation is less a form of speech than a cable operator's decision as to which programs it chooses to present to its viewing audience.

To the extent that the district court relied on the argument that Cockrel's conduct was not speech because she had no advocative purpose when bringing industrial hemp enthusiasts to her class, this was also error. The Supreme Court has held that films, radio programs, and live entertainment are all protected by the First Amendment. Moreover, to have constitutional protection, those who choose to show the film or stage the play need not show that they intended to convey a particularized message in doing so, nor that they approved or disapproved of its content, for such activities are inherently expressive and entitled to constitutional protection.

The district court points to Judge Milburn's concurring opinion in *Fowler v. Board of Education*, in support of its argument that Cockrel's conduct should not be considered speech. In *Fowler,* a high school teacher, at the request of her students, showed them *Pink Floyd—The Wall,* an ''R''-rated film containing nudity and a great deal of violence, on the last day of school while she completed grade cards. The teacher was later terminated for showing the film. The teacher then brought suit, claiming that she was terminated in retaliation for exercising her First Amendment rights.

Judge Milburn, writing only for himself on the issue of whether the conduct of showing the film to the class constituted protected speech, stated that, because the teacher had never seen the movie before and had no idea of its content, her decision to show the film could not be considered ''expressive or communicative'' in nature. Thus, Judge Milburn concluded, the teacher's conduct in showing the film was not entitled to First Amendment protection.

Judges Peck and Merritt disagreed with Judge Milburn's analysis of whether the teacher's showing of a film could be considered speech. Judge Peck, while concurring in the outcome of the case, stated that the expressive conduct cases used by Judge Milburn to analyze the teacher's showing of the film were ''inapposite.'' Judge Merritt, noting that books, movies, and music that are purely for entertainment value still receive First Amendment protection, argued that the teacher's decision to show the film clearly was protected speech.

While Judge Milburn's analysis in *Fowler* is not binding on this court, even if it were, the facts of this case are clearly distinguishable from *Fowler*. Unlike the teacher's showing of a film the content of which she knew nothing about, Cockrel's decision to bring in industrial hemp advocates did have an intent to convey a particularized message. Cockrel, who in her complaint states that "[s]he was a teacher trainer in the state sponsored Kentucky Agriculture and Environment in the Classroom project from 1993 to 1997[,]" worked at designing methods to integrate agricultural topics into her fifth-grade curriculum. She had, on at least three occasions before the Harrelson visit, brought in speakers who advocated the use of industrial hemp to conserve trees and other natural resources. Viewing the facts in the light most favorable to Cockrel, we cannot state, as the district court did, that it was not until "some point during or after the presentation [that] Plaintiff may have developed an approval or disapproval of the use of industrial hemp[.]" Instead, the evidence shows that Cockrel was well aware of the arguments for industrial hemp, and that this was a message she wanted delivered to her students.

Thus, while we believe that Cockrel had an advocative purpose in bringing in speakers who presented her students with information on the environmental benefits of industrial hemp, even if Cockrel did not have such a purpose when organizing these presentations, her decision to present these speakers to her class still constitutes speech.

b.   Is Cockrel's Speech Constitutionally Protected?

Given our determination that Cockrel's decision to bring industrial hemp advocates into her class is speech, the next question we must ask is whether that speech is constitutionally protected. As stated earlier, speech of a public employee is protected by the First Amendment only if it touches on matters of public concern, and only if "the employee's interest in commenting upon matters of public concern . . . outweigh[s] the interest of the State, as an employer, in promoting the efficiency of the public services it performs through its employees." If Cockrel's speech cannot meet both of these standards, then her First Amendment retaliation claim cannot go forward.

i.   Does Cockrel's Speech Touch on a Matter of Public Concern?

In determining whether Cockrel's speech touched on a matter of public concern, we turn to *Connick v. Myers,* 461 U.S. 138, 103 S. Ct. 1684 (1983), the Supreme Court's most instructive case on this issue. In *Connick,* the Court stated that matters of public concern are those that can "be fairly considered as relating to any matter of political, social, or other concern to the community[.]" *Id.* at 146, 103 S. Ct. 1684. There is no question that the issue of industrial hemp is a matter of great political and social concern to many citizens of Kentucky, and we believe that Cockrel's presentations clearly come within the Supreme Court's understanding of speech touching on matters of public concern.

In support of this conclusion, we first turn to the district court's opinion, which unequivocally stated "that the issue of industrial hemp is politically charged and of great concern to certain citizens." Second, in the past year alone, industrial hemp advocacy in Kentucky has made news on several occasions, revealing the significant extent to which industrial hemp has become an important and publicly debated issue in the State. In October, presidential candidate Ralph Nader, in a campaign stop in Kentucky, spoke out in favor of the legalization of industrial hemp and of the benefits it would have for small family farmers. In December, after the Drug Enforcement Agency confiscated industrial hemp being grown on the Pine Ridge, South Dakota Indian Reservation, members of the Kentucky Hemp Growers Association, including former Kentucky governor Louie B. Nunn, traveled to South Dakota and, in a ceremony at the base of Mount Rushmore, delivered legally imported industrial hemp to the tribe as a sign of its solidarity. These examples only scratch the surface of the extent to which industrial hemp has become an issue of contentious political and economic debate in Kentucky.

While discussion of industrial hemp plainly meets the broad concept of "public concern" as defined by the Supreme Court, some courts have focused on other portions of the Supreme Court's *Connick* decision in concluding that a teacher's classroom speech does not touch on matters of public concern. These cases pay particular attention to the following portion of the *Connick* Court's holding:

> [W]hen a public employee speaks not as a citizen upon matters of public concern, but instead as an employee upon matters only of personal interest, absent the most unusual circumstances, a federal court is not the appropriate forum in which to review the wisdom of a personnel decision taken by a public agency allegedly in reaction to the employee's behavior. *Connick,* 461 U.S. at 147, 103 S.Ct. 1684.

Based upon this language, the Fourth and Fifth Circuits have determined that a teacher, in choosing what he will teach his students, is not speaking as a citizen, but rather as an employee on matters of private interest.

We believe that the Fourth and Fifth Circuits have extended the holding of *Connick* beyond what the Supreme Court intended. Under the courts' analyses in *Boring* and *Kirkland,* a teacher, regardless of what he decides to include in his curriculum, is speaking as an employee on a private matter. This essentially gives a teacher no right to freedom of speech when teaching students in a classroom, for the very act of teaching is what the employee is paid to do. Thus, when teaching, even if about an upcoming presidential election or the importance of our Bill of Rights, the Fourth and Fifth Circuits' reasoning would leave such speech without constitutional protection, for the teacher is speaking as an employee, and not as a citizen.

The facts in *Connick* indicate that the Fourth and Fifth Circuits have read the Supreme Court's language too broadly. In *Connick,* an assistant district attorney, following a disagreement with a supervisor, prepared a questionnaire seeking the opinions of her co-workers on issues such as "office transfer policy, office morale, the need for a grievance committee, the level of confidence in supervisors, and whether employees felt pressured to work in political campaigns." *Connick,* 461 U.S. at 141, 103 S.Ct. 1684. Connick was later fired for circulating the questionnaire on the grounds of insubordination. *Id.* The Court held that, while many of the questions simply reflected the plaintiff's efforts to gather information to use against her supervisors in her private employment dispute, Myers's question regarding the pressure to work on political campaigns *did* touch on a matter of public concern. *Id.* at 149, 103 S.Ct. 1684. Thus, the Court held that, even though Myers was speaking as an employee out of her private interest in combating her supervisors' decision to transfer her, the fact that one of her questions dealt with the fundamental constitutional right not to be coerced into campaigning for a political candidate was enough to make this particular issue touch on a matter of public concern. *Id.*

If the Fourth and Fifth Circuits' interpretation of *Connick* were correct, then any time a public employee was speaking as an employee, like Myers was when she asked her question about employees being pressured to campaign, the speech at issue would not be protected. As the Supreme Court made clear in its analysis, however, the key question is not whether a person is speaking in his role as an employee or a citizen, but whether the employee's speech in fact touches on matters of public concern. *Id.* 148–49, 103 S.Ct. 1684. Thus, even if a public employee were acting out of a private motive with no intent to air her speech publicly, as was the case with Myers, so long as the speech relates to matters of "political, social, or other concern to the community," as opposed to matters "only of personal interest," it shall be considered as touching upon matters of public concern. *Id.* at 146–49, 103 S.Ct. 1684.

In Cockrel's case, although she was speaking in her role as an employee when presenting information on the environmental benefits of industrial hemp, the content of her speech, as discussed *supra,* most certainly involved matters related to the political and social concern of the community, as opposed to mere matters of private interest. Thus, contrary to the analyses in *Boring* and *Kirkland,* we hold that Cockrel's speech does touch on matters of public concern.[5]

---

5. While Cockrel, in teaching her students about the environmental benefits of industrial hemp, was arguably speaking both as an employee and as a citizen, we do not believe that this case is best analyzed as a "mixed speech" case. In mixed speech cases, the employee at issue speaks not only as both a citizen and an employee, but the content of her speech involves matters of both public and private concern. In this case, while the very nature of Cockrel's profession entails that her speech on matters of political and social interest is likely to be made both as an employee and a citizen, the content of her speech is not mixed. Instead, rather than concerning, in part, an employee grievance or some other private dispute, as was the case with the professor's speech in *Bonnell,* Cockrel's speech relates to matters particularly of public concern. Even if we were to apply the mixed speech analysis, so long as "any part of an employee's speech, which contributes to the discharge, relates to matters of public concern, the court must conduct a balancing of interests test as set forth in *Pickering v. Board of Education,* 391 U.S. 563, 88 S.Ct. 1731 (1968)." As we will discuss in more detail later, because Cockrel's speech does relate to matters of public concern, and because this speech, at least in part, contributed to her discharge, a balancing of interests under *Pickering* is in order.

ii. *Pickering* Balancing

Having held that Cockrel's speech touches on matters of public concern, we must now weigh the employee's interest in speaking against the employer's interest in regulating the speech to determine if the speech is constitutionally protected. In *Pickering v. Board of Education*, 391 U.S. 563, 88 S. Ct. 1731 (1968), the Supreme Court endeavored to strike a balance between a public employee's speech rights on matters of public interest (in that case a public school teacher's speech outside of school) and the State's interest as an employer in maintaining a productive workplace. In accordance with the balancing test created in *Pickering*, public employee speech, even if touching on matters of public concern, will not be constitutionally protected unless the employee's interest in speaking on these issues "outweigh[s] 'the interest of the State, as an employer, in promoting the efficiency of the public services it performs through its employees.' " In striking the balance between the State's and the employee's respective interests, this court has stated that it will "consider whether an employee's comments meaningfully interfere with the performance of her duties, undermine a legitimate goal or mission of the employer, create disharmony among co-workers, impair discipline by superiors, or destroy the relationship of loyalty and trust required of confidential employees."

Before engaging in a "particularized balancing" of the competing interests at stake in this case, *Connick*, 461 U.S. at 150, 103 S.Ct. 1684, it is important to note that "if an employee's speech substantially involve[s] matters of public concern, an employer may be required to make a particularly strong showing that the employee's speech interfered with workplace functioning before taking action." In this case, it is clear that Cockrel's speech did substantially involve matters of public concern, and thus the defendants will have to make a stronger showing that their interests in regulating plaintiff's speech outweighed Cockrel's interests in speaking.

Weighing in plaintiff's favor in this analysis is the fact that her speech substantially involved matters of significant public concern in Kentucky. Defendants claim, however, that their "interest in maintaining loyalty, efficient operation of the schools, and workplace harmony" outweighs the plaintiff's interest in speaking about industrial hemp. We first note that the defendants do not claim that Cockrel's presentations on industrial hemp meaningfully interfered with the performance of her teaching duties. Defendants would have a difficult time making this argument, however, considering they openly acknowledged in a public statement to CNN that there was "educational value" in teaching students about industrial hemp as an alternative crop. We further note that defendants' purported interest in "maintaining loyalty" is inapposite in this case. While this circuit has stated that it would consider in its balancing whether employee speech operated to "destroy the relationship of loyalty and trust required of confidential employees[,]"a public school teacher, we believe, is hardly the type of confidential employee the court had in mind.

Thus, any loyalty concerns that the defendants may have will not be taken into consideration in our weighing of the competing interests at stake.

Turning to the defendants' proffered interests in an efficient operation of the school and a harmonious work environment, there is evidence that plaintiff's speech has led to problems in both of these areas. For example, following Harrelson's first visit to Simpsonville, numerous members of the school's faculty and staff circulated and or signed letters addressed to school officials criticizing Cockrel's actions in advocating the use of industrial hemp to her students. Cockrel thereafter expressed her displeasure with her co-workers' sentiments on several occasions. As discussed earlier, following D.A.R.E. officer Yeager's criticism of the Harrelson visits, Cockrel no longer wanted the officer in her classroom instructing her students. Cockrel asked Slate to find a replacement for Yeager as well. Cockrel's termination letter detailed several instances of disputes Cockrel had with co-workers, including an instance in which Cockrel jerked a phone away from a co-worker who had signed one of the letters speaking out against the Harrelson visit, and an incident in which Cockrel told two co-workers "not to waste their breath after they said 'good morning' to [her.]" At least one of these co-workers had also signed a letter critical of Cockrel's decision to speak about industrial hemp.

Many parents and members of the school community also expressed great concern over Cockrel's decision to invite speakers to her class who advocated the use of industrial hemp. Parents wrote letters to Principal Slate and Superintendent Mooneyhan in opposition to Cockrel's industrial hemp presentations, and a small number came to Simpsonville Elementary to protest on the final two occasions Harrelson was scheduled to visit. In addition, the PTA passed a position statement recommending that Cockrel no longer teach in the Shelby County School District.

Although this evidence of a contentious and periodically disrupted work environment weighs in favor of the defendants, the amount of weight we should give this evidence is an entirely different question. We are troubled by the fact that, whereas school officials gave plaintiff prior approval to host all three of the industrial hemp presentations at issue in this case, defendants now forward concerns of school efficiency and harmony as reasons supporting their decision to discharge Cockrel. Principal Slate approved all of Harrelson's scheduled visits in advance, and Slate openly stated that he had no problem with Cockrel teaching her students about industrial hemp. Cockrel also met the conditions of the new visitors policy implemented after the initial Harrelson visit, including obtaining the permission of each student's parents before a child could participate in the presentation. We do not believe that defendants can use the outcry within the school community protesting Cockrel's speech, speech that was approved by school officials in advance, as a shield for their decision to discharge her. While ordinarily we would give substantial weight to the government employer's concerns of workplace efficiency, harmony, and discipline in conducting our balancing of the employee's and employer's competing interests, we cannot allow these concerns to tilt the *Pickering* scale in favor of the government, absent other evidence, when the disruptive consequences of the employee speech can be traced back to the government's express decision permitting the employee to engage in that speech.[6]

Accordingly, we hold that, on balance, the defendants' interests in an efficient operation of the school and a harmonious workplace do not outweigh the plaintiff's interests in speaking about the benefits of industrial hemp, an issue of substantial political and economic concern in Kentucky. Thus, because Cockrel's speech touches on matters of public concern and because the balancing of interests under *Pickering* weighs in her favor, her speech is constitutionally protected.[7] We now proceed with an examination of the remainder of the elements of plaintiff's First Amendment retaliation claim.

c. Did the Plaintiff Suffer an Injury as a Result of Her Speech That Would Chill an Ordinary Person From Continuing to Engage in Such Speech?

For the next element of Cockrel's retaliation claim, she must show "that the defendant[s'] adverse action caused [her] to suffer an injury that would likely chill a person of ordinary firmness from continuing to engage in that activity[.]" There is no question that, by being terminated, Cockrel has suffered an injury that would chill an ordinary person from continuing to engage in speech on the environmental benefits of industrial hemp.

d. Was the Decision to Terminate Cockrel Motivated, at Least in Part, by Plaintiff's Decision to Speak About Industrial Hemp?

* * *

Although there certainly is significant evidence that Cockrel's behavior at school, apart from the industrial hemp presentations, was often inappropriate, we believe that Cockrel has presented enough evidence such that a reasonable jury could find that the defendants, in terminating her, were at least partially motivated by her decision to speak on industrial hemp. * * *

After examining this evidence, we conclude that a jury could find, by a preponderance of the evidence, that the defendants' decision to discharge Cockrel was motivated, at least in part, by her decision to teach her students about industrial hemp. The temporal proximity between the

---

6. This circuit has noted, with minimal explanation, that an unconstitutional dilemma may exist for a teacher whose controversial speech is approved ex ante by school officials, but used ex post, in the wake of parental and or community dismay with that speech, as the reason for the teacher's discharge.

7. Rather than apply *Pickering,* several circuits have chosen to apply the Supreme Court's analysis of students' in-class speech rights in *Hazelwood School District v. Kuhlmeier,* 484 U.S. 260, 108 S.Ct. 562 (1988), to cases in which teachers' in-class speech rights are at issue. The *Pickering* balancing analysis has been consistently applied to cases of teacher speech in this circuit. *See, e.g., Bonnell* [*v. Lorenzo*] (applying *Pickering* to a college professor's speech); *Leary* [*v. Daeschner*] (applying *Pickering* to elementary school teachers' speech). We see no reason to part from *Pickering* when deciding cases involving a teacher's in-class speech, nor have either of the parties in this case argued that *Pickering* should not apply.

Harrelson visits and Cockrel's series of unscheduled evaluations, as well as the influence the parent and teacher complaints appeared to have on the defendants in the wake of the Harrelson visits, constitute sufficient evidence for Cockrel to establish the causation element of her First Amendment retaliation claim.

* * *

We are well aware that Cockrel's decision to speak cannot immunize her from an adverse employment decision arising out of inappropriate workplace behavior unrelated to her protected speech. * * * [However,] [i]n this case, the defendants have not met this burden, and we believe that a genuine issue of material facts exists from which a reasonable jury could conclude that Cockrel would not have been terminated had she not engaged in constitutionally protected activity. Thus, this matter should be resolved at trial rather than at the summary judgment stage.

III. SUMMARY

For the foregoing reasons, we REVERSE the district court's decision granting defendants' motion for summary judgment, and REMAND to that court for further proceedings.

NOTES

1. The U.S. Supreme Court recently revisited the question of the parameters of public employee rights in this area when it decided *Garcetti v. Ceballos,* 547 U.S. 410, 126 S.Ct. 1951 (2006). In *Ceballos,* a deputy district attorney argued that his First Amendment rights had been violated when he was allegedly subjected to a series of retaliatory employment actions as a result of internal memos he had written to his supervisor. In the memos, Ceballos complained that a search warrant that was central to a case he was prosecuting contained numerous inaccuracies and reflected shoddy work by law enforcement officials. In a sharply divided opinion, the Court ruled 5–4 against Ceballos. The Court looked primarily to *Pickering* and *Connick,* and distinguished the fact pattern from that in *Pickering* by noting that in this case "the controlling factor...is that his expressions were made pursuant to his duties as a calendar attorney" and concluding that in such a context he did not have First Amendment protection. "We hold," Justice Kennedy wrote, "that when public employees make statements pursuant to their official duties, the employees are not speaking as citizens for First Amendment purposes, and the Constitution does not insulate their communications from employer discipline." 547 U.S. at 421, 126 S.Ct. at 1959–1960.

While the prospective impact of the *Ceballos* decision to K–12 educational settings remains unclear, basic principles derived from *Pickering* and *Connick* appear to have been affirmed. And *Ceballos* explicitly identifies a distinction between teacher speech and that of a Deputy District Attorney writing an internal memo, expressly mentioning teaching as an area where "some expressions related to [their] job" are in fact granted First Amendment protection. *Id.* However, it may be the case that future disputes regarding teacher freedom of expression will indeed turn on how broadly courts define the term *statements pursuant to official duties*. Are such statements to be construed as only those that are made in front of class in a formal setting, for example, or should they also include open houses, back-to-school nights, parent-teacher conferences, field trips, and other settings of a similar nature that may be much more informal? Where should the line be drawn?

2. In *Mayer v. Monroe County Community School Corp.*, 474 F.3d 477 (7th Cir. 2007), a non-tenured probationary teacher argued that her First Amendment rights had been violated when she was let go at the end of the 2002–2003 school year because of comments she had made in a formal classroom session during a lesson on current events. According to Ms. Mayer, she answered a pupil's question "about whether she participated in political demonstrations by saying that, when she passed a demonstration against this nation's military operations in Iraq and saw a placard saying 'Honk for Peace', she honked her car's horn to show support for the demonstrators." The Seventh Circuit upheld the lower court ruling in favor of the Blooming-ton, Indiana school district, relying on principles from both *Pickering* and *Garcetti v. Ceballos*:

> * * * [We need not] consider what rules apply to publications (scholarly or otherwise) by primary and secondary school teachers or the statements they make outside of class. It is enough to hold that the first amendment does not entitle primary and secondary teachers, when conducting the education of captive audiences, to cover topics, or advocate viewpoints, that depart from the curriculum adopted by the school system. *Id.* at 480.

It should be noted, however, that the lower court in the *Mayer* case did explicitly recognize that teachers interact with students in a variety of settings and need not limit their conversations in the same manner that they might be required to do in a formal classroom setting. Indeed, the Court stated that it would be appropriate for the district to provide "teachers and students the opportunity to engage in discussions about the war [in this manner] elsewhere on school property." *See Mayer v. Monroe County Community School Corp.*, 2006 WL 693555 (S.D. Ind.) at *12.

WEINGARTEN v. BOARD OF EDUCATION OF THE CITY SCHOOL DISTRICT OF THE CITY OF NEW YORK

2008 WL 4620573 (S.D.N.Y. 2008)

MEMORANDUM OPINION

Lewis A. Kaplan, District Judge.

Plaintiffs, the president of the United Federation of Teachers (the "UFT") and three New York City public school teachers, claim that two sections of the New York City school chancellor's Regulation D-l30 (the "Regulation") violate their rights under the First Amendment and the New York State Constitution. Specifically, they contend that it impermissibly bars teachers from (1) wearing political campaign buttons in Board of Education ("BOE") buildings, (2) posting candidate political materials on bulletin boards designated for union use in BOE buildings, and (3) placing candidate-related political materials in staff mailboxes in BOE buildings. The matter is before this Court on plaintiffs' motion for a preliminary injunction seeking to enjoin enforcement of the offending sections of the Regulation.

Facts

Section C.1 of the Regulation, which has been in effect since at least 2004, provides, under the heading "Conduct of Officers and Employees" that, "[w]hile on duty or in contact with students, all school personnel shall maintain a posture of complete neutrality with respect to all candidates."

Section B.3.a, under the heading "Use of School Facilities and Equipment," provides:

"No material supporting any candidate, candidates, slate of candidates, or political organizations/committees may be distributed, posted, or displayed in any school building. * * *

[In late September 2008,] * * * Michael Best, general counsel to the chancellor, informed the UFT that the Regulation barred the wearing of campaign buttons and the distribution of any political materials. On or about October 1, 2008, the BOE followed up with an electronic notice to all school principals. It reminded principals of the importance of compliance with the Regulation in light of the upcoming presidential election * * *.

Plaintiffs DelMoor, Thompson, and Pecoraro maintain that the BOE's position has deterred them from wearing political buttons and/or displaying union campaign posters on designated union bulletin boards. They claim also that they all have worn campaign buttons, and witnessed others doing so in the past, without incident. * * *

Discussion

* * * [T]he motion turns entirely on plaintiffs' likelihood of success on the merits.

C.   *Likelihood of Success on the Merits*

(1) Candidate Campaign Buttons

* * * In *Hazelwood School District v. Kuhlmeier,* the issue was whether a public school principal had violated the First Amendment rights of students by insisting upon the removal from a newspaper written and edited as part of a high school journalism class of two pages containing articles that the principal found were inappropriate. * * * [The U.S. Supreme Court] began with the proposition that " '[t]he determination of what manner of speech in the classroom or in school assembly is inappropriate properly rests with the school board,' rather than with the federal courts." It reasoned that "school officials may impose reasonable restrictions on the speech of students, teachers, and other members of the school community" unless the school facilities had become a public forum as a

result of having been opened "for indiscriminate use by the general public". Concluding that the school newspaper was not a public form, it held that "school officials were entitled to regulate [its] contents ... in any reasonable manner" and that "this standard, rather than [its] decision in *Tinker,* ... govern[ed the] case." It then went on to draw a critical distinction between the type of personal student expression at issue in *Tinker,* "personal expression that happen[ed] to occur on the school premises," and speech that "members of the public might reasonably perceive to bear the school's imprimatur," such as the newspaper published as part of the journalism class. "Educators," it ruled, "are entitled to exercise greater control over this second form of student expression to assure that participants learn whatever lessons the activity is designed to teach, that readers or listeners are not exposed to material that may be inappropriate for their level of maturity, *and that the views of the individual speaker are not erroneously attributed to the school."* Accordingly, it held that "a school may refuse to lend its name and resources to the dissemination of student expression ... [and that] educators do not offend the First Amendment by exercising editorial control over the style and content of student speech in school-sponsored expressive activities so long as their actions are reasonably related to legitimate pedagogical concerns."

Hazelwood thus altered or, at least, rendered more complex the analysis that governs this case. Here, defendants' stated concern is the maintenance of neutrality in political campaigns, a concern that is born at least in part of a desire to avoid having the political expression inherent in the wearing of partisan political campaign buttons by teachers "erroneously attributed to the school." And while plaintiffs argue that no reasonable person could conclude that the messages borne by teacher-sported buttons reflect the views of the Board of Education, the cases to have considered this question have applied *Hazelwood* to uphold public school actions identical or comparable to the button ban at issue here.

California Teachers Association v. Governing Board of San Diego Unified School District[21] is directly in point. The San Diego school district there prohibited teachers from wearing political campaign buttons at work during work hours. The teachers' union challenged the ban on First Amendment grounds. The California Court of Appeal began with *Hazelwood's* observation that schools have a "great deal more authority" to regulate speech that could be perceived by members of the public as bearing the school's imprimatur than they do when regulating a student's personal expression. It concluded that public school teachers, at least when teaching, and administrators act with the imprimatur of the school district and that, within the "intimate and deferential environment" of the classroom, "public school authorities may reasonably conclude it is not possible to both permit instructors to engage in classroom political activity and at the same time successfully disassociate the school from such advocacy." Indeed, the court reasoned that the very attributes of a

---

21.   45 Cal.App.4th 1383, 53 Cal.Rptr.2d 474 (1996).

successful student/teacher relationship make it reasonable for school officials to determine that restricting teachers from engaging in political advocacy during instructional activities is the only practical way to dissociate a school from political controversy. Accordingly, it rejected the union's challenge to the button ban.

California Teachers is noteworthy here not only for its application of *Hazelwood* to the wearing by teachers of political campaign buttons in school. Implicit in its analysis is the court's deference to the school district's determination that the wearing of the buttons might be viewed as lending the imprimatur of the district to the wearers' views * * *.

The recent decision in *Mayer v. Monroe Community School Corp.*,[26] while involving somewhat different facts, is essentially to the same effect. [sic] In that case, the school declined to renew the contract of a probationary elementary school teacher, allegedly because she took a political stance during a current events class. In rejecting her First Amendment challenge to that action, the Seventh Circuit held that teachers have no "constitutional right to determine what they say in class," essentially because "the school system does not 'regulate' teachers' speech as much as it *hires* that speech." Echoing *Hazelwood,* it added that "pupils are a captive audience," that "majority rule about what subjects and viewpoints will be expressed in the classroom has the potential to turn into indoctrination," and that "if indoctrination is likely, the power should be reposed in someone the people can vote out of office, rather than tenured teachers." * * *

Mayer and *California Teachers* together demonstrate that (1) the governing boards of public schools are constitutionally permitted, within reason, to regulate the speech of teachers in the classroom for legitimate pedagogical reasons, (2) the maintenance of neutrality on controversial issues is a legitimate pedagogical reason, and (3) [our pre-Hazelwood case law] has been undermined seriously by more than three decades of subsequent decisions.[a] This case, in my view, therefore comes down to whether there is a reasonable connection between defendants' political button ban and political button ban and their legitimate pedagogical concern with the maintenance of neutrality.

There is no evidence in this record that would permit a finding, as a factual matter, that students and parents would view the wearing by teachers of political buttons in the classroom as carrying with it the imprimatur of the Board of Education upon the messages those buttons convey. In consequence, the case turns upon whether and to what extent defendants are entitled to deference on that issue or, instead, bear the burden of proving it as an empirical matter. * * * [In other words, the

---

26.   474 F.3d 477 (7th Cir.2007).

a.   Judge Kaplan also emphasizes throughout this opinion that a 1977 Second Circuit decision relied upon by plaintiffs—*James v. Board of Education of Central School District of the Town of Addison,* 461 F.2d 566 (2d Cir. 1972)—has been discredited both explicitly and implicitly since Hazelwood was decided by the U.S. Supreme Court in 1988.

question] would be whether the defendants' view that the opinions conveyed by teacher-worn political buttons "might reasonably [be] perceive[d] to bear the school's imprimatur" or otherwise interfere with the accomplishment of defendants' public role should control here.

While the question is not free from doubt, I conclude that it should. Our public schools are attended by students ranging from toddlers to 17– and 18–year olds whose range of intellect and sophistication spans the entire spectrum from very low to extremely high. We trust the chancellor and the Board of Education to understand the needs, capabilities and vulnerabilities of that population and to design and implement programs to teach the skills and knowledge required in life. We do so because defendants are expert in those matters. As an initial matter, therefore, their view is entitled to the respect commanded by expertise.

That is not to say that deference is blind. Any determination by school authorities that impinges on free expression is subject to judicial review. But that review must respect not only professional expertise where the determination rests, at least in part, on a judgment as to the manner in which particular activity may affect the students whom we entrust to the care of school boards, but also the sensitivity of the judgment to First Amendment values. In other words, school officials may not take a sledge hammer to freedom of expression and then avoid all scrutiny by invoking alleged professional judgment.

In this case, the Regulation is content-neutral, i.e., it is justified without reference to the content of the regulated speech. Teachers plainly have ample alternative channels for the communication of their views, especially given that there is nothing special about schools that make school venues intimately connected with the messages that the teachers wish to communicate. And plaintiffs have not suggested any less restrictive means by which the defendants could avoid the risk they perceive. While a majority of students, particularly older students, presumably would understand that the views expressed by their teachers' campaign buttons are personal rather than institutional, there is a clear relationship between the regulation and defendants' legitimate interests in avoiding both the inevitable misperceptions on the part of a minority and, perhaps even more important, in avoiding the entanglement of their public educational mission with partisan politics.

* * * I find for purposes of this motion, that the Regulation in this respect reflects a good faith judgment by the defendants in their professional capacities about the impact of teachers' political campaign buttons in the school rather than a covert attempt to favor one viewpoint over another or a willingness to paint with too broad a brush. In light of *Hazelwood* and its progeny, that is all that is required in these circumstances. I therefore hold that plaintiffs are unlikely to prevail on their claim * * * .

(2) School Mailboxes and Union Bulletin Boards

* * *

[The Court went on to find, however, that while the plaintiffs were unlikely to prevail in the dispute over the candidate campaign buttons, they were in fact likely to prevail in the dispute over the use of school mailboxes and union bulletin boards. A preliminary injunction was issued prohibiting the enforcement of "the Regulation to the extent that it prohibits (1) posting materials containing candidate-related political content on UFT bulletin boards located in areas closed to students and (2) placing materials containing candidate related political content in staff mailboxes."] * * *

Notes

1. It should be noted that *Garcetti v. Ceballos* was not mentioned at all by Judge Kaplan in the *Weingarten* opinion.

2. As referenced by the Sixth Circuit in its *Cockrel* decision, *supra,* note 7, some courts have found the principles in *Pickering* to be most directly applicable to the teacher freedom of expression disputes of this era, while others rely on an expansive application of *Hazelwood*. *Cockrel* is an example of the former approach, while *Weingarten* is an example of the latter.

Indeed, for some time, now, federal appeals courts have differed in their approaches to this area. Many have applied *Pickering* and *Connick*, noting that *Pickering* in particular directly implicates educator speech. Others apply principles from the K–12 student freedom of the press case, *Hazelwood v. Kuhlmeier*. Some apply principles from both. *Pickering* is often viewed as applying to a greater extent to speech outside of the classroom, focusing more directly on the teacher as citizen. *Hazelwood,* on the other hand, with its focus on "legitimate pedagogical concerns" and the extent to which the speech may "bear the imprimatur of the school," is often seen as more directly applicable to teacher expression in a formal classroom setting.

Many have concluded that it is possible to reconcile the approaches of the various appeals court decisions and identify a broad range of guidelines that educators would be wise to follow anywhere in the country. All courts would undoubtedly agree, for example, that educators are expected to act professionally when interacting with their students. Viewed traditionally as important role models, they are indeed often held to a higher standard. In a formal education setting, they are expected to keep to the education process. They may not engage in the political, religious, or social indoctrination of their students, and they may not act counter to official school district policies. But outside of the classroom—within the parameters of the above guidelines— they arguably need not feel that they must severely curtail lawful expression…so long as they do not engage in activities that would disrupt their work environment or interfere with the collaborative nature of faculty and staff interaction.

C. "ACADEMIC FREEDOM" AT THE HIGHER EDUCATION LEVEL

UROFSKY v. GILMORE

216 F.3d 401 (4th Cir. 2000)

WILKINS, CIRCUIT JUDGE:

Appellees, six professors employed by various public colleges and universities in Virginia, brought this action challenging the constitutionality of a Virginia law restricting state employees from accessing sexually explicit material on computers that are owned or leased by the state. * * *

I.

The central provision of the Act states:

Except to the extent required in conjunction with a bona fide, agency-approved research project or other agency-approved undertaking, no agency employee shall utilize agency-owned or agency-leased computer equipment to access, download, print or store any information infrastructure files or services having sexually explicit content. Such agency approvals shall be given in writing by agency heads, and any such approvals shall be available to the public under the provisions of the Virginia Freedom of Information Act. Va.Code Ann. § 2.1–805.

Another section of the Act defines "sexually explicit content." When the district court ruled, and when the panel initially considered this appeal, the Act defined "sexually explicit content" to include:

(i) any description of or (ii) any picture, photograph, drawing, motion picture film, digital image or similar visual representation depicting sexual bestiality, a lewd exhibition of nudity, as nudity is defined in § 18.2–390, sexual excitement, sexual conduct or sadomasochistic abuse, as also defined in § 18.2–390, coprophilia, urophilia, or fetishism. Va.Code Ann. § 2.1–804.

Following our panel decision, the Virginia General Assembly amended the definition of "sexually explicit content" to add the italicized language:

content having as a dominant theme (i) any lascivious description of or (ii) any lascivious picture, photograph, drawing, motion picture film, digital image or similar visual representation depicting sexual bestiality, a lewd exhibition of nudity, as nudity is defined in § 18.2–390, sexual excitement, sexual conduct or sadomasochistic abuse, as also defined in § 18.2–390, coprophilia, urophilia, or fetishism. Va. Code Ann. § 2.1–804 (emphasis added).[3]

---

3. Section 18.2–390 provides in pertinent part:

(2) "Nudity" means a state of undress so as to expose the human male or female genitals, pubic area or buttocks with less than a full opaque covering, or the showing of the female breast with less than a fully opaque covering of any portion thereof below the top of the nipple, or the depiction of covered or uncovered male genitals in a discernibly turgid state.

As its language makes plain, the Act restricts access by state employees to lascivious sexually explicit material on computers owned or leased by the state. But, the Act does not prohibit all access by state employees to such materials, for a state agency head may give permission for a state employee to access such information on computers owned or leased by the state if the agency head deems such access to be required in connection with a bona fide research project or other undertaking. Further, state employees remain free to access sexually explicit materials from their personal or other computers not owned or leased by the state. Thus, the Act prohibits state employees from accessing sexually explicit materials only when the employees are using computers that are owned or leased by the state and permission to access the material has not been given by the appropriate agency head.

None of the Appellees has requested or been denied permission to access sexually explicit materials pursuant to the Act. Indeed, the record indicates that no request for access to sexually explicit materials on computers owned or leased by the state has been declined.

Appellees maintain that the restriction imposed by the Act violates the First Amendment rights of state employees. Appellees do not assert that state employees possess a First Amendment right to access sexually explicit materials on state-owned or leased computers for their personal use; rather, Appellees confine their challenge to the restriction of access to sexually explicit materials for work-related purposes. Appellees' challenge to the Act is twofold: They first maintain that the Act is unconstitutional as to all state employees; failing this, they argue more particularly that the Act violates academic employees' right to academic freedom.

II.

It is well settled that citizens do not relinquish all of their First Amendment rights by virtue of accepting public employment. *See United States v. National Treasury Employees Union* [hereinafter *NTEU*]; *Connick v. Myers,* 461 U.S. 138, 142, 103 S. Ct. 1684 (1983); *Pickering v. Board of Educ.,* 391 U.S. 563, 568, 88 S. Ct. 1731 (1968). Nevertheless, the state, as an employer, undoubtedly possesses greater authority to restrict the speech of its employees than it has as sovereign to restrict the speech of the citizenry as a whole. * * *

---

(3) "Sexual conduct" means actual or explicitly simulated acts of masturbation, homosexuality, sexual intercourse, or physical contact in an act of apparent sexual stimulation or gratification with a persons clothed or unclothed genitals, pubic area, buttocks or, if such be female, breast.

(4) "Sexual excitement" means the condition of human male or female genitals when in a state of sexual stimulation or arousal.

(5) "Sadomasochistic abuse" means actual or explicitly simulated flagellation or torture by or upon a person who is nude or clad in undergarments, a mask or bizarre costume, or the condition of being fettered, bound or otherwise physically restrained on the part of one so clothed.

Va.Code Ann. § 18.2–390(2) to–390(5) (Michie 1996) (emphasis omitted).

The threshold inquiry thus is whether the Act regulates speech by state employees in their capacity as citizens upon matters of public concern. If a public employee's speech made in his capacity as a private citizen does not touch upon a matter of public concern, the state, as employer, may regulate it without infringing any First Amendment protection.

* * *

To determine whether speech involves a matter of public concern, we examine the content, context, and form of the speech at issue in light of the entire record. *See Connick,* 461 U.S. at 147–48, 103 S.Ct. 1684. Speech involves a matter of public concern when it involves an issue of social, political, or other interest to a community. *See id.* at 146, 103 S.Ct. 1684. An inquiry into whether a matter is of public concern does not involve a determination of how interesting or important the subject of an employee's speech is. Further, the place where the speech occurs is irrelevant: An employee may speak as a citizen on a matter of public concern at the workplace, and may speak as an employee away from the workplace. *Compare Rankin v. McPherson* (holding public employee's discharge was violative of First Amendment when based on comment by employee as a private citizen on a matter of public concern made at work), *with DiMeglio v. Haines* (recognizing that speech by a public employee outside the workplace was made in the employee's official capacity).

The Supreme Court has made clear that the concern is to maintain for the government employee the same right enjoyed by his privately employed counterpart. To this end, in its decisions determining speech to be entitled to First Amendment protection the Court has emphasized the unrelatedness of the speech at issue to the speaker's employment duties.

* * *

The speech at issue here—access to certain materials using computers owned or leased by the state for the purpose of carrying out employment duties—is clearly made in the employee's role as employee. Therefore, the challenged aspect of the Act does not regulate the speech of the citizenry in general, but rather the speech of state employees in their capacity as employees. It cannot be doubted that in order to pursue its legitimate goals effectively, the state must retain the ability to control the manner in which its employees discharge their duties and to direct its employees to undertake the responsibilities of their positions in a specified way. * * * The essence of Appellees' claim is that they are entitled to access sexually explicit material in their capacity as state employees by using equipment owned or leased by the state. Because, as Appellees acknowledge, the challenged aspect of the Act does not affect speech by Appellees in their capacity as private citizens speaking on matters of public concern, it does not infringe the First Amendment rights of state employees.

III.

Alternatively, Appellees maintain that even if the Act is valid as to the majority of state employees it violates the First Amendment academic freedom rights of professors at state colleges and universities, and thus is invalid as to them.[9] In essence, Appellees contend that a university professor possesses a constitutional right to determine for himself, without the input of the university (and perhaps even contrary to the university's desires), the subjects of his research, writing, and teaching. Appellees maintain that by requiring professors to obtain university approval before accessing sexually explicit materials on the Internet in connection with their research, the Act infringes this individual right of academic freedom. Our review of the law, however, leads us to conclude that to the extent the Constitution recognizes any right of "academic freedom" above and beyond the First Amendment rights to which every citizen is entitled, the right inheres in the University, not in individual professors, and is not violated by the terms of the Act.

"Academic freedom" is a term that is often used, but little explained, by federal courts. As a result, decisions invoking academic freedom are lacking in consistency, and courts invoke the doctrine in circumstances where it arguably has no application. Accordingly, we begin with a brief review of the history of the concept of academic freedom in the United States.

Prior to the late nineteenth century, institutions of higher education in this country were not considered centers of research and scholarship, but rather were viewed as a means of passing received wisdom on to the next generation. "Faculty performed essentially fixed if learned operations within a traditional curriculum under the sanction of established truth.... [A]cademic freedom as we know it simply had no meaning." Additionally, American universities during this period were characterized by "legal control by non-academic trustees; effective governance by administrators set apart from the faculty by political allegiance and professional orientation; [and] dependent and insecure faculty." This began to change, however, as Americans who had studied at German universities sought to remodel American universities in the German image.

The German notion of academic freedom was composed primarily of two concepts: *Lehrfreiheit* and *Lernfreiheit*. *Lehrfreiheit,* or freedom to teach, embodied the notion that professors should be free to conduct research and publish findings without fear of reproof from the church or state; it further denoted the authority to determine the content of courses and lectures. *Lernfreiheit* was essentially a corollary right of students to determine the course of their studies for themselves.

---

9. Appellees assert that the Act infringes on academic freedom by hindering professors' ability to perform their employment duties, particularly teaching and research. The facts alleged in the complaint illustrate the type of restrictions with which Appellees are primarily concerned. Melvin I. Urofsky, the lead plaintiff in the district court, alleged that he had declined to assign an online research project on indecency law because he feared he would be unable to verify his students' work without violating the Act. Appellee Terry L. Meyers contended that he is affected by the Act because his ability to access Virginia's database to research sexually explicit poetry in connection with his study of Victorian poets is restricted by the policy. Appellee Paul Smith's Web site has been censored as a result of the Act. And, appellees Dana Heller, Bernard H. Levin, and Brian J. Delaney maintained that they were hesitant to continue their Internet research of various aspects of human sexuality.

In 1915, a committee of the American Association of University Professors (AAUP) issued a report on academic freedom that adapted the concept of *Lehrfreiheit* to the American university. In large part, the AAUP was concerned with obtaining for professors a measure of professional autonomy from lay administrators and trustees. The AAUP defined academic freedom as "a right claimed by the accredited educator, as teacher and investigator, to interpret his findings and to communicate his conclusions without being subjected to any interference, molestation, or penalization because the conclusions are unacceptable to some constituted authority within or beyond the institution." Significantly, the AAUP conceived academic freedom as a professional norm, not a legal one: The AAUP justified academic freedom on the basis of its social utility as a means of advancing the search for truth, rather than its status as a manifestation of First Amendment rights. The principles adopted in the 1915 report were later codified in a 1940 Statement of Principles on Academic Freedom and Tenure promulgated by the AAUP and the Association of American Colleges. The 1940 Statement since "has been endorsed by every major higher education organization in the nation," "through its adoption into bylaws, faculty contracts, and collective bargaining agreements."[12]

Appellees' insistence that the Act violates their rights of academic freedom amounts to a claim that the academic freedom of professors is not only a professional norm, but also a constitutional right. We disagree. It is true, of course, that homage has been paid to the ideal of academic freedom in a number of Supreme Court opinions, often with reference to the First Amendment. *See, e.g., Regents of the Univ. of Mich. v. Ewing*; *Regents of the Univ. of Cal. v. Bakke* (opinion of Powell, J.); *Keyishian v. Board of Regents*; *Sweezy v. New Hampshire* (plurality opinion); *id.* (Frankfurter, J., concurring in the result). Despite these accolades, the Supreme Court has never set aside a state regulation on the basis that it infringed a First Amendment right to academic freedom. *Cf. Minnesota State Bd. for Community Colleges v. Knight* (stating that the Court has not recognized a First Amendment right of faculty to participate in academic policymaking).

---

12. In view of this history, we do not doubt that, as a matter of professional practice, university professors in fact possess the type of academic freedom asserted by Appellees. Indeed, the claim of an academic institution to status as a "university" may fairly be said to depend upon the extent to which its faculty members are allowed to pursue knowledge free of external constraints. *See* [Richard Hofstadter & Walter P.] Metzger[, *The Development of Academic Freedom in United States*] (explaining that the authors of the 1915 AAUP report believed "that any academic institution that restrict[ed] the intellectual freedom of its professors . . . cease[d] to be a true university"). Were it not so, advances in learning surely would be hindered in a manner harmful to the university as an institution and to society at large. However, Appellees fail to appreciate that the wisdom of a given practice as a matter of policy does not give the practice constitutional status. *See Minnesota State Bd. for Community Colleges v. Knight* (concluding that "[f]aculty involvement in academic governance has much to recommend it as a matter of academic policy, but it finds no basis in the Constitution").

Additionally, we note that we are not here called upon to decide the wisdom of the Act as a matter of policy. That an enactment may be utterly unnecessary, or even profoundly unwise, does not affect its validity as a matter of constitutional law.

Moreover, a close examination of the cases indicates that the right praised by the Court is not the right Appellees seek to establish here. Appellees ask us to recognize a First Amendment right of academic freedom that belongs to the professor as an individual. The Supreme Court, to the extent it has constitutionalized a right of academic freedom at all, appears to have recognized only an institutional right of self-governance in academic affairs.

* * *

This emphasis on institutional rights is particularly evident in more recent Supreme Court jurisprudence. For example, in *Bakke* Justice Powell discussed academic freedom as it related to a program of admissions quotas established by a medical school. Relying on *Keyishian* and on Justice Frankfurter's concurrence in *Sweezy,* Justice Powell characterized academic freedom as "[t]he freedom of a university to make its own judgments as to education." Similarly, in *Ewing* the Court described academic freedom as a concern of the institution.

Significantly, the Court has never recognized that professors possess a First Amendment right of academic freedom to determine for themselves the content of their courses and scholarship, despite opportunities to do so. * * *

Taking all of the cases together, the best that can be said for Appellees' claim that the Constitution protects the academic freedom of an individual professor is that teachers were the first public employees to be afforded the now-universal protection against dismissal for the exercise of First Amendment rights. Nothing in Supreme Court jurisprudence suggests that the "right" claimed by Appellees extends any further. Rather, since declaring that public employees, including teachers, do not forfeit First Amendment rights upon accepting public employment, the Court has focused its discussions of academic freedom solely on issues of institutional autonomy. We therefore conclude that because the Act does not infringe the constitutional rights of public employees in general, it also does not violate the rights of professors.

* * *

MURNAGHAN, CIRCUIT JUDGE, dissenting:

The majority's interpretation of the "public concern" doctrine makes the role of the speaker dispositive of the analysis. Specifically, the majority states that "critical to a determination of whether employee speech is entitled to First Amendment protection is whether the speech is 'made primarily in the [employee's] role as citizen or primarily in his role as employee.'" The majority then rejects the plaintiffs' First Amendment claim because "[t]he speech at issue here ... is clearly made in the employee's role as employee." Because an analysis of *Connick v. Myers,* 461 U.S. 138, 103 S.Ct. 1684 (1983), and its progeny reveals that the majority has adopted an unduly restrictive interpretation of the "public concern" doctrine, I respectfully dissent.

I.

A.

In *Connick,* the Supreme Court held that, as a threshold matter, if a public employee's speech "cannot be fairly characterized as constituting speech on a matter of public concern," then a court does not balance the employer's interests with those of the employee. *Connick,* 461 U.S. at 146, 103 S.Ct. 1684. The Court broadly defined speech of public concern as speech "relating to any matter of political, social, or other concern to the community." *Id.* The Court also stated that "[w]hether an employee's speech addresses a matter of public concern must be determined by the content, form, and context of a given statement, as revealed by the whole record." *Id.* at 147–48, 103 S. Ct. 1684. Nowhere in *Connick,* however, did the Court state that the role of the speaker, standing alone, would be dispositive of the public concern analysis.

Indeed, the facts of *Connick* belie this suggestion. Sheila Myers, an Assistant District Attorney, was discharged for distributing a questionnaire to the other attorneys in her office. In general, Myers' questionnaire asked her peers what they thought of the trustworthiness of certain attorneys in the office, the morale of the office, and the office's transfer policy. *See id.* at 141, 103 S.Ct. 1684.

The Court held that these questions "do not fall under the rubric of matters of 'public concern,'" because they were "mere extensions of Myers' dispute over her transfer to another section of the criminal court." *Id.* at 148, 103 S.Ct. 1684. Myers' questionnaire, however, also asked whether her fellow attorneys "ever feel pressured to work in political campaigns on behalf of office supported candidates." *Id.* at 149, 103 S.Ct. 1684. This question was in the same form and context as Myers' other questions—an internal questionnaire distributed by an employee complaining about on-the-job conditions. The question thus was *speech by an employee in her role as an employee.* The Court nevertheless held that this question did "touch upon a matter of public concern." *Id.* The majority's formalistic focus on the "role of the speaker" in employee speech cases therefore runs directly contrary to Supreme Court precedent.

B.

Post-*Connick* decisions of this court also make it clear that the role of the speaker does not control the public concern analysis. In *Piver v. Pender County Bd. of Educ.*, the plaintiff, a high school teacher, circulated a petition to his students during class urging retention of the school's principal. The plaintiff undoubtedly was speaking in his role as an employee, as he was being paid by the State and using State facilities (classrooms) to carry out his employment duties (instructing students). The court nevertheless held that the plaintiff's speech was on a matter of public concern because it was a "matter in which the community ... was vitally interested." The court also stressed that the speech was "of much wider importance than a mere 'private personnel grievance,' " that would not be of public concern.

In *Piver,* the court relied on the "public concern" analysis set out by this court in *Berger v. Battaglia.* In *Berger,* the court interpreted the public concern doctrine as excluding from First Amendment protection only those matters of purely personal interest to the employee.

> *Pickering,* its antecedents, and its progeny—particularly *Connick*—make it plain that the "public concern" or "community interest" inquiry is better designed—and more concerned—to identify a narrow spectrum of employee speech that is not entitled even to qualified protection than it is to set outer limits on all that is. The principle that emerges is that *all* public employee speech that by content is within the general protection of the first amendment is entitled to at least qualified protection against public employer chilling action except that which, realistically viewed, is of purely "personal concern" to the employee—most typically, a private personnel grievance.

Furthermore, the court stated that when analyzing whether speech is upon "any matter of political, social, or other concern to the community," *see Connick,* 461 U.S. at 146, 103 S.Ct. 1684, "[t]he focus is ... upon whether the 'public' or the 'community' is likely to be truly concerned with or interested in the particular expression, or whether it is more properly viewed as essentially a 'private' matter between employer and employee."

Berger's broad approach to the public concern doctrine, focusing on the public importance of the speech, stands in stark contrast to the majority's singular focus on the role of the speaker—regardless of the public import of the speaker's message. *See also Arvinger v. Mayor and City Council of Baltimore* ("Although the *Connick* court did not elaborate on the relative weight to be accorded these three factors, this court has held that 'content, subject-matter, is always the central aspect.' ").

C.

The majority justifies its singular focus on the role of the speaker by citing to language from *United States v. National Treasury Employees Union* ("*NTEU*"). In *NTEU,* the plaintiffs were executive branch employees challenging a law prohibiting federal employees from accepting any compensation for making speeches or writing articles, even when the speeches or articles did not have any connection to the employees' official duties. The Supreme Court held that the plaintiffs' speech was on a matter of public concern. In doing so, the Court stated that "[t]hey seek compensation for their expressive activities in their capacity as citizens, not as Government employees.... With few exceptions, the content of respondents' messages has nothing to do with their jobs and does not even arguably have any adverse impact on the efficiency of the offices in which they work."

The majority's analysis of this language attempts to push *NTEU* where it did not go. The Court in *NTEU* stated that the plaintiffs' speech was on a matter of public concern in part because it was unrelated to the plaintiffs' employment; however, nowhere in *NTEU* did the Court state the converse: namely, that *if* the plaintiffs' speech was in their role as employees, then it automatically would not qualify as speech on a matter of public concern. Therefore, at best, *NTEU* suggests that the role of the speaker is a *factor* in a public concern analysis. But even a broad reading of *NTEU* does not suggest that the role of the speaker is the *only* factor to consider in a public concern analysis, despite the majority's claims to the contrary.

The majority also relies on our decision in *Boring v. Buncombe County Bd. of Educ.* In *Boring,* the plaintiff, a high school teacher, was transferred by her principal for producing a student-acted play that addressed controversial topics such as lesbianism and teen pregnancy. The plaintiff alleged that the County violated her First Amendment rights by transferring her in retaliation for producing the play.

A majority of this court framed the issue in *Boring* as only "whether a public high school teacher has a First Amendment right to participate in the makeup of the school curriculum through the selection and production of a play." The majority held that the plaintiff's selection of the play was not a matter of public concern and was merely an "ordinary employment dispute." As their framing of the issue shows, however, the majority's reasoning was not based on the fact that the plaintiff's production of the play was in her role as a school district employee. Rather, the majority answered the narrower question of whether a teacher has a First Amendment right to participate in the makeup of the curriculum.

Judge Luttig's concurring opinion in *Boring* also illustrates that the majority's holding did not deal with the broader issue of whether speech by an employee in her role as an employee can qualify as speech on a matter of public concern. Judge Luttig stated that

> [the dissent] fails to recognize the elementary difference between teacher in-class speech which is curricular, and teacher in-class speech which is noncurricular, because it assumes that every word uttered by a teacher in a classroom is curriculum. *In the latter context of teacher in-class noncurricular speech, the teacher assuredly enjoys some First Amendment protection.* (emphasis added)

Presumably, Judge Luttig meant that teacher in-class noncurricular speech could be speech on a matter of public concern. As stated previously, however, a teacher's in-class speech is speech in her role as an employee, whether the speech is curricular or noncurricular. While students are under her care and supervision in the classroom, a teacher surely cannot be regarded as a "citizen" rather than an "employee" merely because she is discussing something other than trigonometry. Thus, *Boring* must rest on something other than the principle that speech by an employee in her role as an employee never qualifies as speech on a matter of public concern. *See Boring* (Motz, J., dissenting) ("Because the majority does not attempt to explicitly hold that the role in which an employee speaks is determinative [or overrule prior precedent], this reasoning must not be the basis for its conclusion that Boring's speech does not relate to a matter of public concern."). *Boring* therefore does not compel a finding that the plaintiffs' speech is not on a matter of public concern, merely because the plaintiffs' speech occurs in their role as employees.[1]

D.

Because speech by an employee in her role as an employee can qualify as speech on a matter of public concern, the issue thus becomes whether, in the instant case, the plaintiffs' speech is on a "matter of political, social, or other concern to the community." *Connick,* 461 U.S. at 146, 103 S.Ct. 1684. The plaintiffs' speech easily meets this test. The Supreme Court has stated that "[s]ex, a great and mysterious motive force in human life, has indisputably been a subject of absorbing interest to mankind through the ages; *it is one of the vital problems of human interest and public concern.*" (emphasis added).

The Act restricts over 101,000 state employees, including university professors, librarians, museum workers, and physicians and social workers at state hospitals, from researching, discussing, and writing about sexually explicit material. As the district court noted, "the Act's broad definition of 'sexually explicit' content would include research and debate on sexual themes in art, literature, history and the law, speech and research by medical and mental health professionals concerning sexual disease, sexual dysfunction, and sexually related mental disorders, and the routine exchange of information among social workers on sexual assault and child abuse." These topics undeniably touch on matters of public concern.

The Commonwealth's recent revision to the Act limiting the definition of "sexually explicit content" to materials and descriptions that are "lascivious" does not change the analysis. Many works of public import could be classified as lascivious; in fact, many were specifically intended to have such an effect. For instance, the works of Toni Morrison and many themes found in Victorian poetry, including the material researched online by one of the plaintiffs, Professor Myers, could be classified as lascivious. Also, the application of the Act to "lascivious" e-mail discussions by psychologists and social workers implicates topics of public import, because the public has an interest in unfettered discussions by State professionals concerning the abnormal sexual behaviors of their patients, in order to better diagnose and understand sexual deviancy.

Finally, the form of the plaintiffs' speech, Internet and e-mail communications, makes the speech of special public significance. In the information age, electronic communications may be the most important forum for

---

1. In any event, to the extent that *Boring* controls the public concern analysis in the instant case, and I do not agree that it does, I would revisit that holding. Judge Motz persuasively argued in her dissent in *Boring* why the majority's approach to public employees is at odds with *Connick* and its progeny.

accessing and discussing topics of concern to the community. This court should be wary of allowing the State to regulate this important medium of communication without requiring a legitimate justification for the regulation.

* * *

PROBLEM 55: DISCIPLINARY SANCTIONS AT THE HIGHER EDUCATION LEVEL

A.   Assume the same set of facts as set forth in Problem 54, above, except that the setting is a public college or university. Is it conceivable that Professor Marcos would have been sanctioned for similar behavior? If so, why? If not, what modifications in the existing fact pattern would be required before the professor might have been disciplined?

B.   If the professor were indeed disciplined in some fashion under the same or a similar scenario, and subsequently filed a lawsuit, would he prevail? Under what theory or theories?

Assume that the institution's faculty code of conduct contains the following pertinent provisions:

- The types of discipline that may be imposed on a member of the faculty are as follows, in order of increasing severity: written censure, reduction in salary, demotion, suspension, denial or curtailment of emeritus status, and dismissal from the employ of the University.

- The *Types of Unacceptable Conduct* listed below are examples of types of conduct which are presumptively subject to University discipline.

Teaching and Students: Types of unacceptable conduct

1.   Failure to meet the responsibilities of instruction, including:

* * *

(b) significant intrusion of material unrelated to the course;

2.   Discrimination, including harassment, against a student on political grounds, or for reasons of race, religion, sex, sexual orientation, ethnic origin, national origin, ancestry, marital status, medical condition, status as a covered veteran, or, within the limits imposed by law or University regulations, because of age or citizenship or for other arbitrary or personal reasons.

* * *

4.   Use of the position or powers of a faculty member to coerce the judgment or conscience of a student or to cause harm to a student for arbitrary or personal reasons.

5.   Participating in or deliberately abetting disruption, interference, or intimidation in the classroom.

The University

* * *

7.   Serious violation of University policies governing the professional conduct of faculty, including but not limited to policies applying to research,

outside professional activities, conflicts of commitment, clinical practices, violence in the workplace, and whistleblower protections.

E. EMPLOYMENT DISCRIMINATION

In general, the area of public sector employment discrimination includes a very large number of cases, statutes, regulations, and relevant policies. Many of the issues that arise in an education context are not necessarily education-specific, and these issues are often resolved by the application of broad overarching principles contained in employment discrimination law.

There are, however, a significant number of employment discrimination cases exemplifying disputes that are uniquely linked to education settings, and these cases raise very specific education-related questions. This section provides an overview of notable decisions in this regard, highlighting litigation that alleged discrimination on the basis of race, gender, LGBT status, religion, age, and disability.

1. RACE/ETHNICITY

In *Wygant v. Jackson Board of Education*, 476 U.S. 267, 106 S.Ct. 1842 (1986), the Court addressed the question of "whether a school board, consistent with the Equal Protection Clause, may extend preferential protection against layoffs to some of its employees because of their race or national origin."

> In 1972 the Jackson Board of Education, because of racial tension in the community that extended to its schools, * * * [added] a layoff provision to the Collective Bargaining Agreement (CBA) between the Board and the Jackson Education Association (Union) that would protect employees who were members of certain minority groups against layoffs. * * *
>
> * * * After [subsequent federal and state litigation], the Board adhered to [the layoff provision,] Article XII. As a result, during the 1976–1977 and 1981–1982 school years, nonminority teachers were laid off, while minority teachers with less seniority were retained. The displaced nonminority teachers * * * brought suit in Federal District Court, alleging violations of the Equal Protection Clause, Title VII, 42 U.S.C. § 1983, and other federal and state statutes. *Id.* at 270–72.

Unable to muster a majority, Justice Powell announced the judgment of the Court and delivered an opinion in which The Chief Justice and Justice Rehnquist joins, and in all but Part IV of which Justice O'Connor joined. In the decision, the Court ruled in favor the plaintiff:

> Petitioners' central claim is that they were laid off because of their race in violation of the Equal Protection Clause of the Fourteenth Amendment. * * * This Court has "consistently repudiated '[d]istinctions between citizens solely because of their ancestry' as being

'odious to a free people whose institutions are founded upon the doctrine of equality.' " "Racial and ethnic distinctions of any sort are inherently suspect and thus call for the most exacting judicial examination." * * *

The Court of Appeals, relying on the reasoning and language of the District Court's opinion, held that the Board's interest in providing minority role models for its minority students, as an attempt to alleviate the effects of societal discrimination, was sufficiently important to justify the racial classification embodied in the layoff provision. The court discerned a need for more minority faculty role models by finding that the percentage of minority teachers was less than the percentage of minority students. * * *

[T]he role model theory employed by the District Court has no logical stopping point. The role model theory allows the Board to engage in discriminatory hiring and layoff practices long past the point required by any legitimate remedial purpose. Indeed, by tying the required percentage of minority teachers to the percentage of minority students, it requires just the sort of year-to-year calibration the Court stated was unnecessary * * * .

Moreover, because the role model theory does not necessarily bear a relationship to the harm caused by prior discriminatory hiring practices, it actually could be used to escape the obligation to remedy such practices by justifying the small percentage of black teachers by reference to the small percentage of black students. Carried to its logical extreme, the idea that black students are better off with black teachers could lead to the very system the Court rejected in *Brown v. Board of Education,* 347 U.S. 483, 74 S.Ct. 686 (1954) (*Brown I*).

Societal discrimination, without more, is too amorphous a basis for imposing a racially classified remedy. The role model theory announced by the District Court and the resultant holding typify this indefiniteness. * * * *Id.* at 273–76.

It is important to note that not even four justices joined all parts of Justice Powell's opinion. What is the precedential value of *Wygant* in the aftermath of *Grutter* (*supra,* chapter 5)? Can an argument be made that *Grutter* limited the scope and impact of the *Wygant* ruling? Why or why not?

2. GENDER

In *Cleveland Board of Education v. LaFleur,* 414 U.S. 632, 94 S.Ct. 791 (1974), the Court was asked to rule on the lawsuit brought by Jo Carol LaFleur and Ann Elizabeth Nelson, junior high school teachers employed by the Board of Education of Cleveland, Ohio:

Pursuant to a rule first adopted in 1952, the school board requires every pregnant school teacher to take maternity leave without pay, beginning five months before the expected birth of her child. * * * A teacher on maternity leave is not allowed to return to work until the beginning of the next regular school semester which follows the date when her child attains the age of three months. A doctor's certificate attesting to the health of the teacher is a prerequisite to return; an additional physical examination may be required. The teacher or maternity leave is not promised re-employment after the birth of the child; she is merely given priority in reassignment to a position for which she is qualified. Failure to comply with the mandatory maternity leave provisions is ground for dismissal.

Neither Mrs. LaFleur nor Mrs. Nelson wished to take an unpaid maternity leave; each wanted to continue teaching until the end of the school year. Because of the mandatory maternity leave rule, however, each was required to leave her job in March 1971.[3] The two women then filed separate suits in the United States District Court for the Northern District of Ohio under 42 U.S.C. § 1983, challenging the constitutionality of the maternity leave rule. * * *

Susan Cohen, was employed by the School Board of Chesterfield County, Virginia. That school board's maternity leave regulation requires that a pregnant teacher leave work at least four months prior to the expected birth of her child. Notice in writing must be given to the school board at least six months prior to the expected birth date. * * *

Mrs. Cohen * * * filed this suit under 42 U.S.C. § 1983 in the United States District Court for the Eastern District of Virginia. * * *

We granted certiorari in both cases in order to resolve the conflict between the Courts of Appeals regarding the constitutionality of such mandatory maternity leave rules for public school teachers. *Id.* at 634–38.

Justice Stewart, writing on behalf of the majority, explained that the Court "has long recognized that freedom of personal choice in matters of marriage and family life is one of the liberties protected by the Due Process Clause of the Fourteenth Amendment":

By acting to penalize the pregnant teacher for deciding to bear a child, overly restrictive maternity leave regulations can constitute a heavy burden on the exercise of these protected freedoms. Because public school maternity leave rules directly affect 'one of the basic civil rights of man,' the Due Process Clause of the Fourteenth Amendment requires that such rules must not needlessly, arbitrarily, or capriciously impinge upon this vital area of a teacher's constitutional liberty. The question before us in these cases is whether the interests advanced in support of the rules of the Cleveland and

---

3. Effective February 1, 1971, the Cleveland regulation was amended to provide that only teachers with one year of continuous service qualified for maternity leave; teachers with less than one year were required to resign at the beginning of the fifth month of pregnancy. * * *

Chesterfield County School Boards can justify the particular procedures they have adopted.

The school boards in these cases have offered two essentially overlapping explanations for their mandatory maternity leave rules. First, they contend that the firm cutoff dates are necessary to maintain continuity of classroom instruction, since advance knowledge of when a pregnant teacher must leave facilitates the finding and hiring of a qualified substitute. Secondly, the school boards seek to justify their maternity rules by arguing that at least some teachers become physically incapable of adequately performing certain of their duties during the latter part of pregnancy. By keeping the pregnant teacher out of the classroom during these final months, the maternity leave rules are said to protect the health of the teacher and her unborn child, while at the same time assuring that students have a physically capable instructor in the classroom at all times.

* * * But * * * while the advance-notice provisions in the Cleveland and Chesterfield County rules are wholly rational and may well be necessary to serve the objective of continuity of instruction, the absolute requirements of termination at the end of the fourth or fifth month of pregnancy are not. Were continuity the only goal, cutoff dates much later during pregnancy would serve as well as or better than the challenged rules, providing that ample advance notice requirements were retained. Indeed, continuity would seem just as well attained if the teacher herself were allowed to choose the date upon which to commence her leave, at least so long as the decision were required to be made and notice given of it well in advance of the date selected. * * *

We * * * conclude that the arbitrary cutoff dates embodied in the mandatory leave rules before us have no rational relationship to the valid state interest of preserving continuity of instruction. As long as the teachers are required to give substantial advance notice of their condition, the choice of firm dates later in pregnancy would serve the boards' objectives just as well, while imposing a far lesser burden on the women's exercise of constitutionally protected freedom.

The question remains as to whether the cutoff dates at the beginning of the fifth and sixth months can be justified on the other ground advanced by the school boards—the necessity of keeping physically unfit teachers out of the classroom. There can be no doubt that such an objective is perfectly legitimate, both on educational and safety grounds. And, despite the plethora of conflicting medical testimony in these cases, we can assume, arguendo, that at least some teachers become physically disabled from effectively performing their duties during the latter stages of pregnancy. * * *

While the medical experts in these cases differed on many points, they unanimously agreed on one—the ability of any particular pregnant woman to continue at work past any fixed time in her pregnancy is very much an individual matter. Even assuming, arguendo, that there are some women who would be physically unable to work past the particular cutoff dates embodied in the challenged rules, it is evident that there are large numbers of teachers who are fully capable of continuing work for longer than the Cleveland and Chesterfield County regulations will allow. * * *

We conclude * * * that neither the necessity for continuity of instruction nor the state interest in keeping physically unfit teachers out of the classroom can justify the sweeping mandatory leave regulations that the Cleveland and Chesterfield County School Boards have adopted. While the regulations no doubt represent a good-faith attempt to achieve a laudable goal, they cannot pass muster under the Due Process Clause of the Fourteenth Amendment. * * * *Id.* at 639–48.

3. LGBT STATUS

No education cases addressing alleged discrimination on the basis of LGBT status have reached the U.S. Supreme Court, but the Court did address LGBT-related discrimination in *Lawrence v. Texas,* 539 U.S. 558, 123 S.Ct. 2472 (2003). And in the years immediately prior to *Lawrence,* several cases were litigated by LGBT educators under antidiscrimination principles.

For example, in the Fourteenth Amendment Equal Protection Clause case of *Glover v. Williamsburg Local School District,* 20 F.Supp.2d 1160 (S.D. Ohio 1998), the Court considered the allegations by openly gay teacher Bruce Glover that the decision not to renew his teaching contract at the Williamsburg Local School District was discriminatory "based on his sexual orientation, his gender, and the race of his partner." *Id.* at 1162. Defendants denied these allegations and claimed that "Glover was not renewed because of deficiencies in his teaching skills." *Id.*

The Court determined that "[h]omosexuals, while not a 'suspect class' for equal protection analysis, are entitled to at least the same protection as any other identifiable group which is subject to disparate treatment by the state." *Id.* at 1169. The Court explained:

> [T]he principle would be the same if [plaintiff] had been arrested discriminatorily based on [his] hair color, [his] college bumper sticker ... or [his] affiliation with a disfavored * * * company. Furthermore, a state action which discriminates against homosexuals and is motivated solely by animus towards that group necessarily violates the Equal Protection Clause, because a "desire to effectuate one's animus against homosexuals can never be a legitimate governmental purpose."; *Romer* [*v. Evans*] ("If the constitutional conception of 'equal protection of the laws' means anything, it must at the very least mean that a bare ... desire to harm a politically unpopular group cannot constitute a legitimate governmental interest.").

* * *

The Court finds that the evidence, taken together, demonstrates that the Board's purported reason for Glover's nonrenewal was pretextual, and in fact the Board discriminated against Glover on the basis of his sexual orientation. The Court can only speculate as to exactly why the Board acted as it did. Perhaps the Board feared that a gay teacher would act inappropriately or somehow be a trouble-maker. Or perhaps the Board was responding to perceived disapproval in the community of having a gay teacher at Williamsburg. Regardless of the Board's reasoning, Glover had established that he was an above average first-year teacher who was more qualified than the woman chosen by the Board to replace him. Glover's successful showing of pretext, together with the other evidence introduced at trial, supports a finding that the Board's decision was motivated by animus towards him as a homosexual. * * *

* * *

Therefore, the Court hereby orders the Board to reinstate Glover as a full-time teacher at Williamsburg Elementary School with a two-year contract, beginning with the 1998–99 school year.

Glover is also hereby awarded compensatory damages for back pay as well as emotional distress. * * * [A]s a result of the Board's wrongful actions, he has suffered considerable anguish as well as humiliation in the community. Glover's psychological injuries also had physical effects, including anxiety, sleeplessness, and digestive problems for which Glover has been receiving treatment since the Fall of 1996. * * *

Therefore, the Court hereby ORDERS the Board to provide the following relief to Glover: (1) reinstatement as a full-time teacher at Williamsburg Elementary School with a two-year teaching contract, beginning in the 1998–99 school year; (2) compensatory damages in the amount of $71,492.00, which includes back pay and emotional distress; and (3) attorneys fees and costs. * * * *Id.* at 1169–76.

In *Weaver v. Nebo School District*, 29 F.Supp.2d 1279 (D. Utah 1998), the Court considered the case of 19–year veteran teacher and volleyball coach Wendy Weaver—a person with an "unblemished" record and a reputation as "an effective and capable teacher"—who acknowledged that she was gay when asked by a senior team member. *Id.* at 1280. She was subsequently admonished "not to make any comments, announcements or statements to students, staff members, or parents of students regarding [her] homosexual orientation or lifestyle." *Id.* at 1281. In addition, she was removed from her position as volleyball coach.

Ms. Weaver brought this action challenging the school district's decisions under both the First Amendment and the Fourteenth Amendment. The Court found that Plaintiff's acknowledgement of her sexual orientation outside the classroom would not, and indeed did not, result in a material or substantial disruption in the school, and "to the extent [that the letters to her] limit her speech in this area, they violate the First Amendment." *Id.* at 1285.

Turning to the Equal Protection Clause claim, the Court also found in favor of the plaintiff:

The Fourteenth Amendment of the United States Constitution entitles all persons to equal protection under the law. It appears that the plain language of the Fourteenth Amendment's Equal Protection Clause prohibits a state government or agency from engaging in intentional discrimination—even on the basis of sexual orientation—absent some rational basis for so doing.

The Supreme Court has recognized that an "irrational prejudice" cannot provide the rational basis to support a state action against an equal protection challenge. * * *

The question then is whether bias concerning Ms. Weaver's sexual orientation furnishes a rational basis for the defendants' decision not to assign her as volleyball coach. The "negative reaction" some members of the community may have to homosexuals is not a proper basis for discriminating against them. So reasoned the Supreme Court in the context of race. *See, e.g., Brown v. Board of Educ.,* 347 U.S. 483, 495, 74 S.Ct. 686 (1954) (declaring that racial school segregation is unconstitutional despite the widespread acceptance of the practice in the community and in the country). If the community's perception is based on nothing more than unsupported assumptions, outdated stereotypes, and animosity, it is necessarily irrational and under *Romer* and other Supreme Court precedent, it provides no legitimate support for the School District's decisions.

The record now before the court contains no job-related justification for not assigning Ms. Weaver as volleyball coach. Nor have the defendants demonstrated how Ms. Weaver's sexual orientation bears any rational relationship to her competency as teacher or coach, or her job performance as coach—a position she has held for many years with distinction. As mentioned earlier, it is undisputed that she was an excellent coach and apparently, up until the time her sexual orientation was revealed, the likely candidate for the position. Principal Wadley's decision not to assign Ms. Weaver (a decision reached after consulting with the other defendants) was based solely on her sexual orientation. Absent some rational relationship to job performance, a decision not to assign Ms. Weaver as coach because of her sexual orientation runs afoul of the Fourteenth Amendment's equal protection guarantee.

Although the Constitution cannot control prejudices, neither this court nor any other court should, directly or indirectly, legitimize them. * * * *Id.* at 1287–89.

* * *

At the time the *Lawrence* case was litigated, 13 states still prohibited consensual relations between people of similar gender in the privacy of their own home. The Court's 6–3 decision on behalf of the petitioners removed the presumption of criminality that still shadowed LGBT educators in 2003 and severely impacted their rights in the public sector, both under the law and as a matter of educational policy.

The privacy right relied upon by Justice Kennedy in the majority opinion is located at the intersection of the Due Process Clause (liberty interest) and the Equal Protection Clause (equality interest). Kennedy focused primarily on the liberty interest, but also emphasized the relevance of the equality component:

> Equality of treatment and the due process right to demand respect for conduct protected by the substantive guarantee of liberty are linked in important respects, and a decision on the latter point advances both interests. 539 U.S. at 575.

Building on privacy-related precedents in this area that date back to earlier decisions on marriage, procreation, contraception, and abortion, the Court concluded that the government has no place interfering with the private consensual conduct of adults in the privacy of their own homes. "Petitioners," Justice Kennedy wrote, "are entitled to respect for their private lives. The State cannot demean their existence or control their destiny by making their private conduct a crime."

The Court addressed the morality question head-on. Kennedy stated directly that many people still have "profound and deep convictions" based on interpretations of certain "moral principles" that lead them to disapprove in some way of "homosexual conduct." But, Kennedy explained, "the issue is whether the majority may use the power of the State to enforce these views on the whole society through operation of the criminal law. Our obligation is to define the liberty of all, not to mandate our own moral code." Justice O'Connor, concurring in the decision, added even stronger language in this context. "Moral disapproval of this group," she wrote, "is . . . insufficient . . . We have never held that moral disapproval, *without any other asserted state interest,* is a sufficient rationale to justify a law that discriminates among groups of persons."

Moreover, *Lawrence v. Texas* included language reminiscent of an analogous discussion of stigma in *Brown v. Board of Education*. It noted the many ways that U.S. law has stigmatized gays and lesbians, and concluded in no uncertain terms that this can no longer be the case. It also addressed the dignity of individuals, within the context of equal treatment and "equal worth." The Court explained that when homosexual conduct is criminalized, it "demeans the lives of homosexual persons . . . The stigma this statute imposes, moreover, is not trivial . . . it remains a criminal offense with all that it imports for the dignity of the persons charged." *Id.* at 560, 571–578, 582.

The scope of the *Lawrence* decision remains unclear, and it is likely to be some time before its applicability to the variety of prospective fact patterns can be determined with any degree of certainty. Commentators and jurists have already wrestled extensively with these questions, and arguably a consensus has yet to emerge. Interpretations range from the narrow view that the decision stands for nothing more than a determination that anti-sodomy laws are unconstitutional to the expansive view that *Lawrence* represents a sweeping recognition of equal rights and privacy guarantees for all LGBT persons in every possible context.

Read together with the growing number of victories in federal courts across the country, however, the decision can only bolster the position of gay and gender non-conforming persons. *Lawrence* was the second U.S. Supreme Court decision within an eight-year period to rule unequivocally on behalf of gay plaintiffs under the Fourteenth Amendment, and in so doing it also expressly overruled a 1986 U.S. Supreme Court decision that had gone the other way.[a] The sweeping and deferential language of both Justice Kennedy's majority opinion and Justice O'Connor's concurrence regarding the importance of honoring the "dignity" of gay persons and "respect[ing]" their private lives explicitly situates LGBTs in a very different place within U.S. constitutional jurisprudence than they had been before.

4. RELIGION

While protections against discrimination on the basis of religion have been clearly established at public colleges and universities, the situation at the K–12 level has been much more uneven. Many school districts and school site administrators continue to express concerns that openly religious educators may have an undue influence on their younger, more impressionable students.

The Supreme Court has not directly addressed this question in an education setting, but lower courts have been wrestling with these issues for some time. The question of whether and to what extent teachers can wear religious clothing or accessories has often served as a focal point of this controversy.

In *Nichol v. Arin Intermediate Unit 28*, 268 F.Supp.2d 536 (W.D. Pa. 2003), the Court addressed the discrimination claim of Instructional Assistant Nichol, who was suspended for refusing to comply with her supervisor's request that she remove or conceal a small cross she regularly wore on a necklace. Plaintiff argued that the Religious Affiliations policy under which she was suspended violated the Free Exercise Clause. The Court found in favor of the plaintiff, distinguishing prior inconsistent decisions by other federal judges:

---

a. The 1996 case decided on behalf of LGBT persons was *Romer v. Evans,* 517 U.S. 620 (1996), which invalidated a Colorado constitutional provision that would have prevented gays and lesbians from being able to obtain explicit protection against discrimination in that state. Amendment 2, the broad and sweeping provision at issue in the case, was added to the Colorado Constitution by the voters in 1996. The 1986 case overruled by *Lawrence* was *Bowers v. Hardwick*, 478 U.S. 186 (1986).

ARIN's Religious Affiliations policy is openly and overtly averse to religion because it singles out and punishes *only* symbolic speech by its employees having religious content or viewpoint, while permitting its employees to wear jewelry containing secular messages or no messages at all.

ARIN's Religious Affiliations policy thus displays, in purpose and effect, decided hostility toward religion, without any important or compelling state interests served, and violates the Free Exercise Clause of the First Amendment. * * *

* * * [The] policy is decidedly not neutral, and has both the effect and the express purpose of discriminating against religion. * * *

Elementary school children as a group are more impressionable than high school or college students, to be sure. However, the impressionability of elementary school students is not a sufficient reason for discriminating against the First Amendment rights of ARIN employees unless the employees are doing something that is likely to influence the students by exploiting their impressionability. * * *

Given the inconspicuous nature of plaintiff's expression of her religious beliefs by wearing a small cross on a necklace, and the fact that other jewelry with secular messages or no messages is permitted to be worn at school, it is extremely unlikely that even elementary students would perceive Penns Manor or ARIN to be *endorsing* her otherwise unvoiced Christian viewpoint, and defendants certainly presented no evidence to support such a perception. Merely employing an individual, such as plaintiff, who unobstrusively displays her religious adherence is not tantamount to government endorsement of that religion, absent any evidence of endorsement or coercion.

* * *

Defendants' strongest argument is that the Garb Statute, pursuant to which its Religious Affiliations policy was promulgated, was upheld in *United States v. Bd. of Educ. for the School District of Philadelphia (Philadelphia Bd. of Educ.),* 911 F.2d 882 (3d Cir.1990), which found that the preservation of an atmosphere of religious neutrality was a compelling state interest. The Garb Statute was enforced in that case to prohibit Alima Reardon, a Muslim teacher, upon pain of prosecution, from wearing identifiable Muslim garb which fully covered her entire body save face and hands. Pursuant to her belief, Amilia Reardon regularly wore a head scarf covering her head, neck and bosom, leaving only her face visible, and a long loose dress which covered her arms to her wrists.

Ms. Reardon mounted a Title VII employment discrimination challenge on the basis of religion, [but the challenge failed]. * * *

Moreover, in the course of discussing a First Amendment challenge to Oregon's garb statute, the Court of Appeals in *Philadelphia Bd. of Educ.* specifically and approvingly highlighted the Oregon Supreme

Court's observation that *"offending dress ... would not include dress that communicates an ambiguous message, such as, for example, the occasional wearing of jewelry that incorporates common decorations like a cross or a Star of David."*

Thus, *Philadelphia Bd. of Educ.* is factually and legally distinguishable, and does not constrain this Court from engaging in an unrestricted Establishment and Free Exercise Clause analysis. Moreover, the Court's analysis today is supported by "subsequent doctrinal developments" in the First Amendment precedent of the Supreme Court, as explicitly recognized explained by the United States Court of Appeals for the Third Circuit only last year.... In the current legal landscape of the Establishment Clause, it is unlikely that the Garb Statute would withstand the heightened scrutiny and endorsement analysis to which it now must be subjected.

For all of the foregoing reasons, the Court holds that ARIN's Religious Affiliations policy violates the Free Exercise Clause of the First Amendment, and that its suspension of Ms. Nichol pursuant to that policy cannot stand. *Id.* at 548–55.

5. AGE

Employment discrimination claims on the basis of age are generally brought under the Age Discrimination in Employment Act (ADEA). In *EEOC v. Board of Regents of the University of Wisconsin System*, 288 F.3d 296 (7th Cir. 2002), the Court considered the allegations of the Equal Employment Opportunity Commission (EEOC) under section 7 of the Age Discrimination in Employment Act (ADEA), 29 U.S.C. § 626:

> The University of Wisconsin Press is a nonprofit organization associated with the UW Graduate School and under the direction of the UW Board of Regents. * * * The EEOC's case is based on claims by four "charging" parties: Rosalie Robertson, who was 50 years old at the relevant time; Mary Braun, who was 46; Joan Strasbaugh, age 47; and Charles Evenson, who was 54. * * * Finding evidence of "ageism" in the terminations, the EEOC filed this action. * * *
>
> In an age discrimination case, we evaluate whether there is evidence that the employer discriminated against the employees "because of" age. Our task, then, is to examine the record to see whether there was evidence from which a reasonable jury could conclude that the "charging" parties were terminated "because of" their ages.
>
> A claim of discrimination can be proven by the direct or indirect methods of proof. * * *
>
> * * * [U]ltimately * * * what we are looking for is proof of intentional discrimination based on an examination of all the evidence in the record viewed in the light favorable to the nonmoving party. * * *
>
> * * * The unavoidable fact is that the four oldest employees were the only ones terminated, and the terminations occurred under circum-

stances from which one could, in fact, draw an inference that they were chosen because of their ages. These workers were terminated and the responsibilities were taken over either by other employees or by replacements brought in from the outside, which supports an inference of discrimination. Robertson was terminated from the acquisitions department, and 2 weeks later the Press hired Sheila McMahon, who was in her mid-twenties, to work in acquisitions. Strasbaugh was 47 when she was terminated as assistant marketing manager. Her duties were assumed by a woman in her twenties or thirties, whose contract was renewed and extended shortly after Strasbaugh's termination. Evenson was 54 years old when he was terminated from his position as a senior marketing specialist, while 23–year-old Rebecca Gimenez was retained. Other people in their twenties and thirties were brought into the acquisitions and marketing departments as well. * * *

Although the "Justification" was said to be an assessment of the skills and experience of the various people working at the Press, neither Bethea nor Salemson spoke with the charging parties about their skills. The two men did not solicit the opinions of managers regarding who should be let go. There were no formal employee evaluations. Documents they did look at included out-of-date resumes which had been on file at the Press, and these were not looked at until April, after the termination decisions had already been made.

The "Justification" can be read to show that they held the charging parties to a higher standard than the younger workers. It claims that Evenson would have to take courses to get "up to speed" on "Webpage programming or the electronic transfer of data and images." In the document there is no indication whether Gimenez, the preferred younger employee, herself had taken such courses. The facts show she had not. Gimenez also received credit in the "Justification" for things she had not done. It says she created the Webpage, but, in fact, it had been created before she began working at the Press.

A reasonable jury could believe that the "Justification" uses code words which reflect an age bias. It refers to Evenson as having skills suited to the "pre-electronic" era and that he would have to be brought "up to speed" on "new trends of advertising via electronic means."

The UW also justifies the termination decisions by saying that the job titles of the newly hired younger people were different from those of the charging parties. Some of the people were hired as "limited term employees." We do not think that hiring individuals under less desirable terms can necessarily overcome the inference that the persons being replaced were replaced because of their ages.
* * *

In addition to finding discrimination, the jury also found that the discrimination was willful. Under the ADEA, an employer's violation of the statute is willful if the "employer knew or showed reckless disregard for the matter of whether its conduct was prohibited by the ADEA." A plaintiff does not need to show that the employer's conduct was "outrageous," nor does he need to provide direct evidence of the employer's motives. An employer who truly violates the ADEA without knowing it and whose ignorance is not reckless is protected from a finding of recklessness. As one might imagine, given the length of time the ADEA has been with us, a finding of nonreckless ignorance is rare.

* * *

* * * We have previously said that "leaving managers with hiring authority in ignorance of the basic features of the discrimination laws is an 'extraordinary mistake' " from which a jury can infer reckless indifference.

* * *

The judgment of the district court is AFFIRMED. *Id.* at 299–305.[b]

6. DISABILITY

In *School Board of Nassau County v. Arline*, 480 U.S. 273, 107 S.Ct. 1123 (1987), the Court reached a landmark decision construing Section 504 of the Rehabilitation Act of 1973, which prohibits a federally funded state program from discriminating against an individual with disabilities solely by reason of his or her disability.[a] On behalf of the majority, Justice Brennan wrote:

> This case presents the questions whether a person afflicted with tuberculosis, a contagious disease, may be considered a "handicapped individual" within the meaning of § 504 of the Act, and, if so, whether such an individual is "otherwise qualified" to teach elementary school.

---

b. In *Kentucky Retirement Systems v. EEOC*, ___ U.S. ___, 128 S.Ct. 2361 (2008), the Court considered the question of whether a state pension plan that included differences in eligibility based on age, years of service, level of hazards encountered, and disability status was violative of the ADEA. By a vote of 5–4, the Court found on behalf of the defendants:

> * * * [O]ur opinion in no way unsettles the rule that a statute or policy that facially discriminates based on age suffices to show disparate treatment under the ADEA. We are dealing today with the quite special case of differential treatment based on *pension status*, where pension status—with the explicit blessing of the ADEA—itself turns, in part, on age. Further, the rule we adopt today for dealing with this sort of case is clear: Where an employer adopts a pension plan that includes age as a factor, and that employer then treats employees differently based on pension status, a plaintiff, to state a disparate treatment claim under the ADEA, must adduce sufficient evidence to show that the differential treatment was "actually motivated" by *age*, not pension status. And our discussion of the factors that lead us to conclude that the Government has failed to make the requisite showing in this case provides an indication of what a plaintiff might show in other cases to meet his burden of proving that differential treatment based on pension status is in fact discrimination "because of" age. 128 S.Ct. at 2369–2370.

a. It should be noted that the decision uses the now outmoded terms "handicap" and "handicapped," which were employed in that era. Today the terms "disability," "disabled," and "persons with disabilities" are more routinely and appropriately used.

From 1966 until 1979, respondent Gene Arline taught elementary school in Nassau County, Florida. She was discharged in 1979 after suffering a third relapse of tuberculosis within two years. After she was denied relief in state administrative proceedings, she brought suit in federal court, alleging that the school board's decision to dismiss her because of her tuberculosis violated § 504 of the Act.

* * * Arline was hospitalized for tuberculosis in 1957. For the next 20 years, Arline's disease was in remission. Then, in 1977, a culture revealed that tuberculosis was again active in her system; cultures taken in March 1978 and in November 1978 were also positive.

* * * After * * * her third relapse in November 1978, the school board suspended Arline with pay for the remainder of the school year. At the end of the 1978–1979 school year, the school board held a hearing, after which it discharged Arline, "not because she had done anything wrong," but because of the "continued reoccurence [sic] of tuberculosis." * * *

Id. at 275–76. Documenting the history and the parameters of Section 504, the Court explained:

In enacting and amending the Act, Congress enlisted all programs receiving federal funds in an effort "to share with handicapped Americans the opportunities for an education, transportation, housing, health care, and jobs that other Americans take for granted." To that end, Congress not only increased federal support for vocational rehabilitation, but also addressed the broader problem of discrimination against the handicapped by including § 504, an antidiscrimination provision patterned after Title VI of the Civil Rights Act of 1964. Section 504 of the Rehabilitation Act reads in pertinent part:

No otherwise qualified handicapped individual in the United States, as defined in section 706(7) of this title, shall, solely by reason of his handicap, be excluded from participation in, be denied the benefits of, or be subjected to discrimination under any program or activity receiving Federal financial assistance....

In 1974 Congress expanded the definition of "handicapped individual" for use in § 504 to read as follows:

[A]ny person who (i) has a physical or mental impairment which substantially limits one or more of such person's major life activities, (ii) has a record of such an impairment, or (iii) is regarded as having such an impairment.

The amended definition reflected Congress' concern with protecting the handicapped against discrimination stemming not only from simple prejudice, but also from "archaic attitudes and laws" and from "the fact that the American people are simply unfamiliar with and insensitive to the difficulties confront[ing] individuals with handicaps." To combat the effects of erroneous but nevertheless prevalent perceptions about the handicapped, Congress expanded the definition of "handicapped individual" so as to preclude discrimination against "[a] person who has a record of, or is regarded as having, an impairment [but who] may at present have no actual incapacity at all." *Southeastern Community College v. Davis,* 442 U.S. 397, 405–406, n.6, 99 S.Ct. 2361, 2366–2367, n.6 (1979).[4]

In determining whether a particular individual is handicapped as defined by the Act, the regulations promulgated by the Department of Health and Human Services * * * are particularly significant here because they define two critical terms used in the statutory definition of handicapped individual. "Physical impairment" is defined as follows:

> [A]ny physiological disorder or condition, cosmetic disfigurement, or anatomical loss affecting one or more of the following body systems: neurological; musculoskeletal; special sense organs; respiratory, including speech organs; cardiovascular; reproductive, digestive, genitor-urinary; hemic and lymphatic; skin; and endocrine.

In addition, the regulations define "major life activities" as

> functions such as caring for one's self, performing manual tasks, walking, seeing, hearing, speaking, breathing, learning, and working. *Id.* at 277–80.

The Court then went on to analyze Arline's claim within this statutory and regulatory framework:

> [W]e must consider whether Arline can be considered a handicapped individual. According to the testimony of Dr. McEuen, Arline suffered tuberculosis "in an acute form in such a degree that it affected her respiratory system," and was hospitalized for this condition. Arline thus had a physical impairment as that term is defined by the regulations, since she had a "physiological disorder or condition ... affecting [her] ... respiratory [system]." This impairment was serious enough to require hospitalization, a fact more than sufficient to establish that one or more of her major life activities were substantially limited by her impairment. Thus, Arline's hospitalization for tuberculosis in 1957 suffices to establish that she has a "record of ... impairment" within the meaning of 29 U.S.C. § 706(7)(B)(ii), and is therefore a handicapped individual.

> Petitioners concede that a contagious disease may constitute a handicapping condition to the extent that it leaves a person with "diminished physical or mental capabilities," and concede that Arline's hospital-

---

4. See *id.,* at 39 ("This subsection includes within the protection of sections 503 and 504 those persons who do not in fact have the condition which they are perceived as having, as well as those persons whose mental or physical condition does not substantially limit their life activities and who thus are not technically within clause (A) in the new definition. Members of both of these groups may be subjected to discrimination on the basis of their being regarded as handicapped"); *id.,* at 37–39, 63–64.

ization for tuberculosis in 1957 demonstrates that she has a record of a physical impairment. Petitioners maintain, however, that Arline's record of impairment is irrelevant in this case, since the school board dismissed Arline not because of her diminished physical capabilities, but because of the threat that her relapses of tuberculosis posed to the health of others.

We do not agree with petitioners that, in defining a handicapped individual under § 504, the contagious effects of a disease can be meaningfully distinguished from the disease's physical effects on a claimant in a case such as this. Arline's contagiousness and her physical impairment each resulted from the same underlying condition, tuberculosis. It would be unfair to allow an employer to seize upon the distinction between the effects of a disease on others and the effects of a disease on a patient and use that distinction to justify discriminatory treatment.

Nothing in the legislative history of § 504 suggests that Congress intended such a result. That history demonstrates that Congress was as concerned about the effect of an impairment on others as it was about its effect on the individual. * * *

Allowing discrimination based on the contagious effects of a physical impairment would be inconsistent with the basic purpose of § 504, which is to ensure that handicapped individuals are not denied jobs or other benefits because of the prejudiced attitudes or the ignorance of others. By amending the definition of "handicapped individual" to include not only those who are actually physically impaired, but also those who are regarded as impaired and who, as a result, are substantially limited in a major life activity, Congress acknowledged that society's accumulated myths and fears about disability and disease are as handicapping as are the physical limitations that flow from actual impairment. Few aspects of a handicap give rise to the same level of public fear and misapprehension as contagiousness. Even those who suffer or have recovered from such noninfectious diseases as epilepsy or cancer have faced discrimination based on the irrational fear that they might be contagious. The Act is carefully structured to replace such reflexive reactions to actual or perceived handicaps with actions based on reasoned and medically sound judgments: the definition of "handicapped individual" is broad, but only those individuals who are both handicapped *and* otherwise qualified are eligible for relief. The fact that *some* persons who have contagious diseases may pose a serious health threat to others under certain circumstances does not justify excluding from the coverage of the Act *all* persons with actual or perceived contagious diseases. Such exclusion would mean that those accused of being contagious would never have the opportunity to have their condition evaluated in light of medical evidence and a determination made as to whether they were "otherwise qualified." Rather, they would be vulnerable to discrimination on the basis of mythology—precisely the type of injury Congress sought to prevent.

We conclude that the fact that a person with a record of a physical impairment is also contagious does not suffice to remove that person from coverage under § 504. *Id.* at 280–86.

Finally, the Court considered the remaining question of whether Arline was "otherwise qualified for the job of elementary schoolteacher":

> To answer this question in most cases, the district court will need to conduct an individualized inquiry and make appropriate findings of fact. Such an inquiry is essential if § 504 is to achieve its goal of protecting handicapped individuals from deprivations based on prejudice, stereotypes, or unfounded fear, while giving appropriate weight to such legitimate concerns of grantees as avoiding exposing others to significant health and safety risks. The basic factors to be considered in conducting this inquiry are well established. In the context of the employment of a person handicapped with a contagious disease, we agree with *amicus* American Medical Association that this inquiry should include
>
>> [findings of] facts, based on reasonable medical judgments given the state of medical knowledge, about (a) the nature of the risk (how the disease is transmitted), (b) the duration of the risk (how long is the carrier infectious), (c) the severity of the risk (what is the potential harm to third parties) and (d) the probabilities the disease will be transmitted and will cause varying degrees of harm.
>
> In making these findings, courts normally should defer to the reasonable medical judgments of public health officials. The next step in the "otherwise-qualified" inquiry is for the court to evaluate, in light of these medical findings, whether the employer could reasonably accommodate the employee under the established standards for that inquiry.

Because of the paucity of factual findings by the District Court, we, like the Court of Appeals, are unable at this stage of the proceedings to resolve whether Arline is "otherwise qualified" for her job. * * * Accordingly, the resolution of whether Arline was otherwise qualified requires further findings of fact.

We hold that a person suffering from the contagious disease of tuberculosis can be a handicapped person within the meaning of § 504 of the Rehabilitation Act of 1973, and that respondent Arline is such a person. We remand the case to the District Court to determine whether Arline is otherwise qualified for her position. The judgment of the Court of Appeals is *Affirmed*. *Id.* at 287–89.

*

INDEX

References are to Pages

ACADEMIC FREEDOM
Generally, 927, 960, 963
See also Free Speech Rights of Educators, this index

ACCOUNTABILITY
Charter schools, 497
Home schooling, regulatory accountability, 703, 705
No Child Left Behind Act, this index
Quality of Education, this index
Race-conscious quality accountability, 464
School accountability report cards (SARC), 447

ACRONYMS
ADA, 98
ADEA, 981
AFT, 887
AYP, 462
BICS, 507
CALP, 507
CCTV, 107
CDA, 807
CIPA, 807
COPA, 807
COPPA, 112
EAHCA, 551
ED, 550
EEOA, 512
EHA, 552
EL, 460
ELD, 506
ELL, 522
EMR, 550
ESD, 506
ESEA, 465
ESL, 506
ETS, 382
FAPE, 549, 552
FEP, 531
FERPA, 95
IDEA, 7, 98
IDEIA, 554
IEP, 549
LD, 550
LEA, 467
LEP, 520, 522, 531
LGBT, 10, 170
LM, 531
LRE, 549, 552
LSAT, 320

ACRONYMS—Cont'd
NCLB, 45
NEA, 887
NET, 853
OCR, 98
OSP, 866
PBMAS, 523
SARC, 447
SAT, 381
SDAIE, 506
SDC, 550
SEA, 467
SES, 319

ADEQUATE YEARLY PROGRESS (AYP)
No Child Left Behind Act, 462

AFFIRMATIVE ACTION
Diversity standards, 332
Higher education
Generally, 317 et seq.
K-12 standards compared, 332
Preferences litigation, 317
K-12 school districts, 332, 339
Law schools, 319
Medical schools, 322
Political opposition, 334
Preferences litigation, 317
School choice programs, 491
Title IX compliance, 393

AGE DISCRIMINATION IN EMPLOYMENT ACT (ADEA)
Educator protections, 981, 983

AMERICAN FEDERATION OF TEACHERS (AFT)
Generally, 887

AMERICANS WITH DISABILITIES ACT (ADA)
Generally, 549, 597
Bar exams and disabilities accommodation, 619
Employment discrimination, 983
LSAT and disabilities accommodation, 619
Medical school students, 604
Reasonable accommodation
Generally, 558
Athletic programs, 389
Higher education, 597
Learning disabilities, 612
Licensure, 619

AMERICANS WITH DISABILITIES ACT (ADA)—Cont'd
Reasonable accommodation—Cont'd
Testing, 591
Records of students, FERPA protections, 98

ATHLETIC ACTIVITIES
Generally, 382 et seq.
Disabilities discrimination, eight semester eligibility rules, 387
Drug testing of college athletes, 95
Drug testing requirement, 94, 95
Eight semester eligibility rules, 387
Eligibility rules
Generally, 382 et seq.
Transfer students, 383
Equal educational opportunity, 382 et seq.
Fundamental right, participation as, 383
Injuries, tort liabilities of schools
Higher education, 66
K-12 schools, 23
Interscholastic and intercollegiate, 382 et seq.
Prayers, 644, 662
Privacy expectations, athletic vs nonathletic extracurricular activities, 90
Racially disparate transfer rules, 386
Reasonable accommodation of students with disabilities, 389
Safety of students during
Higher education, 66
K-12 schools, 23
Safety-related equipment, 28
Scholarship athletes, liability for acts of, 66
Steroid drug testing, 95
Title IX standards, 391
Transfer students, eligibility standards, 383
Transgender students, 415

ATTENDANCE
Compulsory, religious objectors, 696, 769

BIBLE STUDIES
See Religion and Education, this index

BILINGUAL EDUCATION
See English Learners, this index

BISEXUAL STUDENTS
See Lesbian, Gay, Bisexual, and Transgender Students, this index

BULLYING
Generally, 226, 278 et seq.
See also Peer Harassment, this index
Cyberbullying laws, 235
Deliberate indifference of authorities, 125, 296
LGBT students, 290 et seq.
Title IX protections, 290

BUREAUCRACIES
Change conflicts, 4

CENSORSHIP
Child Online Protection Act (COPA), 807
Child pornography, internet access to, 799
Children's Internet Protection Act (CIPA), 807
Communications Decency Act (CDA), 807
Curriculum, 942

CENSORSHIP—Cont'd
DMCA censorship concerns, 869
Homosexuality studies, parental objections, 772 et seq.
Internet filtering, 791 et seq.
Obscenity, internet
Students, 799
Teachers, 960
Parental objections to classroom materials, 763
Public libraries, 801
School libraries, 747
Sex education, parental objections, 783 et seq.

CERTIFICATION
Charter schools, 480
Moral turpitude dismissals, 913
Teacher qualifications, NCLB, 477

CHARTER SCHOOLS
Generally, 486, 497 et seq.
Accountability, 497
Authorizers, 497
Constitutional challenges to programs, 500
Curriculum, 499
Disabilities law compliance, 501
Fiscal impact on public schools, 501
For-profit managers, 499, 500
Founders, 497
Funding, 498
Gender-segregated, 491
Governance standards, 499
Labor relations, 901
Political support and opposition, 426, 499
Self-segregation problem, 488, 501
Skimming problems, 484
Teacher certification, 480
Teacher union conflicts, 501
Voucher programs compared, 498

CHILD ONLINE PROTECTION ACT (COPA)
Generally, 807

CHILD PORNOGRAPHY
Free speech conflicts, 120
Internet site censorship, 799

CHILDREN'S INTERNET PROTECTION ACT (CIPA)
Generally, 807

CHILDREN'S ONLINE PRIVACY PROTECTION ACT (COPPA)
Generally, 112

CHOICE, SCHOOL
Generally, 482 et seq.
See also Voucher Programs, this index
Affirmative action, 491
Charter Schools, this index
Desegregation plan conflicts, 494
Development of programs, 486
IDEA options, 495
Magnet schools, 356, 486
NCLB provisions, 492
Persistently dangerous schools, NCLB rights, 45, 492

CHOICE, SCHOOL—Cont'd
Preferences to achieve balance, 491
Private school financing, constitutional chal-
    lenges, 492
Private schools accepting vouchers, regulation
    of, 495
Reforming school reform, 483
Segregative effects, 491
Skimming problems, 484
Transportation, NCLB provision, 493
Unsafe school choice option, NCLB, 45

CIVIL LIABILITIES
Communicable disease dangers, duty to warn
    students of, 233
FERPA, private actions to enforce, 103
Foreseeability and duty to protect, 47, 232
Fraternity hazing, 64
Free speech rights
    Defamation liability, 122
    Expressive activities, tortious, 127
    Remedies for deprivations, 148
Hazing, 60
Higher education facilities, 46 et seq.
LGBT students, protection from bullying, 291
Malpractice litigation, 428
Peer harassment, 283
Privacy invasions, 123
Qualified immunity, 298
Safe schools laws, 42
Safety-related supervisorial duties
    Generally, 13 et seq.
    See also Safety of Students, this index
Special relationship doctrine
    Higher education, 46
    K-12 schools, 20
Threatening behavior, duty to intervene, 227
Title VII hostile environment claims, 282
Vicarious liability, 61
Warnings duties, 47
Willful and wanton negligence, 36

COACHES
See Athletic Activities, this index

COLLECTIVE BARGAINING
See Labor Relations in Public Education, this
    index

COLLEGES
See Higher Education, this index

**COMMUNICATIONS   DECENCY   ACT
(CDA)**
Generally, 807

COMPULSORY ATTENDANCE
Public school attendance mandates, 769
Religious objectors, 696

CONSENT DECREES
Monitoring implementation of, 356, 431
San Francisco Desegregation Decree: A Case
    Study, 356

CONSTITUTIONAL LAW
Bilingual education, 509
Charter school program challenges, 500

CONSTITUTIONAL LAW—Cont'd
Corporal punishment, 44
English learners programs, 509
Equal educational opportunity, 6
Free Speech Rights of Educators, this index
Free Speech Rights of Students, this index
Fundamental Rights, this index
Judicial review standards, 301
Privacy Rights, this index
Private school financing, constitutional chal-
    lenges, 492
Public Fora, this index
Quality of education
    Fundamental rights, 440, 449 et seq.
    State constitutional standards, 437
Religion and Education, this index
State and federal standards, 437
Tenure, constitutional rights, 907

COPYRIGHT LAW
Generally, 4, 809 et seq.
Attribution rights
    Fair use doctrine, 826
    Professional publications, 815
Clickwrap agreements, 849
Copying services, liability of, 836
Coursepack sales, fair use doctrine, 836
Criminal law penalties, 852 et seq.
Criticism, fair use doctrine, 833
Digital Millennium Copyright Act, this index
Digital technology and fair use, 847
Educational materials for classroom use, 819
Facilitation of infringement, 861
Fair use doctrine
    Generally, 821 et seq.
    Amount used, 826
    Attribution, 826
    Burden of proof, 834, 840
    Coursepack sales, 836
    Criticism, use in, 833
    Digital technology, 847
    DMCA and, 872
    Effect on ownership, 827
    Four factor test, 822, 834
    Guidelines for classroom copying, 840, 845
    Intent to infringe, 826
    Internet use, 822
    Market harm, 836, 838
    Multiple copies for classroom use, 836, 843
    Nature of copyrighted work, 826
    Nonprofit educational purposes, 824, 842
    Plagiarism detection archives, 848
    Reading assignments, copies made for, 836
    Safe harbor guidelines, 840, 845
    Same and different uses, 825
    Statutory factors, 822, 834
    Substantiality of use, 826
    Tests, 829
    Willful infringement, 836
Free speech rights and copyright infringe-
    ments, 126
Guidelines for classroom copying, 840, 845
Higher Education Act enforcement provisions,
    885

COPYRIGHT LAW—Cont'd
Intent to infringe
    Generally, 860
  Fair use determinations, 826
Internet activities
    Generally, 110
  CSS and DeCSS, 864
  Digital Millennium Copyright Act, this index
  Fair use doctrine, 822
  File sharing on campus, 872 et seq.
  Grokster litigation, 873
  Higher Education Act enforcement provisions, 885
  Napster litigation, 872
  No Electronic Theft (NET) Act, 852 et seq.
  Online service provider (OSP) liabilities, 866
  Open courseware, 848
  Peer-to-peer file sharing, 853 et seq., 872 et seq.
Lecture notes, ownership rights, 812
No Electronic Theft (NET) Act, 852 et seq.
Nonprofit educational purposes, fair use for, 824, 842
Plagiarism detection archives, 848
Professional publication attribution rights, 815
Public rights conflicts
    Generally, 811
  Fair use, below
Reading assignments, copies made for, 836
Rights of ownership, 810
Testing materials
  Fair use doctrine, 829
  Secure material copyrighting, 832
Unpublished works, protection of, 833
Willful infringement
    Generally, 860
  Fair use claims, 836
Work for hire
    Generally, 815, 816
  Educational materials for classroom use, 819
  Faculty exception, 821

CORPORAL PUNISHMENT
Constitutional law challenges, 44

CREATION SCIENCE STUDIES
Generally, 755

CREATIONISM
    Generally, 671, 755
Curriculum, this index
Religion and Education, this index

CRIMINAL LAW
Campus safety
  College campuses, 47
  K-12 schools, 29
Copyright law penalties, 852 et seq.
Expressive activities violating, 127
Hate speech, 217
Threats, 234, 237 et seq., 251
Weapons, this index

CURRICULUM
Achievement gap, curriculum gap and, 373
Bible studies, 762
Bicultural classes, segregation issues, 539
Censorship, 747, 942
Charter schools, 499
Creation science studies, 755
Creationism classes, 671
Ethnic studies classes, 39
Evolution, 755
Freedom of ideas and information, 745 et seq.
HIV-AIDS prevention education, 786
Home schooling curriculum control, 770
Ideas and information, freedom of, 745 et seq.
Internet filtering, 791 et seq.
LGBT-related content, 772 et seq.
Library censorship, 747
Low-track classes, 370
Math standards
  Gender stereotypes, 403
  NCLB, 467
No Child Left Behind Act, this index
Parental objections to classroom materials, 763
Quality of Education, this index
Reading standards, NCLB, 467
Regents diplomas, 371
Religious expression in classwork assignments, 725
Sex education, parental objections, 783 et seq.
Track system of student grouping, 365

DELIBERATE INDIFFERENCE
LGBT harassment, 296
Peer harassment, 125

DEPARTMENT OF EDUCATION
Establishment of, 7

DESEGREGATION
    See also Equal Educational Opportunity, this index
Multi-faceted Desegregation, 356
Quality standards, 433
Resegregation
    Generally, 346, 355, 360
  English learner programs, 538 et seq.
Safety-related racial issues, 36
San Francisco Desegregation Decree: A Case Study, 356
School choice rights, desegregation plan conflicts, 494
Supreme Court mandate, 307, 540

DIGITAL MILLENNIUM COPYRIGHT ACT (DMCA)
    Generally, 864 et seq.
Censorship potential, 869
CSS and DeCSS, 864
Exempt activities, 866
Fair use doctrine and, 872
Free speech concerns, 869
Grokster litigation, 873
Librarian of Congress, rulemaking authority, 869
Online service providers (OSP) liabilities, 866

DIGITAL MILLENNIUM COPYRIGHT ACT (DMCA)—Cont'd
Peer-to-peer file sharing, 872 et seq.
Political opposition, 869
Safe harbor, 872
Take-down notices and responses, 883

DISABILITIES, STUDENTS WITH
Generally, 549 et seq.
ADHD, 612
Americans with Disabilities Act, this index
Appropriateness challenges, IDEA, 560
Athletics, eight semester eligibility rules, 387
Charter schools. compliance with disabilities laws, 501
Higher education
Generally, 505, 549, 596 et seq.
ADHD, 612
Professional schools, 598 et seq.
Reasonable accommodation, 597
Rehabilitation Act protections, 598
Individuals with Disabilities Education Act, this index
IQ testing challenges, 583 et seq.
Learning disabilities, 612
Minority students in separate special education classrooms, 583
Models of Historical Treatment, 597
NCLB testing requirements, 591
Parochial schools, assistance to
Generally, 676
Loans of remedial education teachers to, 635
Private school IDEA placements, 572
Records, FERPA protections, 98
Rehabilitation Act, this index
Segregation vs mainstreaming, 550, 572 et seq., 583
Special day classes (SDC), 550
Standardized testing, 584 et seq.
Testing, reasonable accommodation, 591

DISABILITIES, TEACHERS WITH
Employment discrimination, 983

DISCIPLINE
Academic and non-academic, 66
Hate speech regulation, 205
Higher education facilities, 66
IDEA discipline issues, 550
Zero-tolerance statutes, 44

DISCRIMINATION
Affirmative Action, this index
Don't-ask-don't-tell policy, 739
Employment Discrimination, this index
Equal Educational Opportunity, this index
Equal Educational Opportunity Act, this index
Equal Protection, this index
Gender Discrimination, this index
Racial and Ethnic Discrimination, this index
Solomon Amendment, 739
Wealth discrimination, 312

DISCRIMINATORY DISCIPLINE PRACTICES
Blaming the victim
Harassment victims, 54 et seq., 278 et seq.
LGBT victims, 183 et seq., 296 et seq.
Rape victims, 52 et seq.
Cultural sensitivity, 42
Push-Out Policies and Practices, De Facto, this index
Race, ethnicity, and low expectations, 42
San Francisco Desegregation Consent Decree, 357

DISMISSALS OF EDUCATORS
Generally, 911 et seq.
Advocacy, First Amendment protection, 942
Contracts of employment, termination for cause, 920
Discrimination. See Employment Discrimination, this index
Due process, 920, 924
Free Speech Rights of Educators, this index
Insubordination dismissals and free speech rights, 942
Labor Relations in Public Education, this index
Moral turpitude, 913
Motivation for discharge, 952
Tenure Rights, this index

DRESS CODES
Free speech rights of students, 157
Transgender students
Generally, 416
Disruptive behavior, 412

DROP-OUT PREVENTION
English language learners, 520, 524 et seq.
Students with disabilities, 360, 560, 572 et seq.
Within-school segregation, 356, 360, 363 et seq.

DRUG AND ALCOHOL USE
Campus alcohol problems, 92
Free speech rights and drug use advocacy, 148, 157

DRUG TESTING
Generally, 71, 87 et seq.
Athletic activities requirement, 94, 95
College athletes, 95
Consent, coerced, 88
Epidemic use problems, 92
Extracurricular activities requirement, 88
In loco parentis, 89
Intrusiveness, 90
Privacy rights, 90
Probable cause, 88, 92
Reasonableness, 88
Safety concerns justifying, 92
Special needs doctrine, 95
Steroid testing, 95

EDUCATION OF ALL HANDICAPPED CHILDREN ACT (EAHCA)
Generally, 551, 560

EDUCATORS' RIGHTS
Generally, 887 et seq.
Advocacy, First Amendment protection, 942

EDUCATORS' RIGHTS—Cont'd
Attribution rights, 815, 826
Certifications of Educators, this index
Collective bargaining, 887
Contracts of employment, termination for cause, 920
Copyright Law, this index
Dismissal litigation, 911 et seq.
Dismissals of Educators, this index
Due process, 920, 924
Employment Discrimination, this index
Free Speech Rights of Educators, this index
Gender stereotypes in the profession, 888
Highly qualified teachers, NCLB, 479
Insubordination dismissals and free speech rights, 942
Labor Relations in Public Education, this index
Lecture notes, ownership rights, 812
Peer review systems, 894
Professional publication attribution rights, 815
Publication and tenure, 815, 819
Quality evaluations of teachers, 893
Tenure Rights, this index
Work for hire doctrine, copyright law, 815

ELECTRONIC COMMUNICATIONS PRI-VACY ACT (ECPA)
Generally, 112

ELECTRONIC RECORDS
Family Educational Rights and Privacy Act (FERPA), 97
Technology and privacy rights, 104 et seq.

ELEMENTARY AND SECONDARY EDU-CATION ACT (ESEA)
Generally, 465

ELEMENTARY SCHOOLS
See K-12 Schools, this index

EMPLOYMENT DISCRIMINATION
Generally, 971 et seq.
See also Dismissals of Educators, this index
Age, 981
Disabilities, 983
Dismissal litigation generally, 911 et seq.
Ethnicity, 971
First Amendment rights of teachers, 753
Free Speech Rights of Educators, this index
Gender, 972
Gender stereotypes in the profession, 888
Hostile environment, Title VII claims, 282
LGBT status, 913, 975
Racial, 971
Religion-based, 979
Title VII, 282
Viewpoint discrimination, 753

ENGLISH LEARNERS
Generally, 506 et seq.
Adequacy concerns, 531
BICS programs, 507
Bicultural classes, segregation issues, 539
CALP programs, 507
Castaneda three prong test, 514, 521

ENGLISH LEARNERS—Cont'd
Constitutional rights, 509
Dual immersion programs, 506
ELD programs, 506
ELL programs, 514, 522
Equal Educational Opportunity, this index
Equal protection rights, 509, 529
ESL programs, 506
Federal mandates, 509
Funding disputes, 513
Immersion programs, 527
LEP programs, 522
NCLB and EEOA requirements, 517, 519
NCLB requirements, 517
PBMAS systems, 523
Political opposition to bilingual education, 526
Program choices, 506
Quality of programs offered, 531
Resegregation, 538 et seq.
SDAIE programs, 506
Segregation issues, 538 et seq.
Sheltered immersion, 527
Transitional programs, 506

EQUAL ACCESS ACT
Generally, 175, 180

EQUAL EDUCATIONAL OPPORTUNITY
Generally, 303 et seq.
See also Equal Educational Opportunity Act, this index; No Child Left Behind Act, this index
Admission standards
Generally, 304 et seq.
Gender discrimination, 396
Affirmative Action, this index
Assignments
See also Curriculum, this index
Inter-school segregation, 363
Low-track classes, 370
Quality vs equity issues, 427
Track system of student grouping, 365
Athletics
Generally, 382 et seq.
Transfer students, eligibility standards, 383
Bussing and integration, 360
Classroom assignments and inter-school segregation, 363
Consent decree operations, 356, 431
Constitutional bases, 6
Department of Education, establishment of, 7
Desegregation and quality standards, 433
Desegregation mandate, 307, 540
Detracking, 370
Developing standards of equality, 304
Development and achievement of gender equity standards, 396
Diploma testing, validation of, 375
Equal access rights, NCLB challenges based on, 464
Financing, discriminatory
Generally, 309 et seq.
See also Financing Public Education, this index
Adequacy vs equity theories, 435
Fundamental rights infringements, 311

EQUAL EDUCATIONAL OPPORTUNITY
—Cont'd
Financing—Cont'd
    Judicial review of finance-based decisions, 376
    Rural/urban financing discrepancies, 310
    Wealth discrimination, 312
Fourteenth Amendment rights, 6
Fundamental rights infringements
    Generally, 7, 316
    Financing, discriminatory, 311
Gender equity, 305
Gender identity issues, 409
Higher vs K-12 education
    Generally, 303
    Affirmative action, 332
Inter-school segregation, 363
LGBT students, 405
Low-track classes, 370
Magnet schools, 356
Military academies, gender discrimination, 397
Multi-faceted desegregation, 356
NCLB challenges based on equal access rights, 464
Needs meeting standards, 303
No Child Left Behind Act, this index
Placement of students, 304 et seq.
Preferences litigation, 317
Quality
    See also Quality of Education, this index
    Desegregation and, 433
    Equity/quality issues, 427
Race issues, 304 et seq.
Race-based classifications of students, 339
Race-conscious quality accountability, 464
Resegregation
    Generally, 346, 355, 360
    English learner programs, 538 et seq.
Separate-but-equal era, 307, 540
Socioeconomic status (SES), 319
Standardized testing controversy, 375
Supreme Court desegregation mandate, 307, 540
Track system of student grouping, 365
Tracking, disparate racial effects of, 380
Transgender equality issues, 405
Undocumented students
    Generally, 416
    Political resistance, 421
    Resident vs nonresident tuition fees, 424
Unitary districts, 339, 341, 434
Wealth discrimination, 312

EQUAL EDUCATIONAL OPPORTUNITY ACT (EEOA)
    Generally, 512 et seq.
Castaneda three prong test, 514, 521
Congressional intent, 521
Mandates and funding, 513
NCLB and, 517, 519

EQUAL PROTECTION
    See also Equal Educational Opportunity, this index
Educational rights protections, 6
English learners, 509, 529

EQUAL PROTECTION—Cont'd
Gender segregated facilities
    Higher education, 397
    K-12, 402
Gender-based distinctions, judicial review of, 401
Identifiable minorities entitled to, 295
IQ testing, racial disparities, 583 et seq.
Judicial review of gender-based distinctions, 401
LGBT students, 10, 169, 294
Military academies, gender discrimination, 397
Sexual orientation protection, 295
Sliding scale approach, 316
State vs federal equal protection standards, 455
Supreme Court desegregation mandate, 307, 540
Undocumented students, 416

ESTABLISHMENT CLAUSE
See Religion and Education, this index

ETHNIC STUDIES
Bicultural classes, segregation issues, 539

ETHNICITY
English Learners, this index
Racial and Ethnic Discrimination, this index

EVOLUTION
    Generally, 755
Curriculum, this index
Religion and Education, this index

EXPRESSION, FREEDOM OF
Free Speech Rights of Educators, this index
Free Speech Rights of Students, this index

EXTRACURRICULAR ACTIVITIES
Athletic vs nonathletic privacy expectations, 90
Drug testing requirement, 88
Safety of students during, 23 et seq.

FAIR USE OF COPYRIGHT MATERIALS
See Copyright Law, this index

FAMILY EDUCATIONAL RIGHTS AND PRIVACY ACT (FERPA)
    Generally, 95 et seq.
Disabilities, records of students with, 98
Electronic records, 97
Enforcement, 103
Exempt records, 96
Immigrant student' records, 96
Inspection of records by students, 96
Mental health records, 97
NCLB provisions, 96
Peer grading of tests, 99
Private actions to enforce, 103
Report cards, 98
Safety-related justifications for access to records, 96
Technology and privacy rights, 104 et seq.
Test scoring by students, 99
Transcripts, 96, 98

FEDERAL EDUCATION LAW
Age Discrimination in Employment Act, this index
Americans with Disabilities Act, this index
Bilingual education requirements, 509
Child Online Protection Act (COPA), 807
Children's Internet Protection Act (CIPA), 807
Children's Online Privacy Protection Act (COPPA), 112
Communications Decency Act (CDA), 807
Copyright Law, this index
Department of Education, establishment of, 7
Education of All Handicapped Children Act (EAHCA), 551, 560
Electronic Communications Privacy Act (ECPA), 112
English learners, federal mandates, 509
Equal Access Act, 175, 180
Family Educational Rights and Privacy Act, this index
Fundamental right, classification of education as, 7
Gun-Free Schools Act, 43
Higher Education Act, 885
Individuals with Disabilities Education Act, this index
Military recruiters, campus access, 738
No Child Left Behind Act, this index
No Electronic Theft (NET) Act, 852 et seq.
State law and generally, 2

FIELD TRIPS
Safety duties, 21

FINANCING PUBLIC EDUCATION
See also Voucher Programs, this index
Accountability standards, quality, 447
Adequacy standards, 446
Adequacy vs equity theories, 435
Bilingual education funding disputes, 513
Charter school funding
    Generally, 498
    Fiscal impact on public schools, 501
Choice programs financing, constitutional challenges, 492
Efficiency standards, 439
English learner program funding disputes, 513
Equality standards
    Generally, 309 et seq.
    See also Equal Educational Opportunity, this index
    Fundamental rights infringements, 311
    Judicial review of finance-based decisions, 376
    Rural/urban financing discrepancies, 310
    Wealth discrimination, 312
Equity vs adequacy theories, 435
Fundamental rights infringements, 311
Judicial review of finance-based decisions, 376
Monitoring of school quality performance, 447
NCLB funding qualifications, 462
NCLB unfunded mandate challenges, 463
Parochial school aid, 674 et seq.
Private school financing, constitutional challenges, 492

FINANCING PUBLIC EDUCATION— cont'd
Quality and cost
        Generally, 435 et seq.
    Accountability standards, 447
    Adequacy standards, 446
    Efficiency standards, 439
    Fundamental rights analyses, 440
    Monitoring of school performance, 447
    State constitutional standards, 437
Rural/urban financing discrepancies, 310
State constitutional standards, 437
Unfunded mandate challenges, NCLB, 463
Wealth discrimination, 312

FIRST AMENDMENT
    Generally, 118 et seq.
Free Speech Rights of Educators, this index
Free Speech Rights of Students, this index
LGBT students' constitutional rights, 169
Privacy Rights, this index
Religion and Education, this index

FLAG SALUTE CEREMONIES
Generally, 705 et seq., 768

FORESEEABILITY
Tort liabilities, 47, 232

FOURTEENTH AMENDMENT
See Equal Protection, this index

FOURTH AMENDMENT
    Generally, 71 et seq.
Drug testing, coerced consent to, 88
Electronic surveillance laws, 106
Probable Cause, this index
Searches and Seizures, this index

FRATERNITIES
Hazing, tort liabilities, 64

FREE EXERCISE CLAUSE
See Religion and Education, this index

FREE SPEECH RIGHTS OF EDUCATORS
    Generally, 927 et seq.
Academic freedom
        Generally, 927
    College and university faculty, 960
    K-12, 941
Action vs speech, 945
Advocacy protection, 942, 954
Anonymity rights, 113
Chilling effect of adverse action, 952
Citizen vs employee, speech made as, 950, 953
Civility and free speech, 212
Content-based and content-neutral regulation, 119
Copyright infringements, 126
Curriculum censorship, 942
Curriculum choices as matters of public concern, 942, 948
Defamation liability, 122
Dismissal litigation, 911 et seq.
Employment discrimination, 753
Fighting words doctrine, 121, 212

FREE SPEECH RIGHTS OF EDU-CATORS—Cont'd

Higher education vs K-12, 927
Ideas and information, freedom of, 745 et seq.
Inciting violence, 121, 212
Insubordination dismissals and free speech rights, 942
K-12 vs higher education, 927
LGBT teachers' constitutional rights, 169
Motivation for discharge, 952
Obscenity internet site censorship, 960
Overbroad restraints, 119, 208
Pickering balancing
    Generally, 927, 931
    Citizen vs employee, speech made as, 950, 953
Political activity, 954
Privacy right conflicts, 123
Public concern, rights in matters of
    Generally, 927, 931
    Curriculum choices, 948
Public Fora, this index
Retaliation for exercises, 930, 944, 952
Sexual orientation and moral turpitude based dismissals, 913
Tenured teachers, 942
Threat responses, First Amendment issues, 249 et seq.
Threats, this index
True threats, 125, 249 et seq.
Vague restraints, 119, 208
Viewpoint discrimination, 753

FREE SPEECH RIGHTS OF STUDENTS

Generally, 118 et seq., 927 et seq.
Adult vs student rights, 152
Anonymity rights, 113
Anti-war activities, 129, 214
Armbands, expressive, 129
Bible studies, 762
Campus speech codes, 134
Child pornography, 120
Civility and free speech, 212, 214
Clothing regulations, 157
Content-based and content-neutral regulation
    Generally, 119
    Internet filters, 795
Copyright infringements, 126
Creation science studies, 755
Criminal acts, expressive activities constitut-ing, 127
Defamation liability, 122
Digital Millennium Copyright Act (DMCA), 869
Disruptive speech
    Generally, 412
    Test-score rule, 161, 162
Dress codes, 157
Drug use advocacy, 148, 157
Education-related speech, 144
Establishment Clause conflicts, 192, 720
Expressive activities constituting criminal acts, 127
Fighting words doctrine, 121, 212
Flag salute ceremonies, 705 et seq., 768
Free speech movement on campuses, 118

FREE SPEECH RIGHTS OF STUDENTS
—Cont'd

Fundamental right, free speech as, 132
Gay slurs, 159
Gay-Straight Alliance Club, 175, 180
Gender expression, 411
Harassment law conflicts, 124
Hate-speech, 204
Heckler's veto
    Generally, 174, 181
    Tinker rule, 182
Higher education freedom of expression stan-dards, 186 et seq.
HIV-AIDS prevention education, 786
Homosexuality policies of religious groups, 723
Homosexuality studies, parental objections, 772 et seq.
Ideas and information, freedom of, 745 et seq.
Inciting violence, 121, 212
Inflammatory slogans and images, 157
Internet activities, 164
Internet filtering, 791 et seq.
K-12 level freedom of expression standards, 127 et seq.
K-12 vs higher education standards, 118
LGBT students' constitutional rights, 169
NCLB access rules, 738
Newspaper censorship
    Higher education, 192, 197, 720
    K-12, 141
    Political censorship, 197
    Religious censorship, 192, 720
Obscenity
    Generally, 120
    Internet censorship, 799
Overbroad restraints, 119, 208
Parental objections to classroom materials, 763
Patriotism expressions, 705 et seq.
Pledge of Allegiance, 705 et seq.
Political expression, 129
Political opinion
    Generally, 188
    Newspaper censorship, 197
Privacy right conflicts, 123
Public Fora, this index
Religious advocacy and disparagement
    Generally, 158
    Higher education, 186
Religious freedom
    Generally, 695 et seq.
    See also Religion and Education, this index
    Bible studies, 762
    Censorship of library books, 747
    Creation science studies, 755
    Evolution, 755
    Facilities access, 732
    Flag salute ceremonies, 705 et seq., 768
    Homosexuality policies of religious groups, 723
    Ideas and information, freedom of, 745 et seq.
    Library censorship, 747
    NCLB access rules, 738
    Parental objections to classroom materials, 763

FREE SPEECH RIGHTS OF STUDENTS
—Cont'd
Religious freedom—Cont'd
    Patriotism expressions, 705 et seq.
    Public fora free speech standards, 736
    Work assignments, religious expression in, 725
Safety concern conflicts
    College campuses, 118
    K-12 standards, 127
    Threats, responses to, 157
Sex education, parental objections, 783 et seq.
Sexual innuendo, 135
Sexual orientation slurs, 159
Socially appropriate behavior, teaching, 136
State vs federal jurisprudence, 145
Threats, this index
Tinker rule
    Generally, 129
    Heckler's veto, 182
    Religious expression in classwork assignments, 725
    Sexuality expressions, 186
    Threats, 134, 267
    Verbal assault rule, 162
Tort remedies of students, 148
Tortious activities, expressive activities constituting, 127
True threats, 125, 249 et seq.
T-shirt cases, 157
Vague restraints, 119, 208
Verbal assault rule, 160, 162

FUNCTIONAL LITERACY
Generally, 379

FUNDAMENTAL RIGHTS
Athletic participation, 383
Education
    Generally, 7, 316
    Equal opportunities, 311
NCLB as creating, 316, 464
Privacy, 785
Quality education
    Generally, 440, 449 et seq.
    See also Quality of Education, this index
Religious practice, 698
Students,' 132

GAY STUDENTS
See Lesbian, Gay, Bisexual, and Transgender Students, this index

GENDER DISCRIMINATION
Admission standards, 396
Affirmative Action, this index
Athletic activities, Title IX standards, 391
Charter schools, gender-segregated, 491
Classroom assistance, 403
Differential feedback, 403
Employment of educators, 972
Equity, gender, development and achievement, 305, 396
Judicial review of gender-based distinctions, 401
Military academies, 397

GENDER DISCRIMINATION—Cont'd
SAT tests, 381
Segregated facilities
    Charter schools, 491
    Higher education, 397
    K-12, 402
Stereotypes
    Educators, 888
    Students, 402
Teacher attention, 403
Transgender equality issues, 405

GUN-FREE SCHOOLS ACT
Generally, 43

HARASSMENT
Free speech conflicts, 124
Hate-speech proscriptions, 204
Hostile environment sexual harassment, 282
Sexual
    Generally, 278 et seq.
    See also Peer Harassment, this index
Threats, this index

HATE SPEECH
Campus regulations, 205
Criminal sanctions, 217
E-mail, hate-related, 249
Internet proscriptions, 204

HAZING
Fraternities, 64
Negligence liability, 60

HIGH SCHOOLS
See K-12 Schools, this index

HIGHER EDUCATION
Academic Freedom, this index
Alcohol problems, 92
Campus facilities, religious access to, 732 et seq.
Campus forums, religious access to, 720 et seq.
Campus safety, 47
Disabilities, students with
    Generally, 505, 549, 596 et seq., 619
    ADHD, 612
    Professional schools, 598 et seq.
    Reasonable accommodation, 597
Discipline, 66
Drug testing of college athletes, 95
Equal educational opportunity standards
    Generally, 303
    Affirmative action, 332
Fraternity hazing, 64
Free speech, K-12 vs higher education standards, 118
Freedom of expression standards, 186 et seq.
Gender segregated facilities, 397
Hate-speech proscriptions, 204
Hazing, 60
K-12 compared
    Collective bargaining by educators, 891
    First Amendment rights of educators, 927
    Legal principles applicable, 2
Law schools, affirmative action, 319
LGBT students' rights cases, 183

HIGHER EDUCATION—Cont'd
Military academies, gender discrimination, 397
Military recruiters, campus access, 738
Negligence liability, 46 et seq.
Political organizations on campus, 188
Reasonable accommodation of students with
    disabilities, 597
Religion on campus
    Equal Access Act, 175, 180
    Facilities, access to, 732 et seq.
    Forums, access to, 720 et seq.
    Group activities, 192, 720
Resident vs nonresident tuition fees, undocu-
    mented students, 424
    Generally, 46 et seq.
    See also Safety of Students, this index
Sexual harassment, 54
Solicitation proscriptions on campuses, 742
Solomon Amendment, 739
Threats
    E-mails, 251
    Statutory prohibitions, 233 et seq.

HIGHER EDUCATION ACT
Copyright law enforcement, 885

HOME SCHOOLING
Curriculum control, 770
Regulatory accountability, 703, 705
Religion and education, 703

HOMOSEXUALITY
See Lesbian, Gay, Bisexual, and Transgender
    Students, this index

HOSTILE ENVIRONMENT
    Generally, 125
Sexual harassment, 282
Title VII claims, 282

IMMUNITY OF SCHOOL DISTRICTS
Qualified immunity of administrators, 298
Tort liability, 14, 21

INDIVIDUALS WITH DISABILITIES ED-
    UCATION ACT (IDEA)
    See also Disabilities, Students with, this
        index
1997 amendments, 553
2004 amendments, 554
Appropriateness challenges, 560
Assistive services, 563
Civil rights legislation and, 7
Deaf students, 561
Discipline problems, 550
Education of All Handicapped Children Act
    (EAHCA), 551, 560
Eligible students, 560
Emotionally disturbed (ED) students, 550
Enactment, 549, 551
Free appropriate public education (FAPE) re-
    quirement
    Generally, 549, 552, 555
    LRE and, 580
Hearing rights, 562
Individualized Education Plans (IEP), 549

INDIVIDUALS WITH DISABILITIES ED-
    UCATION ACT (IDEA)—Cont'd
Interpreters for deaf students, 561
Learning disabled (LD) students, 550
Least restrictive environment (LRE) require-
    ment
    Generally, 549, 552, 556, 572 et seq.
    FAPE and, 580
Minority students in separate special education
    classrooms, 583
NCLB alignment, 554, 557
Parochial schools, assistance disabled students
    in, 676
Prioritization, 560
Private school placements, 572
Records, FERPA protections, 98
Rehabilitation Act requirements, 558
Related services, 563
School choice options, 495
Segregation, de facto, of minority students, 583
Segregation vs mainstreaming, 550, 572 et seq.

IN LOCO PARENTIS
Drug testing, 71
Safety duties, 20
Searches and seizures, 71

INTEGRATION
Desegregation, this index
Equal Educational Opportunity, this index
Segregation, this index

INTERNET
    Generally, 104 et seq.
Academic freedom and access restrictions, 960
Anonymity rights, 113
Bomb-making information, 234
Carnivore program, 106
Child Online Protection Act (COPA), 807
Children's Internet Protection Act (CIPA), 807
Children's Online Privacy Protection Act
    (COPPA), 112
Clickwrap agreements, 849
Communications Decency Act (CDA), 807
Copyright infringements
    Fair use doctrine, 822
    Free speech conflicts, 126, 164
    Infringements by students, 110
    No Electronic Theft (NET) Act, 852 et seq.
    Open courseware, 848
    Peer-to-peer file sharing, below
    Plagiarism detection archives, 848
CSS and DeCSS, 864
Cyberbullying, 105, 235
Digital Millennium Copyright Act, this index
Electronic Communications Privacy Act
    (ECPA), 112
Electronic surveillance laws, 106
E-mail, hate-related, 249
Employees, monitoring of internet use by, 111
File sharing on campus, 872 et seq.
Filtering, 791 et seq.
Free speech rights and copyright infringe-
    ments, 126, 164
Grokster litigation, 873
Growth, of benefits and dangers, 791, 795

INTERNET—Cont'd
Hate-speech proscriptions, 204
Higher Education Act copyright enforcement provisions, 885
Instant message threats, 267
Monitoring of student activities, 110
Napster litigation, 872
No Electronic Theft (NET) Act, 852 et seq.
Obscenity censorship
    First Amendment rights of students, 799
    First Amendment rights of teachers, 960
Online service providers (OSP), copyright liabilities, 866
Open courseware, 848
Peer-to-peer file sharing
    Generally, 110, 853 et seq.
    DMCA, 872 et seq.
Plagiarism detection archives, copyright implications, 848
Privacy rights, 104 et seq.
Protection of children, 791 et seq.
Public fora free speech standards, library access as, 804
Public library censorship, 801
Stalking, 105
Threat communications, 261
True threats e-mails, 251

JUDICIAL REVIEW
Standards of, 301

K-12 SCHOOLS
Academic freedom rights of teachers, 941
Affirmative action, 339
Bible studies, 762
Campus facilities, religious access to, 732 et seq.
Campus forums, religious access to, 720 et seq.
Campus safety, 29
Censorship of library books, 747
Desegregation law, 337
Equal educational opportunity standards
    Generally, 303
    Affirmative action, 332
Freedom of expression standards, 127 et seq.
Gender segregated facilities, 402
Higher education compared
    Collective bargaining by educators, 891
    First Amendment rights of educators, 927
    Free speech standards, 118
    Legal principles applicable, 2
Homosexuality studies, parental objections, 772 et seq.
Internet filtering, 791 et seq.
Library censorship, 747
Negligence liability, 13 et seq.
Parental objections to classroom materials, 763
Peer sexual harassment, 283
Race-based classifications of students, 339
Safety
        Generally, 13 et seq.
    See also Safety of Students, this index
Search and seizure law standards, 72 et seq.
Sex education, parental objections, 783 et seq.
Socially appropriate behavior, teaching, 136
Tenure rights of teachers, 906

K-12 SCHOOLS—Cont'd
Threats. statutory prohibitions, 261 et seq.
Unitary districts, 339, 341

LABOR RELATIONS IN PUBLIC EDUCATION
    Generally, 887 et seq.
    American Federation of Teachers (AFT), 887
Charter schools, 501, 901
Collective bargaining
        Generally, 887
    Statutory regulation, 889, 903
Dismissal litigation, 911 et seq.
Employment Discrimination, this index
Gender stereotypes, 888
National Education Association (NEA), 887
NCLB mandates, 905
Policy considerations, 888
Reform efforts, 896
Right to strike, 890, 895
Statutory regulation of collective bargaining, 889, 903
Takeovers and reconstitutions of local districts, 896, 905
Tenure Rights, this index
Unionization of teachers generally, 887

LESBIAN, GAY, BISEXUAL, AND TRANSGENDER (LGBT) STUDENTS
    Generally, 406
Athletic activities, transgender students, 415
Bullying, 290 et seq.
Constitutional rights generally, 169, 170
Deliberate indifference of authorities, 296
Disruptive behavior, transgender student dress as, 412
Don't-ask-don't-tell policy, 739
Dress codes, transgender students, 416
Dressing room facilities, transgender students, 415
Educators, sexual preference employment discrimination, 913, 975
Equal opportunity, 405
Equal protection rights, 10, 294
First amendment rights to gender expression, 411
Free speech rights and sexual orientation slurs, 159
Gay-Straight Alliances, 175, 180
Gender identity issues, 406, 409
Harassment, 183
Higher education rights cases, 183
Identifiable minorities entitled to equal protection rights, 295
Judicial review of discrimination claims, 301
LGBT-related content in the curriculum, 772 et seq.
Parental objections to K-12 homosexuality studies, 772 et seq.
Peer harassment, 290 et seq.
Prom dates, same sex, 171
Protection from bullying, 291
Records, transgender students, 415
Religious groups' homosexuality policies, 723
Religious rights analogies, 183
Safety of transgender students, 413

References are to Pages

LESBIAN, GAY, BISEXUAL, AND TRANS-GENDER (LGBT) STUDENTS—Cont'd
Supervisorial liability for bullying, 291
Teachers, sexual orientation employment discrimination, 913, 975

LIBRARIES
Censorship, 747
Child pornography internet sites, 799
Copyright Law, this index
Internet filtering, 791 et seq.
Obscenity internet sites
  Students, 799
  Teachers, 960
Public fora free speech standards, applicability to library internet access, 804
Public library censorship, 801

LITERACY
Functional literacy, 379

MAGNET SCHOOLS
  Generally, 356
Choice programs, 486
Equal Educational Opportunity, this index

MALPRACTICE, EDUCATIONAL
Generally, 428

MIDDLE SCHOOLS
See K-12 Schools, this index

MILITARY RECRUITERS
Campus access, 738
Student records, access to, 96

MILITARY SCHOOLS
Gender discrimination, 397
Hazing, 60
Prayers, 664

MORALITY
See Religion and Education, this index

NATIONAL EDUCATION ASSOCIATION (NEA)
Generally, 887

NEGLIGENCE LIABILITIES
See Civil Liabilities, this index

NO CHILD LEFT BEHIND (NCLB) ACT
  Generally, 461
    See also Equal Educational Opportunity, this index
Accountability standards
  Generally, 466
    Policy considerations, 461
    Race-conscious, 464
    Statutory standards, 475
Adequate yearly progress (AYP), 462, 467, 472
Bilingual education, 517
Choice of schools provisions, 492
Corrective actions, 471
Desegregation plans, school choice rights conflicts, 494
Disabilities, testing students with, 591
Disaggregation of test scores, 462
EEOA and, 517, 519

NO CHILD LEFT BEHIND (NCLB) ACT
—Cont'd
Elementary and Secondary Education Act (ESEA), 465
Enactment, 427
English learner program requirements, 517
Equal access rights, challenges based on, 464
FERPA records requirements, 96
Fundamental right to education, 316, 464
Funding qualifications, 462
Highly qualified teachers, 479
IDEA alignment, 554, 557
Labor relations conflicts, 905
Math standards, 467
Military recruiters' access to student records, 96
Persistently dangerous schools, 45, 492
Policy considerations
    Generally, 7
    Accountability standards, 461
Prayer provisions, 663
Proficiency benchmarks, 467
Public fora access rules, 738
Purposes of Act, 470
Quality of Education, this index
Race-conscious accountability, 464
Reading standards, 467
School choice provisions, 492
School improvement standards, 471
Sex education, 785
Special education student testing problems, 591
State law and federal law conflicts, 2
Supplemental educational services, 462
Teacher qualifications, 477
Test scores, disaggregation of, 462
Unfunded mandate challenges, 463
Unsafe school choice options, 44, 45

NO ELECTRONIC THEFT (NET) ACT
  Generally, 852 et seq.
Facilitation of infringement, 861
Felony violations, 862

OBSCENITY
Free speech conflicts, 120
Internet site censorship
    Students, 799
    Teachers, 960

OFFICE OF CIVIL RIGHTS (OCR)
Athletic programs, Title IX compliance, 392
Student record guidelines, 98

PARENTAL OBJECTIONS TO CLASS-ROOM MATERIALS
Generally, 763

PAROCHIAL SCHOOLS
Private Schools, this index
Religion and Education, this index

PATENT LAW
College and university inventorship, 810

PEER HARASSMENT
  Generally, 226, 278 et seq.
  See also Bullying, this index

PEER HARASSMENT—Cont'd
Deliberate indifference of authorities, 125, 296
Hostile environment sexual harassment, 282
K-12 sexual harassment, 283
LGBT students, 290 et seq.
Sexual harassment, 278 et seq.
Supervisorial duties of schools, 283
Title IX protections, 290
Tort liabilities, 283

PLEDGE OF ALLEGIANCE
Generally, 705 et seq.

POLICY CONSIDERATIONS
Generally, 1
Litigation and change, 5
No Child Left Behind Act (NCLB)
    Generally, 7
    Accountability standards, 461
Threats, 261
Zero tolerance doctrines, 261

POSTGRADUATE EDUCATION
See Higher Education, this index

POVERTY
Equal Educational Opportunity, this index

PRIVACY RIGHTS
Generally, 12
Anonymity rights, 113
Balancing of school and student interests, 75
Closed circuit television, 107
Drug Testing, this index
Drug testing demands, 90
Electronic Communications Privacy Act (ECPA), 112
Electronic surveillance laws, 106
Employees, monitoring of internet use by, 111
Expectations of privacy, 75, 79
Family Educational Rights and Privacy Act, (FERPA), this index
Free speech conflicts, 123
Monitoring of student activities, 110
Safety conflicts, 12
Searches and Seizures, this index
Surveillance cameras, 106
Technology and
    Generally, 104 et seq.
    See also Internet, this index
    Electronic surveillance laws, 106
    Surveillance cameras, 106
Tort liabilities for invasions, 123

PRIVATE SCHOOLS
Home Schooling, this index
IDEA placements, 572
Parochial schools. See Religion and Education, this index
Voucher programs and regulation of, 495

PROBABLE CAUSE
Drug testing, 92
Searches of students, 76

PUBLIC FORA
Generally, 143, 200, 736
Internet, library access as, 804
Military recruiters, campus access, 738
NCLB access rules, 738

PUSH-OUT POLICIES AND PRACTICES, DE FACTO
Generally, 466
Discriminatory Discipline Practices, this index
Drop-Out Prevention, this index
Inappropriate placement in schools, programs, and classrooms, 360, 519 et seq., 550
School-to-Prison Pipeline, this index

QUALIFIED IMMUNITY
Tort liabilities of administrators, 298

QUALITY OF EDUCATION
Generally, 426 et seq.
    See also Curriculum, this index; No Child Left Behind Act, this index
Accountability
    Generally, 447
    Charter schools, 497
    Home schooling, 703, 705
    No Child Left Behind Act (NCLB), 461
Adequacy standards, 446
Appropriateness challenges, IDEA, 560
Bilingual education, 531
Charter Schools, this index
Competition through voucher programs and educational quality, 483
Consent decrees
    Monitoring implementation of, 356, 431
Constitutional standards, 437
Defining quality education, 427 et seq.
Desegregation and quality standards, 433
Diploma testing, validation of, 375
Educators, quality evaluations of, 893
Efficiency standards, 439
English learners programs, 531
Equity vs quality issues, 427
Financial constraints
    Generally, 435 et seq.
    Accountability standards, 447
    Adequacy standards, 446
    Efficiency standards, 439
    Fundamental rights analyses, 440
    Monitoring of school performance, 447
    State constitutional standards, 437
Fundamental rights analysis
    Generally, 440, 449 et seq.
    State vs federal equal protection standards, 455
Grouping conflicts, 427
Home schooling, regulatory accountability, 703, 705
Identifying quality education, 427 et seq.
Malpractice litigation, 428
Monitoring of school performance, 447
Race-conscious quality accountability, 464
Reform movement, 426
Reforming school reform, 483
Regents diplomas, 371
School accountability report cards (SARC), 447
State constitutional standards, 437

QUALITY OF EDUCATION—Cont'd
State vs federal equal protection standards, 455
Supplemental educational services, NCLB, 462
Takeovers and reconstitutions of local districts, 896, 905
Unitary district quality standards, 434
Voucher competition and educational quality, 483

RACIAL AND ETHNIC DISCRIMINA-TION
Affirmative Action, this index
Athletics, racially disparate transfer rules, 386
Disabilities, students with, 583
Disaggregation of test scores, 462
E-mail, hate-related, 249
Employment of educators, 971
Equal Educational Opportunity, this index
Ethnic studies classes, 39
IQ testing challenges, 583 et seq.
K-12 school districts, race-based classifications of students, 339
Quality accountability, race-conscious, 464
Safety-related ethnicity issues, 36
Safety-related racial issues, 36
Self-segregation problems in school choice programs, 488, 501
Separate-but-equal era, 307, 540
Special education students, 583
Stereotyping problems, 42
Tracking, disparate effects of, 380

REASONABLE ACCOMMODATIONS
See Americans With Disabilities Act, this index

RECONSTITUTION
Generally, 356, 898 et seq., 905 et seq.

RECORDS, STUDENT
Family Educational Rights and Privacy Act, this index
Office of Civil Rights (OCR), student record guidelines, 98
Transgender students, 415

REFORM EFFORTS
Charter Schools, this index
Education Reform Movement, 426
Equal Educational Opportunity, this index
Labor relations tensions, 896
No Child Left Behind Act, 427
Quality of Education, this index
Reforming school reform, 483
Takeovers and reconstitutions of local districts, 896, 905
Voucher Programs, this index

REFORM MOVEMENTS
Bureaucracies and change, 4

REHABILITATION ACT
Generally, 588
Educators, employment discrimination, 983
Higher education protections, 598
Higher education students, 598
IDEA and, 558

REHABILITATION ACT—Cont'd
Medical school students, 604
Reasonable accommodation
Generally, 597
Learning disabilities, 612
Scope of protections, 601

RELEASES
Tort liabilities, 21

RELIGION AND EDUCATION
Generally, 622 et seq.
Athletic activity prayers, 644, 662
Bible studies, 762
Campus facilities, access to
Generally, 732 et seq.
Equal Access Act, 175, 180
Campus forums, access to, 720 et seq.
Censorship of library books, 747
Classwork assignments, religious expression in, 725
Coercion test, 654 et seq.
Creation science studies, 755
Creationism classes, 671
Disabled students in parochial schools, public assistance to, 676
Effects inquiries, 625 et seq.
Employment discrimination, religion-based, 979
Endorsement test, 637 et seq.
Equal Access Act, 175, 180
Establishment Clause
Generally, 622 et seq., 678
Facilities access, 732
Free Exercise Clause and, 622, 671
Free speech conflicts, 192, 720
Lemon test, below
Parochial school aid, 674 et seq.
Patriotism expressions, 705 et seq.
Prayers, establishing effect, 630
Teacher, remedial education, loans of to parochial schools, 635
Evolution, 755
Flag salute ceremonies, 705 et seq., 768
Free Exercise Clause
Generally, 695 et seq.
Employment discrimination, religion-based, 979
Establishment Clause and, 622, 671
Facilities access, 732
Fundamental rights, 698
Home schooling, 703
Prayer rights of individuals, 671
Public school attendance mandates, 696, 769
Free speech rights and religious speech on campus
Generally, 158
Higher education, 186
Fundamental rights to free exercise, 698
Graduation ceremony prayers, 655
Higher education religious groups, 192, 720
Home schooling, 703
Ideas and information, freedom of, 745 et seq.
Internet filtering, 791 et seq.

RELIGION AND EDUCATION—Cont'd
Lemon test
　　Generally, 624
　　Creationism classes, 671
　　Parochial schools, direct and indirect aid, 685
　　Purpose inquiries, 670
Library censorship, 747
Military academy prayers, 664
Minutes of silence as prayers, 631
NCLB prayer provisions, 663
NCLB access rules, 738
Neutrality principle
　　Generally, 674 et seq.
　　Campus religious activities, 192, 720
　　Classwork assignments, religious expression in, 725
Parental objections to classroom materials, 763
Parental rights, 703
Parochial schools
　　Direct and indirect aid, 685
　　Disabilities, assistance for students with, 676
　　Public funding, 674 et seq.
　　Public school attendance mandates, 696, 769
　　Voucher programs, participation in, 684, 691
Patriotism expressions, 705 et seq.
Pledge of Allegiance, 705 et seq.
Prayers
　　Generally, 626
　　Athletic activities, 644, 662
　　Free exercise accommodation of individual rights, 671
　　Graduation ceremony, 655
　　Military academies, 664
　　Minutes of silence as, 631
　　NCLB provisions, 663
　　Under God language in Pledge of Allegiance, 705 et seq.
Public fora free speech standards, 736
Public funding of parochial schools, 674 et seq.
Public school attendance mandates, 696, 769
Purpose inquiries
　　Generally, 625 et seq.
　　Lemon test, 670
Sex education, parental objections, 783 et seq.
Solicitation proscriptions on campuses, 742
Songs, religious, 639
Teachers, religion-based discrimination, 979
Teachers, remedial education, loans of to parochial schools, 635
Voucher programs, parochial school participation in, 684, 691

RIGHT TO PUBLIC EDUCATION
　　Generally, 6, 303 et seq.
See also Equal Educational Opportunity, this index; Fundamental Rights, this index

SAFETY OF STUDENTS
　　Generally, 12 et seq.
Assaults on campus
　　College campuses, 47
　　K-12 schools, 29

SAFETY OF STUDENTS—Cont'd
Athletic activities, 23 et seq., 27
Coaches' duties, 23 et seq.
Columbine incident, 29
Communicable disease dangers, duty to warn students of, 233
Control duties of schools, 20
Crime prevention
　　College campuses, 47
　　K-12 schools, 29
Dangerous play activities, 16, 17
Deliberate indifference of authorities, 125, 296
Drug testing, safety concerns justifying, 92
Duty standards, 15
Ethnicity issues, 36
Extracurricular activities, 23 et seq.
Federal laws, 43
FERPA records protection, safety-related justifications for access, 96
Field trips, 21
Foreseeability and duty to protect, 47, 232
Fraternity hazing, 64
Free speech-safety concern conflicts
　　College campuses, 118
　　K-12 standards, 127
　　Threats, responses to, 157
Gun-Free Schools Act, 43
Hazing, 60
Higher education facilities, 46 et seq.
Immunities of school districts, 14
In loco parentis, 20
Internet protection of children, 791 et seq.
Intervention duties as to dangerous students, 55, 227
K-12 schools, 13 et seq.
LGBT bullying, supervisorial liability, 291
Monitoring of student activities, 110
NCLB unsafe school choice options, 44
Negligence law principles, 14 et seq.
Nonstudents injured by students, 20
Off-campus supervisorial duties
　　Colleges, 65
　　K-12 schools, 15, 19
Peer harassment, tort liabilities, 283
Persistently dangerous schools, 45, 492
Playground supervision, 17
Privacy rights conflicts, 12
Racial issues, 36
Releases and school tort liabilities, 21
Releases forms and school tort liabilities, 21
Right to safe schools laws, 42
Searches and Seizures, this index
Segregation, de facto, on violent campuses, 36
Sexual harassment, 54
Special relationship doctrine
　　Higher education, 46
　　K-12 schools, 20
Supervisorial duties, 14 et seq.
Third parties injured by students, 20
Threatening behavior, duty to intervene, 227
Threats, this index
Tort law principles, 14 et seq.
Transgender students, 413
Unsafe school choice option, NCLB, 45
Unsafe school choice options, 44

SAFETY OF STUDENTS—Cont'd
Violent crime prevention
    College campuses, 47
    K-12 schools, 29
Virginia Tech incident, 55, 97
Warnings duties, 47
Weapons on campus
    College campuses, 47
    K-12 schools, 29
Willful and wantonly negligent supervision, 36
Zero-tolerance statutes, 44

SCHOOL-TO-PRISON PIPELINE
Implicated practices at the K-12 school site
    level, generally, 42, 356, 360, 519 et seq.,
    550, 560, 572 et seq.
Push-out Policies and Practices, De Facto, this
    index
Special education placement, 360, 550, 560,
    572 et seq.

SEARCHES AND SEIZURES
Generally, 71 et seq.
Electronic surveillance laws, 106
Expectations of privacy, 75, 79
In loco parentis, 71
K-12 standards, 72 et seq.
Probable cause, 76
Reasonableness, 73, 78, 84
Special needs doctrine, 80
Special relationship between teacher and stu-
    dent, 79
Strip searches of students, 84

SECOND LANGUAGE STUDENTS
See English Learners, this index

SEGREGATION
See Equal Educational Opportunity, this in-
    dex
Bicultural classes, segregation issues, 539
Choice programs, segregative effects, 491
Classroom assignments as
    Disabilities, students with, 572 et seq.
    English learner programs, 538 et seq.
Consent decrees, monitoring implementation
    of, 356, 431
Disabilities. segregation vs mainstreaming of
    students with, 550, 572 et seq.
English learner programs, segregation issues,
    538 et seq.
Inter-school segregation, 363
IQ testing challenges, 583 et seq.
Multi-faceted desegregation, 356
Resegregation concerns
    Generally, 346, 355, 360
    Choice programs, 491
    English learner programs, 538 et seq.
Self-segregation problems, 488, 501
Supreme Court desegregation mandate, 307,
    540

SEX EDUCATION
Generally, 783 et seq.
HIV-AIDS prevention education, 786
Parental objections, 783 et seq.

SEXUAL HARASSMENT
Peers
    Generally, 278 et seq.
    See also Peer Harassment, this index
Supervisorial duties, 54

SOCIOECONOMIC STATUS (SES)
Generally, 319
See also Equal Educational Opportunity, this
    index

SOLOMON AMENDMENT
Don't-ask-don't-tell policy, 739

SPECIAL EDUCATION
Generally, 505 et seq.
Disabilities, Students With, this index
English Learners, this index
NCLB testing requirements, 591

SPECIAL NEEDS DOCTRINE
Drug testing, 95
Search and seizure, 80

SPECIAL NEEDS STUDENTS
See Disabilities, Students With, this index

SPECIAL RELATIONSHIP DOCTRINE
Higher education, 46
K-12 schools, 20
Searches of students, 79
Supervisorial duties of schools, 20, 46, 68
Threats, duty to intervene, 230

SPORTS
See Athletic Activities, this index

STATE LAW
Federal law and generally
    Generally, 2
    Free speech rights of students, 145

SUPERVISION OF STUDENTS
Safety-related supervisorial duties
    Generally, 13 et seq.
    See also Safety of Students, this index

SURVEILLANCE CAMERAS
Generally, 106

SUSPENSION AND EXPULSION
See also Safety of Students, this index
Gun-Free Schools Act, 43
Threats, expulsions for, 261
Threats, suspensions for, 233
Zero-tolerance statutes, 44

TENURE RIGHTS
Generally, 906 et seq.
Academic freedom, 927
Advocacy, First Amendment protection, 942
Constitutional rights, 907
Contracts of employment, termination for
    cause, 920
Dismissal litigation, 911 et seq.
Employment Discrimination, this index
Insubordination dismissals and free speech
    rights, 942
Publication and tenure, 815, 819

TENURE RIGHTS—Cont'd
Sexual orientation and moral turpitude based dismissals, 913

TESTING
Adequacy vs equity financing theories, 435
ADHD, 612
Bar exams and disabilities accommodation, 619
Blind persons, 620
Copyright law applicable to testing materials
    Fair use doctrine, 829
    Secure material copyrighting, 832
Diploma testing, validation of, 375
Disaggregation of test scores, 462
Educational Testing Service (ETS), 382
Functional literacy, 379
IQ testing challenges, 583 et seq.
Learning disabilities, 612
LSAT and disabilities accommodation, 619
Multiple choice testing, 375
No Child Left Behind Act, this index
Peer grading, FERPA challenge, 99
Reasonable accommodations of disabilities, 591, 619
SAT gender bias, 381
Special education student testing problems, 591
Standardized testing
    Generally, 584 et seq.
    Criticisms, 375, 835
Tracking, disparate racial effects of, 380
Validation of diploma testing, 375
Validation of test materials, 832

THREATS
    Generally, 226 et seq.
Criminal penalties, 234, 237 et seq., 251
Direct, 271
Duty to intervene, 227
E-mail, hate-related, 249
Expulsions for, 261
Fiction writing perceived as threatening, 271
First Amendment conflicts with responses to, 125, 157, 249 et seq., 271
Foreseeability and duty to protect, 232
Instant messages, 267
Internet communications, 261
Intervention duties as to dangerous students, 55, 227
Intimidation element, 260
Negligence liability, 227
Policy considerations, 261
Reasonable percipient perception of, 265
Special relationships creating duty to intervene, 230
Statutory prohibitions
    Higher education, 233 et seq.
    K-12, 261 et seq.
Suspensions for, 233
Third party duties occasioned by, 227
Tinker rule, 267
Tinker rule applicability, 134
True threats
    Generally, 125, 249 et seq.
    E-mails, 251
Zero tolerance policies, 226

TINKER RULE
See Free Speech Rights of Students, this index

TITLE IX
Affirmative action remedies, 393
Athletic activities, 391
Bullying, 290
Development and achievement of gender equity standards, 396
Hostile environment harassment, 125
Office of Civil Rights (OCR) compliance guidelines, 392
Peer harassment and mistreatment, 290

TITLE VII
See Employment Discrimination, this index

TORT LIABILITIES
See Civil Liabilities, this index

TRANSCRIPTS
Family Educational Rights and Privacy Act provisions, 96

TRANSGENDER STUDENTS
    Generally, 409
See also Lesbian, Gay, Bisexual, and Transgender Students, this index

UNDOCUMENTED STUDENTS
    Generally, 416
Development, Relief and Education for Alien Minors (DREAM) Act proposal, 425
Political resistance to equal protection of, 421
Resident vs nonresident tuition fees, 424
Student records, immigration authorities' access to, 96

UNIONS
See Labor Relations in Public Education, this index

UNITARY SCHOOL DISTRICTS
See Equal Educational Opportunity, this index

UNIVERSITIES
See Higher Education, this index

VALUES
See Religion and Education, this index

VICARIOUS LIABILITY
Generally, 61

VIOLENCE, SCHOOL
Safety of Students, this index
Threats, this index
Weapons, this index

VOUCHER PROGRAMS
    Generally, 482 et seq.
    See also Choice, School, this index
Charter schools compared, 498
Competition and educational quality, 483
Parochial school participation in, 684, 691
Political support for voucher programs, 426
Private schools accepting, regulation of, 495
Self-segregation problem, 488
Skimming problems, 484

VOUCHER PROGRAMS—Cont'd
Unsafe school choice option, NCLB, 45

WEAPONS
Bomb-making, internet information, 234
Campus safety duties
    College campuses, 47
    K-12 schools, 29
Gun-Free Schools Act, 43
Zero-tolerance statutes, 44

WOMEN
See Gender Discrimination, this index

WORK FOR HIRE DOCTRINE
See Copyright Law, this index

ZERO TOLERANCE
Development of policies, 44
Policy considerations, 261
Threats, 226

†